I0085146

Anonymus

Horse Breeding in Ireland

Minutes of Evidence

Anonymus

Horse Breeding in Ireland
Minutes of Evidence

ISBN/EAN: 9783742805157

Manufactured in Europe, USA, Canada, Australia, Japa

Cover: Foto ©Thomas Meinert / pixelio.de

Manufactured and distributed by brebook publishing software
(www.brebook.com)

Anonymus

Horse Breeding in Ireland

COMMISSION ON HORSE BREEDING, IRELAND.

MINUTES OF EVIDENCE

TAKEN BEFORE THE

COMMISSIONERS

APPOINTED TO INQUIRE INTO THE HORSE BREEDING INDUSTRY IN IRELAND.

WITH APPENDICES.

Presented to both Houses of Parliament by Command of Her Majesty.

DUBLIN:
PRINTED FOR HER MAJESTY'S STATIONERY OFFICE,
BY ALEXANDER THOM & CO. (LIMITED).

And to be purchased, either directly or through any Bookseller, from
HODGES, FIGGIS, and Co. (LIMITED), 104, Grafton-street, Dublin; or
EYRE and SPOTTISWOODE, East Harding-street, Fleet-street, E.C.; or
JOHN MENZIES and Co., 12, Hanover-street, Edinburgh, and 90, West Nile-street, Glasgow.

1897.

CONTENTS

INDEX TO WITNESSES,
INDEX TO APPENDICES, .
MINUTES OF EVIDENCE, .
APPENDICES. . .

INDEX TO WITNESSES.

Name.	Page.	Name.	Page.
1. Anderson, Thomas,	120	59. Lane, B. H.,	107
2. Arcdale, E. M.,	67	60. Lawrenson, B. D.,	258
		61. Legard, Rev. Cecil,	408
3. Bainbridge, W.,	365	62. Longfield, R. E.,	163
4. Barry, J. H.,	139		
5. Begley, R. B.,	209	63. Maloney, James,	131
6. Blennerhassett, Arthur,	36	64. Macafee, Thomas,	85
7. Bamford, J. F.,	257	65. Major, John,	321
8. Burdett-Coutts, W., M.P.,	346	66. Malone, R.,	325
9. Butler, James,	159	67. M'Cutcheon, T.,	219
10. Brooke, Sir Douglas,	370	68. M'Donnell, Henry,	133
		69. M'Kinley, Robert,	273
11. Carden, R. G.,	168	70. M'Mahon, Thomas,	116
12. Carew, T. M.,	250	71. M'Meekin, James,	391
13. Collier, George,	153	72. Melody, Thomas,	384
14. Comerford, T.,	239	73. Mills, W. L.,	1
15. Connellan, Major,	197	74. Miller, George,	139
16. Conyngham, Sir W. L., K.C.B.,	110	75. Milward, Dawson A.,	261
17. Corrigan, Thomas,	202	76. Morton, Nathaniel,	70
18. Coventry, The Earl of,	403	77. Morton, Alexander,	298
19. Craddock, T.,	279	78. Moss, R. J.,	233
20. Dalton, R. H.,	457	79. Newman, Henry,	377
21. Daly, James,	232		
22. De Robeck, H.,	217	80. O'Brien, Thomas,	389
23. Dickson, John,	139	81. O'Malley, Richard,	206
24. Dixon, Scarf,	425	82. O'Reilly, J. B.,	16
25. Donnellan, Capt.,	146		
26. Donovan, St. John,	157	83. Pallin, William,	281
27. Donovan, T.,	311	84. Pringle, R. H.,	36
28. Drage, Vet.-Lieut.,	334	85. Pritchard, Professor,	380
29. Dunne, W.,	361	86. Purdon, John,	265
30. Dunlop, J.,	94		
		87. Reynard, F.,	416
31. Ebrington, The Viscount,	153	88. Reynolds, H.,	317
		89. Richardson, George,	420
32. Farrell, William,	103	90. Roberts, S. Usher,	41
33. Fetherstonhaugh, Capt. C.,	60	91. Roberts, William,	296
34. Fife, Capt. W. H.,	141	92. Robinson, U. A.,	259
35. Fitzgerald, Desmond,	167	93. Russell, David,	63
36. Fitzgerald, Peter,	170	94. Russell, George,	269
37. Flynn, Richard,	235	95. Rutledge, W. E.,	303
38. Frost, J. C.,	200		
39. Forster, Rev. A. N. Haire-,	113	96. Sampey, H. B.,	259
		97. Shelly, P.,	216
40. Galbraith, James,	276	98. Slacke, Sir Owen R.,	315
41. Gale, George,	284	99. Smithwick, Capt. W. F.,	193
42. Giltrap, E.,	230	100. Spaight, Col.,	130
43. Going, R. E.,	178	101. Sproule, Alexander H.,	121
		102. Stevenson, Clement,	370
44. Hallen, Col.,	373	103. Studdert, Major G. W.,	31
45. Hanson, S. L.,	434		
46. Hammond, W.,	85	104. Talbot, R. N.,	148
47. Harris, G. M.,	175	105. Thompson, Richard,	93
48. Henry, Col. F.,	156	106. Tottenham, George L.,	293
49. Hetherington, John,	459	107. Townshend, Capt.,	223
50. Heaven, George,	161	108. Tredegar, The Lord,	348
51. Holtby, William,	413	109. Trench, William Thomas,	181
52. Hunter, R. Todd,	78	110. Trotter, W. B.,	391
		111. Tuthill, Capt. J. F.,	55
53. Ingram, T. A.,	96		
54. Irwin, Rev. A. Staples,	135	112. Warren, Herbert,	204
		113. Watson, Gen. Sir John,	364
55. Johnston, S.,	135	114. Webb, Charles,	257
56. Johnston, R.,	305	115. Webber, T. W.,	183
		116. Widger, John,	338
57. Kelly, John M.,	194	117. Wimbush, Barton,	188
58. Kennedy, Edward,	212	118. Winter, E. C.,	180
		119. Withers, H.,	438

INDEX TO APPENDIX.

Appendix.	Subject.	Page.
A.	Reports on Horse Breeding and aid given by the State in—	
	1. Austria and Hungary, .	465, 469
	2. France, .	470
	3. Italy, .	471
	4. Prussia,	480
B.	Resolutions of Kerry Grand Jury, . .	485
	Petition presented by a Deputation of Ratepayers at Dingle,	485
	Resolutions of Agricultural and other Societies, .	485
C.	Letter from Col. St. Quintin to the Earl of Dunraven with reference to the purchase of [illegible], ...	486
D.	Tables of Expenditure furnished by the Congested Districts Board, - .	488
	Number, Names, Breed, and Distribution of Stallions belonging to the Congested Districts Board, ...	489
	Number of Mares served by each of the Board's Stallions since 1892, .	491
E.	Extract on American Exportation handed in by Mr. James Daly, .	492
F.	Return of Stallions in the hands of Private Owners standing in Ireland in the year 1896, compiled by the Land Commission from reports furnished by the Constabulary, ...	493

COMMISSION ON HORSE BREEDING.

MINUTES OF EVIDENCE.

FIRST DAY.—TUESDAY, OCTOBER 20TH, 1896.

Oct. 20, 1896.

Present:—THE EARL OF DUNRAVEN, K.P., in the Chair; LORD RATHDONNELL, LORD ASHTOWN, SIR WALTER GILBEY, SIR THOMAS ESMONDE, M.P., HON. HENRY W. FITZWILLIAM, MESSRS. J. L. CAREW, M.P., F. S. WRENCH, and PERCY LA TOUCHE.

MR. HUGH NEVILLE, Secretary, was in attendance.

Mr. W. L. Micks.

Mr. WILLIAM LAWSON MICKS was called and examined by the Chairman.

1. You are the Secretary of the Congested Districts Board, Mr. Micks?—Yes, my lord.

2. How long have you occupied that position?—Since the Board was established on the 5th of August, 1891.

3. What are the matters which come under the cognizance of the Board—was it instituted amongst other things to improve the breed of horses?—Yes. They were authorised by the Act of 1891, amongst other things, to take such steps as they might think proper for the breeding of live stock in the congested districts.

4. [illegible]

5. You have that authority ever since the Board was instituted?—That was the Act which formed the Board, and which gave that authority amongst others to the Board.

6. Can you point out the geographical positions of the congested districts?—[illegible]

7. Mr. FITZWILLIAM.—That portion coloured blue is congested?—Yes.

The CHAIRMAN.—What is the proportion to the area of the whole of Ireland?—[illegible]

8. [illegible]

9. I suppose it changes from time to time?—[illegible]

10. [illegible]

12. [illegible]

13. Practically then you may look upon this map as correct?—[illegible]

14. Can you give the Commission any statistics on the subject of horse breeding in the congested districts?—The number of horses in congested districts I can give.

15. What do you mean by "horses"?—I classify them.

16. Well?—The total number of horses in the congested districts is [illegible].

17. When were these statistics made out?—The present year. [illegible]

18. [illegible]

19. [illegible]

20. [illegible]

21. [illegible]

22. From what date are those figures taken?—[illegible]

23. No particular date?—[illegible] before May, early in the spring of this year, I should say.

24. Well?—In the whole of Ireland there are [illegible].

25. Mr. J. L. CAREW.—[illegible]

A

and under two 94,384. Of the horses two years old and over 338,497 are used for agricultural purposes, for traffic and manufactures 46,583, and for amusement and recreation 35,351. For agricultural purposes there are 83,000 in the congested districts, 255,000 in other parts of Ireland; that is about one-fourth of such horses of Ireland in congested districts, and, taking it according to area (about one 3,000,000 acres in the congested districts; half of which is waste and unprofitable land), and having regard to the waste and unprofitable land there are proportionately as many horses in congested districts as in other parts of Ireland, if not fewer.

26. CHAIRMAN.—What is the proportion as regards the working horse to which horses are put?—I do not quite understand.

27. If you compare horses used for agriculture in the congested districts with those similarly employed in other parts of Ireland what is the proportion?—Considerable.

28. And how would it be as regards those used for recreation?—That would be about one-fifth.

29. And for manufactures and traffic?—About one-forty-fifth.

30. Where do these returns for all Ireland come from?—They are collected for the Agricultural Statistics of Ireland by the Constabulary officers for the Registrar-General.

31. Have you any other figures?—No other statistics are kept.

32. I suppose you are not in a position to give us any information as to the character and nature of the horses in the congested districts?—Only from my own observation—I know nothing personally of horses. I know the size of the animals and the general appearance of them.

33. Well, perhaps, you would give us what you saw in each district? They vary a good deal. In the northern part of Donegal——

34. Mr. CAMPBELL.—Of Donegal?—Yes; in the northern part, Inishowen, heavy horses—heavy, hairy-legged horses from Clydesdale, that are often met with; then lower down—Glenties and Dunfanaghy districts—they are more of the pony class, thin, lean, light, and the same applies to the rest of West Donegal. In West Mayo, on the sea-coast, many are very small, poor, thin, little ponies; and also in Erris and Belmullet (including the island). Then in Achill the ponies are of a better class, better shaped and stronger ponies. Then in this island—Achill (including Clare Island)—there are not so many horses; the people there use donkeys more than horses. I can give you the exact numbers.

35. Mr. FITZWILLIAM.—What do you call what district?—East Mayo about Swinford; it takes in a little bit of Roscommon and Castlerea; this is the Swinford district. In this part of Mayo—South Mayo (including?)—Louisburgh, there are rather good ponies, and there you have the Connemara ponies here; then down here in Clare (including) the horses are distinctly better than in Mayo and Donegal, larger, stronger and better, still they are less enough.

36. The CHAIRMAN.—Most of them are small?—Small as compared with the ordinary horse.

37. Mr. FITZWILLIAM.—And not of an agricultural breed like the northern ones?—No, but I fancy they are good enough for [illegible].

38. Sir THOMAS ESMONDE.—These heavy horses in the north, are they used in the locality?—They are.

39. Lord ROSSMORE.—Is not the soil there better in Derry very much the same as up there (indicating)?—The mixing is middle.

40. In the [illegible] better; the [illegible] of it is much better land than any other congested part of West Donegal.

41. Lord ARDILAUN.—In Tyrone?—I am sure they get far more crops out of it.

42. Sir THOMAS ESMONDE.—In these farms in the congested districts can they use them to any better?—Yes, and they sell them to East Donegal which is a very good agricultural part of the country, as good as Tyrone.

43. Then their market would be in other parts of the North of Ireland?—They do.

44. Do they export any of these?—I cannot say.

45. The CHAIRMAN.—They are donkeys; do they use mules much?—Very few.

46. Would they be included in horses?—No, but I can give you the numbers; there are very few mules in Ireland.

47. Mr. J. L. CAREW.—Can you distinguish the nature of the soil in different districts? In Donegal West there is grazing, in the southern part there is rather richer; in the northern part of Mayo some of it is grazing, and very little limestone; there are in Ireland [illegible].

48. Where is the limestone in the congested districts?—There is very little in any large tract.

49. The CHAIRMAN.—Are you well acquainted with the geological formation?—No, I just know it in a rough way.

50. Lord ROSSMORE.—Is there any limestone in the north?—Very little at all in the congested districts.

51. The CHAIRMAN.—What inquiries were made by the Board before starting operations?—The Board issued a number of queries. It issued them sometime up the 5th of August, 1891. In the same week different residents in the congested districts, who written to, and asked different questions with horses and bulls and other matters relating to the districts.

52. Have you a list of the questions?—I have the answers.

The CHAIRMAN.—You can put them in.

Witness (reading).—Mr. W. Hamilton, J.P., Lord Conyngham's Agent, West Donegal, writing generally of Glenties Union, in reply to the query:—

"What class of stallion would you consider most suitable for improving the local breed of horses?"

Said:—

"I am myself in favour of a Hackney stallion."

And in reply to the query—"By what class of stallions are the mares usually served?"

He replies:—

"Generally by a bad mongrel, consequently the ponies of this locality—once they were celebrated for their good qualities—are very much degenerated."

Mr. James Maguire, J.P., the Lodge, Carrick, Co. Donegal, is in favour of "good Hackney ponies or Welsh ponies."

Mr. Wybrants Olphert, as regards the union of Dunfanaghy, is in favour of "a strong high stepping cob, 14 to 15½ high: a Cleveland bay if procurable."

Mr. George Hewson, J.P., Bunbeg, Nr. Letterkenny, as regards the union of Milford, says:—

"Hackney horses are very scarce in Ireland, but I think that a Norfolk trotter crossed with country bred mares would get suitable foals."

The Earl of Leitrim, as regards the union of Milford, is in favour of "the Hackney Suffolk Punch, but if got large enough, with plenty of bone, the Welsh pony."

Mr. W. Sinclair, M.P., Drumbeg, Lever, Co. Donegal, as regards the union of Donegal, suggests "good thick-bred ill-for general work."

Mr. James P. Murphy, Dunfanaghy, as regards part of the unions of Dunfanaghy and Letterkenny, is in favour of "Suffolk Punch and Norfolk breeds for the heavier districts, and Welsh stallions for the mountain parts."

Mr. J. O. Fowler, J.P., Lowtherstown, Ballinasloe, as regards the unions of Achill and Newport, [illegible] a good large horse, either thorough or three-quarter bred animals, the former preferred."

[illegible] M'Cullagh, J.P., [illegible], Co. Monaghan, as regards the [illegible] of Castleblayney and Donegal, is in favour of "a stallion that would get good weight carrying hunters and harness horses."

[illegible] The Chairman.—[illegible] the [illegible] [illegible]—No [illegible] to [illegible]. Mr. William [illegible], as regards the [illegible], without [illegible] the breed, says:—

"A well bred small sire is required."

Mr. William Norwood, J.P., [illegible], as regards the unions of [illegible], [illegible], [illegible], and [illegible], favours "small Clydesdales."

Mr. John [illegible], as regards the union of [illegible], suggests "good strong thorough-bred horse with good action."

Mr. S. F. [illegible], [illegible], Mayo, as regards the union of [illegible], north and south, favours "half bred stallion or Suffolk Punch."

Mr. John E. [illegible], Cork, as regards the union of [illegible], writes—"Small Suffolk Punch."

Mr. J. [illegible], as regards the [illegible] union, favours "a strong serviceable cob."

Mr. George [illegible], J.P., [illegible], as regards the unions of [illegible] and [illegible], writes: "Good half bred horse, 15 hands, as the lands [illegible], but there are several of the larger farmers who greatly want a thoroughbred."

Mr. Hugh M'[illegible], county [illegible], as regards [illegible] union, says:—"The land is too poor and the mares too bad to cross with a thoroughbred [illegible] a large three-quarter bred horse would be [illegible], or a sire capable of getting good [illegible] animals."

Mr. John [illegible], J.P., [illegible], as regards [illegible] union, favours "pure Clydesdale and pure thoroughbred."

Mr. George [illegible], [illegible], Listowel, county Kerry, as regards Listowel union, favours "a [illegible], [illegible] and [illegible]. There are enough thorough-breds for present wants."

In addition to these [illegible] [illegible] to people in the locality, the Board also sent [illegible] in England and elsewhere who have a reputation as to the breeding of horses.

Major [illegible], [illegible], county [illegible], writes to Mr. Wrench as follows:—

"I enclose Lord Londesborough's reply, which [illegible] [illegible] to come on this week. I have no doubt his promised enquiry will enlighten us as to [illegible] the [illegible] and [illegible]. My 'marked' paragraph agrees with what I told you [illegible] 'there are hundreds of that [illegible]' No. [illegible]. I [illegible] [illegible] 14 hands the standard, as in [illegible] the 'Hackney Stallion' if that height, would suit admirably, but must be above that standard."

This is the enclosure from Lord [illegible]:—

"[illegible], [illegible],
"[illegible], 1891.

"Dear Major [illegible],—[illegible] little [illegible] under 15 hands, and [illegible] of that [illegible]. The Welsh pony [illegible] the country [illegible] of [illegible] is that he is a very fast [illegible]. [illegible] on the hills in [illegible]. My [illegible] of [illegible] the [illegible] of [illegible] in the [illegible] of Yorkshire 'Hackney.' [illegible] for [illegible], as they have better shoulders. My 'Show' is on this week, and I will make enquiries of the animal you write about.

"Yours very truly,

"(Signed), [illegible]."

Mr. W. L. [illegible]

Lord Leitrim writes:—

"Mulroy, Milford, Co. Donegal,
"[illegible] Dec., '91.

"[illegible],—I think the replies to the accompanying Query Sheet pretty well answer the questions in your letter to me. My stallions, two Clydesdales in succession, thoroughbred sire Young Artillery and an Arab [illegible] that was General [illegible]'s charger at the battle of [illegible], have all filled up, or perhaps I should say [illegible]. I charged people who were not my tenants [illegible] for Young Artillery, and used to get a good many, and always charged [illegible] double for [illegible] people who are not my tenants. My first Clydesdale was a special favourite. I think a Hackney and Pony Stallion would be made good use of in these parts.

"(Signed), Leitrim."

Mr. Thomas M'Mahon writes from [illegible] House, Castleblayney, 12th December, 1891:—

"Dear Sir,—In reference to your letter, I think Norfolk or Cambridgeshire is the best place to get Hackney stallions. You can get them there from 15 hands to 15.3 hands, or you can get them at York or Beverly or at Bradford, but I prefer Norfolk for the best goers, but they must be bought with lean neck, and good shoulders and good quarters, and they are the best cross for Connemara ponies. If you like I will buy one for you and charge you nothing but my expenses, as I can buy it cheaper than you can, as I know the country so well, I can get you any height or any colour you choose. I can go any day after Friday, 18th of this month."

Mr. [illegible], writing from [illegible], London, on the [illegible] December, 1891, says:—

"Dear Sir,—I am much obliged by your letter, which I have received on my return from America. I will very gladly be of any service in my power to the Congested Districts Board, in supplying [illegible] [illegible]. I send you herewith a copy of the book which I have recently published on the subject of what I call the 'new departure' in horse-breeding, and I think that you will find, if you have time to read it, that the principal [illegible] in England [illegible].

"It is rather difficult for me to advise you definitely, without being acquainted with the exact type of [illegible] from which it is desired to breed, and without knowing what class of horses will find the best market in the [illegible] districts.

"Assuming, however, [illegible] two points—(a) That the [illegible] will consist of [illegible] of both quality and action, and, in addition, [illegible] and [illegible]; and (b) that it is desired to raise the standard of [illegible] that while the stock produced will be more serviceable for the ordinary purposes which are [illegible] [illegible], [illegible] also [illegible] an opportunity of [illegible] here and there a horse with [illegible] action and [illegible], which would fetch good prices from the [illegible] [illegible] a better class of [illegible]. There is [illegible] in strongly advising the use of the Hackney stallion.

"I do not believe in the Arab, nor do I think the [illegible] would be in any way [illegible] by the [illegible] of a small thoroughbred. The thoroughbred [illegible] not the [illegible] to get [illegible] in [illegible] out of [illegible] [illegible], [illegible] the [illegible] of the [illegible], [illegible] all [illegible] [illegible] [illegible].

[illegible]

to get them high on the leg and light of bone. The Hackney corrects the latter deficiencies, gives width, strength, weight-carrying, and draught-power, and in addition, gives action.

"It goes without saying that you must get the right sort of Hackney, because there are a great many of the wrong sort.

"Now as to the question of price which I had better deal with at once.

"I do not think that it would be wise for you to attempt the experiment with the Hackney, unless you are [illegible] to give £50 more per horse than the stated price. Even then, £100 at the present time would not buy any stallion worth his keep. If it were not for the lack of bone that the [illegible] which you mention [illegible]. If your Board will consider how quickly the extra £50 is [illegible] in making some [illegible] I think, hardly imperil the success of the experiment by this amount.

"There are very many important considerations in choosing a Hackney, such as black-blood, reliability, endurance, &c., which must be added to those you mention of action and shape.

"I am, as you know, much interested in the industrial progress of Ireland, and I should be extremely glad to see this experiment made successful. I consider it extremely [illegible] in the right direction, and I would spare no trouble in contributing to have it started upon what, in my opinion, would be the most promising lines.

"I am greatly occupied at present, but if you would suggest any means whereby, in the limited space of time which would be at my disposal for such a purpose, I could have personal inspection of the average type of horses or ponies which it is desired to improve, I would endeavour to make time to select some of the stallions for that purpose. If you will kindly look through the books that I am forwarding herewith, I may, perhaps, to hear from you again on the subject."

54. Mr. Fitzgerald.—What is the price?—He says £200 would be little enough.

55. The Chairman.—Have you got the letter that was in reply to?—I have not.

56. When you put the questions asked—he seems to be giving his own opinions very much?—The questions were these:—

"(1) What class of stallion would you consider most suitable for improving the breed of horses?

"(2) By what class of stallion are the mares mostly served?"

Witness (continuing to read).—The Right Hon. Henry Chaplin writes as follows from [illegible], S.W., on the 1st January, 1892:—

"It depends entirely on what the produce is wanted for. With my present knowledge, I should say Yorkshire Hackneys, not Norfolk. The former has more [illegible] and are a hardier race. Sir W. [illegible], [illegible], is a first-rate judge of Hackneys, and [illegible]. In Ireland I imagine Lord Waterford is one of the best authorities and would [illegible] with horses, but there are many others whom Mr. Wrench will know quite as well or better than I do. You may send him this."

57. Mr. J. T. Carew.—Did it [illegible] Lord Waterford?—Yes. (Continuing to read). Mr. George Wetherell, writing from [illegible], Easingwold, Yorkshire, on the 13th January, 1892, says:—

"In reply to yours I would most strongly advise your using one Yorkshire Hackney stallion in preference to an Arab Stallion. What you want to get is action, and you will get this if you put a well-bred pony about 14½ hands high or 15 hands high to a good Yorkshire Hackney Stallion—at least this is my experience."

Sir Walter Gilbey, writing from Elsenham Hall, Essex, on the 2nd January, 1892, says:—

"I do not anticipate any great difficulty in obtaining Spanish (Andalusian) Stallions.

"It is possible you are correct in your belief, the people themselves would prefer a small good stepping Hackney, and I am sure the cross will produce, and which *will pay for breeding.*

"I did not answer your question as to cost. Good Hackney stallions can be obtained at about £150 to £200. If you care to know, I have no doubt a chance can be arranged for inspection, &c. General [illegible] has been purchasing for the Government, for India, and could assure you I have every reason to believe."

58. Mr. Warren Greene.—I would like to know the date these questions were sent out?—In the end of 1891.

59. The price is very different now from what it was then.—The next came in from Mr. [illegible] T. Tennant. Writing from [illegible], Bedford, January 4th, 1892, he says:—

"I am in receipt of your letter concerning Stallions for your congested districts. As you well know I was strongly opposed to the introduction of Hackney blood into Ireland, but the majority of the Royal Dublin Society thought otherwise, and have allowed the English Hackney to set foot on Irish soil. As far as ponies are concerned, there is only one horse to improve them, and that is the Hackney, and I should much prefer those Stallions which are bred in a certain district of Yorkshire, as they are of much finer quality than the Norfolk horses. Arabs are faulty in every respect, except the way in which their [illegible]. Small Thoroughbred Stallions are worthless [illegible], and, therefore, would most likely get nothing but worthless weeds. If you should decide on buying Hackney Stallions I shall be most happy to do [illegible] in the way of procuring them, as I know every breeder in the country, and might, perhaps, save you some hundreds in their purchase."

Mr. Tennant is an English gentleman who has judged the Hackney classes at the Dublin Horse Show on several occasions. The next letter is from Mr. [illegible]. Writing from [illegible], Co. Cork, 3rd March, 1892, he says:—

"I see in the Farmer's Gazette of the 20th ultimo, that Hackney stallions have been purchased by the Board, and I consider it right that you will [illegible] as to what terms they will be supplied.

"There is not a part of Ireland to my knowledge that requires a [illegible] of good blood more than this district. The breed is greatly going down, and [illegible] principal [illegible] but one [illegible] horse [illegible] (Hackney), as they are [illegible] there.

"I was recently [illegible] of [illegible], I purchased the thoroughbred stallion '[illegible]' in the autumn of 1891, and, though I could not [illegible] working [illegible] to give him [illegible] well-bred horse, however, [illegible] to find the great demand for improvements there is in the horse-breeding [illegible], and could I afford it I would keep six or seven stallions, as I consider nothing that would do the country more good. Going about amongst the farmers, as I do, I find the [illegible] for good horses, but no power to [illegible] it.

"I have long felt that the 'Hackney' is just the class of stallion for this country, and with this view I went over to London last March, to the great Hackney Show, and got an introduction to Mr. [illegible], who very kindly showed me his principal stud

Oct. 26, 1894. Mr. W. L. Micks.

Hackneys, but I was unable to afford his prices as he asked me £250 for a two year old stallion."

"To buy a badly bred stallion would be to do the country more harm than good, so I had to return without one."

60. The Chairman.—Is he residing in a congested district?—Yes, my lord, Skibbereen.

(Continuing to read). Mr. Richard Barter, St. Ann's Hill, Co. Cork, wrote on the 6th December, 1892—

"I was in Norfolk in October and had a look at some of the Hackney Studs there. I feel sure they are well calculated to vastly improve our mountain ponies. I think it would be both useful and interesting to watch the breeding of pure Hackneys in this country, and would I think still more stimulate their use if the farmers saw some good mares and their gets. I would be glad to co-operate with your Board in this direction. I have now three pure-bred Hackney mares, two of them winners of several first prizes in Norfolk; and if your Board would place a good blood Hackney stallion in the Macroom scheduled district that could be used with them, I would then be glad to arrange to show the mares at some of the most important fairs, or any other place suggested.

"Would you kindly bring this matter under the consideration of your Board?"

61. Mr. Percy La Touche.—That is Mr. Barter of Blarney, Co. Cork?—Yes.

(Continuing to read). The Clerk of Donegal Union, writing on the 28th February, 1893, says—

"There is a very great desire in this neighbourhood to secure the services of a stallion—either Hackney or Suffolk Punch—if you think there would be any use in our applying for one, would you kindly have the necessary forms sent to me."

The Earl of Zetland, writing on 3rd January, 1894, from Aske, Richmond, Yorkshire, says—

"I must thank you very much for your most interesting letter, by which I am glad to see that your scheme for improving the breed of horses in Ireland is getting into shape. I think you are working on quite the right lines, and shall be glad to hear in course of time the decisions arrived at by the Committee of the Royal Dublin Society. I am also very glad to hear that the Hackneys are doing well. I hope that you quite understand that my former remarks about them were not intended to disparage the Hackney stallions, but only to express my idea that they should be kept apart from the Hunter breed, I have always thought that they would prove most valuable animals in the congested districts, when they replace stallions of a very inferior quality.

"I am very glad there is so good a demand for their services in the congested districts, and feel confident that they will make their mark before long, if they have not already done so."

62. The Chairman.—What are the former remarks that he alludes to?—A former letter, I presume, written to Mr. Wrench.

63. Not the letter you have read?—No.

64. Mr. Percy La Touche.—What is the date of that letter?—[illegible] January, 1894.

65. The Chairman.—What is the letter from?—Lord Zetland.

66. Mr. Wrench?—What is the date of the other, from Mr. Richard Barter?—December, 1892.

The Chairman.—Those were letters received from the Congested Districts Board before they decided their [illegible]. I do not think we want letters received [illegible].

Witness.—The letters up to Lord Zetland's were in the [illegible] stage—the others [illegible].

67. The Chairman.—Before you begin the letters, is there any information in any of the letters received from gentlemen living in the congested districts that would be useful to us—first of all what were the questions sent out?

Witness.—First—"What class of stallion would give satisfaction most suitable for improving the breed of horses in congested districts?"

68. Was any information received in the letters as to the character of the local breed of horses?—[illegible] of the letters do contain that.

69. Mr. Wrench.—Was not there a second question as to the character of the stallions in the district?—Yes, the second query—"By what class of stallion are the mares usually served?"

70. The Chairman.—All you have told us was as to the character of the stallion recommended?—Yes.

71. I understood from Mr. Wrench there was a second query as to the existing stallions?—Yes, I am coming to that afterwards. If you do not wish to hear any further letters from [illegible] I will go to the second question.

The Chairman.—I don't think we need have any more of the letters.

Witness.—Well, the second query was—"By what class of stallion are the mares usually served?" And in reply to that Mr. Wm. [illegible], Donegal, writes:—

"Generally by a bad mongrel; [illegible] of this locality, [illegible] for their good qualities, are very much depreciated."

Mr. James [illegible], Donegal, writes:—

"Common mongrel breed, [illegible] of good quality."

Mr. W. [illegible], Donegal, writes:—

"The very worst sort."

Mr. [illegible], Sligo, writes:—

"Ordinary country stallions."

The Earl of Leitrim writes:—

"Common badly bred stallions, except those owned by Lord Leitrim [illegible] Clydesdale [illegible] stallions [illegible] 1887, 1888, and 1889."

Mr. W. Sinclair, J.P., Donegal, writes:—

"Indifferent halfbreds."

Mr. James F. Murphy, J.P., Donegal, writes:—

"Class of stallions are improving of late; mares are generally served by [illegible]."

72. The Chairman.—Where is that (sic)?

Witness.—[illegible], Donegal. (Continuing to read).

Mr. F. C. [illegible], [illegible], writes:—

"[illegible] stallions."

Mr. James McCullagh, J.P., Monaghan, writes:—

"Underbred horses, which attend fairs and markets."

Mr. Wm. [illegible], [illegible], Donegal, writes:—

"Small mountain class."

Mr. Wm. [illegible], J.P., [illegible], writes:—

"Broken-down weedy thoroughbreds."

Mr. John [illegible], [illegible], writes:—"Common bred, horses not fit for anything."

Mr. [illegible], Sligo, writes:—"[illegible] stallions of the most common class [illegible]."

73. Lord Ardilaun.—What part is that from?—[illegible], Sligo.

(Continuing to read.)—Mr. John E. [illegible], [illegible], writes:—"No special class."

Oct. 30, 1896. Mr. W. L. Mills.

Mr. Townsend Trench, Kenmare, writes:—"Hackney horses."

Mr. George O. Malley, Mayo, writes:—"A cross, small, but class, when crossed with Arab or Connemara ponies, giving a roomy, but stout."

Mr. Hugh M'Kenna, [illegible] writes:—"Half-bred Clydesdales."

Mr. John Cuffey, Derry [illegible] writes:—"Half-bred Clydesdale and thoroughbred."

Mr. George Harman, [illegible], Kerry, writes:—"Light thoroughbred stallions and half-bred hunters."

[illegible] (continued) with regard to those the Board sent out Inspectors of their own to make inquiries in different parts, not solely about horses but different matters.

T1. The Chairman.—Agricultural matters?—Yes, but the questions of horses included.

T2. Also cattle improvement?—Yes, as a rule.

T3. And they reported separately?—Yes. Mr. [illegible] Roche, as regards Kenmare, County Kerry, reports:—

"This breed of horses has deteriorated from the use of weedy thoroughbred stallions. The introduction of good Hackney stallions would be very beneficial."

And as regards Cahir, County Kerry:—

"A better class of stallions, Hackney for choice, are very necessary in this district."

Mr. F. G. Townsend [illegible], as regards Fanad, County Donegal, reports:—

"There are a large number of horses in the district, many of them large coarse animals, but few are suitable for the farmers who own them. I believe Lord Leitrim has a Clydesdale stallion at Milford; but it is not a breed at all suitable for the peasantry, even when crossed with their small ponies. A stallion Hackney or Suffolk Punch, located at Rosnakill (a central point and not a "Congested" Electoral Division), would be of immense advantage in the parish."

Major Ruttledge-Fair, as regards Carna, county Galway, reports:—

"There are a good many mares in this district, and I think the village of Kilkieran would be a good centre to place a Hackney the next season. It is only eleven miles from Cashel, where a Welsh stallion stood this season."

And as regards Clifden, county Galway:—

"A small Hackney sire, about 14½ hands, with good bone and action, should next year be sent to this community. There are a large number of mares, good size, in that part of the district, and if another good Welsh sire could be procured, he might be sent there."

And as regards Louisburgh, county Mayo:—

"There are a large number of mares, and one or two Hackney stallions, about 15½ hands, with good bone, would soon effect an immense improvement."

And as regards Renvyle, counties Galway and Mayo:—

"There are a large number of mares in this district, Tourmakeady, where there is a police station, and which is very central, would be a very good place for a Hackney stallion. With the exception of Louisburgh and Ballycroneely, I do not know a district where a good stallion is so much required."

He reports in a few months later, that the horses were well stood:—

"It is almost universally admitted that the introduction of small Hackney sires has been generally appreciated by the people, and the arrangements having, as a rule, been satisfactorily carried out.

"The only district where, as far as I can learn, the scheme has not worked well is at Clonbur, in Co. Galway. The Hackney—'Ensign Bell'—placed there this year, is thought by some, sufficient quality for the class of mares generally found in that district. It may be remembered that Clonbur is within better neighbourhood than most of the congested districts, and there is only seven miles from Ballinrobe, one of the best districts in the West of Ireland, where the services of really good thoroughbred sires have always been available.

"Complaints have also been made as to restrictions imposed in the Letterfrack district. It appears that the services of the stallion should have been available for only a short period each day. The stable where the horse was located being more than three miles from the police barrack was, I presume, the reason why this rule was made. Next year stabling might be secured either in the village or close to Letterfrack, where the police barrack is situate.

"The Arab stallions did not take so well, being considered too weedy and light by the majority of people. The Barb, 'Awfully Jolly,' did very well at Cashel, Co. Galway.

"Two of the very best horse-breeding districts were this year left without stallions, viz., Louisburgh, Co. Mayo, and Ballyconneely, Co. Galway. In both these districts horse-breeding is one of the chief resources of the people. I would recommend that Hackney stallions be sent to both these stations next year. Perhaps a Barb also might be sent to Roundstone, in the Clifden Union, as there are fine thoroughbred mares in that district."

Mr. J. R. Baldry, as regards Ballinskelligs, county Kerry, reports:—

"Horses are small and poorly bred; a Hackney stallion would do much good if stationed in Cloghane."

And as regards Cahirciveen, county Kerry:—

"The ponies are small, badly bred, and much deteriorated. The introduction of a few good Hackney and Arab sires would be advantageous."

And as regards Waterville, county Kerry:—

"The breed of horses is poor and deteriorated from breeding from generations of bad sires. There being no stallion in this district, a Hackney stallion in Loughcurrane Electoral Division, and another at Waterville, in Caherdaniel Electoral Division, would produce a much required improvement in the breed of this and surrounding districts."

Mr. Henry Doran reports as regards Swinford, county Mayo:—

"A good stallion in every village for service to the small farmers' mares would be a boon. The service fees which they could give would not repay anyone for the keep of a good horse. The mares are small and ill-shaped, and of no fixed character. They are not strong enough to mate with thoroughbred stallions unless such be possessed exceptionally strong bone. To improve the way for a special class of horse in this district, I think the most suitable horse would be the best description of what are commonly called 'cob horses,' stout—possessing good bone, good action, and as much breeding as can be got. For many of the mares a Cob or Hackney stallion would be more suitable."

The same gentleman reports as regards the district of Ardnaree, counties of Sligo and Mayo:—

"Previous the service of the many Thoroughbred and non-qualified sires in the district and sometimes good Cob or Hackney stallions, with good quarters and shoulders and action, and plenty bone. There are a great many Cob mares in the district. They have bad quarters and straight shoulders, and are bad movers."

And as regards the district of Ballaghaderreen, counties of Sligo, Mayo, and Roscommon:—

"The mares are of a mixed class, and few of them good. The light weak ones would beget useful stock if crossed with small Suffolk Punch stallions. Others if crossed with a Cob or Hackney stallion would produce good roadsters. The best of the mares should be crossed with thoroughbred horses of good bone and action."

Major D. P. Gaskell, as regards the district of Dunfanaghy, county Donegal, reports:—

"These are a small, useful, active class, wanting only an infusion of good blood to produce a saleable breed. Among them are mares well suited for carrying out the object of the Board in sending a fine Hackney stallion into the district. Unfortunately the distance of these three Electoral Divisions from Carndonagh, where the horse is stationed, appears to be a bar to full advantage being taken of his services. There are only two foals by 'Lord Tennyson' in this district. Both are particularly good specimens. One of them was sold by the breeder to a neighbour for £8 at seven months' old, at the same time that the other ordinary local foals fetched from £4 to £7; the other of the two is now for sale, and the owner says he has refused £8 for him. Whether the small means, poor pastures, ill-fenced enclosures, and rough appliances at the disposal of the small farmers will enable them to rear and manage the high-spirited progeny of the Hackney stallions is a question which the future must determine. Some of the colts have already shown remarkable leaping proclivities and powers. The average price of the yearlings hitherto may here be taken at £6."

77. The Chairman.—Are these all the reports? Witness.—Yes.

78. Do you know how these gentlemen were selected?—Appointed by the Board; two or three of these gentlemen are still in the employment of the Board.

79. I want to know if they would be available as witnesses?—Mr. Redmond Roche is dead, but I think all the others would be available.

80. Would you be able to give us their addresses? —Yes.

81. Is that all you have to say on the subject of the inquiries you have made?—That is all.

82. The Chairman.—Perhaps, before I ask any more questions, it may be convenient for the Members of the Commission to put any question they have to ask on that point.

83. Sir Thomas Esmonde.—I would like to know if you have any means of giving the prices charged for the stallions, the native stallions, before the introduction of the Congested Districts Board's stallions into those districts?—I am afraid not.

84. In one of those letters, I think some reference was made to the price charged for the stallions?—Yes, there was one letter from Lord Lalarin, saying what he charged.

85. And some other gentleman?—The other gentleman was from the county of Cork. He said he charged two guineas, that he could not afford to charge less than two guineas. I believe the usual fee was 10s., 15s., or £1, payable a year after, if the mare foaled.

86. Can you tell us from your own experience, has the price of a stallion anything to say to his popularity? —I don't think the local people know the prices of our stallions.

87. No, but the local stallions?—No, I can't say.

88. The Chairman.—Perhaps, better answers can be got from some other witnesses on that point.

89. Mr. La Touche.—When you were sketching the different congested districts, and discussing them in reference to horse-breeding schemes, do horse-breeding schemes exist in every part of the congested districts? —No. This (map) shows roughly where the horses are stationed.

90. Do not the [illegible] practically cover the whole of the congested districts?—Ridges of mountains and other barriers come in between, and exclude some localities from where the horse is.

91. Mr. [illegible].—What is that district near Roscommon?—That is Woodford.

92. Mr. La Touche.—These statistics you have given us of the number of the horses and the different uses they are put to, were selected from the Registrar-General's statistics, I take it?—Not from any published statistics yet.

93. They are the statistics collected by the Constabulary for the Registrar-General?—They are.

94. Do you know, or can you tell, how many horses, two-years-old and over, are classed as agricultural horses?—No, I can't say.

95. Because there are many horses used for agricultural purposes up to three years old, and then used for [illegible] and [illegible] afterwards, and it does not seem to me that there is any [illegible] by which the Constabulary can decide which horses are purely agricultural, and which horses are intended for [illegible]?—I don't think people in congested districts keep horses for amusement. They only keep them for agricultural purposes.

96. But a man may breed horses for [illegible]?—No, I don't think so.

97. Would he keep [illegible] them for [illegible] only?—He would sell them for profit only.

98. You read for us a number of replies to questions sent out by the Congested Districts Board to gentlemen who reside in the congested districts as to the best sort of stallion for those districts. Did you tell us how many are in favour of the Hackney stallion?—About one half, roughly speaking. I did not enumerate them.

99. Then you read us a number of letters from different gentlemen and it would appear these were not in reply to any circular, but in reply to letters written to them directly?—By Mr. Wrench, some of them.

100. Are those letters in existence?—Yes, they can be got.

101. The Chairman.—It may be well to hand in any letters to which the letters you have already read are answers?—Yes, any [illegible].

102. Mr. La Touche.—Then Mr. [illegible] apparently recommended £300 as the lowest price at which a suitable Hackney stallion could be purchased. Can you tell us the prices that you paid for these subsequently?—Yes, I am coming to that.

103. The Hackney stallions were under 15 hands high?—Of course, that appears from the records.

104. Well then, I see a number of those gentlemen who made statements and wrote letters referred to the former stallions in the district?—Yes.

105. I ask in respect of the replies they speak of the thoroughbred stallions that were in those districts as having [illegible] thoroughbreds, and it does not appear from any of those replies that a respectable thoroughbred horse ever did stand in those districts?—Lord Lalarin had one. He mentions the horse "Conservancy."

106. Mr. [illegible].—No, that is another horse?—Lord [illegible] had one also, "Young Ardchoy" he was called.

107. Mr. [illegible] said he had a thoroughbred "Conservancy," and that his [illegible] was quite full?—Yes, and another gentleman said that there were enough of thoroughbreds in the district.

108. Mr. La Touche.—But it seems to be a general consensus of opinion amongst these gentlemen that the thoroughbred stallion thus [illegible] in

the question was a horse dealers would asked?—Yes, it appeared that the local stallions were of bad and inferior.

109. You mentioned several of the inspectors who were sent round to these different districts. Will you give us any idea of the instructions given to these different inspectors?—Yes, they came to see the Board, and they had conferences with the Board, and with members of the Board separately, and then heading of instructions were given to them.

110. The Chairman.—Can you furnish us with those letters of instructions?—I think I have. The letter was merely a covering letter with a string of queries, but I can furnish the queries quite easily.

111. I suppose they were all the same?—All the same, my lord; it was a circular letter.

112. Mr. La Touche.—It struck me, as rather strange certainly that, although not more than [illegible] the number in the queries as are [illegible] as the [illegible] [illegible] reference in [illegible] made to Hackney stallions in the report of every one of the inspectors, and I wish to know whether the inspectors were instructed previous to this, in favour of the Hackney stallions by the Board?—No.

113. In every case it [illegible] to the [illegible] of Major Gaskell, and in the report of Major Gaskell he speaks of the breeding possibilities of the [illegible].

114. Now, these gentlemen, Mr. Reade, Major Rutledge Fair, Mr. Henry Dixon, Mr. [illegible], Major Gaskell, and the others, did they [illegible] any qualifications connected with agriculture as well as horse breeding?—I should say, and other [illegible] [illegible] [illegible].

115. Do you think that they all possessed knowledge of horse breeding?—Some of them had. Mr. [illegible] Reade and Mr. [illegible], Major Rutledge Fair, I believe, and Mr. Henry Dixon. I cannot speak for Major Gaskell's qualifications personally. Mr. [illegible] I believe is a man who knows horses, but I don't know much about that.

116. Now, as travelling [illegible] these persons, you had [illegible] from the [illegible] of being in the congested districts?—Yes, [illegible] them [illegible]. I think them [illegible].

117. Were all these [illegible] the [illegible] selected by the Board to the [illegible] of queries?—I don't know. I should say not.

118. The Chairman.—Can you find out for us?—Yes, I can easily.

119. Mr. La Touche.—Then you read letters from several other gentlemen from Lord Zetland, Sir [illegible], Sir Walter Gilbey, and others. Do you know how many gentlemen with practical knowledge [illegible] [illegible] horse breeding were consulted in England, and how many in Ireland, for I noticed that all the letters you read were from England?—No, there were letters from Major Rutledge Fair, Lord [illegible], and others.

120. Didn't Major [illegible] say he was ready [illegible] [illegible] to convey the views of Lord [illegible]?—"Hackney stallions, 15.2 to 15 hands high." Major [illegible] says, "I would not [illegible] [illegible] many of them are above that standard." And there were letters from Lord [illegible], Mr. [illegible], [illegible]; Mr. Townsend, Mr. Richard [illegible], the Clerk of the [illegible], and Lord [illegible].

121. Mr. Richard [illegible] has himself a stud of thoroughbred Hackneys?—I think so.

122. The Chairman.—Possibly we can get the definition of a horse for an agricultural horse and a horse for [illegible] better from the Registrar General's Office than from you?—You can.

123. When these gentlemen were [illegible] to report to the Board do you know had the Board [illegible] any conclusion as to the [illegible] [illegible] best to send to the congested districts?—Not that one [illegible] for as far as I know. I think the conclusion was come to after [illegible], at that time, the [illegible] [illegible] of an [illegible] to the Board.

124. Do you know whether these gentlemen were selected chiefly for their knowledge of agriculture in general or for their knowledge of horses in particular?—For [illegible] [illegible].

125. The [illegible]. I [illegible] they were selected, as [illegible] with any special view to horses, but [illegible] of [illegible] [illegible] knowledge of the country and its conditions.

126. They [illegible] not [illegible] known than [illegible] of them were not [illegible] with horses?—Yes.

127. Do you consider yourself capable of saying whether they were or not?—My only means of knowing was their [illegible] reputation, and they have the reputation of knowing about horses.

128. Do you know why Lord [illegible] was not asked for [illegible]?

129. Was it with regard to the [illegible] of Welsh ponies being [illegible] similar to ponies in the congested districts?—I think it was as to Welsh ponies.

130. Do you know whether any [illegible] [illegible] [illegible] [illegible] which class of [illegible] had been [illegible] by the [illegible] and New Forest ponies?—No; I have not heard anything as to [illegible] or New Forest ponies.

131. Then the Board having [illegible] these [illegible], [illegible] I suppose to [illegible] [illegible] [illegible] [illegible] was to [illegible]?—They started with [illegible] [illegible] horses. The first year they had [illegible] [illegible] to the last [illegible].

132. That is in 1892?—Yes. In 1892 they started with [illegible] [illegible], one Cleveland Bay, [illegible], [illegible] [illegible], and the [illegible], 12 Hackneys.

133. That was in 1892?—Yes.

134. How many in all?—[illegible], the first year.

135. How many have you now?—[illegible] [illegible] of fifty, including ponies. Some of the fifty are no longer in the Board's [illegible]. Some were sold, and [illegible] got rid of, some have died, and [illegible]. Altogether the Board bought thirty-six Hackneys. They are [illegible], [illegible], [illegible], [illegible], [illegible], [illegible] II., Lord [illegible], [illegible], [illegible], [illegible], [illegible] II., [illegible], [illegible], [illegible], [illegible], [illegible], [illegible], [illegible] Duke of York, [illegible] I., [illegible], [illegible], [illegible], [illegible], Lord [illegible], [illegible], Lord [illegible], [illegible], [illegible], [illegible], Lord [illegible], [illegible], [illegible], [illegible], [illegible], [illegible], Lord [illegible], [illegible] and [illegible]. These were all the Hackneys that they bought.

How [illegible]?—Thirty-six.

136. [illegible] [illegible] [illegible] of [illegible] [illegible] of the [illegible], [illegible] [illegible] and [illegible] [illegible], were bought by the Board, and [illegible] and [illegible] [illegible] [illegible] [illegible] [illegible]?—Yes.

137. Mr. La Touche.—You [illegible] [illegible] of the Hackneys altogether?—Yes; they are on that list.

138. Chairman.—And there are [illegible] [illegible] including what you bought, bred, and [illegible]?—Yes. There are fifty [illegible] altogether. The [illegible] are —[illegible] Bay, [illegible], [illegible], [illegible] [illegible], [illegible], [illegible], [illegible], [illegible], [illegible], [illegible] and [illegible]; [illegible], [illegible], [illegible], [illegible] IV., and [illegible]; [illegible] [illegible] [illegible] and [illegible]; and two [illegible], [illegible] and [illegible].

139. Can you tell us where the [illegible] were placed?—[illegible] was in [illegible] in 1893 and [illegible] in 1894, and in [illegible] in 1895. [illegible] [illegible] [illegible] in 1892, [illegible] [illegible] in 1893, and [illegible] in 1894; he was in [illegible] in [illegible] [illegible], and was in [illegible] [illegible] in 1893, and [illegible] in 1894. [illegible] [illegible] was in [illegible] in 1892 and 1893, and in [illegible] in 1895. [illegible] [illegible] in [illegible] in 1893, was in [illegible] in 1893, and in [illegible] in 1894, 1895, and 1896. [illegible] III. was in [illegible] in

1893, in Kilmacrenan in 1888 and 1894, and in Tyrone in 1889 and 1896. Lord Gough was in Letterkenny in 1891, in Carrigart in 1893 and 1894, and in Glenties in 1895 and 1896. [illegible] was in Dunglow in 1893 and 1895, and in Carndonagh in 1894. Lord [illegible] was in Belmullet in 1893, and at Achill Sound in 1895. [illegible] II. was in Swinford in 1891, 1893, and 1894, and in Kenmare in 1896. King [illegible] was in Oughterard in 1893, and in Cahirciveen in 1893 and 1894. Lord Templemore was in Carndonagh in 1892, in Ardara in 1893, 1894, and 1895, and in Letterkenny in 1896. Highgate Performer was in Clifden in 1893 and 1894, and in Dungloe in 1895. Hercules II. was in Belmullet in 1893 and 1896, at Achill Sound in 1895, and in Castlerea in 1894. Guy Earl III. was in Bantry in 1893 and 1894, and in Swinford in 1895 and 1896. Earl of [illegible] was in Carndonagh in 1893 and 1894. Flying Flemming was in Dunfanaghy in 1894, 1895, and 1896. Lord [illegible] Duke of [illegible] was at Belmullet in 1893 and 1896. Chancellor I. was in Letterkenny in 1895, and in Clifden in 1896. Maidstone Stallion was in Donegal in 1894. [illegible] Performer was in Glenties in 1895, and in Louisburgh in 1896. [illegible] Molino was in Skibbereen in 1895 and 1896. Lord Lexington was in Killarney in 1894, in Donegal in 1895, and in Carndonagh in 1896. Young Dane was in Clifden and Letterkenny in 1893. Lord Rupert was in Newport in 1895, and in Clifden in 1896. Lord Sheridan was in Letterkenny in 1894, and in Newport in 1895. Maryfield was in Newport in 1896. Clarendon was in Belmullet in 1893 and 1896. Derwent was in Achill in 1894, and at Achill Sound in 1895. [illegible] Duke was in Bantry in 1895, and in Kenmare in 1896. Galloway Performer was in Louisburgh in 1895. Flockbury Cup was in Clifden in 1893. Lord Middleton was in Carndonagh in 1893, and in Carrigart in 1894. Sir Teller was in Dunfanaghy in 1895, and in Ballyshannon in 1894; and Gentry was in Ardara in 1892. These are the Hackneys. As to the others, the Cleveland Bay, Blue Ruin(?), was in Kilkenny in 1893 and 1894, and then he was sold. The Brick, Arabella(?), was in Clifden in 1893 and 1895, in Carrigart in 1894, and at Achill Sound in 1895 and 1896. All Bele was stationed in Belmullet in 1893; he was only hired for the season. Thoroughbreds were stationed in Achill in 1893, and were in Achill again in 1894, and in Belmullet in 1895 and 1896. [illegible] was in Clifden in 1893, in Belmullet in 1895, and in Dunfanaghy in 1894. Electricity was in Louisburgh in 1893 and 1895, and in Carrigart in 1893 and 1894. [illegible] was stationed in Letterkenny in 1893, and was there also in 1894, and again in Oughterard in 1895 and 1896. Signaus IV. was in Ballyconneely in 1893 and 1894, and in Rath, Achill Island, in 1895 and 1896. Prince Llewellyn was in Oughterard in 1893, in Rath Island in 1894 and 1895, and in Carndonagh in 1896. Welsh Tommy was at Achill Sound in 1893, in Swinford in 1894, and in Killorglin in 1895 and 1896; and Mountain was in Carrigart in 1893, in Tralee(?) in 1894, and in Clare Island in 1895 and 1896. The thoroughbred St. Aidan was the Good Prince, where he mixed with ponies, and Guide Rein was stationed in Bantry in 1896.

140. Do you know how the selections are made as to particular horses being stationed in particular places?—It is discussed by the Land Committee of the Horse Committee of the Board. They make up a list of places, and then they consider and discuss amongst themselves where to put each horse, and then the list is drawn up, and put in print.

141. Upon the subject of selecting the breed of the horse, do they decide upon that themselves?—That is all discussed at the Committee meeting.

142. That is without any reference to the wishes of the people of the locality?—Oh yes; the wishes of the people of the locality largely come into it; people write letters.

143. The horses of different breeds are stationed at the same station in the same locality?—Yes, we have a Hackney and an Arab stationed in the same place some years.

144. Would you have a Hackney and a thoroughbred?—At Bantry, yes. The Hackney was taken the past year.

145. Mr. Le Terrier.—But have you a Hackney and a thoroughbred standing in the same place?—No; the only place where a thoroughbred is is in Bantry.

146. The Chairman.—Then the Board has had no direct opportunity of seeing whether a Hackney or thoroughbred would be preferred by having them both in the same place at the same time?—The only place where a thoroughbred is put is in the country in at Bantry.

147. Mr. Watson.—Do you know how there has been any request from the people of Bantry with regard to the thoroughbred?—I don't remember.

148. Mr. Clarke.—Do you know why Bantry was fixed on?—I really forget. I am only there in an official capacity; I don't know anything about horses, and I don't take note of such considerations very much.

149. The Chairman.—Do you know the number of services given by the stallions?—Roughly several 172 mares.

150. Lord Ardilaun.—In the four years?—Yes. That is an average of forty-three per annum.

151. Lord Rathdonnell.—Would it be possible to give from the year 1893 downwards the services by each breed, by the Hackneys, the Arabs, and the other sires?—I can give the total number for each year; they have not always stood in the same place. I can give the total number of Hackney services for the whole of 1893, 1895, and so on, but I have not the return made out in the way referred to. It is quite easy to prepare it. I have here the total number of services for each horse since he was acquired by the Board, and then I have the average number for each season.

152. Could you not take the Hackneys for 1893 and say how many services there were of Hackneys in 1893, how many of Arabs, how many of thoroughbreds, and so on?—That is one way to get at it, and I can easily have it for you.

153. You see we want the number of services of each class of horse for each year, that is, Arab, Clydesdale, Barbs, Hackneys?—Yes, I can easily prepare that.

154. The Chairman.—You could let us have that information?—Yes.

155. Lord Ardilaun.—Where Arabs and Hackneys were standing together, which were preferred?—My recollection is that they both filled. I am pretty sure they both filled.

156. Mr. Green.—Can you give me the prices paid for the thoroughbreds?—No.

157. The Chairman.—There is no objection to give us the figures as you have got them, Mr. Micks?

158. Mr. Watson.—You have not the individual services for any stallion?—No, I have the total number over all the years and the average for each year.

159. What Lord Ardilaun would like is a return where two horses stood together, a Hackney and an Arab, a return of the services given by each horse?—Very well.

160. The Chairman.—What are the prices charged for services?—I can give the total number of the services. The number of services at 5s. was 5,590, at 10s. 147, and at £1 the number was 209, making a total of 5,978.

161. What makes the variation in the charges?—It is the poverty of the small farmers.

162. You charge 5s. to some and £1 to others for the same horse?—Yes. The 5s. fee amounts to 93½ per cent. of the whole.

[illegible] 163. LORD ARDILAUN.—Is it [illegible] by reductions?—Yes. The 10s. fees are 24 per cent. of the whole and the £1 fees are ever given are 4 per cent. In addition there are 132 free services as prizes for horses at local shows. The total number of services would be 6,043. A further number of 1,344 has been served this year up to the present, and then with the 5,275 up to the end of 1895, the 1,344 during the present year, and 112 free services, make 6,043 as a total, and of these 4,392 services were Hackney services.

164. MR. [illegible].—Up to the end of last year the services were 5,799 taking the free services?—Yes, and of these 4,398 were by Hackneys.

165. THE CHAIRMAN.—As I understand, the same fee is charged to the owners of mares, whether for the services of a Hackney or pony or [illegible] or thoroughbred?—That is so. This year the Board in some cases fixed a higher fee—a 10s. fee in some places—specially where they were sending a very good horse, but I think as far as I can judge the Board are not inclined to continue the higher fee.

166. There is no definite rule on the subject?—Yes. The rule is that a poster is sent out with each horse, and full particulars are given in the posters.

167. There is no definite rule of the Board as to the fees charged, and it may be varied?—It is fixed for each horse and it is practically the fee every horse with two or three exceptions hardly worth taking into account.

168. Have you anything further to tell us on this point?—I think not.

169. This system has been practically in operation since 1892?—The Board started in 1891. The Board began in the autumn of 1891, and they had 17 horses out for the season of 1892.

170. Are you in a position to give the Commission any information as to the general results of the working of your Board in your opinion?—The Board issued a series of queries to 31 people in the congested districts and a summary has been made of their evidence, a short summary. (Reading.) "The first query is:—At what ages do small farmers in the districts usually dispose of the foals or horses which they breed? The replies to this question indicate that in the western or Connaught districts, it is usual to sell in foals of from six to eight months of age. On rare occasions sale is deferred until one year or one year and a half, but this is [illegible] confined to large [illegible] or to those who are in better circumstances than the ordinary small holder. Munster is said to be [illegible] from [illegible] of [illegible] farmers who retain their young stock till two or three years of age. In the north-west or Donegal district six out of eight reports [illegible] the usual age for sale as being at least one year. Sales, as foals of six months old, are, however, not infrequent, while [illegible] farmers are stated occasionally to keep colts till two or three years of age [illegible]. No explanation is given to show why this [illegible] [illegible] [illegible] in the age of sale, but it may be inferred that there is considerable difference in the ability to keep [illegible] by the occupiers of land in the north-west. Not only may this difference reveal itself in more ample means but in the extent of land occupied by farmers, [illegible] to the holdings proper or the area of [illegible]. In that [illegible] sales usually take place from one to two years of age. [illegible] and [illegible] sales are [illegible], and these may be [illegible] either to [illegible] poverty in the one case or prosperity in the other. Summarising the evidence, as received from the whole area of congested districts, it is quite apparent that the general rule is to sell, either as foals after weaning or as yearlings. Those who retain till yearling or over three years old, although they may occupy land in congested districts, can hardly be described as in circumstances constituting, as individuals, a portion of a congested population. They are [illegible], but not of it, and their system of farming and general mode of life differs materially from that which pertains to the small and very poor farmers, for whose benefit the scheme was originally instituted."

171. THE CHAIRMAN.—Were these queries sent out this year?—Yes.

172. Are they sent out each year?—No; this year was the first season. The next query and the replies were as follows:—(Reading) Query II. (A.) What prices have been obtained by small farmers who have used the Board's stallions for the past few years for the produce of these stallions? (B.) How do these prices compare with the prices obtained during the same periods by similar classes of farmers for horses not bred by the Board's stallions? Five reports state that the foals by the Board's stallions will realise no better or very little better than those got by ordinary country stallions. In Clifden and Roundstone districts the absence of increased value appears to be especially marked, but it must be observed, that the reports in these instances refer to the produce of the Barb rather than of the Hackney sire. In some parts of Donegal the stock by the Clydesdale or half-bred Clydesdale is said to be as popular and valuable as that by the Board's sires, the reason assigned being that the Clydesdale stock is the more fit for work. Fully every other district the use of the Hackney, Barb or Arab has resulted in an increased value of produce. In few reports the increased value is specified in figures, but described in modified terms, such as "a slight gain," "a gain," "a good deal." With these exceptions a substantial increase in price is reported. The price of foals from six to eight months old has increased from 10s. to as much as £5, irrespective of the saving on service fee amounting to, say, 10s. For one and a half year olds, an increase varying from £2 to £6 is recorded. A fair average would be £3 10s., to which must again be added the saving on service fee, making a total increase of £4. Two year olds, by the Board's sires, where such have been sold, have realised from £4 to £6 over the ordinary horses, exclusive of the saving in service fee, and this increase in value continues to augment with age, the [illegible] reference to three year olds, from £8 to £12 is mentioned as having been gained in the selling price. The evidence in point of increased value is so divergent in character, that it does not afford material for any precise comparison or statement. The results of a few (in most reports very few) individual sales can hardly be taken as sufficient to form a key to the whole position. But there appears to be no room for doubt that in [illegible] of the districts where the Board has introduced sires, the value of young horses, whether sold as foals, yearlings, two year olds or three year olds, has been very considerably increased to those who have made use of the new stallions. In Connemara there seems to have been among the dealers a combined and successful attempt to undervalue or ignore the improving effects of the new blood, which, in many instances, such as at Ashill Bonnet and Kenly, the Board's stallions would appear to have left but little behind them. It is important to observe that the willingness on the part of purchasers, to pay more for the new type of horses, is as well defined for two and three year olds as for foals and yearlings—rather more so if anything."

173. THE CHAIRMAN.—As regards the price of foals from six to eight months?—The price has increased from 10s. to as much as £5, irrespective of the saving on service fee amounting to, say, 10s., that would be from £1 to £5 10s.

174. Is £5 a common price to give?—I believe there were some exceptional prices for some of the produce of the Barb "Awfully Jolly."

175. Are the Commissioners to take it that the prices increased generally to this extent?—No. £5 is a very large price?—It is.

176. LORD ARDILAUN.—You say a horse [illegible] was got from the Barb?—Yes. I think there was [illegible]

English [illegible] for [illegible] foals. It is a celebrated [illegible] [illegible].

177. The Chairman.—[illegible] mean to say that the former price was 10s. and the present price was £5? —Yes. The foals used to run from about £3 or £4 to £5. The paragraph is—"The price of foals from six to eight months old has increased from 10s.," it should be by 10s., "or as much as £5, irrespective of the saving on service fee amounting to, say 10s."

178. It does not seem very clear. The increase was not from 10s. to the present price of £5. That is not what you mean?—No.

179. How many queries were there?—Five. That was in the answer to the second. The third query is (reading)—"Query III.—Is the demand for the Board's stallions increasing or otherwise? Of [illegible] replies to Query III., [illegible] are in the affirmative; [illegible] in the negative; [illegible] are in the indefinite; one says demand is stationary." The replies apparently refer to the whole period which has elapsed since the commencement of the scheme, and when considering them, it is well to recollect that once the limit of mares is reached, there can be no further increase. This has taken place in many districts, and the fact may have given rise to misapprehension as regards increase or diminution [illegible]. There can be no doubt, however, that the dimensions of service fees generally made [illegible] by the Board customers, while, in a few instances, the stallion has either failed in his duties or, for some other cause, failed to please, and accordingly lost custom and credit. The lowness of fee is frequently quoted as an important factor in bringing mares to the Board's stallion. Query IV.—Are local farmers disposed to retain colts bred by the Board's stallion for breeding purposes? The replies indicate a distinct desire on the part of those who can afford it, or who have sufficient land and other necessities for young horses, to retain those by the Board's stallions. Many are compelled, [illegible] think [illegible] by reason of poverty, to sell what they would otherwise keep. At the same time there are some without any principle in breeding, who have no doubt sold when they might well make [illegible]. Query V.—What [illegible] (if any) in the number of inferior stallions has followed the action of the Board? From the evidence, it would appear that the presence of the Board's stallions has [illegible] most markedly on the number of ordinary and inferior sires in the congested districts. [illegible] the old breed of horses is [illegible] out. In other localities they have been eliminated. Elsewhere they have been sold or left the country. In some localities they no longer exhibit. They get less mares and are made to do farm work. Their fees are greatly reduced in order to compete with the Board's horses. Data showing the number of stallions for the years 1891-96 could probably be obtained from some reliable source, and such evidence would be superior to the replies given to query V."

180. Those are all the questions?—Those are all the questions.

After the adjournment.

181. The Chairman.—I think you mentioned some stallions as being sold?—I did, my lord, some of them were sold.

182. What were they?—"Rokeby," Hackney, "[illegible]," Hackney, "Zion," Hackney, "King [illegible]," Hackney, "Highgate Performer." I am not sure that he was not a [illegible] horse, but he ceased to belong to the Board.

183. Do you know why they were sold?—A couple were sold because they were not considered suitable, [illegible] and [illegible] of them I think the Board sold to advantage, getting a good price for them.

184. Do you know to whom they were sold, what [illegible] of them?—The Indian Government.

185. They went out of the country?—Yes, to India.

186. They all went out of the country?—They went to India.

187. What became of the others?—They were sold at a low price.

188. Did they remain in the country?—I don't think any of them remained in this country. Just before the adjournment I gave a general summary of the evidence as regards the prices that were obtained for the young horses produced by the Board's stallions. I can give the names of the people whose evidence is summarised, and I can give the prices that they mention as having been got for the young horses if you wish. Mr. [illegible], District Inspector, Ardara, County Donegal, says that the young ones sold at about six months old from the Board's horses fetch from £5 to £8, except about Glenclomakill, a parish in his district, where the prices have not been so good on account of the smallness of the animals; £3 10s. was the highest price ever got before by the ordinary foals of the country. At [illegible], Mr. [illegible], District Inspector, reports that the horses sold at one and a half years fetch from £8 to £18, the produce of half-bred Clydesdales used to realise about the same. At Carrigart Mr. [illegible] states that the young ones from the Board's horses go from £7 to £10 10s. in 1893.

189. Lord Enniskillen.—What age?—About one and a half years old, and that these are higher prices; the demand for them much higher than the produce of the country stallions. Mr. [illegible], [illegible], says that for yearlings the Board's go from £4 10s. to £7, [illegible] two years old £8 10s. to £19, or exceptional [illegible] up to £14, for two and a half year olds £14 to £17, and sometimes as high as £30. For ordinary bred foals of similar ages prices are about 20 per cent. under those obtained from Hackney sires, except [illegible] half-bred Clydesdales that sell well, as they are ready for work early. The produce of Hackneys are about £3 on an average higher than those of country stallions. Mr. Boyle, Dunglow, states that the [illegible] there are generally sold under a year, and for year olds and under, the prices for the Board's young ones is about £5 to £9, and for the ordinary ones from £3 to £4. Major Purdon, [illegible].—Foals sold at six months fetch from £5 to £10, the produce of the Board's horses; [illegible] foals from other stallions [illegible] from £3; [illegible] not say to what height they go. Mr. [illegible], [illegible], county Donegal.—Animals sold at a year or a year and a half old, for yearlings from £6 to £8 during the last three years; for one and a half years old £10 to £18, ordinary local country horses, yearlings, £3 to £7, one and a half years old, £5 to £11. [illegible].—Mr. [illegible] says there is very little difference in the price of all foals; in a few instances the prices for produce of Board's stallions have exceeded the usual price for other breeds. Ballinamore.—Mr. J. [illegible] says: Very little difference in price. Mr. [illegible], [illegible].—Hackney [illegible] foals and foals by Board's stallions sold at about six months old fetched from £5 10s. to £8 10s., [illegible] £7 10s.; [illegible] £5 to £5 10s. During the same period foals got by Board's stallions fetched £4 10s. to £7 10s., £6 being an average price. [illegible], county Mayo.—Mr. [illegible] says foals by the Welsh cob "[illegible]" averaged £3 15s., from local stallions £3, foals by the [illegible] "[illegible] [illegible]" averaged £3 5s., but from local stallions for that age, six months old, £2 10s. Mr. J. Hughes, [illegible], near [illegible], county Galway, says in 1893 the Board's young horses fetched from £4 to £5 10s. for foals, and those by country bred stallions £3 to £4, in later years £5 to £8 for foals and ordinary country stallions, produce about the same prices. There is a note to this witness's report "Owing to the greater number being sold at Connemara [illegible] the prices of foals have varied little. In latter years the Board's horses were Hackneys, and sales at foals have seldom occurred." Mr. [illegible], Clifden, £3 10s. to £4 the average price for foals, and from local breed the foals fetch £3 10s. to £4. Mr. O'Hara, [illegible], foals six months old from Board horses £4 to

C 2

£1 10s., at one year to one and a half £3 to £7, foals from "Welsh Tommy" fetched £3 10s. He does not give any particulars about the local horses. Mr. Moore, Newport, county Mayo, says the local horses sell at about £1 a head under the Hackney foals. Mr. Sullivan, [illegible], for one and a half years old prices ranging up to £13. Mr. [illegible] Board's horses, average price for one and a half year olds got by Board's horses, £7. Mr. J. Baker, [illegible], for foals fifteen months old, £6 to £9 freely got, from the Board's stallions, from local stallions [illegible] lower than the produce of the Board's stallions. Mr. [illegible], Dingle, average price for one and a half year olds from Board's stallions, £12; £5 to £8 from other stallions. Mr. Watson, [illegible], [illegible] sold £30 and upwards at three years old, three year old colts of no special pedigree £12 to £14. Mr. Wilson, [illegible], Kenmare, price of foals vary from £6 to £10 at one and a half years old down to six months, prices for yearlings got by Board's stallion slightly lower; he does not mention the amount. [illegible], Mr. [illegible] [illegible] by "[illegible] II." sold for £5 10s., and one and a half year old by "[illegible] II." sold for £8 10s. in [illegible], 1896. These particulars are given in those several cases, the names of the buyer and seller is given, I can hand in that.

190. The Chairman.—I don't think you told us what was the price given for the Hackney stallions?—That will be the next head of my evidence, my lord.

191. I should like you to take it as you have got it, as far as you can. The return of the horses in congested districts for the year 1896 shows a distinct increase over the number of horses in preceding years in those districts. There are eight congested district counties, and in eleven of them [illegible] the number of horses [illegible]—are these counties entirely in the congested districts?—No; there is one county very little in the congested districts—Co. Cork—and there there is a falling off; it is the only district that is partially congested where there has been a falling off. In the remainder of Ireland—the non-congested counties—in eight cases the [illegible] and in sixteen there has been a decrease.

192. Lord Ardilaun.—That table refers to the whole county, not the congested parts?—Yes. I have not got them separately, but in the counties which are partly congested all, except one, have increased; in the case of [illegible] in the counties which are not congested there has been a decrease in the case of two [illegible] have decreased, the remainder has increased.

193. The Chairman.—Can you not hand in the Agricultural Statistics?—The agricultural statistics—a published return. I am now about to give, my lord, some particulars about the expenditure that the Board has incurred on horse-breeding schemes from 1st August, 1891, to 31st March in this year. The expenditure is divided into two classes—capital expenditure and annual maintenance. Capital expenditure is as follows:—For the purchase of forty-two stallions, £[illegible] 1s. 2d.

194. Have you got the average?—No, my lord, this is not a return exactly, it is a form of account. For the purchase of eight mares, £1,[illegible]. There is also no expenditure for mares, and also for donkeys; I can take off the amount spent on ponies and donkeys later on.

195. Lord Rathdonnell.—The number of mares?—Eight Hackney mares.

196. Lord Ardilaun.—What is Spanish donkeys?—Two Spanish donkeys, £[illegible] 1s. 3d. Then there are a variety of items in the account which don't exactly refer to the horse breeding; I have here an item which was used for the pony, a stallion pony, introduced to the island of [illegible] [illegible] horses for the Stud Farm was £[illegible], and these [illegible] foals were bought in the country, last year, for experimental purposes, they were the produce of the Board's horses, and some foals were bought to enable [illegible] Board [illegible] how they turned out.

197. What was paid for them?—£75 10s.

198. Lord Rathdonnell.—What year was that?—They were bought in different years.

199. What is the oldest one?—Three, I think.

200. Sir T. Esmonde.—Where are they kept now?—At [illegible], county Dublin, on the Dublin and Bray line.

201. Then the eight mares purchased, are they there also?—They are also at the Stud Farm; the Board besides hired a couple of stallions. Hire of stallions, £129 3s. 8d.

202. Mr. La Touche.—In one year?—No; the total hiring, carriage, and maintenance of stallions, £910 13s. 2d. Then the cost of the buildings, cost of Stud Farm and buildings, £4,100, furniture, £65 11s., implements, £175; transmission of water supply, £123; fencing, 19; fitting up stables in the country, £678. Total capital expenditure, £[illegible] odd. Now the annual expenditure is divided into four columns, 1892–93, 1893–94, 1894–95, 1895–96. I can give these separately or the total of the four. Transport expenses, for bringing the stallions to and from the Stud Farm to the country, 1892–93, £[illegible] odd, 1893–94, £[illegible]; 1894–95, £[illegible]; 1895–96, £[illegible], total, £976. Keep in the country and forage while at the central Stud Farm, £[illegible], £1,[illegible], £1,[illegible], £1,[illegible], total, £[illegible].

203. The Chairman.—I suppose the amount you have kept about the same?—I can give the amount per head separately. I have separate columns for the shoeing, veterinary fees, medicine, &c., £[illegible], £[illegible], £[illegible], £[illegible], total £[illegible]. Wages of managers and grooms, £[illegible], £1,274, £1,183, £1,300, total, £[illegible]. In the instance where the stallions are in the country stations, these are performed by the Royal Irish Constabulary and sergeants, and remuneration is paid to them as follows:—£[illegible], £[illegible], £[illegible], £[illegible], total £1,322 odd. For the Stud Farm, that is the time where the horses are kept in 1893–94, £7[illegible] 3s. 6d., that was the first year. Rent and taxes, 1893–94, £[illegible]; 1894–95, £[illegible]; 1895–96, £[illegible], total £[illegible]. Insurance on horses, 1892–93, £[illegible]; 1893–94, £[illegible]; 1894–95, £[illegible]; 1895–96, £[illegible] odd, total £[illegible] odd. Coal, oil, &c., £[illegible] 15s., £[illegible], £[illegible], £[illegible], total £[illegible]. For inspection of mares for serving, advertising the horses, insurance of horses, &c., £[illegible], £[illegible], £[illegible], £[illegible], total £[illegible] 3s. 7d.

204. What do you mean by inspection of mares?—Before a mare is served I believe she has to be examined to see whether she is suitable.

205. By a veterinary surgeon?—Generally I believe a District Inspector of Police, and sometimes a veterinary surgeon.

206. Sir T. Esmonde.—Then if the mare is not sound?—She is not allowed to be served, I understand.

207. That is the [illegible] provision?—I believe so.

208. The Chairman.—Is the Inspector of Police paid a fee for examining the mare?—I don't think he is; he is just paid his [illegible]; he gets a small lump sum for his services in each year that would be included.

209. Mr. [illegible].—Then the mares that are served by these particular stallions have all of them passed, they are all examined?—They are always examined.

210. Lord Ardilaun.—As to soundness or as to shape or suitability?—I am afraid that question had better be asked of someone else, but they are examined.

211. Sir T. Esmonde.—Can you say are the Board's stallions examined every year by the same veterinary surgeon?—Oh, yes, there is a highly qualified man constantly there, one of the veterinary surgeons of Dublin, Mr. Daly, visits the Stud Farm very often.

212. Are the stallions passed sound every season?—I cannot say, but I know they are carefully

being looked after by Mr. [illegible]. Thus the total annual maintenance expenditure, 1891–93, was £2,[illegible]; 1893–94, £4,2[illegible]; 1894–95, 3,[illegible]; for 1895–96, £4,15[illegible]; total expenditure on maintenance, £14,[illegible]; gross total expenditure on both capital and maintenance, £31,[illegible] 5s. 11d. [illegible]

[illegible]

213. The Chairman.—Do you know anything [illegible]

214. Lord [illegible].—You said £14,[illegible] [illegible] From 8th August, 1891, to the 31st March of this year, the end of our financial year.

215. The Chairman.—[illegible]

[illegible]

217. Could you furnish us with the **actual price** that was given for each one?—Yes.

[illegible]

224. In making this comparison, [illegible]

225. I mean in that comparison based on the [illegible]

226. Lord Ardilaun.—And in **the other way you** charge interest on capital?—And **their proportion of** rent, [illegible]

227. The Chairman.—[illegible]

[illegible]

Oct. 18, 1895. Mr. W. L. Micks.

240. The Chairman.—Are you in a position to say at all why the Board did anything, or can you only tell us what they did?—Well, I heard some of the discussions.

241. Mr. La Touche.—I was going to ask you the number of mares served by each horse, but I believe the subscriptions are not very generally full?—Most of them were, they run from about 60 the lowest I saw to something over 60 or 70, yes, 77 is the highest.

242. Lord Ardilaun.—What regulations being full?—Different horses have different numbers assigned to them according to age and other considerations.

243. Mr. La Touche.—Then you say the total number of services as far as I take it up to 1895 was either 3,798 or 3,042, I forget which. Do you know anything about the number of foals?—Nothing.

244. Have you any returns from the District Inspectors of Constabulary as to the fruitfulness of these horses, the number of foals left by them?—I have not got any official returns about these things at all, I think the number has been reported, but I have not any record.

245. You said that a thoroughbred horse stood at Bantry, it was the only place the Board sent a thoroughbred horse to, I think that there are Hackney sires sent to the same district?—Not at the same time.

246. Could you tell me where was the nearest?—I suppose, Castletown or Schull would be the places where they had a Hackney?—Yes.

247. How far is it from Bantry to Schull?—I don't know.

248. Mr. Wrench.—Did it at all come before you that there was an application from the people of Bantry to send back a Hackney instead of the thoroughbred horse?—No, that did not come before me.

249. Mr. La Touche.—Do you know what price "Uncle Sam" stood at?—No, or "St. Aidan," but I could ascertain it at once.

250. Lord Ardilaun.—Did you not say that all the stallions stood, to all intents and purposes, at the same price?—Oh, the fee is the same; I thought it was the price Mr. La Touche was asking.

251. The Chairman.—You said they all stood at the same price, and the price was fixed according to the valuation of the tenant?—Yes. Ninety-one per cent. are 5s. fee.

252. Lord Ardilaun.—A man can have a choice of a sire at that fee bringing to his mare?—Yes, but he is practically limited to the sire that is next to him.

253. The Chairman.—The fee charged for the thoroughbred stallion at Bantry would be the same as the fees charged for Hackney stallions to similar persons in their districts?—Yes.

254. Lord Ardilaun.—Varying according to valuation?—Yes.

255. Mr. La Touche.—You are sure of that?—I am sure of it; if it was not so I would have heard it.

256. The Chairman.—It would make no difference to the man whether he sent his mare to the thoroughbred at Bantry or to the Hackney at Schull?—It was a thing he might be obliged to do, but I think it would depend on the parish district he was in. For convenience the farmers are inspected according to the parish districts.

257. Lord Ardilaun.—Do you mean the parish would practically recommend a sire?—Oh, no, but it is the same as if a man was in one parish he would then get the service of the parish horse.

258. Would he be allowed to go to any place else outside that district?—He might. I never heard the question raised, but they keep fairly to the district.

259. The Chairman.—The Commission wants to know whether an individual farmer has a free choice whether he would send his mare to a Hackney or a thoroughbred horse, as far as prices are concerned, but as far as the horse is concerned he may have no opportunity of sending it to the horse that he likes.

260. Lord Ardilaun.—The districts to which the horses are sent—how are the horses selected to be sent into particular districts?—They were selected by the committee of the Board who dealt with the matter, they discussed with themselves "where shall we send such and such a horse, he has been two years in such a place, where shall we send him now."

261. Mr. La Touche.—It appears, taking it all round, to be the general practice in the Congested Districts Board to sell the produce at less than two years old?—Yes, generally, I think they may say under a year.

262. Have you any idea what becomes of these horses?—No, I cannot follow them, the dealers go and buy them, I don't know what they do with them.

263. They are not retained in the Congested Districts?—Oh, certainly not, except some few, they are taken off in large quantities.

264. And the result of the introduction of these horses has been according to your report that the value of these young animals under two years old has increased, and you wrote that stallions stood in these districts at smaller fees before the introduction of the Congested Boards' horses?—I think the fees were higher, they only had not to pay at the time was the only thing, they had to pay the following year.

265. And you have got no evidence as to the value of the sires displaced by the Congested Districts?—Oh, yes, I have a variety of accounts about them which, they were worthless.

266. A description of them, but not anything touching the prices paid for them?—No.

267. Well, you say of the stallions that were sold, some remain in Ireland. Then you go on to some reports as to the improved price of horses, and that many of these persons stated that prices were better now than the prices of animals got by half-bred Clydesdales. What year did these reports deal with?—They dealt with all the years, they were obliged to deal with every year from the start.

268. They were sent in this year?—They were sent in this year.

269. I don't know whether they specified that the prices had been gradually increasing or that they had been from the moment that the Congested Districts Board began to get foals there that the prices of foals and horses increased?—They became increased in some districts.

270. A gentleman writes from Bantry and says that the average price of the yearling, I think, was from £13 10s., an enormous price, and then you say that the number of farmers in counties which contain congested districts has increased. Is there any evidence to show that they have increased in parts of those counties that are congested?—No, they are not divided, but the proportion is very much larger. For instance, in the County Mayo a portion is very largely congested, in Donegal a very large proportion is congested, and in Galway a large proportion is congested.

271. Then we come to the expenditure. The average cost of these stallions was about £190, and you say that the Board have bought two foals at an average price of a little over £2. What became of those foals?—They are at present at the Stud Farm at Slane.

272. How old are they?—I think the oldest is over three.

273. Have none of them been sold?—None of them sold as far as I know.

274. Do you know how any of them have been offered for sale?—I don't think any have been offered for sale. I think some have been broken.

275. Are they valued in the assets of the Congested Districts Board?—Oh, they are, of course; I don't think there is anything more than their cost price put down, until they are actually sold.

276. Lord Enniskillen.—Do you know the cost price?—Oh, yes, I gave it, £23 10s.

277. That was the average?—No, that was the total for two foals.

278. Mr. La Touche.—There is an item that you have read in the annual expenditure, the inspection of mares, &c.; you said that the District Inspector inspected these mares previous to their being passed?—Before they get the service cards.

279. Are you sure that you are correct in saying that?—Well, that is my belief.

280. Do they inspect the mares do you know, to judge of the fitness of the animal to be served, or to judge of the qualifications that the owner of the mare has?—Well, I cannot say—that witness will be able to tell you that distinctly.

281. You said the average cost of the stallion was £150 per annum; what annual charge do you put for depreciation of capital cost made there?—Is the amount spent on the horse?

282. No, but the annual depreciation in value of the horse?—I know that cost price there, the horses may either increase in value, or depreciate in value; there is no certainty of knowing that.

283. Don't you write off something for depreciation each year?—We could not write it off, we might have to add something for the additional value.

284. My experience of horses is they don't show much increase in value?—Some of our horses have distinctly increased in value. If his produce becomes well thought of, he will increase in value as a pound.

285. Well, you don't, in fact, take anything off for that?—No.

286. Lord Ardilaun.—Is the depreciation on capital, is that depreciation on horses or on buildings?—No; it is buildings. Practically our capital expenditure was caused over the buying, so far as buildings are concerned we have a number of them still, when coming on, we have been steadily moving and some making on.

287. Mr. La Touche.—Surely you charge interest on the capital invested in the horses, £1,000?—We have no such capital account under audit regulations.

288. At any rate you don't think it is necessary to charge such interest with the percentage of depreciation. In that manner, one by the result of the sale of the horses that you have sold since the Board has been in existence?—On a couple of horses we got a substantial increase; on a couple we lost.

289. You said [illegible]?—Did I say twelve? I think they were sold.

290. It seems to me that if you invested £16,935, that you ought to charge [illegible] somewhere or [illegible] with some interest on that?—I don't exactly understand in what way. Do you mean for bookkeeping purposes?

291. Lord Ardilaun.—No; the sinking of the capital?—If we were providing an account such as that, we should have to do so.

292. Mr. La Touche.—The total expenditure in the scheme the Board has been working on capital and maintenance of the horse breeding establishment has been £31,000?—£31,[illegible].

293. And the result has been that 8,[illegible] mares have been served?—Or, including the present year, over 9,000.

294. And you claim that by the action of the Congested Districts Board's horse breeding scheme you have improved the value of young horses—some horses say £5 or £6 per head, and other people say up to £8 or £9 a head. Is not that the gist of the report?—Yes; that is what it comes to.

295. Taking an average of £5 a head and assuming that 8,000 [illegible] produced 6,000 foals you have increased the [illegible] in these congested districts to the extent of £30,000?—Yes, that is assuming they are all sold as foals. The increase would be greater the older the young one is when sold.

296. I take it that the enormous majority of horses are sold as foals?—Yes, the large majority, but not [illegible] the [illegible].

297. Therefore you appear to have expended £31,[illegible] in doing £30,000 worth of benefit?—That would be hardly so, because that £31,000 is divided into two heads of expenditure, capital and maintenance.

298. You have invested £16,000 capital and you have expended £15,000 in maintenance?—Yes.

299. And the benefit that has accrued by this expenditure appears to amount to about £30,000?—I should not say that, I should say that would be a very low estimate indeed.

300. Do you think then that the horses in these districts have improved to a larger extent than £5 a head?—I should say very much larger taking the whole thing, taking the value of all the different ages that they are sold.

301. Of course if this had been in a country where horses are maintained for the use or amusement or necessities of the people who live in it you would have made a permanent improvement, but these congested districts appear to be places in which horses are not kept?—They are kept for breeding in a very large number of cases.

302. Your report seemed to prove that it had not tended to keep the mares in the country?—I think the evidence is that a very large number of the fillies are kept for breeding.

303. I took a note when you were making out the evidence that the result of the increase of foal and the improved value of the horse had not tended to induce the farmers to keep their mares?—That is not my impression of the evidence.

304. Lord Ardilaun.—As far as I remember he said that in a large number of cases people had sold what ought to have been kept?—Yes.

305. Mr. La Touche.—As a matter of fact the great majority of horses that are bred there leave the country when they are a year or two old?—Yes, the great majority of them; some of the fillies are kept for doing their work.

306. Lord Ardilaun.—What you want to get at is whether they sell the mares and keep the filly?—There is a tendency in that direction, and everything the Board can do is being in that direction, they are doing, giving prizes for fillies kept in the country.

307. Mr. La Touche.—I understand that item for cost of inspection includes prizes for mares and foals and the establishment the Board allows?—No, there is a further sum of £[illegible] for brood mares, prizes at brood mares, and with merely prizes, but expenses on inspection, this item includes.

308. Is that included in the £15,[illegible]?—It is only it was included. I did not observe it until now; it is an extra item of £[illegible].

309. Mr. [illegible].—Mr. Micks, you mentioned, or rather in your report there is an item of remuneration to the police of £1,302 for their trouble?—Yes.

310. A large item, can you give us any details of that?—The police acting [illegible] in charge of the horse from the time it goes down to the district in the country. He makes all the arrangements for the keeping, he has charge in respect of the horse, he inspects the mares who are brought to the horse, except where there is a qualifying surgeon employed, there is a great deal of writing up and keeping service books and [illegible] that sort. They are doing the [illegible] of the clerk, and that saves the Board the [illegible] of District Inspectors, as many as there are horses in fact, and those officers each have got some slight remuneration. That is what it comes up to; it comes to about £[illegible] a year.

311. They send you in a return of these horses and a return of the fees that go to them?—Yes, and keep the service book, and give the orders to the people who choose just [illegible] the mares.

312. And practically what the mares who are allowed to go to this horse?—Well, [illegible] the mares, they [illegible] it, I suppose.

Oct. 18, 1897. Mr. W. L. Micks.

313. Mr. La Touche.—I suppose to have them [illegible] would cost a great deal more money?—It would, I think, be cheap for the work they do; they have a great amount of correspondence and business to do.

314. The Chairman.—But the value of the services the police render you does not appear in your accounts, there is a certain sum, but that does not represent the value of the work they do for you?—That represents what they get for it.

315. But not the full amount of the value they give you?—No, but we make an acknowledgement to them in our report every year.

316. And if you had not the services of the police you would have to pay a great deal more for the same services?—I think we would.

317. I think you said that the bulk of the produce of your stallions was sold under one year old?—Yes.

318. And that the majority of them were not kept in the district?—Yes.

319. I think you said you did not know where they went to?—I have heard of buyers buying them in different other parts of Ireland.

320. Do you know to all who buy them?—Dealers I believe, I don't know positively.

321. Then, according to you, the bulk of the produce of these Railway stallions is distributed all over Ireland?—I cannot follow the distribution.

322. At any rate it does not remain in the district?—Not much of it.

323. At the same time the number of horses in the congested districts is increasing very rapidly?—It is.

324. And at the same time all the produce of your stallions are sold under a year old?—Yes.

325. And not sold in the district, how do you account for the increase?—It is possible that those young fillies being kept may account in a large measure for it.

326. Mr. W. Gilmour.—You have no actual figures of the number sold have you?—No, we have not.

327. Lord Rathdonnell.—Can you tell the increase?—Yes.

328. The Chairman.—There has been a large increase, according to what we have in evidence, in the counties which contain congested districts?—Yes.

329. And a decrease in the counties in Ireland which do not contain congested districts, is not that so?—That is so. In 6 counties they have increased, counties in which there are congested districts, they have increased in Kerry by 813, in Galway by 173, in Leitrim by 123, in Mayo by 448, in Roscommon by 251, in Sligo by 609, and in Donegal by 780, a total increase of 2,483.

330. Mr. Wrench.—Might not the explanation of that be that horse breeding in the congested districts was paying better and that it was worse in other parts of the country?—That occurs to one as a possible explanation of it, I have not followed it up, I merely take the figures and give them to the Commission.

331. The Chairman.—I suppose you never entered into any calculation as to what fees you would have to charge if this was a private business?—No.

332. Would you be able to give us any idea, the fees would be your only asset, your only property and no occasional sale?—I have not an idea really.

333. You have given us the capital expenditure and the annual expenses, can you give us what the annual receipts amount to?—I can in a very few minutes, there are 6,191 at 5s., 197 at 10s., and 260 at £1 and over, about £2,700.

334. I think you said there was a tendency on the part of the occupiers to sell their mares, and that the Board were trying to devise means of counteracting that?—The Board are encouraging them to keep the fillies to breed out of.

335. How do they encourage them?—They give prizes for fillies kept in the country, they brand the fillies as prize winners at the Show, and if that filly is produced in the subsequent year they give a production prize for it.

336. Have their efforts been successful?—I think there are being higher payments under it.

337. Mr. La Touche.—I have seen a great many of these mares, but I never saw a filly branded, are you sure they go on branding fillies?—Mr. Wrench could answer that.

338. Speaking roughly, you say the receipts from fees amounted to £2,700, while the expenditure on maintenance was £11,607, so as a trading concern the Congested Districts Board seems to have sustained a dead loss of £11,897 on the expenses of £16,635?—If you put even your sum of £10,000 on to that that would suffice us.

Mr. La Touche.—Yes, as a philanthropic concern, but not as a trading concern.

Joseph B. O'Reilly, D.L., examined.

Joseph B. O'Reilly, D.L.

339. The Chairman.—You are a member of the Council of the Irish Harness Horse Society?—Yes, my lord.

340. And of the Royal Dublin Society?—Yes.

341. How long have you been a member of the Harness Horse Society?—Since its foundation.

342. When was its foundation?—It was founded in the spring of 1895.

343. And with what object?—Well, the objects were to encourage the breeding of harness horses in districts where it did not interfere with hunter breeding. Its objects were to encourage generally the breeding of harness horses and to assist in filling classes of the Royal Dublin Society, the classes had fallen off very much in 1894 in the harness classes, [illegible] filling off and there was disappointment felt by some members at the action of the Horse Show Committee of the Dublin Society in throwing out the Hackney classes for stallions from the prize list of 1895, particularly as that class had been very well supported and well spoken of by the Judges that had come over [illegible] in the Society they had congratulated the Society on introducing that breed of horses into the country. Then again there was a feeling amongst [illegible] interested in harness horse breeding that the Royal Dublin Society and other agricultural associations gave little encouragement to Irish breeders in the harness [illegible] direction, that a valuable industry might suffer unless some society was formed to encourage Irish breeders. All the prizes at the Royal Dublin Society were being carried off by English exhibitors and English breeders, and our society was formed to assist the Royal Dublin Society and other associations in furthering the interests of Irish breeders of harness horses.

344. Your object was to encourage generally the breeding of harness horses in Ireland?—Yes.

345. But as I understand merely in such districts as would not interfere with hunter breeding?—Yes.

346. Who were the original promoters of the society?—Mr. Thomas Talbot Power, Mr. Fowler, Mr. Dames Longworth, Lord Bellew, Lord Ashtown, Colonel Lindsay Gore, and Sir Douglas Brooke, Mr. Wrench, and myself I think were the first promoters.

347. Were there any societies in existence at the time of your foundation dealing with the subject?—Not specially for harness purposes, the only extent that other societies recognised it as such is that the Royal Dublin Society used to give open classes for harness horses, but they did not give special classes, they failed to recognise the importance of establishing special classes for stallions, thoroughbred or otherwise with action best suited for harness purposes and for getting harness horses, nor did they give us classes for mares with action specially suited for harness purposes.

248. Have you got a prospectus of the **society**?—Yes (produces it).

249. Perhaps you better read it?

Witness (reading)—"Objects of the society to promote and encourage the breeding of harness horses, with action, in Ireland. To publish for the information of breeders, a list of any stallions in Ireland specially suitable for that purpose. To publish for the information of buyers a list of breeders of such harness horses. Gradually to form a register of mares specially suitable for breeding harness horses. And generally to promote the exhibition of harness horses at agricultural shows and elsewhere. To attract public attention to this important subject, and to spread knowledge of the principles upon which harness horses may be bred. The society has been formed to foster and strengthen a trade which it is believed will prove profitable to Ireland. There is a constant demand in England and Scotland for harness horses with action, and these are now largely supplied by foreign breeders. Many of those are bred out of foreign mares mated by stallions imported from England. There is no reason why Ireland should not produce such animals better than they can be produced in any other country, without in any way interfering with the breeding of hunters—especially as many of the mares are too light and weedy to be mated with a thoroughbred horse. The Irish Harness Horse Society urges that combined efforts should be made in Ireland towards the improvement of Hackneys, in the production of which this country should excel, and for which she has acquired her reputation as a Horse-breeding country. At the same time it is submitted that the interests of the farming classes ought to be taken into consideration, and every opportunity afforded them of making Horse-breeding more profitable. There is little doubt that a large class exists who would find a ready sale for a shapely Harness Horse with action, that could be worked at an early age on the land. There is plenty of room in Ireland for the production of both Harness Horses and Hunters, and there is no reason why it should not excel in both departments. The Irish Harness Horse Society further submits that in view of the continued depressed condition of agriculture, and the impossibility of those being very remunerative and easily marketed at prices of ordinary agricultural produce, a favourable opportunity now exists for placing before the farming classes of Ireland, means and facilities by which they may be encouraged and enabled to effect a decided improvement in a branch of their business, hitherto either comparatively neglected or imperfectively carried out. It is not contended that a Hunter can be produced by using a Hackney Sire, the Hackney being purely a Road and Harness horse, but this Society has particularly in mind the breeding of harness specially adapted to harness or roadster purposes by similar methods to, and concurrent with, those which have been successfully employed in the improvement of Hunters by the Royal Dublin Society under their Horse-breeding scheme. In the Harness Classes at the Horse Show of the Royal Dublin Society, the prizes are too often carried off by English exhibitors, or with horses bred in England. This ought not to be, and without in any way interfering with the Hunter and the Thoroughbred, or concerning the breeding of Harness Horses, in Hackney lines, it is submitted that more encouragement should be given to the breeding of high class Harness Horses in Ireland, and more facilities afforded to Irishmen favourably situated for the production of such animals in this country."

250. What action has the Society taken to carry out its objects?—Well, up to the present, the Society has confined itself chiefly to promoting exhibitions of harness horses bred in Ireland at the Royal Dublin Society and other agricultural shows, and also in the organising shows of ponies and fashionable equipages in the Park, and at the Show, to attract public attention to the importance of this industry. In conjunction, too, with the Royal Dublin Society, we instituted two new classes at the August Show of 1895 and 1896, and for each class we provided the prize money. In Class A the harness horses shown in harness, not exceeding six years old, bred in Ireland and exhibited by residents in Ireland, we gave £30. And for Class B, young horses suitable for harness not exceeding four years old, shown in hand and bred in Ireland and exhibited by a resident in Ireland, we gave £15 and the Society's silver medal to the best prize winners in both these classes. And also with the concurrence of the Royal Dublin Society, we organised a meet of carriages at the August Show, and in the absence of a prize list, we gave handsome silver mounted whips to the drivers of each of these carriages, and this parade formed a leading feature of the Show. To the North-East Agricultural Show at Belfast we gave a cup, value 10 guineas, and a silver medal for young horses suitable for harness, not exceeding four years old, bred in Ireland and exhibited by residents in Ireland. At the Enniskillen Agricultural Society's Show, we gave a cup, value £5, for the best young horse bred in Ireland, suitable for harness, under three years old, open to all classes in the Show. At the Galway Show we gave a silver cup, value £5, for young horses, three to four years old, and under 15 hands high, with style and action, suitable for hunting, to be shown in harness. At the Mullingar Show we gave a cup valued £5, or if preferred, a silver medal and £3 for the best Hackney or harness horse bred in Ireland. For the Ballinasloe Agricultural Society we gave a silver cup for the best young horse not exceeding four years old, with style and action, suitable for harness, bred in Ireland. And to the Tullamore Agricultural Show we gave a silver medal. I think that was about all we were able to manage with the funds at our disposal.

251. Have your efforts been well supported throughout the country—have you received good support?—Yes; we have received from some breeders in Ireland very handsome individual donations of £5 through the columns of our society, and also the classes that we have given in the country shows were all well supported, and the newspapers speak very strongly indeed of the satisfactory exhibits and the exhibitions that were supported and to be given in similar lines. The entries also at the Royal Dublin Society's Show—which had fallen, as I said, about 40 per cent.—have risen in 1895 and 1896 per cent. over 1894, and in 1896—this last year's show—they rose 75 per cent. over 1894.

252. Do you consider the breeding of harness horses an important industry in the country?—Yes; I think it is a very important industry. Dealers come over here from the other side to look for harness horses, and they say they can never get them. I know that there is a great demand for horses with action. I think there is a greater demand now for getting horses with style and action; there is more demand for now than a couple of years ago. I know an Irish dealer myself who has got an order for eighty harness horses at £100 each, and finds it very hard to get them.

253. Where are they mostly produced?—I think all over Ireland. I don't know that there is any special part, except the south of Ireland has got a greater name for harness breeding than any other I know of. The Vale of Clwyd, in Tyrone, is a great fair for dealers to go to looking for harness horses more than anything else.

254. You don't think any particular part of the country is more suitable for breeding this class of harness than any other?—No, I would not say so exactly. I think that where hunters are not bred harness horses might be very well developed and bred.

255. Where are the districts where hunters are not bred?—Chiefly in the north, there is very little hunting in the north. They encourage the harness class more in the North-East Agricultural Society's

[illegible]

[illegible] in Ireland. They have more go for harness there than in any other part of the country.

358. And you think the industry is capable of being largely increased?—I think so. I think there is a great demand for good harness horses, and I don't see why it should not be increased in those districts where there is scope for them, and where people have a taste for it I think they ought to be encouraged, as well as other breeds.

359. How are they bred, these harness horses in the north?—Mostly from thoroughbred hunters, some from Hackneys.

360. Do you think the supply of stallions is sufficient and suitable?—No, I think the stallions would be improved very much. We want more action in the thoroughbred horses, and when there is less [illegible] action for harness, in whatever breed of horse you use, we require action. Action is essential for harness.

361. Your society has not done anything towards [illegible] this?—We have not had funds at our disposal, but you may take that it is in our programme. We fully intend to move on, if we have funds enough, a system of registration of stallions, thoroughbred, or any other pure breed with action and bone and marketability for getting harness horses, and subsidising breeders by such a registration of sound horses and also of mares. It was our intention also to have classes for mares, and to work more or less similarly to those the Royal Dublin Society had instituted for hunters in those districts.

362. To have mares registered?—Not registration of mares, but to have shows of mares suitable for harness in those districts where harness horses were bred, without interfering with hunter breeding in the least, and if the mares were suitable, if we had money in our disposal, or if there was a government grant for that purpose that those mares that were suitable for harness should get nominations to stallions on the register, leaving the breeder his own choice of what stallion he might go to.

363. Giving him a nomination fee?—Not necessarily free but at a price for so much, leaving him free to choose his stallion.

364. When you don't, I understand, recommend any particular breed of stallion over another?—No, we have an open policy as regards the breed of stallions. What we do recommend is that they should have action, which is essential for harness, and also that they should be pure-bred of their own class—that is pedigree bred and sound.

365. Any other information you wish to lay before the Commission?—I don't think so, my lord. Except I think that on the broad principle, without interfering with the hunter breeding industry, harness horse breeding has claims for encouragement in those districts where the particular trade is carried on and found more profitable than hunter breeding. So many more men want a good harness horse for twelve months in the year as the one that wants a hunter for six months in the year. I think on the broad principle that the wants of the majority should have equal if not greater claims to encouragement than the wants of the minority.

366. Mr. F. Wrench.—Have you any idea which is the larger trade in Ireland: the breeding of the hacking horse or of the harness horse?—Oh, the hunting horse, there is no doubt about it.

367. Much larger?—Oh, much larger.

368. You could not give any figures?—I could not give any figures, but I should say the exportation of horses is so great that it is nearly the hunting they are exported to Scotland, nearly all the horses in England are bought as harness from this country.

369. The Chairman.—Have you any figures you could give the Commission as to the number of harness horses that are exported?—I have not, it would be very hard to give, as they go away on going from this country before they are bought for harness, and may be trained to hunting or harness purposes when they leave the country. The exportation of horses has increased immensely, it reaches 34,000 a year, or 700 a week.

370. How do you obtain funds?—Donations from those interested in breeding, and also subscriptions from the members, annual subscriptions, but we are sadly in want of funds to work what our original programme intended; we should look for some government assistance to do all we should wish.

371. Mr. Whitworth.—What are the means that you hold out to improve breeding horses?—By encouraging stallion ownership.

372. Yes, but how are they bred?—Well, they may be bred by thoroughbred horses, if they show sufficient blood and quality with action for harness, they may be mated according to the opinion of the breeder. If he thinks they will make better with a Hackney-bred horse he will go to the thoroughbred horse if his mares want quality.

373. I am not talking of the kind here, where are the mares breeding?—They are mostly from the one breed, the size the neighborhood in our side.

374. Any admixture of Clevelands or anything of that kind?—I don't think there is any Cleveland in this country at all.

375. Not in the North of Ireland?—Not that I am aware of, there is some carriage blood mixed, no doubt, what we call cart blood.

376. Agricultural?—Yes, agricultural horses.

377. Mr. F. Wrench.—Can you say why it is that you think that there are more hunters sold than harness horses, do you know any reason why the trade should be bigger?—I think there are more foreign dealers coming over looking for hunters, at the same time there are a great many looking for harness horses, but the majority are looking for hunters.

378. Have you any idea why they come more for hunters?—Because this country is so specially adapted for breeding hunters, it is the greatest industry of this country.

379. Lord Harrington.—There is one remark you made, you said there was no class in the Royal Dublin Society's Show for harness horses also?—No, no special class for harness horse show, there is a class for [illegible] calculated to get hunters or harness horses.

380. I think so?—Hackneys, but nothing special for harness horses.

381. But still it is open to harness horses?—It is directly.

382. Directly I think?—Well, breeders of harness horses look upon action as the essential attribute of the harness horse and of the sire that is calculated to get them, and we don't look for that in the hunter, we don't look for harness action, which we want to breed a harness horse.

383. Well, to breed a harness horse or a hunter you must breed for action?—For a hunter not harness action, but it is not the same action as you want for harness horses.

384. Do you mean you prefer up and down action?—Not necessarily, but you want them to use their shoulders well and step up with knees, and carry their head and tail [illegible].

385. You yourself I fancy have bred a great many horses?—I have bred a great many horses, with thoroughbreds and others.

386. What sires have you used as a rule?—I have used altogether thoroughbred sires for hunting purposes, I have used Hackney lately on some mares and I have been very successful so far. I have had the first prize winner in the harness class at the Dublin Show. I never was able to bring into the ribbons in this class in the Dublin Show until I put my mares to a Hackney sire, and I got first prize this last Show with the result of the produce, four years old.

387. You also, I think, sell the horses you breed for every kind—all kinds—of horses [illegible]

breeding in Ireland, as well as breeding the hunter?—Yes.

386. Now, do you think that the increase of Hackney sires will do any harm to Ireland if they spread from the districts where they are at present in districts like Meath and the best horse breeding districts of Ireland?—I don't think there is any danger of that. I think that is a sentimental grievance. I don't think you will find where Hackneys at present are making that there is the slightest danger of the class of mares that are going to these Hackneys being taken up by breeders of hunters. They have not got the points of the hunter, and I think they will be easily avoided for hunter breeding.

387. You think they will remain in the districts where they happen to be bred?—I do; they won't go into the hands of breeders of hunters, because I don't think any breeder of a hunter would like to have any of the Hackney blood in his mares.

388. Have you ever heard it said that the young mares, fillies by the sires imported from Wales, the Hackney, from any the original districts remaining are sold at their age?—Yes; I have certainly heard that they were sold.

389. Did you ever find out what way they went?—No; I have no means of telling you that.

390. I know they must have disappeared, they went and could not tell you; I have no idea.

391. If there happen to be fillies crossed, then that we will only cannot only keep the fillies at home, therefore, some of the fillies must go from there—what becomes of them?—But I take it that the mares that would be sired by these Hackney sires in the congested districts would be a class of mare that would be a long way off the class of a great hunting, and it would be a long time before the breeding of a hunter would take her into his stud to breed a hunter from.

392. Then you think everybody who buys young stock of this sort is not likely to put the mare to a horse to breed one with stamina?—No, I don't think they would put it to a horse to breed a hunter, they might have been sold to.

393. You don't think a small farmer would if he had such a mare?—I don't think so.

394. Mr. Clarke.—You agree that the breeding of hunters is by far the most important branch of the horse-breeding industry in Ireland?—I think so.

395. And you would not care to interfere with it?—No, far from it.

396. How would you arrange the operations of your society so as not to interfere with the breeding of hunters?—I should have a special registration of horses available for breeding harness horses with action, and I think if there were sires held in those districts where the harness industry should be encouraged, and those of course held there, I think if something were to admit the mares that were suitable harness, and they had them at their disposal to give them proper opportunities, that is mating them with Hackney sires, that they would be put to any breed of sire that is an ornament of the Harness Society.

397. Do you think there would be danger of infusing hunting breeding?—I do not think so. I don't think the blood of the Hackney is at all inferior. I would not consider it as a hunter to any extent, but I don't think there is any inferior comparison with Irish hunters blood or Shire or Clydesdale or any of this sort blood, and hunting could have not the same risk in the majority of hunting instances with that blood as they would with the Hackney.

398. What do you mean by the Irish cart-horse?—Very often they mean the agricultural horses that are bred by small farmers on their farms cart-horses.

399. You have no idea how they are bred?—No. There is a great deal of thoroughbred blood in them; they are mixed horses.

400. Mr. La Touche.—You **said you thought your** society would do a great deal of good in certain districts in Ireland which were not suitable for the breeding of hunters?—Yes.

401. And in the prospectus of your society you say there is no reason why Ireland should not produce animals that are better than could be produced in any other country without in any way interfering with the breeding of hunters, are we to infer that if you think the operations of your society were carried on in a county where hunters were bred it might possibly interfere with the breeding of hunters?—I don't think so.

402. Why did you particularly specify as the Clydesdale those districts in the north of Ireland?—I say those are the districts where the breeding of harness horses is more extensively carried on; the others are in combination with hunter breeding. In the north they breed very much for harness purposes, and the others; in the south and in the midland counties they breed altogether mostly for hunters.

403. Then, in the first paragraph of the objects of the society, "especially as many of the mares are too light and weedy to be mated with a thoroughbred horse." Is not that rather wholesale condemnation of the thoroughbred horse; it may be within your experience, you have seen thoroughbred horses with as much bone as any other horse?—Yes; but if you have a mare that is weedy you cannot put a thoroughbred on to her again, or the result will be a lack of bone and substance.

404. If the thoroughbred horse you put on her has more bone and substance than any other horse you would not be likely to get a weedier animal then from any other horse?—If he had more bone and substance than any other horse, you would not, but most of the thoroughbreds in this country have not as much bone and substance as is desirable for breeding.

405. Some of them?—A great many of them.

406. Then this ought to read "especially as many of the mares are so light and weedy to be mated with a light and weedy thoroughbred horse"?—We want both bone and substance and action, for harness, as much thoroughbred blood as you can get, but not the action you want.

407. Supposing you have the action and the bone and substance in the thoroughbred horse would you prefer him to any other breed of horse?—I would decidedly.

408. I suppose you admit that you have seen thoroughbred horses with as much bone and action as required?—I have seen them but they are very scarce.

409. Well you say that a harness horse is very hard to get, but it appears from some information that I received, I think, two years ago, in connection with the Royal Dublin Society, that the principal dealers in England get their best carriage horses in Ireland, at least so they say at any rate. And these dealers condition that the horses they have found most suitable for their purpose were got by thoroughbred horses and were bred in the south of Ireland, not the north of Ireland. And I also take it that you particularly specified that you thought the breeding of good harness horses should be encouraged, and you say that even in the most good harness horses are directly bred by thoroughbreds and some by Hackneys, have you any practical experience of which, see the most valuable, they are sold at sales I suppose?—If the previous show action, style and quality it would make no difference whether they are by a thoroughbred or a Hackney sire.

410. How about price? No, I have one Hackney sires' produce in Ireland from some of the Dublin classes. I can give you an instance, at the last show a Hackney horse who got the first prize and champion cup was sold for £300 to a Paris dealer.

411. Mr. Clarke.—That is exceptional?—Well, the year before the horse that got first prize was sold for £300, by the same man and of the same sort, he also won by a Hackney the cost of a mare bought in Dublin.

[illegible]

Joseph M. O'Reilly, Esq.

[illegible] O'Reilly, Esq.

412. How was the mare bred?—You could not say, it is very hard to trace the pedigree of any mare in Ireland.

413. Mr. La Touche.—Do you think the ordinary mare in the country is calculated to produce a good carriage horse?—Yes, if she has action she is, but without action she is not.

414. Do you think action is one of the qualities of the ordinary mare?—I think the present style of the day is for action in harness.

415. Do you think action is one of the attributes of the ordinary mare of the country?—No, not harness action.

416. Then I may take it you would hold that the ordinary mare of the country is not at present adapted to breed good harness horses?—Not the general run of them, no, but unless the sire has exceptionally good action, you may get it then.

417. I suppose while the price of a very tip-top harness horse is likely always to keep up, the price of an inferior harness horse is very likely to fall?—Yes, I should say so.

418. By the introduction of bicycles and motor carriages. Do you really think the majority of those horses that are sold in Ireland are hunters?—Yes, decidedly.

419. Would you say two-thirds?—I should say more—that are exported, I mean.

420. You said there are 33,000 horses exported from Ireland every year, do you mean to say there are 20,000 hunters sent out of Ireland every year?—I would not be surprised.

421. I think you would probably find that the Messrs. Widger, of Waterford, are the largest exporters of horses from Ireland, and I should think a very small proportion of the horses they send are hunters, or intended for hunters?—I think they are very large buyers of horses of all sorts. It is very hard to trace a horse when he leaves there always—what he is to be used for—but I know all the best hunters in England are Irish-bred.

422. I cannot imagine that 20,000 hunters a year are sold out of Ireland?—That may be a little over the mark.

423. You said you bred the first prize winner in the Harness class at the Dublin Show last year?—Yes.

424. And it was by a Hackney?—Yes.

425. How old was it?—Four years old.

426. Had you had the dam any time?—Yes, I have had the dam for a long time, six or seven years.

427. How was she bred?—I bought her in Ireland; I don't know her pedigree, never could trace it; she got first prize herself in the Harness class in the Dublin Show.

428. As a brood mare?—As a harness mare.

429. Do you think she was an Irish mare, or an English mare, or a Hackney mare?—I could not say, it is very hard.

430. Had she bred anything for you before?—This was her first foal, this one that got the first prize.

431. Of course you put her to horse since then?—I have.

432. Did you use the same sire? No, I have not used it the last two years; I put her to my own sire. I keep an American trotting horse, a standard American trotting horse, and I have put her to him for the last two years.

433. Does your Harness Horse Society propose to introduce stallions into Ireland at all for the purpose of breeding?—Our Society would like to see horses introduced into Ireland with action calculated to get harness horses, no doubt, but we have no funds at our disposal.

434. Are you disposed to look favourably on this American horse of yours; have you seen his stock?—Yes; they promise very well indeed, but they are too young yet to form any opinion.

435. Mr. Wrench.—You have never made any calculations, Mr. O'Reilly, to see exactly what the probable requirements of all the different hunts of the United Kingdom would be so as to test what really the hunting trade would be, have you?—Well, I was doing that last night. I got the return in last week's *Field*. It gave the different hunts in England, foxhounds, staghounds, and harriers, and I totted them all up, and made them 300 hunts.

436. And how many horses per hunt did you allow for replacing horses sold?—Well, I did not go in very closely to the whole thing, but I was doing it in a rough way.

437. I only wanted to arrive at some point in reference to Mr. La Touche's question as to your evidence that there are 20,000 hunters sold from Ireland?—If there are 300 hunts you can take an average of 100 horses there.

438. And in that way you arrive at the 20,000?—Yes.

439. I think you had a good deal to say to the Royal Dublin Society?—Yes.

440. And have been present at all their shows?—I have.

441. Have you any particulars at all as to how the horses were bred that have generally won the prizes for harness in the Dublin Show?—Yes; they were nearly all bred, as far as I could see, the majority at any rate, by Hackney sires. As I said regarding the Irish Harness Horse Society, I mentioned that all the prizes were going to England, and the horses that came over from England were invariably bred by Hackney sires. I don't think you can point to any one by a Queen's premium sire that came over here in the harness classes.

442. With regard to thoroughbreds I think you mentioned that you were against crossing thoroughbreds with weedy mares, have you any information as to the thoroughbreds in the country, whether they are sound or the reverse?—I know the Dublin Society are doing their utmost to extinguish the unsound sire by the registration system, and I think they are gaining ground every day in that direction. I think the registration scheme of the Dublin Society is a very fine scheme. It is better than any stud book, because the stud book don't require soundness, but the Dublin Society requires soundness before they register the sire.

443. Would you be inclined to increase that registration and make it include mares or not?—No, I would not go so far as that, I don't know on what foundation you could start a registration of mares in Ireland.

444. Then you think all the registration that can be attempted is at present the registration the Royal Dublin Society carry out?—I think it can be further developed in the registration of stallions carried on to a larger extent and supplemented by the importation of stallions or by exciting private enterprise in the purchase of stallions of the right stamp.

445. In your evidence I think you said you dislike the half-bred sire?—I do immensely, I should not have anything to say to him either for harness or hunter breeding.

446. Why?—Because he is neither one thing or the other, and you can never rely on his get, he may throw back to the bad side instead of the good side.

447. Then you would not approve of any suggestion to register half-bred sires?—No, I would be dead against registering half-bred sires.

448. Mr. Fitzwilliam.—What do you mean by half-bred exactly?—When I say half-bred I mean what they call hunter-bred in this country, that is by a thoroughbred stallion and a dam not in the stud book.

449. Still a well bred one?—Yes.

450. Lord Ashtown.—Is that a horse three-quarter blood?—Yes.

451. Sir W. Gilbey.—I believe you are interested in the improvement of the breed of horses generally

in Ireland. You are on the Council of the Royal Dublin Society, and you also support the [illegible] Society?—Yes.

4[illegible]. You have no prejudice as to the breed, because [illegible] you hold your [illegible] a pure breed, and you keep a stallion yourself [illegible]?—Yes.

[illegible]. With regard to the breed of mares which are shown in the Dublin Show, which [illegible] have been for many years [illegible], [illegible] the "breeding unknown" in so many cases, even when there are prizes given for brood mares. How do you account for that?—They know the breeder, but they don't know the sire or the dam [illegible] hunter in the country [illegible] pedigree, but it [illegible] that [illegible] distinguished himself [illegible] a very fine pedigree. I think really the answer to the question is that [illegible] young [illegible] very [illegible], and [illegible] all the horse [illegible] and the size that has the [illegible] as to his purchase straight off, [illegible] there is [illegible] of [illegible].

[illegible]. But there would not be much difficulty in getting that information?—I think there is immense difficulty.

[illegible]. If the exhibitor is known and the breeder why should they not know the name of the [illegible]?—Yes, [illegible] they know the name of the breeder [illegible] breeders [illegible] good [illegible] and they [illegible] good opinion.

[illegible]. You know what an infusion [illegible] every [illegible] the fact that the English [illegible] in London [illegible], if they [illegible] a good horse, [illegible] Irish horse [illegible] pedigree [illegible] whether [illegible] very [illegible] and if the horse [illegible] against [illegible] it is a [illegible] I don't [illegible] the blood, it is [illegible] against the Irish horse.

[illegible]. Mr. Clancy.—You are [illegible] in half-bred [illegible]?—Yes, for getting hunters or [illegible] horses, I think they ought to be [illegible] to their own [illegible].

[illegible]. Are not the best hunters [illegible] with thoroughbred sires?—Yes.

[illegible]. Then how do you propose to maintain, if you [illegible] half-breds, how do you propose to maintain the half-bred [illegible], they [illegible] the [illegible], because [illegible]?—Not by changing your strain of blood, and [illegible] with [illegible] strain, you [illegible] very much [illegible].

[illegible]. What do you mean by changing the strain, [illegible] thoroughbred [illegible] thoroughbred [illegible] necessarily, but I don't [illegible] breeding [illegible] would [illegible].

[illegible]. But I am talking of horses, [illegible] that the best hunters are [illegible] crossed with thoroughbred sires, if you [illegible] in half-breds [illegible] of half-bred [illegible] you might [illegible] thoroughbreds, they would become [illegible] and [illegible] bone and substance [illegible] is going on for generations in the [illegible], and the [illegible] has not [illegible], it has rather improved.

[illegible]. [illegible] the [illegible]?—No, but they [illegible] back [illegible] thoroughbreds [illegible].

[illegible]. You want something [illegible] in a family?—Yes, [illegible]. But I don't think there [illegible] of you [illegible] thoroughbred [illegible] in [illegible], you [illegible] very [illegible] back [illegible] the [illegible]. Keep the biggest and [illegible] and the mares with the best bone and [illegible] with a thoroughbred horse you will get them.

[illegible]. But if you go on breeding from a thoroughbred [illegible] the produce of the [illegible] in the [illegible], and [illegible] you [illegible] the [illegible]?—I [illegible] that [illegible] would [illegible], we don't [illegible] that we have lost size or substance [illegible], in that I think the [illegible] has [illegible] in size and substance.

[illegible]. Lord Ardilaun.—Suppose you had a half-bred mare and put her to a thoroughbred horse you would get a [illegible] filly, would you cross that filly with a half-bred horse?—I would not like to [illegible] that, it might be done successfully, but I would not like to [illegible] that theory. I think it is done very often successfully, but as [illegible] it may be the reverse, it may throw back to the wrong side.

[illegible]. Would you object to breed a hunter from a mare that was a [illegible] three or four crosses of blood put to a half-bred horse?—I would not object [illegible] was [illegible], but I should not like to try it.

[illegible]. Mr. Wrench.—I see from your evidence here that you [illegible] the different parts of Dublin [illegible] different systems of breeding, do you think that could be carried out [illegible] you could breed [illegible] horses in one [illegible], hunters [illegible] in another [illegible]?—[illegible] the county Dublin there [illegible] of [illegible] breeding [illegible] of Dublin, and on the [illegible] hunters and [illegible].

[illegible]. What I mean is do you think these different systems of breeding can be carried on without interfering with each other?—I think so, decidedly, I don't see any danger in that.

[illegible]. Do you think that [illegible] with the [illegible] that they are [illegible] in [illegible] of [illegible]?—I think so, the breeder ought to be the best judge [illegible] what he is going to do, [illegible] to satisfy the [illegible], but in the [illegible] the [illegible] opinion of [illegible] that is to be [illegible]. I don't think the [illegible]'s opinion is worth anything, if [illegible] breeder's opinion [illegible] worth [illegible] to [illegible] the [illegible] and [illegible] the [illegible] in [illegible].

[illegible]. As a rule you think the pedigrees of horses that are entered at the Dublin Show and [illegible] of the catalogue are [illegible]?—I think so decidedly, I think you can [illegible] them [illegible] the [illegible].

[illegible]. You cannot suggest any remedy? Would you prevent a man from [illegible] his horse and [illegible] a pedigree where he did not know the breeding?—I think you would [illegible] at [illegible] your [illegible], it would [illegible] to [illegible] altogether.

[illegible]. You think it is [illegible] pedigrees [illegible] of all?—I think it would [illegible] if you [illegible] to verify all the breeding of the horses [illegible], I think it would be very hard to [illegible] it [illegible].

[illegible]. Lord Ardilaun.—What would you say to not printing the pedigree in the catalogue if the breeder was not known?—I think it would look very bad.

[illegible]. If they could not [illegible] pedigree [illegible]?—You could [illegible] but I think a great many [illegible] to [illegible] pedigrees [illegible] to verify them and that would be a very bad thing to do.

[illegible]. Mr. [illegible].—[illegible] suggestion as to how it could be [illegible] or [illegible] or improved by the Dublin Society, supposing there was a [illegible] class, [illegible] in which a man need give no information as to breeding and [illegible] class [illegible] could only enter [illegible] would authenticate the breeding of the animal, [illegible] I know the show [illegible] young [illegible] I [illegible] at the [illegible], I am only [illegible] of [illegible] out of 100, you

on the breeder without the pedigree or the pedigree without the breeder, what reliance is there on that, it goes for nothing. Would it not be possible to leave it out?—I don't think it would further the interests of the show to leave it out, it may be the best for buyers.

476. Mr. WRENCH.—Are you aware whether many American horses are being imported into Ireland at present?—There are a good many American horses unfortunately, I think, being imported. I saw one shipload when I was in Belfast. I saw a shipload landed the day I arrived there. I also saw some sold in Dublin.

477. Mr. FITZWILLIAM.—What class of horse?—A very poor class of horses.

478. Harness horses?—They were broken to harness; flat-sided animals, very poor; sold for very small money, and certainly were no advantage coming into this country, rather the reverse.

479. Lord RATHDONNELL.—Many mares among them?—A good many amongst the lot I saw in Belfast.

480. Mr. WRENCH.—Were they sold in Belfast?—Yes, I waited for the auction; they brought from £7 up to £13 or £14; the best mare in the whole lot fetched £30.

481. You don't know whether there were any American horses shown in the Dublin Show?—There were some in the Fast Trotting class.

482. You don't know whether there were any in the Hunters' class?—No; I don't think so.

483. The CHAIRMAN.—About your own society, I gather from you that your general opinion, the opinion of your society, is that the breeding of hunters is and will remain the principal part of the horse-breeding industry of Ireland, taking it as a whole?—Certainly.

484. But certain districts, especially in the North, are more suited for breeding harness horses?—Yes, where there is no hunting, and no markets for hunters.

485. As you say the fashion being for action, I should like to know, in your opinion, whether the action is not better obtained by Hackney sires than any other means?—Certainly; I think the characteristic of the Hackney is action, no doubt about it.

486. Although you have no prejudice one way or the other, would the breeding of harness horses be more likely to be improved by the introduction of Hackney sires than in any other way?—I think it would be improved very much by the introduction of Hackney sires, with a judicious mixture of blood in the mares. I think the Hackney sire would improve the harness horse very much from instances I have seen myself. I have seen an instance of a hackney cross here in Dublin. I saw a mare by a Hackney sire sold by this carman at three years old for £60; it was an exceptionally fine goer, and £100 was refused at our show immediately after.

487. But you don't think it would be an equal improvement, or any improvement at all, in producing hunters?—Oh, no; I would not like to see it in the hunter at all, in any shape or form—the Hackney is a harness horse.

488. But you do think the Hackneys could be introduced in the North without any danger of the Hackney strain being spread over the country, and damaging the production of hunters?—I do; I think the hunting men know how to protect themselves.

489. You think a man could detect a strain of Hackney blood after a generation or two?—I think if he cannot detect it there is not more harm in it than cart-blood in the hunter that he cannot detect at present.

490. There is no danger of the progeny throwing back?—No.

491. You think the Hackney blood would be discernible in the mare?—Yes.

492. And it would be the breeder's own fault if he could not discover it?—Yes.

The Commission adjourned.

SECOND DAY.—WEDNESDAY, OCTOBER 21st, 1896.

PRESENT:—THE EARL OF DUNRAVEN, K.P., in the Chair; LORD RATHDONNELL, LORD ASHTOWN, SIR WALTER GILBEY, SIR THOMAS G. ESMONDE, M.P., HON. HENRY W. FITZWILLIAM, MESSRS. J. L. CAREW, M.P., F. S. WRENCH, PERCY LA TOUCHE, and COL. ST. QUINTIN.

MR. HUGH NEVILLE, Secretary, was in attendance.

JOSEPH R. O'REILLY, further examined.

493. The CHAIRMAN.—As a member of the Irish Hackney Society, have you any more information you would like to give the Commission—as representing that society?—No, not here, I think I gave all I had yesterday.

494. Sir THOMAS ESMONDE.—On the general question of horse breeding, have you any experience whether there is much breeding in Ireland, from [illegible] of stallions?—From my experience in a number of the County Dublin Horse Breeding Committee, I [illegible] a great many [illegible] small mares that came before us for registration at the county shows; and [illegible] the registration of stallions the society found it very hard to get suitable stallions [illegible] for the use of the country; this led to the alteration of the original scheme which was the same as that in England—subsidising stallions, giving them £100, and asking them to serve [illegible] tenant farmers' mares.

495. But afterwards?—It was found that the mares that went to these stallions were [illegible], as a rule, and stallion owners were not pleased. There were several reasons for giving it up; that was one of them.

496. What system do you think the best?—I have no doubt that the best system, and the best principle, is registering sound stallions, and giving [illegible] to farmers to bring suitable mares to those sound stallions. A farmer's mare ought to be inspected [illegible] necessary [illegible] the [illegible] also, and I don't think there can be a better principle than to have soundness on both sides [illegible]. The Royal Dublin Society in 1894 employed a scheme [illegible] the stallions to be registered [illegible] and the mares to be inspected at the county shows and passed sound by a veterinary surgeon.

497. Did you find that scheme popular?—It worked well in some districts, but it required time, and I do not think the society gave it sufficient time to work in the country. The registration of stallions at that time was not complete, and had not arrived at the same standard as at present; [illegible] mares [illegible] sound were [illegible] when they

... before their county committees, that farmers begin to breed. That machinery must be established by degrees, and it is my strong opinion that this principle will become the best.

498. How long is that system in operation?—That in 1892, carried on with slight alterations till 1896; in 1896 a new scheme was adopted, and 1898 was the ... in 1899.

499. Mr. La Touche.—With reference to the evidence you gave yesterday I understand you to say you approved of breeding from any pure bred stallion, but you objected to any scheme of registration of half-bred stallions—what do you mean by a pure bred stallion?—Thoroughbred—I would say stallions that are in Weatherby's Stud Book, Hackneys that are in the Hackney Stud Book, and Americans that are in the Standard Register, the American Trotters.

500. Why would you call a horse entered in the Hackney Stud Book a pure bred horse instead of what is usually known as a half-bred?—You can only trace them on their sire side; in the Hackney Stud Book they are traced on both sides for many years. I believe that altogether there are twenty volumes of the Hackney Society's Register containing, I think, the pedigree of 14,000 stallions and mares.

501. I think in the Hackney Stud Book was first published in 1883 or 1885; that extends over a period of fifteen years. Do you think that is long enough to constitute a pure breed?—The breed was in the country for years before; it is traced back to 1755; I believe the Hackney breeders were to be found very much in the Eastern counties of England and Yorkshire; it was kept very much to themselves in the same way that we in Ireland keep a particular breed of hunting horses.

502. I take it that you prefer a stallion from the fact of its being entered in a Stud Book for eighteen years to a stallion got by a thoroughbred, out of a dam that had been covered by a thoroughbred horse and whose dam and grand-dam have for years been got by thoroughbreds?—You can trace it better with the Stud Book; you can go back in that case for a longer period; it is easier traced. You have no Hackney Stud Book to go back to, you can only go by Weatherby's for the thoroughbreds.

503. Mr. La Touche.—Thirteen years is not a long period to constitute a pure breed?

504. Mr. Wrench.—Is it not a fact that although the Hackney Stud Book was only published in 1883 it reproduces the records kept for many families in Yorkshire and Norfolk for the last 100 years?—That is so.

505. Yesterday, I think, you said with regard to American horses that you had seen some in Belfast, and that you believed a great many American horses were imported, and that you thought they were of a worthless class?—Yes, from what I saw, but it is right to state that I only saw two ugly beasts.

506. Do you think that it would be prejudicial to Ireland to have those horses spread over the country?—I do, most certainly.

507. Have you at all considered, or do you suggest that there should be any way of marking those American horses?—Some are branded; the Southern American horses are properly branded—particularly for this country—but some come from other parts of America without a brand. It is easy, however, to recognise them by their flat sides and lanky appearance.

508. With their tails cut off, do you think it possible to recognise them?—Well, if they were in condition it might be difficult to recognise them.

509. Do you suggest there should be a marking of foreign horses?—I certainly think it would be a great advantage.

510. I think you said you would like to see the registration of horses greatly extended?—Yes.

511. That applies to horses of all pure breeds?—Of all pure breeds.

512. Take for instance a county where the Dublin Society's scheme is not in operation, how would you ascertain what class of horses you would have registered?—I should certainly say that each county should have some representative—the Horse-breeding Committee in the county should be able to know the class of horses that would suit best for the county, and the sire that would suit the mares of the county; the selection should rest very much with them.

513. Have you thought how you would form a County Horse-breeding Committee?—Breeders should be represented on the committee; that would be a matter for the counties themselves, the farmers ought to select.

514. Would you leave it to the county to select the particular class of horse they required?—Yes, I would.

515. Sir Walter Gilbey.—In England all the thoroughbred horses that receive premiums are examined at the Spring Show by specially appointed veterinary surgeons. May I ask what system is pursued in Dublin?—The horses are all examined by veterinary surgeons; in 1893 they were sent down all over the country, a considerable expense to examine the horses that were put on their register, and they were not put on unless passed by them as sound, and passed by the County Committees as being suitable sires to produce hunters or useful horses.

516. Do you think that is a preferable system to the one in practice in England?—Yes, I think it far better.

517. Any veterinary surgeon can examine?—The Royal Dublin Society send specially to examine, and to make sure they are satisfied with the opinion of the veterinary surgeons of the Society; but in many cases they send direct, particularly in cases where there might be any suspicion.

518. You have said it was the practice in the Dublin Society to have an examination of mares. You are aware this system is not carried out in England; stallions on the show yards are examined, it has been going on for years; there is a committee appointed to the Society where these stallions are, but there is no inspecting of mares; it is left to the discretion of the owner?—I don't think that is sufficient; I think examination should be on both sides.

519. The Chairman.—You are a member of the Royal Dublin Society?—Yes.

520. And on the Council?—I am on the Council; the agricultural portion of the Council.

521. And you have taken a very active part in the affairs of the Society?—I have taken a great interest in all the doings of the Society.

522. When did the Society first turn its attention to the question of horse-breeding?—In 1887 they turned their attention to working the Government grant; they were granted £5,000 for the improvement of the stock of this country, and they devoted £3,000 to the improvement of the breed of horses for the farmers in the country; the other portion went towards bull premiums.

523. And on what system did they apply this grant?—First, in 1887, on lines similar to those at present in use in England, exhibiting stallions; that was changed in 1892 to registering sound stallions and issuing nominations to the value of £3 to farmers' mares, only available to horses on the Society's register, and these nominations were only given to sound mares.

524. And did you find that worked well?—We found it worked extremely well; that the money went into the farmers' pocket first, and then went back to the stallion owners—first into the farmers' pocket in the shape of nominations, and then it went to the stallion owner, so that both sides were benefited, the owner of the mare and the owner of the stallion.

525. Is that scheme of the Society in operation throughout the whole of Ireland, both scheme operation

throughout the whole of Ireland up to 1894; there it was altered, and I may tell you, as chairman of the County Dublin Horse Breeding Committee, that my committee unanimously reported this year asking the Royal Dublin Society to revert to the system of 1894.

526. To revert to it in what way?—The system of giving nominations; the County of Dublin Committee were unanimous in recommending a revival of the system of 1894, and have asked the Royal Dublin Society to revert to it.

527. What is the present system?—Of giving prizes to mares, and foals to the nominee; the other system was giving nominations in the spring before the service season; the present system gives prizes to mares allowed to registered stallions, and to mares with foal at foot, and their prizes for foals got by registered stallions.

528. That is the system since 1894?—Yes.

529. And the system up to 1894 was what you have already described?—Yes.

530. And your county wish to revert to the system up to 1894?—My county committee want to revert to the 1894 system as being the best suited to our county. It is more satisfactory to distribute [illegible], and we think the money goes much further, and besides that more parties are benefited under it. In the present system the prize winners alone are benefited, and they are smaller as compared with the nominations. In our county we get £300, and we issued fifty nominations. Under the present system we had only thirty prizes, so that at the most not more than thirty could be benefited, and there were not thirty [illegible] because the foals were given prizes as well as the mares, and of the mares that got prizes their foals also got prizes, so that the number of farmers benefited was much less. I should say the proportion would be twenty to fifty.

531. Why was the old system ever altered?—I think it was because a number of mares that were up in some of the shows were considered not of the quality they ought to be, and the nominations were not all issued by the county committees. I don't think there was a general wish to alter it; it was the wish of some societies, no doubt.

532. Did any other county, recently, give the county of Dublin, express any opinion as to the present system?—I can only speak for two other counties. Cork and Wexford, that I know, have expressed it, but the majority will be coming in now; we are expecting them every day.

533. And how will they be guided as to their decision?—I could not answer that question.

534. Do you think yourself that the former system was better than the present?—Most decidedly.

535. And do you think that the efforts of the Dublin Society have had any marked effect upon the improving of the breed of horses in Ireland?—I think so; from what I have seen at the last show the mares which are brought before the county committees are better, and they are younger mares.

536. You attach great importance to the soundness of mares?—Very great importance indeed.

537. And in your opinion are the farmers inclined to sell their best mares?—If they get a good price they very often do, but there are a great many other good mares in the country.

538. Is there not a great tendency to sell the good mares and breed from inferior mares?—I do not think a farmer will sell a good mare if the produce is bringing him in a good return. I think the market very much regulates that.

539. You are very much interested in the breeding of harness horses?—I take an interest in the breeding of harness horses.

540. You have bred all classes of horses?—Yes, but I breed thoroughbreds now more than any other class.

541. As regards the possibilities of breeding harness horses in the future, has it ever occurred to you that the value of horses for all purposes may diminish, owing to the introduction of motor traction?—[illegible] I hope we will not see motor cars here for a very long time, at any rate.

542. In breeding hunters, the produce of which might not be good enough for that purpose, would they be good enough for general utility purposes and harness horses?—Very often.

543. Would what I might call the inferior produce of Hackney stallions be of equal marketable value?—I think so for harness purposes—more so, in fact, than the others.

544. Lord Ashtown.—You object to half-bred sires being taken on the register of the Royal Dublin Society?—Yes.

545. For what reason?—Because I think you are on unsafe ground. You may be successful, but it is risky to go outside thoroughbred registered stock—pedigree stock.

546. Would you be averse to a register of horses being formed, so as to try and get half-bred sires with a guaranteed pedigree?—I think it would be hard to establish a register of horses. I don't know what [illegible] you would take. Would it be the sires that you thought would breed a hunter or half-bred [illegible]? Pedigree does not make a hunter or otherwise.

547. Don't you think that some sire is necessary under the scheme besides the thoroughbred?—Yes, more for harness; I don't think so. I do think that in many places you want a thoroughbred horse with more bone for getting hunters.

548. What would you do with the light filly?—If I found a filly would not breed a profitable animal from the thoroughbred I would get rid of her, or send her to a Hackney, and try my luck there.

549. Mr. Thomas Kennedy.—Do you know anything of the operation of foreign commissions?—I have not visited foreign studs.

550. Do you know if there are many Irish mares bought by foreign breeders?—Yes.

551. Not so many now, I believe, as formerly?—Not so many as years ago. I could not, however, answer that question as well as others might.

552. Can you say what qualifications were necessary in mares to entitle them to premiums of the Royal Dublin Society?—They must be [illegible] and suitable for producing hunters, and [illegible] as they are.

553. Lord Rathdonnell.—With reference to your remarks about the change of system in the Royal Dublin Society, under the old system was it not a fact that a number of farmers were obliged to send their mares to certain horses in the district—that they had to choose; they were obliged to send them?—Yes. The 1894 system was the registration and nomination system; that is, the system was that of selecting stallions, giving them £50, and obliging them to serve fifty mares of some such qualification. In 1894 they were sent to certain set horses. They had to send their horses to the shows, only in their own district.

554. Under the present system is that abolished?—They can go to any sire in Ireland on the Register.

555. There is a remark that you made about hunters and I would like to ask you a question. Suppose a half-bred horse of the stamp of the "Lawyer" or "Revenge," would you prefer to breed from them or to a Hackney stallion and try your luck?—If breeding for a hunter, I would certainly send her to the "Lawyer"; if for a harness horse, I would go to the Hackney.

556. You would go to the Hackney for action only, when the action of the "Lawyer" or "Revenge" is good?—I would, in preference; you would be certain of it, his characteristic is action, and that he transmits it to his get, almost without exception, is my experience.

557. Mr. J. L. Carew.—You said you were principally for the breeding of thoroughbred mares?—Yes.

[illegible]

555. **You have bred from Hackney sires?**—I have.

556. Have you given them up?—No, but really my system of breeding is breeding thoroughbreds for hunting sires.

557. You said in reply to Lord Ashtown that you would send the light filly to a Hackney stallion for preference?—Yes, to produce a harness horse.

558. Not a hunter?—No.

559. Colonel St. Quintin.—What class of harness horse would you propose to get by that cross—an ordinary or light trap horse?—You would get a light harness horse from a weedy mare crossed with the Hackney, the result would be a good deal more bone, there would be the mare [illegible] by the Hackney sire, you would get bone and action.

560. A useful agricultural horse or light trap horse?—It might be either, it depends on the sire, if the horse be a powerful animal or of a smaller stamp.

561. Would you be able to breed what they call a light van horse?—I don't think [illegible] that you might get a class of hunting mares; I don't [illegible] they were very light, about the same substance as would breed a hunter. I saw very fine van horses bred in this way in this country.

562. Mr. La Touche.—Why do you think the light weedy filly is more likely to breed a carriage horse than a hunter?—With the Hackney you would get bone and action which you will not with the thoroughbred with a very light filly.

563. Why should you get more bone from the Hackney than the thoroughbred if the thoroughbred had more bone?—The result is generally more bone from the Hackney than it is with the thoroughbred.

564. A particular class of thoroughbred?—Probably you would have a great deal to say to it; it is hard to get a thoroughbred with a considerable amount of bone.

565. I have not had very much experience of [illegible] Hackneys, but I should not think I had ever seen a Hackney that would transmit more bone than the sire?—I think there are plenty of them that would.

566. I suppose an unsound thoroughbred would [illegible]?—Certainly.

567. Is it not laid down by authorities that the bone of a thoroughbred is of a harder and denser nature than any other?—It is of the very best, I should say.

568. Then it comes to this, that if a Hackney and thoroughbred are of equal measurement of bone, the weedy filly is just as likely to produce a bony horse by a thoroughbred as by a Hackney?—I don't go so far as that. I don't think you will get bone as often with a thoroughbred as with a Hackney.

569. Of course the thoroughbred with bone of this description is much more expensive and much more valuable and not within the reach of Irish farmers?—Yes, that is so.

570. If such horses were put in the reach of Irish farmers the value of horses would be more increased than by bringing in a new strain?—Decidedly.

571. You would not accept the pedigree of the Irish horse through to his family for 200 years, as they said, of the breeding of half-bred mares?—I would take it as it is known, as the saying is.

572. You would not consider him a pure bred horse although he produced records for 100 years?—I would not.

573. Mr. Wrench.—Have you ever met with an Irish farmer who could produce records for 100 years?—No.

574. Or 50?—No.

575. Or 20?—I suppose there are some families that could go back a good many years—the larger farmers.

576. Are you aware that in portions of England Hackney mares were looked upon as being so valuable that they were actually held by breeders in their wills as their mares?—I was not aware of that.

577. Is it not a matter of fact that the action horse of a Hackney is derived from that of a thoroughbred as a rule?—I would not go so far as that.

578. You have not studied that question?—I might not say it was.

579. With regard to the breeding of harness horses and hunters do you think the harness horse comes quicker to a valuable age than the hunter?—The Hackney comes very quick. You can put them to harness at three years old.

580. Therefore they are an early marketable horse?—Yes; you would market a three-year-old, though it is done in some parts of Ireland.

581. Do you think it a great improvement that under the Scheme of 1894 the examination is not only for soundness but also for suitability?—Yes, most decidedly.

582. Before that it was only for soundness?—In 1892 they were inspected for soundness and suitability.

583. The mares?—The mares.

584. Not stallions?—The stallions put on the Register were certainly inspected but not inspected so very carefully as at present.

585. Had you any doubt as to the suitability of any stallion before he was put on the Register?—Under the 1892 scheme we sent down to inspect them.

586. It was not done so carefully then?—Not [illegible], that is why I say the registration has advanced so much during the last few years that it is getting more valuable every year.

587. And the registration has been very much more perfect for the last two years?—Decidedly, very much more so.

588. Mr W. Gilbey.—You said yesterday you had experience in breeding successful Hackneys, and won prizes at the Dublin Show this year; what is your experience of breeding from harness mares, have you tried the cross made with thoroughbred stallions and Hackney stallions [illegible]—I have only got harness mares [illegible].

589. The mares that bred these prize winners are harness mares?—Yes, my experience in Ireland is the county of Dublin on [illegible] Hackneys.

590. The dams of these prize winners, were these Irish bred mares?—I could not follow their pedigree because they were bought at auctions, and really you could not find in what you would be likely [illegible] the pedigree of Hackneys is limited to two [illegible] of the Hackney breed.

591. The Chairman.—The Hackney Stud Book is in existence for sixteen years?—Yes.

592. And it was compiled then from records by the breeders of owners?—Yes, the general one.

593. You do not think an Irish Hackney Stud Book in Ireland could be compiled in the same way?—It would be too big a matter entirely. I calculate there are 100,000 brood mares in Ireland alone, and there you could not trace the pedigree entries.

594. You think that could be done in England but not in Ireland?—I don't know that it could be done in England either.

595. You have no knowledge yourself, personally, of the registered [illegible] Hackneys?—No, only hearsay.

596. Lord Rathdonnell.—There is one question with regard to the alteration of the Spring Show, which I think you said you were in favour of—as the Autumn Show, the reasons for which I believe to be that those who inspected should be able to see the produce and their dams?—That was one of the reasons; that was suggested as an improvement to be able to see the foals, but that could be equally well achieved if funds were sufficient to continue the system at Spring Shows, and to supplement with it to give prizes to yearlings got by the registered stallions.

Oct. 23, 1896. Joseph B. O'Reilly, B.L.

In that way you would see the results of the scheme, and also encourage the farmer to nurture his young horses, because success really depends to a great extent on the way the colts are fed. It would be of vast importance if farmers were trained to feed their horses the first year. If properly fed the first year there is a chance of their turning out well, if not there is no chance.

597. You said also there was rather a difficulty of tracing pedigrees in Ireland, and you were not sure it would not be difficult in England also?—Yes, but specially difficult in Ireland because horses changed hands so often; it is almost impossible, you can carry on the name of the sire but you cannot trace the dam side at all.

598. Do you see any difficulty in showing yearlings at all?—No, I don't see any difficulty in showing yearlings at the Spring Show in conjunction with a show of mares for nomination.

599. You think there could be no alteration—no change of the premium?—No, not without the knowledge of the county committees; it would be quite impossible.

600. The CHAIRMAN.—The Royal Dublin Society's scheme is not in operation in all counties?—To the best of my opinion it is in every county.

601. Mr. WRENCH.—It is in operation, but not much used in some and more in others; is not that the case?—Yes, it is being supported in some counties; it is more applied for. Some counties are stronger than others in horses. According to [illegible] figures it varied in 1896 from £140 in some counties, and the county of Cork got £[illegible].

602. In one class, commonly a premium over from the fund of the Society [illegible] being [illegible] ?—There is a [illegible] every year.

603. And it is generally expended in providing stallions?—Yes, which the society used to buy [illegible] which they think wants a stallion; if the breeder writes to the Royal Dublin Society and asks them to send a stallion, they generally buy one and sell him to the applicant on the instalment system.

604. And the society is [illegible] would not in this case [illegible] to acquire a good stallion?—That is so; I think they bought two. [illegible] at the [illegible] in the back of any [illegible].

605. The CHAIRMAN.—What is that scheme you quoted from now?—The Society's Horse Breeding Scheme for 1896.

606. That is the latest?—Yes.

607. Mr. LA TOUCHE.—All those horses purchased by the Royal Dublin Society were thoroughbreds?—Yes, without exception.

Mr. R. Hunter Persse.

R. HUNTER PERSSE examined.

608. The CHAIRMAN.—You are the secretary of the Irish Hunter Horse Society, I see.

609. For how long?—Since the 13th of May this year.

610. When was the society started?—All I know on that subject is derived from the information on the minutes. I know it was founded in the spring of 1895.

611. Can you give us any information as to the affairs of the society when you took office?—Yes, sir. On my accession to the secretaryship, the books of the society and the affairs generally were in arrears. I believe that this was entirely due to the fact that the secretary for the preceding year had left Ireland, and the post had been vacant or practically so. On the 13th of May no steps had been taken to collect the annual subscriptions for the year or to secure any new members.

612. How many members were there when you took office?—For 1896 there were eleven life members and forty-six annual members, total fifty-seven.

613. That was in 1896?—Yes, that represented the strength of the society at the time I became secretary.

614. You published an annual report?—We did, sir.

615. Would you put it in?—This is put in, sir. I gave Mr. Neville some twenty copies for 1895.

616. Will you publish a report for this year?—Yes, sir.

617. When is it published?—The report for 1895 was prepared by myself, consequently it was very late in the year, it was in May, but if I am instructed by the council to do so I see no difficulty in preparing an annual report for 1896 in December.

618. Well, if your council approve of that we should like to have it?—Very well, sir; let them give me the order, and I will see to it; I have got the whole of the financial department here before me, and I can give you any information that you would like, which would otherwise appear in the report.

619. I don't think it would be of value to us. What we want rather to know is what practical steps your society takes to further its objects in improving the breed of hunters in Ireland?—The practical steps that we have taken last year are detailed in the annual reports so far as they exist in connection. I can tell you what has been done this year.

620. Yes, tell us.—Would you like, in the first place, to hear the change that has taken place in our membership?

621. Yes, I should like you to give us any information you think useful?—Comparing 1896 and 1895, our membership has altered as follows:—Life members remain as before, eleven; the annual members have been increased from forty-six in 1895 to seventy in 1896, an increase of fifty-six per cent. Our annual subscriptions for 1895 amounted to £46 5s.; for 1896 they amounted to £84 [illegible]. Recently one gentleman [illegible] by mistake, and I kept it. We have since then had a donation of £2 which a gentleman who sent it said was by mistake, and I kept it. I used it as a receipt for it in the shape of a receipt for a donation, which he seemed quite pleased with. Then as to what we have done. This year we gave prizes at the Royal Dublin Society's Show in August in Class A and Class B, the same as the year before, and precisely the same amounts—£15 in all, and one silver medal, which cost £3. We gave this in hunter horses shown in harness, one [illegible], not exceeding six years old, bred in Ireland, and exhibited by a resident in Ireland. We gave £10 in Class B for young horses suitable for hunting, [illegible] and upwards, not exceeding four years old. We also, as in 1895, organised and arranged for a parade of winners, [illegible] preceding the winners of their class with a [illegible]. The whole parade of 1896 cost our society in all £15 [illegible]. That society's total of £[illegible] [illegible], did [illegible] the Royal Dublin Society's Show. We also rendered assistance to the breeding and improvement of hunter horses in Ireland by giving prizes and grants at provincial shows in the following manner and order:—To the North Eastern Agricultural Association, which held its show at Belfast, for Class 11, "For the best young horse or mare, 15.2 or over, not exceeding four years, bred in Ireland and exhibited by a resident in Ireland, to be shown in hand," we gave £20 and a silver medal. The £20 was divided into three prizes of £[illegible], £[illegible], and £[illegible]. To the Ballymoney Society, Class [illegible], "For the best [illegible] or hunter horse bred in Ireland, gelding or mare, three years old or upwards," we gave a cup value £5, or, if preferred, a silver medal and £[illegible]. The cup was taken. We also gave £10 towards the completion of the driving track in Ballymoney show grounds.

612. Where is the Ballymoney Agricultural Show held?—In County Mayo, in Connaught. We gave to this £10, because we thought it was a good and deserving object for us to support. To the Ballymena, Ballyclare, and Whitehaven Agricultural Society, which holds its show at Sligo, we gave "For the best horse, shown in hand, suitable for harness, bred in Ireland, under four years old and over 14.2 high," £5. As a matter of fact we offered £20 at that show, but I think the judges did not think the horses were up to the mark. To the County Fermanagh Agricultural Society we suggested a class for harness horses, and we gave £5 for that class. The class was "For the best harness horse, gelding or mare, not exceeding four years old, 14.2 or over, bred in Ireland. To be shown in hand." To the Ballinasloe Agricultural Society, Class 10—"For young horses, not exceeding four years old, with style and action suitable for harness, bred in Ireland and exhibited by a resident in Ireland, to be shown in hand," we gave a cup value £5, or if preferred a silver medal and £5. To the Clones, Co. Cavan, Agricultural Society "The Irish Harness Horse Society gave £5 to be divided between Classes 11 and 12, as a means of encouraging the breeding of horses suitable for harness purposes." Class 11 was—"Driving. For the best single harness horse, [illegible]." Class 12. "Driving. For the best single harness pony, [illegible] 14 hands 2 inches." The summary of our expenditure in aid of harness horses and their breeding and improvement in the year 1896 shows a total expenditure of £117 4s. 6d., as against £103 13s. last year, an increase of £14 11s. 6d. In prize money awarded. In 1895 we gave to the Royal Dublin Society £70 14s. 6d. This year we only gave £66 14s. 6d., or a decrease of £4 per cent. That happened to be because there were fewer entries to make up. Instead we had taken a reduction, in that leaving the monies that we paid the horses that did not come under this year. In 1895, on the other hand, we gave to local societies £31 15s. 6d. This year we increased our donations to local societies to £50 10s., being an increase of £18 14s. 6d., or 59½ per cent.

613. The main difference is that you have given larger support to the local societies?—Yes, that we have increased our membership, we have got more money (as well we have given more money out), and we have altogether done wisely, which we did think. I got that additional donation of £5, that we did not win it, and we thought we did this well in the one with this year.

614. And I suppose, if you had a larger amount of money at your disposal, you would be able to do more?—Yes, sir, we would be delighted to do so.

615. Did you consider the results of making your efforts to the local shows satisfactory?—I cannot say, the information at the present, begin to the [illegible] of all the societies we supported, and their results I have been. They pointed out to the fact that the horses in the competition were not in fairly satisfactory. We think—I am speaking of it for the committee—that they might be greatly improved both in quality and number. In Belfast we had a good show in quality and fifteen entries, being two more than for Class 12 at Tubbercurry. In Enniskillen we had 15, Ballinasloe 6, Ballyshannon 18, Clones 11 (in all classes—10 and 7). At Bray I never could exactly tell the number of entries; there seemed to be some confusion on the part of the stewards, and the horses did not turn up at the time they should have.

616. Then in your opinion, and in the opinion of your society, the entries are not quite satisfactory, either in point of numbers or in point of quality?—I really would like to express an opinion on behalf of the society. I am not sure that the question was ever [illegible] to council, but I certainly, if I can speak for [illegible], think there is certainly room for considerable improvement, both in numbers and quality.

617. I think you said you got reports from the secretaries of the local shows?—Yes, sir.

618. Perhaps you would let me look at this and see if they would be useful to us. Do they speak of the quality as well as of the quantity?—I [illegible] a circular with the questions.

619. And what said?—This is from the Secretary, Mr. R. J. Kelly, of the Ballinasloe Agricultural Society. The questions were:—"1. Have the interests of exhibitors for the class or classes for which the Society has given prizes been, in any way, advanced?—Answer, 'No.' This refers to 1895. "2. Were the exhibits generally speaking of a good quality, or did you, on the contrary, observe a marked want of improvement? If so, kindly state in what directions?—Answer, 'Of fair quality, considering the district and the novelty of the class. A marked want for improvement is only noticeable.' "3. Horses should be more of a harness class and quality and conformation, should be attended to. 4. Are you of opinion that the exhibition of harness horses is deserving of support, and with a view to popularising and improving the breeding of animals of this description, are you prepared to recommend continued action on the part of this Society on these similar lines?—Answer, 'Yes.' This society has found exhibition with to a great extent this season where breeders find foreign horses are classed in sheep, and a distinct market thus afforded. Breeders in Ireland are only being induced to breed this more useful for a hunter by encouragement or otherwise."

620. And the other letters are more or less similar to this?—Yes, sir, I think so. I think there is one of those hardly deals with the point, but it happens to be in my bag, and I will go on with the others.

621. These are all for 1895?—All for 1895.

622. There are only six similar questions this year?—Yes, sir, I was not instructed to do so. The time is hardly over, but I shall certainly do so soon.

623. In general, you seemed to be in a position to say whether the quality is improved or not?—I will answer this question, sir, to the best of my ability.

624. On the whole, perhaps you can answer it, if you have not the replies?—I attended some of those shows, and speaking in a good many lots myself, and I have had enormous letters, but in answer to any formal question. Although, at each of every show some animals of merit as harness horses, there is, in the opinion of those qualified to express one, great room for improvement, especially in the counties of action. At Clones there was not one single horse with good action. Only two out of seventeen had any pretensions to action. At Ballymoney only the prize winners were worth looking at as animals in harness; whilst Bray it appeared to me to be a very poor class. What might not be quite so bad the good harness invariably belonged to gentlemen or businessmen farmers or neighbours, whereas the exhibits of the farming classes were shuffling, clumsy, and only half broken to the or something gear. I lived in the Ballymoney district for eleven years—from 1873 to 1884—and consequently I do know something about that district. Contrasting that time with the period 1873 to 1884, I should say the harness horses in Ballymoney district had distinctly deteriorated. This may, however, be due to the fact that formerly every country district was supplied, and there were plenty of good time pots. So far as the Bessborough is concerned, I believe the type of harness horses is worse than it was.

625. You heard there is more demand?—I think the best youngsters are sold, and the children kept, in a greater extent than was the case before agricultural depression had set in. I think that is one of the causes that is operating.

626. Is that all you wish to say on that point?—Yes, sir; that is all I have on that point.

627. What part of the country does your society principally confine its operations to?—All over Ireland.

E 2

Oct. 29, 1896. Mr. [illegible]

637. Do you consider any particular parts of Ireland more naturally adapted to breeding than others? — I am not the man that [illegible]. I think it is more [illegible]. Certainly in the North of Ireland they are far more [illegible] towards horse breeding than in Leinster.

637a. They breed fewer hunters and more heavier [illegible] in the North, and more hunters and [illegible] horses in the South? — Yes; I should think so. I can tell you. I have got some statistics on that subject which may be of some use. I understood in response to Mr. Neville to do anything I could in the way of statistics, and I have tried to do so. I can give you the supply in Ireland and the percentage of the various purposes for which horses are kept.

638. Where do you take these statistics from? — They are all taken from the agricultural returns for Ireland, and I have placed the different classes in different columns, and calculated the weight of the percentages myself.

639. Perhaps you would give us the percentages — the number [illegible], etc. The returns relate to 1895. I am putting out of account anything under two-year-olds, because I think the percentages that apply to two-year-olds and upwards would apply to the others so far as the purposes for which they were bred, kept, or used. In Ulster 88 per cent. of the two-year-olds and upwards are bred, kept, or used for agricultural purposes; 8·8 per cent. are bred, kept, or used for purposes of trade and manufacture; and 3 per cent. for purposes of amusement and recreation. I calculate that there is one brood mare to every [illegible] horses in Ulster. I arrive at that conclusion in this way. I take the number of horses under one year, and I take the basis which I believe was laid down by the Royal Commission on Horse Breeding in England that 40 per cent. of mares go barren [illegible]; and there is no difficulty whatever in taking that, and working upon that, and finding the number of brood mares.

640. On that supposition? — Yes, on that supposition.

641. Do you divide the province into counties? — I have it [illegible] in counties too, etc.

642. Can you give us the same percentages and numbers for counties? — Yes, I can, etc.

643. I think that will be valuable? — I have got every county by itself, and every single column has got a space for each county.

644. Can you give us the counties of Ulster? — I will put in any document if you like. I only finished it last night, and I have not got it properly bound, but I hope your lordship will allow me to add them.

645. We will go on with the provinces? — Yes, sir; and if at any time you should wish I will be only too delighted to give you a copy. In Leinster 7[illegible] per cent. of two-year-olds and upwards are kept, used, or bred for agricultural purposes; [illegible] per cent. for trade and manufacture; and 2[illegible] per cent. for amusement and recreation. In Munster 8[illegible] per cent. are for agricultural purposes; 7·[illegible] for trade and manufacture; and [illegible] for amusement and recreation. In Connaught [illegible] per cent. are kept for agricultural purposes; [illegible] for trade and manufacture; and 5·[illegible] per cent. for amusement and recreation. I do not absolutely carry out the decimal figures in all cases, but I think you will find that I account for 99 per cent. and over of all the horses two years old and upwards, and if you like to do so I can very easily account for the 100 per cent. It is [illegible] carrying out the figures a little further.

646. I suppose those used for trade would be heavy draught horses? — I think it means van horses, dray horses, lorry horses, bakers, butchers, cart horses [illegible] trade and manufactures. If you would like the figures for Ireland as a whole I have them. The total number of horses, two years old and upwards, in Ireland is 464,608. The percentage engaged in agricultural purposes is 83·6, in trade and manufacture 9·6, and in amusement and recreation 6·61. Total 99·97. I have submitted these figures because I think they will give you an indication of the different interests in Ireland, and your lordship will take note of the fact that the agricultural interest appears to be of overwhelming importance.

647. Mr. Fitzwilliam. — Can you define what amusement and recreation means? — I cannot tell you what amusement means; it is a very wide term.

648. The Chairman. — Are many horses sold out of the country under two years old? — I am afraid we are very far behind the world in these statistics. I have got the Board of Agriculture Returns for 1895, and I have looked through them, and I am not very sure that they specify two years old. They don't. They specify stallions, mares, geldings, and the average importation to Great Britain. That is all I can tell you — the importation to Great Britain from Ireland. The average for 1893, 1894, and 1895 was 39,478.

649. Of all kinds? — Mares and geldings, that is excluding stallions.

650. Mr. La Touche. — What does "export" mean? — Export from Ireland, import to England; these are English agricultural statistics.

651. The Chairman. — Can you give us the number of horses in each province? — I can. I can give you the number of horses under one year, one year and under two, and two years old and upwards. I can also give you the total number of horses in each province.

652. Give us the numbers for each province of two years old and upwards? — Ulster 161,339; Leinster 140,606; Munster 113,613, and Connaught 49,031. Total 464,608.

653. Can you give us also the total number of horses in Ireland of all ages by provinces? — Yes, I can. Ulster 193,661; Leinster 207,181; Munster 161,101; and Connaught 76,912. Total 639,112.

654. There are no statistics, you say, to show the export of horses over two years old? — There may be, but I am not aware of them. I really have not asked Dr. Grimshaw myself, I had not got time.

655. You will be able to put in statistics the same as these for the counties? — Yes; I have got everything before me here.

656. We will not trouble you to read it. Have you any other statistical information? — I made out this: I think it may be of some use to you. It is more or less an adaptation of the figures on that sheet. I made out this as indicating the different tendencies in each province, breeding or buying. I have found that in Ulster breeders sell largely under one year old. Taking the figures in that table as fair averages, one year with another, the horses under one year old in Ulster exceed those over one and under two years old by 6,0[illegible] or 37 per cent. That is to say those under one exceed those over one and under two by 37 per cent. Ulster, therefore, I take it, breeds and rears largely for sale at an early age. There are 193,661 horses of all ages in Ulster, of which 27,631 are calculated as being brood mares — that is, one in every seven horses in Ulster is a brood mare.

657. You don't mean kept exclusively for breeding? — Well, of course, it is more or less a manipulation of figures. I calculated the number of brood mares as well as possible without any absolute information, and then I divide the number of horses of all ages by the number of brood mares, which gave one in seven. In Leinster the foals bred in the province are evidently not sufficient for the requirements of the horse keepers of Leinster. The horse supply therefore is supplemented from other districts. The number of those over one and under two years old exceed those under one by 11·125 or just exactly 33 per cent. Leinster, consequently, has not such strong claims as Ulster to be considered a purely breeding and rearing province. She has to find 11,125 yearlings outside her own boundaries. There are in

Leinster 207,783 horses of all ages, of which 38,827 are believed to be [illegible]. In Munster [illegible] under two [illegible] by 6,081, or 23 per cent. Munster, accordingly, is unable to supply her own [illegible] less than Leinster, though [illegible] In Munster there are 161,234 horses of all ages, of which 34,838 [illegible] In Connaught the [illegible] Connaught may therefore be [illegible] Of the 76,398 horses of all ages in Connaught, 21,819 [illegible] This is doubtless due to [illegible]

[illegible]

873. Your contention is that Ulster is the great breeding [illegible]—Yes, and that they sell [illegible]

874. I want to point out this—that of two year olds and under in Ulster there are 161,559 [illegible]

[illegible]

876. You have an explanation?—No; I am simply taking the figures as they are before me.

877. Lord Ashtown.—You say that Ulster [illegible] into Leinster [illegible]

878. The Chairman.—[illegible]

879. Mr. Chaine.—[illegible]

[illegible]

[illegible]

730. Mr. La Touche.—They are classified?—Only as mares and geldings and stallions. They go back to the year 1852. I have got the book and the average of the last three years.

731. The Chairman.—We will take those back.

Witness.—Do you want me to include stallions, or just mares and geldings?

732. Everything.

Witness.—180 stallions were imported into Great Britain from Ireland last year; of mares, 13,371 were imported, and of geldings, 13,023; making a total of mares and geldings of [illegible], or a total of stallions, mares, and geldings of [illegible].

733. Mr. Wrench.—Apparently that would not include any horses that were taken to other countries from Ireland?—No, sir; there are no particulars in the agricultural statistics of Ireland, neither are there in the agricultural returns from Great Britain, as the export of horses from Ireland to foreign countries, so far as I can see.

734. Sir Walter Gilbey.—In many of these depots where Irish horses are sold, as there are no figures to guide one, what was your experience of the class of horse that was sold? Take York, London, the eastern counties; they are a mixed class for hacks, hunters, &c.?—Yes, they are just that sort of indefinite and very difficult to be described animal which we have throughout very large portions of Ireland. They will do for a variety of purposes. If they happen to be big enough I suppose they may go to trams or buses. I should say that a very great many of them find their way to hansoms and cabs. The ordinary animal that I have seen in the fair in the west of Ireland, and the ordinary animal—putting aside high-class hunters—that I have seen sold as Irish horses in England—it is very difficult to define what they are. They are suitable for various purposes.

After the adjournment,

Major G. W. Studdert examined.

735. Chairman.—Major Studdert, I understand you are a resident in County Clare?—I am, my lord.

736. What part of the county?—Within six miles of Ennis, a place called Cragmoher, near Corofin.

737. You are a breeder of horses yourself?—I am.

738. What class of horse have you been breeding?—Thoroughbreds. I bred a great many half-bred hunters.

739. You have acted as judge, I think, at a number of shows in this country as well as in England?—I have.

740. I take it that you have had a considerable experience in breeding horses yourself and a large experience of horses generally?—Yes, I have over forty years' experience.

741. You have also attended markets and fairs in the country?—Yes, I have, my lord, all those years.

742. And in Great Britain?—I have, yes; in Great Britain, not so much, of course, as much as in this country. But I have attended fairs and markets on the other side.

743. Taking the larger area, I think, the whole country of Ireland, from your experience, have you formed any opinion as to what class of horses it is most profitable to breed?—I have.

744. What do you think?—I think high-class hunters.

745. What do you mean by high-class hunters?—A lot of horses are bred in my own county and the [illegible]. He pays from £20 to £100 [illegible] hunters, and a great many of them would make very good [illegible].

746. The same class of horse, in fact, as the hunter?—Very much.

747. How would they be bred?—I think, without exception, by thoroughbred horses.

748. Out of what class of mares?—Well, out of rather well-bred, good-boned [illegible] mares, [illegible]. In some parts of my own county, the land is very good, and they produce very good [illegible] by thoroughbred horses, most of them by what we would call old Irish mares.

749. We have heard that expression used several times, and I [illegible] understood by most members of the Commission. Possibly, I think, you could give us some explanation of what is meant by an old Irish mare?—My idea of what I would call an old Irish mare is a big, lengthy mare about 15.3, with good neck, head, and shoulders. She would have some hair on her legs, too. She is a mare that can go eight Irish miles twice a day (in which we call a [illegible]) [illegible]

750. How are they produced?—They are produced from old Irish blood, with some crosses of thoroughbred blood. They have a light, clean head, [illegible] mostly all of them.

751. Have they Hackney or Clydesdale [illegible] blood in them?—I don't think they would do [illegible] if they had Clydesdale or any Hackney blood in them, from my own experience.

752. Have you any experience of Clydesdale or Hackney horses?—Yes, I have experience. I have [illegible] Hackneys in England.

753. You never bred from them?—No. I rode and drove in Suffolk, [illegible] Yorkshire and Norfolk Hackneys.

754. In your opinion what would be the effect of the introduction of Hackney or Clydesdale blood in producing the class you describe—high-class hunters and harness horses?—I have an [illegible] opinion [illegible] it would be [illegible] in that class of horse, and a great [illegible] of [illegible] the Irish hunter.

755. [illegible]

756. Then you would consider that [illegible]

757. And [illegible] the use of thoroughbred sires?—[illegible]

758. [illegible] Hackney [illegible] Royal Dublin Society [illegible]

[illegible]

748. Then you think if Hackney blood was largely introduced into this country it would have a prejudicial effect upon the hunters?—I am sure it would.

749. We have had the opinion stated in evidence that the Hackney strain would be so easily detectable that there would be no danger of its having any effect upon the breed of hunting produced in this country unless the owners of mares chose to make use of it—what do you think about that?—I don't think that. A man who has been brought up to breeding and is a good judge would perhaps be able to detect the made hind quarters and straight shoulders and knee action, without any obvious action, but the vast majority of those who buy hunters are not what I call judges of horses, and I don't see how they could detect it.

750. What I want to ascertain is whether in your opinion, assuming that in certain districts the introduction of Hackney blood might be useful in those districts, there would be any probability that the blood would spread throughout the country generally, and act prejudicially in other districts more suitable for the breeding of hunters?—I think it quite possible and quite probable that it would spread.

751. And that it would not be detected by the average farmer?—No, certainly not.

752. Are many remounts of the Government bought in your part of the country?—The English Government?

753. Yes.—One two Government buy on the average I think about 60 or 70 horses a year from the Ennistymon district.

754. Are they also bought by other countries?—Yes, some remounts for the French, Italians, French, and Belgians.

755. How are they bought?—They are bought by dealers; Messrs. Widger and Mr. Mahony. The Widgers are the largest buyers, but there are others buying too.

756. What class of horses are they?—They are a good kind class of horses, particularly those that are bought for foreigners. They are mostly three year-olds. There are more half-bred ones. Some beautiful colts and fillies go away with them.

757. Would you consider that the introduction of Hackney blood, for instance, would have a prejudicial effect upon those horses also?—Certainly. I think it would have a wonderful effect upon the foreign buyers. I have spoken to several of those and they told me so.

758. Have you any idea what objection they would have to the Hackney stallion?—They all look upon them as a kind of cross that a horse does [illegible]. A man is anxious that you can sell him in one day what would take him time to get back. I mean they have no staying power. They are all very well for show purposes, striking up and down, or for ticking up and down a street, but I think any man of experience would agree as to the conclusion that they are a lazy one-horse breed.

759. What class of sires have you in county Clare?—We have a nice class of well bred mares. They have everything improved since the Royal Dublin Society started. As Mr. O'Reilly explained to you, though we had a fewer number of mares at the show this year, they were an immense lot of good mares.

760. Do you think the Royal Dublin Society has had a good effect?—I think it had a very good effect, but I agree with Mr. O'Reilly in thinking, however, that the previous system had a better effect than the present system. I think if it was altered perhaps ... a little different then it would have a very marked effect on the class of horses Ireland would produce in a very few years.

761. Have you formed any opinion as to the relative value approximately of the breeding of hunters or harness horses—the export value, I mean?—Well, in my own county I think sixty and ninety guineas. In the fair generally, with very few exceptions, the high priced horses are three year olds. I think they are almost equally bought—either high class hunters horses and other high class animals. The harness horses go for quite as much money as the colts bought for hunters.

762. What kind of stallions are there in your county?—All those horses I tell you of were got by thoroughbred stallions.

763. What thoroughbred stallions are there in the county?—I know a good many of them. I could run over a good many of them.

764. Are they well adapted to the class of mares you have in the county?—Well, I don't think they are, my lord. I think there might be a few more good horses there.

765. What is the matter with them?—I think a good many of them are weedy, not leggy, and they are not thick enough. I think the horse we would want in my county is a thick short-legged horse, with good knees and hocks. I think that is more important than perhaps size, even in producing good sized hunters.

766. By thoroughbred horses?—I mean thoroughbred horses.

767. What kind are the fees there?—Well, from £3 to £5. £5 is the highest. That brings nearly sixty guineas.

768. Do you think the price has very much effect upon the farmer in determining the stallion to which he sends his mare?—Yes. There can be no question about that. If the farmer could get a thoroughbred horse for the same price as any other class, I should think I am quite safe in saying that each 95 per cent. would go to the thoroughbred horse.

769. Have you any halfbred stallions in the county?—Yes. I think I am underestimating when I say 95 per cent. of the farmers would go to the thoroughbred. It is the money that prevents them sending to the thoroughbred.

770. They would like a good horse, but they cannot afford to pay for him?—Yes; they like a thoroughbred horse.

771. It would not pay a man as a commercial enterprise to have a good thoroughbred horse?—That is just it, and that is the reason the first system of the Royal Dublin Society was the better one. I think the first system, with a little modification, is what the country would require.

772. What age are they sold at—two year olds?—Yes, and lots of yearlings and two year olds are sold too. Nearly all buy them year olds. The farmers that are comfortable, the large farmers of over fifty acres, generally keep their horses if they are promising until they are three year olds. Of course they must then sell them as two year olds and yearlings.

773. How do they treat their young stock—do they treat them well?—They do not treat them as well as they ought. I am always preaching to them, and I am getting them into it a bit, and they are feeding them better the first year now. You cannot get a poor farmer to treat his horse as he ought. If they would only feed them well the first year they would make a great deal of everything. Some of the land is very good, and some of the horses grow well, though not put into a house in winter. Some may get a bit of hay. That is all they get.

774. Are they housed in winter?—They are not housed at all. It is a mild country.

775. Do you think the farmers generally appreciate the necessity of treating them their best?—I do, my lord. But it is really very seldom a poor man is kept without the means with no pocket. Nearly all the good mares are sold for hunters, or if they have plenty of size they are sometimes bought to make hunters of them, or go as remounts to other countries. Some [illegible] go away [illegible]. Consequently I think if young mares could be encouraged it would have a wonderful effect. I have been always saying that.

776. How would you propose to do that?—My idea would be to have a show every year for mares, to give

[illegible]

Dec. 11, 1894.
Major C. W. Blacker.

districts as there used to be?—I think there are quite as many.

805. Is there any improvement or deterioration in the soundness of the mares about you?—No, I don't think there is very much.

806. Or vice versa the other?—I don't think there is any deterioration very much in the breeding of horses. I think Ireland produces as many good horses.

807. But in soundness?—There are certainly more horses rejected now than forty years ago, but I don't think there are so very much more unsound ones, but I think the veterinary surgeons find out things now that they did not know anything about before.

808. Breeding societies where they are breeding these could meet?—Yes, they do.

809. You spoke of stallions in your district, and the absence of thoroughbred stallions for high-class carriage horses, and the hunters?—Yes.

810. Do you think the stallions could be improved?—I think they could.

811. A better class?—I think some of them are very good; but, as a rule, they could be very much improved.

812. There is room for a better class of stallion?—Yes.

813. Do you think the price of the stallion has very much to do in determining the farmers to which to send their mares?—I think very much.

814. You think that is the most important thing?—Yes, it is the most important thing.

815. (Lord Ribblesdale.)—I think you stated you have several times ridden and driven Hackneys?—I did.

816. Were many of those that you rode or drove thoroughbred animals, either prize winners or sires in other words?—I cannot tell you about their being prize winners; they cost a good deal of money. It was in Suffolk, with my wife's people, with whom I used to spend a good deal of time. The pace is good, generally, but altogether they were very good.

817. What was your experience there—what would you say as regards their shape and action, first as regards riding and then as regards driving; say first, as to riding?—Rather too much action, I think, for pleasure riding. They went up and down a lot, almost all of them I knew; they shook you about a good deal. My idea of a riding horse is a horse I could get up and ride along at eight or nine miles an hour, but I could ride one of them that I could ride there, miles without giving them a good walk, and I was then a younger man than now. I had only seven miles to go from this old gentleman's place to my brother-in-law's place, and they certainly had not much humour in those coming back after that long ride.

818. Had you under the saddle?—Yes, but it was just the same with the harness. It was a heavy, sandy soil, I think you, in Suffolk. They might suit in the gill in grass country always.

819. (Mr. Garnett.)—Is it not your experience of Hackneys that they are made rather a mistake about, on the road?—Yes, after they are worn out they lose their action.

820. Is not the superiority of the Irish to the English horse due to the superior Irish blood?—In my opinion, certainly.

821. I think you said that you bred from two year old mares?—Yes.

822. What in your experience of breeding from them at that early age?—I think they are just as likely to produce a good animal without injury to the mare herself—I am talking of half-bred animals and thoroughbred or other mares.

823. Would you give them a rest after the second foal?—No, I think if you want to keep them on for breeding you need not give them any rest at all.

824. If you did not want to keep them on for breeding, but wanted to make them into hunters or harness?—I would not breed from her as a three year old. I would let her run up till she was made and breed her in the spring.

825. It would tend to weaken her?—Yes.

826. You said that the Royal Dublin Society has worked well and that with a little modification the old system if reverted to would be a great improvement?—I think it would.

827. What is the modification?—I would revert to the old system of subsidizing mares. I can name myself that the committee in my own county are of that opinion, and I believe they wrote to the Royal Dublin Society to that effect, because as Mr. O'Neill so clearly put it, you get very nearly 50 per cent. more mares, at least you get 50 mares instead of 30—you enable 50 farmers instead of 30 to get their mares covered by a thoroughbred stallion.

828. (Col. St. Quintin.)—Talking of mares and the trying to keep good mares in the country you say you would give prizes to two year old mares instead of three year olds?—Yes.

829. Would it not be better if you could increase the age and give a prize which would make it worth a man's while to keep his mare for a four year old with a foal at foot?—Yes, certainly.

830. If it could be carried out would not that be better than giving a prize for two year olds?—Yes, but my idea is to encourage them to give two year old prizes in the first instance. If they kept a good foal from her they might be tempted to give her another chance. They might think it is keeping a good well bred mare. It would be all the better if the money was there.

831. If it could be arranged to give a breeding premium for two year olds and a high premium to the four year olds it would carry the inducement still further?—Yes, and have a better effect.

832. Then, with regard to stallions, you spoke of a half-bred stallion, which we take to mean a horse with a strain in it—would you suggest any rule by which a horse of that class must qualify before he is admitted as a stallion?—Oh, yes; I should think the horse should be passed by a board of three or five really qualified competent men. I think it would be very likely to have a most ruinous effect if you let a horse of that kind slip in without the greatest supervision.

833. Unless you actually knew his breeding?—Unless you knew all about him, and that he and his dam had no taint of Hackney blood.

834. With regard to the advice you would give the farmer if he wished to breed a horse himself and also to get rid of him at a remunerative price, there have been discussions as to the class; and, putting the thoroughbred class aside, there are two or three classes which have been introduced into the country which are largely such as the Hackney, the Clydesdale, and the Shire horse. If you wanted a strong draught horse—I am speaking more or less personally, because I only want draught horses, and I cannot obtain them in Ireland—if you wanted what I would call a really high-class, active agricultural horse, would it pay the farmer best to breed from the Hackney, the Clydesdale, or the Shire?—I should think from neither of the three.

835. Not of the three?—None of the three. I should breed from a horse out of a thoroughbred mare, with a certain amount of breeding in him. There are some of these in Ireland—what you call half-bred horses—strong, half-bred horses, one of our ordinary Irish cart mares got by a thoroughbred horse with great size and bone, some of them.

The Chairman.—You didn't answer Major St. Quintin's question as to which of the three you would prefer.

Col. St. Quintin.—He said he would not breed from any of them.

836. And weight?—And weight, as you say.

837. The Chairman.—Which of the three would you prefer, if you are confined to the three?—I should say the Clydesdale, that would be the lesser evil of the three, if you force me to choose the lesser evil. I would

by the class of horse you talk of is a class of horse I never saw any breed or breeding.

838. Col. St. QUINTIN.—It is now bred in England?—No.

839. I don't think you can breed him in Ireland?—No.

840. A great distinction has been apparently going on in reference to the Hackney horse—do you think that a cross of the Hackney, from his conformation and action, is likely to breed a horse that you can possibly rise to anything as a hackney hunter?—I don't think so at all.

841. Or as a heavy draught horse?—No. He has not size or length for an agricultural horse, nor is he suitable for riding. The class of horse you talk of is not bred in Ireland. All Irishmen breed with a view of getting a hunter, or a harness horse or, perhaps, a jumper. That is the ambition of every little farmer in Ireland if they can get money to send their mares to a thoroughbred horse.

842. Mr. La TOUCHE.—You describe the old Irish mare as a long, low, good looking animal, with good neck and shoulders, and good legs and feet. I suppose it is only from a sense of patriotism that you claim the title of an old Irish mare, if nonexisting?—I think the type are still to be found in great numbers in Kerry, Cork, and Limerick, particularly where there they are breeding them. You see them going about with the old type of head, neck, and shoulders. They are not generally so nicely made behind, but they have all the characteristics. I think there are a great many of them left yet. They are bred in families from generation to generation. Somebody said that the Irishmen does not keep up the breed to-day. My experience goes against that. I know strains of blood that have the same breed in their families for generations keeping on a mare always from the old stock.

843. Usually crossed with a thoroughbred horse?—Yes.

844. In answer to Mr. FitzWilliam, you said you could buy a horse in England and that you could sell the same horse in Ireland for 50 per cent. more. Have you mean in England owing to the prestige of the Irish horse. Do you mean by that only the prestige, or do you not mean the superior excellence?—I mean owing to the superior excellence of the Irish animal, because the Englishman has found it out.

845. It is really owing to excellence more than prestige?—Yes.

846. The excellence precedes for it prestige?—Yes.

847. You say you think it would be advantageous in subsidising young mares with the view of inducing farmers to keep them to breed from, and that the shows of the Royal Dublin Society would be best devoted to that purpose; but are you aware that the whole sum available by the Royal Dublin Society is only £3,200 a year or £100 a year for each county in Ireland. Giving a prize of £10 to each young mare that would only subsidise ten young mares in each county?—I said if the Society had the money. I am not at all throwing a reflection on the Society for what they have done. That is the way for them to put it out if the money is there. If the money is not there, I think it would be better to subsidise the mares rather than the present system of giving prizes to horses and foals.

848. When you say subsidise you mean give them premiums?—Give them premiums as you did at first. I think the old system of giving premiums would do more to do good than the present.

849. You think it would be better to give £100 in the horses than to give £100 in twenty [illegible]?—I do.

850. Mr. WRENCH.—You are only breeding thoroughbreds?—Yes.

851. Do you find that breeding thoroughbreds pays better than breeding half-breds in Ireland?—I do not.

852. You do it as an amusement?—Yes.

853. It has not paid nearly so well?—Up to the present it has not paid at all. I won't say that, for I have got £1,000 for a three-year-old.

854. How long have you been breeding thoroughbreds?—Only four years.

855. You have hardly had time to reap the results?—I hope I will.

856. Your land is some of the best in Ireland for horses?—I think it is.

857. Perhaps the best?—It is certainly the best that every thoroughbred I breed has extraordinary bone.

858. That you attribute a great deal to the land?—A great deal to the land.

859. In the experience you have had of Hackneys the personal experience confined to the Hackney you rode belonging to your relative in Suffolk?—Except what I have seen in shows. My one of them was confined to those horses.

860. Do you know how they were bred?—I don't know.

861. You don't know whether they were Norfolk or Yorkshire bred?—I think they were both.

862. Were they pedigree horses?—I think they were.

863. Do you know by what stallions?—I don't. I know he gave £250 a piece for some of them.

864. Is it possible they were not pure bred Hackneys?—It is quite possible. They were the usual type of Hackneys, quite as good looking as I have seen at these shows.

865. You have no particulars as to their pedigree?—No. I should not place much value on it if I had.

866. You would not place much reliance on a Hackney having two or three crosses of the thoroughbred?—The cross would be too extreme, and I don't think it could ever hit.

867. If you a Hackney horse having two or three crosses of thoroughbred blood, you would not place any value on that, but would much prefer him to one that had not.

868. Are you aware that a great many horses sold as Hackneys in Yorkshire have a large admixture of thoroughbred blood?—Yes.

869. You prefer that to not having any?—Yes.

870. You don't think the Hackney blood puts something the thoroughbred blood?—No.

871. You would modify your opinion of the Hackney if he had a good deal of thoroughbred blood?—It would make him better than if he had not. I am not contemplating cross breeding. If a man likes to make a fool of himself as I do breeding thoroughbreds, or if a man likes to amuse himself bringing over Hackneys, well and good. But I do think that where money has been given by the State, it is a great thing to encourage the breeding of horses of that class. They may be very nice and very valuable. We know they have fetched great prices, though my impression is that the price is entirely going down, and that it will go down entirely. They are very nice to drive about, but they only tend to do injury to the breeding of high class hunters and harness horses.

872. You are speaking only from personal experience?—What can we speak from except personal experience?

873. It is rather a sweeping condemnation to talk of them as hackney animals at the present time when you have only had experience in England?—I form my opinion from the type of animal I see at shows, that they are thoroughly unsuited to in any way improve the breed of hunters or high-class horses. If you ask Mr. Woodcock or Mr. —— whom he selects highest priced carriage horses he will tell you he gets them all from Ireland, and there is no Hackney blood in them.

874. At the same time you don't profess knowledge as to the breed of the Hackneys in Yorkshire?—Certainly not.

[illegible] [illegible]
[illegible]

[illegible]. You said you would register a certain class of hackneys with only a stain in their pedigree if they passed a competent Board?—Yes.

[illegible]. Do you think that those animals that have so much of the thoroughbred in their breeding [illegible] advantage over the pure thoroughbred horse?—No, if you could get a [illegible] horse with that strength.

[illegible]. Could you buy that horse cheaper?—You would have to breed that class of horse. I don't see where they are to be got now; [illegible] the Lord [illegible] asked me about.

[illegible]. You don't know many of that class of horse?—Years ago there were a good many in the South of Ireland where they were [illegible]. Thirty years ago at Cahirmee Fair you would have [illegible] or fifty better stallions than those that [illegible] in this season and were [illegible] all the winter.

[illegible]. There are few of those left?—Very few.

[illegible]. You would not register any horse with only a small stain, say one or two thoroughbred crosses and no matter how good his stock?—I would not.

[illegible]. You draw the line at horses with only a stain in their pedigree?—I say the great difficulty is to draw the line.

[illegible]. Would you follow the lines laid down by the Hackney Improvement Society in England?—Yes, I think I would.

[illegible]. CHAIRMAN.—Do you know what the lines laid down by the Hackney Improvement Society are?—I know that there was some [illegible] of that sort.

[illegible]. Or the exact conditions?—I remember when reading the qualification at the time that I considered they were well thought over.

[illegible]. Mr. WRENCH.—Do you think it would be possible to obtain many reliable records where there are [illegible]?—Yes, if you had anybody that you might depend upon in the country. I think [illegible] are very [illegible]. I have had [illegible] years experience buying and selling horses in large [illegible] and I have not got a [illegible] pedigree [illegible] in my life.

[illegible]. You are pretty well known?—I am pretty well known. If you get a [illegible] pedigree [illegible] I [illegible] proceedings in [illegible] instances.

[illegible]. If the Royal Dublin Society had the funds at their disposal would it be worth their while to try and find out the records of those mares so that they could form the [illegible] knowledge?—[illegible]

[illegible]. I would not go so far as that, but when any records would be found that they should be registered and kept,—would it not put up the value of the [illegible]?—It would be a good thing to do but an expensive thing to do, and I don't know that it would repay for the trouble and expense.

[illegible]. Would not foreigners give more for animals if they knew their pedigree?—I don't think they would.

[illegible]. Sir WALTER GILBEY.—With regard to the breeding of horses that was given at the last Dublin Show—I am sorry I have not the catalogue—there were [illegible] the breed [illegible] for any other class of animal, and yet that class was very [illegible], and there was no record with regard to the breeding of the animals. They would be what you call a heavy Irish mare, a [illegible]. The owners do not seem to know how the animals are bred—[illegible] to the majority [illegible] to know [illegible]. I [illegible] speak from experience, because I was judging [illegible] class. I have never been judging the [illegible], but I am always judging at the show. I think you have got pedigrees with some of the mares. I thought most of them did get their pedigree in the catalogue.

[illegible]. Even in the [illegible] last year and [illegible] there are [illegible] entries there are many of the mares whose pedigrees are unknown—[illegible]—It is. I should have thought you would have had the pedigrees of most of them.

[illegible]. Is it not rather strange that the Royal Dublin Society should give large prizes without the name of the breeder being insisted upon?—I think it ought to be. If you get the [illegible] and the [illegible] you might certainly tell where you got the mare.

[illegible]. It is a general topic of conversation, with those who visit the Dublin Show, the want of pedigree with regard to the breeding of Irish horses?—I think it would be better to have a very [illegible] without a pedigree than to give a pedigree without the name of the breeder. Of course if you give the pedigree without giving the name of the breeder you cannot prove anything.

[illegible]. You have visited districts that you claim to be equal to the Irish horses. You seem to know [illegible] as to whether they are not bred from other blood, different from the way Irish horses are bred; have you any knowledge of it, as to the way those animals were bred?—I know only the knowledge that they were [illegible] bred ones.

[illegible]. I don't know of half a dozen breeders in England that breed a [illegible] horse [illegible] by thoroughbred horse?—That is the question which has [illegible] the breeding [illegible]. I cannot tell you about that.

[illegible]. What is the extent of your experience about those [illegible] in England?—[illegible] in Cheshire. I saw many of them. I [illegible] twenty years ago.

[illegible]. Was that the time you speak of as having been in Suffolk?—I have been in Suffolk a good deal since. I [illegible] in Suffolk [illegible].

[illegible]. You are not sure those animals you describe as Hackneys were not [illegible] Suffolk horses?—Quite certain. [illegible]. He had [illegible] on his farm.

[illegible]. Was it possible they might [illegible] in condition when you saw them, [illegible]?—They were in [illegible] condition enough.

[illegible]. I think you will admit that at a public inquiry, and in the case of a great authority like you, making such statements, I should consider myself remiss unless I put these questions to you. [illegible]

[illegible]. That is the [illegible] I [illegible] to draw. I [illegible] a good many of them thirty miles [illegible] in London, and I [illegible] that state of things. [illegible] English bred. I [illegible]. [illegible] you said [illegible] were [illegible] in [illegible]. [illegible] responsibility from the hands of [illegible] gentlemen? [illegible] you [illegible]. [illegible] a [illegible] of five or six [illegible], [illegible] a [illegible] responsibilities [illegible], and I don't think you will get men [illegible] it if you [illegible]. I think the men you [illegible] to be perfectly independent of the country.

[illegible]. The society [illegible] be [illegible] if those [illegible] gentlemen gave [illegible] and [illegible] of the [illegible]. It is always [illegible] a particular [illegible] bred. [illegible] you think they would be [illegible] a [illegible] their [illegible]?—You know it is not [illegible].

[illegible] any man to mind his stallion [illegible] and although [illegible] in [illegible], still if you mate a mare and a stallion properly they are more likely to produce a good animal than if not mated properly. If a mare is bad in one or two points I think it is a bad thing to give her a stallion having the same bad points. The only way you can do that is to have two good points. Great care should be taken in the [illegible] selected. They should know their business [illegible] [illegible] do it. That is the most sensible way. I think it would be a very good plan if it could be done.

901. Chairman.—You have had a very long and a large experience, speaking generally, but confining yourself to the hunters and high class horses which you have spoken of, would you think there has been any deterioration in the quality during, say, the last twenty years?—Well, I don't think there is, my lord, but it is the general opinion that there is, but I think there is not. [illegible] it is impossible to find [illegible] now. I think what leads people to say that is that there are [illegible] people looking for hunters now [illegible] looking for them thirty years ago. There were certain localities in Ireland where we used to go [illegible]. There is hardly a district in Ireland now where buyers don't go.

902. The demand has very much increased?—Yes.

903. Increased much more largely than the supply?—Yes.

904. And the quality has not deteriorated?—There are as many good horses bred in Ireland as [illegible].

905. There are more horses bred?—There are more horses.

906. If the quality is maintained there ought to be very many more good horses?—Yes, there are more hunters and [illegible]. Every county has [illegible] three gentlemen who make or deal in horses. That was not in [illegible] of thirty years ago.

907. What kind of horses are used for purely agricultural purposes in your part of the country?—Light active horses. Heavy horses would not do. The farmers have such distances to draw their hay, and go to markets, and [illegible] would [illegible] that heavy horses could not do. These little horses being [illegible] [illegible] [illegible] and think nothing of it.

908. Do you think the produce of the Hackney stallions of the [illegible] Thoroughbred have [illegible] [illegible] [illegible] [illegible] [illegible] [illegible] [illegible] [illegible] [illegible] [illegible] [illegible] [illegible] [illegible] [illegible] them [illegible] four pounds apiece. I believe they were [illegible] [illegible]. That is all I can tell you. They said they were by the stallions.

909. What became of them?—They were bought up by the [illegible] at three and four pounds apiece.

910. Yearlings?—[illegible] foals. It has been a [illegible] for a great many years. They [illegible] them in [illegible] of thirty or forty over the country selling them as they go along.

911. Have you any personal knowledge of the [illegible] of the [illegible] under the Congested Districts Board?—Well, I know the Connemara pony—what used to be the Connemara pony. I have been through Connemara three or four times. It is a very beautiful country all through it, through the mountains, and I saw the animals there.

912. You never bought any?—Oh! I have had several Connemara ponies. I bought them for the children. I had them when my children were young. They were nice little animals. They had beautiful [illegible] [illegible] as [illegible], rather plain headed, a [illegible] not well [illegible], but good animals. I don't think you could breed anything but a pony in Connemara, you know. In fact I think it would not pay them [illegible] better to breed something else—[illegible], or something of that sort.

913. Mr. Wrench.—Have the foals of [illegible] deteriorated very much during the last fifty years?—No, those with a good [illegible] [illegible] [illegible] [illegible].

914. It is much easier now to buy [illegible]?—[illegible] [illegible] cheaper.

915. There has been a fall in second class hunters?—Certainly, in the third class horses.

916. While good horses are [illegible], the very third class horses are very much cheaper?—Yes.

917. Do you know if there is a [illegible] stallion standing in [illegible]?—I don't know him.

Mr. Wrench.—[illegible] [illegible].

918. Mr. La Touche.—The farmers who bought the foals at three and four pounds apiece have been in the habit of buying foals?—Yes, they come every year, dozens of them. They come to the nearest place to [illegible] and might [illegible] two or three [illegible].

919. What do they do with them?—They are bought by the small [illegible] farmers [illegible] up in the hills, and they are bought by the [illegible] in the [illegible] of [illegible] who [illegible] with them.

920. Do they use the fillies to breed from?—Yes, they are too small.

921. Lord [illegible].—Do you attach any importance to the light weedy animals on the farm you go to?—I do not know that there [illegible] [illegible] [illegible] [illegible] light horses.

922. Do you know what I [illegible] light [illegible] class?—Yes, I [illegible] would not [illegible] [illegible] [illegible] [illegible] [illegible] [illegible] [illegible] [illegible]. I [illegible] [illegible] [illegible] [illegible] [illegible] [illegible] of horse.

923. Are there plenty of them about?—There are plenty of them about.

924. And also the other class, the [illegible] [illegible] legged [illegible]?—Yes.

925. Suppose a farmer has a mare that won't breed to a thoroughbred would you recommend her being with a half-bred horse?—The one [illegible] [illegible] [illegible] [illegible], [illegible] [illegible] [illegible] [illegible] between which I could [illegible].

926. It is rather hard to say that the farmer [illegible] [illegible] [illegible] [illegible] [illegible] a [illegible] should not [illegible]?—You know that if he can not [illegible] to get a hunter on a good [illegible] [illegible]—if he does not [illegible] [illegible] [illegible] [illegible] [illegible] [illegible] [illegible].

927. I would like to ask [illegible] [illegible] [illegible] would give the farmer a [illegible]?—I give him every chance. If you give the farmer a thoroughbred horse at the same price as you give the other [illegible], every [illegible] of them will go away from the thoroughbred horse.

928. Mr. Wrench.—Do you know Mr. [illegible] [illegible]; don't you know his [illegible]?—He told me he had [illegible] thoroughbred horses, he [illegible] to have two or three.

929. Do you know that [illegible] [illegible] to [illegible] [illegible]?—I do not.

930. Don't you know he refused a big price for [illegible]?—I don't know anything about that. I know he has been [illegible] [illegible] [illegible] [illegible].

931. The Chairman.—Is there anything you would like to add [illegible] [illegible] [illegible] [illegible], my lord. I am at your disposal. I will answer you anything I [illegible] I can with pleasure.

932. Lord [illegible].—I think you said if there was a small [illegible] [illegible] you would not object to its [illegible] [illegible] [illegible] [illegible] [illegible] [illegible] if passed by the Board?—If the Board were a competent [illegible].

933. I think that would rather answer Lord [illegible] [illegible] about the half-bred [illegible]?—Yes.

934. The Chairman.—[illegible] [illegible] you [illegible] [illegible] to [illegible] [illegible] [illegible] [illegible] [illegible] or [illegible], [illegible] [illegible] [illegible] [illegible] [illegible] [illegible] [illegible]. If the [illegible] could be examined and passed by some competent authority you would not object to a [illegible] [illegible]?—[illegible] [illegible].

935. Have you any idea of what the general value of a thoroughbred stallion in your district would be—the cost price?—It is what they are worth?

936. What was given for them or what they are worth?—I should think there was not much given for

what were bought—a big price has been offered for one. I think something like £300 guineas. There are some of those you would not like to give so much for.

909. Mr. La Touche.—You would get a good one for £100?—Yes, if you went judiciously about it. They are a common animal to buy. I would not like to take a contract to get me good thoroughbred stallions for £100.

910. Col. St. Quintin.—Don't you think the thoroughbred horse to get hunters is a better sire for the money—which is half the price, and he is probably a big boned, short legged useful animal. He is the very horse you want to get into this district. If he is found as a two year old a little wanting to pass, he is castrated and turned into a hunter?—Yes, very often. If you get that sort of horse and it is wanted to be sound, the foreigner steps in as another horse [illegible]. I bought a horse at Newmarket and a foreigner offered me £300 profit on him the next morning, but I refused.

911. The Chairman.—You have not done that very often?—I was acting for the Royal Dublin Society. I did [illegible] since I did. That poor horse was killed on his way back. I was very near telegraphing to the Society to know what I would do.

[illegible], D.L., examined.

912. The Chairman.—You are resident in the **county Kerry?—Yes, sir.**

913. And a Deputy Lieutenant for the county?—Yes.

914. What part of the county do you live in?—Three miles from Tralee.

915. I suppose that part of the county is not in the congested districts?—No; it is not in the congested districts.

916. Are there many horses bred in that part of the county?—Yes, there are a good number.

917. Who are they bred by?—Bred by the farmers chiefly.

918. Small farmers?—Yes, large and small.

919. What would be the usual size of the holdings and the condition of the people?—Well, the holdings are not very large about there.

920. Do you breed horses yourself?—Yes; I have for nearly the last twenty years.

921. What class of horses?—Well, lately I have been breeding from thoroughbred horses altogether.

922. And what formerly?—I did formerly an American horse, an American trotter, and I got rid of him; he was not at all suitable.

923. Mr. La Touche.—Why?—Because his produce were not at all; very bad.

924. The Chairman.—You are breeding from thoroughbreds?—Thoroughbred sires altogether.

925. And half-bred mares?—Half-bred mares.

926. You had an American horse of your own?—I had, he was a very fine horse, but the produce were very bad indeed; they were not suitable, and the farmers about that hated him; and not at all like the produce—they could not sell them for any price at all.

927. What were they deficient in?—They had big heads and were slack in the loins, and had bad looking horses altogether.

928. The sire was a good looking horse?—The sire was a very good looking horse, and a sound horse; but a great number of the [illegible] unsound, although the mares were sound [illegible].

929. In what way unsound?—They had curbs and spavins particularly.

930. Do you know how the horse was bred?—I bought him in America; he was in the American Trotting Stud Book, I believe.

931. Then you returned to the thoroughbred?—To the thoroughbred.

932. Have you a thoroughbred horse of your own?—I have.

933. What are the general kind of mares in your part of the country?—There are some thoroughbred horses; there are some good, [illegible] and half-bred horses; very [illegible] half-bred mares.

934. What do you mean by not [illegible]?—Well, there are some Shire horses and Clydesdales.

935. Any Hackneys?—I believe there is a Hackney at Dingle and at Cahirciveen.

936. Well, Dingle and Cahirciveen would be some way from you?—Yes, it is a good distance.

937. Have you any personal knowledge of **what** they have produced, the Hackneys?—Well, I **have** seen some of the young ones sold. I saw some last August sold at Killorglin fair; the oldest, I think, was two years old, and they fetched wretched prices.

938. Rather bad prices?—Very bad prices.

939. What kind of prices?—I saw the second prize yearling sold from Cahirciveen for £8 10s., and I asked the price of a two-year-old myself, the man asked me £8 10s. I am sure he would have taken less.

940. I suppose you don't know at all what kind of mares they were?—No; I don't know what they were out of.

941. Were **there many of them** at Killorglin fair?—Well, I **saw four or five myself.** I was not looking for them.

942. And what is your experience, so far as you know, of the produce of the Clydesdales?—Two come into Tralee, and stand in Tralee one day a week, and then the other days they stand at their owners' places.

943. What kind of mares are put to them?—All descriptions of mares.

944. And, as far as you can judge, with what results?—Well, I think, with bad results; the farmers prefer the thoroughbred horse, but they don't like paying the fee.

945. What are the fees charged for thoroughbred horses?—Three pounds, I think, is the fee for all thoroughbred horses about there.

946. What do they charge for these Clydesdale horses?—I did not mention Clevelands, my lord, but Clydesdales, from 10s. up to 30s. for all the others, the half-bred sires and the [illegible] horses, [illegible].

947. Which do you find the farmers prefer, the half-bred or the thoroughbred? I think you said they [illegible] the same?—I think they go mostly to the half-bred ones, they seem to think that the thoroughbred are [illegible] heavy.

948. What do they want for agricultural purposes?—They want a light horse.

949. I think you said there were two such horses?—Two come into Tralee, but there are more about.

950. How long have they been in the country?—Well, these particular ones have been here [illegible] years, I think, but there were others not known before that.

951. Then there must have been a certain amount of demand for them?—But I think they would always go to the thoroughbred horse if they could get him at the same price.

952. Do you suppose that would apply equally to the Hackney?—How do you mean, my lord?

953. I mean if they could get the thoroughbred at the same fee as the Hackney, you think they would prefer the thoroughbred?—Oh, certainly.

954. Then you think that the fee is a very important consideration?—I think it is a very strong item.

955. What kind of mares have you in your district generally?—Well, I generally notice [illegible] that mares they only send to the [illegible] cannot sell.

956. Who do they sell them to?—Dealers come down to all the fairs; Cahirciveen is a large fair, and

are dealers from all parts of Ireland there, and foreigners buy horses there, too.

987. Do the foreigners buy through dealers, or by themselves?—I think they buy themselves there.

988. In your opinion, has the breed of hunters and horses of that class deteriorated in your district, or are there as many good horses produced as formerly?—No; I don't think there are as many good horses produced in Kerry as there used to be, and I think the reason is there is not so many thoroughbred sires as there used to be, and there are a great number of very bad sires [illegible].

989. You have said just now that the farmers are very much inclined to sell their best mares, would not that have a very bad effect?—Oh, yes, I think that certainly has; if they could be induced to keep their good mares it would be a very great thing.

990. What would you suggest to improve the breed of horses?—If there is some inducement held out to the farmers to keep the good mares, and to have good thoroughbred stallions there, I think that would greatly improve the breed.

991. It would be impossible, would it not, for private enterprise to supply what you call a thoroughly satisfactory thoroughbred stallion in competing prices with the cart horse and others?—It would not pay anyone to have a good thoroughbred stallion there, because they would always go to the cheap horse in preference.

992. Are the class of [illegible] to pay the [illegible]?—Some of them, I think, are [illegible], but there is a great number who [illegible].

993. They are tempted by the cheapness of the inferior horse?—That is it, I think.

994. Can you suggest any way of inducing them to keep their mares?—Well, I think if good prizes were given for young mares in foal, it might be an inducement. In fact, I think, the scheme of the Royal Dublin Society of 1904—I think that was the year when mares were nominated—I think that was much better than we had for the last couple of years, that was when the mares were nominated.

995. Do you know whether any recommendation to that effect has been made by any society in Kerry?—No, I haven't; I was not on the committee myself.

996. I suppose there is a society of that kind, is there not?—Oh, yes.

997. Lord [illegible].—You say you have been breeding horses about twenty years yourself?—Yes.

998. So that you ought to have a pretty good idea by this time what is the most paying horse to breed?—Yes.

999. And what class of mare would breed that horse?—Yes.

1000. Do you think the mares in your district are really capable of breeding horses that would pay the farmer to breed them in any size?—I do; there are good, large mares there. [illegible] and Dingle way, there are smaller horses, but about Tralee it is very good land, limestone land.

1001. Is there much tillage?—There is a fair amount of tillage.

1002. And, I suppose, they want a light quality horse to work the land?—Yes, light.

1003. But you say the Royal Dublin Society's scheme, the best scheme, [illegible] which is the scheme that you think is the better, to nominate the mares instead of giving prizes?—Well, because I think [illegible] and so go to their registered sires then.

1004. When they got nominations don't you think it helped the mare owner to keep a better class, to get

part of the [illegible], they don't want the thoroughbred horse so much now at all, they go in the [illegible] now.

1005. In fact you think the old [illegible] thoroughbred sires for the farmers?—Yes, it would make them go to the good sires more than they do now.

1006. Sir T. [illegible].—Horse-breeding is a large industry in your district?—Yes, there is a great deal of it.

1007. But you say you have not a sufficient number of suitable stallions?—No, I don't think there are enough suitable horses in the county.

1008. Are there many of the old breed of mares there still?—There are some.

1009. They are deteriorating?—They are, certainly.

1010. Have they been bought?—No, I think they are more dying out now.

1011. What class of horse do you mainly produce?—Hunting horses and harness horses.

1012. Which are the principal fairs with you?—Castleisland is a large fair, there are two or three large fairs in the year there, and Killorglin fair on the 11th August, that is I suppose the biggest horse fair.

1013. What class of horses are sold at those fairs now, do you notice whether they are better than they used to be or worse?—Well, I don't think they are as good as they were fifteen years ago, but I think they are getting a little better again, the last few years they have been getting better.

1014. Is that owing to some care being taken in breeding horses?—I think the scheme of the Royal Dublin Society has helped the breeding there a good deal.

1015. And you said that a good many horses are bought by foreigners at those fairs?—Yes, I have seen foreigners buying there.

1016. What kind of horses did they buy?—Well, the younger class mostly, I think, and some better class.

1017. Are there many horses suitable for troopers produced down there?—Oh, yes, there are a good number, a good number of troopers bought in the county.

1018. Lord [illegible].—You said just now that you preferred the Royal Dublin Society's scheme of 1904, in which they nominated mares to stallions, to the present scheme?—Yes.

1019. What reason do you give for that?—Well, supposing the horse was standing at £3, the stallion owner was paid £2 by the Royal Dublin Society and the farmer had only to pay £1 for the service of the thoroughbred horse; now he has to pay [illegible] for the service of the thoroughbred, so he goes to the cheap horse and there is not so much breeding from thoroughbred horses as there was then.

1020. Then you liked the nominations, don't you?—Yes.

1021. You give prizes there in Kerry?—We do.

1022. They are served by a registered stallion?—Yes.

1023. Did you have many mares at the last show?—No, we have not had many for the last couple of years.

1024. Not since this system came in?—No, we have had very few mares sent in for prizes, I don't think all the money was given away in prizes at all, there were not mares enough to give it to.

1025. Under the old system you mentioned £2 as the price of the stallion?—That is the price the stallions were in Kerry.

1026. And £2 paid to the owner of the stallion?—From the Royal Dublin Society.

1027. And the owner of the mare had to pay £1; did you ever know that the stallion owner paid any of the £1 to the farmer, thus making the fee less money?—I have heard of it, but I have no proof of it in any way.

1028. Col. St. [illegible].—You had a very celebrated breed of ponies in Kerry for many years?—Yes.

[illegible]

Col. M., [illegible]
Arthur [illegible]

1029. In certain parts of Kerry?—Near Killorglin.

1030. Are they still as celebrated in the same numbers as they were?—No, they are dying out. The ponies, you hardly ever see a pony there now.

1031. What has replaced them. How have horses replaced them?—Well, there is a very mixed breed there now.

1032. Did it used to be a very lucrative trade for the farmers who originally bred these ponies, was it not; they used to sell their ponies well?—Yes.

1033. Which is their usual industry there. Do they breed other animals in their place?—I think they gave up the ponies, I don't know what they do in stead. The one more small things, you cannot call these ponies, they are small horses that are very little value now.

1034. Would that country that used to produce those ponies produce anything better?—Well, when those ponies were there I don't think it would. I think the ponies are the most suitable thing for that place. It was from up in the mountains beyond Killorglin that those ponies used to come. It would not suit a horse.

1035. Mr. La Touche.—The part of Kerry you live in is not under the department of the Congested Districts Board Lands.

1036. How far are you from a congested part?—Well, Dingle, I think, is the nearest to me.

1037. All to the west of you beyond. Tralee?—That is the congested district.

1038. Are you acquainted with those parts of your county?—Well, no, I have not been out there.

1039. Have you been to Cahirciveen?—No, not lately.

1040. Do you know the part down south of you about Kenmare, Waterville, and Sneem?—No, I don't know that part.

1041. You have been engaged in horse breeding in the county Kerry the whole period you say?—Yes.

1042. Are there many resident gentlemen in the county Kerry who carry on horse breeding?—No, very few.

1043. Do you know of any to the west of you?—No, I don't know anyone in that district. Lord Castlerosse breeds horses near Killarney for the last six or seven years.

1044. May I take it that you are probably the most western resident gentleman in Kerry who is engaged in horse breeding?—Yes, I should think I am, certainly.

1045. In fact there is no gentleman, no landed proprietor, who lives west of you?—Oh, there are, but they don't breed horses.

1046. Mr. Hanley, of Dingle, I suppose?—Yes, and Lord Ventry; he is at Dingle.

1047. He is south of you?—South-west.

1048. You say there are Hackney stallions, the property of the Congested Districts Board, at Dingle and Cahirciveen?—I believe there were last season.

1049. Do you know by whose recommendation these horses were sent down to your county?—No, I don't.

1050. Were you yourself consulted as to the most suitable horses to send down there?—No, I never heard anything about it.

1051. Are you aware who was responsible for the recommendation of the Hackney horses there in your county?—No, I am not.

1052. You said in answer to Col. St. Quintin that the breed of ponies which came down from the mountains near Killorglin had deteriorated?—They have gone out altogether, you hardly ever see a pony there now.

1053. I take it that that is owing to the use of improper stallions?—I think so.

1054. Is it your impression that the use of Hackney stallions in Kerry is to raise the breed to the former condition?—No, certainly not.

1055. Do you think that a small short-legged thoroughbred horse put down into those parts of Kerry standing at St. [illegible] would be more calculated to improve the breed?—I certainly think it would.

1056. Do you think the stock would be able to stand hard there, the stock got by a thoroughbred horse would exist as well there as stock got by a Hackney?—I think they would be just as hardy as if got by a Hackney.

1057. As a matter of fact the animals bred there in the western part of Kerry don't have to spend the winter there; they are generally sold as foals?—The greater part of them are; foals and yearlings.

1058. You yourself are not aware of any gentleman engaged in horse-breeding in Kerry who was consulted as to the best sort of stallions to be sent there to improve the breed of horses?—No, I was not.

1059. Mr. Wrench.—That is rather a wide question of course, but you think the produce of the thoroughbred would be equally well able to stand the climate and conditions of Kerry as the Hackney; you don't speak from experience, I suppose?—Well, I have never had Hackneys myself.

1060. You don't speak from personal experience?—No, certainly not.

1061. You have been breeding horses for the last twenty years, have you found it pay?—Yes; I did not find the American trotter pay.

1062. But such you have taken to thoroughbreds you have found it pay?—I have found it pay fairly well; Yes.

1063. Did you happen to be at the Agricultural Show at Tralee on the 14th?—I was.

1064. You were not judging were you?—No, I was not.

1065. Did you see a class of yearlings that were there for which Colonel Conolly gave a special cup?—I really did not; I was engaged at the judging rings of the day; I had not time to go; I had to go round with one of the judges who was not judging horses, and I really had not time to go through the horses properly at all; I had very short time.

1066. You did not see that class?—Yes, I did see it, but I did not take much notice of it.

1067. Do you know how many animals there were in it?—No, I don't.

1068. You don't know whether there were twelve or thirteen animals?—No.

1069. Do you know what won the first prize, and what was the reserve?—In the class for the Challenge cup I think the winner was by "Wanderer."

1070. And what was the reserve?—I don't know.

1071. You don't know that the reserve was by the Hackney stallion at Cahirciveen?—No; I don't.

1072. You are speaking, I suppose, of the Show of Tralee?—Yes.

1073. I think you said that the farmers there would use a thoroughbred horse only that the horses they used [illegible]?—Yes.

1074. Do you allude to the one horse that was registered under the Dublin Society's scheme?—No; there are three horses I think there registered.

1075. Do you know the fee they, the farmers, would pay those [illegible] used to go there to [illegible] was not aware of it.

1076. You don't know what it is on their product?—No, I don't; they are not supposed to take the [illegible].

1077. I suppose if they put it on their posters that is prima facie evidence what they do?—I have not seen the posters.

1078. The Chairman.—When you say that you think the produce of the thoroughbred is as well capable of standing the climate as the produce of the Hackney of course you are speaking generally from what you know and have heard of the relative merits of the thoroughbred and the Hackney?—Yes, my idea.

1079. You think, in your opinion generally, the thoroughbred is as hardy and lives as much condition.

[illegible] the Hackney?—A great deal [illegible].

1050. [illegible] Hackneys [illegible]—No.

1051. Mr. [illegible].—Have you heard the [illegible] of the [illegible] Kerry?—No, I have not, personally.

1052. The Chairman.—Do you know how long the Hackneys have been standing in Kerry?—I believe the oldest [illegible] is [illegible] years old.

1053. [illegible] it is—[illegible].

1054. Lord Ashtown.—[illegible] of the Royal Dublin Society, I suppose you may take it for granted that [illegible] at the show, [illegible] the last show [illegible], and I did not [illegible].

1055. [illegible]—Yes.

1056. [illegible] and they did not [illegible] a long distance.

1057. [illegible] of the [illegible] for breeding a valuable [illegible] under the scheme?—Well, they were [illegible], they were not [illegible].

1058. They [illegible]?—Yes, [illegible].

1059. The Chairman.—I would like to ask you [illegible] the Kerry ponies that have disappeared, that is to say they have ceased to [illegible] demand for them [illegible]? [illegible] I think there used to be a good demand for them, but I think they got some [illegible], and [illegible] the breed.

1060. What did they want to breed these bigger for if they had a good demand for them?—Well, I don't know; I suppose they thought they would [illegible].

1061. They have not succeeded?—No.

1062. Mr. [illegible].—Was that the [illegible] of trying an [illegible]?—I think so.

1063. Trying a [illegible] which happened to [illegible]?—They [illegible], and I think that spoiled the breed, and they were neither [illegible].

1064. Lord Ashtown.—[illegible]?—That is [illegible].

The Commission adjourned.

Holiday note in margin: [illegible]

THIRD DAY—THURSDAY, OCTOBER 22nd, 1896.

Oct. 22, 1896.

Present:—The Earl of Dunraven, K.P., in the Chair; The Hon. Henry W. Fitzwilliam, Lord Ashtown, Sir T. H. G. Esmonde, M.P., Lord Rathdonnell, Mr. J. L. Carew, M.P., Colonel St. Quintin, Mr. F. S. Wrench, and Sir Walter Gilbey.

Mr. Hugh Neville, Secretary, was in attendance.

Mr. Samuel Thomas Roberts, c.e., examined.

Mr. Saml. Thomas Roberts, C.E.

1065. The Chairman.—Mr. Roberts, you are a member of the Horse Breeding Association?—I am, my lord.

1066. Are you also a member of the council of the Royal Dublin Society?—Yes, I am.

1067. And of the committee on Horse Breeding?—I am.

1068. Have you acted as judge in horse shows in Ireland?—I have for some years acted as judge in a great many provincial shows in Ireland.

1069. Have you acted in England at all as judge?—No.

1100. Are you personally interested in the subject of horse breeding?—Do you breed horses yourself?—[illegible].

1101. When was the Irish Horse Breeding Association formed?—The Irish Horse Breeding Association was formed in the early part of August [illegible] the first time [illegible] for the purpose of forming an association.

1102. Can you explain to us the object of the association?—The object of the association, as they [illegible], [illegible] evidence [illegible] horse breeding, and [illegible] with regard to the [illegible] Hackney [illegible] in Ireland, [illegible] in different parts of the country, with a view to [illegible] before you [illegible] your being thoroughly well informed on the subject.

1103. Does the association propose to make a [illegible] to ask the Commission to [illegible]?—We have not come to any determination on that. We have collected a large amount of information, which we will be glad to place at your disposal; as to what [illegible] will be a [illegible] consideration for [illegible].

1104. And you [illegible] position [illegible] to the Commission [illegible] all the information [illegible].

1105. He is coming before us probably [illegible] to-day.

1106. Have you yourself a general knowledge of Ireland—the whole of it as regards horse breeding?—Yes, I have lived in Ireland [illegible] in Ireland, and have great many different [illegible]. I have taken a great interest in horse breeding; I [illegible] the Royal Dublin Society [illegible] the improvement of horse-breeding I have taken a very active part in it.

1107. Would you be able to give us generally a description of the different types of horses bred in different parts of the country?—I think [illegible] Ireland, in regard to horse breeding, is divided into three [illegible] districts—one consisting of the southern and western; and midland counties, the other [illegible] the northern counties, and the third, the western portions of the counties of Kerry, Galway, Mayo, and Sligo, and Donegal, [illegible].

1108. And how about the [illegible] would have [illegible] the southern, western, and midland districts; the northern districts and the western district [illegible] part of Kerry, Galway, Mayo, Sligo, and Donegal?

[illegible]

[illegible]

1109. How do you distinguish the different types of horses produced in these districts?—The first district I have referred to, that is what I may call the midland, southern and eastern counties, that is in reality the great horse breeding district of Ireland; it is to a great extent governed by the nature of the soil, and in a slight extent by the habits and pursuits of its people; that is the great horse breeding district, and it is in that district, with few exceptions, all the high class hunters, harness horses, and army remounts which have made this country so well known as a horse breeding country, are bred. Of course there are exceptions; I am only speaking in a general way.

1110. What is the peculiarity of the soil?—Both the limestone soil that is so instrumental in producing good bone.

1111. As to the northern districts?—In the northern district the breeding of horses is confined more to what may perhaps be roughly termed utility horses—that is horses for harness purposes and general agricultural and market purposes; it is a little bit but a horse breeding district, but is the district in which a high class of horses is bred.

1112. The western districts?—That is what I may call the pony district; there is a portion of it with which I had a good deal to do, and about which I am very well informed—I mean Connemara and a portion of Mayo; I lived for many years in the west of Galway—for five and twenty years—and there was at that time an extremely hardy wiry class of pony in this district, showing a good deal of the Barb or Arab blood. Without exception they were the best animals of their size I ever knew, good shoulders, good hind legs, good action, and good stamina. In the performance of my duties in the west of Ireland I have had occasion to drive long distances, and I have always considered them the most wiry and useful animals I ever knew.

1113. What size?—They were seldom over 14.2; I never knew one of them to have a spavin or splints, or to be in any respect unsound in his wind.

1114. And you say there was Arab blood in them?—There was a strong trace of Arab blood which I always understood came from the introduction, into Connemara, of the Barb or Arab by the Martin family many years ago; you could very easily trace it in the Connemara ponies at the time I speak of.

1115. That was probably the Andalusian horse crossed with Arab?—No, I have always understood that Colonel Martin, the owner of Ballinahinch, introduced Arabs and Barbs into the country with a view to improving the class of ponies and keeping up the breed, in measure had that effect.

1116. To what do you attribute the difference in the types in these three districts?—In a great measure to the soil and climate, and to some extent the habits and pursuits of the people, and to the fact that in the southern, eastern and midland districts you have numerous packs of hounds which induce farmers to breed hunters.

1117. Would you say taking it generally that these districts produce the type of horse which is best calculated to produce from the soil and climate?—I think so.

1118. And how about the sires in these different districts; do you think they are best suited for the requirements of the districts?—Well, the sires in the district which I have referred to, comprising the southern, eastern, and midland counties, include a very large number of good ones. I confine my observations to the sires on the register of the Royal Dublin Society; there are something approaching 250 sires on the society's register and the greater number of these are stationed in the district I have referred to. Many of these horses are very good class indeed, as good as money can buy; some are not so good and might be better. Outside that I think the class of sires is not good. I am of course speaking of thoroughbreds.

1119. That is to say that the sires put on the register are practically the best?—We put no sire on the register that is not a good horse, and calculated to improve the breed of horses; he may not be as good as we would wish, but if a sound horse, and we have got any information as to his stock being sound, we put him on the register.

1120. Do you know what proportion, taking the south and midlands, the other stallions bear to them on the register?—I could not say, my lord, in that particular district. We have, I think, something over 700 thoroughbred stallions in Ireland; I am afraid that may not be correct; as in the agricultural returns many are returned that are not thoroughbreds. The horses on the Dublin Society Register are all in Weatherby's Stud Book; that is the rule of the Society.

1121. Speaking for yourself would you have any objection to half-bred sires?—I do think there is a want in the country of other than the strictly speaking thoroughbred horse. I speak of that particular district I referred to comprising the southern, eastern and midland counties, of the farmers. I know a very large number of farmers are anxious to get a horse with more substance, bone, and size than the ordinary thoroughbred sire, and I do think a half-bred sire under certain restrictions might well be admitted to a separate register and recommended for the use of farmers throughout the district—something on the lines of the Hunters' Improvement Society in England might be followed in this country.

1122. Under what restrictions?—I certainly think they should have a good strain on the dam's side of pure blood, and be got by a thoroughbred horse.

1123. That would have to be determined by some authority?—That, and many other matters, if I may be permitted to make a suggestion, would have to be determined by some committee or board of men with technical knowledge of their business in inquiry; somehow based on whose competency and knowledge the breeders of the country would have confidence.

1124. What are the steps taken by the Society now before a stallion is put on the register?—First, as regards the soundness of the horse, we require the owner to produce the certificate of a qualified veterinary surgeon; then if we have any reason to be dissatisfied with that certificate we send our own veterinary surgeon to examine him, and if the horse on further inspection is found to be sound we send our inspector to report upon the horse's suitability as a sire for producing the class of horse suitable for the district, and so on, each of these reports we get. It requires inquiry & scrutiny we have to make. But the committee generally appointed very carefully consider, not only the veterinary surgeon's certificate, but also the information from the county committee and otherwise as to the character and class of the stallion, and, in addition to that, our own inspector's report on the examination of the horse.

1125. Then, on the whole, taking the southern, midland, and eastern districts I gather that you consider a thoroughbred sire, or properly selected half-bred sire, with a considerable strain of pure blood on the mother's side, and got by a thoroughbred sire, to be the most suitable description?—I think so. I think the farmers and horse breeders in that particular might be divided into three classes in considering this matter. There is one class of very small farmers who now breed a weedy, worthless animal. I don't think that class of farmer ought to be encouraged to breed any, except what is required for his own particular use. They breed a worthless class of animal that cannot be sold at any price that would repay them, and which remains on their hands for a considerable time, entailing a heavy loss to them. I was lately in Cork during the ing of the great horse fair, and I stood at the entrance in the fair green in order to see the class of horses that were there, and I was astonished to see the number of weedy wretched animals. I did not think there was such rubbish in the country; they cannot be sold; they are no advantage to the country; they require a certain amount of feeding, and the money they are put at would be the better for the country.

1118. That is the small class?—Yes; they cannot afford to pay for a good stallion, and they go to the nearest horse they can get without regard to his qualifications, and don't they much care which class of animal they breed.

1127. Do you think they would continue to breed unless it paid them?—I don't think it pays with a large number of small farmers; they breed horses.

1128. But probably it pays them?—I don't think it does.

1129. Then what would be best for?—A man buys a mare, and thinks that he ought to breed, but he will find if he keeps an account that he has not made anything by the progeny.

1130. Do you not think that evil, if it is an evil, is likely to cure itself?—I think it will, and I think it is improving itself now, but these wretched animals will remain in the country for a considerable time, because they will have to be knocked about from fair to fair before they are got rid of.

1131. What do you attribute their wretchedness to?—Breeding a bad class of animal.

1132. Do you attribute it more to the bad mare, or to the fact that the owner cannot afford to pay for a good sire?—He won't go to a good sire, and he has a bad mare to begin with.

1133. Do you mean he cannot afford?—Well, he is unwilling to spend the money; [illegible] a good horse as a very [illegible] and a bad horse standing close to him, and the farmer has gone to the bad horse in order to save five shillings. Then there is the class of the well-to-do farmer, Class II., who has, as a general rule, a good class of mare. I have seen [illegible] a good class of mare exhibited, and have been surprised to find that farmers think it worth their while to send those mares to shows; the only object is to gain a prize, and I have been surprised that they send those mares long distances for such a prize; the middle class farmer as a rule has a good class of mare—good, thick, short-legged mares, and breed a good many very good horses. Take Clonmel, the centre of the largest horse-breeding district of Ireland. At their [illegible] I think more horses are sold there than at any other fair in Ireland, and a very good class of horses.

1134. What kind of size holding would they have?—A holding with a valuation of from £100 to £500.

1135. Do they keep mares specially for breeding?—Many of them do; they all breed their mares; they do mate where I think makes it an object to breed a good class of horse, and know that if they fail to produce a good class for hunters or harness purposes very likely the animal will fall in for some other purpose. The object ought to be to aim at breeding a good horse, and if not quite successful having made that attempt they will find that the animal will be good for other purposes and that they will get a price for it that will pay them, and when they succeed to breed [illegible] remarkably well.

1136. The third class of man do, in your opinion, [illegible] themselves of the services of the best stallions they can get?—A great many of them do, but a great many of them go to a cheap horse. As a rule, however, that class of farmer is anxious to get a good stallion.

1137. At what age do they sell them?—They prefer to keep them long, but it is very seldom they keep a horse until four years. Three years is the age at which they are looked for by the English dealers.

1138. Do they treat them properly in their early life?—[illegible] they are fairly well and fairly fed.

1139. Well, then you come to another class?—Yes, the third class. The third class would be composed of the larger farmers and gentlemen who breed horses in the country, and they of course [illegible] breeding the highest class of horse they can, the either hunter or harness horse, and [illegible] a high character for good horses; they can afford to keep a good mare and go to the best stallion, and also keep the young stock well.

1140. Is all this district you speak of sufficiently supplied with suitable thoroughbred stallions?—I don't think it is. There are many parts where they are badly in want of a good stallion. The Royal Dublin Society have endeavoured to [illegible] they have [illegible] funds were available applied them to the purchase of stallions and [illegible] them on the [illegible] principle in premium. Being in the [illegible], the principle they have gone upon is to secure a good horse, for this district though it may be attended with considerable loss in [illegible] the purchase money. For instance, we bought "Marsden" the other day and paid £400 for him; he is a beautiful horse and would carry 14 stone with hounds; we gave £400 and we sold him for £200, leaving [illegible] so that the £200 was capital [illegible] to the farmers at a moderate rate.

1141. Did the Society select the mares?—No.

1142. How are they bred?—In the Dublin Society's scheme for horse breeding now there is no selection of mares; the money is given as prizes to young stock.

1143. I understood you to say you made it a condition that he was to serve a certain number of mares at £3?—They did not select the mares; that was left quite open to the farmers of the district.

1144. [illegible]?—Well, of course [illegible].

1145. Do you know what he was charged for that horse?—£3.

1146. I don't quite understand, you made it a condition that he was to serve a certain number of mares at each guinea?—Yes, and beyond that he was not restricted as to price.

1147. What would be the ordinary charge?—He is a horse that would ordinarily stand at 5l., and the [illegible] £5 or £10; he was quite a first class horse.

1148. You made it a condition that he was not to charge more than £3 until the purchase money was repaid?—Yes, that he was to serve farmers' mares at a fee of £3 until the purchase money was repaid; he then became the property of the owner, and we did not make any further conditions after that.

1149. Mr. Fitzwilliam.—What was the breeding of the horse?—Thoroughbred.

1150. The Chairman.—In this district do you know any [illegible] Cleveland?—There are a good many half-bred horses that have got good stock that stand in that district. There is a horse called "Blackthorn" in the county of Clare; he is not in the Stud Book; he is a highly-bred animal, and has got more valuable horses than any other half-bred horse in Ireland probably.

1151. I was not referring so much to that breed as to whether there were any pure Hackneys [illegible] in this district?—No, I don't think so.

1152. Do you think that [illegible] the introduction of Clydesdales and Clevelands would be a benefit?—I think it would ruin the horse breeding in that district.

1153. On what do you found that opinion?—My objection to Hackneys is this, that I think they are

[illegible] [illegible]
Mr. [illegible]

unsuited to produce either hunters or high-class harness horses; I think it ought to be the aim of every one to produce one or the other, and I think that a Hackney is wholly unsuited to producing one or the other.

1154. Do you form that opinion from experience?—Of course outside Hackneys, my knowledge is the [illegible] and information collected from various sources from time to time; I may say with regard to collecting information, that we have received several [illegible] on the subject, extracts from which I will read if I may be permitted to do so.

1155. Would that exclude horses from this country?—They would, very likely.

1156. As to the high-class harness horses, I think we had it proved in evidence the other day by Mr. O'Reilly, that there was no special class for stallions intended to get harness horses, given at the Royal Dublin Society's Shows, and I see, on looking at the catalogue, that Class I is for "thoroughbred stallions under sixteen years old, to get weight-carrying hunters or high-class harness horses." Then, I presume, I am correct?—We hold that a thoroughbred horse is suited in every respect to get high-class harness horses. As a matter of fact, a very large number of the harness horses that go to England are from thoroughbreds with half-bred mares; we have the evidence of the London dealers that the best carriage horses they get, the five-year-old colts they buy in Ireland, are the produce of a thoroughbred horse out of a half-bred mare.

1157. Then I am correct, I think, in saying that this [illegible] there was only that there was no class for stallions calculated to get harness horses was not quite correct?—No, it was not.

1158. It would only be correct to say that there was no class exclusively for stallions likely to produce harness horses?—No, the wording of that class was put in after very careful consideration by the committee.

1159. Speaking of the medium, ordinary, cart horses, cobs, and all the work-horses of the country farmer, and so on, I suppose the majority of them are not thoroughbreds?—No, I should say that probably quite as many of them are sold for harness horses as hunters—I should think quite as many.

1160. Mr. Wrench.—Is that Class 3 or 4?—Oh, Class 3; Class 1 comprises all the horses whose [illegible] I want ought to be got.

1161. Class 3 or 3 Irish?—Class 3, I am speaking of.

1162. The Chairman.—You think as many are sold for harness as for hunters?—I think so. I have seen at Cahirmee fair numbers of colts, three or four years old, with an admixture in the harness that were out of the fair, and magnificent horses they were—[illegible] horses, 16 hands high.

1163. Mr. Fitzwilliam.—The eighty-seven stallions chosen by the Royal Dublin Society, are they chosen to the whole, with a view to the breeding of general purpose animals or hunters?—General purpose animals, that is the object.

1164. Can you tell us how the mares are bred in those classes 3 and 4?—No, I could not tell, I have got no information as to that, but as a general rule they are well-bred half-bred mares.

1165. No evidence of cart blood of any kind?—They are free as a rule, from any appearance of such blood.

1166. Also those half-bred horses you have named, may be bred almost in the same way as the thoroughbreds?—This is the half-bred I recommend.

1167. You say there are a great number in the country?—Yes, very well bred horses that have probably three or four strains of pure blood on the dam side, and got by a thoroughbred horse, some probably not so well bred, and thirty others perhaps only nearly thoroughbred.

1168. Lord Arnott.—Do you include in the district any of the western counties?—Part of Galway—the west part.

1169. And I suppose Roscommon?—Yes, a certain part of that, and a part of Sligo.

1170. Mr Tierney Rehearse.—You said you thought small farmers could not breed horses of a proper. Would you be any limit to the size of the farm in which farmers could breed with profit?—It very much depends on the character of the land, but I think a farmer holding a farm valued under £30 [illegible] do [illegible] breeding.

1171. Not a man above that rating?—I think so.

1172. Do you think that good stallions at a cheap rate would be a help to small farmers?—They would do better than they are doing, but I don't think you can expect to get a good class of animal bred by that class of man; heretofore there has been a market for what I might call the weedy horse, but I think the market is disappearing rapidly—the bicycle and the motor car will do away with it altogether, and they will become a drug in the market.

1173. You think high class horses will only pay in future?—Every breeder ought to aim at breeding the best horse he can; if he does not [illegible] succeed the [illegible] will make it for some lower purpose.

1174. Breeding all round conduces to the success of the system of selection?—Oh, certainly, if you have the means of doing it. I think ultimately public money be given to provide a stallion for a district that ought to be compulsorily a means of selecting the mares to be served by that horse.

1175. That is the system of the Congested Districts Board—they select the mares?—That is the right system, no doubt.

1176. Have you come across any specimens of the old Irish mares?—Yes, I have, numbers of them in different parts of the country.

1177. Are any records of pedigrees from the[illegible]?—I [illegible] I do not think the records of [illegible] [illegible] [illegible] for that class of old Irish mares—mares with plenty of [illegible], show [illegible] and action, plenty of stamina.

1178. Do you find there are fewer of them?—I would not say, but I think there are quite as many; there are a great many farmers who try to keep on the old blood, and do keep the same blood in their families for many years.

1179. A great deal of care is taken then of gold [illegible] make a great deal of care of it.

1180. Colonel St. Quintin.—I should like to ask you what is your objection to the Hackney as a sire for a [illegible] of this particular breed—do you consider that the confirmation of the Hackney is an inferior conformation?—I do for the hunter or high class carriage horse.

1181. Do you consider his action is a good action and a useful action?—I do not.

1182. Do you think the introduction of that one cross would increase the size [illegible] I am sure it would ruin it.

1183. Do you think it would benefit the [illegible] [illegible]—The Hackney one cross?—I am sure it would not.

1184. Mr. Wrench.—You said that, under more [illegible] conditions, you would register some so-called half-bred [illegible], would you register any of these small farmers' [illegible] once proved to be good?—I would; if the horse is well bred, if his [illegible] is good, and if I thought that in every other respect he was [illegible] to get good stock. If he did not come up to the [illegible] I would get rid of him.

1185. What would you call sufficiently near to thoroughbred—how many crosses?—I think there ought to be at least three crosses; it would be a very [illegible], once which you would be justified in [illegible] a horse with less than three crosses.

1186. You have stated that in your opinion [illegible] [illegible] cannot produce high class harness horses?—That is my opinion.

1182. You have been at the Royal Dublin Society's Show?—Yes.

1183. [illegible]

[illegible]

1209. Sir W. [illegible]

[illegible]

[illegible] Evidence. [illegible]

[illegible]

1225. I don't quite understand what you said in reply to Mr. Wrench. Do you know whether any Hackney stallions have been used in this northern, midland, and eastern districts?—I don't know any. I know there are Hackney stallions in it.

1226. You know there are?—There are.

1226a. You don't know what they are?—No.

1227. Nor where they are?—No.

1228. I think you told us they had already produced some harm?—I did.

1229. How did you detect that?—I merely gave that as my opinion. I have no way of detecting it.

1230. Do you think harm has been done because you know the fact that these stallions have got the approval of his ... or have you any demonstration of it?—I have no demonstration of it.

1231. You believe the Hackney is injurious, and, as the Hackney is there, you therefore think harm must be done?—Yes; it is the inference I draw.

1232. Now, there is one of the other districts—the northern or western—The western district is where the ponies are. This district is altogether suited for breeding ponies?—Almost so; it is the western district. It is a mountainy district, a poor soil, and a rather bad climate, and that, I think, is suited only for ponies.

1233. That, I understand, covers the whole of the west?—It is pretty nearly the whole of the west, taking it up from Kerry; it does not take in Clare, but it takes in the whole of the western part of Galway and Mayo. That is the district I have the most information about.

1234. Now, this district is only adapted to raise ponies?—Altogether adapted to raising ponies, and no other class of horse, I think.

1235. We had evidence the other day that in Kerry the class of ponies disappeared altogether?—Yes, I was aware of it.

1236. That is to say, the ponies disappeared, and a larger animal was produced, but nearly as valuable as the pony—isn't that so?—I believe so.

1237. Do you know what they were crossed with?—I don't know.

1238. Your experience of the western part of the country extends over a great number of years?—It does.

1239. For about how long?—I have known Galway and Mayo since the year 1850 very well.

1240. Is there any marked change in the character of the ponies produced there in the last thirty years?—Oh, yes. Up to the time I left Galway, in 1874 or 1875, the ponies of that western district had deteriorated very much indeed.

1241. Mr. Wrench.—From 1850?—From 1850.

1242. The Chairman.—Up to what time?—Up to 1875; up to the time when I left Galway.

1243. To what do you attribute that?—That was attributable to the want of good stallions. The stallions they used were bad, what is called a mongrel stallion, and I attribute the deterioration in the quality of the animals altogether to that.

1244. The stallions were inferior to those used formerly?—They were inferior. The hap-hazard way they were breeding from stallions bred in the district and without any care.

1245. Your practical knowledge of that part of the country ceased in 1875?—Yes.

1246. What class of stallion do you think best suited for all that part of the country?—I think for the greater portion I would fall back on what produced the good animals before, that is the Barb or the Arab. I think for certain parts of the district the Welsh pony would be the hardier animal and more suitable, but I think for the other portions of the district either the Arab or the Barb or a small thorough-bred short-legged horse would be best suited for the district.

1247. In your experience were many ponies sold out of this district?—Yes, very large quantities of them were sold out of the district in my time; you could see droves of ponies going through the midland counties—a hundred or two hundred of them—bought at the fairs of Oughterard, Clifden, Westport, and other places, and taken up by jobbers and driven through Ireland and sold as high as they could.

1248. They remained in Ireland?—A great many of them went to England, and a great many of them went to the coal mines.

1249. For work underground?—Underground.

1250. Do you know whether the same quantities of them are sold now in that way?—I can't say, but if the same number are bred now they might be sold, because I don't think the country could support them.

1251. Well, of course, you have not any practical knowledge of that part of the country since the establishment of the Congested Districts Board?—No, I know nothing of it.

1252. And you cannot tell us from your practical knowledge what effect the Hackney has had there?—No.

1253. From your general knowledge do you think the Hackney would be suitable to cross with these ponies?—No, I don't think it is. The Hackney is not a suitable sire to cross with ponies.

1254. They don't produce as valuable produce?—No, I am sure the produce which will find its way into the midland counties and other horse breeding districts, and will be bought, perhaps, by the small farmers there, and when tested out no good hard and given to fine, and that will make its way and be used as brood mares for breeding hunters or carriage horses, and that will tell on the breed of those animals. That, to my mind, is the great danger of introducing the Hackney blood, for you cannot by any means prevent it from penetrating to those districts in Ireland where horses of the well-bred class are bred. Of course, it is quite possible to build a wall around them in a certain district and breed the Hackney there, then they will do no harm.

1255. Mr. Wrench.—And you quite agree that would not keep them in?—We have heard of their leaping powers.

1256. The Chairman.—Do you think Hackney blood would improve ponies?—I don't think it is the right way to improve them. I am quite sure the Barb or the Arab will produce better animals of ponies. I saw instances of it. I was judging at Ballinasloe Show, and I saw a very beautiful pony mare, bred out of a ... by an Arab, good shoulders, good hard legs, and good feet, and all the appearance of a hardy, wiry animal, with great stamina, and showed a great deal of breeding. She had a two year old and a yearling got by a Hackney sire. They were as bad a couple of young horses as ever I saw. They were heavy-legged, and they had no redeeming feature that I could see.

1257. When was this?—This year.

1258. You can give us the name of the animal?—I cannot give the name of the mare, but it was a filly by "Fireaway," an animal owned by the Congested Districts Board.

1259. Sir Walter Gilbey.—What sort of action had those two animals?—Nothing peculiar as to action.

1260. The action was not good?—No.

1261. The Chairman.—Although you said you had no recent experience of those western districts you have some practical experience of the produce of a Hackney stallion there?—Oh, yes, I go very frequently through the country. I have some knowledge of it, and I have judged at the shows in Galway and Ballinasloe.

1262. Can you give us any more information about that subject, as I thought you were speaking pretty theoretically, and that you had not seen the produce of Hackney sires?—Those are the only ones that I can call to mind. Those are the only ones I saw.

[illegible]

[illegible]

1295. Were most of the animals in your time sold as foals?—They were always as foals. Well, not as foals, they were sold as yearlings and two year olds.

1296. They were kept only up to two years old at that time?—Yes.

1297. That was prior to 1874?—Yes.

1298. You know the pony foal is a small animal?—Yes.

1299. You and I may not agree about Hackneys altogether, but I think you will agree with what we have clearly [illegible] in this [illegible] district of Connemara. [illegible]?—Yes.

1300. And we have evidence of Arab blood?—Yes.

1301. And you have also [illegible]. Which ponies in other districts?—I don't know, but I take it for granted that what you say is quite correct. I have not been in the district since you stationed the sires there.

1302. Are you aware that where we sent a Hackney sire to Clifden in the same district the people themselves preferred to have the use of the Hackney?—I would like to answer that question. I saw the Arabs that you bought, three of them, and I think two were the very worst class of Arabs. I saw the three Arabs in [illegible] stables—one of them had come from the Queen's stables—and two were quite unsuited for breeding purposes. There was one grey, I must say, was a good one.

1303. What did you think of Lord [illegible] Barb?—The [illegible] that was a very good horse.

1304. What do you say as to the [illegible] [illegible], but I [illegible] as to two of the Arabs I saw they were a bad class of [illegible].

1305. One was the Queen's?—[illegible] particularly. I [illegible] the progeny of that animal, and [illegible] as bad as the sire.

1306. The Chairman.—Assuming the fact that it is claimed that the farmers prefer Hackneys to the [illegible], you would not be surprised, because you say you don't think the Arabs were good at their [illegible]?—On that point I say it is impossible to apply a definite answer to a [illegible] question.

1307. I think I can satisfy you with evidence on that point?—[illegible]. We were [illegible] in the Royal Dublin Society, before the Congested Districts Board proceeded to improve the breed of horses in this district, to send suitable sires into those western districts, since the Dublin Society —and we purchased one small thoroughbred called "Welsh Spring." [illegible] and we sent him into one of the districts. We [illegible] him for a [illegible] [illegible] [illegible]. We paid £150 for the horse, and we sold the horse for the same money to him, undertaking to pay him £50 a year for three years for the service of the horse for [illegible] [illegible] in that district, on the understanding that he was to charge only like the [illegible] [illegible], and [illegible] for [illegible] mares.

1308. The Chairman.—Where was the sire sent to?—To Connemara, to Recess. The Congested Districts Board placed their stallion very shortly afterwards in the same district, and since that time the [illegible], and the result is that the farmers went to the [illegible] horse, for they said "These are the thoroughbred [illegible] [illegible] best [illegible] in the world, and we will go to the cheapest," and they went to the cheap horse and left ours to a great extent idle. There you have the result of the Government Department managing horse breeding.

1309. Mr. Wrench.—You don't suggest that the horse was sent specially to Clifden on that account?—No, I don't say so.

1310. Are you aware that it was by arrangement that [illegible] were sent to this district?—No.

1311. Do you know that [illegible] [illegible] the [illegible] the [illegible] [illegible] pony in Connemara?—Well, I don't know.

1312. But you think that is the ordinary fee?—Yes, that is about it.

1313. In 1874, when you left, the class of stallion to you was very much deteriorated, and you knew that the farmers were breeding from their own animals and produced a very bad class?—Yes.

1314. You don't know what foreign blood brought in the larger animal?—No.

1315. You did not trace the exact origin of the Connemara pony beyond the time that Col Martin introduced the Arab blood?—No.

1316. Do you know that they were traced behind that?—No.

1317. Sir Walter Gilbey.—The history of the pony before the time to which you refer you know nothing about?—Yes.

1318. The produce was there in the year 1850?—Yes.

1319. You know the district?—Yes.

1320. It is a mountainous district?—Yes.

1321. I suppose you know that it was exposure and the quality of the herbage that made the animals there degenerate from a larger breed?—I can't say that.

1322. Because you must know that in the last century there were a very great number of Arab stallions not only in Ireland, but in England?—Yes.

1323. And previous to Colonel Martin having drafted in that particular breed there, there was some of the breed in the place?—I have no doubt it was.

1324. You have mentioned the Welsh ponies. Do you know the breed of the Welsh ponies?—No; I don't know anything about them, except that I have seen some very nice ponies belonging to the Congested Districts Board.

1325. You are not aware that the Welsh breed of ponies, going back fifty years, was very largely an [illegible] from the Norfolk Hackney?—I daresay it is.

1326. That is a very well known fact?—Yes; and I suggested their use in many exposed districts where only a very hardy horse would live out the winter.

1327. Frequent reference has been made to Arab and Barb blood. What definition do you give to Barb?—I cannot define it.

1328. Are not both Eastern horses?—Yes: both are Eastern blood. The Barb has generally more substance than the Arab.

1329. Only [illegible], I think?—Yes.

1330. What they call Barbs?—Yes.

1331. Mr. Wrench.—Do you remember the Welsh cob taking first prize at the Galway Show?—The chestnut.

1332. The bay?—Yes.

1333. And that is the class of animal you would think suitable for Connemara?—Yes, for some parts.

1334. For Ballyconneely and Carraroe?—Yes.

1335. The Chairman.—What became of "Welsh Spring" that the Dublin Society sent down to the district?—He is there still. We have effected the object for which we localised him there. I saw some of his stock at the Ballyconneely Show, and they were extremely good. One, I recollect, got first prize.

1336. Have you reduced the fee?—No, we cannot now regulate the fee charged as the horse has been paid for and he belongs to the owner of the Ballynahinch property.

1337. Do you know what is charged now?—I don't know what is charged now.

1338. Mr. Fitzwilliam.—Do you know the breeding of "Welsh Spring"?—Got by "Sterling."

1339. Isn't it by "Springfield"?—Yes, you are right, by "Springfield."

1340. The Chairman.—Turn now to the northern district?—The northern district is the one perhaps I know less of than any of the other districts, and what I know of it strictly is that it is generally confined to the breeding of carriage horses and what I would call the general utility horse. There are very few thoroughbred stallions on our register standing in the North of Ireland. [illegible] I believe I am [illegible] in saying that as a general rule the northern dealers and the northern horse owners are in the habit of buying in the southern districts, in Cahirciveen or Limerick or Roscrea, the colts are brought up and trained in the North of Ireland, and then they are sold as hunters and high class carriage horses. A great number that are shown at the Dublin Show by breeders from the North of Ireland have been bought at Spancil Hill, Roscrea and Cahirmee, purchased at three years old and then brought back to the show five years old and sold as hunters. They don't breed that class of horse so much in the North of Ireland.

1341. In your opinion what class of stallion do you consider most suitable in the North of Ireland?—I would strongly recommend a thoroughbred horse specially selected as suitable for getting carriage horses.

1342. And the general utility horse?—And the general utility horse, either a thoroughbred horse or a half-bred horse, with the qualification I have referred to.

1343. Assuming that it would be possible to confine the blood to the North of Ireland would you have the same objection to Hackney blood to produce [illegible] or generally utility horses?—I think the value is very much better.

1344. Mr. Wrench.—The halfbred stallion?—Yes.

1345. The Chairman.—That is halfbred with the qualification you have mentioned?—Under the condition I have mentioned.

1346. This paragraph [illegible] I gather generally you think a suitable thoroughbred or a half-bred selected under conditions you have mentioned is better than a Hackney to produce any kind of horse that is produced in Ireland?—Yes, that is my opinion.

1347. Objecting generally you would not consider it so objectionable in the North of Ireland as in portions of the west, south, midland, and east?—Yes.

1348. You also object, as I gather, to this strain of blood being introduced into any portion of the country on the ground that the strain would spread throughout the country?—Yes, that is the danger I apprehend.

1349. Is that the principal danger you apprehend?—Yes, the principal danger.

1350. You say as the strain is not quickly detected you would not prevent the farmers using it?—I don't see how it is possible to detect it no matter how good a judge a man may be.

1351. Taking the whole country generally you have a long experience, and do you see any deterioration in the class of horse produced in [illegible]?—No. There is no deterioration I am glad to say, and I am sure there is a marked improvement in the shape and quality of the horses bred in Ireland.

1352. There are more horses bred than there used to be?—There are more horses bred than there used to be, and there are more highly shaped horses sold by dealers and go to England—I suppose two to one or three to one—more than there used to be.

1353. I think I gather from you that you anticipate that the demand for inferior classes of horses, for the general utility horse, will be less in future?—I think it will die out to a large extent, that is the demand for hacks or utility horses kept for ordinary use. It is dying out as it is. I know great numbers of people who have sold their horses and ride their bicycles.

1354. More people keep bicycles now?—Yes.

1355. But the general demand for hunters and carriage horses will maintain itself?—I think it is on the increase. I have more hunt now for one who hunted ten years ago, and consequently there is a larger demand for hunters, and I am glad to say as to high-class horses from Ireland there is always a demand for them.

1356. Consequently you think, taking the industry as a whole, it is advisable that the attention of the producers should be directed to producing these high-class carriage horses and hunters?—I think so. Nov. 8, 1899. [illegible]

1357. Have you any further information you can give or any suggestion, taking the matters in the order in which you took yourself at the beginning?—Yes, I should like to suggest that I think the basis upon which the horse-breeding interest depends in Ireland is the registration of stallions. I think, whatever class of stallions are to be used in Ireland, they ought to be registered, and they ought to be registered by a board, a competent body, in whom the public would have confidence; and then, as to getting rid by legislation of bad horses, that is the only way by which you can minimise the danger of having bad stallions in the country. We have in the Dublin Society been trying to effect the registration of stallions, with the result that already a very large number of bad horses have been sold and left the country. We found that the horses were marked by not having a place on our register, and the owners got rid of them, and so their place got better ones. I attach the greatest importance to, and I think any expense in moderation incurred in adopting such a complete and satisfactory registration of stallions would be well spent. I think the scheme of the Dublin Society of 1894 in regulating the various conditions in which mares was a good one. I would be in favour of giving assistance to mares, and giving substantial prizes to young mares put to stud. I think if you register the stallions then you will secure a sufficient number of sound, good horses in the country, and then if you could induce men to put young mares of a good class, two or three years old, to the stallion and make it worth their while to do it by offering these substantial prizes, you will in that way secure a very marked improvement in the breed of horses in Ireland. Of course the difficulty in the scheme, if it is to have any sensible effect, is that it will cost money; it can't be done otherwise.

1358. Am I to gather from you that you prefer the system in operation in the Dublin Society up to 1894 to the present?—Yes. I would like to see in part the 1894 scheme combined. I would like to see registration combined with prizes to young mares put to stud.

1359. Have you anything more that you would like to put before the Commission?—No, I don't think so at present.

1360. Mr. [illegible].—You think registration of the stallions is a matter of vital importance?—I do.

1361. Have you any knowledge of the [illegible] of foreign countries in this matter?—No. Nothing beyond what I have read, I have no personal knowledge.

1362. Mr. Wrench.—With regard to the registration of stallions you would only register thoroughbreds and half-breds such as you have described?—Yes.

1363. That is all you recommend?—Yes.

1364. That is that thoroughbreds and half-breds should be the only registered stallions?—Yes.

1365. What would you do with stallions outside that class? Would you require a licence of registration, or would you leave stallions as at present?—You would require legislation for that.

1366. Would you recommend any legislation?—No. I would not approve of stallions being required to have a licence for standing. I would have nothing to do with them if they were unsound. I would rather get rid of them altogether, and limit the stallions to the class I have referred to.

1367. You would limit the public to thoroughbreds and half-breds under carefully considered conditions?—Yes.

1368. Do you know anything about the introduction of the American horse into Ireland?—No. I have seen the horses imported into Ireland. I don't know much of them.

1369. They have not ever [illegible]. Do you think it is a good thing for the country or a bad?—I think it is a very bad thing. I have seen a Clydesdale [illegible] at the Horse Show, and it was very good.

1370. I referred to the American horses brought in here and offered for sale. Are they very bad in quality?—Yes.

1371. And you think they will do great harm?—I do.

1372. Do you suggest in any way the limiting of such imports?—I think it would be very good.

1373. You think there should be limiting of the American horses that are brought in here?—Yes, I would do anything that would prevent this [illegible] in every way.

1374. Sir WALTER GILBEY.—Were you not suspicious that some of the animals exhibited at the last Dublin Show were imported from America?—We were suspicious.

1375. And your remarks all point to the importance of keeping the Irish hunter breed pure?—I think it is a great advantage.

1376. And so you are this party are you in favour of the registration of pedigrees if it can be carried out?—If it can be carried out I would be very glad, but it is a tremendous undertaking.

1377. Mr. WRENCH.—It would be too much for the resources of the Royal Dublin Society?—It is a tremendous undertaking.

1378. Sir WALTER GILBEY.—Failing that it is not undertaken by the Royal Dublin Society, do you think if the Dublin Society would give in the class for two-year-olds [illegible] prizes for reliable pedigrees that could be carried out?—I am not quite prepared to say whether that would be practicable or desirable or not, but it could be done of course.

1379. I suppose you notice in the catalogue the [illegible] comes in the classes for two or three year olds where you would imagine the pedigree should be known, that in many, a very large number of cases, the personality of the breeder is unknown and the pedigrees are nil?—I don't think there are any two year olds at any show.

1380. Well, in the three and four year olds?—Yes, the reason of that is that the owner of the horse was not quite certain of the breeding. He may have purchased the horse, and he may have been given the breeding on assumption, but not being quite certain of it, unless he had documentary proof, he did not put it in. Some people are very slow about giving a pedigree unless they are in a position to prove it.

1381. The breeders are unknown, but the pedigree is known?—Yes. Very often a two year old horse is sold in a fair, and quite correctly the dealer is told that he is by "Victor," out of a dam by "Warren Hastings," and the horse then passes through two or three hands, and it comes to the show at last, and the man who bought the horse last has lost all trace of the breeder, and he is, therefore, unable to give the breeder's name though the pedigree is carefully handed down.

1382. If the system of insisting on the breeder's name being given is carried out in future it will make purchasers more careful?—I quite agree with you that it is desirable.

1383. I am very glad you think so, because it has always appeared to me such an omission in reading the catalogues of your show?—I attach the greatest value myself to breeding, and I think anybody buying a horse would wish to be perfectly satisfied about it.

Lord ASHTOWN.—Registering the mares would do that.

Captain C. FETHERSTONHAUGH examined.

1384. The CHAIRMAN.—You are a member of the Irish Horse Breeding Association?—Yes, my lord.

1385. And you take a general interest in the subject of horse-breeding?—Yes; I may say I take a very deep interest in horse-breeding in Ireland generally.

1386. Have you had any personal experience in horse-breeding?—Well, I may say I have had a good deal of experience; I have been breeding horses ever since I was twenty, and I have also been an owner of a stallion for a considerable number of years; had several stallions, and I have acted as judge at shows, and in various ways I have had a good deal to say to horse-breeding.

1387. In what districts of the country has your experience been gained?—I can only speak for the midland counties; I live in Westmeath, and can only speak for that part of Ireland. I have not had any varied experience in other parts of Ireland, except I have acted as judge at shows in other parts of Ireland, and seen the class of horses bred there.

1388. Speaking for your own district, which you know well, do you think that the quality of the horses has deteriorated at all?—Well, no; I am certain the contrary has taken place. I think that undoubtedly there are a great number of inferior animals, perhaps a greater number than ever there were in the country, but I attribute that chiefly to the greater number of horses that have been lately bred in the country, and, of course, the more horses that are bred the more misfits must be bred. For the last few years horse-breeding has paid very well, up to the last two or three years it has paid tremendously well; but latterly it has not, and consequently the fairs are now very full of horses of an unsaleable and unsound description, for which there is no market.

1389. You are speaking of breeding what class of horses?—I am speaking of breeding from half-bred mares with thoroughbred horses, and the same class of mare crossed with the ordinary stallion of the country, which is of a nondescript description.

1390. That would be horses for hunting?—Every farmer's object in my country when he breeds a horse is to breed him for a hunter, for if he is not suitable for a hunter he goes as a trooper or to a lower grade.

1391. Would the same remark apply to the whole country, so far as you know it; I mean that there has been no general deterioration?—I am confident there has not been; that a greater number of good horses are bred in the country than ever there were, and there is a greater demand for them, and horses are taken at an earlier age than ever they were before.

1392. There are more horses bred altogether?—Yes; I consider there are a great many more horses bred in the country, and more good ones. Yes; I think there are certainly more good horses bred; at the same time, there are a great number of indifferent animals bred in the country.

1393. Well, can you tell the Commission on what facts you base that opinion?—I consider there must be more horses bred in the country, because I see the fairs are full of an unsaleable class of horse; there are enormous numbers of them which they take from fair to fair, and especially the unsound horses would be sold for anything that would be offered for them, but they are of an indifferent description; the best class of horses never comes into the fairs at all, at least great numbers of them are bought privately.

1394. These horses you speak of as now unsaleable, do you mean they were formerly saleable?—Yes, I consider that they were three or four years ago, they were then sold and were shipped to England, but there is not a demand for those horses now.

1395. Do you account for that in any way?—Yes, a great many people have given up keeping horses and taken to bicycles; the middle-class people keep less horses than they used to—they keep bicycles, and don't keep small horses for their own pleasure that they used to keep.

1396. May I take it that you think the demand for superior animals is as great as ever it was?—I think it is greater.

1397. And the supply?—And the supply is greater than ever it was but the supply is not equal to the demand by any means.

1398. But the demand for the inferior animals is less?—It is absolutely nil.

1399. Well, you think that supply is likely in a comparatively [illegible] to that, that is to say, that the production of the inferior animal will naturally fall off?—I think it is bound to, because the breeding of that class of horses is not paying the farmer, and I think he will gradually drop it, that is the small farmer.

1400. Did you hear Mr. [illegible] evidence?—I did.

1401. Do you generally agree with him as to the [illegible] of the small class of farmers breeding?—I do; I think many farmers breed from ponies which are bound to be a loss to themselves and to the country at large. I don't think they are capable of breeding an animal that will ever pay for feeding; but, I think, they are beginning to realise that—they are not breeding them in such numbers as they did.

1402. They can breed a class of animals which was [illegible] some years ago but which is not saleable now?—I think there are a great number of very good mares in the country, excellent mares, and I judge that principally from mares that I see exhibited at shows where they, at the same time, there are a great number of a bad class of mares that are principally in the possession of small farmers—the good class of mares are usually owned by the better class of farmers, who keep their stock better.

1403. And as to the stallions?—There are a great number of very good thoroughbred stallions standing in the country, but they are standing at fees which are more or less prohibitive for the smaller farmers of the country, and outside those there are an enormous number of what are called draught stallions, which have been comparatively used by the farmers lately.

1404. What do you mean by that?—Horses with a great admixture of cart-horse blood.

1405. You are speaking of the mixture of cart-horse type?—I am speaking of the [illegible] particularly.

1406. What do you mean by cart-horse blood?—I mean a cross of Shire, or Clydesdale, or Clydesdale.

1407. Have they become more common in your district than formerly?—I think they have; I think there are a good number of them.

1408. They belong, of course, to private owners?—Oh, yes.

1409. Would they be introduced if there was not a demand for them?—Oh, there undoubtedly is a demand for them for the use of the more [illegible] description of farmer.

1410. What kind of fees do they charge?—I think from 15s. to 2l., and, I suppose, in some cases less.

1411. And what are the general fees charged for thoroughbred stallions in your district?—The average fee would be 3l., 3l. 3s., from that up to 5 guineas.

1412. Could you form any opinion as to whether the farmer prefers the cart-horse stallion to the thoroughbred stallion on account of the lower fee or because he thinks it makes a more saleable animal?—I think the farmers in this country breed from the cart-horse, chiefly because they get them cheaper, and also because he gets more size in the progeny; but they are chiefly men who breed to sell the produce at two and a-half years old, and for that purpose they want size.

1413. What are they sold at do you know, I mean for what purpose?—They are bought by English dealers and shipped over. I have been told that they are bought chiefly for putting to tradesmen's carts in provincial towns in England; they get them to harness at a very early age, and if they turn out good, they turn a [illegible] or three and replace them with another one.

1414. What kind of a horse do they use for light cartage purposes about you?—They use a light description of horse, a heavy agricultural horse is not required, we have very small tillage in the country, and a heavy horse is not suited at all, the light description of horse is able to bring a reasonable weight of hay and straw, [illegible] loads compared with the size of the animal.

1415. Then in your opinion is the produce of the Shire horse generally sold out of the country or kept in the country?—I think they are chiefly sold at an early age.

1416. And generally do you think the class of stallion in your country is the best it can be for the purpose?—I think the class of half-bred stallion that I mentioned is a very bad class of stallion, and I don't think it pays the farmers to breed from them, besides the thoroughbred stallions, I consider are very good, but there are not enough of them and the fees are too high.

1417. By the class of stallion you speak of do you mean the draught stallion?—I mean the draught stallion, the [illegible] with a large admixture of cart-blood.

1418. Have you any opinion as to how an improvement can be made in respect of the stallions?—I am of opinion that it would be a great advantage to the country if more thoroughbred stallions were put at the disposal of the farmers at a small fee. I also think that a class of stallion is required in this country other than a thoroughbred horse for the use of small farmers whose mares are of a weedy description, I think a half-bred horse, that is to say a horse with a good admixture of thoroughbred blood and bred from what is called a country mare, an old Irish country mare, would be the best sire for use in the country.

1419. Have you any suggestion to make as to how that could be brought about?—Well, I think that of course it can only be brought about by state aid; if a demand arose for that class of horse they would be bred.

1420. You think it would not pay a private person as a commercial speculation to introduce that kind of horse?—I don't think it would, because they would not be of a recognised breed, and they would not be registered, which, I think, is a very necessary thing. I think all stallions serving should be registered and certified sound, and of proper formation.

1421. Have you had any practical experience of the working of the Royal Dublin Society's scheme?—Yes I have; I have acted as chairman of my county committee.

1422. And what do you think of the scheme?—I think it has done an incalculable lot of good to the country, especially in some counties.

1423. Especially in what counties?—I should say especially in the counties Meath, Kildare, and Mayo. I think the horses have improved enormously at the shows there. I have acted as judge at Ballyshannon for the past five years, or more, and every year I see a marked improvement, and the younger horses better, which shows they are steadily improving.

1424. Can you explain why the scheme has had a better effect in those counties than in others?—In my own county I know the reason it has not been a success is that there are not a sufficient number of thoroughbred registered stallions at the disposal of the farmers, and what there are are standing at too high a fee.

1425. Well, there have been various schemes, have there not, of the Royal Dublin Society from time to time; have you any preference for one over the other?—The schemes were originally subsidised, and for the last two years the money has been given in prizes to mares to be bred to those registered stallions.

1426. Which of those schemes do you prefer?—I think if the two schemes were worked in conjunction it would be the best.

[illegible]

Captain C. [illegible]-borough.

1427. That would be to——?—That would be to give the farmer facilities in neighbourhood stallions, so that the owner of the horse could have his own stallion. Formerly there was only one registered stallion in the country, that is up my place was one registered stallion, and he was not sufficient for the mares that had to be covered. I would then suggest that the money should be given in prizes to old mares, and premiums [illegible] should be given to young mares [illegible] the years old; and these would require to be a substantial sum, to encourage the owner of the mare to keep them for the purpose of breeding instead of selling them abroad.

1428. Do you think they do sell their mares largely abroad?—I am quite certain they do. They mare that has a valuable animal to sell, don't retain, except those [illegible], not nearly such mares to breed young ones.

1429. You think possibly there is a tendency to sell the best mares and breed from inferior ones?—Anything that is valuable is ordered.

1430. And you would suggest giving a prize of a sufficient amount to counteract the inducement to sell?—Yes, that would encourage the farmer to keep his young mares to breed from.

1431. I think you said that the demand for hunters and high class carriage horses is increasing?—Yes, I certainly consider it is; every horse of any value at all in any part of the world is immediately bought up when offered for sale.

1432. Do you think the supply is increasing in proportion to the increased demand?—Well, I don't think it is. I think the demand always exceeds the supply, and the consequence of that is the high price at which horses are selling in Ireland.

1433. Then in certain districts you think there is a scarcity in Ireland for horses?—I think there is undoubtedly, though a great number are bred.

1434. And besides what you have already said, can you suggest any means whereby the production could or should be encouraged?—I don't think, except by local shows and prizes being given to encourage farmers to put their good mares to good horses, I don't see which would be done in addition to the registration of stallions, which I look upon as very important.

1435. I think you said that the quality of horses is [illegible] so good as it used to be?—No, well I [illegible] there is many horses of the best class not getting into the farm at all, they are bought up before ever they get into work in addition to that the local dealers have also taken the cream of the horses, which used formerly to be sold in fairs, and now don't readily reach them at the fairs.

1436. Then in your opinion, the farm cannot be looked on as their criterion of the quality or the quantity?—No, I don't think so.

1437. What class of horses have you bred yourself?—I have always aimed at breeding a high class hunter or steeplechase horse. I don't think myself that it pays to breed anything else.

1438. And what kind of a sire?—A thoroughbred sire.

1439. I think you said that in your district the farmers had bred hunters from their horses?—Oh, I don't say that they breed hunters, my lord. They have bred animals which they have sold to go to England at an early age, at one and a half years of age, they go by the name of "yearlings" in the country, they are sold at fairs.

1440. You don't know what becomes of them?—I think they are shipped to England, I don't know for what, unless they eventually find their way as team horses.

1441. Then you have no experience yourself of horses bred by a sire with Hackney blood?—No, I have not, indeed, I don't consider that a horse with cart blood in him would be any use in this country.

1442. Why do you think not?—Because I think that it takes an exceptional horse to carry a man to hounds in this country. I think that a horse must have great stamina and power of endurance, and I don't think any cart blood in him would conduce to that.

1443. Would that same remark apply in England?—Well, I suppose it would, quite so.

1444. As far as breeding is concerned, I gather you would not approve of any strain of cart-horse blood?—No, I would be entirely against it.

1445. Or Hackney blood?—I should be entirely against any with blood, and I consider Hackney blood would come under that denomination.

1446. How about horses used for harness purposes?—My experience of harness horses is that horses that are used for hunters are equally good harness horses, and there is no class demand for these, and if they have a certain amount of action that there is good [illegible] a sale for them as they are used for harness purposes as for hunters, and I see them sold at local fairs, Mallow, [illegible], and other fairs with which I am acquainted, and they make just as much money for the purpose as for hunters.

1447. Action, I suppose, is an important factor in a harness horse. Action and colour influencing them a great deal?—If they are good colour and have a bit of action they are almost immediately bought for harness horses.

1448. Don't you think the Hackney would be useful in giving action?—Well, I don't think that sort of Hackney action—I don't consider it is true action, it is extravagant and may be very good for some purposes or for teams, but I don't think it is for general purposes. I think the action is extravagant and is hard on the wire.

1449. Putting aside your own personal opinion on the matter and looking at the matter economically, do you think the introduction of Hackney blood would produce a valuable horse?—I don't think it would, because if the buyer got wind of [illegible] Hackney blood in it I think he would be all the more likely to [illegible] shy.

1450. Have you any experience of [illegible] used in a cavalry regiment. For some years and I have always taken a great interest in remounts, and I have on various occasions sold [illegible] fit for the purpose.

1451. They were by thoroughbred horses?—Invariably, I never knew them anything else.

1452. Do you hold the same opinion as regards Hackney and cart-horse blood in relation to army remounts?—I do, most strongly; I am of opinion from my experience I may have known remounts that had not got thoroughbred blood in any [illegible] would be of little value, would not have sufficient endurance.

1453. Have you any opinion at all as to the advisability or practicability of the remounts being bought direct from the breeder instead of through a dealer?—It is of course a very good thing if it could be managed, but at the same time I think it is a very difficult thing to do and would require a much larger organisation than is put at the disposal of the Army Remount Department in Ireland. It is the practice of the dealers and has been for many years, for [illegible] years, to buy the horses for this purpose, and I think there would be a great difficulty in any private individual or body buying them outside of the dealers.

1454. Some suggestions have been made to the Commission that it might be a good thing if the old troopers were in some way distributed throughout the country, do you think that would be a good thing from your experience of the country and of the army?—I don't think it would; I think the cast trooper as a rule is an old and hard fed animal that I think would be unlikely to breed well, of course they have bred well in some instances, but I don't think as a rule they would breed well. They have been fed many years on hard feeding without a mouthful of grass, and it would be some years before they threw an animal of any class.

1455. They would not be cast, I suppose, while they had many years left?—No; and it would require two or three good fillies [illegible] very likely.

1456. You heard Mr. Roberts' evidence?—I did, my lord.

1457. Do you generally agree with what he has said, or have you any remarks to make?—I agree entirely with Mr. Roberts' evidence in every point.

1458. Lord Ashbourne.—Don't you think small [illegible] in your district [illegible] a horse with a double object, [illegible] good and so on [illegible]?—I think on a [illegible] of [illegible] which [illegible] for that purpose and [illegible] the province.

1459. An uncommon and [illegible] price [illegible]?—Yes.

1460. And might not that be the reason why they [illegible]?—I agree with you. I think that is the reason why they do [illegible] so many [illegible], but at the same time I think if a good class of thoroughbred [illegible] registered as has been described [illegible] throughout, I think they would [illegible] them for the [illegible] they would have to provide.

1461. Do you think they would do the work on the land as well [illegible], and the chances are that the [illegible] would be much smaller.

1462. How would you be disposed to have a registry of [illegible] kept as well as of sires?—I think it would be a great advantage to the country if it could be worked, but I think it would be a very complex business and would entail an enormous amount of [illegible] verifying the pedigrees, and it would take a long time before it was thoroughly established; I think if it was once established it would then go ahead.

1463. And put money into the pockets of the breeders?—It would, and would enhance the value of [illegible] in the eyes of foreigners.

1464. You admit that the Hackney is good for town work, do you?—I think that he is a good animal to [illegible] up and down.

1465. No gain money?—There are always a class of [illegible] who will give money for him.

1466. The question is which is the most valuable [illegible] horse—the [illegible] horse or the ordinary [illegible] horse?—I consider the Irish hunter, sired by the thoroughbred horse, is far and away the best animal [illegible] in this nation.

1467. What proportion would you put of those?—I think if thoroughbred stallions were purchased and [illegible] through the country and bought with [illegible], I think many thoroughbred stallions in the country have [illegible], but there is certainly a great want of good thoroughbred stallions in the country with size and [illegible], and I am certain they would be bought in England.

1468. Another thing you say, you find the farmers don't keep their young mares if they can get a good price for them, that means practically that if the filly [illegible] more than the mare they [illegible] they [illegible] keep the filly [illegible] the [illegible].

1469. Unless they thought the filly would sell for less than the mare?—Unless the filly was injured or blemished or [illegible].

1470. Mr. F. [illegible].—You think it would be a public advantage if there were more stallions [illegible] the country?—I think it would be of the greatest advantage; what is really wanted is to oust the mongrel and bad stallion that is going through the country now, and I think the only way to do that is for the State to be applied to in placing sound stallions through the country which would eventually oust these mongrel and badly-bred brutes that are now covering mares throughout the country.

1470a. And of course you would think it advisable that these stallions should be supplied to the farmers at a low fee?—At the fees they are now giving for the mongrel stallions, that is the only way to get rid of the mongrel animals that are in the country now.

1471. Lord Rathdonnell.—I think you stated that there is a scarcity of [illegible] in Ireland, and by scarcity of [illegible] in Ireland do you mean that there are [illegible] good horses [illegible] formerly [illegible] namely more than the demand for them in [illegible]?—I merely mean that the demand is greater.

1472. Now in addition to your answer to Lord Ashbourne, is not the demand for Clydesdales and Shires [illegible] consequence of the [illegible] and [illegible] horses for [illegible]?—Undoubtedly, what they [illegible] is they [illegible].

1473. If a good half-bred stallion of more or less suitable [illegible] stood [illegible] by a Clydesdale or Shire stallion and they were standing at equal fees, to your opinion, to which stallion would the farmer send his mare to get [illegible]?—I think the [illegible] stallion would be [illegible].

1474. Mr. Crean.—You would [illegible] thoroughbred and half-bred?—I would have thoroughbred blood [illegible] in the stallion.

1475. That is thoroughbred for blood and half-bred for [illegible] substance?—Yes, and [illegible] for the use of the [illegible] farmer who would want to work their mares on farms.

1476. That is the [illegible] in the beginning?—They work them on [illegible] and then [illegible] in later, harrowed and ploughed.

1477. Mr. Wrench.—You said you would have all the stallions registered, by that I suppose you mean thoroughbred or approved [illegible]?—That is the only class I would admit to register.

1478. In addition to the registry would you think it wise that there should be a license, that all stallions [illegible] should be obliged to take out a license that their stallions [illegible]?—I think the registry would be sufficient in the [illegible].

1479. You think so many stallions would be registered under the scheme that there would not be a large balance remaining throughout the country [illegible]?—I don't think there would be, especially if there were enough stallions scattered throughout the country that would [illegible] the [illegible] of the horse we want to put in the country.

1480. You think all the steps that would be necessary with regard to stallions would be to supply thoroughbred and half-bred stallions?—That is my view.

1481. And that they would [illegible] all the [illegible] [illegible] of the country?—I think so.

1482. Then you said you consider Hackney blood [illegible], do you think that in any way those [illegible] [illegible]?—I cannot say that I have had any experience beyond what I have actually seen. I have [illegible] a Hackney stallion, but I am only [illegible] the [illegible] of [illegible] of the [illegible] and [illegible] throughout Ireland that I have come in contact with, [illegible] that the introduction of Hackney blood might prove [illegible] to the horse-breeding industry, at any rate in that part of the country.

1483. Did you merely take that opinion from what you heard?—I merely took that opinion from what I have heard.

1484. Do you think supposing there was any very [illegible] of breeding harness horses with [illegible] that that would pay as well as breeding hunters, I think you said that the harness [illegible] not as much money as the [illegible] hunters?—They do undoubtedly.

1485. You think there is as good a demand for harness horses with action?—Just as good a demand.

1486. That it would be as paying an industry?—Not as paying.

1487. And do you think that harness horses can be sold at as early age as hunters?—No, I think the harness horse can be sold at [illegible], and the hunter is [illegible] to make a [illegible] at [illegible] age.

1488. Lord Ashbourne.—[illegible] [illegible] them [illegible] on [illegible]

1489. Mr. W[illegible].—You think you can sell a three-year-old for a hunter to the same advantage as you can sell a four-year-old [illegible]—I [illegible] going at just the same rate.

1490. You said you thought it was of great importance that [illegible] through the country should have good action?—I do think it is very important.

1491. Do you think the thoroughbred horse has not all the same powers of [illegible] action as the Hackney stallion has?—Well, I cannot say that [illegible] I have never had any experience in breeding from a Hackney.

1492. Col. St. Quintin.—Do you consider that the Hackney action is [illegible]—[illegible] and I also think it is a class of horse that is [illegible] in the requirements of this country.

1493. Mr. W. [illegible].—The best horses bred in Ireland [illegible] Dublin [illegible]—I think they [illegible].

1494. You [illegible] that a thoroughbred stallion and one of the old breed of Irish mares would be [illegible] the half-bred [illegible]—I think that is [illegible] wanted [illegible].

1495. But would you not insist any qualification with the mares, because you have [illegible] the country; [illegible] mares good enough?—There are [illegible] plenty of good mares [illegible] plenty of them; it is the [illegible].

1496. Would you insist on qualification for these mares, that they should have either won races or [illegible] or have something about the breeding?—I think that would have to be left to the discretion of the body who were appointed to select these mares for the purpose.

1497. You keep thoroughbred stallions?—I do.

1498. Do you find any difficulty in getting stallions; [illegible]—I [illegible] knee-action, but principally shoulder action.

1499. Which you would term a daisy-cutter, or would he [illegible]—No, he must have knee-action in conjunction with shoulder action.

1500. Have you found great difficulty in getting horses of this description thoroughbred?—Well, I think there is a certain amount of difficulty; but I think at the same time there are plenty of them to be had if they are looked for.

1501. You have [illegible] in London, I suppose, of thoroughbred stock?—I have, at Newmarket.

1502. And York, and other places?—Newmarket, and Doncaster, I have [illegible].

1503. Have you ever been able to see there the [illegible] that would be good enough to breed from, with a knee-action that would [illegible] for the purpose?—Oh, I have seen plenty of them.

1504. In the locality in which you reside there is a demand only for thoroughbreds, you say?—The [illegible] of mares are sent to thoroughbred horses entirely.

1505. Do you find no difficulty in [illegible] of thoroughbreds than you [illegible] for hunters?—I think that [illegible] have rather [illegible] off the thoroughbred horse; I think that they want to [illegible] with more substance and bone than the thoroughbreds.

1506. But that you know, that you [illegible] [illegible] you describe?—[illegible] I could [illegible] is a [illegible] horse.

1507. In answering Mr. W[illegible] you said you know nothing of the [illegible] breeding of the Hackney?—No, I don't know anything about the Hackney.

1508. You don't know that he came originally from the same source as the thoroughbred?—I understand a great many of them have two or three crosses.

1509. One had [illegible] in the one [illegible] thoroughbred dates back in 2 or 3, [illegible]?—No, I have no knowledge of Hackney breeding.

1510. You have not used the Hackneys for [illegible] ing?—No.

1511. What do [illegible] action?—I [illegible] an extravagant action.

1512. Horses that can get away with that action go up to fifteen or eighteen miles an hour, do you call that [illegible] action?—I should say they do [illegible] they have tremendous action for a short journey, but I should [illegible] could not possibly stay on.

1513. But you have no experience of it?—No; I cannot say I have.

1514. Mr. W[illegible].—Have you [illegible] thoroughbred horse [illegible] before?—I have [illegible].

1515. Do you ordinarily think he has sufficient action to get harness horses?—I said in my evidence that he had not got as much knee action as I would wish.

1516. [illegible]—I [illegible] him as a hunter sire, I would prefer him [illegible] action.

1517. The Chairman.—I take it that what you have [illegible] Hackneys in [illegible], you have had no practical experience?—No, there are none in this [illegible] part of Ireland at all.

1518. I suppose you have seen them at shows?—I have frequently.

1519. And I gather from you, that if it could be managed you think that the registration of mares would be a good thing?—I think it would be a very good thing, I think it would enhance the value of Irish horses.

1520. You think the registration of stallions would be sufficient and that the licensing of stallions is not necessary?—I think it would have to be done by Act of Parliament.

1521. There is a great difference, registration is voluntary and licensing is compulsory?—I think if sufficient [illegible] at the disposal of the Committee of [illegible] it would [illegible] the [illegible] would [illegible].

1522. That is what I wanted to ascertain from you [illegible] the State to assist these [illegible] stallions [illegible] would be [illegible], but it would be [illegible] do you [illegible]—It is a [illegible], I would [illegible] that at [illegible] the effect [illegible] the [illegible] of doing it [illegible] would [illegible].

1523. And would produce this [illegible] result?—I think it would be likely.

1524. Mr. W[illegible].—Is it not a fact that the mares in Westmeath are about the best mares in any county in Ireland?—I think without saying that they are the best, I think they are as good as any in any part of the country.

1525. Of a very high standard?—Of a very high standard.

1526. And you have a lot of stud there who are intelligent enough to mind their mares to the best stallions?—Undoubtedly, but I consider that class of [illegible] don't require to be legislated for.

1527. It has not therefore been [illegible] upon you [illegible] that people have had the mares in the country can have?—I think of course in every county there are a certain number of bad mares. I don't think we have a preponderance of bad mares in Westmeath.

1528. You have a preponderance of good mares?—I think we have, which would also apply to [illegible] and Kildare, the further the distance the poorer the class of mares.

1529. Mr W. Gilbey.—With regard to the half-bred [illegible] you would have [illegible] the [illegible] thoroughbred?—Undoubtedly, I would [illegible] to have mares [illegible] registered, if possible.

1530. And that would be done [illegible] to be having been bred under a suitable sire such as [illegible]?—That is, [illegible] would be [illegible] registered stallions; that is the system I would work on.

1531. Lord Ashtown.—And it would be necessary to register each of the mares to have their progeny registered as well?—Certainly, I am all for registration.

1532. I may be quite wrong, but I think about two years ago I saw your name down in the prize list at [illegible] for a colt by a thoroughbred out of a [illegible]?—You are quite right, but the horse's name was "[illegible]," but he is a thoroughbred horse named "[illegible]."

1533. Mr. Warren.—There was a Cleveland Bay at [illegible], were there not?—There was, some years ago, at Castlepollard, not recently; I have often heard that the stock were of a valuable description, and that they were good-looking. I cannot say whether they had stamina, I have never seen them.

1534. It was a long time ago?—About thirty years ago.

1535. Mr. Carew.—You have a thoroughbred sire called "Delight"?—We have, who has got some good stock there [illegible] other horse in the country.

1536. The Chairman.—Are you a member of the Royal Dublin Society?—I am.

1537. Are you on the Council?—No, I am not; I am on the Horse-breeding Committee, an additional member of it.

1538. Mr. W. Carew.—I notice in the Dublin papers I have looked at, and also observed it at the show, there was a three-year-old gelding shown as a thoroughbred gelding—you give prizes for thoroughbred geldings, but no prize for two-year-olds and three-year-olds—and I questioned the gentleman [illegible] what horse is getting, and I said, "Which is your [illegible]?" He said, "There are no prizes given for two or three year olds, otherwise I would have kept him; he was a colt [illegible] yearling"?—That is a fact, but if the [illegible] had been encouraged that horse would not have been [illegible], he would have been kept for a [illegible] stallion.

1539. He was thoroughbred, it [illegible] in this country, [illegible] a large price to go abroad?—Nearly all thoroughbred horses are gelded in this country; they are bred principally for the purpose of making steeplechase horses, and they are nearly all cut as yearlings.

1540. Mr. Carew.—Just to make him quiet for training?—There is a prejudice against stallions for steeplechasing.

1541. Mr. Warren.—As a matter of fact, there are very few half-bred horses now kept as stallions?—Very few, very rarely. In former days people used to ride stallions as hunters, but now it is an exception.

1542. If the present race of half-bred horses die out, there are really not young horses in the country to replace them?—Not half-bred horses; I only know of one half-bred stallion hunter in Meath now, and he is the property of the Master of the Meath Hounds.

1543. Chairman.—How do you account for that change?—By fashion; it has become unfashionable to ride a stallion.

1544. Mr. Warren.—But if these horses were registered, and a register adopted for half-bred horses, don't you think it might then become more fashionable?—Undoubtedly.

1545. Lord Ashtown.—And also do good?—We anticipate it would.

1546. Lord Rathdonnell.—Have you ever heard it stated as a fact that a stallion ridden to hounds, or raced, if he is over-pressed, is never quite so kind a horse again?—I have, and I believe it to be an undisputed fact.

1547. Has not that something to say to the castrating of some of these horses in the case of hunters?—I think it has; and also that a half-bred stallion is not a saleable animal; people would not have him in their stables, as a rule they are troublesome horses; and in any case they require an enormous amount of work and exercise to keep them fit, more than their legs will stand.

1548. Mr. Carew.—They require to be isolated in boxes?—They require to be isolated as well.

Captain [illegible] examined.

1549. Chairman.—You are, I believe, secretary to the Irish Horse Breeding Association?—I am, my lord.

1550. And you a member of the Royal Dublin Society?—I am also, my lord.

1551. Do you do any work for them in any way?—I do; I act for them as inspector under their horse-breeding scheme for the registration of mares throughout Ireland.

1552. Sole inspector?—I believe I am the only one.

1553. And, on their behalf you would visit stallions?—I do; I attend shows throughout Ireland, and report to the Dublin Society accordingly.

1554. Can you give the Commission any information as to the objects and scope of the Horse-breeding Association?—Yes, my lord. It was formed on the 13th of August of this year, and was the outcome of a deputation that waited on His Excellency on the 8th of May. This deputation was the outcome of a petition against Hackneys being imported into this country by [illegible]. This is a copy of the letter that was issued asking opinion upon it, and this is a copy of the petition:—

"Dear Sir,—The enclosed will show you my object in writing. I have been requested to ask you, [illegible] authorities, on the subject of the importation of Hackney stallions into Ireland. You will oblige us very much if you will write a letter stating your experience and opinion with regard to these animals, as [illegible] on the breeding of carriage horses their introduction into English counties has produced. Will you kindly allow me to make use of your letter when the deputation waits on His Excellency the Lord Lieutenant a fortnight hence?"

This is a copy of the petition.

1555. To whom did you send those letters asking for opinions?—To the judges that chiefly act [illegible] in the shows in Dublin, and to the leading dealers throughout England.

1556. You sent them to the leading dealers in England. Did you not send them to people in Ireland as well?—I did not; practically this letter is [illegible] a letter of my own; perhaps I should say it is a letter of Mr. [illegible] J. M'[illegible], of [illegible], County Meath.

1557. But written on behalf of your Society?—It was before the formation of the Society; that letter was dated 1st of May.

1558. That formed the basis on which you petitioned?—Yes, my lord.

1559. Perhaps you would read us the petition?

"Hackney Stallions.—We, the undersigned, are strongly of opinion that the introduction of Hackney stallions into Ireland will prove a serious injury to the breed of Irish horses, and that it will be impossible to maintain the position of Irish horses in the [illegible] markets: we, therefore, humbly petition His Excellency the Lord Lieutenant to use his influence against public funds being applied to encourage Hackney stallions."

That was very largely signed, indeed, and laid before His Excellency on the 8th of May last at the Castle.

1560. And this petition was the cause of the formation of this Society?—Yes, my lord.

1561. We shall be very glad to hear any information as to the objects of the Society, and what steps were taken to carry out those objects?—The Society having been formed on the 13th August, [illegible], I beg to submit a copy of [illegible] in the present [illegible]; [illegible] still [illegible].

1862. Is that material to our inquiry?—These names are drawn from every part of Ireland—representative people—thoroughly conversant upon the subject of horse breeding.

1863. What we chiefly want to know is, what the object of the Society is, and what means you take to carry out that object?—Perhaps I ought to read the letter that was sent in answer to one we received from your Secretary upon the subject.

1864. Give us the information any way you like; I only want to know what were the objects of the Horse-breeding Association?—Then here is the letter, my lord:—

"11, South Frederick-street,
"Dublin, 26th Sept., 1896.

"Sir,—In reply to your letter of the 11th inst., requesting information as to the scope and work of the Irish Horse-breeding Association, and its expression of its views on several matters connected with the subject, I am directed to state that at present the primary object of the Association is to collect such information and evidence in regard to horse-breeding in the different parts of the country as they deem it important to submit for the consideration of the Commission. The Association includes among its members, a list of which is enclosed, a large number of gentlemen who take a deep interest in maintaining and improving the high character of Irish horses, not only as hunters, but for all other useful purposes. They felt that it was only through such an organisation as theirs being formed that the information and evidence which they deem it desirable to submit for the consideration of the Commission could be prepared in a satisfactory form, and they trust the action which they have taken may be useful to the Commission in connection with the arduous inquiry they have undertaken. The Association does not contemplate taking any steps for the registration of stallions. That most important duty, as far as it relates to thoroughbred horses, has been carried out for the past two years by the Royal Dublin Society in connection with their horse-breeding scheme, and has been attended with most satisfactory results, which will, no doubt, be fully explained to the Commission by the officers of that Society; it is, therefore, right here to observe that the Horse-breeding Association attach the greatest importance to the registration of sound and suitable stallions, and are of opinion that that duty should be entrusted to the Royal Dublin Society, and sufficient means placed at their disposal to carry it out in an efficient manner, and that the registered stallions in every class of stallions which it is considered by competent and independent judges desirable to encourage in every district of the country. The Association is in favour of giving premiums to registered stallions under such conditions as will ensure suitable sires being available for the service of mares of farmers of limited means at a moderate or nominal fee. If such an arrangement could be carried out in conjunction with the giving of substantial prizes in each county for young mares and for stud purposes, and young stock got by registered stallions, on the system now adopted by the Royal Dublin Society in the administration of the Government grant placed at their disposal for the improvement of the breeding of horses, it would be attended with satisfactory results. The word 'half-bred' stallions requires consideration. Stallions purebred on one side and on the other having several crosses of pure blood have been used with advantage, and the Association is of opinion that such half-bred stallions, if considered suitable, from their performances, their own conformation, and action, should be encouraged and included in the register, and that their stock should participate in the same benefits as stock got by registered thoroughbred sires. There is another class of individual stallions, which may be termed 'mongrels,' that have little (if any) breeding on either side, and which, notwithstanding, are largely used by farmers, as the service fee is small; the produce of such sires is, comparatively speaking, worthless. The Association is not in favour of the introduction of Clydesdale blood into the country. The crossing of a Clydesdale mare with a thoroughbred horse is not to be recommended, in the hope of producing useful hunters or harness horses. It is possible that the crossing of a brood mare of Hackney blood, with a thoroughbred stallion may produce useful stock, but there is throughout the country a deep-rooted objection to the introduction of Hackney blood in any form; and it is alleged, in support of this view, that English and foreign dealers, who buy horses largely in Ireland, object to it in the strongest manner. The Association submit herewith the names of gentlemen who are prepared to give evidence on the several points referred to in this letter, and trust the Commission will be good enough to hear and examine their statements."

That embraces chiefly the objects of the Association, which was formed with a view to getting evidence generally by letter and by query form, a copy of which I wish to hand in, throughout the country, the information that could be got regarding the different breeds of horses throughout the country.

1865. To whom was that letter addressed?—That was sent to the Commission some three weeks ago.

1866. Then you issued a series of questions?—We issued a series of questions which I have handed in, and entered into correspondence with people upon the subject of horse-breeding generally, and obtained answers generally.

1867. Yes; we we will be very glad to hear the opinions of this society you represent through you or through anybody else that the association likes to send, but I don't see how we can take in evidence anything in the nature of reports of your association which are based upon the answers to a series of questions without calling before us the people who answered these questions?—The bulk of them, my lord, will be prepared to come forward here and support their statements.

1868. But there are more than a hundred of them?—I have summed it and brought out their opinions, and if I may state it, as to the breeds in which it is given, as regards the different breeds of horses, if I may state that in bulk.

1869. Let me look at it. We shall be very happy to have any facts, any opinion, any information of that kind that you can give us now, but I think we will have to consider if your society wishes to give in a report founded on the opinion of a great number of people, we shall have to consider how to deal with it. We obviously cannot take fiction on an information the gentlemen who sent answers to your inquiry?—May I put in copies of replies received from some different dealers and gentlemen on the subject?

1870. No, I think not.—May I read those original letters?

1871. You have got the letter that you sent to the Commission, I think you better give [illegible] the evidence you have got, and whatever do I will submit the members of the Commission as to how they shall deal with the other matters. Have you any statistical information?—Certainly.

1872. There were certain reports and things Mr. Roberts mentioned that he said he thought would come better from you in this association, and this based entirely upon obtaining information from the country upon the subject of horse-breeding generally.

1873. All I want you to understand is that we will be perfectly ready to hear that evidence, but it must come from somebody whom we can examine and cross-examine?—We shall be very pleased to submit to your lordships a great number of gentlemen. I have already handed in a list of names of parties willing to be examined.

1874. Yes, but in the meantime have you got any information you can give us from yourself?—I am quite at your service to answer any question.

[illegible]

rent of the very bad class, the unthoroughbred class, that are responsible for the extent that it has been said your industry appears in the face to the country.

1603. That I hope does not apply to the whole of the 3,000?—I am not speaking with reference to the whole of the 3,000, of that there are nearly 800 thoroughbreds, I am speaking chiefly of the half-breds and unthoroughbred class.

1603. Of course all you register are thoroughbred?—They are all thoroughbred and sound.

1604. Can you give any general information as to the thoroughbreds that are not registered? Is it their [illegible] reason for not being registered owing to [illegible] that in the first place they are not sound, or that more applications would appear so that [illegible] to be registered, they are not able, I presume, to put forward a sound certificate, many of them. Of course there are some people [illegible] very hard to get to register, at the present day. There is really no money inducement held out to any registered stallion like there was in the first year that came out of Captain's premiums.

1605. The only advantage of registration is the assistance that has been [illegible] by adding his [illegible] from year to year to a marked extent, the farmers are anxious now to go to a stallion where they can [illegible] that way to give the fee, but unfortunately the fee is the stumbling block, that is what prevents the farmers going to these stallions in many cases in [illegible] comparatively to the cheaper and also to the unsound stallions.

1606. May I take it that your opinion is, in view of the figures which you have given us, that the quantity of stallions is sufficient?—The quantity I should say is ample if the quality and conformation and soundness were right, we have ample stallions in the country as regards numbers.

1607. Do you think as a general rule that the stallions are the best adapted for the different districts they serve in?—No, I do not.

1608. Have you any suggestion to make as to how the quality of the stallions generally could be improved, and how they could be better selected as suitable for the various districts?—By registration.

1609. Registration involving a certificate of soundness, and also of suitability?—Yes.

1610. With reference to mares, what is your opinion?—The experience that I have gathered mostly has been from the Mare Shows that I have attended in the last three or four years, and from those Shows that are inaugurated by the Dublin Society in connection with their horse-breeding schemes.

1611. And what opinion have you formed?—In some counties and they differ to a very marked extent; in some counties the mares are particularly good, good size and good bone and of a good hardy breed, whereas in other counties they are not—I can't give a sweeping statement, but I say, to a large extent, in some counties, they are not fit to breed from.

1612. Not fit even for the breed demand for agricultural purposes?—There are a great number that are unfit for this purpose, both from size and constitution, &c. [illegible] the farmer breeds in the poorer districts, from that, that he cannot sell, [illegible] from accident or unsoundness, he puts them to the cheapest horse in the hopes of making money, that is where the downfall has been, and the [illegible] has appeared in the [illegible] as a result.

1613. You think the quality, so far as you could judge by them, has deteriorated?—It has in some places. I think the [illegible] ahead of the [illegible] as regards the quality, of course in some counties they are very [illegible] about going to a good horse.

1614. I am talking now about the mares, it has been suggested that there is a very great tendency on the part of the farmers, especially small farmers, to sell their best mares to [illegible] and breed from inferior ones?—I think that is so, they sell their filly to a foreigner who will give a better price for a three year old, and they sell them as [illegible] instead of keeping them. A great number of fillies go for remounts, I have heard it stated up to 65 per cent.

1615. Do you mean remounts for foreign armies?—For every where; it is thought at least 65 per cent. I think we provide remounts for the Italian, and Dutch and French, and other governments.

1616. Is your experience long enough to enable you to form an opinion as to whether the mares are as good as they used to be, the general stamp of them?—My experience doesn't go over very many years, but, certainly in the last ten years I would not say in some counties they had deteriorated at all; in fact I would say they had improved. I speak now more of the Counties Meath, Kildare, Tipperary, and Wexford.

1617. You think they have improved there?—Yes.

1618. Well, as to other counties?—I think they have deteriorated to some extent.

1619. Have you any idea of the cause?—The cause is from what I stated before, my lord, that I think they have sold the good ones, and they have kept them to breed from that they could not sell from some reason, that I have before mentioned, accident or unsoundness.

1620. I forget whether in your letter to the Commission you made any suggestion as about registration of mares?—We did not.

1621. Or dealing with the question of mares in any way?—Not to my knowledge or recollection.

1622. Have you any suggestion in that direction in mind generally?—I think that the old scheme that the Dublin Society had in 1894 was a better scheme than the present one, but I quite hold with Captain Fetherstonhaugh that if the two could be worked together in conjunction, that is by giving nominations to the mares and subsidising the stallions to some extent, it would work better. I think the money is spread over a large number of mares, and you get them to touch with them. But the present system of giving prizes to mares works particularly well in Kildare, and works well in Tipperary, at least about the Clonmel district it does; they are keener about horse-breeding in some counties than they are in others, but that may be owing to the fact that they have a better demand in those counties.

1623. In the questions you have about the mares did you submit questions on these points?—They asked questions as to the class of mare, and as to what size would be considered best suited to mate their mares with, and it was on that point that I wished to give you that table as to the replies received; I have not reduced [illegible] from the total amount of replies that has come in, and I find that 75 per cent. were in favour of the thoroughbred.

THE CHAIRMAN.—We will go into that question another time.

1624. Lord ARDILAUN.—Don't you think one of the reasons for going back to the old scheme of the Royal Dublin Society was that the Society previously gave [illegible] the stallion owner part of the fee?—I believe they did.

1625. Would not that encourage the owner to keep better sires, to guarantee his fees; it is only [illegible] guarantee him now?—But by the altered scheme of 1895, the money was more spread over the districts, and I think in that way as this better.

1626. Mr T. [illegible].—Can you say what steps are taken to ensure soundness in the stallions [illegible] for the premium by the Dublin Society, and there are some such [illegible] that certificate [illegible] to be forwarded with the application, before they entertain it at all, of soundness from a qualified veterinary surgeon, and if they have any doubt, [illegible] they send their own qualified veterinary surgeon to give a certificate.

1627. Is that done every year?—Yes, not quite. There are some points raised, and it is considered necessary to go further into the matter.

[illegible]

1 5

1659. [illegible] could not have been one of the judges? — No, but three of our own [illegible] in the district; I was giving a [illegible] [illegible] Hackneys. I was also at the [illegible] show this year, and observed the [illegible] competition there. I was struck [illegible] [illegible] [illegible] [illegible]; they were [illegible] [illegible] Hackneys [illegible] [illegible] [illegible] [illegible] [illegible] years ago.

1660. The Chairman. — [illegible] [illegible] [illegible] [illegible]; it was by [illegible] [illegible].

1661. Did you see many specimens of the produce of the Congested Districts Hackneys at Kenmare? — I did. I suppose I saw quite forty; [illegible] by "[illegible]" [illegible] so many [illegible] [illegible].

1662. Were they ready for sale? — I could give you the exact number. I think there were about thirteen yearlings, fifteen foals, all by "[illegible]" [illegible]; the yearlings were not so good as the [illegible].

1663. Two-year-olds? — There were twelve [illegible]; they were very [illegible], and [illegible].

1664. Were any of them sold? — Oh, yes, but not at the show; they are sold in that district, and bought by men who take them up into the southern parts of Limerick and part of Cork; I know the names of the men who take them up.

1665. Are they bought as foals? — They are bought as foals and yearlings.

1666. You don't know what prices are given for them? — Yes; as foals and yearlings they go at about £4 or £5, and beyond that age £8; they seldom keep them as [illegible], although [illegible] [illegible] that were going to keep their [illegible]; they had taken prizes at previous shows and were branded, and [illegible] they were to get a free service, and [illegible] an inducement to go back to that breed.

1667. Are any of them put into the [illegible] parts of Limerick and Cork? — Yes.

1668. What are they bought for? — They are bought by the small farmers for working purposes, and [illegible] generally for jumping.

1669. That is only a supposition, you don't know? — I have not seen them back there. They are also bought in the west in the Connemara districts and they are brought up to Edgeworthstown and Longford and up to Strokestown, which are all hunter-breeding districts.

1670. Lord Ardilaun. — They buy these horses as foals down at Kenmare? — They buy them as foals and yearlings.

1671. Mr. Wrench. — What did you think of the mares at Kenmare? — With some few exceptions they were not a good lot.

1672. A great many common and coarse? — Yes, they were common, still I thought that if mated with a horse with really good shoulders they might have produced useful animals.

1673. Did you notice that they were very much in-kneed the mares? — Some of them, some of them were calf-kneed.

1674. Do you know that the two year olds had been left out on the mountain? — Yes, some of them had some cow disease, I don't know that they had come off the mountain, but I don't think that would alter their flat-sidedness.

1675. It is a very poor district? — I would not say that altogether, there is some of it good land, I drove some portions of that quite capable of feeding horses.

1676. On which side? — On the north-western side of Kenmare.

1677. Where were you going from? — I went over the suction crossing and turned to the right and went to a lot of farms up that road, and then turned and came back to the right, right round the valley.

1678. It was all fairly near the town? — I did not go too far out, I saw a number of stock on the land that enabled me to judge, I saw stock by other horses too on the land outside.

1679. Sir W. Gilbey. — At these fairs I suppose there were many foals? — There was a show, there were only foals by the Board's stallions that stood there the year before.

1680. The Chairman. — Were there any foals by any other stallions except Hackney stallions? — I saw some but not at the show, there would only be allowed at that show what were got by the Board's stallions.

1681. But the Board have other stallions? — They had only the one stallion there that year.

The Commission adjourned to November 17th.

FOURTH DAY.—TUESDAY, NOVEMBER 17TH, 1896.

Present:—Lord Rathdonnell in the Chair; Mr. Wrench, Mr. Percy La Touche, and Colonel St. Quintin.

Mr. Hugh Neville, Secretary.

Captain Tidswell recalled.

1682. The Chairman. — Captain Tidswell, I think you have some documents you wished to hand in to the Commission as part of your evidence — please state what they are? — Yes, my Lord, in accordance with the promise given by me I will put them in. They are copies of letters received from different people in England on the subject of Hackney breeding. They are from Lord Coventry, J. M. Richardson, Willoughby de Broke, Owen C. Wallis, Lincoln, Garrard, W. [illegible], [illegible] Chapman, [illegible] and Co., [illegible], J. Hooper, A. J. Brown, J. [illegible], F. A. [illegible], H. C. Brown, [illegible], Arthur [illegible], Henry Ford, George [illegible], John [illegible], W. Chambers, Alfred Withers, H. and W. Milton, John Darby, Joseph [illegible], [illegible], John Johnson, John J. Thompson, George [illegible], G. [illegible], F. P. [illegible], George [illegible] Miller, [illegible] and Sons. These letters, [illegible] I have received from the same people, I have [illegible] relating to the breeding of horses in Ireland, and [illegible] of them [illegible] [illegible] on the question of the introduction of Hackney sires. Their opinions are strongly against the Hackney blood being introduced, and they say the introduction of Hackneys in Yorkshire has ruined it as a hunter and horse breeding county. I have made a [illegible] as to the [illegible] annually on horses for hunting and [illegible] purposes bought in Ireland by English buyers, who have communicated with our Association on horse-breeding and who are opposed to the introduction of Hackney blood into the country. They amount in figures to £[illegible] — a very large [illegible]. I also beg to lay before you [illegible] the original resolutions of the following [illegible] [illegible] and Irish [illegible] of the [illegible] of [illegible] into this country. These [illegible] are [illegible] by [illegible]

[illegible] Captain J. F. [illegible]

for two [illegible], four-year-olds by him this year [illegible], and I got [illegible] in Dublin for one of them. [illegible] used to be ridden by Lord Waterford [illegible].

1705. Mr. Wrench.—Do you know how many [illegible] the kind of thoroughbred blood?—I do not. [illegible] from the south. The [illegible] of Wicklow [illegible] the last two years. One of the best hunters we have in [illegible], now ridden by [illegible], Mr. [illegible], a thoroughbred horse by "[illegible]." He [illegible] but [illegible] too long for him.

1706. All the [illegible] you gave [illegible] the [illegible] of thoroughbred [illegible] in Ireland. You gave them from the [illegible] returns, did you not?—Yes, I did, from the Agricultural returns of [illegible].

1707. Have you any reason to believe they are [illegible] every reason to believe they are not [illegible] as to thoroughbreds.

1708. [illegible] as to the [illegible] of the [illegible] of thoroughbreds [illegible], you would not say that is correct?—I would not like to set myself against the [illegible], but I know what the [illegible] was in my own [illegible].

1709. But you did not give these figures [illegible] correct?—I gave them as quoted from [illegible].

1710. Then you would not wish them to be accepted as the actual number of animals [illegible] in Ireland?—I would not dispute a [illegible] to [illegible] that.

1711. In your opinion is it correct?—I did not [illegible] it myself, and I would not [illegible] it.

1712. You have not made any inquiries to find [illegible] correct?—Well, I know. I have been trying to make up a [illegible] of [illegible] in every county.

1713. And have done [illegible] with the record [illegible] the blue-book?—I can't get the [illegible] and I find there should be an increase in the [illegible] and all other [illegible]. For instance, [illegible] "To be registered?" [illegible] registered [illegible] in a stud-book. If [illegible] registered [illegible] the thoroughbred [illegible] in the Book.

1714. The Chairman.—Is there any further statement you wish to make?—[illegible]. I have been in the [illegible] through Ireland, at Cork, Limerick, and [illegible], and [illegible] through Ireland, and I have been at [illegible] and [illegible] this year, and could tell [illegible] about the stock I saw there.

Mr. David [illegible].

Mr. David [illegible], [illegible], Ballymena, Co. Antrim, **examined.**

1715. The Chairman.—You are a farmer, **and live** in the County Antrim?—Yes, my lord.

1716. Have you any [illegible] experience of the breeding of horses?—I have been breeding for about eighteen years.

1717. What class of sires have you generally used, and what breed?—I have used thoroughbred sires, Yorkshire coaching horses, [illegible] Hackney, and half-bred horses, and the [illegible] have been what we call the old Irish breed.

1718. As to the dams?—Well, they are half-breeds I have been using, [illegible], that is to say the result of thoroughbred horses and an ordinary half-bred [illegible], which I can [illegible], but a [illegible] of [illegible] the produce of [illegible] probably of a thoroughbred, and it may have been a Cleveland, Yorkshire, or [illegible].

1719. You say you have used the half-bred sire, what has been your experience in using such animals and the half-bred sire?—Well, it [illegible] a fairly strong [illegible] of 15.3 to 16 hands, they got good [illegible] stock.

1720. Can you give us any information as to the half-bred sire [illegible]?—Well, he was [illegible] from a thoroughbred horse, but it is very very hard to describe the [illegible], that is to say, [illegible] probably from a thoroughbred and from a Yorkshire coaching mare, or what we call the old Irish [illegible] has been in our [illegible] for generations.

1721. Have you tried a Hackney sire?—[illegible] twice.

1722. What was the result?—Well, I sold the horse [illegible] and he [illegible] to turn out fairly well. I have one two-year-old at present, and I have [illegible] a [illegible] Hackney. That is my only experience in Hackney breeding.

1723. Are many horses bred by the farmers in your district or neighbourhood?—A great many.

1724. Can you give any description of the type of mare usually bred in your part of the country for breeding purposes?—Well, they are usually from 15 to 15.3 hands in height with lots of muscle, good [illegible], very active, sharp, with plenty of go and [illegible] [illegible], and as a [illegible] fairly clean legs and not much hair on them.

1725. Have you had any experience of breeding from two-year-old mares?—Yes, very [illegible].

1726. Can you give us any opinion on that?—Well, I do not think it desirable from my experience to breed from a two-year-old mare unless she is [illegible], and then I would only breed from her at a very early age, that is at a very early part of the season, I would not put her to the horse later than the month of May, my reason for so saying is that otherwise the [illegible] and as a rule they don't milk well unless they feed well, and the foal won't winter well if it is a late foal; the mare has not been developed thoroughly at two years old. That is my experience.

1727. Have you bred from a three-year-old mare?—Yes, I always follow, and I find three-year-old [illegible] the [illegible] is better able to nourish [illegible], and they are better able in [illegible] and [illegible] [illegible], than [illegible] a three-year-old mare, that has been served at three years old, [illegible] at four.

1728. Have you found any difference in the amount of milk a two-year-old mare can give as compared with a three-year-old mare?—Nothing further than the appearance of the foal. That is to say the foal always appears better nourished. It seems to be a better foal and more muscular, but as to a given quantity of milk that is a thing I could not say.

1729. Do the farmers appreciate a good sire, and are they willing to pay a fair price to [illegible] in your part of the country?—They [illegible] to be [illegible] [illegible]. [illegible] they did not appreciate a good sire—they [illegible] to appreciate the quality [illegible]. That is to say, they did not seem to [illegible] to pay too high a fee for a [illegible] if they got a good one.

1730. Do you think now they would pay?—I think [illegible] owing to the [illegible] held out by the Royal Dublin Society, [illegible] at [illegible] and [illegible] better [illegible] of [illegible], [illegible] better [illegible]; the [illegible] of [illegible] in the market.

1731. Have many Hackneys been bred in your neighbourhood [illegible]?—[illegible] years ago there was a good many bred. [illegible] [illegible] the last [illegible] years. There are [illegible] bred now.

1732. You say it is [illegible]?—I should not say so. This was a particularly good [illegible] [illegible].

1733. Have you a sufficient number of [illegible] in your district?—Well, I should not say [illegible], [illegible], but I think they might be improved [illegible].

1734. What class of sire is generally used in the [illegible]?—Well, half-bred horses.

1735. You mentioned the Royal Dublin Society

[illegible] purpose; have you had any experience of the benefit derived from the Royal Dublin Society's scheme?—Yes. I am the owner of a sire under the Royal Dublin Society's scheme, and I know one instance where a man put his mare to my sire, and as a two-year-old [illegible] [illegible] Royal Dublin Society's scheme [illegible] [illegible] class of mares.

[illegible] Do you think the poorer farmers derive any advantage from the scheme?—Yes, decidedly [illegible] from 30 to [illegible] acres [illegible] They are the class who [illegible] [illegible]

[illegible] Now, what class of horses do you think your district was found to the best advantage?—Would you say, my lord, for the particular wants of the farmers or from the financial point of view, to sell? [illegible]

[illegible] Well, take the financial point of view—what class of horse should a man breed?—I think, from a [illegible] thoroughbred horse, an [illegible] thoroughbred horse.

[illegible] Well, from the other point of view?—They get a very useful horse from a half-bred or Hackney. [illegible] farming work. They are able to do that kind of work and the [illegible] [illegible]

[illegible] Have you any suggestions to make to improve the horse breeding in your district?—I think there might be something done by offering some valuable prizes to the owners of [illegible] [illegible] The Royal Dublin Society, according to the present scheme, [illegible] [illegible] Royal Dublin Society.

[illegible] Mr. [illegible] [illegible]

[illegible]

[illegible] Yes.

[illegible]

[illegible] In Dublin.

[illegible] [illegible] Yes, or private [illegible]

[illegible] You said that about six years ago [illegible] Hackneys [illegible]

[illegible] To what do you attribute the giving up of the breeding of Hackneys six years ago?—The failure of the [illegible] [illegible]

[illegible] They did not get sufficiently good prices for their young stock?—Yes, and I think they [illegible] [illegible] "[illegible]" [illegible] Hackney [illegible]

[illegible] He was, you think, an exceptionally good horse?—Yes.

[illegible] A Hackney?—Yes, a Norfolk Hackney.

[illegible] Are there any thoroughbred Hackney mares [illegible] thoroughbred Hackney mare I think Mr. [illegible]

[illegible] You said that the produce of one of [illegible] as a three-year-old sold for [illegible] [illegible] show.

[illegible] What was it got by—by "[illegible]"?

[illegible] A thoroughbred horse?—Yes.

[illegible]

[illegible] Colonel St. [illegible]

[illegible] The light class of horse—light [illegible]

[illegible]

[illegible]

[illegible] He is a [illegible] horse?—Yes, a good [illegible]

[illegible] You were speaking about breeding from two [illegible] [illegible]

Nov. 17, 18[illegible]

Mr. [illegible]

the foals between two and three-year-olds?—Yes, those from two-year-old mares are smaller and not so well nourished, and we observe while we are weighing the foals that [illegible] from the two-year-olds than we get from the three-year-olds.

1774. They don't develop in [illegible] like large animals as those from the three-year-olds?—No, certainly not, for the first two years. It will take a year longer to develop.

1775. Mr. Wrench.—You said you have for your own purposes a thoroughbred horse and a Yorkshire coaching horse?—Quite so.

1776. How many mares do you allow the thoroughbred to serve?—Eighty.

1777. That is rather above the average of people who keep horses?—Yes.

1778. He is a good server?—Yes, a very good foal getter.

1779. What price do you get for the service? I get [illegible] and the groom's fees, and [illegible] the foal, but that of course throws a great many [illegible] for the money, and if they have no foal they have paid their money.

1780. And if they like to wait till the chance of a foal they pay [illegible]?—Yes, I should say more [illegible] go in for the system of the money than for the foal. I have a larger percentage of mares now than I have going in for the foal.

1781. That applies to both horses?—Yes.

1782. How many do you let the Yorkshire horse serve?—[illegible]

1783. Not [illegible]?—He would serve more but he did not get more. He is capable of serving any amount.

1784. They like the thoroughbred best?—Yes, [illegible]. They [illegible] like horse-breeding schemes. There are three [illegible] at Ballymena—under the horse-breeding scheme.

1785. Your own horses; what class of mares do you breed mostly?—[illegible] I have one mare I breed from 15.3, and one [illegible], and [illegible] two and three-year-olds that stand about 15 hands.

1786. They are not mares of breeding?—No, I have just a thoroughbred horse.

1787. Have you crossed any of those with the thoroughbred horse again?—Yes.

1788. Do you find they are getting lighter in bone?—I do, very much, I think they are deteriorating.

1789. Then you think it is necessary to bring in a new horse to correct the perpetual breeding with a thoroughbred horse?—Quite so, that was my reason for getting the Yorkshire coaching horse to get size and more bone.

1790. I think you told [illegible] Norfolk Hackney, was that Hackney in such cases?—Yes.

1791. Did you sell one as a four-year-old?—Yes.

1792. What price did you get?—£65.

1793. That was unbroken?—Yes, broken to ride.

1794. Have you a two-year-old coming on bred in the same way?—Yes.

1795. Out of the same mare?—Yes, out of a different mare.

1796. And that practically is your only experience of breeding from a Hackney?—Yes.

1797. Have you seen many Hackneys?—Yes, I have seen a good many [illegible].

1798. You consider "[illegible]" a good horse?—Yes, of his class.

1799. Rather heavy head?—No, [illegible].

1800. Not much quality?—No, but a fine mover.

1801. I think you talked about the mares of the old Irish breed; can you trace in any way that old Irish breed in your neighbourhood?—Well, no, I could not trace it. I could not go back, but it is generally admitted that those mares have not been imported much. They must have been crossed with Yorkshire or thoroughbred.

1802. I suppose they were practically kept [illegible] because the necessities of [illegible] did not require [illegible]?—Yes, that is it.

1803. Any heavy mares, blood like those in Clydesdale, is not required there?—They are not wanted in the district.

1804. You think they would do harm?—I think the farmers would not mind it there, would not find them adapted to work their farms.

1805. There are not many Clydesdale stallions in your district now?—No, [illegible] Clydesdales.

1806. But there are a great many so-called half-bred horses?—Quite so.

1807. And a great deal of rubbish?—A great deal indeed. I may say the bulk of it.

1808. Is there any way of knowing if these half-breds are sound?—There is no way of knowing, indeed, there is a way of knowing that they are not sound.

1809. You say, I think, that farmers of twenty or thirty acres comprise fifty per cent. of the horse breeders in your district?—Yes, that is so.

1810. Do you think that the opinion of these men should be taken as to the class of sires they would require [illegible] to be provided by public money?—I certainly think the opinion of these men should be taken as to their own requirements; as a rule, they are intelligent, hard headed, shrewd people, quite capable of knowing what kind they require.

1811. And you think there ought to be some way of taking their opinion as to the best class of horse for them?—Yes, I think so.

1812. When you say that the best market is Dublin, I suppose you mean for the class you yourself breed?—Yes, I breed some here and sell them here.

1813. You generally bring them to the show and sell them in the show?—Yes.

1814. That is your market?—Well, I have sold [illegible] and in Dublin.

1815. What would you consider the best market for the small farmer?—Ballymena, and a fair called [illegible].

1816. What buyers are there there?—Scotch, English, and Belfast men.

1817. Chiefly?—Yes.

1818. Some of these big carriage horses that these men buy are bred in your district?—[illegible] there may be an occasional one but only an odd one.

1819. What age do they sell those horses at?—Four or five years; they give them light work at two years, [illegible] work them on regularly, and sell them as four or five-year-olds as they find a market.

1820. Are there many people in your district who buy horses in the South of Ireland and bring them down and fatten them?—There are a good many.

1821. Bought in the South and then fed and sold at the May as four or five years old?—Yes.

1822. The Chairman.—You used the expression Yorkshire coaching horse, is that any recognised breed as distinct from Hackney?—Yes, there is quite a distinct stud book.

1823. And the horse you have, what is he?—He is a pure Yorkshire coaching horse registered in the stud book.

1824. In your opinion do some of the four and five-year-old [illegible] sold in your district go to Scotland and England for work [illegible]?—In Scotland and England chiefly.

1825. Mr. Wrench.—Talking of those small breeders who have twenty or thirty acres, don't you think that [illegible] is a very valuable [illegible] to the breeding?—Yes, I think so.

1826. Is not that what the country [illegible]?—Yes.

1827. And [illegible] with [illegible] account?—Yes, it is most necessary.

1828. Does [illegible] a valuable [illegible]?—Yes.

1830. Colonel Sir [illegible].—To the purchaser or the seller?—I don't quite understand your question.

1831. Would the horses be more valuable to the seller or buyer [illegible]?—I should say to both, because the purchaser [illegible] the seller.

1832. Mr. W[illegible].—Have you been able to form any opinion as to whether a Hackney with good action gets a [illegible] better action than the thoroughbred?—[illegible] which I would compare their action with the ordinary Hackney [illegible] as they become [illegible] and [illegible] away, which I don't think it will from the Hackney, because it is [illegible].

1833. You think the Hackney would be able to produce stock that when it developed would have better action?—That is higher action.

1834. [illegible].—Yes, I quite agree with you.

1835. Do you think if there were better horses in the country the farmers might be developed of breeding [illegible] horses?—I think it is very desirable [illegible] better class of horses for getting up-to-date and high priced horses [illegible].

1836. You think it would pay?—I think there would be a demand for a good, sound, upstanding harness horse. I think the country is glutted with poor, small horses, not fitted for [illegible] and the [illegible] are [illegible] as be a glut on the market.

1837. Have you been in many fairs recently?—Not recently.

1838. In the last few months?—No.

1839. You don't know whether it is a fact that there are a great many horses [illegible]?—There are a certain class, but I think the good class horses [illegible].

1840. You think those people who do produce [illegible] [illegible] to produce a better article?—Yes, [illegible] the larger farmers who can afford to pay a good fee, it [illegible] for the use of a sire.

1841. Mr. [illegible].—You speak of breeding the [illegible] horse—how would you [illegible] [illegible] to breed them from a high class horse to begin with, and a mare with a Yorkshire horse [illegible] with high action.

1842. Mr. W[illegible] asked you about getting the opinion of the small farmers [illegible]—Don't you think the opinion of men who live in the country [illegible] as valuable as that of [illegible]?—I don't know. That is an [illegible] question.

1843. Don't you think, you know the requirements of the [illegible] [illegible]?—I don't know, I should not say that they are [illegible] [illegible] than I could do [illegible].

Mr. [illegible].—You take a [illegible] view of your [illegible].

1844. CHAIRMAN.—Have you got any scheme in your own mind as to obtaining the views of the [illegible] in [illegible]?—No, the only scheme I would suggest is the [illegible] for [illegible] be a [illegible] for me to keep my [illegible] that I will be able to [illegible] by getting a valuable prize [illegible].

1845. Your scheme would be on the lines of the present scheme of the Royal Dublin Society?—Yes, I would make the prizes more valuable.

1846. Colonel Sir [illegible].—Would you [illegible] the [illegible] with [illegible]?—I think that the [illegible] [illegible] for this [illegible] [illegible] with a registered [illegible] that has been [illegible] on the [illegible] be [illegible]. [illegible] a [illegible] that once has £5 or £6 [illegible]. The [illegible] of the registered [illegible] the certificate. I would suggest that the [illegible] would be when the veterinary [illegible] [illegible] that the [illegible] was [illegible] on the [illegible] of [illegible].

1847. Mr. W[illegible].—You think there are some [illegible] horses have got prizes?—Yes, I am afraid there are.

1848. Of prize [illegible] [illegible] horses from which they get the certificate?—I am afraid so; [illegible] at all, they [illegible] £5 [illegible] may have been [illegible] £2, and [illegible] [illegible] [illegible] for the [illegible].

1849. CHAIRMAN.—[illegible] with the Royal Dublin Society?—I understand that the certificate [illegible] the Local Committees [illegible] the money. I am aware the Local Committees are empowered to [illegible] the [illegible] of a [illegible].

1850. You [illegible] [illegible] [illegible].—I am quite [illegible] of this.

1851. Have you paid the [illegible]?—Yes.

1852. You are [illegible] all the money to [illegible]?—[illegible] to [illegible], [illegible] the [illegible] of [illegible].

1853. To be [illegible] for what purpose?—For [illegible] with [illegible], [illegible], [illegible] [illegible] for the [illegible] of the Royal Dublin Society, 1890 or 1891.

1854. [illegible]—[illegible] should be [illegible] to [illegible] [illegible] to the Local Committee to [illegible] [illegible] [illegible]?—[illegible]. I think, from the [illegible] of [illegible], I [illegible] it was [illegible] [illegible] [illegible] [illegible] [illegible] [illegible].

1855. In order to [illegible] [illegible] [illegible] would be [illegible] [illegible] [illegible] to get [illegible] very [illegible]?—I don't [illegible] would follow.

1856. You [illegible] [illegible] [illegible] [illegible]?—[illegible] before [illegible], and I think [illegible] [illegible] would want to have your [illegible] [illegible] [illegible] Hackney.

1856a. Mr. W[illegible].—[illegible] [illegible]?—Yes.

Mr. THOMAS MACARTNEY examined.

1857. CHAIRMAN.—You live in the Union of Ballymoney, County Antrim?—Yes.

1858. You are an Assistant Land Commissioner?—Yes.

1859. Have you any experience of horse-breeding?—I have been breeding, off and on, nearly for the last thirty years.

1860. What stallions have you used and on what sort of mares?—I have bred from thoroughbreds, Clydesdales and Hackneys.

1861. Have you been successful in your horse-breeding?—I have had a fair measure of success, I have bred a few good ones.

1862. What stallions did you say you used?—Thoroughbreds, Clydesdales, and Hackneys.

1863. Which class of horse have you succeeded best

[illegible]

Mr. Thomas [illegible].

with?—I have only bred two from a Hackney sire, a number from thoroughbreds and a few Clydesdales. I didn't breed very many Clydesdales; I had a good mare and put her to thoroughbred sires. I have bred from half-bred mares, and latterly altogether from thoroughbred and Hackney sires.

1864. Which have you been most successful with?—If I have a good stamp of mare I like to breed from the thoroughbred, because if you can breed a good one it is all right, though if you miss it is altogether wrong.

1865. What has been your experience with regard to the Hackneys?—I have sold my colts from thoroughbreds for 60 to 75 guineas at three years old, and I have sold a half-bred Hackney colt at the same money.

1866. Do dealers appreciate horses got by Hackneys, or do they fight shy of them?—Hackneys are not very long introduced into the north of Ireland—five or six years ago, I think; the first Hackney sire I remember was about six years ago. The last witness said he got some stock from him that was not very good. I think that is owing to the fact that he got a good many mares that did not suit him; he was a fine class of horse and he got a class of mares that should not have been sent to him. I considered myself very well paid when I can sell one of his stock at £50, untrained, as a three year old. I don't object to breed more on the same terms; the same horse was subsequently sold at Sewell's for 100 guineas, though in the condition he met with some slight accident.

1867. Do many farmers breed horses in your neighbourhood?—A good many farmers do.

1868. With what results?—The class of horse they usually breed is the ordinary work horse.

1869. Is the breed stuff?—It is largely clay stuff; the great tendency with the farmers in my neighbourhood is to breed a horse that is able to work for his meat when he is two years old. They won't take the thoroughbred horses because they are too light to do that; if they happen to breed a good horse so to be they won't run the risk again. They breed a class of horse that will be useful, and that if there is anything wrong with it they can work.

1870. What sort of mare do they use?—Generally speaking a cross between an ordinary mare and a half-bred Clydesdale or Clydesdale horse, mares with plenty of bone, and not too much hair on their legs; the description Mr. Russell gave was very fair.

1871. What do they mate them with?—They mate them with a half-bred horse; that may be a horse with a variety of breeds; if a horse with colour, and fair size and action, and let at a low fee, the tendency is to go to him. My experience of thoroughbreds in the district is that it is hard to get a good one. I may say that I patronize Mr. Russell's horse myself, and I have to send my mare 35 miles to him, and if I want another thoroughbred I must send to Limavady. There is no thoroughbred sire in the district within 20 miles except Mrs. Anderson's, and she may not let to a half-bred mare at all, or charge a fee that farmers would not pay.

1872. Are the stallions of a type that are not required?—A large number are a type that should not be encouraged anywhere. I am pleased to say a great many of them have got little to do this year, and a great many of them are not stallions at the present time.

1873. With regard to the Royal Dublin Society scheme, is that working in your part of the country at the present time?—The Royal Dublin Society scheme so far as registered stallions are concerned, does not work well for me or any farmer in the neighbourhood who wants to patronize a Royal Dublin Society horse, because as I told you we are 30 or 35 miles from any registered sire. Mr. Russell did give us an advantage this year, because he very kindly sent his sire to Ballymoney by train, but for that we would not have had a registered stallion within 35 miles of us.

1874. Can you suggest any way of getting these stallions that would suit you and the farmers in your district?—I don't know. The Royal Dublin Society had a plan a few years ago of sending sires into the poorer districts, but our experience of this class of horse was that anyone who cared for breeding a good class of horse would not send their mares to him. I would rather pay the fee to Mrs. Anderson's [illegible] thoroughbred. In the [illegible]; and the experience of the owners of horses in our locality is that they got so little patronage for thoroughbreds that they gave up keeping them. I hold the opinion very strongly that if the Royal Dublin Society, or the Government want to benefit the class of farmers described by Mr. Russell they must adopt a different system. Your registered thoroughbreds may be all very well [illegible] but the farmers won't patronise them; they are quite sensible enough to know what suits them. So far as village [illegible] horses are concerned they [illegible] what pays best. I think the Royal Dublin Society should register any good-bred horse—Hackney, thoroughbred, Cleveland, or Clydesdale—so that a farmer may know they are sound. If these horses are let out at a moderate price it will have the effect of crushing out the [illegible] sort of horse that an owner will let at any fee he can get.

1875. What class of stallion would your district require?—I have consulted a good many farmers, and they all unanimously say they won't breed from thoroughbreds unless they have a good class of mare; and the only horse they will send the rest with is what will likely get a good strong farm horse of a type [illegible] such as one of the Commissioners described a few minutes ago in his question.

1876. What class of stallion do you suggest?—One [illegible] is the Clydesdale, which in [illegible] for getting a good class of farm horse. The Hackney with style and action, I think, would be [illegible].

1877. You have heard of the breeders getting the half-bred mares—would that kind of horse suit?—Yes; if he has strength and action he would take very well. I have known one or two horses of that class to get very good stock.

1878. Are there any standing in your district?—Very few of that stamp got by a thoroughbred. Mrs. Anderson has a good class of horse got by a thoroughbred sire out of a half-bred mare. There is a [illegible] likely to [illegible] a horse got by a Clydesdale or a Cleveland horse, or something of that stamp.

1879. Mr. De Robeck.—You said that you bred from thoroughbred sires and Hackney sires, but you apparently only bred two Hackneys?—Yes.

1880. You only sent two mares to a Hackney?—I generally keep two brood mares.

1881. And those are the mares that you have been in the habit of sending to thoroughbred sires, you sent them to Hackney horses?—No, I did not. I had a mare about half-bred or three-quarters bred that I was driving myself. I sent her to a Hackney simply because I thought she had not size enough about her for a thoroughbred horse. I am a strong believer in successful breeding in studying carefully the class of mare you mate with a certain class of horse. I thought this mare was too small for a thoroughbred and I sent her to a Hackney with very good results. I sold the mare afterwards, and that was the only reason I did not continue to breed from Hackneys. If I had the same mare still I would continue to mate her to Hackneys as long as I found it suited her.

1882. What is the ordinary style of mare in that county, a big mare?—No, a medium class mare.

1883. Bigger than this mare you described?—Oh, yes, stronger with more of the character of the Clydesdale.

1884. The ordinary mare of the country is bigger and stronger?—Yes, taking them generally.

1885. You said the farmers had sent a number of [illegible] mares to the Hackney sire "Excelsior"?—Yes, that is the [illegible].

1886. What is your opinion [illegible] as to a suitable mare for a Hackney sire?—A big rough half-bred Clydesdale mare, she is not the sort of mare to stick in a Hackney sire.

1887. What sort of mare would you put her to?—If she was a strong half-bred Clydesdale mare with good shape and plenty of action, I would send her to a thoroughbred horse or to a horse with two or three strains of blood, if I could get a good one.

1888. You don't think an animal bred that way would be suitable for a Hackney mare?—I don't think a half-bred Clydesdale is the sort to breed to a Hackney at all; I think if you have a good sharp, tight little mare with clean bone and a good deal of breeding in her, and if you have a very light thoroughbred horse, she would make a Hackney as well as any if the action is right.

1889. You say there is a great dearth of thorough-bred stallions up in your country so that you must [illegible] twenty-five miles?—Yes, and they depend altogether [illegible] for a [illegible] of patronage.

1890. Where were thoroughbred horses at one time there?—When I remember twenty-five or thirty years ago we had no difficulty in getting two or three thoroughbred horses in the district.

1891. What sort of horses were they?—They were horses in the [illegible].

1892. I mean were they good horses?—Fairly good.

1893. What sort of fees did they serve at?—Generally from £2 to £3 10s. at that time.

1894. Have you any idea what the owners of those sires gave for them?—I have not any idea.

1895. Is the fee of the ordinary stallion in the country much less than that?—There are some, I suppose, that if you had a half-sovereign in your pocket the fellow would serve your mare for it rather than let you go to his neighbour standing in the next box. I don't think very much of the type of horse that would do that, in what I may say.

1896. Do you think good strong thoroughbred horses have ever been within the reach of the farmers in your district?—No, I think the very good thorough-bred horses are hardly within the reach of the small farmer, that is the farmer with from twenty-five to forty acres of land. I think that as things go the farmer thinks twice before he will pay two or three sovereigns for the service of a horse, but leaving the question of the sale, the farmers seem to have a fairly say that it is a rather risky thing breeding off a thoroughbred horse.

1897. Do you think that feeling may have arisen in consequence of the inferiority of the thoroughbred horses within their reach?—I think it has arisen really from practical experience, breeding off a thoroughbred horse and finding that they had a thing that did not take in the market when they went to sell it. I think the worst thing a man could have is a weedy thoroughbred horse that when he goes to the fair and you begin to show him round he is tired at the knees [illegible] his feet about. I think two or three experiences of that is enough to prevent a small farmer continuing that breeding.

1898. I conclude that the thoroughbred horses they did breed from were weedy?—I think not any than at all.

1899. You speak of weedy thoroughbred horses, are there any weedy horses of any other sort?—Certainly, there are weeds in all breeds, but I think the worst weed of all is a weed bred from a thoroughbred.

1900. I should think the fact of his being a thorough-bred was something in his favour as all [illegible] experience of sales that I have been watching of thoroughbreds and more that were very near thorough-bred have been very nearly the opposite. You can sell a weed of any other breed except a thoroughbred. You can sell a horse that is not up to the mark if he is big enough, because you will get a man that will buy him to [illegible] or to plough.

1901. You said just now that some of these stallions had less to do than they had formerly, do you mean the farmers are not breeding horses as much?—I think they are breeding quite as many.

1902. Then they are getting more particular about the sires they are sending to?—No, but the tendency has been growing in [illegible] the country to breed a class of [illegible] to work the [illegible] from he is two years old.

1903. But I was thinking speaking about thorough-bred horses you said there were a [illegible] of stallions of every sort and breed, thoroughbreds, Hackneys and every description of stallion in the country, and you were glad to say a great many of them were not doing as much as they did?—I heard said the hackney this year was to breed [illegible] that class of horse was not getting so much support, and I think that is largely owing to the fact that farmers have not been selling so well, especially young horses.

1904. You think they are not breeding so much?—I don't think this year there have been so many mares served of the ordinary type. I think men who have good mares and good horses are breeding as much as ever they did, but I think the small class of farmer with a poor mare going to these poor horses have not been doing so much this year from any information I have been able to gather from the men who keep them, and I know one or two veterinary surgeons told me they have got a good many of that class of brood mares not breeding this year, which they took as a signal something as it would be more or less a sign that they did not get the support they did formerly.

1905. Col. St. Quintin.—You heard I asked a question, and you noted it apparently, of Mr. Russell, putting the thoroughbred horse on one side, supposing the small farmer breeds with two objects, either to sell or to use himself.

1906. Suppose that, as you say, he breeds to sell, he may have an animal on his hands that he cannot sell, and therefore he likes breeding an animal that may be useful to him if he cannot get rid of it in the market?—Certainly, that is the one great object he has in view.

1907. Then putting the thoroughbred horse on one side, what the small farmer wants for his own use, as I gather, with this light soil, is not a very heavy weighty horse, but a horse that can work the soil and take him to the fair, a smallish, fairly strong, useful horse?—Yes, I said at first in answer to a question that my district of the country is largely heavy soil.

1908. Then you like the big heavy horse?—Yes.

1909. Can you say do you grow the big weighty horse there as well?—Oh, yes; there is no horse gets more support than a good Clydesdale. I know two or three Clydesdale horses, and they do more in my immediate neighbourhood of country than any horses that stand in the fair or market. I know one horse, and I have a foal off him this year myself, and I have known that horse serving as many as 200 mares in the season.

1910. And they get you a class of horse that is useful throughout the district for the actual farming work of the smaller farmers?—Yes.

1911. Do you think that the Hackney horse which is a lighter horse than him, and a horse with more action, will get the same useful class of horses as the other?—Yes, but I think that a farmer who has a suitable mare and goes to a Hackney horse will get a horse that is able to work the [illegible] from two years old to four years old, and then he has a chance of having a horse that he can take to a fair that will attract the attention of buyers, and he will get a fair price for him.

1912. There is a great deal of talk about the action of a horse, and everybody likes to see action to a certain extent; but in the Hackney action is useful action. The small farmer's horse is for the big [illegible], supposing he [illegible] sell him?—Yes, but you must bear in mind that there are very few farmers in the

[illegible] 17, 1898.

Mr. Thomas [illegible].

Jan. 27, 1896.

Mr. Thomas [illegible]

North of Ireland **that have pure bred Hackney mares.**

1913. I know, but the cross [illegible] am [illegible] to that. An ordinary farm mare [illegible] action. [illegible] of the class of Hackney [illegible], and if you put a Hackney [illegible] mare [illegible] you get the medium action between the two, which is a [illegible] thing at a fair.

1914. I was trying to arrive at the [illegible] to the farmer of [illegible] the [illegible] produce [illegible] you [illegible] of mare I am speaking of to the Hackney [illegible] you have too much action for any [illegible]. If you take a [illegible] to a pure bred Hackney horse you have too much action for a farmer, and there is only in [illegible] Hackney [illegible] in [illegible] for that reason.

1915. Then you would not [illegible] action [illegible] the ordinary mare of the country [illegible] Hackney [illegible]—I don't think you would, and my experience of [illegible] horse [illegible] is that a [illegible] with straight action was generally the man who [illegible] what he wanted for it.

1916. There is [illegible] action, and there is this extraordinary [illegible] action [illegible] different thing [illegible]. If a horse goes straight he goes straight [illegible], this is a different [illegible] of action. [illegible] you have very many men with [illegible] either in the North of Ireland or any other [illegible] than you will breed horses of that very high class here. I think [illegible] be bred by [illegible] the action on both sides like the [illegible].

1917. There is very little **cart work** necessary [illegible]. Those in all the [illegible] necessary on a farm.

1918. [illegible]—There are [illegible] to [illegible] than the [illegible] in [illegible] horses.

1919. [illegible] that they [illegible] light [illegible] on the road [illegible]. Certainly, they all have [illegible] driving to drive to market [illegible]. I don't know any [illegible] of [illegible] that [illegible] his [illegible] down.

1920. [illegible] the horse [illegible] for [illegible] in the general [illegible]—The [illegible] a farm [illegible] all [illegible].

1921. Mr. [illegible]—[illegible] you [illegible] very [illegible] generally [illegible] large [illegible] with [illegible] ordinary horse of the country [illegible]. I think that [illegible] one of the [illegible] that any man going to select a [illegible] from a number of horses will [illegible] to [illegible] to them.

1922. And do you think that if a thoroughbred happens to have a specially good action that he is as likely to transmit it as a Hackney, a horse that has been bred for generations for action? Which do you think would transmit it, [illegible]—My opinion is you may get a thoroughbred horse that has particularly good [illegible] to [illegible], and if you go back [illegible] generations [illegible] may be [illegible] action, and I think it is questionable whether that will be brought into the [illegible]. The [illegible] the Hackney [illegible] has been [illegible] into the [illegible] you [illegible] to have it.

1923. It is true, a fact that it is a drawback to the thoroughbred to have high action, or the power of getting it [illegible] I would [illegible] thoroughbred horse with Hackney action.

1924. To [illegible] a thoroughbred horse [illegible] for **speed** [illegible]—Yes.

1925. You said you have bred a few good horses. [illegible] you [illegible] particulars of any horses you bred, [illegible] sold for?—[illegible] in Ireland, I [illegible] Hackney [illegible] good [illegible] I [illegible] anything that I have bred [illegible] have been successful, and I have sold [illegible] a [illegible] good [illegible] bred by [illegible] from £200 to £250. I sold him [illegible] cost at £75 that he sold [illegible] months afterwards for £150, and he [illegible] to a gentleman in the [illegible] House that sold him three years after [illegible] for £300.

1926. Then you do occasionally breed good horses in the North of Ireland?—Yes, we try to breed good ones. And a friend of mine sold [illegible] this year at the Royal Dublin Society's Show [illegible] in the [illegible] class, and he sold a [illegible] that was brought [illegible] good [illegible]. We are very fond of breeding [illegible] horses, the only thing is that we have not the [illegible] they have in other parts of Ireland. If we had the soil of Meath, and Kildare, and King's Co. and Queen's Co., we would be just as anxious to breed these thoroughbreds and as [illegible] there are [illegible] now living in those districts.

1927. And is horse-breeding **a considerable industry in your part of the North of Ireland?—Yes,** [illegible].

1928. And all over Ulster?—All over Ulster.

1929. Do you agree with Mr. [illegible] that a very large number of the horses are bred by men who hold from 20 to 30 acres?—Yes, well, I would give it a wider limit than Mr. [illegible], I would say from 20 to 50 acres.

1930. You think the larger proportion of horses is bred by men holding under 50 acres?—Yes, a good proportion.

1931. Do you think these men are qualified to form an opinion for themselves as to which they [illegible] have [illegible] than [illegible].

1932. And you think they ought to be consulted if there was any public grant in aid of horse-breeding, you think that might be the [illegible] way of getting the opinions of these people?—I do.

1933. Have you [illegible] in which you would take it?—I think there are two ways you could bring it, by having a [illegible] of all the farmers of from 20 to 50 acres, through the Constabulary. Or you could bring it in a way that I think would give you the matter in [illegible] either way [illegible] the opinion of the farmers. If the Royal Dublin Society would send a thoroughbred horse down into the district or town and let him stand there, and take a Hackney horse with a fair quality of action, and let him stand in the same town, you would very soon find which of the two the farmers would patronise. [illegible] I saw [illegible] yesterday, and I don't [illegible] you would find [illegible] if you sent a thoroughbred horse [illegible] there. I [illegible] in any [illegible] four or five [illegible] to the [illegible] thoroughbred would get in this district I came from.

1934. [illegible] the [illegible] in your [illegible] the [illegible] you [illegible] anything about [illegible] has [illegible] by [illegible] people "the old Irish mare," this [illegible]?—I don't know what you would call an old Irish mare. It is a question of going back for a generation or two to find what they were or how they were bred. [illegible] but I saw in the evidence given [illegible] a [illegible] given by a witness with regard to what constituted an old Irish mare, and all I know is it would not be very hard to pick up plenty of mares or horses in the North of Ireland that would come up to that qualification at any rate.

1935. I forget which qualification that [illegible]—A mare that would carry a [illegible] weight [illegible] and [illegible] at the rate of five or six miles an hour, and do it [illegible] day for months.

1936. You think there are plenty of these mares in the North?—I do.

1937. And do you think any of the people that have these mares [illegible] breeding?—I don't think it, they [illegible] attention [illegible].

1938. [illegible] farmers in your district that [illegible] good [illegible] as a general [illegible] for [illegible] for years?—There may be [illegible]

[illegible]

1939. Do you know how these mares [illegible]—It is a horse I bought [illegible] of Ireland.

1940. Do you think that a [illegible] thoroughbred horse would produce stock strong enough to work on the farms in your district?—I do.

1941. What becomes of the horses chiefly [illegible] in your district?—Well, when a horse comes to four or five years of age [illegible]

[illegible]

Dec. 12, 1896. — Mr. Thomas Martin.

head this year, and Mr. Taylor, of Colraine, gives two special prizes for the best hunter horse in the show. If we could get these things supplemented, the the result of their giving these prizes has been to double or treble the number of horses of the particular classes shown. It is hardly fair however to ask us to send from one end of the county to the other to compete for those Government prizes at present, it is rather against the Ballymena gentlemen who are present to say this, but I think it is only fair it should be distributed a little more over the county.

1956. CHAIRMAN.—You used a peculiar expression as regards certain farmers in Ulster, you said they had horses, I presume you mean they buy them, and take them down there and then sell them again?—Yes. The plan on which they work is, to some particular districts they go down to the fairs in the South or Midland Counties, and they buy raw colts, and bring them up and feed them in the very best way as I would feed twenty or thirty bullocks.

1957. They do that with an eye to selling purposes; where do they sell chiefly?—The great bulk of those horses are sold to mere gentlemen. Englishmen who come over. I mentioned the fact that two men that I know intimately sold all their horses to Hurt, they would not sell a horse to you or any other gentleman until Hunt had first taken his horses out of them, all they called him; then there are other men who feed them, and sell the great bulk of their horses in May.

1958. Where do these horses go?—To England, and France, and Scotland.

1959. They don't travel much, then?—Oh, I don't think it.

1960. Colonel St. Quintin.—I was going to ask the same question. The bulk of those horses, as far as I gather, are bought by the farmers and fed in that way?—Yes, they are.

1961. There are a great many bought by small dealers in Belfast and all round there, brought during the winter, and then chiefly find their way into the May, is it from the Belfast district across the water from Belfast?—They do.

1962. And they go, the greater bulk of them, to the foreign governments as remounts?—Yes, it is a great question. We have a lot of men who act as dealers, and go down to the fairs in the South and Midland Counties, and bring up the horses in the colts, and sell them to the local fairs to farmers who buy two three, or three horses, and feed them, and then they sell them as you describe in the May Fair or in Belfast district, and they all leave the country.

1963. They never come down here again?—I don't think one in a thousand horses sold in Ulster ever comes back to any other province. There was just one remark I wanted to make with regard to the exhibition of mares and foals, according to the arrangement at present you have only one class, that is up to £100 valuation.

1964. CHAIRMAN.—Who have only one class?—They are, only exhibit up to £100 under the Royal Dublin Society for mares and foals. I think it would be a great improvement if you would cut the class in two, and make a class that would suit smaller farmers, and then a class without any limit that would suit the larger farmers, because, as it stands at present, these men you have heard so much evidence about, holders of twenty or thirty or forty acres have to compete against large farmers who can afford to buy a very much better mare and feed the produce better. I was present at the last show of mares and foals at Ballymena, and I thought the small farmers there were more or less shut out, though they had quite as good a right to win the money as the big farmers.

1965. Mr. Wrench.—What division would you make?—Up to £50 or £75. I would give a small class up to a moderate sum that would give the small farmer a chance of competing and getting a share of the money, and then I would make an open class of all the others.

Nathaniel Waugh examined.

Mr. Nathaniel Waugh.

1966. CHAIRMAN.—You live at Brookville, Ballymena, County Antrim?—Yes.

1967. Will you describe the district in which you reside, the nature of the country, the soil?—Well, the soil for the most part in the neighbourhood is of a light nature, and the district all round about is peopled by small farmers, small in comparison with the farmers in other parts of Ireland and England, but they are a very hard-working and very intelligent set of people, and they are nearly all well-doing, and all in good circumstances.

1968. Do you consider it adapted to the breeding of horses?—Well, whether it is naturally adapted or not I don't know whether I am qualified to say, but the fact remains that a great many are bred there, and even bred by some farmers who occupy very small holdings, and what they cannot do for their colts and young stock in grazing they supplement with other feeding.

1969. You have been a successful exhibitor at the Royal Dublin Society's Show?—I think I may claim to have been fairly successful, I won the jumping championship of the Show three times, I don't think anyone ever did that before. I also won the champion Stone Wall Jumping event often and often, and in large classes with 60 or 70 horses competing I have had the good fortune to get first and second on more than one occasion.

1970. A great many horses pass through your hands annually?—Yes, I am very fond of passing them on.

1971. What class of horses do you refer to?—I like most of all, and above all, and beyond all, a good blood hunter.

1972. Where do you procure them chiefly?—Well, I have got some of them in the North of Ireland, I have bred some of them myself, but I got a great many from the South and West of Ireland. I don't know whether I am right in saying West, I am not very clear in my geography, but from such places as Cahirciveen, Cork, Hardway, Ballinasloe, and Mullingar, and all the fairs of note.

1973. Now with regard to the mares in your district, are they a good class of mares, are they as good as formerly or are they going back?—In my opinion there is no such thing as a typical mare, I mean to say there is no type, they are of all sorts and conditions, and they breed from every sort of thing there is, that is much to be regretted but it is so, they will breed from great leggy brutes that should be slaughtered, and they will breed from little common ones, and they will breed from all sorts, but among them they have a great many good mares. If a good hunting mare comes from the South of Ireland, or any part of Ireland, and any accident happens to her she passes into the hands of a small farmer, and he at once proceeds to breed from her.

1974. Are the stallions you have sufficient in number, and are they of the right stamp for your part of the country?—I think much good could be done for breeding if we had still more stallions spread over the country and put within the reach of small farmers at small fees.

1975. I mean to say it would not pay private owners to procure good enough stallions and put them at the disposal of these people at fees that these people would give or could give?—I think the Government could help them very much by scattering good stallions over the country at low fees.

1876. What class of stallion, what breeds?—I don't know. I think if you take two or three descriptions of stallions and get the best examples of their own breeds within reach of the people that you might fairly trust them to find out what were the best to breed from, and what were the most paying ones to breed from. I would not mind if there was a Cleveland Bay, a Yorkshire coaching horse, a very good Hackney, and a very good thoroughbred, all in my own neighbourhood; I think the people can find out for themselves the one that it would pay them to breed from, and I hold that no one can know how a stallion will breed you can tell anything about him until you see his stock. I heard a gentleman at the beginning of this inquiry say he would advocate, if I understood him aright, the withholding of the registration of stallions until the horse had proved himself. I think he was speaking of stallions with a stain, whose produce there might be some doubt about, but I would go further than that and say that should apply to thoroughbreds, and I will tell you why. I have known many thoroughbreds faultlessly bred, and fashionably bred, and yet as a matter of fact no matter what mares was put to them they only produced a wretched weed. I have known other stallions with perhaps no great claims to an expensive [illegible] thoroughbred, and yet everything they got turned a good thing.

1877. Your remarks, I suppose, refer to half-bred mares put to the stallions you are speaking of?—Well, you see so very few (most thoroughbred) that it may be taken as referring more to half-bred mares. Will you pardon me referring to this. Mr. Russell in his evidence to-day said he had a couple of years ago, I forget which, a very handsome thoroughbred stallion, I think he was a Government registered one or a Royal Dublin Society registered one. He was a particularly well-bred horse, and he was very much fancied. Well, he has gone now and I don't think Mr. Russell will blame me for saying so everything he got was small. As a matter of fact he would have been a great horse for Mr. Russell if he had kept him. Since the contrary applies to the present horse he has got now, yet if you had taken their pedigrees and appearance you would have chosen one just as fast as the other, and that is why I say if it were possible to do so I would defer the registration of the stallion until he had proved what stock he had got or was likely to get.

1878. Have you had any experience with regard to the breeding of Hackneys?—None.

1879. How in your opinion will the introduction of Hackneys affect the trade in Irish hunters?—Well, I don't think there is any cause for the alarm that is so generally expressed at all. I don't think there is the slightest. I have heard it said that mares bred from Hackney horses in the congested districts will [illegible] the hunter-breeding districts and do a great deal of harm. I don't know why they should do so any more than the mares that were bred there before the introduction of Hackneys, and they were acknowledged not to be good mares.

1880. Have you any suggestions to make with a view of bringing farmers to breed horses, any scheme?—I really cannot say that I have formulated any scheme or thought that matter out sufficiently. I think a few shows where farmers might have brought to their work, and they would find out something very good and very needful as a result of their inspection. I think, generally speaking, that it would be a good thing to try to establish more local shows and give prizes for breeding, and try to encourage farmers who have really very good and approved mares to keep breeding. Mr. Manning suggested that if there were more money taken to the Clonmel Show it would be an advantage. I have no doubt it would. I think if there were more money offered for produce in Ballymena a larger show would be formed for the people in the district, and probably a very nice little show could be got up there; and I think that an increase of shows throughout this country would stimulate in general horse-breeding generally, it would bring people together and let them exchange ideas and allow them to see the results, and where they had made a mistake they would have some enough left to repair it.

1881. Are there as many horses bred in your district as formerly?—I think there are a very great number bred in my district.

1882. More or less than formerly?—I think there are quite as many now as nine times were. I think the people are trying to breed now from better horses because they find that moderate or low priced horses won't pay them.

1883. Is the soil in your district adapted for raising good stock?—I think we have some very good soil in the district, in parts of Ulster. In my own district there is some very good grazing, quite as good as in other counties; there is none of the old pastures for which Meath and some other counties are famous, but there is very good grazing that can grow large stock.

1884. Any limestone?—There must be limestone in the district, and down towards the west there is a great deal of limestone, there is plenty of old grazing in the neighbourhood of Loane and Carnmoney, which is 10 miles from Ballymena; it is really over limestone quarries, lots of it.

1885. There was a question, which has been asked and answered, about half-bred sires, have you any experience of half-bred sires?—Yes. I don't know one horse, he probably was located nearer Mr. Russell's residence than mine, but he was known in our neighbourhood as Ferguson's "Blood Royal," unfortunately that horse was wrong in his wind, and still more unfortunately, a certain percentage of his stock were wrong in their wind, but I can say that the ones of his stock that were sound were in my opinion priceless; they were worth their weight in gold; better hunters never were bred in any corner of the kingdom; and, as a matter of fact, I have myself the champion cup in the Dublin Show with a four-year-old got by him, beating all ages and winners there.

1886. What breeding was he?—He was by the real "Blood Royal," a horse by "The Baron," a horse, if I remember him right, with rather a Hackney sort and not the best head, and he was out of a mare by "Fugit," and as I understand he was not a clean bred horse, but I know that it was quite a byword in our country that anything got by "Fugit" had unlimited endurance, the dam of this "Blood Royal" I think of was got by this "Fugit."

1887. You don't know what sire, what sire the dam?—I do not, I could not particularize the sire. I daresay it would be possible to ascertain them, but the man who bred and owned him is dead, and whether it could be ascertained reliably or not I am afraid to say. Do you happen to know a horse called "Victorious"?

Captain Riddell.—The Chairman is this man.

Witness.—There is there one "Victorious"?

Captain Riddell.—He is dead, he was that name horse.

Witness.—I am afraid I refer to "Victorious," could you tell the owner?

Captain Riddell.—I don't know; he was a Limerick bred horse.

Witness.—I had a colt by Victorious and I sold him as a young two-year-old, I rarely knew of his first [illegible], 4th, and I heard he gave the greatest satisfaction.

Mr. Lawrence.—There was a Victorious that belonged to Ferguson.

Witness.—I am speaking of the Victorious by Victory, if I heard the name right. I would remember it because I had been a correspondent with him about sending him some mares of my own to him.

1888. The Chairman.—In former evidence given it was stated that half-bred stallions under certain

[illegible]

restriction would be desirable animals to have in the country, are you of the same opinion?—As a matter of fact I did not see particularly the [illegible], because I have been from home. I have only just returned from England and was not giving the matter much attention, but I should be of opinion that if you were sure they got good ones they might do [illegible], but I would be far more particular about what they got there, whether they had [illegible] or too fine means of blood. For instance, I [illegible] "Royal Mayo" [illegible], I would then [illegible] that I could feel that would pass muster in the wind.

1980. Mr. La Touche.—Then you say that you consider there would be a great [illegible] upon the farmers?—That is quite so.

1981. And it would not pay a man to buy good thoroughbred horses and let them out to the farmers at the fees that a farmer would be prepared to pay?—I question very much if it would, to work it that way, at those [illegible] within a [illegible] that can [illegible], but of those were sufficient for the district, and it would [illegible] the fees would have to be so low that it would not pay any private individual.

1982. You would not expect to get a useful thoroughbred [illegible] for less than £200 or £300?—I have seen thoroughbreds sold at all sorts of prices.

1983. Do you keep a horse yourself for stud?—I have had more than one thoroughbred horse. I have a couple of Hackney stallions at present, I have [illegible] and I have a pony stallion.

1984. Have you got any thoroughbred stallions at present?—I have not, and I will tell you why. The last one I had was a Royal Dublin Society's [illegible] prize [illegible] as good as any thoroughbred in the North of Ireland, some of which I have [illegible] [illegible].

1985. Was he a good foal getter?—I am telling you I was [illegible] his stock [illegible] any thoroughbred horse [illegible]. Well, my best Hackney [illegible] for him.

1986. Then, as a matter of fact, [illegible] the farmers that the [illegible] would not send their [illegible]?—I would like to show all his [illegible] produced from any other [illegible].

1987. Do you think the stock out of [illegible] more valuable [illegible]?—[illegible] I would hardly tell you; [illegible] and I hope to have [illegible].

1988. You can compare [illegible]?—I have [illegible] a Hackney [illegible] for a [illegible].

1989. The thoroughbred horse [illegible] the farmers [illegible] any other thoroughbred horse in the north of Ireland?—I think so.

1990. But you would not [illegible] as good as [illegible] Hackney horse?—They are [illegible] a large majority of [illegible]. It is only [illegible] Hackney horse that I am speaking of.

1991. You say that it is only the stock of an exceptional Hackney that would be more valuable than the stock of the thoroughbred horse?—I mean by that a Hackney with very good legs and [illegible] action, [illegible] would be [illegible] a special purpose.

1992. What I want to get at is, you said you would not [illegible] a farmer to send his mare to this horse [illegible], while at the same time you say his stock [illegible] good [illegible]. Will you tell me what I should [illegible]?—I think [illegible] that horse [illegible] of [illegible]. I did not know myself that his stock would be as good as they turned out. I think that is the [illegible] of the matter.

1993. What did you do with him?—I sold him and gave him away.

1994. You keep your Hackney stallions, you have not given them away yet?—No, I [illegible] one of them.

1995. Have you been breeding from them for any length of time?—I have been breeding a great many kinds of horses for a great many years.

1996. No, but those Hackney stallions, have you been breeding from them for any length of time?—I don't know; I think only [illegible] three years, about three years.

1997. Have you sold any of their produce?—I don't think I have [illegible] any of them.

1998. You did not send any over to [illegible]?—No, [illegible] of doing so, [illegible] and [illegible]. That is a question of [illegible].

1999. In answer to Lord [illegible] you told him you did not think that the Hackney [illegible] the [illegible] of this [illegible] being any [illegible] upon the [illegible] in the south of Ireland, did you not say according to that [illegible]?—I think I would think it a very great thing for a man who [illegible] to [illegible] a bad [illegible] [illegible] from that to [illegible], high class [illegible]; I cannot imagine why they should do such a thing.

2000. You don't think that in the South of Ireland it would [illegible] is very [illegible] from the North of Ireland as the North of Ireland?—No, [illegible] from the South of Ireland to the North, [illegible] the North of Ireland [illegible] and if the South of Ireland were [illegible] they would be [illegible] for a market for [illegible].

2001. Do you think this Hackney strain is a good hardy strain to introduce?—I think good Hackneys are as good and game animals as are living and [illegible] as long as [illegible].

2002. Speaking generally of the blood, is it a good hardy blood?—I think there is a great deal of [illegible] among the Hackneys, and in the [illegible] and I think the [illegible] in the [illegible] and any other breed you can think of, but there are Hackneys as good and as [illegible] as there [illegible], with [illegible] this breed is [illegible].

2003. Have you a large herd of [illegible]?—We have a [illegible] every year.

2004. Driving?—Yes.

2005. Have you got a [illegible]?—We have.

2006. [illegible] in Dublin.

2007. [illegible] Dublin [illegible].

2008. How long has it been [illegible]?—[illegible].

2009. Did you take an active part in the [illegible] of [illegible]?—I did.

2010. Did you express any opinion about the [illegible]?—I never think it desirable to have a show [illegible] horses [illegible] for long, [illegible] and I will tell you why. If you are looking at horses [illegible] and you want to see their [illegible] them to go to a distance and out of the [illegible] of [illegible].

2020. Don't you think you can see a horse's action better on a long straight piece than when he is always on the turn?—I think you can see a horse well enough in a ring the size of Dublin and you can see him well on a track less than Dublin. I know when I went to judge at [illegible] where they had unlimited space they went out of the range of my vision, we had to bring them into a smaller circle. It does not seem that you must keep them going for a long time but they are more under the command of your eye, you see them all the time.

2021. If they are nearer you a smaller number of circuits would give you the same opportunity of seeing them as a larger number of circuits?—That is so.

2022. Did you express an opinion on the buying out of this trade that the demand was so large that horses got by Hackneys could not go round twice?—I did not, I know what you refer to, but it is a misconception of what I said.

2023. There was a witness here someone who told us he could buy these poor ships in England at forty per cent. cheaper than he could ever buy; and if he was a dishonest man he could buy horses in England and bring them over here and sell them at forty per cent. profit?—I am sure he was not dishonest, that gentleman, he would do no such thing.

2024. Not all quite, but do you agree with him?—I really don't know, I hardly ever saw a pair in England worth buying, and I have had the luck to have had several of them myself and I always wished I had put their throats on the other side and left them alone.

2025. Do you think the Irish horse owes any of its [illegible] to the fact of his being almost invariably got by a thoroughbred horse and that he has not got by a thoroughbred horse?—But I don't think he is invariably got by a thoroughbred horse, and I don't know where the good is then it is.

2026. There is no proof of course, but don't you think, or do you think that an English dealer is prepared to give a better price for an Irish horse than he would for a horse bred in his own country from the belief, as they say, that the animal he is buying in Ireland is got by a thoroughbred horse and is not got by a thoroughbred horse?—I think the fact remains, and I am proud of it, that Irish horses sell better than English horses and that English dealers will come and buy them and be very glad to do so in Ireland when they get the opportunity.

2027. Do you think they would give the same price for high class Irish horses if they had reason to believe that their Hackney blood is [illegible] among them at all?—That is a question I could not answer, I think the English dealers will buy what they like when they see it and they don't ask particularly how it is bred.

2028. Do you go down to the South of Ireland to buy horses?—Very seldom.

2029. Galway and Clare?—I have been there, but that is all, I have no time to go to them.

2030. You are aware that although these horses don't come out of the province of Ulster into the southern and eastern provinces of Ireland horses do come out of the congested districts in the West of Ireland and more in Galway, Clare and Limerick?—I don't know anything about what happens there, I don't know anything about them whatever, I am not qualified to give an opinion, I have never been there.

2031. You did give an opinion just now, you said you did not think that the crossing of the congested district mares with Hackney horses would have any effect on the breeding of hunters?—I repeat I don't see why it is to be treated so much as some people think it is.

2032. But at the same time you have not much experience of those particular districts?—I have no experience of the congested districts, I don't pretend to have.

2033. Mr. Warren.—What are the horses chiefly bred in your district by the farmers; what class do they chiefly try to breed?—They breed to hire and principally to sell them, they want to make their profit during the period of their maturing and to sell them afterwards.

2034. And when they sell them is action a very great consideration?—It is an absolute necessity.

2035. It is an absolute necessity that a horse should have action to realise any paying price?—Of course.

2036. Have you formed any opinion as to whether a Hackney is best able to produce action, or whether you can get equally good action from a thoroughbred with good action himself?—Well, I can only say that as a matter of opinion I think the Hackney would be more likely to produce action than a thoroughbred.

2037. Do you find the animals that are bred by your Hackney stallions now from half-bred mares have more action than ordinary action?—Well, I hardly like to answer that question because it means running my horse, as a matter of fact they have.

2038. And with regard to the mares; you don't think that any such [illegible] action, in any sense in Ulster, as an old Irish breed?—Well, it is certain in Ireland as well as around in Ulster, and that the mares have been [illegible] places but they have drifted there coming from the south as hunters and leaving once would accidents have been carried [illegible].

2039. Then a great many mares that are kept in Ulster have come from the south?—Undoubtedly. Mr. Macaulay tells you that the mare he bred his high-priced hunter from came from the south.

2040. If you were looking for a thoroughbred sire as a sire for hunters, would you consider it against a horse to have very high action or not?—It depends entirely on the nature of the action; if it is true, straight action from the shoulder in front and the hocks well flexed behind, and no dishing or throwing in of the feet, no [illegible] on the knees or anything of that kind, I think good action is to be preferred to that of an animal that goes along digging his toes in the ground and making you think that he is going to fall and break your neck coming home.

2041. Do you think Hackneys have good action from the shoulder?—There are some of them have most charming and magnificent action, and others have the worst class of action, propping their legs up and down in the same place and knocking their fore to pieces.

2042. And I think you said there were Hackneys that had as good staying powers as any horse?—Yes.

2043. Have you had any experience yourself of driving horses bred by Hackneys?—Yes, both pure bred and half-bred ones.

2044. For long distances?—Very long distances.

2045. What do you call long distances?—I think a horse that goes 40 miles in some time in a day, and some during the time you drive him and there is no [illegible] [illegible] pulling, a touch of the whip or being spoken to, that he is a very good one.

2046. Have you had Hackneys that did that?—Yes, decidedly.

2047. Do you think breeding harness horses is equally paying with breeding hunters?—Well, a high-class harness horse is worth a deal of money, and is much sought after; but the ordinary harness horse, I hardly see how the Irish farmer can breed him to compete with American opposition.

2048. Is the American opposition very strong?—The American opposition is very strong, and American horses are being brought into Ireland in big batches weekly.

2049. Do you know at all what become of those?—I fancy they go into carriages and they go into heavy harness work, and parcel van work, and all that sort of thing.

2050. And if they are [illegible] and [illegible] and grass, is it easy to distinguish them from Irish horses?—A man of considerable experience will do it.

Nov. 11, 1886. Mr. Nathaniel [illegible].

[illegible]
Mr. [illegible] Mason.

with wonderful certainty, but a great many of them are unsuitable to sell.

2047. Would you suggest any [illegible] or branding of foreign horses that came into this country as a protection?—I don't know that it could be carried out, but I think it would be a very great matter if they were branded or marked, because I know that many of those [illegible] and [illegible] will be sold as Irish horses [illegible] those Hackney horses you speak of.

2048. But the class of horses bought by the London dealers, high-class carriage horses, they are not bred, surely, in Ulster?—No, they are not bred much in Ulster; where they are bred is [illegible] or [illegible].

2049. They have not the means?—These horses are bought in the fairs that [illegible] have talked of—[illegible], [illegible], and all these fairs; they are bought there as three-year-old colts by [illegible] farmers, who just bring them through a process that they call finishing them, which, as Lord [illegible] has said, is something difficult to understand; but it means fitting them for sale. These men buy them at three years old and bring them to my neighbourhood. These people have been within four miles of my place, and [illegible] about one hundred in the year [illegible] a family will spend 15, 18, or 20 horses. He keeps them all so [illegible] [illegible], [illegible] and keeps them for nearly twelve months in a small [illegible], and if you looked into it you would [illegible] [illegible] [illegible] locality. [illegible] with special [illegible] and [illegible] under [illegible] [illegible] or [illegible], the fact is when you come to see them [illegible] before [illegible] to buy them you are astonished beyond measure at what they have grown into, and it [illegible] what a man once said, that "the horse of the [illegible] is by the [illegible]." If they have got [illegible] good horses to begin with [illegible] by their [illegible] they [illegible] a [illegible] the money. I have given [illegible] from £80 to £120 for them as four-year-old [illegible].

2050. And you think it really is the [illegible] they get during that last year that has more effect on their growth than their previous feeding?—I think the men that feed them in [illegible] could not tell the [illegible] if they saw them.

2051. They grow to an extraordinary extent in the year?—They do.

2052. I don't suggest that the Hackney is at all the horse to produce a hunter, but have you ever heard of the [illegible] of [illegible] produced by Hackney stallions [illegible] [illegible] [illegible] and [illegible] [illegible] [illegible]?

2053. Have you heard of any that sold for large prices?—I know Mr. [illegible]'s "[illegible]," that won first prize at [illegible], and [illegible] at the Royal Show, was out of a [illegible] mare by a thoroughbred horse. I further know that Mr. John [illegible], of the [illegible] in [illegible], bred a [illegible] horse, which he sold for 300 guineas to [illegible], of [illegible] [illegible], the horse was [illegible] two [illegible] [illegible] the [illegible], and [illegible] 300 guineas at a public sale [illegible], and it is said changed hands after at a higher price. That horse was got by "[illegible]," acknowledged not a very good Hackney.

2054. Do you know what mare?—It was a good mare, an [illegible] thoroughbred in [illegible]. And I also know that Mr. Charles Wilson, of [illegible], Master of the [illegible] Hounds, that his famous horse "[illegible]," known all over the North of England, was bred in the [illegible] by a Hackney stallion. I [illegible] a good judge that both horses were [illegible] "[illegible]" and [illegible] [illegible] with [illegible].

2055. I think you said that you considered the farmers in your district very intelligent, and you think that [illegible] farmers, holding under 50 acres,

who breed horses, any encouragement to give as [illegible] [illegible] [illegible] would suit them?—[illegible].

2056. And you think that in any plan to give [illegible] and [illegible] ought to be [illegible] as to the [illegible] on which the aid should be given?—If you give them the aid in a way they don't like, they won't accept it; they are not [illegible], but they are very independent, and if they don't like it they won't have it; they will tell you they are much obliged to you, but it is no use to them and they will not trouble you.

2057. Have you ever noticed any colts in [illegible] [illegible]?—No; I have known [illegible] in [illegible]. I have [illegible] [illegible] at [illegible] and [illegible] [illegible] [illegible].

2058. You think you have seen as many [illegible] and [illegible] among thoroughbreds [illegible] [illegible] [illegible] Hackneys?—I think there are a [illegible] [illegible] thoroughbreds. That should not be allowed to get stock of any kind.

2059. And you think it would be well if [illegible] [illegible] took to breeding thoroughbreds for stock instead of simply breeding them for racing?—I [illegible] that would be very [illegible], but I [illegible] [illegible] [illegible] [illegible] [illegible] is the stock [illegible], and [illegible] [illegible] [illegible] [illegible] [illegible].

2060. Therefore, you would not register?—[illegible] I would not [illegible] [illegible] [illegible] [illegible] however well bred or good-looking unless I had a [illegible] of what he got; of course I would willingly [illegible] [illegible] the [illegible].

2061. [illegible] [illegible] [illegible] [illegible] [illegible] [illegible] of [illegible] [illegible] [illegible] [illegible] [illegible]?—Well, it [illegible], [illegible] [illegible] [illegible] [illegible] [illegible] [illegible] [illegible]. I am making some experiments myself [illegible] [illegible] [illegible] to the [illegible] of the Hackney question and to find out whether it is going to do the harm which [illegible]. I have got my Hackney [illegible] [illegible] [illegible] [illegible] [illegible] [illegible] [illegible] [illegible] this year, and had very [illegible] [illegible], but I [illegible] [illegible] [illegible]. I have [illegible] [illegible] a thoroughbred mare. I [illegible] [illegible] [illegible] [illegible] [illegible] [illegible] thoroughbred [illegible], and I am going to [illegible] [illegible] [illegible] [illegible]. I [illegible] a [illegible] [illegible] that Hackneys are going to destroy everything, as other people have done, [illegible] [illegible] [illegible].

2062. Do you know anything of a horse that Lord [illegible] had, called "Broad Arrow"?—I can't say at the moment that I actually saw him, but now that you have [illegible] him, I bought a horse [illegible] by him called "[illegible]" at [illegible], a [illegible] horse and a typical weight-carrying hunter, and I sold him to a [illegible] dealer for 300 guineas and he was sold, as I heard, to [illegible], of [illegible], who won first prize with him at the [illegible] [illegible] Show, and then sold him for a very big price. I bought that horse's own brother, that [illegible] [illegible] [illegible] [illegible] [illegible] I bought him, [illegible] years old, [illegible] [illegible] [illegible] [illegible] [illegible] [illegible] [illegible] [illegible] and [illegible] [illegible] [illegible], and I showed him at the Dublin Show, and I believe he would have won only he had [illegible] [illegible]. [illegible] [illegible] [illegible] [illegible] [illegible] [illegible] [illegible] [illegible] being [illegible], and was bought by a [illegible] [illegible] for £130 as a hunter. These were by "Broad Arrow" out of a [illegible] of [illegible] [illegible].

2063. And "Broad Arrow" was a Hackney?—Yes.

2064. Did he do much to improve the horses in that district?—I have always heard so. It is [illegible] [illegible] [illegible] in the [illegible] [illegible], and [illegible] in the [illegible] [illegible] [illegible] [illegible].

2065. [illegible] types.

Mar. 18, 189[illegible]. Mr. [illegible] [illegible].

2091. Have you ever found that when you give a horse to a buyer of two year old and three years old that he is [illegible] a year's rest themselves?—I have no experience except this one example, and it is as you say.

2092. Chairman.—Do you believe in the show-yard as being a means test of the breeding?—Well, I don't quite know what form you want the answer to come in. At such a show as Dublin I take it that a man is very happy if he can sell whether he thinks a horse or not, with the opportunity he gets to buy a horse there, especially if he sees him in the jumping competition.

2093. But without the jumping competition?—My opinion is that all the horses that passed the [illegible] should be tried for the purpose for which they are ostensibly offered.

2094. Now, there was a horse that you mentioned that was got by a certain Hackney stallion that got first prize, I think you said, at the Royal Show in England?—And at the Great Yorkshire.

2095. Did that animal ever show a quality?—That I cannot tell of my own knowledge, but I am mentioning, I got the information from a very reliable friend in a letter which is in my pocket at this moment; if you care to hear it I will give it in his own words.

2096. Mr. Wrench.—You can hand the letter in privately?—With pleasure. The letter was an ordinary private letter, with no thought of being produced here whatever. I may tell you before [illegible] finishing my reading the letter it comes from a man of acknowledged position in England, a great hunting man, a man who has a big stud of hunters always, and he has four daughters, the finest horsewomen I ever saw in any country, so he knows what he is talking about. I asked him the question, could he give me any particulars of any hunters that had Hackney blood in them, and had any more [illegible]. He says:—"I don't think I can give you any special particulars about Hackney bred hunters that are not already well-known. Certainly several of our best and most successful show horses are so bred, namely Mr. Cookson's Cherry Girl, who was first, both at the Great Yorkshire and the Royal, she was out of a Hackney mare. John Rogers's champion hunter that he sold in Dublin for £300, and was afterwards sold by private [illegible] for over three hundred, after going with the Queen for two seasons, and again changed hands at, I believe, a still higher price, he was got by [illegible], a [illegible] very good Hackney, and out of a blood mare. This I know of my own knowledge, as he was bred near me. Again Charles Wilson's celebrated Ambrose is the same way bred, and both of them were first through the High Leicestershire, and could stay with the very best; indeed the champion horse was not only the fastest, boldest, and most brilliant hunter I ever saw, but the highest class looking one. I don't say but these two are exceptions, but it is reasonable to say that a bit of good Hackney blood goes a great deal in a hunter; if a horse gallops in good jumping form, and gives you a good feel, of which each man must be his own judge, and can stay, and I have known, and you have known, Hackneys that are as good [illegible] and as good as any blood one, I think he is none the worse, but rather the better of a dash of the big Hackney, as he will bring you home after a long day without digging his toes into the ground. Of course we all like them as near thoroughbred as possible if they can carry the weight, but I would much rather have a bit of a cross of good Hackney than a great [illegible]. Yorkshire coach horse or Cleveland Bay or such cart horse, though I have seen good and valuable hunters bred from a quarter-bred, [illegible], Clydesdale mare; indeed, the third cross is best, if the mare is wisely mated, often results in a good weight carrier. We in England have none of what you call big, old Irish mares with no cross of any other blood, unless the I think you have, and if all the Dublin winners and other good hunters were [illegible]. Ireland could only tell their real pedigrees, it would open the eyes of the sticklers for pure breeding. If they would admit their Hackneys, big ones with good shoulders, and quality and action, they would do good to the hunter breeders in Ireland and not harm."

2097. Chairman.—Who is that?—Mr. [illegible] Turner, of Warren Grange, [illegible], Justice of the Peace for Lancashire, an important man, well known in the [illegible].

2098. It is usually acknowledged that the Irish-bred horse is stouter than the English-bred horse?—I think so.

2099. Why should this be?—I don't know the reason, except from the system of soft pampered feeding they give them in England; the very grass they have, the pastures in Yorkshire, is that thick, and loggy stuff, that they can always be filled with, and it does not seem to give bone or put mettle into them at all.

2100. You said you wished you had cut the throats of certain horses you sent to England?—I meant they were of no value and were unsaleable.

2101. Do you suppose if they had gone through a course of hunting in the North of Ireland they would be picked up by Mr. Wimbush or Mr. [illegible]?—They were not of the type he buys, but I have no doubt they [illegible] go somewhere else in England, but I must beg you to remember that that [illegible] process belongs only to a certain class of animal and to a certain class of man. I would consider it a stupid thing to do with a hunter; I would consider it the worst treatment possible with a hunter; it is only done with these horses to make them into big good-looking horses for London carriage horses.

2102. Would you do it with Hackneys?—I would not, I think. You would grow them into very useful looking [illegible], that would show very little quality if treated like that.

2103. What would happen, would they get coarse?—Nothing stands what we call forcing so well as the thoroughbred horse.

2104. Why is that, is it because the stamina and [illegible]?—I don't know that I could give an intelligent reason for it; I know it to be so, but I could hardly tell you why.

2105. Mr. Wrench.—Nothing stands forcing in what way, how do you mean?—You can force [illegible] a blood horse with plenty of nourishment; he looks all the better the more you throw on him; if you have a common bred horse and load him up with condition you get a bullock.

2106. Chairman.—Do you mean that would happen in the case of Hackneys?—Well, I don't think it would be to the advantage of Hackneys to keep them big and pamper them with feeding; I don't know why it should be so.

2107. In answering Mr. LaTouche you said you were comparing the value of the produce of a thoroughbred stallion and the produce of a Hackney. Are the stock you named as the produce of your Hackneys not being so valuable, was that stock pure bred Hackney mares or from a Hackney stallion crossed with half-bred mares?—The [illegible] I have had have been pure bred mares.

2108. In answering Mr. La Touche you mentioned [illegible], and I wanted to know whether it was the pure bred hackney stallion and the pure bred Hackney mare you referred to?—I really don't know how it works out. I mentioned the case of those two horses bred by the [illegible] horse, they were by a Hackney horse out of an Irish mare, one I sold for £[illegible], and the other went to Sewell's for £[illegible], when he was finished and seasoned; that shows they were fairly valuable.

2109. Bred from a half-bred mare?—They were from a [illegible] of Ireland hunting mare, out of [illegible], Charlemont's Blood Arrow.

[illegible] 1[illegible], 18[illegible].
Mr. [illegible] [illegible].

2110. Now as to the pure bred?—I think I have some pure bred Hackneys that I value more highly than my half-bred ones; I was referring to ones in particular that I think have exceptional action above them, but there are others I think that are [illegible] valuable.

2111. Mr. Wrench.—You have had your Hackney stallion standing at Ballymena for three years, have you not?—Yes.

2112. In your experience then if you let the services of your Hackney stallion only for £1 [illegible], your [illegible], would you get a great many more applications from farmers than if you put a good thoroughbred horse at the same price?—I think so; the farmers at present [illegible], without attempting to say whether the people are right or not, they would certainly go for the Hackney.

2113. You can get enough services taken up at £1 now?—A fair many at £1 [illegible].

2114. And you could not do that with a thoroughbred horse?—One gentleman tried it. [illegible] brought over some beautiful mares, thoroughbred, and of the highest pedigree, and sent the whole lot to my Hackney horse with the idea of trying to breed high-class carriage horses.

2115. Of course you have got no results yet?—No, I think he will this year [illegible].

2116. Mr. La Touche.—You said in answer to Mr. Wrench that you thought the farmers ought to be consulted and their opinions taken as to what would be the best means of improving the breed of horses, [illegible] you not?—Well, I don't know whether I put it in those words or not, but I did say that whatever [illegible] you offered them did not [illegible] them as a [illegible] they would not accept it.

2117. Then that is what you think the farmers would not be very much inclined to accept anything [illegible], they would [illegible] what they liked in the end?—They would tell you what they wanted if you cared to carry it out.

2118. But they would not engage that they would follow the advice you gave them unless your advice [illegible] with their [illegible], they would not take your advice?—I think my experience of North of Ireland farmers is that you cannot persuade them against their will. I don't suggest that you cannot lead them, if you can show them an improvement they will pick it up very quickly and adopt it, and adopt it [illegible].

2119. At the present time the prejudice of the small North of Ireland farmer is in favour of the Hackney stallion as opposed to the thoroughbred horse?—I would not say as much as that, some of them will breed from a thoroughbred and prefer it and some will breed from a Hackney, a great deal will depend on the nature of the mare. There are other thoroughbred stallions that are getting a fair amount of mares now, Mr. [illegible]'s stallion, [illegible] within three miles of my place and he has a fair number of mares.

2120. Then you don't contend that the farmers are prejudiced in favour of the Hackney stallion?—I don't say so particularly, but they are very fond of action, they want [illegible], they don't want anything weedy, they want an animal that they can put [illegible] in work and sell at four years old, and if it misses this [illegible] to the [illegible] they like it to [illegible].

2121. Have you got any thoroughbred **Hackney** mares?—Yes.

2122. That you brought to England, I suppose?—I [illegible] I bred. I have bred a good many.

2123. Have you sold any Hackneys of your own breeding?—I don't know that I have, I don't think I have ever offered any.

2124. Is there not a Mr. Kirk in your neighbourhood who breeds Hackneys?—Yes, all the mares were with my horse this year, four of them, but I would not call them high class Hackney mares, I think there were only, perhaps, two pure bred, if that many, one was [illegible] which he had been breeding from, and another was [illegible] that he had bred from a Hackney mare and a horse of the Prince of Wales.

2125. Do you know if he sold a Hackney mare to England to be sold?—I know he sent some this year and was offered very high prices for them.

2126. Have you sold any of your Hackneys in England?—I did.

2127. Did you get good prices?—Very bad.

2128. To what do you attribute that?—I think they were not good ones to begin with and they got no attention whatever at the sale, they were simply sent over to an auction [illegible] in the field without [illegible], and nobody was with them, for I did not care [illegible] of them, but I think [illegible] that [illegible] anything; for I was present at the sale [illegible] where I saw [illegible] thoroughbred mares sold for five guineas and another for £3 10s.

2129. Mr. Wrench.—Where was that?—At [illegible], [illegible]'s sale, one was sold for five guineas and [illegible], a black mare, that he gave 300 guineas for, sold for [illegible], for which he paid twenty sovereigns for the service of a horse, was [illegible] before my eyes for £7 10s.

2130. Were there many other thoroughbreds sold?—Yes, all sold at equally slaughtering prices. I was present at York when I saw some very fashionable thoroughbred [illegible], for [illegible] prices such as that, so what horses make at an auction sale under exceptional circumstances, I think, proves nothing.

The Committee adjourned until [illegible].

Mr. Robert Todd Heston.

Mr. Henry Tom [illegible] examined.

2131. CHAIRMAN.—You are a veterinary surgeon, practising at [illegible]?—I am.

2132. To what extent is horse-breeding carried on in your neighbourhood?—There is a good deal of horse-breeding.

2133. What class of horse does the farmer generally breed?—A harness horse. I might say altogether a harness horse. From the better class of mares they breed a good coaching horse, or a double harness horse, if you understand.

2134. From what sort of mares?—From very good, [illegible] mares—good-going mares with a certain amount of quality about them, and those horses are got by a thoroughbred horse.

2135. MR. WRENCH.—The mares?—The harness horses I spoke of are got out of those mares by a thoroughbred horse.

2136. CHAIRMAN.—Then the mares that are used in the district are chiefly thoroughbred?—No; chiefly half-bred. The mares I now speak of are a very small proportion of the mares that are bred there.

2137. What is the other proportion?—They are a [illegible] class of mares—light-legged, with fine action; and the farmers prefer to put them to half-bred horses.

2138. What do you mean by a half-bred horse?—A half-bred horse is a horse got out of a [illegible] mare by a thoroughbred horse.

2139. How could half-bred sire breed?—He is generally got by a thoroughbred horse—almost invariably got by a thoroughbred horse, and out of these class mares—that is, a useful and perhaps a better class than the usual run of them.

2140. Do you keep a half-bred stallion yourself?—I do; he is got by "[illegible]," and his dam a very [illegible] horse, and out of a [illegible] well bred mare. He was the property of the late J. A. M. Cope, of [illegible]. I don't know how she was got, but she was a very strong and well-bred animal. He bought the animal in [illegible], and trained it himself, and he was a very heavy man, [illegible] in weight. He bought her for riding purposes.

2141. Would you know the sires [illegible] got by a thoroughbred horse?—I would not know that mare was by a thoroughbred horse. I would not say. She was a very good-going mare and might possibly have had Hackney blood in her.

2142. Have you had any experience in the breeding of Hackneys?—Yes, Hackneys?

2143. Yes?—I have.

2144. Give us your experience?—The best mares at present in our neighbourhood are mares that the farmers bred themselves by a horse—I don't know whether he was a thoroughbred Hackney or not. He was the property of the late Lord Charlemont—"Bend Arrow." Then there was the late Lord Caledon's "Character." Both these horses had Hackney blood in them. The mares from these are the best mares, and when bred with thoroughbred horses got the best stock in our neighbourhood. Any farmer who has one of those mares would not part with them for money.

2145. Mr. WRENCH.—What do you say about the produce?—They are better than [illegible] any mares in the country; they are [illegible]. But the mares got by those horses are one kind of harness; and got the best stock that is in our country when served by a thoroughbred horse, particularly when served by a thoroughbred horse that suits them. The unfortunate part of it is, that the horses that have come to our neighbourhood have not been horses calculated to get harness horses—they have been short horses; I am speaking of the thoroughbreds there under the Royal Dublin Society's scheme.

2147. CHAIRMAN.—You say in answer to question [illegible] that you know very [illegible] people who have [illegible] by the Royal Dublin Society's scheme?—I do, sir. These are men that had [illegible] mares [illegible] thoroughbred horses, they were too light-boned, and had not action enough; and these farmers put them to the Government horses when they came, fancying these horses would get wonderful stock. They had [illegible] half-bred [illegible] got [illegible] from the half-breds than from the Government horses when these arrived, because the mares were not suited to the Government horses.

2148. What class of horse do you consider pays the breeding farmer in your district?—A good harness horse; it is worth £100 and over when it is four years old, and that amount is easily got for it.

2149. With regard to the horses you gave to question 25, have you ever used in studies the result of the cross you recommend by a thoroughbred out of a Hackney mare?—I would say these [illegible] those horses—Lord Charlemont's "Bend Arrow" and the Earl of Caledon's "Character"—would have been got by [illegible] sires they were. And there is another stallion in [illegible] moving in the district out of a thoroughbred horse by Lord Caledon's "Character," and he is one of our best half-bred sires at present.

2150. Mr. WRENCH.—What is he out of?—He is out of a thoroughbred mare, "Nancy Gale"; he is an old horse now.

2151. You don't know that Lord Charlemont's horse was a pure Hackney?—No; I understood that there was Hackney blood in both Lord Charlemont's and Lord Caledon's horses, and for all I know one or other might have been thoroughbred Hackneys.

2152. CHAIRMAN.—What sort of horse [illegible] suited to, and with what results?—To the second class of country mares not suited to a thoroughbred horse, mares of lighter bone, with not sufficient action or quality to go to a thoroughbred horse.

2153. You say the bulk of the stock is more like the [illegible] than [illegible] sire, and therefore recommend the thoroughbred as a sire?—Yes, in the half-bred horse most decidedly.

2154. Would not the desired result be more likely to be produced if both [illegible] were thoroughbred?—Well, no; because, you see, you require to mate by a half-bred horse; you must introduce something to put bone and action into those country mares. If I put a thoroughbred horse on these light, weedy mares [illegible], the stock is worse than the mare itself; and, I contend, that in order to improve the breed of horses the mares should be served in such a way that the stock will be better than themselves. That is at present not being done in our district, and I say it

[illegible]

2177. Don't you think it would be better to cross it out?—I don't think it is possible to cross it out. You have the animals there and you must deal with them. By crossing those mares with horses of fine strains of Hackney or thoroughbred blood, however, you would eventually, if you crossed them with horses of their stamina, probably get mares that would go to a thoroughbred. That is my idea, to cross the strain in such a way that eventually we will have mares to go to a thoroughbred horse, and I say it is necessary to give prizes to the farmers to keep these good mares, because they will keep their good mares if they have them. I would wish them all up to go to the thoroughbred horse, except the cart horses, for I don't think you would hardly ever weed them up to breed good hunters from the half-bred Clydesdale mares.

2178. Then the mares should be allowed at this time [illegible] would go to thoroughbred horses eventually?—Eventually; that is my idea. And to get a large majority of the mares, at present being bred, [illegible] to go to a thoroughbred horse, it will be necessary to introduce Hackney blood.

2179. You think the Hackney blood is preferable to what you call the half-bred stallion; would you prefer a half-bred stallion got by a thoroughbred out of a Hackney mare?—There I have the grandsire of my stock out of a thoroughbred horse.

2180. Would you prefer that to a stallion got by a thoroughbred horse out of a half-bred mare?—Yes, if the half-bred mare pleased me.

2181. Out of a hunting mare?—Out of a good hunting mare if she had action as well. I would prefer her to a Hackney mare, but they are very hard to get.

2182. Colonel St. Quintin.—Have you an equal objection to the Cleveland and the Shire as you have to the Clydesdale?—I don't like the Clydesdale at all, because there are so many diseases follow the Clydesdale horse.

2183. You object particularly to him, but you also object to the introduction of others. There are different classes of mares and different classes of horses, and you want to get hunters and [illegible] horses. Putting the thoroughbred and the Hackney on one side do you object to the Cleveland or the Shire horse, or the Yorkshire coaching horse?—I don't like the Cleveland at all.

2184. Or the Yorkshire coaching horse that we heard of yesterday?—I object to the Cleveland [illegible] of those I have seen I object to. I don't like them as coaching horses at all, they would not cross with our mares. There is generally a want of muscle about their thighs and [illegible] which the Hackney has. As a rule they are not as good goers as the Hackney. I speak of these two horses, Lord Clonbrock's "Royal Arthur" and Lord Cloncurry's "Chamation." These horses I know. They have bred horses that are still in our country, and are our best mares. From practical experience I am speaking.

2185. Mr. Carew.—You say the halfbred sire you would prefer would be one by a thoroughbred out of a Hackney mare?—Yes.

2186. For bagging purposes?—Altogether. We have no good mares in our district calculated to get hunters.

2187. So that you would **not like that for the** hunter breed?—No.

2188. You are speaking entirely from the farmers' point of view?—Yes. If we have a hunter in our district it has to be sold in the Royal Dublin Society's Show or at the Ballinasloe fair.

2189. Between the Hackney class and the half-bred class, if the latter had good action you would prefer the half-bred class to the Hackney?—I would.

2190. Mr. Wrench.—What becomes of the horses that are chiefly sold in your district; where are they bought, and by whom?—The best class of coaching horses are bought from the farmers by dealers that live in our country, and Mr. [illegible] [illegible], Dublin, and [illegible] [illegible], and those men attend at those dealers' places and buy them in lots of from fifty to a hundred.

2191. Are those the class produced by the people you call here "Class I," valued at over £150 value each?—[illegible].

2192. These animals are bred by that class of breeder?—Yes, and when that class of breeder has a very good mare he puts her to a half-bred horse if he gets a horse that goes off with that idea; but they are principally got by thoroughbred horses out of the good mares, and those are the class we ought to try to encourage, and get every breeder if possible to breed that will breed that class of horse, for those will pay them.

2193. Then you take your class, so called two. Do you say the mares are not good enough to go to the thoroughbred horse?—No, not the half-bred horse made these horses.

2194. Those class thereof?—A very poor lot of mares.

2195. Should you think a Hackney is required there to enable them to produce good mares for breeding there in future?—Yes. Those two would require to be mated there by a half-bred horse in order to get produce fit to go to a thoroughbred horse. They there would require to be mated perhaps two or three times before the produce would be fit to go to a thoroughbred horse, but we should always want [illegible].

2196. You say the best mares that are now go to a thoroughbred are the mares got by the best horses you named?—They are.

2197. You cannot say of your own knowledge whether they were bred Hackneys?—They call them Hackneys in the country, that is all I know. And I know perfectly well if you could bring "Brand Arrow" back today to our district and se[illegible] people with him there is not a farmer in the district would sell a mare by him they have such an opinion of him.

2198. Had some of the animals bred by "Dunk Acorn" pleased?—Magnificent cattle. That is their great point. He started to serve at ten shillings a cover, and, before he was done this practice was the charge, and the farmers willingly now consider fix the service.

2199. You consider action requisite to enable a hunter to gain a good price for a horse?—Yes, for a horse hore.

2200. You think that breeding hunters here in Ireland would pay farmers better when trying to breed hunters?—You must change all their world before they can breed hunters, and I don't see how you can make them pay until we make them fine hunters.

2201. Are they sold to other parts of Ireland or out of the country?—Some go to other parts of Ireland. We bring a lot of horses from the north to our district and sell them again in Ireland. As a rule all our farmers keep their horses on until they have [illegible] months of their old [illegible]. They sell them worth a month, somewhere [illegible]-and-a-half.

2202. With regard to the Clydesdale blood, do you think it would be [illegible] to the animals you want to breed from than a cross of Hackney? When you want to produce a harness horse you don't like Clydesdale blood?—No, I don't. Clydesdale blood would do cheap horses.

2203. And there many Clydesdale stallions in the north?—Yes, and doing a great deal of harm.

2204. Would you be in favour of requiring people to take out a license for stallions?—They would not.

2205. To pay so much for a license to allow their stock stallions to be shown. Are there not many[illegible] [illegible] at present?—The bulk of the stallion [illegible] [illegible].

2206. In some counties they are obliged to take out a license to show that their stallion is sound. Would you approve of that?—Certainly.

2207. You think it would be a good system?—Yes.

2208. Do you think people would object to it?—Any man with an unsound stallion would object.

2209. Does the public generally would approve such a regulation?—I believe they would.

2210. If the farmers knew there was a guarantee that a stallion was sound would they appreciate that?—They would to a certain extent. But the great point is this: the farmers go to the cheap sires, and we must give them a good sire at the same price they are getting the bad sires for if we are to do good.

2211. What class horses have the [illegible]?—[illegible] twenty-five years.

2212. Are there a good many **horse** breeders among them?—There are.

2213. You think it would be quite impossible to stop that class of farmer from breeding horses?—I don't see how that would be done.

2214. You would not agree with some of the witnesses that these farmers ought not to be allowed to breed horses?—I would not indeed. If a man can do it profitably, and if he is given a horse to suit his mare, it could be done profitably.

2215. You think he could make a good profit from breeding, if he had the proper class of sire placed within his reach?—Yes. In my recollection [illegible] there were over 200 mares served by very inferior half-bred horses of all shapes and kinds; and if these farmers had got good half-bred horses at the same price as they got those inferior horses it would certainly improve the breed of horses.

2216. Do you think a Shire horse would be too heavy for the mares or the work required in your district?—I don't think so.

2217. You think he would mix with the [illegible] mares?—Yes; there is a great inclination at the present time to put a heavy horse on more of the mares than there was some years ago, owing, I suppose, to the depreciation in the price of horses. The year before last at the end of the season I [illegible] half-breds that were mixing in the district. This year I [illegible] a distinct falling off in the number of half-bred horses.

2218. Can you give any definite suggestion as to how you would take the opinion of these people as to the class of horses that should be sent to their district?—I think the local committee would be an exceedingly good judge.

2219. How would you select your local committee?—The Royal Dublin Society would suggest a very good committee. I could suggest no better committee than we have.

2220. Would you leave that selection to the Royal Dublin Society?—I would not have the slightest objection.

2221. Are there on your local committee who represent the small farmers?—We have men who know their wants, and men who during the working of the Royal Dublin Society scheme have seen their district thoroughly, and seen their stock, and who know exactly what the farmers want.

2222. Would you recommend that the Royal Dublin Society should register other horses besides thoroughbreds?—I should decidedly, yes.

2223. Would you lay down any definite number of mares that half-bred sires have to produce before he is registered?—Well, of course, a half-bred sire necessarily should be judged by the get he produced [illegible].

2224. But how many mares would you require on the stud-book?—I would not require any number if the horse was what was required.

2225. Would you register the horse before he was known what stock he would get?—No; I don't think so.

2226. You would wait to see whether he was a good stock getter or not?—Yes, I think it would be a good plan to [illegible] the stock got by the horse before he was registered.

2227. Do you know anything about these American trotting sires, they say are brought into this country?—I have seen a great many of them.

2228. In your own district?—No, about Dublin.

2229. Are they calculated to do good or harm?—They will reduce the price of Irish horses and are doing so.

2229. Will these animals be of any use to the farmers as brood mares?—No.

2230. You don't approve of the cross?—No; [illegible] about their legs.

2231. Would you suggest that they should be banned in any way?—Yes, I would, most decidedly.

2232. You think that would be an improvement?—It would.

2233. You think that people would be slow to buy branded horses?—They would.

2234. Chairman.—With regard to Clydesdales and Shires and Clydesdale and cart horses generally, with regard to their bone, although bigger to look on, it is not much coarser and [illegible]—a great deal.

2235. More liable to fly and break?—Certainly.

2236. Do you know from experience what the difficulty with which breeders of heavy horses have to contend in their land, and the horses [illegible] with their feet?—Yes.

2237. Is that the chief thing?—Yes, with Clydesdales; but I don't think it is so much the case with the English Shire horse—he is a much sounder horse than the Clydesdale, and that is why I suggest him.

2238. If a half-bred horse is, in your opinion, approved of and registered by some competent board, who standing in the same [illegible] as a Clydesdale, Clydesdale, Hackney, or any horse, getting mares of the same kind, to which stallion would the farmers in your district send their mares?—The bulk of them would send them to the half-bred horse. I say it would take two half-breds to do the work in my district as the thoroughbred or one Shire horse. If you had these two better, something in a district, it would take the two, a half-bred and a Hackney, or two half-breds, to do the work of one of the others.

2239. You include the Hackney, then, in **the same** class as the half-bred horse. If I had **two half-breds** got in the right way, I would prefer **them to** the Hackney.

2240. In your district are the [illegible] or do the farmers retain them for breeding purposes, and sell the [illegible] if they can?—As a rule they part with their mares' fillies; as the fillies come on [illegible], they are parted with.

2241. What will that lead to in the long run?—If they were satisfied that these fillies would breed well, I am quite sure the farmers would keep more of them. They change their horses very frequently in this way, and they change their mares [illegible]. A few of them breed from two or three-year-old mares, and they take them [illegible] and they sell [illegible].

2242. Where do they go to replace the mares they sell?—You mean the mares that would probably replace the two-year-old filly that was going away?

2243. Where would they get that mare?—They would breed it.

2244. If it turns out sound?—They would breed a filly or two and sell it again.

2245. At what age?—They would sell it at about the same age—three-year-old or four-year-old.

2246. Have you had any experience in breeding from two-year-olds and three-year-olds?—I have. I think it is good practice. I think that [illegible] two-year-old. She then gets over it well, and it takes her a couple of years to pick up again. The farmers generally have to keep that mare one year longer than they otherwise would to have her ready for the market. Breeding from a three-year-old, I think, does no harm.

2247. Mr. Cameron.—What do you say as to the stock from a two-year-old?—They are not as big or as strong, but numbers of them do well.

[illegible]

[illegible]

2266. [illegible] whether the sire or the dam is most inclined to give action?—By the thoroughbred horse undoubtedly a great deal of the action is got from the dam, but with a bad going thoroughbred horse there are many good harness horses bred where the dam has good action.

2267. Then you think that in very many cases the action in the dam has a great deal to say to it?—It has, undoubtedly.

2268. You said that the best harness horses in your country were bred from mares that were as a rule supposed from the south?—I would fancy most of them are.

2269. Do you know how they are bred at all?—I do not.

2270. You imagine they are got by a thoroughbred horse?—I would fancy so, coming from the south. The big farmers go south to buy them themselves, and bring up an exceedingly good mare.

2271. Mr. Wrench.—Is that class No. 1?—Yes.

2272. Mr. La Touche.—And you think these mares as a rule are got by a thoroughbred horse?—I would fancy so.

2273. You think they owe their excellence as brood mares very much to the fact that they are got by a thoroughbred horse?—I would not doubt it at all, but then they are out of the right class of mare evidently. That mare is of the right class; if got by a thoroughbred she must be of a good class, not a class of mare that we have as a rule.

2274. Do you know anything about the class of mares in the congested districts, south and west, served by these Hackneys?—I do not know anything.

2275. Do you think the spread of the Hackney strain through the south and west is likely to have any effect on the class of horses farmers buy?—I have no idea of what class of mares are in the south. I am speaking for my own district only.

2276. You cannot give an opinion?—If they are the same class as ours, I don't think it would do the south any harm. I suppose it would benefit them in a slight way.

2277. Do you think your big farmers would be able to get as good mares in the south if they contracted some of the Hackney blood as at present?—I hold that a dash of Hackney blood does some good.

2278. That is your opinion on that subject?—Yes.

2279. Mr. Carew.—Can you name any of the fairs in the south most popular with northern farmers?—They attend nearly all the southern fairs. Our large farmers as well as being breeders are feeders. They go south and fetch eight, ten, and twelve horses annually. They are all off at the fairs now. They buy them, bring them up, and feed them during the winter, and have them ready for March, April, or May. They attend all the fairs in the south.

2280. What do you mean by the south?—South of Dublin.

2281. You would not call the county of Meath south?—No, they don't buy many there.

2282. Skryne, in Meath, would you call that south?—A good many go there. It is a good fair, but they prefer further south—Cahirmee and French Park.

2283. French Park, County Kildare?—Yes; that is a popular fair.

2284. What are the fairs to which the congested districts horses go?

Mr. Wrench.—He doesn't know.

2285. Chairman.—Have you anything else you wish to tell the Commission?

Witness.—I don't think so.

Mr. W. Hammond, Ballyarnett House, Londonderry, examined.

2286. Chairman.—You are a land agent, I believe?—Yes.

2287. How large is the area under your control?—The area that I manage is about 60,000 acres.

2288. What are the chief characteristics of the soil in that district?—A great part of the locality is mountain, and the farms are very small, and all worked by the spade; I don't think in all that locality there is a single plough, the farms are all extremely small and the land generally soft, rather too soft for horse work. In the harrowing in of their seed they don't put a horse as a general rule on the land at all; they cover their oats in with large rakes worked by hand. Of course there are some districts where the land is better—where there is a little more clay; then they can use horses on the land for assisting in the work.

2289. Are there any horses bred down in your district?—Oh yes, I am speaking now particularly regarding the western seaboard of Donegal and of all that district which is called congested.

2290. You have had some considerable experience in horse-breeding?—Yes, for a considerable time in a small way.

2290a. What stallions have you used, and with what results?—In the west of the county of Donegal the stallions were of an inferior description; there were no local stallions at all. There were travelling stallions that came from a distance, and the breeding of these animals was very bad—indeed a kind of mongrel race. I never saw a good stallion coming into Rosses, west of Donegal, to my knowledge. Of course the people took advantage of what they could get, and bred from them to a certain extent, but the produce was never good.

2291. Have you any idea of the breeding of the stallions?—I think there was a good deal of Clydesdale blood in some of the heavy, coarse-bred, ugly kind of horses; some of them may have had a little blood in them, but the generality of them were unsuitable to the small mares in the locality. I never saw a stallion I could approve of—that is previous to the last five or six years.

2292. Do you remember a different state of things?—I have known the locality for thirty years, and the breed of horses—or ponies rather—has been seriously degenerating. In days gone by I heard of a good class of ponies called the Rosses ponies, extremely enduring, plenty of life and plenty of go in them; they have died out, I don't think there is a remnant of them remaining.

2293. Have you any idea how they were bred?—I have not been able to find out. This was a small class of ponies. I have been endeavouring to find out where the sire came from, but failed; they were 14·2 high with white legs, white face and white eyes; a better or tougher class of pony could not exist; I had one myself and sold it to a lady who took a fancy to it. It turned out a remarkably good pony; and the lady took it from Ireland to Scotland, to Wales, and to England, until it was done up. I don't know a single good pony of that description at the present time; twenty-five years ago there were a number of them.

2294. You cannot tell how that pony originated?—I cannot tell where the sire came from.

2295. Mr. Carew.—Is this what you describe as the Rosses' pony?—Yes.

2296. Chairman.—It was a well-known breed?—It was a breed that everyone knew and everybody appreciated, and they always went at high prices.

2297. You don't know whether they had any cross of Arab or Barb in them at any time?—I cannot say.

2298. Can you give any reason for the deterioration of stock that you speak of in your locality?—The want of good stallions, decidedly; if the breed had been kept up of those ponies by good sires, I believe the race of horses in that part of the country would be superior in the present time to which they are now.

2299. I believe that you and some friends of yours imported a stallion?—Yes, that was the year previous to the Congested Districts Board sending stallions to the country; two friends and myself saw the necessity of getting a good stallion, and one of them who was in England looked out for the most suitable stallion he could pick up, and he purchased this "Little Wenlock" in Norfolk. We brought him over and he stood between Dungloe and Gweedore for a season; the produce was not numerous, the people did not seem to appreciate him, some, however, reared good foals and sold them at from £10 to £17 each as foals, that of course was the highest at about eight months old, they didn't all go to that.

2300. What class of stallion do you consider would be best in that locality?—Decidedly the Hackney. I don't know any horse more suitable for the small mares to improve them, give them bone, and spirit and endurance as well. I know no horse better calculated to do it than the Hackney, and the people themselves appreciate the Hackney stallion extremely. I don't think they would exchange him for any other at the present time. I made inquiries from a person that is not very much interested and he wrote to me as follows:—

2301. Is it in answer to a question you asked?—I asked what the people thought of the foals out of the Hackney horse.

2302. Mr. Wrench.—What district?—Dungloe district. This gentleman writes to me as follows—it is only a sentence from a letter (Reading) 'Regarding the foals from the Hackney horse they are turning out splendid, but I understand that the first Hackney sire which came here was the best. His produce is now three year old past and they are reckoned the best and most suitable for our district. I have a three-year-old of the breed of horse and he is a grand pony. I purchased him from Mr. James Sweeney. He took first prize at the Horse Show in Dungloe last year, then two years old.'

2303. Chairman.—Who is that letter from?—Mr. James O'Donnell from Burtonport.

2304. Is that the only stallion the Congested Districts Board have sent?—They send one every year. This was the first, and I think he was there for two seasons.

2305. Mr. Wrench.—A horse called "Real Gentleman?"—Yes.

2306. The Chairman.—Have they sent any other class of sire?—All Hackneys; one season they sent an Arab.

2307. What was the name?—"Teresito," the one presented by the Queen.

2308. A Barb has never been sent there?—No, and the Arab was not appreciated at all by the people in comparison with the Hackney.

2309. Was the Arab altogether a well-shaped animal?—Oh, yes; a nice little animal, but too light for the class of mares in that country. I dare say if put to a large-sized mare the produce may have been good, but there are no mares of that class in that country.

2310. You imported "Little Wenlock?"—Yes, with two friends.

2311. What stamp was he?—A small thoroughbred.

2312. Who selected him?—Major Gordon.

2313. And you thought him a good stamp?—He thought he was, but when we saw him we didn't care much about him. I don't think his produce have turned out well.

2314. How did the produce of the Arab turn out?—Very light. I remember seeing one especially, and it was extremely light in the bone, it would just remind you of a deer about the legs. It was very shapely, very neat, and very nice, but no strength in it.

2315. Are there any other stallions in the neighbourhood besides?—I don't know of another stallion in the neighbourhood.

[illegible]

Mr. W. [illegible]

2325. What would you suggest as a means of improving the breed there?—I would suggest the continuation of the Hackney stallions, and endeavouring to make the people—small farmers—keep their fillies for breeding. Until they do that no permanent improvement can take place. With these old and weedy [illegible] the same thing over and over again, and no matter how good the horse may be the produce will not be good; that is the drawback, and if some inducement was held out to the people to keep their fillies we would have a better class of horses.

2326. You say the farms in your district are worked by spade and hand?—Altogether.

2327. What then do they use the ponies for?—Back-loading; some have carts; back-loading, carrying [illegible] and seaweed, and bringing [illegible] from the market. Many of them, of course, have no carts, and [illegible] on the horse's back.

2328. You don't require a large animal for that?—No, a large animal would be out of place there. Their farms would not feed them. They don't take the same particular care of their horses in that locality, and if you give them a large highly bred horse they cannot feed them.

2329. Do you consider the Hackney a [illegible] sire?—Yes, a most [illegible] animal. I had one myself [illegible] that I used for eighteen years, and it [illegible] animal [illegible]. She had action, [illegible], and a spirit up to anything. I used to drive [illegible] in a day, and she would come home as fresh as she went out.

2330. Have you any experience of Welsh ponies?—I had one at one time, small, 13.2, [illegible] animal with splendid action, and I liked him.

2331. [illegible] in harness [illegible]; I [illegible] from a [illegible] I had him [illegible] and [illegible] him to [illegible].

2332. I suppose the stallion [illegible] was the best bred [illegible]?—A small [illegible], bred from a horse called [illegible]. It was the most [illegible] I could get at the time to put this pony to, and she [illegible].

2333. The [illegible] of the pony was [illegible]?—Yes.

2334. And they grew well under [illegible]?—[illegible] [illegible] would be the height of them, they were both [illegible] [illegible] in [illegible] and [illegible] had the [illegible] of the Hackney, which was a high, [illegible] action, and the other [illegible], although [illegible] and [illegible], [illegible] were good and both good [illegible], the same, [illegible] the same [illegible] of the [illegible].

2335. Do you think a stallion of the Welsh stamp, [illegible], would be a good cross with the Kerry pony?—[illegible] height [illegible], and anything under 13 hands would be small [illegible] to [illegible] their height and their [illegible] [illegible].

2336. What is the usual height of the Kerry pony?—13.2.

2337. Do you wish them higher than that for [illegible]?—They might be up to 14. Then it would not [illegible] give the people an opportunity of [illegible] their [illegible] they would sell better; [illegible] people look out for a good cob, and if they get a good [illegible] it is a matter of money [illegible] with them.

2338. [illegible] in the county of [illegible]?—[illegible] or [illegible] in the [illegible].

2339. And in that [illegible] you think the class of ponies has [illegible]?—On the contrary, I think it has deteriorated very much.

2340. The [illegible] of a pony with white eyes and white legs, a good [illegible] pony?—Yes.

2341. That was [illegible] in the district?—Yes.

2342. [illegible] has disappeared?—Yes, it has. I think one of the last I had myself, and that was [illegible] by a lady to whom I sold it.

2343. What sort of sires did the people in use when you first went to the district?—Those nondescript ponies that used to travel the country.

2344. Their white-eyed ones?—[illegible] I [illegible] no record of finding out where they came from.

2345. At any rate the ponies of 40 or 50 years ago were better?—Undoubtedly, far better.

2346. What became of "Little Wonder"?—[illegible] [illegible] the Congested Districts Board sent their [illegible] everything [illegible] to him, and "Little Wonder" had nothing to do. He was given to a [illegible] in [illegible], where there was larger scope and which is a better district, and had broken his [illegible] [illegible] and was shot.

2347. I suppose when the Congested Districts Board stallions came they got all the work?—Altogether.

2348. Was the fee that the Congested Districts Board charged much lower?—Oh, yes.

2349. Considerably lower?—Yes, considerably lower.

2350. I suppose those nondescript ponies didn't charge more than five shillings?—They did not.

2351. But the Congested Districts Board's fee is five shillings?—Yes; but the people would prefer to get a good horse at 5s. than a bad one.

2352. Then it is not on account of the lowness of the fee, but on account of the excellence of the horse?—Yes; they would take the Hackney in preference to the [illegible] at the same figure.

2353. What you mean to say is that the Congested Districts Board's horse has got the custom from its superiority, and not through its [illegible] [illegible] of the fee; the people appreciate the Hackney, and would rather have him at a higher fee.

2354. Do you think the people understand the requirements of horse-breeding?—I think the people know what [illegible] remarkably well.

2355. But they have allowed their horses to deteriorate for twenty or thirty years?—But they have had no good stallions that would have kept up the breed.

2356. You think they had stallions twenty or thirty years ago that they have not had since?—There was a better class of pony.

2357. How do you account for the good class disappearing?—It was not the fault of the people. No person in that part of the country could afford to bring in sires. The people were too poor, and the landlords certainly were not inclined to do anything in the way.

2358. Do you think they could afford to keep [illegible] twenty or thirty years ago?—I [illegible] very [illegible] [illegible] for the [illegible], so far as the [illegible] of the people are concerned.

2359. What I want to get at is how you account for the people allowing their horses to deteriorate so much [illegible] twenty or thirty years?—[illegible] their [illegible]. If they had had good sires coming to the country they would have taken advantage of them.

2360. But previous to that they must have had them good sires?—Very good, indeed.

2361. And they must have been brought in by the people?—I [illegible] [illegible] [illegible] where they came from.

2362. [illegible] very people who allowed the breed to deteriorate [illegible] twenty or thirty years are now highly appreciative of the Hackney horse?—Certainly.

2363. You thought it would be advisable to use a bigger horse than the Welsh cob [illegible] think so. I don't know the size of the [illegible] Welsh cob, but anything [illegible] 15 hands would be [illegible].

2364. Do you think it would be advisable to breed an animal more than 14.2 in the Rosses?—I would say up to 15. The 15 hands horse will go on the [illegible] [illegible] than the 14.2.

2365. [illegible] they were [illegible]?—Yes, [illegible] to the [illegible] [illegible] the Hackney [illegible]. I consider [illegible] [illegible] the [illegible] breed, and [illegible] [illegible]. [illegible] has a kindly disposition, and is easily broken to be anything in the thoroughbred. The people there generally break in their own horses, and if they have a thoroughbred one they can do nothing with it—they spoil them to fret.

2357. Your experience is that the Hackney is more suited than the half-bred thoroughbred?—Yes.

2358. You have had experience of both?—I have had a little experience, but not so much of the Hackney as I would wish. This grey mare that I spoke about was a Hackney. I took the trouble to send her as through to try to breed from her.

2359. Was she a thoroughbred Hackney?—Yes.

2360. Did you buy her in England?—I bought her from a dealer in Ireland, and I sent her to a thoroughbred Hackney from Norfolk belonging to the City. Mr. Johnston, in Dublin—"Breakaway" he was called. She was, unfortunately, barren, and would not breed.

2361. Was she in the stud-book?—She was not.

2362. Are you quite certain she was a thoroughbred?—I believe she was, from what I know myself, and from what others said, and from her appearance.

2363. You only know by personal appearance?—Yes, personal appearance. I had no record of what she was.

2364. There is a great deal of posting work in the county of Donegal?—Yes, a good deal at Buncrana, Letterkenny, Dungloe, and Glenties.

2365. There is a good deal of such work?—A good deal of posting.

2366. What are the animals that are used?—Animals which are generally purchased in fairs outside the district. For posting purposes and for heavy carting purposes, they generally go to Strabane, Derry, or Milford to buy suitable horses.

2367. Are there any reared in the district?—They are all too small and unsuitable for work of that description.

2368. And you think with a cross of a Hackney stallion you can breed the same horses?—Yes, if you can breed them up to fifteen hands they would be very fair post horses.

2369. As a matter of fact have you any idea how the present horses are bred?—I could not say.

2370. But they have no appearance of being highly bred?—I consider they are bred from the country mares, larger and heavier than in the Rosses, and probably of half-bred stallions.

2371. And you think that for general purposes and suitable use that the Hackney stallion is superior to any other?—I do for that locality.

2372. What advantage do you think the Hackney has over the horse that might be got by the thoroughbred horse, out of mares themselves got by thoroughbred horses?—I think he is a more compact animal. I think he is stronger in the loins, with any amount of spirit, a showy horse, and a more enduring horse. I think there are qualities that you would not have in the half-bred.

2373. Occurrence of spirit is not an essential quality for carrying creels up a mountain?—It is an essential with those people who want to sell them.

2374. You think he would be more saleable?—Yes, I think so; if they have got a horse they can get good money for, they won't put a creel on his back.

2375. They sell them as foals?—Yes, but latterly they are anxious to hold on a little longer to realise than they may get a better price.

2376. How do they keep them in the winter?—They house them at night, and allow them to run out in the day.

2377. This would be the bigger farmers?—And the smaller ones, too, give them a little hay and meals during the nights. It takes a hardy horse to live and [illegible] under these circumstances, especially with the small farmers.

2378. Have you any reason to say that horses got by a Hackney stallion are more capable of bearing these trials and privations than horses got by a thoroughbred out of a half-bred mare?—No, because our experience is narrow.

2379. Are there any other thoroughbred horses in that district?—None, except the one I mentioned.

2380. Where did he stand?—Between Ardara and Glenties.

2381. Did you find his stock were hardy in the country?—No, I didn't hear that any of them did.

2382. They were able to endure during the winter?—Yes; they would not keep up the same condition in the winter as the produce of the Hackney, they are thinner in the skin, and thinner in the hair.

2383. Do you think that the Hackney has got more bone?—Yes, certainly.

2384. And why do you think so? If the Hackney measures eight inches below the knee, and the thoroughbred measures eight inches, why do you say that the Hackney has more bone?—I am not acquainted with those large thoroughbreds; I never measured them, but from appearance it is obvious that the Hackney is the stronger; I think that is generally admitted.

2385. I have not seen many Hackneys myself, but is that any experience of the stock I have seen. You think that the Hackney would impart more bone?—Yes.

2386. Than any thoroughbred you know?—Yes.

2387. Mr. Greene.—You have no experience except the one you owned yourself, the eighteen years, which you didn't know was a Hackney?—That is so.

2388. The Hackneys in your district, have you to [illegible] themselves?—Yes.

2389. Mr. Wrench.—Do you know anything of the Welsh cob?—Do you know the most of them of the best quality are largely crossed with Hackney blood?—No, I am not aware.

2390. You don't know anything about the breeding of Welsh cobs?—No, I do not.

2391. And you think if any horse is supplied in these districts to satisfy the people and fairly the requirements which exist, that there is nothing more suitable than the Hackney?—I would; I know the people of the district are well satisfied with the Hackney as an animal.

2392. Do you know, if they have sold the produce at higher prices than they sold the produce of the mongrels?—Yes, at eight or nine months old up to £32.

2393. Is that the produce of the Hackney?—Yes.

2394. In that parish higher than before?—I never knew them to get more than £6 heretofore, and more than they sold for half-bred prices. I remember some being sold for £4.

2395. And as apple of that horse have been getting double for the last few years?—Very highly.

2396. Don't they also require horses they can trust at an early age?—Yes.

2397. Two years old?—Yes, they put them into work when they are two years old.

2398. And work them from that on?—Yes.

2399. In horse breeding a considerable industry amongst the people in that district?—Yes, it forms during the time the mares are rearing the foal they work her and work her up to the very day she foals.

2400. And this is a considerable source of income?—Yes.

2401. You would not agree to any recommendation that those people should not be allowed to breed from—I think it would be a great hardship, but I would do everything to advise them to improve their breeding again, that is a thing the Congested Districts Board will very soon have to look into and to try and find some remedy why the people should keep the filly and get rid of the old mares.

2402. Have you any suggestion to offer?—I was thinking if the Board charged a higher figure for service to the old mares, and gave the young mares a [illegible] it is a small colt [illegible] will induce these people to do what will turn to their advantage in the end; it is a thing that might be considered.

2403. You would make a difference in the treatment between the young and old mares?—The old mares one would [illegible] give any assistance at all, and the young filly [illegible] from a Hackney I would give her assistance.

2404. Do you think the land is good enough to encourage people to breed from their fillies as two years old?—I think it stunts the growth of the animal, and I don't see how one can find the [illegible] at two years old at [illegible].

2405. You think it better they should not be encouraged to breed until three years old?—I think so.

2406. I think you said that the [illegible] in [illegible] the large side?—Yes.

2407. On the larger side as compared with their sires?—Yes.

2408. Have you a clear recollection of any of the [illegible] stallions in the district before the Congested Districts Board sent their stallions?—I have a recollection of two.

2409. Can you describe them?—A coarse blooded small sorry looking one, a half-bred; he was kept by a person of the name of Phillips; he used to ride and drive him; he was a black horse with [illegible] legs and [illegible] body.

2410. What kind of stock did he produce?—Very inferior. I remember another, a black horse, that they charged half-a-crown for the service of; he was so [illegible] he was hardly able to draw a cart; he was [illegible].

2411. Then practically the stallions were of the worst description?—The worst description, and that has been the great drawback to horse-breeding in that part of the country.

2412. Not I think before the Board took any steps they asked you and a good many people down there for information?—They sent a list of queries to people who had the interest of the district at heart, and who were well acquainted with the locality.

2413. You know the whole of these districts?—The whole of the congested district and a large part of the county as well.

2414. Chairman.—Was it not in order to get over this big size [illegible] in your locality, with the small [illegible] the sheep little ponies disappeared?—Yes.

2415. It was in order to get size that they used this large size of cross-bred [illegible]?—Well, they had no [illegible]; they could not afford to go long distances, and took the [illegible] of those that came through the country to fairs and markets.

2416. But was it in order to get size?—It was in order to get a [illegible] of [illegible] work.

2417. Would it be possible to breed polo ponies in your district?—I believe it would. I believe that from the old type of animals in [illegible], and that they breed from the Hackneys, I believe they could be bred.

2418. [illegible] you want a good sire?—Certainly.

2419. In order to breed polo ponies you want to breed an animal not above 14.2?—Yes.

2420.—It would be of some advantage to the farmers to breed polo ponies?—It would, if they could do it.

2421. Don't you consider a thoroughbred or Arab or small thoroughbred, would be more likely to get the sharp polo pony?—You must improve the type before you do anything; the Hackney stallion is the only animal that I am aware of that will improve the breed; when it is improved you might use other sires to advantage.

2422. Are you not afraid that you will get your mares too large with the Hackneys?—You might be [illegible] certainly, but the largest stock mares now would not be higher than 14.2, and they are down to 12.2.

2423. Mr. Wrench.—Is it not a fact that a large number of the polo [illegible] are [illegible]?—Yes.

2424. Are not the [illegible] got by Arabs and [illegible] and some thoroughbreds [illegible] than those got by Hackneys? They would [illegible] at a smaller price?—Yes.

2425. And is it not a fact that most of the polo ponies that produce good ponies only produce large ponies when [illegible]?—Yes.

2426. And they don't bring the profit so much in the [illegible]?—No. It might [illegible] a [illegible] [illegible] polo pony or cob; but they would never [illegible] it.

2427. In those places where those people sell [illegible] animals is not [illegible] a good advantage?—The poorest man in the country will look to [illegible]; it is one of the things [illegible].

2428. Chairman.—In former days are you aware what price they got for their ponies—the good ponies that you speak of as the Kerry breed?—I cannot answer that question definitely.

2429. I suppose they were sold at [illegible]?—Yes; the same [illegible] animal then as at the present time. They then sold them at fairs. Some by necessity; some expecting to make money kept them a little longer, kept them on and sold them [illegible].

2430. Mr. La Touche.—Do you know what became of those ponies that were bred in the Kerry and sold in the [illegible] of Donegal and [illegible]?—Strangers came from Donegal, Strabane, Stranorlar, and other places, and purchased them and took them away.

2431. That one man buy a batch of them here, one would buy two or three of them at a time; but mostly they were picked up individually.

2432. One man would buy all one [illegible]?—Yes, and take it away and either keep it or sell it.

2433. Is it to your knowledge that they grow bigger when they get down into a good country like [illegible]?—I should say so.

2434. Then the foal that would probably attain a size of 14.1 or 14.2 in the [illegible] would grow to 15 hands in another place—the county of Cavan for [illegible], or something else [illegible]; but I have had no experience and cannot give any evidence.

2435. Chairman.—There is just one [illegible] I should like to ask you—Whether or not there has been any industry up there in the way of mule-breeding?—No.

2436. They don't breed mules?—No.

2437. They never try?—No.

2438. Are there many mules in that country?—I only know one.

2439. I suppose there are plenty of donkeys?—Oh, yes. There was a Spaniard out there [illegible]; the Congested Districts Board sent him down.

2440. What sizes are the donkeys; big or small?—Very small; [illegible] diminutive, but extremely useful.

2441. Don't you think they might grow mules there?—Yes, I think so. At the time the Congested Districts Board sent the Spaniard out I was anxious they should try [illegible] for mules, and he [illegible] to [illegible].

2442. By mules I mean [illegible] as well?—Yes, they are both useful, and no doubt, would [illegible] poor country like that. They are easily kept, and, if good, they are of great value.

2443. Mr. Wrench.—Have you any experience as to whether they sell as well as the produce of the Hackney?—No, certainly not. They cannot be so profitable; but for the use of the poor man they are just as valuable; but certainly not for selling. Therefore, I think the people would not take to breeding them so much as ponies.

2444. Chairman.—What is the highest price you have heard paid for a colt?—My experience is very limited; I think the most I refer to, [illegible] have got has been £8 or £9.

[illegible]

The Commission adjourned to next morning.

SIXTH DAY.—THURSDAY, NOVEMBER 19TH, 1896.

Present:—The Earl of Dunraven, K.P., in the Chair; Lord Rathdonnell, Lord Ashtown, Mr. F. S. Wrench; Mr. J. L. Carew; Sir T. H. G. Esmonde, M.P.; and Colonel St. Quintin.

Mr Hugh Neville, Secretary.

Mr. R. M. Archdale, D.L., Ballinamallard, Co. Fermanagh, examined.

[illegible]

[illegible]

[illegible]?—I [illegible] with a great many a good deal, but I can [illegible] many [illegible] were [illegible]. I don't know the [illegible] of any [illegible] except my own. I sold to a [illegible], of Tipperary, Rugby, for many years, and a great many of [illegible] have gone to [illegible]. I won the [illegible] [illegible] [illegible] out of eight times by horses bred by myself which were sold as hunters.

2439. How were they bred?—By a thoroughbred horse out of a well-bred mare.

2440. Would you call your district a hunter producing district?—No, not a hunter producing district. There is no [illegible] for hunters there. They have to come to this country for hunters. The dealers get the hunters down here and they make the principal profit.

2441. Have you any opinion yourself as to what effect the [illegible] of Hackney blood would be likely to have upon the trade in Irish hunters generally throughout the country?—I think it would do it good. I think it would give bone and substance, and do away with a lot of the soft [illegible] they are getting from the Clydesdale at present.

2442. I think you said, in answer to a question, that the mares have improved in your district?—Not; I think they are improving. I think the Royal Dublin Society's scheme is improving them. The prizes are tempting them to keep on the mares, instead of selling them as they used.

2443. Do you attribute the improvement entirely to that cause or to any other cause?—Entirely to that cause, and to the people taking a little more interest in breeding and in [illegible] principally. As a rule, the [illegible] that is fit for nothing else is [illegible] [illegible] in our country—[illegible], [illegible] [illegible] [illegible] [illegible].

2444. I think you said that you have bred out of a thoroughbred mare and your own Hackney stallion?—Yes; I have; but the produce is only two years old at present.

2445. And from half-bred mares, too?—Yes; I have bred from half-bred mares and from pedigree Hackney [illegible].

2446. What is the sale?—Yes; [illegible] are [illegible] years old, the oldest of them; I am driving [illegible] year olds, but I have not tried to sell any yet. They do not sell well until they are five years olds down in our part.

2447. Not until five?—That is the time to get the best price, if you can keep them until then.

2448. Can you compare at all the prices you got for the stock of the Hackney stallion and the stock of the thoroughbred stallion?—I have not sold any yet; but two [illegible], who sold a four-year-old mare and horse, got better prices than [illegible]. They told me they were well satisfied. They got £[illegible] [illegible], at [illegible], in May last, and a [illegible] called [illegible] [illegible] got £[illegible] prize at [illegible]; another man got £[illegible] for a three-year-old off my horse—a mare called [illegible]. That was much more than they could have got before.

2449. Are there many high-class harness horses bred in your district?—There have been a great many horses bred; very good [illegible].

2450. I am asking about harness horses?—Yes; I think a good many good horses.

2451. At what age would they be sold to the dealers?—They would be sold at three by the bigger farmers. The small farmers sell them coming two.

2452. What price would they fetch?—£[illegible] and £[illegible].

2453. Do you think that the farmer would prefer harness horses got by a Hackney to hunters horses got by a thoroughbred?—If they could get a harness horse by a thoroughbred with [illegible] [illegible] I dare say they would prefer it.

2454. [illegible] [illegible] [illegible] [illegible] [illegible] the harness horse a profitable kind to breed?—Yes, I think so. I think it is the great [illegible] for the [illegible]. I have sold harness horses by a thoroughbred to Glasgow dealers, and I got about £[illegible] or £[illegible] for four-year-olds. I sold several over there.

2455. You said, in answer to a question, that [illegible] that the number of persons who benefited by the Royal Dublin Society's Scheme was small, because they are obliged to use only registered stallions?—Yes; I am on the County Committee of the Royal Dublin Society's Scheme. We have never been able to get mares enough for the prizes. During the whole time the Dublin Scheme has been in operation in Tipperary we have never been able to use the whole of the money. We never got mares enough.

2456. How do you account for that?—They don't care to go to the stallion in order to get prizes. They require a different class of the Dublin horse, and they would prefer to go to another horse, pay more, and lose the prize, than go to the Dublin horse.

2457. You think they ought to be allowed to choose their own stallion?—That is my own opinion. I think all suitable stallions, of whatever breed, as long as they are pure-bred, should be registered, and men allowed to go to whom he selects their own stallions.

2458. Do you think that stallions other than thoroughbred ought to be registered?—I think so.

2459. Half-bred stallions?—No; I don't approve of half-bred.

2460. You mean pure-bred?—Stallions belonging to some recognised stud-book.

2461. Are not any half-breds? No. I am opposed to half-breds, and the majority of the stallions in the County Tipperary are half-bred [illegible] [illegible] [illegible] [illegible].

2462. Have you any idea of the number of stallions in the county?—I have no idea. I saw [illegible] [illegible] [illegible] [illegible] [illegible], [illegible] I do not know the number.

2463. Are there many thoroughbred stallions about your own place?—There are. A man called [illegible] has got three, Sir [illegible] [illegible] has one. I think there are about four or five in the county now.

2464. Is the farmer very much influenced by the question of prizes in selecting a stallion?—Very much. Price and [illegible] are the two principal things, I think—that is, with the small class of farmers, who are the principal breeders.

2465. And the large class of farmers—do you think they are affected by prize?—If he saw a valuable stallion he will send to it.

2466. But in the case of the small farmer the price is a great object to him?—Very great—very.

2467. Are you in a position to give any opinion, prices being equal, what kind of stallion they would select?—I think, now, they would go to the Hackney stallion if they got him. I think the Hackney stallion is the favourite class of stallion in the county at the present time. I am getting mares from men who own thoroughbred and half-bred stallions. They are sending them to my Hackney, instead of giving them to their own horse for nothing at all.

2468. Was there any Hackney in your county before yours?—Mine was the first.

2469. You have had experience of the [illegible] for the last few years—do you think they would prefer a Hackney sire to a good thoroughbred sire, the fees being equal?—Yes; I think so, undoubtedly.

2470. Colonel St. Quintin.—A great many of the horses sold to the big carriage horse dealers command, you say, from £[illegible] to £[illegible] and £[illegible]?—£[illegible] to £[illegible], I said.

2471. How were those horses you speak of got?—Some by thoroughbred, and the majority by half-bred Clydesdales. I have known them sell a stallion that was got by my own thoroughbred horse out of a Clydesdale mare, and I have known the produce got by that horse go for £[illegible] or £[illegible] to [illegible] dealers at the [illegible].

2472. What class of carriage horse was that?—Sixteen hands high.

2473. Showing quality?—Showing a great deal of quality considering his size. The mare must have been a light well-bred mare. [illegible] [illegible] [illegible] wonderful [illegible] of quality. I saw one horse I remember quite well.

2474. You also told us that there had been people who crossed thoroughbred and half-bred stallions who had been crossing to your Hackney stallion, which was only a short time ago?—This year.

2475. That, I should imagine, was an experiment?—Yes, they are good colts by the Hackney stallion now there in sound condition and better than what they could breed otherwise. I imagine that.

2476. It is not from any general [illegible]?—No.

2477. You also said that the people in the district object to go to the Royal Dublin Society's stallions?—Yes.

2478. Why is that?—I don't know. We are very hard put to it to get enough of mares this year. After a lot of [illegible] we got the Dublin Society to give consent to our giving a £10 prize, which is more than the other [illegible]. We gave Dublin money to try and induce more mares to come.

2479. What was the objection to those stallions?—I fancy they might [illegible] had proved so profitable to them.

2480. Lord Rathdonnell.—You say the mares in your district have improved. Are they bred or bought?—A good many have been bought. Some mares have been bought in the north since the Society began to give prizes. Our farmers get mares in the north, feed them until they become four and five year olds, and then sell them to the London dealers.

2481. I am referring chiefly to mares?—They keep some of the mares when they get good prizes; they keep some of them in order to try and get a prize, they then sell them afterwards.

2482. Do you find that the sound foals are [illegible] up by the dealers, and the unsound ones left in the country as a rule?—Very much so; it is doing the greatest damage in our horses I think.

2483. Have you any scheme in your mind as to how that could be stopped, as to how the sound mares could be kept?—I have often thought of that, but I have not seen the [illegible] only of giving the prizes. They do to a certain extent enable [illegible], as the mares must be sound in order to obtain a prize.

2484. What thoroughbreds are in your district?—[illegible], the winner of the [illegible], and [illegible] and [illegible] was there, but he has gone this year.

2485. How far apart are they, are they "[illegible]" in the adjoining [illegible]?—Well, they are not very far [illegible] as a rule. [illegible] and [illegible] are near [illegible]. [illegible], the [illegible], stands his horses, and there is "[illegible]" close to [illegible]. There are a good many close to [illegible], but some in the other parts of the county.

2486. You mentioned about the half-bred sires in your district. What do you mean by half-bred sires?—I mean a sire got how I could not tell; it is not a Clydesdale, a Shire, nor a thoroughbred; it is nearly always got by a thoroughbred from a heavy cart mare which they think great bone.

2487. Where do these heavy cart mares come from, are bought from dealers?—No, they were in the country as a rule.

2488. How are they crossed?—They are bred by a Clydesdale sire out of a country mare.

2489. What do you mean by a country mare?—A light mare 15·1 or 15·2, no bone and bad shoulders.

2490. Is it your opinion that they have gone in for Clydesdale to get bone?—Yes, that is what they do it [illegible]. They have a good reason, and they seem to me to know which horse they would put her to. They always neglect the thoroughbred. They stand the mare is too light, and think they want a produce with bone; they want a little quantity.

2491. Is it your opinion as regards bone, that the Clydesdales, Shires and Clevelands, although bigger to look at, the bone is much more porous and more inclined to fly?—Yes. I do not agree with the theory at all that the Clydesdale and Shire will give bone. I think they spoil the horse.

2492. You don't like the Clydesdale cross?—I don't like any cart cross in a mare except for farm work.

2493. I think you kept a horse called "Forlorn Hope"?—I owned him for many years.

2494. Was he a thoroughbred?—He was bought as a thoroughbred, he was bought from [illegible], but Weatherby would not put him in the book; he was supposed to be by [illegible] out of [illegible] by [illegible].

2495. He was not in the Stud book?—He was not; he was for some time, but Weatherby could not verify his pedigree after Mr. [illegible] died.

2496. You have a horse called "Revenge"?—Yes, sold.

2497. Was he a thoroughbred?—He was in the same sort of way I believe really a thoroughbred, but not such a thoroughbred.

2498. He was a half-bred?—I should not call those horses half-bred.

2499. He had a stain?—Yes.

2500. Would you object yourself to horses which have stains of that kind?—I should be very glad to get them to run.

2501. You think a half-bred stallion of breeding, bone and substance would be acceptable to the people in your district?—A half-bred stallion like "Revenge" would be acceptable. No one would look upon him as a half-bred.

2502. If he is not in the Stud Book he must be a half-bred?—I mean to say the people would not look upon him as half-bred.

2503. If a half-bred of that description, approved of by some competent Board, registered in fact, was to stand in the same locality as a Clydesdale, or Hackney, or a Cleveland, at a good figure, and were going at the same fee, to which stallion would the farmers in your district send their mares?—At the present time they would go to the Hackney. I think it would be a close run between the Hackney and a stallion like that if they got to know his merit. I had a thoroughbred stallion "[illegible];" he was the winner of a good many races. The farmers at first might did not care about him, he being rather high on the legs. But his produce turned out so well that he was very acceptable afterwards.

2504. Do Messrs. Hunt and Winthrop, and large dealers like them buy many horses in your district?—They do not come near us. All the good horses go to the fair.

2505. They spend a great deal of money in this country?—Yes, a great deal.

2506. If Messrs. Hunt and Winthrop were to state that they dislike the cross of the Hackney would you still be inclined to use the Hackney?—Yes, because I don't think they know the harm or know what the horses are got by that they get.

2507. But if they knew that the Hackney stallions were had been used do you think there would be any danger of their keeping their money away from you?—I think hunters but, if they got a suitable horse they would buy it no matter what it was got by; even if got by a Clydesdale to their knowledge, if it looked good enough they would buy it.

2508. Mr. Cassidy.—You said you sold some horses yourself in Glasgow for £60 or £70. Was that recently?—About four years ago.

2509. They were got by Hackneys?—No, by a thoroughbred, by "Forlorn Hope."

2510. What age?—Four-year-olds.

2511. Do you think you can improve on the price by the produce out of the Hackney?—I hope so, with some I have got now, two-year-olds coming three, I think they are.

2512. You said that as between the Hackney and

Nov. 14, 1896.
Mr. [illegible]
[illegible]

the thoroughbred if the thoroughbred had high action you would prefer it?—I would prefer it, but when I speak of the breeding of the Hackney class I do not speak of my own mares so much; only two are good stout mares with plenty of breeding.

2513. With those qualifications you would prefer the thoroughbred?—Yes.

2514. If the mares in the country were like yours you would prefer the thoroughbred?—I think the Hackney would bring plenty of good stock, but that the thoroughbred would bring stock too. I have been [illegible] thoroughbreds and Hackneys for about six years. They talk about the staying powers of the Hackneys. I drive one thirty miles and never touch her with the whip, that is the pedigree Hackney mare that I have been breeding at the same time.

2515. You said you think the introduction of Hackney blood through all the country would improve the breeding and, [illegible]?—I would like to qualify that. I would not like to introduce the Hackney into Meath or Kildare, or any hunting district at all. I would keep it in places like our county where they have small, light mares unfit to produce big stock.

2516. Col. Sir [illegible].—Your county, is not that class of country that you would breed hunters?—No, we are not the natural part at all.

2517. Mr. W[illegible].—I think in addition to being on the Council committee of the Royal Dublin Society you are also on the Horse-breeding Committee of the Dublin Society?—Yes, I was.

2518. I think you are also the practical manager of the [illegible] Farming Society, that you have managed the County Society for many years?—Yes, I have been managing for fifteen years.

2519. And you were master of the Fermanagh Harriers?—Yes, I was about five years master.

2520. So that you have exceptional opportunities of knowing the farmers, and the horse-breeding of the district?—I don't think any one knows the farmers in Fermanagh better than I do.

2521. You have mentioned you had a horse called "[illegible]"?—Yes.

2522. Was he not a horse with exceptional bone below the knee?—Yes, very good bone.

2523. Did he not measure nearly 9 inches?—Yes, within one-eighth of an inch of 9 inches. He measured over 9[illegible].

2524. Above the knee?—Yes.

2525. A big upstanding hunter?—Yes, a horse 16·1.

2526. Therefore you had experience of breeding from the type of thoroughbred you recommend?—Yes, my father bought him specially for that purpose from Newtown.

2527. Do you think a thoroughbred horse is calculated to produce action with the same certainty as a Hackney stallion?—I am afraid not. I have never found that he could.

2528. You think the Hackney produces bad better action than any thoroughbred?—Yes, undoubtedly.

2529. Have you had any experience of the West of Ireland—Donegal, or any of those western districts?—I know the west of Donegal very well—Ardara, Killybegs, and all that part from Bundoran to North Leitrim.

2530. You have been around the west coast and know the west coast of Donegal?—I know it very well indeed.

2531. Do you know the class of mares that they have in that district?—Small, light, undersized mares, about 13 or 14 hands, up to 14.

2532. What horse do you think best calculated to mate with those mares?—I think no other horse but the Hackney would get a good stock out of them.

2533. Do you think that the people there ought their mares to be [illegible] into a stronger and more saleable class of mare?—Undoubtedly.

2534. You think that the [illegible] in Fermanagh?—I think in a great many places of Fermanagh. The mares in Fermanagh want bone. I don't find them

practice of crossing the bred with the Clydesdale, which they want to do. I think the Hackney will put the Clydesdale cross out of it.

2535. You don't consider that there is anything in this allegation that Hackneys are soft?—My experience is that they are quite the reverse. They are wonderful, as far as I have found.

2536. Do you know how they are bred, if there is anything in their breeding that can give any force to that statement?—I think the origin of the Hackney—a thoroughbred cross on an old nag [illegible]—ought to make them hard, and they are very particular in all the stud books to keep the cart cross out of it.

2537. You think that there is a considerable crossing of the cart horse in Ireland now on the mares of this country?—There is a tremendous amount in Fermanagh of the cart horse with the mares. Many mares are served by cart horses than by any other sire. Ten times as many are served by cart horses than by any other particular horses.

2538. We have heard the old Irish horse spoken of. Are you of opinion that there is any particular type of Irish mares still existing?—They are not in our country. I saw the mares described, but I never saw one in my life.

2539. Was not your father a large breeder before you?—Yes, a large breeder, and he used to judge at shows in Dublin and in England and other thoroughbreds, horses and hunters.

2540. Of those mares any means of that sort, he would be likely to have had them?—I fancy so.

2541. His mares were especially good?—They were very good mares.

2542. When you are carrying out any scheme with public money to improve the breed of horses in a district, do you think that the people themselves ought to be consulted?—Well, I think they ought to be consulted to a certain extent. I think they know perfectly well themselves what they would go for. There is no good in driving them against their wishes. There is no use in forcing them [illegible] what they would not.

2543. Do you think they would know the type of horse they would want?—More certainly.

2544. Would you agree with the opinion that the small farmers, say of £30 valuation, should not be allowed to breed horses?—No, I should not, because that would prohibit the horses in Ireland out of the country.

2545. Is not the breeding of horses a source of considerable profit to a great many men of that description?—Yes, they do not throw life [illegible]; they rear them and would rear nothing, and it does them no harm.

2546. Would you register any so-called hackney horses?—No, I would not.

2547. In addition to the horses that you mentioned as having been bred in Fermanagh have many high class race horses been bred in Fermanagh?—Yes, the best horse in England at the present time, has been bred in Fermanagh, [illegible], [illegible], [illegible], [illegible], was bred by us in Fermanagh.

2548. Therefore it is a county that has bred good horses and can breed good horses.

2549. And your opinion of the breeding of hunters is that hunters always ought to be got by a thoroughbred horse?—Yes, I should certainly think so.

2550. Supposing that Hackney blood did spread up well up from the West of Ireland into other parts of Ireland to the injury of the horses of the country, do you think it at any possible bad results that then might be with regard to action could be got by being crossed by a thoroughbred?—I think they would make typical brood mares for crossing with a thoroughbred horse.

2551. You don't think there would be any disadvantage in galloping or moving, or in any other way?—I cannot see any disadvantage. I do not believe the action would be too high for fast going.

2552. Did you hear that it had been stated by a witness here that farmers could be relied on as a rule to give a true pedigree of their horses?—If you knew that they would, not otherwise.

2553. If you knew them they will tell you the truth about the horse?—Yes, I think if you know them they will.

2554. Did you hear that the classes which were started to have back the horses which have given Ireland a name for good Irish horses were the gentry and the farmers over £200 valuation?—I saw that in print; I think it was Mr. Roberts said it.

2555. Then if these people get a statement from the farmers how their mares were bred, do you think there would be the same danger, when they wanted to buy a mare to breed a hunter, to their buying a mare that was got by a Hackney stallion, if they did not want one?—They would know if they bought the mare over there what she was got by.

2556. It was a danger they could guard against?—They could guard against it. If they went to a distant fair to buy from a stranger they would not get a true pedigree; they would simply see the horse and buy it from its appearance.

2557. You were asked if Messrs. Kerr and Windsor, dealers, who buy these high class hunters in [illegible] a large supply in your district?—They buy a great many at [illegible] fair.

2558. Then it is a very large market from which to buy that class of horse?—A great many small dealers buy. A man called Maguire, of Fermanagh, buys 200 or 300 every year and ships them to England.

2559. And are there other dealers in the North?—Yes, from Derry and places come down to Dunbar[illegible] and Clones.

2560. If Messrs. Kerr and Windsor found a good looking horse that went well they would not be particular about the pedigree?—I don't think they care much about pedigree; they look to every stock.

2561. Did you know as a matter of fact that Messrs. Kerr and Windsor have bought a great many American horses?—From my own knowledge I could not say.

2562. Do you know anything about the importation of American horses into Ireland?—I saw two Canadian horses, the highest class of Canadian horses; they belonged to a [illegible] of Lord Lansdowne, and were bought by a friend of his . . . . . . I think they are very much preferable to them. They have very fine shoulders and great [illegible] very bad hind quarters and the rump fell away altogether, and I suppose they were the pick of Canadian horses; I never saw Canadian horses before.

2563. Do you think it would be to the advantage of traders in Ireland if the American horses or foreign horses were branded in any way so as to distinguish them?—Very much, I think.

2564. You would be in favour of branding?—Yes, if they could be distinguished without being disfigured.

2565. Do you think that would put up the price of Irish horses?—I think they would do them good. It would prevent the Irish character being taken away from them entirely. I like all foreign goods marked, more especially.

2566. CHAIRMAN.—One or two questions so as to be quite sure that we have got your meaning correctly. You said in answer to Lord Rathdonnell that you considered the improvement in your district partly to the fact that a better class of mare had been imported from other parts of the country?—Partly to that, in order to obtain the Royal Dublin Society's prizes the people were anxious to keep good mares. It was the Dublin Society's Scheme and their prizes for mares that kept good mares in the country instead of their being sold.

2567. You mean that the improvement is due to keeping better mares belonging to each district and also to the importation of a better class of mares; not to the introduction of a new strain of blood or anything of that kind?—Not to the introduction of a new strain of blood at all I think. It is solely due to keeping better mares.

2568. Well, then, I think you mentioned in connection with the staying powers of the Hackney horse that you got your own cob of a pedigree mare [illegible] is the mare I referred to; she is a pedigree Hackney mare and also a four-year-old trotting one of hers which I am driving ditto, by "Danegelt," a celebrated Hackney. I am driving both of them now.

2569. Do you think there is anything like what might be called a market [illegible] of being created in your country by breeding horses by pure bred Hackney sires and pure bred Hackney mares?—I think there would be a very good market about Belfast, not in my part of the country. I don't think there could be a market for them in this part of the country, not for the pedigree mares.

2570. Do you attribute the staying qualities of the pony that you cannot to its being pure bred on both sides?—I don't know which to attribute it to, I thought it was the natural Hackney blood. They are from old generations of Norfolk mares.

2571. You think the Hackney blood is likely, generally speaking, to transmit staying qualities to the produce?—I can only speak from my own experience, I have these Hackney mares now and they all, I find, are very hard.

2572. You would not desire the introduction of Hackney blood into Meath, Kildare, and other places of that kind?—It is certainly not.

2573. And you said that Messrs. Kerr and Windsor, and others—I did not quite understand whether it was that they did not care, or could not distinguish the Hackney blood?—I do not think they could distinguish, and even if they could, they would not care; if they saw a suitable horse they would not care what it was got by.

2574. Do you think the breeders in these counties you mention would be able to distinguish whether the mares have a strain of the Hackney blood in them or not?—I am sure they would not. I have seen Hackney mares that one would hardly tell from a thoroughbred mare.

2575. Then if you think the Hackney strain is undesirable in those counties how would it be kept out?—I think it would be kept there [illegible] of the mares they get out. I should prefer a hunter out of a thoroughbred horse to a hunter by a Hackney, but I think the Hackney sire would produce a better class of mares to breed from to get a good hunter.

2576. Are there many ponies in this part of Donegal that you are acquainted with?—The ponies are nearly all what you call pony sized. We buy a great many polo ponies there, all the English dealers come to my country to buy polo ponies.

2577. What kind are the stallions?—Some of them are light, well-bred stallions as a rule. All the mares have been clearing this way a lot kept down their size so much.

2578. Would you call those ponies a distinctive breed?—No, I think not. Lord Enniskillen, a member of the Commission, bought a Fermanagh pony for some sires, and he got splendid ponies.

2579. Do you think the Hackney sire would improve the breeding of these polo ponies?—No, I don't think it would; I think it would be a bad cross for a polo pony.

2580. What would you recommend?—I think the polo pony breeding is all on chance. I am breeding myself all polo ponies. I have got [illegible] and I am putting them to a thoroughbred horse, "Ratcliffe Plain." The dams originally of the mares were polo ponies, well-bred mares. I could not get their pedigrees; it would not be correct.

2581. As far as polo ponies are concerned, you would not cross these West Donegal ponies with the Hackney?—Not to get polo ponies. I don't think there are any many in West Donegal as there are about Fermanagh. I don't think they would breed anything

9th Jan. 1896.
Mr. E. M. [illegible]
[illegible], J.P.

Dec. 15, 1896.
Mr. E. D. [illegible], D.L.

in West Donegal suitable to buy; they are all very bad shouldered and very light in bone.

2582. You must have misunderstood me—you don't mean to say that the produce of these ponies of West Donegal are sold as polo ponies?—I gave a wrong answer if I said that. I don't think their produce are sold as polo ponies at all. I have tried to buy polo ponies up there very often, and I never got one yet.

2583. What class of mares did your father keep?—Hackney bred mares with two or three crosses of the thoroughbred in them. I have known him sell some Clydesdale crosses for high-class horses; I would not like to buy them myself.

2584. You evidently prefer, I gather from you, the Hackney to the Clydesdale, or any other cart blood?—Very much, and they much also to the Cleveland. There is a Cleveland in one end of our own county; I don't like it at all; I don't like the colour by it.

2585. It is specially for giving them substance and action?—Bone and substance is the principal thing.

2586. Would you prefer the Hackney to the thoroughbred; I mean a suitable thoroughbred, bone and sufficient bone?—If a thoroughbred could be found to give the same characteristics, I would prefer the thoroughbred. I have never yet seen the thoroughbred that would.

2587. And you think in the case of small farmers under £20 valuation, that the breeding of horses is profitable to them?—Yes, certainly; very much.

2588. Do you think they can afford to pay a suitable fee, one large enough to obtain the services of a good horse?—I am afraid they could not pay a high fee—or they would not, rather. But with the Dublin Society prices they can do well enough.

2589. And as regards the registration of half-bred horses, I understand you to say that you do not approve of it as regards what you call half-breds; but you would not object to some horses which are not in the Stud Book being registered after careful selection?—I would not object to any stallion in the Hackney Improvement Society's Stud Book; as a matter, I think, they register.

2590. And you think the foreign horses should be branded in order to be distinguished?—I think it would be very desirable in the interests of the Irish horse.

2591. Why if those horses like Mount Kent and [illegible], and others we are on, to know how the horses are bred, what difference would it make if the horses came from America?—I don't think it would make much difference, but it would prevent the character of the Irish horse being taken away. Those other horses, I think, are not well-bred.

2592. Colonel Sir [illegible].—Talking of these farmers under £20 valuation, what price at the various ages do you think would pay the farmer; what is the usual age at which they are usually sold?—One and three-quarters, coming two.

2593. What price does he get, and what price would pay him?—He gets £10 as a rule, from that to £16.

2594. Would that pay his expenses?—Yes, I think it would. I think if he got £20 coming two, it would pay him very well indeed. They do not give them any sort of care; they work the mare up to a few days of foaling, and they work her again shortly after wards. There is no rearing them at just the keep of the colt up to a year.

2595. Suppose the farmer keeps them until they are three or four, what would you put it at for them years?—I always consider you could not do it under £10 a year at the lowest. £40 for four year olds would be the lowest that could make any profit, that is without any finding at all.

2596. Well, then, there is a great deal of talk about Hackney action, do you think that excessive action is desirable from farmers?—No, I do not.

2597. Does not excessive action constitute waste of power?—I think it is power wasted; I would call any waste of power.

2598. Waste of power, I beg pardon?—Waste of power.

2599. That must necessarily stop power of endurance and give less power?—Yes, I should think so.

2600. You have been a hunting man all your life. You understand what riding a horse is, and you say you don't think that Hackney action interferes with a horse in galloping or in getting over the ground fast?—I would not hunt a pedigree Hackney, but I think the mare got by a Hackney stallion out of the ordinary country mare would get a good mare to breed from with a thoroughbred. I am speaking of the hunter class. I mean a hunter?—I would not like a hunter to have Hackney action.

2601. You don't think the Hackney can gallop?—No.

2602. You said you did not think the action interfered with the galloping power?—I mean the action of the cross of a thoroughbred stallion with a halfbred Hackney mare, in that case the action would not be potent enough to interfere.

2603. Have you ever seen a Hackney gallop?—Yes, I have.

2604. Do you think the general formation of the ordinary Hackney is calculated to get safely over the country?—There are Hackneys and Hackneys. My own Hackneys cannot be kept in; they will jump anything, they are rather too much of the Norfolk Hackney.

2605. Do you think he would go quickly and safely over a Meath double?—He would go safely over a Meath double, but he would not go too quickly. But I think if a thoroughbred stallion were crossed with him the produce would go both quickly and safely over it.

2606. With regard to the conformation of the shoulders of the ordinary Hackney do you think it is a conformation that is either comfortable to the rider as a riding shoulder, or that is likely to gallop and get quickly and safely over the country?—All the Hackneys I have seen have splendid shoulders. I ride my own Hackneys very comfortably.

2607. Do you like Hackneys with broad withers?—I do not care about broad withers.

2608. How many have you seen with riding shoulders?—A great majority of them, I think the Norfolk Hackney has not riding shoulders, and I would not have them brought into the country, but the Yorkshire is much more of the thoroughbred.

2609. Do you think that that cross is likely to give a good conformation for a riding horse?—No, I would not encourage the Hackney if I could get a good thoroughbred. I think the Hackney is far better than the Clydesdale or the Shire cross which people are using to get a big brood mare.

2610. Lord Ravensworth.—What breed was your mare?—A Norfolk mare, curiously enough.

2611. I thought you said you did not care for them?—No, and if I had money enough I would buy a Yorkshire mare and sell her.

2612. You said you have seen Hackneys that you could not distinguish from thoroughbreds?—Yes.

2613. And I think you also stated that you would not like to see any of this breed introduced into Kildare and Meath?—No, I would not like to see the Hackney stallion in Meath or Kildare. I would like to get the mares there crossed with a thoroughbred.

2614. Suppose the foals produced by the Congested Districts Board's stallions were to get into Meath and Kildare, is there any danger of them doing some harm?—I don't think so. I don't think they would do any harm.

2615. You are rather fond of trying experiments, I think?—I am afraid so.

2616. Your father was a very successful exhibitor and breeder?—Very successful.

2617. Have you any of his stock left, his horses?—Yes, I have. I have only one now, that is a descendant, of course. She is a brood mare.

2618. He also had a lot of shorthorns?—Yes.

2619. What have you now?—Polled Angus.

2620. He also had sheep—are they the same?—They are the same, what there are of them. I sold them all last year.

2621. You have changed everything?—I intend to return to the sheep as soon as the land is cleared.

2622. You have got rid of all the successful articles?—I was much more successful in sheep than my father.

2623. And then you have got rid of them?—I have got rid of them to let the land rest for a year or two. I had too many sheep, and I could not get a good shepherd.

2624. Still you like experiments?—I think it is no experiment resting the land from sheep.

2625. Mr. Gahan.—You say that the Royal Dublin Society's Scheme has improved the stock?—Yes.

2626. It is due largely to importations from the south of Ireland?—Not altogether. It makes people keep a good mare. If a man goes down south and gets a good mare he keeps her.

2627. These are half-bred mares?—Altogether.

2628. You play polo in Fermanagh?—Yes; we have a very successful polo team.

2629. You think that in the case of the farmers who sell their produce at fairs it would pay them to produce an animal of a class suitable for polo ponies?—It would pay no man to produce a polo pony. The producer gets no price; it is the man who makes the pony who gets all the benefit.

2630. From the small farmers' point of view the producing of polo ponies is not profitable?—Not profitable at all. I think polo pony breeding is entirely a matter of chance.

2631. Mr. Wrench.—You were asked about the excessive action of the Hackney, do you think that the Hackney, if he has excessive action, must always produce that excessive action when crossed with an ordinary country mare?—No, I think not; he makes her lift her legs and gives her straight action.

2632. If a horse has got to be crossed with country mares, excessive action is not a drawback in that respect?—He requires good action to counteract the bad action of most of the country mares in our parts.

2633. Most country mares have bad action now?—Very bad.

2634. You think that the existing breed of harness horses in your district can be improved with ordinary care?—Yes.

2635. You think action is one of the chief requisites of a harness horse?—One of the chief requisites in order to enable it to sell well.

2636. I think you have seen the Hackney stallions of the Congested Districts Board?—I remember them well.

2637. Do you think them a suitable type to introduce into Ireland?—They are a splendid type; I don't like the Welsh ones.

2638. I was referring to the Hackneys?—I think the Hackneys are a very good type.

2639. A class of horse calculated to improve the Irish small farmers' mares?—I think so. I don't like the small Hackneys the Congested Districts Board have got as well as the large ones. I don't like the cob horse.

2640. You prefer the large ones?—Yes.

2641. Are their shoulders well made?—Some of the shoulders are most excellent; you could not wish for better shoulders.

2642. You stated to me before that you think these big breeders have it quite within their power not to buy mares that have any blood to which they object?—They can buy from men near them, and be sure of the pedigree.

2643. It is only at the fair far off that they are not sure of the breeding?—Yes.

2644. Chairman.—Have you anything more you would like to say to the Commission?—No, my lord; I don't recollect anything.

Mr. Richard Thompson, Brookeborough, County Fermanagh, examined.

2645. Chairman.—You live at Brookeborough?—Beside it.

2646. Are you engaged in farming?—I am, sir.

2647. And do you breed horses?—I do, sir.

2648. What class of horses?—I go in for breeding hunters and [illegible] harness horses.

2649. Have you got any sires of your own?—No.

2650. What kind of mares do you breed these hunters from?—The mares is very nearly clean bred, and a class as a person would choose to ride to hounds.

2651. And what horses do you put them to?—Thoroughbred horses.

2652. How long have you been breeding horses?—I have been breeding them constantly these ten years, and off and on within the last thirty years. I breed from three to six young horses every year.

2653. You have invariably used thoroughbred sires?—Yes, I breed from thoroughbred sires.

2654. You had no experience in breeding Irish any other kind?—I have no experience breeding from others but pure thoroughbreds. They sometimes chance to have a fair horse, but very often they do not.

2655. Why have you never tried, perhaps you are not fond of trying experiments?—No.

2656. Why?—I cannot afford to try experiments.

2657. Is your part of the country sufficiently supplied with suitable thoroughbred stallions?—There are a lot of them, but there is not a good one in the whole lot according to my notion. I would not call any of them good ones. They are old, wornout race horses and little horses. They could not very well get a saleable horse of them.

2658. Are there any Hackneys or Clydesdales in your part of the country?—There is no Hackney horse in my side of the country.

2659. Is there any reason why you have always used a thoroughbred sire, or did you prefer it?—I preferred it.

2660. Do you think that the Hackney or any of those other horse sires are suitable to the mares in your district?—They might do for some, but if a man has a mare suitable for a hunter I prefer giving him a thoroughbred horse.

2661. Have you formed any opinion as to the selling price of high-class carriage horses the produce of thoroughbreds, compared with the produce of Hackneys?—I have no experience of that; [illegible], I know a neighbour of mine to sell two horses together at £130. One of them was the produce of a Hackney—a Hackney of Mr. [illegible]'s, I think he was.

2662. Do you consider your district suitable to breed hunters?—I do.

2663. Do you think the introduction of the Hackney blood would be advisable?—That is a question on which I could not give a decided opinion. My experience has not been so great that it would enable me to pronounce a decided opinion.

2664. I think you said there were no such horse stallions in your district at all?—Not within seven or eight or nine miles of where I live.

2665. Is the Royal Dublin Society's Scheme at work in your district?—It is.

2666. What do you think of it?—I think it is an improvement on the old system.

2667. You think it has done good?—I think it has. If we could get a better class of stud horse I think it would be an admirable system.

2668. Are you in the habit of attending Dublin Horse Show?—Yes, occasionally. I sell all my horses there in the May.

Jan. 29, 1896.

Mr. Richard Thompson.

2669. Have you seen many of the [illegible] of the Congested Districts Board's horses?—I could not say I have ever seen one of them.

2670. Have you any opinion as to the advisability of breeding from two-year-olds?—I would not do it, nor from a three-year-old.

2671. Nor a three-year-old?—No.

2672. Do you think the breed of horses generally is improving or not in your district?—Well now I think it is at a [illegible] still. I have had as good horses thirty years ago as I would get now.

2673. Are the farmers inclined to sell their best mares and breed from the worst?—I am sorry to say they are too much inclined to it. The mistake I think is that I do not breed from young mares. I beg a [illegible] that in [illegible] breeding properly, they make a good farm mare and breed a better horse than young [illegible]. Another objection I have is that is [illegible] the breeding of horses, breeding from very young ones. If a mare is bred from a three-year-old she will not make so good a [illegible] of mare as if bred from a five-year-old. It is killing the goose for the golden egg.

2674. Do you think anything could be done to make the farmers breed from better mares?—I do not see how it could be done, except that those who do breed from good mares, when they see the results, it might be an object lesson to them, otherwise it is no use in talking to them.

2675. Lord Rathdonnell.—What is the nature of the soil in your district?—There are different varieties. About the lake side it is a heavy clay loam; further out, where I live, there is a gravelly limestone land. There is limestone, sandstone, and peat on my farm, still it is suitable for breeding, and there are [illegible] good horses on it.

2676. Where did you buy the horses you had?—[illegible] places I happened to get them, at Gorey, and I have gone south to Ballinasloe, and even as far as Clonmel. I would spend £10 looking for good ones before I would buy one that did not fit me.

2677. Is the present run of mares good in your district, not suitable to cross with thoroughbreds?—There are a good many that would be quite suitable to breed from, but unfortunately a lot of mares are breeding in harness they are not suitable for. I think a half-bred horse, or a Hackney would be better to put one of those [illegible] mares to.

2678. Is it because of lack of bone or size?—A little of both sometimes.

2679. You made use of the expression just now "half-bred horse"—What would you describe as a half-bred?—Any horse short of a thoroughbred.

2680. Do you think if a horse of that description were standing down in your neighbourhood, and breeding, [illegible] a Clydesdale, a Hackney, or a Cleveland, or anything of the sort horse type, for which of the horses would the farmers send their mares?—I think they would send them to the half-bred horse that would be nearly thoroughbred. As for their opinion of Hackneys I would not like to bind to anyone to, as I might not be doing them justice. I do not know all their minds upon it. I myself have bought colts from farmers who have bred from half-bred horses or horses nearly thoroughbred, and they produced magnificent horses. There was a horse in my neighbourhood called "Young Heron" from Lord Caledon's Old Heron—unfortunately he was castrated at five years, and we did not know his value until his services were over.

2681. How was he bred?—From one of those old celebrated Irish trotting mares, he had splendid action, very nearly like a Hackney.

2682. Have you any experience of the cross between the country mare and the Clydesdale?—I believe a good pure-bred Clydesdale would pay the farmer to breed from, if a person had a mare nearly thoroughbred, but unfortunately we have not many mares of that kind. I know there is a demand for tip-top Clydesdale horses, but our country is not the best to rear them in.

2683. Have you found that in a mare with a Clydesdale cross the bone is softer and more apt to fly?—I think the people in our country are somewhat deceived about bone. The Clydesdale has a lot of hair on his legs and big feet. When people see this they say "there is a good horse, he has a lot of bone," but when you take the hair off you will often find a thin shank below the knee—it is a very small bone. I have colts myself pure-bred, you would think their shank was small, and when you catch it under the knee you would be surprised at the thickness of it.

2684. Mr. Green.—You say that in your district they breed from hunt mares that are past their work?—Yes, or carriage mares.

2685. You mate them with thoroughbreds?—Yes, and we get a good hunter and a good harness one as well, a good horse to sell. There was one mare of that kind I bred from, and the first time I put her to a thoroughbred horse, "Rob'in the Rocks," I got a colt that I got £100 for before he was four years old, and the dealer got £30 more for him before he paid me.

2686. You think you could breed a hunter or a harness-horse from that as well as from a Hackney?—I would rather chance it.

2687. What was this horse by?—Young Heron. How was the dam bred?—That is about thirty years ago, but as far as I can find out she was an Irish mare celebrated for her fast action in harness.

2688. A sire of that description you would approve of?—It would do good in any country; it never got an unsound horse.

2689. Had good bone and substance?—Yes, beautiful quarters, fine back, and all that.

2690. You would not breed from a mare of three-year-old?—No.

Not before a four-year-old?—Yes, and then they are worth too much to breed from. If they are the right sort, that is, for a farmer like me, we are not millionaires.

2691. If a mare is good for a fair price the [illegible] not be kept for breeding?—No, that is what is injuring the breed of horses.

2692. The good ones are sold out?—Yes and that would be remedied if you have an equal share of a good type, and they will breed horses that the first year old.

2693. In the produce of a four-year-old mare?—I never saw a good one; it is not very much. [illegible] any other that I know not a good one.

2694. Mr. Thomas Robinson.—Are there any of the old Irish mares known in your district?—I do not think there is a lone [illegible] one, but there might be descendants of some, their closest [illegible] people's eye.

2695. They have practically disappeared?—They are so much mixed up with other breeds it is difficult to find them.

2696. Do you find a difficulty in getting good bred mares?—I can always get those when I want them.

2697. What size did you say you prefer for breeding?—A thoroughbred horse.

2698. For both hunters and carriage horses?—I like a [illegible] thoroughbred horse, with plenty of heart, with [illegible] action. These crosses of mine horses that are realised at two years old, sold to the country [illegible] trading, I do not think they are serviceable in this country, I would like one of the half-breds I spoke of in preference.

2699. The present style of thoroughbred sires, that is not suitable?—We have some good ones; Robin the Rocks, for instance; but some of them are thin and light.

2700. The same sire that would breed a good hunter would breed a good carriage horse?—I think so.

2701. Mr. Wrench.—Do you think it would be easy to find the thoroughbred horse you describe?—I have never done any business in buying thoroughbred horses, but it is the kind I would like.

2702. Have you seen many?—Yes, Royal Meath, [illegible] the [illegible], and a few more.

2703. That class of horses would cost a good deal of money?—They would, but I think it would pay, always a little more.

2704. Do you think the people would pay an extra service fee?—I think that if the Society gave a little assistance a good many people would use them.

2705. You attend May fair, Mr. [illegible]?—Yes, I sell most of my horses there.

2706. Have you bought many horses there?—I bought a horse there at £30 a couple of years ago, and sold him nine months after for £100.

2707. Do you remember anything of the [illegible] of [illegible] horses that used to stand there?—I saw a great many of them about this country.

2708. What kind were they?—High stepping horses but very bad about the [illegible] and [illegible]; weedy things. If not for their action they were not worth a £10 note in my opinion.

2709. Did they sell well?—They did.

2710. The [illegible] action does a great deal for the sale of a horse?—Very much.

2711. Do you think it pays better to breed hunters or harness horses?—Hunters of course, but only it is not a [illegible] the getting value for hunters, I have had as good hunters for the price of harness horses. Besides that buy hunters do not come to our district like them.

2712. But the dealers think harness horses are the [illegible]?—They do.

2713. Would you register any sires but thoroughbred horses?—I would not register them [illegible]. There would be a lot of bad horses registered, and I have no doubt there are some good horses that are not registered.

2714. I suppose you have seen instances of thoroughbred horses producing very bad stock?—I have seen them produce horses very hard to be sold.

2715. Would you be in favour of not registering any horses there who had been proved in the stud [illegible]?—I would.

2716. Have you seen any American horses?—Very little; there are not many in my neighbourhood, I saw some at [illegible].

2717. What do you think most of the horses produced in Ulster are sold?—Some of them are sold in Dublin at the Horse Show.

2718. There would be buyers?—Well, they buy carriage horses there, too.

2719. Yes, but [illegible] to the [illegible] [illegible] [illegible] to Ballinasloe for harness horses, though they are classed as hunters in the Show. My opinion is that the horse that would make a good hunter would make a good harness horse if it has action.

2720. Do you think many horses are sent to other parts of Ireland from Ulster?—Not so many as used formerly be sent to Ballinasloe and Mullingar.

2721. Most of them are sold in the north to English and Scotch dealers?—Yes.

2722. And go out of the country in that way?—Yes. The produce might go miles, sometimes in shows, in May fair.

2723. May fair is practically the best monthly fair in Ireland?—I think it is.

2724. Chairman.—You attend fairs all over the country?—I used, but I do not travel so much now as I used; I am getting too old.

2725. When did you first attend in the north?—I have not been in the south these ten years.

2726. Perhaps so that you had considerable experience of the horses all over the country?—Yes.

2727. Colonel St. Quintin.—You told us that besides what you bred you had occasionally bought some young horses?—Yes.

2728. Did those horses chiefly come from the south?—Some of them; but some I got about my own neighbourhood; some at fairs.

2729. With regard to those horses, what class of [illegible] generally did you buy them?—Whenever I have a loose [illegible] I look out for something to put in its place.

2730. But since you do prefer young horses bought in the early seasons in the south and taken up to your country and sold in the spring?—That is so.

2731. Can you tell me what cost their horses you sold during that time?—Well, it would be about fifteen shillings a week and £5 for training and all the [illegible] expenses.

2732. You always train them?—Yes; always train them to ride.

2733. Mr. Wrench.—What do you feed them on?—Good grass hay, a little oats, and a little [illegible].

2734. A little turnip?—No.

2735. Any boiled [illegible]?—No.

2736. No boiled wheat?—No. Some boiled [illegible] [illegible]; a small quantity to keep their bowels open.

2737. They are fed up well, I suppose?—I would not do it. I have a horse I give four [illegible] of oats in the day.

2738. They are kept in a dark house, I believe?—Some people who do not know their business do that; but I do not see anything to be gained by it.

2739. Colonel St. Quintin.—They are generally very well turned out when they put in May fair.

Witness.—We turn them out as well as we can. We like to show the customers what we have there. I have been selling to the same customers for the last thirty or forty years.

2740. Chairman.—Is there anything you would like to say as to how the breed of horses could be improved generally?—I think the thoroughbred horse is the best breed to get carriage horses and hunters from, and the others might be got from the half-bred or the [illegible].

2741. Col. St. Quintin.—Would you tell us who the dealer is that generally buys from you?—There are several principal buyers; Mr. [illegible], from [illegible]; Mr. [illegible], who lives at [illegible], a [illegible]; I sell also to Tom [illegible], and to Mr. [illegible], of [illegible].

2742. Do they go for hunters?—They buy them as harness horses or hunters.

2743. Could you give us any information about horses sold to foreign dealers and exported, not to England?—There is one dealer named [illegible], near [illegible]; he would sell nearly a hundred horses in a season to foreign dealers.

2744. You do not know to what countries they go?—To France, Switzerland, and Belgium; some to Italy, and I believe to Germany too. A dealer would come and buy maybe fifty horses from him at a time; another dealer might come when he had a good many. Mr. [illegible], of [illegible], sells I think, most more horses to the same class of exporter.

2745. Lord [illegible].—Do the foreign dealers have to buy a more or a [illegible] [illegible] before they are [illegible] of [illegible].

2746. Col. St. Quintin.—Some are bought by dealers and [illegible] by Governments [illegible] at a fixed price. Do you know that the Governments [illegible] [illegible]?—I should think not two of them. Some think and [illegible] [illegible] high as £30 and £35 for this class of horses they buy, [illegible]. [illegible] they [illegible] [illegible] horses and they would give from £40 to £50 for a good one, that is, if they happened to get them from their [illegible].

2747. Lord Arnold.—The bargains they buy at Dublin?—Yes.

2748. Col. St. Quintin.—Do you know about the Dublin dealers?—No.

2749. Mr. Wrench.—About the class of horses sold by Mr. Maguire and Mr. Robinson, are they mostly troopers and [illegible] troopers prices?—The greater part of them, yes.

2750. They are about £40?—Yes; but there is always [illegible] in [illegible] for a better class of horses too; some of them are three-year-old colts, of course they [illegible] [illegible] [illegible] [illegible] [illegible] they go to their [illegible], [illegible] [illegible] [illegible] and [illegible] [illegible] them back again.

Mr. T. A. [illegible], [illegible] House, Dunfanaghy, County Donegal, examined.

2751. Chairman.—You live in the County Donegal?—Yes, in the north-west of the county.

2752. You carry on the occupation of a farmer?—Yes.

2753. You are a land agent also?—Yes, I have some agencies.

2754. You are well acquainted with the north-western portion of the county?—Yes, I know nearly a whole barony. I know the district from Gweedore to Letterkenny, that is about thirty miles.

2755. You breed horses yourself?—I do.

2756. Do you consider your district a suitable one for horse-breeding?—We are in a thoroughly congested district.

2757. That is not quite an answer to the question whether it is suitable for horse-breeding?—In the parts of it away west towards Gweedore it is not suitable for horse-breeding, the land and grass are poor.

2758. What is the general nature of the soil in your district?—Where I live myself it is a strong clay soil with gravel through it, and as I live near the sea shore it is very sandy.

2759. What is the class of horse in the country?—They are nearly all ponies, light ponies. There are some few exceptions. The better class of farmers have heavier and stronger horses.

2760. What class of horse do you breed, yourself?—My horses are all between 15 and 16 hands high. I keep five horses. I always keep one brood mare, and I am obliged to send to Letterkenny, Derry, Strabane, or Raphoe to a horse. My valuation qualification charges me too high a fee for the Congested Districts Board's horses. I go elsewhere.

2761. You breed them for sale?—Some for sale and some for my own use on the farm.

2762. The greater number of the farmers in your district have small holdings?—Yes, and avail themselves principally of the Congested Districts Board's horses.

2763. What class of horse do they require for their farm work?—They are almost all from about 13½ or 14 hands high, the horse of the locality.

2764. In your opinion would a heavier horse be more suitable?—The Congested Districts Board's horse has been very much availed of, and I think there is no inclination for a heavier horse.

2765. What class of horse is most suitable for the use of the farmers in your district?—I do believe the Hackneys are very suitable for our horses, which are light little mares and [illegible] limited.

2766. You have not availed yourself of the Congested Districts Board's stallions?—No, I have not.

2767. Why?—The fee you pay depends on the valuation qualification.

2768. What fee would you have to pay?—£2, [illegible]; consequently I do not pay that. I went further.

2769. You have sent your mares some distance?—Not less than twenty miles. This year we have another horse in the district, and I have not sent so far.

2770. Have you any objection to say what fee you paid? You sent them to a thoroughbred horse?—The trustees of Lord Leitrim have brought a pure bred Suffolk Punch from England, and I send to that horse, a good many others went as well.

2771. You sent all your mares to a thoroughbred horse [illegible] of late years?—I was not very successful when I did, and I did not send again. I have very [illegible] to send, and a good deal of expense.

2772. Do you prefer the Suffolk Punch to the Hackney, or do you send to the Suffolk Punch because the fee is less? Supposing the fee to be equal, which would you prefer?—If I had a Hackney close enough, I would send to a Hackney at first or any horse. The first horse we got was a small horse and did not breed large. The second was a large horse, and had a white face. He stamped some of the foals with this, and I think there is an objection to him on that account, but he breeds good horses. I had experience of the Suffolk Punch on the Leitrim Estate. He did well, and we are trying it again.

2773. Are there suitable stallions in the district?—Quite the reverse, nothing but weeds, except the Congested Districts Board horses.

2774. Do you know whether the horses of the Congested Districts Board stallions get bigger prices than others?—Yes, larger than what was paid before they came.

2775. In answer to one of the questions we sent out to you, you said the native [illegible] active, clean, and hardy, the want of size being the principal drawback?—Yes.

2776. You think larger horses might be reared?—I think so.

2777. How long has there been a Congested Districts Board stallion in the neighbourhood?—1892 was the first year.

2778. What was there before then?—Just the greatest cross-bred mixture of the country, a good deal crossed with the Clydesdale.

2779. And if you had your choice what breed would you select as the most suitable for your district?—Something stronger and bigger than the Hackney for my district.

2780. For the district generally?—I think the Hackneys will answer fairly well in north-west Donegal.

2781. Do you know what becomes of the young stock when sold?—The majority of them are taken out of the country. Some of them are sent as far as Milford, twenty-four miles away, and sold.

2782. I take it that as you send your own mares to the Suffolk Punch you consider his produce satisfactory?—Yes, from the experience I have noticed of the same kind of horse before. They are strong, and are cleaner limbed than the Clydesdale. They have good action sometimes too.

2783. In answer to question 26, you recommend breeding from pure bred horses; what do you mean by a pure bred horse?—I include the Suffolk Punch as pure bred. We are [illegible] obliged to breed from the Clydesdales with our mares. We get a few crops from them. At six quarters old they get a fair price in the fairs.

2784. By pure bred horse you mean a pure bred horse of any breed?—Yes.

2785. Have you any experience in your district of the produce of a small thoroughbred horse?—We have very little experience of the produce of a thoroughbred horse where I live. In Raphoe and Strabane I have seen them, that is in the district which is the richer part of Donegal.

2786. Have you sufficient experience to be able to compare the produce of a small thoroughbred horse with the produce of a Hackney stallion?—No; because the thoroughbreds are so seldom used there.

2787. Is it the custom of the farmers to sell their best fillies?—I am sorry to say it is. The best fillies go out of the place.

2788. Can you suggest any way in which that might be prevented?—Except by giving them premiums for good mares, that is all I can suggest.

2789. Do you buy mares yourself in other parts of the country?—No; I get one or two brood mares; I have one from Clones, County Monaghan, at present.

2790. What do you sell your horses at?—I have got £50 for some of my horses.

2791. Do you sell them as carriage horses?—Generally farming and driving horses.

2792. I think you said there was an admixture of Clydesdale blood?—A good deal, in the locality in which I live.

2793. Where is the Clydesdale stallion?—The late Lord Leitrim owned him; he was sold before the Suffolk Punch came.

June 12, 1900.

Mr. T. A. Lagan.

2794. Do you approve of that breed?—They have bone and substance, they have very well, and are sometimes fairly good sleeping horses.

2795. The work generally on the farms in your district is I believe of a light character?—Very light indeed.

2796. Would it be any advantage to the farmers for their own work to breed heavier horses than there now is the country?—Well, I can hardly tell; they seem quite satisfied with the Hackneys even. they are in the country, but the bettor class of farmers do go in for breeding to get bigger horses.

2797. For the advantage of breeding bigger horses for sale or agricultural purposes, it would be for sale they would breed them.

2798. Lord Rathdonnell.—The part I saw the district called the Rosses?—Yes.

2799. Is that your district?—I happen to be agent for Lord [illegible], it is near the one district, and any doing there longer we [illegible] after a [illegible].

2800. Is it near you?—between thirty and forty miles away.

2801. The nature of the soil where you live is quite different from the nature of the soil in the Rosses?—It is a good deal better, there is very poor soil in the Rosses.

2802. We had [illegible] yesterday that all the farming work is done by hand in the Rosses?—Yes, digging. Very few horses or [illegible] [illegible] the Rosses.

2803. That is not the case in your district?—No.

2804. What is the usual size of the breed horses in your district?—From thirteen and a half to fourteen and a half hands; some few go to fifteen.

2805. Are they ponies or cobs or small cart horses?—I would call them cobs more than anything else; there are ponies as well; they are good cob horses the majority of them.

2806. That is the class of animal you work on your farm?—Yes.

2807. In the soil not so light fairly is a fair, strong, dry soil a [illegible], but towards the west end that district is [illegible], and nothing but pretty mountainy soil, as towards the Rosses and Gweedore a boggy soil.

2808. These thick cobby animals are they adapted for working the farms?—They are most useful horses.

2809. You do not want these to [illegible] to sires?—The farmers who breed for sale would prefer them in [illegible] also to gain a better price.

2810. Are they sturdy, quick, ponies?—They are sharp, hardy horses, and there is great endurance in them. There are no better hardy little horses.

2811. Have you ever thought of using a Barb or an Arab?—I understand there was an Arab sent to the Rosses but we never got one.

2812. Do you think it would be a suitable cross?—No, the late Earl of Leitrim got an Arab there and his stock was a remarkable failure.

2813. What about the produce of that stallion; did people breed from that?—I never knew anyone to breed from it. They were sold out of the place; they were not a success by any means.

2814. Mr. Ganly.—What sort of a sire would you recommend to mate with your mares?—I think if we had a strong Hackney it would do well enough with our mares.

2815. Have you any experience of the Hackney?—Only what I saw of the Congested Districts Board's the last time.

2816. How long is that?—Since 1893.

2817. Have you seen any of the produce sold?—Number of them.

2818. What price do they bring?—The yearlings bring £8 to £9, the two-year-olds will go from £9 to £10 and £12; a very good one would go £1 higher; the three-year-olds would go to £16, and exceptionally good ones as high as £20.

2819. Sir Thomas Esmonde.—What price do the farmers of your district pay for the service of a horse?—About £1, or £1 2s. 6d. perhaps.

2820. They have no difficulty in getting a suitable horse at that figure?—No, but there is the discount as put in him.

2821. How is that?—Landlords would take cheaper place; the breeders are English sales from where I live.

2822. Do find in your immediate neighbourhood there is a want of horses?—There are some twenty horses in the locality that get two shillings; some places will go in high because they are married at high.

2823. You think these horses get as much profit because they are so cheap?—I do; I know it.

2824. Mr. Wrench.—I believe there are very large numbers of horses bred by the people in the Donegal you live in, and of Gweedore?—There are a great many.

2825. They use the horses chiefly for carrying sea-weed, manure, and turf, and carrying themselves in almost?—Yes, they bring all their [illegible] in panniers, and bring stuff to market on the horse's back.

2826. That is very severe on horses?—Yes, it is very severe on the horses, but they do it.

2827. There is a great deal of work for a horse there?—Yes.

2828. Horse-breeding is an industry there?—Yes, largely, in my district.

2829. And the sale of the foal is a considerable item in the receipts of every farmer?—It is it is.

2830. You do not think it possible to get those people to give up horse breeding?—No.

2831. Can you suggest any horse more suitable than a Hackney for improving those mares?—I think if you had a horse of a larger kind; Hackneys are nice horses, but they would like a larger horse.

2832. Would the produce of a Suffolk Punch not be too large to work on the small farms in the congested District?—No; I would say it would be too much going west in Gweedore, but not in the other direction to Letterkenny and Milford.

2833. Your experience of horses got by the Congested Districts Board, I suppose, is with reference to Carrigart and Dunfanaghy?—Yes, and so far as Dunfanaghy district; the stallions of the Board were there too.

2834. As a matter of fact, I believe people have got much higher prices for their produce than before the horses went to that district?—Yes.

2835. Do you remember any of the country stallions in the district before?—I do; I remember back for twenty-five years.

2836. Were they not very common, underbred, miserable looking brutes, generally bad Clydesdales, with the native mare of the country?—Yes.

2837. The reason they used those sires was simply to get bigger foals?—Yes; and they come to market earlier. A three-quarter Clydesdale they would plough with in the spring and then try to sell. They generally work their horses that they breed at three-quarter, nearing two years old.

2838. It is necessary in supplying any horses to improve the breed of that district, to have hardy horses to stand a great deal of hardship?—It would require them. The mares are in very good, except in some places. They are certainly hardy horses what we have in that district.

2839. I suppose in a great part of that district the horses are housed, they are housed with the people in the house?—Yes; and under the conditions with the poorer people, I am sorry to say.

2840. I think you said Lord Leitrim's experience with the Arab was not a success?—Yes, that is my opinion.

2841. And if you got an Arab stallion the people would not use that?—I do not think they would. He might be better than what Lord Leitrim's people had, but there was no success breeding from him.

2842. Lord Rathdonnell.—Was he generally a good stamp?—He had a tendency to breed very small foals.

2843. Chairman.—I do not know that we have

O

[illegible] quite get what your own opinion is as to the breed of stallion best suitable for your district? You have told us you cannot compare the produce of the Hackney with the thoroughbred in your own district, as there is no thoroughbred horse?—There is no thoroughbred horse nearer than twenty miles.

2944. Supposing the Board provided a sound thoroughbred stallion and a Hackney stallion, have you any strong opinion which they would prefer?—I believe they would have the Hackney stallion. Our mares are too light to match with the thoroughbred horse.

2945. You think that would be the general opinion of the farmers of the district?—Yes.

Mr. James Dunlop, V.S.

JAMES DUNLOP, V.S., Downpatrick, examined.

2946. CHAIRMAN.—You are, I believe, a veterinary surgeon, living at Downpatrick?—I am.

2947. How long have you lived there, or in that locality?—Between thirty and forty years.

2948. Are there many horses bred in that district?—Yes; a great number.

2949. Do you breed horses yourself?—No, I don't [illegible]

[illegible]

2881. I mean if you were to consider how the breed could be best improved, would you turn your attention rather to the preservation or introduction of better mares or better stallions?—Better mares. I would try to improve the mares; there is no want of good stallions with us.

2882. You say the prices of horses are very low?—Very low.

2883. Since when?—They have been falling for the last four years, and they are lower now than ever.

2884. Has the price got so low that it has ceased to be profitable to breed?—I believe it is unprofitable now, unless with a particularly good mare.

2885. You mean that the very high-class hunters [illegible] can still be bred profitably, but an ordinary general utility horse cannot?—No; it cannot be bred profitably now.

2886. And you think that, I understand, a good deal to the importation of foreign horses?—Yes.

2887. Have you seen many of these foreign horses?—Yes, I have seen a few of them landed in Belfast, [illegible], they were the Canadian horses.

2888. Where are they landed generally?—I think they are landed at Liverpool and brought across to Belfast.

2889. What is your opinion of those?—I was told by the dealers they are not going to bring any more, they certainly will not compare with the Irish horses, [illegible].

2890. Are they sold as Canadian horses?—They are sold as Canadian horses.

2891. Do the buyers know their origin?—They do.

2892. No claim to any distinction?—No [illegible].

2893. Then the deterioration in the value of horses that you speak of would not be affected in any way by these foreign horses, whether branded or [illegible] in any way?—I don't think it would, but it might prevent people from breeding from them, and if these passed into other hands they might be sold again for Irish horses; it would [illegible] the character of the Irish horse [illegible] if they were breeding.

2894. You think the first buyer who recognised them as being Canadian or American horses might pass it off [illegible] as an Irish horse?—He might.

2895. In what way do you think they are inferior to the native bred ones?—They don't stand the journey so well. I am speaking about them [illegible], though. I have experience of one myself. I put it off the road to a very short [illegible] they did not stand the road so well as this [illegible].

2896. The horses you have seen, are mostly landed, they have not [illegible]?—There might be something in that.

2897. Speaking in your professional capacity have you any fault to find with them?—They look very well, some of those horses, particularly well.

2898. Can you suggest any way in which this competition could be legitimately stopped?—No, that is just what I complain.

2899. Has the breed generally improved in your district of late years?—No, they have not improved. There are more bad horses in the district now than I saw twenty-five years ago.

2900. How do you account for that?—Farmers selling all their good mares.

2901. Where do they sell them to; do they go abroad or where?—They mostly go to England and Scotland, the dealers buy them and take them across there, and sometimes they take good mares themselves across to the English fairs.

2902. I gather that you attribute the deterioration in the breed a good deal to the mares. Have you anything you can suggest to induce farmers to keep their best mares in the country?—I think those prizes for [illegible] giving for the mares is inducing some to keep better mares, it might be a check upon the deterioration.

2903. Do you think there has been a greater tendency of late years among farmers to sell their best mares and breed from the worst than there was in the past than there has been previously?—There was always that tendency, I think. It is intensified now on account of the agricultural depression, the farmers are very depressed, and hard owing to the bad prices.

2904. Could you describe the general class of mares in your district?—There are a good many mares with a good deal of the Clydesdale blood, about 15 hands; and then you have mares with a little more breeding in them, about 15.2, and so on; and then you have a lot of useful mares got by thoroughbred horses, and lighter; they have not been sold, and the farmers keep them for breeding; and they will put them first time to a heavier horse if they want to breed again, perhaps a Clydesdale horse; and when light next time they send to the thoroughbred horse and then sell them as well as they can. They have a horse very well [illegible].

2905. Lord Rathdonnell.—How many stallions have you kept usually at your place?—I have five stallions just now.

2906. What are they?—I have three Hackneys, one thoroughbred, and one young Yorkshire trotting horse; but these last three years I have tried some of them with Hackneys on account of the depression in breeding.

2907. Have you bred many horses yourself?—Six [illegible] for Hackneys.

2908. You are a Scotchman, I think?—Yes, sir.

2909. What district of Scotland?—Ayrshire.

2910. Have you any experience of breeding there?—Yes.

2911. What class of horses?—They were mostly all Clydesdales in the district I came from.

2912. Have you ever lived in the south of Ireland?—No; but I have lived in Norfolk. I was in practice in Norfolk for some time when a young man.

2913. Then I suppose you came in contact with the Norfolk trotting horse and Hackney?—Yes, but I could not say that [illegible] on the Norfolk; they have some breeding in their foundation.

2914. But you have no experience of all of the south of Ireland or the class of mares bred there?—No.

2915. I suppose you have seen some south of Ireland sires that have been brought northward by buyers?—Remarkably few.

2916. Have you ever sold any of the produce of your Hackney stallions?—No; they are young ones.

2917. Have you ever tried to sell any?—Well, I tried to sell one filly which was two years old; but I did not get a sufficient offer for her.

2918. That is all you have tried?—Yes.

2919. You mentioned, I think, that there are half-bred stallions standing in your district, County Donegal?—Yes.

2920. What class of horse is that?—They are generally about 16 hands or 15.1, and, as a rule, they are very good-looking horses. There is a class of horses called the Hackneys, and it is remarkable how they have [illegible] during the last three years.

2921. Do you know anything about the breeding of those, how they are bred, what strain?—Those Hackney horses are got by half-bred mares.

2922. How was Hackney bred?—They are not what you would call a violent cross, for years they have been bred very much of the same type.

2923. What breeding?—If you go to the foundation it is thoroughbred and Clydesdale; but for the last [illegible] years they have not made a violent cross. The [illegible] of them half-bred horses and not produced by a violent cross.

2924. Then that is not the Hackney quite?—Yes; the Hackneys have been put to half-bred mares very much like themselves, and they have been able to maintain their characteristics.

2925. I thought you said the Hackney cross was a good cross?—It is coupled like the half-bred.

2926. And that is a cross you think superior of—

Mar. 16, 1896. Mr. James [illegible], &c.

Jan. 1[illegible], 18[illegible]. — Mr. James Dunlop, V.S.

Clydesdale and thoroughbred?—Clydesdale and thoroughbred would be the foundation if you would go far enough back.

2927. Mr. Cairns.—What are the mares to which the Harkaways would be put?—The Harkaways are about 16 hands and nearly all chestnut in colour, and they never keep one that does not come true to the type.

2928. Lord Rathdonnell.—May I ask you how Harkaway was bred?—There was an original blood horse; but Mr. Farrell will be able to give you an answer, as he has one.

2929. I understand from you that Harkaway sprang from a Clydesdale and a thoroughbred originally?—They always go back to the Clydesdale to get strength. If you continued to breed to the blood they would get too light, and all our horses would go back to the Clydesdale and thoroughbred.

2930. Chairman.—Was not Harkaway a thoroughbred?—The original Harkaway; but that is many generations away.

2931. How do they get their name?—They were in the country when I came.

2932. Lord Rathdonnell.—Do I understand you to say that you don't approve of the Clydesdale and that class of heavy horse crossing?—The Clydesdales are rather rough. I would rather increase their strength by something finer than the Clydesdale—something like the Cleveland Bay—and then they would get the strength up without having so much roughness as the Clydesdale.

2933. Do you consider that the Clydesdale, although his bone is, perhaps, to the eye bigger than the thoroughbred horse, do you consider his bone is as good as the thoroughbred bone?—The bone is not so good, but they have more bone; it is thicker.

2934. You mean to say the same amount of bone in the one would weigh heavier in the other?—In the cart horse it is more spongy, more liable to fly. The Clevelands have the hardest bone of any horse of weight, their bone is nearly as hard as the thoroughbred, and the cross with them and bloods are about the most handsome horses. You will see them in Yorkshire.

2935. And you maintain that the bone of the Cleveland is equal to the bone of the thoroughbred?—No, it comes next to it in quality.

2936. You have not bred Clydesdales, have you?—I was bred on a farm where I saw them bred in Scotland.

2937. Have you any experience of the breeding of them?—I was bred up on a farm where they were bred.

2938. Did you find any difficulty as regards their feet, and the bones connected with their feet?—No, the Clydesdales have much better feet than the Shires.

2939. I did not compare them, but did you find any difficulty with their feet?—A little more grease than a thoroughbred horse.

2940. Are they at all liable to side bones?—All heavy horses are liable to side bones.

2941. Then there is more difficulty in keeping a heavy horse on his feet than a lighter animal?—Yes.

2942. You have heard certain half-bred horses mentioned or seen in the evidence given that certain half-bred horses would be acceptable to dealers as sires?—Yes, they patronise them very well.

2943. That is with clean legs, good bone, nice action, and so on?—Yes.

2944. If a horse of that description, without any heavy cart-horse blood in him was standing in the neighbourhood of Downpatrick, for instance, do you suppose the farmers of that district would patronise that horse in preference to the heavy cart-horse?—It would depend on what kind of a mare they had. If they had a very light mare, and wanted, perhaps, a heavy worker on the farm, they would patronise a Clydesdale horse; another time if they wanted to breed a hunter horse they would go to the half-bred one.

2945. Still you yourself would prefer the lighter and sharper horse with good sound bone and action to the Clydesdale?—Yes.

2946. Are there many horses sold out of your district?—Yes, a good number.

2947. At what age are they sold?—They are sold principally as four-year-olds to the dealers.

2948. Where do they come from, are they bred in the country or brought into it?—Mostly bred there; they breed a great number there.

2949. Have you any experience of what they call the Norfolk trotting horses?—Yes.

2950. Then the horses you refer to are not [illegible] until four years?—A good many of the better class of farmers keep their horses until they are four years old, since they have [illegible], and there are other farmers buy horses at three-year-old, feed them during the winter, and sell them at four years.

2951. Where are they sold?—They are sold to dealers to go to England.

2952. From the farm or the fairs?—The better class of horses are sold on the farm, the dealers or their agents come round and buy the horses there, and the remainder go to the fairs.

2953. Where do they chiefly go to, where are they chiefly bought for?—Most of them go to England.

2954. Do any come North?—Very few; mostly all to England.

2955. I suppose the dealers buy the [illegible], and leave the [illegible] to [illegible]?

2956. That happens in the case of mares?—In [illegible].

2957. Where do they find their mares for keeping up the breed, do they breed from the [illegible] ones?—Yes, they breed from all kinds of mares.

2958. Mr. F. Bosanquet.—Are there any horses bought by foreign dealers in your part of the country?—They come to the [illegible] and buy horses in Downpatrick fair.

2959. What price would they give?—A [illegible] over [illegible].

2960. Do they buy many [illegible]?—Some times they buy a good many, other times you don't see them for awhile again.

2961. I suppose you have no means of knowing what country they buy for?—[illegible]

2962. You spoke of American horses, what is your experience of American horses?—My experience of [illegible] is that they are rather light, [illegible] and the [illegible] power of their horses.

2963. What are they used for?—The heavier class of them for vans, the lighter class for gigs.

2964. Have you seen any of them used [illegible]?—No.

2965. They would not suit carriages?—Yes, the American trotting horse would suit a carriage very well.

2966. But you don't get many American [illegible] horses?—No, they are seldom [illegible].

2967. You think [illegible]?—All the animals I have seen [illegible].

2968. Are they as useful as our horses?—Yes, they are fairly sound, I suppose it would not pay them to send unsound ones.

2969. Legs good?—Fairly good legs to look at them, don't wear as well as they look.

2970. But you think that the importation of these horses has injuriously affected the horse trade?—[illegible]

2971. Have you any idea what the number of American horses imported would be annually?—[illegible]

2972. Do you know any of these horses bought by the English Government?—[illegible]

[illegible] Mr. [illegible] — I think you said you have been over [illegible] years [illegible] — [illegible]

[illegible] belonging to Lord [illegible] "[illegible]" [illegible]

[illegible] Have you [illegible] of the [illegible] — [illegible]

[illegible] But you have had experience of Hackneys, you say, when you were in Norfolk? — Yes.

[illegible] Is it your experience that they are both [illegible] or not? — I think the Norfolk horses are rather [illegible] than the Yorkshire.

[illegible] Do you think the [illegible] horses are at all [illegible] in [illegible] power? — I do not.

[illegible] Would you be inclined to register any other [illegible] the thoroughbred horses that are [illegible]? — Yes.

[illegible] What would you register? — I would register a horse [illegible] if he [illegible] is a good [illegible] in shape, I would register him as a [illegible] [illegible].

[illegible] Would you register a horse [illegible] that [illegible] to be a good [illegible]? — [illegible] would be better if [illegible], but [illegible] would be a difficult thing to do.

[illegible] Would you also register [illegible] Hackneys and Clydesdales and [illegible] horses? — Yes, and I would [illegible] prizes to [illegible] that [illegible] until they were [illegible] to [illegible] their [illegible].

[illegible] And you believe that a horse bred in Ireland [illegible] England, [illegible] — I have seen [illegible] horses in Yorkshire than I have ever seen in Ireland.

[illegible] To what do you attribute that? — They [illegible] which you see in a Yorkshire farmer [illegible] Hackney mare, [illegible] a Hackney horse, [illegible] Cleveland horse, [illegible] that [illegible] better.

[illegible] The Yorkshire [illegible] a good deal [illegible] for it.

[illegible] What is the size of the farms [illegible] of the farmers who breed horses chiefly in your district? — [illegible] of them that have not more than fifteen acres would breed [illegible], but those that have [illegible] would [illegible] three or four [illegible] for breeding.

[illegible] Do you think that it would be possible [illegible] those smaller people from breeding [illegible], they have a great taste for breeding horses?

[illegible] Then you think it was [illegible] to giving them [illegible] of [illegible] like larger people? — Certainly.

[illegible] And you think the people who occupy the small farms are competent to form an opinion as to what horses suit their [illegible]? — They are [illegible] judges of horses.

[illegible] Have you thought at all how you would take the opinion of those people with regard to any public grant made for the improvement of horses, how would you ascertain from them what kind of horse they would like? — [illegible]

[illegible] They do [illegible] the [illegible] — Yes, [illegible]

[illegible] And of your [illegible] which [illegible] — [illegible] "[illegible]" horse, [illegible] Yorkshire Hackney by [illegible] has been very largely patronised.

[illegible] Are his [illegible] good? — Yes, very good, very [illegible].

[illegible] And you think that a Hackney [illegible] is more [illegible] to [illegible] the [illegible] than a thoroughbred horse? — Yes.

[illegible] I think you said that you had seen these horses [illegible] selling at a very small price lately? — Yes, I have seen [illegible] selling at [illegible] price of late than ever I saw since I came to Ireland.

[illegible] What do they [illegible] horses of all kinds? — All kinds of them are selling [illegible], especially light ones.

[illegible] Is it a fact that the light mares by thoroughbred horses [illegible] by [illegible] to breed [illegible], [illegible] horses they have been [illegible]? — Yes.

[illegible] Do you think that the thoroughbred [illegible] is as likely to produce action [illegible] as a Hackney? — No.

[illegible] What is your opinion as to the condition or soundness of horses in your district, do you think [illegible] in [illegible] or the reverse? — I don't think it is [illegible], the stallions are [illegible] sound.

[illegible] You think the stallions are [illegible] sound? — They are [illegible] to the mares.

[illegible] Would you be in favour of [illegible] stallions [illegible] licence [illegible]? — Yes, it would be a very good thing.

[illegible] You think there would be [illegible] in favour of the public? — Yes, [illegible] that [illegible] they [illegible] — [illegible] him.

[illegible] Is there practically a class of stallions [illegible] in the early season they bring them out [illegible].

[illegible] And the [illegible] whether the stallion is sound or not? — They [illegible] whether the [illegible]

[illegible] You think [illegible] that the mares in your district [illegible] thoroughbred horse would [illegible] — They would.

[illegible] CHAIRMAN. — Those farmers you speak of who sell horses [illegible] — They are mostly [illegible] to the [illegible], and [illegible] they go up to [illegible] and [illegible] them and bring them [illegible] and [illegible] them.

[illegible] They don't come from the south, any of them? — Some of them might come from the south, but they are mostly bred in the county Down.

[illegible] About these foreign horses, I am not quite clear that I understand exactly what your opinion is. Do you think that the price of horses has been [illegible] down in your district by the general [illegible] in horses, that is to say, by the importation of foreign horses into Ireland? — Oh, certainly.

[illegible] Not specially by the importation of foreign horses into your district? — No.

[illegible] [illegible] — No, [illegible].

[illegible] Then it is merely the general effect upon the market that you complain of? — Yes.

[illegible] And you don't think a sound thoroughbred [illegible] for your district? — Oh, yes, they are very [illegible], they would [illegible] good [illegible], but they will get a [illegible] light [illegible]. When they come [illegible] they will [illegible] [illegible] they always [illegible] a [illegible] of [illegible].

[illegible] Lord [illegible]. — You say that the Yorkshire Hackney is better than the Norfolk? — Yes; there are a great many of the Norfolk Hackneys [illegible] of little [illegible] and [illegible] of their [illegible].

[illegible] But they don't [illegible] — [illegible] of the Yorkshire is [illegible] than is [illegible] in the [illegible] of [illegible].

[illegible] You [illegible] in Norfolk, [illegible] in Norfolk.

[illegible]

Mr. James Dunlop, V.S.

3016. Have you ever lived in Yorkshire?—No; but I have spent sometimes a fortnight at a time among the shows.

3017. But you have no practical experience of the Yorkshire Hackney except what you bought yourself?—I have bought hundreds of them in Yorkshire.

3018. [illegible]

3019. When you talk of the Yorkshire bred horse, in what class do you refer, [illegible] Hackneys out of the question?—They breed all kinds in Yorkshire, hackneys, Yorkshire coaching horses, Clevelands, and Shires.

3020. Now as regards the hunter class of horse that you have had experience of in Yorkshire, have you ever heard it said that the Yorkshire hunter has deteriorated in later years?—No. I went over several years to see the Great Yorkshire Show, and I observed in every year an improvement in the Yorkshire Hackney breed, they are gaining more quality.

3021. Hackney?—Yes, an improvement in the Hackney.

3022. I spoke as regards hunters?—I have no experience except at the shows, and they certainly showed very good hunting horses at the shows.

3023. But you never heard that the hunting class had deteriorated there?—I saw it in the newspapers yesterday, that is all I know of it.

3024. Have the produce of your Hackneys fetched high prices?—They have brought very good prices; not so high as some of the thoroughbreds and not so low as some of the thoroughbreds have gone; not so many high ones.

3025. What age are they sold at?—They are sold at four year old.

3026. The produce of your present stallions?—Yes.

3027. What prices did they fetch?—The first ones of them brought £50 and fifty good mares about £30, but the prices have been falling ever since the produce of my Hackney horses came into the country; the prices have been gradually [illegible]; the depression in prices commenced as the produce was coming into market, so it was unfortunate.

3028. [illegible]—The prices are not nearly so good as when I bought those horses first; if the prices had been maintained those horses would have been most successful.

3029. You say a great many horses for hunting purposes are bought from Mullingar and other fairs you consider this north, don't you?—Yes.

3030. Colonel Sir [illegible].—Could you, do you think, with any cross, breed a weighty draught horse in your country?—Yes, if you take the heaviest of the mares and put those to a Shire or Clydesdale or the heavier class of horse they could breed a weighty horse.

3031. Would it be one of those heavier dray horses or a light van horse?—None of our mares would breed heavy enough for the brewers, but they would breed van horses.

3032. And light van horses?—They might breed a heavy one.

3033. And bus horses [illegible].

3034. You would not get much beyond that, would you?—No.

3035. You say there has been a great falling off in the demand for horses on account of these American horses in the price, and therefore that practically means the demand—do you think that this utility horse is being interfered with by the cycling?—Yes, I do.

3036. Then you think this may possibly the demand for these medium draft horses will get less instead of more?—That will depend on how the automobiles are perfected.

3037. But there is undoubtedly a falling off in the price and demand for the lighter draught horses?—Oh, a very serious falling off in prices that has been going on for the last four years or more—the last four years.

3038. Mr. [illegible].—Do you know any of the prices which these American horses fetched at the sale at Islington which you attended?—Oh, yes; about £30.

3039. What ages were they?—About four or five years old.

3040. Was there any other country exhibited horses for sale?—[illegible] ponies.

3041. What were they like?—Miserable looking animals.

3042. What did they fetch?—Very low prices.

3043. Mr. Weston.—Do you think that a Hackney stallion crossed with the light mares in your country would tend to produce a stronger and more useful mare from which valuable animals could be bred afterwards?—Yes, I do.

3044. Do you think other stallions are more calculated than a Hackney to produce that result?—From a pure bred Cleveland you would get a heavier animal with more quality, but you would lack the beautiful action of the Hackney.

3045. Is the Cleveland at all as well ribbed up as the Hackney?—Not as a rule, but they are lengthier and more muscular in their quarters.

3046. More blood quarters?—They are lengthier than blood horses with longer quarters.

3047. You have been among the Yorkshire farmers and seen their studs?—I have.

3048. And found them an intelligent people?—A very canny people.

3049. Do you know why they have begun to give up breeding the coaching horse and to breed Hackneys to a greater extent?—It is because of the showy action of the Hackneys; there is more demand for the Hackneys.

3050. They have given up the coaching horse, a type of horse that Messrs. East used to buy, because they found it pays better to breed Hackneys?—There is more demand for them.

3051. You said the price of your horses had fallen for the last four years, I suppose that applies to all horses?—Yes.

3052. And other horses have fallen in a corresponding or greater degree?—Yes.

3053. And the horses below that class very often are almost unsaleable at present?—Yes, almost unsaleable.

3054. Chaplin.—You know Yorkshire pretty well?—I have been through a great deal of it.

3055. I gather from what you said, that although you have seen it in the newspapers stated that the Yorkshire hunter breed has deteriorated that that is not your opinion from your personal observation?—Not at the shows—they show very good hunters.

3056. Assuming that these motor cars and such inventions are successful, and that the demand continues to decrease for these general utility horses, what breed of horses do you think would take their place in your district?—I don't quite comprehend your question.

3057. Well, you said that the demand is falling off for the general utility horse, but I suppose you would admit that the demand for very high class hunters and carriage horses generally is not falling off, is it?—No; I believe that they will have to breed from their very best mares to supply a good class.

3058. In your district if the demand decreases it will cease to pay to breed the general utility horse?—It has ceased to pay to breed a low class of horse.

3059. What horse could be bred with advantage?—The very highest class of horse, a hunter or carriage horse.

3060. Would your district be suitable to produce that kind of horse?—Yes.

3061. And would you recommend the Hackney horse as the best sire for the production of that class?—For the production of the harness horse I would, but for hunters I would prefer the thoroughbred horse.

3062. Lord Ampthill.—Have you got the mares in your district at present to produce this high class of hunter and harness horse?—We have a few mares, but not many.

3063. But the general run of the mares?—They would not be good enough.

3064. CHAIRMAN.—You said in reply to Mr. Wrench that, taken in Yorkshire, they have to breed the Hackneys because it pays better, that is to say there is more demand I suppose for a horse with showy action?—Yes.

3065. In your opinion is the Hackney principally valuable on account of the showy action, or is it valuable also on account of other qualities?—Yes, he is very good both for quality and endurance and action; the Yorkshire Hackney is the best I think.

3066. Lord BATTERSBY.—With regard to high class harness horses, have Messrs. East and Messrs. Wimbush stated that they did not like the cross of the Hackney, and preferred the thoroughbred cross in their high class harness horses, would you take their opinion or not?—I would not.

3067. Although they spend several thousands of pounds in the country, you would not be afraid of losing these thousands?—No, I would not.

3068. This is the letter from Messrs. East and Co. —"Replying to your letter of the 1st inst., we do not think we can do better than repeat the letter we wrote last year about this time in answer to a similar inquiry, which was as follows:—In our opinion the introduction of Hackney stallions into Ireland for the purpose of breeding carriage horses would be most disastrous in its effects to the business in young horses now done by that country. We believe it would result in a greatly inferior stamp of horse being produced unsuitable for carriage horses such as we require. And our experience with regard to Yorkshire horses confirms this, as we find since the Hackney stallions were introduced there that we can obtain but a very small number of our horses from that country. We hold that it is most essential the sire should be thoroughbred, but with good action rather than speed." Now, Messrs. Wimbush and Co. say—"We beg to acknowledge the receipt of your letter. The fine handsome, well-bred bay carriage horse for which Yorkshire was so famous in our recollection, is very rarely to be met with now, while formerly nearly all our best London carriage horses came from Yorkshire and were bred there. We attribute this decline to the introduction of Hackney stallions, and we should be sorry to see them introduced into Ireland, as that country still produces a fair number of first-class carriage horses, and if Hackney stallions take the place of the thoroughbred sire, we have no doubt but that a similar decline of valuable carriage horses will be the result." They spend a great deal of money in Ireland in buying. Do you think is there any fear of our losing that money if we use the Hackney stallion?—No, I think not. The Hon. Somerset Ward drives a pair of Hackneys got by "Romeo," half-bred ones, and they are by far the prettiest that came into Downpatrick. There is a style about them that you will not see in those got by a thoroughbred sire.

3069. Then you would place your opinion against that of Messrs. East and Wimbush?—I believe they are wrong in their estimate of the Yorkshire Hackney.

3070. Although they buy the article?—Yes.

3071. Mr. WRENCH.—But is it not a fact that the Yorkshire men have given up breeding coach horses because they did not find it pay?—I heard so, that there was more demand for the Hackneys when I was there.

3072. Do you know as a matter of fact that there used to be a large trade with America in Yorkshire coach horses, chiefly through Stericker Brothers, and that that has been given up?—Yes, and they were very beautiful horses. The prettiest horses I have ever seen in my life were the Yorkshire coaching horses.

3073. Do you think Hackneys are at all likely to take the place of thoroughbred sires, or will they be only used with mares that thoroughbreds would not suit?—I think they would be used with mares suitable to them.

3074. And the mares with which Hackneys would be used would not be suitable for thoroughbred sires?—They would need heavier mares to thoroughbred horses generally.

3075. Therefore you do not think the fear that Hackneys will take the place of thoroughbreds will be realised?—I think not.

3076. And is not the trade of Messrs. East and Wimbush and men who buy 16 hands horses in your county comparatively small compared with the trade carried on by other men, such as Mr. Hotherall and other dealers?—Yes, the parties you speak of don't buy many in our county; you don't hear their names mentioned.

3077. Mr. Hotherall buys largely?—Yes.

3078. The CHAIRMAN.—These letters refer of course to the whole of Ireland, and I gather from you that you attribute the falling off, of which they complain in Yorkshire, in the class of carriage horses which they require to the fact that, there being a greater demand for the Hackney, the attention of the people has been directed to breeding Hackneys rather than to other classes of horses?—Yes.

WILLIAM FARRELL, examined.

3079. CHAIRMAN.—You live in the County Down, I think?—Yes, sir.

3080. In what part of the county?—I live in East Down.

3081. Have you any experience yourself in horse-breeding?—I have been breeding horses or taking a deep interest in horses for more than 20 years.

3082. Do you breed horses yourself?—I do.

3083. What class of horses do you breed?—I breed from thoroughbreds and half-breds with a slight stain in them, nearly thoroughbred, and lately from a Clydesdale.

3084. Do you judge at Horse Shows sometimes?—I do.

3085. In England as well as in Ireland?—No; I have only judged at Banbridge and Downpatrick; Banbridge is a very large show, but Downpatrick is a local one, and I have been through all Lecale judging green crops on farms, and I was always looking about me to see what I could and learn what I could.

3086. Are you pretty well acquainted with horse-breeding through Ireland?—Not all through Ireland but the North. I have been at Ballinasloe.

3087. Do you know the South?—I do, I have been up here two or three times, and Ballinasloe twice, and at the Moy once a year anyway.

3088. Do you farm yourself?—I farm.

3089. Do you breed for your own use on your farm or to sell?—I usually have two or three mares having foals every summer.

3090. I think you said you breed from a thoroughbred?—I do, a half-bred and a Clydesdale; I usually take one from each, or sometimes two from the half-bred and one from the thoroughbred, sometimes one each horse.

3091. And what class of mares do you use?—Well, for a Clydesdale horse I use a coarse, rough, strong mare that I think would not suit a thoroughbred, and for a thoroughbred horse I use a Hackney mare, a long lengthy mare with good bone, wide of her ribs, good

Nov. 25, 1896.

Mr. William Pyper.

action, a sweet-looking mare. Then if I have a blood mare I put her to a half-bred horse to bring bone, so what we call half-bred horses that have either two strains of the thoroughbred on the dam or the sire's side.

3092. What do you do with the produce of the Clydesdale?—I work him on the farm or sometimes sell him for a cart. We have a sort of a mare, a good, short-legged, strong mare, we call an Irish cart mare, and we can breed a very good cart horse from that sort of mare, and there is a very good demand for them for heavy work in Belfast, not just the very heaviest but middling, up to two tons.

3093. At what age do you sell the produce?—Four years old, sometimes five.

3094. What price do you get?—We used to get a little better price, but if we had a good horse we could still get the better price. I have got £75, and £40 or £35 would be about the lowest.

3095. What do you do with the produce of the thoroughbred sires?—I try to sell it either as a harness horse or a hunter, if not good enough for a hunter it usually makes a harness horse.

3096. And the same I suppose with the blood mare and the thoroughbred horse?—Yes, my lord.

3097. And which pays you best?—Both pay equally well. I don't breed just exactly thoroughbreds. I had one last year and I have one this year, but you see when we cross the thoroughbred horse ——

3098. I don't mean the thoroughbred; but which pays you best of the others?—If you could breed a good hunting horse it would pay the best.

3099. Is it a good district for horse-breeding, in your opinion, that you live in?—It is very good.

3100. And a good quality of soil; what is the soil?—Heavy clay, and some of it light, and some of it touches limestone a little, and our farms are pretty well cultivated. We go in a good deal for green crops, and use town manure, and I think it helps the bone of the animal besides when it comes to graze on it.

3101. What kind of mares have the farmers?—Good, useful, short-legged mares, with plenty of bone, very hardy, about 15·3, some of them a little more.

3102. Do you buy yourself any mares in any part of the country?—None, unless if I get a good hunter broken down. We cannot afford to go in for expensive mares; we would like to do it.

3103. Is it the custom to breed from two-year-olds?—Well, we do in our district.

3104. What is your opinion about that?—Well, we have bred some very good animals from two-year-olds and three-year-olds. I would not like to be longer starting to breed than three-year-old, and then you can take a couple of foals; and sometimes you are inclined to sell the mare, and you have a couple of good foals left. Sometimes they breed from them at four-year old, and you have a foal at five. Breeding from a two-year-old is very severe on the mare; it takes her a year to come up again, but on the three-year-old it is not so severe.

3105. How is your district off for stallions?—We are well supplied.

3106. With suitable stallions?—Well, they are pretty good all over, generally speaking; there are some bad.

3107. What are they?—We have some half-breds not just the thing, and some Clydesdales not the thing, but still they breed some of them pretty well. Whenever they don't breed the people have to part with them, for they don't get anything to do. Our farming people out there are pretty apt to know very soon what sort a horse suits for, and they don't very often follow up a middling horse.

3108. Are there any Hackney stallions in your district?—We had a few, but they were not very successful in my immediate neighbourhood, and I think they hardly paid their way.

3109. Are there any there now?—None in my immediate neighbourhood, none nearer than Downpatrick; we used to have them within about a mile of us, but they have ceased to keep them; they would not take the place of the Harkaway horses.

3110. Are there any cart-horse sires?—We have some very good cart-horses in the neighbourhood; we have three Clydesdales or four; we have one Clydesdale got by the famous Clydesdale horse, "The Prince of Wales"; we have another, a very good one, and they are all breeding pretty well.

3111. You think their produce is successful?—I do, where land is hilly and hard to labour, it takes you to have strong horses on the farm or you could not work it.

3112. You think, on the whole, from your experience, that the mares in the district are improving?—Deteriorating.

3113. How do you account for that?—Well, now, they have to be turned into money; the people cannot afford to keep them, that is just all there is about it, and the people have ceased to breed lately; they are not breeding so much as they did.

3114. Why is that?—In the first place, I suppose, the mares not being so good they did not get just as good an animal; and the middling-priced horse has gone down, while I think the high-priced horse is just as dear as ever, if we could get them. I was in the last May fair, and if you had the right good horse you would get as much money as ever.

3115. But the medium horses have gone down in price?—They have.

3116. Can you account for that?—I think the mares are not so good.

3117. When I said that the prices had gone down I meant the prices had gone down, the quality of the animal remaining the same?—Well, you know you can't always breed a good one, and for a misfit you used to get a middling good price, and now if you have a misfit you cannot get any price at all. Troopers last year in our neighbourhood were brought at £18 to £20 or £22; the men that got that won't breed any more. If the Government would come and give us £30 or £35 we would breed more.

3118. How do you define a half-bred horse—what do you consider a half-bred?—The Harkaway horse you heard mentioned there by Mr. Dunlop I could give you the outline of, with your permission. That is our half-bred in Ulster; that is the horse that has kept the people in their places in the County Down—he has paid the rent all the time. "The King of Trumps," a thoroughbred horse, came to Ireland about sixty years ago; he was shipwrecked on the way, and came here blind. He was crossed with a sort of Irish mare. I knew the descendant of the man that had the mare that the horse was crossed with, and from the cross came a chestnut horse, and that is what they call a Harkaway; and that horse has been crossed with a good sort of mare, and then they sometimes turn back to the thoroughbred mare, and that is how we keep up the character of the half-bred horse, but the great mistake was that there was no stud book got up for him. If there had been a stud book for that Harkaway breed so that they could be sold in America and other places—I could have sold some myself in America if they were registered in any stud book.

3119. Is the Royal Dublin Society's scheme in operation in your district?—But little, not much.

3120. Has it had any effect?—It had an effect where they give prizes to mares more than to the sires, because we have enough of private enterprise to get plenty of sires; gentlemen in the neighbourhood bring the sires and speculate in them, looking to these to pay them without any prizes.

3121. You think the scheme of the Dublin Society has had a good effect?—It has where it was given to the mares and of course to the sires as well.

3122. Have you had any experience as to the effect of the importation of foreign horses?—It has hurt the price of low-priced horses.

3123. In your opinion has it been the [illegible] of [illegible] horses and [illegible]?—Not so much, unless where they alter them and bring them down to [illegible] and [illegible] them over to England, [illegible] the price of [illegible] has been [illegible].

3124. Do you sell horses in England?—I sold one [illegible] a young horse. I went over to the [illegible] [illegible] with a young horse, a Hackney horse.

3125. You sold him there?—I sold him, he is not [illegible] enough yet, the classes are not properly [illegible]; I exhibited him in the [illegible] class as a [illegible]-year-old [illegible]. I was exhibiting him against older [illegible] that were [illegible], and I had not the right chance; he was in the wrong class, but I think he will come right in the end.

3126. You yourself have had no experience of the breeding from Hackneys?—None, I don't touch them.

3127. And they are not bred here in your district?—A little, not much; I have seen some of those crossed with a good thoroughbred mare, or a [illegible] thoroughbred, with good enough results.

3128. What is your opinion of the thoroughbred?—I think the thoroughbred with a very good mare would do well enough, but I would not approve of a [illegible] [illegible]. I have an example not very far off me, and I don't think in the [illegible] [illegible] the [illegible] will be as good.

3129. Do you think it pays to breed in your district as well as it used to?—I think, my Lord, if we could [illegible] a good horse, as I said before, it would pay as well as ever, as we would get as much if we could get the good animal, and there are some very good animals in our district at the present time, young horses.

3130. Have you any suggestion to make as to how it could be made to pay better?—Well, there is one suggestion I would make, as to the buying of troopers [illegible] the Government [illegible] to the breeder [illegible] or other [illegible] like a [illegible], [illegible] would [illegible] for [illegible], and in breeding troopers they might get a good one and [illegible]. [illegible] [illegible], all good; but [illegible] the Government [illegible] the people they will get very few troopers in the district I am in, or in the County [illegible].

3131. You think the Government should buy direct from the breeder?—I think the [illegible] [illegible] gets an [illegible] profit in the [illegible] for buying him from young [illegible] of mine sold a trooper for £35, [illegible] [illegible], [illegible] had a [illegible] of his [illegible]; that [illegible] a very good man [illegible] would not think of [illegible] for [illegible] again.

3132. Lord Harrington.—Mr. [illegible], I think [illegible] that he thought Clydesdale and thoroughbred was the foundation of the Hackney blood, do you [illegible] that in the [illegible]?—I think Mr. [illegible] made a mistake, because he did not know, [illegible] [illegible] in the country; the [illegible] is wrong [illegible].

3133. But he did not seem to mind it?—No, the [illegible] Hackney was from a thoroughbred horse, and what we call [illegible] [illegible].

3134. You don't know the breeding of the mare?—I do not, it is a [illegible] over fifty years ago, but a strong [illegible] mare, a [illegible] mare I believe—I got a description of the mare—a good [illegible] [illegible], I was not old enough to know the [illegible] that owned the horse, but I knew the family. He [illegible] [illegible] and [illegible] him, and was [illegible] on a [illegible]; and he would [illegible] him [illegible] [illegible], and [illegible] his [illegible] up to the [illegible] and [illegible] [illegible] there, and then drive back again from [illegible], [illegible] miles, and not hurt him; he was [illegible] as a [illegible]. "King of [illegible]" was the first foundation of the Hackneys.

3135. One of the old Irish strain of mare?—Yes.

3136. Colonel St. Leger.—I should like to ask you with reference to the troopers, you say that there are a suitable number of mares; you are always [illegible] trying to breed to the highest possible standard, as ought to be?—That is what we want to get at.

3137. And every man who breeds, breeds with the view of getting the best animal he can?—Yes.

3138. Then you have what you call a [illegible] [illegible] that [illegible] up as [illegible] [illegible], an animal that may be perfectly sound, but not of a good appearance to command a high price. For these what price do you expect to get?—He might get £30 or £35, or you might get £100, and then if he is not a good looking animal he [illegible] is for a trooper if he is sound; they won't take anything that is not sound.

3139. You say the remounts have been making from £35 to £25 to Government?—Yes, to the men who bought them for the Government.

3140. Do you know what Government **they were** sold to?—I believe to the English.

3141. To the English Government [illegible] [illegible] [illegible]?—[illegible] [illegible] buys them for the English Government.

3142. When were they sold?—He [illegible] round to people's houses; he [illegible] up what we [illegible] a [illegible] or [illegible] [illegible], [illegible] [illegible] like 5£ 1s. for [illegible] him to a [illegible]; he comes to the [illegible] and [illegible] round for twenty or thirty miles of the district, and buys the horses [illegible] [illegible] [illegible] the [illegible].

3143. They are like that [illegible] of the people, [illegible] as [illegible] as they can?—If the Government wants to encourage us they must give more than that.

3144. Do you know that the English Government hardly ever buys a trooper north of the Boyne?—I did not.

3145. What class of horses are you speaking of, were they riding horses, or draught horses, or [illegible] for both work?—Principally riding, they would do both work; but there were good heads to them, good [illegible] legs, and fair action.

3146. They were riding horses?—Yes, but not good enough to make a hunter, not enough quality about them.

3147. Then you think nearly anything you breed is good enough to be a trooper?—I think so.

3148. What price would you propose should be given for these troopers?—I think if they would give the breeder from £30 to £35 he would try and breed them.

3149. Would anybody try and breed a trooper?—I think they would in the course of breeding a good horse.

3150. And then they would not give it to the Government?—Oh, no.

3151. It is very like trying to breed a polo pony, no man would try to breed a trooper unless he was [illegible] a [illegible] to Government, and if he was a good one he would sell it for a higher price elsewhere; but if he is a [illegible], he is good enough to go as a trooper to Government?—That is so.

3152. Mr. Clancy.—What you mean is, if you breed a trooper you are not going to give it to the Government, you don't want to [illegible] the army on Ireland?—No.

3153. Colonel St. Leger.—You would give them your rubbish, but you ask them to come forward and support you, and get the money in your pocket, the [illegible]?—It is our rubbish, and unless they give us some encouragement, we won't give them anything at all.

3154. Mr. Clancy.—You mean if **the Government** gave you £30 or £35 for your [illegible] **you would sell** it to them?—Yes, or even £30.

3155. But you would like to **get £35** for [illegible] [illegible] as troopers?—Yes.

3156. Have you any of the Hackney blood in your district?—Yes, we have three or four sires [illegible]; I [illegible] say that they are as good as they [illegible], but we try to keep them as good as we can.

3157. Is one of those Hackney mares [illegible] [illegible]?

Rev. [illegible]
Mr. William [illegible].

Jan. 18, 1896.
Mr. William [illegible].

with a good thoroughbred while this bad employment, do you think it would reproduce these qualities?—That is the way we get the best hunters from a thoroughbred horse and a Hackney mare, or a thoroughbred horse and a [illegible] mare; but we prefer the Hackney mare, because they give strength.

3158. You would approve of registering a sire, like the Hackney, half-bred?—Certainly; I think they deserve it as much as the thoroughbred.

3159. You say that Hackneys have been bred in your district, and lately they are not popular; they are being discouraged?—They are being discouraged, we say (as strong every man has his own opinion); we consider them rather soft, and we consider the Clydesdale a soft breed.

3160. Sir T. Esmonde.—Would you say there were any of the old Irish breed of mares left in your country?—They did, would have a little manner—we have some very good mares, no doubt about it; some men are inclined to keep as good mares as ever they did, and you would wonder at the pictures of some of these mid-sized mares.

3161. Would you approve of a system of registering this old breed of Irish mares?—I would; something like the way the Hunter Improvement Society are doing.

3162. On the question of young remounts, are there any troopers bought by foreigners in your district?—Any of the foreigners that buy there do not discover the local dealer usually gets them first; there is such a man at Mallow, he gives a good price, and it would be nothing to him—he gives up to £100, the foreigners take most of the good mares away.

3163. Mr. Wrench.—You say you would be in favour of establishing a Stud Book like that of the Hunter Improvement Society?—Yes, that.

3164. Would you lay down any definite number of crosses that you think necessary?—I would like two or three crosses of blood on the dam's side or the sire's side, take two of blood.

3165. On the dam's side or the sire's side you would not mind which?—Either.

3166. And you think if such a Stud Book or register was established it would put up the price of half-bred horses?—All I know is I could have sold more horses I had in America, an American friend wrote to me, and would have sold those well for me; but they were not registered in any Stud Book and they would not take them in America.

3167. Therefore if they had been registered you could have sold them?—Yes, for two or three times as much as I could get at home.

3168. Talking of America, I think you said there were some American horses in the Dublin Show; [illegible] could there were, it would not be right for me to answer that question.

3169. I would not ask you?—I know there were American horses sold in Dublin Show as Irish hunters and had Irish pedigrees.

3170. And Irish horses sold?—A friend of mine bought one in Mallow, gave a very low price for it, he took it to England and sold it as an Irish hunter for £50 of profit in a few months, and in every English fair lately there have been a few Americans sold as Irish horses; I hold this spoils the character of Irish horses, because in the hunting field they have not the same staying power our horses have.

3171. With reference to the Hackneys in your district, where were they stationed in Mr. Empey's? In the lowest sense, the Hackney most probably have spent their time at twice, they don't keep them now, that is Mr. [illegible] of [illegible], near Clonmel.

3172. They are not there now?—No.

3173. But you don't know whether they were pure Hackneys?—I would give the pedigree of one shown he used to Tipperary, "The Wildman," bred by Lord Masters, and in the yearling class at that same show I think we had real Hackneys.

3174. The Chairman.—Are **you speaking of** stallions standing at those places?—Yes, this was one of them; I think he went last year to Glasgow.

3175. Mr. Wrench.—This was one of the horses whose produce they did not care about?—They did not, and he was the best shouldered one I ever saw, but he did not seem to take with the people.

3176. Did he win any prizes in Ireland?—He got a third. If he had been a success in the way of getting mares I don't think he would be away, because there are none of the very apt to part with anything that [illegible].

3177. That was the only Hackney here though?—He had a little Yorkshire hackney stallion, "The Squire," sometime ago; a very nice looking horse he was.

3178. Lord Rathdonnell.—In answering Mr. Wrench, with regard to registration, don't you mean that you would register the stallion and not all the produce of the stallion?—I don't think it would be necessary to register the produce of the stallion unless some of the produce wanted to be kept as a sire; if you wanted to keep the produce as a sire you would have to register it to keep it for a half-bred horse.

3179. Do you mean to say you would register anything that had not proved himself to be a good animal?—Indeed I don't think I would.

3180. Therefore you would not register **all the** produce?—I would not.

3181. But you would register a stallion although half-bred if he proved himself to be a good [illegible]?—Yes; but I don't think I would register any stallion with too much of the Clydesdale in him.

3182. The system of registration would have, I suppose, to be left to some competent Board, you would not object to that?—Oh, no.

3183. If a competent Board was formed, and they came to the conclusion that the sire and produce of a certain half-bred stallion were good and desired to register him, that is what you would like to see done?—Yes, my lord.

3184. But you don't favour indiscriminate registration of produce?—No.

3185. Lord Ardilaun.—Even if you were selling this produce, how would you be able to prove that it was the produce out of a registered sire and registered dam in America, for instance?—That would be a trouble again, I suppose, the body could decide that better than I can tell you here.

3186. Lord Rathdonnell.—Under the scheme of registration that I brought you since there would not be such a thing as a registered dam?—No, there would be nothing of the sort.

3187. There would be no registered dam, all you would register would be the horse that proved himself to be a good foal getter, is that what you mean?—That is all I mean.

3188. Lord Ardilaun.—Would you be in favour of registering mares?—I think if the mare was from a thoroughbred horse or from something good, you may go a little back, but not too far. I don't know exactly how such books are got up, if I did I would have one got up long ago.

3189. Sir T. Esmonde.—If it could be discovered there were any of these old Irish mares left, would you be in favour of having some kind of registration of them?—I would if you could get them.

3190. Mr. Wrench.—Do you think you could get these?—It would be a question, I think it would be hard to get.

3191. Lord Rathdonnell.—Don't you think it would be very costly?—It would.

3192. Sir T. Esmonde.—With reference to the American horses and their being sold as Irish horses in the English market, do you think it would be a good thing to stand them?—I think they should be sold for what they are. If they are American horses let them be sold as such. When they come here they [illegible] who should get them. Now they have to be sold under cover. You heard Mr. Inglis quoted a large number of people who had American horses, and they would not have them at all now.

3193. The CHAIRMAN.—Do you think these American mares are brought at all to breed from in the country?—I could not say, if you got a good mare it might; I don't know much about them, but I don't think they should be sold as Irish horses if that could be managed; if we had a fair field to fight them it would help our position greatly.

3194. Is there anything you would like to suggest to the Commission as to how breeding can be improved in Ireland generally?—Well, if you could give a little more to the people who keep good mares, begin to give prizes at three year old, because when a mare comes to three year old the people think of selling her; if you gave a premium for good mares, and made a man keep a mare in the country, that would be the only step I could think of at the present time. I think if you could give us any encouragement to keep the mares by good premiums, there is not so much required for the horses, it is mares we want more than anything else.

3195. Mr. WRENCH.—Do you keep more than one horse?—I keep just one.

3196. Lord RATHDONNELL.—The inference drawn from what you have just now said is, that the good mares are drafted out of the country by the farmer having money offered him by dealers?—Yes.

3197. And away goes the good sound mare?—After they come to three year old they are in danger; if there is a prize offered at three year old you have a chance to keep them a few years.

3198. Any scheme that would keep the sound mares in the country would meet your approval?—If you could help us in that way it would.

The Commission adjourned to next morning.

SEVENTH DAY.—FRIDAY, NOVEMBER 20TH, 1896

Present:—THE EARL OF DUNRAVEN, K.P., in the Chair; LORD ASHTOWN, MR. F. S. WRENCH, SIR T. H. G. ESMONDE, M.P., MR. J. L. CAREW, M.P., and MR. PERCY LA TOUCHE.

MR. HUGH NEVILLE, Secretary.

E. M. LUSK examined.

3199. CHAIRMAN.—You reside in the county Londonderry?—North Derry.

3200. Do you consider the district you live in a horse-breeding district?—The breeding of horses is.

3201. What classes of horses?—Cart horses and harness horses.

3202. They breed a good many of them, do they?—They do.

3203. Do you breed horses yourself?—I do.

3204. For some time?—Yes, for a good many years off and on.

3205. Which class of horses do you breed yourself?—Principally cart horses. The largest cart horses we can breed for dray purposes, and for harness purposes we use the Hackneys.

3206. Have you got a stallion of your own?—Not just at present.

3207. And are these the general classes of horses that are bred in that part of the country?—Well, largely, and altogether.

3208. Where are they sold, this class of horse?—The cart horses are principally sold to Scotch dealers, the harness horses are bought by the principal Dublin dealers, local dealers buy them and send them to England.

3209. Then, I take it, that very little attention is paid to the breeding of hunters?—Practically none.

3210. What class of stallion have you been yourself?—Well, I have had a share in keeping. I never kept a horse entirely on my own account. Generally a few of us together in the neighbourhood got the very best horse we could, and we join together to keep a really good horse. In that way I have owned a horse, had a share in him. We keep the best Clydesdale blood we can get, and the Hackney.

3211. How long have you had Clydesdale blood in the country?—A long time.

3212. Have you had any stallions of any other breed except the Hackneys and Clydesdales?—Yes, I had a share in a thoroughbred stallion at one time, but he did not take.

3213. And the Clydesdale you use for the cart horse and the Hackney for the harness horse?—Yes, my lord.

3214. How long have there been Hackneys in the country?—Well, in the immediate neighbourhood, about eight years. Of course Lord Charlemont, in the neighbouring county, had a Hackney a good many years ago, "Donald Arrow." He left a lot of good stock I believe.

3215. Do you know anything of "Donald Arrow's" stock?—I have seen a good many of them.

3216. Do you like them?—Yes, any that I have seen were good.

3217. What Hackney sires have you got now in your neighbourhood?—There is "Yorkshire Fox," belonging to Mr. Moulton. We had up to recently, when we sold him, a horse called "Dandy," a Yorkshire bred Hackney, and we had also one "Excelsior," who was a very celebrated sire.

3218. Before the introduction of these Hackneys how were the harness horses bred?—Well, they were bred from a sort of half-bred horses, some of those from Yorkshire horses, coaching horses I have known to be in the country, said to be Cleveland Bays, whether pure bred or not I would not undertake to say. They were stated to be Cleveland Bays, they were this class of horse, big, clean legged horses of no distinct type.

3219. In your opinion is the Hackney superior?—I think so, for the class of mares we have in our country.

3220. What kind of mares have you?—They are rather plain; in fact there is no distinct type of mare in the country. The great want in my opinion is the mares. I think there should be more encouragement given to try to keep the good mares in the country than there is, because in the want of good mares that is a great necessity in improving the breeding of good horses.

3221. Do you think the mares are getting worse?—I don't think they are as good as they were.

3222. Can you attribute that to any particular cause?—I think there has been a great foreign demand for the good mares; any really good mares are picked up by foreigners at once.

3223. What step would you suggest to induce the farmers to keep their good mares at home?—If

Oct. 22, 1896.

Mr. R. H. Lamb.

the money that was spent in subsidising the stallions was spent in some way in giving prizes to mares locally, and mares in mares generally. By that I mean to say that the mares which should not get their grant get the money for the mares. I think that [illegible] the small farmers from competing with their [illegible]. I should think that some regulation that would prevent the same horse getting the prize money frequently, or any more than once, would be very useful.

3224. What sized farms are there, generally speaking, about you?—When I live the farms are very large, from 600 acres down to 100 or 150 acres. In a little distance away the farms get smaller, and average 30 or 40 acres.

3225. Do the smaller class of farmers do much in horse-breeding?—They do; a great many of them always breed a horse.

3226. What class of horses do they use for their own farm work?—A sort of half-bred grade or heavy. They use the Clydesdale very largely; there is a good deal of Clydesdale blood in them.

3227. How about prices, have the prices gone up in these last five years?—A good horse is always worth money, but at the present time a middling horse is unsaleable.

3228. Is the good horse worth as much as ever he was?—I think he is, but the middling horse is very hard to sell.

3229. How do you account for that?—I think that there is not the demand, and I think the foreign horses that are brought into the country have cut down what you might call the second or third class horse, or the third class horse, greatly because they come into competition with them and have reduced the prices.

3230. And do you think the introduction of the Hackney sire will increase the value of the produce?—I should think so as a harness horse, decidedly.

3231. Give them better action?—Better action. Of course there are Hackneys and Hackneys, as there are horses of all descriptions; some Hackneys I would not breed from at all, but I think a Hackney of a proper description, a big horse with quality and good bone, there is a really great want of horses bred in this [illegible].

3232. Have you a share in any Hackney stallion at present?—No.

3233. Where did you get your horse from?—The last horse that we got that we sold the other day we got him in Yorkshire.

3234. Have you any preference?—I am inclined to think the Yorkshire blood is better than the Norfolk, has more quality.

3235. Is the Royal Dublin Society's scheme in operation about you?—Not at all. There is a registered stallion I think in the county Derry. I believe, according to the returns, I was looking them up, that in the counties Down, Antrim, Derry, Tyrone and Donegal there are 158 stallions, and of them only 11 are registered.

3236. How do you account for that?—I think that if it were in the hands of some local society like the North-East Society in Belfast it would be more popular.

3237. Do you think they would be more likely to register if it was all conducted by a local society?—I think there would be more interest taken in it. In the county Derry there are very few thoroughbred stallions at all. In fact just at the present moment I don't know that I know of a thoroughbred stallion standing except perhaps one or so in Derry.

3238. On the whole in your opinion is the class of stallion you have in Derry well suited to the district?—I would not say that at all, because I think if you speak generally there are a good many unsound stallions in use, horses that should not be allowed to serve at all. I have an opinion or view that there should be a license duty put upon stallions and every man with a stallion for hire should have to pay a license of so much a year, and if his horse passed a board of veterinary surgeons it should be reduced; if he chooses to keep an unsound stallion let him pay for it, there are very many unsound stallions in use.

3239. You think a penalty of that kind would be sufficient to wipe out the unsound stallions?—I think it would go a long way towards it.

3240. Sir T. Esmonde.—On the point of unsound stallions, you have strong views that they are extremely objectionable?—Most undesirable.

3241. And do you think, from your experience of this country, it is necessary to take steps to deal with that question?—I do indeed, I think it would be a very essential thing if it could be carried out, as there are unsound stallions being used. I may say that when we began to go into horse-breeding we invariably insisted that every stallion that we took was to be sound, and had a certificate from two or three veterinary surgeons of his soundness and advertised him to be sound. And that I observe, whether truthfully or not, has been followed by several instances where I see stallions being advertised, at the bottom of their card it says they have been examined by a veterinary surgeon and passed sound.

3242. Was your mare breeding every season?—No, not every season unless we competed; there was something [illegible].

3243. Do you think there is much breeding from unsound mares with you?—Indeed I think there is, they are very careless about the mare they use still, seem to think anyone is good enough to breed from.

3244. Do you think it is equally important to have a sound mare as it is to have a sound stallion?—Equally.

3245. You would be in favour of some system to remedy that?—I don't see how you can prevent it; if a man chooses to serve his mare, whether she is sound or not, you cannot prevent him; but with regard to giving premiums, I would insist on sound mares.

3246. You are not aware I suppose of the practice of foreign countries in respect of this question of sound or unsound horses?—No; I have heard that in France there is a duty on stallions, and only sound stallions are licensed.

3247. Mr. De Robeck.—You say you think the mares have deteriorated a good deal in your country?—I think they are not as good as they were.

3248. And that there are hardly any thoroughbred stallions that you are aware of in this county?—I really don't know that I could name a thoroughbred stallion in Derry just at present; there may be one or two.

3249. Do you think the mares have deteriorated from the absence of thoroughbred blood?—Well, no; I don't know that it is attributable to that; the good mares are sold because they bring the most money.

3250. I suppose that was always the custom, wasn't it?—I suppose, perhaps, it was, but I think the mares are not as good as they were, for some reason or other.

3251. But you think there used to be more thoroughbred stallions in the country before the introduction of these Clydesdales?—Well, in my recollection I don't think there were; there was generally one or two thoroughbred stallions.

3252. What were the ordinary mares in this country when the mares were in a better state, were they all half-bred?—Half-bred, I understand, as far as I recollect.

3253. What is your definition of a half-bred?—My definition of a half-bred would be from a thoroughbred horse in that line, or from any thoroughbred, a half-bred, I would consider, since the race on one side, but the half-breds that are in the country are not that at all, they are a sort of nondescript, which, perhaps, would be a better description to give them.

3254. Then you cannot keep any idea how they were bred, the crossbreds you speak of?—I have not any idea at all; I should say they were bred in every way.

3255. What sort of horse do you expect to breed by a Hackney stallion out of the ordinary mares of the country?—If cross your mare to a big weak-kneed Hackney, you may breed a Yorkshire [illegible] horse, you may breed him, if you don't you will breed a horse that is fit for a van, which is a fairly selling horse; and if he misses that, of course, he is only a harness.

3256. Do you really expect to breed mares big enough for vans?—Certainly, if you breed with the right sort of stallion. I would never think of breeding him under 15·3 or 16 hands.

3257. Are your good Hackney stallions up there 15 hands?—Certainly. The last horse we had was 16 hands high.

3258. Is the mare of the country big enough to produce that sort of animal?—Oh, yes, my experience is that very often a small mare produces the biggest horse.

3259. Mr. Wrench.—Practically you would divide the mares in your district into classes, one to be crossed with a Clydesdale or cart horse, and others to be crossed with a Hackney to produce harness horses?—Yes.

3260. Do you think, with regard to the latter class, if the principal mares that exist in the country were crossed with a good Hackney stallion they would in time produce a much better class in the country if the produce were kept?—I think it would.

3261. When "Excelsior" was crossed with a cart-bred mare, did he get good animals, then?—He did, "Excelsior" was a Norfolk bred Hackney, and my opinion about the Norfolk Hackneys is that he requires a better quality of mare than a Yorkshire Hackney. I may say that I bred by "Excelsior" out of a mare that was nearly thoroughbred the first [illegible]. I bred a horse that is in Cheshire, and the [illegible] [illegible] [illegible] [illegible] on the [illegible] said he had never [illegible] by no horse in that country. I sold him to [illegible], of Chester, and his dam was nearly thoroughbred, a small mare not 15 hands, and he is over 16 hands, according to the papers in the paper now. I sold him at six years old.

3262. Do you remember, I think it was the year before last, a [illegible] mare [illegible] in the heavy-weight class in the Dublin Show got by "Excelsior"?—Yes, I know that mare very well, that mare was on the [illegible] next to my place.

3263. How was that mare bred?—That mare was bred out of a well-bred mare which I believe came from the West of Ireland, and "Excelsior." And I will tell you an extraordinary thing about that. The year before that the light weight champion hunter in the show in Dublin was out of that mare by a thoroughbred horse, and the next year a mare out of the same mare by the Hackney horse was in the heavy weight class, she was either first or second, I forget which.

3264. Then you think that if the people thought the position of the Hackney stallions they are suitable, or look on them as another class of horse?—Certainly, nothing else.

3265. You said you had a thoroughbred horse there at one time?—Yes, but he was not patronised much.

3266. Got a good class of thoroughbred?—We thought him very good.

3267. Mr. La Touche.—What was he?—A horse called "[illegible]," by "[illegible]," he had been [illegible] and [illegible] well.

3268. Mr. Wrench.—He was a powerful horse?—A good horse he was but not very strong.

3269. Plenty of bone?—Plenty of bone.

3270. I think from some of your answers you would recommend that other stallions besides thoroughbreds should be registered by the Dublin Society in the County Derry?—I would say so, certainly.

3271. Would you recommend that these other kinds of stallions or Hackney stallions should be registered?—Certainly.

3272. Would you recommend that half-bred stallions should be registered?—I don't think so, I would not breed from a half-bred stallion at all, you don't know what you may get.

3273. And I think this is the question which you answered in the Commission you gave some recommendation about buying stallions?—Yes, I think if there could be some scheme devised by which farmers could register their mares in some way that it could be more [illegible] brought under the eye of the Government Board of [illegible] would be a good thing, because at present I should say the farmers, as very few, sell their horses for remounts direct to the Government, they nearly all pass through the hands of dealers.

3274. And you thought it would be possible to arrange some system by which they would be bought direct from the breeders?—I think so. I think that if they were registered, and then when the Board or whoever was buying for the Government came down they could know where to go, or they would give notice that they would be at a certain place on a certain day to those men who thought they had horses suitable for remounts, and get an opportunity of seeing them gathered together.

3275. Are many hunters bought in the North of Ireland?—I could not say very much about that myself, but I believe there are a good many bought in the [illegible].

3276. Is Derry a good horse fair?—Oh, no.

3277. When you kept different classes of stallions do you think the farmers were fairly intelligent as to mating the right mare with the right horse?—I think so.

3278. You think the farmers in their districts would be able to give a very good opinion as to their own requirements?—Generally they would, undoubtedly.

3279. And would you rather—in offering you advice as to carrying out any scheme for the improvement of horses—would you prefer that it should be done through the local shows than through the Royal Dublin Society or a body like that?—Yes, I think that a body like the Northwest Society in Derry, or the Newtownards Society in Derry know much more about what the neighbourhood really requires, and the class of horses that will take in the district, and take more interest in it.

3280. Then you think that if any Government aid was given in the direction of improving the breed of horses that it ought to be worked through a local society in preference to the central society?—I should think so.

3281. Chairman.—Do you know at what age these horses for remounts are generally sold to the dealers?—Invariably when they are bought by the Government, the dealer does not keep them long on hand as a rule.

3282. I would like to understand a little better what your opinion is about the deterioration of the horses; because you have told us that prior to the introduction of the pure-bred Hackneys and cart horses the country generally was served by those mongrel sires which were referred to the year [illegible] time, yet at the same time you say that the produce, as far as the horses remaining in the country are concerned, has not been improved. And [illegible] the average as you know, in Derry with the [illegible] of Hackneys has only been introduced within the last seven or eight years, so that really there is no time to prove what the result of their breeding would be, and all you can tell of them is the horses that have been bred and sold, you are not in a position to judge from practical experience what the results in improving the breed may be, but certainly they are good saleable horses. It is my experience that if you put a thoroughbred horse again a cart mare you will get an animal with perhaps thoroughbred [illegible] and each Kingsworthy or [illegible], the most useless sort of animal for any purpose; there is no class of [illegible] the Hackney.

3283. Is there anything you would like to say to the Commission, any suggestions as to the way in which the industry could be improved in your part of the country?—I don't know that there is anything I could suggest except some scheme for providing the use of sound stallions in the country could be [illegible], and a scheme that would give an inducement for the keeping of a better class of mares.

3284. I take it that you think the latter is almost of the same importance as the former?—Certainly; a good mare is quite as essential as a good horse.

Colonel Sir WILLIAM LENOX CONYNGHAM examined.

3285. CHAIRMAN.—You live in the County Derry?—I do.

3286. In what part of the county?—The south east.

3287. Are you interested in horse-breeding?—I don't breed any horses at present, but formerly I did breed a good many at one time, and I take a great interest in the welfare of horse-breeding in this neighbourhood.

3288. When did you cease breeding horses yourself?—About eight years ago.

3289. Do you consider that your district is well suited, generally speaking, for horse-breeding?—Yes, it is a very fair district for breeding, a great many horses are bred in it.

3290. What kind of soil?—It varies considerably, it is gravel and clay, a loamy soil.

3291. What is the kind of horse that is produced?—Harness horses principally, and occasionally hunters, you get occasional hunters, I have known some very good hunters produced in the country some years ago.

3292. What do the farmers generally aim at producing?—Oh, harness horses, a horse they can sell at the May fair in the best way to dispose of.

3293. Then you consider the production of harness horses to be the most profitable form of horse-breeding?—Yes, the farmers certainly do.

3294. Are there large farms in your district?—Probably from 50 to 100 acres, and below that again.

3295. And do the farmers generally turn their attention to breeding horses [illegible], horses almost entirely.

3296. They look upon horse-breeding as a profitable business?—A good many of them do.

3297. What mares did you breed yourself?—I used to breed from thoroughbreds. Unfortunately at one time I tried from a son of Brown Ainslie and I got three of the greatest rubbish that anybody ever saw, all of [illegible]; the other one which was got by a horse called [illegible] and her dam was by Minuet, and she [illegible] looked a very well bred mare but I could never find out how she was bred.

3298. You have bred entirely from thoroughbred sires?—I bred from a horse of Lord Charlemont's called Mr. O'Neill, a [illegible] for hunting purposes. I bred from Purchase, and I bred from a horse called Chevalier by Cavalier.

3299. What class of mares?—I had two mares at one time, one was a great big, said to be a well-bred mare, did not look it, but she bred very badly. The other was a small mare and bred very well.

3300. Are there any thoroughbred stallions in your part of the country?—There are two or three horses; there are two horses standing in Magherafelt said to be thoroughbreds, one horse I was standing, he is a horse called King of the Village by Pirate Chief.

3301. Are there any half-bred horses carrying on the district?—Yes, there is one standing there got by [illegible] out of a mare said to be by a horse called Prince Warden [illegible] near Derry, a very good-looking horse and his stock are very good-looking.

3302. Do you approve of breeding from half-breds?—I would not do it myself, I don't like them, I would rather have pure bred ones.

3303. Are there any such horses or Hackneys ones in your part of the country?—There is one such horse supposed to be a Hackney horse.

3304. Have you any experience of breeding from Hackneys?—None.

3305. Have you seen any of their produce?—I have seen some of them in my neighbourhood, and when I was walking to [illegible] I have asked a great many of the farmers about my neighbourhood whether they approve of them and they invariably condemn them, and say "Don't send us Hackneys whatever you do."

3306. It is merely second hand evidence, but have you any idea what induced them to form that opinion?—Two of them especially are men who deal in horses and buy them in the neighbourhood, and they won't have them at any price.

3307. You heard the evidence that was just given to us by Mr. [illegible]?—Yes, I heard it.

3308. Then you would not, I take it, agree with his opinion as to the improvement likely to arise from the introduction of Hackney blood?—I don't agree with it at all.

3309. Do you think the farmers appreciate a good stallion?—They do thoroughly.

3310. And are you satisfied with the class of stallions in your part of the country?—I am not, indeed, there are two horses that have been brought out lately from Yorkshire said to be Cleveland Bays. I have only seen one of them, he is a very good looking horse and I think will improve the breed very much, [illegible], beautifully coloured horse with very fine action.

3311. What class of stallion would you like to see introduced into the country?—A large, strong thoroughbred.

3312. Do you think the farmers would pay for his services?—They would, I think, if it was not too high.

3313. You think that is the kind of horse they would prefer?—I am sure they would.

3314. Have you ever heard if there is a demand for such a horse, as stallions of that kind have been brought into the county?—Some of the Dublin Society's horses have been sent down. There is a horse called "The Wait" there. Four or five years ago they would not have that horse at any price. He went to Magherafelt for a season; I don't think he got four mares; I don't wonder at it, the fee was not at all suited to the country.

3315. Is the Royal Dublin Society's scheme in operation in your part of the country?—Not now; it was.

3316. And how did it answer?—The result was "The Wait" was sent down there, and it did no good.

3317. Have you any suggestion as to any better course that could be taken than that now taken by the Dublin Society?—I think if the neighbourhood was represented in the choice of the horses it would be better; for the selection of the horses is made by people who don't know the wants of the neighbourhood at all, and consequently we would be better without these light horses like "The Wait." It would be far better not to send a horse down at all; it only brings the thoroughbred into contempt.

3318. Have you any hunters bred that are occasionally bred in your district?—There were very good horses got by a horse called "Ulysses" that stood in our district; he was a "Blue Ribbon" horse. I am speaking of a good many years ago. A horse called "Fire-brand" got some very nice horses.

3319. Are you pretty well acquainted with Ireland generally as to horse-breeding?—I know the North of Ireland—Derry and the neighbourhood—very well, and I know the neighbourhood of Clonmel pretty well, but that is the only place I can say.

3320. Have you formed any opinion of the probable effect of the introduction of Hackney blood in the country?—From personal experience I cannot say anything about it, but individually I don't like Hackney sires; I think they go off their action, and in breeding up their horses they don't see their condition.

3321. How about the mares in your district?—They are very indifferent. I am not absolutely certain that is all [illegible], what is perfectly useless for anything else, "Oh, she will do capitally to take a foal from."

3322. Are they getting worse or better?—I think they are getting worse.

3323. How do you account for that?—Where the mare is a tolerably good one the people think her like money.

3324. Was not that always the case?—I don't think it was so many years ago; I think they kept better mares. There was a great run, especially upon brown mares—it is a great many years ago now though—by the Austrian Government, and that drained us of our best mares.

3325. Do you mean that the farmers don't understand that a good mare is important to breed from?—They certainly understand that they have a better chance of good produce from a good mare, but at the same time, if they can get a long price for a mare, they will pass it [illegible] and not wait for the produce.

3326. And that, in your opinion, is harmful to the industry?—Oh, no question whatever about it.

3327. Can you suggest any way of checking that?—I would suggest that if possible the Government should send down through the country to the farmers [illegible]—on what conditions I am hardly prepared to say—good mares from the artillery. The reason I say that the mares in this country would be of use to farmers because they would work, and absolutely, if I may say so, good mares, [illegible] that have worked for a certain time, and that there is a great deal [illegible]—mares that we will say have served seven or eight years in the artillery. If they were given among the farmers, and to be bred from, conditionally that the Government should have the refusal of their produce, or something of that sort, I think that would be of use.

3328. You mean that they should be distributed gratis or sold cheaply?—Gratis would be the most attractive way no doubt, but I would sell them cheaply, it would perhaps come to the same thing. I was told the other day that the French are instituting a plan. They are taking their mares after three years' service [illegible] the country, giving them to the farmers and putting them in the stallions that are kept in the French haras, with the arrangement with the farmers that the produce is to go to the Government; that I think has been always the case when they breed from the horses in the haras, that the Government have the claim on the produce; and I was told [illegible] some years ago.

3329. Suppose this would be done don't you think there would be a great deal of dissatisfaction? If a man had an animal worth £40, should be obliged to sell it to the Government for half the money?—I don't see why they should; when he gets the mare for very little and makes a condition at the same time, I don't see why he should; if he is [illegible] £20 or £30 for a three-year-old, I think he would be very foolish not to try it.

3330. They would have to be sound I suppose for this scheme?

3331. Yes, I [illegible] to say [illegible] with veterinary surgeon would hardly pass those mares after six or seven years in the Artillery.

3332. Mr. Clarke.—Sound in wind?—Yes, sound in wind of course—and [illegible].

3333. Chairman.—Can you suggest any means by which suitable stallions could be brought to your district?—I think the Royal Dublin Society's plan is as good as any if they could get the right horses.

3334. I take it from you that any encouragement or aid given by the Government or by a society ought to be conducted by a local committee?—I think, say, under the superintendence of the Royal Dublin Society. I would not leave it more directly to the local society.

3335. Lord Arthur [illegible].—The mares in your district, can you give us any information about the size and quality, what they are like?—They vary; some of the farmers have fine big mares, some smaller ones, and the big ones are very good.

3336. Have the small mares got any bone?—Yes.

3337. Does the land grow bone?—Some of it does, not all of it.

3338. Do you think the majority of the mares are fit to breed a hunter?—Certainly not the majority, the minority by far.

3339. Then the thoroughbred horse that you would cross would want to have plenty of bone?—He would want to have plenty of bone.

3340. And short legs and [illegible]?—Short legs.

3341. Failing that, that horse, which is a very hard horse to get, what would you suggest?—Then I would rather [illegible] the Clevelands [illegible] and get a [illegible].

3342. Sir Thomas Esmonde.—On the question of stallions you say there is a want of suitable stallions in your district?—Yes, there is.

3343. And for the purpose of selecting a good stallion for that or any other district would you be in favour of some system of selection by [illegible] of the kind of stallion they would want?—I would, under certain supervision.

3344. Then on the question of price, what would be an average price for the service of a stallion? What do you think the farmers would pay for the service of a stallion?—Well, I kept a stallion for a season myself, and I had great difficulty in getting £2, and then they used to make a bargain that there should be a foal; that is a very common practice that you don't pay unless there is a foal. In my instance the foals did not appear, but they were sold afterwards for considerable sums of money.

3345. Then you think that £2 is the outside price that a man would be disposed to pay?—Yes.

3346. Would he pay £3?—Yes, the same man would be likely to breed good horses would pay £3.

3347. Are there any remounts bought in your district?—There are [illegible] in May fair, principally by foreigners.

3348. What price do they give as an average?—From five and twenty to thirty pounds is the French price.

3349. What would be the average price of the remount bought by the Home Government?—£30 to £35 and £40. The foreigners will give more money for an inferior horse than we will for a remount.

3350. Do you find that they buy [illegible] to English taste?—To English taste, oh, decidedly. There was a horse, I don't know whether he is alive or not, called "Galanthus" that stood in my district, and the French buyers would buy almost all his produce, any horse they thought was got by him. They had a great opinion of him. He was a thoroughbred horse got by "Arbitrator" by "Faugh-a-ballagh," a plain heavy horse, but a very powerful good one. He came to the county by accident. He had met with an injury, and I am sorry to say he has left it.

3351. Mr. Clarke.—I think you said, Sir William, that you had some of "Rural Dean's" stock?—I had them a [illegible] of his.

3352. He is a Hackney?—He was a Hackney.

3353. And the produce was very disappointing?—Very disappointing. I have two got by "Rural

"Arrow." One of them is a very old mare. She was a perfect beauty, and most beautiful goer, but I am told that after 5 or six miles you must press her.

3354. That is about the length of her limbs, she would require pressing after that distance?—I cannot say that from personal knowledge; I only heard it; and the other mare was a brown mare, a very handsome mare that didn't like a long day either.

3355. Do not the dealers in your district entirely disapprove of the Hackney?—Yes.

3356. And those dealers are largely interested in the trade?—They are; they sell a good many in Moy fair.

3357. Do you know how much they spend in the country in the purchase of horses, those dealers?—No, I may not say; they generally have from 6 to 7, 8 and 10 horses at a time; one of them especially.

3358. Then you are in favour of a large strong boned thorough-bred horse?—Yes.

3359. For getting harness horses?—Yes; there was a horse called "Nimrod."

3360. Mr. La Touche.—A brother to Excelsior?

Witness.—Oh, dear, no, a much older horse; he was by "Quicksilver" out of "Charm." Mr. H. H. O'H. O'Hara, of Clogher, brought him over to this country; he belonged to Mr. Walter Wynne, who had ridden him seven years with hounds, riding 17 stone; that horse stood in the country for a good while, and left his mark; but it is a long time ago, it must be 40 years.

3361. You don't know what his breeding was?—No.

3362. Mr. Carew.—How many years ago was that would you say?—Forty years.

3363. Was he a thoroughbred?—Yes; got by "Quicksilver," afterwards "The Emerald." "Quicksilver" was by "Messenger," and "Nameless" dam was a mare called "Charm." I think she was not in the stud book, but she was said to be a thoroughbred. He was a tremendously powerful horse. I never saw so strong a thoroughbred.

3364. You spoke of a half-bred by "Bluestocking," who had good stock?—Yes.

3365. Would you not be in favour of a half-bred for those mares?—I think this horse I spoke of has hardly a stain in him.

3366. He is not in the stud book?—No, his dam is not.

3367. Mr. La Touche.—Do they sell many foals, the farmers in your country, or keep them for three or four years?—They sell a good many of them as foals.

3368. Sell them in our market?—They are sold in the fair at Moneymore, a great many of them.

3369. Does one man buy a lot of them?—No, generally one.

3370. They buy one each?—One at a time is sold generally; sometimes the English dealers buy them there.

3371. Buy the foals?—Yes; that is not often; and sometimes they are [illegible].

3372. Reason for two Hackney stallions a good deal in your district?—One Hackney stallion which from the town of Magherafelt having the season; he comes from Limavady, Mr. Lecky's people; they like him pretty well. One of the men who objected to the Hackneys was a man who had kept a Hackney stallion himself, a Yorkshire Hackney.

3373. Did these people give any reason?—They don't like their action; they say it is a lifting action; and that they go off their action, and that it is a great effort with them to go.

3374. Does the pedigree finish a good many?—No, only I know [illegible] other horses. But I object to any pedigree that this stallion which I knew was a Hackney I don't think anyone would care much about him—no matter how much in favour he might be with Hackneys; he was a hobby-horse headed style of brute with bad carriage, I don't wonder they do not breed from him.

3375. Mr. Warren.—The Hackney you are specially alluding to was a son of "Broad Arrow"?—I don't specially allude to him except breeding from him myself and having a very bad horse from him.

3376. But you said he was a son of "Broad Arrow"?—Yes.

3377. Do you know what mare he was out of?—Said to be a Yorkshire cart mare.

3378. He was not a pure Hackney?—No, he was not.

3379. And this other Hackney which you think no one would breed from, how was he bred?—I don't know, he was a blood horse, he came from Limavady.

3380. You don't know whether he is a pure Hackney?—He was said to be.

3381. He is the horse that has been sold?—I don't know.

3382. You say that the trade in your district is practically entirely harness trade?—Yes, a harness trade.

3383. Then the demand for other horses is small?—It is, except locally for farm horses.

3384. That is general utility horses?—Yes.

3385. But the harness horse is the best class they try to produce?—Yes, that is what they want.

3386. I suppose you think action is a very great consideration in a harness horse?—No doubt.

3387. How have you formed your opinion as to Hackney action being bad, as you generally see Hackney action?—I don't like it myself. I don't like that style of action.

3388. Where have you seen it?—At a show in Cambridge where there were said to be very good Hackneys; I don't like their style of action.

3389. Where else?—And this horse "Excelsior" in Limavady.

3390. Then your experience is confined?—My experience is limited of course, but I don't like the action.

3391. It is practically confined to what you saw at Cambridge and the Limavady horse?—Yes, horses.

3392. I think you also bred from a horse called "Dr. O'Toole"?—Yes.

3393. Did you find his stock good?—Thoroughly bad.

3394. He was a thoroughbred?—Yes.

3395. Your aim was to breed hunters?—Yes.

3396. Did you find it pay?—out of that one mare I cannot complain of her not paying me.

3397. She was a specially good mare?—Yes, except those three of "Broad Arrow's" which did not pay me well, but a horse by "Crusader," and one by "Kate? Selta," and one by "Normanby" paid me well.

3398. You think the mares are bad in your district?—No doubt about it.

3399. And you think that an effort should be made to improve them so that they would be fit to cross with a thoroughbred horse?—Yes.

3400. How would you propose to improve the mares there?—With Clevelands.

3401. You alluded to two Clevelands in your district?—Yes.

3402. Have you seen them?—Only one of them.

3403. You only speak of the other by hearsay?—By hearsay; this horse I have seen last season was his second, and the other one was his first.

3404. Have you seen any Clevelands in other places?—At shows, and one or two in the county of Derry a long time ago.

3405. What shows?—Belfast occasionally.

3406. Pure Clevelands?—Said to be.

3407. Then your experience of Clevelands is confined to what you have seen in shows in Ireland?—Yes.

3408. And to the one horse in your own district?—Yes.

3409. I think also in your report you recommend that the horses that should be used should be strong thoroughbreds or Clevelands?—Yes.

Sir William Lowe, examined.

3410. So that your recommendation regarding Clevelands is only based on what you have seen yourself?—Yes; I have seen Clevelands elsewhere; a great many years ago there were a great many Cleveland carriage horses in my neighbourhood.

3411. You don't know if they were pedigreed?—No.

3412. Would you be inclined to register what you call a half-bred sire?—A half-bred sire with barely a stain in him, but I would not register an extreme cross such as a thoroughbred with a Hackney or Clydesdale.

3413. But what class of half-breds would you register?—One that you could not absolutely trace his pedigree in the stud book, but that spoke for himself as a thoroughbred.

3414. Then you would register on appearance?—Not entirely on appearance, because you can trace them.

3415. How many crosses would you think necessary in a half-bred horse to be registered?—I would do it where the dam and sire did not appear in the stud book, but were known to be thoroughbred.

3416. You would not require any definite particulars of thoroughbred cross?—I would not.

3417. I think you said you spoke to two dealers who disliked Hackneys very much?—Yes.

3418. I was just going to ask you to put the names of those two dealers in privately to the Chairman?—Yes.

3419. Were they large dealers?—Yes; they deal in a good many good horses in Moy fair.

3420. You don't know what experience they have had of Hackneys except that one kept what was called a Hackney stallion at one time?—No, that man was not a dealer, he was a veterinary surgeon.

3421. You don't know if these men have had any experience of Hackneys?—No, except they bought some of the produce, and didn't like them.

3422. CHAIRMAN.—I take it, Sir William, that what you would prefer to improve the breed of horses is a strong, sound, thoroughbred stallion?—Yes.

3423. And that you think it would improve the mares to cross them with a Cleveland Bay?—Yes.

3424. Would you prefer a Cleveland Bay to a Hackney?—I would on account of the great cross with a thoroughbred; I think a Cleveland is more like a thoroughbred than a Hackney; if you go in for breeding harness horses, I think you will be much more likely to have hunters from Clevelands than——

3425. How do you think the mares could be best improved—by a cross with what, as regards harness horses?—For harness horses I think the Clevelands are more likely to produce a big, upstanding carriage horse than the Hackney.

3426. And your opinion of the Clevelands and your opinion of the Hackney is arrived at from what you have seen, what you have heard, and what you have read?—Yes.

3427. Lord ARDILAUN.—You prefer a Cleveland for harness purposes, for these purposes, to the Hackney?—Yes; I think he is more of a thoroughbred looking horse.

3428. Do you prefer his action?—I think his action would take you over the ground faster than the Hackney.

3429. You mentioned a horse called "Ranelagh." Do you like his action?—I do not.

3430. Do you think, supposing you would breed a horse with his action, you would not get a high price for him?—I should say you would sell them well enough, but I would not like to buy him.

3431. Would you not get a better price for a horse like "Ranelagh," a harness horse, than for a Cleveland?—I do not. I don't think he would be so big or so useful.

3432. Still you would get a good price for a harness horse like "Ranelagh"?—Yes; any a horse like "Ranelagh" would pay right well.

3433. So that, although you don't personally like them, still you say it would pay the farmer to breed them?—It would pay them to breed a horse like "Ranelagh"; it would pay very well indeed.

3434. And with that action?—I wouldn't say that. So far I am convinced I would not be bothered with him.

3435. CHAIRMAN.—Is there anything else you would like to say to the Commission, Sir William?—I don't think there is anything I have got to say except to try to keep the mares in the country; it is a very important matter, more important perhaps than the sires; you have a fair chance of getting the thoroughbred horse because there are so many of them [illegible], but the difficulty is getting the farmers to keep [illegible] best mares.

3436. Lord ARDILAUN.—In the horses you saw was the thoroughbred you would want to improve the [illegible] to get them fit for it?—Yes; but even with the [illegible] that we have I think you have a better chance with a thoroughbred than with anything else.

3437. In the hunter line?—Yes.

3438. Mr. LA TOUCHE.—You agree with the London dealers that the best upstanding carriage horses are got by thoroughbreds?—I do.

3439. And you think that the big upstanding carriage horse is more likely to be produced by the thoroughbred than any other?—I think so. I was told recently up in the train the other day by a man who knows a good deal about the matter, that [illegible], the dealer, says that if Hackneys are introduced in Ireland it will spoil the carriage horse, of which he buys £14,000 worth each year.

3440. CHAIRMAN.—This is rather [illegible]. We can get it more directly?—I know that Hack? [illegible] are very good looking ones, whatever he might think.

The Rev. A. E. [illegible] Forster, J.P., examined. Rev. A. E. [illegible] Forster.

3441. CHAIRMAN.—You live in the county of Monaghan?—I do.

3442. In what part of the county?—The northern end of it, near to the town of Clones, bordering on Fermanagh.

3443. Can you give the Commission an idea of the character of your district, soil, and so on?—It is generally wet heavy clay.

3444. What kind of sized holdings?—Very small, from twenty acres down, some as low as five or six acres.

3445. Are many horses bred by the farmers of the district?—Not many; they say always that their farms are too small; they have no stalls for them.

3446. What kind of horses do they breed and from what class of mares?—A very low, small mongrel sort of mare that it would be difficult to describe, and from whatever stallion they can get easiest, and at the lowest rate.

3447. Do they breed for their own purposes or for sale?—For sale if they can get the price.

3448. What kind of stallions are there in the district?—For the most part stallions brought about to fairs; some call them half-bred; there are some thoroughbreds in the county, but the small farmers would not pay the service fee as a rule; there are several registered by the Royal Dublin Society but very few avail themselves of them.

3449. The fee is too high?—Too high, and also they do not like the stamp of the animals; those that are good the fee is too high, and the others they don't like.

3450. Are there any large farmers in your district who breed?—So far as I can say the larger farmer does not go in for it.

[illegible]

3451. Are you interested in the subject of horse-breeding yourself?—Yes, I have been acting for the Royal Dublin Society since it started in the county.

3452. Were you at the Clones show last autumn?—I was.

3453. What kind of show was it—I mean the stock exhibited?—A very fair young stock; they only have them up to three-year-old—a mare and foal, yearling, two-year-old and three-year-old, if in the hands of breeder.

3454. How were they bred generally?—By thoroughbreds, many by the registered stallions of the Royal Dublin Society.

3455. Have you been engaged in breeding of horses yourself at all?—Every year a little, for some twenty years with whatever mares I used on my farm, had one, two or three foals each year.

3456. What horse do you generally put them to?—The thoroughbred I can most easily approach.

3457. Is there any suitable thoroughbred near enough to you?—I have had two or three of the Royal Dublin Society's not far from me—kept by Colonel Thompson at Rockcorry, latterly three years, and before that, "Future Hope," in the county Fermanagh, kept by the Archdales, I found the most successful.

3458. What do you think influences the small farmer most—the fee or proximity?—Proximity and low rate of service, but what I find they lay more stress on than anything is the guarantee of the foal—no pay no foal; they don't like paying any fee absolutely.

3459. I suppose they are able to judge what class of horses would be best for them—supposing they can afford the fee?—They would like the horse they could sell best.

3460. You said I think you never had a quite sound horse?—I said that with a cart mare and a farm horse I never had a sound one.

3461. Lord Arnrown.—Never a sound one?—Between a cart mare and a thoroughbred—when the cross was a very distinct one, in that case I never had a sound one produced from the same mare that had always bred sound ones with a horse of her own class.

3462. Chairman.—Are there any Clydesdale stallions in your county?—I don't know that in this county, Monaghan, there is a Clydesdale; in the adjoining counties there are.

3463. Or Clevelands or anything of that kind?—Latterly there has been a Cleveland, within the last three years I should think.

3464. Have you formed any opinion as to the advantages and disadvantages of crossing mares with a Cleveland for producing hunters?—Not the least.

3465. No experiments?—From anything I do know I should not like to try the experiment.

3466. How about the Hackney?—Not with a view of producing a hunter, I would not run the risk; all horse-breeding on the best lines is very risky; taking every precaution that one can you will be often disappointed.

3467. Mr. Carew.—It is a speculation?—Yes.

3468. Chairman.—And you don't think that the risks would be lessened by the introduction of Cleveland blood?—Not for hunters.

3469. And how about the introduction of Hackney blood?—I know very little about it; anything I do know so far as my experience goes in breeding is against them. Having bred from the same mare by a thoroughbred horse and also by them, but only four or five foals—I had a little mare, practically a thoroughbred, that got weight-carrying hunters from "Future Hope," and absolutely worthless foals from a Hackney—a little more, her produce went for £250 in England as a weight-carrying hunter. I tried to sell a four-year-old—a horse by a Hackney—and I could not get £20 for him.

3470. What Hackney sire?—"Prince George;" he was standing in Fermanagh.

3471. Mr. Wrench.—He was a small horse?—He was, and there my knowledge of Hackneys ends, except so far as breeding from that one.

3472. Chairman.—Your personal knowledge?—That is all.

3473. Speaking generally, what do you consider the best class of stallion?—Undoubtedly the thoroughbred of the right type, get a thoroughbred with bone.

3474. You have described the mares as being very mongrel?—Yes; and as a rule if the farmer has a filly foal he cannot sell he keeps her to breed from. He only keeps her to breed because he cannot get the price.

3475. Can you suggest what, in your opinion, would be the best way to improve the mares?—I am in hopes that the plan which is in work now with the Royal Dublin Society will do it—giving prizes to men to keep the mares. I was always in favour of that, but I have been disappointed that they won't pay the service money. The class of men who have these poor mares won't go in for the service of the thoroughbred, because they have to pay too much. If they could combine somewhat of the two systems it might have a good effect—rewarding the farmer for keeping a good mare, and helping him to get the service of the horse. In my locality that is what I have observed.

3476. To improve the breed of the mares (to make them more suitable, and thereby produce more valuable carriage horses and hunters), do you think it would be advisable to introduce any other cross?—Not so far as I know, if you could get a thoroughbred with good enough bone.

3477. And the Royal Dublin Society's scheme has not, in your opinion, been very successful in your county?—Not in my immediate neighbourhood, in the end of the county nearer Dublin—Carrickmacross and Castleblayney—there is a larger class of farmer with better mares, and they are making good use of it. They are crossing now with mares got by the sires that they were helped with the service of in years gone by, and getting prizes for those mares.

3478. We have heard it in evidence several times that the demand for the general utility horse has declined, and the price declined, although the prices for good hunters and good carriage horses keeps up—do you think the small farmers, under any circumstances, would be able to breed valuable horses?—Sometimes with these unaccountable mares an odd cross hits well, and they get a horse which pays them fairly.

3479. If it be true that the demand for the general utility horse is declining, in assisting small farmers to breed, would it be assisting him in endeavouring to encourage him in what was bound to be an unprofitable business?—That is a very difficult question; if the price continues to fall of the middling or worse than middling horse, it is a question if it would pay him.

3480. Do you know if the foreign competition has any effect on the middling or worse than middling horse?—I know the dealers say they can get a foreign horse much cheaper. There are several causes to pull down the price.

3481. What are they?—The foreign competition, and a number of people have given up horses that made use of them formerly, together with the fact that a class of people who kept horses as a luxury are being deprived of the means of keeping them.

3482. A good many people who kept horses cannot now afford it?—Yes, that is one cause; they are taking to bicycles and other means of conveyance, and the foreign competition; I think these three things have pulled down the prices of horses.

3483. Are many horses sold for remounts in your part of the country?—Yes, in the fair of Clones; I think a couple of hundred in every fair.

3484. Did you hear a suggestion made by a former witness that it would be a good thing if Artillery mares could be distributed among the farmers?—Yes, I heard it, but I am not competent to say. But those [illegible] from everywhere, the dealers said to [illegible] for [illegible] from many parts. Dealers bring them to [illegible] from [illegible] and other parts of [illegible]; it is a place that a [illegible] of horses from all parts and dealers come from everywhere to it.

3486. Mr. [illegible].—[illegible] of ponies in your district?—[illegible] very [illegible]; there is no such thing as a pony [illegible] to the [illegible] that I know of.

3487. Is the [illegible] adapted to the breeding of ponies?—I should think it would, but the question is if they would be able to command a price. I don't think they would [illegible] anything that would [illegible] them.

3488. You have had no experience of the breeding of ponies?—The only [illegible] I have bred a good many.

3489. How did you find they paid?—I had a [illegible] mare [illegible] and [illegible] being [illegible] in foal. I sold some and got £20 or £30 for them.

3490. What were they by?—[illegible] I bred from was a [illegible], a pony of Lord Dunsandle's.

3491. What was he, a pony?—Yes, a [illegible], they call him a pony.

3492. Have you any **experience of the Barb or Arab?**—No.

3493. They have never been tried up with you?—They have; [illegible] Lord [illegible] [illegible] an Arab, but I don't know much about the result.

3494. Have you ever seen any of his produce?—I have seen some but I don't know that I can form any opinion; they were very young when I saw them.

3495. Mr. [illegible].—I think you said your only experience of [illegible] was with "Royal George"?—That is all.

3496. You would not call him a good specimen of a horse of any kind?—No, was more of a pony; he was not 15 hands.

3497. And the mares you bred [illegible] good mares [illegible] before you crossed with "Royal George"; and when you [illegible] [illegible] a thoroughbred [illegible] with a [illegible] thoroughbred?—It was always from a thoroughbred that I bred before.

3498. I gather the thoroughbred you bred from before was a good deal bigger than "Royal George"?—Yes, he was 16 hands at least.

3499. And with a big thoroughbred you produced a good result?—Yes.

3500. And with a small [illegible] you produced a bad result?—That is all I can say.

3501. In your recommendation as to what class of horse would be [illegible] what shape, you say, "I like a small compact thoroughbred with good bone and action under 16 hands, anything over 15.3"?—With fair action.

3502. Would it not be better for these farmers to breed [illegible] horses than to [illegible] to breed hunters?—I think it would.

3503. A horse with good **action does sell well generally** [illegible] the one thing **that does sell a horse** [illegible].

3504. Clones is one of the chief monthly fairs in the North of Ireland?—[illegible] [illegible] fair, it is the best monthly fair in Ireland. I don't know any [illegible] places there are twelve fairs [illegible] Clones and May. [illegible] are [illegible] fairs, [illegible] you understand, but [illegible] I think the only [illegible] it is May.

3505. [illegible] Clones [illegible] the county Fermanagh, a considerable district where horses are bred?—Fermanagh is a great horse breeding county, [illegible].

3506. Especially [illegible] the town of Clones?—Yes.

3507. [illegible] a good [illegible] horse bred in your district [illegible] in the [illegible]?—[illegible]. Fermanagh is [illegible] horse-breeding county.

3508. And your experience [illegible] [illegible] [illegible] does not [illegible]?—[illegible], without exception, [illegible].

3509. Therefore in trying to improve the stock of small farmers' mares, the [illegible] [illegible] for [illegible] the [illegible] I think so.

3510. Do you think a thoroughbred horse would be [illegible] to all the [illegible] your [illegible]?—Well, I suppose so; [illegible] I think [illegible] through [illegible] for the good of the [illegible].

3511. If a man must keep a mare [illegible] breeding as a [illegible] of profit, [illegible] [illegible] ought not to be [illegible] with a thoroughbred horse, [illegible] and [illegible] I think they ought to be [illegible] anything.

3512. You would stop them altogether from breeding?—I would.

3513. [illegible] the breeding of horses is concerned, do you think that is [illegible]?—[illegible] as it is now.

3514. You said a better class of horse was coming from the [illegible] and [illegible] district, from that end of the county?—Yes.

3515. You don't attribute that to the size of the farms?—Large farms are able to get a better class of horse by keeping large farms.

3516. [illegible] think [illegible] [illegible] [illegible] in [illegible] [illegible] and up to [illegible] [illegible] where there are large farms.

3517. But is it not a fact that the [illegible] round Clones are much larger, as a rule, than about [illegible] and [illegible], except just round that district?—That is the only district from which the men [illegible] to make use of the Royal Dublin Society's grant; that is the only reason I know of [illegible].

3518. Do you think any grant [illegible] through the Royal Dublin Society or other society would be expended through the local society, such as Clones?—[illegible] they [illegible] by a [illegible] [illegible] I don't [illegible] [illegible], the Royal Dublin Society [illegible] by local committee.

3519. Don't the Royal Dublin Society name their own committee?—Well, I can only tell you as my own county; they asked me would I act as [illegible] and to appoint my own committee.

3520. You think that is a better way than asking the people to appoint a committee?—That I don't know.

3521. You said you thought the people [illegible] [illegible] to form an opinion as to which they want for themselves?—Yes.

3522. At present they have no voice in the selection of the committee?—No.

3523. Chairman.—Is there anything you would like to say to the Commission?—I have heard a [illegible] about [illegible] [illegible] [illegible] [illegible]; if there be a horse [illegible] a thoroughbred, who had proved himself a [illegible], I think such a horse as that might be [illegible] [illegible] has proved himself, because if he [illegible] a horse [illegible] [illegible] [illegible] what sort of [illegible] he will produce; I think there is an ideal horse, which might not be a thoroughbred that ought to be [illegible] [illegible] he has proved himself.

3524. That is approved of by **some competent** authority?—By the [illegible] he got; **by his produce** only.

3525. But somebody must judge of that?—The only proof [illegible] is his produce; if [illegible] a [illegible] one, and if he was [illegible] to continue the [illegible] of the Royal Dublin Society I know of no better thing for the country—namely, encouraging the farmers to keep a good mare, and helping them also in the service of a good horse. [illegible] [illegible] paying for the service of the horse; they [illegible] and gave all the money in prizes to the mares. If it were [illegible] to [illegible] [illegible] of [illegible] [illegible] I think it would [illegible].

3525. Mr. La Touche.—Do you think mares in your county are fit to be bred from to all with a suitable thoroughbred horse?—I do.

3526. Do you think that the mares that are not fit to be put to a thoroughbred are not fit to be put to a horse of any sort or kind?—I do. I think it is not worth the cost.

3527. Mr. Wrench.—Then you think you would go on breeding their produce with a thoroughbred horse?—I should think so.

3528. And you don't think the result in their would be a lot of weeds?—Well, but we have [illegible] that we have got rid of the worst of them.

3529. Then you say that out of the mares that might not be bred from are fit to be crossed with a thoroughbred horse?—But then as to crossing again I really know nothing.

3530. You don't pretend to say you would go on crossing with thoroughbred horses?—I myself have [illegible] with a thoroughbred, then [illegible] got by a thoroughbred; then I have sent them again to a thoroughbred. I found them always fairly satisfactory.

3531. You found you got good prices for them also?—Yes.

3532. Then, of course, your mares are perhaps exceptionally good, better than the farmers have in the district?—Oh, they are, of course they are better.

3533. You think you could go on breeding from thoroughbred horses without bringing in any stronger strain?—I would prefer it. I would rather do it myself.

3534. And you think the produce would be as suitable to work on the farms, and do the work of the people when they are required?—Oh, if you want farming I would go to the Clydesdale.

3535. No, but it is not necessary on the small farms that you speak of always to have a horse of the same strength as the Clydesdale, is it?—No, they want the horse to go to the market and for general purposes.

3536. Or for light carts?—Yes.

3537. But you think a horse with two or three crosses of thoroughbred blood in him would be a suitable horse for that purpose?—I have seen them do very well with them.

3538. Mr. Carew.—If you desired a change you would go to the half-bred horse that you would register?—I would have no objection to one that had proved himself.

3539. The thoroughbred and the registered half-bred you would go to?—I am in favour of registering nothing but a pure bred and an exceptional case of a horse that had proved himself a valuable sire.

3540. And if you wanted a change from the thoroughbred with these good mares you have you would prefer to send them to a half-bred that was registered, when he had shown by his produce he was a good one?—Yes, I should place him then in the category of a thoroughbred for use.

3541. Mr. Wrench.—Would you register any horse of a pure breed except a thoroughbred?—I know nothing about any other.

3542. In answer to the query "What breed of stallion do you consider most suitable to mate with the mares in your district," Mr. Forster says, "Any sound compact stallion with bone and action out of some pure breed, thoroughbred, Clydesdale, Cleveland, or Hackney"?—Any pure breed I would register.

3543. You register any of these three breeds that you have named there if they were suitable?—I would.

3544. Chairman.—That is quite different to what I understood you to say before. I should like to know what your opinion is, because I asked you some time ago a question whether to make the mares in your district more suitable to be crossed with a thoroughbred sire you thought the introduction of Clydesdale or Hackney blood would be of service. I understood you to say you did not think so. Now I gather from this you approve of the Clydesdale and Hackney, provided they were pure bred?—Clydesdale I always approved of for farm purposes, and often bred from them.

3545. The distinction is you do not approve of them for hunters and carriage horses, but you do approve of them for farms?—Or even for farmers to get a price. The small farmer when he breeds wants to have something to sell in the first instance, and they do not sell so well.

3546. Mr. Wrench.—What do not sell so well?—The produce of the Clydesdale.

3547. Chairman.—May I put it this way that as regards breeding hunters or high class carriage horses you would consider that the introduction of the Clydesdale or Hackney blood, even from a pure bred Clydesdale or Hackney stallion, would be of no advantage?—That is my opinion.

3548. But as regards horses for farming purposes and a certain class of carriage horse that you think the introduction of that blood, provided the sire was pure bred, would be an advantage?—It might be, but I have no experience of the Hackney beyond what I have stated, and of the Clydesdale, except for farm work, for which I think it is very valuable.

Mr. Thomas M'[illegible], examined.

3549. Chairman.—You live in the county Monaghan, I think?—Yes, sir.

3550. What part of the county?—Castleblayney.

3551. Are you occupied in farming?—A little bit, I have seven farms of land round Castleblayney.

3552. You breed horses?—A little.

3553. Do you deal in horses?—Yes.

3554. And you know the whole county pretty well as regards horsebreeding?—Oh, yes, I know several countries—I know Ireland, England, and America.

3555. Do you keep a stallion yourself?—Yes, sir.

3556. What kind of a stallion?—Different kinds I kept.

3557. Oh, you have got several?—Yes, had several.

3558. How many have you got now or how many have you had altogether?—I could not tell you I had so many.

3559. Of all kinds of breeds?—All kinds of breeds—no, I never had any Clydesdales or Arabs.

3560. How many have you got now?—I have some racing now that I am going to keep as sires, but I have got three sires at present at home in my place.

3561. What are they?—Thoroughbred.

3562. All thoroughbreds?—Yes. I had a Hackney about twenty years ago and he died with me, I had him three years.

3563. Have you ever had a Hackney since?—Yes, I went to the London show and I bought a Hackney there, a thoroughbred, I gave [illegible] for him, I bought him for my own purposes; he was a fine Hackney 15.3 hands, made like a hunter, good neck and shoulders, could carry you with hounds I think if he would gallop enough.

3564. What became of him?—I sold him the day I landed him from London to an American with [illegible] of profit. I thought a nearly thoroughbred was [illegible] wanting for a stallion, and so I took it, and I was very sorry for it after; I bought him purposely to keep as a sire.

3565. What is the size of the farms in your neighbourhood, small or large?—There are some of them small and some not very large, I think I have the largest farm I know of myself for a good while.

[illegible] What class of horses are bred—saddle horses, hunters, or what?—I think there are more carriage horses bred about there except a few. I breed myself.

[illegible] What kind of horse does the farmer go in for producing?—Really, I could not answer the question, but I think all the farmers would be a pony for a [illegible], or something cheap, and as [illegible] of [illegible] when they are bringing the mare into the [illegible] they don't [illegible] at all, only to [illegible] something cheap. As a rule the farmers round where I live would just give as much for a [illegible] as they would for a salmon.

[illegible] What kind of mares do they breed from?—I could not tell you the pedigrees of them.

[illegible] No, I don't suppose you could, but you might give us an idea of what they are like?—Some of them are pretty big; and if they got a good mare they would breed a very useful horse; if they were crossed with a good thoroughbred stallion, in the first place, with short legs and plenty of bone, and went straight to his work, and stepped a little high, not a very big or leggy thoroughbred stallion, only a horse about [illegible], with plenty of bone, good shoulders, and tail on the top of his back. Then there is the Hackney. If you want to breed from a Hackney with the [illegible], you must have a Hackney with good [illegible] shoulders, good [illegible], legs and feet, a short back, and the tail on the top of his back with action; if you put that upon a half-bred mare in any country, I will guarantee you will breed a good riding horse. I had a [illegible] when I sent her to a Hackney [illegible] and I got a [illegible], and it is as pretty a riding [illegible] as ever I saw, one of the best [illegible].

[illegible] Have you sold any produce of your mares by the Hackney [illegible]?—Oh, yes, I did, when I had it, but it is 10 or 12 years ago, I could not tell you so much about it. The Hackney stallion's name was [illegible]; I [illegible] him [illegible] years, and I bought [illegible].

[illegible] Have you any knowledge or any experience of the produce of the [illegible]?—Well, it is a thing I don't take much interest in, I cannot tell you about that, I don't go round [illegible] the farmers to see what they have got.

[illegible] You buy and sell horses, don't you?—Yes; [illegible], when I am [illegible] buy any one has [illegible] me [illegible], let them not think I am [illegible] buy [illegible]; I am only a [illegible].

[illegible] What is your opinion of the half-bred stallion?—I cannot answer the question; I never had one.

[illegible] You have no opinion as to whether a half-bred sire is better or worse than a thoroughbred sire?—I cannot answer the question, because I never had one; and when I had not I could not answer [illegible].

[illegible] You have no opinion about anything unless you have had personal experience of it?—Yes, and [illegible] to see the [illegible] or more than a half-bred. I often [illegible] some very good hunters out of half-bred [illegible] got by thoroughbred [illegible]; and I got three or four very good ones that were got by a Hackney stallion, [illegible] 17 or 18 years ago, and I sold them at large prices, but the [illegible] in England at that time. [illegible]; [illegible] any [illegible], a [illegible] you take to market to sell. If it has not [illegible] just like a bull without a [illegible], it is very little use.

[illegible] Have you got a horse named [illegible]?—I had him; he is dead, which I am very sorry for.

[illegible] Was he in the Stud Book?—He was got by [illegible]; I bought him of [illegible], [illegible], Cheshire.

[illegible] What breed of stallion do you consider the best calculated to produce high-class harness horses and leaders?—Thoroughbreds **will produce the best** horses.

[illegible] What about a harness horse?—I said [illegible] [illegible]. I sent them to England last Monday; I sold them last Thursday week; I sold the [illegible] to [illegible] at [illegible] a piece, and there was [illegible] of this lot got by Hackneys. I gave the [illegible] [illegible].

[illegible] What am I to deduce from that **as your** opinion?—I am only telling you what is the way you [illegible] the [illegible] what they were got by, in [illegible] the [illegible] of [illegible].

[illegible] I am asking you which you prefer. If you have not got any opinion you have only to say so. I was asking you whether you would prefer a Hackney or a thoroughbred or any other sire to produce high-class carriage horses?—If you have a right strong [illegible] and has [illegible], she will get the best carriage horse with a thoroughbred horse, but if you have a good mare with good shoulders and [illegible] of a Hackney, he will get as good a one as the thoroughbred, [illegible], for [illegible], for they will have better [illegible], and they [illegible] [illegible] in London that used to buy big horses they [illegible] to get them now from [illegible] to under 16.

[illegible] [illegible] has a large effect upon the price, has it not?—It is everything to the harness horse, but not to the hunter.

[illegible] I am talking of the harness horse; do you think a horse is more likely to be obtained from a Hackney sire than any other?—I am sure the Hackney sire will produce better action if he gets a [illegible] [illegible], and the Hackney sire to be a good sound one with good shoulders and [illegible], and plenty of bone, and above everything [illegible] of his [illegible].

[illegible] What class of a horse do you think it pays best to breed [illegible]?—I [illegible] [illegible] a [illegible] for [illegible] [illegible] a thoroughbred; and if you want to ask me I prefer [illegible] a thoroughbred.

[illegible] [illegible], [illegible] yourself?—That **was** [illegible], but when you asked me what was **my opinion** I have given it to you.

[illegible] [illegible] the Commission to understand that you think the best thing the [illegible] in your district could do would be to breed thoroughbred [illegible]?—[illegible] the farmers cannot afford it; [illegible] [illegible] [illegible] for the [illegible] [illegible] in.

[illegible] I think you said you had some experience in America?—Yes, a little; I was there seven times, [illegible] horses out there and back fifteen [illegible].

[illegible] Have you sold many horses to America?—Yes.

[illegible] And imported [illegible] from America?—Yes. I was given [illegible] for a Hackney four-year-old, called "The [illegible] of [illegible]," when I took him to America.

[illegible] Is there much demand for Hackneys **in** America?—Yes, sir.

[illegible] What do they use them for?—For breeding purposes, if they are stallions.

[illegible] And you have imported horses from America?—Oh, yes.

[illegible] What [illegible] of horses?—I bought them from [illegible] to [illegible] a piece.

[illegible] And what became of them?—Some of them died on the [illegible] home, and some of them died [illegible], and some of them I sold at a very good price. I sold one the other day at [illegible]. I gave [illegible] for [illegible] in America, and it made [illegible]; and I sold one [illegible] I gave [illegible] for, and it made [illegible], so I am just telling you a little [illegible] about my trade.

[illegible] Where were they landed, these horses from America?—In Liverpool; I bought them in Chicago. I want to tell you where I bought them; and then I took them from Chicago to New York and shipped them by the White Star Company.

[illegible] You selected them yourself, I suppose?—Oh,

[illegible] Mr. Thomas [illegible]

you see, I am satisfied, if I get the worth of my money, at buying it.

3600. It has been mentioned in evidence by a good many witnesses that they think the importation of American horses has knocked down prices a good deal; is that your opinion?—That is my opinion, exactly, and I often saw 700 horses of a day in Chicago for sale, and I would not pick [illegible] out of the 700 to pay the expense of taking them home.

3601. Do you think the quality of the mares in your district is improving or getting worse than fifty years? —Well, I think there is a difference in them; there were a great deal better brood-mares so many years ago than there are now, I am sure.

3602. How do you account for their falling off?—If a farmer in my country had a mare three years old that would make from £30 to £40 [illegible] he will sell her, [illegible] the Government [illegible] got and bred [illegible].

3603. [illegible] not always [illegible]—No, years ago they did not [illegible] the [illegible] very pretty well off, they would keep a good brood mare and breed from her, but now they cannot afford it, the small farmers, I am not talking of large farmers.

3604. Do you think anything can be done to stop that?—Oh, yes, I think a great deal can be done to [illegible] and encourage the farmers in this country.

3605. In what way do you think they could be helped?—In the first place to tax every horse that comes out of America to be landed in England, the same as every horse that comes from us and everything else that comes from America [illegible] have to pay duty on; I had to pay as much as forty per cent. for taking horses there. That is the first [illegible] would encourage the farmers [illegible] I heard other gentlemen suggested to get them branded, that would not do [illegible] for the sort of horses they breed in this country, because these Americans are all sold for hard work, [illegible] and [illegible]. Seven years ago I paid £15 a head for them coming from New York to Liverpool, and this year I paid £3 10s in a better ship and I will tell you what we had, we had 331 horses, 800 [illegible], 9,000 sheep and 15,000 tons of dead meat in the "Georgic."

3606. Then you would recommend that these horses should have a duty put upon them?—Yes, a duty on them and on cattle. Seven years ago the [illegible] [illegible] for a [illegible] and [illegible]. If we sent carriage horses or [illegible] to America we have to pay forty per cent. on them when they go there, and there is no way at all to encourage farmers in England or Ireland only to make the American horses pay duty as we have to pay there on everything except animals for breeding purposes, then they let it go free if we can show them [illegible] is a stud book.

3607. Supposing that cannot be done can you suggest any other way in which the breed of horses can be improved?—There is no way the breed of horses can be much better improved than to give every farmer the price of a useful mare and [illegible] not give her to him and make him pay as much a year until she is paid for; sending her to him without the money for five years and he pay so much a year until she was paid for.

3608. On the instalment system?—Yes, the Jew system.

3609. Where would the mares come from?—You can buy plenty of them in England after the hunting season, broken down mares, in England or Ireland too, mares with good [illegible], [illegible] good bone, supposing they are broken down in their [illegible] or [illegible], by hard work this is the right class of mare for a farmer to breed from.

3610. Do you suggest any way by which the farmers can be induced to keep their best mares in the country?—There are plenty of mares, I may say, mares, and mares I know in plenty of regiments, there are plenty of them would do a farmer well for hard work on the farm and to breed a very good foal.

3607. But supposing they did breed a good foal you say the farmers are much more inclined now than they used to be to sell their best mares and keep the worst ones, how would you prevent that?—The farmers are pressed so much, they are getting such a bad price for their wheat, corn, and flax, and every such thing as that, they have their bills to meet, and they must sell what will get them the money, that is what I hear them talking. I often pressed them to borrow money and pay interest on the money and keep their good mares, that they never could make money out of horse-breeding unless they had good mares.

3608. Do you think anything can be done by offering prizes?—That would be very good, and I think it has done a great deal of good, but still the poor man what prize he gets cannot induce him to keep what he can sell for from £35 to £40 and he has the money to pay.

3609. Sir T. Esmonde.—You mentioned about the cheapness of the rates from America, you mentioned that you can bring a horse over for £3?—That is what I paid.

3610. Have you any idea how the American rates compare with the Irish railway rates?—Oh, yes, every way, you can get five tons of stuff from New York to Liverpool for five shillings a ton and you will pay fourteen shillings a ton from Liverpool to Dundalk.

3611. Then you consider that the Irish railway rates are excessive?—I am talking of the steamboat now, I brought thirty horses nearly 1,100 miles in one carriage for $30 dollars, £30, and I suppose they would charge about five times that much in England, or more.

3612. Then as to the quality of American horses you say you have had a good deal of experience in American horses, you have bought there and sold them over here?—I have got some of them yet and I could sell you a couple or three very good ones too.

3613. Do you find taking them generally they are as good as the Irish horses?—I don't say so, they are not, but for some purposes they are very good, but they are not as good as the Irish horses at all.

3614. For what purposes are they good?—For harness and going quick.

3615. That is the American trotter?—I don't call them the American trotter at all but the American harness horse.

3616. Then you distinguish between the harness horse and the trotter?—They are two different classes.

3617. And you have no experience of the American trotter?—I have, and I have one of them now, if you come down I will lay a wager with you and trot you for some money if you like, but he has as good action as any harness horse in Dublin, but if you loose his head and let him go he will touch the ground, and if you get hold of him by the head and drive him along he will step out. If you want a horse to step you must get hold of him by the head and not let him go slithering along.

3618. For harness purposes you think the American horses are as good as the Irish?—I say not, they are not worth as much money, not but I bid 1,450 dollars for a harness horse got by a Hackney stallion, and he was bought by a millionaire in Chicago, he went for 1,650 dollars, that was £330.

3619. And I think you also said that you would not approve of branding American horses, you thought that would do no good to the horse purchaser?—I think not, I don't think anything you could do with him, brand him or not, it would not rise him or fall him because they are only for a certain class. Out of 700 horses that you will see in Chicago in a day perhaps you would not buy ten; perhaps, one day you might might buy ten and you might be a week there and you would not buy one, I was out with them buying [illegible] horses.

3620. Yes, but I mean American horses brought over here and sold in England as Irish horses?—I never knew any of them to be done that way.

3621. Do you think if they were branded that would be prevented?—I don't know, I cannot answer the question, everyone would know then that they were American.

3622. Mr. Carew.—You spoke of breeding from a Hackney?—Yes, sir.

3623. The mare that you would mate with a Hackney would require to be a better shape and make than the one you would mate with a thoroughbred?—It would, with better neck and shoulders and well ribbed and straight on her legs with plenty of bone.

3624. So far as you are concerned, you would prefer the thoroughbred produce to the Hackney produce?—I prefer a thoroughbred horse for getting hunters, for a Hackney, in my opinion, won't get any hunter; but a Hackney, if he gets mated with a good sort of mare, will get a [illegible] carriage horse.

3625. It is more difficult to mate with the Hackney than with a thoroughbred?—There are plenty of thoroughbreds that if you mate them with Irish mares you will get nothing but weeds. I keep three thoroughbred stallions at present, and I would not let them cover any mare unless she pleased me, because it only gives your horse a bad name, they are bringing wretches of mares there, and I would rather give them £5 or £10 and let them go somewhere else; in fact, I would not let them have the service of the horse.

3626. Mr. La Touche.—You say you have had no experience of breeding from half-bred horses?—I have not.

3627. I suppose you have bought horses that were by half-bred horses?—Indeed I did, and sold them for horses at big prices; I heard it after.

3628. You have no particular objection to horses got by half-bred horses?—Not the least.

3629. Don't you think a stallion that was got by a thoroughbred horse out of a mare got by a thoroughbred horse is just as likely to be as good a stallion as a Hackney?—A first rate stallion for harness horses, but not to get hunters; we don't want any stallions in this country to get harness horses, we only want them to get hunters, or stepping horses with plenty of bone.

3630. Do you agree with Messrs. East and Wimbush, for instance, who say that the best matching carriage horses are got by a thoroughbred horse?—I dare say that is, but I think there is got as good by Hackney horses as there is got by thoroughbred horses.

3631. You are aware that East and Wimbush, who are carriage horse dealers, have expressed a strong opinion contrary to the advantage of introducing Hackneys?—I know East and the whole breed of them these fifty years, many men have many minds; I sold them horses.

3632. You are aware they have expressed that opinion?—I am not aware of anything, I did not see it in the paper, or look at it; my chief point is to buy cheap and sell dear.

3633. Would you agree with such an opinion?—I would, they have great experience, because every horse they buy from me they must have the pedigree from me or from my son, they take them all down, and they have a better right to know than anybody else, but I don't know what they said or suggested.

3634. You said you sold twenty-six harness horses?—Yes, but I did not tell you who I sold them to.

3635. I don't want to know?—I will put it in writing, but I won't make it public; I will put in writing what I got for them, and I will put the two together.

3636. You sold twenty-six harness horses, at any rate, at an average price of £90, that was all round?—All round; some of them perhaps as high as £110, some at £65 to £70, but the round number was £90 a piece.

3637. Out of the twenty-six, five were got by Hackneys?—Yes, and they got Hackney pedigrees.

3638. The other ones were got by thoroughbred horses?—Everyone of them by thoroughbreds [illegible] to my opinion.

3639. So that there were five bred by thoroughbreds to one got by the Hackney?—Decidedly.

3640. And those were all harness horses?—They are all harness horses, and most likely I will get some of them back, and they will go, according to harness, and I will make hunters of them.

3641. You say there are a lot of mares in the country quite unsuitable to put to the ordinary thoroughbred horse, and that would produce nothing but weeds?—My opinion is, that if the thoroughbred horse is [illegible], with plenty of bone and [illegible] legs, and has good standing action, they may put it, and unless the horse is that I would think it a very bad one to put them to.

3642. Do you find a good brood mare is invariably a good-looking animal?—Yes, but the looks of a mare or horse is nothing until you try them.

3643. Do you mean to say you can stand over them and say that mare will be a good brood mare, and her produce will be worth £80 as a three-year-old?—I would say nothing until I saw her going.

3644. But if you saw her moved?—Then I would give you my opinion.

3645. Don't you think mares that you [illegible] very good things, very often a big, [illegible] standing mare with [illegible] and style never produces anything so good as herself?—They must be mated with the right kind of horse.

3646. You do think you can judge a brood mare by her personal appearance?—Yes; and if I knew the breeding and saw her appearance, the [illegible] and the way she stands and walks, and if she was mated with a thoroughbred horse that suited her, or a Hackney horse.

3647. Have you ever attended any of those shows of the Dublin Society to select mares for prizes?—I think I did.

3648. Could you always pick out the mare that had [illegible] to be the best brood mare by looking at her?—I give my opinion, you cannot always do it, [illegible] along with me; [illegible] not do it.

3649. Do you think of those many mares that the mare that has got first prize is always the best [illegible] in the country?—[illegible] many [illegible] a [illegible] and after she has gone [illegible] walking. Personal appearance is all very well, to have good bone and legs, there is nothing like to [illegible] with, and action—[illegible] if they have not, I would not be breeding from them only for a hunter.

3650. Mr. Wrench.—With regard to those five that were got by Hackneys, were they as good as the other ones?—They were not worse; I think they were mostly at an average. Some were extraordinary good [illegible] and so good, but I think they were worth on average perhaps £80 a piece.

3651. Have you sold any horses in England on this trip [illegible] from America—any American horses that you brought to England?—No, I never sold an American, and I never [illegible] in England since.

3652. Have you sold any American horses in Liverpool to [illegible] [illegible] which question, I think, [illegible]? Well, when you ask it, I will [illegible]; out of the forty-six I only picked [illegible], I thought I would have bought the whole of them, and instead of that I only picked [illegible]; [illegible] did not [illegible] them.

3653. And do you think the fact of dealers being able to buy the American horses in England prevents them coming over to Ireland to buy horses [illegible]. [illegible] a [illegible] [illegible] horse [illegible] more

Nov. 19, 1896.

Mr. Thomas M'Kane.

cheaper in America than it is in Paris, where I used to get the best prices. I could buy a pair of good carriage horses in London, and give a good price for them, and sell them in Chicago, New York, Philadelphia, or Boston for more money than they would bring in those places.

3654. The good horses are dearer in America than here?—Yes, but the commoner horses sold for the working classes are cheap in America.

3655. So that it is the commoner horses in America that are missing the superior horses here?—They are missing the farmers of the country.

3656. There is no trade for bad horses?—The farmers cannot get any price for their horses; where they used to get £50 they are down to £7 or £10 a piece these three years.

3657. Do you think the trade in harness horses is as profitable to the trade as hunters?—No; if you had the customers for the harness it is a good deal the best.

3658. Which is the standard trade?—Of course the hunter trade; there are some dealers buy harness horses, and give good prices, and they hardly ever buy a hunter, the hunting trade is a trade by itself.

3659. Can you always sell a good harness horse?—Yes, you can.

3660. If he has good action?—Action is everything; there is too long a time having a harness horse without action; buy them if you can that would step as high as wild geese can fly; then you will sell them.

3661. Then you don't think a horse could step too high for sale?—No, if he goes straight.

3662. You think it is not wise a guide for farmers to breed horses with good action as to breed hunters?—A farmer might have more faith, and he might not have a hunter out of the grown mare he might breed another horse and have, generally take horses, and he would get a fair price for three out of the mares.

3663. That it is more certain although you don't get so big a price?—I think for the farmer it is easier for him to breed harness horses than it is to breed hunters; in the beginning if you want to breed a hunter to go across country you must have good horses and then they are bred and reared again, and you must keep them well and train them well. If a farmer has a hunter horse only half trained he can sell him, but there is no gentleman or dealer that wants to buy a hunter if he is not thoroughly trained to ride with hounds.

3664. And if you see a good looking horse in a fair with good action do you stop to find out how he is bred before you try to buy him?—I did not even recognise if he had action and looks to please me how he was bred; I would not bother the man to ask him, because every man out of ten would give you a pedigree that the horse never was bred by at all.

3665. Do you think other dealers follow your opinion, and buy what they see and like?—I won't answer for any other dealer's opinion but my own.

3666. You yourself would not think of asking how he was bred unless if I liked the horse, not even a hunter, if I liked the way he walked and galloped, because there is a power of them sold with false pedigrees.

3667. You think that so long as good looking, good horses to look at, are bred in Ireland people will come over to buy them, no matter how they are bred?—No matter how they are bred.

3668. You have heard that some people object to the introduction of Hackney blood into Ireland; do you think the mere fact of there being a few Hackney stallions in Ireland would prevent people coming over to buy horses, and giving as big prices for a good horse as before?—Twenty years ago the best coaching horse that could be found was in Yorkshire, and when they started to introduce this Hackney blood they all gave up breeding coachers, and turned to the Hackney breeding.

3669. Why?—Because they made more money out of it; I bought over 100 Hackneys myself, sires and mares, and took them out to America.

3670. What did you find the result of the Hackneys in America?—I found that I made them well, got a good price for them, and got a profit, and I did not care what they done with them then. In Chicago any kind of a dead horse, if he is got by a Hackney, will bring more money than any other class of horse.

3671. And have you formed any opinion as to whether a good Hackney stallion, such as you describe, or a Cleveland Bay, would be a more suitable horse for Ireland; how do you like the Cleveland Bay?—I don't know anything at all about them, I never saw a Cleveland Bay only some years ago, when I was in Yorkshire, and I was very sorry I did not buy him; he was a cracking stallion, and the man wanted me to buy him and I did not; I was very sorry for it, and went back to buy him, but he was then bought by a dealer, who trained him and sold him to Mr. Winans for £1,500 as a carriage horse.

3672. Have you formed any opinion why Ireland produces much better hunters than any other country?—I will give you my own opinion—we have the air, we have the water, and we have the ground they are bred on, and my opinion is that for pace, or horses, or beasts there is no better place in the world, if they had only encouragement and could straightforwardly, than Ireland, to breed anything.

3673. You think they are from the world in breeding horses?—Yes, or cattle, or even Christians, if they only considered themselves; they breed them with bone and strength, and they can stand more hardship than any other man in the world, unless a nigger.

3674. And I think you said that the big job-masters, like Tilbury and Wimbush, and these men, are going to give a higher class of harness horses than formerly?—So they told me; I used to buy horses for different people and I used to buy them 17 hands high, and 17·2 some, and they say that the carriages that they are building in London, and through England, are all on a smaller scale, with lighter springs and lighter wheels, and they like them horses to be all under 16, from 15·3.

3675. With good action?—Oh, must have action.

3676. I think you said you had sold good geldings long ago by a Hackney [illegible], [illegible]?—Yes.

3677. Do you know anything about the mares, were they small mares, or what kind of mares?—I knew one very nice little black mare, 15 hands high, and the man paid me £25. for the services of [illegible], and she bred a little chestnut horse, 15·3, with great action; he kept him for a year for that season; I bought him when he was 5 off, and gave him £200 for him, and I got him carefully, and sold him the April following to a Frenchman to go to Paris, he paid me very well, and he was a very nice horse.

3678. You got a good price for him?—He paid me very well.

3679. It was stated, I think yesterday, that there were not many troopers bought south of the Boyne?—Might I ask you where south of the Boyne is, is that the farm they call "The Boyne Water," that is north of Drogheda. I saw troopers bought in Derry for the Government, I saw them bought in [illegible] fair; I saw them bought in Armagh, [illegible], Ballybay, Armagh, Navan, and Limerick.

3680. And they are still bought in those fairs?—I have not been very much in the fairs in the Northern [illegible] months.

3681. But within the last few years?—Yes, they still come to the North and buy them; I saw the General that is dead about a year ago, General Ravenhill, I saw him several times in the May buying troopers, light troopers and artillery horses—and blacks for the Queen's Life Guards.

3682. That I think, in answer to Mr. La Touche, you said you had bought very good horses got by half-bred horses?—Yes, by half-bred horses, I think is out after; they turned out to be very good horses to the people I sold them to.

3083. Do you think these half-bred horses would get animals with as good action as a good Hackney stallion?—No, they won't get as high action or as true action.

3084. They would get better hunters?—Yes; unless some of these half-bred horses you talk about could step as high and true as a Hackney, but if they did not, they would not get good harness horses.

3085. But if they could step as high it would be too high for a hunter?—Yes, a hunter wants to walk well and trot straight, and give you a good feel when you are on his back. Nov. 23, 1896.

The Commission adjourned to November 24th.

EIGHTH DAY.—TUESDAY, NOVEMBER 24TH, 1896.

Nov. 24, 1896.

PRESENT:—MR. PERCY LA TOUCHE, (in the Chair), HON. H. W. FITZWILLIAM, SIR T. H. G. ESMONDE, M.P., MR. J. L. CAREW, M.P., COL. ST. QUINTIN, and MR. F. S. WRENCH.

MR. HUGH NEVILLE, Secretary.

Mr. ALEXANDER H. SPROULE, Dunnamanagh House, Tyrone, examined.

Mr. Alexander H. Sproule.

3086. CHAIRMAN.—You are a justice of the peace and live in county Tyrone?—Yes.

3087. You have had considerable experience in horse-breeding?—Yes.

3088. What class of horses have you usually bred?—Thoroughbreds, Hackneys, Shire horses, and Clydesdales.

3089. Have you some thoroughbred mares of your own?—Yes, I had.

3090. You have not any now?—Not at present.

3091. Have you got thoroughbred Hackney mares?—Yes; I have at present.

3092. Do you keep a stallion?—Yes.

3093. What breeds is the stallion?—I kept a thoroughbred stallion, a Hackney stallion, and a half-bred stallion.

3094. Have you got them all now?—No.

3095. What stallions have you now?—I have none now.

3096. You have no stallions at present?—No.

3097. Are you still breeding horses?—Yes.

3098. How many years have you been breeding horses?—For the last nine years I have been breeding horses myself, thoroughbred Hackneys and half-bred Hackneys.

3099. What mares do you put the Hackneys to?—I put the Hackney mares to the Hackney horse, and I put the half-bred mares to a horse got by "The South Palestine"; he was half-bred by "Numismatist" by "Touchstone." I put the half-bred mares to him, and I put the common mares of the country to the Hackney horse.

3100. Do you keep the young stock yourself, or do you sell them?—I generally keep them until they are three or four years old.

3101. And then you sell them?—Yes.

3102. I suppose the product would be harness horses?—Yes; harness horses generally, and fairly good action.

3103. Do the farmers in your county generally sell their horses at four and five years old?—The young class sell them younger, at two or three.

3104. Where do they sell their horses?—In the fairs.

3105. And where do they go to, do you know?—They are bought up, some of them, by men who feed them and take them over to the fairs afterwards. They keep them until they are five years old, and they are taken to the Dublin fair.

3106. You mean the local ones?—Yes.

3107. As far as you know do the young horses that are sold by the farmers stay in the same neighbourhood until they are four or five years old?—They do.

3108. Do they breed much horses from Hackney stallions in your neighbourhood?—Yes.

3109. They use them chiefly?—Yes; at present that is so.

3110. They do not breed many hunters there?—They tried to breed them, but the class of horses the Royal Dublin Society sent down there—I have yet to see a good one out of them—I have seen nothing but weedy brutes out of them.

3111. They are not good horses?—The sires may be the farmer's fault, but as a rule the mares are not good.

3112. Are there any registered mares under the Royal Dublin Society's scheme there?—Yes; a few are there.

3113. Registered?—Well, they are supposed to be registered.

3114. Are they advertised as registered?—Yes.

3115. Do you know if many horses are bred in your county or district for the purpose of being turned into hunters?—It is not a hunting district.

3116. I know, but will horses of any quality leave it?—Any horses that are bought are generally bought in the Bog and brought up here to Dublin. It is more of a draught class of horse that are reared in the North.

3117. Are there many Hackney stallions in your part of the country?—There is quite a few in the present day there.

3118. Good horses?—Yes, fairly good horses.

3119. What are they?—The stallion horses I know; Paragon, ... Queen ... The Hackney Stud Company. I don't know what the name of their horse is, but he was a very good looking horse. There is a bay horse there ... Donegal or Derry, ... Hackney breed.

3120. Do farmers usually use those Hackney stallions?—Yes, they do, they are more suitable to them. I may state that I was all my life in favour of thoroughbred horses myself. I have been paying particular attention to the breeding of horses for the past twenty or thirty years, and I was always in favour of thoroughbred blood. I bought thoroughbred stallions and tried the experiment, I could be beaten though in the North of Ireland, but I found the animals of the North of Ireland were too coarse with the half-bred foals, they are tender and cannot stand the cold. As a rule they are not suitable for farming purposes; our farmers are rather small there. There is ... the Clyde horse ... the popular class of farmers, and the Hackney is what you might call the "general-purpose" horse better suited for the class of horse they have there.

3121. Have you any experience of what are called half-bred cart horses that are got by a thoroughbred

K

Jan. 16, 1896. Mr. [illegible]

horse?—Yes, I bred a half-bred horse which stands now at Derry. I do not care for breeding from a half-bred unless you mean, that he comes from a Hackney horse and a thoroughbred mare—a stallion from that I consider a capital good horse to cross the country mares with.

3725. But you would not approve of a cross between a thoroughbred horse and a mare got by a thoroughbred horse?—No, that is a thing I was quite satisfied if the mare had a strain of Clyde or common breeding in her. As a rule when they are crossed out the mixture you begin to cross again, you throw up curious, queer, and extraordinary animals.

3726. Have you any experience of a stallion got by a thoroughbred horse out of a Hackney mare?—Well, no, I have not, I cannot speak to that.

3727. You think it would make a useful sire?—I am speaking of Hackney horses bred from thoroughbred mares and a Hackney horse.

3728. Have you any experience of such a stallion got by a Hackney horse out of a thoroughbred mare?—That is what I was speaking about.

3729. You know of one?—Yes, I do.

3730. You think he is a good sire?—My experience of that horse and of the Hackney horses in the country is this—I have not seen 5 per cent. of foals bred from Hackney horses, of any description, that is of good thoroughbred Hackney horse and a half-bred mare, I have not seen 5 per cent. of the foals with any unsoundness whatever; and beyond all doubt, I am not afraid of contradiction in saying it, that I have seen badly thoroughbred horses put on Hackney horses, and their foals came out perfectly sound.

3731. You do not consider that the Royal Dublin Society's scheme works well in your district?—I do not. But I do not blame the Royal Dublin Society, but entirely the rules. The valuation is by far too high. The fixing of it at £150 is not for the benefit of those people who are [illegible] for the public. If the valuation was put at £50 then it would benefit the poor man, but now on the contrary you are benefiting the man who is quite independent. The value of the horse now must be not to exceed £150.

3732. You consider that to be too high?—Yes, far too high.

3733. The smaller farmers have no chance or a bad chance against the big man?—They have no chance at all.

3734. Do many of the small farmers breed horses?—Yes, a very large number do.

3735. You do not know as a matter of fact what the registered sires are in your district?—I do not know the names, I know the horses. There is a horse from Fermanagh—the owner is Mr. Mitchell—a fairly good horse too—a thoroughbred horse. There is a horse bought from Ardboe—a decent horse, but I do not think very much of him. But in fact we have not the class of mares to breed to a thoroughbred horse in my district.

3736. What would you suggest as the best means of getting a better class of horse in your district or of improving the breed of the horses?—Well, as I said before, the offspring from the thoroughbred horse and the class of mares that are in the district in which I reside are of no value whatever as the majority of the small farmers are farming; their land is heavy and their farms are small. The Clydesdale horse's offspring is too big, the farmers consider, and he would require too much feeding, and he is too soft to stand out in the winter. The Hackney horse is a hardy horse, which I know from experience by having him and of the Hackney, of the thoroughbred, and of the Clyde, and seeing them running together. The Hackney horse meets the purposes of the poor farmer, and he is a horse he can take to fair and sell, and if he cannot sell him to one he can to another.

3737. And I take it you consider that the best means of improving the horse in your district will be the use of the Hackney stallion?—By all means, and then you will have a class of mares that will be worth breeding from.

3738. Have you any experience as to the importation of American horses in the North?—Yes, I have seen a great many of them, and I have great experience of American horses, and I consider them very unsuitable for Ireland—he is too long in the back, too long in the legs, and too short at the ribs, and too wide at his kidneys.

3739. Are they scattered about your country?—Quite a few.

3740. They are bought in Belfast?—Yes, and brought up.

3741. Have you any suggestion you would like to make as to these imported horses?—I think that as to all American horses—in my opinion we should take a leaf out of the American book, we should [illegible] the horses coming in from America, and by all means put a duty on them. I should also think as far as stallions are concerned in Ireland, stallions, bulls, rams, and pigs, and everything else, there should be a license for keeping them, and they should pass an examination. The majority of the poorer farmers have not the means to pay for a good horse, and they breed from inferior horses, leaving a very bad class of animals in the country.

3742. Mr. Gason.—You say, Mr. [illegible], that Hackneys are the best kind for your district—[illegible] they are?

3743. And that is only the Hackney horse?—For farming and harness horses.

3744. Nothing more?—Yes, I think you can get fairly good hunting horses from them.

3745. You think so?—Yes, I am sure of it. I have seen some fairly good hunters from a thoroughbred mare and a Hackney stallion, generally a good short-backed horse.

3746. Can you give us any idea of the prices obtained for the Hackney produce in different fairs?—They are different, and range from £25 to £60.

3747. At what age?—At five years old.

3748. Can farmers in your district keep them so long?—The poorer farmers cannot.

3749. At what age would they be obliged to sell them?—Well, three years. I can only speak I suppose from what I have seen.

3750. Yes, from your experience?—I have seen some sell from £8 to £12 coming off very poor ground in my district.

3751. Where would they go to?—They are bought up by the bigger farmers.

3752. Who feed them and sell them at bigger prices?—Yes.

3753. And you did, I think, you said that the produce of thoroughbred and half-bred is rather soft and not so durable for your district?—I have tried them myself. I have an island on Lough Erne, and I was breeding extensively, and I went in extensively in breeding horses long before I thought of any Hackney horses, and I was opposed completely to Hackney horses, but I was advised to try them, and I put the colts on this island, and they all, during the summer, did fairly well; I had thoroughbreds, Hackneys, and half-bred thoroughbreds, and some Clydesdales, on this island. I found, as to the half-bred foals and young colts, at the latter part of December, I had to take them in and house them. The Clydesdale colts I had to take them all in in March; they could not stand out at all. They all got hay on the grass, and the Hackneys kept all the winter, and were in better condition, actually, than the colts turned out of the stables after housing them, and that was the first thing turned me to Hackney horses. I consider them hardier horses, and can stand more cold.

3754. Then you disapprove of thoroughbreds crossing with half-breds?—I disapprove of a thoroughbred mating with our class of mares.

3755. You do not think your class of mares which

[illegible]

3762. How would you improve these mares?—By mating with a Hackney horse.

[illegible]

3770. They go up from your district to the May?—Oh, yes.

[illegible]

R 2

[illegible]

3785. Then I gather from what you have said you think the small [illegible] require more help than the big man over £100 valuation?—I consider a man with a valuation of over £100 in my district would not help themselves, as a rule they are generally fairly [illegible] men.

3786. And you think it would be quite within the power, remembering which the different breeds of horses in his district, to guard against using any of those breeds in the [illegible]?—Yes, I think so.

3787. You think there would be no danger of Hackney blood, or Clydesdale blood, or any other blood was allowed to be [illegible]. You think there would be no danger of the [illegible] blood among [illegible] they were breeding would not like to answer that question. I think there should be no special limit to the number of mares [illegible] by the Royal Dublin Society. I think, as I said before, if the horses are owned by the Society or Government and were let [illegible], something that there would be [illegible] and the fee of that horse they were served by the horses, then you will have a chance, and no more to be served by a man whose valuation is up to £100. I would say put the valuation at £50 and a fee of £1 and you will be serving more benefitting the poor man.

3788. Would you touch on the mares that are put to these horses being sound?—I would.

3789. You would not give any privilege to the man who had an unsound mare?—Well, I would. I have [illegible] unsound mares breeding very good foals.

3790. Where would you draw the line?—[illegible] I would not breed from breeding unsoundness.

3791. You would disqualify all mares if they proved to have breeding [illegible]?—Decidedly I would.

3792. I think you said you found the Hackneys hardier. Do you find they come to maturity sooner?—I find they come to maturity much sooner, and [illegible] they are very saleable.

3793. And very hardy?—And very stylish. I have got to [illegible] of Hackney horses. I cannot think of one that I have seen yet.

3794. Chairman.—You said you had no objection to the [illegible] a cross between the pure [illegible] on the thoroughbred mare and the Hackney horse on the thoroughbred horse and the Clydesdale mare?—I think it would help to improve the breed very much.

3795. What is your opinion regarding a pure-bred [illegible]?—I consider a thoroughbred horse which is registered in the stud book is a pure-bred horse, and I consider the Hackney horse which is registered in the Hackney stud book is a pure-bred horse.

3796. Why do you consider the Hackney a pure-bred horse, you know the stud book has not been in existence long?—Yes, they are, like the Shire, [illegible], but we count them pure-bred.

3797. Do you think the fact of their being in the Hackney stud book constitutes a pure breed?—I do not, as the first thing they introduced [illegible] they allowed some to be registered in the [illegible] and in the stud book, but that is done away with now.

3798. But it is quite possible the produce of those horses that are registered are now in the stud book?—I look upon a [illegible] horse as a [illegible], and a registered horse is as pure breeding as they can get.

3799. Have the horses in your district improved or deteriorated?—Since the introduction of the Hackneys I am quite an improvement.

3800. I see in your replies to queries you say that your opinion that they have deteriorated?—That is the reason here.

3801. They have deteriorated?—They have.

3802. You attribute that to the farmers selling their best stock, I suppose?—They do, they generally sell off their best young stock [illegible].

3803. As you are the owner of [illegible] whose opinion you consider very valuable on the subject of what horses they should, you have offered these animals to Clydesdale?—Well, I think there is great [illegible] in many ways; until lately the majority of horses were kept by a certain class, and of course the farmers were obliged to put their mares to those horses or else select the poorest horses in the neighbourhood, whatever horses they would get for the cheapest money, and they allowed their mares to deteriorate, that is the reason I would place a [illegible] on them. Those are horses travelling the country, and all they want is to be sold for Canada, they are certainly running the breeds of this country.

3804. Do you believe that apart from the [illegible] the opinion of the farmers of the district that they have allowed their mares to deteriorate by the use of these horses?—Well, yes, it does.

3805. Mr. Wrench.—Do you find, as a matter of fact, that Hackney stallions in your neighbourhood are popular with the farmers?—Very. I would have Hackney stallions at the present time I might state to you, but I was not in Canada and had my horses sold before I went away. I would like to keep a Hackney horse and a thoroughbred horse. I believe they are the only horses fit for the country, but the Hackney horse is the only horse for the North of Ireland, that is my opinion.

3806. Mr. Gilmour.—You say the farmer is quite competent in the case of Government horses being kept there to select good ones [illegible]?—I would not say they are quite competent, but they get such a [illegible] by these horses that were kept in there by Royal Dublin Society's horses, that at [illegible] there were three—[illegible]. I am sure all the horses of the Royal Dublin Society [illegible] and during the whole season I don't think these three horses served nine mares, the farmers were so much against them.

3807. Mr. T. Robinson.—What was that owing to?—Owing to the breeding of some of the horses. [illegible] a good horse [illegible] I like him. I consider him a little light, but a first-class animal.

3808. Had these animals been in the country before?—Yes.

3809. They had been for some years in the country?—Yes.

3810. And the farmers did not approve of their progeny?—Not at all.

3811. At what age are horses usually sold with you?—At the May Fair from two to four years old upwards.

3812. You don't sell them under four years old?—No, they would not be bought.

3813. What would be the average price that a farmer would get for a four-year-old of that kind?—What class of horse would you mean?

3814. The majority of horses that are bought in the country now?—I would say the average price might be £35 for a horse.

3815. Mr. Casey.—I think you said to me it is £35?—Yes, that is a good class of mare from big farmers.

3816. Mr. T. Robinson.—Do you think £35 for a four-year-old pays a man to breed horses?—I think it does not pay a man unless he works his horses when young, but the majority continue to work their horses when two-year-olds, the poorer class of farmers.

3817. Mr. Grubb.—You said you preferred to breed from the pure blood on both sides?—I would have pure blood on both sides to breed from.

3818. There was a witness here the other day who said that the breeding from the [illegible] [illegible] on either side [illegible] [illegible] [illegible] [illegible] by the [illegible] [illegible] [illegible] of [illegible] and [illegible] the [illegible]?—Well, my experience in [illegible] breeding [illegible] is [illegible] [illegible] you will [illegible] [illegible] [illegible]. If you [illegible] [illegible] a [illegible] horse and a [illegible] mare, on a [illegible] you will [illegible] the [illegible] [illegible] to the [illegible], [illegible] the [illegible] [illegible] upon the [illegible] side, or whichever side has the [illegible] [illegible] you will find the [illegible] [illegible] [illegible], but if you breed from a [illegible] horse and [illegible] [illegible] [illegible] through [illegible] [illegible], you don't know what you are going to get.

3819. Mr. [illegible].—These horses that you say are [illegible] [illegible] they are [illegible] or [illegible] years old, [illegible] what [illegible] are they put in [illegible] [illegible]?—To [illegible].

3820. And they are [illegible] [illegible] for that particular purpose?—Yes.

3821. You [illegible] they would [illegible] the [illegible] [illegible] of the [illegible] [illegible] [illegible] [illegible] for [illegible]?

3822. I mean horses that are sold in the Fair of May which you say are not sold until three-year-old or later?—Four or five, they are not sold under four; generally [illegible] in the [illegible].

3823. What I asked you was what are those horses used for?—After they are sold?

3824. No, before they are sold?—Well, a great many of those horses that are sold in the May, a large percentage, if you talk of the horses raised in the district I could [illegible] [illegible] [illegible]—

3825. I am speaking of the horses [illegible] in the district?—A great many of those [illegible] [illegible] [illegible] [illegible] and [illegible] up [illegible] by [illegible], who, when he [illegible] a [illegible] [illegible] [illegible] [illegible] [illegible] [illegible] [illegible] [illegible] [illegible] [illegible] [illegible] [illegible] and takes [illegible] to the May and makes money of him.

3826. Chairman.—There [illegible] [illegible] [illegible] in this district, I suppose, bought for the purpose of [illegible] [illegible] [illegible] [illegible] [illegible]?—They do.

3827. You have been to Canada, I think, you said?—Yes.

3828. What is your opinion of the Canadian [illegible] [illegible] the [illegible] of the [illegible] [illegible] [illegible] [illegible] [illegible] [illegible] horse.

3829. How are they bred?—They are bred from a [illegible] [illegible] [illegible] of [illegible] than we [illegible] in this country, and there they are [illegible] [illegible] [illegible] [illegible] brought out [illegible] [illegible] [illegible] again. In the first place there was a class of [illegible] in the [illegible] [illegible] [illegible] [illegible] [illegible] of [illegible] [illegible] [illegible] [illegible] something like to what you have in the north of England; then they [illegible] [illegible] [illegible] [illegible] [illegible] [illegible] horses, and they have got a very good class of [illegible] horses in the north-west territory. But the [illegible] [illegible] [illegible] the United States is [illegible] [illegible] [illegible] class of horses.

3830. That is the horse that [illegible] [illegible] **here?**—Yes, there are a good many of the north-west **horses** coming over.

3831. You think they are [illegible]?—They are [illegible] good [illegible] horses [illegible], [illegible] [illegible] [illegible] [illegible] [illegible] [illegible], but they are a fairly good [illegible] and [illegible] horse, they have good [illegible].

3832. I suppose you would suggest that they should be [illegible] as well as the others?—[illegible] I [illegible], I would [illegible] everything coming [illegible] there; and I would [illegible] a [illegible] [illegible] on all [illegible] [illegible] [illegible] in the country, I would put on a [illegible] [illegible] and if they passed a [illegible] [illegible] examination I would reduce the licence.

3833. Mr. [illegible].—You would put on a [illegible] [illegible]?—I would put on a [illegible] licence [illegible] all stallions serving mares that had not passed a veterinary surgeon's examination.

3834. Have you thought at all of the amount?—I would not [illegible] [illegible] [illegible] [illegible] £1[illegible] unless he passed a veterinary surgeon.

3835. And when he had passed that **you would** reduce this to a nominal fee?—I would.

Rev. A. [illegible] [illegible], [illegible] [illegible], examined.

Rev. A. [illegible] [illegible].

3836. Chairman.—You live at [illegible], near [illegible]?—Yes.

3837. Do you breed horses?—Yes, I breed eight; that is the extent of my breeding.

3838. What class of horses have you bred?—With [illegible] [illegible] from [illegible] to [illegible]. [illegible] [illegible], but the last I sold was very well able to carry [illegible].

3839. How have you bred them?—My first attempt at breeding was from a purchased "[illegible]" [illegible]. Long [illegible] [illegible] [illegible] [illegible] [illegible] [illegible] [illegible]. This mare had [illegible] a foal to the [illegible] horse "[illegible]." I [illegible] this particularly, and [illegible] this in mind, "[illegible]" was a thoroughbred horse, [illegible] [illegible] [illegible] [illegible]. She had a foal [illegible] to a [illegible] horse, a rather [illegible] [illegible], but I saw [illegible] [illegible] [illegible], one [illegible] [illegible] when it was a [illegible]-year-old and the other when it was [illegible]-year-old, and they were both [illegible]. The [illegible] [illegible] I [illegible] [illegible] is this, I [illegible] [illegible] [illegible] a [illegible] to [illegible] [illegible] [illegible] [illegible] [illegible] [illegible] [illegible] [illegible] [illegible] [illegible] [illegible]. I [illegible] [illegible] [illegible] [illegible] [illegible] [illegible] [illegible] [illegible] [illegible], and we were [illegible] up [illegible] [illegible] [illegible] [illegible] [illegible] [illegible], and one of the [illegible] in the [illegible] I [illegible] [illegible] [illegible] [illegible] [illegible]. I said, "Well, that is a beautiful [illegible]." "Ah, yes, that mare has had two foals." I thought she had [illegible] [illegible] she was a little heavy [illegible] [illegible] [illegible]. And when we came [illegible] from the [illegible] [illegible] [illegible] [illegible] [illegible] we [illegible] [illegible] [illegible] [illegible] [illegible]. And one of them was such a [illegible] [illegible] [illegible] [illegible] a foal." I [illegible] [illegible] [illegible] [illegible]. The other foal was a very good foal. And I said, "It is a [illegible] to put [illegible] [illegible] [illegible] [illegible] [illegible] [illegible] up to Lord [illegible]'s horse '[illegible],' and have some of that class of foal." [illegible] [illegible] [illegible] to Lord [illegible]'s horse, and she [illegible] [illegible]. Next year I [illegible] to go [illegible] [illegible] the [illegible] [illegible], and [illegible] him [illegible] to make the [illegible] [illegible], and [illegible] [illegible] to [illegible], and the old [illegible] was [illegible] [illegible]. [illegible] [illegible] [illegible] [illegible] [illegible] [illegible] [illegible] [illegible] [illegible] [illegible] [illegible]. I said, "It is a shame [illegible] [illegible] [illegible] [illegible] [illegible] [illegible]; I will give you a [illegible] [illegible] [illegible]." "[illegible]," said the [illegible], and I [illegible] [illegible] [illegible]. I [illegible] [illegible] [illegible] [illegible] [illegible], [illegible] I [illegible] [illegible] [illegible] [illegible] the [illegible]. I [illegible] a [illegible] [illegible] [illegible] I [illegible] [illegible] [illegible] [illegible] [illegible] [illegible] [illegible] [illegible] a [illegible] [illegible] [illegible] [illegible] [illegible] and a thoroughbred [illegible], as I [illegible] [illegible] [illegible] [illegible] [illegible] [illegible] Lord [illegible] [illegible] [illegible] [illegible] [illegible] [illegible] by a thoroughbred horse [illegible] [illegible] [illegible]. [illegible], but a [illegible] [illegible] [illegible] all [illegible] [illegible]. The [illegible] [illegible] [illegible] [illegible] [illegible] [illegible]. [illegible] [illegible] [illegible] [illegible] [illegible], [illegible] [illegible], [illegible] the [illegible] [illegible] [illegible] [illegible]. I [illegible] [illegible] [illegible] [illegible] [illegible] [illegible] [illegible] [illegible] [illegible] [illegible] [illegible], [illegible] [illegible] [illegible] [illegible], and [illegible] [illegible] [illegible] [illegible] [illegible] for [illegible] [illegible] [illegible] [illegible] [illegible] [illegible] good. I [illegible] this particularly for my theory, [illegible] [illegible] [illegible] [illegible] [illegible] [illegible] [illegible] [illegible] [illegible] [illegible] [illegible] [illegible] [illegible] or less, and that is [illegible] [illegible] by the [illegible] of the [illegible] who had a [illegible] in [illegible] [illegible] by a [illegible], and had a foal in this [illegible] [illegible], and it was brought [illegible] back to Ireland, and [illegible] [illegible] when the [illegible] [illegible] [illegible] her foals had the [illegible] [illegible] on the [illegible]. And we all know that if a [illegible] [illegible] [illegible] [illegible] [illegible] [illegible] [illegible], her foals [illegible] [illegible] [illegible] [illegible] [illegible]. Well, [illegible], my [illegible] [illegible] of breeding—you [illegible] [illegible] [illegible] [illegible] [illegible] of what they did. My [illegible] [illegible] of breeding was by "[illegible]" with a [illegible] [illegible], as the late Lord Mayo or Lord Naas would have [illegible]. I am a very old man and remember these things. This mare, her foal was hunted with the Ward Hounds for nine years.

3840. Mr. Gibson.—What was her foal by?—Her foal was by "Blarney," a thoroughbred. He hunted nine years with the Ward Hounds, never made a mistake, frequently gave them the lead, and frequently left them, [illegible], and had [illegible] to himself, was never tired at 15 years; he was sold in England, and he went then to Yorkshire and won the Point to Point Steeplechase, five miles, 15 stone up.

3841. Chairman.—He was a good horse. I conclude those mares of yours were above the ordinary class of mares kept by the farmers in the country?—Well, now we have come on to that, I live in a country of chalk formation which is very much superior to the [illegible] formation, for this reason, that practically there is a good deal of lime in the ground, which is largely absorbed by the produce of the ground, the hay and grass, and produces a finer kind of bone than the lime will.

3842. You think the chalk formation is better adapted for breeding horses than the limestone formation?—Very much superior.

3843. Is the chalk formation all over this particular district?—It is not over the whole district, it is a [illegible] peculiarities, it only occurs in my [illegible] six square miles.

3844. And are there particularly good horses bred on that particular formation?—I have bred nine there on that formation, and two of those that have been sold have been winners, one won at Punchestown last spring.—Rock of Cashel.

3845. Do the farmers living on those farms always succeed in breeding?—They don't attempt to breed high-class horses, or they would deserve to attempt it, because they won't feed their horses as mares. I feed my brood mares well always, and I feed my foals.

3846. What condition do the farmers generally use?—They don't feed their mares when they are rearing their foals. The better class of farmers certainly like a strong thoroughbred stallion.

3846. I suppose the horses are small, are they not?—They are fair but they are not so small.

3847. Are there good stallions in your neighbourhood, good thoroughbred stallions?—Not near in the immediate neighbourhood.

3848. Do you think the horses have deteriorated or improved, as a rule, in your district?—Well, I think they are improved because we have had some good horses in the neighbourhood. There was one remarkably good horse that I bred from Cashel, by Normanby out of Pamela by Dundee, a very fine horse, a good walker, trotter, and galloper.

3849. Have you any experience with regard to breeding from Hackney sires?—Well, I have seen a little of it but I never think much [illegible] in it. We have had a very good Hackney horse in my neighbourhood a couple of years ago, and the progeny I did not like.

3850. I suppose the farmers in your neighbourhood use them a good deal, don't they?—No, they don't like them much. Last year we got two very good coaching Yorkshire horses into the neighbourhood, and I think they will take in the country and do good, they breed a better class of horse and bigger horses. Our neighbourhood produces heavier horses and they breed a better horse with better [illegible]. The Hackney horse produces a round leg, the coaching horse is more of a blood horse, he produces a good flat leg with the sinew a good distance away from the bone.

3851. Do you think that the introduction of the Hackney blood will have any effect on the breeding of Irish hunters?—Well, I don't know, I think the Irish hunters that get the prizes in Dublin are plenty much of the Hackney class. I really do.

3852. Have you any suggestions you would like to make with a view of encouraging farmers to keep better mares?—Yes, my suggestions would be to have a prize for a mare of positive quality, not of a comparative quality, because if you compare two bad things together, one very little better than the other, the better of the two is no use at all. I would therefore largely [illegible] the liberty of the subject, and I would allow no stallion to be used that was not registered.

3853. And sound?—Oh, of course, that I mean, sound and registered as sound—that is, without any hereditary defect that would be likely to pass on.

3854. And I conclude other considerations, with good bone and action and shape?—Oh, of course, but I have to say what very few breeders have to say, that I never bred a weed, and never bred an unsound one, and I was able to follow my horses, and I never knew one of my breeding for years to go unsound except one.

3855. Are you breeding now?—Yes, and I have [illegible].

3856. What are you breeding from now?—I am breeding now, and have been breeding for the last nine years, from a mare by Fitzjames out of a horse by [illegible], an old mare now, from Cashel by Normanby out of Pamela by Dundee. Now Dundee I consider the very best blood there can be.

3857. This horse Cashel is the sire you use?—Cashel is the sire of the last five foals I have bred.

3858. He is in your country now?—He is.

3859. Is he a registered horse, do you know?—Oh, no, he before your registered horses.

3860. But he might have been registered this year?—Oh, he is an old horse now, he is a very fine horse. I remember riding him. He was bred by a syndicate of farmers at Belfast. I don't know how it was he happened to come this way, [illegible] years old from Newmarket, where he was in training, and I happened to ride him, the [illegible] never saw a better horse.

3861. Is he called Rock of Cashel?—He is the sire of "Rock of Cashel." Well, I say not only that I never bred an unsound one or a weedy one, but all mine were, for the size of their parents, bigger in every way than their parents, and I suppose that was in consequence of the soil and, perhaps they were reared upon, and the good feeding [illegible].

3862. Mr. Fitzwilliam.—Could you tell us what class of mares are in your neighbourhood, and those that you know yourself, but what is the average class of mares?—The average class of mares in the neighbourhood is not a good class.

3863. Do you mean they are small and light?—They are fair height, but they are [illegible] mares, small legs, weedy.

3864. How have those mares been bred?—They have been bred from weedy thoroughbred sires, and weedy mares.

3865. And are they in the hands, do you think, of farmers who can breed a good horse, I mean financially—are they in the hands of very small farmers?—There are plenty of men with good large farms, but who will not give a price for a good mare.

3866. Then they only keep their mares they sell their foals?—Unfortunately, anything as good enough to breed from. My mare that I bred from was 16 hands high. Yesterday, [illegible] for today, I got a standard and found a year and three months old by the stand 15.2½ high.

3867. Mr. Gibson.—What was it by?—By Cashel, and [illegible] the horse [illegible] whole [illegible].

3868. Mr. Fitzwilliam.—Do you think that it pays these very small men to use good blood horses, or do you think they do themselves any good by trying to breed horses, the very small farmers?—Oh, they do.

3869. Do you think it is wise of them to try and do it?—There has been a very great patronage given to the Yorkshire horses, the coaching horses, two remarkably good horses in my neighbourhood now.

3870. What do they breed with these carriage horses?—There are a good lot of good upstanding carriage horses, and that is the class of horse that should be bred in the country. There is no use in breeding little horses, more than by breeding good sized horses, the farmer can get some little use of him when he is two off in light harrowing and that kind of thing, and then [illegible] and can sell him until four, and he then gets some payment as he goes along.

3871. What fees do these new horses that you say have come into the country, these coaching horses, what do they stand at, what fees do they serve at?—About £2 for the Yorkshire horses.

3872. And as a rule will the farmers go to the cheapest horse?—No, not with us.

3873. He will go to the good horse?—Yes, but the fee must not be extravagant. When I say extravagant I mean that it must not be anything over £2.

3874. Sir Thomas Esmonde.—What would you consider a proper fee for your district?—I think that if the Government gave some help it would be better to have a fee of not more than 10s., but it is really not the [illegible] that is the trouble.

3875. Do you find that the brood mares are diminishing?—They are not up to the [illegible].

3876. Can you give any explanation why the brood mares have disappeared?—Oh, they were [illegible] them.

3877. Then you have never seen any of those old [illegible] mares that we have heard about?—I have seen some at Mullingar and at Ballinasloe; but there [illegible] but there is a great difficulty in getting a good mare [illegible] there.

3878. In your district I suppose they are all small mares?—No, they measure a certain height; but they are [illegible]. I have great faith in the [illegible], although I have seen great exceptions to that rule.

3879. Is that there want of care in breeding them, or that they have no means?—When they have a [illegible] they sell it.

3880. Are there many mares sold to foreign dealers?—We sometimes get good mares from the south or west of Ireland; they are bred there, made into condition, and sold in May fair, and at a particular time of the year the foreign dealers buy them frequently. The Hungarians [illegible] buy them and take them away and the produce of those mares will come back to [illegible] in consequence of the Government [illegible] in Hungary to buy [illegible], which, I think is a false economy. I have had some little experience of American horses in the neighbourhood, but they don't make [illegible].

3881. Chairman.—You don't think well of them?—No.

3882. Mr. [illegible].—You spoke of the Yorkshire [illegible] that was done by the half-bred [illegible] by Lord Caledon?—Yes.

3883. And two foals bred from her were sold at eighty guineas each?—No, one was sold at 105 guineas, a four-year-old, and another at eighty guineas, a three-year-old.

3884. How was this half-bred of Lord Caledon's bred?—Bred by the late Lord Clonmel out of a Clydesdale mare by a thoroughbred horse.

3885. What was the thoroughbred?—I don't know, but he was called "Chevalier," because he came to stand [illegible] in the north. He was a beautiful [illegible], and got [illegible] in the North [illegible] to get [illegible] horses.

3886. You spoke of a "Freeholder" mare?—Yes.

3887. Was she a thoroughbred?—No.

3888. How was she bred?—I don't know anything about her breeding except that she was by [illegible] "Freeholder," out of a half-bred.

3889. Was "Freeholder" a thoroughbred?—Yes; he was a remarkable horse.

3890. Then the mare with a thoroughbred [illegible] mated with "Disney."

3891. And produced this great weight-carrying hunter?—Yes. "Disney" was by "Clove" out of "Magnum" by "Playfair."

3892. So that you approve of sending half-bred mares with thoroughbreds to produce hunters?—Yes.

3893. And you disapprove of Hackneys?—I disapprove of them entirely. I would not let them into the country; they have long legs, [illegible] and always greasy. You cannot better my horses. You cannot [illegible] their legs or that kind of thing, and although they look light, some of them will [illegible] horses, they measure big; for instance there was a horse of mine exhibited at the Show last summer. An eminent dealer in Dublin said "My friend, you have put him in the wrong class; this should have been in Class 9, instead of Class 10"; he was bigger than the horse that got the prize in Class 10.

3894. You spoke of a [illegible] which you [illegible] experiments you took before coming up here?—Yes.

3895. He is by "[illegible]" out of what sort of mare?—A half-bred mare; she is practically a thoroughbred mare by "Freeholder," out of a dam by "[illegible]." I should say that, although I have only bred this, I have been an observant man of horse breeding, and have had a good deal of guiding of other people in their choice of mares for [illegible].

3896. Mr. Wrench.—What was the name of the Hackney stallion you referred to in your district?—I quite forget.

3897. Who did he belong to?—Mr. George; he is dead now; he was burned to death; his house was burned; but Mr. George has now a very fine Yorkshire horse.

3898. You cannot remember the name of the horse?—"Performer;" he was bought in England—Yorkshire—some time ago.

3899. Do you know whether he was a pure bred Hackney?—He was a pure bred Hackney in the Hackney Stud Book.

3900. And had you experience of other Hackneys there?—No, there was an old Norfolk trotter. Was he a Hackney?

3901. Not the Hackney I am speaking about?—There was a great Norfolk trotter in this neighbourhood—the sire of the late Lord [illegible] "Royal Arrow"—"[illegible]" was in my neighbourhood for twenty years or something like that.

3902. He got very good stock?—Undoubtedly; they [illegible] over 15.3, 15.3, and 16.3, but beautiful horses.

3903. Did they sell well?—Yes, but [illegible] very useful afterwards in the [illegible] business, because they required a great deal of it [illegible].

3904. Have you any other experience of Hackneys?—No, I never saw any except these here.

3905. And therefore anything you have stated is founded on that experience and nothing else?—They were never good.

3906. You have had no experience among them?—None.

3907. How long have these two Yorkshire coaching horses been in your district?—We have had no experience of their breeding yet—they are only there this year.

3908. You have not seen their foals?—No.

3909. Anything you say is imaginary as to what their produce will be?—Only from the [illegible] like; [illegible] is quite as good as Hackney action with much better shape.

Nov. 22, 1895.
Rev. A. Stephen Bruce.

[illegible]
Mr. John Dickson.

Mr. John Dickson, Clogher, County Tyrone, examined.

3840. CHAIRMAN.—You live in the county of Tyrone?—Yes.

3841. And you farm land?—Yes.

3842. And breed horses?—Yes.

3843. What kind of horses have you been breeding?—We have bred from thoroughbreds and from Yorkshire horses.

3844. You mean what they call a Cleveland Bay or Yorkshire coaching horse?—Yorkshire coaching horse.

3845. You keep stallions?—Yes, sir.

3846. What sort of stallions?—A Yorkshire coaching horse at the present time.

3847. How long have you had him?—Two seasons.

3848. You get foals by him?—Yes, there are six or seven months old now.

3849. How do you like them?—They look uncommonly well; good [illegible] and [illegible] and [illegible] appearance, more like thoroughbreds but stronger.

3850. Is this horse of yours in the Yorkshire Coaching Horse Stud Book?—Yes, I have a certificate to that effect.

3851. Do the farmers breed hunters in your district at all?—As a rule not, they have not mares to breed hunters.

3852. Do they try to breed carriage horses?—They have been breeding different horses; the reason of it [illegible] light [illegible] wanting in height and bone, and they have bred different horses—and [illegible] [illegible].

3853. Do they breed a good many troopers?—A good many.

3854. Bought in the fairs?—Lately they have not been paying; they used to get £30 and £40 for a [illegible] [illegible], now he is not worth more than £16 or £18, the same horse.

3855. In that connection horses have deteriorated or that the prices have gone down?—In my opinion the horses have deteriorated.

3856. What do you attribute that to?—Lately the farmers have had a good deal [illegible] a couple of thoroughbreds in the neighbourhood that have brought a good many light horses and mares. One was "The Knight," and the other "[illegible]," this last [illegible] [illegible]. With the mares of the district they brought light stock.

3857. The same direction—do you think they have deteriorated [illegible] [illegible] they have.

3858. That you also attribute to the use of improper sires?—Yes, that would be the proper answer.

3859. How long have they been in the habit of breeding from thoroughbred sires?—There have been thoroughbred sires in the country for the last twenty years. [illegible] good [illegible] [illegible] and [illegible] [illegible] to breed horses with size and bone, but as [illegible] they were not fit to breed from thoroughbreds; [illegible] [illegible] the foals were not very good.

3860. What would you suggest respecting the [illegible] [illegible] [illegible] be [illegible] [illegible] [illegible] under the control or supervision of the Royal Dublin Society, and that the farmers should get [illegible] [illegible] [illegible] [illegible], at [illegible] [illegible] [illegible], or [illegible] [illegible], and that they would [illegible] [illegible] [illegible] [illegible] [illegible] [illegible] [illegible]. I think that would help to get farmers to keep their best fillies.

3861. As a rule now they sell their best foals?—As a rule they do.

3862. Is there a good class of stallions at present in your district?—I [illegible] [illegible] [illegible] [illegible] [illegible] a horse—a Yorkshire [illegible] [illegible] [illegible] about the middle of the country last year [illegible] [illegible], owned by Mr. George, and the horse I own myself.

3863. What is Mr. George's horse?—A Yorkshire coaching horse.

3864. The same breed as your own?—I believe so, but I have not seen him.

3865. They are popular horses with the farmers?—I can say that [illegible] [illegible] [illegible] [illegible] [illegible] views last year, that they are very fond of them.

3866. Your horse has got plenty of mares?—Yes, [illegible] [illegible].

3867. How many?—He served 105 mares this season. I don't know whether that is might be [illegible].

3868. You spoke of these two horses, yours and Mr. George's, as being the main [illegible]. I suppose that is not a sufficient number for the requirements of the farmers?—There are a great many other horses of no particular breed; there is no Hackney in our district; there is a thoroughbred horse at [illegible] [illegible].

3869. There appear to be only two thoroughbreds registered in the county at present. I suppose there are some other horses [illegible] in those neighbouring counties?—Yes, there are.

3870. Do you think if those were good thoroughbreds the farmers would use them?—They would seem to be very heavy and strong, and as the [illegible] [illegible] [illegible] the [illegible] in the district in which I live I don't know a mare fit to be put to a thoroughbred [illegible] [illegible] being a good [illegible]—a hunting horse or carriage horse of any good.

3871. Do you think that a good mare would be more likely to breed a useful horse by a Yorkshire coaching horse than by a thoroughbred?—Well, all I can say is that it was not until after [illegible] [illegible] with a gentleman of long experience [illegible] Mr. [illegible], that I bought this coaching horse for the sake of benefiting the country as well as [illegible] [illegible].

3872. Have you any suggestions to make with a view of improving the horses in your district?—I think what I spoke of about the [illegible] [illegible], [illegible] with a little [illegible] and a better class of horses, is likely to improve the breeding.

3873. Getting a better class of sires?—Yes.

3874. What do you consider a Yorkshire coaching horse would be [illegible] [illegible] [illegible] a [illegible] [illegible] [illegible] horse, [illegible] [illegible] [illegible] [illegible] [illegible] [illegible] [illegible] a good back and good quarters and [illegible] [illegible] [illegible], altogether a lovely horse, and would get very good horses.

3875. Would you prefer him to a thoroughbred of the same [illegible] [illegible] [illegible] [illegible]—The [illegible] [illegible] [illegible] [illegible] [illegible] [illegible] a [illegible] thoroughbred of the same [illegible], but it is hard to get [illegible].

3876. Have you any experience of Hackney stallions?—I have seen some at the [illegible], and have seen [illegible] of them; but they [illegible] not [illegible] [illegible]. They are more of a [illegible] [illegible]. A horse that ought [illegible] a [illegible] [illegible] [illegible] [illegible]. I never knew of any high prices being given for them.

3877. Do people of the farmers sell their stock at foals?—The [illegible] [illegible] [illegible] they are not able to keep them until they are of age.

3878. Do American buyers come about your [illegible] a [illegible], they come as far as Belfast, and they would not [illegible] [illegible] through the country.

3879. Do you approve of the suggestion made by other witnesses that they should be branded?—[illegible] [illegible] they are doing harm by the [illegible] [illegible] of Ireland; they are so good; they go to [illegible] [illegible] they would not do to [illegible] [illegible] [illegible] [illegible] [illegible] [illegible]. I [illegible] [illegible] of them.

3880. What sort of horses are generally bred in your district?—Generally harness horses, single and double.

3881. Are they improving in price?—[illegible] [illegible] [illegible] [illegible] the last [illegible] or three years.

3882. Do you think it pays the ordinary small farmer to breed a animal [illegible] [illegible] [illegible] [illegible]—If they start to work, [illegible] as [illegible] [illegible] I think [illegible] to get £30 for a four-year-old is better than buying a £10 horse and selling him for nothing [illegible].

3953. Mr. Fitzwilliam.—Then I think that you have introduced into the country [illegible] either Yorkshire coaching horses, or is it with a view to breeding [illegible] horses or agricultural horses, or what?—I think they have strength enough to be used for agricultural purposes, and they have shape to make [illegible] horses or saddle horses, and according to the [illegible] they got they very [illegible].

3954. Do you think that the sires round about [illegible] anything of your sort [illegible] enough to breed first class horses [illegible] they are, the average of mares may be [illegible] 15 hands, or may be 15½.

3955. They are fairly strong animals?—Yes, the [illegible] are light; they are generally [illegible] from those thoroughbreds that I have spoken of, [illegible] "Knight" and "[illegible]"—and are generally [illegible]. All the [illegible] I have seen from the [illegible] have been strong enough, and [illegible] by [illegible] anything.

3956. Sir Thomas Esmonde.—Did you say, Mr. [illegible], there were a sufficient number of good sires [illegible]? I don't think I answered that question. I think there are not a sufficient number of good sires in our part of the country.

3957. And have you formed any opinion as to the sort that would be most suitable?—[illegible] talking about this Yorkshire coaching horse, but as I said it was only after the most [illegible] consideration that he was bought and brought [illegible]. I don't know how he produces [illegible] are looking well, and he looks well enough himself, but I [illegible] any other horse.

3958. This horse was bought by a number of gentlemen?—Two other gentlemen and myself.

3959. Of course you consider your own opinion in arriving at the conclusion as to what would be most suitable?—Of course I had a voice in the matter, but [illegible] knowledge than I have.

3960. Do you think it would be advisable if the question of improving [illegible] Ireland [illegible] the different [illegible] what they would be best?—I think it would be [illegible] the different [illegible] have [illegible]. I don't think they [illegible] is capable of giving a proper opinion, but there are men in every locality [illegible] as to the proper horse.

3961. You think by [illegible] you would [illegible] as to what would be the most suitable horse?—That is my opinion.

3962. Mr. Gilmore.—You said there was no Hackney in the district?—Not just now.

3963. Was there ever any?—"Performer," that was owned by the Rev. Mr. [illegible].

3964. How was he bred?—I don't know; he came from Yorkshire and only stayed there a few years.

3965. Where?—I expect he is dead two years.

3966. Did he [illegible] until he died?—Yes, until he died.

3967. And he has not been replaced by any other Hackney?—No.

3968. What sort were his progeny?—Very variable [illegible] of different types and colours, and I am saying that he never grew a horse to be worth more than £10.

3969. That is at full age?—Yes, at full age.

3970. The experience of [illegible]'s stock has not induced any other breeder to [illegible] a Hackney?—No. They are not fond of them in my district.

3971. Mr. Quinn.—Do the small farmers around you breed for sale or for their own purposes?—A good many of them sell as year olds and two-year olds; a good many sell their young stock at an early age.

3972. Do you think their idea is to utilise them or do they breed as an industry for sale?—They breed as an industry for sale, I think.

3973. You say the price of those smaller horses has gone down very much?—Yes.

3974. Can you account for that?—There are different reasons given; some say that owing to the introduction of bicycles so many horses are not required, and others say that the American horses have supplied the places of the Irish horses; no doubt both have contributed.

3975. What do you say has brought it down?—The use of bicycles, the importation of American horses, and the lack of quality in what is being bred.

3976. Supposing there is a still further decrease owing say to the introduction of motor cars and the use of bicycles and the importation of American horses, would it pay the farmer to breed, or would he breed only for his own purposes?—Only for his own purposes if things go on like this.

3977. Mr. Watson.—Where did you buy your coaching horse?—From a gentleman called F. H. Stericker, of Pickering, Yorkshire.

3978. Then I think you said your experience of Hackneys was confined to a Hackney called "Performer"?—Yes.

3979. Who did he belong to?—Mr. Gabriel George.

3980. What was he?—A farmer.

3981. A rich man?—Well, he is in good circumstances; he owns a good sized farm.

3982. You don't know how that horse was bred?—No, I could not say; I don't know anything about his pedigree.

3983. In the questions that were sent out to you by the Commission, in answer to the question "What are the most popular stallions in your district?" you say—Two gone by "The Bounding Willow" and Yorkshire coaching stallion?—One of those gone is very old, he was a popular stallion in his day.

3984. What is he?—His mother was got by "Blarney," the property of the late Lord Charlemont. He is by a horse called "Bounding Willow."

3985. And he has been a very popular stallion?—Yes.

3986. He served for a good many seasons?—Yes, but not exactly in my district.

3987. What were his stock like?—Generally good, but under-sized.

3988. "Bounding Willow" was a Hackney stallion?—Yes, with a good touch of Arab in him. He may have been entered in the Hackney Stud Book.

3989. Then I think you said the average of the height of mares in your district was about 15 hands?—Yes, about 15 hands; a good many are under 15—14.2 and 14½. I should say 15 hands is the average.

3990. Would not the cross of a Yorkshire coaching horse on those 14.2 mares be rather a violent cross, an extreme cross?—I don't know that it has any tendency to do any harm.

3991. What height is your horse?—16.1½.

3992. It would be rather extreme?—They would be two extremes.

3993. Is it your opinion that the best results are obtained by using an extreme cross like that?—When you get the mare 14½, that is under the average.

3994. The average you say is 15?—The average.

3995. I am not talking of the big mares, I am talking of the small. Would you not think it an extreme cross for them?—I have seen many small mares breed very nice horses of a good size.

3996. You have no experience of his stock yet?—Nothing more than yearling year-old foals.

[illegible]
Mr. John [illegible]

[illegible]

Colonel [illegible], Derry [illegible], [illegible], examined.

3996. CHAIRMAN.—You live in the county of Clare?—In the county of Tipperary, but my [illegible] [illegible] in Clare.

3997. You have had considerable experience of horse-breeding?—I have had [illegible] [illegible] years' experience since the breeding of horses, and my brother, [illegible] [illegible] for a long time; he [illegible] a great interest in it.

3998. What sort of horses do you breed?—Hunters and carriage horses [illegible].

3999. Do you breed them in the same way?—I would breed [illegible] in the same way as [illegible] [illegible]; I have had a long experience of [illegible] and [illegible], and I [illegible] to breed horses out of really good mares; I think that [illegible] in my county [illegible] [illegible] [illegible] they can breed out of anything, and make a good [illegible] by doing so.

4000. You say you breed hunters and harness horses; do you use the same stallions?—I would; I [illegible] thoroughbred stallion [illegible] all circumstances, [illegible] I think the great mistake that people make is [illegible] that any [illegible] is good enough to breed from, and I think if any encouragement could be given to farmers to keep their mares [illegible] it would be a good thing; they sell now the better class ones, and think anything is good enough to breed from. I think if they could be induced to keep the better class of mares, and that some premium could be given to them [illegible] they would do it—a very little would make them do it. I would suggest giving [illegible] to them to keep the better class mares. They are tempted by a small [illegible] to sell them, and think anything good enough to breed from. If there were some small premium or [illegible] [illegible] [illegible] [illegible] giving a small thing, say five [illegible] for [illegible] [illegible] of [illegible] [illegible] [illegible] [illegible] [illegible] [illegible] [illegible]. I think [illegible] [illegible] [illegible] [illegible] keep the good ones and they [illegible] [illegible] [illegible] [illegible] [illegible] [illegible] [illegible].

4001. You would give premiums for young mares?—I have [illegible] [illegible] [illegible] [illegible] [illegible] and [illegible] [illegible] [illegible] [illegible]. I think if farmers were to breed from [illegible] horses they [illegible] [illegible] and [illegible] they would [illegible] [illegible] [illegible] something of them. [illegible] [illegible] I [illegible], [illegible] have got a [illegible] of [illegible] [illegible] the [illegible] [illegible] [illegible] young, and [illegible] [illegible] [illegible] of them.

4002. But the Industry [illegible] [illegible] [illegible] in any part of the country: [illegible] [illegible] [illegible], but I don't think [illegible] [illegible] [illegible] [illegible] [illegible] [illegible] [illegible] [illegible] [illegible] [illegible] [illegible] [illegible] [illegible].

4003. Are there many good stallions in your district?—Yes, in Limerick, [illegible] [illegible] good stallions, but not very many.

4004. Do you approve of half-breds?—I don't believe in them at all. I believe only in breeding from the thorough-bred you can get, and I don't think [illegible] [illegible] [illegible] [illegible] [illegible] [illegible] [illegible] [illegible] [illegible]. I have known [illegible] [illegible] [illegible] [illegible] [illegible] [illegible] [illegible] [illegible] [illegible] [illegible] horses and [illegible] [illegible] [illegible] [illegible] [illegible], [illegible] [illegible] [illegible] [illegible] [illegible] breeding.

4005. Do you think the Royal Dublin Society's scheme has been a success so far?—[illegible] [illegible], I think they have done very well; [illegible] [illegible] [illegible] [illegible], I think the [illegible] [illegible] [illegible] [illegible] [illegible] [illegible] [illegible] [illegible] they are [illegible] good.

4006. And as regards giving premiums to mares, that ought to be extended?—I don't think anything would do so much to improve the breed of horses as giving the farmers some encouragement to keep their [illegible].

4007. That is done under the present scheme; they give prizes [illegible] [illegible] [illegible] to farmers [illegible] [illegible] [illegible] [illegible] [illegible] [illegible] [illegible] [illegible] [illegible] to [illegible].

4008. [illegible].—Do you [illegible] [illegible] [illegible] [illegible] [illegible]?—I think that if some [illegible] encouragement could be given by letting the [illegible] [illegible] [illegible], and if some inducement could be held out to the farmer to hold on to his best filly instead of selling [illegible] [illegible] [illegible] [illegible], [illegible] [illegible] [illegible] [illegible] [illegible] would do more than anything to improve the breed of horses. As long as you keep the good mares you will have the good foals.

4009. Do you think the horses in your district have improved or deteriorated?—I do not think they have; I think that [illegible] [illegible] [illegible] a good [illegible] [illegible] in the old days than [illegible] [illegible].

4010. You think they have deteriorated then?—I would not say that; I think we are at a standstill.

4011. Are prices as good for young stock?—I don't think so; if you get a really good animal you will always get a good price for it. I [illegible] a [illegible] [illegible] [illegible] with the object of improving the breed [illegible] [illegible], and I think we are [illegible] [illegible] [illegible] [illegible] [illegible] [illegible] [illegible]. I [illegible] [illegible] [illegible] [illegible] [illegible] [illegible].

4012. At what age do the farmers sell their [illegible]?—They generally sell them at [illegible] [illegible] [illegible] [illegible] half years.

4013. The [illegible] [illegible]?—The [illegible] [illegible] [illegible] them [illegible].

4014. And sell them at about [illegible] [illegible] years old?—At [illegible] years old; they [illegible] [illegible] [illegible] [illegible] [illegible] a half years very [illegible] at light farm work.

4015. Are these horses chiefly got by thoroughbred horses?—Yes, got by thoroughbreds. A great many are got by [illegible] [illegible] [illegible]; that, perhaps, [illegible] [illegible] [illegible] [illegible] [illegible] [illegible]. The [illegible] [illegible] [illegible] [illegible] [illegible] [illegible] [illegible] [illegible] [illegible], and the [illegible] [illegible] [illegible] a great difference to a great many farmers; they put them [illegible] [illegible] [illegible] [illegible] [illegible] [illegible] [illegible] [illegible] [illegible]. If you could get good stallions, and farmers can be induced, by [illegible] [illegible], [illegible] [illegible] [illegible] [illegible] [illegible] [illegible], I think it would [illegible] [illegible] [illegible] [illegible].

4016. You think the farmers [illegible] the [illegible] [illegible] [illegible] [illegible]?—I do.

4017. Do the farmers take good care of their brood mares and young horses?—They do; they [illegible] [illegible] [illegible] [illegible]. If they [illegible] [illegible] [illegible] [illegible] [illegible] they [illegible] [illegible] [illegible] [illegible] [illegible]. The [illegible] [illegible] [illegible] [illegible] [illegible] [illegible] [illegible]. A good [illegible] [illegible] [illegible] [illegible], [illegible] [illegible] [illegible] [illegible] [illegible] [illegible]; [illegible] of a good breed of horses.

4018. Have you any experience of breeding [illegible] [illegible]?—No; I [illegible] [illegible] [illegible] [illegible] [illegible] [illegible] [illegible] [illegible] [illegible] [illegible] [illegible] Board [illegible] in the West of Ireland, but I didn't breed them at all.

4019. You don't [illegible] [illegible] [illegible] for the [illegible] [illegible] [illegible] of the country?—[illegible] [illegible] [illegible] in my part of the country, but I don't believe in [illegible] [illegible] [illegible] useful; they are good for [illegible] [illegible] and [illegible] and light work, but they would [illegible] [illegible] [illegible] [illegible].

4020. Do you think if they were introduced into your county they would affect the value of the hunters?—I cannot say, because I have had no experience of them myself.

4021. The [illegible] [illegible] of horses from the [illegible] came into your district?—Oh! no, not now, some years ago they used to, but not now.

4022. I think you said at the beginning that you had experience of breeding horses in [illegible] [illegible]?—Yes, in [illegible]. I [illegible] [illegible] a few years abroad, and [illegible] [illegible] [illegible] [illegible] [illegible] [illegible] [illegible] [illegible], [illegible] generally [illegible] [illegible] [illegible] [illegible].

4023. In India?—The [illegible] [illegible].

[illegible]. You bred Barb stallions?—Yes.

[illegible]. Was the issue of any particular breed [illegible] Barb stallions and bred from the mares of the country a very useful class of horses. We used them for riding purposes principally. We had no [illegible] and used them for [illegible].

[illegible]. Were they small horses?—Well, about [illegible].

[illegible]. What class of horses do you suggest would be best for the farmers in your district to breed? [illegible]

[illegible]

[illegible]. Mr. [illegible].—You don't reply [illegible] of your own?—[illegible].

[illegible]. In your district, a horse-breeding district?—Yes. I think there is a good deal of horse breeding, and a great many good horses bred in the district.

[illegible]

[illegible]. You are speaking of the blood?—Yes. [illegible]

[illegible]

[illegible]. And one takes a very different view of horses?—The Hackney might do in some parts of the West of Ireland. [illegible] I think in all the breeds of Ireland you can breed a much superior class of horse.

Mr. [illegible]

Mr. James MacClancy, Milltown Malbay, examined.

4033. Chairman.—You live in the west of Clare, I think?—Yes, sir.

4034. Do you farm lands?—I do.

4035. And have you some experience in horse-breeding?—Well, I bred horses for the last fifteen or seventeen years.

4036. Would you describe to us the breed of horse that you tried to produce?—I bred from the [illegible] mares with the thoroughbred, the best thoroughbred in my district.

4037. You think that the thoroughbred horse is the most suitable horse?—Yes; I think so. In my district, sir, in the west of Clare, the holdings are very small, and they cannot afford to keep good mares, they sell their best fillies and mares.

4038. At what age do they generally sell the horses, the farmers in your district?—The larger class of farmers keep them to three and four-year-olds, and the smaller class one and a-half year-olds to two-year-olds.

4039. Do you think your district is a good horse producing district?—Very much so, it is famous for breeding young cattle of every kind.

4040. And what class of horses do you think could be produced that would be most likely to be remunerative?—I would say the larger class of farmers would produce a hunter or good harness horse.

4041. Are they useful mares, the ordinary run of mares?—The larger class generally keep a useful mare, but the smaller class cannot afford to do so, they are very weedy and defective, very light.

4042. Do the farmers take any trouble about mating their mares as a rule?—Latterly they seem more interested in the breeding of horses than formerly, they were rather indifferent, latterly they are rather more inclined to take more trouble.

4043. What class of stallion do they like?—Generally thoroughbred, they are most popular and more useful I think.

4044. Are there plenty of suitable stallions in the

Mr. James MacClancy.

Apr. 13, 1896. Mr. James [illegible].

[illegible]?—Rather the small stallions, but of a very indifferent quality, I think.

4045. Do you think they would be improved?—Very much so.

4046. What would you suggest in that direction; how would you suggest the improvement should come?—I would recommend for the larger class of farmers a good thoroughbred with plenty of substance and bone; and for the smaller class a half-bred or Hackney stallion I think would do very well.

4047. Have you had any personal experience of breeding from a Hackney stallion?—Not myself, but there is a Hackney in my neighbourhood, and he seems popular enough with some of the farmers.

4048. Have you seen his stock?—Yes, I have seen some of his progeny.

4049. Do you consider that they are good useful horses?—They are suited for the farmers, for their own work, and they are [illegible] than they would the produce of the thoroughbred perhaps; they develop earlier, and become more useful.

4050. Do the farmers in your district breed principally for the purpose of sale or for their own use?—Well, some of them breed for sale and some for their own use.

4051. Are there many horses sold out of your district annually?—A great many, every farmer there seems to have a horse, and they generally keep a mare, and whether it is good or bad they breed from the mare and get a foal from her.

4052. What age do they generally sell them at?—The small farmers sell at half a year old and some from that to a year and a half, and the bigger class keep them to three or four years old.

4053. Have you any experience of the Royal Dublin Society's scheme working in your district?—I have. I believe the people have a greater interest in the breeding of horses since it was introduced, but as far as the Royal Dublin Society is [illegible], I think, we are placed at a great disadvantage in the West of Clare, it is very [illegible] and expensive to take horses from there to the [illegible]; very often I know a farmer to have a good horse and he is deterred from [illegible] the expense [illegible] he might not sell him to advantage.

4054. You mean as regards the Shows?—Yes. I think the scheme is working very well.

4055. Just as regards the [illegible] scheme?—It is working reasonably; [illegible] to [illegible] horse breeding, it would be a benefit if we had more shows and prizes given to the farmers to keep their good mares and fillies, for really no matter what sire we have we won't produce good horses from the mares we have there.

4056. But still the scheme is in operation in your district?—It is.

4057. And the mares are shown and prizes given to mares that are considered most suitable?—Yes.

4058. There is a local committee I conclude [illegible]?—Yes.

4059. And those mares are brought to certain places and judged and prizes given accordingly?—Yes.

4060. Do you think [illegible] works satisfactorily?—I think so, but it might be improved if we had more of them; it is rather remote [illegible] parts of the county, it is generally held in Ennis, and that is very far away from the west of Clare.

4061. Do they sell many troopers in your district?—They do, they are quite satisfied with those young horses if they grow up to be troopers.

4062. If you think the breed is improving?—Yes, but I can say [illegible] very few would sell as troopers, they are not about enough or heavy enough.

4063. Have not the farmers bred?—Generally from the mares we have and half-bred sires; all the horses in my neighbourhood are half-breds, the thoroughbreds that we have there are some twenty-five miles from where I live, and further from other districts in Clare.

4064. There are some few thoroughbred horses in your immediate vicinity?—The nearest is about twenty-five miles, Major Studdert's.

4065. Do the farmers take good care of their mares and young stock?—I think they take greater care now than heretofore, they are more interested, and they are becoming more intelligent I think in that respect.

4066. Do you keep a stallion yourself?—No.

4067. What stallion do you think is most suitable for the mares in your neighbourhood?—I think for the larger farmers the thoroughbred with plenty of bone and substance would be the best.

4068. A good thoroughbred?—A good thoroughbred, and for the smaller I would say a half-bred or Hackney would do very well. I would rather myself breed from the thoroughbred.

4069. Do you think the introduction of the Hackney blood would have any effect on the sale of hunters from your part of the country?—I cannot speak from experience, but from what I have heard I believe it would, there is a prejudice against it, and people who seem to know better than I do say they have not spirit enough or stamina as well as our Irish bred or thoroughbred, which I believe.

4070. You think that the present Irish breed of horses is good?—I think so, much better than the Hackney breed.

4071. Mr. Fitzwilliam.—Which would you prefer to breed from in your district, the half-bred, and when I say the half-bred I mean a well-bred thoroughbred cross, what I think is usually understood as a half-bred, a good half-bred or a good Hackney?—I think that a good half-bred would be better, I would prefer a good half-bred at any rate to a Hackney.

4072. You think that they would be obtainable if there was a demand for them?—I think so.

4073. Then we understand you prefer that for the mares in your district to the Hackney or to any other breed like that because of the people in my district are not suited to the Hackney, they say that he develops earlier and is very easily handled.

4074. Still you yourself would prefer a good well-bred half-bred to any other after the thoroughbred?—I would, but the great thing in our district is to improve the breed of mares, I would say the sires are good enough in a way but the mares are very defective.

4075. Can you make any suggestion for improving the mares?—If you had prizes given to the farmers to keep the best fillies and mares I would say it would be a great thing, and then shows in the localities. You could have a show in each barony and a few prizes for the best mares, they are much interested and very anxious to keep them, but they are so poor they would sell anything they have to try and make ends meet.

4076. Local shows you mean, prizes at local shows for mares who have bred foals?—Yes, for the owners or who might have young foals that they would keep to breed, to encourage them to keep them because their best fillies are now bought by foreigners, and anything they have in the shape of a good horse or good young beast of any kind they sell them to make the money and make ends meet, they want some encouragement to keep them; the best sires in the world would not produce a good foal from the mares they have at present.

4077. Sir T. Esmonde.—Are there many of those fillies bought by foreigners?—All the best likely fillies are bought by foreigners, as a matter of fact when a man has a good filly he is bound to sell her through poverty.

4078. I suppose they buy them at any cost?—They buy them at any cost.

4079. Did you notice a suggestion made by some witnesses before this Commission that the old mares used by the Army Service Corps and the Artillery, when their work was done and they were no longer fit for use, should be distributed among the farmers in breeding horses?—I would not approve of it.

4079. Why not?—I would rather breed from younger mares.

4080. You believe in breeding from young mares?—I do.

4081. Mr. Gannon.—Would you breed from a two-year-old?—Yes, I have bred myself from a two-year-old.

4082. And found it successful?—And found it successful.

4083. Then the purpose of your evidence is that for the [illegible], with a good mare, you would breed from a thoroughbred?—Entirely.

4084. And you prefer a good half-bred sire to a Hackney?—I do. I think the Hackney might do fairly well, and some of the people like Hackneys; they mature earlier and are saleable at a year or a year and a half old.

4085. Are they good workers on the farm?—They are good workers on the farm, very handy and useful animals.

4086. You suggest that brood mares should be kept for the purpose of improving the breed?—Yes, it would be a great improvement.

4087. And if the breed of mares was improved you would have all that was desired as far as sires are concerned, you have good enough sires in the district if you have good mares?—I think so, the want of good mares is a great thing, but we want sires badly.

4088. You would be in favour of registering every sire?—Every sound sire.

4089. If you register them he could be discarded?—I would prefer, if I could, every unsound sire kept away from breeding at all, because it is a [illegible] for the country as far as breeding is concerned.

4090. Mr. Wrench.—You would be in favour of registering every kind of sire?—Only the sound sires.

4091. You would not object to what breed it was provided it was sound?—Provided it was sound.

4092. The subject of the larger and smaller class of farmers, what do you call the larger class of farmers, I mean up to what valuation?—I would not say [illegible]; I would say he would be of the [illegible] class of farmers.

4093. You would draw the line at £50?—At £50.

4094. The smaller those above £50 the larger?—Yes, as you might put it down to £30; any person with £30 valuation is hardly able to mind [illegible]; they are [illegible] independent.

4095. Are there many farmers in your district above £50 [illegible]?—Yes, most of them; say from £30 to £50 [illegible] most of them; they would keep a brood mare and they generally keep a mare, and say they will have a foal out of her, to [illegible] for [illegible] ploughing.

4096. Then any suggestion as to preventing these men from breeding would not be [illegible]?—Unless they [illegible] I would not prevent them breeding.

4097. Provided they had sound mares you would [illegible] people to be allowed to breed?—I think [illegible] they are breeding from very bad classes.

4098. And unsound, diseased?—I daresay they are, but they are [illegible].

4099. What fairs in your district do they generally sell their horses at?—[illegible] fair; [illegible] a great [illegible] in our country; we have several local fairs [illegible] and have a [illegible] fair and [illegible] fair.

4100. Do you find horses with good action sell well?—Oh, very well; if they have good action they are bound to sell well; they must be shapely too.

4101. Can you say from your own experience whether Hackney horses get horses with better action than half-bred horses?—No.

4102. You have not much practical experience of Hackneys?—No.

4103. Therefore, though you have a preference for a half-bred sire, you have never bred from a Hackney stallion yourself?—Never.

4104. Have you ever bred from a half-bred sire?—Never.

4105. You have only bred from a thoroughbred?—Yes.

4106. And I gather from your evidence that you think it would be better if more prizes were given to brood mares?—I think so, to improve the breed of horses.

4107. Do you [illegible] got up by local committees?—Well, yes, in connection with the Dublin Show, and horses generally.

4108. And the Royal Dublin Society's Committee, do you know how that is appointed or [illegible]?—I do; I know the members.

4109. Do you know how it is appointed?—Well, but I think there would be [illegible] in touch with [illegible] in my district; [illegible] the people [illegible] to go to Dublin.

4110. Is Dublin the only place?—Dublin is the only place in my county that I am aware of.

4111. And you think that the smaller class of farmers [illegible] require more help than the larger class?—I think the larger class of farmers are able to help themselves, but the smaller class require help.

4112. Chairman.—Any other suggestions that you would like to make to the Commission, Mr. M'Donnell?—Well, I don't know, sir, except we find that we don't benefit much from the Royal Dublin Society's Show in Dublin; we are too remote and terribly handicapped in the west of Ireland, with railway fares and our expenses; if they could be subsidised in some way by the Government it would benefit us; we are terribly handicapped compared with places near Dublin. I attended the Dublin Show with horses with a friend of mine. If you don't sell well they are [illegible] altogether, [illegible] expenses to bring them back, and, as a matter of fact, I could hardly tell you [illegible] I was sure of selling my horse [illegible].

4113. Mr. Gannon.—What do the railway companies charge from [illegible]?—I would not [illegible], but it is rather heavy, and you have to [illegible] a week with your horse, and [illegible] would cost the price of the horse altogether if you don't sell well.

4114. Sir T. Esmonde.—Do you find the railway rates have an injurious effect on the trade?—Oh, undoubtedly; if you have not a good horse and cannot sell well, you simply lose the money; there are plenty of people who could not afford to run the risk of paying up.

4115. Do you think the trade could be developed if the railway rates were put in [illegible]?—No doubt about it; people would be anxious to improve their breed of horses, and would strive to get a good market for them if they could do it in a [illegible] way.

4116. That should be done?—They ought to do it now, from the experience of those of us who would not think of doing it.

Mr. Harry M'Donnell, [illegible], examined.

4118. Chairman.—You live in the county Galway?—Yes, sir.

4119. You are a land agent and farm land there?—Yes, sir.

4120. You are well acquainted with a considerable portion of the county?—With the Connemara portion of Galway.

4121. And you think the soil is suitable for horse-breeding?—I do, sir.

4122. Do many farmers breed horses?—Nearly everyone keeps a mare, mostly all the small farmers.

4123. What class of mares?—From 14 to 15 hands, the Connemara pony.

4124. What sort of stallion do you think is most

[illegible] Welsh cob would suit the country very well.

[illegible]

4122. [illegible]

4123. [illegible]

4124. [illegible]

4125. [illegible]

4126. [illegible]

4127. [illegible]

4128. [illegible]

4129. [illegible]

4130. [illegible]

[illegible] Welsh [illegible]

[illegible] Royal Dublin Society [illegible]

[illegible] "Wonderspring" [illegible]

[illegible] Congested Districts Board [illegible]

[illegible] "Wonderspring" [illegible]

[illegible] want to get a horse in our country at all; they only want to get a pony.

[illegible] At Clifden and Westport, those are the principal fairs.

[illegible] a horse called "Lioness" [illegible]

[illegible]

[illegible] Congested Districts Board, a horse called "Sultana." [illegible] Welsh [illegible]

[illegible] "Wonderspring." [illegible]

[illegible]

[illegible] would be a good thing in future to rehabilitate the Connemara pony?—It may be, I think it would be. [illegible] I would rather have the Welsh [illegible].

6173. By the Welsh [illegible] do you mean the English thoroughbred, of suitable [illegible] shape, and [illegible]?—[illegible].

6174. Sir T. [illegible].—With regard to your suggestion of licensing the stallions, would you license every stallion?—The stallion should be brought before a committee, and then any stallion that was fit for it should get a licence, and the others should be sent away, and if such a stallion was [illegible] the owner should be fined.

6175. Would you have the stallions examined by a veterinary surgeon [illegible]?

6176. Would you consider that necessary in your system of licensing?—Yes.

6177. They should be sound stallions, free from any hereditary disease?—No doubt.

6178. The Chairman.—You knew [illegible] "Tamworth," was he highbred?—He was.

6179. Did you [illegible] of his [illegible]?—I have only [illegible] years of age.

6180. Had his produce good?—Very good [illegible] horses. I have [illegible] of them [illegible] a day.

6181. Did you ever see him?—Oh, I remember seeing him.

6182. Was he a good horse?—Yes, big [illegible], a big black horse.

6183. Mr. Wrench.—[illegible] one of the best [illegible] in the United Kingdom [illegible] for the last [illegible] years [illegible]

6184. You have not been in [illegible] when he was standing there?—[illegible].

6185. Were they big enough?—They appeared to [illegible] for this country. [illegible] £8 for the [illegible] had to sell [illegible].

6186. They did not grow big enough?—They [illegible] enough.

6187. Do you know that the people of [illegible] were [illegible] about the time they [illegible] "Welshpring" [illegible] I don't think they know much about "Welshpring" until lately.

6188. I am speaking of two years ago?—I don't think they knew anything of "Welshpring" [illegible] two years ago, and did not know how the foals would turn out.

6189. Has he not been in the country five years?—No, only four.

6190. Have you not seen any of his produce sold?—No, I have not.

6191. Did you know the horse himself?—I did. Mr. [illegible] bought him [illegible].

6192. Do you think he has been long enough for the success of the country [illegible]?

6193. You say the [illegible] public [illegible] this [illegible]; they [illegible] into the country to buy a class of pony [illegible] but the [illegible] prefers them bigger.

6194. Who are the [illegible] public?—Different people who want to [illegible] and who [illegible] a low price.

6195. That is polo ponies?—Yes, sir.

6196. Then it is the people who want for [illegible] ponies [illegible], the [illegible] don't know what they are there for.

6197. The people themselves, the farmers that breed these ponies, what class [illegible]?—The Welsh cob, [illegible], they [illegible] very big, they [illegible] it is all [illegible] on the [illegible].

6198. Can you say whether the produce of the Welsh cob or the [illegible] are the best?—I think the Welsh cob.

6199. And you have seen both?—I have seen both. I think the Welsh cob with Connemara [illegible] is a [illegible] black horse.

6200. Can you [illegible] any [illegible] except this one?—No.

6201. And you have never been [illegible]?—I have [illegible], I bought [illegible].

6202. Chairman.—Is there any further suggestion you would like to make?—I think not.

6203. You think the Welsh cob is the most suitable animal for your district, and you think the stallions should be licensed?—I think so. You could not improve the breed of horses in the country if everyone was allowed to keep a stallion, because the country people will go to the cheapest.

Mr. [illegible] Johnston, [illegible], examined.

6204. Chairman.—You are a [illegible] living in [illegible]?—Yes, sir.

6205. Are you live in the [illegible] side of the county?—[illegible].

6206. Do [illegible] horses [illegible]?—Yes, they are bred largely.

6207. Do you breed horses yourself?—I do.

6208. What class do you breed?—I breed them for [illegible] and good weight-carrying hunters. I approve of the thoroughbred horse, the best thoroughbred horse that can be got with good bone and substance, and [illegible] horses [illegible], but I believe good half-bred horses are very useful for my district. What I mean by half-bred is the thoroughbred horse and the good old Irish mare, which is very rare now, but is [illegible] for the [illegible] if [illegible] the [illegible].

6209. What is your definition of this old Irish mare?—A good old breed of Irish mare, [illegible], good [illegible] good sloping shoulders, [illegible] in fact the animal to [illegible] able to [illegible] a [illegible].

6210. How is she bred?—Well, there was an old breed in the country. I [illegible] where it [illegible], unfortunately. You [illegible] good [illegible] of [illegible], but [illegible] they were very good hunters [illegible] the [illegible] kind of [illegible] blood, I [illegible] where it [illegible], but they [illegible] the old class [illegible] very well known, and [illegible] of them [illegible] weight-carrying hunters [illegible] half-bred, the [illegible] part of the [illegible]. [illegible] of [illegible] of [illegible] There must be a [illegible] in the [illegible] thoroughbred, the [illegible] of [illegible], a [illegible] and all that sort of thing.

6211. You say you breed hunters and [illegible] carriage horses?—Yes.

6212. And in [illegible] hunters you use a thoroughbred horse, what sire do you use to breed carriage horses?—Well, in breeding from a [illegible] mare with a half-bred horse, [illegible] a carriage [illegible]; [illegible] carriage horse [illegible] you get a great many [illegible].

6213. What is the usual class of horse [illegible] by the farmers in your part of [illegible]?—I [illegible] the [illegible] horse, the [illegible] by the small class of farmers; they go to [illegible] of the [illegible] Board, [illegible] of that kind, and they [illegible] a very bad [illegible]. [illegible] a large [illegible] and [illegible], [illegible] keep the [illegible] and generally keep [illegible].

most people who have them keep them to five years old. I very often break them myself, and from them hunting, and try to get them to as much as I can.

4214. Then I presume the large farmers generally aim at good size, and the small farmers only [illegible] the small farmers are greatly afraid [illegible] the small farmers in [illegible]. Then, as a rule, these people sell them as a year and a half old and [illegible]. Some keep them to two years old, and then they get those little weeds out of them, which is of course very injurious to the breed. They begin to work them at one and a half years old, and ruin them by that, and they try to sell them at two and a half years old, and many sell at three years old, but of course the large farmers who have large lands let them run from three to four years old without ever touching them.

4215. What sort of mares do the farmers [illegible]?—As a rule they are [illegible] and weedy; we want something to increase the size. Indeed, we want more improvement in the mares than in the sires, as far as that goes.

4216. How would you suggest to improve the mares?—We have a very good lead there in my locality, which has been worked up wonderfully by some of the local gentry. Lord Ardilaun is at the head of it, and he has given [illegible] for it at [illegible], and there has been a good deal of good effected by keeping these mares and giving good prizes for the good ones. But I would suggest going further, and it would be this, if possible, to induce the owners of these animals, by giving them premiums, to hold them on, to keep them for [illegible]. Well, that is rather a difficult question, or at least a difficult problem perhaps to recognise, but I think that would be one way it could be done. It would be by giving them certain good prizes, and then, when the good mares are selected by the Government or Royal Dublin Society, let them have the marking of them, [illegible] competent veterinary surgeons to go and [illegible] down the [illegible] of the mares that would take those prizes, [illegible] would be kept [illegible] from the farmers that they would keep them for a certain number of years, a certain time after getting the prize, and the feeling of getting the service grant, I think, would [illegible] and induce the farmers to keep them.

4217. You think it is absolutely necessary to give additional facilities to farmers to induce them to keep their mares in more expensive and valuable condition?—I believe that would be a step in the right direction.

4218. Is the Royal Dublin Society's scheme working in your part of Galway?—Yes, it has effected a great deal of good, and has given people more taste for getting the right horses and getting into the good [illegible].

4219. Do you think the small prizes given to these mares of £5 and £10 has the result of inducing farmers to keep their mares?—I believe it has, and would more, if attached one further, as I suggested, if they keep up these mares and give a regular guarantee to keep them for a certain number of years, then to allow them to have the service grant. I believe it would be a step in the right direction.

4220. Are there plenty of suitable sires do you think in your part of Galway?—No, we have not many suitable sires in my locality, [illegible] what I consider one good thoroughbred horse belonging to [illegible], a very well known old horse called [illegible], one of the best bred horses in Galway, bred by one of the Dukes of [illegible], one of the old [illegible] breed, got by [illegible] I think. There is another good horse about six miles from [illegible], on the other side, owned by Mr. [illegible], a horse called [illegible], that is a good thoroughbred horse, [illegible] about the end of [illegible]. On the other side of [illegible] also there are a few good horses; there are a couple of good horses owned by Mr. [illegible]; there is a good old horse also of the [illegible] breeding, [illegible], I think that is one of the best thoroughbred horses in Ireland, one of the best bred thoroughbred horses I ever saw, but he is an old horse now.

4221. Are the [illegible] good half-bred [illegible]?—[illegible] they are, I have seen some of them very good, I never bred from him myself.

4222. What horses do you use yourself?—I [illegible] a half-bred horse myself, but he is [illegible]. [illegible] I cannot follow his grandam's pedigree far enough, and he is out of [illegible], he was got by [illegible], by [illegible], and his dam by [illegible]. I could not follow the breeding of the dam far enough, but the horse is getting very well.

4223. And in your opinion what sires do you consider most suitable for the ordinary mares of the district, you spoke of the mares being light and weedy?—Yes, as a rule a great many of them are. Well there are three classes of horses I would recommend for the district, there would be the thoroughbred for those who can afford to wait for the progeny to come up to the proper age and afford to keep them, and who can afford to have the proper mares as far as the thoroughbred horse. Then the half-bred for the man who would be inclined to pay [illegible] and unable to sell the produce [illegible] the thoroughbred would not [illegible]. I think they would be very useful for the class of farmers who would not give [illegible] of the thoroughbred [illegible] would be much more expensive [illegible]. To improve the size of the small mares you want something big and useful for agricultural work; I believe the Clydesdale [illegible] the size for agricultural purposes, but [illegible] large horses [illegible].

4224. Then the Clydesdale you would recommend with the thoroughbred, a good half-bred, and the Clydesdale?—Yes, and the half-bred would [illegible] in the first cross from the thoroughbred horse and good old well-shaped [illegible] mares of the district, the good [illegible] free from hereditary taint.

4225. Have you always lived in Galway?—Yes, since I was born.

4226. Do you see any difference in the breeding of the horses there now, do you think they are improving or deteriorating?—Well, considering when I began to know these horses first in my boyhood, I think the horses were better then, and I think they fell away for a considerable time, and generally, and for the last ten or eleven years I think there has been an improvement. I think there are better animals, and I attribute that very much to the interest taken in the breeding of horses by the Royal Dublin Society and those connected with it.

4227. Do the Clydesdale [illegible] in Galway?—We have an occasional Clydesdale [illegible] and they [illegible] useful. They are for [illegible] work and small [illegible] work.

4228. Did you ever breed hunters out of [illegible]?—Yes; I have bred one of the best hunters I ever had out of a Connemara mare by a thoroughbred horse, [illegible] by [illegible].

4229. Have you any practical experience of breeding out of Hackney horses?—I never have, but I have seen some in my locality, there are a couple

Nov. 16, 1896.

Mr. Samuel Johnson.

owned by my neighbour Lord Ashtown, one of them, I consider one of the best specimens of the breed that could possibly be shown by anyone.

4230. And their produce?—I saw a good many with Lord Ashtown, and they look to be nice animals, but the people about I think do not seem to have availed themselves very much of the sires.

4231. The farmers don't seem to be favourably disposed to the Hackney stallions?—No, they don't care about them; personally I don't like them.

4232. You have bred a hunter out of a Connemara pony by a thoroughbred horse?—I have a good one.

4233. If that Connemara pony had been got by a Hackney stallion would you have expected to have bred as good a hunter?—I think not. I am sure there was not a drop of the Hackney in her. There was nothing known about Hackneys in that district at the time. It was a good many years ago. She seemed to be of a good old type. She may have had a cross of the Arab in her; something very good in the animal. My idea of the Hackney is that he cannot get a good hunter. I don't see how he can from his action.

4234. Not himself but the mare got by the Hackney stallion, do you think she would be likely to produce a good hunter?—I don't like the drop for hunting at all. I am sure they are useful in a way, and they are very showy nice horses about a park or town, and I think they might go nine or ten miles very well, but if you wanted them to go fifty or sixty you would be a long time coming to the end of your journey.

4235. Do you think the introduction of the Hackney blood in Connemara is likely to affect hunter breeding in Galway?—To a certain extent. If they come to a size in Connemara they might be brought farther into the country, and I consider that would do a great deal of harm. I would be very sorry to see it get in. I think it would spoil our western Irish hunters altogether if the Hackney blood got in. They may be useful in their own way, I suppose they are, but I don't think they can have power of endurance from the great high knee action they have. I think they must wear themselves out. They pound too much, and another thing that action appears to me to come more from the knee than from the shoulder. That I consider must wear the animal out, and they cannot have the power of endurance of a horse with the ordinary fair level action. I like the even action, more low than high.

4236. Mr. Carew.—Too great a waste of power?—That is it, altogether too great a waste of power.

4237. Mr. Fitzwilliam.—You say you think the blood of the Hackney is a soft blood; you say that you think that he is all very well for going eight or ten miles, but that he would not do the long journey that we are in the habit of doing with the hunt car horse of the present day?—That is my opinion of him.

4238. Do you think that if this blood was introduced in a large way in the district that it would in course of time tend to produce a softer bred animal than you have got at present?—I am perfectly certain it would and they would not be nearly as saleable in the district as the animals that would be bred from a good half-bred horse.

4239. And if so it would tend to deteriorate the breed and it would also tend to damage the prestige that the breed now has got as being courageous with good stamina?—I am sure it would.

4240. Sir T. Esmonde.—Have any of these American horses reached your district?—No, not exactly my district, but I have seen a couple of them in Roscommon, at least I have seen two Argentine horses.

4241. Chairman.—Not stallions?—No, they were geldings, they were brought over there to hunt, and most useless brutes they were, cross made animals with no shape or power.

4242. Sir T. Esmonde.—Did they try to hunt those animals?—They did, they were a complete failure, no more of them came, and those were done away with as soon as possible.

4243. You have not seen any of the North American horses?—No, I have not.

4244. Col. St. Quintin.—You say that you have seen some of the stock got by Lord Ashtown's Hackney horses?—I have.

4245. What ages were they?—I have seen them as foals and one and a half year old.

4246. No more than that?—Not more than that.

4247. So you could not really judge what they would grow into?—I could not be sure what they would do as trained horses.

4248. I want to try to arrive at what class of animal they would grow into, for what purpose could they be used whether as riding or driving horses, or both combined?—They struck me as being more like harness horses, any of them I saw, I thought that would be about what they would be suitable for.

4249. Mr. Wrench.—Do you know of any other instances of hunters being bred out of Connemara ponies besides the one you had?—I have often heard of people having good hunters out of Connemara ponies.

4250. Then you think that Connemara ponies are brought into your district and used as hunter brood mares?—No, sir, they are not generally, it is only a very isolated case.

4251. Do you think that Connemara would be suited for a thoroughbred horse, do you think that the produce would be sufficiently hardy?—I think not.

4252. You think they would require some stronger and coarser horse?—I believe so.

4253. Presumably your opinion of the Hackneys has been formed on Lord Ashtown's horses?—It has. I know very little about them unless what I have seen of Lord Ashtown's horses, one of them is a beautiful horse to look at and one of the best movers I ever saw, a horse called Marmaduke, a chestnut horse, perhaps you have seen him.

4254. You like him the best of the two?—Well, that is a matter of opinion, for myself I don't think he might be as useful as the other one, perhaps not, but he is more showy to look at.

4255. Is your opinion as to the breeding of Hackneys formed on what you have been able to learn from Lord Ashtown?—Oh, I have seen Hackneys before I saw them there, but I have not been watching them as closely as I have since Lord Ashtown got them, for I drive a good deal past by the road where those horses are, and I take a look at them over the fence and form my own opinion. But of course I have seen Hackneys before, and my opinion is that there is too much waste of power about them for endurance.

4256. You think they would soften the blood in the native horses?—Yes.

4257. Where does the soft blood in the Hackney come from?—I believe from their action and the way I have seen them get so heated in work that they would not have anything like the endurance power of our horses.

4258. Where have you seen them get heated—in shows?—No, in the ordinary work, of course I don't mind it in shows.

4259. Where?—I have seen them in some parts of England.

4260. Animals you knew to be Hackneys?—Yes.

4261. Where do you think the soft blood comes in?—I know nothing about the breeding of Hackneys, I may admit that I have never had any experience of them, only I formed that opinion.

4262. You have not seen Hackneys that have not got extravagant action, but only ordinary action, and can use their shoulders?—I have seen some Hackneys that had not as high action as others, I believe it is not natural to the Hackney to use his shoulders properly, I believe he is not made for that.

Mr. Samuel Johnston

4263. But that is only your opinion from a limited experience?—From a limited experience indeed, but from what I know of them I would not breed from them.

4264. Do you think the Clydesdale is a good cross with the Irish mare?—You want something to throw weight and strength into these weedy mares, and I believe he is the truest blood to do it, and he is always a good stepper as a rule.

4265. Then you think action is a desirable quality in a horse?—Of course it is, now I am talking of that low class horse, principally for agricultural work, and of course it is a great point to get the agricultural horse to walk well.

4266. Are the Irish mares deficient in action as a rule, the common mares of the farmers?—Well, there are a good many rather crooked with straight thick shoulders and a great many of them cross-made. The people say: "We will have something out of the mare and we will send her to a sire and she will do our work along with breeding a foal;" it is a great inducement to them to get something out of her. As a rule they require to breed some animal that they can work on their farms in addition to breeding for sale, I believe that is the only way that horse-breeding would be profitable to the small farmer.

4267. Have you seen many of the produce of the Clydesdales and the mares of your district?—I have, a great many.

4268. And are they a fairly nice animal to look at?—I would rather have the second or third cross away from the Clydesdale.

4269. You would rather breed back again to the thoroughbred?—I would, because I think from the first cross they perhaps get too heavy and big and clumsy.

4270. Too like the sire?—That is so, but a drop throws great strength into the small mare and her progeny.

4271. In the half-bred stallions that you would register would you require any particular number of crosses?—I would not go further than the first cross of the thoroughbred horse on to a good well-shaped old Irish mare, that would be my idea of what the half-bred horse should be.

4272. And would you register a horse like that until he had been proved by his stock?—Well, I think I would when you have good judges to look at them, of course I would have them properly examined as to their soundness and shape and everything of the kind, and then I would register him without going any further.

4273. And you think it is safe when you are selecting a sire to judge by his appearance when you have no back pedigree to go upon?—Well, it goes a long way, of course, as a rule like begets like.

4274. Even when the breeding is uncertain?—Of course I would like to know as much as possible about the breeding.

4275. Would you not think the result would be much more likely to be certain when you were able to trace his pedigree back for several generations?—Most certainly.

4276. But at the same time you would register a sire without being able to trace his pedigree?—I would if he was a really good looking one and there was no unsoundness, and good shape.

4277. Do you think in your district it would be easy to find many good half-bred sires?—I know of a few. There is one horse, the best horse I ever knew, in my district, and he made more money for the people than any horse I ever knew, that was Thunderbolt.

4278. How was he bred?—A half-bred horse by Old Thunderbolt, which was thoroughbred, and by [illegible], one of the best horses we had in our country for getting weight-carrying hunters.

4279. He was a great big-boned horse?—Yes.

4280. A big-sized horse himself?—Yes, 16 hands.

4281. Is he in the country still?—Yes, the last [illegible] horse is within two miles of Wicklow, a farmer named Flanagan owns him, he is an old horse now.

4282. Do you think there are many horses of this type?—No, there are not, this is a horse that got [illegible] useful horses, [illegible] good hunters, and sometimes farmers' horses and a great many [illegible] as a rule were [illegible] with no hereditary disease unless there was something very wrong with the mare. I have got £10 for them [illegible] by that horse, I have got £140 for a four-year-old hunter by him, [illegible] a four-year-old [illegible] hunter. I have sold them at £120, £200, and £150.

4283. But these were out of well-bred mares?—Yes, good half-bred mares.

4284. Was there a Clydesdale standing in the same district?—Yes, there has been a Clydesdale all through my memory within nine or ten miles.

4285. Which horse would be most popular with the farmers, a horse like Thunderbolt or the Clydesdale?—Thunderbolt by far, he got too many mares, his produce were easily sold, they did the farm work and [illegible] and they could be sold at four and five years old.

4286. But don't you think there is a necessity for some horse like the Clydesdale?—I do, I believe that the ordinary small farmer won't pay the fee of a good half-bred horse, not [illegible] of a thoroughbred horse, so he must have something at a low figure, and then to supply that want I think I would give him the Clydesdale before anything else rather than these mongrel breeds that are in the country at present.

4287. I suppose there are a great many bad stallions in the country at present?—It is [illegible] with them, it would be very well to have them [illegible], I believe thoroughly in that.

4288. Would you put a general tax on entire horses [illegible] or have you arrived at any particular plan?—It would be interfering very much with the rights of the subject to say "you must get rid of a certain class of horse," saying to a man "you must do this" or "you must do that," and making away with his property, I don't believe in that, but I would certainly put a good tax on a bad horse, and then [illegible] it would be proved sound and all that [illegible] at a nominal figure.

4289. And you would not put any tax on [illegible]?—No, I don't think there would be any occasion to do that. I think if the system I propose [illegible] adopted [illegible], that the [illegible] at local shows and get prizes should [illegible] in order to induce the owners to keep [illegible] the service of the best [illegible] by Government [illegible], I think nothing would have more effect than that.

4290. Would you [illegible]?—No, because that might interfere with the value of them afterwards to the farmer.

4291. How would you be sure that the same sire was [illegible]?—I would be almost sure, I would first have the owner give a guarantee, and then have veterinary surgeons and competent men to examine those mares properly and keep a proper record of them, and I don't think there would be very many mistakes in the matter.

4292. You have not heard of such instances as having happened of [illegible] being painted different colours to come in and get the service fee?—I have heard of a good deal of scheming, but that could be [illegible] by a [illegible] looking officer.

4293. Do you think that it is easy to ascertain the correct pedigrees from the farmers when you are buying horses from them?—It is not very easy to get at the correct pedigrees unless you know some of the neighbours in the district. I often buy horses from the farmers, and when I do I make inquiries about them, but you cannot believe all you hear from the owners.

4294. Do you think they are taking more trouble about keeping the pedigrees of the animals they have?—I think they are more interested in horse-breeding altogether, and more anxious to do the thing well though they have been getting bad prices.

4295. But the prices of all horses, except the very best ones, have fallen steadily during the last four years?—Very much, and there has been very little demand for remount horses. At the great fairs of Ballinasloe and Banagher where we used to sell a large number, there were very poor prices this year.

4296. Even from foreign Governments?—It was very hard to sell them.

4297. Were there plenty of remounts to be sold?—There were a great many, and people had to sacrifice them or bring them home.

4298. What becomes of these remount horses when they cannot be sold?—I suppose they must be sold then for agricultural purposes and [illegible] at a very small price. I think I had seven of them myself at Banagher fair, and out of the seven I only sold one, they were all suitable for remounts I think, at least all but one which was too small and I could not get them away unless at a sacrifice; they were only three years old, so I said I would let them remain on the farm and see what they would do at four years old.

4299. Would they pay for the breeding?—They would not pay at the price I was getting, because I take more trouble than most people do about foals, in my district a great many people take no trouble about foals but let them run about the farm during the winter and let them pick up what they can, and, as a consequence, they never grow as they should, but I stand my foals during the winter and give them plenty of oats and hay, and let them out in a dry field during the day and put them in the shed at night and let them have oats in the morning, and they grow bigger as a rule. I don't believe these horses I speak about would have grown so much only for having fed them as foals.

4300. Mr. Carew.—What age is **Thunderbolt**?—He must be over 20 years of age.

4301. Mr. Fitzwilliam.—There were two Thunderbolts, one belonging to Mr. Alexander, I forget who the other belonged to, one was a very speedy horse?—A big brown horse.

4302. I think it was by Blackmail?—Well, that is not the horse I alluded to, this other horse was bred by the late Mr. Lewis, of County Galway.

4303. Mr. Carew.—You don't know what **he** was by?—By Bow Bells.

4304. Sir T. Esmonde.—Do you possess any of these old Irish mares?—I do, I have a couple of them with a great deal of that old type.

4305. Then you believe it is a really genuine race of ponies?—I believe it is, some of those old mares died with me, and I kept their breeds, I kept their daughters to breed from.

4306. Do you think it would be possible to preserve that breed [illegible]?—I am afraid it is rather too far gone.

4307. I suppose really we have no definite history about it?—No, I don't think so, it is a thing nearly everyone knows something about, but still we cannot go far back to trace it, the fact remains that it is a splendid breed.

4308. With you are there any farmers that have breeds of horses like that in their families for generations?—A great many, and would not part with them.

4309. Mr. Wrench.—You have never driven Hackneys yourself?—Never.

The Commission adjourned to next morning.

NINTH DAY.—WEDNESDAY, NOVEMBER 25TH, 1896

Present:—Mr. Percy La Touche, (in the Chair), Hon. H. W. Fitzwilliam, Mr. J. L. Carew, M.P., Col. St. Quintin, and Mr. F. S. Wrench.

Mr. Hugh Neville, Secretary.

Mr. John H. Barry, Ballyvourney, Dunmanway, Co. Cork, examined.

4310. Chairman.—Mr. Barry, you live in the County Cork?—Yes.

4311. You have **bred yourself?—I hold land** myself, yes.

4312. You have had considerable personal experience of the breeding of horses, I think?—Yes; since I was a boy I was more or less mixed up with them.

4313. Will you tell us what sort of horse you breed?—Well, I breed all a good class of horse.

4314. What class of stallion?—Always a thoroughbred stallion.

4315. When you speak of a good class of horse, you mean a more or less a thoroughbred horse?—Yes; possibly one has one or two crosses of the thoroughbred horse, that I only mean. I find they produce the very best hunters.

4316. Are these mares chiefly of your own breeding or do you buy them from the farmers?—Well, they are chiefly of my own breeding, and if I buy them from the farmers I know their breeding. I may buy young ones which may go into [illegible] work. I find, if I can get a mare of that class that works nicely on a farm, that she produces a very fine hunting foal and, generally sound.

4317. Are those mares that you buy usually bred from a thoroughbred horse, do you know?—Yes, certainly they have one cross of the thoroughbred.

4318. Some witnesses have spoken to us of what they call the old Irish mare; does that convey anything to you?—The old Irish mare—I happened to come across some old documents—what I call the old Irish mare was a mare there remained in the country, that was generally got by a good class of horse, a hunter class of [illegible]. I just happened to have the [illegible]. It is a very old bill that will show you the class of horse. The strain remained in the country—the Andrew strain, the Mighty Andrew strain.

4319. What is popularly called the old Irish mare is usually a mare got by a half-bred horse?—Got by a half bred horse without anything at all of what we call the English breed—Clydesdale, Suffolk Punch, or any of those breeds.

4320. Mr. Carew (referring to the bill produced by the witness).—This is an advertisement of March 22nd, 1828:—"A horse owned by Mr. Edmund B. Barry, a pedigree horse, Mighty Andrew, got by Old Andrew [illegible] with [illegible] Old Andrew nearly as elegant a hunter as ever was mounted, and for which owner in this year [illegible] 150 guineas were refused. He is a dark bay, and from his symmetry of shape and great strength, and known to be of the best hunter blood in Ireland; is allowed by some of the best judges to be one of the most promising [illegible]

[illegible]
Sir John B. Barry

ing sires in this county, many of whom have already subscribed to mind (?) mares, but no mare to be served after the 20th of July, and any mare which misses this season shall be served next year. Two guineas and a crown for the groom."

Witness.—I had a direct descendant of that horse until a short time ago, when she died.

4331. CHAIRMAN.—"Merry Andrew," by "Andrew." Was Andrew a thoroughbred horse?

Mr. CAREW.—Hunter sire, "Old Andrew," it says.

Witness.—Here is another old document. This is a funny thing.

4332. Mr. CAREW, referring to document.—This is in writing—"'Merry Andrew,' lately purchased from Sir Edward O'Brien, Bart., by Mr. George Clancy, of Cratloe, County Clare. He is to stand at Ardsallis, in the said county, from the 20th of March to the 10th of August next, and is to be let out to mares at two guineas a leap as trials, and a crown for the groom, the money to be paid down before the horse is let out of the stable. He was bred by his Grace the Duke of Bolton, and was got by 'Fox.' His dam was full sister——" and so on * * "His great-grand dam was by Mr. Place's White Arabian, out of a thoroughbred mare of Mr Tregonwell. 'Merry Andrew' won the 700 Guineas' stakes at Newmarket in April, 1733, and the Thousand Guinea Stakes in October after, from twelve of the best horses in England; and in the year 1734 he won His Majesty's Plate at Lewis, near Canterbury.—Sir Edward O'Brien, Bart." That is tracing back.

Witness.—That is the strain so far as a hundred years ago, and I thought it would be interesting.

4333. Mr CAREW.—It is getting somewhat at the root of the old Irish mare.

Witness.—What I call the old Irish mare was descended from that class of horse; they remained in the county and the farmers would speak of "the old strain and the old mare." They generally kept one of the old mares in the family. The Andrew strain was one particular strain in the country. There was another strain, a horse called "Diamond," got one of a Diamond mare.

4334. CHAIRMAN.—A half-bred horse?—No, I think it must have been a thoroughbred horse.

4335. They breed a good many horses in your district?—A good many horses have been bred in my district, and if you ask me our district, which I call North Cork, or the Duhallow hunting district—if I was put to it I would go to it before any district I know in Ireland to get a really good hunter, and I attribute that very much. I have another old document that I thought would be interesting. There was an old gentleman, a Mr Hotchkiss, who was a bachelor and a man of means, and his fad, if you think it so, was his great passion and love for horses. I happened to have all these (indicating documents), and I put them by as a matter of curiosity. In August, 1839, this old gentleman sold 73 horses. He called an auction and sold 73 horses, and they were all one better bred than the other, all thoroughbred horses. A great many of these horses remained—some of them were sold very low—a great many remained in the county scattered about. I could trace the pedigree of several to horses purchased at this auction.

4336. Mr. CAREW.—What was the chief strain in those horses?—Virginia, grey mare, Washington, Regent, Oakstick, Potamia.

4337. CHAIRMAN.—Do you think the farmers are sufficiently careful about breeding from their best mares; about keeping the best mares?—No, I am afraid not. I am sorry to say that latterly the farmers have been selling their good mares when they have been offered fair prices. The French bought a few years ago a great many of our good mares.

4338. Do you think the mares have deteriorated in your country?—I am afraid yes. The good mares are picked away and the rubbish bred from. Sometimes a thoroughbred or a Hackney, a few might put a hunter; she was generally put to stud and generally produced a paying sort.

4339. Otherwise they only breed from the mares they could not sell?—In many cases yes.

4340. Do you think that the farmers show a discrimination in selecting the sires for their mares?—I am afraid not much.

4341. What do you think influences their selection?—Cheapness, friendship and [illegible]. They patronise friends. We have had some wretched horses.

4342. Do you think that the scheme of the Royal Dublin Society has worked well?—Well, it has worked very well, but I think it might be improved a little.

4343. In what way?—Well, I think you might make some alterations in the prizes you give.

4344. In what way would you suggest?—I would give more encouragement to induce farmers to keep [illegible] a very good class of mares. I would give substantial prizes for good four year old mares. I don't think I would go further.

4345. Do you approve of breeding from two-year-old fillies?—Not as a rule. I tried it in a few instances myself and I didn't find it successful. The two-year-old mares [illegible] sufficiently good mares. I kept [illegible] two-year-olds with rather [illegible] and they afterwards bred a good foal. The great thing in the country. Unless they mate the first year you cannot have substance [illegible]. They are always weak.

4346. And you think that some substantial prizes to four-year-old mares would be the greatest inducement to farmers?—I think I would give more substantial prizes to four-year-old mares, good [illegible] mares either [illegible] to a thoroughbred [illegible] stallion, or with foal at foot got by a thoroughbred stallion. I think, now for instance, supposing a man had a good promising three year old mare, and he thought he would get £40 for her, [illegible] he would get it easily for a [illegible], for a good [illegible] mare. If that man thought he would get a £30 or a £20 prize, he would say "I will [illegible]." I think that man would consider before he would sell the mare. I don't think it would give prizes for old mares.

4347. You would only give a prize to a mare that was covered by a thoroughbred horse or had a foal at foot?—Only to a mare covered by a good thoroughbred horse or with a foal at foot.

4348. Don't you find that some of those half-bred horses—horses of the same class as "Merry Andrew"—still exist in your country and breed very good hunters?—Yes, very good hunters, but I think the thoroughbred better. You have more reliability in him. You may breed very good hunters from the half-bred, but I think the thoroughbred is more reliable.

4349. There was a horse called Clonsilla, a half-bred, in the county Cork?—He is by [illegible] I [illegible] of. He was got by "[illegible]" [illegible], and "[illegible]" was a "Sir Hercules" horse. That was a very good strain of horses.

4350. There was a horse called Hotchkiss' "Hercules"?—That was Mr Hotchkiss' horse [illegible]. One of those very horses, Mr. Hotchkiss [illegible] a [illegible] thoroughbred horse. This thoroughbred horse [illegible]. That was thirty years ago.

4351. Was Hotchkiss' Hercules a thoroughbred horse?—He was by the Sir Hercules.

4352. I thought he was a half-bred horse?—He was by Sir Hercules out of a mare got by Foliage. [illegible] Foliage is one of those [illegible].

4353. Have you had any personal experience of breeding from Hackneys or Clydesdale stallions?—No, I have just seen Hackneys and admired them [illegible]

[illegible] horses, but I have very little experience of Hackneys, there are not much in the south.

4344. Do you think that the introduction of the Hackney blood into West Cork would have any effect upon the horse breeding in North Cork and the other hunter breeding districts of Cork?—Well, I think that if you breed at all you must try to breed the very best. You will have plenty of misfits, do your best; I don't think anything you breed from a Hackney will be anything more than a misfit. You will have plenty of misfits and do your best.

4345. I was not at all referring to breeding in the hunter producing parts of Cork, but I want to ask you whether you thought that the introduction of the Hackney blood into the West of Cork would have any effect upon the horse breeding in East Cork or North Cork?—I suppose not, but I think what we ought to encourage would be the breeding of the best and most paying animal. I don't think there would be [illegible] class horse would pay. If we do anything we ought to encourage farmers to breed what will pay best.

4346. Do you know West Cork?—Not much.

4347. You have been there?—I know it of course; I think the class of horse there is very poor.

4348. Have you been in Bantry?—Yes.

4349. You know the class of mare that you see there?—Well, I have friends living in the district. If they wanted anything they would never think of looking for a horse there in that country; if they wanted a good hunter or saddle horse they would come to our country.

4350. There are very few horses coming up from West Cork into your district?—Very few; there are a few about Bandon which sometimes used to come—a few.

4351. But there are a great number of horses bred in West Cork?—I believe so, that is about Bantry. I don't think they extend beyond Bandon—a good class of horse, as beyond Bandon [illegible].

4352. What becomes of the bad class of horses bred in the mountain side?—I think they live and die there.

4353. I take it that you consider the thoroughbred horse is the most suitable sire for getting a hunter or high-class horse?—Yes, decidedly. I think that is the horse we ought to encourage. It's much like to breed from the Hackney in his own business. If half-bred [illegible] of them do not really get good, I would not [illegible] that class of horse, I think the thoroughbred is the proper one—a well bred, sound horse.

4354. Mr. Cassidy.—What height?—The height for any [illegible] of a good horse, I suppose; I have known them get a big horse.

4355. Chairman.—Are you in favour of the idea that has been propounded to us by several witnesses that stallions should be registered and examined and passed sound before they are permitted to serve?—I think so, and I think I would give as an encouragement three money prizes, and I think then to [illegible] horses I would give an encouragement to thoroughbred stallions at say £3 a mare and pay the difference. I would say to the farmer "you take your mare to a thoroughbred horse; you will get less money for a pound and we will pay the difference," and I would have an understanding with the people to breed the stallions. I think that would be a useful thing.

4356. You think there is a sufficiency of good stallions, sound thoroughbred stallions?—I think we are very well off for stallions. There is a Mr. [illegible], of [illegible], very enterprising; Mr. [illegible], of Mallow, has some good horses; and a Mr. [illegible] has some horses. I think there is plenty of private enterprise to keep good stallions if they are encouraged.

4357. You think, as a matter of fact, that at the present time there is a sufficiency of good, sound, suitable stallions in North Cork?—I think there are enough of stallions in North Cork, and I would encourage those people who keep these stallions by giving them, either by obliging people to send mares to them, and obliging them not to go to them, or by giving them an option of [illegible] them.

4358. You are in favour of registering sound stallions, and merely well-shaped thoroughbred horses?—Yes, that would be an inducement; the very fact of registering a stallion, it being known that it is registered, and that the stallion is entitled or eligible to go in for prizes, that is an encouragement to the owner of the stallion.

4359. Would you, under any circumstances, register a half-bred sire?—I hardly think I would; I would not.

4360. You think it would be better at least to draw the line between the thoroughbred horses?—The thoroughbred is one. If there is a half-bred suitable sire he would be [illegible], because people will have these easily [illegible], they will send them to him.

4361. Is there any other suggestion that you would like to make, Mr. Barry, with reference to the improvement of horses?—I don't know about this question as to valuation. I don't know that the better class of farmers in the higher valuations should be excluded from competition. They take a little pride in it, and although a man may have a high valuation his rate are comparatively high, and he may be just as needy as a man on the small scale with a very low valuation, and I think any man who is farming would take a little pride in it. For instance, if we go in for prizes for cattle or butter, it is not [illegible] a man is valued at £200 or £300 that he is excluded. Why should a man in keeping horses be? The valuer is [illegible] and his [illegible] and his [illegible] to take pride in getting a prize. It would be a pity to exclude him.

4362. The idea is, no doubt, that a farmer of over £150 valuation is able to take care of himself?—I am sorry to say that I know some of high valuations that are just as needy and just as anxious to make a few pounds as a man of £50 valuation.

4363. You would be in favour of the limit being removed?—I think so. I don't know that I would limit it at all. People take a little pride in it; and, apart from money reasons, they like the credit; they take a little pride in it.

4364. And you would be in favour of giving substantial prizes to young mares, of subsidizing stallions to a moderate extent, and of giving the owners of the prize mares a very low figure for the registered stallions?—Yes.

4365. And the establishment **and registration of** thoroughbred horses?—Yes.

4366. And the removal of limits?—Yes.

4367. Mr. Cassidy.—Do you think that breeding in Ireland from a thoroughbred would produce stock strong enough for the work on the farms?—I do. I have seen well-shaped, sound thoroughbred stallions [illegible] [illegible] fit to do a [illegible] heavy [illegible] [illegible], I think—"Regulator," [illegible] something [illegible] hands high. I have seen [illegible] [illegible] horses of [illegible] [illegible] good big horses.

4368. Mated with thoroughbred mares?—No, not with thoroughbreds, but with good plain half-bred mares or [illegible].

4369. Don't you think it would be very necessary to have a well-bred half-bred horse with a great many crosses of the thoroughbred blood in him?—I think it would be useful. I am not sure that I would encourage those much. I think the thoroughbred horse is far more reliable.

4370. Would you be in favour of every man who has a stallion taking out a licence?—I think yes; I would encourage that; it would be a kind of information to the people, you know, to go to a sound stallion.

4371. The fair of Cahirmee is in your district?—It is in my district, a very fine fair.

4372. One of the largest in the South of Ireland?—Yes.

Mar. [illegible], 1896. Mr. [illegible] Barry.

4373. Do you see any deterioration in the class of horses they breed there?—There are horses I was going to say all Cobbs[illegible] people rather inbreed.[illegible] these farmers have tendency, they are all spoiled and they often bought in private paddocks by English horse-dealers. They don't wait for the Cobbs fair fields, [illegible]. Men will go and buy them at farms.

4374. You say the valuation is too high?—I don't say it is too high.

4375. What would you fix it at?—I would take it off altogether, and let every fellow go in for it.

4376. Is it necessary in order to improve the breed to encourage the big farmers as well as the small farmers?—Yes, I would not prevent the[illegible] farmer. As I told you it is only the money prize or much on the prize in it.

4377. Are there any horses now with the Merry Andrew blood in your district?—Yes, there are. You can trace them, I think I have some mares with it; I have two Victor mares, they were beautiful hunters, and I can trace through their dam back to the Andrew blood.

4378. Colonel St. Quintin.—You have in your district, I suppose, a great number of very small holdings, small farmers?—There are now a great many very small ones.

4379. They are all capable of bringing up their young stock, are they, do you think?—Not all. You know if a man has a good colt he is sure to get a good price for him.

4380. Would you encourage breeding with the very small farmers?—Well, I would, yes, if they had a good mare. I do not care to whom a good mare belongs, be he rich or poor. I should encourage breeding from a good mare.

4381. What would you say was a sufficient holding to give him a chance of bringing up his colt well?—If a small farmer has a good valuable animal, he will [illegible] in feeding, if it is good enough he will get good for his horse; or he will manage to some way if it is pure enough, or sell it for a good price. I know a [illegible] farmer who bred a good colt. The colt was sold as he thought for a good price, £20 or £30, as a two-year-old. That animal was sold back to the neighbourhood again. I saw it the other day sold for something under £100, about £80 under £100, a four-year-old horse got by this mare. It was a Republican.

4382. Do you think he would breed him with any particular object—beyond desiring an animal to breed to any type at all, has he any idea of what the animal is likely to grow into—he will put the mare to the first horse he comes to, won't he, or will he try to breed a high class horse?—I am afraid the small farmer will go to the cheapest horse; he won't go to a dear horse but to a convenient horse.

4383. And he does not mind—the man who has got a certain strain of blood—he does not know what blood the animal is going to be, or even as long as he puts [illegible] or the sire—he does not know whether a hunter or a riding horse?—The small farmer does not [illegible] in the a foal.

4384. Mr. Wrench.—Mr. Barry, I think you said that these old Irish mares—you thought that they were descended from the hunting strain in the country before any English blood came in?—Yes.

4385. By English blood you mean?—What we call the Clydesdale. The very heavy cart horses, none of those have come into our country; there have been below us.

4386. Do you know there are Clydesdale, cart horse stallions and half-bred, cart stallions in the county Cork?—I did not know there were so many. I know there are some.

4387. Could you fix the time that these animals first came into this country?—I am afraid not, so long I remember there was an old one here and there.

4388. Even before the famine?—I could not go beyond the famine.

4389. You don't remember their introduction?—No.

4390. Do you think it would be possible to get the pedigrees of any of these mares bred from the horse you mentioned. Do you think any of the farmers have kept their pedigrees?—I am afraid not.

4391. Then you don't think it would be possible from the mares in your district to breed up any horses of the same breed, the same strains?—Well, as I told you, I have a mare got by a horse called Old Victor, and I can trace her pedigree back to the Andrew.

4392. To this horse called Andrew?—Yes, to the Cork Merry Andrew, that is to the main Andrew, and exactly to this horse but to the cousin got by a horse called Merry Andrew; he belonged to a man in the west of the county near Kildinnery.

4393. Do you think there are many other people who can do so?—No, I am afraid not.

4394. So that it would be impossible to try to trace up a lot of horses, more of the old blood?—I am afraid it would be.

4395. You would not register any thick-bred horse?—I would not. I would let a half-bred horse fine that breed; if he was good he would be sought after.

4396. These animals that were bred out of those good mares by a thoroughbred horse if perpetually crossed by a thoroughbred horse would they not in time become too fine—would there be any danger of that?—I have seen very fine well bred thoroughbred horses.

4397. You mean in Cork, grown on good land?—I don't think they do deteriorate much. The fillies do if they are badly cared.

4398. But you are referring to animals grown on good land?—Reared on good land and well kept, and I think the first year or two has a great deal to say to the animal.

4399. The first winter?—The first winter, and the milking qualities of the dam too.

4400. Do you think that horses bred now for the [illegible] good hunters—are as good as the horses used to be?—I think they are as good as you can get in the world.

4401. As good as they used to be thirty years ago?—Just as good.

4402. You think that the men who bred horses have been able to keep some of this improved blood?—I think they have. I have come across some of these good looking horses with their dam with some of the [illegible] blood or something of that kind in them, and I found them very safe.

4403. You yourself have been able to keep some of them?—I kept some of them. I might not think of keeping them. If I saw a colt or mare I liked some of that kind of thing, I would not buy him, but if I had the misfortune of buying him I would get rid of him as soon as I could. I would not like to sell him myself.

4404. Would you take the trouble to find out how the animal was bred before buying it?—Always. I try to go back as far as I can, but it is not always very reliable information when you get.

4405. You would not breed from a two-year-old filly, I think you said?—No.

4406. Do you think it is safer to get a filly in foal as two years old than at three years old?—It is very risky.

4407. And that is the chief recommendation in your opinion, is it?—I don't approve of breeding from two-year-old fillies.

4408. You don't think it would be a good thing to encourage the farmers to breed from two-year-old fillies?—No.

4409. So as to get a foal out of a good filly?—No, I would discourage, as much as I could, the breeding of two-year-old animals; I don't know what we will do with them.

4410. Mr. Carew.—The chief objection is that they are not likely to be good mares?—Yes.

Nov. [illegible]
Mr. John R. Barry.

4411. Mr. Wrench.—In recommending thoroughbred horses, I understand you are referring to your own district, and you don't pretend to make any suggestion for the congested districts on the west coast?—No, I don't. I confine my own experience of Hackneys is very limited.

4412. And you think the system adopted by the Dublin Society now of registering stallions, thoroughbred stallions—do you think that is a good one?—It is a very good one.

4413. And you think that the people who have thoroughbred stallions in your district would like to have them on the Dublin Society's list?—I think so, if they have good sound stallions.

4414. I see that a great many of the thoroughbred stallions in Cork do not appear to be on the list?—I am afraid there are a great many unsound thoroughbreds in Cork. If a man has a sound stallion, and if he thinks he is perfectly sound, he would be glad to have him on that list.

4415. You appear to be very well supplied in Cork; you have 22 thoroughbreds on the register and 10 off the register?—I think so, yes.

4416. Do you think that many people who have stallions which are sound would like to have them on the register?—I think any man having a sound stallion would like to have him on the register.

4417. Colonel Sir Gregory.—I would like to ask you, with regard to these small farmers who you say hardly know what they are going to produce, do you think that the opinion of a man of that class, who only goes for a foal, is worth taking, as to the class of horse that would suit his neighbourhood?—I think those weedy inferior horses are not worth breeding at all; they are not worth their oats. I would not encourage any man that would not try to go in for a really good class of horse. Do your best, you will have plenty of misfits. I don't know what you will do with that weedy kind of horse since bicycles and all these things came in.

4418. I don't quite mean that; I mean with regard to the individual himself, the small farmer—is his opinion worth taking as to the class of horse that should stand in his neighbourhood, if he only breeds for the sake of getting a foal and does not know what he is going to breed—if there was any grant of money for his district is his fancy to have any weight in that way?—I don't think it ought; if a man breeds at all he ought to breed a good article.

4419. You would legislate for him and not allow him to legislate for himself?—Yes.

4420. His actual opinion is not of very great value?—No value.

4421. Mr. Wrench.—Do you think the opinion of the small farmers of the west coast of value—don't they know what they want for their own use?—I have no experience of the west.

4422. Therefore, you are not speaking of them?—I am not speaking at all of them. I know nothing of the west.

Mr. R. E. Longfield.

R. E. Longfield, Longueville, Mallow, examined.

4423. Chairman.—You are deputy-lieutenant of the county Cork?—Yes.

4424. You breed horses yourself?—Yes.

4425. What sort of horse do you breed?—Hunters from hunting mares.

4426. You breed entirely from hunting mares?—I bred some cart horses, a few cart horses.

4427. By Clydesdale stallions?—Yes.

4428. What class of horse do you think your part of Cork is particularly adapted to produce?—I agree with what Mr. Barry said that they can produce the very best, I think I can grow horses to their full size. I think well bred horses develop fully and better than cattle do.

4429. A good many farmers I suppose breed horses?—A good many, yes.

4430. Do you think they take any trouble about getting the best mares?—No, I don't think they do. I think they have got extremely bad mares now.

4431. You think they have deteriorated?—I think they have.

4432. Do you think they take sufficient trouble investigating the stallions to mate them with?—No, I think not. I think they go to the nearest or the cheapest, or to a stallion belonging to a friend in many cases. Of course there are [illegible].

4433. Are there many cart stallions in your district?—No, there are more thoroughbred stallions than anything else in my immediate neighbourhood, I think.

4434. Do you think there is much cart blood since many were crossed?—Oh, yes, I think there is been and there.

4435. Do you attribute the deterioration of the horse in any way to this cross, do you think there is more cart blood than there used to be?—Yes, I think a great number of cart horses were brought over thirty years ago or six.

4436. And the farmers used them with a view of getting more size?—Some of them did.

4437. There is a certain amount of this cart blood [illegible] through the country?—I think so. I think that they and the old Irish hunters were good on account of the absence of that cart blood.

4438. Do you think the hunters of the present day are as sound as they used to be?—I think they are very unsound. I think an enormous proportion of them are unsound, and I think a great number of stallions are unsound.

4439. You have a greater proportion of unsound stallions now than a great number of [illegible]?

4440. Chiefly whistling?—I think that is the commonest unsoundness.

4441. Do you attribute that to the stallions?—Principally; yes.

4442. Have you any experience of breeding from half-bred sires?—No, I have only bred from one.

4443. Do the farmers use them much to produce hunters?—There are very few in my neighbourhood. In other districts, more often away to the east, there are, for instance, in the [illegible] district about fifteen miles to the west of me I believe there are no thoroughbred horses.

4444. There are a certain number of half-bred ones?—A great number of half-bred horses.

4445. Do they produce good hunters?—No, I don't think they do as a rule.

4446. There are not a great many good horses bred in the [illegible] district?—No, I don't think so.

4447. Do you think that the Dublin Society scheme works well?—I think it is a very good thing to register sound horses. I think that is a very good thing, and I should suggest that a great many of the horses not registered are not sound.

4448. Do you agree with some witnesses who suggested that a horse that did not pass a veterinary examination should not be permitted to serve?—I think if it were possible it would be a very good thing.

4449. For the breeding of stallions, it has been suggested to us that a heavy license should be put upon stallions which would be unsuitable unless they passed an examination for soundness?—I think that is a thing that ought to be done, to prohibit them, if possible, but I do not know the way it ought to be done.

4450. With regard to the cattle, do you think the Dublin Society's scheme works well?—I think that a number of local shows would be useful, with, as they have, considerable prizes for young mares.

Nov. 9, 1896.

Mr. R. E. Longfield.

4451. Do you think there is any object in giving prizes to old mares?—I would rather give them to young ones, I think.

4452. When a mare is old she has to be a brood mare?—Yes, she is merely done then.

4453. Do you think that the registration of horses—I suppose you know most of the registered horses in your part of Cork—do you think that they answer all the qualifications necessary for a stallion? I have known one very bad one. I believe he was a sound but extremely unfortunate stallion; he was a very mischievous stallion; he covered a great deal.

4454. A registered horse?—Yes.

4455. Do you mean he didn't get foals, **or that he** got bad foals?—Got bad foals.

4456. Mr. Cameron.—Covered?—Yes, **many of** them.

4457. Chairman.—Do the farmers generally sell their horses at their own places, or do they part with them at fairs?—It depends upon the class of horses. If the farmer has a very good colt, the dealer will go to him; if he has a very valuable colt, he cannot take him to the fair.

4458. What sort of stallion do you think is most suitable to be encouraged in your district?—I should like the thoroughbred one.

4459. Do you think the farmers would appreciate a really thoroughbred horse if they got him at a reasonable fee?—I think so.

4460. The ordinary farmer only pays a very small fee.—It is very hard to say what they pay for the service. I believe some stallions serve for what they can get pretty well.

4461. Have you any suggestions that you would like to make with a view of improving the breeding of horses in West Cork?—I should like to keep out the mongrel stallions and encourage the good ones; but it is a very difficult question.

4462. What would you suggest that these mongrels should be—what rule would you suggest?—Well, there has got to be some regulation for stallions. I am hardly prepared to say.

4463. Prizes for mares and registration of any sort of sound suitable stallions?—Registration, yes.

4464. Have you any experience of breeding from Hackney horses?—No, none.

4465. Do you think that the introduction of Hackney blood into West Cork would have any effect upon the horse-breeding in your part of the country?—After a time it might, if the mares got by Hackney horses got scattered about the country.

4466. Do they, as a matter of fact, move mares from West Cork into North Cork?—It is very hard to say; I don't suppose they often do.

4467. Do you know West Cork personally?—Yes, pretty well; I know the neighbourhood of Bantry and Glengarriff. There was formerly a very good breed of ponies about there, and they have produced an extremely good breed of ponies.

4468. Do you think that that **breed has disappeared**?—Entirely.

4469. On account of the farmers using unsuitable stallions?—Oh, I fancy they sold off their ponies to the dealers, I think so.

4470. They disappeared so long ago as that?—They did not quite disappear then because we had some of them, extremely good ponies that came from Glengarriff; I think one of them had some Arab blood in it, at least a pony or 2 or 3 of them.

4471. What would you suggest as being the best means of restoring that breed?—I don't know, I am sure.

4472. You don't know what stallion because it would have to be done by the introduction of a suitable stallion—what stallion do you think, from your knowledge of the ponies of Bantry and Glengarriff, would be suitable?—I think a great deal of that country is only suitable for breeding ponies. I think the Arab blood did good there, but you would not do good entirely on that. I think the Arab blood was brought there many years ago. Mr. Bernard was said to have had an Arab there a great many years ago.

4473. You would suggest the reintroduction of the Arab blood?—No, I think it would be a country that Welsh ponies would do very well in.

4474. Do you think that the Hackney stallion is calculated to benefit the breed anywhere in the South?—I do not think so.

4475. Have you any experience of Hackneys personally?—I have seen them and heard a great deal about them. I never owned one.

4476. You can only speak of their general appearance then?—Yes.

4477. And from what you have seen of their general appearance, do you think that they would be suitable stallions to put to these ponies?—I think if you can breed any animal as big as that I would try to have something well bred. I don't like their shoulders. The country that owes fine animals of that size I think might breed something better.

4478. Mr. Fitzwilliam.—There are a good number of cart stallions down in your part of the country?—There is a Shire horse—there is a horse used but in the Shire Horse Stud Book, that I have used.

4479. Are they used a good deal by the farmers do you think?—I have heard that the farmers lately have been getting mares to them in order to get colts of size and substance that they will sell young.

4480. And breeding from those cart stallions I suppose that the produce is rather easy to sell, there is the more blood in him?—Oh, it would be.

4481. If you used up these any other blood, equally as what I should call pure blood, but one that you might trust to bring up a colt from the appearance, do you think it would be disappointing to the country or not?—I think it would. I think any country was found the very best. You cannot always tell each year. I should like to read a resolution passed by the County Cork Agricultural Society on the 14th September. It belongs to the history for many years. May I read it?

"That we the members of the Committee of the Cork Agricultural Society, protest in the strongest manner against the introduction of the breed of Hackney horses into Ireland by the aid of state funds as being detrimental to the best interests of the farmers and the good of the country at large, as we so definitely that breed of horses for which Ireland has hitherto been justly celebrated."

4482. Chairman.—That was the General Body?—No, the County Cork Agricultural Society, a very large Society. I think there are over 500 members.

4483. Was there a large attendance at that meeting?—I think so. It was passed unanimously.

4484. Were you present?—I cannot remember whether I was or not. I remember its being passed, whether I read it or whether I was there. I go to a great number of the meetings.

4485. Are the names of the proposer and seconder there?—No, I have not got them.

4486. Would it be unfair to be passed unanimously?—Yes.

4487. Is that the official record?—No, it is a copy that I have from the official record.

4488. Mr. Fitzwilliam.—With regard to half-bred stallions, would you advocate the use of half-bred stallions if they were sound and suitable to mares?—If there was a very little strain on them I don't think it would matter.

4489. But you would not object to some of a half-bred or cold with a thoroughbred or had some far back, if he had proved himself a good breeder.

4490. If what?—If he had been well he might be useful. I think of the stories men might recall it would not matter. However, I would not register him if he had not proved himself a good breeder.

4491. Mr. Cameron.—You said that you were a member of this agricultural association?—Yes.

4492. You know that a great many farmers in the County of Cork are members [illegible], yes, a great number.

4493. And that they approve of this resolution?—Yes, it was passed unanimously.

4494. Have you any experience of the Hackney class, have you seen them?—I have seen them; I saw them at the farm at [illegible] yesterday, and often at shows.

4495. Your objection is that there is not much action in their action?—Well, years ago I asked a gentleman who is a very good judge, what he thought of the Hackney, and he said—"There is nothing they can do that a thoroughbred cannot do a great deal better."

4496. That is the thoroughbred can get all the animals they can get, and in addition the hunter?—Yes, and there is a very important matter in a hunting country, that is farmers very often sell an account of horses very well, because they were good hunters. I have known two tenant farmers sell animals for a large sum in a fortnight which were both unsound; they were lucky horses, but such good hunters that people put up with them.

4497. You say the deterioration of horses is due in great measure to farmers selling their young mares?—I think they sell their good mares and have a very bad lot now.

4498. And the great consideration is **to offer them** some inducement to keep them?—Yes.

4499. And also the deterioration is due to the number of bad stallions in the country?—I think many of the stallions are very bad and very unsound.

4500. You would approve of insisting that every one who keeps a stallion should take out a licence?—Something of that sort.

4501. And that the licence should show on the face of it whether he was sound, and what the defects were?—Something of that sort.

4502. You also approve of registering the bulls [illegible] there was very little [illegible]—Yes.

4503. Colonel St. Quintin.—I should just like to ask you if you know anything about the other with the small horse round about you. What class do you put them to? Whether it supplies the needs of the farmers for their agricultural work? Whether it is large enough for them, and not too large?—There are a good many thoroughbred stallions now, and I only know one really cart horse, there are not many of them.

4504. And does it prove a very heavy horse in your district?—Most of the farmers have lighthish horses with more quality in them.

4505. Yes, but the produce of the [illegible] in your country doesn't grow a great weighty animal, it grows a [illegible]. There are some big animals but not a great many of them, there are infinitely more thoroughbred stallions than cart stallions.

4506. You don't know what class of horse the Shire or Clydesdale throws, is it not a big weighty draft horse?—Not many of the very big ones. I have got good myself, but as a rule the more [illegible] farmers breed from do not breed big heavy horses.

4507. That is what I expect. They are useful farm horses for that part of the country, I suppose?—Yes.

4508. Mr. Warren.—When you say there are infinitely more thoroughbred stallions than cart stallions, you are speaking of your own neighbourhood?—Yes, for miles around.

4509. And not of the county generally?—No.

4510. Do you think the sports have deteriorated?—Yes, I am afraid they have.

4511. In what way, have they become more coarse or weedy?—Some are more coarse, and I am afraid they are more unsound.

4512. And you think as good hunters are bred now as used to be bred, in your neighbourhood?—I fancy a smaller proportion are as good. There are some just as good but not so many.

4513. Not so many on an average?—No, I should think not. The smaller proportion would be very good, but an immense number of the young horses you see at fairs are unsound.

4514. And you attribute that to the unsoundness of the sires?—The unsoundness of the sires and the badness of the dams.

4515. I think you said you would advocate the registering of sires. It has also been suggested that we should have no one stallions to be confined to a certain man if sound. Would you approve of any suggestion of that description?—I am not prepared to say that would be the best **way** to do it. I should like to encourage good ones.

4516. Your suggestion is **to** give prizes to young mares?—Yes, and local shows.

4517. Would it not take a lot of money to make that work?—I think it is worth spending money on it.

4518. Do you think a man would keep a mare for £10 if he could get a big price for her. I should give him more. I don't think £10 would be enough.

4519. Do you know what class of mares there are about Bantry and in West Cork?—No, I cannot say, I have not looked particularly at them.

4520. You cannot speak of that country with a view to horse-breeding?—No.

4521. Do you know anything of the [illegible] of the produce of Hackneys as compared with thoroughbreds?—I cannot say I do.

4522. Talking of the resolution to which you referred, do you know as a matter of fact there are no Hackney stallions in the whole of the County of Cork?—They don't want to have them there.

4523. Are there is not one?—No, I dare say not.

4524. And perhaps the people who passed the resolution know very little about them?—A great many of them are in the habit of going to shows.

4525. Do you think any of them breed from Hackneys?—I should say not.

4526. You have had a great experience of Ireland as a Grand Juror, and doing the [illegible], and in many other ways?—Yes.

4527. It is not very hard to get a sufficiently good mare, and pass it [illegible] anything?—I think these people know what they are about; **we** have a very good show in Cork; the judges there told me they could find a better show of young horses.

4528. Did you ever hear it suggested that Hackneys should be sent into the good parts of Cork?—No, if they came to our part I believe they would spread to the other parts.

4529. Do you think now that any of the good hunters in your district are bred out of mares from Castletownroche, and Bantry and those parts of the [illegible]?—It is not likely.

4530. And you don't think the Hackney is such a wonderful animal that he is likely to breed hunters that will be sought after as hunter breed, unless he [illegible]?—I suppose it is very hard to tell.

4531. Do you think that is likely?—Of course.

4532. Mr. Fitzwilliam.—Would you be afraid if there were Hackney stallions largely used in the adjoining districts that in course of time the blood would filter into your district and do harm?—I think it would spread immensely; it would be very hard to tell how much, but I think it would spread by degrees.

4533. Chairman.—Do you **think the effect of its** spreading by degrees would **have an effect on the** hunter breed?—Yes, I think so.

4534. A deteriorating effect?—I think so.

4535. Mr. Warren.—I presume you don't know how the Hackneys are bred, those that you are referring to?—No, I don't know whether they are very old bred or not.

4536. You don't know anything about their origin?—No, I don't.

4537. Col. St. Quintin.—What is it you object

Mr. G. F. Langfield.

to about a Hackney, is it his appearance or breeding?—I don't like his appearance, and I have always understood that he was very soft, I don't like his shoulders, I don't like anything about him.

4538. He is supposed to have great action?—I am told he goes for a little while, then he does not go much further. Someone said that he was a good horse to drive out, but a bad horse to drive home.

4539. But you object to his shoulders, and do you think it would improve the mares of the country to get harness horses by such a sire?—No, I don't think so.

4540. That they would get better harness horses with that action and formation?—I don't think so.

4541. Mr. Warren.—Have you ever driven a Hackney?—No.

4542. Have you ever acted as a judge at any Horse Show?—No.

Captain Donnellan, M.P.

4543. Chairman.—You live in the county of Cork?—Yes, sir.

4544. In what part?—East Cork, near Midleton. I might mention in the course of a breeding district.

4545. Mr. Carew.—What breeds have they chiefly? They have their hunters at Midleton, and indeed I think East Cork may fairly be said to hold its own ... with North Cork which has been praised so much, and I must say justifiably praised.

4546. Chairman.—Do you breed horses yourself?—Yes, I do; chiefly hunters. In fact, I may say hunters are chiefly bred in East Cork.

4547. What sires do you use?—Well, I use a thoroughbred ... for breeding purposes.

4548. And what class of mares?—Well, I think that the only class of hunter that pays to breed at present is the weight-carrier. I think the light weight hunters are now practically unsaleable, and to breed the weight-carrying hunter you will require the thoroughbred horse and a good roomy well bred mare or half-bred mare.

4549. Being a thoroughbred horse?—Yes, I should say so, if possible, ... the half-bred may be ... with a high-class stock, but, as a rule, Irish farmers don't keep such a class of mare, because she would not be any use for a farmer. Provided the sire be in the stud book, I think conformation and soundness are of greater importance ... than any particular strain of blood.

4550. Do you regard it as essential that he should be a thoroughbred horse?—Well, as a general rule, there are exceptions. I know cases in which half-bred horses have been ... from good ...

4551. Do the farmers in your country breed many horses, around Midleton?—Yes, I should think so; it is practically as good a district for horse breeding as any in the county of Cork.

4552. Do you think that the class of horses bred there has improved or ...?—I don't think the system adopted by the Royal Dublin Society has improved the breed of horses in my district.

4553. Has it the present system?—I think the class of horses ... better now than before the system of premiums ... was adopted.

4554. ... since 1886, that, speaking generally, ... marked difference in the horses bred ... in the neighbourhood of Midleton, do you think they are better or worse ... than they used to be twenty or thirty years ago?—I think the mares have been deteriorating gradually, because as farmers have ... they have not been able to keep as good a class of mares, they are ... the best of the ... Farmers are always in need of money, and only keep mares they cannot realise a good price for.

4555. Have you any suggestions you would like to make towards extending the Royal Dublin Society's scheme?—Well, I have a suggestion which, with your permission, I would like to read to the Commission. I am satisfied myself that some such plan must be adopted before the breed of Irish horses can be substantially improved.

4556. I would like to know if this suggestion which you are going to read is one that meets with your own approval?—Most certainly.

4557. Mr. Carew.—It is not an original suggestion, but you have adopted it as your own?—Yes. I ... in mentioning the name of the author, ... on this subject in the south of Ireland.

4558. Chairman.—Will you be so kind as to give the name of ... —Mr. ... Furlong, of Fermoy, who is well-known as a judge of ... that ... objected ... in the first place:—

"That some should be directed towards improving the breeding mares, for, without suitable mares ... to breed ... [illegible] should be devoted to this purpose. None should be given ... there are plenty of ... in Ireland with capital and enterprise to ... high class ... if there is a demand for their ... [illegible] ... the chance of winning a premium ... should be to improve breeding ... giving prizes of £5 or £6 to thirty or forty mares ... [illegible] ... Royal Dublin Society to ... this ..."

and in order to ... this, this gentleman suggests the following scheme:—

"... That the £5,000 per annum now given away in ... should be expended in buying ... from ... in England and Ireland ... [illegible] ... would, therefore, pay ... a year ...

... be distributed throughout Ireland, ... by Local Committees ... upon the following terms:—

(1.) That they should be served by sires chosen by their Local Committee.

(2.) That these mares should be distinguished and ... and each farmer should pay for the ... of the ...

(3.) That the property of the mare should be in the ... of the ...

(4.) That the ... may ... a year to the Local Committee.

(5.) That these Committees should have the power to ... from any farmer ... and ... to other farmers upon the same terms."

and then he goes on:—

"It may be assumed that these mares would be ... for breeding ... of four ... years, and, therefore, by adopting this plan the Royal Dublin Society, instead of parting with £5,000 per annum, ... premiums, would in ... years ... £5,000 ... under their own control, and ... to produce ... than the ... now bred in Ireland."

I think there is a great deal in that worth favourable consideration.

4559. It has been suggested by a witness that the Government should contribute ... to the farmers ... breeding purposes ...

[illegible] of that kind?—Provided they were only [illegible] for [illegible].

4558. Have you any experience in buying [illegible]?—No, I know nothing about them.

4560. I suppose a certain number of troopers are bought round about [illegible]?—Oh, yes, no doubt. I think it would be a great advantage if the military [illegible] were brought more into contact with the farmers, but I have not thought out any scheme.

4561. You would suggest the troopers should be bought direct from the farmers, and, if possible, do away with the middleman?—If possible, I think it would be very desirable. With reference to Hackney sires I might mention that I perfectly agree with Mr. [illegible] and Mr. [illegible] on that subject; there is a very strong feeling in the county of Cork that they would tend to deteriorate the breed very much. I have no personal experience myself, but I have talked over the matter with men who understand horse breeding, and the various classes of horses that are suitable for the English market, and they all agree that Hackney sires would not be suited certainly for the county of Cork, because we are in a very favourable position in the greater part of the county to produce a good class of hunter, suitable for the English market, and [illegible], I think it is [illegible] class of hunter.

4562. Do you think that the effect of Hackneys [illegible] in [illegible], [illegible], and [illegible] would have any effect on the breeding of horses in [illegible]?—I think, as Mr. [illegible] said, that in the course of time in [illegible] it would, but it would not be immediately apparent.

4563. You think some of the blood would [illegible] through?—In course of time I am sure it would.

4564. Is there any importation of ponies and small [illegible] from the [illegible] to your own [illegible]?—Not that I know of. Of course [illegible] might produce [illegible] horses, [illegible] [illegible] [illegible] and I think the [illegible] of the county of Cork would be [illegible] [illegible] present [illegible] [illegible] [illegible] I think it would be rather risky, and there is not much chance, so far as [illegible] [illegible] [illegible].

[illegible]

[illegible] for you keeping up?—As far as I can understand light weight horses have reduced very much in value. A large dealer in the county of Cork told me not long ago that light weight horses have [illegible] in value as much as 50 per cent. within the last four or five years.

4571. Light weight hunters?—Light weight hunters he was talking of.

4572. Mr. [illegible].—Reduced how much?—Very nearly 50 per cent. I think what he said was that you would buy as good a light weight horse now for [illegible] as you would give £[illegible] or £[illegible] for [illegible] years ago; perhaps 50 per cent. would be more like the [illegible].

4573. CHAIRMAN.—I am sorry to say I don't find it so.—There is no doubt they have reduced very much in value. I am not talking now of a horse with character; a horse with character will always sell well. I am talking of the present average.

4574. You mean the light-weight [illegible]?—Yes, I only mean the average light-weight [illegible] [illegible].

4575. Mr. [illegible].—What fees do [illegible] the farmers give [illegible] for the services of a stallion, of course they will go to the cheapest [illegible], but what do they give usually, do you think?—The service fee of the best class thoroughbred stallion [illegible] [illegible]. I don't think there is anything over [illegible].

4576. A horse standing at that rate would not be likely to get a great many mares, would he [illegible] from gentlemen and well-to-do people?—[illegible] [illegible] [illegible] horses standing at that fee would [illegible] well patronised; now, I think that owing to [illegible] [illegible], farmers would consider that [illegible] high.

4577. The farmer who would give £[illegible] for the services of a stallion would be a man who would [illegible] [illegible] [illegible] [illegible] [illegible] [illegible] [illegible] [illegible] [illegible]. I think it is [illegible] [illegible] [illegible] [illegible] [illegible] the county of Cork in order [illegible] [illegible] for their [illegible] [illegible] [illegible] [illegible] keep [illegible] [illegible] [illegible] [illegible] [illegible], I am [illegible] [illegible] [illegible].

4578. And yet they will [illegible]?—[illegible] [illegible] [illegible] [illegible] [illegible] [illegible]—now I fancy that would be [illegible] [illegible].

4579. Mr. [illegible].—You said in [illegible] [illegible] [illegible] by Mr. [illegible] you recommend that the [illegible] of [illegible] should be the absolute property of the farmers?—Yes.

4580. Why do you recommend [illegible] [illegible] [illegible]?—The mares were always [illegible] the property of the Royal Dublin Society, [illegible] [illegible] [illegible] [illegible] [illegible] [illegible] [illegible] [illegible] [illegible].

4581. [illegible] [illegible] [illegible] [illegible]?—Yes, [illegible] [illegible] [illegible] the Royal Dublin Society [illegible] [illegible] [illegible] [illegible] [illegible] [illegible] [illegible].

4582. Don't you think that would [illegible] a great deal of [illegible]?—[illegible] would depend on the constitution of the local committee.

4583. Don't you think that the farmer [illegible] would [illegible] [illegible] [illegible] [illegible] [illegible] [illegible] [illegible] [illegible] [illegible] [illegible] [illegible] [illegible] [illegible] I don't think it would [illegible] [illegible] [illegible] [illegible] [illegible].

4584. Mr. [illegible].—[illegible] good [illegible] [illegible]?—Yes.

4585. Mr. [illegible].—[illegible] [illegible] of the introduction of Hackneys?—Yes, the breeding [illegible].

4586. Hackneys would only be [illegible] for

[illegible] [illegible] [illegible] [illegible] [illegible] [illegible] [illegible] [illegible] [illegible] [illegible] [illegible] [illegible]

[illegible] Cork. [illegible]

breeding hunters [illegible]?—I presume so; I have no personal knowledge.

4587. Don't you think a mistake [illegible] a hunter would make a good harness horse?—I think the shape [illegible] make one very different. I presume you require action for harness horses.

4588. Don't you find the thoroughbred will breed good enough action for harness purposes?—As a rule, I don't think the thoroughbred has a high [illegible] action.

4589. Well, sufficient action for harness purposes? —Certainly, for [illegible] purposes.

4590. Do you agree with Mr. Barry and Mr. Langfield that everyone who keeps a stallion should take out a licence?—Yes, certainly.

4591. And that the defects of wind or limb should be shown on the face of the licence?—Yes.

4592. Mr. Wrench.—With regard to these [illegible] to Mr. [illegible] scheme, I think you said that you would leave the entire control with the local committee. I mean that practically everything not the [illegible] would be left with the local committees?—Yes.

4593. Who would have to inspect, and change the [illegible] if necessary?—Yes.

4594. Would you leave the local committees [illegible] to proceed, or would you give the people who are breeding by the scheme any voice in the selection? —That is a detail I have not considered.

4595. You have not thought that out?—I have not.

4596. I think you said, with regard to Hackneys, that you thought [illegible] the blood might [illegible] through?—Yes.

4597. And that you considered their action objectionable?—I think their action in this [illegible] the [illegible].

4598. As I understand you, you live in one of the [illegible] districts, and you wish to keep the [illegible] of the [illegible] up, and you don't want any other blood?—Yes, that is so.

4599. And I don't know that it has been suggested that you should have any other blood, therefore, if you are breeding hunters you would not object to [illegible] to breed from that had very high knee action? —I don't know that it would be a very strong objection if she had very good shoulders, [illegible], and [illegible], and in every other respect was suitable.

4600. You would not [illegible] her having extravagant action?—I think I would take the chance.

4601. And you think that could be corrected by the thoroughbred horse?—Yes, I think so.

4602. Do you think it any drawback for a [illegible] to have extravagant knee action—does it not, to a certain extent, [illegible] galloping power?—I think so.

4603. Therefore, in selecting a [illegible] sire, as long as he had [illegible], straight action, you would prefer him not to have knee action?—I think he should have sufficient action to travel safely from [illegible] to [illegible] along the road without stumbling; anything beyond that is not necessary.

4604. With regard to harness horses do you think action is a valuable commodity [illegible]?—I [illegible] [illegible] is guided to a very large extent by action.

4605. You think a horse with good action is more quickly picked out [illegible] than a horse that has not?—Yes, for harness purposes.

4606. Then putting the Hackney [illegible] altogether, and suppose some [illegible] were [illegible] to be useful to the people in the very poor districts of Ireland, would you deprive those people of that advantage on account of any imaginary injury to the [illegible] that were well able to take care of themselves?—I cannot speak of the congested districts, or any poor districts, in Ireland, but I imagine a good deal of [illegible] might be [illegible].

4607. I am only saying supposing they had been tried, and it was found a [illegible] class of animals suited them, don't you think the people who breed hunters in your district are very well able to look after the class of mares they breed from?—You are referring to other parts of the county of Cork.

4608. I am referring to Midleton. Your people would not be likely to bring mares from [illegible] or [illegible] or other parts to breed hunters from in Midleton?—I think, of course, there might be an exceptional case in which mares might, but as a general rule I think not. But there is a very strong feeling in the whole county of Cork against the introduction of Hackney sires.

4609. When you say the whole county do you include the congested districts?—I think I do. Mr. Langfield referred to the resolution of the County Cork Agricultural Society—a resolution was also passed by the County Grand Jury at the last Spring Assizes—unanimously protesting against the introduction of the breed of Hackneys.

4610. You don't know that as a matter of fact they had a thoroughbred standing in one of the [illegible] districts, and we were asked to send down the Hackney which [illegible]?—In West Cork?

4611. Yes?—No; I was not aware of that.

4612. Personally you have no experience of Hackneys?—I have no experience of Hackneys at all. The proposer and seconder of this resolution are men of considerable experience in horse-breeding.

4613. Chairman.—Mr. Wrench asked you if some particular horse was most suited to the peasants in the congested districts whether you would deprive them of the use of that horse for fear of some [illegible] injury to a hunter-producing district, don't you consider that [illegible] in those cases [illegible] than the hunter-breeding interests of the [illegible] districts of Cork?—Certainly, and I might go so far as to say throughout Ireland. Of course, I am only speaking for the county of Cork, but Ireland is the great nursery for hunters for the English market.

4614. Mr. Grace.—In view of these new [illegible] of [illegible], the value of the hunter is not likely to be improved?—I think it will hold its own.

4615. Chairman.—From your knowledge of the congested districts—have you been in West Cork at all?—Simply visiting; I cannot speak as to the conditions of [illegible] there at all.

4616. But you have met the inhabitants, and do you think they possess sufficient intelligence to be able to tell what sort of horse is best adapted to their needs?—I think myself the welfare of the community should be considered in this matter before any particular district.

4617. Mr. Wrench.—I think you said the [illegible]-breeding [illegible], was more valuable. Can you say as to the amount of the [illegible] of the men who breed hunters in your district. What class of farmers?—In East Cork we have such a very large proportion of very small farmers, and I think as a rule the small farmers of my district very frequently endeavour to breed a hunter themselves, even the smallest one.

4618. You don't quite agree with some of the witnesses who told us that the horses that generally [illegible] the [illegible] are [illegible] bred by the gentry and men of some [illegible]?—I do not; many small farmers frequently breed a horse that turns out a good hunter.

4619. That is in your district?—Yes.

R. H. [illegible], [illegible], Queen's County.

[illegible] Mr. R. H. [illegible].

[illegible]. The CHAIRMAN.—You live in the Queen's County, I think? [illegible]

[illegible]. You have had considerable experience in horse breeding?—I have been at it about twenty years. I have had both thoroughbred horses, Norfolk trotters, a Hackney sire, a Norfolk Punch, and a Shire horse, from time to time.

[illegible]. Have you got any stallions now [illegible] [illegible], besides [illegible] going to the stud [illegible] [illegible] a [illegible] [illegible]. I believe he is in the Hackney Stud Book. [illegible] [illegible] is his name.

[illegible]. Is he a Yorkshire or Norfolk Hackney?—He is in the Hackney Stud Book; he is [illegible] [illegible], and is by a horse called "[illegible] [illegible]." I bought [illegible] from [illegible] at the [illegible] Show.

[illegible]. What horses do you breed yourself personally?—I breed from thoroughbred [illegible] [illegible].

[illegible]. What horses are generally bred in your district?—At the present time it is very hard to tell what they breed from. They go very often to the cheapest and nearest horse, and if, as they say in the country, a [illegible] [illegible] [illegible] to a certain horse, the whole townland will follow him.

[illegible]. Mr. [illegible].—What is a [illegible] [illegible] man?—That is a man who is a [illegible] [illegible], or [illegible] [illegible] [illegible] as [illegible] [illegible]. If such a man goes to a certain stallion, all the neighbours will go after him, irrespective of anything else. Of course the horse must be cheap.

[illegible]. CHAIRMAN.—Are there good mares in your district?—No; the mares have I think gone from bad to worse, even, for the last few years. In fact the small farmers cannot afford to keep a good mare. If they have a good mare they will sell her. They can get no price for a bad mare and they [illegible] them [illegible]. They are going from bad to worse, [illegible], and everything else.

[illegible]. You think the mares are deteriorating in [illegible] of the want of money on the part of the farmers?—Yes; I do.

[illegible]. Do you think that farmers appreciate the value of a good sire?—I am sure they should. Any of the farmers that I know are fairly well off and they always send to a good thoroughbred horse, and very few of them have really good mares. When I had "[illegible] of [illegible]," he always got [illegible] fifty or so only [illegible] mares every year, and he did a lot of good to the [illegible] round about; they got from [illegible] to £70 for the produce as three-year-olds.

[illegible]. Do you think the farmers are generally influenced by the [illegible] of the horse or by the [illegible] of the service fee?—Some of them are influenced by his appearance and [illegible] [illegible]; many are influenced by their friends; and a good many of them will send their mares to a horse and they will never pay him.

[illegible]. They don't pay at all?—No, not at all.

[illegible]. Then it does not matter what the fee is?—[illegible] no; they would rather send their mares on a [illegible] to you; that is my experience.

[illegible]. Are there many mares in your neighbourhood that you consider suitable to put to the sires of the [illegible]?—Well, there are a few—some fairly good [illegible] [illegible]. I think the curse of Ireland is [illegible] of these half-bred sires. Half of what they call half-bred sires are made up with [illegible] pedigrees.

[illegible]. You don't approve of half-breds?—No, sir; because they are not really half-bred. They may be [illegible] by a thoroughbred horse, and if the [illegible] [illegible] [illegible] a good-looking colt they won't cut him, but will [illegible] [illegible] by [illegible], the [illegible]; a good many are said to have been got by "[illegible] of [illegible]," and I [illegible] [illegible] the mares never came to the horse.

[illegible]. Would you approve of breeding from half-bred horses really got by "[illegible] of [illegible]"?—I would like to have the dam of best above [illegible] [illegible] [illegible], that is, you should go back as far as the great grandsire.

[illegible]. And that the grandsire and the great grandsire should be thoroughbred?—[illegible] be thoroughbred. If they were got by what they call the old Irish horse they would make good hunters.

[illegible]. What do you mean by the old Irish horse?—I could not exactly describe the breed. There was one in this country [illegible] [illegible] [illegible], a [illegible] horse called "Mr. Henry," who got very [illegible] [illegible]. He was [illegible] [illegible] the old Irish draught horse—very light, without much [illegible] on his legs, with really good bone, about 15.3 high. He got very valuable hunters, as far as [illegible] were concerned, and he got some [illegible] that could always be sold.

[illegible]. Have you any idea how he was bred?—I have not. His name was "Mr. Henry;" I know the man that had him for years, his name is [illegible].

[illegible]. Do you know the horse himself?—I often saw the horse and his produce. He is dead now.

[illegible]. What [illegible] did his appearance give you?—He gave the idea of being [illegible] a bit [illegible] than half-bred. He had no [illegible] hair and did not [illegible] any of the characteristics of the draught horse at all. He had great action, and very good [illegible] and very good [illegible] bones, and a fine [illegible].

[illegible]. You think the Royal Dublin Society's [illegible] has been beneficial in your part of England?—It has been beneficial in this way. The small [illegible] people always like to know if the [illegible] [illegible] [illegible] is sound, and it is a good thing to have a certificate of his soundness.

[illegible]. You approve of registration?—Yes, I do.

[illegible]. Do you think [illegible] [illegible] [illegible] have been [illegible] in selecting really suitable horses for [illegible] [illegible]?—I think so. In the Queen's county there were only [illegible] that were registered, and I think one of these, even, "[illegible]" is dead.

[illegible]. Such horses as you know that are registered are in your opinion suitable horses?—They are, to get really good [illegible] or high class [illegible] horses, because if they don't breed a hunter you can [illegible] [illegible] and sell it as a harness horse.

[illegible]. What is your opinion as regards the prices of horses bred in your district?—The prices have, at the very [illegible] dropped forty per cent. on all sorts of horses, as far as I know.

[illegible]. What class of horses has been particularly affected by the depreciation of value?—I think it is mostly the [illegible] and in the light harness horses, in the light [illegible]. From the [illegible] [illegible] the farmers [illegible] [illegible] [illegible] [illegible] [illegible] [illegible] [illegible] [illegible] and [illegible] a [illegible] [illegible] [illegible], and so [illegible] [illegible] to [illegible] them—some [illegible] [illegible] would [illegible] £14 or £15, [illegible] years ago, would not get more than £7 now.

[illegible]. Who buys them?—They are all bought by the [illegible], who come down to Kilkenny to purchase. Nearly all these horses go up North, but I don't know for what purpose.

[illegible]. Are there [illegible], as many horses in your district as [illegible] [illegible] [illegible]?—I don't think so.

[illegible]. What do you attribute that to?—The bad prices. I did not put any of my half-bred mares to a horse at all this last season.

[illegible]. Are there many [illegible] [illegible] in your part of the Queen's county?—There are.

[illegible]. You don't like them?—I do not.

[illegible]. You don't [illegible] any of them of the same [illegible] "Mr. Henry"?—No, they are not. Most of them are said to be got by "[illegible] of [illegible]," "[illegible] of [illegible]," or by "[illegible] [illegible]." They may be [illegible] [illegible] [illegible]; the pedigrees they are [illegible] [illegible], and [illegible] they [illegible] [illegible], I [illegible].

[illegible]. You don't think they are suitable horses to improve the breed in your district?—No, I don't.

[illegible]

[illegible] And there was a good many mares of [illegible] a few years ago [illegible] there [illegible] "[illegible] Arran" [illegible] I [illegible] three years [illegible] the [illegible] [illegible] In the [illegible] the [illegible] of [illegible] [illegible] they didn't mind [illegible] registered in the stud book.

[illegible]. CHAIRMAN.—Can you trace "[illegible]" pedigree back [illegible] generations?

[illegible]. She was of the same blood as "[illegible]"—She was [illegible] the same way bred as "[illegible]," by "[illegible]," out of "[illegible]," by "[illegible]" out of [illegible] by "[illegible]." That is as far as I can go; that is as far as Mr. [illegible] could get it; [illegible] But I asked Mr. [illegible] this mare, and he said [illegible] get their horses in the stud book [illegible] of their [illegible] they [illegible] [illegible] [illegible].

[illegible]. Mr. FITZGERALD.—Do they do that now?—There is no [illegible] now.

[illegible]. Col. St. QUINTIN.—You say the prices have dropped very considerably in the last two or three years?—Yes.

[illegible]. Do you think they have dropped equally in the very high-class hunters and [illegible] horses [illegible] [illegible] good weight carrying [illegible].

[illegible]. And in the harness horses?—The [illegible] horses I have [illegible] experience about.

[illegible]. Do you think a [illegible] good thoroughbred [illegible] with sufficient bone [illegible] [illegible] get as good [illegible] and good [illegible] a [illegible] [illegible] as any [illegible] stallion of any other breed?—I think so, [illegible].

[illegible]. [illegible] a lot of those [illegible] the [illegible] to the class of the high-class hunter [illegible] capable of making high-class hunters [illegible]?—They [illegible].

[illegible]. And there is a great demand for those in the market?—Yes.

[illegible]. Do you think the price of [illegible] has dropped?—[illegible] as [illegible] of [illegible] I [illegible] sold one.

[illegible]. You have no personal experience, but [illegible] the breeding country [illegible] [illegible] the [illegible] [illegible] [illegible] I don't know anything about [illegible] at all.

[illegible]. With regard to the [illegible] going from the [illegible] and other [illegible] to the farmers, which [illegible] the [illegible] you think a [illegible] should be [illegible] to the farmer [illegible]?—I have known very good [illegible] to be sold [illegible] that were got to the stud at [illegible] years of the [illegible].

[illegible]. You didn't quite understand me. What is the greatest age that you would [illegible] a mare to the farmer [illegible]. Say sixteen years of age?—Yes. I would say twelve years of age.

[illegible]. [illegible] the difficulty of [illegible] with the [illegible] [illegible] [illegible] they don't [illegible] until they are [illegible] years of age. Would you consider that too old?—Too old, in this way. Very probably the mare would [illegible] the first year she would be put to a stallion, [illegible] and the mare [illegible] to [illegible] to grass.

[illegible]. There is some difficulty [illegible] to induce the farmer to take her [illegible]?—[illegible] and [illegible]. Of course she might [illegible] the [illegible] year, and it is [illegible] she would [illegible] the first year.

[illegible]. Mr. WRENCH.—Your only experience about [illegible] is with regard to [illegible] you and your father have had?—That is all.

[illegible]. One was a Norfolk [illegible] of [illegible] Norfolk.

[illegible]. The other [illegible]?—Yes.

[illegible]. He does not appear to be in the [illegible] stud book [illegible] I don't know whether he was in it or not. I [illegible] pedigree. He was sold to me with his pedigree [illegible].

[illegible]. He is an old horse?—A very old horse now, he is eighteen or twenty years.

[illegible]. CHAIRMAN.—Are there any observations you would like to make on the subject of [illegible] breeding?—I have nothing else to say.

[illegible]. Mr. FITZGERALD.—Can you suggest anything with a view to [illegible] [illegible]?—[illegible] the present state of [illegible] of everything in Ireland. As a farmer, I know that everything has gone down, [illegible] horses, cattle, sheep, [illegible], and everything else [illegible]. With [illegible] of the [illegible] the [illegible] for the [illegible] they have the [illegible] [illegible] if they [illegible] good [illegible] and they are very glad to [illegible].

Mr. WILLIAM [illegible], [illegible], Queen's County, examined.

[illegible]. CHAIRMAN.—You live in the Queen's County, and have [illegible], [illegible] in horse-breeding for a good many years?—Yes.

[illegible]. What class of horse do you principally breed?—Thoroughbreds and half-breds.

[illegible]. You have bred half-bred horses?—Yes, [illegible] the last four or five years. I always [illegible] good number of half-breds. I always kept [illegible] of four mares working on my farm, and I always [illegible] them [illegible] thoroughbred horses.

[illegible]. You always used a thoroughbred [illegible]?—Always.

[illegible]. [illegible] you put to these mares [illegible] thoroughbred horses?—[illegible] [illegible] [illegible] [illegible] [illegible] [illegible] [illegible] belonging to my father. [illegible] [illegible] [illegible] [illegible] [illegible] [illegible] [illegible] by horses with [illegible] of the [illegible].

[illegible]. How do you define an Irish horse—a [illegible] Irish horse?—I [illegible] good-looking, [illegible] [illegible]. You [illegible] of them [illegible] the County Wexford [illegible] [illegible] [illegible].

[illegible]. How [illegible] they bred?—[illegible].

[illegible]. Mr. [illegible].—There is thoroughbred blood in them, you think?—It would be [illegible] what I would say about that. I [illegible] [illegible] them at all. I have always [illegible] [illegible] of horse, just as I have a [illegible] class of cattle that I look on as old Irish blood. I can't tell you why, and I have never heard [illegible].

[illegible]. CHAIRMAN.—Do the farmers [illegible] [illegible] good [illegible]?—[illegible] but they are [illegible] [illegible]. [illegible] [illegible] [illegible] [illegible] [illegible] [illegible] the breed. What we want a Commission [illegible] [illegible] [illegible] of horses in Ireland? [illegible] breeding has declined [illegible], it is not because the blood is [illegible], but because there is nothing for the [illegible].

[illegible]. Mr. [illegible].—[illegible] before the breeding [illegible]; I think the breeding

[illegible] Mr. William Dagan.

has not gone off. I think there are as many good horses bred in Ireland as ever there were.

4709. CHAIRMAN.—You think the horses have not deteriorated, but that the value has depreciated?—I am perfectly certain of it. I don't know whether this may be connected with this inquiry or not, but if you will allow me I will tell you what I think are the prices of horses now in comparison with what they were ten or fifteen years ago. There are three fairs round us, and they are typical Irish fairs. They are held at Rathdowney, Frankfurt, and Castletown. I am perfectly certain that in those three fairs this year there were not ten three-year-old horses sold for £40 each, and I think I am over it a good deal in saying there were not ten. I don't think any three-year-old, unless there is something remarkable about him, is worth £40 in the public market now. Fifteen years ago I saw £90 offered for a three-year-old in Rathdowney one day; and I am perfectly certain that the fall is in the price of the horse and not in the value of the animal. If the best three-year-old in a fair is not worth £40, what can the average three-year-old be worth? Certainly, I would say not £20. This is what we farmers are asked to go on breeding horses for, and when we have them bred there is no market for the ordinary horse. Consequently I myself and a good number of other men are dropping out of breeding. It is better for me and others to go to the fair and buy a horse if we want it than to breed it.

4710. What do you attribute the falling to, to lack of quality?—I don't think so; I can get as good a three-year-old horse now as I have ever done.

4711. That is, you can get as good a horse for £40 now as you should pay £90 for some years ago?—Yes.

4712. MR. CAREW.—That is, the average of the three-year-olds?—Yes. More than that, you will now get a 12 stone hunter for 50 or 60 guineas as well as any that you paid £120 for some time ago. Widger told me that. He told it to me in explanation in a conversation we had when I was remonstrating with him on the price he was offering me for a horse. I am quite sure of that myself, for my own experience is the same.

4713. CHAIRMAN.—You are quite sure it is not owing to any deterioration in the horses themselves?—No, I don't think it is. There are as many good horses in the country as ever; there may be some bad ones. I don't think that in my county this present scheme of the Royal Dublin Society has done any use.

4714. What class of horses do you think your part of the Queen's County is best adapted to breeding?—Thoroughbreds.

4715. Clean thoroughbreds?—Yes.

4716. You would not suggest that the farmers should breed clean thoroughbreds?—I meant sires. Will you ask the question again.

4717. What class of horses do you think your part of the country is best adapted to produce?—Hunters. I have never known them do anything else. Any fellow who thinks at all of what he is going to breed from has a hunter. I know nothing at all about harness horses. I never saw a harness horse buyer in my country.

4718. In attempting to breed hunters they very often breed something that is not a hunter?—That is particularly so just now. There is a horse that is getting rather good stock, I noticed them in the show the other day in Maryboro'; his produce looked as no more like harness horses than hunters and the sire is the only creditable registered sire in the country.

4719. Is it a thoroughbred sire?—Yes; "Early Bird."

4720. Do you think that the mares that the farmers use have deteriorated, to your knowledge?—I heard you ask that question of one or two of the other witnesses. As a matter of fact until these mare shows were held, as far as I myself was concerned I did not know, and I think that hardly anyone else had an opportunity of knowing the mares in the country. Until these mare shows of the last four or five years, I never saw all these mares. I saw them gathered together at the last summer show, and I say that it was the best. This year I was asked to judge in Longford. I never saw so good a class of mares in my country as in Longford. As far as judging goes, I don't think myself that any man can say what is a good brood mare until he sees the produce.

4721. What?—Until they see their produce. The only really certain good brood mare I ever had of my own was a mare that if she were entered in a class would be hurried out of the ring with the first lot when the judging was on in her class. She would not sell for more than £10 I think, but I never sold a colt out of her for less than £200 as four-year-old.

4722. Do you mean that she would not get a prize in a show?—I say if she was the only one in her class you would not give a prize to her for want of quality.

4723. MR. WATSON.—How was she bred?—I bred her myself, by a stallion that had a good deal of Clydesdale in him out of an old Irish mare.

4724. CHAIRMAN.—Have you any suggestions as to improving the mares?—They are not of a very high standard. I have not; but I have this suggestion to make, and in that I think I will disagree with almost all the witnesses here. The only way you can improve the breed of horses is to go to the sires. In the latter scheme that the Royal Dublin Society are now working under, one of the rules is that no prize can be over £5. The prize to the sire has been done away with. You can hardly imagine, or I can't imagine any man keeping a mare for the purpose of, or buying a mare for the purpose of, taking a chance of getting a prize at some future time of £5 and no more. That is at present what you are doing. Under the system also a man may get a prize out of this mare when the foal is about two years old; and the prize he may get is £5. I am thoroughly convinced that at present, in my county at least, there is not a mare more put to the stud than there would be if the Royal Society did not give a shilling of this money.

4725. You don't think this scheme had the effect of inducing farmers to keep their good mares?—I am perfectly certain it didn't. All the Royal Dublin Society is doing now is giving a man a chance of £5. I know of my own knowledge of lots of men who had intended sending in mares to the shows in the Queen's County, and merely because it was a fine day and a good day for working on the farm, they didn't send in the mare on a chance of getting £5 by doing so, and I think they were quite right.

4726. They would not lose their day's work?—They would not lose their day's work. I am very strongly of opinion that there is not an extra mare in the Queen's County sent to a sire more than there would be if there were none of this money of the Royal Dublin Society going.

4727. Do you think that the farmers have got a sufficiency of suitable sires?—No, that is exactly what they have not got. I am a friend of some here, and I would be very sorry to say anything hurtful to any of his sires, but I can't help it really. The sires in the Queen's County last year, were "Almoner," "Bel Demonio," covering at thirteen guineas, "Harbinger," "Early Bird," "Oracle," at ten guineas, "St. David," at thirteen guineas. They were, I think, put in here (referring to a document) as an advertisement. I know "St. David" and "Bel Demonio" would not serve half-bred mares—I expect Mr. Blake put them in as an advertisement for his sire and a very good advertisement. That leaves three other horses. "Almoner" has got race horses, but I don't think he has size to get hunters nor do I think that either of the others are much. In that way I think we are wretchedly served with sires. I would almost say that unless there was something superlatively good in the mares I don't think they could get very high class produce. It is rather serious to talk of all these horses belonging to friends of my own, but a man must say what he thinks.

4728. Do you suggest that the sires should be registered?—I do, and I can speak on that with a certain amount of experience. It so happened that I was asked to go and judge at the first show of premium sires in England at Newcastle, and a wretcheder lot of horses I never saw in a show-yard. I never was more disgusted in my life than I was with that lot. Six or seven years afterwards I was asked to go again to another show, I think one held at Islington, and I was amazed at the class of horses that were in it. I never saw a finer lot of horses in my life in a show-yard, even putting the Royal Dublin Society in. I never saw so good a class, speaking of it as a class, in Ballsbridge as I saw on that day.

4729. Mr. Fitzwilliam.—Was that the class for premium sires?—Yes, the premium sires. I asked Captain Fife "How do you account for this wonderful improvement?" "Well," he said, "it is worth our while you know now. We are getting £200 a year for these horses now, and we can afford to go and buy them." There is another man I know very well—Dr. Blackwood, of Buxton. I have to go to Buxton now and then, and he has rather a fad about horses. When we made each other out when I first went there, and he asked me to look at his stud. He had two or three wretched beasts. Later on when I went there again he had five excellent horses. I was one of the judges who gave three of them £200 each at Islington. He said to me:—"It is a real good game now. I can afford to go and buy horses. I can give £400 for a horse now, and I can send him out, and it pays me well if he only lives two or three years." They have stuck to this one scheme from the beginning in England, and in my opinion it has done an immensity of good in the shires. It has done that in the sense, that good sires must produce better foals than bad ones.

4730. Mr. Fitzwilliam.—There is not a great number of them?—There is not one extra one in Ireland. Do away with the whole of the Dublin Society's Scheme, and you won't do away with a sire in Ireland, nor in my opinion will there be a single brood mare the less. With the quantity of money you have, you can't divide it over the mares at all. You have one [illegible] upon one side you can give it all to, on the other side you must divide it amongst fifty or sixty mares, and that brings it down to nothing. When this scheme was going on in Ireland I knew a man who went to England and bought a good horse on the chance of his getting £200 a year in this country from the Royal Dublin Society. He paid a good price for that horse, but then the next year the Royal Dublin Society changed their rules, and ran another scheme for a year, and then changed that to another scheme, and they seem to be changing it from year to year. I think they are chucking their money away.

4731. You approve of the idea of registering untried stallions?—I heard you ask that of each witness, and it is possible that you mean that every man who has a stallion in Ireland must register it.

4732. As far as the Royal Dublin Society is concerned?—Yes.

4733. You do approve as far as the Society is concerned?—Yes.

4734. There is also a suggestion that all stallions should be licensed?—That is a most drastic idea—unless they are sound they won't be licensed, they will be driven out of the country, in fact.

4735. The suggestion is that a heavy fee at any rate should be placed upon such horses as are not certified to be sound and suitable?—But does that apply to thoroughbred stallions covering thoroughbred mares? According to that you know "Ormond," if he came to this country, would be hurled out.

4736. Mr. Fitzwilliam.—It need not apply to any horses except those entering under a scheme?—[illegible] I think it would be interfering, it would be very strong indeed.

4737. Mr. Green.—"Ormond," was sold out of the country [illegible]?—The horse I am thinking of is a horse that is standing in Ireland at the highest fee for the past two years. I think this would be a very strong measure.

4738. Chairman.—Which you approve of?—I should not say I would.

4739. Then the requirement you would suggest to the Royal Dublin Society is to register thoroughbred [illegible]?—Yes, and then stick to it.

4740. You would approve of the [illegible] of [illegible]?—They had not passed a resolution to that effect at our society meeting this year.

4741. You would only subsidise thoroughbred sires?—Certainly; I would only subsidise thoroughbreds; I would draw the line hard and fast. Mr. Fitzwilliam asked a question about half-breds that were almost thoroughbreds. Of course I look upon "Mayboy" as a thoroughbred horse. It so happened my father was one of the stewards who acted in the [illegible] case, which disqualified him from the [illegible], but [illegible] [illegible]. There was a horse called [illegible], one of the finest horses I ever saw, a [illegible] horse, and so [illegible] that he was a [illegible] of [illegible] [illegible]. I believe that he was really a [illegible].

4742. Mr. Fitzwilliam.—He was [illegible] by Sir Tatton Sykes, if I remember right. In the [illegible] of [illegible] [illegible] [illegible] [illegible] had a great deal to do with a great number of horses [illegible] in the [illegible] of Yorkshire?—He was a [illegible] [illegible] [illegible] [illegible]. I [illegible] him a lot of [illegible], but I never got anything [illegible]. He [illegible] in [illegible] for two or three years.

4743. I didn't think [illegible] [illegible] to [illegible] [illegible] [illegible] [illegible] [illegible] [illegible] [illegible] [illegible] [illegible] [illegible] afterwards.

4744. He was in Wexford afterwards, but he didn't [illegible] [illegible] [illegible] [illegible] [illegible] [illegible] [illegible].

4745. Chairman.—"Mahony," of course, [illegible] [illegible] in the [illegible] book?—I don't know anything about him.

4746. You would suggest that the Royal Dublin Society only recognise thoroughbred horses?—Yes.

4747. You agree with Admiral Dixon that the thoroughbred horse is the best horse in the world for Ireland, that the thoroughbred animal of any sort is [illegible]?—I have [illegible] [illegible] that it is almost impossible to breed from a half-bred of any sort—pigs, cattle, dogs, or anything. You may breed [illegible] [illegible] [illegible] [illegible] [illegible] [illegible] [illegible] [illegible]. We [illegible] the [illegible] [illegible] [illegible] and the [illegible], [illegible]; they are very [illegible] animals, but if you [illegible] to breed from them, you would [illegible] [illegible] [illegible] [illegible] [illegible]. It is like [illegible] [illegible] [illegible] [illegible] [illegible] [illegible]. If you attempt to go [illegible] [illegible] [illegible] you get [illegible] [illegible] [illegible], [illegible] [illegible].

4748. Mr. Fitzwilliam.—I think what you say about the [illegible] [illegible] [illegible] [illegible] [illegible] [illegible]?—Well, you can [illegible] [illegible] [illegible] [illegible] of [illegible] [illegible], from a half-bred horse with a [illegible] [illegible]. [illegible] [illegible] [illegible] the number of [illegible] [illegible] [illegible] [illegible] [illegible] [illegible] [illegible] [illegible] [illegible] [illegible] [illegible] of thoroughbreds.

4749. Chairman.—[illegible] [illegible] [illegible] [illegible] [illegible] [illegible] [illegible] [illegible] [illegible] [illegible] [illegible] [illegible] [illegible]. I [illegible] [illegible] [illegible]. I don't think I [illegible] [illegible] [illegible] [illegible] [illegible] [illegible], or [illegible], or some of the [illegible] of those days, and I [illegible] [illegible].

Nov. 26, 1896.

Mr. William [illegible].

[illegible] Wynne.

when we were younger we thought some of the horses we saw then.

4750. Admiral Rous said that the thoroughbred horse increased an inch in stature in every twenty-five years, and that, in fact, the average height of a thoroughbred horse is a hand higher than it was 100 years ago?—I don't know about 100 years ago, but I don't think he is anything higher than he was twenty-five years ago. I am quite sure he is not.

4751. He said that in 1853 that the average height of a thoroughbred was a hand higher than it was 100 years before?—I can just as [illegible] twenty-five years ago as I can now.

4752. Do you think thoroughbred horses are more [illegible] than they used to be?—I think they are in England, not in Ireland.

4753. Do you think there is any other breed of horse that would remain as sound if subjected to the same trials as the thoroughbred horse is subjected to?—I don't think so.

4754. Therefore you consider that a particularly sound breed?—Much the soundest of any one single breed that I know of. I don't know anything at all of these Norfolk trotters we hear so much about; but as for Clydesdales and all that sort of animal, I am sure that the thoroughbred is the soundest; if people took the ordinary care of not breeding from unsound ones.

4755. Admiral Rous says "The stature of the thoroughbred horse has increased since the year 1700 an inch every twenty-five years, and whereas the average size of a horse then was 13.3 hands, the average is now 15.2 hands, and that in carrying power they can carry twice as much weight as they could 100 years ago"?—What age is the horse that the average size of is 15.2?

4756. He does not say?—Certainly the average height of a full grown horse is bigger than that now.

4757. Mr. Gibson.—In the licensing scheme that every horse should be licensed it is not at all suggested that [illegible]. It is suggested that the object of a license is that the defects from which a horse ought to be suffering should appear on the face of the license, and let the farmers have the option of going to that animal or not, as they like?—What will be the effect if the horse is not licensed.

4758. It will not be licensed for shape and make; it would get rid of the bad horses [illegible]. Is it as easy as he [illegible] to be licensed?

4759. It is that every one who owns a sire must get a license?—Yes, but if he does not get a license.

4760. What harm has it had [illegible] from, that is, an expert [illegible]?—But that is a bad way of doing now. You are registering horses now but that is all you propose though, under this scheme as well as I understand it. You will register any one that [illegible] to get his horse registered; if he then [illegible] it is his own lookout. For instance, [illegible] the best horse in the Queen's County is [illegible] thoroughbred horse "Wildreamer." I have sent a lot of mares to him this year because he is there. What is your scheme?

4761. To [illegible] the mongrel breeds going about the country?—But your scheme won't do that.

4762. In this way, if so much is charged for a license a great many would not keep horses?—But you are penalising the good horses.

4763. But this good ones, I should say?—But the good ones won't take out a license.

4764. The owner of a good horse would only be too willing to take out a license, because the bad ones will be got rid of?—Why should you ask him to do so? You are doing the [illegible] of my [illegible]. I was for giving [illegible] £200 and you want to make him pay something.

4765. No, in the first place you would want a committee to select the proper style of horse according to the shape and make, [illegible] of that horse by breeding from any patent defects, it should be stated on the face of the license. The farmers should have the opportunity of seeing that, and of going if he liked to that horse knowing that they are not going to charge the sire owner for that. That would be sensible.

4767. What would you suggest as a remedy for the evil that undoubtedly exists of bad shaped sires in this country?—The good ones at a low fee in [illegible]. I am perfectly [illegible] of them. [illegible] to Dublin Society sires.

4768. But if the Dublin Society suggest any improvement of any value they should stick to it?—I see very strongly of that opinion.

4769. And they should increase the premium?—If they could. I think if they could give one good sire in every two counties, besides what are in them. They have done nothing in my opinion up to the present. The money that was given in my county is absolutely in my opinion thrown away, and if they gave us a sire at a cheap rate, or any a sire [illegible], it would be much good, but it will be more than we are getting.

4770. You said when breeding half-bred with half-bred there is generally bad results?—It is too [illegible] to say that it would be unsound. I would not breed from a half-bred horse on any terms; they are mongrel.

4771. How would you propose to maintain the size and substance of the mares?—Put a good thoroughbred sire with a good well boned mare.

4772. But how will this sire be bred. Would she be a thoroughbred?—My own experience with mares is that as many horses a good mare bred. he was the produce either by thoroughbreds or half-breds.

4773. Mr. Wrench.—Did you hear it argued this morning that if the Dublin Society were to give prizes up to £50 the prizes that would keep the good mares in the country. Do you think that is a practical scheme at all?—No, I don't. Think of all they could not do it for [illegible] I look at it in this light. In their own view a farmer is not going to keep a mare on the chance of getting £50. He may get it one year; if he has a good mare he would get it every year unless you prevent him getting it the second year, [illegible] to that effect, then he will have his £50, and he will sell the mare, and will say to the foreigner who comes to buy the mare, "That's a good mare, I want £50 more for her, for she will get first prize this year, she got first prize last year." But if you give the one prize year after year, the other fellows won't send in their mares. They will say, "What is the use of sending in against him?"

4774. Chairman.—Are there any other suggestions you would like to make as to improvements in the breeding of horses?—I [illegible] think [illegible] want to improve the breeding of horses, [illegible] want to improve the price of [illegible], and the only way to do that I think is for the military authorities to buy yearlings and two-year-olds. If that could be done it would do a lot of good, because it is very hard on a farmer with only thirty or forty acres of land to keep his horse up to four years old, to be sure now.

4775. Colonel St. Quintin.—Why do you put it down to the military authorities? Why would you not say the Government should?—The Government would do it for the military.

4776. The military are only a small amount in the country, and there are certainly not so [illegible] they [illegible] to deal with?—I should think they would be making money by doing it.

4777. It would want a large establishment?—If they bought the yearlings and two year olds and had them properly fed and kept up to four years old what an improvement there would be in the horses in the army. As a matter of fact, you are now making money by them; you are buying them for less than their rearing costs. But you can't expect the farmers to be such fools as to go on doing this. You can't expect the class of troopers you are now getting for £35 after five or six years.

1778. That is for the Government?—But the Government don't want horses except for the military.

1779. But they are the people who should legislate. As a commercial transaction you would not go into that yourself. You would not set up a big establishment and take the risk of all the animals from yearlings and those eighteen months old up to four year olds?—I think it would be well worth the military authorities while to look forward and make provision. It is all well enough now, but how are we going to get on later on if the Irish farmers leave off breeding horses?

1780. But the British Government bought these horses [illegible]?—[illegible] in Ireland.

1781. They [illegible] indeed. Have you any idea how many they took in the year?—[illegible]

1782. This year I bought 730 horses up to the present time?—And where did you get all the rest.

1783. I don't think [illegible] bought more than a thousand in the year?—I thought it was a great deal more.

1784. I can get as many as ever I like in the [illegible] of the highest possible class. It is a very, very small thing in the export of Ireland?—Yes, if they only get a thousand a year.

1785. It does not affect the breeding of Ireland at all?—Very [illegible]. I certainly thought there were more [illegible] bought.

George Collins, Dingle, **examined.**

1786. Chairman.—You come from Kerry?—Yes.

1787. Are you much interested in horse-breeding?—Yes.

1788. What part of Kerry do you live in?—Dingle.

1789. What class of horses have you bred?—Oh, some from thoroughbreds and some from half-breds.

1790. What class of horse do you find most profitable?—The horses are used for general work. Very few people keep more than one horse, and he has to do every kind of work. The stamp at present, I think, [illegible]; they are almost altogether the produce of very inferior thoroughbreds.

1791. The mares are?—Yes, thoroughbred or half-bred, and the thoroughbreds are very inferior ones.

1792. Were there many thoroughbred stallions standing in the neighbourhood of Dingle?—[illegible] without one for some years back. There [illegible] years there has not been one. One [illegible] last year, but I don't think he has got much to do yet.

1793. I consider the Congested Districts Board horses have taken the place of all other stallions there, have they?—It is the [illegible].

1794. And gets much the most custom?—Yes, and his produce are very much [illegible] to what we have been accustomed to for a long time.

1795. How old is the produce now?—We have had the Hackney stallion for three years, I think.

1796. They are two year olds?—Yes. I have not seen many [illegible] altogether, but I have seen a number of yearlings, and they are fine and very superior to anything we were accustomed to.

1797. Do the farmers sell a good many of the produce at a year old?—They do, and sell foals; they sell the good ones almost always.

1798.—As foals and yearlings?—And when they are [illegible] years old and four.

1799. They sometimes keep them as long as that?—Yes.

1800. Where do they go to?—They are bought in the neighbouring fairs; they never go to a fair outside [illegible] the county.

1801. You don't know who buys them?—No; a good many are bought locally, and pass about from hand to hand, sometimes for [illegible] of the [illegible] go to the fairs and are passed away out of the county altogether.

1802. I suppose the small farmers in the neighbourhood of Dingle breed horses more for the purpose of sale than for their own requirements?—No, [illegible] they keep them for their own use, but when a horse gets a good price he is tempted to sell.

1802a. Are the owners of the mares very small farmers, as a rule?—Yes.

1803. Then they [illegible] work them [illegible]?—Yes, and [illegible]; they sell their colts and fillies.

1804. Then they must breed a good many more horses than their require for their own requirements?—They breed one almost every year.

1805. Surely that [illegible] for sale?—But you find the [illegible] a horse that would be suitable for his neighbour's [illegible].

1806. You approve of the Hackney horse and his produce in your district?—Yes, sir; they are a wonderful improvement on those we have been accustomed to.

1807. Have you any experience of breeding from Clydesdale or English Percheron or Shire horses?—Well, I had a mare got by a half-bred Clydesdale, but a very good one, that I refused £60 for one time.

1808. Do you approve of the Clydesdale sire?—I should like them better than the thoroughbreds we have been accustomed to, but I should prefer the animals [illegible] half-bred Clydesdale. I think he is a bigger type, thicker and more suitable to our requirements.

1809. Do you think that the class of horse in your district has deteriorated in your own knowledge?—Yes, sir.

1810. Used to be better?—Yes.

1811. To what do you attribute that deterioration?—To those poor thoroughbreds and their half-bred offspring.

1812. What sires used the farmers use formerly?—Before then they were mostly half-bred from [illegible], Suffolk or Clydesdale or some of the common horses about the country [illegible] pedigree very few could [illegible] up, but they were stronger horses and larger animals.

1813. The [illegible] stock by those was inferior?—Yes, rather inferior, [illegible] from those inferior thoroughbreds.

1814. Have you any suggestions you would like to make as to the best means of inducing the farmers to breed a better class of horses?—I think if you keep [illegible] the present breed the Hackney would [illegible] the Commission to give us some [illegible], good class, that might be put at thoroughbreds, [illegible] them who prefer that class of horse [illegible] would be of the right kind. But I think if [illegible] thoroughbreds [illegible], even though [illegible] a lot of suitable [illegible] work.

1815. You would get them too light?—Yes.

1816. Mr. Fitzgerald.—What do you say the horses [illegible] which you have been accustomed, [illegible] What were they?—The [illegible] thoroughbreds [illegible] got by thoroughbreds out of any mares.

1817. But I mean were they very weedy ones?—Almost always.

1818. Very bad?—Yes.

1819. Were they often unsound?—Yes.

4520. Then you prefer a good Hackney to a bad thoroughbred, is that what you mean?—And at the present time I should prefer a Hackney to even a good thoroughbred, I think they are likely to give us a supply of [illegible] good [illegible] to breed from.

4521. If the thoroughbred was of the same calibre as the Hackney?—Well, even then, I think he would be more likely to get light horses than the Hackney would.

4522. What do the stallions there usually charge for covering a mare?—There is no uniform charge, a lot of them follow their friends, and they pay less down in almost nothing.

4523. And the mares are extremely small and weedy too, I suppose?—Yes.

4524. So that they are not worth breeding from?—Not worth breeding from.

4525. And you think you can [illegible] that class of animal into a class of mare that is worth breeding from?—Well, your mark is to improve, and, as I apprehend, we have not very good mares to make better, we have bad ones we should like to improve, and I think the way to do it would be to make them heavier first of all.

4526. Mr. Clarke.—All the thoroughbreds that have been serving in your district were weedy ones?—Yes, though one was the winner of the Grand Steeple Plate in Cork, he was perhaps one of the worst in the lot.

4527. At getting stock?—Yes.

4528. Then you approve of the Hackneys for the purpose of increasing the size and substance of the mares and then breeding by thoroughbreds?—When you have a foundation of good dams I imagine the thoroughbred will find his way without any special assistance, the results experienced from him will always find him out, and the breeding ultimately generated there would in a very short time produce a lot of horses [illegible] in the [illegible] of the farmers.

4529. You think that mares may be improved by mating with the Hackney sires?—I do, sir, and then when the mares are improved you could go back to the thoroughbred.

4530. Colonel St. Quintin.—You don't require a very large breed of horses, do you, there?—No, sir.

4531. You want a thick set, active useful horse?—Yes.

4532. Up until now you had a very good breed of ponies and small animals in the country and they were bought at a considerable rate?—The company does not [illegible] so far [illegible] at that time, I have heard of their breeding in the neighbouring [illegible] more than the one I [illegible], my company does not take me back to the pony class.

4533. Do you think the country itself is capable of producing a horse that would sell to advantage outside its own county?—Oh, I do. I heard a gentleman say a while ago that £40 was a good price for a three-year-old; I refused £60 for a three-year-old this spring got by a thoroughbred, but a good one out of what is known as a common mare. There is plenty of good feeding down there for horses, but I should say it would not be a thoroughbred breeding country.

4534. The [illegible] same class of mountains will grow size and others will not, do you think your country is capable of growing size?—I don't think so, sir.

4535. In your [illegible] you cannot grow size?—No, and with difficulty maintain the [illegible] we bought there.

4536. Mr. Wrench.—Do you find the produce of the Hackney sires hardy?—They have not been amongst us long enough yet to know whether they are going to be hardy horses; they have the appearance of hardy horses.

4537. But I mean hardy young horses to lie out during the winter?—Yes, I have heard no fault found with them in that way.

4538. And you have had no experience yet as to whether they eventually become [illegible] or [illegible] quiet and I have heard it remarked by some people that they were likely would be very easy to break.

4539. Have the produce of these Hackneys sold at better prices than the produce of the [illegible] you have had before?—I don't know that many of them have been put on the market at all.

4540. I mean in the neighbourhood where they have changed hands so far [illegible] enough to give an idea as to what the general value would be.

4541. Are the Hackneys and the two-year-olds or whatever age, are they superior in appearance to their dams?—I only saw a considerable number of yearlings and they were certainly very much superior.

4542. To their dams?—Yes, and to everything that we were accustomed to see.

4543. And would you suggest any other horse being sent there in preference to the Hackney or would you rather have the Hackney?—I should rather see the others discontinued, those we have; I should like to see the bad ones [illegible] and put off altogether.

4544. But you think the Hackney is very suitable for your district?—I do.

4545. And do you think the people of the district share that opinion?—I am quite satisfied they do.

4546. That is the general opinion of the district?—Yes.

4547. Are those people as intelligent people capable of forming an opinion on what suits them best?—I suppose they know their own business.

4548. The Kerry people are fairly shrewd, are they not?—I should think so.

4549. And it has been suggested here that it is useless for small farmers of that type to breed horses; would it be possible to prevent them breeding?—I don't know what the law is capable of, but [illegible] would not prevent them breeding.

4550. And as a matter of fact it pays them to breed, they get more profit?—Oh, yes, the mare is never idle.

4551. It is an industry that pays them?—Yes.

4552. And an industry that they will carry on?—Certainly.

4553. Colonel St. Quintin.—You say that these are some of the Hackney breed sufficiently advanced for you to be able to form any opinion as to whether they are a hardy horse or not, or a useful horse, they are only young?—No, sir, they are only young.

4554. Then you are not speaking from any experience, it is only your fancy or idea that this will be an improvement?—It is more than fancy, in so [illegible] apparently they are a sounder horse than those bred from thoroughbreds.

4555. But it does not necessarily follow that because a horse is larger [illegible] the same [illegible] than a small or lighter horse, therefore you have no actual practical knowledge that a Hackney will produce a horse that can do more, it is only your idea that it will?—I know those we have from thoroughbreds are very bad, and I am very hopeful that those we have from Hackneys will be good.

4556. Quite so, but it is only hope at present?—Only hope at present.

4557. Mr. Wrench.—Do you think you could suggest any improvement in the scheme?—I don't know, sir, the removal of restrictions on the [illegible] supplied by public bodies I think would be desirable, based on valuation or anything that way. I never heard a mare that was blemished or did not [illegible] for good shape [illegible] the mares of the Hackney down there, and I don't think that is the proper way to proceed, I imagine it would be better to let all who would come to him.

4558. Would you let the unsound mares go if they are [illegible]?—I would, they will go to some horse and they might as well go to a good one.

4559. And you would leave the restriction as to valuation out and let everybody have the same opportunity at the same fee?—Yes, at present the [illegible] valuation [illegible] a county [illegible] of the same [illegible] county [illegible] [illegible], [illegible] work, you would be giving [illegible] to a class of farmer that was much more likely to [illegible] a good [illegible] commercially.

[illegible]. You would be bigger farmers in?—Yes.

[illegible]. You know as a matter of fact that all the [illegible] were taken up?—Yes, and in consequence of the [illegible] of valuation I am aware that [illegible] the property of farmers with larger valuation were [illegible] put to the horse, that is to say they were put in the [illegible] of farmers of smaller valuation.

[illegible]. So that the object which the Board desired was not arrived at?—No; I think if you [illegible] with the inferior mare very few people would be [illegible].

[illegible]. Are they [illegible] in any way the [illegible] stock of the district?—Well, they have [illegible] [illegible] since the Hackney made its appearance, but perhaps you cannot [illegible] to [illegible] horses. All only the [illegible], and if you [illegible] a horse to [illegible] and be [illegible] I think you would [illegible] get rid of all the [illegible].

[illegible]. You think it would be an improvement?—Yes.

The Commission adjourned to next morning.

TENTH DAY.—THURSDAY, 26TH NOVEMBER, 1896.

Present:—Lord Ashtown (in the Chair); The Hon. Henry W. Fitzwilliam, Mr. J. L. Carew, M.P., Colonel St. Quintin, and Mr. F. S. Wrench.

Mr. Hugh Neville, Secretary.

Mr. [illegible] John [illegible], [illegible], [illegible], examined.

[illegible]. Chairman.—You are a [illegible] of the [illegible] in the County Kerry?—Yes.

[illegible]. You live near Tralee?—Yes, within a few miles of it.

[illegible]. You take a considerable interest in horse-breeding?—I take a great interest in horses and hunting.

[illegible]. Do you breed any horses yourself?—In a very small way, personally. I have bred a little.

[illegible]. What class of horses are bred around your neighbourhood?—There are two or three classes; there is the hunter and the draft horse; but the hunters are rather light to Tralee and district.

1870. You mean they breed more of the draft than the hunter?—No, they breed more hunters, but the hunter stallions are rather light.

[illegible]. The sires used are rather light?—Yes.

[illegible]. What class of soil is there?—Rather [illegible] in parts.

[illegible]. Is it suitable for horse-breeding?—Oh, yes.

[illegible]. Are the farms large or small?—They are generally [illegible]. You would call them small, [illegible] at any rate. Thirty acres is about the average [illegible].

[illegible]. Are there many [illegible] in your district?—There are a fair number within a radius of two miles [illegible] about [illegible].

[illegible]. Are they suitable for **the wants of the district?**—No, the [illegible] the **hunters are too light,** and [illegible] not sufficient bone.

[illegible]. What class of sires, as a rule, are they?—Thoroughbred, mostly. Of course, we have some of the [illegible], [illegible] [illegible], and some [illegible].

[illegible]. Have you any experience of the Hackneys introduced by the Congested Districts Board?—Not personally, nor have I had a chance of seeing them, because they are out of my district. I have not seen the young horses, and cannot give you an opinion as to them, but from what I have heard, they are not giving much satisfaction.

[illegible]. You have not yourself seen any of the young horses got by those horses?—I have not.

[illegible]. Do you think their introduction would have any effect on the [illegible] of horses in your district?—I think it would affect the breed of hunters.

[illegible]. In what way, granting that?—Well, from what I can learn. I have no personal knowledge. I am speaking only from what I have learned from the people who have used the Hackney in the district.

[illegible]. That is the general opinion of the people?—Yes, I think that is the opinion of the farmers around.

[illegible]. You cannot say yourself whether the horses are suitable for the district or not?—Not from personal knowledge.

[illegible]. Do you think the farmers would avail themselves of stallions [illegible] being placed in the district?—They would, they are very anxious to [illegible] if they [illegible] at a fee they could pay, but the fees [illegible] and [illegible] are high for a good horse, and they will not take them.

[illegible]. What is the general fee?—£3 or [illegible].

[illegible]. What fees are charged for ordinary country [illegible]?—£3 or £5 for a good-class horse. Personally I had to pay £4. I am not sure what the farmers have to pay. I think it is about [illegible] shillings.

[illegible]. For the ordinary half-bred?—Yes.

[illegible]. And they charge you £5?—Yes.

[illegible]. Mr. [illegible].—The ordinary country stallion?—No, the thoroughbred. I have not bred from any of the half-breds myself, but to the farmers I believe the fee is from a pound to thirty shillings.

[illegible]. Chairman.—What class of mares are there in your district?—The mares are rather weedy and light. We have some good old mares, but the farmers are not breeding. They are [illegible] to rather too light.

[illegible]. What do you mean?—They are keeping them too light, not [illegible] out for the purpose to make [illegible] properly.

[illegible]. How would you suggest the breed should be improved?—Well, if there is a good stallion of a [illegible] they will come on.

[illegible]. Keeping the fillies?—Yes.

[illegible]. What sort of stallion would you suggest as suitable?—I think the thoroughbred for a hunter; a horse with plenty of bone and [illegible].

[illegible]. You would not approve of the half-bred stallion?—I do not think so. They do not [illegible] so well. We have a Yorkshire carriage horse there [illegible], and he is doing rather well. I have seen [illegible] of his foals, two year olds, and they are [illegible] [illegible]. What they will turn out afterwards I do not know, because they have not had time to be [illegible].

[illegible]. Are there any registered sires in your district other than the Royal Dublin Society [illegible]?—I think [illegible], but he [illegible] away. That is the only one in my [illegible] district.

[illegible]. Do they [illegible] in the [illegible] in

operation?—We had a horse show this year, but the Royal Dublin Society only gave a small grant to us.

4898. Is this scheme doing good in your district?—It has not been availed of by us in our immediate district.

4899. The farmers have not taken it up?—No.

4900. Do you approve of the present scheme?—I think it will do good in time, but it will take time.

4901. Mr. FITZWILLIAM.—Why do you think the farmers have not taken up the scheme of the Royal Dublin Society?—Well, I do not know. There is no special reason, only that they are slow to take up anything strange.

4902. They have no radical objection to the scheme?—No, not to my knowledge.

4903. Mr. CHEERS.—You say the farmers are charged £2 for the service of a horse?—From a pound to thirty shillings for the common breed, and £2 for the thoroughbred.

4904. That is much too high?—It is too high. Our farms are small. A large farm would be thirty acres in our district.

4905. You think the introduction of a good thoroughbred sire with bone and substance would improve the breed?—I am certain of it.

4906. At a reasonable fee?—Yes.

4907. The farmers are quite enough alive to their own interests to see the advantage of producing a more desirable horse, or a better horse?—I think so, and I think every stallion should be licensed, they ought to be registered, and pass a thorough examination. In connection with as there have been many blemishes.

4908. Unsoundness in wind and limb you mean by blemishes?—Yes.

4909. Mr. WRENCH.—Your part of Kerry is better than the rest of Kerry, Mr. Donovan?—Yes, it is the better portion.

4910. There is good land around Tralee, I believe?—Yes.

4911. What size are the ordinary mares belonging to the farmers?—They stand from 14.1, an average size.

4912. There are many a good deal smaller, of course?—Yes.

4913. Have they deteriorated or not lately?—For the last few years I do not think they have deteriorated so much.

4914. Have they improved?—No, they are just stationary.

4915. Do you say their greatest fault is that they are weedy?—Yes.

4916. Do you think they are strong enough to go on breeding from thoroughbred horses with these mares?—Not with these mares. There are some of the farmers who have very few mares, but when they are older they do not breed from them. When they are young they sell them; that is, when they have a good mare. They realise the money instead of keeping the mare and making money out of her if she got a good one.

4917. You do not think a thoroughbred would be the right horse to breed from with these weedy mares?—I do not think so.

4918. What horse, then?—A good half-bred would do better.

4919. Then you would approve of a half-bred horse?—For these weedy mares.

4920. What would you call a half-bred horse?—If you could get one out of a real old Irish mare by a thoroughbred sire.

4921. You would be in favour of registering horses bred in that way?—I would.

4922. Do you think there are many of what you call real old Irish mares in the country?—There are in our district a fair number.

4923. You could trace how they are bred?—Yes.

4924. How long has this Yorkshire coach-horse been in that district?—Two or three years.

4925. He is a pedigree Yorkshire coach-horse, is he?—Yes.

4926. What size is he?—About 16.1½.

4927. He would be rather large for some of the smaller mares?—Yes.

4928. Rather a strong sire?—Yes, but his stock are good, and I have seen some from small mares and they are promising well.

4929. Were you at Tralee Show last September?—I was.

4930. Do you remember the class of colts entered for a cup offered by Colonel Cradock?—Yes.

4931. Do you remember the first and second animals there?—Yes; that is Murphy's, I think; I do not well remember.

4932. Were they a good class?—If it is Murphy's you mean—

4933. I am asking was it a good class, those particular animals?—I think so.

4934. Those two?—Yes.

4935. Do you know how they were bred?—I think the one that got the prize was by Waterloo, one of the thoroughbreds standing in the district?—And out of an old Irish mare belonging to a man named Murphy.

4936. And do you know what the reserve horse was by?—No, I do not.

4937. Was he a sire horse?—I can not actually say, because I was not near that class at the show; I had some other things to perform. I was on another committee.

4938. You did take part in the show?—Yes.

4939. What is a good show?—A very fair show.

4940. Was there a good class of mares there?—Well, fair; it was the first we have started for some years time.

4941. A fair number of exhibits altogether?—Yes, a fair number.

4942. Were there many sires exhibited?—Three were shown.

4943. Any cart horses?—Yes, some Clydesdales, three or four.

4944. Practically all the congested districts you do not profess to have much experience?—No, I am not in a congested district myself.

4945. CHAIRMAN.—I take it that you suggest the best sire for the best mares in your district would be the thoroughbred horse?—A thoroughbred is good for them.

4946. And for the inferior class of mare a good half-bred?—Yes.

4947. Mr. CHEERS.—You are strongly in favour of registration?—Yes.

4948. Mr. WRENCH.—I think you have stated that the tendency of the farmers is to sell their good mares?—Yes, when they have a young good-looking mare they generally sell her.

4949. Can you make any suggestion that would tend to make them keep the good mares and breed from them?—I suppose if there was a prize for a certain class—a good brood mare with foal at foot. That would induce people to keep the good ones.

4950. CHAIRMAN.—Something like the Royal Dublin Society's Scheme at present?—Yes.

4951. Thanking you for what you have told us, we—

4952. When you say you are in favour of registration, do you mean for sires as well as mares?—I think so.

J. BUTLER, Waterville, County Kerry, examined.

4953. CHAIRMAN.—You live at Waterville, County Kerry?—Yes.

4954. Have you had any personal experience of horse-breeding?—Considerable experience for the last twenty years. I have bred a lot of horses myself and kept a [illegible] some time ago.

4955. What class of horses did you try to breed?—A good class of horse; I have bred some Hackneys also. In my country it is very little use to try to breed a good horse; a heavy horse in fact, when you have them you could sell them.

4956. What sire did you keep?—A Shire horse, but he did not do very well. The people did not take to him and I got rid of him.

4957. How many [illegible] had several years' [illegible]?—I think about ten mares, very few. I had him only for three years, the people thought him too big and heavy for the district. The small farmers [illegible] a good many. The majority of the farms around are not small. They average from £10 to £20 or £30 a year.

4958. What class of mares have these farmers?—Useful, hardy, active, [illegible] mares.

4959. What size are they?—From 14.2 to 15 hands, the majority of them.

4960. Are there many sires in the country suitable for those little mares?—There has been no sire for some time at all suitable for them, until the Congested Districts Board sent one to Cahirciveen.

4961. You live in a congested district?—I live in the centre of the most congested District in Ireland, I think, certainly the most congested district in the South of Ireland.

4962. Do you consider those sires the most suitable for the district in which you live?—They have done considerably good in the district. They have given the small farmers of the district an animal that will be useful to him for his own work, that is a small, strong, active horse, quiet and easily trained, and he is suitable for the farmers' own work in that district.

4963. What do the farmers do with the horses?—[illegible] work, and for going to market, and drawing light loads, seaweed and sand, that is what they are [illegible].

4964. But do they work the produce on the land before they sell it, or those horses' progeny?—They either keep the foal or sell it at fifteen months old.

4965. They do not work them before they sell them?—They either work or sell them when they are two years old or fifteen months old.

4966. Are the horses in your district improving or [illegible]?—I think they are getting well as animal will.

4967. No difference one way or the other?—Yes, the years there has been nothing but the worst class of [illegible] until quite lately. At first there were [illegible] and only breaking at all, standing in the district of Cahirciveen and around it. There is no thoroughbred horse, except this that one [illegible] years. He [illegible] for three years, but he did not suit the district, though he was a very good horse in his way; "[illegible]" was his name.

4968. Are these young horses sold at fairs or to dealers who come round?—They are principally sold at fairs for local use; bought by the small farmers from [illegible].

4969. They are kept in the **district?—A great many of them.**

4970. Are the prices improving?—The principal fair where farmers sell at is Puck Fair, held at Killorglin every August. I have seen a great many of those sold for the last few years; £25, £26, £27, or £28 would be given for yearlings.

4971. Where were those got by?—A great many of them by the Hackney horse standing in Cahirciveen, that is the third season he has been there. A small farmer, for his own use, when he could get one of those Hackney horses, he preferred it.

4972. You said you had been a Hackney?—The [illegible] I have got by him are only three years old. I have three of his foals.

4973. Do you like the look of the progeny?—Yes, for certain purposes.

4974. What purposes?—Harness work.

4975. Do you think the Hackney stallion introduced into your district will affect the other districts of the county?—Very slightly, indeed.

4976. You think the horses bred in your district are kept in your district, and do not spread to the rest of Kerry?—A great many of them are. It is not what you call a horse breeding country, and the horses bred there are for the very little except for the use of the farmer.

4977. Has the Royal Dublin Society horses been working in your district?—No, not within fifty or sixty miles; there is no horse belonging to the Society.

4978. You do not know anything about the working of it?—I am only of the Congested Districts Board working it there.

4979. Do you think it is working satisfactorily?—No, I do not think the farmers are taking to it. They do not send mares to the horse. It is very up-hill work trying to work it in Kerry.

4980. Have you a sufficient number of sires?—We have three, at Tralee, Castleisland, and Killorglin, but they do not send their mares, and much so [illegible] out to the stallion. In time, I have no doubt, it will do good.

4981. Have any of the farmers in your district got what you would call a really good mare, or are they all those ponies?—I do not know a mare in my district that you would choose if you wished to breed a hunter, with perhaps one or two exceptions.

4982. You think the best fillies are taken away from the district?—They are; consequently, even if they are not good enough to leave the district, the majority of them.

4983. Mr. FITZGERALD.—You say the majority of the farms in your district are extremely small?—Yes.

4984. Are there a great number of those horses bred; do all the farmers breed?—No, not every year, or a year; every second or third year only; and they breed chiefly for their own requirements rather than to sell the progeny when it is a year or a year and a half old.

4985. Where do they sell?—At the local fairs.

4986. I think you said the stallions that had hitherto stood in the district were exceedingly bad?—There are four of them in the district at present, and one of the four, there of them are no bad, as they can be, and the other is a fair horse. That, there has been a Hackney sent down by the Congested Districts Board.

4987. Of the four local stallions there is only one that is of any use?—There are three bad ones in addition. I am not speaking of the Congested Districts Board horse at all.

4988. But there has been one **sent there?—Yes,** for four years now in the district.

4989. How do the fees of the stallions of horses compare? What do they charge for the services of those animals?—For a small farmer usually the fee will be [illegible] or [illegible] shillings for a quarter of a [illegible].

4990. What does the Congested Districts Board [illegible]?—A nominal [illegible] for the mare, of five shillings.

4991. That is what the farmer pays?—Yes.

4992. Are any of the sires of the Congested Districts Board horse [illegible] for work?—Yes, [illegible]. I know one or two [illegible] year old, that [illegible] there, and they are working.

4993. Do they ever [illegible]?—Yes, and they [illegible] them in light carts.

Mr. J. [illegible].

5998. You have seen these [illegible]?

5999. Would you approve of a half-bred horse [illegible] down to your country, [illegible] shape, make, and action [illegible] horse for that district would be what I call a [illegible] size, a [illegible], [illegible] well [illegible] and [illegible].

6000. If you could you would like to have the produce of one of these [illegible] mares?—A very good [illegible], and a good [illegible] a good class of horse.

6001. [illegible] to [illegible].

6002. Mr. Chairman.—Rather than the Hackney [illegible]? Yes, I think [illegible] the Hackney [illegible] would be the most suitable, and a good [illegible] in the district.

6003. A well-bred half-bred [illegible] with a good dash of thoroughbred blood [illegible]. [illegible] why the horses are so bad [illegible] the first year or year and a half they are not properly fed. Unless you feed a horse well while he is young, he will never turn out well, in my experience.

6004. Are you in favour of registering stallions? [illegible] should be registered by the Government, [illegible] certificate to say that they are free from hereditary disease.

6005. [illegible] the certificate?—Anything hereditary. I would do away with all the [illegible] if possible; [illegible].

6006. Mr. Wrench.—You kept a [illegible] stallion [illegible]?—I did, eight or nine years ago.

6007. [illegible]?—No.

6008. Do you think a Clydesdale would be more [illegible]?—[illegible].

6009. [illegible] a more suitable [illegible] than a Hackney for [illegible]?—I think [illegible].

6010. But you think the Hackney is the right cross to begin with?—For the present.

6011. [illegible]?—Yes.

6012. [illegible] in addition to your own [illegible]?—Yes, I have [illegible].

6013. [illegible] much the same [illegible]?—Yes, sir. [illegible]. The [illegible] is a better class of [illegible].

6014. [illegible] good [illegible] will be able to go through very hard [illegible]?—Yes.

6015. [illegible] something that will do hard work and not [illegible]?—Yes, and be [illegible] quiet and easily handled.

6016. And you think the Hackneys do that?—So far as I can see they do.

6017. Have the fees charged for the local stallions been reduced since the horse was sent there by the Congested Districts Board?—They would not reduce their [illegible]; they charged ten shillings and sometimes [illegible].

6018. The owners of local stallions [illegible] for the [illegible] of [illegible] shillings?—Yes, they take it as they get it.

6019. Whereas the Board charge [illegible] shillings on the [illegible]?—Yes, [illegible].

6020. So the people like [illegible] as well as the [illegible]. They would [illegible] the ten shillings to pay as they like, than the five shillings on the spot?—Yes. I think there have been [illegible] in [illegible] the Board's horse [illegible] every year [illegible].

6016. He has got his full number?—Most years. I do not know about this year, but I know the first year he could have got a great deal more than his number. They would not be taken.

6017. Do you know whether they have got better prices for the produce of this stallion?—They have got from £1 to £1 10s., sometimes £2 more for the produce of the Hackney than for the produce of the ordinary sire.

6018. And the price of horses has been falling all the time?—The price of that class of horse has not fallen as much as the others, it was always very low. That class is bought by small farmers for their own use.

6019. How did the produce of the Hackney look as compared with their dams?—They are stouter, and a considerable improvement as far as shape and [illegible].

6020. Were you at [illegible]?—I was.

6021. Do you remember the class I asked Mr. [illegible] about?—Yes; I have a catalogue here.

6022. Was it a good class all round?—It was a very fair class, very good considering.

6023. Do you remember how many horses there were in the class?—Twelve entries for "two year olds [illegible], suitable for [illegible] purposes." The class was for horses over two and under three.

6024. Do you know how the horse that took first place was bred?—By a sire called Wanderer, a thoroughbred.

6025. And the second?—The [illegible] or Second [illegible] was got by "[illegible] the Second," a horse bred at [illegible] by a Hackney. It was by King [illegible].

6026. Have you any scheme you would suggest by which people could be induced to keep their best [illegible]?—I think the great thing for improving the breed is to have good sires. If you keep on having good sires you will improve the breed eventually. [illegible], they [illegible] good, but I have no suggestion to make to induce them to keep them.

6027. You think the sire is the chief thing, and you know of no practical way to induce the people to keep their best mares?—No practical way.

6028. Chairman.—As far as I gather, you had some idea of the horse for the district was that the Hackney [illegible]; have you any special reason for putting the Hackney [illegible]?—The Hackney [illegible] a [illegible] amount of [illegible]. My idea would be to get [illegible] from a [illegible].

6029. You would choose the Hackney [illegible]?—I would take the horses [illegible].

6030. Mr. Fitzwilliam.—You think suitable [illegible] might be produced if there was a thoroughbred, half-bred [illegible], with a good dash of thoroughbred blood in them, for the purpose of [illegible] these different [illegible]?—I think it would be very hard to [illegible].

6031. If the demand were created, do you think it would soon be supplied?—If the demand were created, and the man who bred that class of horse were induced to keep them without selling them—if the demand was there, you would get the horse.

6032. If you could get them you would prefer them to any other?—I would, for this district.

6033. Mr. Wrench.—Do you know of any [illegible]?—No, not in that district; I have [illegible].

6034. Do you know of any special horse you would like to [illegible]?—Not that I can name at the present moment.

6035. The [illegible] you suggest should be bred [illegible]?—I think so.

6036. He does not exist at present?—[illegible].

6037. At present?—I am afraid not.

6038. Chairman.—Have you any suggestion to

make as to how you would encourage the breed of him?—I think if such an animal was there he would be bought. If he was there certain men would breed from him.

5038. Would you be in favour of the Royal Dublin Society taking half-bred sires on their register?—For the congested districts I would, but not for ordinary service in what you call horse-breeding districts. For districts like Mallow and Fermoy and around there, I think nothing more suitable than a good thoroughbred, but in my district a thoroughbred would be no use.

5039. Mr. Wrench.—Do you think the hunter sire would be as good as the Hackney for action?—I think a great deal of the Hackney action is much, and they are better without it.

5040. Do you think the foals have too much action?—No, not too much.

5041. Mr. Carew.—At the time of the introduction of the Hackney into your district, you would have preferred a hunter?—Yes.

5042. Chairman.—Have you any other suggestion to make?—Nothing; but I am afraid the introduction of bicycles and motor cars will injure the Hackney.

5043. Mr. Wrench.—Is Kerry a good county for bicycling?—The finest in Ireland.

Jan. 9, 1900.
Mr. J. Barker.

Mr. George Hewson, Drumshanbo, County Leitrim, examined.

Mr. George Hewson.

5044. Chairman.—You live in Leitrim and have [illegible] on the borders of Leitrim and Sligo.

5045. You are a land agent there, and own some property yourself?—Yes.

5046. Do you breed horses yourself?—I keep them, two or three brood mares as a rule.

5047. Are there a great many horses bred round your district?—A great many have been. The farmers are rather going out of breeding lately.

5048. What is the reason of that?—The reason of it, in my opinion, is that it is so very difficult to sell anything now, unless [illegible] up to weight.

5049. What class of horses have you bred yourself?—I have, up to [illegible] great [illegible] bred from a thoroughbred horse out of a half-bred mare. I have [illegible] years ago a Hackney in a [illegible] a fairly bred mare to try what would come of it.

5050. What was your experience?—I have been [illegible] [illegible] the produce. I have [illegible] [illegible]. On [illegible] occasions the mare did not hold, on one the foal died, and I bought [illegible] [illegible] [illegible] with the other one.

5051. That is your personal experience?—Yes, I have also been looking at the foals got by Hackney horses.

5052. What is your opinion of the foals?—In my opinion the Hackney horse does not do with the ordinary country bred mares. I do not like the look of the foals. They are a heavy, lumpy sort of animal without any action. I think very likely with a small, fairly bred mare the Hackney would do well.

5053. What class of mares are in your district?—A good many half-bred mares, and farmers [illegible] [illegible] a good many. In Sligo there are a great many good mares, but I do not think the farmers are sufficiently alive to the fact that they should be mated. I think they will breed from a good-looking mare, [illegible] [illegible] [illegible].

5054. Are they small or big?—From 14.3 to 15.2 in Leitrim; 15 to 16 in Sligo.

5055. Do they work those mares on the land?—[illegible] country. Many [illegible] a few [illegible]. There are a good many small farms and big farms as well.

5056. You do not think the Hackney suitable for your district?—No, I do not.

5057. At what age do they sell the horses, as a rule, from neighbourhood?—Smaller farmers sell foals. The farmers mostly want to sell them at sixteen-year-olds; now they have to wait till they are three or five.

5058. This is the bigger farmers?—All farmers who breed horses, [illegible] keep them to work on their farms.

5059. Work them first and then sell them when they get aged?—You start working them at two old.

5060. Do you think it is [illegible] them to break in [illegible] [illegible] as [illegible]?—[illegible] [illegible] [illegible] [illegible] [illegible] [illegible] [illegible] entirely in the back.

5061. What class of horses would you recommend the farmers to breed?—I would be [illegible] by a thoroughbred horse out of a half-bred mare, and [illegible] this should be done by all breeders. I do a great deal of driving busy [illegible]. I prefer driving any kind than [illegible] of horse. They are excellent [illegible] general [illegible] purposes. They do not [illegible] me well as four or five year olds. In fact I cannot get anything like the prices I got ten years ago for them.

5062. If you wanted the farmers of your district to make money by breeding, what course would you suggest they should take?—In the first place the Government should assist them by giving them a market for their lighter horses, which in my opinion would do very well for troopers.

5063. You think they will be troopers?—Yes, I think so.

5064. Don't they buy troopers in your district?—Yes, they are bought by dealers who make their own market, and give nothing like the full value.

5065. You mean the Government should send a representative directly themselves and buy?—To a great extent, yes; but I think depots should be formed in various districts where suitable horses of this class are bred, and the horses should be bought direct from the farmers. If the Government cannot [illegible] [illegible] them as three-year-olds, I think they should buy them from the farmers and send them to these depots for a year. That would get over the difficulty entirely.

5066. What class of land is about you?—A very mixed class of land. It is very [illegible] land around me, a great deal of limestone, and a great deal of boggy country over the limestone. The latter I think [illegible] horses.

5067. The cattle bog on limestone?—Not exactly bog; but [illegible] [illegible] limestone land [illegible] [illegible] years gone by [illegible] [illegible] and has been reclaimed.

5068. You prefer to breed horses on that rather than limestone?—I have both classes of land, and I find my horses do a great deal better on that than on a purely limestone farm.

5069. In what respect?—They grow bigger, and have better limbs. I know that is against the general theory, but it is what I have found in practice. There is limestone all round of the farm I talk of.

5070. What class of sires are in your district?—Around my district we only have two or three sires. In Sligo they have an excellent lot. "Sir George" has got most excellent weight horses, and "[illegible]" who has just been sold out of the country, was in my opinion a beautiful horse. Sir George is now old, a good thoroughbred is much wanted.

5071. Is that a thoroughbred horse?—Yes, the sire of "Drum Forgan." In my opinion he was rather too light for the country. I think what we [illegible] is a nearly thoroughbred, giving a better weight horse than the light thoroughbred.

5072. A heavy thoroughbred?—Yes. This is Mayo, where I bought a good many horses, they had a most excellent strain of horses got originally by "Blackbird" and by "[illegible]," who got first-class stock.

Nov. 12, [illegible]. — Mr. George [illegible].

5073. Are you on the borders of Meath?—No, but I very often go there, and I have bought horses in Dublin.

5074. Are there any half-bred horses in your district?—There was one, and he was a very good horse, and there were two or three more. I don't suppose [illegible] the good one was called "Dandy," belonging to a man named Dixon. I bought his breeding, but he got good stock.

5075. Would you be in favour of the Royal Dublin Society subsidising good half-bred sires?—Yes, under certain conditions. Give them a license and subsidise them as well. You cannot prevent any man keeping any sire he likes, but if a man applied to the Royal Dublin Society to have his horse registered, and got a subsidy of £15 or £20 a year for keeping him, it would enable him to give that horse cheaper to the farmers, and by degrees they would use the suitable sires.

5076. Would you agree to these horses being registered under the same conditions as thoroughbreds are, provided they pass good horses?—Yes, while on that subject I do not think the present scheme of the Royal Dublin Society is nearly as good as the old one, which was subsidising sires. A good many mares used to go to the local shows when a subsidy was given to the sire, and they got the service at a cheaper rate. Now it is a matter of speculation when farmers have to go to a thoroughbred horse, [illegible] the chances of getting a prize at the local shows, the prizes don't work. At our local shows, for instance, at a place called Mountnugent, speaking for Leinster only, we had three aged mares, three young mares, and three foals to show. In another district, Mullagh, we had only two young mares, three aged, and a foal. In Carrick we had only one mare. Originally, while the sires were subsidised, we had a great deal better showing. I should like to say also on that question that the Dublin Society's plan was not altogether a good way of registering such stock. In any application that came to them I understand, if the horse was sound they registered him as a Government sire without practically seeing the horse as to whether he was really suitable for the district.

5077. I think we had it in evidence that that was not the case?—I was surprised to think [illegible] the amount of [illegible] horses, one being a very [illegible] powerful horse, and the other a very weedy horse that was not suitable at all for the country.

5078. Mr. Wrench.—Are they on the register now?—One of them is, the other is not.

5079. Mr. [illegible].—Which is on the register, the [illegible] one?—Yes, I think so. The [illegible]. The [illegible].

5080. Mr. Wrench.—Is that in Leinster?—I should not like to say which county it is.

5081. Chairman.—Have you any other suggestions to make about the Royal Dublin Society scheme?—No, but I would like to say that I think the Horse Show in Dublin has very much spoiled the country markets. All you can sell is a made hunter, and it becomes necessary to the small farmer to send up a horse to the Show. The entrance fee is under £10, which takes a considerable amount of the price of an average horse. I think if the local shows were encouraged, and that a class at the local shows was opened for troopers, a trooper class, and if there was a trooper class at the Royal Dublin Society Show, it would assist the breed of the ordinary horse very much. I am very much afraid that [illegible] will go [illegible] of breeding horses for the reason that they cannot dispose of their [illegible] horses, and that in the course of [illegible] a lot of [illegible] being [illegible] will not be [illegible] longer.

5082. If it cost you £10 for bringing a horse to Dublin, it would hardly be worth bringing it to get a trooper price?—I am only speaking of the [illegible] to have local shows for troopers, but I think it would pay the Dublin and Meath men to send to Dublin Show if there was a class for troopers.

5083. Do you mean to suggest that the money given by the Royal Dublin Society for the improvement of horses should be sent to local shows?—Yes, but I say the Government should give a considerable amount more than now for that purpose. Of course the argument is that the army estimates are framed on certain lines, and, your army estimates, you cannot spend more than a certain amount on troopers, but if the Government came to the rescue in another department, I think it could be done.

5084. What stallion do you think most suitable for your district?—I think the strong thoroughbred is.

5085. You would be in favour of a good half-bred being used too?—In my neighbourhood the difficulty is that these good thoroughbreds are fourteen and fifteen miles away, and in the districts where that is the case, such as mine, I think the Government should send down a horse if possible.

5086. Then you do not think there are a sufficient number of suitable sires in your district?—No, there are not; they are all huddled up in one spot a long way off, and people have too far to go.

5087. Are there any registered sires near you?—The nearest is fourteen miles, and a farmer will not go that distance.

5088. Is there a ready market?—There used to be an excellent market ten or twelve years ago. I brought a string of young horses into Boyle fair, for instance, and friends of mine have done the same. There we used to sell at £30 or £40 apiece for a three-year-old; now you would not get anything like that price.

5089. For what purpose were they sold?—Mostly as troopers. Now you go to the same Boyle fair on the 1st of October, which was our great market for getting rid of that class of long-tail, and we cannot sell them at all. I had one horse, a four-year-old mare, by a horse called "Dalhousie," and should not have had the slightest difficulty in getting £35 ten years ago. I asked £30 and did not get a bid. I told my man to ask £10, to see if he could induce anyone to bid. I should not have sold her at it, of course, but there was nobody to make a bid. At Ballinasloe fair I sold a five-year-old mare, by "Duncombe" by "Sparalvan," sound and a good jumper—I sold her to Byrne for £22, when I could have got £30 for her ten years ago.

5090. Mr Fitzwilliam.—Have you any suggestion to make with regard to trying to keep the good mares in the country?—No; I think it is an impossibility, as things go at present. I think if you go in for breeding from a better class of horse, you will by degrees get a better class of mare, and they will stop in the country whether you will or no. If you improve your mares up to a better standard, you will have a great many more good mares to keep.

5091. If you have only a limited amount of money, should you prefer to spend it on subsidising good stallions throughout the different districts?—I think it would pay a great deal better, spending the money on the stallion. The stallion owner has much the greater risk. It costs a lot of money to get his stallion and to keep his stallion, as well as advertising and everything else.

5092. In England, under the Queen's Premiums, the arrangement is to give £200 to the stallion owner, and the horse is obliged to cover a certain number of mares in his district at a certain price—£2, I think?—I think that would be a most excellent arrangement in Ireland. They allowance to our county duty arrangement, which has to go to several stallions. I think if there could be such an arrangement as there is in England it would tend to improve the class of horses in this country.

5093. What breed of stallion would you suggest as the best?—I think, in the first instance, a strong thoroughbred, certainly. Later on, I should say a [illegible] half-bred by a thoroughbred horse out of a really nice [illegible], well [illegible], and [illegible].

[illegible]. And you think there would be calculated [illegible] things [illegible] class [illegible], [illegible] I will say, the [illegible] is [illegible] to the [illegible]?—Yes, and as a proof of that, I may say I have [illegible] of [illegible] at the [illegible] fair, in the [illegible], which is the great [illegible] for the North, and I had no [illegible] in [illegible].

8097. What sort of [illegible] do you think a good stallion [illegible] would, or [illegible] a thoroughbred [illegible] half-breds, what fee do you think he would [illegible] to pay from about £4 to £5, but I think the farmer would pay [illegible] if the horse was [illegible], and I think that would be [illegible].

8098. Mr. Carew.—You say there is a great depression [illegible] within the last [illegible] years?—Yes.

8099. Was [illegible] to the quality of the [illegible] compared with the one you sold [illegible] ago?—No.

8100. How do you account for that depression?—The very fact that the ordinary [illegible] horse is [illegible] you would [illegible] frequently, and that he has gone [illegible]. The heavy-weight horse, of course, is a [illegible] and will always command a big price, [illegible].

8101. You suggested the Government should open [illegible] in the different districts for [illegible], and [illegible] them out?—Yes.

8102. Mr. Watson.—You say the mares in your district are from 14.3 to 15.3?—Yes.

8103. Have they much [illegible] blood, or any [illegible] blood?—A few of them have. I have a Clydesdale mare I bred from, and bred very good foals from a thoroughbred horse.

8104. Do you think, as a rule, the mares would be [illegible] a thoroughbred horse?—[illegible].

8105. He would be the most generally useful horse at the present time?—Yes.

8106. You gave an opinion to the Congested Districts Board that a Norfolk trotter would be a good horse to [illegible]?—Yes, but I have changed my mind from seeing the foals of the [illegible] horse.

8107. Have you seen any foals from the horse [illegible] or these two years [illegible]?—No.

8108. [illegible] from the horse there now?—Yes; I saw my own foal from the horse that was in [illegible] last year, but I do not think it would be a fair [illegible] to [illegible] him. The [illegible] small [illegible] half-bred mare [illegible], and [illegible]; but I think the size of the foal was the mare's own fault. She had not milk enough for him, and he died.

8109. Did you know that the horse he sent there before, [illegible], was the only [illegible] of Norfolk blood [illegible]?—I think [illegible] was supposed to be a Yorkshire.

8110. Was [illegible]?—[illegible] you are right. That is the horse you allude to.—Yes. I think the cross between the Hackney and the really fairly bred mare would probably get a good [illegible] for the [illegible], but the [illegible] that there is so very limited I do not think it should be encouraged generally.

8111. Do you think the farmers would send to a thoroughbred horse if it was sent there?—I am perfectly certain they would, if they had popular prices.

8112. At present I believe Leitrim is the only county in Ireland where there is not a thoroughbred horse standing?—I think so; we are very badly off for that reason. It is a long narrow county, and a horse at the northern end would not be [illegible] at the southern end.

8113. The horses come to Sligo?—Yes, and in North Leitrim we go to Sligo a good deal.

8114. Do you know any half-bred horse in your county that would be worth registering?—The [illegible] of [illegible] if he was alive.

8115. You do not know how he was bred?—No, he got excellent stock, [illegible], big [illegible] and [illegible].

8116. He was a half-bred horse?—Yes.

8117. This horse you offered for £50, was also a well-bred [illegible]?—Yes, a well-bred four-year-old. What I want to emphasise is that the [illegible] in this country have [illegible] in the last, something must be done to create some kind of a [illegible]. Though we are [illegible], I [illegible] this question. I think the [illegible] is really the [illegible] one.

8118. The people must breed some animals for their own use?—Yes.

8119. That must go on whether there are [illegible] and [illegible] or not?—I think so, certainly.

8120. A certain amount of breeding must go on, and the question is how that can be [illegible]?—Quite so.

8121. Would you call it a paying business to breed from your own mares animals only good enough for [illegible]?—What I find is that for ordinary [illegible] purposes, you will get a big horse out [illegible] of the same horse and the same [illegible] and possibly a small one the next year out of the same horse and mare. It is those smaller horses that take the place of the [illegible]. Whatever you make on the big one you lose on the small. That is really what is [illegible] the [illegible] in my county of breeding.

T. W. Watson, Kellyville, Athy.

Mr. T. W. Watson

8122. Chairman.—You live in the Queen's County?—Yes.

8123. And you have bred a good many horses yourself?—Yes, I began thirty years ago, and have bred nearly every year since.

8124. What class of horses?—Every sort. I have bred every kind.

8125. What kinds have you tried to breed?—Principally the hunter; our county is suitable for hunters.

8126. Is the [illegible] able to breed a good [illegible] with plenty of bone?—Yes. The difficulty is to get plenty of bone.

8127. Will you describe to us some of the difficulties?—I have bred from good hunter mares I have [illegible], up to fourteen stone. I put them to the best thoroughbred and got a light-weight [illegible] up to no weight and worth about £30 generally; in one case out of [illegible] I got a first prize horse at the [illegible] of quality, but the majority [illegible] light; that is, when bred from the hunter mare and the thoroughbred, the only way I can succeed in breeding a hunter is to have a [illegible] or [illegible] mare from the old Irish mare; I have got two of them now that I breed from with the best horse I can get, a horse called "[illegible]." He is a tremendous big horse and the mares are [illegible]; they are the old Irish breed, as near as I can get them; perhaps they may have one cross of the thoroughbred. I consider, [illegible], [illegible] of the [illegible] with the old Irish mare is the best; that is the only way you can get a weight carrier; [illegible] light [illegible] that you cannot get a weight-carrier for hunters with thoroughbred sires.

8128. What do you mean by an old Irish mare?—In my younger days there were plenty of the [illegible] at the Athy [illegible], and the old Irish [illegible]; that they would not part with for anything, and they bred their grandmothers and great grandmothers; they said they would part with the [illegible].

[illegible]

Mr. T. W. Walsh.

the mares and they considered so long as they kept the old stock of mares they would do well, but they found in many cases that the difficulty was to get the stallions of the same breed. There are very few of the old Irish stallions existing now because the Royal Dublin Society has discouraged the Irish breeds and given only prizes for the English breeds, consequently he is scarce in the country.

5128. You mean the old half-bred stallion?—I don't call him a half-bred, I call him the old Irish stallion, they used to exist, but now there are very few owing to the failure of the Royal Dublin Society to encourage the old Irish breed; it is very hard to get now, but I still believe it could be done if prizes were given, and I think in time you would get up a stock of them.

5129. You mean to make a sort of half-breed?—I would not call it a half-breed.

5130. Can you get them with pedigrees to rely on?—If you search, I believe you can find them. You can only take the animals as you see them, as near as you can possibly get to what you want, and if the progeny goes wrong you reject the bad ones and keep the good ones.

5131. Do the farmers round about you breed many horses?—A vast number.

5132. What stallions do they use?—They used the thoroughbred till they got sick of him; they cannot get the old Irish stallion and they have to take to the Shire horse.

5133. What class of mares have they got?—The progeny of the old Irish mares; the old Irish mares I look on as the parent stock of the famous Irish hunter, they have been crossed for years with the thoroughbred, and they have got too small, and the farmer has found that it does not pay him to breed, and he has had to mate with the clumsy Clydesdale or Shire horse in order to get size.

5134. Would you advocate breeding from the Clydesdale or Shire horse?—Certainly not, if I could get the old Irish horse; I prefer the old Irish horse stallion.

5135. These are mares still?—They are the mares that got most of the progeny, and the farmer finds it does not pay him to breed from the thoroughbred unless he has got a very big mare; the mares are getting smaller and he has to go to the Clydesdale or Shire for size.

5136. Do they work the mares?—Yes, they cannot afford to breed unless they do.

5137. They don't work the young ones?—No, they are broken into harness, three or four years old.

5137a. Are there a sufficient number of them in your district?—I think there are plenty.

5138. Do they sell the animals?—There are too many thoroughbreds—and half-breds plenty of them, and the great thing that is wanting is the old Irish stallion. I have got a Shire stallion myself, and he is rough enough of himself, he is clean legged and has good action. I find most of his progeny has been sold as heavy hunters, and I know a few hunters they will breed good hunters with good action. I know one or two that are likely to take very well before the judges at the show as weight-carriers.

5139. You don't know how they will turn out in the field?—The Dublin Society can't in any way guarantee that a horse will stand up in the field.

5140. What chiefly influences a farmer in your district in sending his mare to the stock?—The farmers are influenced by cheapness; they will send to the nearest horse whatever he may happen to be, and will give £1, but the better class who have a fancy for breeding and have been breeding for a great number of years are very particular about their sires.

5141. They don't mind the fee if they get the right sire?—They don't mind the fee; they will give £5 readily and £3 in other cases.

5142. Was there not a horse in your district called "Prince Imperial"?—Yes.

5143. Can you describe him?—He is pretty near the old Irish stallion; a big Irish cart horse; clean in the heels, over 16 hands, he has good action, and is able to carry 15 stone to hounds.

5144. What sort of stock has he got?—I have seen a good many of his foals; I have got one myself; they are not sufficiently old to tell what they are going to turn out, but they look well; they are rather disappointing in size, but then may be because of the farmers putting small mares to the horse believing him a big horse.

5145. Where did he come from?—He belongs to Mr. McMahon, of the Cahir Stud Farm. He had his father have owned stallions for years, and he told me he got this horse from some place in the mountainous district of Tipperary, and he gave me his pedigree; no doubt he may not be a pure old Irish stallion, but he is the nearest thing to it; he has got none of the Clydesdale or Shire in him.

5146. A clean legged cart horse?—Yes, that is what you want.

5147. Have the prices gone up or down in your district?—The price of good weight-carrying hunters is as high as ever. I was at a fair last week, and they were asking £200 for their three-year-olds, and they bought from the farmers; the price for them is as good as ever and better, but the price for small horses is not so good.

5148. A good horse is easily sold?—A good horse is readily sold. There is a buyer for Mr. Rhodes, of Leamington, buying up good weight-carrying horses as fast as he can get them.

5149. What is your opinion of the half-bred?—I don't think the half-bred exists in this country; they are all mongrels.

5150. You would not put the old Irish horse you talk of under the definition of a half-bred?—No, the half-bred is a sort of mongrel; nobody knows how he is bred, he may have a cross with a thoroughbred in him; they don't exist, I think. What I would understand by a half-bred is a first cross between a Clydesdale and a thoroughbred, or a first cross between a Shire and a thoroughbred, or a first cross between a Hackney and a race horse.

5151. Anything else is a first cross between two pure breeds?—Yes.

5152. Would you be in favour of the Royal Dublin Society registering some of these stallions you tell about?—I would not exactly put it that way. I would be in favour of establishing a stud book for weight-carrying hunters. I have written to the *Field* and also to other papers as much as twenty-five years ago upon the subject, advocating the formation of a stud book for weight-carrying hunters, and the method I proposed was that the Royal Dublin Society should give prizes for weight-carrying hunters to be entered. I consider a good deal of money is thrown away by giving prizes to weight-carrying hunters that nobody recognises their sires; it doesn't encourage anything, and there no good except getting the owner a good price for his horse. It would be much better if they gave some of the money to weight-carrying hunters on the sires, observed for breeding, and entered in the stud book for weight-carrying hunters.

5153. You would register mares as well as males?—Certainly. The principle of forming a breed is recommended by this and the like—the same principle that is adopted in breeding every kind of stock; the shorthorns were bred from an original family; they only mated them and them; in the various breeds of sheep it is the same and then, and the Hackneys, who have a complete Stud Book very originated in a small number of animals, and now they are breeding a pure breed; also the race horse was not a pure breed originally; bred originally from four different sources, the Arab, the Turk, the old English mare, and the Barb.

5154. You suggest forming a breed of hunters?—Yes, in the same way that you form a breed of cart horse, breeding in from the members of the same family until you get a breed of a permanent type in the same way that Booth and Bates bred shorthorns from a small family until they got them to be a permanent type, and until they got excellence and size, and everything else.

5153. The land about your district apparently doesn't breed bone?—It doesn't; part of it does; it is not the breeding altogether that makes the bone; it is the grass as well.

5154. Horses bred on most of your district are not inclined to breed bone?—Half and half. You must give your young horses oats in the winter to make them grow, a good deal in limestone land where horses will grow to a good size with plenty of bone.

5155. Do the farmers treat their young horses well?—They do, those that buy breeding. Of course there are some poorer fellows that cannot afford to do it, but those who follow their own horses treat them well, and keep them out all the winter on the winter grass, and give them plenty of hay and some oats occasionally.

5156. Mr. Fitzwilliam.—You talked about the old Irish stallion—I forget if you told us if you could trace his pedigree in any way, how he was originally bred?—He was originally bred very simply, he was the old Irish pack horse that was bred on the mountains, and was used for carrying packs. There was no introduction of English blood, but they have been crossed so often that it is hard to find the old Irish blood, but there is a good deal of it still.

5157. Do you think it could be traced?—Yes, I think so. I believe I could pick out a half-dozen myself.

5158. And this horse "Prince Imperial," you say you have got this horse's pedigree—can you give it?—No. You will have to ask Mr. M'Mahon for that.

5159. Without knowing the names of the animals he is bred from you know how he is bred?—He told me he was bred in a mountainous part where they had a good deal of the old Irish stock.

5160. Yet you say his foals are small?—I could not judge from one individual of that class, but I have known several old Irish horses that got magnificent big horses; there were some in the district around me some years ago, the old Irish, and they got splendid big horses, that were very good for troopers and also the mares for breeding hunters.

5161. You say the mares round you have deteriorated you think in size, don't you think that to a great extent is from the farmer selling the good produce and keeping the bad?—I think it is the want of large sized stallions.

5162. Is it a fact that they have sold their best mares—that they don't keep their best mares?—I don't think they do; they like to sell their colts; if they have a good mare they will work her on the farm and keep her for breeding, but the difficulty is to get the mare big enough owing to the scarcity of old Irish blood.

5163. Suppose you cannot obtain the old Irish blood, would you object to an animal—a half bred—but you seem to think there is no such thing?—I don't know what you would describe as that.

5164. What I should call a well-bred hunter—would you object to breed from that?—No, I think he is a good animal but he requires improving on the system I have recommended by giving prizes for weight-carrying hunters—entire—you would have to subsidise them in some way.

5165. I think you would have to subsidise the rider too. I don't think you would get any great number of gentlemen to hunt these entire horses?—You would not require a very great number of them and they would not be kept for hunting; it would be a limited class; a small number would be sufficient to start the breed. I think that for breeding weight-carrying hunters the first way is the best, and that would be to have a stud book for them and register pure bred of them; but the second best way is to breed from the large Irish mare from the thoroughbred; but your difficulty is to get a large Irish mare, and you cannot get that without encouraging the Irish breed.

5166. To make up a new breed would take a long time?—It would.

5167. How many years—how many generations would you require?—I wrote an essay for Lord Cadogan twenty-five years ago in which I advocated the establishment of a stud for weight-carrying hunters of pure breed, and I think if adopted then for more than thirty years the breed would have become pretty well established by this. But the prize for that essay was given to the mongrel system of [illegible]—accidental mating—which I condemn. When you breed [illegible] you don't [illegible] the bloodhound with the [illegible] to produce the [illegible]—you breed from [illegible] and [illegible], and therefore you get a pure-bred animal that will propagate his race. Why not have the same principle when dealing with the most valuable animal of all, the horse.

5168. Mr. [illegible].—You say there are some Irish bred mares in the country now?—Yes, a few.

5169. You know [illegible]?—There is one in my district. I heard of several some years ago.

5170. You would like those for propagating this breed [illegible] with the Irish draught mare?—Yes, I think so, but they could not [illegible].

5171. You have old Irish bred mares?—Yes.

5172. How are they bred?—I bought one of them off one farm; a farmer who had had the breed for generations, and this was a [illegible] got by a Welsh horse. I consider that the Welsh [illegible] is the nearest thing to the old Irish, and that the old Irish would [illegible] be improved by the [illegible] of the Welsh [illegible] not so heavy as the English [illegible], and not so heavy as the [illegible]. You might very safely use [illegible] for establishing a breed similar to the old Irish breed; that is, a breed of horse good in [illegible], with [illegible], which [illegible] jumping powers, which [illegible]. The [illegible] "Knight of St. Patrick" [illegible]. I believe he was an old Irish horse.

5173. A hunter sire?—Yes, a hunter horse.

5174. And you think if the Royal Dublin Society established this form of breeding it would improve the breed of horses generally?—Yes, they might improve them by a cross with the Welsh cart horse. I have seen the progeny of the Welsh cart horse—that is a big strong horse with plenty of bone and activity to go up and down mountains which gives the jumping power.

5175. And you find that there is no great prize obtainable for the weight-carrying hunter now as ever?—Yes, [illegible]. I make another suggestion—this is with regard to Connemara ponies.

5176. You had better keep to your own district?—Because I am asking these questions, and I am asking about my [illegible]. I buy them young, [illegible] a [illegible] than [illegible] of [illegible]. I buy two or three every year. I have got some now [illegible] to [illegible]. I can show you two that I don't think can possibly be improved upon for carrying [illegible] weight over country safely and fast. If you could encourage that type of [illegible] and Connemara pony it would be a great thing, and I think the Royal Dublin Society would do well to give prizes for Connemara ponies of that stamp and encourage their breed as much as possible, and stick to type, the breed. I could show photographs of those ponies.

5177. Mr. [illegible].—Have you got these with you?—No, but I could send them to the [illegible]; [illegible] his galloping is quite fast enough. I don't think any

Nov. 18, 1897.
[illegible]

[illegible] Mr. [illegible] Pennington [illegible].

5210. [illegible] for having good Hackneys?—[illegible] a very large [illegible].

5211. This is [illegible]. You will be glad to hear that we have not [illegible] any of the Hackneys [illegible] in regard to the [illegible] of the Hackney. I think the Hackney is a splendid [illegible] for the North of Ireland [illegible] horses, but if you want to [illegible] the racing horses or [illegible] I would not [illegible] of them.

5212. If it was decided to buy any of these old Irish stallions, do you think it would be possible to [illegible] them?—I think it would.

5213. They still exist?—They do; it would take a good deal of [illegible] out, but there are [illegible] who still keep the old breed. [illegible] the Welsh [illegible] would help.

5214. I think you said a good many [illegible] were [illegible]?—A good many.

5215. Do you think it [illegible] to say that a horse is [illegible] by a thoroughbred in order to [illegible]?—I think the farmers speak [illegible] what they [illegible] by.

[illegible]

[illegible] how they were bred?—You might make plenty of [illegible], but as a rule they would get [illegible] by going to their houses and talking to them.

5220. You would [illegible] of the Royal Dublin Society—you would [illegible] horses [illegible]?—Yes, [illegible] to be [illegible] for breeding.

5221. Would you [illegible] to be shown [illegible] for other horses [illegible] thoroughbred [illegible]; why should you [illegible] other horses and only admit the [illegible]?—I would [illegible] the best [illegible].

5222. You think [illegible] good thoroughbred [illegible] is [illegible]?—[illegible].

5223. [illegible] breeding [illegible] you must [illegible] and [illegible] that you find [illegible] breeding too [illegible] from the [illegible] that you have [illegible]. The average of the [illegible] horse is [illegible] inches below the knee, the average of the [illegible] horse is [illegible] inches; [illegible] inches.

5224. [illegible] a half inches [illegible]?—I would like to [illegible] and a half inches. All the [illegible] in the world [illegible] unless it is in the [illegible].

5225. [illegible]

[illegible]

Mr. [illegible], Turlough Lodge, Castlebar.

[illegible]

[illegible] What part of the county are you in?—Turlough, near Castlebar.

[illegible]

over by Mr. Mitchell, who lives in Tourmakeady, and I used him with small Connemara ponies, and got wonderful good ponies, about 13.2.

5245. What horse was that?—Star of the West.

5246. Did you sell any of this stock at all?—No, I have got some now. They are all good; there is one of them the best I ever followed in my life.

5247. In the trap?—In the trap or as a hunter; he used to carry one of my sons, 10½ stone, with the stag hounds.

5248. Do farmers in your district appreciate the advantage of good stallions?—I think they do. The Royal Dublin Society's stallion is too far away from them to use down there in any direction. I suppose he is fourteen or fifteen miles away.

5249. In your immediate district?—In my immediate district. They are, as I said before, some of these half-bred horses. Some half-bred horses from Lothario, a thoroughbred horse; some from "Ballinafad," another thoroughbred horse; and from "Saga," down there now.

5250. Will they pay a decent fee for the sire?—Well, I could hardly say that. I should say they would be willing to pay £1. I am speaking of the farmers.

5251. Take the ordinary farmer, is he more influenced by the fee than by the making of the horse?—I think so.

5252. More by the fee?—I am sure the small farmers will not put their mares to any horse, no matter how good he is, if they have to pay large fees. The foals are sent away at six months old. A large number of foals are sold in the market at six months old, and go away in droves.

5253. The thoroughbred horses you have got, are they close to you?—I suppose about nine or ten miles.

5254. Do you think they are suitable for the district at all?—I think they are. I am speaking now of the sire that belongs to the Royal Dublin Society.

5255. Do you think he will suit well for the mares of the district?—I think he would. There are not a great many mares; there is a great dearth of mares suitable for breeding hunters.

5256. Is the Dublin Society Scheme in operation in your district?—It is; I think it does good, but I think it is a mistake to have them always located in the one place. I think the Dublin Society's horse, the Government horse, ought to be moved about from one part of the district to another each year, so that each part might get a fair chance. Of course the present system is to register the horses that are suitable to get good produce indiscriminately of where they are. We have a great number. There was Mr. Blake, down at Ballinafad, used to breed any number of horses, and kept good sires. Unfortunately we have lost him, and there is a dearth of thoroughbred sires.

5257. Have you any experience of the work of the Congested Districts Board Scheme in your neighbourhood?—I think they have done a great deal of good.

5258. Do you think the people are getting a better price for the young stock since the Hackney stallion was introduced?—I can hardly say that, because the large majority of the foals go away at six months.

5259. Do they get a better price for the foals?—Perhaps a few shillings. Say a half sovereign.

5260. And you think the Hackney stallion is suitable to mate with mares in the district?—Very much so. I think the thoroughbred horses would not suit at all to be put with these mountainy ponies. I think you would have a number of weeds.

5261. Do the farmers keep the best mares?—No, I am sorry to say they don't; they sell them, the best looking fillies are all sold away, and the very worst are kept.

5262. Have you any suggestion you could make to remedy that?—The only thing I can think of is giving premiums to mares of, say, four or five years old.

5263. Mr. Fitzwilliam.—You say these Mayo ponies, do you call them Mayo or Connemara?—They are usually called Connemara ponies, it is the district on the seaboard.

5264. Years ago you say they were the perfect thing?—Of a perfect type.

5265. And you would like if you could to reproduce that type?—I think it would be far superior to what they are now, but I do not think there is any likelihood of its being done.

5266. You would like to do it if it could be done?—I should, they were a perfect pony; in fact very much like the Welsh pony, but there is hardly one of this class got now.

5267. You think the introduction of the Welsh pony blood would be a good thing?—Well, the mares now are such real scrub that it is very hard to say, and we all know how mares throw back. It is very hard to say what the progeny would be from the Welsh sire.

5268. They were you say derived from a perfect type of pony?—Originally.

5269. And they will throw back to that good type, won't they?—I am afraid we will have to wait a long time before we get back to that type.

5270. But you must make a beginning. How would you set about it?—I think these Hackneys are very suitable for the mares they have now.

5271. And you would prefer them to the Welsh?—I think so.

5272. Why?—So far as I can see of the ones I have got myself, the produce of the Hackney, they have very good action, good knee action, reaching, and good hock action.

5273. And they were a breed which had a great deal of the Arab blood in them?—There was Arab blood in them originally, far back.

5274. And do you think the grafting of this new blood into them would be a good thing?—I think it will produce certainly a more useful animal than is there now.

5275. But if you say they were nearly perfect and they were like the Welsh pony, why do you not like the idea of grafting the Welsh pony blood on to them again?—I dare say that ought answer. I have not seen any of the produce from the Welsh sire. The ones I have seen were from the Hackney.

5276. And you base your opinion on the produce of the Hackney that you have already seen?—Yes; what I have seen.

5277. What number of these have you seen?—I suppose I have seen fifty or sixty of them.

5278. What age?—Some are coming four—they will be four in May next.

5279. And do you believe that the old breed of Connemara pony can be resuscitated?—I should hardly say that. It would take a very long time to do it.

5280. Then you are going to strike out a new breed of them?—The ones that are there now are real scrub, taking the big majority of them. Now and again you can pick out a good pony, but taking the majority they are scrub.

5281. Do you think they are beyond redemption?—Well, I won't say that, it is never too late to mend.

5282. No, and if you are going to mend them would you not rather try to mend them on the old lines—try to reproduce them on the old lines so far as you know?—You are speaking of the ponies.

5283. Yes; these Connemara ponies that you have been talking about all the time I understand?—Quite so; the same remark applies to the New Forest ponies, they have deteriorated, and they are trying to reproduce them again.

5284. You would get him to re-introduce the Arab strain again with a view of getting courage?—I do not think the Arab is suitable for this cross. I saw a good deal of the Arab blood in Queensland, on the

Bone there. When the Arab was crossed with a strong well bred mare, you got almost a perfect pack back, but when you put the Arab to thin mares [illegible] and when they are here I do not think it would answer.

[illegible]. You do not call the Connemara pony a non-descript breed?—Now I do, because they have gone away from the original [illegible] and you can not call it anything [illegible].

[illegible]. And you think it is impossible?—I think as the old farmers produce the old Connemara pony, but they were sometimes [illegible] from 12 to 13 and 13½ hands high.

[illegible]. Mr. Chase.—What has caused this deterioration in the Connemara pony?—It is chiefly by the introduction of half Clydesdale and half Clydesdale, that has been brought in to increase the strength of them. I consider myself that all these ought to be [illegible].

[illegible]. Is there a Welsh cob in the district at all?—I believe there is one, but I am not quite sure, I have not seen any of the produce.

[illegible]. All that you are acquainted with now is the produce of the Hackney?—I am speaking of the Hackney that I have seen.

[illegible]. And as far as you have seen the introduction of the Hackney blood has improved the breed?—They are a very useful class of horses certainly, with action [illegible].

[illegible]. You have got some yourself?—I have.

[illegible]. What age are they?—I have one two, and another eight, another five, and another four.

[illegible]. Not all by the Congested Districts Board sire?—Not all; some by the Congested Districts Board sire and some from Mr. Midwell's horse. He imported Hackneys into the district some time before. His Hackneys were larger than the Congested Districts Board. I suppose the horse I speak of was about [illegible].

[illegible]. Now we come to the registration. You are in favour of registering all sires?—Strongly in favour of registering all sires.

[illegible]. You would register young stock?—I would, a certain class of mares, I would register breeding mares.

[illegible]. Mr. Wrench.—You practically know Connemara and all the district of [illegible]?—Yes.

[illegible]. So that you really know all these cases where the Congested Board have their horse-breeding arrangements going on?—I do.

[illegible]. And you know the names of the districts?—Certainly.

[illegible]. Both at [illegible] and [illegible]?—Yes.

[illegible]. Do you know that the Board have had Hackney stallions at [illegible] and [illegible] in the same [illegible] Hackney and the Arab?—[illegible].

[illegible]. You don't know that?—No. It has not been put there at the time.

[illegible]. And you know there has been a Welsh pony in addition?—Yes.

[illegible]. And also where the Welsh pony is?—Yes, a Welsh pony at [illegible].

[illegible]. You know the country?—Yes, the greater part of it.

[illegible]. And they are very much the same both at [illegible] and [illegible]?—Pretty much the same, they might be a little better at [illegible] than [illegible].

[illegible]. But you have not looked into the produce of them?—No, not at [illegible].

[illegible]. And you know there was a Welsh pony at [illegible] before the Board?

[illegible]. You say you have got three of these animals yourself from the Congested districts?—Yes.

[illegible]. Have they plenty of durable action?—They have a good striding action, knee and hock action.

[illegible]. You don't see anything in their action to find fault with?—Nothing.

[illegible]. With regard to the other Hackneys you speak of bred from Mr. Midwell's horse, have you been able to test their staying powers?—Indeed I have.

[illegible]. Then you think they are a stronger breed as far as your experience goes?—As far as my experience goes, that is crossed with the Connemara pony. I have one of the old original Connemara ponies now, over [illegible] years old, one of the kind I speak of.

[illegible]. A very fine horse.

[illegible]. But you have been able to test the goodness of these Hackneys as far as staying goes?—I have.

[illegible]. And I think you said your son rode them?—Hunted them with Mr. Fitzpatrick's staghounds.

[illegible]. Would they hold their own in the hunting field?—I think there that were there could speak as to that.

[illegible]. You think they could, I suppose, trust in keep?—Certainly, quite well, up to the front.

[illegible]. And jump?—And jump any amount.

[illegible]. We are not suggesting them as [illegible] but I merely wanted to know?—Oh, no. In fact this pony I am speaking of is a remarkable jumper, it has been [illegible] by the large [illegible] a half [illegible].

[illegible]. What height is she?—[illegible].

[illegible]. Is the breeding of horses a considerable industry among the people along that seaboard?—It has been up to this, but I think the prices have diminished so much lately that I don't know whether they will continue it so much, but up to this they have been all breeding every year.

[illegible]. Well, they have to breed a certain number of horses in order to carry on their work?—Certainly.

[illegible]. And are you suggest any other class of stallion you would recommend to be tried there?—You mean another?—Well, no, I certainly would not at present.

[illegible]. You think the type the Board is sending there now is suited?—At the present time.

[illegible]. You don't think the time has arrived to make any change?—Not yet.

[illegible]. What do you think of the half-bred horses there?—Well, I have known some very good horses got by half-bred sires, but think there are half-bred sires that are [illegible].

[illegible]. And would you rather have a half-bred sire that is [illegible] or would you prefer a half-bred sire with a [illegible]?—I would rather have the high breed, as the breeding [illegible] may make the horse go on the side of the [illegible].

[illegible]. You would like to have your sires as purely [illegible] as possible?—I would, as long as I could get them strong.

[illegible]. A gentleman told us this morning that he bought some ponies from a dealer in Connemara. I suppose when you bought your [illegible] you saw the [illegible] in Newport and Westport fairs?

[illegible]. You saw them there, and were they got by horses belonging to the Board?—I got a certificate.

[illegible]. They had their certificates with them so that there could be no doubt about [illegible] them. Mr. [illegible] asked you if you thought the produce of reclaiming the original breed was impossible?—I would be inclined to think it was.

[illegible]. Now, could you yourself at the present time point out to any animal in that district like your old [illegible]?—Out of that type I spoke of, about fifteen years ago there was one or two of them.

[illegible]. But for the last five or six years, might have practically disappeared?—I have not seen any of that type.

[illegible]. And their place has been taken by a larger class of animal, well [illegible] than those of [illegible]?—Yes, a good deal of half-bred or half Clydesdale, with a large body and no legs.

[illegible]. And the chief cause there is mainly the Board's [illegible] the Board as [illegible].

5336. And the foals from these brood mares, [illegible] looking [illegible]?—[illegible]; they are taken away; we don't see them after they go to the fairs and they are taken away; it is very hard to say which is the best [illegible].

5337. Do you know how many foals were bred from Mr. Blake's thoroughbred horse with Connemara ponies?—No, I don't know that; one with the Connemara ponies, but a good class of mares were put to Mr. Blake's horse.

5338. But you don't know that the Connemara ponies are crossed?—I never heard that.

5339. You did not know about a cross of ponies bred in that way recently?—No, I did not.

5340. And you would be inclined to keep all horses registered?—I'd have certainly registered.

5341. Do you mean by that horses of every breed?—[illegible].

5342. Would you register any [illegible] else or only the [illegible]?—I don't believe in [illegible].

5343. You would register a pure-bred of any kind?—I would; our great [illegible] is want of mares for breeding hunters [illegible].

5344. Of course you don't think these [illegible] would be at all likely to be bred, as far as I understand that they would be likely to be bred from them [illegible], not at all.

5345. Do you think there is any danger of the [illegible] of these mares in [illegible] into districts where the hunters are [illegible]?—[illegible] I should not think so; I should think a man's own judgment would be able to detect the [illegible]. I think [illegible] a type you can see the [illegible] type.

5346. That is your experience?—That is my experience.

5347. And you have seen some of the produce of Mr. [illegible] before any [illegible] were sent there by the Board?—Oh, yes.

5348. Do you know whether they sold for good prices?—Some of them very good prices, and in [illegible] very good prices in [illegible]. The [illegible] a bigger type than the Congested Districts Board's horses.

5349. CHAIRMAN.—As far as I understood what you are talking Mr. [illegible] [illegible] clearly [illegible]?—The [illegible].

5350. Are there many hunters raised [illegible]?—[illegible] a few hunters.

5351. Have they got good mares for breeding hunters?—They [illegible] a great deal of [illegible].

5352. Have they good sires for breeding hunters?—Up to this we had, because we had Mr. Blake's horse to go to.

5353. That is about three years ago?—About three years ago; there are no thoroughbred horses [illegible].

5354. There is a dearth of good sires?—There is a great dearth of good sires.

5355. What is the nearest horse under the [illegible] Department's scheme?—I should think about [illegible] miles.

5356. You don't know anything about the [illegible] of it?—No, except that people [illegible] to go to [illegible], and I don't think they can make use of him for that reason.

5357. What sire would you recommend for the hunter-breeding districts for the mares, if [illegible] the necessary [illegible]?—Well, I should recommend a strong low [illegible] type of horse, thoroughbred horse with plenty of bone.

5358. And you would be averse to any half-bred horse?—I would be averse to any half-bred thing.

5359. And you, with the [illegible], would be in favour of the [illegible] in the [illegible] districts and the thoroughbred in other districts?—Quite so.

5360. MR. [illegible].—You don't think there is any danger of the breed [illegible] in that way?—[illegible]. I think if any scheme could be adopted for [illegible] by [illegible] the mares that would be [illegible] in the [illegible] and [illegible] to give them out to the [illegible] farmers on condition that they keep them for a certain length of time.

5361. Of course that only applies in the poor districts where they would be able to find a good animal?—Quite so, I am speaking now of the [illegible].

5362. And you would give these mares in [illegible] of the farmers?—I would give them to the [illegible] that were able to feed them, on condition that they kept the foals for a certain time, [illegible].

5363. CHAIRMAN.—Do you think a certain [illegible] of [illegible] a certain number of years [illegible]?—[illegible] to breed hunters. I would give every [illegible] to keep that mare in the country.

5364. MR. [illegible].—And you would [illegible] by [illegible]?—Certainly [illegible]; the only thing we can go by is the best of our judgment to [illegible] what we want.

5365. But there is a great dearth of thoroughbred sires since the death of Mr. Blake's?—There is and a greater dearth of mares.

5366. CHAIRMAN.—Any other suggestions you would like to make?—I don't think there is anything more.

5367. MR. [illegible].—You spoke of [illegible] to your district; did you see him?—I saw a [illegible] of his, I did not care very much about them.

5368. You never saw himself?—No, I never saw himself.

PETER FITZGERALD, Prospect, Limerick, examined.

5369. CHAIRMAN.—I think you live in the County Limerick?—Yes, my lord.

5370. And have had some experience there in horse breeding?—Yes.

5371. Have you bred yourself?—Yes.

5372. With good success or otherwise?—I have not bred to a very great extent, but I have been successful in those that I have bred. I have bred for other people and for myself.

5373. What do you aim at breeding?—High-class hunters or high-class carriage horses, which are the only things, I think, that pay in this country, and what, I think, everybody ought to aim at doing.

5374. You know something about Kerry, too, I believe?—Yes; I am a native of Kerry.

5375. We will take Kerry afterwards. Referring to Limerick, what sire do you think they can adopt to breed a [illegible] horse in your district?—The thoroughbred and the half-bred, [illegible] himself a good [illegible] that has proved himself [illegible].

5376. The thoroughbred, practically, within [illegible] in his pedigree?—Yes.

5377. And your district is suitable for breeding high-class animals of all [illegible]?—Yes.

5378. Are the people suitable for breeding [illegible] horses, too?—Of course, there is a great [illegible], and there are excellent [illegible] in the country.

5379. What part of Limerick do you come from?—I have lived [illegible] in Adare, which is [illegible] in the centre of the county.

5390. Would you describe the mares?—It is very hard to describe them, there are such a variety.

5391. Give us some idea of the general type of mare?—I should call them the half-bred mares, they have all, or nearly all, got a cross of thoroughbred.

5392. Suitable for breeding hunters and high-class harness horses?—Certainly.

5393. Are there a sufficient number of suitable sires in your district?—I should say so.

5394. You approve, you say, of breeding from half-bred sires?—Where they are known to be good sire-producers, such as some I could mention:—Traverser, Mackintosh, Archer, Mayboy; of course Mayboy is practically thoroughbred, but he is not in the Stud-book.

5395. Would you approve of these sires being registered by the Royal Dublin Society?—I should; their colts have fetched some of the highest prices in the district.

5396. Do the farmers generally round breed a good class of horses?—Yes; of course there is a good deal of rubbish, but I should say the best horses in Ireland come from my district.

5397. Do they breed there from two-year old fillies?—No, I don't think they do; they did breed from two-year old fillies, but they found that some of the mares died, and they thought that caused their death.

5398. You mean the fillies after having foaled died?—Yes.

5399. And did you breed yourself at all from two-year olds?—No, never.

5390. Would you approve of it or otherwise?—I should disapprove of it. I don't think you ought to breed from anything under three, at least the class of mares that farmers keep.

5391. Are many of the best mares sold out of your country?—Yes.

5392. If the farmers get a better price for the good mare, they keep the bad one and sell the good one?—Certainly.

5393. Have you any suggestion to make to the Commission how you would encourage them to keep those mares?—I think the system adopted by the Royal Dublin Society has done good, but I think it might be improved upon, for instance I should suggest having spring shows instead of summer shows.

5394. Spring shows of mares?—Yes, and give the mares, young mares, nominations to any registered sire at £2 or £3 a head. I don't know whether it might be considered interfering with the liberty of the subject, but I should like to put a tax on all young mares going out of the country.

5395. And all the young mares are bought by foreigners?—Yes.

5396. Would you suggest licensing the stallions?—Yes, certainly.

5397. And taxing or prohibiting unsound stallions from serving in the country?—Yes.

5398. Now the Royal Dublin Society's scheme you say has improved the stock, and in the same way I suppose it has benefited the breeders in your district?—Yes, I am chairman of the committee for the last two years under the Royal Dublin Society's Hunter Improvement Scheme, and speak from experience.

5399. At what ages are the horses generally bought?—A great many of the best horses are bought as three-year-olds and four-year olds; I may mention that seeing it stated that there was nothing but a hunter trade in this country and thinking that there was a very large trade in harness horses—untrained harness colts, I wrote to Messrs. East and Co., of London, to ask them what their experience was, and with your permission I should like to read a letter which I have received from them:—

"7 Curzon-street, May Fair,
"London, W., June 25th, 1896.

"Sir,—Replying to your letter of the 22nd inst., addressed to Mr. George East, we are afraid we can give you [illegible] Ireland. What we can say however is that for high class carriage horses, [illegible] we consider Ireland [illegible]

"As to the [illegible] stallions in Ireland, [illegible]

"[illegible]

"Yours faithfully,
"East & Co.

"Peter Fitzgerald, Esq.,
"[illegible], Limerick."

5400. [illegible]

5401. What class of mares are there in that district?—[illegible] I was at the Congested Districts show and I was surprised [illegible] good mares [illegible] I should say there were 12 good mares amongst them [illegible]

5402. Have you seen any of the stock of the Congested Districts Board stallions. I suppose you did at that show?—Yes, [illegible] and I have gone into that district and seen a great many of them.

5403. Have you seen the sires?—Yes, I have [illegible] I have seen their progeny which I think is more important.

5404. What is your opinion of them?—I don't like them. I don't think they ever will develop into anything like a good horse, [illegible]

5405. What age were the horses you saw?—[illegible] yearlings, and two-year-olds.

5406. What is the ordinary stallion used [illegible]

5407. What is their progeny like?—Bad.

5408. Half-bred, or [illegible] the Congested Districts Board sires?—They are so bad that I don't think you could [illegible] I have seen better [illegible] than any of the Congested Districts Board sires.

5409. Would they make [illegible]?—They might [illegible]

5410. What would you suggest as the best means of improving the horses in those districts?—I believe [illegible] a good thoroughbred sire and a half-bred mare [illegible] Congested Districts Board [illegible] I think it would do a great deal of good, and from my knowledge of it I believe a very great number of [illegible] County Cork, [illegible]

5411. [illegible]

5412. [illegible] young

Mr. Peter Fitzgerald

[illegible]

5439. There is a great difference between Kerry and Limerick?—I think the Kerry land is capable of producing a horse as big as they, and it has done so, I have seen instances of it.

[illegible]

the hands I presume of a Board of some kind?—Yes.

[illegible]

few good stallions in Kerry such as "Double Dink," "Royal Charter," and "Watchful" is, I believe, [illegible]

[illegible]

5458. You would not see the foal at foot of the mare [illegible] now?—It is impossible to judge [illegible]. I think you have a lot of foals at ages varying [illegible] any show in a difference of a month or two in every foal, which makes a great deal of difference, and it is impossible to compare foals.

5459. But if you knew the age of the foal, don't you think it is possible to form some opinion?—You can only form a guess; but it is very hard to form any opinion as to his future prospects, or as to his being better than a foal that is two months younger.

5460. Then you would simply have [illegible]?—Yes. I should not object to having a foal show.

5461. I cannot [illegible] a good foal [illegible] the [illegible] show with a view of giving [illegible].

5462. You said, I think, that you would [illegible] that were out of the country?—Yes.

5463. That is, that the [illegible] should pay a [illegible]?—Yes.

5464. Would not [illegible] would be [illegible]?—Then the [illegible].

5465. The [illegible] would gradually become [illegible] profitable?—[illegible] would not be so [illegible] for [illegible] purposes.

5466. Would you like to [illegible] American horses?—[illegible] I think they ought to be [illegible] as [illegible] horses.

5467. You would approve of branding American horses?—Yes.

5468. Have you seen any American horses?—No, I have not; I have seen [illegible] in America [illegible] of them [illegible] the progeny; but I [illegible] any of them [illegible] American horses.

5469. You said [illegible], do you know how many horses [illegible] in Ireland in this year?—[illegible] in Ireland in the year in buying horses [illegible].

5470. Do you know how [illegible] horses that [illegible]?—They pay £200 [illegible].

5471. But they only buy a very high class of horses?—Yes.

5472. And most of those horses are bred out of [illegible], I suppose?—They are bred by thoroughbred sires I think.

5473. They require a big class horse, don't they, up to 16 hands?—Yes.

5474. Therefore it would not [illegible] small horses [illegible]?—I don't [illegible] small [illegible] good [illegible] it [illegible].

5475. [illegible] Cahirciveen [illegible]?—I [illegible] only [illegible].

5476. Is there a good [illegible]?—Not [illegible].

5477. [illegible], are there [illegible]?—I [illegible] there is a lot of small [illegible] in Cahirciveen district.

5478. It has been suggested that a Clydesdale [illegible] in the Cahirciveen district, would you be in favour of having Clydesdales there [illegible]?—I don't think they are wanted, but I should prefer them to the Hackneys.

5479. Why?—Because they are more distinguishable, they are not such an [illegible] breed.

5480. I thought you said that there was [illegible] Hackney [illegible] dent distinguishment is it not?—I mean there is no fear of the produce of the Hackney being mistaken for a hunter, if he is only likely to develop into a bad cabby?—I should think not.

5481. Therefore you don't want any animal that will stamp its breed more than at present, that you will always know?—Yes.

5482. So your argument in favour of the Clydesdale—putting that argument aside—do you think he would be a suitable horse for the district?—I think the only object of having a Clydesdale would be for agricultural purposes, and I think the agricultural requirements can be met by producing mules, or a farmer can buy a horse to do his farm work for a very small price; I myself have bought farm horses for £14 or £15 good enough to do any work in the Limerick district, and good enough to do any work in the Cahirciveen district, so I don't think you can breed anything that would pay at that price.

5483. So you practically don't want the heavy horse?—I don't think you do.

5484. I think you said the average height you thought of the mares about Cahirciveen was 13 hands, do you think it is as much?—I should think so.

5485. You have measured them, have you?—No, but I can judge, I have seen them constantly.

5486. For instance take those mares that we had at the show in Cahirciveen, do you think they were an average of 13 hands?—Above it I should say, there were some smaller certainly.

5487. I think you say you would suggest stud farms in several centres in Ireland?—I should breed horses for the district, you could buy up some of the mares that would otherwise be sold away, keep good stallions for the use of the stud farm, and for the use of the district.

5488. And what would you do with the mares that you bought up?—I should breed from them and then sell the progeny to farmers, if they turn out well, at a cheap rate for breeding purposes.

5489. Would you take any steps to ensure farmers keeping those mares?—I think it would be necessary to do so.

5490. Have you ever thought how you could do that?—It could be easily done, I would let farmers have the use of the mare and get progeny himself, it could be easily seen that they did not dispose of them or did not treat them ill.

5491. Do you see any objection to having these mares branded?—I think that would be a good thing.

5492. When you say this produce will only develop into a cabber, you have never kept any of these animals yourself I suppose?—I had one.

5493. For long?—No, I sold it as soon as I could.

5494. That was not a fair test?—I tried him well first, I bought him for £45, he had beautiful action in front.

5495. What age?—Four-year-old.

5496. Anything to say as to the horses sent by the Congested Districts Board?—Oh, no, he was by a Hackney horse.

5497. I was talking of the produce of the horses sent by the Board?—Oh, no, the oldest in that district, I think, is two-year-old, they may be there in that immediate district.

5498. I wanted to know had you any experience of them?—No, except that I saw them at Puck fair, where I saw several of them sold, I saw the third year yearling sold for £8 15s. I saw the first prize two-year-old of the show of the preceding day offered for sale at £13 and he was brought home.

5499. Did you hear this morning a gentleman say he had offered a very well bred four-year-old filly by a thoroughbred horse for £10 and had not received a bid for it at the fair at Rosscommon?—I did not hear him say so, it is quite possible.

5500. You know that prices are very bad now,

Dec. 12, 1895.

Mr Peter Fitzgerald.

don't you know the prices for certain classes of horses in [illegible]?—The class of horses sold by small farmers, yes.

6502. And are high and in [illegible] [illegible] [illegible] [illegible] [illegible]?—Of course there was a great many horses that were not sold.

6503. At any price?—Yes, some always are [illegible].

6503. The animal you referred to that was not sold belonged to Mr. Sullivan, the schoolmaster in the Island?—Yes.

6504. [illegible] [illegible] [illegible] [illegible] [illegible] [illegible] [illegible], which he would you take?—He said he was, I [illegible].

6505. I suppose you will believe him if he says he [illegible] would not dispute it.

6506. [illegible] [illegible] [illegible] [illegible] [illegible]?—Yes.

6507. Chairman.—Can you tell [illegible] [illegible] [illegible]. [illegible] [illegible] [illegible]?—[illegible], I [illegible].

6508. Mr. Fitzgerald.—I should rather like to have some experience of the Hackney that you bought [illegible], although it did not come from the [illegible] [illegible]?—I [illegible] [illegible] [illegible] [illegible], and when I had [illegible] about [illegible] [illegible] I thought I was going to [illegible] [illegible] [illegible] [illegible], but I found [illegible] [illegible] I was [illegible].

6509. Chairman.—Where did you buy the animal?—I bought him in Limerick.

6510. Mr. Wrench.—What was he by?

6511. Chairman.—Are you sure he was by a Hackney?—I believe so.

6512. Mr. Wrench.—What was he said to be by?—By a horse called [illegible].

6513. I am afraid we could hardly call him a Hackney?—Perhaps not. He may not be a pure-bred Hackney, but [illegible] Hackney blood.

6514. Mr. Fitzgerald.—He was eventually [illegible] [illegible] [illegible] [illegible] [illegible] for half the price I gave for him.

6515. Mr. Wrench.—You want to [illegible] [illegible] [illegible]?—That is a [illegible] of the County Limerick Horse Breeding Committee.

6516. Chairman.—Does it refer to the Dublin Society's scheme?—Yes. It is as follows:—

1895.

"Report of the County Limerick Horse Breeding Committee.

"November 13, 1895.

"[illegible]

"[illegible]

"[illegible]

"[illegible]

"[illegible]

"Peter Fitzgerald,

"Chairman, Co. Limerick Committee."

6517. Mr. Wrench.—You mention prizes to yearlings, did you propose that the prizes should be given at the same time that the mares are inspected in spring?—Yes.

6518. Immediately after the winter?—Certainly, you could not judge during the summer as to the way the farmer had fed his colt during the winter.

6519. Just one show and that show would be for mares and yearlings?—Yes.

6520. Mr. Fitzgerald.—Was that a resolution?—That was the report of the county Limerick Committee. Then we have a resolution that was passed at the Limerick Horse Show and Agricultural Society on the question of Hackneys.

6521. Do you agree with it?—Oh, yes, entirely, I was present at the meeting and the meeting was unanimous, it was largely attended.

6522. Chairman.—Is it your own opinion?—It is, and I voted on it.

"That we the Members of the Committee of the Limerick Horse Show and Agricultural Society protest most strongly against the State aided introduction of Hackney stallions into any portion of this country, as we believe the blood will seriously deteriorate the class of horse now bred in this country, and in this opinion we are supported by the best judges in England, where the experiment has been tried and proved a failure, and we suggest the substitution of thoroughbred horses with bone and substance, or of sires as nearly thoroughbred as possible, which have proved good colt getters.

"Passed unanimously.

"(Signed), Jas. P. Gaffney,

"High Sheriff, Chairman.

"3rd Oct., 1895."

6523. [illegible] [illegible] [illegible] [illegible] [illegible]?—[illegible] [illegible] [illegible] [illegible] [illegible] [illegible] [illegible] [illegible] [illegible] [illegible].

6524. You don't mind the Hackney blood in your district [illegible]?—[illegible] [illegible].

6525. The original Connemara pony, you think, [illegible] [illegible] [illegible] [illegible] [illegible] [illegible] [illegible] [illegible] [illegible] [illegible] [illegible].

6526. Do you think there is any number of farmers [illegible] [illegible] [illegible] [illegible] [illegible] [illegible]?—[illegible] [illegible].

6527. Mr. Wrench.—And you think that any of the gentlemen who proposed that resolution has had any experience themselves of Hackney breeding?—Everyone of them had experience in horse-breeding [illegible]

5528. In breeding from Hackneys?—I cannot say. No, I should not say they personally had. Mr. O'Brien, the horse-dealer of Limerick, whose evidence you probably will hear, I suppose knows what a Hackney is. He was there. If I might read you a letter which I have received from Mr. O'Brien.

5529. CHAIRMAN.—Have you any more to tell us yourself?—I have nothing more to add. I should like to say one word—I think it is rather an important thing—that my reason for saying that a thoroughbred and a half-bred would do well in Kerry is that in old times there was a good many thoroughbreds in Kerry, and at that time Kerry and Puck fair in particular was famous for the class of cobs that came out of it. In those days they had a horse called "Priam," "Porto Rico," "Daniel O'Connell," sire of "The Liberator," "Touchstone," a horse called "Mocky Prem" that, I believe, was by "Priam." I don't think it was the "Mocky Prem." This horse was by "Priam," out of a mare got by an Arab which Lord Kenmare introduced into Kenmare some forty years ago.

5530. Does that refer generally to Kerry or parts of Kerry?—That refers generally to Kerry. Of course the district around Cahirciveen has always been badly off for horses. In fact, I remember my father used to send mares off to a sire thirty-five and forty miles away, and some of the farmers have taken their mares to the sire forty miles away, and brought them back again.

5531. Are the mares in Kerry now as good as they were in those days, [illegible]—I should say not, but I think it ought not to be very difficult to [illegible] good [illegible].

5532. You would have to [illegible] with the [illegible]—I don't see why you should not [illegible].

5533. That is rather a big order?—They could be got very cheap in mare [illegible] from the [illegible]. There was one thing I forgot to say. It was [illegible] at [illegible] shown. I should like very much if they could be [illegible].

5534. You mean the district shows?—I mean the Limerick Show. I know from experience that they are not paying their way, and if they are not [illegible] along they cannot go on. They are most useful in the direction of horse-breeding, and I don't think that they would be the least [illegible] with the Dublin Show. [illegible], I think they are not [illegible] in connection with the question of horse-breeding generally, I think that we ought to [illegible]. For instance, Mr. Widger, I know, spends £100,000 a year in Ireland in buying horses. I think that in [illegible] the [illegible], I think, the great point in [illegible]. I come to say the people who spend the money ought to be [illegible].

Mr. GEORGE M. HARRIS examined.

5535. CHAIRMAN.—You live in the County Limerick?—Yes.

5536. And you have considerable experience in horse-breeding?—Yes.

5537. Tell the Commission what sires you bring [illegible]—My father kept [illegible] in the County Limerick for the last fifty years. [illegible] We had such horses as "Old Victor," "Peter Eden," "Consternation," and many others. [illegible]

5538. Mr. [illegible].—In what class [illegible]?

5539. CHAIRMAN.—The district you live in is [illegible] the highest class of horses [illegible]?

5540. What horses do the farmers breed?—The [illegible] and high class hunters.

5541. Are the mares good in your district?—Very good mares as a rule; there are some bad ones.

5542. Do they breed from two-year-old fillies?—It is not usual to breed from two-year-old fillies, but they have tried it with very good success, and some of the best [illegible] bred in Limerick were from two-year-old mares. The colt that got the first prize in the yearling class last year at Limerick was from a two-year-old mare.

5543. Was this colt a thoroughbred or half-bred [illegible]?—The yearling was half-bred, it got first prize and also got the Hunter Improvement Society's medal as the best [illegible] in the show, and it was bought by Mr. Henry Thompson, I think he [illegible].

5544. You approve then of breeding from two-year-olds?—Under certain circumstances, if the [illegible] [illegible] a good [illegible] I would approve of breeding from her, and I say that it is better two and three-year-old, [illegible] if possible. If [illegible] bred from the mare, if the foal is at all good, is kept and probably [illegible] again in the [illegible], if she is not [illegible] at a two-year-old [illegible] of three or three or four [illegible] [illegible].

Mr. George M. Harris.

5545. Are the farmers about you particular about mating their mares?—Latterly they are paying more attention than they did ten or twelve years ago, they were breeding in a haphazard fashion, took any sire and any mare and they found they lost money by it, and they have stopped that system. Now they are paying more attention and will only breed from a good sire, and they are breeding from good mares and keeping some of them.

5546. What sires are the stallions in the district?—There is nothing within 15 miles of Kilmallock but thoroughbreds, I know of only one half-bred, except Mr. Gubbins' "Mayboy," he is within seven miles.

5547. He is practically thoroughbred?—He is more thoroughbred than many thoroughbreds, he is the sire of "Clem-clem," the favourite for the Cesarewitch the other day, that is out of a half-bred mare.

5548. Is the Royal Dublin Society's scheme in your district?—Yes.

5549. Is it doing good?—I think it is doing a great deal of good, and I was sorry to hear they are thinking of changing it this year and going back to the nomination system.

5550. You approve of giving the prizes to mares?—Altogether, and to limit it to mares of three or four years old, I see some mares getting prizes at 15 years of age, these mares are kept for breeding purposes and nothing else, and there is no use in giving those mares prizes, twenty prizes of £5 each would be better than five prizes of £20 each; I would give those prizes to mares of two and three years old served by a sire.

5551. Or three and four?—Two, three, or four, I would divide those £5 prizes amongst these mares. If the mare has a foal and the foal is a good looking one, the foal is kept in the country and the farmer gets rid of the old mare, but if he can continue to win prizes with the mare at the show he will get rid of the young ones.

5552. A large number of horses are bred in your district, are they bought in fairs or from the breeder?—Chiefly from the breeder, the country is scoured by members of fox-hounds, they stay in the country and go round and see the young horses and take them away.

5553. At what age?—Three and four years.

5554. And good prices?—They get £100 and £120

Dec. 12, 1895.

Mr. George H. Rowe.

for a three-year-old, the prices are not so good now as they were ten years ago.

5555. What do you think of breeding from half-bred sires to get hunters?—I had one half-bred sire myself by Old Victor, and he was one of the best horses I had. I hunted him regularly, and I sold him to Mr. Donovan, in Cork, the dealer, who refused £1,000 for him afterwards. He was by a thoroughbred horse from a half-bred mare—that is, a mare with two or three crosses of thoroughbred blood.

5556. Would you approve of the Dublin Society registering half-bred sires?—As to the registering of sires, I would not only register them with the Royal Dublin Society, but I would register all sires and mares used for breeding purposes, and in this connection I may say that it can be done very cheaply. In following the evidence given I saw that the registering of sires and the registering of mares would cost a great deal of money; I believe you have all the machinery at hand, and it can be done at a minimum cost. All sires and mares could be registered with the Petty Sessions Clerk, just the same as you register dogs, and the registry could be open to the public. I would register all sires—Clydesdales, Hackneys, and thoroughbreds, it did not matter whether they were half-breds or thoroughbreds. I would have a register in every district of the sires and mares; that register would be open to the farmers, and they could see whether the sires were registered with a veterinary certificate or not, and they could see whether they were registered with the Royal Dublin Society or not. At present they have no means of knowing whether the horse is sound or not. The Dublin Society have at least 25 per cent. of their horses registered that are unsound, and the farmers have no means of finding that out. You go to the owner, and ask him is his horse sound. "Why, he is registered; is not that enough for you?" Well, the horse may be unsound. I know several—I know dozens—that are registered by the Society that are unsound; I think at least 25 per cent. of them are. I would also register all the produce annually of every mare.

5557. You mean you would keep a sort of stud-book?—Keep a stud-book in every district, and then the Clerk of Petty Sessions could issue a certificate that the mare was served by such and such a horse and a certificate of the produce.

5558. You would leave it to the breeder what sire he would select?—Exactly. I would register them in every district, and the farmer could see was the horse sound, and who signed the certificate, and the date. Take every horse and register him in that district.

5559. But then you would leave it to the breeder altogether to select shapes and breed of horse and everything?—Exactly; I would not confine him at all. At present he is altogether in the dark; he does not know whether the horse is sound or not, he simply has to take it as granted by the Royal Dublin Society.

5560. Are there any cart sires in your district?—Not one.

5561. Or Hackney sires?—No. My father introduced a Hackney about five years ago—a small one, about 14.3—and it only got six mares; they would not have it at any price. About thirty years ago he introduced a Norfolk trotter, and had to get rid of it, they would not have it at all. It is altogether a horse-producing district, and breeding harness colts for Messrs. Windsor and Messrs. Kerr.

5562. Mr. Fitzwilliam.—Do you believe the stallions you have now in the country are the best calculated for producing these?—Yes.

5563. Thoroughbred or nearly thoroughbred?—Thoroughbred altogether.

5564. You think they are quite sufficient?—Quite sufficient. The best sires we ever had were light weedy sires, with very little bone. Old Victor was a horse with 7½ inches of bone.

5565. But they get good bone in their produce?—Extraordinary bone. It is the mares, not the sires; the sires are good enough for anything. It is the mares of the country you want to improve, not the sires.

5566. You mean improve the mare through the sire?—Well, keep the young mares—that is the way to improve them.

5567. Is not the object of giving these prizes to induce the keeping of mares in the country in good breeding order?—It occurs to me that [illegible] if a man has an old mare [illegible] good brood mare it would be a good thing to keep her in the country. If the mare is a good brood mare I certainly would be inclined to give her a prize, but if she be a good looking mare the farmer won't get her at any price; but I know one mare that won first prize in Dublin; she has won several times in the County Limerick, and she is not worth a hundred, and her produce are the most worthless brutes that ever were bred.

5568. Chairman.—You have to give prizes according to shapes; it would be hard to go into the breed?—Exactly; that is why I say keep the young mares in the country. I have heard it urged that the [illegible] old hunter mares, or good mares [illegible]; well, any improvement in breeding is [illegible] an old mare [illegible]. A farmer will keep his old mare for ten years, and drive her and work her, and then say she is good for nothing but breeding—and she is not much good for that—[illegible] the stallion. The young mares are the proper ones to breed from, and if you can keep them in the country you will improve the breed of horses materially.

5569. Mr. Wrench.—You think, then, that the foals that are bred out of a mare during the first years of her life are the best?—[illegible]

5570. With regard to your suggested register, have you thought at all how you would enforce the registering? Do you suggest that it be made illegal that a horse should be registered like a dog?—Exactly. Make it an offence not to do so, punishable by fine or imprisonment.

5571. Would you put on a tax, large or small?—I would put on a tax; I would make it compulsory on every man keeping a sire or mare for breeding purposes that he should register the pedigree, and if he failed to do that I would have him heavily punished. Then in after generations you could go back, and if there was a Clydesdale or Hackney cross you could go back and trace it.

5572. And when you registered them the first time you would have as full a description of the animal as possible?—Yes; it would be entirely the business of the [illegible], and the [illegible] of the Petty Sessions Clerk, and that could be covered by fee of 1s. for each one.

5573. And if you could keep up a pedigree for the first, do you think that farmers would get more money for the animals?—I am sure they would. I know a man whose dealer bought a horse from a friend of mine on the 12th of July. It was a bargain between him and the dealer that he had a [illegible] and he [illegible] Light Weight Hunter. [illegible] pedigree [illegible] the mare [illegible].

5574. You think that is a strong argument [illegible] that horses sold on pedigree as they are [illegible] in Holland?—There is a good many sold [illegible], and I think the Royal Dublin Society should not accept a pedigree for publication in their stud-book without the breeder's name and address being known.

5575. You think, then, [illegible] it would be very much [illegible]?—I think the only [illegible] way is by registering them in every district.

you have got the machinery at hand, and you will have no trouble; but to send down a register, and the Clerk of Petty Sessions would have the certificate of pedigree, with the names given at time of birth.

5578. You think many of the horses on the register of the Royal Dublin Society at present are not sound?—I know it.

5579. How would you have their soundness decided, would you send down a vet. from Dublin, or allow the men to select their own vets.?—I am afraid it is almost impossible to trust a horse for soundness in case of the local veterinary surgeons in Ireland, and he never saw a sound horse yet; or, in other words, he never saw a horse he would not spin.

5580. How would you remedy that state of affairs?—I would register them in the district, and let the farmers see the Committee what qualities they have, what they have done, who signs the certificate, and the rest of it.

5581. You would not require any special examination by a special body?—No, because I know the farmers in our district are some of the keenest judges of a horse, and they can pick the points of each horse; I know one small farmer who has travelled the County Cork looking for a sire.

5582. Are they good judges of sires, too?—Oh, they know the sires, which is why I say when they would have the vet.'s certificate, and the dam of it, they would know what pedigree they would place on it.

5583. CHAIRMAN.—You say you get some of the best horses from those county sires, don't you think the land has something to do with that?—I think it has, for in the County Limerick we grow some of the biggest mules, and biggest horses, and biggest bullocks in the world.

5584. Have you any other suggestion to make to the Commission?—There is one matter, I think if you were doing the Queen's Plates, you know numerous Queen's Plates given in racing every year, that is £1,700, and those Queen's Plates are usually won by one or two racing men. They are given for the improvement of the breed of horses in Ireland, but they are no value, I think, as a means to that end. In 1891 Mr. Linde won seven, in 1895 he won ten of them, in 1893 he won eight, and, I am sorry to say, in 1896 he only won two. He won twenty seven out of sixty-eight plates in four years—that is £3,700.

5585. What would you suggest to do with that, would it help to make a registry of sires?—Either that, or give it to the different county shows. If £100, the value of one plate, was given to Limerick—for in Limerick we have been losing money for years since the show was started; it is the same in Cork, and I believe everywhere else—if that £100 was given as prizes for young horses at the different shows I think it would be a great means of inducing the farmers to keep their young mares and exhibit them there.

5586. Do the farmers send their mares to the Royal Dublin Society's show, Mr. Moore?—They do not to the extent to which they ought to do.

5587. You don't remember the number of mares that put in an appearance?—I was at Dublin Show this year. I judged at Dublin Show this year and last year, and the brood mares there this year were far better than the ones there last year. I believe that is because the farmers saw they had not the slightest chance with the rubbish they brought there the year before.

5588. It has done good in that way?—It has done good in that way. Then the class of Shetland were confined to horses under three years. I was very glad to see them doing that.

5589. In the County Limerick?—In the County Limerick; Mr. Fitzgerald has told you all about that, I agree with him altogether.

5590. Is there anything else you want to say?—Just one thing. I was surprised to hear the Congested Districts Board's stallions had covered something like 100 mares last year.

5591. Is it handy in your district?—I don't know whether it is a fact or not, but I think there is nothing so injurious in horse-breeding as an overdone stallion.

5592. That would not exist in your district?—It does prevail to my knowledge.

5593. You are not in a congested district?—No; but as to stallions being overdone, I have known several stallions who in the first season got extraordinary good foals, the first crop of them. Their name is made on the show, and the stallion was overdone, the owner of the stallion would not turn away any mares, and some of the horses covered as many as 150 mares; their produce afterwards was utterly worthless, and I think you should devise some means to prevent stallion owners allowing more than sixty or seventy mares to their horse.

5594. Mr. WRENCH.—Do you know as a question of fact that Hackneys are able to cover a much larger number of mares than other horses?—I think a horse if you let him will go on covering for ever.

5595. Do you know that stallions in Yorkshire cover 100 mares in a year, and none of them 150?—There are no overdone stallions.

5596. CHAIRMAN.—You mean to infer that if the stallions are not limited the progeny is inferior, after a bit?—Unless they are limited.

5597. Mr. WRENCH.—What would you limit stallions to as a rule?—Not more than seventy. A stallion serving 200 mares, which I have heard of, means at least 250 covers, and as the covering season is only three months, it is at the rate of four a day.

The Commission adjourned to next morning.

Nov. 27, 1896.

ELEVENTH DAY.—FRIDAY, NOVEMBER 27TH, 1896.

PRESENT:—LORD ASHTOWN (in the Chair); LORD RATHDONNELL, THE HON. HENRY W. FITZWILLIAM, MR. WRENCH, COLONEL ST. QUINTIN.

MR. HUGH NEVILLE, Secretary.

Mr. B. E. Gould.

MR. B. E. GOULD, Grange, Newport, examined.

5558. CHAIRMAN.—You live in the County Limerick but [illegible] in Tipperary, just on the borders of the County of Limerick.

5559. You have considerable experience in horse breeding?—Yes.

5560. What class have you chiefly bred yourself?—Half-bred horses—that is, horses mostly crossed thoroughbreds.

5561. What do you call horses [illegible] with a couple of crosses of thoroughbred blood. Some have only half-bred blood, but mares of the breed [illegible] and have proved themselves good hunters.

5562. That is the class of horse you breed from?—Yes, and I have also bred from one or two [illegible] mares who have been breeding on and doing fairly well—and I have bred once or twice from Clydesdale stallions and good mares and I have also bred from mares crossed with Clydesdale blood.

5563. With what result?—Thoroughbred [illegible].

5564. Have you bought any horses?—Yes, a considerable number.

5565. At what age do you chiefly buy?—Four years. I have bought younger, but as a rule, four.

5566. What do you do with them?—Sell them again.

5567. What class of horses is chiefly bred in your district?—Well, they aim at breeding hunters. The small farmers, I don't think, have any very clear idea as to what they are trying to breed.

5568. What class of horse is most suitable to breed in your district?—I think hunters—high-class hunters—and carriage or harness horses.

5569. And what class of sires?—Hunter sires.

5570. Do they work the mares, or do they keep them simply at home?—They work them, they are out in the field. As a rule, they work them, but some farmers keep them simply for breeding.

5571. What sires do they chiefly use?—Thoroughbred ones.

5572. Altogether?—They generally do. The farmers that aim at breeding the best horses only breed from thoroughbred sires. Of course they may breed from horses with [illegible] sires. The smaller farmers breed from half-breds, and a larger number of them breed in a haphazard kind of way from anything they get cheap.

5573. Do they breed from two-year-old fillies?—I don't think they do much. I don't think in that locality the two-year-old fillies would be able to breed; they are [illegible].

5574. You don't approve of breeding from two-year-old fillies?—It depends altogether on the country where it is tried. If it is tried in a very rich country—Kildare or Meath, or in a good part of Limerick—it may be very successful, but not in the North Riding of Tipperary. I don't think the farmers feed the fillies enough to make them able to breed at that.

5575. Do they take any trouble about mating the sire and the mare together?—Some do, but I think [illegible] in that kind of a breeding country they would [illegible]. They are poor judges of [illegible] they send to, and they do whatever the man [illegible] tells them.

5576. Are they influenced by the [illegible] of the fee?—[illegible] Well, the small farmers are guided very largely by the lowness of the fee, but I know some farmers who are quite ready to pay £2 10s. or £3, and I know farmers to give as high as £5, but I think that in the [illegible] that [illegible] of fee would go [illegible].

5577. Do you know [illegible] from [illegible], Clydesdales or [illegible]?—No, I don't think so. About [illegible] part of Tipperary, of which I know [illegible] a good deal, they have a sort of half-bred Clydesdale, but I don't know of any pure-bred Clydesdale there.

5578. Is the scheme of the Royal Dublin Society operating in your part of the country?—In other parts of the district I know it is.

5579. How is it taken up at all?—I don't think it has done any good. I think the district is not suitable for it to do much good.

5580. Do the farmers send the mares to the [illegible]?—Well, I believe they do, but I don't think it does much good. I don't think it is sufficiently used to have any great effect for or against.

5581. What breed of stallion do you recommend for that district?—Thoroughbred sires. I should not object to a very high class, I mean if a horse is [illegible], such a horse as [illegible], or [illegible], I would not object to such horses, but as a general rule, I recommend thoroughbreds.

5582. Would you allow the half-bred horses you have mentioned [illegible] the registered horses of the Royal Dublin Society?—Yes, I would not object to their being registered, but to the ordinary half-bred sires, which [illegible] generally called half-bred sires in the country, I would object very much.

5583. The [illegible] half-bred?—Yes, to a thoroughbred horse which [illegible] as a thoroughbred, but is [illegible] thoroughbred, I would not object.

5584. Do the farmers sell their best mares, or do they keep any good mares in your district?—They sell them.

5585. If they can get the money for them?—Yes.

5586. Can you suggest any way of preventing the farmers from doing that?—No, I don't think it would be possible. I don't think if a farmer has a mare sufficiently good to keep her as a hunter breeding mare, I don't think he could possibly refuse the price that that mare would be worth. If offered £60 or £70, no farmer in my district would refuse that for a mare out of the [illegible].

5587. There is no scheme that you can suggest to tempt the farmers to keep their good mares?—Not to keep their fillies; I have [illegible] scheme [illegible] that has suggested to me.

5588. Will you kindly read those headings—

SUMMARY AND SUGGESTIONS FOR IMPROVING HORSE BREEDING IN IRELAND.

1. That Ireland [illegible] peculiarly suited for the breeding and rearing of high class hunters and harness horses, [illegible] horse-breeding should be [illegible] as the [illegible] of these classes [illegible]. 2. That [illegible]. 3. That [illegible] as to [illegible] the price [illegible]. 4. That [illegible] a high class [illegible] for their work [illegible] should be bought in England by the [illegible] Society and distributed to districts by means of local committees. 5. That the mares be paid for [illegible] for two years. The [illegible] to give annually for the

[illegible]

Mr. [illegible]

money. 6. That only Irish bred mares be bought for this purpose. 7. That arrangements be made for placing mares quite enough for work with small farmers, and mares made for sale with farmers able to afford life breed mares. 8. That a registry of mares be opened, and all approved brood mares now in Ireland, together with those to be bought, be entered therein. 9. That thoroughbred sires be registered as at present, but that a higher standard of excellence be adopted, and that each year the least good sires be removed from the register. 10. That a horse with a stain in his pedigree but having proved himself to be a good sire, or having run well on the turf, be eligible for registration. 11. That the fee proposed to be charged for each stallion be approved of by the Dublin Society, having regard to the circumstances of the farmers in that district, and that the society pay half that fee for all registered mares going to the stallion."

5559. That is your scheme. You say only buy Irish-bred mares, but if you go to buy mares in England it would be very hard to say that they were Irish-bred mares?—It would be very hard to be absolutely certain in every case, but I don't think it would be impossible to work it if you were in touch with the large dealers. There are several big dealers who buy a good many hunters in Ireland; I think they would be very happy to really honestly assist in anything in the way of getting to know where these mares went to. If, for instance, a mare was broken down, as is often the case in the first season's hunting, I think the dealers in communication with a central society would pick up that mare for them for breeding purposes. I don't mean old, worn out, and utterly broken down animals, but mares that have met with an accident.

5560. You mean that the Government should give an extra grant for the supply of a better breed of mares in the country?—I suppose some extra grant would require to be given, but I don't think the money given in prizes does a great deal of good.

5561. You think the present system of giving prizes is not working well?—I think the other system would work better. The thing that really attracts a man to horse breeding is not getting a prize of £5 or £10 and it is only a chance if he gets the prize—but in the other case they can all get colts, and if they sell them they are sure of the money. In the first case it is only a chance of getting the £5 or £10.

5562. Do you think as to the stallion fee that the farmers would pay a sufficient fee to enable the owner to keep a good stallion?—I know in a good many districts in the North Riding of Tipperary generally I don't think it would pay to keep a good stallion for the fees that can be got, and that is the part I am talking about principally.

5563. That is why you mention that a certain portion of this fee should be supplied?—Yes, but at the same time I think if these farmers had better brood mares and had sold good colts it would encourage them to give higher fees, but then of course that is looking a good way into the future.

5564. Mr. Fitzwilliam.—What fee do you think the farmers in your district could be fairly expected to pay for the service of a good stallion?—I don't think it would pay a man to import a really good thoroughbred stallion and keep him for mares under these systems.

5565. What do you think in the market, either here or in England, a stallion suitable for the mares in your district could be bought for—have you formed any idea?—No, I have not, because I believe there are very few classes of animals in which there are greater variations of price than in stallions. A stallion worth very little as a race horse might be got very cheap as a hunter sire.

5566. They are very cheap just now?—Well, I don't think a bad thoroughbred stallion would be any advantage.

5567. You would not object to a well bred half-bred stallion?—No; a horse with a name. I know some of them who have got extremely well. The horse "Mackintosh" in Limerick, I was for years under the impression was a thoroughbred, but he is not, and he gets uncommonly well.

5568. He is not a thoroughbred?—I was for years under the impression he was, and I would have [illegible] next to him as a thoroughbred.

5569. You would like to see the money spent on mares, in a general way, and in small sums to individuals [illegible] a certain number of mares at a low fee [illegible], I would look, I think, to the mares. The mares are the main point.

5570. You think the mares are the main point?—I don't think the stallions, no matter how good they may be, can do much good in the country unless the standard of the mares be kept up.

5571. Do you think, looking at the small number that is now distributed for mares, that the present system is a satisfactory way of utilising the money that is available?—I must say that it has affected my district poorly, but I have heard that it works well in other districts.

5572. Should you be afraid of the blood of the Hackney or Clydesdale stallions which stand at a distance adjoining yours penetrating your district, and do you think that this cross so produced would eventually do harm to the breed of horses [illegible]?—I think they would. Possibly they would not come [illegible].

5573. No, but if they came into the district on half-bred mares [illegible]?—Well, I would rather they did not come in, and I think it is very likely they would come in. I know some years ago an effort was made by Scotch farmers in North Tipperary to bring over Clydesdale and Shire horses, and they bred a good many of those, and I believe they did a great deal of mischief. The first cross was undoubtedly a heavy looking horse that nobody could mistake. Generally, they crossed with a thoroughbred and then they got a [illegible] looking horse, very often as nice as you would like to ride, but in the [illegible] it was always a [illegible]. I am certain that a great deal of mischief has been done in the Dublin Show by the [illegible] putting down [illegible] I have [illegible]. They have been brought up and trimmed and look well, and an Englishman [illegible] "These are the Irish horses we hear so much about," and [illegible]. Very good looking horses [illegible] at the Dublin Show and they were exceedingly bad horses. There are three cases in my [illegible] of exceedingly bad horses and yet they have won prizes again and again at the Dublin Show, and they looked [illegible] the prize list. I don't think any judge could have picked them [illegible] in the ring, and at the same time they were extremely bad horses.

5574. Then you believe it would be a dangerous experiment to introduce any foreign blood into Ireland that had not a strong admixture of thoroughbred?—I would prefer not seeing it introduced for the reasons I have stated.

5575. Mr. Wrench.—In answer to the last question you stated that you would prefer that no blood should be introduced into Ireland that had not a strong admixture of thoroughbred? Are you aware that the Yorkshire Hackney have a strong admixture of thoroughbred blood?—I was not speaking of Hackneys.

5576. I know, but Hackneys were referred to. I understand that you do not yourself know that Hackneys have a strong admixture of thoroughbred blood?—I do not.

5577. You don't know much about their breeding?—No, I do not.

5578. Do you know whether the three horses that turned out so badly, that were really bad horses and got prizes at the Dublin Show, had much Clydesdale blood in them?—I have a strong suspicion that two of them had. My impression is that the horses were not bred as they were stated to have been bred.

2 A 2

3409. That is not an uncommon thing?—I don't know. I should say not.

3410. You could not detect it by looking at them?—No, I don't think I could. That is where the mischief lies.

3411. Therefore horses may be bred out of a Clydesdale and you would not know there was such a strain in them?—I believe they could.

3412. In those suggestions you have made, in the first of them you say you would only give State aid to those owners of horses that produce high class hunters or harness horses?—Yes.

3413. You would give no State aid to small farmers who either because of their circumstances or land could not breed good horses?—I don't think so in the case of the very small or very poor farmers. It may be worth his while to breed polo ponies, but I really don't know much about polo ponies—in fact I know nothing at all about them—but I don't believe in the case of small farmers it would ever be worth while to assist them to breed horses.

3414. Therefore you would not help them at all?—I would, I think, assist them to breed ponies, but I would not assist them to breed horses. I don't think it is in their interest.

3415. In No. 6, you suggest that a registry of mares be opened, and all approved mares now in Ireland, together with those to be bought, be entered therein. Have you considered when you opened the registry how you would work it?—Well, I don't see why it should not be worked on the same lines as the registry of stallions is now worked. I believe the way it is done is that an Inspector is sent down, and he makes a return of the stallions inspected.

3416. Would not that be a huge work for the Dublin Society to undertake to register the number of good mares in the country?—No. I think the mares could be collected at the shows, and they would send down an Inspector.

3417. Would you propose to leave it to the central body and not to the counties?—I think they should work through the county committees, but they might send the Inspector down. Of course these are matters of detail.

3418. I thought you might have considered the details?—Well, I have. My idea generally would be to collect the mares at the shows, very much as is done for the prizes that are given now, and if the mare was known to have bred good colts it would be registered.

3419. In the first instance, you would register them by appearance?—Or by having bred good colts. I would be chary about registering any except high-class ones.

3420. In the registry you could obtain particulars of how the different mares were bred?—Yes.

3421. They would be recorded in the books kept?—Certainly.

3422. If a registry of mares were adopted, would there be any danger of unsuitable blood getting in amongst the brood mares of the country?—After registering them?

3423. Yes.—Well, I think the registry would not prevent unsuitable blood creeping in.

3424. Could not it be traced then?—It would simplify the tracing of it.

3425. Having the registry established you would be able to trace the breeding of the animals?—I think so.

3426. Do you think it would put up the price of animals of that class if the dealer or buyer could tell how the particular animal was bred?—I certainly think if the dealer was absolutely sure of the breeding of the animal he would give more for it.

3427. Do you think it would put up the price of hunters in Ireland?—I think a great many horses would fetch higher prices.

3428. Do you think that a good deal of general information given as to animals in the catalogue of the Dublin Show is not absolutely reliable?—Well, I don't see how it could be absolutely reliable, because I have seen in the catalogue "breeder unknown," "pedigree so and so," and how is the exhibitor to get the pedigree if the breeder is unknown.

3429. And do you think if the breeding of the mares was registered the pedigrees could be traced?—Yes.

3430. CHAIRMAN.—When you formed your registry of mares would you register the produce of those mares?—Well, that is forming a Hunter Stud Book.

3431. Would you do that?—I think it would be a very good thing to do.

3432. If you did not do that you would not get any further?—I don't see any objections to doing that.

3433. When you had formed the register of sires and register of mares you would be in favour of entering the produce of those mares by registered sires?—Yes, I would; that is very much on the lines of the Hunter Improvement Society in England I believe.

3434. So that there could be a guaranteed pedigree given of these horses?—Yes.

3435. MR. WRENCH.—I want to ask you one more question—you think that the first step in improving the horses in your district is improving the brood mares?—Unquestionably. I don't believe it is possible to work it altogether through the sires to improve from a very bad stock, and I believe the registration of mares would do a great deal of good.

Mr. E. C. W[illegible], v.s., examined.

3436. CHAIRMAN.—You are a veterinary surgeon and live in the county of Limerick?—Yes.

3437. Have you any personal experience of the breeding of horses?—Yes, I have bred some horses, and my father bred horses, and my brother is still breeding them.

3438. What class?—Hunters and high-class harness horses and coach horses.

3439. What sires do you use?—There are various sires, there was a sire, "Prince of Peru," who, I am sorry to say, did a lot of harm in the district.

3440. Were they thoroughbreds?—Yes, with one or two exceptions.

3441. You have bred from half-breds?—Yes, and with very good results.

3442. Is the climate and district in your county suited for breeding horses?—Very well suited; it is good limestone land.

3443. What is the general class of horses bred about that district?—I should say half hunter colts and half good harness colts; it is one of the districts that supply the London job masters principally.

3444. Have the farmers got good mares as a rule?—In parts of the County Limerick they have, in the County Clare they have not, in parts of the Counties Cork and Kerry they have not, and in the extreme west of the County Limerick they have not good mares, but round the Limerick district and towards Cork, in the Golden Vale district, they have very good mares.

3445. Taking them generally do they feed their young stock well?—They do not, and I think if any inducement could be offered to them to improve their young stock in the way of premiums for foals, yearlings and two-year-olds it would be a step in the right direction, they starve their horses, anything is good enough for a horse, because it is a dairy country principally.

3446. They give the cows the best of it?—Yes, and they put the horses where the cows won't do.

3447. Do they work their brood mares?—Yes,

[illegible]

ing in the South of Ireland for the last five years as before, farmers have given it up.

5664. If these half-bred sires got good stock why were they not patronised?—Many farmers gave up breeding.

5665. Do you approve of the Royal Dublin Society's Scheme?—Not in its entirety. I believe they have taken a step in the right direction in registration. I don't approve of subsidising stallions, because it has been greatly abused, and is bound to be abused.

5666. How do you mean?—For instance when the Society paid half a registered stallion's fee I have known cases were that was the only money paid to the stallion owner, and they were glad to get it. I have known horses bought for £40 and £50 in days gone by to get £200 premium.

5667. In those days the horses were not registered?—Yes, they were, they were shown here and awarded premiums, I call it registration.

5668. What scheme would you suggest?—I would suggest that if practicable every stallion of every sort be registered, and, if possible, every brood mare, every stallion of every breed in Ireland be registered, and also every brood mare.

5669. You would insist on their being sound, would you?—Decidedly. I believe that has been one of the curses of horse-breeding in this country, breeding from unsound stock, not so much stallions as mares, because if it gets abroad that a stallion is unsound people will shun him unless he gets exteriorly good stock.

5670. You think there are a number of unsound mares in your district?—I know it, I live on it.

5671. The young stock are more unsound or are they getting sound?—I think they are improving for the last three or four years slightly.

5672. Are there any other sires in your district, besides half-bred and thoroughbred?—There are a few nondescripts, and there used to be a good many more.

5673. We will call those half-breds, but are there any other pure-bred like Suffolk Punches or Hackneys?—There are some Hackney sires, there is a Hackney sire in Clare, and there is a Hackney sire at Galway Castle. I don't know whether it is in Limerick, Cork, Tipperary, it is near the whole three.

5674. What is his name?—I cannot tell you, he belongs to Mr. Abel Buckley. There was a Hackney sire called King of the Forest that stood at Kilmallock for two years, he was leased by the late Mr. Harris, I think, and there are some Hackney horses in Galway.

5675. Have you seen the stock of King of the Forest?—Yes, I saw the foals which were very pretty; I thought the yearlings were not so nice as they should be, and I did not like the two-year-olds.

5676. They deteriorated each year?—I thought they did. I have seen some very nice Hackneys, but they have been exceptions, one in a hundred, and I don't believe in the half-bred stallion.

5677. You don't believe in the cross between the Hackney and the ordinary Irish blood mare?—I do not.

5678. You advise the farmers to breed hunters and hunting horses, what sire would you use?—They are the only horses that will pay, and I recommend them to get big-boned thoroughbred sires; if they cannot get them, I would not object to a half-bred sire; I mean a horse with three-quarters English thoroughbred blood in him.

5679. You are in favour of registering mares as well as sires?—I should like to insist on it if possible.

5680. And would you register again the progeny of those mares?—Yes, like individuals are registered, register the birth of every foal and keep a record of it, and have that record available on the payment of a small fee, 6d or 1s, by anybody who wanted it.

5681. Mr. Fitzwilliam.—Don't you think that mode of registering would cost a great deal of money?—I think it would be a very simple matter by insisting on the owners of stallions registering the service of every mare who comes to them, there is no need of

improve the mare before you can improve the breed. How would you propose to improve the mare, do you think you would improve her by putting a foreign horse to her or a thoroughbred horse?—I don't think there is any necessity at least to other countries to improve our breed, if we could retain the fillies that I am [illegible] every day, and destroy the weeds, [illegible] that they [illegible] from now, because they cannot get any one to buy them at any price.

5720. Do you think, if you could do away with the inferior thoroughbred without any bone or shape or [illegible] about them, if you did away with them and could introduce into the country a really high class thoroughbred horse with plenty of bone and substance and power about him, that he would be a better horse than any of the Shires or Clydesdales or Hackneys and those horses, and that you could build up the breed again better than with any other class of horse?—Decidedly. I would not let a Clydesdale, Shire, or Hackney into the country to be used generally through the country if I could stop them. I believe if we could keep our own fillies, without outside [illegible], and the question of the sires would regulate itself, it pays no man to keep a bad sire, a weedy thoroughbred horse, whatever his [illegible], will pay no money.

5721. Don't you think there is a good deal of wrong impression amongst many farmers with regard to bone and substance, they will see an underbred big boned horse and they will think that he is a much more powerful and larger boned horse than a higher well-bred one?—Decidedly, that is through the ignorance I spoke about before, and that wants to be overcome. If you can, they want to be protected from themselves. They will choose strong horses in my country, and if they have a weedy mare they come out with these and get a [illegible] which they [illegible] worthless.

5722. Is that in them not partly owing to [illegible] into them which he gets in hock and [illegible]?—[illegible], with [illegible], bad legs, and bad feet, they get [illegible] to those [illegible] which [illegible] to [illegible] their [illegible] and go wrong generally. And on the question of [illegible] I think it is a mistake the Royal Dublin Society have not taken it up, it is not one of these hereditary diseases, and I don't know anything more hereditary.

5723. Mr. Webster.—Do you mean the neck itself or the formation of the hock?—The formation of hock and the tendency to crack.

5724. The horse may have a curb and a very good hock?—That is what I mean.

5725. You mean a curby hock—that is [illegible] curby hock ought to come under the list of hereditary diseases?—Decidedly.

5726. When you are talking of horses being bred from these animals that produce curbs and spavins and ringbones, I think you are speaking generally with regard to Shires and Clydesdales?—I think any horse or mare for stud purposes should be rejected for curbs and unsoundness.

5727. But when you say that these outside-bred horses produce them, were you referring to Hackneys or not?—I think Hackneys give a decided tendency to curbs—particularly the half-bred Hackney—and bone weak hocks, all of them.

5728. From what experience are you speaking with regard to that hock [illegible]?—Several I have seen in the country—several colts got by him and some got by the other Hackney I have spoken about; and the general formation of the Hackney hock is what we call a curby hock—a weak hock.

5729. Was that other Hackney you spoke of a pure Hackney?—Yes; he was in the Hackney stud book.

5730. You don't remember his name?—King of the Road.

5731. You would not call that a good specimen of a Hackney?—I would call him a very [illegible] Hackney.

5732. Practically from these two your chief experience is derived?—Yes, and from the general formation of the half-bred Hackney's hock, which is a weak hock, and liable to crack on the slightest strain; but I would reject thoroughbred horses with a curb as well—all horses with curbs.

5733. You said, I think, that you had done very well with a good many small half-bred horses that got good stock?—Yes.

5734. You think that is a pity?—I do.

5735. And you think that some of these horses ought to be registered?—I think they should be registered, but I would have them on a separate register and as a distinct thing from the thoroughbred horse.

5736. In your register you would mean as far as possible the breeding of each horse?—As far as possible.

5737. How would you propose to carry it out; it was suggested yesterday through the Petty Sessions Clerk?—It would be a very good way.

5738. And you think that would be carried out, and it would be worth the expense?—I think it could be done very cheaply through the stallion owner and the Petty Sessions Clerk.

5739. You cannot suggest any better way?—No, I cannot.

5740. If that registration was carried out would not the breeder be sufficiently capable of taking care of himself, and seeing that he did not breed from any blood he objected to?—No; you want to protect the majority of breeders in Ireland from themselves.

5741. But if the register was carried out everybody who bought a horse could find out what it was bred?—That would be the object of registration.

5742. Then if anybody objected to any particular blood he could avoid it?—That would be the object of registration, and the Irish breeders are getting a bad name, as a good many horses are sold as Irish hunters that were never bred at all in the country. I know horses bought from England to Ireland, and taken back again to England as Irish hunters.

5743. Is it a fact that horses come over from England to the Horse Show?—Yes.

5744. You have seen them at Ballsbridge, perhaps?—I am not at liberty to give any names of individuals, but I know it. I have known horses entered for the Dublin Show with their pedigrees, and bought subsequently to the entry, say, entered as a bay horse six years old, got by Yankee or something else, and the man that has gone and bought the horse after he made his entry—a horse he had never seen or heard of before, I have known several instances. He entered the horse before he knew whether he would buy him or not, got him in on the single fee, and then went to look for the horse.

Mr. William Thomas [illegible], B.A., Lorrha, examined.

5745. Chairman.—You live in the Co. Tipperary?—Yes.

5746. Near Borrisokane?—Near Parsonstown.

5747. You take a considerable interest in horse-breeding in your district?—Yes.

5748. Do you breed any horses yourself?—Yes, I do, thoroughbreds and half-breds.

5749. Are there many horses bred round you?—Yes, it is a large horse-breeding district, North Tipperary.

5750. What class of mares have the farmers?—Well, I suppose they are what you would call border-bred mares, many of them, they are half-breds, but I should think there is every breed almost represented there.

5751. Mongrels in fact?—Yes, there is a great deal

of thoroughbred blood through the country, and that thoroughbred blood in unison with the blood of what would half-bred stallions bred with Clydesdales and with English Hackneys and Shire horses. I don't altogether [illegible] much [illegible]. I am not much of these being any Hackney stallion in our part of the country.

6752. Do they work the mares as their [illegible] or [illegible]?—They are all worked, the farmers all work their mares.

6753. And the stallions in your district, what are they?—The stallions, I think, are chiefly thoroughbreds in North Tipperary, but there are others hunters, half-bred and [illegible].

6754. And are they suitable to the mares in the district, do you think?—No, I don't think they are.

6755. What class have you?—I keep a thoroughbred stallion myself.

6756. Do you approve of half-breds?—Yes, I think the half-bred would be a decided improvement, if we had good half-breds.

6757. Have you any suggestion to make as to how good blood you would want or any qualification to be known?—I think it ought to be selected by experts first of all, but I don't think appearance would be sufficient unless they were tested in some way or other, either in the hunting field, or to jump or go [illegible], or in public before the [illegible]. Supposing a horse had got good shape I should be quite satisfied with that. If a horse got good stock I think it would be the very best test whatever his appearance was.

6758. Have you ever considered the question of introducing the Hackney?—Not to any very great extent, but I believe it is necessary to have some cross, if you go on using nothing but the thoroughbred you will end in weeds; you must have a cross at some time, when that cross should be in another thing, at present the cross is Clydesdale and to a certain extent the half-bred, and I think if you would improve the half-bred you would do away with the necessity for any other cross, you would do away with the Clydesdale and you would do away with the Shire horse.

6759. Is the Royal Dublin Society's scheme working in your district?—Yes.

6760. Is it doing good do you think?—I don't think it is.

6761. Do farmers avail themselves of it?—To a very limited extent.

6762. Do you think the young stock has improved in the district since the scheme was started?—I cannot see any improvement, I should say it had not.

6763. Would you have any suggestion to make for a change in the scheme?—I should give prizes for the horse that got the best stock.

6764. Thoroughbred or half-bred?—Whichever it was.

6765. Would you be in favour like some of the other witnesses of registering mares?—Yes, I think I should, I think it would give a great deal of trouble, but if it could be carried out I think it would be very [illegible]. I think it would put down bogus pedigrees to a great extent, which is very desirable.

6766. You mean you would say "Bred in a [illegible] bred in such and such a way," and point to the registered [illegible]?—Yes, I think that would be very useful.

6767. Do you think the horses raised in your district now are as good as they were some time ago?—Yes, I should say quite as good.

6768. Not inferior?—No, I would not say that they are inferior to what they were, a large proportion of them are very bad, but that must always be the result of mare breeding.

6769. You mean breeding from a mare of any type and a sire of another?—Yes; you cannot tell [illegible] and neither of these the type you want to produce.

6770. Do the farmers feed their stock [illegible] they used to?—No, I don't think they do as well as they ought to.

6771. The stock would be [illegible]?—[illegible] not at all.

6772. Do you breed from them yourself?—I have once or twice.

6773. Are you in favour of it?—No, I think it dries the filly, and you are breeding from an unmatured animal which I think is objectionable. I would rather breed from an old mare with [illegible] than from an unmatured animal, if I knew the old mare was a good one.

6774. Do you think the farmers take any trouble about mating their mares, or are they guided more by the fee?—Some of them are very particular about the horse, but I don't think, as a rule, in our part of the country they have much judgment. I agree very much with what Mr. Wilson said that I think they ought to be taught, a great many of them.

6775. You say the stock in your district you don't consider suitable for the district?—No, I think there are very few good sires in the district.

6776. Have you any suggestions to make for improving the stock in your district?—I would refer you to the answers to the queries sent to me which I would suggest.

6777. Will you read it now please?—Perhaps I might read the conclusion. I venture to suggest the following:—First, that local shows should be held in the spring at which prizes would be awarded to the best yearlings, the property of farmers. At these shows let the result of each stallion be exhibited separately, so as to give breeders an opportunity of judging of the characteristics of each horse by his produce. Secondly, award substantial prizes to the sires of the best groups of yearlings, say twelve in each group. These sires would be [illegible] for the purposes of competition. They would not be favoured by dealers, who would prefer that the best stock should be kept in the hands [illegible] by them. As a result of these shows I would anticipate that some of the best mares would be kept at home, and that the pick of the half-breds would be used to perpetuate their species. I think the shows being held in the spring would encourage the farmers to keep their stock well during the first winter, the most important period of a horse's life. I would abolish the registration of sires, and as far as possible let each sire stand on his own merits as judged by his stock, of course the registration of sires at the Dublin Show would still continue. 3rd. Roaring: In order to discourage the use of roaring sires I would have a register kept by the Dublin Society of all horses winning races (not being [illegible] races) [illegible] in public. This list possibly might not be perfect, but it might easily be nearly complete, if the Society employed a veterinary surgeon at a yearly salary at each of the principal training grounds. These veterinary surgeons would report to the Society as to each horse's wind, a matter which is perfectly well known to every stable boy in the locality. This list would not be published, but any breeder would, on payment of a fee, be informed whether any particular horse was on the list of those [illegible]. In that way [illegible] horses would be discouraged, and in course of time we should cease to breed our half-bred stock from horses of roaring blood. The unsatisfactory working of the present system of voluntary veterinary examination of stallions I need hardly remark upon, the plan I have suggested would I hope do away to a great extent with this. In conclusion, I think we ought to try to breed our hunting sires. If we could begin by breeding them the best looking hunting mares should be selected by a [illegible] of the Agricultural Department. The Americans have established a breed of trotting horses [illegible] as our Grand National thoroughbreds [illegible], and there is no doubt we can breed our hunters to any type and standard we please. The thoroughbred [illegible] a hunter [illegible] is generally preferred to a hunter stallion. I have already suggested that

Nov. [illegible]
Mr. William Thomas Tuthill.

[illegible] C. [illegible]
Mr. William [illegible]
[illegible]

breeders might be induced to keep their colts better. Had the difficulty not existed we should have had a distinct breed of hunters long ago. But though we might breed good-looking hunters in this way we could never expect to bring them to a high standard of excellence as regards performance unless they were brought up to speed, galloping, and weight-carrying powers. I entirely agree with Count Lehndorff that it is the test of the winning post which has made the English thoroughbred what he is, and our hunters must be tested similarly if they are to excel in this respect.

5778. In fact you would like to register mares and start a Registered Hunters Book?—Yes, and they would have to be tested.

5779. In your district does the land grow good bone or do it [illegible]?—I think the horses in my district are inclined to be light in bone; they are very hardy, the land is limestone and it is light soil, the horses have wonderful stamina, you never get a [illegible] from our part of the country.

5780. What sire would you recommend in your district?—I recommend a good thoroughbred [illegible] and a half-bred sire with a certain amount of thoroughbred blood in him.

5781. Mr. Wrench.—How do you account for the excellence of the horses in your district, do you think soil or climate has anything to do with it?—I think that has a good deal to say to it, and also there is a good deal of thoroughbred blood running through the mares.

5782. And then you say that all these stallions should be tested?—Might I add I think it is wise that the mares are put to extremely hard work, and the farmer won't keep a mare if she is not hardy and healthy and able to do a long day's work and a furrow [illegible].

5783. Therefore you think it is an advantage resulting from mares that undergo a great deal of hard work and hardship?—Yes.

5784. And would not the hunting field be the best practical test of these horses that you suggest should be tested?—I think it would, but I think point to point races might do something towards it; it is very difficult in all of the private matches in the hunting field, it depends very much on the rider.

5785. But still it would be some test if he did a long run?—Yes.

5786. Mr. Fitzwilliam.—You would not look on the test of the hunting field as equal to the test of the racecourse?—By no means, but I think the test of the racecourse is very often omitted in the thoroughbred stallions we use, they are simply bought by their pedigrees, horses entirely useless on the turf, and that perhaps never have been raced, are used as hunter sires.

5787. And then, although they may not have been raced, these sires are doing very probably what?—A great many of the horses that have never been raced, I think half the horses in the Stud Book have never been tried, never been publicly tried, nobody knows anything about their performance.

5788. Mr. Wrench.—Would you be satisfied to breed from a horse that had not proved a success on the racecourse himself, provided he was bred from parents both of whom had been very successful on the racecourse?—I would rather have a horse that was a good performer himself.

5789. Do you think it is very hard to buy the right kind of thoroughbred stallion at present?—I can hardly say that, I should say it was not very hard.

5790. You think you could buy a good class of thoroughbred stallion now at a reasonable price?—It is a matter of what you would call a reasonable price, maybe £300.

5791. Do you think you would have to give up to that extent?—I would put that as an outside sum to give for a hunter stallion, from £100 to £150, perhaps.

5792. But as a rule are not the majority of the thoroughbred stallions that come over to Ireland bought for very much less?—I believe for very much less.

5793. There are very few of that class of hunting gentlemen in the country?—Very few.

5794. Do you think it would be easy to find suitable horses there now?—No, I don't think it would, they seem so [illegible].

5795. As sires they don't exist?—They don't exist. If you could have your pick of the south of Ireland you would have a very fine class of hunter sires, or if you could have the prize geldings of the Dublin Show as stallions you would have a very fine breed of hunters.

5796. But up to the present it has not been [illegible] in got them?—No.

5797. And they would have to be hard. Taking such a hunter type with action that would be too fine and weedy for a thoroughbred horse; what mating would you employ?—I think the best horses are certainly thoroughbreds, I think the Hackneys are perhaps too much the best horse.

5798. Have you any personal experience of Hackney breeding at all?—The best hunting I ever rode was by a Hackney out of a Connemara pony, and I believe he himself was Hackney, but I don't think one swallow proves anything. Mr. Wilson stated yesterday he had ridden a Hackney, and could not get him over the first fence, all I can say is that this horse, and a good many people remember him in my part of the country.—I never saw a man too long for him; he was not very fast, but if it was his first fence he was and so on at the end of a long run, he could jump anything, he had very bad action.

5799. His high action did not make him go?—No, he went close to the ground, but he had beautiful shoulders and never came down.

5800. If you could get a suitable Hackney for very weedy mares with some thoroughbred blood in them you would not object, I mean, in your district where you cannot get a thoroughbred horse and cannot buy a hunter sire?—I have seen the Hackneys at the Hackney Show in London, but there are very few of them one would like to put to a mare. If one could get them like that they would do (producing picture), that is a fancy picture, there (producing picture) is the reality.

5801. He is not a very well bred Hackney?—He was a prize winner at the London Show this year.

5802. I think you said that at the Dublin Show you would give prizes to the young stock, no matter by what sire they were?—I think I said I would give prizes to the best, no matter to what breed he belonged.

5803. I understood it was the stock?—No, my object is to encourage the sires that produced the best stock. I think that it is very doubtful whether it is very much use to give prizes to the best-looking sires. Some little time ago I compared a list, went through the prize lists of the Royal Dublin Society's Show, and, examining the pedigrees, to the extent which, perhaps is rather a large percentage, but presuming them to be correct in the majority of instances—I found out that in the twenty years from 1868, when there was a regular list kept, until 1888, that the sires that had got the most of the winners had never been shown, with the exception of one, and he had been rejected; and that three sires, two of whom had never been shown and the third had been turned out of the ring, had got more prize winners than all the prize stallions put together. These three got 41 between them, and all the prize stallions in the Dublin Show for 20 years had only got 38. This (producing) is that list, and I think you will see the horses at the top of the list were deserving of a good deal more money than some of the others.

5804. Practically you would let all the prizes be given according to the result and not to appearance?—In the first instance, I think I should give a good looking horse a prize, and then he has proved himself afterwards. I would give him a start for his looks, for you have the valuable opinion of the judges as to his appearance, and that carries out Mr. W[illegible]'s plan of educating the farmer and instructing him.

6909. In the [illegible] Ring, in those classes where mares are shown with foal at foot in a thoroughbred [illegible], would you submit them to veterinary inspection?—I don't think you can judge a foal at all; there is no [illegible] in that class.

6910. Would you submit mares in foal by half-bred [illegible]?—I would prefer not giving an opinion; I think [illegible] either way or the other.

6911. You have [illegible] suggested of [illegible], and also it has been suggested it should be carried out through the Petty Sessions Clerk; do you think that is a practical proposal?—Yes; I don't see any objection to it.

6912. And you think that any expense that was incurred by that would be well worth while?—I am inclined to think it would.

6913. Can you think of any better proposal than carrying out local registration?—No; I don't think there could be anything better. I think there should be a register kept some way or other. I think the stallion owner ought to be obliged to register all the mares that come to his horse as far as he knows them, but I think some of the stallion owners don't know what mares their horses cover.

6914. But still you think registration might be carried out, and it is quite a practical proposal through the Petty Sessions Clerk?—I think so, or the Constabulary; the Constabulary now-a-days have very little to do, I am glad to say. I just wish to say with regard to making sure that there are none of the [illegible] Irish stallions at the present moment that are supposed to be sound. I won't mention names because I don't know whether I might not be laying myself open to an action for libel or not; but I think it is very objectionable that nobody should be able to say for certain whether the horse he sends his mare to is sound or otherwise. [illegible] I suppose it will be considered confidential.

6915. CHAIRMAN.—Suppose a horse makes a noise [illegible] the [illegible], he might be perfectly sound all the [illegible], but he might have [illegible] again.—I should ask the question if he had been at public up to three or four year old and came sound all the [illegible]; I don't think you can go any further than that.

6916. Lord [illegible].—That is if he had a [illegible]?—I don't know whether it would be [illegible] to go into that question. I should not like to go into that question, but I should not like to see a horse with a long neck like a giraffe; he would be [illegible]; but if he went through [illegible] up to four-year-old, I think he would be very [illegible] to breed a roaring stock.

6917. CHAIRMAN.—You mean if a horse came [illegible] off the turf, you would not ask any questions?—[illegible] up to [illegible] years of [illegible].

6918. Lord [illegible].—I think you said that you would be in favour of registration rather than making a stud-book for hunters?—No, I did not intend to say that. I think registration and the making of a stud-book, there is a very great distinction between them.

6919. I just wanted to know what was your [illegible]?—I did not intend to distinguish between them.

6920. You have no preference for one above the other?—I think registration would perhaps be best.

6921. But a stud-book has to be closed sometime or other?—No; you start by entering in the first instance.

6922. How do you admit afterwards?—In [illegible] Weatherby's Stud-book you must trace back to a sire and dam in the stud book.

6923. That is because it is closed, but if you made a stud-book, you must close it, I fancy?—I have not looked so far ahead as that.

6924. That is why I wanted to know if your [illegible] preference for registration over a stud-book?—I should close it except to thoroughbred blood, of course.

6925. I notice that a rule in the English Hunter Improvement Society:—"The mare is eligible for entry which has been awarded a prize, been reserved or highly commended in hunter classes at any show in the United Kingdom." [illegible] whether you would be inclined to admit mares that way?—I should say [illegible] not so much as I would; I think the system on which the Hunter Improvement Society was [illegible] was necessary, but I don't think it was [illegible] to be [illegible].

6926. You also said, with regard to the registration of stallions, that you would like to abolish the registration of sires?—The present registration of sires, I mean, under the Royal Dublin Society.

6927. What harm does it do?—I think horses are registered that ought not to have been [illegible]; I think it has discredited the system, because horses have been registered which they don't consider, and I think rightly don't consider, to be worthy of registration.

6928. So you would not examine or inspect any horses in [illegible] of [illegible]?—I am not prepared to say that, but I think I would have them all examined at some local centre.

6929. You would not abolish the registration, but I understand you to say you did not see that there was any use in having them registered?—What I mean was under the present scheme, as it stands at present.

6930. Then [illegible] of [illegible], I suppose, in those?—I think there is very little, I have seen so [illegible] horses not to be registered; I cannot understand on what principle they were allowed to pass—I have known horses [illegible] in the same [illegible].

6931. Did they come off the turf sound?—I cannot tell you that, nobody [illegible] that, we are all kept in ignorance at present about unsound [illegible] horses, I am sorry I can't throw a little light on it.

6932. Mr. W[illegible].—You think it would be possible to throw light on it in the way you suggest by having a veterinary surgeon appointed to watch horses on the training grounds?—Yes, I cannot see any practical difficulty; the trainer of a horse might, when he is sent back in a matter of necessity, which is published in the papers occasionally with regard to certain horses, and I often get them out for my own information.

6933. Suppose we advertised Mr. W[illegible] to spend his time on the training grounds do you think he would be a very popular man there?—I think Mr. W[illegible] would be very glad to undertake the business, I don't think it would be a question of popularity at all, if you go to [illegible] you will generally find out about a horse's wind.

6934. Mr. [illegible].—But I think you often know that they are roarers when they are not so?—I saw it stated the other day that [illegible] was roarer and that was [illegible] next week; I know it anybody goes out and listens on the training ground he will learn a good deal about horse's wind, or if you listen when horses come back to the paddock. I have heard horses roaring in the paddock, and I have seen them advertised with a veterinary surgeon's certificate afterwards as perfectly sound. I could give you some curious instances in my own experience, although it is very limited indeed.

Mr. R. G. [illegible], J.P., Barrinleigh, examined.

5631. (Chairman.)—You live in Tipperary and have had considerable experience in the breeding of horses I understand?—Yes, I have been breeding horses for the last ten years, from 10 to 15 mares each year.

5632. Can you tell us what success you have had?—I have won a good many cups and prizes in England and Ireland for animals principally bred by myself, and I sold some for high prices in some cases; in 1893 to 1895 I won [illegible] for the Produce Cup at the Dublin Society's Show, and this year I won it, and sold the winner at a good price. I have acted as a judge of [illegible], hunters and hackneys and [illegible] as well as shown in England and Ireland.

5633. What class of mares have you bred from and what sires have you used?—I principally bred from half-bred mares and to a few mares from thoroughbreds, but the stallions I have used have been to thoroughbreds, but occasionally I have used half-bred stallions.

5634. What class of horse is there the most demand for in your District?—The district is [illegible] I think of producing the best class of horses of the [illegible] hunters [illegible], but owing to the demand in the [illegible] for [illegible] harness [illegible] I consider [illegible] to [illegible].

5635. Are many horses bred in the district [illegible]?—There are a great number of horses bred in the district. The people who chiefly breed the horses, [illegible] of the [illegible], are the small agricultural tenants and working farmers who generally keep one or two brood mares, with which they do their light work and from which they breed a foal as a rule every year. The class of mare [illegible] is a half-bred animal from 15.0 to 15.3 hands high, whose principal faults are [illegible] of their [illegible], [illegible] of bone and what is commonly called [illegible].

5636. In breeding from [illegible] [illegible] [illegible]?—[illegible] I think if a two-year-old shows [illegible] bone and substance she may be covered with advantage at three years by a half-bred [illegible], or a very strong thoroughbred.

5637. Is there a sufficiency of stallions in your district, are they suitable for the [illegible]?—The thoroughbreds in any classes are fairly good, but in [illegible] they are [illegible] and [illegible], and also very [illegible]. The half-bred stallions [illegible] in most instances they are the result of the cross of a thoroughbred or half-bred sire on a mare whose pedigree can [illegible] be traced, and [illegible] of [illegible] pedigree [illegible] of [illegible].

5638. Have the mares deteriorated, and if so, from what cause?—Yes, I think they have [illegible] [illegible]; the [illegible] with the farmers [illegible] been [illegible], they [illegible] years ago.

5639. Can you give any reason for that at all?—Yes, I consider that mostly due to the fact that [illegible] thoroughbred sires have been used instead of half-bred sires of good breeding.

5640. What is your opinion of the so-called half-bred [illegible] with regard to his suitability as a sire?—I consider that the correct type of half-bred sire that should be used in the country [illegible] to [illegible] [illegible], [illegible] in a very few cases, and consequently they would have to be bred.

5641. You don't approve of the present class of half-breds?—No; not as a rule.

5642. Have you any observations to make with regard to the Royal Dublin Society's scheme in your district?—[illegible] the scheme has been [illegible] a failure in Tipperary. The young mares shown in the recent shows, with one or two exceptions, have been quite useless for breeding purposes, and if mated with any registered horse I know could not possibly produce a hunter to carry more than ten or twelve stone. The number of mares shown at the shows has decreased within the last two years.

5643. Have you any experience of breeding from a Hackney sire?—I never bred from a Hackney sire myself, though if I could get one of good breeding quality and hunter shape I should unquestionably put some of my hunter mares to him in preference to many of the half-bred sires of doubtful pedigree in the country.

5644. Do you think it is a desirable thing to introduce Hackney blood into a hunter district?—In the exclusively hunter districts such as Meath I would not be in favour of introducing a Hackney sire, but in districts which produce harness horses as well as hunters, I think they could with advantage be used, as a complete system of registration of every breed of horses in Ireland would prevent any mixing of the breed.

5645. Do you think a Hackney is likely to get a hunter?—I should not advocate Hackneys for producing hunters, but I would not go so far as to say it would be utterly impossible for a good shaped one to do so.

5646. Do you think he would get a good harness horse suitable for London dealers?—From what I have seen of Hackneys I think they are very suitable, for nearly all the prize winners in the harness classes at the shows in England and Ireland are pure-bred Hackneys.

5647. Would they be suitable for getting army horses?—I have no experience, but I should think it probable that the progeny of the Hackney would not be less suitable than the misfit of an animal bred from a thoroughbred for a hunter and failing to be one. I consider the cross of the Hackney on the weedy mares of the country would be better than the cross of the thoroughbred at present available.

5648. Have you any suggestion to make to encourage the farmers to keep their good mares to breed from?—I consider if State aid was given Government Stud Farms should be started in different parts of the country, and that these studs should be formed with a view of improving horse-breeding, whether with a view of producing hunters or harness horses as will be most suitable to each district. Mares should be bred from at these studs which could be sold at public auction to the farmers, or that the farmers could obtain them at a fixed price, with a view to breeding from them, these mares should also be branded so as to prevent the farmers disposing of them, and they should be covered free by whatever stallion at the Government stud, whoever was in charge of the stud should consider most suitable, this combined with a very strict system of registration would, I think, in time, greatly improve the breed of mares in the country.

5649. You would not leave the selecting of the sire to the farmer?—I certainly would not leave it to the farmer, my experience of the farmer is that he takes his mare to a stallion simply because he happens to be friendly with the owner, quite irrespective of the question of whether the sire is suitable to the mare or not.

5650. You think the Government ought in fact to supply at a low price the mares to the farmers who have not got good ones?—I think the farmer should be able to go to these studs and either buy a mare there or be able to claim her at a fixed price, for the purpose of breeding from her, and I might say also, that I think at these studs—of course there would naturally be colts as well as fillies produced there—a very good type of half-bred sire would probably be produced.

5651. You recommend, I think, that the half-bred sire would have to be bred, that there are very few of them in the country at present?—Yes.

[illegible]

[illegible]

Dec. 8, 1896.
Mr. T. G. Conlon.

nearly thoroughbred, the class you mentioned just now?—Yes.

5890. The horse you would really like to breed from for producing hunters and the horse you think would be most useful in Ireland would be a roomy horse that has a very large admixture of thoroughbred provided that he is sound?—That is in the hunter-breeding districts, not the harness horse districts.

5891. Lord Rathdonnell.—When you say the harness horse districts, could you define the harness horse districts in Ireland?—Well, I think from my experience there is really only one hunter-breeding district exclusively, and that is the county Meath. I think all the rest of Ireland breed both hunters and harness horses.

5892. And Meath is the only one for hunters, exclusively I mean, for hunters?—I think it would pay in the rest of Ireland to breed harness horses as well as hunters.

5893. Col. St. Quintin.—You attribute the decrease in the value and the quality of the animals to the cross with the light thoroughbred?—Yes.

5894. Do you think that the introduction of half-bred horses like the Shires and Clydesdales, of which there are a good many in the country, have had anything to do with it?—Well, not in my experience, though I certainly would be very strongly against a Shire or Clydesdale.

5895. Do you go round many of the fairs in Ireland?—A certain number.

5896. Well, walking through these fairs, when you have looked carefully over the animals don't you think you can detect the cross without any difficulty between what is a high class animal and one that has been crossed with a half-bred, namely, the Shire or Hackney, at least I know very little about Hackneys, but what I call the agricultural horse?—Yes, I think one can detect them in this way, that as a rule the highest and weediest animal to be seen in the fairs is probably, if you inquire into the pedigree, got by a thoroughbred horse.

5897. Don't you see a very large number of what I call three-cornered brutes, useless for anything, with great heads badly set on to their necks, bad shoulders, bad legs, bad temper, in fact bad everywhere, that class?—Unquestionably you do.

5898. One you not in a measured way that that class of horse has got into this class from the introduction of other blood, other than the thoroughbred?—Yes, not perhaps directly, but I should probably imagine if I saw an animal of that description that it is one in that might have had a soft strain of Clydesdale, Shire, or Suffolk Punch blood.

5899. Yes, but if you go through the fairs and go with your eyes open you can see them by hundreds?—Well, quite admit that.

5900. And you can detect that that is not the thoroughbred that has done that?—I don't say it is, but I say it is the low-priced, not quality of a thoroughbred of the cart horse bloods you mean.

5901. I don't say the direct cross, not the first cross, I am only speaking of the introduction of the blood that has altered the shape of what was a nicely turned thoroughbred horse, and he has grown a most three-cornered useless animal?—I don't think there are so many strains of cart horse blood now of late years being used as there had been formerly.

5902. That I am not speaking of, but can you not detect the cart-horse blood and the coarse formation of the animal in the fairs now you go to, surely?—You can.

5903. Undoubtedly there are animals that one would from thoroughbred sires, but they are a much more shapely animal, and though they are a lighter animal, they are an animal you possibly could do something with, they would make a light hack or light harness horse?—As a rule, if an animal is strong even if he has bad shapes, you will find sale to buy him, whereas an animal may be of good shape but light, and nobody will buy him.

5904. What will he buy them for, and at what price?—Of course at a low price, but one class of animal is practically unsaleable.

5905. They will sell a cart for the machine, or pull the manure out of a farmer's yard, but he will not get anything for the animal?—No, a poor price.

5906. And that is through the introduction of half-bred blood?—Of cart horse blood.

5907. There are certain breeds of cart horse you would not prize?—Yes, I suppose so, every animal of its own breed is prized if it is suited to the kind of work of the breed.

5908. Would you advocate the introduction of any coarse blood into the country to increase the size of the animals?—No cart horse blood.

5909. You very seldom get that heavy size without putting a certain coarseness in the blood?—With reference to what are you talking about.

5910. You get a big bony horse?—Stallions, do you mean.

5911. He has generally got some coarseness in his blood?—Yes.

5912. Would you advocate bringing any of that coarse blood into the small mares of Ireland to improve her, to get strength and size?—I would not try to get strength and size by bringing in coarse, heavy blood into the country, I mean, Shires, Clydesdales, or Suffolk Punches.

5913. Don't you think, or rather do you think, with the really good horse, clean thoroughbred sires with good bone, a powerful horse you could build up the present breed of animals in the country?—If they were procurable I should say so, but I don't think they are procurable.

5914. That is the question, but if they were procurable, don't you think you would do it better with that than by introducing any other blood?—I should agree so in hunting districts if you wanted to breed a hunter.

5915. Or even harness horses?—Well, I differ from you there.

5916. Will you take the men who deal in harness horses, their opinion upon it as of a certain amount of value? But with regard to the harness horses, you say all the prizes at shows are taken by the Hackneys; say you have a class of four or five Hackneys, what do you give the prize for for a Hackney—do you give it for his conformation or his extraordinary height of his action?—General conformation and action.

5917. Which do you think gets the greatest number of points in the judge's eye, action or shape?—Personally speaking, I have given about an equal number of points in my opinion, when I have been judging them.

5918. It is not necessary that the highest action gets the prize?—By no manner of means; in fact I think Hackney men attach too much importance to high action.

5919. It is a physical fact that any extra action beyond what is required to carry the animal safely and well must necessarily be a waste of power?—That is a very debateable point to give an opinion on; I would not like to say that as an absolute fact.

5920. Well, it can be proved?—As a law of nature.

5921. As a law of nature, a physical fact, and it is a very essential one in a certain way with regard to the staying power of the animal, because, given two animals of equal staying power, if one has got that extravagant high action it cannot last as long as the other, it is physically impossible?—I drove behind a Hackney in Donegal, a pure-bred Hackney in the spring; I drove that horse from twenty to twenty-five miles, and coming back you dare not touch that horse with a whip.

5922. There are Hackneys and Hackneys, that I don't deny for a moment, I wanted to find from you whether you did consider that the present breed in the country might be improved and built up by selecting to use thoroughbred, if you could give the early high action breed, with bone and strength, as well as by the introduction of any other blood?—I agree with you there, but I do not think it possible to procure it.

[illegible]. But if it was procurable you would prefer it?—Certainly.

[illegible]. Mr. WARBURTON.—Do you think hunter mares generally make good harness horses, have they got enough action?—As a rule, the animal bred as a hunter and not coming up to the requirements in the work of his being too light for that purpose; such animals are sold for little money, and would certainly be unsuitable as good harness horses.

[illegible]. Do you think the horses that you see in the fairs now are deficient in action or not, what class of action have they?—Their action, as a rule, is bad, and they often they are inclined to dish; taken on the whole, improvement in action, I should say was required.

[illegible]. And what do you think is the most valuable commodity in harness horses?—Action, certainly.

[illegible]. Do you think that a thoroughbred horse is as likely to transmit action, as a Hackney Stallion?—I should not say so.

[illegible]. We have heard a great deal about this peculiar action that a Hackney has, you have seen a good many Hackneys, what do you think of Hackney action?—I think there are two distinct types of Hackney action:—The Yorkshire Hackney, which gets his fore-legs well out in front his shoulders, and spreads well at his hocks; and the Norfolk which produces a flashy, more showy action, but is rather inclined to [illegible].

[illegible]. Which do you prefer?—I should certainly prefer the Yorkshire.

[illegible]. You have seen a large number of the produce of Hackneys, have you not; do you find that their action is objectionable in any way?—I have seen a large number of the progeny of Hackneys, and when they have been of the Yorkshire type I have not considered their action too high; as a matter of fact, I have seen some Hackneys coming to the [illegible] and they would [illegible] their action was no higher than the ordinary horse one sees.

[illegible]. You have watched those as young Hackneys?—Yes.

[illegible]. What do you consider are the points that those weedy horses that you have described in your district are most deficient in?—As I said before, straight shoulders, light of bone in the leg, drooping rumps, and indifferent action.

[illegible]. What cross do you think would be likely to correct that?—An exceptionally big, strong-boned thoroughbred, which, however, is hard to get; I consider a well-bred, hunter-shaped Hackney as being the next most suitable.

[illegible]. And if Government aid was given would you leave it to the farmers to say which class of stallion they required?—No; if, as I suggest, they were to get their brood mares at a reasonable price and free service of Government stallions, I should leave it to the head of such stud, who should be an authority on horse-breeding, to decide the mare which stallion stallion, in his opinion, would be most suitable to her.

[illegible]. I think you said that in your district the farmers had used nearly thoroughbreds very largely, and that you attributed the deterioration in horses to that?—Yes.

[illegible]. Are they at all falling into the opposite in breeding now, and using coarse horses in order to get size?—Yes; farmers are evidently beginning to find, as a rule, the progeny of the thoroughbred horse is practically unsaleable before he reaches the age of three years, they are consequently inclined to go to half-bred stallions of perhaps doubtful pedigree.

[illegible]. I think you said you would like thoroughbred sires to have three crosses on the dam's side, do you think it is possible to buy those horses in this country now?—I think a certain number of good, sound ones might be procurable, but not anything like the number that would be required in the country, and, in default of there being a sufficient supply, I should be quite content for such a hunter-shaped Hackney with a sufficient strain of thoroughbred blood in his pedigree.

[illegible]. Would you use one for your own mares?—Yes; I would to one I considered too light to put to a thoroughbred.

[illegible]. And you think it would be a distinct advantage if it was used in your district with carefully selected mares?—I should say so.

[illegible]. Do you know at all how Yorkshire Hackneys were bred?—Yes; I believe the foundation of the breed was the cross of the thoroughbred horse with a Yorkshire roadster mare, which is of a distinctly stepping type, and before railways were invented the Yorkshire farmer had to depend solely on his horse for means of locomotion; I believe there are great records of their endurance and staying power.

[illegible]. They were bred, as far as you could hear when in England, from a very stepping mare?—I believe so.

[illegible]. A mare that did very long distances?—I believe so.

[illegible]. You have described the results of the Royal Dublin Society's schemes in your district, and I think you said that the produce of mares were disappointing, as the stallions?—Oh, yes; they are.

[illegible]. To what do you attribute that?—I think they don't use the thoroughbred sires as much as they used to, and therefore they are not eligible to come under the scheme.

[illegible]. And do the young horses that are brought and shown under the scheme show an improvement?—With a very few exceptions, the young horses shown in the classes held this year were quite unsuitable to breed any useful horses.

[illegible]. What class of farmers would you consider should be helped in Stallion assistance; we have had it suggested this morning that only the farmers who [illegible] very high class hunters or harness horses should be assisted by the State, do you agree with that?—I think it is the poorer farmers should be assisted, say the farmer whose valuation is under £10, or perhaps £15; I think the better class are able to take care of themselves.

[illegible]. And as a rule do those farmers want to breed the produce heavy stock that can be easily reared?—Oh, yes. It very often happens that they have no house accommodation to winter them in at all, they have to let them run out all the winter.

[illegible]. Then I think you have heard it advocated that there should be a very complete system of registration, and I understand you agree with that?—Yes, a complete system of registration, and I should go as far as establishing a stud book of such breed.

[illegible]. A stud book of horses alone?—Of every breed that is [illegible] that has not already a stud book.

[illegible]. And you would call it a breed of Irish horses?—I would call the particular breed Irish hunters.

[illegible]. And you have heard it stated here that some people view with alarm the introduction of Hackneys, that it may effect an injury to the Irish hunters, do you think there is any real ground for their alarm?—I think if the registration and stud book were carried out, as I suggest, I don't see how the limited crossing [illegible] could be injurious, and I think there is quite room enough in the country to breed the three distinctive breeds of [illegible].

[illegible]. Is it difficult to find harness horses now?—If I wanted a pair of harness horses tomorrow, I should not quite know where to go to look for them in this country.

[illegible]. Do you know that the trade in those big [illegible] that has been referred to is really a very limited trade, as compared with the whole trade of England. We heard of one dealer yesterday who stated that bought 250 horses a year?—I should consider it an extremely limited trade.

[illegible]
Mr. [illegible]

[illegible]. Of course there are others, but the [illegible] is [illegible] by [illegible] [illegible] in a limited trade?—I should say so.

[illegible]. They cannot be produced in large numbers?—I should say not.

[illegible]. Have you attended any sales of thorough-bred horses?—Yes, I attended the [illegible] sales [illegible] several times.

[illegible]. Do you think it is hard [illegible] to find thorough-bred [illegible] with plenty of bone?—I should say it is very hard, [illegible] December [illegible] [illegible] [illegible] [illegible] [illegible] to purchase a horse.

[illegible]. And generally [illegible] in breeding thorough-bred [illegible] [illegible] to [illegible]?—I [illegible] [illegible] [illegible] [illegible] [illegible] [illegible] [illegible] of their [illegible] and the [illegible] of whether they will break [illegible] of races or [illegible].

[illegible]. Have you been [illegible] for the congested districts?—Yes, I have been to Clare, Kerry, and Donegal.

[illegible]. On **more than one occasion?—Yes, the last two years.**

[illegible]. Judging **at the** [illegible]—Judging **at the** shows.

[illegible]. Have you had an opportunity of seeing the mares there and their produce?—Oh, yes, I [illegible] there, the [illegible], and it was [illegible] [illegible] [illegible] the good-looking foals running at their foot would be the progeny of such mares.

[illegible]. And in addition to the foals did you see older produce?—Yes, yearlings, two-year-olds, and three-year-olds, they all [illegible] a good [illegible], on the contrary [illegible] of mare found in the [illegible].

[illegible]. Have you seen the produce of different stallions out of the same mare?—Yes. This year in [illegible] [illegible] [illegible] [illegible] [illegible] [illegible] [illegible] [illegible] [illegible] good enough to [illegible] a prize [illegible] [illegible] [illegible] [illegible] [illegible] [illegible] [illegible] [illegible] a thorough-bred, a [illegible] by a [illegible], and [illegible] [illegible] [illegible] Hackney, neither the [illegible] nor the [illegible] [illegible] [illegible], and the [illegible] [illegible] by the Hackney stallion was [illegible] in its class and [illegible] [illegible] [illegible].

[illegible]. Lord [illegible].—Was that foal?—The Hackney was a yearling.

[illegible]. Mr. [illegible].—When you were in the congested districts have you seen any of the [illegible] that used to be [illegible]?—Yes, I have. One of the [illegible] I saw was [illegible], [illegible], [illegible], and [illegible].

[illegible]. I believe he was a very popular animal in the district?—Yes, as [illegible].

[illegible]. He [illegible] [illegible] [illegible] [illegible] [illegible] [illegible] [illegible]?—He did.

[illegible]. If you had to advise the Congested Districts Board, what stallions would you recommend them to send into those districts?—Unquestionably the Hackney. I have seen the [illegible] of the Welsh cob and Arab there [illegible], and I think they are by no means so [illegible] [illegible] as the [illegible] got by the Hackney.

[illegible]. Do you think it would pay the Hackney [illegible] to breed from them [illegible] the Arab?—No, not like the Arab at all.

[illegible]. You don't like the **Arabs or Barbs for that district?**—No.

[illegible]. You think they would [illegible] a [illegible]?—Yes.

[illegible]. But at the same time if good [illegible] [illegible] exist you would try them?—I think I should.

[illegible]. [illegible] [illegible] [illegible] [illegible], you consider the Hackney the best?—I [illegible] [illegible] [illegible] [illegible] [illegible] I should use the Hackney; for I think he would give them [illegible], which they [illegible] very badly, he would give them action [illegible] [illegible] any [illegible] [illegible] [illegible].

[illegible]. You would use the Hackney in the first instance?—I think I should.

[illegible]. Have you, as a matter of fact, seen any of these Hackneys that [illegible] [illegible] those districts by the Board?—Yes.

[illegible]. What do you think of them?—I think they are a very good [illegible] kind.

[illegible]. Have you seen, when you have been in those districts, [illegible] to the people, [illegible] class of [illegible] they themselves like?—Yes, as [illegible], in the [illegible] [illegible], the country people told me they would have nothing except a Hackney; the [illegible] thorough-bred horse [illegible] [illegible] and [illegible] [illegible] [illegible] [illegible] [illegible] [illegible] the Hackney had been.

[illegible]. Was he a good class of thorough-bred?—No, [illegible]. I thought [illegible] a good [illegible] of thorough-bred. [illegible] he was good enough to win a good number of prizes at shows.

[illegible]. I think he did a good **deal of racing too?—** Yes, he won several races.

[illegible]. We have heard [illegible] that there is [illegible] [illegible] [illegible] the Hackney [illegible] is only animal I [illegible] in [illegible] particular [illegible] that happened to be in the South of Ireland, but from your experience of the [illegible] you have [illegible] [illegible] Hackneys, [illegible] [illegible] [illegible] of Ireland do you think they [illegible] [illegible] [illegible] [illegible] [illegible] [illegible] [illegible] [illegible] [illegible] [illegible] [illegible] of the Hackneys I have seen in both Ireland and England have very good heads.

[illegible]. And do you know whether they [illegible] a [illegible] horse or not?—I believe them to be a sound horse.

[illegible]. But you have no experience of that?—No, I have not.

[illegible]. I think you were [illegible] of the [illegible] [illegible] in which you and [illegible] Hackneys [illegible] [illegible] [illegible], [illegible] you know as a matter of fact that all the [illegible] [illegible] in the Dublin Show [illegible] [illegible]?—In the [illegible] [illegible], yes.

[illegible]. And for the last five or six years the majority of the prizes have been won by Hackney bred horses?—Yes.

[illegible]. Lord [illegible].—I should like to ask a question or two. I know you know the [illegible] of a [illegible] [illegible] and [illegible] as [illegible], I would like to get your opinion as to the Hackney generally—not the Hackneys that may happen to be in Ireland at the present moment, but as a general rule I should like to know your opinion whether they have good shoulders as a rule?—I think the Yorkshire Hackneys have very good shoulders, and the Norfolk [illegible] [illegible].

[illegible]. Do you think as a rule that the Hackney is [illegible] [illegible] to [illegible] [illegible]?—No, I should say not.

[illegible]. You stated just now that you didn't like the Hackney [illegible] very [illegible] back?—A good shaped back.

[illegible]. Strong good shaped back as a rule?—Yes.

[illegible]. Do you consider that they [illegible] as a rule [illegible] good [illegible] [illegible]?—Well, I think that is [illegible] [illegible] [illegible] the two types of Hackney differ. I think the Yorkshire have, and the Norfolks are [illegible] to [illegible] [illegible] [illegible] [illegible].

[illegible]. What do you consider these [illegible] below the knee to be as a general rule?—I consider the Yorkshire Hackney have very good, I may tell you that I think there is a [illegible] difference between the two types of Hackneys.

[illegible]. You think that the Yorkshire Hackney is [illegible] below the knee as a rule?—I do.

[illegible]. If they don't happen to be [illegible] very good [illegible] [illegible] [illegible] [illegible] on a [illegible] [illegible]?—The [illegible] [illegible] of them are, but if [illegible] is very [illegible] of horses, you will find animals deficient in certain points.

[illegible]. You don't think they require much [illegible] up with [illegible]?—I don't think so.

[illegible]. Mr. [illegible].—Do you know any [illegible] [illegible] [illegible] [illegible] up [illegible] Hackneys?—I think they [illegible] [illegible] [illegible] [illegible] [illegible] [illegible].

5996. Colonel St. Quintin.—You only advocate him to get harness horses?—Oh, yes, and I should advocate a good well-shaped Hackney to be used with some of the weedy mares of the country.

5997. To get riding horses?—Yes, in default of being able to procure a good half-bred stallion.

5998. Would you ride an actual Hackney yourself?—I have never ridden one.

5999. You say you advocate the formation of Government studs?—Yes.

6000. Could you give us any idea as to how you would set about that, and whether you would have one large stud or in different provinces?—It is a complicated question to go into.

6001. Would you give us your idea with regard to the formation of Government studs?—I think studs should be formed with the idea of improving whatever breed of animal is most suitable to the district, in Meath I should only have good thoroughbred horses, if they could be got, and also thoroughbred mares, or perhaps strong half-bred mares, so that sires and mares suitable to breed hunters might be bred there. In the north I should have it almost entirely for harness horses, and in the south I should have studs to breed both sorts of animals, harness and hunter.

6002. How would you propose that that should be initiated?—That Government should buy the best procurable stallions of their respective breeds, they should also buy the best mares that would be likely to produce mares suitable to breed hunters from, or mares suitable to breed harness horses from.

6003. To do that they would have to take up a certain amount of ground and put up a certain amount of buildings?—They would.

6004. Would you recommend anything as to the number of brood mares they should keep and sires in the different establishments?—That would greatly depend on the amount of money that they would be prepared, if they did it at all, to give. [illegible]

6005. Have you ever thought [illegible] of what the scheme would cost the Government?—No, because I don't know what Government would do it.

6006. What benefit do you think it would be to the country, how do you propose that the country should get the benefit of it?—I think it would give the [illegible] [illegible] [illegible] [illegible] [illegible] [illegible] [illegible] [illegible] [illegible] [illegible] [illegible] [illegible] a question of improving the [illegible] in the country it would take considerably longer than three years to improve the breed [illegible] of the country.

6007. Your proposition is that Government should keep the [illegible], and breed the [illegible] [illegible] [illegible].

6008. What is to become of the young stock?—That of course would be a question of arrangement, either that the animal should be sold by public auction, the mares I am talking of, or that the farmers should be able to [illegible] [illegible] [illegible] at a fixed price, and [illegible] [illegible] [illegible] [illegible] would be a fair price, whether the Government would [illegible] [illegible] [illegible] [illegible] [illegible] [illegible] [illegible] [illegible] at that price.

6009. But then only a few farmers could take advantage of this?—Yes.

6010. How many foals are you going to breed?—It would begin in a small way, but [illegible] [illegible] they would be [illegible].

6011. Don't you think there would be a great outcry, that the farmers who had got bad young stock would say "The Government is breeding good stock, and we cannot sell our bad stock?"—I don't think people would object to that in the long run.

Captain W. F. Sh[illegible], [illegible], examined.

Captain W. F. [illegible]

6012. Chairman.—You live in the county [illegible]?—Yes.

6013. Have you considerable experience in horse-breeding yourself?—Yes, I have been breeding horses for twenty-five years.

6014. You buy horses?—I keep a good many.

6015. And sell them again, what stallions have you generally used yourself?—I always use my own thoroughbred.

6016. What prices have you got for your young horses when you have sold them, did they pay you well?—I think they have paid me very well, I got generally £100 and £130 and £160 for horses under [illegible] years old, around [illegible].

6017. What mares were they out of?—The mares were half-bred mares.

6018. The ordinary half-bred mares of the country?—Yes.

6019. You say you buy young horses, what age do you generally buy them at?—I generally buy them young [illegible] when I can.

6020. Do you break them?—[illegible] them [illegible], and keep them a bit, and sell them.

6021. What class of horse is most suitable for your district?—I think the thoroughbred horse is most suitable. I don't know a bad class Hackney. I have never bred them and cannot say anything about them, [illegible] recommend to any part of the country.

6022. Are many horses bred by the farmers in your neighbourhood?—Not [illegible] [illegible] [illegible] and I think really that the chief cause of the [illegible] [illegible] [illegible] [illegible] is due to [illegible] [illegible], if you go to the [illegible] [illegible] [illegible] [illegible] [illegible] [illegible] [illegible] [illegible] [illegible] [illegible] [illegible] [illegible] [illegible] [illegible] I don't think they have [illegible] [illegible] [illegible] [illegible] price of these has got very low, of course the [illegible] [illegible] [illegible] [illegible] [illegible] [illegible] [illegible] [illegible] [illegible] [illegible] [illegible] [illegible] than [illegible] one-third what they did, and there is a great [illegible] [illegible], I think it is [illegible].

6023. You think it is because there is too many horses?—Yes.

6024. Surely there is always a sale for high class horses?—Yes, but they cannot find sale for the [illegible] class.

6025. Do you breed at all from two-year-olds? I only put to horse [illegible] [illegible] two-year-olds, and they turned out fairly well, but from all I have heard I think it is not desirable, but should be [illegible] a thing as a two-year-old [illegible] [illegible] in any part of the country.

6026. Do they feed the young horses well?—I think they do, but they do not break them [illegible] year old.

6027. Are the stallions in your district generally suited for the wants of the district?—I think the stallions are quite good enough [illegible] [illegible] the horses that want to be improved; the only thing that [illegible] [illegible] [illegible] [illegible] [illegible] [illegible] [illegible] [illegible] [illegible] [illegible] [illegible] the class of mares, a small [illegible] class of mares; they [illegible], the [illegible] [illegible] a great [illegible] [illegible] of the mares are not worth anything—they are useless.

6028. Can you suggest anything to enable them to buy better mares?—I made a suggestion [illegible] [illegible] [illegible] [illegible] [illegible] [illegible] [illegible] [illegible] [illegible] [illegible] bought by the Royal Dublin Society or in some other way and distributed [illegible] the country, and if they [illegible] [illegible] [illegible] [illegible] the farmers on the [illegible] [illegible], those [illegible], it would [illegible] [illegible] [illegible] [illegible] of [illegible] [illegible] in [illegible] [illegible]. I think [illegible] would be an advantage, and it would give them a far superior class of mares; they would easily get security. I myself would go security for a great number of farmers if they wanted to buy mares, and I think you might get very good mares, far superior to what they have, for £15 or £18 ...

6029. If they had those good mares, would they be suitable enough to mate them with good horses?—I think they would, I think the horses are quite good enough; what we want is to help the farmers to improve the mares, I don't think there is the smallest possibility in life of getting them to keep a good young one unless you make them do it, and then I don't think you would, for a great many rich people would sell their mares if they got a good price, and would not keep them for breeding.

6030. What age do they sell them at?—As a rule, three-year-old and younger; rarely keep them longer, and that is a great mistake [illegible] the half-bred horse, because foals and yearlings got by a half-bred will look very often better than those got by a thoroughbred; and I think in that way they are encouraged to breed from half-bred horses.

6031. Is the Royal Dublin Society's scheme working in your district?—Yes.

6032. Has it done good?—I don't see it has done the smallest piece of good; I don't see how it can, when I mention there was £15 spent for mares in Nenagh district last year, that would not make much difference either one way or the other; there were five mares registered in Nenagh district, and I don't see how that could affect them in any shape.

6033. In fact, you practically say you cannot improve the breed of horses in your district with the present class of mares?—It is the mares you must go at, I can see no other way, no, I can see no other way of improving the mares except by supplying them; you should possibly make the farmers keep their good mares.

6034. Is the land good around you?—Yes; some of the best horses in Ireland have come from there—Wild Man from Borneo came from my place, and The Lamb.

6035. Do you think the farmer's mares at present are totally unsuitable?—I do; I think they are the worst [illegible].

6036. What stallion would you recommend for your district?—A strong thoroughbred stallion.

6037. Lord RATHDONNELL.—I think just now you said that the Royal Dublin Society's scheme had done no good in your district?—None that I can perceive.

6038. Are you aware that it only deals with the small farmers under a certain valuation?—Yes.

6039. Not with the farmers of Ireland generally?—Yes. How could it be expected to do any good for £15 for the whole of the Nenagh district?

6040. You say you cannot devise any means to keep the good young mares in the country?—I don't see any possible means of doing it. I have never heard any suggestion yet that was in the slightest way practicable.

6041. Are you aware that under the Dublin Society's scheme money is offered for foals?—I don't think any prize that can be given will ever make any difference.

6042. Are you aware that money is given to young mares, fillies, two or three-year-old in foal or stinted to a registered sire?—Where was that given, in Dublin?

6043. No, in the districts?—It has never been given, I did not know that it was offered.

6044. It is open to give it, the local committee can give it under the rules of the Society, there is a rule to that effect. Now, supposing a two-year-old filly or a three-year-old filly was in foal, is it likely that a dealer would buy it to take away even if it was sound?—I don't think so, a dealer would never think of such a thing.

6045. Do you think that might prevent dealers from taking all the sound fillies out of Ireland, if they happened to be in foal at that early age?—I don't think it would, I don't think it would be an advantage to prevent dealers buying. I was reading Captain Dugdale's evidence, and he seemed to advocate the very thing I have thought of, of buying up the mares and distributing them through the country at a low rate, of course the farmers have no opportunity of attending these sales and they have no other way of getting a brood mare except by keeping a worthless thing, they have no other way of getting them. I think broken down hunters might be bought, I don't know much about omnibus and tram horses, they may be useful, I don't know, and perhaps cast troopers.

6046. Mr. WRENCH.—You think the farmers in your neighbourhood would take advantage of such a scheme if it was put within their reach?—I think they would take advantage of it, I am certain they would, we had a meeting of the North Tipperary Farming Society, and I proposed this scheme, and the meeting was very largely attended by the horse-breeding farmers, and they all seemed to take it up, and unanimously thought it was the best thing that was proposed, and they would be delighted with it I am certain.

6047. Would you suggest that those mares should be branded or marked in some way?—I don't see any necessity.

6048. You don't think there would be any danger of those mares being sold again?—I don't think so, they would not be sold for anything but brood mares, the only way they could sell them would be amongst themselves, and if they did that it would be no disadvantage.

6049. You heard it suggested that there should be a register of all horses and brood mares in the district, would you approve of that?—I have not considered that, I think a Hunter Stud Book would be of great use in time to come, but it would be a long time before we could see the effect of it, I think a Hunter Stud Book is what we want because you would then get the intrinsic qualities of the horse, now if you get a half-bred horse he is always left to be a stallion without knowing what he is, he is an untried horse not selected for anything but because a man chooses to have him.

6050. You think it would be worth the trouble of starting a Hunter Stud Book in Ireland?—I think in future it will be of use, but I don't think we will see the advantage of it, it takes a number of years to make a horse eligible.

John M. Kelly, [illegible], examined.

6051. CHAIRMAN.—You live in Westmeath, I believe, and are a magistrate for that county?—Yes.

6052. What experience have you had in the way of horse-breeding?—I have been breeding horses all my life, and my father before me, and I have a stud at present, and I keep some thoroughbred brood mares, and two or three half-bred mares.

6053. Are many horses bred by the farmers in your district?—Oh, yes, a great many farmers breed now.

6054. What class of mares do they generally keep for breeding purposes?—Half-bred mares.

6055. What class of sires do they mate with?—When they can accomplish it they always go to the thoroughbred sires.

6056. Do the farmers appreciate the advantage of a suitable sire to mate with their mares, or by what considerations are they influenced when selecting the sire?—If they can manage the price they always go to the thoroughbred horse. If they can manage the mixing they will always go to the best horses, but unfortunately the great majority are not ... they are getting more enlightened every day as regards the thoroughbred.

6057. In your district are the horses travelling at a reasonable fee mostly?—Well, the thoroughbred horses are £3, and the half-bred horses and some thoroughbred horses perhaps less, a little less, I don't know really.

6058. There is a sufficient number of suitable stallions in the district?—There are now, there are a good many stallions in the locality, years ago there were a great number of good horses but they fell away, and I attribute [illegible] in the falling off in the mares to the want of good horses, there are bad half-bred horses, and the want of thoroughbred horses. Now for the last few years they are [illegible] up again and there is more thoroughbred blood in the country.

6059. When do the farmers sell their young horses, and are the prices as remunerative as the farmers want?—If a farmer has a good horse now, he may be bought up at the [illegible] from him or at the fairs, there are plenty of men to buy them. But really what has filled up our fairs with those wretched horses is they have come up from the West, they have come up within, within the last ten days I have seen 200 of these wretched foals coming from the congested districts, from Galway, and they are brought from Ballinasloe through the country.

6060. You would think these at the fairs?—At the large fairs in Mullingar I saw these wretched little horses, and I think they have done an enormity of mischief, when they were [illegible] years they were very good, but now I think they have deteriorated [illegible] and [illegible] our horses.

6061. Have you had any experience in the breeding of Hackneys?—No, I never bred from them and would not breed from them. There was one Hackney in my locality and I would not breed from him at any price. I saw a most remarkable thing with regard to one of his get, I knew the mare, she had a foal from this Hackney horse, and she was sent to a thoroughbred horse the following year, and it is the most remarkable thing the difference between the two foals, one of whom is now a year and a half and the other two and a half years old, one you would [illegible], the other you would not [illegible].

6062. Colonel St. Quintin.—Which one would you keep?—The one by the thoroughbred horse.

6063. Chairman.—What class of stallion do you consider most suited for breeding high class hunters horses?—The thoroughbred, I think the thoroughbred stallion is before anything in the world, the success of the thoroughbred horse is to be preferred to that of any other [illegible] in the world. I think the Hackney and these Clydesdale and Yorkshire horses have ruined the country wherever they have come into it.

6064. Do you consider the Royal Dublin Society's scheme has had any beneficial effect in your neighbourhood?—I think it had a good effect, because in the first place it registers the stallions, and the farmers when they have a registered horse near them go to him, because they say he is a sound horse, he won't be registered unless, and I am glad to see registered horses are going out very fast. As for their scheme as regards the mares, I think the premium scheme is not so good as it ought to be. I think that instead of giving prizes to mares in the month of October, I believe in seeing the mares brought up in the spring, and then have them judged and give them nominations to thoroughbred horses or registered horses, the farmer paying some of the money, and then they would go to the good horse. I have been judging the mares for the last five years in the King's County, at Tullamore and Parsonstown, for the Royal Dublin Society, and I don't think it is working, I think there were only two young mares in each place this year.

6065. You have heard the evidence about the half-bred stallion, what is your opinion as regards those?—What is called the half-bred may be quite as good as the thoroughbred, although he is not in the stud book. I would not turn him out; there are a great number of them with a slight stain, and I certainly would not object to those, but [illegible] everything in the world. I think stallion owners will be [illegible], if you will, the [illegible] unsound mares, I think they should be more [illegible], I think they should reject unsound mares, and if they did you would find the [illegible] would wear away very quickly. I know I for one would reject all unsound mares, and I have done so.

6066. Do you think that the horses in the district are as good as they were in former years?—I do not, and I attribute it to the bad half-bred horses and the want of the thoroughbred blood. In my recollection years ago we had plenty of well-bred horses in it, and the mares and the class of cattle were far better than they are now. There was no end of good horses. [illegible] and [illegible], all those good horses went away, and these half-bred horses cropped up, and the farmers [illegible] them whenever they could. [illegible] from the good horses that I distinctly remember, but now there are a good many horses spread over the country throughout, and I hope now through the Royal Dublin Society there will be more; I think really their scheme is a very good one if they would improve it so that [illegible] in this matter [illegible] have been neglected.

6067. How would be more [illegible] of the two schemes?—It might be that [illegible] farmer pay £1, and instead of giving a prize let the Royal Dublin Society pay the balance, it would work better than the present scheme.

6068. Have you any other suggestions to make with a view of encouraging the industry of horse-breeding?—Well, I certainly would like to see good sires go down to the congested districts, because we see the nuisance in the Midland Counties with those wretched little foals coming up and bought at from £3 to £4 each, and the farmer when he gets a foal at £3 he will be seeking to keep him on, and when he is three years old he is not worth £4, not worth anything; you will see the fairs crowded with these wretched animals. I saw at least 200 come up this year and bought at the stations and then have come up in a large droving, turning on a [illegible] and bought by farmers and shopkeepers in towns, and then they come into the fairs and they are looked on as being horses bred in the country while we have had nothing at all to say to them.

6069. When in the [illegible] you have seen them come up?—Only from this year's foals, I have seen a [illegible] of hundreds of them, this year coming up at £3 [illegible] apiece, and I think if there were good sires down in those parts we would have a chance of good foals, because those people sell their foals, I understand, and they come up to us. When they [illegible], the [illegible] were very good, but now they are not [illegible] as they were.

6070. Mr. Fitzwilliam.—What do you think in your part of the country the farmers would be able and willing to give for the service of a good class of horse?—I am very sure they would give £1 a mare; many of them would give more, as I said they are getting more enlightened every day, and the first thing they do is to inquire whether a horse is sound, and whether he is registered and that sort of thing.

6071. I think you said that the horses that stood there were [illegible] half-bred [illegible] about £3?—Well, there may be some thoroughbred horses, I believe there are, they [illegible] a little less, a well-bred thoroughbred horse [illegible] because he [illegible] a good deal himself.

6072. My question referred to a good class of stallion in the [illegible] district [illegible] the farmers [illegible] I suppose, they'll go on that class of horse [illegible] of which [illegible] what they [illegible] do it.

Nov. 29, 1896. Mr. John M. Kelly.

6073. They don't go to them that charge £3 a mare?—A few of them do, I have reason to know that.

6074. You say the foals come up out of the west in large numbers and enter your district, and you think through the breeding of the district is deteriorating?—I am quite sure they do.

6075. Whatever animal nothing was sent down into the west I suppose it would be the same thing?—They will sell all their foals, there ought to be a good thoroughbred horse sent down to the west, I would say.

6076. And for that reason you think there might to be a good thoroughbred horse sent down there?—Yes.

6077. And you would infinitely prefer if possible a thoroughbred to any other?—Certainly.

6078. And if you could not get enough thoroughbreds would you like a half-bred?—Well, if there was a well-bred half-bred horse with very little stain to him, and there are a good many of them spread about the country.

6079. If this half-bred horse was out of a thoroughbred mare and a thoroughbred sire would you think they would be preferred to a short stock?—I think they would, you will always be able to buy thoroughbred horses.

6080. Colonel St. Quintin.—I gather from what you say that there has always been an influx of a certain number of animals from the west into the centre of Ireland?—Yes.

6081. And you think that will always continue, and that whatever is bred in the west must permeate through into the centre of the country?—Quite sure, I am certain it will; for years they are sending and their foals brought up by dealers, mostly to Birr at a time. When they were grown they were only good animals, now the animals that are coming are very indifferent, and if there was a good sire or three in that part of the world I think it would do an immensity of good.

6082. You would not confine any particular animal to a particular district?—I don't know, it is difficult for me, but I would not have the Clydesdale or those other breeds on my conscience.

6083. I mean supposing any particular animal was brought into a certain part of the country you don't think it would be confined there, it must filter through to the rest of the country?—I think it must.

6084. Mr. Wrench.—Where do the foals come from?—I really cannot tell you, I know they come on through Galway and Ballinasloe, and up the country.

6085. You don't know where they come from?—They come from the west mountainous, the mountainous districts, I always heard.

6086. You have no personal knowledge as to the districts they come from?—I have not, I think they come from all the west down with dealers.

6087. Up to the present you have only seen the foals?—Well, up to 1½ year old.

6088. You have seen nothing older than 1½ year old?—Certainly not.

6089. Then it is more anticipation that you think they will only grow up to be worth £4?—I have seen them over and over again that they could not be sold when they are three and four, I have seen them in our fairs.

6090. But do you know that there are no animals got by the Congested Districts Board stallions that are four year old, they have not been long enough in the country, so you are speaking of animals that came up before that time?—I am looking at them coming up for years, and it is very hard to sell them when they come to age, they are so badly made you know them at once.

6091. You are speaking of what was in the past, not what will be in the future?—Say for the last ten years.

6092. But you know the Board's stallions have only been in the country four years?—Yes.

6093. And these foals you think are not likely ever to be worth more than £4 or £5?—They look very badly now, it is very hard to judge of foals.

6094. But you think these will grow into animals only worth £4 or £5?—Those I have seen for the last few years, I have seen them in the locality and they were worth absolutely nothing or £4 or £5.

6095. These are what you have seen at five or six years old?—Yes.

6096. Then, as a matter of fact, you know that these could not have been by any of the Hackney stallions?—If they are only four years then they could not.

6097. None of their produce is older than three years?—Then I cannot say I saw them.

6098. Then you are merely speaking about the animals from the west and not specially about the animals got by the Hackney stallions?—Oh, I am only speaking of them as they came up to us.

6099. And you don't know how they are bred?—I don't know how they are bred.

6100. Are any of these animals used as hunter brood mares?—Oh, well, I should say not.

6101. So there is no danger of the Westmeath farmers making use of them in that way?—I daresay the farmers may breed from them.

6102. But you don't think they would produce valuable hunters?—Any of them I ever saw would not.

6103. As a matter of fact are not the mares in Westmeath as good mares as any in Ireland?—They were very good.

6104. But are they not at present?—I am afraid not, and I give my reasons, they are bred from bad half-bred sires for some time past, and there has been a want of thoroughbred blood, but the last three years a good many thoroughbred horses have come into the country and I really hope for better animals from thenceforward.

The Commission adjourned to the following Tuesday.

TWELFTH DAY.—TUESDAY, DECEMBER 1st, 1896.

Dec. 1, 1896.

PRESENT:—THE EARL OF DUNRAVEN (in the Chair); LORD RATHDONNELL, MR. [illegible] WRENCH, and MR. HUGH NEVILLE, Secretary.

Major J. H. CONNELLAN, Coolmore, Thomastown, Co. Kilkenny, examined.

Major J. H. Connellan.

6105. CHAIRMAN.—Major Connellan, you are resident in the County Kilkenny?—Yes, my lord.

6106. What part of the county?—[illegible] south of the middle of the county.

6107. You are a Justice of the Peace for the county?—Yes.

6108. Have you had personal experience in horse-breeding?—Yes; I have been breeding for [illegible] years, and I have [illegible]

6109. What class of horses?—Well, I have bred a good many from thoroughbred horses. I have bred [illegible]

6110. What do you mean by the country-bred horse?—What they call the country horse [illegible] blood in him, [illegible] Clydesdale and other stock.

6111. Clydesdale?—Clydesdale. Some of them have got the Clydesdale blood [illegible] It is very hard to define [illegible]

6112. Do you know where they got the Clydesdale [illegible]?—[illegible] Clydesdale blood.

6113. Are there any there now?—Yes; a couple of them.

6114. Have you a good opinion of that cross?—[illegible] as a rule.

6115. Do you consider [illegible] suitable for the breeding of hunters?—Yes; particularly the [illegible] end of the county.

6116. What is the character of the soil?—The greater part of it is limestone.

6117. And do the farmers breed much [illegible]?—They breed a great deal in the southern part of the county. [illegible]

[illegible]

6124. Do you think there has been any falling off in the quality of the horses generally in the district?—[illegible] I saw it in the exhibitions under the Royal Dublin Society's scheme.

6125. To what do you attribute this falling off?—If you will allow me, I will not give the history of [illegible] The old Irish horse, [illegible] in the early part of the century, and up to the middle of the century. At that time, the early part of the century particularly, [illegible] very small things; they were generally [illegible] and a strong horse. [illegible] Clydesdale [illegible]

[illegible]

6133. What would you put them to?—I would put them to a thoroughly sound half-bred horse, or to a horse with a good deal of blood in him, three-quarters bred or a really good half-bred horse.

6134. Would you prefer that to the Clydesdale or the Hackney?—In our county there is only one Hackney, and it has been there only a short time, so that so far as our mares are concerned I would not say anything about the Hackney. I think a good half-bred with bone, with good style and square about him, will sometimes be better than a thoroughbred horse, particularly as some thoroughbred horses are light of bone.

6135. How long has the Hackney been in your country?—Only two years, we cannot judge what his stock are yet.

6136. Do you know the horse yourself?—I don't know him, I have never seen him, I only know what others have said about him.

6137. You cannot express any opinion as to the value or reverse of Hackney blood?—No, so far as my own county is concerned. I have seen them in England. I have had some experience of them in England in a large manufacturing town that I lived near for some years. They bred a certain class of Hackney to do a spin on a bank-holiday, and that kind of thing, and he was not a good horse.

6138. Would you like to express any opinion to the Commission as to the probable effect generally of the introduction of Hackney blood into the country?—Not except in this way—that I think generally we ought to pause before we do anything to introduce any particular breed which is likely to oust the thoroughbred horse. Beyond that I am not prepared to say anything. We live very far from any congested district in our part of the world.

6139. In your opinion, Major Conolan, is there a tendency on the part of the farmers to part with their best mares, to sell them, and breed from an inferior class of mare?—Decidedly, and in certain districts very much so. In other districts the farmers seem to understand breeding better, and they often stick to a good mare. Down in the southern end a good many of them do, but taking the whole country all round they are far too apt to get rid of their good mares and to breed from old inferior mares.

6140. Is that tendency greater than it used to be?—I think it is. I think they sell their young mares more readily than they used to.

6141. What is your opinion, as to the desirability of breeding from sound good mares?—I think that any good young mare from three years old and upwards is worth keeping by any farmer if he can make any use of her.

6142. I mean, rather, relatively to the importance of the stallion. Do you think it is equally important to breed from a good mare as it is to breed from a good sire?—Oh, certainly.

6143. And can you suggest any way in which farmers can be induced to keep their best mares?—Yes, I can. Perhaps if you would allow me I would read some ideas that I put down on the subject of that, and of the thoroughbred horse as well. They are not altogether my own ideas, they are partially derived from the hints of other people and partly from my own observation. There are some points on which I think some remedy might be found. First, I would have a more rigorous selection of thoroughbred sires, and I would register none that got a weedy or unsound stock. This would entail some expense and some trouble, but it would prevent much misconduct, for some of the registered stallions I know of have been notorious for getting unsound stock. I would class these as Class I. on the register. I would have a classified register. I would make a second class, and would register in it three-quarter-bred sires—that is, sires having three thoroughbred crosses in one strain, provided the sire had good action and shape and was sound. Third, I would have all sires examined, if possible, and to those which were sound I would award a certificate of soundness and suitability, provided they had good shape and action. This would let in some of the country sires which had been getting a very valuable stock and which the farmers like to use, and I think it would gradually drive out the unsound and nondescript stallion. I would put these as Class III. on the register, but I should be inclined to say that the first two only might be subsidised. The third class I would leave to be used by the farmers as they liked, but would give them a certificate of soundness and suitability. Fourthly, I would give premiums to all sound, well-shaped mares from three to ten years old covered by one of the registered thoroughbred stallions, or possibly by one of the second class. Fifthly, I would register the foals of such mares, giving the owner a certificate as to its breeding, and giving its colour and any marks tending to identify it, so that the owner could produce a warranty as to its breeding when he was selling it. This would enhance the value for sale, and would do away with fictitious pedigree-making, and it would be more easily carried out than at first it may appear. I would subsidise all selected sires, so that small farmers owning the premium mares I mentioned could have their services at a low fee—that is, all selected sires of the first two classes. I would leave the farmers themselves to deal with the third class. I am aware that none of these remedies taken by itself would have any great effect, but I believe if all these suggestions were adopted a more saleable horse would come into the market than is now the case, and this in a few years time.

6144. You think that in selecting the sires, as I understand, they ought to be selected not only in view of the soundness of the horse itself and its qualifications, but in view of the stock that he has got?—I do, and I am driven to that conclusion by knowing stallions which were registered—and I have got one particularly in my mind—and which were notorious for getting unsound stock. Nearly all the stock were unsound. That horse is not registered now, and he is still in the country, I am glad to say, but there are others besides.

6145. If you take the stock into consideration and that it turns out bad, what would you do—deprive the horse of his certificate?—Yes, I should do that. His continuing on the register, and continuing to get unsound stock cannot be a good thing for the country.

6146. You propose to grant a certificate to the stallion, not anything in the nature of a licence?—Well, a licence would lead to legislation of course. You could not do that without legislation, but at the same time I think the effect of giving a horse a certificate for soundness and suitability—for his shape as well as his soundness—would help in time to drive inferior and unsound stallions out of the country.

6147. By what machinery would you suggest that all this should be carried out?—It could be done in an simplified way under the scheme of the Royal Dublin Society by amplifying the existing scheme to a certain extent. It would entail some money and some trouble.

6148. Do you think it should be done by the Royal Dublin Society?—That I am not prepared to say. The scheme of the Royal Dublin Society has worked very well in some districts, and not so well in others. It has worked unequally it seems to me. That may be the fault of the farmers, not the fault of the Royal Dublin Society. But in some cases the mares exhibited have been very poor. In others they have been very good. Very often the farmers don't like the distance; they say they have got to go so far. If they have got to go 20 miles with a mare you don't get at the best mares sometimes. I have heard some farmers with good mares say "we don't like to go so far; it is a very long way; we might not get selected when we go there."

6149. It would be a rather formidable undertaking to do this all over the country?—Yes, but I think unless something very drastic is done you [illegible] in [illegible] [illegible].

6153. Assuming that some scheme of that kind would be undertaken, do you think it ought to be carried out [illegible] by local societies?—Yes, by local societies and, no doubt, inspectors would have to be appointed, I suppose, and veterinary surgeons would have to be got for the [illegible] of these animals.

6154. I mean if there was any money grant or money from the Royal Dublin Society or some central body, do you think it ought to be committed to local people?—Yes, I do, because I think the local people would be more likely to get at the horses. They would know the breeding.

6155. Do you think the farmers generally in your district are good judges as to the best sort of sires to suit their mares, and so on?—Yes, I think the farmers in the [illegible] part of the county breed with a good deal of judgment, and they have always done so. They have got a taste for horse-breeding. In the northern part of the county they have not got it so much. They go for the low class of sire, and the proximity of the [illegible]. That is what governs a great many of them.

6156. Do you think generally that the quality and the quantity of the horses have improved or [illegible] or remained about the same?—Well, I think there are just as many horses bred to-day. You can see from the local fairs. You see a great many horses there, but you see an enormous preponderance of horses not sold at all. They have a great many [illegible] of horses I can [illegible] the [illegible] number of dealers in the country by whom they are picked up before they get into the fairs. Before all [illegible] to the fairs, [illegible] a great many of the horses are picked up before they get into the fairs. You don't see many [illegible] horses in the fairs now; they are nearly all from two to four years old.

6157. Do you think that the price of the better quality horses, the hunter and the harness horses, have [illegible] up [illegible]. For the high class horses the price probably is as good as ever; but the second class horse—the harness horse of the [illegible] class there is a [illegible] depreciation—a depreciation of £5 to £6 per head. I know that from buying and selling myself. At the same time I will say this, that if a horse has got some style and action he will find a dealer; there will be a market for him, he will be bought.

6158. Almost these [illegible] sires, would you have them registered also?—Well, they certainly ought to be examined I think so, I think, [illegible].

6159. You would not endeavour to eliminate them out of the country?—No, I don't think I would, because there are some of them that get a very good stock—thoroughly good and sound. But [illegible] them generally I think think they have been a good [illegible] for that part of Ireland. They didn't suit the [illegible] [illegible] some I think at all.

6160. Mr. [illegible].—What are the chief selling fairs in your district?—Well, there is Kilkenny and New Ross, and there is Waterford and [illegible] Clonmel, that a great many of the Kilkenny horses go into.

6161. [illegible] is the chief fair for the good horses?—Yes, but there are a good many sold in New Ross in the county of Wexford. It is a large horse fair.

6162. Would you be in favour of registering any of these half-bred sires that have not been proved by their stock?—No, I would say that every horse should be judged by his stock as well as by his appearance.

6163. So that you would make good stock a sine qua non?—Yes, I have been driven to that conclusion in the breeding trade.

6164. I think you said you would [illegible] set up [illegible] of [illegible]?—Yes.

6165. Have you thought by what machinery you would carry out the registration?—No. I think that would be a [illegible] consideration [illegible] to work [illegible] at the same time it would do away with what everybody would like [illegible] of the fairs—the [illegible] of pedigree making that goes on. It would be a sort of [illegible] on the [illegible].

6166. Did you hear it has been suggested to us by [illegible] witnesses that the registration should be carried out by the Petty Sessions Clerk?—I have not heard that.

6167. Do you think that that would be a practical suggestion?—It might be [illegible] in many [illegible] the more mechanical part of it. But of course the horses would have to be examined by somebody else.

6168. [illegible] or [illegible] to suggestion?—Yes, as [illegible] suggestion. I think he would do very well.

6169. Do you think that if registration was established the people would fall in with it?—Yes, I think the farmers would see the advantage of it if they got a good [illegible].

6170. Do you think that being able to give a [illegible] pedigree of a horse in selling to a dealer would put his value up?—Yes, and I think it would put the value up to the man who bought him; if a dealer bought him he might add to his [illegible] in selling again by saying "I have a certificate of the [illegible] of this animal."

6171. You said you would give premiums to mares to encourage the farmers to keep their good mares?—Yes.

6172. Have you thought of the amount of the [illegible]?—No, that would depend upon the amount of money available for the purpose.

6173. Say for a premium of £10—do you think a premium of £10 would make the farmer keep a valuable mare if he were offered a good price for her?—Yes, I think it would tend to do so. It might not in every case, but many farmers would do it.

6174. Do you think that pedigree is a valuable factor in selling a dealer any horse?—Dealers look for certain.

6175. CHAIRMAN.—Has the Royal Dublin Society's scheme been in operation in your part of the country?—Yes.

6176. Is it generally successful?—Yes. I was talking yesterday to Mr. Chairman, Mr. [illegible], who knows as much about the breeding of horses as any one in Ireland, he is an excellent judge himself; he said that in some districts it had been successful, but he said he was afraid that they didn't keep their best mares, and that they didn't come up; he never saw [illegible] in the fairs within the last two or three years; there was a better class of foals bred; but taking it all round he thought the best mares had gone abroad, and that the class of mares they had in [illegible] [illegible] [illegible] not so really good as those over in the country.

6177. Do you know how much the Society have to spend in your district?—I think it is from £50 to £60 a year for [illegible], but I am not quite certain, I did know, but I forget.

6178. I gather from you that the question of the registration of sires would be a purely voluntary matter?—A purely voluntary matter. I may state that that was a suggestion made to me. I thought of something of the kind myself, but it was made to me by a man who thoroughly understands the breeding of horses, and whose father for fifty years bred as high class horses as any man in the country.

6179. You think it would pay the farmer to be able to produce this registration—that he would get a better price?—Yes; it would make people confident that the pedigree was right.

6180. And as to the stallions, that would be voluntary also; if a man wished to have his stallion examined he would get a certificate; if he did not choose he would not [illegible] and [illegible], but the [illegible] are that he would if the stallion was sound.

6181. As to the mares, you would give a direct premium?—I would give a direct premium for the mares.

6182. And the effect of that would be to tend to

[illegible]

Mr. John [illegible], [illegible], examined.

[illegible]

make a living by having an inferior animal—very often they give him not cheap.

6208. What age do you generally sell your produce at?—I generally let them run until they are four-year-olds. I bring them in, train and break them, you may say, until they are five. They are five when I sell them.

6209. Do you sell them at fairs or direct to the dealers?—Well, I sell to dealers, or sometimes gentlemen buy from me and take them over to England. I have sold a good many to dealers.

6210. Do you breed from two-year-olds?—No, sir, I would not approve of that at all; it ruins them; it makes weeds of them; they never grow. My idea is that the nourishment that would go to support the foal—that the mother would require it for herself to develop her. I would breed from a three-year-old and then she would have a foal at four.

6211. Is it not customary in your part of the country to breed from two-year-olds?—Yes, a great many of them do. They are under the idea that a three-year-old mare will not breed, which is a fallacy. They are under the idea that a two-year-old will, and that a three-year-old will not, but I have found them to always.

6212. What class of horse do you use on your farm—do you breed your own farm horses?—No; I have very little tillage, and I have a common old horse that does this for me. I would rather pay for the tillage being done than keep a bad horse.

6213. Are there small holdings or large holdings about you?—A good many of them are small—50, 60, 100, 150, and 200 acres. Some of them are smaller than that; I mean are 50 acres.

6214. Do the occupiers of the small holdings of twenty or thirty acres—do they breed?—They do, if they have a mare. They are under the idea that it is a good thing to have a mare to foal and knowing what the offspring may turn out, and then they might make money some day or other at the fair.

6215. Do you think that the mares in your district are as good as they used to be?—Yes, we have some very good mares in that district; they are good mares.

6216. Are they as good or better than they used to be?—Well, they are more weedy than they were. I don't think they have altogether the same amount of bone. They are of a different class. They are longer in the legs and longer in the bodies than the old class of mare that I remember.

6217. Not such good bone?—Not as good bone.

6218. Would you consider that to be a falling off in the quality or not?—Well, I would not.

6219. And as to the sires, are they mostly all thoroughbred sires?—Well, most of them are.

6220. I don't want to specify particular sires, but are the general opinion?—Well, I don't know. Oh, there are some of them—I would not say they all are. A great many of them are bad.

6221. Are they as good as they used to be in former days?—I think not. They may have bigger pedigrees, but I don't think they are as good as some of the old sires.

6222. Do you think the farmers are more inclined than they used to be to sell their best mares, and to breed from inferior ones?—Oh, yes.

6223. Why is that?—Poverty. They are so poor they cannot afford to keep them.

6224. Do you think that it is on account of the industry being poorer, or on account of the fact that foreign or other governments will give more money for the mare?—No; to depression in all sorts of produce. They cannot afford it. And then the landlord impulses his rent, and they think if they ever £100, and they can get £30 or £40 for a good brood mare, they will pay the landlord—that is if they are honest—but a good many of them are only thinking they have it to hold, and they will have a balance of £10, and then come to pay the shopkeeper.

6225. That mare have always been the most necessary, has kept them home, I think. It is going to ruin.

6226. Do you know where those mares go to—do they go abroad?—I think they go to the foreigners.

6227. Within your recollection have the foreigners been more keen to buy?—I think he buys more mares than ever he did.

6228. Do you house and feed your **young stock in** the winter time?—No, sir.

6229. Out there the time?—Yes.

6230. Are they, you said they are from year-olds?—Until they are four-year-olds. From the time they are weaned I let them run. I think it is the very best thing. I don't approve of pampering animals at all. I let them run and it develops their muscles, of course giving them a little feeding. I would not do that on the top of a mountain. I would like to have them in a place of shelter. I have particularly good shelter myself. Perhaps what I do would not suit everyone. I have very good shelter, and I have houses the doors of my stables, but they would rather stay out than go into the houses.

6231. Do you hand-feed at all?—Nothing, except during a bad winter I give them a little hay. They have plenty of grass to live on the land, and a fine run.

6232. Are there any Clydesdale or Hackney sires in your part of the country?—No, sir.

6233. And you have had no experience of breeding from Hackneys or Clydesdales?—No, I have not, sir.

6234. Is the Royal Dublin Society's scheme in operation in your county?—Yes, sir.

6235. What have been its effects in your opinion?—Well, I think I cannot say it is doing very much. It does not give enough money. £100 in the County Wexford is a very poor thing. I believe it is very difficult to get the money, as we must be thankful.

6236. Do you know how long it has been in operation in the County Wexford?—Three or four years, I think.

6237. As to prices that you got for the stock you produce, are you getting as good prices as you did fifteen or twenty years ago—bigger prices or less prices?—Less prices. I got more now then. I think then, demand and supply, most of the good horses go to England.

6238. Do you know what kind of prices they get for an inferior class of horse—at the price of good as is used to be?—Oh, no, sir, a very bad price. The one more for an inferior class of horse, they are worthless.

6239. They are not worth now as much as they were?—No, sir.

6240. Do you think anything could be done to persuade the farmers the breeders to keep their best mares to breed here instead of selling them?—I think by giving larger prizes, and by allowing a longer time for going in for these mares. I would limit the age to fifteen instead of five. A great many people may have a mare who may be a very useful mare, she may be kicked until she is broken, or [illegible]; and then she breaks down, it would be very hard to put her out of there. I would limit it to fifteen years.

6241. Did you hear what the former witness said with regard to giving certificates of soundness and registering foals?—Yes, sir.

6242. Do you agree with him at all?—I would allow no stallions in my country without paying a license. I would license them all. I think it would do away with all the weeds and bad ones.

6243. You would not allow a stallion to be in the country without he was licensed?—I would not. What is the use of allowing those to the country to breed inferior animals?

6244. What authority would you suggest with the duty of licensing those which you would have licensed?—Oh, I would have a local committee that, [illegible]

Dec. 1, 189[illegible]. Mr. John Charles [illegible].

[illegible]

think. It might not be a very pleasant thing for the local committee to do, but at the same time I think a local committee would know the bad ones better than a stranger. There is no use in letting a bad stallion go along through the country.

6245. But would not the local committee be perhaps more or less interested in the owners of the stallions?—They may, and if they do not give licenses to men they may come across the themselves. It is very hard to know, but I certainly would have a local committee and a veterinary surgeon.

6246. And as to the registration of foals, do you think that is practicable, or would it be any use?—I think it would be the very best thing to register them. I would give a half-crown or five shillings to register them, and have a man registered in each county. I would have them examined there when they were twelve months old, and I would see if they were sound or likely to go on well. I would have them examined at two years old and up to three years old, and any of them that were showing any unsoundness or anything of that sort I would reject them out. It would be a guarantee to everyone as to the breeding of the animal; but some people do not think much importance to the breeding.

6247. I was going to ask you are the dealers who buy your horses particular as to the pedigree of them; the breed of them?—Some of them are; but I was selling a horse to a dealer at one time. I thought I would get more money by telling him how he was bred. The turned around, and said, "I did not ask his breeding; leave that to me. I can find a pedigree for that fellow if it suits me."

6248. In your opinion can the farmers in your district be trusted to select the most suitable sires for the mares they have got, provided the sires are there?—Yes, they are very keen, some of them. But the popularity of the sire owner goes a long way with them, at least amongst the lower class—the small farmers and that sort.

6249. The popularity of the sire or the owner?—Oh, the popularity of the owner. If he gives credit, and if he treats the customers to a few glasses now and again, he will be very popular amongst a certain lot.

6250. Are there a sufficiency of sires in your county, enough of them?—Do you mean thoroughbred?

6251. Yes?—Yes, there are, but they belong to local people.

6252. Have the farmers to go a long distance to get to them?—No, in my district they have not—not perhaps more than ten miles.

6253. What is the general fee charged?—£3 and £2, and down I suppose to half a sovereign.

6254. Are there many horses bought for the cavalry purposes in your part of the country?—Not many, sir.

6255. Mr. Wrench.—Do you keep your mares entirely for breeding—the brood mares you refer to?—I never work them.

6256. Keep them entirely for breeding?—Yes.

6257. You don't believe in finding your foal well the first winter?—No.

6258. You have never tried that?—I never did. They go on well enough for me without trying that.

6259. It is very good land?—Oh, well, it is rough land, but suitable land; it is good land, sound land—a good run on it for them.

6260. But you have never tried feeding the foals well the first winter to see how they would do in comparison with those you did not feed?—I tried one; he was delicate; he did not do well; he never grew.

6261. You have he was delicate in the first instance?—Yes, I thought I would do better for him; he was the only foal I ever fed.

6262. I think you said you were in favour of a local committee; how would you select your local committee for the constitution of it?—Well, I would say that the chairman of our Waterford agricultural, Captain Maxwell, who is a horsey Judge, he would be a very good man, and let him associate those on that with himself.

6263. I am not talking of individuals. Would you leave it to the chairman of the county committee to select his committee?—Certainly, leave it to him.

6264. You would not give the breeders any voice in the selection?—Of course, I would take in two or three breeders, large farmers.

6265. As regards the farmers themselves, would you give them any voice in the selection of the committee—the ordinary farmers who breed the horses, the breeders—would you let them have a voice?—Of course I would.

6266. You would take their opinions?—I would, of course, sir; they ought to be the best judges of what would suit themselves.

6267. Have you any experience of selling to foreign buyers?—I sold a few, sir.

6268. Did they generally ask you about the pedigree?—Yes, latterly they have asked me. Not in the beginning. Latterly they have.

6269. You think it would be an advantage to be able to give true pedigrees for the foreign buyers?—Yes, I wrote it down for them and they took it.

6270. They attach importance to the pedigrees?—I think so, sir.

6271. Did you sell many hunters horses?—No; I generally go for hunters.

6272. Chairman.—Have you any suggestions, Mr. Poole, that you would like to give the Commission as to how the industry of horse-breeding can be improved in your locality; anything that you consider would be done?—Try and encourage the farmers to keep their good mares, and I said to extend the premiums to them.

6273. You think as far as the sires are concerned?—You would have an opportunity of seeing the young stock of a mare if she comes up for a prize.

6274. And you think that the sires should be licensed?—Oh, I think the sires should be licensed, and the half-breds done away with at any rate.

6275. Anything else you would like to say, Mr. Poole?—Except—I think I said it before—if we could get more money for the county than £100 a year, it would be an encouragement to give more money to the owners of good mares. It would be an encouragement to them. I would do away with the valuation altogether, rather than we value it to £100. The man whose valuation is £100 a year would be more likely to keep a good mare than the man whose valuation is only £10.

Mr. Thomas Carrigan, Maplestown, Rathvilly, Co. Carlow, examined.

Mr. Thomas Carrigan.

6276. Chairman.—You live in the County of Carlow?—Yes.

6277. Are you farming there?—Yes.

6278. And you breed horses yourself?—Yes.

6279. Have you done so for some time?—Well, I have been breeding on my own account for 15 or 16 years, and my father bred a good many horses.

6280. What class of horse do you try to produce?—A good many classes—hunters, working horses, and harness horses.

6281. Do you breed any hunters?—Yes.

6282. What do you find pays you best to breed?—I think, taking a given number, that the strong heavy horses pays best.

6283. The strong heavy horses, what are they used for?—The agricultural horse.

6284. Are there many horses bred about you?—There are a good many.

6285. Mostly for agricultural purposes?—I don't think so. They are pretty mixed—hunters and harness horses and a good deal of very low class.

6216. What kind of mares do you use yourself?—I have one three-parts-bred mare and a couple of plain bred mares as described.

6217. Do you think the quality of the mares is as good as it used to be throughout your county?—I think not, it is not as good. I am certain of it.

6218. You think the farmers are selling their best mares out of the country altogether?—I do.

6219. What breed of stallions are generally used—thoroughbred?—Both thoroughbred horses and some draught horses.

6220. Draught horses?—Yes.

6221. What are they?—Clydesdale.

6222. Is there a Clydesdale sire standing near you?—Yes—within 10 miles; there is one in [illegible].

6223. Are there many of those in the county?—Not many.

6224. Any Hackneys?—No, sir.

6225. Have you bred from the Clydesdale any produce you have sold as hunters or harness horses?—No, sir, not as hunters or harness horses; I don't think you could breed them that way.

6226. Have you bred from Irish draught horses at all?—No, sir; I bred some from the Cleveland horse with small well-bred mares, and I found them a very useful horse.

6227. Do you think the Cleveland and Clydesdale are suitable for your county?—I think the Cleveland would be a suitable horse with some of the small mares. I think he would be a more suitable horse than the Clydesdale.

6228. Do you know anything about the Hackney?—No, sir, nothing except what I heard talked about him. I don't know what a Hackney is.

6229. Is the Royal Dublin Society's Scheme in operation in your county?—Yes.

6230. How long has it been in operation?—I think somewhere about three years.

6231. Has it done any good do you think?—I think not much.

6232. Not had much effect?—I have not seen any.

6233. Are the horses produced in your part of the country as good as they used to be?—I think not at all.

6234. How do you account for their not being so good?—I think it is a great deal from the good mares being sold out of the country, and people breeding from things that are not able to sell.

6235. Do the prices keep up?—For the high class of hunters I think the prices are as good as ever; for any other class, I think they have gone down considerably.

6236. Have you bred from any half-bred stallions?—I have, from what are called half-bred stallions. I would not breed from them now again.

6237. You mean you would prefer a thoroughbred?—Certainly, if I had a mare to suit him.

6238. Are there a sufficient number of thoroughbred stallions in your part of the country?—I think there is a very good number of very good horses in our part of the country.

6239. Are many horses in your district bought by the Government?—At Castleblayney fair there are a good many bought sometimes.

6240. What do you think could be done to keep the best mares in the country?—I think by giving good prices for the hunt horses, unless it might cause a tendency to keep them in the country; it is a great thing. I think it is a want of capital that causes the people not to take good care of and how to manage that class of horse.

6241. There good mares that so many of the witnesses complain of as leaving the country are they fetching bigger prices than they did twenty years ago?—No, I think not that class.

6242. I mean the good horses?—The really good high-class hunters would be worth as much.

6243. I mean the mares?—I think not.

6244. Where do they go to?—The foreign governments take a fair number of them.

6245. In your opinion do you think the foreign governments are buying more of our good mares than they used to?—I don't know that; I could not say.

6246. Lord Rathdonnell.—Would you approve of what is called the half-bred sire, with a good deal of thoroughbred breeding if he had bone and action?—Certainly.

6247. What would you yourself use, a half-bred of that description or a Clydesdale or Cleveland?—It would depend on the class of mare; if I had bone enough I would rather use a horse with breeding; but if I had a light well-bred mare, I would rather mate her with a Cleveland.

6248. I am talking of the half-bred sire with plenty of bone and action, which would you send to?—I don't exactly understand.

6249. I mean the half-bred sire I am speaking of with a certain amount of thoroughbred running in his blood, and bone, and was a strong and active horse, which would you send to—him or a Cleveland?—I would rather send to the half-bred horse.

6250. With regard to riding horses, have you bred many large mares that you have hunters from?—No, not large enough; I like it very to breed a horse of twelve and a half stone hunter, but not bigger; I can get blood enough, this not bone.

6251. The usual mare you have bred from is a small type?—Yes.

6252. Mr. Wrench.—Your evidence is that it pays best to breed strong draught horses?—Yes; I think a plain stronger horse all round, they leave you more profit than the other horses.

6253. Referring to riding horses, you are chiefly referring to thoroughbreds?—Yes.

6254. Have you bred many hunters here?—Not many.

6255. Have you sold them at good prices?—Yes, some of them.

6256. Do you find it easy to get action?—No; it is not so easy to get good action.

6257. If you had good action would it be of any use to you?—Oh, certainly.

6258. You think it is a good thing?—It is the chief point with the harness horse.

6259. The class of horse you see in Castleblayney fair, are they much worse than they used to be?—The greater part of them are decidedly worse.

6260. What is the average price they are brought down to?—The most of the best class I have seen this year sold at £10, and some of them as low as £8.

6261. Do you know how any of those horses were bred?—No.

6262. You say they generally sold at £9 and £10?—Yes.

6263. And Castleblayney is considered the best fair in that district?—Yes.

6264. Are many foreigners bought there?—There are, a good many.

6265. Are they bought direct from the breeders or by dealers?—By dealers generally.

6266. Do you know what prices the breeders get for them?—I don't know; they get very different prices.

6267. Did you see many sold?—Not personally.

6268. Then you say the mares from Clydesdales by that you mean that they have got weedy and smaller?—Yes, and [illegible] up, and [illegible] every way.

6269. Do you think it would be a good thing that all horses should be registered?—Yes.

6270. So that it could be ascertained how they were bred?—Yes.

6271. You think the farmers would fall in with that idea and carry it out?—I do—I think they would.

Dec. 5, 1896.

Mr. Thomas Corrigan.

Jan. 1, 1896. Mr. Thomas Corrigan.

6272. The CHAIRMAN.—Is there anything else that you would like to say to the Commission?—I think in this district I would not confine them to one class of horse; it may suit some to breed from the thoroughbred, while others may be inclined to breed from another sort of horse, and I think at the present time, with the class of fillies in our country—that is with the mares they have—if any horse were sent into the county, the Cleveland would be the best horse and most likely to improve the breed of horses. I don't say that would be the way to improve the breed of hunters, but it would be the way to improve the present [illegible]

Mr. Herbert Wrench.

Mr. HERBERT WRENCH, Garrendenny Castle, Queen's County, examined.

6273. CHAIRMAN.—You live in the County Carlow?—Queen's County, my lord, but I am intimately acquainted with the county Carlow.

6274. Have you a farm in the county of Carlow?—Yes.

6275. Mr. WRENCH.—Which district in Queen's county do you live?—The eastern portion, between Kilkenny and Carlow.

6276. CHAIRMAN.—You live in Queen's county?—Yes.

6277. Which are you best acquainted with—Queen's county or Carlow?—Both, equally so.

6278. Did you hear the evidence of the last witness with respect to the part of Carlow that he is acquainted with?—Yes.

6279. Do you agree mainly with what he said?—Fairly so; I believe the difficulty myself is that the thoroughbred we have had in the country has ruined the breed of horses.

6280. What is the matter with the thoroughbred horse?—At least 50 per cent. of the thoroughbreds will never get a weight-carrying hunter. A horse with about seven inches or eight inches of bone below the knee, and possibly able to carry 15 stone, will never get a hunter except out of a Clydesdale mare.

6281. Do you breed horses yourself?—Yes, my lord.

6282. In both places?—In both places.

6283. What kind of mares do you breed from?—From all kinds. I like the mare with a cross or two of thoroughbred blood the best.

6284. And you bred for what?—I attempt to breed hunters; I have also used Clydesdale sires to well-bred mares, and they have no other failure.

6285. Was it a failure?—Yes, my lord.

6286. And as far as the hunter is concerned, you found the thoroughbred the best?—Oh, undoubtedly; the failure in that instance [illegible] the mares being too small.

6287. You think the mares have deteriorated?—I think they have.

6288. Not so good as they used to be?—I don't think they are.

6289. I gather from what you said you attribute that to the inferiority of the thoroughbred sires?—I think that is largely to blame. Very much so. They are light-boned and small, and the occasional large one you see is such a success. I have several large thoroughbreds having been bred by [illegible] and have produced stock singularly successful.

6290. Do you think the deterioration is due as well to the best mares being sold out of the country?—It is, undoubtedly; but I blame the sires just as much as selling the mares.

6291. Do you know about these foreign governments buying these mares more than they used to?—They don't come to the fairs for them; the occasional foreign purchaser is purchased by the dealer.

6292. I mean, that foreigners are more inclined to give good prices and breed from inferior mares than they used to do. I mean in that way to whom that tendency is due, whether it is that they are offered larger prices or what?—They are not offered large prices for them; as a hunter of that quality equal quality is worth more than the big.

6293. You don't think the thoroughbred stallions in the parts of the country you are acquainted with are so good as they ought to be?—Undoubtedly not.

6294. What is your opinion of the half-bred stallion?—I think the half-bred stallion is very useful.

6295. Provided of course that he is sound and suitable?—Oh, undoubtedly.

6296. What is your opinion as to the Clydesdales, Cleveland, or any other breed?—Is there not a great contrast between the Cleveland and Clydesdale? I really think in much the Cleveland is a useful horse, and that the Clydesdale is hardly wanted, except in very heavy tillage land where they are required with the plough, in parts of Kilkenny and parts of Kildare.

6297. There are Clydesdale sires in your part of the country?—There are.

6298. Are there any Cleveland sires?—No.

6299. Any Hackney sires?—No, not [illegible].

6300. Have you any experience of Hackneys?—Yes.

6301. Where did you gain that?—In this country [illegible], and in America principally.

6302. Have you ever bred from the Hackney sire?—I have.

6303. And with what results?—Well, I lay great stress on the choice of any alteration in the breed but in the choice of the individual, thoroughbred or Hackney; I believe there are very charming horses in the Hackney Book, and I believe these are [illegible] but [illegible]; I think the Hackney with a cross or two of thoroughbred is a most useful animal.

6304. As a stallion?—Yes, as a stallion; that is to say a stallion out of a thoroughbred mare by a [illegible] Hackney. Is it not a fact that thoroughbred horses can be entered in the Hackney Book, and not as a matter of fact; and also that horses of two or three crosses of thoroughbred blood are eligible to be entered?

6305. I only wished to find out what you mean. You think a stallion would be useful crossed between a thoroughbred and a Hackney?—Yes, my lord.

6306. Have you seen such stallions?—I have.

6307. And their produce?—And their produce.

6308. Whereabouts in your own part of the country?—In America.

6309. And you approve of them?—I do, my lord. I think they are a useful all round animal, and I think a mare of that breeding would be a valuable animal crossed with a thoroughbred sire—her produce, I mean.

6310. Then you, consequently, have no objection to the introduction of Hackney blood into your part of the country?—None, if he was of right type. Some of these are very short and cocky, and with short pasterns. They are, undoubtedly, bad animals; ours I preferred, are long [illegible] from their hip to their tail.

6311. Is the Royal Dublin Society's scheme in operation in your district?—For years.

6312. Has it done any good?—It has done harm.

6313. In what way?—It has put a thoroughbred sire before the small farmer, which is a calamity, considering the cost to him, and that is the reason one hears of three and four-year-olds being sold for £10, £15, and £20. If they had a proper sire they would be worth £50 and upwards, but the miserable thoroughbred sires which have been in the country, and which have been too cheap to the small farmer, has ruined him; he has had the use of a horse with a long pedigree for £1, and it has done harm.

6314. What class do you think he ought to go to?—

[illegible] Mr. [illegible]

a [illegible] horse, and I would have it in the [illegible] something between a draught horse and a thoroughbred. The Clydesdale is no use for that animal; she doesn't breed anything large enough. I would suggest a Cleveland or a good Hackney.

6315. There is no Hackney anywhere [illegible]?—No, my lord.

6316. Lord [illegible].—Is the soil generally of a light nature about you?—Well, perhaps, I should say [illegible].

6317. Then the heavy horse is not required?—Not required.

6318. You mentioned about Hackneys; do you consider the Hackney a stout breed of horses?—I do.

6319. Good staying power, I am talking of his staying power; that is what I mean by stout?—He makes very as long as a thoroughbred horse, but I don't know that is a point that will touch the smaller farmer, who wants to sell when he grows. He would like to produce an animal that would produce the [illegible] money.

6320. Would you advocate using a stallion that has not very much staying power?—But the poor man, I would allow him to use the horse the produce of which would make the most money.

6321. Do you think that breeding would go on bringing him in money or be likely to fall away in staying power?—I think the cross of this Irish blood with the thoroughbred would do away with all the weakness of the Hackney.

6322. Supposing there was a stallion of the half-bred which you have mentioned out of the old Irish mare with two or three crosses of thorough breeding, if he had bone and substance and action, would you consider him a good sort of horse?—Yes, better than the Hackney.

6323. And you think it would be likely to do good to the small farmer if he had a horse of that description?—I do.

6324. In preference to any heavy horse of any breed at all?—Well, mares vary so much; but on the whole I would say yes.

6325. Do you consider the bone of the Clydesdale as good as the thoroughbred?—It is larger, but not so hard.

6326. Mr. [illegible].—Have you ever seen a half-bred horse, such as you speak of, with as much action as the Hackney?—Never.

6327. Do you think that class of sire would be likely to breed as good action?—The Hackney will get the best action.

6328. Do you know at all how the Yorkshire Hackneys are largely bred?—No, I do not.

6329. You know that a good many have a thoroughbred cross in them?—I do.

6330. You know that in Yorkshire they used the thoroughbred horse very largely in producing Hackneys?—I have heard so.

6331. But you don't know out of what class of mares they are bred?—I do not.

6332. Have you seen the result of the cross of the Hackney with the country-bred animals in [illegible] [illegible]?

6333. And what class of animals do they produce?—A useful all round animal with action that would be [illegible] useful and a price.

6334. Were the mares very angular and narrow in chest?—No, they were not.

6335. What were they like?—Not a wild mare by any means, or perhaps a mare of very considerable size. The [illegible] I refer to had mares of considerable size, but I could not say what breed they were.

6336. Were they weedy?—Not weedy.

6337. Was the production of the Hackney better than the Cob?—The production was better, but the Hackney was a good one with a couple of crosses of thoroughbred blood—a [illegible] looking horse.

6338. You lay very much against the Clydesdale blood?—Altogether; I think it has done harm in Ireland.

6339. And you don't think it is required on the farms in your district?—No.

6340. A lighter horse would do as well?—Yes.

6341. Have you had any success in breeding horses?—Yes, considerable.

6342. What mares did you breed from?—Half-bred mares, and what you might call common mares. I have a couple of [illegible].

6343. You don't know how they were bred?—I know nothing about them.

6344. I think you said you had seen a good many bad as well as good Hackneys?—I have.

6345. And have you seen as many bad thoroughbreds as good?—I have—more.

6346. So that it is not a peculiarity of any breed that there should be a good many bad animals in it?—It seems to be rather the reverse.

6347. And you think that giving prominence to the thoroughbred over any other has necessarily done an injury to the farmers of your district?—I should modify the word you make use.

6348. I understand you to say that your objection to the Royal Dublin Society's scheme is that they only subsidise thoroughbreds, that there are no suitable thoroughbreds in your district, and that they had encouraged the farmers to go in for thoroughbreds in preference to the horse that would suit them?—Quite so, but the farmers are not judges.

6349. The farmers are not judges?—No.

6350. You think the horse ought to be selected for them?—Yes, without telling them so.

6351. You heard a good deal about registration?—Yes.

6352. Do you think it practicable that every horse and mare should be registered?—There might be difficulty with the mares; I would license all sires.

6353. Would you do that with a local organising or central body?—By a central body; I would not trust a local committee very much.

6354. You think the influences are too great?—You don't get half the men you want breeding horses know nothing about it.

6355. You would prefer a committee of experts?—Yes.

6356. You think it is practicable to register horses as suggested?—I think it would be very easily managed.

6357. Do you think it would put up the price of horses?—I don't know that it would.

6358. Are they very particular about pedigrees in America?—Yes, very.

6359. And you can generally ascertain there how the horses are bred?—Yes, you can.

6360. And when they are put up for auction their pedigrees given are generally correct?—Yes.

6361. Chairman.—What part of America are you acquainted with?—The North Western States—Iowa, Minnesota, Dakota, Nebraska.

6362. And you spent a good deal of time there?—Yes, three years.

6363. Were you farming?—Yes.

6364. Did you breed horses there yourself?—Yes.

6365. What do they try to breed in those States?—They only aim at breeding the utility animal to do all kinds of work.

6366. For their own purposes?—Yes, for their own purposes.

6367. It is an enormous district, if you can speak of it as one—all those States and Territories—but what kind of sires are there there?—Portion of those States are agricultural—not like Montana, with cattle ranches—they are agricultural and require horses.

6368. What kind of sires?—Several kinds—Clydesdales, Hackneys, Shire, Suffolk Punch, American trotters, and thoroughbreds, and French and German.

6369. Can you tell us at all which succeeds best out of all that lot?—In America?

6370. Yes, those parts you are acquainted with?—It is very difficult to say; I liked the [illegible] better with lots of thoroughbred blood better than any that [illegible].

6371. Those [illegible] you spoke of had got a strong cross of thoroughbred blood?—Yes.

6372. What were they used for?—They were used for [illegible]; but they were fine driving horses with good action; some of the [illegible] I refer to were used for the [illegible].

6373. I suppose the saddle horse is not so much used in those parts?—No, the pony is used.

6374. I think you said you thought the [illegible] should be [illegible] to be [illegible] for the farmer?—I do.

6375. Do you think the farmer would approve of that?—What I meant by that was to place the desirable kind of sire in the country.

6376. And by the [illegible] that you said you had been so successful in breeding, what sires did you use?—They were all by thoroughbred horses; I think that crossing a thoroughbred on a thoroughbred is often [illegible]; if you want to breed a horse to carry some [illegible] you will have to begin with a mare of [illegible] and she will [illegible] more than [illegible] will give you to believe. I might say that I bred one specially good colt, and his dam [illegible] by a Norfolk trotter.

6377. His grand-dam?—[illegible] Norfolk blood was [illegible] there were [illegible] of thoroughbred. That horse when [illegible] sold [illegible] England.

6378. Lord RATHDONNELL.—Did you ever [illegible] him?—He was [illegible] about the [illegible] when [illegible].

6379. He went to England as a hunter?—Yes; he was bought by [illegible].

6380. CHAIRMAN.—Have you any suggestion to make as to what [illegible] could be done to improve the breed of horses in your part of the country?—I have heard a great many suggestions, and I think Major Cressidge, the last witness, made some useful suggestions. It means a lot of trouble and expense to choosing the man to do it. A very simple thing to do would be to [illegible] the sires and not touch the mares. What the small farmer wants is the sire. You cannot [illegible] [illegible] give them to him, consequently you want to give him a sire between a thoroughbred and a Clydesdale that will produce him [illegible] that will be [illegible] with a thoroughbred cross.

6381. Lord RATHDONNELL.—You don't mean a cross of the thoroughbred and Clydesdale?—No; I mean a distinct animal.

6382. Did you not say you approved of the half-bred horse out of the [illegible] mare [illegible] by a thoroughbred hunter?—Yes; I do. The great thing that is wanted is [illegible] to make money.

6383. Mr. [illegible].—You would [illegible] by [illegible] the [illegible] horses with a stronger class of stallions?—Yes, certainly.

6384. And when graded up you would use the thoroughbred?—Yes.

6385. Lord RATHDONNELL.—Mr. [illegible] suggested that the [illegible] of the [illegible] of stallions and mares should be [illegible] in yearlings, or two-year-olds, and as three-year-olds; and then if [illegible] should be [illegible]?—I would leave that altogether to the buyer, and [illegible] him to find out the [illegible].

6386. You would not register them?—I would [illegible] [illegible].

6387. Mr. [illegible].—You would register them as to pedigree, but you would register the sires as to soundness?—And the mares, too. If you are going to register a foal, I would register his dam.

6388. You would register the [illegible] as to breeding, but would register the stallions as to soundness?—[illegible]; I would [illegible] unsound horses to the country. Public opinion will support the Royal Dublin Society in [illegible] unsound horses.

6389. CHAIRMAN.—Would you [illegible] registration to [illegible]?—I would [illegible] as well, the [illegible] will [illegible] [illegible] the owner who had an unsound one.

6390. Lord RATHDONNELL.—In the case of a filly—you would register that filly as a foal. When would you fix it [illegible] and [illegible] if she was [illegible] in the country?—[illegible] a [illegible] give the [illegible] [illegible] to [illegible] her [illegible].

6391. I thought you would not examine her?—I would examine the dam before I registered her, and then the [illegible] which would probably be sound.

6392. You would leave [illegible] to [illegible]?—Yes.

6393. CHAIRMAN.—Have you any other suggestion to make?—I don't think so, my lord, except that I would have no [illegible] from the opinion of one of the Queen's Plate [illegible] who said the mares are good enough.

6394. When was that?—A few days since. I don't like to [illegible]; he said he considered the [illegible] and mares good enough, and to improve the price, I think that—that is putting the cart before the horse, [illegible] if you improve the [illegible] you get the price. I would give [illegible] [illegible] a [illegible]; if he has got a good [illegible] he will make [illegible] and get enough [illegible] and the money. I would give no [illegible] [illegible] is [illegible].

6395. Lord [illegible].—You would [illegible] [illegible]?—I would prepare the [illegible] [illegible] in the county, and there will be no [illegible] or objection to that; the public would like to have the unsound [illegible] [illegible].

6396. CHAIRMAN.—But what about the [illegible] of unsound animals?—

6397. Mr. [illegible].—They would be a great [illegible]?—Yes; you see [illegible] [illegible] that has been a [illegible] in the [illegible], so I think the [illegible] you would have to give a man for [illegible] with his [illegible], [illegible] him to a [illegible], would be [illegible]; [illegible] [illegible] [illegible] and [illegible] [illegible] producing [illegible] [illegible], but I think [illegible] [illegible] [illegible] clear of them, though indeed I am [illegible] to say that I know of a [illegible] [illegible] of a mare, [illegible] from a [illegible], producing some [illegible], all of which were [illegible] from [illegible], and sold at five years old at over £100 each.

6398. You don't know how they ended their career?—No.

6399. Lord RATHDONNELL.—It is not possible [illegible] [illegible] in [illegible] [illegible]?—Possibly; it did [illegible] [illegible] [illegible].

Dec. 3, 1896.

Mr. Edward O'Reilly.

them, and then each of these two and a half year olds only does half a day's work, and that brings them into a good working condition afterwards for me.

6403. What kind of mares do you breed from?—Clydesdale and Shire mares.

6404. And what kind of stallion?—I prefer the Clydesdale stallion to the Shire; I think he is a better horse, he has better bones and frame, he goes better; with the Shire horse, to my mind, his forepart went well away, but his hind part was carrying after him. I don't like a horse of that stamp if he does not go straight, and I think they are a hardier and better horse, with flat and cleaner bones.

6405. Then may we take it that you have practically given up breeding hunters?—Practically given up breeding hunters for the last five or six years.

6406. Do you breed from two-year old fillies?—No; I did in some cases and I did not approve of it; I think it weakened the constitution of the two-year old by breeding at that young age, that what went to mature the dam was taken away by the foal, and I further proved in some cases that I thought the mare was very much liable afterwards to weak bowels, and that they were not quite as strong after breeding; it might be, perhaps, imagination, but I have passed that remark on some of them, that I could not keep them as strong that way without hard dry feeding as those that I never bred from as two year olds.

6407. You breed from them at three year old?—I bred from a three-year old, but I find that it is somewhat more difficult to get the three-year old in foal than to get a four-year old or a two-year old. I could not say what the cause is though.

6408. Are there any thoroughbred stallions about you?—There are, under the Royal Dublin Society's scheme; there are some in Clogherne, some in Swords, some about Balrothery, and more about my own neighbourhood.

6409. Any half-bred stallions?—There may be some, but I do not approve at all of the half-bred stallion, I would like them pure of any breed. I find, from seeing the result of horse-breeding by half-bred stallions, that the crosses were inclined to run slacky and to form the back in a round form and not a proper cup on the back.

6410. When you bred hunters what stallions did you use?—Thoroughbred stallions and a Clydesdale once. I have bred a Clydesdale horse to a thoroughbred mare that I was made a present of by Mr. Wardell, the owner of Ben Battle, and I gave my Clydesdale horse to that mare, and at three-year old I sold a colt by it for £105, a hunter. I then followed the next year, and it bred a mare, and I think it was £60 I got for her; she had a slight curb at three-year old.

6411. As to the general quality of the horses in your district, do you think they are improving?—I think they are about the same for the last twenty years—that is, in agricultural horses.

6412. In the hunting horses?—In the hunting horses, any hunters I see around me I think they are equally good as they were years ago; you will get them at all times bad, sometimes you will get a mare that may breed a good foal or two, and then she may have not as good a one; she may breed a soft horse or a very hardy horse one year, and the contrary the next year.

6413. Have you anything to say about the Royal Dublin Society's scheme?—I think it is working very well all over the country; the only thing that I have got to say is that we have not got money enough in the Royal Dublin Society; there is a grant of £5,000, and I think that perhaps the public labour under the idea that we are spending that all on the horses; that is not the case, we only give £3,500 to horses, and £1,500 to bulls and other animals; but I think that if we had double the amount of money at our command now that we have, we could do far more good; and I am of opinion, perhaps I am not correct, that no other body of men could do as much good as the Royal Dublin Society are doing, and will do, because the gentlemen there give their time free, and the County Committees under them, as their guiding side, never take any fees, and go out to inspect all the ... everywhere, with their time and money and everything.

6414. Lord Carysfort.—Did you follow up the young horses you bred and sold of the hunting class, that were got of the Clydesdale horse by the thoroughbred mare?—I heard about, I think, four or five of them.

6415. Did you ever follow them up in their after career?—No, I did not, but I can give you like an history:—Mr. Kennedy, of Cabra, who owned a thoroughbred horse and my father Orphan served that mare, and he sold the produce of that mare at five-year-old for 600 guineas; got by a Clydesdale—which I can prove. And I have sold a long back all a mare that I have other ... by a Clydesdale, but this Clydesdale horse, my lord, never was beaten. Because he won the Royal Dublin Society's Cup right out; he had beautiful shoulders, and quarters and middle, and everything to make him perfect; he won the Clyde Cup, and he won the Belfast Cup; and when he was only two years old I refused 1,000 guineas for him in the Belfast Show from a Yorkshireman, and his service with me for sixteen years was three guineas to farmers, and five guineas to gentlemen, and every year on an average for sixteen or fourteen years I got served over 100 mares by him.

6416. He was Clydesdale?—He was a Clydesdale, and from that horse I sold two colts to Messrs. Guinness, and those both won our Royal Dublin Society's Cup and within the last eight years. And when they brought all the horses over from Scotland, where they have 120, they would not yield them as good horses as I reared and sold to them.

6417. Mr. Wrench.—You have had a great deal of experience of the working of the schemes of the Royal Dublin Society for a good many years?—I have.

6418. And do you know that the Royal Dublin Society only subsidises the thoroughbred horse to encourage the thoroughbred horse on their exhibition?—Not at all.

6419. Would you be in favour of encouraging any other breed of horse?—Oh, certainly.

6420. What breed?—I would encourage the Clydesdale and the Shire horse, and I would encourage the Hackney horse I think; for in a particular district.

6421. And that he would be very serviceable in different parts of Ireland the more than any other horse that can be introduced?—He has good shoulders, good middle piece, beautiful bone and quarters, and well set ... back and beautiful action; in my opinion he is a model of a horse, and in the proper places, if a man has a small mare, I believe the introduction of the Hackney would be a great service, inasmuch as that he is small, though he would produce an animal from his mare that could work light work on the farm after the autumn time of the year, in light ploughing the same as I do with my Clydesdales and Shires at two and a half years old, he would be a paying one more or less for that small farmer, however, he would not be using the bred of himself. If he were a hunter, the farmer would not make any of that hunter sooner than four or coming up to five year old; and what would forward one very well, giving as it is ... from three to five years old, at least three to five years old? That is how that horse in ... by a Hackney or any other horse you can ... than on a small farm; I think that is where they would be very serviceable.

6422. Which do you think pays the best to breed, hunters or farmers' horses, in your experience? I know the County Dublin in my district a draft horse will pay the best.

6423. Have you any experience of breeding hackney horses?—I have.

Dec. 9, 1896.
Mr. Richard Dunbar(?).

6424. Have you found it difficult to sell them or easy?—If I have the right style of a horse, a good stepper, and a nice mover, he will certainly be bought up at once. In my experience of fairs and places—I read these reports here, from time to time, vouching their easily disposed—that Hackneys have no sale. Well that may be the case, but if I meet a buyer in a fair when I go into it and he has a good style of a horse, a good stepper and goer, I never seek to ask a man what he is going by; I buy him, because if I go away another steps in and buys him.

6425. You have heard it suggested here that all horses should be registered; would you be in favour of that?—I would be in favour of that very much; I would go further, I would allow no unsound horses to serve; I would condemn those horses or put a heavy fine on the man who owned them, for if they are allowed to remain without some heavy punishment on the owner of the horse the small farmer will go to these horses and get a foal, and the produce of that service, perhaps, at three or four years old is an unsound horse and the farmer gets nothing for him; and as long as those unsound stallions are allowed to roam the country I don't think you will ever have horses right. But I would like the Commission to understand that I don't want to father the Hackney with the Hackney, or with any other horse, I want to get for a general all-round horse that is easily available to every part of the country, and in saying so we want to do—that is, the Royal Dublin Society—the smaller farmers, for I hold the larger ones can mind themselves.

6426. You think the smaller farmers are the people that need most assistance?—I believe so.

6427. And you would be in favour then of encouraging pure-bred stallions of any breed in preference to the half-bred?—In preference to the half-bred. You may get from a half-bred a good horse with power and go in him, but they are inclined to have horses with a light quarter, with a bad-formed way to the back, which is very much against the horse. I would be in favour I think of using the Cleveland bay—it would be a splendid thing to get the Cleveland bay to the Hackney mare. You would bring him down, for he is very tall—some of them want plenty of daylight to get up on them. I think if they were thickened down with the Hackney they would breed an excellent class of horse.

6428. Have you any suggestions to make as to encouraging people to keep their best mares?—I have heard it frequently said, over and over, give them a prize, but I do not agree with that, because supposing in your scheme under the Royal Dublin Society you awarded them a prize, and they took this prize and may win it next year—supposing we give them £5 or £10 as prizes of the kind I suggest—I think many of those men who have good mares got the prize this year and maybe were offered £20 or £30 more than they might expect in consequence of their getting it, so pride money would prevent them selling their mare—they will not keep them.

6429. Then have you any suggestion to make as to how public money could be kept in the country?—I really could not say; I believe no matter which prize you offer that, as I have already said, they will not keep them if tempted with money, except a man has a great liking for breeding and will stick to a mare as long as the dealers don't pay him.

6430. Do you know whether many of the mares now belonging to the Tenantry Company find their way into farmers' hands as brood mares?—Several of them, but I cannot tell you.

6431. Is it the custom among a great many of the smaller farmers to buy them?—A great number.

6432. Are there a great many of the brood mares round Dublin come from the tramways?—A great number.

6433. You don't know how these tramway horses are bred?—I don't know anything about them, they must be very much crossed.—I am aware that there is.

6434. CHAIRMAN.—Have you any experience yourself of breeding from Hackney sires?—None; my brothers have bred from Mr. Tommy Power's horse, and he has a perfect beauty in training now.

6435. You have no experience yourself as to whether the Hackney is soft or not?—I have not, my lord; but as I have already said, even with my Clydesdales and other horses I have bred horribly good foals, and I have got soft ones in the same way from the same dams.

6436. I think you said that even if the Hackney was soft, that as far as the sale price or value of the produce was concerned that would not signify?—I don't know did I say that.

6437. It was something to that effect. I want to know what you meant by that if you did not have me to understand that you did not think it a material consideration whether the produce was soft or was not soft so long as it fetched a good price?—With the greatest respect, my lord, I did not mean that. It has been said that the Hackneys are very soft; I am not able to say whether they are or are not; but from the make and appearance and shape it appears to me that they are a perfect made animal, that they ought not to be soft; but I have bred very lovely Clydesdales from a mare, and I have bred from the same mare and by the same horse, brothers and sisters, and some of them were soft and bad—that is what I mean, my lord.

6438. I wanted to know what your opinion on that was. In answer to this—you might produce a very saleable horse that would fetch a good price, but if it turned out to be soft, although that would not affect you immediately, I presume, in your opinion, it would not be a wise thing to encourage?—Are you referring, my lord, to the Hackney?

6439. I was referring to the Hackney?—If it turned out to be soft at eleven your would qualify it, somehow on the farm or in harness work definitely.

(Shorthand notes, by direction of the Chairman, read: Question 6434.)

6440. That gave me the impression it did not signify whether it turned out soft or not?—If I see the style of horse before me that will suit my market I buy him at once.

6441. And if it turned out soft do you think you would buy again with equal confidence?—I would not go to the same place perhaps again.

6442. LORD HARRINGTON.—I notice in giving your evidence you have used the word "we" in reference to the Royal Dublin Society several times and would like to ask you whether you are speaking on behalf of the Royal Dublin Society or are you speaking in my own.

6443. MR. WRENCH.—Can you tell me at all where the suggested soft blood in the Hackneys comes in?—I could not tell, because he is a perfect made animal, as I have already said, and I don't think he can be so soft as some represent him.

6444. Do you know how Yorkshire Hackneys are bred?—I do; there is a good deal of thoroughbred blood in them. I was over at last Hull show, and saw there some of the most beautiful horses I could look at.

6445. LORD HARRINGTON.—Do you think they have very good strong second thighs or ankle?—They have plenty of bone, and good hocks and good pasterns and splendid second thighs and beautiful shoulders, and splendid tail. I think they are a perfect model of a horse, and if I was going to breed a harness horse or anything of the kind a Hackney I would breed.

6446. Supposing there was a good deal of money spent in this country by dealers in harness horses, such as Winholt and Hunt, if they expressed a decided opinion against the Hackney horse, would you still think it advisable to use him?—I still will be in my own opinion, because during my time for the last thirty years I have taken over 600 first prizes at shows all over Ireland, and more than that in second.

prices, and I never consulted any one how I should mate my mare to my horse. If there is a bad place in my mare or a weak spot I watch that in the horse, and that is what I generally go for.

6447. You would not be afraid of losing their money supposing the Hackney stallion was sent when they had expressed an opinion so strongly against him, for it is in evidence already that they have?—It would not influence me at all, not until I had proved it myself.

6448. I mean you would not have any fear of losing their money?—I don't know for that.

6449. Mr. Wrench.—Do you know, as a matter of fact, that the trade of Messrs. Rose and Messrs. [illegible], and those big dealers who object to Hackneys for their big class of horses, is a mere bagatelle as compared with the general trade of the country?—I would say so. I don't know anything about those gentlemen, but I think there is room for every breed of horses.

6450. If you go to an ordinary fair in the country do you see many high-class carriage horses in the fair? —One about for every fifty we see here in this city of Dublin—the remains of old thoroughbreds and weeds turned into traps and cars—and they not able to raise themselves, only hitting the same point of the season. They have no style or elegance or substance.

Oct. 5, 1896. Mr. Richard O'Malley.

6451. Do you know that there has been a great demand in Dublin for harness horses with action?—Quite so. If I have many harness horses or carriage horses I sell them whenever I have them. I have always [illegible] for harness horses or weight-carrying horses of my horses I have to sell.

6452. Lord Rathdonnell.—The chief horses you have bred, though, have been heavy?—Clydesdales and Shires, and hunting and harness horses.

6453. Yes, but your hunters were bred from a Clydesdale and a thoroughbred horse?—Quite so; [illegible] thoroughbred mare, and I had some beautiful fillies from her.

6454. Chairman.—Have you anything you would like to say to the Commission, Mr. O'Malley?—I don't think I have anything more to say, only that I, some years ago, tried [illegible] breeding—[illegible] breeding—the [illegible] of that was [illegible] tried I had only one good result.

6455. In cold [illegible] breeding of what?—Of horses—Clydesdales—they had all misformations [illegible] their [illegible], their legs not right, their backs not right, their [illegible] not right, so I [illegible] it.

Mr. E. B. Begley, Claremorris, examined.

Mr. E. B. Begley.

6456. Chairman.—You live near Claremorris, in Mayo?—Yes.

6457. What is the nature of the district in which you reside?—It is a congested district for the most part—more than half of the Claremorris Union is congested.

6458. Do you breed horses yourself at all?—Yes.

6459. Do many of the farmers near you breed horses?—Yes.

6460. What kind of horses do they breed?—Harness horses and horses for pulling heavy loads, cart horses, and they breed cobs and small ponies.

6461. Where do they sell them?—At the fair of Claremorris, and when they have good ones they take them to the fair of Ballinasloe and dispose of them there; sometimes dealers come into the district and buy them up.

6462. Are the holdings small about you?—In the congested division itself the holdings are all small.

6463. Do you know anything of the Congested Districts Board's stallions?—I don't know anything about the Congested Districts Board's stallions. I know a good deal about the Hackneys. I don't know about the Hackneys that the Congested Districts Board have sent out, but I know about the Hackneys that have been in the district before that; there have been some Hackneys at Mount Perry belonging to Mitchell Brothers.

6464. What are the stallions generally in the district?—Half-bred stallions and some thoroughbred.

6465. And Hackneys?—And Hackneys; the only party who keeps Hackneys in the neighbourhood are the Mitchell Brothers.

6466. What do you prefer yourself?—I prefer for that district—a congested district—a half-bred hunter stallion with strong bone, plenty of muscle, measuring from 15-3 to 16 hands.

6467. You think that he is likely to produce as saleable a carriage or harness horse as the Hackney?—Yes, for the class of mares we have in that district.

6468. What kind of mares are they, do you know?—They are a light class of mare, and the Hackney with those I fancy would not produce a horse big enough, tall enough.

6469. How do the people about you treat their young stock—do they take sufficient care of them, do they house them?—They house them in the winter season, and take fairly good care of them.

6470. Feed them?—Feed them fairly well.

6471. At what age are they generally sold?—Sold at three-year-old, at four-year-old, and at two-year-old, and they sell them as foals.

6472. Are the prices as good as they used to be?—No, the prices are down considerably.

6473. For all kinds?—For nearly all classes of horses in that district.

6474. Are the farmers in your district inclined to sell their best mares and breed from their inferior ones?—Well, no, they are inclined to keep their good mares if they can, but sometimes they have an inferior class of foal produced and they have to dispose of the mare and keep the foal when they want to realise and get some money out of them.

6475. And you think your district is sufficiently provided with suitable stallions?—Yes, I think there could be more stallions sent into the district; the half-bred hunter stallions that are in the district are private property, and the people have to pay so much for the hire of them.

6476. What do you mean by a half-bred hunter?—One that is not a thoroughbred.

6477. When you say the half-bred is a suitable horse, do you mean the half-bred with a considerable strain of thoroughbred?—Yes.

6478. Do you think anything ought to be done in the way of licensing or registering stallions?—I consider it would be a very good thing to register all stallions of every class, and the foals in particular, and at the time of registering I would consider it a very good thing to give certificates to the owners of the foals, certificates of the registration, so that they might pass them over to purchasers later on, and it would be a guarantee that the foals were of the class they described.

6479. Is there a distinct breed of ponies in your district?—Well, there is a ponyish pony—you could hardly call it a distinct pony.

6480. How has that been produced do you know? —Out of the old Irish pony, the mountainy pony, and the hunter; there is a good pony sometimes produced out of the mountainy pony with the thoroughbred.

6481. What are those ponies used for?—They are used in harness, and for different purposes, trapping.

6482. Is there any sale for them out of the country? —Oh, there is.

6583. Mr. Wrench.—Have the mares run down very much in your district within the last few years?—Yes, they have; they have deteriorated considerably.

6584. From what origin do you think?—Well, I believe it is principally from the fact that the thorough-bred horses sent into the district by the Royal Dublin Society were too light, and did not mate properly with mares we had in the district, and produced a weedy class of animal.

6585. Do you think they want more strength, more bone and substance in the sires?—Yes, they want a half-bred sire of the description I gave before, something like 15 hands high, with plenty of bone and muscle, and a class of breeding in him.

6586. When you are speaking of the half-bred sire, what particular district do you refer to?—I refer to the district around Claremorris, the low lands where the tenant farmers are fairly wealthy and able to live comfortably.

6587. And what class of sire would you recommend for the poorer districts beside the mountains?—The Hackney.

6588. Do you think the Hackney is the best sire for that district?—I do; I have had a good deal of experience of the Hackney in that way myself, I have bred from him for the last 10 years.

6589. With what result?—I have got a small pony from an ordinary mountain pony by a Hackney belonging to the Mitchells of Tourmakeady and Montgomery, called Star of the West—she could make an English mile in three minutes.

6590. And keep it up?—Yes, I drove her 24 Irish miles in one day. I have frequently driven her 40 Irish miles in one day and not whipping, and I was two years with her [illegible] Ballyvourney Horse Show. I have hunted her with big men on her back along with the South Mayo hounds, and she performed well almost always.

6591. And could keep up and stay?—And stay.

6592. Chairman.—How was she bred?—Out of a mountain pony by Star of the West, a pure-bred Hackney.

6593. Lord Kilbracken.—How was he bred?—I cannot tell the breeding further than that he was brought over by the Mitchells of Tourmakeady.

6594. Mr. Wrench.—From Yorkshire?—From England.

6595. Has they have had Hackneys in that district for many years?—Yes; I have got ponies by Hackneys that they had before Star of the West, and they were equally good, but not so good as this one by Star of the West.

6596. You think Star of the West was the best sire?—I do; I have known The Wilton, a horse bred by Mr. Tabor, of Ballinrobe, took the championship nearly in all the shows.

6597. He was by Star of the West?—Yes.

6598. He took the prize in Hollymount?—Yes, and at Roscommon and Ballinrobe, and the all round prize in Castlebar; I have [illegible] alongside him and [illegible] through the whole [illegible], and saw him [illegible] in the leading fields and [illegible].

6599. And he was got by Star of the West, was he?—Yes.

6600. Have you known many good animals got by Star of the West in that district?—Yes, I have four animals myself got by Star of the West, and I hunted with the South Mayo hounds, carrying twelve stone, sometimes thirteen stone, and she could jump anything. I have oftentimes put her over a five-foot wall.

6601. Then your experience of animals bred by Hackneys is [illegible]?—Yes; in the mountains I believe there is no breeding them for durability.

6602. Are they sound, do those horses, very sound?—Sufficiently sound.

6603. And really sound?—They really are sound; as easily reared as a donkey.

6604. Is horse-breeding a considerable industry among the people there?—It is.

6605. Both in the lowlands you speak of and in the mountain districts?—Yes.

6606. Then you don't think that any suggestion to prevent these people breeding horses, or rather to encourage them to breed ponies, would be practicable?—I don't think so; I think it would be very useless to them.

6607. You think they would go on breeding?—I believe so.

6608. And do they necessarily sell their animals themselves only on the ground?—They break them in at two years old, and then sell them along the fairs; sometimes they sell them according as they come in for them.

6609. What are the chief fairs there?—Claremorris, Ballina, Castlebar, Swinford, Ballyhaunis, Ballinrobe, and Tuam.

6610. And I think you told you would suggest inspecting the horses and give certificates to the best of them?—Yes.

6611. Have you thought at all how you would get that carried out; you have heard the suggestion that the system should be put in operation through the Petty Sessions Clerks—do you think that would be a practical way of doing it?—I would much prefer to see it handed over to the authorities, the police of the district.

6612. Can you tell us at all about the opinions of the people in your district of the class of sire they would like?—They are all of opinion that the half-bred horse such as I have described already is the class they want about Claremorris.

6613. You don't know the opinion of the people in the poorer districts?—I don't know the opinion of the people in the other districts; but I know what class of pony can be produced by the Hackney horse and the mountain pony.

6614. Chairman.—When you speak of the experience you have had of Hackneys do you mean the experience you have had of this particular horse, Star of the West?—Yes.

6615. How long has he been in the country?—He has gone out of the country about two years.

6616. How long was he in the country?—About five years; they change their horses very often.

6617. Who do?—The Mitchells, the owners of the horse.

6618. Do you know where he went to?—They took him back to England.

6619. What pony replaced him?—There is another Hackney, but I don't know his name.

6620. You don't know why they took him away?—They wished to bring other blood into the district; they mostly get all the good-producing ponies sired by that one, and they buy up the produce of the [illegible], all the [illegible], and ship them away to England.

6621. Yes; but I wanted to know if you could tell us at all, if you have got any idea, why, if that horse was so successful and so much liked, he was taken away?—I cannot say. I suppose the Mitchells could tell that. He was [illegible], and they [illegible] with them as they chose.

6622. Mr. Wrench.—Do you know the name of the horse that was there before "Star of the West"?—"A [illegible]."

6623. And do you know that the present horse is "Lord Rattan"?—That is his name.

6624. And have not the Messrs. Mitchell a good number of Hackney mares of their own breeding at Tourmakeady?—Yes.

6625. They have a stock of their own that they breed with the horses they have there to [illegible]?—Yes, and they also buy all the foals in the district.

6626. Has Mr. Mitchell bought Hackney [illegible] do you know that he engaged in other horse breeding there?—I cannot say. He is not many years in the West.

6528. But he buys up a good number of those bred by the country people from his own horse?—He buys, mostly all, and hardly gives the people a chance.

6528. At long prices?—At prices that pay them well.

6529. Lord Rathdonnell.—What is he? Is he a horse dealer?—I don't know, really. He has a shooting lodge at [illegible].

6529. Chairman.—What does he do with them?—Takes them over to England.

6530. Lord Rathdonnell.—All of them?—Yes.

6531. Chairman.—Do you know what fee they charge for "Star of the West"?—£1, I think, to an outsider.

6532. Mr. Wrench.—And less to his own tenants?—Very little to his own tenants—a few shillings.

6533. Chairman.—You said just now that you have a high opinion of the half-bred as being suitable to the district?—Yes; suitable to the district round Claremorris.

6534. You don't think the Hackney is suitable there, or do you think it is suitable?—I don't think it is suitable.

6535. You think the Hackney is more valuable when crossed with the mountain pony?—Yes, that is my own experience of it. I tried it in that way.

6536. All the produce of this Hackney sire and these mountain ponies, you say, is bought and taken out of the country?—Yes, most of them are taken away, with the exception of a few ponies that may be kept by private parties who send their mares there and get them served by the horse.

6537. Have you any practical experience of the produce of those ponies yourself?—As a three-year-old I took a prize with it in harness, and one of those ponies as a four year old took a prize again.

6538. Yes, you have told me[illegible]; I wanted to know whether the produce is generally taken out of the country?—Oh, yes; the produce is generally taken out of the country.

6539. You cannot tell generally throughout the [illegible] in which this produce came out [illegible] to [illegible] for your [illegible]?—I know several of them that belonged to private parties who kept them and bred for themselves and they were very good.

6540. What kind of a sire was he?—About 15 hands high—"Star of the West" was. He was long and strong.

6541. And these mountain ponies that he was put to?—They were long, low ponies, something of the old Irish breed, as described, with good action and good backs, and well coupled.

6542. Do you know at all what becomes of their produce that is taken out of the country?—I don't know what they do with them afterwards. I got a cob bred by "Star of the West" out of a half-bred mare, and it was a very good one. I sold it at a big price at Ballinasloe.

6543. Anything you would like to say to the Commission?—I think there is nothing particular that I have to say except that we would wish to have horses shown there and supported by Government in my neighbourhood.

6544. Lord Rathdonnell.—Did I understand you to say that you consider that the Royal Dublin Society had done harm in your district?—Yes.

6545. I think then you said it was owing to their having sent down unduly thoroughbred stallions?—Yes, on account of sending down a thoroughbred stallion that did not suit in the district.

6546. What stallion was that?—He was too light in bone.

6547. What stallion was that?—Locksley Hall and The Queen.

6548. What year was that in? Could you give the exact year?—About five years ago.

6549. That was under a different scheme, though, to what they generally act on now?—Yes, it was.

6550. Do you consider that their scheme in working at present in your district is doing harm?—Well, it has done no good; all the animals that are got by them since are weedy.

6551. It is for that reason you would prefer to see a good half-bred stallion, upstanding, with plenty of bone and substance and action?—Yes, because there should have been tried with the half-bred before the thoroughbred came into the district and they have bred a very good class of horses, which have been sold in Ballinasloe at fairly good prices.

6552. What sort of half-bred stallion was in your district that you referred to just now?—A hunter class, a half-bred.

6553. You have some of that class there?—We have some few in that district.

6554. Have you any of what has been described as mongrel breed, half Clydesdale and half common?—There are none of them now in the district.

6555. Are they intended?—Very little, but I believe if there is any change they will be patronised because the people that have bred from these thoroughbreds that have been sent in are so disgusted with the produce that they say they will breed from anything now rather than send their mares to thoroughbreds.

6556. Are there any thoroughbred horses in your district?—There are some.

6557. Are they all bad?—People don't wish to breed from them, they consider what is produced by them is not strong enough, and they are not marketable, although they are too delicate, not able to bear any sort of hardship. As yearlings they cannot dispose of them, as two-year-olds they cannot work them, as three-year-olds they are lying over in their hands and then they have to sell them cheap and keep them. Weedy things bred from them.

6558. What thoroughbred stallions are in your district?—I cannot just think of the names of them now, there are a few.

6559. Chairman.—Is there any stallion belonging to the Congested Districts Board near you?—No, there is not.

6560. What is the nearest?—Swinford, that is 18 miles away.

The Commission adjourned to next morning.

[illegible]

Dec. 2, 1896.

THIRTEENTH DAY.—WEDNESDAY, DECEMBER 2ND, 1896.

PRESENT:—THE EARL OF DUNRAVEN, K.P. (in the Chair), LORD RATHDONNELL, LORD ASHTOWN, SIR T. H. G. ESMONDE, M.P., MR. F. S. WRENCH, MR. J. L. CAREW, M.P., and MR. HUGH NEVILLE, Secretary.

Mr. E. Kennedy.

Mr. E. Kennedy examined.

6561. CHAIRMAN.—You live in the county Kildare, [illegible]?—Yes.

6562. Near Newbridge?—Yes.

6563. At [illegible] Stud Farm [illegible]?—[illegible]; I keep horses there.

6564. Are you the manager of the [illegible] Stock and Hunter-Sale and [illegible] Agency?—Yes, I am.

6565. What is the nature of that agency?—I keep books in which horses from all parts of Ireland are registered for sale. I advertise occasionally in England and write to clients that I know, and sell horses privately in that manner.

6566. Does the business of the agency take you about Ireland a good deal?—Yes; that and other business takes me through all parts of Ireland. I am [illegible] acquainted with nearly every part of Ireland where horses are bred. I don't know the North, but every other part of Ireland I am fairly acquainted with. I know all the horse fairs.

6567. Does your business take you to England?—I am taken to Yorkshire every week for about six months out of the year.

6568. What do you go to Yorkshire for?—I am connected with the cotton trade. I go there once a week for six months out of the year without missing a week.

6569. Do you breed horses yourself?—Yes, rather largely. I keep one thoroughbred stallion.

6570. What kind are your mares?—Nothing but thoroughbred mares.

6571. Nothing but thoroughbred mares?—Yes; I have a half-bred, and I keep her for old friendship's sake more than anything else. I have got rid of all other half-bred mares I had.

6572. What class of horse is generally bred in your part of Kildare?—I think that in Kildare most people try to breed a really good hunter, with the exception of those like myself who prefer to breed thoroughbred horses, but the poorer farmers naturally try to breed hunters.

6573. What class of horse do you think is the most profitable to breed?—For the farmer the best high-class hunter they can breed. It is very hard for a poor farmer who is not very skilful in handling young horses to breed anything but a hunter. He is not [illegible], perhaps, sensible enough to breed thoroughbreds which will sell well, and it is far better for him to confine himself to breeding high-class hunters and high-class carriage horses.

6574. Which do you find pays best—hunters or harness horses?—Oh, hunters, certainly. There are often [illegible] that farmers have got, by thoroughbred stallions, fail in becoming a hunter [illegible] very often becomes a harness horse, provided it is well grown.

6575. Do you keep your stallions entirely for the service of thoroughbred mares?—No, I have one horse which gets very few thoroughbred mares—all half-breds, all farmers' mares almost.

6576. Are there plenty of stallions in your part of Kildare?—I think quite sufficient good horses. Kildare has got the advantage of having the Curragh, which is the headquarters of the turf, and you have the advantage of having thoroughbred stallions always there. Kildare farmers have, I think, exceptional advantages for breeding.

6577. Are there any half-bred stallions serving in that part of the country?—Indeed, there are.

6578. What is your opinion about them?—I don't like them. I think there is very little demand for their stock now. At the same time, the farmers find they are cheap and convenient, and they are very often more fruitful than thoroughbred horses that are not properly looked after or properly exercised; and the farmers go to them accordingly for that reason, too.

6579. To get the hunter and high-class carriage horses in your part of the country you would prefer a thoroughbred?—Oh, certainly.

6580. Are there any other stallions of any other breed in your part of the country?—Not exactly in my part of the country. There is a half-bred, a few Clydesdale horses—not very many; they are more confined to county Dublin than to my immediate neighbourhood.

6581. Would they be used to get horses for the [illegible] of the [illegible] and [illegible] in Dublin?—I think the farmers like that sort of horse, and I think very often that they can sell a rough two-year-old for any sort of work. They can work him as a two-year-old, and sell him after the spring work is over. They are bought for [illegible] and [illegible] at low prices that scarcely pays to produce them.

6582. What do they use for their own farm work?—Some of them use very useful mares that will breed a very useful hunter. Others of them who are ignorant of the advantage of breeding a good horse breed half-bred animals and sell them at a low price, but a great many of the Kildare farmers keep very useful mares.

6583. What kind of mares do they generally breed from?—Mares that are got by a thoroughbred horse out of, perhaps, some of the old native mares that one hears talked about. I mean mares that trace back to the old native mares.

6584. Is the quality of the mares, generally, as good as it used to be?—In my part of the country I really think it is; I am inclined to think it is, but Kildare being near the Curragh is exceptional.

6585. Do you think the farmers are more inclined than they used to be to sell their best mares and breed from inferior ones?—I think the Kildare farmers see the advantage of keeping their good mares more than the farmers throughout Ireland do. They are so near the Curragh, and they see the advantage of the high prices that horses are sold at there. I think a great many of them like to keep their good mares. I know plenty of them who don't like to part with the mares at all that they have been successful with. But I am acquainted with other parts of Ireland, and I know that in those places the farmers always sell, the price is always tempting for them.

6586. Is the price high up as it used to be?—I think that high-class hunters are not cheaper than ever they were—high-class hunters and horses calculated to win races certainly not. I think Ireland, during the last ten or fifteen years, has become the world's market for a really good horse, and I think it is the duty of Irishmen to maintain that reputation.

6587. We have had a great deal of evidence as to the price of high-class harness horses and hunters?—Their price is as good as ever it was.

6588. And we have got evidence that the inferior classes have gone down in price?—Yes, I think the American competition has had as much to do with

Dec. 1, 19[illegible]
Mr. R. Kennedy.

that as the market was glad [illegible]. The enormous [illegible] of horses coming over to London from the Argentine has completely broken down the price of the underbred [illegible] and [illegible]. They can sell their Argentine horses to get a profit at about £[illegible] and in London—I was on those from the Argentine—and it is very hard to compete with that low price.

[illegible]. You have not yourself bred horses specially for [illegible]?—No, never.

[illegible]. I gather from you that that is not generally done in your part of the country?—Certainly not. However a good many farmers there [illegible] to breed light-class hunters, provided they are well-grown and got by a thoroughbred stallion, make very fine hunters, and are very often sold at a good price for that market.

[illegible]. I think you said that there are Clydesdales in your part of the country?—A few. They [illegible] through the country, [illegible] out of the [illegible] parts of county [illegible].

[illegible]. Are there many other stallions of any breed [illegible] half-bred [illegible], with one of the [illegible]; I don't think they get very much to do.

[illegible]. Are there any Hackney stallions?—Not that I am aware of.

[illegible]. Have you any knowledge of breeding from a Hackney sire?—Personally I have never bred from one.

[illegible]. You are very well acquainted with the whole South and West?—Yes, I know it fairly well.

[illegible]. And for how many years have you had experience of this country, generally?—About fifteen years.

[illegible]. Speaking generally, would you say there has been any deterioration in the production of horses?—I think I might say that from 1880 to 1890 the farmers were very careless about breeding. Perhaps it was because breeding in most sections in Ireland was stopped in 1880. I think they thought the demand would slacken and decrease, and they became very [illegible] and [illegible] about what they bred. I [illegible] the efforts of the Royal Dublin Society within the past few years that all that is altered, and they are certainly [illegible] to [illegible] now that [illegible] more than they did before in the breeding that they will do better.

[illegible]. Do you think there is a tendency in the [illegible] to sell their best mares, and that as a consequence the quality of the mares were generally throughout the country is not as good as it used to be?—I can't speak further back than ten or fifteen years. I have not had reason to think that they were deteriorated so much, with the exception, perhaps, that they were rather careless of the breeding [illegible] from 1880 to 1890. It is I think that they, no doubt, sold anything they could [illegible] into money at a reasonable price, but my impression is that they are improving now. Under the system of the Royal Dublin Society I think that the mares are improving very much indeed.

[illegible]. Have you seen any Hackney produce in any part of the country?—The half-bred Hackney produce.

[illegible]. Yes?—Yes, I have seen some fine [illegible]. I have seen half-bred Hackneys in the West.

[illegible]. Could you not tell whether they were or not?—I would not be certain. I was told they were [illegible], I believe they were. I am thoroughly [illegible] with the half-bred produce of Yorkshire [illegible] I am told are directly crossed with Hackneys or from Hackney sires. In Yorkshire and the [illegible] 10 to 15 per cent. of the animals are [illegible] to the [illegible] from the Hackney, I [illegible].

[illegible]. Excluding the North, which you are not acquainted with, do you consider breeding hunters is the most profitable branch of horse-breeding in Ireland?—Well, I think, taking the farmers in Ireland who breed, certainly so. Speaking generally for the whole of Ireland, I should say, most certainly, yes.

[illegible]. That is, the object of the farmer should be to breed the hunter, if he fails to hit that to sell him as a carriage horse, and if he fails in that the horse will go for something else. I think we ought all to try to maintain the reputation we have gained. During the last [illegible] years we have been practically the world's market for the high class hunter.

[illegible]. Have you formed any opinion yourself as to the effects of the introduction of Hackney blood, or any blood other than thoroughbred?—Yes, I have. I don't think we have got in Ireland a market for anything else except a really fairly high class horse, except a carriage horse or a harness horse; we have not got a market for anything else that would pay. I don't think it pays to breed from anything except a horse that can sell at a reasonable price, and I don't think we would be able to sell the produce of Hackney stallions at a reasonable price. I think quite [illegible] per cent. of the foals that are bred in the West of Ireland are sold to go into better countries. I think [illegible] per cent. of them find their way into Leinster. I have seen many hundreds of foals lately go to Leinster of the foals that are bred in the West, and I believe if the farmers find that the foals they buy only turn out small animals and don't grow—the farmers, if they are got by the Welsh ponies imported, instead the farmers will give up buying them, and that the middlemen will also give up buying them in the West. Some of the western foals brought into Leinster grow there into very fine horses. If they were got by big-boned thoroughbreds it would pay the farmers in Leinster to keep them, and growing well and paying very well I think the farmers would go back to the same market. I saw three [illegible] of those [illegible] other day in my own county town, brought up from Newport.

[illegible]. How were they produced do you think?—They were produced from thoroughbred ponies, 14.2 to 14.3 hands.

[illegible]. By what class of sire?—The half-bred [illegible] that is walking about the country. I have seen sires over at Westport, "[illegible]," who has had a most phenomenal success in producing good well-grown horses from those Connemara ponies. He is about fifteen hands and was formerly the property of Lord [illegible], by "[illegible]." He is not absolutely pure-bred, but has a very [illegible] strain that I don't know. The size of his stock from those country ponies is phenomenal.

[illegible]. Mr. [illegible].—Besides, you cannot?—Yes, besides, for the same [illegible], if high-class thoroughbreds were sent there I think they would have the same chance or a greater chance of success.

[illegible]. Chairman.—We have very often heard the opinion expressed, whether rightly or wrongly that in a great deal of the country the mares have deteriorated very much, that they have got small, that they are lacking in bone and substance owing to their being continually crossed with inferior thoroughbred stallions; that a stronger strain of blood should be introduced; that the Hackney would probably supply the size and substance required, that the mares would be improved, and would probably produce better mares than a generation, or which crossed again with a thoroughbred sire?—I have hardly personal experience enough to say that. I don't really think so myself. I believe a big-boned blood horse will get bigger produce than a Hackney.

[illegible]. But are there many of these big-boned blood horses about the country?—I think there are lots of them to be had. This little horse "[illegible]" is not a big-boned horse, yet he has had the most phenomenal success standing at Westport. His produce really is [illegible] valuable horses.

[illegible]. Do you think generally that the supply of [illegible] thoroughbred stallions throughout the country is sufficiently good?—Throughout Ireland do you mean, generally?

[illegible]. Yes?—No; I think there is room for a great deal of improvement.

[illegible] Mr. E. Kennedy.

6612. [illegible] for half-bred mares to breed hunters, and so on?—I think there is room for a great deal of improvement. At the same time I think we are as well off as any country in the world for thoroughbred stallions. There are a great many unsound horses; and I certainly agree with those people who would like to see these licensed by some Government department. I would like to see unsound ones cleared off altogether.

6613. On that point, would you suggest a system of licensing or registration?—I should certainly advocate that the unsound stallions, be they of any breed—that stallions which are not calculated to get fairly sound stock—should not be allowed to serve any but their owners' own mares. I should not like to see the owner of a stallion doing harm by having a worthless brute and letting him out cheap. I think it ought to be the province of an Agricultural Department to see that that would not go on.

6614. Do you think a hunter stud book would be practicable or useful?—Yes; I think it would be of great service to foreign buyers. If a foal was got by a thoroughbred horse it would be registered in the book, and if the owners of these animals had or could obtain certificates from a hunter's stud book, or from a hunter's registration book, I think it would be a great advantage to the owners in selling. I think it would also be a great advantage to the buyer to know what he got. Many horses which go out of this country are thereby sold on the strength of having Weatherby's certificate of being from a thoroughbred horse. I think some animals in this country would be sold if people had certificates.

6615. Do you consider it necessary because of the American horses?—I think it necessary all the more especially when all these American horses are coming into the country.

6616. Do you think these American horses **ought** to be branded or distinguished in some **way**?—Certainly.

6617. By "the country" do you mean England and Ireland?—Yes; I would like to have them branded in both countries.

6618. Do you think many of these horses are imported into Ireland and sold as Irish horses?—It is only hearsay, but I heard that they are being sold in that way. I have never, however, been aware personally of such a case.

6619. Have you experience of the Royal Dublin Society's scheme?—Yes, I have.

6620. What do you think of it?—I think **it is** working most admirably, that is, as far as I can see, but beyond Limerick I have not visited the places under the auspices of the Society's scheme.

6621. You think the system is good?—Certainly.

6622. And probably you think if the Society had larger means at its disposal it would do more good?—I am quite certain of it.

6623. You think the Society **is working on the** right lines?—I do.

6624. I gather from you that you think generally it is the duty of every Irishman to keep up the reputation of the country for producing high-class hunters and harness horses?—I means to include every high-class horse which would sell at a good paying price. I think it should also include the roadster and the [illegible] horse. I think it is the duty of every Irishman to maintain the fairly high repute of Ireland abroad the world's market for a high-class horse.

6625. Do you think it is possible for the small farmers to breed this kind of horse?—I think the small farmers in the west will breed sixty to seventy per cent. of the foals. At this time of the year they come into better condition and have opportunities of developing and growing. I think if they all had thoroughbred stallions they would develop the produce into hunters, and failing hunters they would develop into harness horses or [illegible].

6626. Do you know Yorkshire well enough to give the Commission any information as to the effect of breeding Hackneys in that country?—I have gathered a good deal of information from people I met there, and I find it very much talked. They all very much agree. They like them very much indeed, when they are bred by themselves and are thoroughbreds; but as far as I can find out they don't advocate their crossing. The Hackney breeders in Yorkshire that I met all swear by them as long as they are kept to themselves. They tell me that they don't think they can be successfully crossed. They won't cross with the horses of the country—Yorkshire. That is the opinion I gathered generally in Yorkshire.

6627. Do you think Ireland has got any particular natural advantages for breeding steeplechasers, hunters, and other high-class horses?—Oh! certainly—the limestone land and our good rich pasture land. The many hills as well as the good lands of Ireland, I think the young stock have an advantage beyond any other country.

6628. Do you think we should have an equal advantage in breeding the heavy draught horse and horses of that kind?—I think we have no heavy deep-ploughed land to use the heavy draught horse as they have in England. I think we have already made our mark for high class steeplechase horses and hunters, and I think we ought to keep up the reputation we have already gained. I don't think we have a market for that class of animals you mention. I don't think it would pay the farmers to breed draught horses.

6629. You think it probable that the country having made its reputation by breeding the class of animal that is most useful to breed, it would be wiser therefore to stick to that class?—It would be what I think is stick to what we have been successful at.

6630. Lord [illegible].—You say you know a great part of the South of Ireland from travelling through it?—Yes.

6631. Is not the general cry of the horse-breeder for bone and substance?—Certainly.

6632. Take the farmers, for instance. How do they try to get this?—You mean the smaller farmer throughout the south?

6633. Yes. How do they try to get bone and substance?—Well, I think a great many of them breed from a half-bred—what they call a hunter sire. I think that is their notion of producing bone. I think that they imagine that a horse three parts bred will produce bigger bone than a thoroughbred horse.

6634. Do you approve of that system of breeding?—I would rather have a good class thoroughbred sire. I would like that system of horse well enough, if I could not get a thoroughbred sire, but I would rather have a good class thoroughbred sire.

6635. I think you said just now in evidence that you don't quite approve of the half-bred sire, and I want to know what is the half-bred horse you don't approve of?—A horse with traces of the blood of the Clydesdale or Suffolk Punch in him, such as I described now.

6636. But a horse like "[illegible]" you would not disapprove of?—He has a distant strain that won't be noticed. I don't disapprove of him. I would rather have a horse that is in Weatherby; but if there is a distant strain, such as in "[illegible]" or "[illegible]," I would not altogether object to him on that account.

6637. If a half-bred stallion with great bone and good action of the hunter type was standing in the country, and then next door to him a half-bred Clydesdale, or a Clydesdale, or a Cleveland was standing, which do you think the farmers would chiefly go to, if all were standing at the same fee in the South of Ireland?—

6638. The—I think they would go to the horse with the thoroughbred strains in him. I am certain they would.

6639. With regard to registration, would you go above all the question of registered horses, or would you have each animal examined before registration; that is having each animal shown on its own merits?—I think it would be a very big business to have each animal examined which is, each animal got by a registered sire.

6640. Supposing the mare to be registered, then you would not allow the produce of that mare to be registered without examination?—I would if the produce was got by a registered sire.

6641. Regardless of its soundness or unsoundness?—It would be an enormous business. I think it would not be possible. In my opinion all foals got by the registered stallions should be registered regardless of their soundness.

6642. You think that would be too big a business?—Well, it would be a big business after a few years. It would be hardly possible, but not feasible. If they were out of a registered mare and got by a registered stallion I think that would be sufficient, for unsoundness may be traced as always defined there against unsound animals.

6643. Practically, might, but if a mare were lost in the interim would you register that mare before she is going to breed? Would you have her registered as a mare out of a registered animal, or would you have her examined?—I think it ought to be examined if she is got by a registered stallion out of a registered mare.

6644. Mr. [illegible].—You spoke of "Abdallah" as a hybrid; is he not practically a thoroughbred?—Yes; there is only a distant strain in him.

6645. And that is the style of hybrid you approve of?—Well, yes, if I would approve of any hybrid. I always prefer a thoroughbred, but not being able to obtain a thoroughbred, I don't in the least object to a horse that has got a distant strain you might not trace—"Hackney" for instance.

6646. He is practically a thoroughbred horse?—Yes, he has a distant strain that cannot be traced.

6647. You spoke of Connemara ponies fetching over **my** [illegible]?—Yes, about fifty pounds.

6648. You don't know if they were produced by Hackneys or not?—I asked the question of one man at the last fair in [illegible], who had a number of them, and he said they were not. I asked if he had got any by Government or Hackney horses, and he said "No."

6649. Do you think it would be possible in Ireland to isolate the Hackney breed to the congested districts and keep them there?—Certainly not. They would be purchased with others to be imported into Ireland, which are the [illegible] producing grounds in Ireland, to be sold there.

6650. And you think they would deteriorate the hunting stock in Leinster?—I am inclined to think they would.

6651. Your experience, from what you have heard of Hackney breeding in Yorkshire, is that the breeding of Hackneys is disappointing, or by the well-known hunting?—Say breeders I have spoken to are very fond of their Hackneys when bred to thoroughbreds; they don't go largely [illegible]; they don't approve of the [illegible]; they don't approve of the crossing with the hunting horse in Yorkshire.

6652. You think breeding from a thoroughbred [illegible] with your good hunting stock and [illegible]?—Certainly.

6653. And that it will be more popular with the buyers from England?—Yes, certainly.

6654. Have you any experience of breeding from thoroughbred [illegible]?—[illegible]

6655. Mr. Wrench.—You would have thoroughbred stallions [illegible]?—That is my opinion.

6656. You would [illegible] half-bred horses as well?—I would not like to [illegible]

farmers in certain districts in the north where it is all village from breeding Clydesdale horses.

6658. What about Kildare and the south?—We have an ancient [illegible] for them.

6660. Do you know that out of the fifty-eight stallions in Kildare eighteen are each horse or half-bred?—I don't exactly know the number. I knew there were some there. I didn't think there were so many as that.

6661. Do you know that such horses and half-bred horses form more than one-third of the entire stallions in Ireland?—I am sure they would.

6662. There are a great many stallions in the country that ought not to be in it?—Certainly.

6663. You have referred to the west of Ireland. Does your experience of the west go beyond Westport?—I know Westport and Newport and that country.

6664. Have you been to Achill?—I have not. I have been at Ballina and beyond that country. I think I have been to Belmullet, but not lately.

6665. Have you been in Connemara?—I have been very little in Connemara, not much beyond Galway.

6666. Donegal you don't know?—I don't.

6667. Do you know the western coasts of Kerry and Cork?—Yes.

6668. How far have you been there?—To Dingle, Cahirciveen, Valentia.

6669. In Cork, have you been far?—I don't think I have been far, to Bandon.

6670. You would recommend that the ponies there should be crossed with a thoroughbred horse?—Certainly, the biggest horse and best thoroughbred it is possible; the bigger he is the better for the cross.

6671. Do you know there have been some sales lately of the ponies of that cross in Dublin?—I was not aware of it.

6672. You don't know there were [illegible] and [illegible] got by a thoroughbred horse sold in Dublin at an average of seven guineas a piece lately?—I was not aware of it.

6673. You didn't hear of Colonel [illegible]'s sale of Connemara ponies got by a thoroughbred horse?—I did hear of it, but it didn't pay much attention.

6674. You didn't hear that thirteen of them were sold at an average of 53l.?—I didn't.

6675. That is not a very encouraging result of the cross?—Most discouraging; but I would like it to be understood that my principal reason for advocating the thoroughbred stallion there is that quite the gentlemen of those people adopt them [illegible], and I think if they were got—I will not say by a Hackney—but by any inferior horse, say a Welsh pony, that the farmers up here in Leinster who buy them would never become tired of buying and would not buy them at all.

6676. You think the trade for those ponies is to produce foals, so that if these farm ones went up here people will go back and buy again?—Exactly.

6677. If you found that the results of the Hackneys were bought and produced good ponies you might alter your opinion?—Most certainly. I would rather profit from what I see—Hackneys in the south [illegible] of Welsh ponies which I understand have been very successful in the West.

6678. You would prefer the Hackney to the Welsh pony?—Yes.

6679. Would you prefer the Hackney to the [illegible] or a [illegible]?—I can't say that. I have no experience of cross-bred stock of a Hackney or a Welsh.

6680. You would prefer a thoroughbred to an Arab or a Barb?—Certainly.

6681. I suppose you know that in those congested districts it is necessary to have a sire that will produce hardy stock. I think that the stock that is got has to go through great hardships, the land being very wretched?—Yes; the stock they keep there then has to be hardy.

6682. I think you referred to the Hackney and mentioned well-bred, the country people in Yorkshire

Dec. 2, 1896.

Mr. R. [illegible]

—I have only that as hearsay from the Yorkshire gentleman I meant.

6683. You have not been about through the country districts in Yorkshire to see what these people keep?—I have seen them at fairs.

6684. Are their horses very much cheaper than anything we have in this country?—Yes.

6685. With a lot of cart blood in them?—Yes; a very bad class of horse.

6686. A horse that wants a thoroughbred horse if possible?—I should say so.

6687. They are big and not at all like anything we have in Ireland?—I think they are the worst class of horses I ever saw—the small farmers' horses in Yorkshire. I think that going into a Yorkshire fair, where you see the horses of the country, I have never seen anything so clumsy and underbred-looking in any part of Ireland.

6688. They are coarse and common?—They are coarse bad Hackneys. When I go to Doncaster and see the horses that ply from the station to the course I always wonder how they get so many bad horses together, and most of them are half-bred Hackneys.

6689. You are strongly in favour of licensing stallions, and also of forming a hunters' stud book in Ireland?—Yes; I think it would be a good inducement to buyers from abroad.

6690. How far would you go in registration; would you register every horse, or merely form a hunters' stud book on the lines of the Hunters' Improvement Society in England?—I am afraid I don't know enough about the Hunters' Improvement Society lines in England.

6691. What is your idea of a hunters' stud book?—I would take the registered mares and the produce of registered stallions. It is hard to make a beginning and to draw the line in this hunters' stud book.

6692. Did you hear it suggested by some of the witnesses that every horse should be registered with the Petty Sessions clerk?—Every stallion.

6693. That every horse should be registered in exactly the same way as dogs?—I think that would be a very good suggestion if it was practicable.

6694. If a hunters' stud book was formed would there be any danger of the fact that you anticipate of Hackneys intermixing [sic] ?—If the stud book was formed I certainly think it would lessen the danger, but the danger might still exist.

6695. But how could that be, if the breeding of the animals was registered?—There might be a good deal of fraud in these things. Hackneys might get into the book. I am told that fraud has existed to a great extent in the Hackney stud book in Yorkshire. I was told that only yesterday by a Yorkshire man. I was told that a great many horses have got into the book that are not Hackneys at all.

6696. You think it would be hard to guard against that?—I do.

6697. But it would lessen the danger?—I think the stud book would certainly lessen the danger.

6698. I think you made a suggestion at the end of your opinion here that you were not quite satisfied with what the Government have done with regard to horse-breeding in Ireland up to the present, and suggested that steps should be taken to improve the fairs?—Certainly.

6699. What improvements at the fairs do you think is necessary?—I think the fairs as they are at present are altogether under the influence of the town commissioners. I think the majority of the town commissioners throughout Ireland are drawn from the publicans' interest, and they would like to keep the horses, buyers, and sellers, jogging up and down in front of their own doors in very narrow streets, and a great many buyers find that they cannot get reasonable trials of a horse, and people who have sufficient horses don't like the horses to be taken into their fields in the neighbourhood, and jumped and galloped about there. I think all the good fairs in Ireland should be provided with a field where you can get a good trial of what a horse can do—trot, gallop, jump, and so on. I think this would be an inducement to foreign buyers to come into the country. I think the fairs as they are at present are a disgrace to the people who look after them, to the commissioners of the various towns who look after them, with some exceptions only.

6700. You think if the accommodation was improved it would help the trade in horses?—Without doubt. I think it is a crying necessity to improve the fairs and the markets where the small farmers dispose of their stock.

6701. Do you approve of the present Royal Dublin Society's scheme?—I think it is working very well indeed. I should like to emphasise the fact that I think the fairs in Ireland are very disgracefully managed by the various commissioners who have the province of looking after them, with some exceptions, Limerick and Kilkenny.

6702. Mr. Carew.—Those are the town fairs of course?—The town fairs.

6703. Chairman.—Are there as many horses sold at fairs as there used to be?—I think the high-class horses are sold privately, but the young horses are always sold at the fairs—three and four-year olds.

6704. At what age are they mostly sold in your part of the country?—Four and five-year olds, mostly at those years.

6705. They are out all the time?—Almost all of them are out the whole of the winter.

6706. Are they generally fed at all?—I think they feed them reasonably; not, perhaps, as well as they might feed them.

6707. I gather that you think that in the western districts and the wilder part of the country the best possible stallion would be a good sound thoroughbred with plenty of bone?—That is strongly my opinion.

6708. Do you think the farmers in those districts would ever be able to pay the fee that would have to be charged by private owners for horses of that kind?—I think you can buy very useful thoroughbred stallions almost as cheap as you can buy horses of another breed. For instance, take the Yorkshire horses. I think you can buy them as cheap as a good Hackney stallion. I think you can buy a strong thoroughbred horse of the steeplechase type, perhaps not very fashionably bred, at a reasonable price to allow him to serve at a pretty cheap fee.

6709. You think the Government would have more valuable lines for the same price than they have for the Hackney stallions?—I am not accurately aware of what the Hackneys cost.

6710. Do you think that a thoroughbred stallion of the class you have in your mind can be bought for, say, £200 on an average?—I do, certainly. You might not be able to get him within the month, but take your time, and, I think, you would get a very reasonable supply for £200 each.

6711. You think it would be a good thing if such horses were standing in the same districts as the Hackneys at the same fee so that people could have their choice?—I should like to see them have their choice.

6712. I think I gather generally that your opinion of the Hackney is that the pure Hackney is valuable and desirable, but that the cross is not good?—That is the opinion I gathered from my visits to Yorkshire. All the Hackney breeders there are very strong admirers of the thoroughbred Hackney, and have made very considerable sums of money breeding them.

6713. Assuming there being any money forthcoming for anything more than what is now done at present to try and improve the breed of horses generally in the country, do you think attention should be directed mainly to the improvement of the class of mares?—Well, I should think, certainly, the aim I think if we had good sires, good mares would come in too.—I think in improving the class you would also be improving the mares at the same time. The produce of the sires in time would improve.

6714. It has been suggested that some Government horses might be distributed where the country is most deficient throughout the country?—You think that [illegible] I think it certainly would be useful. I think that all the [illegible] are all generally [illegible] I think they would do good.

6715. Is there anything else you can suggest to the Commission on the subject of improving the breed of horses generally?—Nothing further than my suggestion that all stallions should be registered. All thoroughbred horses should be registered. I should like to see the [illegible] horses of every class registered entirely. Let the owners use them if they wish for their own mares, but not use them to the mares of the public.

6716. You would have certain horses not absolutely thoroughbred—that is, not in the stud book—allowed to be registered—horses like "Mayboy," for instance?—Certainly—horses like "Mayboy."

6717. How far would you go in the direction of registering horses that are not thoroughbred, say, if they were examined and approved?—Yes, and with all stallions I should go rather for performance. If a horse had been a good, unregistered horse, and if he had a strain that could not be traced, I should certainly permit him to be registered in the horse stud book.

6718. You think a horse should not be registered until there was some experience of his stock?—If the horse was right in every other way, say a good-looking well-bred horse, and had been a fine performer, I don't think any one would have any necessity to see his stock.

6719. Lord RATHDONNELL.—You advocate the formation of a stud book?—Or some general system of registration, which could be used by foreign purchasers coming into the country.

6720. You want a stud book, decidedly?—Yes, certainly.

6721. I suppose that has to be started at some time breeding, has it not?—Certainly. Let us start by bringing out a separate volume.

6722. Would not there be a danger in that of excluding animals in the future from entry—[illegible] I don't quite catch your meaning.

6723. Would not there be a danger in that of excluding animals in the future from entry—animals which if only registration were now might be still eligible for entry on that registration?—I don't think you would close a stud book except to bring out various volumes.

6724. How do you propose then to enter in the future if you don't close your stud book?—I would have them entered exactly in the same way as they are entered in Weatherby's stud book.

6725. That is the position of the stud book entirely?—Certainly.

6726. That would exclude animals bred outside the stud book. You would have no chance of entering them?—I would bring in animals got by the [illegible] thoroughbred sire or a horse sire fit to be registered in that way.

6727. If you call it registration?—I am quite satisfied then to alter the name to registration. I would rather like to have a stud book or a general system of registration. Either would perfectly satisfy me. I would like to see them with a certificate they could show to any purchaser who might have already, and who could show the certificate showing what the particular animal. That would, I think, largely enhance the value of many of our horses. For instance, when horses that are "plated" in Kildare are sold abroad, the more of them so having been so plated is preferred by the vendor to the [illegible] and on that certificate the animal is sold. So I think the registration certificate would be extremely advantageous in selling Irish horses.

6728. There is a difference between registration and a stud book?—Well, a general system of registration I would be perfectly satisfied.

6729. Would you limit animals to be registered for breeding horses to such as are got by a thoroughbred sire?—I would, or such sires as "Ataliah" or "Mayboy."

Colonel H. DE ROBECK examined.

6730. CHAIRMAN.—You are Secretary to the Kildare Horse Show?—Yes.

6731. And to the Dublin Society's Horse-breeding Scheme in the County Kildare?—Yes.

6732. You know the county well?—Yes, pretty well.

6733. In your part of the county do the farmers breed much?—Yes; a good many breed. They breed from bad mares, instead of keeping good ones. It would be much better if they bred fewer; it would be much more paying. Small farmers breed, and have no method of bringing the horses or getting good prices for them. I don't see how it pays lots of them to breed.

6734. What do they aim at breeding?—Hunters principally. When they fail as hunters they go off as trade horses or as troopers. We give prizes at the show to farmers under 250l. valuation, as we do to the bigger farmers, but very few of them enter. They say they have not time to waste a day in taking the animals in, I think.

6735. Is the only thing the small farmers can breed this kind of horse profitably?—Some of them do. They can sell them at Kilcullen about the place. I think it is very hard for a lot of the small farmers to do it profitably. They break them and work them to five-year olds, and then try to sell them as hunters. It's a small farmer, but a really good mare people would get to know it, and they would get a hire and buy his young horse.

6736. What are the class and quality of the mares generally?—I think they are well-bred mares, most of them. A lot of them I know about the country have been broken-down hunting or racing mares, or have been given as presents to farmers, who keep them and work them. Any mare that does not breed fairly they send to a cart-horse, and the produce they keep to breed from, and then, I think, the produce is uncertain. One might be one year a good hunter and the next not worth much.

6737. What kind of cart-horses do they send them to?—One man has what they call an Irish cart-horse. He has very little hair on his legs, is a very strong horse, and looks like a cross of the Clydesdale. There is a man who has a horse that gets a lot of mares that are fairly useful. I have often tried to get him to tell what the breeding is, but the man says that he does not know the breeding of the horse or he would tell us. He is what he calls an Irish cart-horse, but it is a good useful stamp of horse to get a farm horse or a useful horse, but it is not a very highly-bred horse.

6738. The produce of these cart stallions put again to a thoroughbred horse?—Yes, is a great success again.

6739. What they produce is somewhat doubtful?—Very doubtful. I bred one myself from a cart-horse—a useful one—and a grey mare that had a certain amount of quality. The first foal is now as good a hunter as ever was seen; the next was bred exactly

Col. E. [illegible]
Mr. E. Kennedy.

Colonel H. De Robeck.

June 2, 1897. Mr. Gerald H. De Robeck.

the colt may get by the same stallion, and is a medium type of a carriage-horse. One showed quality, and the other threw back to something or other.

6740. Is your part of the country well supplied with useful sires—sires suitable to the mares in the country?—Very well supplied; we are very well off. We are so near the Curragh that we have a supply of good stallions.

6741. Have you any personal experience of breeding from these cart-horses?—Only in this way by this one mare who was from one of these cart-horses. I didn't breed from her again after the second time.

6742. Have you bred at all, or have you any experience of breeding from the Hackney sire?—No; the only experience I know of is that of a man who sold a very valuable horse as a hunter and was known as the breeder of valuable animals; he bought a young mare the other day and found out it was a Hackney mare by a Hackney horse, and he sold it; [illegible] the experience would go.

6743. Where did he buy it from?—He bought it somewhere in Galway, I think. The only other thing I know about a Hackney was selling a pony that came from Mayo somewhere; Kennedy got it. I was selling her to a man as a polo pony, and drove the buyer in a trap with her to the station. Twice he looked at her action, and he said he was afraid she had Hackney blood, and he would not take her then.

6744. Then I gather from you that, so far as you can judge, you would not think the introduction of Hackney blood would be beneficial?—I should say certainly not, as far as Kildare is concerned. A certain amount of it is bound to be brought into Kildare where I should say it is certainly not wanted. It would spoil the sale of the horses a great deal. We have tried in our show under the Hunters' Improvement Society to register some of the mares in our part, and have got ten or twelve mares entered into their book, and the gentlemen of many men [illegible] be examined by us. Some of them entered are two and three-year-old mares. One of the two-year-old mares showed last year at Naas for breeding purposes [illegible] have been kept [illegible] mares as three-year-olds. All took prizes this year except one that was [illegible], and the man said he would not breed from it any more. The prizes that induced them to keep those on as brood mares are worth more to them [illegible]. There are five or six prizes in each class. There are also prizes for foals, so that a man may make £10 at the show. That pays for the keep of them, and they are able to work them too.

6745. Do you agree with Mr. Kennedy that the thoroughbred, or a selected and approved half-bred, is the best to get high class hunters and carriage horses?—Certainly; I think a thoroughbred horse the best, or any horse like "Mayboy" who has only a strain of three or four generations ago, which was probably caused more from carelessness than anything else. In Kildare the registered horse is beginning to do good. In the show of '96 only one horse in the whole show got a prize, which was by a horse not registered, and this year there was absolutely none, though several were shown.

6746. You think the Royal Dublin Society scheme works well in Kildare?—Yes; before the farmers went to the nearest horse and the cheapest, now they are beginning to understand that the scheme is really to help them in giving prizes to the mares. Several men have shown their mares every year, and are taking prizes every year. I think that is a good thing, for if a man has got a good mare it encourages him to keep her.

6747. Do the farmers generally appreciate a good sire?—They do, but money has a great deal to do with it. They will always try to bargain with you. A lot of them will pay a lot more on the sight of a foal. Many would rather give £2 on the sight of a foal than £3 or £4 at the service of the mare.

6748. Do they breed from two-year-olds?—Yes; we give prizes for the two-year-olds, and a lot of them breed. We give as much for two-year-olds as we give for the aged mares. There are very few entries up to this in the Naas show, but each year we are getting more. Three years ago it was only three, it is now up to seven or eight. There is a very good class of two and three-year-olds.

6749. Do you approve of breeding from two-year-old fillies?—I think it depends on the shape of the animal to a great degree. Some are backward, but a strong filly one I would not mind breeding from at all. I have bred from them myself. [illegible] old only moderate sized filly—bred a 16 hands high hunter which was sold last year.

6750. Do you think the farmers generally understand the importance of breeding from a good mare instead of breeding from any mare?—They know well enough, but they can't resist getting the money when they can, and then they choose a bad mare. They say "she may be a fairly good breeding mare, and may throw back to the sire and not show her own deformity."

6751. Sir T. Esmonde.—Do you say you have adopted the system of the Hunters' Improvement Society?—We have affiliated with them, and joined them. They enter the mares. They gave us five for examination the first year. Besides that, where we entered mares that didn't get the gold medal or silver medal we got two free into the year, and we have about ten or twelve entered in their book up to this. They are principally young ones. Those young ones—two and three-year-olds—were shown at [illegible], and one won first prize in the open class judged by different judges. They are a good class to keep if we could encourage them to keep them.

6752. Do you think that system will encourage the keeping of good mares?—I think it would do so. I would be for giving more money to really good ones, though I would encourage moderate animals with small prizes. I have no objection to giving prizes year after year to a good [redacted] which means one produces a better one.

6753. You would give the prizes according to merit?—I would give a prize to the best, till a better one turns. A two-year-old mare this year beat all the others—two or three were complaining, saying the same mares were over and over again getting prizes. I tried to tell them if they got a good mare they would be as likely to get a prize as the other man.

6754. Is this the first year you have adopted the system?—This is three years now; but this is the first time we got free registration. Kildare Show has paid for entering in the book two of them mares every year. We have had a gold medal or a bronze medal and £3 which they generally take for the last three or four years, and this year they gave a silver medal for young mares—two and three-year-old mares—as well.

6755. You find that the farmers like the system?—They like these medals very much. Two of them, instead of taking the bronze medal and £3, preferred a gold medal, but they would prefer the silver medal they gave this year, it is much more showy.

6756. They are beginning to understand the system?—Yes; they have asked me would they be more sought for by [illegible] men. It costs more advertising still. They are beginning to find out it is for their own good.

6757. Mr. Cassidy.—You say Hackneys are in the hunters in Kildare?—Yes.

6758. Were many exhibited in Kildare?—Very few; but there seemed to be a strong feeling against them.

6759. You think it would be impossible to keep them out of Kildare if bred in Ireland?—Whatever came by a Hackney may get into Kildare. Other mares we think are well bred may be by Hackneys; you can only go by eye.

6760. Mr. Wrench.—Would you prefer to be affiliated to the Hunters' Improvement Society or could you prefer to have an Irish Hunters' Improvement Society?—I think we ought to have an Irish one.

6761. You would advocate it being started?—It would do a lot of good, I think.

6762. On the same lines?—Yes, and being very careful what is entered in it.

6763. Do you think there would be much danger of not being able to tell how the horses were bred?—I think there is a great deal.

6764. If a Hunters' Improvement Society was started, do you think there would be so much danger?—Yes, a horse who was successful in one part of the country and every horse from that part of the country [illegible] from that [illegible].

6765. You think that practice is likely to continue?—I think it will.

6766. You know that the Dublin Society have [illegible] suggestions to alter their scheme this year. Would you approve of that?—No; I think the Autumn show does very well in Kildare, because you see the produce as well at the same time then. I think it was better for the stallion class that there were nominations. They got better by it, because they got so much for each nomination. The Dublin Society used to give you £3 for each mare you sent in. Now the stallion owner has to make the best price he can with the farmers. At the Autumn show we get now a much better class of mares than at the Spring shows. At one of the shows there were only three animals. At Dundalk a large number came, but that is the only time there was ever a big Spring show. The farmers said they were too busy.

6767. You think it is better to keep to the same system?—I think it is beginning to work very well.

6768. You are rather speaking against your own interest?—I think it is against their own interest. I think they ought to be subsidised—the good ones. Really there is no inducement to register your horse whatever now, except that they are beginning to come more to the better horses and to the registered horses than to the unregistered horses. In fact, the unregistered horses are having a bad time of it in Kildare just now, I think.

6769. They will probably disappear?—I think so, and I will get the blame of it as being Secretary of this scheme.

6770. Chairman.—When you say you are attached with the Hunters' Improvement Society, what do you mean?—I mean the Kildare Hunt Show.

6771. What have you got to do?—We give them £14 a year, and I try to get as many of the people to join as I can. For that they give us a gold medal for a mare and a silver medal for young horses, and they give us free entries into their shows in London. So that they are very liberal, I think. There are [illegible] of the people in Kildare belonging to it now. I think it is a very useful society.

6772. What are the general lines it goes on?—It [illegible] the [illegible] prizes at these shows, and the [illegible] like it, be very carefully entered, if they can be found free from hereditary disease by competent veterinary surgeons. They enter these mares and take a note of their produce, and they will enter them, too, if they can be passed free. Then they have a certain number of stallions to be entered that are not quite thoroughbred. There are various rules for that laid down. I think it is the best [illegible]. I think something on that principle might be worked in Kildare. There are one or two half-bred horses in Kildare got good horses. The late Lord Waterford's "Ragout" got good horses. He was not quite thoroughbred, but very nearly.

6773. You think we ought to have something of the same kind in Ireland?—I think so. If we [illegible] them breeding from the worthless things they do breed, I think it would be a good thing.

6774. Would it not be better if they could get direct assistance?—Whatever one can get does not many [illegible] of it the [illegible].

6775. Do you think, speaking generally, there has been any deterioration in the quality of mares, or their produce in the way of hunters and high-class carriage horses in Kildare to your knowledge?—I think you would see a lot of yearlings going to fairs, and they say they can't sell them: that is principally because they are bad. I think that really good mares, and high-class horses are there still, and men keep the good ones. Dealers come to the same farmers time after time if they have had one good one from them.

6776. Taking it generally, would you say in some part of the country that the tendency has been to sell good mares, keeping their inferior ones?—Some will keep their good ones, but they cannot refuse a good price occasionally, and will try something that has met with an accident or a good-shaped one. There are a lot of mares about the country that have been good hunters or racing mares, and have been lent and passed into the possession of farmers. They are breeding with those now, and they do the farmer's work.

6777. Mr. Gilmour.—They are quite good enough to do the farm work?—Yes; in the south of Kildare there is more tillage, but all about us is light work, and a light animal is able to do it all.

6778. Chairman.—Are you in favour of licensing stallions or of registration?—I should be inclined to license them. Registration is doing a lot of good, but I would be more particular still.

6779. You would consider it a danger if the Hackney producer should drift from the congested districts into the other parts of Ireland; you think that would be prejudicial?—I think so. The dealers are very particular in asking the breeding, and finding out about it. I think it would, certainly.

6780. Have you any idea how they get this prejudice against the Hackney?—They [illegible] in different shows. They see them working, and one dealer remarked to me that the back bone of one horse was the wrong way up. They wanted it curved the other way like a hunter—it is hollow in a Hackney. I have seen in a veterinary surgeon's yard the bone of a thoroughbred and the bone of a Hackney. The [illegible] was porous and light, and the other like ivory and hard, and weighs more, although it looked smaller than the other.

6781. Are you pretty well acquainted with the South of Ireland generally?—I have been in Clonakilty. We had a meet down there—[illegible]—and I was asked about the [illegible] there a great deal. I spent there, and talked about their horses with the farmers. I saw there few of their ponies. I thought they looked well-bred mares. The animals were good small things, but they worked extraordinarily well. They carried large loads, thirty miles a day. They were out a big load—probably not more than fifteen hands. A lot of them were working on the new railway in Cahirciveen, and the contractor paid them six shillings a day. I saw very fine ponies, [illegible] hands high. These did the carrying of the loads of stuff away from the railway to make cuttings and things like that. The contractor seemed very well satisfied. I also saw a very bad class of stallion down there. They were small mongrel animals. If they had a good class of animals there they would get quite good enough animals.

6782. I gather that you approve of the Royal Dublin Society's scheme[illegible] that this is the right manner of giving the money to the [illegible].

6783. Would you suggest any way in which it could be improved?—I would say give more prizes, and hold more local shows, which do a lot of good, because people see the class of animal that is there, and what they ought to breed. They see their friends have a good mare, and send to a good horse, and they do the same. Small local shows would be a good thing.

6784. Do you think, **as a rule, the distribution of**

[illegible] Colonel [illegible]

[illegible]

Colonel H. De Robeck.

mentary prizes, or whatever it might be, ought to be entrusted to local committees?—I think so. We have a large committee in Kildare, under the Royal Dublin Society's scheme. We have six gentlemen, six farmers, and a secretary, and between us we work it somehow or other. In fact it is left to us to distribute the prizes.

6785. How was your committee formed?—The Royal Dublin Society appointed a chairman, and he asked anybody he thought was interested in horse breeding to make up this number. I think it is composed of six gentlemen and six farmers of the neighbourhood that we thought would be interested in it, and would take a little trouble. We asked them if they would serve on the committee, and they all agreed to; we had no refusals.

6786. As vacancies occur do you fill them up by election or nomination?—Anybody would suggest one and we would think of it, but we have had no vacancy yet. Generally the chairman suggests somebody, and he writes and asks if that person will agree to serve on the committee, and the reply is "yes."

6787. You find the farmers are anxious to serve on it?—Yes, and they attend the meetings very well. We don't have many meetings, one just before our show and one the other day to consider a letter from the Royal Dublin Society who asked us to send in recommendations on the scheme; they always attend to anything like that.

6788. Supposing any large system of registration was started throughout the country, what would be the best authority to deal with it—the police or the petty sessions clerk?—I think it would have to be done by a society like the Hunters' Improvement Society, or an agricultural department of the Government. I don't think a petty sessions clerk would have time to do it or be able to do it accurately enough. I should be very particular before entering them in a book. I should find out all about them.

6789. Lord Rathdonnell.—Are you on the Royal Dublin Society's Horse-breeding Committee?—No.

6790. Are you on the Horse Show Committee?—On the Horse Show Committee.

6791. Have you heard that it is likely there will be any alteration in the horse-breeding scheme this year?—A thing came round to the different committees to ask their opinion on the present scheme. I think it was started by the County Dublin Committee, which said this scheme was no good at present. I think the thing is left to the different counties—whatever works in the different counties.

6792. Have you heard it said that it would be left optional to each county committee to select either of the two schemes?—I didn't hear that.

6793. The nomination system or the premium system?—I didn't hear that.

6794. Would you be inclined to approve of county committees having the option?—I think so—certainly. Different districts would want the thing worked differently, I think.

6795. Mr. Wrench.—Do you think many false pedigrees find their way into the Hunters' Improvement Society's books?—I should not say they did. They are very particular. You sign a certificate, and they get it signed not only by the owner, but by the breeder of the mare. They are very particular about it.

6796. If a Hunters' Improvement Society was formed in Ireland they ought to be just as particular here?—I think they ought to be very particular. It would be very hard to start the book, and you would get very few at first. You ought to be very particular in forming a book like that.

6797. It practically would not be very much good unless you could rely on it?—I think not.

6798. The dealers who come into Kildare are chiefly hunter dealers or come from polo ponies? We haven't many polo ponies in Kildare—but what are bought from other places or sold.

6799. But you spoke about a polo pony buyer who came to you?—He was a polo player who came down I had played with him. I trained the pony myself.

6800. You were talking about the horse of a Hack may?—I forget the name of the horse.

6801. Was it in a veterinary yard? Did you see it in Ireland or England?—At Woolwich in England, when I was soldiering, it was our veterinary surgeon got it, I forget the name of the horse at the present moment.

6802. Chairman.—Have you anything you would like to suggest to the Commission?—I think if they could improve and add something for the registered horses and give more prizes to the mares in certain districts—I think that would be a good thing.

6803. You mean the present system carried out more fully?—I think if carried out more fully it would do more good than anything else. I think it is beginning to work well now. Of course it takes some time to get the thing fairly started.

Mr. Thomas Anthony.

Mr. Thomas Anthony, Lewistown, Athy, examined.

6804. Chairman.—You live in the county of Kildare?—Yes, my lord—South Kildare.

6805. Are you engaged in farming?—Yes, very largely.

6806. Do you breed horses yourself?—Not so much now as at one time; latterly I go in more for buying colts than for breeding. I breed draught horses still.

6807. Do you think it pays better to buy than to breed?—I do.

6809. What do you buy?—Four or five or three-year-old colts that would make good hunters.

6810. Where do you buy them?—Largely in the south.

6811. You go about the country looking for them?—Yes.

6812. When do you sell them?—I sell them at four-year-old.

6813. And you still breed draught horses?—Yes, still largely—and must have a heavy horse for that sort of work.

6814. For your own purposes?—Yes.

6815. Do you sell them?—I generally wear them out.

6816. Are they out of your own mares?—Out of my own mares.

6817. What kind of sire?—Usually a Clydesdale horse or a Shire horse.

6818. Do you buy three-year-olds at all in your part of the country?—Sometimes I do, but never from a small farmer.

6819. Three and two-year-old colts?—Under four or five years.

6820. And not one from a small farmer?—Not from a man, I think, who is under £100 valuation.

6821. Do you think the small farmer is unable to breed?—He is not breeding a good horse just now in our district.

6822. What are they breeding?—There seem to be two classes of mares; of course there have always been Shires and Clydesdales in our district—some are heavy and suited for heavy work; the other mares have got weedy and too light.

6823. Some too heavy and others too light?—They look like that.

6824. How long have you been buying in this way?—For some years.

6825. And do you find you have to give the same

price in the market than you used to?—I don't think the price of cobs has changed very much; they are easily bought than they were, but not to any great extent.

6828. Where do you buy generally?—At fairs?—At fairs, or at home if I can hear of a good horse.

6829. As far as the fairs are concerned, do you think they are as good as they used to be?—I think they have deteriorated greatly. All the better class horses are bought at home and never come to fairs—they are bought by dealers, the majority of them.

6830. Are they bought at home before they can be sold?—Yes, the good horses that are in the country don't come to fairs, they are all picked up. You never see a really valuable thoroughbred horse at a fair.

6831. You think the good horses are as scarce in the country as ever they were?—I think so.

6832. Do any ponies come from your district?—There are some good ponies bred in the district.

6833. What are they used for?—I bought some polo ponies in the district which turned out well.

6834. Bought them and sold them as polo ponies?—Yes.

6835. Bred in Kildare?—Not all.

6836. How were they bred?—All by thoroughbred horses, and in some parts of Wicklow by a pony called "The Wasp," a Weir's pony I have heard of. I don't know what they were, but some I got, they had some blood in them.

6837. These were not bred in your county?—Yes; but they seem to be spread over the country to a certain extent.

6838. Do any ponies come from the West?—Yes, a few.

6839. What kind are they?—Useful ponies; they must exceed 13 hands. It is very useful animals for driving. I think the farmers in our district, the larger ones, are very largely helped as regards their driving by Connemara ponies.

6840. Have you bought any yourself?—One or two; but I have never had a Connemara polo pony; if I do buy I try to get ponies to make polo ponies that are not quality enough.

6841. How are they bred?—The of the ponies of the country by a thoroughbred half-bred sort of animal. Many of these Connemara ponies carry legs and grow well in [illegible], and are original breeding.

6842. You said you gave about the same prices as formerly?—I was not buying them until the last six or seven years. In that time I don't think there has been much of a drop in the three-year-old colt.

6843. Do you think the price of high-class hunters and hackneys has kept up?—I think so. The high-class hunter is as good as ever he was; it is as difficult to get him.

6844. But you have the evidence of Colonel De Robeck and Mr. Kennedy?—Yes.

6845. Do you agree generally with them?—I don't agree with them in the condemnation of the Hackney; they think the thoroughbred is the only horse. It is absolutely necessary to have something else.

6846. Why do you think it necessary?—You must have draught horses in the country; you cannot do heavy carting with the thoroughbred horse. You must have some substance, and, I think in breeding hunters you must have bone, and the question is how you are to get it.

6847. Do you think the mares producing these hunters lacking in substance and deficient in bone?—There are very few bred in our district.

6848. You say they must have bone. Do you mean throughout the country generally?—They must.

6849. How do you think that can be obtained?—Supposing you take a good draught mare and cross with a thoroughbred, I think the second would be likely to produce a hunter. If you go any further than that you depend upon bone merits.

6850. You think to prevent deterioration this would be brought in by a cross, with what kind of blood?—I think the half-bred horse, such as you took in hounds, a horse of that class would give the bone. We have many mares too weedy to be put to a thoroughbred, and with a horse with bone of these draught qualities useful might be bred. The fairs are filled with light weight useless animals, no use for anything in these days of the bicycle; some might carry a lady or light weight, but they are all being knocked now, and the price of these animals has deteriorated tremendously.

6851. Do you know the horse that has been described as the Irish draught horse?—I do; we have got two of them about us.

6852. What are the cart **horse** mares in your part of the country like?—I can show that are called Irish draught—good hardy—highish-looking horses, without much hair on their legs, and then, of course, there are the pure bred Clydesdales and Shire horses.

6853. Do you think the mare with the Clydesdale or Shire would be more likely to give the bone you consider necessary than the mare with the thoroughbred—to produce a good hunter?—I think so.

6854. How about the Hackney?—I don't endorse the condemnation so much as some do. To judge of the Hackney stallions I think he would be a great animal, taking the breed I spoke of, a half-bred horse, but I don't see that he is to be put at present; I don't see him anywhere.

6855. You think, speaking generally, that the mares and stallions in the country require something to improve them?—In North Kildare they are pretty badly with it. We don't benefit by the Hackney scheme at all; it is entirely confined to North Kildare.

6856. Then the scheme is not in operation?—Practically it is not in operation in our district; it is entirely confined to the northern portion of the county; there is nothing satisfactory; they have got a better class of stallions. Some people don't think the stallions are good enough.

6857. You do not agree that sound thoroughbred stallions with good bone would give sufficient strength to the class of mares?—To many in quality, and not strong enough. There is not much horse-breeding in our part of the county, and except by large farmers who have got good mares, there are very few good animals bred.

6858. Lord RATHDONNELL.—You say that you would cross a Clydesdale stallion with a half-bred mare, or a thoroughbred horse with a Clydesdale, to give a good hunter?—Not to get a hunter, but that animal might be useful to get a hunter—a thoroughbred put to her again.

6859. I understand you to say a mixed cross would be useful?—Yes, the first cross would be all right to be put to a thoroughbred horse, the first cross a half-bred; I think would be likely to produce a good hunter; if you then use the third cross with a thoroughbred it would be weedy. I don't fancy the Clydesdale. I would rather have an Irish draught mare to start upon as a foundation.

6860. Have you ever hunted **one of these** horses?—I did. I have a **very good horse now**, got out of a Clydesdale mare.

6861. Was there any thoroughbred blood in her?—Irish draught. I don't know how it is got.

6862. Do you know the **name** of the horse?—Which?

6863. The Irish bred horse?—I bought this mare in Wexford, and the mare I have now is out of her by rather a clean-bred Clydesdale I had myself; this old mare I speak of had a good deal of the Irish draught breed.

6864. Do you remember a **horse called "Huntsman"**?—Yes.

6865. In what class would you put him?—The best. I am speaking of—the half-bred horse that

Jan. 5, 1897.
Mr. Thomas Anderson.

would get useful stock in our part.—I would put him to some of the weedy mares I talked of.

6864. He had been trained, and ridden to hounds? —Yes; he would be a most valuable horse.

6865. For hunters?—Yes; very much better to get it that way than by going to the thorough-bred horse.

6866. You prefer him to the straight horse?—Undoubtedly.

6867. Sir Thomas Esmonde.—Would this mare correspond with the old Irish mare?—She would, I suppose, as far as I have heard of them.

6868. Do you think there is such a thing as a special breed of the old Irish mare?—There was undoubtedly some mixed breed; it was a good deal thoroughbred.

6869. It was crossed with the thoroughbred?—I should think so.

6870. You never came across anything you could say was an old Irish mare?—No; I should fancy there always have been thoroughbreds in Ireland; it is only of late years that Clydesdales and Shires were introduced.

6871. Those two mares you talked of you didn't think they had Clydesdale or Shire blood in them?—I could not say; but I think the introduction of Clydesdale is comparatively recent in Ireland.

6872. Mr. Cherry.—You say North Kildare is much better off for sires than South Kildare?—They have a much better class of stallion.

6873. How would you suggest they should be improved in South Kildare?—I think the Royal Dublin Society's scheme is very good as worked in North Kildare. I am a member of the Kildare Horse Show, and have attended every year, and saw a marked improvement in the quality.

6874. Are there many exhibits from the South?—There are none at all from the South—not a single animal.

6875. Are not one fourth of those exhibited from the North?—Not from the Athy district—I am sure of that; there may be from Kilkenny, but not nearer for them that, and that is four or twelve miles away.

6876. Do you think there is too far from the centre of the county?—No, I cannot say I do; when the Society gave premiums we had shows of mares as near Athy as possible, and they were not patronised. The farmers did not send, and they didn't come in much; it takes taken a very long time to get them to catch on to a thing. In County Carlow they are not catching on to it, and though they are following in the old class of roadsters there the class doesn't seem to be improving.

6877. You don't agree with the condemnation of the Hackney?—No, from what I have seen.

6878. You have no experience of Hackneys?—I have not used them or driven them.

6879. Mr. Wrench.—Do you know anything about the West of Ireland?—I know Mayo pretty well; I have never lived there, but have been there there pretty often.

6880. Have you been at the shows of the Congested Districts Board at Belmullet and Achill?—Yes, I have this year.

6881. And had you the experience of seeing the mares and young stock there?—I only saw 300 at one show.

6882. Were you able to form any opinion from what you saw or heard as to what would be the best class of sire to send to Belmullet or Achill?—I was. I think that the Hackney, in the absence of the half-bred horse such as I described, is the best horse for that district.

6883. Would you be inclined to send a thoroughbred there?—No, I don't think so; I think the produce would be too weedy, unless you got good bone in the thoroughbred, which you seldom do.

6884. You would be in favour of sending the Hackney to those districts?—Yes; I would.

6885. You have since seen the sires belonging to the Board?—Yes.

6886. And do you think they are suitable to send down?—With one or two exceptions.

6887. But as a rule?—As a rule, I think they are suitable to the districts.

6888. I think you told you bought a good many horses from farmers in your district?—Yes.

6889. Are they large farmers?—Yes, chiefly; a good deal farms over £100 valuation.

6890. Are they the men that breed good hunters in your district?—I think so.

6891. Do you think there is any danger of these ones, using pony mares that come from the West as hunter brood mares?—I think they would be bred from undoubtedly.

6892. Do you think they would be hard done to breed hunters—the animals you have been seeing from the West—if the mare was mated on good hunt they might produce a hunter; they run up to nearly 15 hands, and have pretty good bone and substance.

6893. Those that came up now?—Yes; those that came up now.

6894. Do you know of many hunters being sold in your district that have Clydesdale blood in them?—I have known of horses being sold with Clydesdale blood in them, and a good deal of it, too.

6895. And those are ones horses had Clydesdales stallions in that part of the country?—Yes, there have been for a considerable time.

6896. Have you formed any opinion about registering horses?—I think mares ought to be registered, and I think the Royal Dublin Society's scheme good as regards giving the prizes to the mares, but I think the stallions ought to be improved; the system of registration of stallions is good, but I think the system of inspection should be more stringent; and a great many horses at present registered by the Society should not be allowed to be registered, most of all otherwise. The system of registering would appear to work good. I know it is very difficult to judge hunters three-year-old colts; they look very good to make hunters, but when they come up two years, you find they are whistlers. That must come from somewhere—it must be hereditary; and as we are told the stallions are sound, it must come from the dams, and I think the mares should be registered, as well as the sires.

6897. You would have them examined for soundness?—Yes.

6898. Is unsound what breeding very great should be limited?—I think it is; the number of horses which should be valuable as hunters, rejected for whistling, is very large.

6899. You have not sold or bred many hunters lately?—I have sold horses which were not good enough for hunters or harness horses.

6900. Do hunters suitable only as much money as harness horses?—No, not as much.

6901. The Chairman.—In buying these three-year-old colts in the South do you ascertain how they are bred?—I always endeavour to get their pedigree.

6902. Do you find any difficulty?—It would be very much easier if the breeder could show you the certificate of the service of his mare, and show you how the dam was bred, and show you a service note saying that the mare was served in such a year, and that this was the produce of the service; at present we have just got to take the statements they are given, and in many cases they are quite untrue.

6903. And for the modern districts that you know you think the Hackney is a useful kind of sire?—I think so from the class of mare the animals bred to the carrying big bone hind from the sea. You must have plenty of bone and a certain amount of strength.

6904. I want to be quite sure that we exactly understand your opinion. I understood you to say you approved of the Hackney, provided you could not get a half-bred horse?—I think that a half-bred horse ought to be provided in the country, and I think it should be done by Government; that horse should be sent through the different districts, and half-bred horses should be placed on the register so that people could use them if they wished.

6905. The thoroughbred sires you are speaking of, what are they?—I don't think the ordinary thoroughbred as we see him—the more valuable animal—would be a good horse for that district. I didn't see the produce in the shows of the Congested Districts Board of any thoroughbred horse, but I saw the produce of Welsh cobs, Arabs, and Barbs, and I don't think any of them as suitable as the Hackney for the purpose.

6906. You said, in speaking of the half-bred, you preferred him to a thoroughbred, provided he had sufficient bone and was sound?—Yes.

6907. So I gather that your opinion is, that for these western districts the thoroughbred, provided he was a suitable thoroughbred, or the half-bred if he had bone, would be as valuable or more valuable than the Hackney?—I would do it in this way, because of the prejudice which seems to exist against the Hackney.

6908. Put away the prejudice—we would like to know your own opinion?—From all I read about the Hackney I would imagine he has good action and good staying powers; if we read the evidence of the dealers they say the produce of the Hackney will not stay, and that they are not any good as hunters. Of course I have no personal experience, but my idea is that a Hackney stallion put to a half-bred mare would produce a very good animal to breed hunters; that would be my own idea.

6909. And put it to the thoroughbred afterwards?—Yes; I would rather have it than the draught blood.

6910. Are there any suggestions which you would like to make to the Commission?—Except about the registration of stallions. If continued by the Royal Dublin Society it would be a very considerable improvement in many districts that the stallions should be improved and the inspection made more stringent.

Mr. Thomas [illegible]

Captain Townshend, Derry, Rosscarbery, examined.

Captain Townshend.

6911. Chairman.—You live in the County of Cork?—Yes, in the south of the County of Cork.

6912. Have you any personal experience in breeding horses there?—I have been breeding them about fourteen or fifteen years. I keep two thoroughbred stallions.

6913. And what class of animal do you aim at producing?—I have been trying my best to produce the high-class hunter ever since I have been breeding—for the last fifteen years.

6914. What class of mare do you use?—I, myself, have always used what I suppose you would call a three-quarter bred mare—a hunter mare.

6915. What do the farmers about you breed?—Till I introduced the thoroughbred stallions they bred a most miserable class of mare, and they have been breeding from that. There are a few better class mares going now.

6916. What kind of stallions were there there before you introduced your thoroughbreds?—It would be hard to say how they were bred. My own experience of what we call half-breds is that they are the most abominable brutes to breed from. "Cortez," who ran and was placed in the Derby is supposed to be a half-bred, so that it is a large term. Half-breds in my district are the most abominable brutes. There was a man in my neighbourhood tried two; they were both supposed to be got by a thoroughbred out of fairly well-bred mares, but I am glad to say he has gelded them both. He did a good deal of service with them at first, and did a lot of harm. The get of one of them were all bad-tempered—wretched creatures altogether—no heart; then he gelded him, then he tried another, and I am thankful to say he gelded him also.

6917. Are you situated in a congested district?—No; I wish I were.

6918. That seems odd; why?—Because I could then get the service of some of the Hackney stallions.

6919. But you are near a congested district?—Not far away; Schull is the nearest, about fourteen miles from me.

6920. Are you acquainted with the stock got by Congested Districts Board stallions?—No, I cannot say that I am; they have been there such a short time—only two years.

6921. Would you use a Hackney stallion if you had access to him?—If I could get at a good Hackney I would put him to several mares. I would not breed from them otherwise.

6922. Why don't you in that case substitute a Hackney for one of your thoroughbreds?—If I could pick one up I would, but they are very expensive—highclass Hackneys. I don't like a low class, but high-class, such as you see at Mr. Burdett-Coutts's, or Sir Walter Gilbey's, or the London show. Anyone who admires a horse must admire them; they have bone and substance and pluck, and are eager for work. I think they are magnificent horses.

6923. Do you think a Hackney is suitable to get hunters?—Oh, no; you must have blood on the top and blood all through, but you cannot grow hunters in all parts of Ireland.

6924. In your part?—I have been doing my best finding them with care since they were foals, and have never grown a really high-class horse yet.

6925. What do you think your district is suitable to produce?—I would like to try the Hackney; from what I have known of them they are a really good horse.

6926. What class of horse would you expect to get?—A saleable horse, with action, for harness purposes; you might get good hacks too. I have been going to fairs for a good many years, and my experience is, that you can sell anything with action no matter if it is not big, whereas those weedy light horses at the present moment are almost unsaleable, whether it is because of bicycles or what, they certainly don't pay to breed.

6927. You would think your district more suitable to breed horses exclusively for harness?—Let people who have the desire try the other one. I would like to see the Hackney as well. I would have the farmers to try whichever they liked. I would encourage both. I think the Royal Dublin Society does a good thing in encouraging a good class of thoroughbreds.

6928. Have you ever seen the Hackney produce around?—I have at present myself what I suppose you might call that class of horse, and he is a good horse. I got him from Yorkshire under the impression that he was a pure-bred Hackney, but I found out afterwards he was not, so I gelded him. I have been working him since, and have found him a most useful horse, a capital horse, unpleasant, no doubt, to ride, but charming in a trap, and draws a common cart with sand and manure; he jolts you to pieces when riding.

6929. How old is he?—Four off. I could have sold him several times; he is a capital good horse and I don't think a bit soft. Of course we have not very long distances in my district. I am eight miles from the railway and he will go there and come back as game as he goes.

6930. He is not quite pure-bred?—No; I understood he was. I bought him from an Irish dealer who went over to Yorkshire, and when I found he was not a pure bred I would not keep him as a stallion.

Dec. 4, 1896. Captain [illegible].

6531. Do you know enough about Hackneys to know that the thoroughbred Hackney is a valuable horse which the half-bred is not?—The only Hackneys I ever knew were good horses, pure-bred. My poor father, who used to drive a good deal, bought once a couple of Hackneys; one was a leader and the other a wheeler; they were magnificent horses. He paid £130 for one and £150 for the other; they were very handsome horses. I did not know what they were until I took to going to shows in England and saw the type reproduced exactly; we knew nothing about Hackneys.

6532. They were pure-bred?—I don't know at all; he bought them from a dealer; we went over to Mr. [illegible]—he keeps stallions at Kilmallock—and he said he was a Norfolk Trotter, but he wasn't so much like a Norfolk Trotter; I saw one like him this year or twenty years.

6533. How do the farmers seem to rear their young stock about you—do they raise them well?—No, I don't think they do. One farmer, a rich man, had [illegible] the best stallion I got, "Crusader," and I think he regularly reared the crushed food in [illegible]. I [illegible] as a thick as [illegible] in [illegible]; [illegible] and [illegible], and at [illegible] he got [illegible] and [illegible] in [illegible]; but there is no doubt he regularly [illegible] the animal. I think now, however, they are beginning to realise that if they breed well-bred stock they must take better care of them.

6534. Where do they sell their horses?—At Ballyboy principally; there is a good fair at Ennis also, and dealers are beginning to come to it.

6535. Are ponies as good as they used to be?—I don't think they are good now.

6536. Do you think that generally your part of the country is capable of producing a high-class hunter or carriage horse with any kind of stallion?—I don't think you can produce a high-class horse on any soil; everything is small, the cattle are small. There is a breed of cattle with [illegible] in the King's County. He [illegible] the young stock at all, and he produces some good, thoroughbred, weight-carrying horses; if I was as [illegible] I would breed as good as I could.

6537. Are there any ponies in that part of the country?—A few, but they are increasing; the poor people prefer them since they [illegible].

6538. But there is no indigenous breed—no native breed?—No, I don't think so.

6539. Lord [illegible].—What stallions did you keep—which were their names?—"Crusader" was the first, "[illegible]" and "Tyrconnel," that I got last year; "[illegible]" is breeding well.

6540. For [illegible] [illegible]?—Well, "[illegible]" was a good deal criticised by opposition stallion owners, but he is getting so well that I [illegible] if he lives he will pay. At one show we had four first prizes out of six horses, belonging to the Royal Dublin Society, and his gets took three first prizes out of a possible four.

6541. I think you said the stock had improved since you imported thoroughbred stallions?—They have, certainly; they are breeding from [illegible] of them.

6542. If you approve of a Hackney stallion, why have you not imported one?—They are so awfully expensive horses to buy; I could not afford it, and I am not going to get a bad looking brute.

6543. I suppose the thoroughbred is you get out of a cheaper class?—You can get thoroughbreds much cheaper than the Hackney, there are so many more of them.

6544. And there is some difference in their size, bone, and shape?—Oh, of course there is.

6545. Have yours got good bone and size?—Yes, "Tyrconnel," the one getting well. I never saw a horse of his size with better bone and back.

6546. What size is he?—Supposed to be 15.3, but he is not quite so much; he has got good bone, large knees, and large hocks. I don't think I have ever seen a better horse foaled in Ireland, and I have ridden a good many good horses in England.

6547. You say the sold in your neighbourhood is not adapted for horse-breeding?—It is very hard to breed a high-class horse. I would not breed horses at all only I am so fond of them; they are not a paying game.

6548. Is there any limestone in your district?—Absolutely none, except near Cork, and Cork is fifty miles from me.

6549. How do you expect to increase the breed?—It is a very open question; by giving and getting the [illegible] horses I can lay hands on, I may improve it in that way.

6550. Without the [illegible], the horse-breeding will?—Of course. I have no [illegible]. There is a farmer near me who has improved his hack very much. He has grown some likely good foals, and got £80 at [illegible] for a three-year-old. He thought it paid him, and was very pleased. I don't think it would pay me the way I find my cattle.

6551. Sir Thomas Esmonde.—Did you say there was a sufficient number of stallions with you?—I think there are too many.

6552. Of good stallions?—I **think we have very** few good stallions.

6553. There are of an inferior description?—A whole breed. One witness said he thought a half-bred stallion bred better. I think that is only because, as a rule, they want them. There are a few good enough. I think good stallions are kept in a more [illegible] way—pampered up and kept in hot stables. I think that is the only reason. I think a well-bred horse would breed just as well, and with more vigour.

6554. What do they charge for the service of those horses?—It is arbitrary. They have minimal fees, but they take anything down even to 5s., and then supply those farmers.

6555. I suppose the farmers go to the cheapest horse?—Generally. Last year a good many came to "Tyrconnel" because he is a high upstanding, nice looking horse. I made no reduction in his advertised fee of 2 guineas. A good many of the strong farmers would pay a good fee.

6556. If they had a suitable horse?—I think so.

6557. You think the reason they go to these bad horses is because they have not got much choice?—A great many of the small farmers would rather they got stallions under the Royal Dublin Society scheme; unless they got him cheaper they would go to an inferior horse.

6558. Mr. Carew.—What recommendation would you make to get rid of the bad ones?—I have always been a believer in the theory, though it is against my own interests to say so, that no private individual should keep stallions, but that we should have Government studs.

6559. Would you be in favour of every owner of a stallion taking out a license?—I don't think that would be a good plan—anything to reduce the [illegible]. There are any amount of "Young [illegible]," in my neighbourhood—most awful brutes. "[illegible]," [illegible] one [illegible] Royal Dublin Society horse, was the first horse that came down to my neighbourhood, we have been so very badly used until the last few years. The Royal Dublin Society only gave one grant for Cork; the [illegible] adjoining county, North Cork, got the advantage of this, and we had none for West Cork until I represented how hard that was, and they then generously gave us a grant for West Cork, and I hope it will do good. The [illegible] certainly are good, but whether they will work out with large premiums is to be seen.

6560. Do you charge the same fee all round—mares, half-bred and thoroughbred?—There are practically no thoroughbreds in that part of the country.

6561. "Tyrconnel" is by "[illegible]"?—Yes, by "[illegible]," out of "[illegible]."

6962. "Chatterbox," is [illegible] of the Lincoln Handicap?—Yes.

6963. Have you got him still [illegible]?—[illegible] sorry to say.

6964. Mr. Wrench.—[illegible] horse-breeding a [illegible] industry among the small farmers?—[illegible] horse is [illegible] them to breed from.

6965. You know a good part of West Cork in addition to your own district?—Yes, pretty well.

6966. Do you think there would be any use in the people there trying to breed hunters?—I don't think so, it would be waste of time; they would grow things that would jump, but could not gallop; they would be as slow as possible. Any [illegible] jump. You can [illegible] a Clydesdale to jump. I have [illegible] jumpers, but they cannot gallop or stay.

6967. Do you think it would pay them better to breed horses with action?—Decidedly; because, as I said before, my experience is [illegible] you [illegible] with action [illegible] up, and the action of the Hackney in good knee action and hock action, it looks so well.

6968. You have not seen much of the produce of the Congested Districts Board stallions there?—No, I have not. I [illegible] to buy one. I [illegible] thinks very highly of those, and who is a capable judge of horses, to buy one [illegible] the Hackney I spoke of [illegible].

6969. Lord Rathdonnell.—Mr. Wrench asked you whether the small farmers made horse-breeding an industry in that part of the country. I want to know what your idea of an industry is?—[illegible] way to keeping the horse and paying rent.

6970. You meant to say they breed [illegible] with us for their own use. [illegible] of the farmers mostly always sell the [illegible]. For instance, the other day I wanted a working horse, and [illegible] of those horses were brought up for me to see; [illegible] they [illegible] them until they are a [illegible]. I think the Hackney would be a good general horse for them.

6971. From your evidence, I should suppose your district was not a natural horse-breeding country, and you could scarcely call it an industry?—I think most of the farmers about breed horses.

6972. They breed horses they have got [illegible] to it?—They have got a mare and they don't find [illegible] up as they say [illegible] to sell.

6973. Where do they sell it?—I [illegible] were [illegible] brought on [illegible], no one [illegible] sold. I have never [illegible] any [illegible] for foals.

6974. What do they do with them?—Work them until they are two off or three, and if they turn out any good and have another young [illegible] they will sell them.

6975. The Chairman.—Is there anything you would like to suggest to the Commission?—I would do anything, I think, to get rid, if one could, of these ugly brutes called half-bred horses that are getting so badly, and then if they could have any way of giving premiums to those who got [illegible] it would be a good thing. Somebody [illegible] giving premiums to stallions without knowing what they [illegible] get [illegible] giving a prize to a [illegible] on the walking [illegible]. I knew a horse—of course it is invidious to mention names, and I won't do it—he was a thorough-bred sold from England because he was getting light; he was brought by a man and brought to Ireland, and has got the [illegible]; he is one of the Royal Dublin Society's registered horses, but it was a bad reason to bring him to Ireland when he was too light for England; he will have nothing to do [illegible] few years.

6976. You say you think private ownership of stallions might [illegible] to be allowed in [illegible]; they ought to be kept by the Government?—Yes, it will [illegible] better for the money; the Government could afford to give a higher price. There is a very good [illegible], as [illegible] "Royal Meath"—being brought to [illegible] by the [illegible] the Duke of Devonshire's property; if he doesn't get well no [illegible] will [illegible]. Of course [illegible] in under Cork, with these [illegible] of the [illegible]. I think a great deal of the agitation against the Hackney is that they know nothing about him. They got up a [illegible] in the County Club at Cork and half those who signed it know nothing at all about Hackneys—[illegible] a [illegible] show.

6977. There is no possibility of [illegible] the produce of [illegible] in Ireland?—No; they [illegible] there a [illegible] in England and [illegible]. I [illegible] the [illegible] last year at the show.

6978. Have you anything further to say?—I might just [illegible] that [illegible] at [illegible]. I saw a good Hackney, I don't know [illegible] and thought he would make a great match for this horse I have. A great many horses were being sold at [illegible], and I thought I would put him near the [illegible] show half the quality of those [illegible]. He was [illegible] when he was [illegible] at [illegible] guineas. They are valuable [illegible] good straight action and substance. He was not more than 15 hands, and if got by a thoroughbred would have given for about 15 guineas, because he was small.

Mr. R. Malone, V.S., Wexford, examined.

6979. Chairman.—Mr. Malone, you are a veterinary surgeon?—Yes.

6980. Living in Wexford?—Yes, Wexford town.

6981. Have you had any experience as regards horse-breeding personally, I mean not professionally; do you breed at all yourself?—Yes, I breed a good deal from thoroughbreds.

6982. Are many horses bred in your neighbourhood?—A great many. I think Wexford is about the largest horse-breeding county in Ireland.

6983. What class of horses do they breed?—Half-breds, and high class thoroughbreds.

6984. What do they aim at—to get hunters?—To get hunters, high class harness horses, and polo ponies.

6985. The polo pony I suppose is a matter of chance?—A matter of chance, yes, but some go in for it specially by a small thoroughbred horse crossing with Connemara ponies.

6986. What is the kind of mare the farmers in the county generally have?—A small mare, generally about 15·1, short legged, thick, with a good deal of quality.

6987. What kind of sires do they use?—Thoroughbred sires with strong bone; big thick horses.

6988. Is the county well supplied with thoroughbreds of that kind?—We are rather short of thoroughbred horses now.

6989. Are there any half bred horses in the county?—A few half-breds, but a great many mongrel horses, underbred horses.

6990. Bred anyhow?—Bred anyhow.

6991. Are there any cart horses there?—Very few; one or two, perhaps three, that is, thoroughbred cart horses, Shire horses, and Clydesdales.

6992. Are they patronised much?—Not in latter years at all.

6993. Do you think the demand for hunters and high class carriage horses is as great as it used to be?—I think it is more so than ever it was.

6994. Is the supply as good as it used to be?—We cannot get them.

6995. You mean the supply is less than it was formerly?—There are too many looking for them, [illegible] Northern men come down in Enniscorthy fair and buy all the yearlings and two-year-olds. They buy a great many at large. I do not believe a good horse was ever bred in the North of Ireland.

6996. Does your county produce as many of these class of horse as it used to?—Yes, they are all bought at a year or two years old. Mr. [illegible], of [illegible], the best buyer of young horses in England, paid £80 for a two-year-old, and £95 for a three-year-old.

6997. At what age are they sold?—A good many of the small farmers sell at a year and two years old.

6998. Does the price keep up?—There is a good price still for a good two-year-old, or a good yearling, if he is a shapely colt, and has good bone. It is only this week I saw a gentleman, Mr. Tighe, give a hundred guineas for a three-year-old only six weeks in breaking.

6999. Those yearlings and two-year-olds that are bought, where do they go to?—To the North of England generally.

7000. Kept there and sold again?—I think the men that come to Wexford county deal in the farmers up there, and they are kept there till they are four or five years old.

7001. It pays your farmers better to sell them young instead of the farmers keeping them till four years old, and break them and deal them.

7002. In your opinion, are the thoroughbred sires in the county suitable [illegible]?—Any horses there that are on the register are sound, and they are suitable, shapely, good horses.

7003. Have you got a stallion of your own?—The last horse I had I lost him. I have a half-bred sire now not a Yorkshire coach horse. One time I had five thoroughbred sires.

7004. Why did you discontinue keeping them?—I was offered a good price for them and sold them.

7005. Are these young horses generally sold at the fairs or picked up by dealers?—There are a great many going round the country looking for them. A great dealer man, [illegible] take at two years old, keep them and break them, they sell them.

7006. What is the character of the soil generally in the county?—Limestone.

7007. The county is a very suitable country for breeding horses?—I do.

7008. Do you consider hunters and high-class carriage horses the most profitable kind of horse to breed?—I do.

7009. How long have you been in Wexford?—All my lifetime. I was born in Wexford.

7010. How long have you been practising?—Twenty years.

7011. In your opinion, are the horses produced in the country deteriorating at all in condition?—No; I think the horses at the present time are very good.

7012. As good as ever they were?—As good as ever they were.

7013. Are the farmers inclined to sell their horses young, or do they see the advantage of keeping them?—Well, they are beginning to keep them now, under the Royal Dublin Society's scheme.

7014. You think the Royal Dublin Society's scheme has worked well?—I do. It is an excellent scheme, but it would want advertising. The farmers do not know enough about it yet.

7015. You approve of the scheme?—I do.

7016. Have you any opinion as to the desirability of licensing or registering sires?—I think the registration that is going on at the present time is first class; quite sufficient. It is working well in the County Wexford.

7017. Do you think any system of registering [illegible] would be beneficial?—I would never go back to the old scheme [illegible] giving premiums [illegible]. At the present time [illegible] I would give up to forty or fifty [illegible] when farmers bring their mares [illegible] they do not like to go the distance [illegible] ing your horses they might meet the same sires again.

7018. Are many horses bred for harness purposes in your district?—A good many. We used to have a good man coming down to Wexford to buy them, Mr. Hicks; he used to buy for East of London.

7019. Are they bred specially, or are they horses that do not turn out quite good enough for hunters?—That is it; horses that do not turn out quite good enough for hunters.

7020. Are many horses bought for the Army?—A great many; Widger buys a whole lot.

7021. Lord Ardilaun.—With regard to supply and demand for horses bred in your district, do you mean to say the supply is not equal to the demand?—It is not.

7022. You do not mean to say there are not good horses bred?—I do not. There are as many good horses bred there as ever, and the farmers are anxious to do so still.

7023. You say there are several half-bred horses in Wexford; what do you mean by half-bred?—Horses got by a thoroughbred horse out of a three-quarter bred mare or half-bred mare. Some of these produce very good stock.

7024. What sort of stamp are they?—A good big horse, [illegible] with quality, standing on straight good legs, good back and thighs, and quarters. We had one very good half-bred sire in the County Wexford, [illegible], a chestnut horse. He produced a whole host of good horses; he was produced from [illegible].

7025. What sort of breeding was he?—They say by a Suffolk Punch out of a pure thoroughbred mare. I only heard that; [illegible] a little bit, everything he produced was really first class.

7026. Then, there are other classes of half-bred sires in the county which you want to disapprove of; how are they bred?—Nobody knows how they are bred; they are bred and [illegible], and you would not know how they are bred.

7027. You also said you had a Yorkshire coach horse; [illegible] a Yorkshire coach horse down [illegible] years ago in York from [illegible].

7028. What sort of produce had he?—He is producing good stock [illegible] with small mares.

7029. I think you said you had—Yes, I have the Yorkshire coach horse still; [illegible] thoroughbreds I had.

7030. Lord Ardilaun.—What makes you think of getting a Yorkshire coach horse [illegible]?—It would be a good cross with the mares in our part to produce [illegible] horses again here.

7031. What is the general class of mares in your district?—A good class of [illegible] mares.

7032. Do they come [illegible]?—They have good bone. There are a great many mares bred by [illegible] of the best blood [illegible].

7033. Do the farmers keep the fillies by the Yorkshire coach horse?—Yes, to breed from them again.

7034. You do not like the general half-bred horse?—I do not. I like a half-bred by a [illegible] thoroughbred, not out of a three-quarter-bred or half-bred mare.

7035. Would you approve of their being registered by the Royal Dublin Society?—Not until I see what their produce.

7036. You would never register such a horse bred like a Cleveland Bay or a Yorkshire coach horse? Would you register any other breed?—I would register half-bred sires if I knew they were producing good stock.

7037. You would not register any grass bred horses?—I would, of course.

7038. Well, you say you will the Yorkshire coach horse [illegible]?—I believe they have a stud book of their own.

7039. You would be in favour of registering them?—Yes.

7040. Sir Thomas Esmonde.—What class of horses is produced in the County Wexford?—Mostly hunters, harness horses, and polo ponies.

7041. Is there a large trade done in those three classes?—A very large trade. There is a good demand for hunters and ponies, in fact I never saw the demand so great.

7042. Which class of horses finds the most ready sale in Wexford?—Hunters.

7043. Which are the principal fairs?—Enniscorthy is the principal one.

7044. And is this fair attended by foreign dealers?—It is; in fact it is a great fair. I think they come from all parts of England and Ireland to Enniscorthy, and of course the Northerns come down there to every fair; they buy all their good horses there.

7045. These horses, I presume, would be bred in the county?—In the county.

7046. What have you to say about the sires in the county?—We want a few more good thoroughbred sires in the county with plenty of bone and quality.

7047. What price would you suggest these sires should be given in fees? you won't get good sires.

7048. Would that be about the average price you would?—I do not think you would get them less than £5; I think the farmers will not give more for any sire.

7049. Apart from thoroughbred horses, what kind of stallions are there in County Wexford now?—A few half breeds, and other breeds; a few Shire horses, and I do not think they are much good; a few Clydesdale horses, and a lot of mongrels.

7050. Nonthoroughbreds. Yes; I have seen as many as forty stallions in Enniscorthy on a fair day.

7051. What price would these stallions be at from a glass of whiskey to five shillings, and perhaps nothing at all but a shake hands.

7052. So Wexford is a good horse breeding county?—It is.

7053. For the size of it. And what have you to say about the brood mares in Wexford?—They are pretty good. They are rather small, but I have seen small mares breed good and big horses.

7054. You spoke of Continental people for producing good stock, do you know how they are fixed?—I have not the least idea. I believe used to bring them down in droves to Wexford years ago, and sold them at those pound-old prices there, and got £6 or £7 apiece for them. They would sell them at prices. They go to £4, £5 or £6 at a good size.

7055. Some of these produce good mares?—I have known Continental people to produce horses that sold at £40 or £50 apiece, by old "Lawyer."

7056. You say the foreign dealers also attended Enniscorthy fair, what class of horses would they buy?—High-class hunters and high-class harness horses; always a good quality horse.

7057. Are there any army remount buyers in Wexford?—Lots of them. Mr. Wedgey buys a lot.

7058. What price does he give for them?—Up to £40 for a good jumper.

7059. That is for the English Government?—Yes.

7060. Do any foreign dealers buy for Foreign Governments?—The Danish Government, I think, buys a lot. The class of horses they buy are rather small, short-legged, active horses.

7061. The Italian Government buys a large number of remounts?—Yes, a whole lot.

7062. Have you any experience of the old Irish horse we have heard a great deal about?—No, I do not understand how she is bred.

7063. You think she is not to be found?—I do not think she is.

7064. Was in Wexford?—Well, if I knew what she is like, but I never heard the old Irish horse described.

7065. Have you any plan for improving the breed of horses in Wexford?—The best plan, I think, would be to go back to the old scheme of giving nominations for mares.

7066. You think the old scheme of the Royal Dublin Society is better than the present one?—I think it is. You would have far more mares shown. Advertise the scheme well. Lots of farmers were putting their mares to mongrel sires thinking they had nothing to do but to go and get a prize for the mares; and it was only when they found out their mistake. They do not know anything about the scheme.

7067. You think if the scheme was more widely advertised it would be productive of more good?—I am quite sure of it.

7068. You say there are sufficient good brood mares in the county?—A good many of the farmers are beginning to get them now.

7069. What would you say to the system of the Hunters' Registration Society; would that be applicable in Wexford?—You mean, to have a registration book for hunters? Yes, I think it would.

7070. Do you think it would encourage the keeping of good brood mares in the county?—It would.

7071. Mr. Cooper.—You say there are a lot of mongrel sires in the County Wexford?—Yes.

7072. Would you approve of insisting on every owner taking out a licence to keep a sire?—Yes.

7073. That would put them out?—Yes.

7074. That, in addition to the registration, would come to a small charge?—Yes.

7075. Wexford enjoys a high reputation as a breeding county?—Yes, I believe it does.

7076. That is from crossing half-bred mares with thoroughbred sires?—Yes.

7077. And a good number of the mares bred out turn out well as harness horses?—Yes.

7078. Dublin trades largely for harness horses with Wexford?—It does.

7079. You know the Wexford harness horse enjoys a high reputation?—It does.

7080. Have you any experience of breeding from a Hackney sire?—Yes; I bought three or four Hackneys.

7081. With what result?—The very worst.

7082. You disapprove of the Hackney?—They are frightful brutes. I [illegible] Hackney stallion one of the best bred in the world.

7083. And the result was frightful?—I bought a pony in Enniscorthy, which came from Connemara. I never set behind anything like her; she won a lot prizes. I could drive her a hundred miles. I sold her for ninety guineas.

7084. A pure Connemara breed?—Yes. The man I sold her to sold her for eighty guineas a fortnight after, and he bought her back for a hundred guineas. She was with a foal and he asked me what he would do. I told him to send her to a thoroughbred Hackney sire, and I never heard of her that I gave a hundred pony, nearly the pride of the breeder.

7085. Sir Thomas Esmonde.—What is the price of the pony?—I would be ashamed to tell you what I paid for it. I kept him for three years and a half. I drove him out to a place eighteen miles away, and on the road I thought he was sick, and I left him at a farmer's house. I gave him another chance. He used to lie out on the road and knocking you might hit him with the butt end of the whip. I sold him in Enniscorthy two shillings for all.

7086. Mr. Cooper.—You are not of opinion that the introduction of a Hackney sire would injure the breed of horses in Wexford?—I do not know, but I suppose it. I have been asking hundreds of people about it and they say they are not. If your lordship would allow me, I was speaking to an English dealer, and had a letter from him which I would like to read.

7087. Chairman.—Who is it from?—From Mr. Topham, a large dealer in horses in Yorkshire, the gentleman who gave me the hundred guineas for the four-year-old mare.

7088. That is the Connemara?—No, a young horse he bought in Wexford. I asked his opinion about Hackney sires in Yorkshire. I wrote to him asking

[illegible]
Mr. R. Holmes,
[illegible]

him what he thought of the Hackney, and if your lordship will allow me I will read the letter I got from him.

7088. **There is no** objection to your reading it.

"[illegible], Thorn Mount-road,
"York, 20. 9. '96.

"Dear Mr. Holmes,—In answer to your inquiry re importation of Hackney sires into Ireland, judging from what I see in Yorkshire it would completely destroy the value and character of the Irish hunter. When the Hackney boom came upon us twenty years ago, every man put his mare to a Hackney sire, and the consequence is that we are now flooded with a lot of common, misfit, jaded brutes of very small value, and only fit to drag a parcel cart, while our fine Yorkshire hunters and carriage horses have practically disappeared. Being in a Hackney district I have had many opportunities of seeing Hackneys crossed with good breeds, chiefly with mares. The result is perhaps the power of [illegible] all the more undesirable properties and weak [illegible] only. As a breeder crossing has been a decided failure here. I have often known a horse so bred to be good without jumping, but never to stay. Why do you wish to make your hunter worse? There is no comparison. Scarcely any hunters are bred in England now. The game is in your own hands. Stick to your [illegible], [illegible], thoroughbred sires, and you will continue to have the finest breed of horses in the world.

"Yours faithfully,
"[illegible] Dawson."

7089. **That letter was** written after you had asked the experiment you were speaking about?—No, yes, I bought a Hackney for Major Dodson, Edward M'Donnell, of [illegible]. He was a Hackney horse. I gave him [illegible] guineas for it. It was a very bad horse too, no mobility about it.

7090. Do you know how it was bred?—He bought it in England the time of the great boom in Hackneys. I think it will ruin this country if you bring Hackneys into it. We are purely and simply the best hunter breeding people in the world, and if you allow a horse to come into the country that has no mobility and no [illegible], [illegible] in [illegible].

7091. Mr. Carew.—The Hackney is brought in not as a hunter, but for [illegible] purposes?—I do not think he is a [illegible] horse at all; I think he is a [illegible] short horse. He is a horse slapping his legs against the ground; he is a good horse to [illegible] from, and [illegible].

7092. Mr. Wrench.—You say good Yorkshire [illegible] [illegible] in getting good stock?—Yes.

7093. And are [illegible] selling well?—Yes, I could sell [illegible] [illegible] [illegible] Mr. [illegible]. He bought a lot of the stock.

7094. They are selling at a good price?—Yes.

7095. As well as the animals got by the thoroughbred [illegible]?—Oh, no.

7096. They have good action?—Fair, nice, graceful action.

7097. Selling at a fair price?—Yes.

7098. You bought him at [illegible]; who did you buy him from?—From [illegible] [illegible].

7099. What is the name of the horse?—[illegible] [illegible]; they call [illegible] after the place where they were bred.

7100. You mentioned having seen a Hackney in one occasion; what horse was that?—I would not like to mention his name, but if you wish I will bring it to [illegible].

7101. Did he stand in the County Wexford?—No. He is a well known Hackney.

7102. I would like the name handed in, I do not want it for any public purpose.

(Witness handed in the name.)

7103. Is Mr. [illegible] a large dealer?—He is one of the largest dealers. He has a house in Dublin now, to buy all his horses in Ireland.

7104. He has opened an Irish branch?—No, he has only come here to buy horses for the English trade. Of course I am not prejudiced against any breed of horse, but I [illegible] that in this country we [illegible] in horse breeding.

7105. Do you approve of registering [illegible] [illegible] stallions, if I know they were producing good stock.

7106. You would approve of registering those as well as thoroughbreds?—If they were producing good stock.

7107. Would you be in favour of having a Hunters' Improvement Society in Ireland?—I would.

7108. Do you think it would add to the value of horses if their pedigree could be certified?—If they could be certified and trusted.

7109. You think that would put up their value?—I think it would.

7110. Would you register all brood mares **in the** country?—I would register the good sound **mares**; not [illegible] [illegible].

7111. Do you think the farmers are parting with their good mares at all now?—They are not, now. They are keeping them now. But if you go back to the old scheme, I think it would do more good.

7112. Chairman. Are there generally large holdings about your part, or small?—A good many large holdings and a good many small too.

7113. Do the small farmers breed also?—They do, and do them well too. They look forward to breeding a hunter; that is the great object.

7114. You think the small farmer is as capable of breeding a hunter as the larger one?—I do. I think they take better care of them. They take care of them like a child. A small farmer got a hundred guineas for two of them, twenty-one thirty, a short time since.

7115. How are the polo ponies bred generally?—Out of the Connemara ponies by small thoroughbred horses.

7116. I suppose the production of the polo pony is a matter of chance?—A great many go in for those on [illegible] now.

7117. Are they fairly successful in that?—Yes, they will get [illegible] or fifty guineas for a good polo pony.

7118. Is it not a matter of chance whether it turns out a good polo pony?—If you get a good small pony mare, with a good small thoroughbred horse, the result is sure to be a good polo pony.

7119. Do those Connemara ponies come in every year?—They do. That is, they bring them down there from Connemara. They are not selling so well for the last two or three years.

7120. Have you seen any you know that were the produce of Hackneys there?—I would tell them the very minute I saw them; [illegible] [illegible] with upright [illegible].

7121. Have you seen any?—They bring them to [illegible] and put them on the [illegible]. They bring them down on [illegible].

7122. Would you have any objection to that?—I think it would ruin the country; putting them on and making brood mares of them by and by. The result would be that we would have Hackney blood there.

7123. You say a mixture of blood, either from a thoroughbred [illegible] or a Yorkshire coach horse, might be beneficial?—Yes.

7124. But you think in all cases the introduction of the Hackney blood would be detrimental?—I do. I do not care very much about very large horses in a hunter [illegible]. I like a horse with [illegible] bone that stands straight on his legs. The horse by a thoroughbred horse is a good deal heavier than the [illegible] [illegible] by the Hackney. You may have a bright [illegible] [illegible] [illegible] is [illegible] [illegible], where [illegible] [illegible] [illegible] in the thoroughbred horse.

7125. Are you acquainted with any parts of the country where the farmers aim principally at breeding harness horses, and not so much hunters?—I do not think there is any part of Ireland where they breed exclusively for harness horses.

7126. Not exclusively; but in the north don't they

principally?—They do, but I never remember having seen a good horse bred in the North of Ireland.

7127. Do you think hereditary disease is as prevalent as it used to be?—I believe there are not so many unsound horses now as formerly.

7128. How do you account for that?—The farmers are paying more attention. They feed them. They tend the young stock well and feed them well.

7129. Mr. Wrench.—I do not want you to tell me the name of the stallion, but do you know that the Hackney stallion you alluded to is a Norfolk Hackney?—They nearly all come from Norfolk.

7130. You know, don't you, that there are two distinct breeds of them?—Yes.

7131. That very horse was a Norfolk Hackney?—I do not know that, but is he not a Hackney?

7132. Yes, but there is a great difference?—They are all the one breed out of the one stud book.

7133. Did you ever own a horse called Stanley III?—Yes.

7134. Was he a Hackney?—No, one of the best half-bred horses. I have him still.

7135. He is a bay horse?—Yes.

7136. Where did you buy him?—In Dublin.

7137. Does he breed good stock?—He does.

7138. Is his produce very good?—He is not long enough with me yet to know, but his two and three-year olds are very promising.

7139. You have him five years?—No, I don't think I have.

7140. How long?—[illegible] I might have him four years.

7141. Are his stock promising?—Yes, his two-year olds and three-year olds are very promising now.

7142. What fee do you charge for him?—Thirty shillings.

7143. Would you be surprised to hear that he was a Hackney?—I would be surprised, because I know he is not.

7144. If he is entered in the Hackney stud book by [illegible], you would think that that is the wrong horse?—He is not in the stud book. My horse is by [illegible] out of [illegible] by [illegible]. He was bred in Wicklow.

7145. Then what is Stanley III.?—He is not my horse, my horse is Stanley I., Stanley One.

7146. He is a half-bred horse?—He is a beautiful horse by [illegible].

7147. What was his dam?—His dam was a half-bred mare, more like a half-bred mare.

7148. Chairman.—Anything you would like to suggest to the Commission?—The only suggestion I can make would be to give the nominations to the [illegible] again, instead of giving the premiums to give forty or fifty nominations, you would have a lot of [illegible] instead of [illegible], [illegible] you would have forty [illegible]; it would encourage the farmers again.

7149. That is to revert to the old system?—Yes.

Mr. T. [illegible], [illegible], Rathdrum, Co. Wicklow, examined.

7150. Chairman.—You live in the Co. Wicklow?—Yes.

7151. What part?—Rathdrum, about eight miles from the town of Wicklow.

7152. Are you interested in breeding horses?—Yes. I am very fond of horses.

7153. Do you breed yourself?—I have [illegible] some [illegible].

7154. What do you breed?—I try to breed hunters. [illegible] a really good horse. I send her to the best thoroughbred I can find within distance. Some of them do not prove very [illegible], but I got [illegible] [illegible], that [illegible] at the last Horse Show in Dublin.

7155. Do you consider your part of the County Wicklow suitable for horse-breeding?—I think we should breed as good horses as they do in Wexford, but we have not got the material. Both the mares and stallions are inferior, especially the stallions.

7156. You think the soil and climate as good?—I do not see any difference really.

7157. The county is not properly supplied with suitable stallions?—No, as my district there are none, at least, not stallions, I would——.

7158. What are the stallions mostly in the county?—I have been obliged to send to Wexford and to [illegible] for my own mares. There were two horses there, "[illegible]" and "[illegible]."

7159. There is no thoroughbred horse near you?—No.

7160. [illegible]?—There may be [illegible] [illegible] [illegible] [illegible] [illegible] [illegible] [illegible] [illegible], I do not know the [illegible] [illegible] [illegible] breed.

7161. Do not the farmers about you breed?—They do, [illegible] horse breed [illegible], but several of the [illegible] [illegible] [illegible] [illegible] [illegible] [illegible] [illegible] [illegible] [illegible] [illegible] [illegible] [illegible] [illegible]. They [illegible] [illegible] [illegible] [illegible] [illegible] [illegible] [illegible] [illegible] [illegible] [illegible].

7162. Would they pay for the service of a good horse?—I think they would, if we got a good, strong, fresh horse, with good hunting action; I do not want a [illegible]. [illegible] would [illegible] [illegible] [illegible] [illegible] or hunters, and he would be highly patronised, provided the fee was not too big.

7163. Are there any core stallions in [illegible] or any of those kinds?—I have seen such stallions going through the country but I do not know where they stand. I do not [illegible] [illegible] [illegible] them.

7164. Lord [illegible].—In your district is it very hilly?—It is very hilly but there are [illegible] [illegible] sheltered valleys—low lying lands.

7165. You know the [illegible] [illegible] [illegible] [illegible]?—There is about eight miles from where I live.

7166. Would you put it down as a natural horse-breeding district?—Well, I have seen some splendid horses bred by [illegible] [illegible]. There were two very good horses bred [illegible] [illegible] [illegible] [illegible]. [illegible] [illegible] [illegible] [illegible] [illegible] year olds.

7167. Do farmers in the district [illegible] [illegible] [illegible] [illegible] to horse-breeding?—Well, I do not think their horse-breeding has been sufficiently successful to induce them to stick to it [illegible] [illegible] [illegible] [illegible] [illegible], whereas, if we had good sires why they should not take to it and breed [illegible]. They are [illegible] [illegible] [illegible] [illegible] [illegible] [illegible] [illegible] young horses [illegible] [illegible] [illegible] [illegible] [illegible].

7168. Is there any [illegible] [illegible] [illegible] district?—No, I do not think there is any [illegible].

7169. Lord [illegible].—The mares, are they good?—They are rather wanting in quality. [illegible] [illegible] mares they were [illegible] [illegible] [illegible] would be good mares.

7170. The present class of mares you think would pay the farmers to breed from?—I think if there [illegible] [illegible] a good thoroughbred horse with good hunting action they would produce good [illegible] or [illegible] [illegible].

7171. You think it would pay the farmers to breed from them?—I do not think it would pay any farmer to breed a horse at less than £[illegible] for a [illegible] horse.

7172. You think they would get that?—I think if they had a good stallion they would, but not with the present stallions.

7173. You would want a good stallion?—A good [illegible] [illegible], a good [illegible] on the [illegible] [illegible] as in the field. The horse I speak of would produce a good carriage horse or a hunter, but mainly for hunters.

7174. SIR THOMAS ESMONDE.—You think the stallions in your district are not good stallions?—The very worst I have had. There is no thoroughbred stallion in the district, and every year there are cheap stallions imported, which means ruin to any man who puts a mare to them.

7175. Are these stallions sound?—Very unsound, I believe.

7176. What is your opinion about breeding from an unsound stallion?—I think it is a ruinous game. They cannot be sold. They will not average more than about £20 apiece as four-year-olds, and very often they hang along, taken to fair after fair, and cannot be sold.

7177. You think a stallion should be examined, and not allowed to serve if not sound?—I think it would be in the interest of the public at large, to prevent unsound stallions from being put to stud purposes at all. A stallion to be advertised for stud purposes should be at least free from hereditary disease.

7178. Near you at Wicklow is not there a very large horse fair?—There is one horse fair in the year. An odd good colt comes in and there are a hundred buyers for him.

7179. Are there many foreign buyers at the Wicklow fair?—Not so much at many of the fairs, but there are any number of buyers for a good horse.

7180. Which is the largest fair in Wicklow?—On the 12th August; there are fairs there quarterly, but they are not attended by buyers or horse trade.

7181. In the other parts of the county are there horse fairs?—On the other side there is a horse fair in Dunlavin[?], I do not know whether it is in Wicklow or Kildare.

7182. There are a good many horses produced in Wicklow?—Yes.

7183. A fair trade done in horses?—I do not know that it is a very profitable one.

7184. There are a good many horses?—Judging from Wicklow fair, there are a good many horses in the county.

7185. You think it could be made more profitable?—Yes, with one good stallion or two.

7186. What about the brood mares?—They are wanting in quality, and I would not expect to breed high-class horses from them at present, but they are sound, and move straight, and are good nurses, and I think they would breed good hunters.

7187. So that the horse-breeding industry in Wicklow is capable of extension?—Yes, and of great improvement. It is nearer to Dublin, and more convenient to dealers than Enniscorthy. There is no reason why we would not breed good horses if we had stallions.

7188. MR. CAREW.—How was the horse you sold at the show for £150 bred?—By Kempton[?], his dam by Lucky Star.

7189. Where does he stand?—At Coolattin.

7190. How many miles away?—About sixteen miles; but when I speak of farmers I do not think they like sending a horse away a long distance; they have to pay for grass.

7191. That is the only thoroughbred horse near you?—Mr. Thompson, of Newcastle, has a thoroughbred horse, "Buckmaster," but that is equally far. There was a horse at Roundwood called Glimmer[?]; he was a fairly good sire but he has left the country.

7192. The only thoroughbred sires near are at Coolattin and Newcastle?—I do not know of any others.

7193. How far is Torpedo from you?—He is at Ballinahill; that would be sixteen miles.

7194. You think the mares are quite good enough to breed from if you got the good thoroughbred sire you spoke of?—As a rule they are sound mares, move straight, and are good nurses. It is very hard to lay down any general rule; there are good ones and bad ones.

7195. There are a good many mongrel sires?—Yes, on account of the scarcity of stallions, these horses I speak of are bought for about £60.

7196. Are you in favour of licensing sires?—I would not allow any owner of a sire receive money for the service of a horse that had not a certificate from the Veterinary Department of the State that he was free from hereditary disease.

7197. You think every owner of a horse should take out a licence before keeping him?—Yes; and should not get a licence for any horse except a sound one.

7198. CHAIRMAN.—Anything else you would like to tell the Commission, Mr. Comerford?—Well, I would not like to see Hackney blood imported into the country where there was hunting stock.

7199. Why have you an opinion against the Hackney?—Because I have seen them: I don't wish to run them down as harness horses; I don't know anything about them as harness horses; they may be very showy and good, but as hunters their hind legs are behind them and their heads up in the air; they frame short and very cloddy. I think it would be ruinous to the production of hunters to introduce the Hackney stallion.

7200. You mean you would be opposed to the introduction of the Hackney sire, or of the Hackney blood?—He has so many faults in him as a hunter, I do not mean to say a word against him as a harness horse. Personally I do not like him as a harness horse, but there are others who do, but as a hunter I think he would be of the worst description.

Mr. R. G[illegible], [illegible]town, Blessington, examined.

7201. CHAIRMAN.—You also live in the county Wicklow?—I live in Kildare, but quite near Wicklow, only about a mile from Blessington, on the border.

7202. Are you acquainted with the county Wicklow?—With the part of it that lies on this side of the [illegible], [illegible] Blessington, I know it very well.

7203. That would be some distance from the district Mr. Comerford was speaking of?—Yes, [illegible]; but I [illegible] going in there, but I know it in a general way.

7204. Do you breed horses?—Yes, for the last twenty-six years I have bred [illegible] every year. I have bought a good many [illegible] too, and though I could [illegible] that way than breeding, still I keep on breeding.

7205. What kind of mares do you breed from?—Every kind. Since I was fourteen years of age I have had experience of them. I [illegible] of horses [illegible] my own, but I would [illegible] or more, and my experience is that the best brood mare to breed weight-carrying hunters is [illegible] by a thoroughbred horse. I don't know what anybody says [illegible]. [illegible] a really good half-bred mare, so far as I know, and my experience is not very big [illegible], but [illegible] a half-bred mare, a mare by a thoroughbred horse, is likely to breed weight, [illegible] plenty of [illegible], a good [illegible] and a good [illegible]; I do not [illegible] a good thoroughbred horse, is the best chance for a hunter.

7206. What is the kind of mare you have bred from yourself?—Well, I have bred [illegible]. [illegible] when I [illegible] mares that had two crosses, or even one by a thorough-bred horse, they have not been as good horses for me. The horse that makes the most money in the long run [illegible]. A dealer does not ask you when you get into the fair what your horse is by. He likes the horse that is [illegible], with plenty of bone.

7207. What kind of stallion do you send your mares to?—Every kind. The last horse in the country was a draught horse; not a Clydesdale or a Shire horse, but a horse of a draught breed. All his stock [illegible] had plenty of money while he was in the country.

7208. What became of him?—He died. He lived up to twenty-two years of age. I was the first that made a [illegible] of him and the like. Richard Brown, of [illegible], bred him and had him. He was one of a fine looking sorts, a half-bred. He was by a big horse that used to [illegible] bridge, a horse belonging to Mr. Mooney, of [illegible]. [illegible] the last few years.

7209. Mr. E. [illegible].—What was his sire?—"Sir William Wallace." The name [illegible] a horse that got [illegible] at [illegible], "Sir Patrick Wallace."

7210. What is he?—The [illegible] horse; he has plenty of bone, a big brown horse.

7211. What class did this horse get the prizes in?—I do not know; I did not go often to [illegible] them. I took no interest in him [illegible] in our neighbourhood. I saw him often, [illegible] a sort of [illegible] drawing [illegible], a fine looking horse with a great back and [illegible].

7212. And the produce of that horse, what were they sold at?—The best [illegible] in the country. I [illegible] from different gentlemen. Some of the gentlemen [illegible]. He [illegible] over and over that [illegible] had been by him. I had some myself, and got £60 and £70 [illegible] by him, and John [illegible] got £60 [illegible], and I was offered £[illegible] for [illegible] bought them [illegible] guineas.

7213. That was a horse by him?—[illegible]. No matter what way you bought a horse you will [illegible], but [illegible] all those horses were worth plenty of money, and you could sell them, young or old, at any age.

7214. When did that horse die?—About three years ago, I think. Not that he was an exception. I do not put it down that every draught horse is able to do that. He bought a Clydesdale from England, and gave a [illegible] of money for him. I had a few from him, and they were the worst horses I ever [illegible] to [illegible]; they were [illegible] for any plough, [illegible] and they had nothing that [illegible].

7215. Have you used a thorough-bred sire at all?—I have had two by a thorough-bred, [illegible] I had by a draught bred [illegible]. I have them by "Heart of Oak," "[illegible]," and other horses. "[illegible]" was the best [illegible] horse ever in our country. He [illegible] half the [illegible]. He would have [illegible] in the country. The [illegible] him [illegible] him [illegible] a few [illegible], and the [illegible] bought them and [illegible] them, and they [illegible]. A lot of the produce [illegible] light and [illegible], and [illegible] young horses, at two or three years old, [illegible] it is light and [illegible]. I sold the [illegible] as [illegible] myself [illegible] for £[illegible], [illegible]. I [illegible] of them [illegible] I gave a big price for myself, simply to breed a foal. I sent her to [illegible] of this [illegible] year, [illegible] had a [illegible] foal. I sent her to [illegible] and then [illegible] a big foal, [illegible].

7216. Have you used a Suffolk Punch?—There is [illegible] that I know of in the country.

7217. Are there any half-bred stallions in your country?—Two or three, and they [illegible] of all. What I call a half-bred horse is, we will say, out of a draught mare by a thorough-bred horse. [illegible] a half-bred horse is [illegible] that has not any [illegible] him. I call them a good [illegible], but a half-bred horse bred from a Clydesdale by a thorough-bred horse, I think that is the worst [illegible] you could get. There was one there by [illegible], a splendid looking horse, and only [illegible] he would have made a splendid hunter. A man named [illegible] had him, and he [illegible] and [illegible] a great many [illegible] him, I did not. [illegible] standing [illegible] big [illegible]. There was a draught horse standing beside him in the same yard, and the owner would get [illegible] the draught horse for the one he would get for this one. The get did not pay.

7218. What are they sold for, generally?—Our district [illegible] of the best horses you would get. There are [illegible] good [illegible] to select from in our part.

7219. What [illegible] they sell at?—For the [illegible] I sold to [illegible] to English [illegible]. For [illegible], I don't suppose I would get anyone to buy them [illegible]. I don't [illegible] when I got a good one I will stick to him.

7220. What do you and your neighbours take of producing; is it hunters or harness horses?—We try to [illegible] hunters, but we [illegible] disappointed if they are not [illegible]. When [illegible] them we go in for [illegible] they are too light. If a horse is not able to carry [illegible] thing, what good is he?

7221. Has the Royal Dublin Society [illegible] done any good to your district?—I think it has, because it is encouraging the [illegible]. I [illegible] I was offered a [illegible] price for. I do not suppose I would keep [illegible] horse.

7222. Do the prizes [illegible] in this: [illegible] a [illegible] good [illegible], perhaps, as much as [illegible], and if you have only a [illegible] one he would not pay for half his keep. A horse that does not pay £[illegible] a year will not pay you for keeping him.

7223. You buy horses [illegible]?—I got [illegible] four years, but before that I bought them.

7224. What age did you buy them at?—I [illegible] one I would buy I would keep my eye on it until the man was going to sell it. I bought him a year old or two years old.

7225. Do you [illegible]?—Yes, and in the Sales of [illegible] in Dublin [illegible]. The [illegible] is the [illegible] of the Sales. It takes the [illegible] for [illegible] hunters. The [illegible] it, on the [illegible] generally get [illegible] than [illegible] anywhere [illegible]. The [illegible] a horse to a gentleman, [illegible] a horse to a gentleman, [illegible] one out of fifty. I bring them to the Sales, and if they are [illegible] horses I [illegible] what they are [illegible] and have a [illegible] and a good [illegible], plenty of bone and [illegible], and [illegible] to buy them. While [illegible] going to the [illegible] I [illegible] them. I would [illegible] a [illegible] thorough-bred [illegible] with a draught horse.

7226. Lord [illegible].—What sire do you recommend for your district?—I [illegible] a [illegible] good animal [illegible], because [illegible]; I don't like the [illegible].

7227. How was he bred?—I do not know; but he was a [illegible] thorough-bred.

7228. Take the ordinary [illegible] in your district. What sire would you recommend him to send to her?—For the average of the [illegible] we have, [illegible] draught horse is paying far more at present than the thoroughbred horse. There is no doubt about it. What would it if I get £100 for a horse, that is only an exception. If I had five others that won't pay me it, taking more than the whole of that, that is my experience. I have never seen a farmer that stuck to thoroughbred [illegible] that had been thoroughbred horses successfully, without mixing with a draught horse—I mean any one of them that became poor. That is the reason I say they should use the draught horse sometimes. Otherwise, with [illegible] horses [illegible] I live by. I am fond of them, but when I am looking ahead in the beginning of the new year I never give any of my horses in worth anything. If one is a good horse [illegible] may be a bad horse to-morrow. Whatever I make in the year by them I get it mainly in the latter end of the year.

7449. That is gambling?—Well, it is. I put it down in that sort of way, because if you have a horse that you think a fortune you don't know when you go out into the field to-morrow something may not have happened. I had a beautiful colt that got his foot through a rough wire and left him a wreck in pieces.

7450. Mr. Thomas Simpson.—What kind of mares do you breed from?—All kinds of mares. The best mare I ever had was one that died in Major [illegible]'s land. She was by the horse I told you of, and out of a [illegible] mare, a [illegible]. I got up to £100 for a three-year-old from her, but they were dear at the time. The mare I took in "Heart of Oak," and got a foal out of her at three years old. The second next year and I put her to work. She worked well at ploughing and other work, and I sent her to him again. She had a big foal that time. I put her again, and I thought I was doing a great thing sending her to Major [illegible]'s great grass which was on the way to the place where the horse was standing. In the morning I got her dying of convulsions. I brought the foal home and pulled it. I have it now, and was offered a big price for it. One colt she did breed. I [illegible] sold into [illegible], and he was a good one.

7451. Do you approve of breeding from young mares?—I have bred from mares two years old. I have a filly this year from "Heart of Oak" by "[illegible]."

7452. All your breeding is from young mares practically?—No; we always keep a mare working and breeding. I would not keep any brood mare unless I knew it was something extraordinary. I got [illegible] a local mare—[illegible]—as if she had no foal.

7453. Have you any opinion as to whether breeding from young mares or old is better?—I think young mares are the best. If you breed from old mares you will find they are apt to have big bellies over the years. My father used this [illegible] that I remember it. You will find it is right. When they fail to feed themselves they fail the foal, and the first year in the year is to make a [illegible]. I never saw a good foal that was starved in the beginning.

7454. Do you think the [illegible] take sufficient care of the young ones [illegible] by a [illegible] horse that I do not give a kind of care a very [illegible]. In the days of the draught [illegible] I did [illegible]. I [illegible] different plans, and [illegible], but you cannot expect a high [illegible] growing on nothing. If you keep a heavy [illegible] with little nourishment, but if you buy a beautiful [illegible] you must feed him well. People used to come and say to me "Your cattle are not [illegible] like yours, how is that?" Well, my father only [illegible]; but my father would be up at five in the morning feeding them and minding them, and if they don't pay for feeding them, it is a fact that they won't pay for starving them.

7455. Mr. Chaloner.—You say the best breed [illegible] for a draught horse out of a well bred mare?—[illegible] but I think in [illegible] breeding [illegible] that want to keep them; keep [illegible] this time. If you go to a draught horse with a bred [illegible] to the [illegible]. I would like to have a thoroughbred sire with a mare with plenty of strength. I would not take a [illegible] of the produce of a thoroughbred horse with a Clydesdale mare. To my opinion you might as well expect a [illegible] out of a [illegible]. [illegible] get a sort with proper legs and back, a[illegible] and well [illegible], and a good man [illegible]. I have [illegible] it, and [illegible] it [illegible], before them and talk about giving [illegible]. I never got a good [illegible] with [illegible] a good big [illegible] neck on [illegible]. Get a horse with the head [illegible], and a big [illegible], and, perhaps, [illegible]. I don't care what horse you go to, [illegible], or the [illegible] horse on the Curragh, it is [illegible] one new will have a bad horn.

7456. Can you give an idea of the breed of draught horse you would select?—The draught horse I would like is one that some people would call a half-bred horse. I would like his legs to be [illegible] and clean breeding. If he was light in the side he should have plenty of [illegible] on the [illegible], and [illegible] [illegible] to a good [illegible] horse with [illegible], a horse with good [illegible]. You may be disappointed, but you are most likely to have a good [illegible]. That [illegible] [illegible] I would like to see coming into the country. I would send him the best mare I have.

7457. That is your description of the draught horse? —Yes, but not a pure draught horse. That is what I would [illegible].

7458. One of a well-bred mare?—I would not say [illegible].

7459. [illegible] thoroughbred blood in the mare?—You [illegible] for [illegible] blood in him. I have [illegible] the big horses and bred them and bought them, and I never got one that I had any pleasure with. I worked several horses when a young boy with my father, I [illegible] a young draught horse to [illegible] they are [illegible]. If you have a horse with a little [illegible] he will nearly do anything you [illegible], with [illegible], you will always have to [illegible]. I am decidedly in favour of breeding from two-year-old fillies. I think a [illegible] would be [illegible], [illegible] [illegible]. For instance, a sheep at two or three years old won't make as good a lamb for me as if she [illegible]. If you give me a sheep [illegible] like that she [illegible] in the sheep that will [illegible] [illegible]. If you put a mare to [illegible] [illegible] developed you cannot expect she will have the [illegible] of milk to give, or breed a foal as well as one that has got up in years. Some will breed [illegible], they are [illegible], [illegible] at fifteen. I would not say a [illegible] [illegible] or [illegible] in [illegible] than [illegible] when they come to twenty I say they are.

7460. Chairman.—Do you consider the breeding of [illegible] a profitable [illegible] in your part of the country?—Most [illegible] if you stick to the [illegible]. I [illegible] on that, I [illegible]. If you breed a [illegible] at three years old it is hard to get £35 for it, and if it was [illegible] draught [illegible] worth [illegible] way. And [illegible] you will get [illegible] [illegible].

7461. Do the farmers about you [illegible]. Is [illegible] bred in? [illegible] they [illegible] a [illegible], and there are a good many [illegible] in the district. Anyone that [illegible] [illegible] would not [illegible] in good [illegible] [illegible] [illegible] [illegible].

7462. You think it pays them?—One gentleman said if he got £[illegible] he would not [illegible]. If I get £[illegible] for one at three years old, or £[illegible] for one at [illegible] old, I think I am well off.

7463. Can you suggest anything that would make it more profitable?—Send us a good draught horse. My idea about a thoroughbred horse I give it to you [illegible]. I think [illegible] [illegible].

[illegible]

The Commissioners adjourned to next day.

FOURTEENTH DAY—THURSDAY, DECEMBER 3RD, 1896.

Dec. [illegible] 1896.

PRESENT:—THE EARL OF DUNRAVEN, K.P., in the Chair; LORD ASHTOWN, MR. PERCY LA TOUCHE, MR. J. L. CAREW, M.P., MR. F. S. WRENCH.

MR. HUGH NEVILLE, Secretary.

MR. RICHARD J. MOSS examined.

Mr. R. J. Moss.

[illegible] CHAIRMAN.—You are the Registrar of the Royal Dublin Society, are you not?—I am.

[illegible]. How long have you held that post?—I have held that post for sixteen years; I have been an officer of the Society for twenty-one years.

[illegible]. Will you give the Commission shortly a sketch of the constitution and objects of the Society?—The Society was founded in 1731, it was incorporated by Royal Charter in 1751, a Supplemental Charter was granted in 18[illegible], and a second Supplemental Charter in 18[illegible]. The objects for which the Society is incorporated are—"The advancement of Agriculture and other branches of Industry, and the advancement of Science and Art." The first Supplemental Charter constituted the Council the governing body of the Society, and directed that the general management and control over the affairs of the Society should be vested in, and exercised by, the Council exclusively. The second Supplemental Charter dissolved the Royal Agricultural Society of Ireland, and transferred its members and its property to the Royal Dublin Society. This Charter also re-organized the Council, and provided that it shall consist of the President, ex-officio officers to be added by By-law, and three Sections, each consisting of an equal number of members, the entire Council, excluding the President, not [illegible]

[illegible]
Mr. R. J. Moss.

are resident in Dublin and the adjoining counties, there is no county in Ireland without several representatives on the roll of Members. Twenty years ago the number of Members and Associates was 1,206; the increase for the period is [illegible] per cent.

[illegible]. What is the difference between a Member and an Associate?—A Member is endowed with the power of voting—he has a vote for members of Council and members of Committees, and for the election of new members; the Associate is not given this power, and his subscription is correspondingly less.

[illegible]. What is the subscription?—The subscription of a Member is two guineas per annum with an entrance fee of three guineas; life composition, £21. The subscription of an Associate is one guinea, except in the case of certain agricultural Associates of small tenancies [illegible] whose subscription is [illegible], and Associates pay no entrance fee. At an early date in its history the Royal Dublin Society endeavoured to improve the breed of horses in Ireland by offering premiums for the importation of stallions and mares.

[illegible]. When was that?—I am uncertain when this practice began. The following extract from the minutes shows that the practice was in operation [illegible] years ago.

Extract from the Minutes of a Meeting of the Dublin Society, February 11, [illegible].

"Ordered:—

"That a premium of £[illegible] be given to Mr. Thomas [illegible] of [illegible] in the County of Tipperary, being [illegible] for importing a stallion fit for the plough, and other country work, and [illegible] imported by him into this kingdom since June last.

"That a gold medal be presented to the Right Hon. the Earl of [illegible] (a member of this Society) in lieu of a premium of £[illegible] for having imported into this kingdom the beginning of last summer, six strong able mares fit for the plough and other country work, and that the said gold medal be presented to his Lordship in lieu of a premium of £[illegible], for having imported at the same time a fine [illegible] stallion. The said medals being adjudged according to a [illegible] which [illegible] than [illegible] premiums granted."

"That a premium of £[illegible] be given to Robert French of [illegible] in the County of Roscommon, Esquire, for a fine black draft stallion imported by him in August last."

Then follows a minute to the effect that a claim for a premium lodged by Mr. Philip [illegible] of [illegible], county Dublin, for importing two mares and a stallion, should lie on the table, and postponing the consideration of another claim for a premium for importing a stallion. I find these claims were subsequently disallowed on the ground that the importation had taken place before the period prescribed in the announcement of the premiums. In the year [illegible] a Farming Society was started under the patronage of the Dublin Society, and it was granted a subsidy of £[illegible] per annum by the Dublin Society. The Farming Society held two shows annually at Ball's Bridge, Dublin, and one at Ballinasloe. In the schedule a premium of [illegible] was offered for the best draft stallion of any kind; and a premium of £[illegible] to any person who shall import the best lot of horses of the Suffolk Punch breed, to consist of one stallion and two mares." The encouragement led to the importation of a number of horses. The Farming Society was not self-supporting, and came to an end. In [illegible] the Royal Dublin Society commenced a series of Agricultural Shows which have been held annually in Dublin without intermission to the present day. At first the Shows were very small. In [illegible] there were only [illegible] head of cattle, six sheep, [illegible] swine, two Spanish asses, and six horses. The horses were agricultural draught stallions of various breeds. These Shows have been [illegible] and the premiums for horses were struck out of the prize list in [illegible]. Agricultural horses were again introduced at the Spring Shows in recent years. It was not until 1868 that the Society held a Show for horses exclusively. At this Show the entries numbered [illegible]. At the [illegible] Annual Horse Show, which was held last August, the entries numbered 1,[illegible]. The Dublin Horse Show is now the largest show of hunters in the world. The prizes awarded at the late Show amounted to £[illegible]; the Show was visited by [illegible] persons, including purchasers from the United States, France, Belgium, Germany, Austria-Hungary, and other countries. I have referred in the briefest manner to the work of the Royal Dublin Society in improving the breed of horses in Ireland, apart from the administration of the funds paid to the Society annually under the Probate Duties Act. Before the Act of Union the Society was the medium through which the Irish Parliament administered grants for agricultural purposes, including horse-breeding. But from the time the Society started agricultural shows in [illegible] to the present day, the shows have been supported out of the private funds of the Society exclusively. I wish to point out specially that not one penny of Government money has ever been spent upon the Horse Show. On the contrary, the Society offers out of its private funds at the Horse Show, valuable prizes which are intended to supplement the scheme of the Commission [illegible] with the administration of the public fund to which I shall refer presently. It is difficult to say what has been the effect of the Horse Show upon horse breeding in Ireland. Concurrently with the development of the show there has been a marked development in the horse trade. There are no statistics of this trade available before [illegible], in which year the Irish Veterinary Department commenced the publication of statistics of the export of horses from Ireland to Great Britain. The last published returns show that the average annual export of horses from this country to Great Britain has been as follows:—

Period	Annual Average
[illegible]	26,[illegible]
[illegible]	33,[illegible]
[illegible]	3[illegible],444
[illegible]	3[illegible],604

These figures show an increase in the horse trade of the period ending [illegible], when compared with the period ending [illegible], amounting to 36 per cent. On investigating the increase in its relation to sexes, I find that the export of geldings has increased [illegible] per cent. in the period referred to, the export of mares has increased [illegible] per cent., and the export of stallions has increased no less than [illegible] per cent. These figures are significant. It is important to note that the number of horses imported by Great Britain from Ireland exceeds the number of horses imported into the United Kingdom from all the countries of the world. For example, in the year [illegible] Great Britain imported from Ireland [illegible] horses, while in the same year the total import of horses from all countries into Great Britain and Ireland was [illegible]. About one quarter of these horses came from Canada, about one-fifth from the United States, Germany supplied another fifth, while Russia, Denmark, and Holland [illegible] in order. A [illegible] the number of horses exported from Ireland [illegible] countries and British possessions. In [illegible] the United Kingdom exported [illegible] stallions, [illegible] mares, and [illegible] geldings, making a total of [illegible] horses. Nearly half these horses went to Belgium, about one-quarter to Holland, while France took the greater part of the remainder. It will be seen from the figures I have given that Ireland has almost as great an export trade in horses with Great Britain as the United Kingdom has with all parts of the world. Or, to put it another way, Ireland is [illegible] of the rest of the world in the horse trade with Great Britain. This development has taken place concurrently with the development of the Horse Show, and must, I think, be largely attributed to the Horse Show.

[illegible]. Before you leave the figures I should like to ask you one or two questions about them. Have you got any returns of the imports into Ireland from Great Britain?—Yes; I can give figures from the British Board of Agriculture returns.

[illegible]. Because some of the imports ought to be

bettered by the importers, ought they not?—Yes; the quality is much.

7260. There must be a certain number of horses that go backwards and forwards?—The horses imported from Great Britain to Ireland in the year ending 1892—very small.

7261. Mr. La Touche.—Does it distinguish the mares and stallions?—Yes; 63 stallions and 1,778 mares, 2,864 geldings.

7262. Chairman.—You gave us just now the increased percentage of the export of geldings, mares, and stallions, and you said the figures were significant; what do you deduce from the figures?—The relative figures of the different sexes; it shows that the geldings are 35 per cent., whereas in the case of mares it is 104 per cent., and in the case of stallions it amounts to 134. It is not in geldings that the main increase has taken place.

7263. Well, the main increase, according to that, is in stallions; what do you deduce from that?—That it is the breeding stock that is leaving the country—mares and stallions.

7264. The stallions would probably include all the young thorough-bred horses?—Yes.

7265. Can you give us the actual number of stallions?—I can.

7266. In judging by percentages it is necessary to have the basis upon them formed?—The number of stallions exported is relatively small; I have calculated the five year periods—they give averages of five year which are perhaps the most trustworthy.

7267. You said the export of stallions had increased 134 per cent. in a certain period; can you tell us how many were exported at the beginning of that period?—Yes; 65 in the first five year period, 80 the second, 72 the third, and 135 in the last.

7268. Do you think there would be more demand for by increased exportation of young thorough-bred stock?—My own opinion simply is, that it shows that the foreigners have been coming here in increasing numbers to get our breeding stock.

7269. You think that the stallions arriving in the country were sold out of it?—Well, yes; but it is impossible to say how many of those are yearlings or young horses taking their own part in the trade; it is impossible to say what the number is.

7270. And can you give us the figures as the case of the mares?—In the case of mares the periods are, ending 1881, 9,902. I should say that that particular period is calculated upon three years figures, because the statistics only begin in 1878, but it is the yearly average for that three years; then the period ending 1886, 11,617; the period ending 1890, 12,098; and the period ending 1894, 14,018. It has gone up from 9,902 to 14,452.

7271. That appears to me more significant than the case of the stallions?—The number of mares is very much larger.

7272. How are these statistics collected; by whom?—The statistics I quote are published by the British Board of Agriculture; they get them, I believe, from forms prepared by the Irish Veterinary Department.

7273. Do they publish the statistics of exports and imports?—They do, from Ireland to Great Britain.

7274. Do you know how they are collected?—I have no direct knowledge of it.

7275. Do you think that they are sufficiently reliable?—I cannot say that at all; I quote them as the only official figures available.

7276. But such as they are, the only official figures, do you think they are sufficient to enable you to form a correct opinion?—I should suppose them to be fairly correct.

7277. Can you suggest any improvement in the statistical information?—Without knowing exactly the method of collecting the figures, I should scarcely venture to express any opinion on the subject, but I have no doubt the department do their best to get the exact result.

7278. They give no sort of any note of the animals, whether they are ponies, geldings, or stallions?—That is all in the public records.

7279. No particulars as to age or breed?—No; I don't know whether such particulars can be obtained in a satisfactory manner.

7280. Have you got any figures as to the number of [illegible] the months during those same periods?—Yes.

7281. Would you give them to the Committee?—I refer to them later on.

7282. Going back. You were saying that the great development of the export went on at the same time as the development of the Horse Show?—Which is the effect is a matter of opinion.

7283. Mr. La Touche.—Are not the statistics of exports prepared weekly; don't the Board of Trade publish a weekly return of exports and imports?—Well, I am not sure what is the shortest period that they are available for; I don't know about that.

7284. There are no figures in that report at any rate, that show?—There are no figures as to stallions.

7285. Can you show the exports of horses for the whole of the Horse Show?—No; I have no doubt that the offices who make the returns have their [illegible] the North Wall.

7286. Chairman.—Will you go on with your statement?—I wish to refer to Lord Calthorpe's proposal some years ago.

7287. What was that?—In a letter to the Times of May 4th, 1876, Lord Calthorpe expressed his belief that no Government would interfere to check the exportation of mares (which at that time seemed to have attracted attention), and that all that was required could be effected by private enterprise. He offered to subscribe £100 per annum if 100 other gentlemen would follow his example.

7288. Which year was that?—1876. He proposed that the fund should be devoted to the purchase of good stallions to be located in various parts of the United Kingdom, and rendered available for farmers at low rates. Referring to horse-breeding in Ireland, he stated:—"The climate and soil are most favourable, the holdings are so small that most men have ample time to look after and educate their colts, and there is no finer breed of horses in Christendom unequalled even in Yorkshire." In the Times of May 9th, 1876, Lord Lucan published a letter strongly supporting Lord Calthorpe's proposal, and offering to subscribe £100 per annum. A committee was appointed by the Royal Dublin Society to inquire as to how Lord Calthorpe's scheme could best be carried out, and the sum of £100 was placed at the disposal of the committee. Prizes were offered by the Society for essays on the best method of carrying out the details of Lord Calthorpe's proposal. The first prize was subsequently awarded to Mr. R. A. [illegible], of [illegible], Kensington, and the second prize was awarded to Mr. [illegible], of [illegible], New Ross. These essays were printed; I have the copies. The financial support necessary for carrying out Lord Calthorpe's suggestion was not, however, forthcoming, and the idea was abandoned for the time being.

7289. Are those essays long?—They are perhaps too long to read.

7290. Suggesting how the scheme might be carried out?—They are interesting now from the historical point of view.

7291. Can you tell us shortly the general effect of them?—It would be very difficult to summarise either of the schemes. The financial support necessary for [illegible] and the like was abandoned.

7292. The scheme throughout the United Kingdom?—Throughout the United Kingdom.

7293. Did the Royal Dublin Society take any action in the matter?—No further action, owing to funds not being forthcoming, the scheme fell to the ground. Acting on the recommendation of the Horse Show Committee, the Society in 1883 approached Lord Londonderry, who was then the Lord Lieutenant, and after some negotiations the Government promised a

Dec. 6th. Mr. R. J. Moss.

[illegible]
Mr. R. J. [illegible]

year of £5,000 to encourage improvement in the breed of horses and cattle in Ireland. This sum is [illegible] [illegible] payable annually to the Society under the Probate Duties (Scotland and Ireland) Act, 1888. I shall here deal only with the administration of that portion of the fund appropriated by the Society to horse-breeding, viz.—£3,000 per annum. It is [illegible] [illegible] to point out that [illegible] £3,000 devoted to the improvement of the breed of horses in Ireland amounts to [illegible] [illegible] of the [illegible] horses in the country, a [illegible] [illegible] [illegible]. Or [illegible] the matter in another way, it amounts to [illegible] [illegible] on every £100 of horse flesh in the country, taking the [illegible] estimate of [illegible] per head as the value of the horses. That is to say, the amount devoted to improving the article is about one-fourteenth per cent. of its value.

7284. What do you want us to deduce from that? —That the result to be obtained from such an expenditure as [illegible] would be proportionate to the expenditure.

7285. But, of course, the more successful you were, and the greater number of horses in the country, the less per head there would be to devote to them?—Quite so; and the fact remains that that is the amount expended per head.

7286. That would be reduced in proportion as you were successful in one point of view?—In the first year, the season 1888, [illegible] premiums of £[illegible] each were offered for thoroughbred stallions to serve not less than 50 half-bred mares, the property of farmers whose tenement valuation did not exceed £[illegible], at a fee of £1 for each mare. Sixty stallions competed for the premiums at the Horse Show in August, 1887. [illegible] were selected as suitable, and placed for the purposes of the scheme. Each stallion owner received, immediately after the Show, £[illegible] on account of the premium. Local committees were appointed to carry out the scheme in their several districts, the [illegible] [illegible]. After careful inquiry the Horse-breeding Committee of the Royal Dublin Society selected [illegible] [illegible] persons to act as Chairman, Secretary, and Treasurer in each district. These officers were [illegible] [illegible]. The Chairmen [illegible] the [illegible] of the persons to [illegible] [illegible] of the committees. The [illegible] appointment of the committees rested with the Society. Each local committee consisted of not less than 5 or more than 7 members, of whom at least 4 were farmers. The local committees held inspections in their districts, and examined 1,748 mares. [illegible] mares were passed as suitable, and 704 were [illegible]. The head-quarters of the several districts were—(1) [illegible], (2) Antrim, (3) Portadown, (4) [illegible], (5) Ballymahon, (6) [illegible], (7) Longford, (8) Kells, (9) Kilkenny, (10) [illegible], (11) [illegible], (12) Templemore, (13) Tallow, (14) [illegible], (15) [illegible], (16) Dunmanway. In the second year, 1889, a similar scheme was carried out; but in the case of stallions serving in districts in which the owner resided, the service and groom's fees were paid over to the Society. This change enabled the Committee to increase the number of districts from 16 to 18. The districts were so arranged, that the head-quarters [illegible] in several cases. They were—(1) [illegible], (2) [illegible], (3) Lisburn, (4) Dungannon, (5) [illegible], (6) Ballymahon, (7) [illegible], (8) [illegible], (9) [illegible], (10) [illegible], (11) Athenry, (12) Parsonstown, (13) [illegible], (14) Kilkenny, (15) [illegible], (16) Rathkeale, (17) [illegible], (18) [illegible]. The selection of stallions for these districts took place at a Show held at Ball's Bridge, February 13th and 14th, 1889. Forty stallions competed for the 18 premiums.

7287. Why do you make these changes in the headquarters?—It would be difficult to give the reasons in each individual instance; the committees had reports before them, and, in some cases, direct information conveyed to the committee by members of the [illegible], which induced them to select other towns more suitable than those they had previously selected. At the shows of mares held by the district committees there were 1,715 mares submitted at fifteen districts; the numbers were not ascertained in three of the districts. Assuming that the numbers in those districts corresponded with the average in the other districts, the total for the eighteen districts would be 2,034. The number of mares actually served was 833. The following year the Society sent a circular to the owners of 690 mares in [illegible] of three districts, 577, being 83 per cent. of the farmers, replied to the circular; and from these replies it was ascertained that 401 foals had been produced, 223 colts, and 178 fillies. 69½ per cent. of the mares served produced foals. In the third year, 1890, several changes were made. Shows were held in the Autumn of 1889 for the selection of stallions, not only in Dublin, but in Belfast, Sligo, Ballinasloe and Cork. At these shows sixty-one stallions competed for eighteen prizes of £30 each, on the condition that the selected stallions should each serve not more than fifty mares, the property of farmers of not more than £200 tenement valuation, at a fee of £3 3s. 6d., of which sum the farmer was to pay £1 2s. 6d. The stallions were assigned to the following districts:—Belfast Centre—(1) Londonderry, (2) Ballymena, (3) Armagh, (4) Belfast, Sligo Centre—(5) Sligo, (6) Castlerea, (7) Clones, Ballinasloe Centre—(8) Ballinasloe, (9) Athenry, (10) Parsonstown; Dublin Centre—(11) Navan, (12) Mullingar, (13) Kildare, (14) Carlow, (15) Wexford, Cork Centre, (16) Dungarvan, (17) Rathkeale, (18) Mallow. In each of these eighteen districts shows of mares were held. Excluding Ballymena, where the number of mares was not ascertained, there were 1,718 mares inspected. Prizes were awarded to the owners of the best mares, divided into two classes—those over five years old and those under five years old. The prizes in each class were £5, £4, £3, and £2, with a free nomination in each case; there was also a fifth prize in each class, consisting of a free nomination, as well as a champion prize of £10 for the best mare in each class. The number of mares served under the scheme was 811. A return, sent in subsequently by 648 owners of mares, showed that 465 foals were produced, 218 colts and 247 fillies. Seventy-two per cent. of the mares served produced foals. In the year 1891 the Society reverted to the selection of stallions at Dublin, and a Show was held at Ball's Bridge on February 7th. Forty-nine stallions competed for sixteen £200 premiums, the selected stallions being required to serve fifty mares, the property of farmers of not more than £100 tenement valuation. The judges of the stallions on this occasion reported as follows:—

"In compliance with the instructions that we should write a report upon the stallions which have been under our adjudication, we have the pleasure to state that in our opinion, they compare favourably with any shown for the Queen's Premiums held previously in Dublin or in England, several of the horses representing a high class, and being thoroughly well adapted for getting hunters and half-bred stock. We had little difficulty in coming to a conclusion that the sixteen selected were qualified to receive the Queen's Premiums. While it is to be regretted that two or three of the horses provisionally selected could not receive premiums, still at the same time exhibitors may be congratulated on the very small percentage out of the great number which failed to pass the Veterinary Surgeon's Examination.

" (Signed), CECIL LYARD.
RICHARD BELL.
C. J. BLAKE."

7288. Why did they give up the system of having shows elsewhere than in Dublin?—I should find it very difficult to give any reason; on the occasion of any change being made the matter is dealt with by a Committee; the individual members of the Committee have their own opinions, and would no doubt themselves differ in assigning a reason for the change.

7289. All you know is the change was made?—All I know is the change was made. The selected sta-

...were assigned to districts of which the head-quarters were—(1) [illegible]; (2) Magherafelt; (3) [illegible]; (4) [illegible]; (5) Boyle; (6) [illegible]; (7) [illegible]; (8) [illegible]; (9) [illegible]; (10) Ardee; (11) Enniscorthy; (12) [illegible]; (13) Macroom; (14) Listowel; (15) [illegible]; (16) [illegible]. The local committees in these districts held shows at which 1,[illegible] mares were submitted for inspection. Five prizes of £[illegible] each were awarded at these shows for mares under [illegible] years old, and five prizes of £[illegible] each for mares [illegible] years old or upwards. There were also champion prizes of £10 for the best mare in each class. At the close of the season the number of mares served was [illegible]. The owners of these mares were subsequently asked to send in a return; [illegible] replies were received, showing that [illegible] foals had been produced—[illegible] males and [illegible] fillies, or [illegible] per cent. of the mares produced foals. In 1903 a new system was introduced. The owners of thoroughbred stallions were invited to register them. [illegible]

[illegible]

...that fewer unsound stallions were submitted for registration, and that several horses rejected in the preceding season had disappeared from the country. [illegible]

[illegible]

[illegible]

those for 1895. The limit of age for stallions in class (a) was extended to four years, and the limit of £5 to the total premiums was withdrawn. The number of stallions presented for examination was 181; 109 were accepted. The returns of the local committees have not yet been completed. So far they show a slight increase in the number of mares and foals competing for the premiums.

7208. If you have done with that part of the subject, there is, perhaps, a question or two I might ask you?—Yes; the rest is statistical.

7209. Prior to 1896 stallions were inspected by veterinary surgeons appointed by the Society, I understand?—Yes; since 1896 by veterinary surgeons appointed by the Society.

7210. And since then, you take the certificate of any member of the College of Veterinary Surgeons?—Yes; but the Committee reserve at the same time the right, when they think fit, of having their own veterinary surgeon, or a veterinary surgeon appointed by themselves, to examine or to re-examine such stallions.

7211. Did they usually employ a local veterinary surgeon, or a veterinary surgeon from a distance, when they did the work themselves?—When they did the work themselves they used to come to Dublin to get the veterinary surgeons to inspect stallions in the districts in which they did not practise extensively.

7212. Do you know how it is now when you take a certificate; is the certificate generally obtained from a veterinary surgeon in the locality?—Frequently it is.

7213. Besides unsoundness you would not register horses that are objectionable in some other way; what are we to understand by that?—Unsuitable to get half-bred horses such as the Committee think is desirable to produce.

7214. You mean when the Society is sending down a veterinary surgeon to examine stallions, you must give him some idea of the class as to what is wanted for examining?—Oh, yes; it would be very difficult to say what the directions are; the directions are not in print; a great deal is left to the discretion of the inspector or veterinary surgeon.

7215. Lord Ashtown.—They are good judges of a horse generally?—Of course they are selected as being suitable men to judge, from the Committee's point of view, what the stallions ought to be.

7216. Mr. Wrench.—Is each stallion submitted to the inspection of a vet, and correspondence dealt with, and returned the form to the Committee?—That is so; the form gives a subject in detail.

7217. So that they actually have all the particulars of the horse that can be given before them?—Yes.

7218. Chairman.—Who decides as to the horse being suitable or not?—The Horse Breeding Committee.

7219. That is not a question for the veterinary surgeon?—No; he only reports as to soundness.

7220. Mr. Wrench.—Do you know that the Committee also ask for a description of the stock the horse has got?—Yes; that is an important element in deciding whether the horse is suitable or not.

7221. Chairman.—They are inspected also by an inspector?—Yes.

7222. Even now that the certificate of any member of the College of Veterinary Surgeons is accepted as to soundness?—Yes, as to soundness. As to suitability the Society send their own inspector to the district with a report, and to see the animal and to judge himself. He sends in all the particulars, and the Committee decide on that decision.

7223. And these horses are examined for soundness every year?—Not since 1893, when the new system was introduced. A certificate dating back to the date which I mentioned is accepted.

7224. I don't quite understand that?—In the year 1895 we accepted the certificate of any member of the Royal College of Veterinary Surgeons, provided it was dated later than February of 1896, as stated before.

7225. Is that to hold good for all time?—This year it would be a year advanced; this year it would be February, 1898, for the year 1899.

7226. Then the horse would have to be examined for soundness every year?—Well, no; the Committee, if they think fit, forego the second examination, if they have evidence before them satisfactory.

7227. Then a stallion need not necessarily be examined for soundness since 1894?—No; but the right to examine is always maintained.

7228. Lord Ashtown.—If a new stallion is wanted to be put upon the register he would have to be examined?—Oh, of course.

7229. Mr. Wrench.—It is only for strong horses, such as horses of a well-known name like "Ascetic" or "Torpedo," that the Committee dispense with the examination?—That is so.

7230. Chairman.—They have very strong reasons when they dispense?—Of course; they don't dispense necessarily with the examination; it is on evidence before them that they dispense with it or not.

7231. You said just now that it was reported that one of the results of registration was that unsound horses were tending to disappear—horses that did not pass?—That is so; that was in the second year of the registration.

7232. Whose report was that?—The report came from more than one source.

7233. Can you tell us whether you have any further returns to the same effect?—I believe the Committee had information sufficiently satisfactory that such a change had been effected by the system of registration; stallions were known to have disappeared which had previously been serving—unsound stallions.

7234. Do you think you could give any figures?—It would be difficult; it might be possible to ascertain them, but it is many years ago now.

7235. In the second year of the registration scheme?—That was in 1893.

7236. It would be very interesting if you could give us any figures on that?—I will look into it and see if the actual figures are available.

7237. Then you said, I think, that in some parts of Ulster there was an excess of nominations?—In some parts of Ulster it was difficult to get a sufficient number of persons to apply for nominations.

7238. What did you do in these cases—were additional nominations given to other parts of the country?—The effect of a circumstance of that kind would be to leave a certain portion of the fund unexpended, and I deal with that afterwards in referring to the statistics—the financial results.

7239. Can you tell us at all why the somewhat sweeping change was made in 1896—was there any particular reason?—There, again, it is a matter of individual opinion of the Committee selected for the purpose of investigating the matter, and the reasons are not recorded upon their minutes.

7240. And as to the effect of these changes you have not yet had time to form an opinion, I suppose?—No.

7241. Mr. La Touche.—I would like to ask you one question—how do the Committee account for the fact that the moment they accept the certificate of any veterinary surgeon the number of stallions accepted and declared to be suitable increased something like 70 or 80 per cent.?—There were other changes made simultaneously; it would be unsafe to assign that increase to the change in the veterinary examination alone.

7242. Chairman.—The fee was abolished?—Yes; the whole system was altered that year.

7243. Mr. La Touche.—How did that affect the system greatly?—It is hard to say how the system of the alteration in the mode of paying the premium of the mares would affect the stallion owners; exceedingly difficult to follow it.

7244. Lord Ashtown.—In that year I think it was

Mr. [illegible]. £47,[illegible], and expenditure on horse breeding, £[illegible], and on cattle breeding, £[illegible]; the balance on 31st December, 1895, was £[illegible], which has since been expended in the current year's work. It will be observed that the cost of administration has charged to the funds. [illegible] what this charge would be, because in salaries and wages the administration of £23,[illegible] costs the Royal Dublin Society £[illegible], or [illegible] per cent. On this basis of calculation the administration of the Private Dublin Fund would cost the Society £[illegible] per annum, but whatever the cost is to be paid out of the private funds of the Royal Dublin Society; it would be difficult for the State to secure efficient administration at more favourable terms. I hand in also the annual statement of the horses to which, under the breeding schemes of the Society, which have been in operation each year.

7365. CHAIRMAN.—Is that all you wish to say on the administration of the grant?—That is all I have to say on that subject.

7366. Owing to the fact that it is administered out of the private funds of the Society, I understand that the whole of the grant is expended for the purpose of horse breeding?—The whole of it. The entire amount reaches the people of those for whom it is intended, the expenses of administration are charged to the funds.

7367. Can you tell us where those stallions were bought?—they are stallions I have got the figures with me. I can get the figures. They have been brought in different places.

7368. At an average of £300?—An average of about £300 a piece.

7369. Perhaps you will let us know?—I will ascertain.

7370. And also the where they were sold?—Yes, certainly.

7371. Can you tell us how it was managed, that they were sold for less than cost price?—It has varied with the different stallions.

7372. How did they select the persons to be allowed to buy them?—By inquiry as to the districts where they would be placed. Almost every year the Society has noticed that in certain districts good stallions are not forthcoming, and they have inquired in those districts as to persons who would be disposed to take stallions on payment by instalments, with certain conditions attached. From the beginning it has always been one of the regulations in the scheme that in the event of persons coming forward and requesting a chance to obtain stallions, that the Society would aid them.

7373. They selected the men that suitable in a district?—That is the way it is really worked. As this has been continued in the regulations almost from the beginning, that in the event of districts not being suitably supplied with stallions, the Society would consider in what way the deficiency could be remedied.

7374. MR. LA TOUCHE.—Have you any record in reference to those stallions purchased by the Commission, as regards the prices they have secured, their popularity with owners, &c.?—I have no doubt information could be obtained on some of those points.

7375. THE CHAIRMAN.—When were they sold?—I have not those figures with me. They have been sold within the past ten years.—Examples very interesting. The third stallion purchased is sold. I have given the details of them here. I am bound to the names of each stallion and the amount paid.

7376. MR. WRENCH.—I think they are all in the returns?—Yes.

7377. At least the Commission can turn to them at some?—They have in a return showing the names of the stallions, when purchased, the amount paid, the amount for which sold, the instalments paid, and the name of the person by whom the stallion was purchased.

7378. THE CHAIRMAN.—Have you anything further you wish to state to the Commission?—I have no more statistics; if desirable I can supply further facts.

7379. You said, I think, that prior to the Act of Union this Society administered whatever grants were made by Parliament?—Yes; sometimes large sums.

7380. Can you give them to us?—It extends over a long period. One of the last Acts of the Irish Parliament was to vote £[illegible] to be administered by the Dublin Society for the encouragement of agricultural industries.

7381. Can you get this information for us?—It would involve a good deal of research, because it extends over a long period; but I have no doubt it can be obtained.

7382. I noticed from some of the records you sent out to us of the early days of the Society, that grants appear to have been given for the importation of horses, and occasionally for stallions?—That is so.

7383. Did that continue long?—I have endeavoured to get the information, but have not been successful, and cannot state positively how long it continued.

7384. You don't know what it was discontinued?—That is the difficulty; the minutes are often very brief, and it is not easy to get information as to points of that kind.

7385. It would rather look as if there was a lack of good sires in this country at that time?—That is distinctly the inference to be drawn from the early years; persons were encouraged to import not only stallions but mares.

7386. As far as stallions are concerned that was limited?—Yes; premiums were given in the latter part of the 18th century for the importation of sires.

7387. Would the records of your Society be able to give any fuller information on that point?—I doubt that it is possible to give any fuller information.

7388. You could not be certain at all as to what kind the sires were?—It would seem that the desire was to get large animals "fit for the plough," as the term was—strong large animals. At the beginning of this century, immediately after the Union, the Society surveyed Ireland—made statistical surveys of 22 out of the 32 counties, and published them in some 25 volumes. I have noticed that in them there are repeated references to the horses of the county. In some of the surveys the class of horse in certain parts of the country is spoken of very highly indeed, and in other cases the horses are described as being miserable, and in two or three reports they are referred to as being barbarously treated by the people—badly fed and cruelly treated.

7389. From your statistical knowledge can you say as to whether the race of horses has been improving in the country of late years?—Well, almost the only data upon which I could personally form an opinion would be from the Horse Show, and most unquestionably there has been an extraordinary development in the horses that come to the Horse Show; the figures show that most distinctly, and then there is the development which I have pointed out in taking place in the horse trade—the exportation of horses from Ireland is increasing, and I think if the breed of horses was deteriorating it is scarcely likely the trade would be increasing. I would draw the opposite inference, that because the trade is increasing the breed must be improving; it must be worth the while of Englishmen and foreigners to come to this country to buy horses or they would not come.

7390. MR. LA TOUCHE.—How do you arrive at the value of a horse at £[illegible]?—I take the official figures; I would not venture to value them.

7391. DR. [illegible]?—Yes.

7392. Are you quite sure you have got that correctly; in the statistics you value horses of different ages at different prices and different valuations?—I have taken round numbers, five millions, for the 600,000 horses; it would not make much difference if you altered the valuation a little one way or the other.

7393. In 1860 or 1861 I collected some statistics

and, adopting Dr. Grimshaw's figures then, I arrived at £15 per horse, yearlings, two-year-olds, and three-year-olds, and the numbers of the respective ages [illegible]. It [illegible] the expenditure upon the article [illegible] ridiculously small. It would become about [illegible] per cent.

7391. I should like to ask you if the Committee or Council have any information showing which of the many schemes adopted by the Society was most popular with the horse breeders?—The Society is [illegible] collecting information on that point, but the returns are not complete. So far as they go, it is pretty much of an equality as to the schemes considered most popular. Some counties prefer one scheme and some another. When I speak of one scheme and another, I mean the system of subsidizing stallions is preferred in some counties, and the system of prizes for mares is preferred in other counties, and at the present moment the Society has in draft a scheme which would afford different counties opportunities of carrying out whichever scheme they preferred.

7392. And you propose for 1897 a new scheme?—It would be practically a choice of either of the schemes formerly in operation.

7393. Are the owners of stallions consulted as regards the popularity of the various schemes as well as the owners of mares?—I cannot say that they have been. I don't know to what extent we have obtained opinions from them.

7394. You are endeavouring to obtain the opinions of the owners of mares?—Well, they are the people for whose benefit the fund is devoted.

7395. Mr. WRENCH.—With the exception of these copies of the Surveys, are there any books belonging to the Society that would be likely to throw any light on the subject of the ancient Irish horse?—I have consulted other works, but I find they are for the [illegible] from the Royal Dublin Society's [illegible].

7396. So that the County Surveys are the only books available?—That is so. I might say that I noticed in one of those Surveys that in the year 1802 there was a scheme for the registration of stallions, and E. J. [illegible], who surveyed that county, recommended getting rid of what he described as the "breed of cart stallions"—that is the horse that pulls a [illegible] or a barrel of wine—and he proposed a system of registration, and that suitable stallions should be [illegible] a fee, except in the case of those recommended by the local Farming Society, in which case the fee should be remitted. That was nearly a century ago.

7397. The CHAIRMAN.—I suppose nothing more of him is known?—Nothing.

7398. Mr. WRENCH.—Have you any more information of that kind or anything of interest you have there?—It is contained through a great number of volumes, and I have not read them all through. I have read a large number, but not the whole lot.

7399. Mr. J. L. THOMAS.—It was not before 1888 that the Royal Dublin Society gave any prizes to thoroughbred stallions, the first inclusion of them [illegible] in 1888?—The scheme commenced in 1887 and 1888.

7400. But they were giving prizes in 1868 at the Horse Show?—The Horse Shows commenced in 1868, and that was the first year the Royal Dublin Society offered prizes for thoroughbred stallions. They gave Cups, Medals, and other gold medals in the [illegible] for draft stallions. [illegible] the Farming Society, discontinuing operations in 1868, the Society commenced them, and prizes were awarded in them up to the year 1888. The horses were for the most part agricultural horses; but I observe, in looking over the catalogues, there were occasionally thoroughbreds.

7401. There were occasionally?—Yes; and apparently hunters on some occasions. The system of giving prizes to horses at the spring shows was discontinued for a couple of years, and immediately afterwards the system of holding a show exclusively for horses commenced.

7402. In the scientific department of the Royal Dublin Society is there any information regarding the ancient Irish horse?—There is not; the best record is in the statistical Surveys.

7403. That was in the middle of the last century?—That was in the beginning of this century; most of the Surveys were published in the first five years of the century.

7404. Is there any information concerning the breeds of the 18th century?—No, there is not; these Surveys in some cases refer to what is called the old Irish horse, described as a "garron"—a [illegible] the native breed is frequently spoken of as a "garron."

7405. The CHAIRMAN.—Amongst all these different changes I think the limits of valuation have remained the same?—In certain counties it has been extended from £150 to £200, it being believed that the best class of mares would be found in those counties in the hands of persons of the higher valuations—a more suitable class of mares.

7406. About these local committees—they were entirely appointed?—Yes, entirely appointed.

7407. Has the Society ever considered whether it would be advisable to have any elected element in them?—You see the sum the Society has been dealing with—£100 per county is exceedingly small—and any system of election would be a costly system. I think the cost of election would exceed the £100.

7408. And for the future I understand you to say that the Society propose to give to these local committees the option of selecting which of the two schemes they like best?—That is the proposal; they have not yet gone into details; it is practically arranged for the coming season, but not quite definitely arranged.

7409. Supposing there was a larger Government grant, have you considered what would be the best way to administer it?—The Society has only dealt with the administration of this fund; what they would do as regards the administration of a larger fund is a contingency that has not arisen, and I could not offer any opinion.

7410. The Society, I suppose, would think itself capable of administering a larger fund?—That is rather a delicate question to answer.

7411. It has been suggested by a good many witnesses that money [illegible] should be expended—a large system of registration—can you give us any idea as to how that could be done [illegible] without any considerable expenditure?—Such a thing could not be carried out without very considerable expenditure.

7412. Probably you have not considered that?—No; the position of the Society has been that we get £3,200 for the thirty-two counties of Ireland.

7413. I was not asking you the question as representing the Society, merely as your own opinion?—Individually I have no opinion.

7414. Is there any other information you can give us, Mr. Moss?—I do not know that there is; if any should occur to the Commission as desirable I shall be happy to furnish it.

Dec. 4, 1896. Mr. R. J. Moss.

Mr. DAWSON A. MILWARD, Lavistown, Kilkenny, examined.

Mr. Dawson A. Milward.

7415. CHAIRMAN.—You live in the County of Kilkenny?—Yes.

7416. You are engaged in farming?—I have been since 1848.

7417. And engaged as a land agent?—Engaged as a land agent and very largely engaged in farming, and have been breeding horses.

7418. You breed yourself?—Yes; I have always

Mr. [illegible] Mr. [illegible] [illegible].

from breeding half-bred [illegible] from my [illegible] mares, and mostly with [illegible] horses, some of them in [illegible] with the half-bred.

7[illegible]. What do you sell them as?—For hunters, and some [illegible] carriage horses. A large number [illegible] into [illegible] good [illegible]; they are [illegible] horses.

7[illegible]. Is your part of the county suitable for horse breeding?—It has always had rather a good name. The south part of the county, which is called the W[illegible] [illegible], has always been noted for a good class of [illegible] horses. The north side is not quite so good, but at the same time [illegible] a good class of horse.

7[illegible]. Is it limestone soil?—The south [illegible] is all limestone, the north [illegible] is not.

7[illegible]. And you think the southern end is better than the northern end?—[illegible] good [illegible] in my opinion.

7[illegible]. You think the limestone soil is not necessary?—It has not been my experience that it is necessary. I may say I was [illegible] who wrote that [illegible] mentioned by Mr. [illegible] just now in 18[illegible], and I had my attention pretty well called to public horse breeding ever since, and I have been a member of the [illegible] Committee for many years.

7[illegible]. It is rather generally supposed that lime is necessary—do you know if the water [illegible]—[illegible] in the County of Kilkenny; the limestone [illegible] the [illegible] of the way [illegible].

7[illegible]. Does the river come from the same place?—They [illegible] in a [illegible] part of the country, and it is a hilly district, [illegible] nothing from drainage.

7[illegible]. Does the river rise in a limestone country?—Yes.

7[illegible]. And so it is possible there is lime in the water?—The water in the district [illegible] from the [illegible] of the hills and those hills [illegible] into the main river, which is a [illegible] river for many miles up, so it would not possibly [illegible] any lime from that.

7[illegible]. What is the general class of horse bred in your part of the country?—Very good; worth from £[illegible] to £[illegible]. They have [illegible] very much indeed. There is a large fair in Kilkenny, and you would not, perhaps, [illegible] three or four £[illegible] horses [illegible].

7[illegible]. To what do you attribute this?—To the [illegible] of mares [illegible] very much. I [illegible] have a good [illegible] buy her. I [illegible] good many horses in [illegible], which is the best fair in the country, and the foreigners almost always [illegible] the best of them.

7[illegible]. You think the farmers have been tempted by the higher prices they get for the mares?—[illegible] I don't think that the [illegible] of [illegible] by the small farmers is worth talking of. The [illegible] may get a [illegible] light weight, but the average horses in those fairs are altogether below [illegible]—[illegible] and delivery [illegible].

7[illegible]. But that [illegible] the price goes down much?—Very much.

7[illegible]. Do you think it does pay any small farmer to breed?—It cannot possibly; [illegible] at £[illegible] cannot pay them.

7[illegible]. Then what do they do it for?—They [illegible] and [illegible] them to the farm, without knowing what they are doing; [illegible] a [illegible] transaction certainly.

7[illegible]. Are there as many horses bred now as formerly?—I think so.

7[illegible]. What kind of mares do you breed from yourself?—The [illegible] half-bred mares—[illegible] heavy [illegible] as if a [illegible] class would go into a [illegible]—they have been [illegible] for my work.

7[illegible]. Do you always put them to a thoroughbred?—Generally. Some of the best [illegible] I have bred were by half-bred horses.

7[illegible]. What do you mean by half-bred horses [illegible] that cannot go into the Stud Book, [illegible] half-bred horse is [illegible] thoroughbred. He has a great many [illegible] of thoroughbred.

7[illegible]. Do you keep stallions yourself?—[illegible].

7[illegible]. How is your county off for stallions?—I think we have quite enough. I think the system of registration has [illegible] it a good deal, but I think it [illegible] well off.

7[illegible]. How has the registration affected it?—[illegible] on the Horse Breeding Committee in 18[illegible], [illegible] partly the origin of the [illegible], [illegible] might be well to give my opinion on that. In 18[illegible] I [illegible] the proposal that it would be [illegible] to give the money to mares, because we thought that there was plenty of stallions in the country, and that the stallion owners were able to take care of themselves. I was very much [illegible] at the time; but subsequently, in 18[illegible], that same proposition was adopted, and later in the [illegible] of the [illegible] change [illegible] has [illegible] in the [illegible] working of the Government grant. Since that I think that system has been [illegible] by the fact that the horses to be used are obliged to be registered. In the registration of those horses—

7[illegible]. Stallions?—Yes, I call them horses; in the registration they are liable to be [illegible] and also to be [illegible] for soundness. I think that the [illegible] question is a [illegible] beyond all doubt—that they should be inspected for soundness; but I am not prepared to say that the inspection for quality is fairly carried out or worth doing. I [illegible] the [illegible] of the thoroughbred show in Dublin, which are supposed to be the [illegible] class [illegible]—very much better than the horses [illegible] for Queen's premiums—horses that would [illegible] the [illegible] of Queen's premiums—that the judgments there were [illegible] and so up and down, that in my mind they have destroyed all confidence. I [illegible] the horse that won first prize this year, having [illegible] been [illegible] last year [illegible] and the [illegible] year [illegible] and so on. Then [illegible] a good deal to do with [illegible] the idea of registering, and prevented many from registering in the first place; the fee for registering was [illegible], but that has been done away with. The [illegible] should not be allowed to exhibit their [illegible] unless in [illegible] registered stallions, [illegible] badly. In Kilkenny there are [illegible] registered, and out of those [illegible] are serving at the [illegible], leaving only [illegible] horses in the county of Kilkenny—which is [illegible] the leading county in Ireland—to be used by the farmers under [illegible] regulation, because they charge only £[illegible]. In other counties I have the statistics showing very much the same sort of thing.

7[illegible]. Where did you get those from?—From the Register of Thoroughbred Stallions of the Royal Dublin Society for 18[illegible]. I have taken all the horses with their fees; the horses are given in each county, and the fee they charge is also given. In the county of Londonderry—take that as an example—[illegible] horse is registered, and the result is that no farmer in that county can [illegible] a [illegible] of any [illegible] or kind. The farmer might go outside the county or he [illegible] the chance, but in his own county he has not the chance. Therefore I say the registering system has rather broken down. The total number of horses that was put on the register was 2[illegible]; [illegible] of these were [illegible] charging over £[illegible], leaving only 1[illegible] horses in all Ireland from which those [illegible] could [illegible]. That, in my opinion, has tended to reduce the [illegible] mares [illegible] to a [illegible] extent. My experience of breeding horses has been that it is exceedingly difficult to judge from the looks of a stallion what he is going to do at stud, and my opinion is that the farmers judge by produce more than by appearance. A farmer would therefore be much better pleased to judge by produce than to be bound to go to one particular horse, and if he had his choice I think we should have a very much larger number of horses exhibited. It has been said by dealers, by owners of brood mares, and by many people, that we want more, we have plenty of stallions, and this with that [illegible] I started this system of trying to get money given to prizes [illegible]; but, as I said just now, [illegible] [illegible] by this registration [illegible] [illegible]. I have here the [illegible] [illegible], and [illegible] [illegible] this [illegible] of registration which I think has done the [illegible].

7442. You think the system as applied to [illegible] has not been as successful as it ought to be, from the fact that [illegible] [illegible] [illegible] enough?—Exactly [illegible] enough.

7443. You object to the system of registration as applied to stallions, and on account of the [illegible] for [illegible], but [illegible] [illegible] [illegible] good deal; I don't think the stallion owner likes to submit his horse to be examined, in other words.

7444. You would not do away with the examination for soundness?—No; I think that is absolutely necessary, and for the [illegible].

7445. And the horse being passed sound you would leave it to the farmer to go to the horse he likes best?—Yes. In my opinion the farmers of Ireland have got that [illegible] breed of horse [illegible] [illegible] [illegible] or [illegible], and I don't [illegible] [illegible]; if we could put a stop to these unsound horses. I have a map showing, as [illegible] and Wexford, the location of these horses.

7446. What map is this?—A map of Ireland on which I have [illegible] down the location of these horses—in Kilkenny the horses are nearly all in the north; the larger part is [illegible] [illegible], so that the [illegible] people have no opportunity of using the registered stallions. No farmer who wants his mare [illegible] [illegible] [illegible] [illegible] [illegible] [illegible] [illegible] [illegible] [illegible] [illegible] [illegible] [illegible] [illegible] [illegible] away and [illegible] there. My [illegible] [illegible] to the day they had; then, if the [illegible] [illegible], they [illegible] and [illegible]; if the [illegible] and [illegible] [illegible] [illegible] [illegible] [illegible] [illegible]. The registration, I think, has [illegible] the [illegible] [illegible] of the [illegible] of the [illegible] [illegible].

7447. Provided the horses were passed sound, you would leave it to supply and demand?—I should; I think any farmer who has [illegible] enough [illegible] [illegible] [illegible] [illegible] enough to go to a good stallion. I don't know whether you would like to take down the way these thoroughbred prizes were awarded.

7448. I don't think so—you mean prizes for thoroughbreds?—Prizes for the horses at the Horse Show; it is one horse one time, and another another time.

7449. Is that the same in every class?—The other classes you cannot judge in that way, because they [illegible] [illegible] [illegible].

7450. What classes were you speaking of?—The thoroughbred stallions; there is a class at the show for thoroughbred stallions. I happen to have one [illegible] here; there were two prizes given—one for [illegible] [illegible] under this scheme, [illegible] [illegible] [illegible] as [illegible] weight-carrying hunters—[illegible] [illegible] [illegible] [illegible] [illegible] [illegible] of that [illegible] [illegible] [illegible] [illegible] of stallions.

7451. I think that would be useful?—Well, in 1893 in the thoroughbred stallions [illegible] for the [illegible] [illegible], and [illegible] [illegible] there was £100 given to the three or prizes—[illegible] [illegible] got first, and [illegible] of [illegible] [illegible].

7452. Mr. Cleary.—What year was this?—1893, and Heart of Oak was also shown. In 1894 Heart of Oak [illegible], [illegible] [illegible], and [illegible] third; and amongst the others, Mont Carlo was also shown, but not mentioned. Next year Heart of Oak was first, King of Trumps second, and the Marshal taking the [illegible] [illegible] [illegible] [illegible] [illegible] [illegible] the year before for a Queen's Plate; Mont Carlo was also shown. In 1896 [illegible] got first, Mont Carlo [illegible], Heart of Oak third, thus reversing the judgment of previous year. In 1897 [illegible] was again first; [illegible], [illegible] [illegible] [illegible] for a Queen's Plate, was second, Heart of Oak was third, and Mont Carlo, highly commended and reserved. In 1898 [illegible] was first, Mont Carlo second, and Royal Marsh was third; Marchaway was highly commended, and Heart of Oak got nothing at all. In 1899 Marchaway got second prize, Telephone first, Royal Marsh third, and Ambition, M.P., and Victorious not mentioned; M.P. and Victorious were bought at large prices by the Dublin Society, to be sent out to the country as [illegible], Victorious having cost 400l. In 1900 Marchaway was put first, leaving Royal Marsh second. In 1901 Royal Marsh was first, Duke of Portland second, [illegible] third; Marchaway being highly commended, and M.P. not mentioned at all. In 1902 Royal Marsh was first, Red Prince second, Duke of Portland third, and Marchaway simply commended. That, I think, shows the ups and downs of stallion judging, and that, in my opinion, it is hardly very much to lose a stallion owner them showing as [illegible] [illegible] [illegible] [illegible] Queen's prizes.

7453. What do you suggest should be done?—I have suggested there should be no judging of stallions, letting the farmer to judge for himself.

7454. Then you object to prizes being given for stallions?—Let the prizes be given as before, things are the Dublin Society giving them and the Queen's premiums at £200.

7455. You object to them?—Yes; if a horse is really passed sound, let the farmer judge for himself.

7456. I don't understand exactly what it is you want?—I want all the money in the [illegible] [illegible] amongst the mares, and let the men owning these mares [illegible] to the local show, let them produce the [illegible] that the [illegible] [illegible], or foal at foot, has been got by a horse passed sound; let him judge for himself if he likes [illegible] registered or unregistered. I have had a [illegible] [illegible] with the [illegible] and I [illegible] with the [illegible]. I had [illegible], the [illegible] [illegible] to my yard one day, and he said, "I think these are the best [illegible] [illegible] I have seen in my life in one yard." They were got by a horse I had given 45l. for.

7457. What prevents the man now sending his [illegible]?—He must go to a registered horse.

7458. What has registration got to do with it, that that apparently does not great [illegible] in [illegible] as the horse [illegible]?—It would tend to show that registration has broken down.

7459. Lord Ardilaun.—I think you mean that the [illegible] of [illegible] the horses [illegible] being shown on this evidence?—Yes, that is what I wish to convey. In 1896 we had shows held in Dublin, [illegible], Cork, [illegible], and Belfast. I find some broken [illegible] all the way from Dublin to Cork, and from that to Belfast, and when they got to Belfast they were found to be good enough, while in Dublin and Cork they were rejected.

7460. Chairman.—What is good enough for Belfast is not half good enough for Cork?—That is it. I would [illegible] [illegible] [illegible] [illegible] [illegible] [illegible] [illegible] [illegible] [illegible] [illegible]. I have always said the [illegible] [illegible] [illegible] [illegible] [illegible] [illegible] [illegible] has been a mistake.

7461. Have you any other suggestions to make, as regards the Royal Dublin Society's Scheme?—I think that is a very important part of it. Thinking, and taking that I think it right to mention. Mr. More seemed not to understand why it was that in 1896 the number of registered horses had [illegible] so much, and I [illegible] to add the [illegible] of the [illegible] [illegible] [illegible] [illegible] [illegible] [illegible] [illegible] the

Mr. [illegible] [illegible] [illegible]

[illegible]

all prizes that all stallions must be registered; that is the reason of the great increase of those stallions that competed for the £50 prize were obliged to be registered; they never were registered before.

7464. Mr. Warren.—And all their stock?—Yes; the result was that brought them in; it runs up the number of registered stallions, but does not help us a bit in the way of breeding horses. A great deal has been said about Hackneys. I am not an advocate of the Hackney in any shape or form. I don't know anything about the Hackney, but I think it should be understood that no one has yet, as far as I am aware, and I have attended a good many meetings of the Royal Dublin Society. I don't think it has been suggested that any part of this £5,000 should be devoted to Hackneys.

7465. Chairman.—*Have you ever bred from anything but a thoroughbred?*—The Irish halfbred. I never bred from a Hackney. We have no Hackney that I am aware of in our county. Major Considine said there was one, but I don't know where he is.

7466. In your district is there a Clydesdale or cart horse?—There are one or two, and they are rather popular, but I don't think they are doing very much.

7467. You have never used them yourself?—No. I don't think the Royal Dublin Society ever intended to introduce the Hackney; in 1891 and 1894 they did give prizes for Hackneys, and it was understood if any person chose to bring a Hackney they should be allowed to come there and show them and allow the public to judge for themselves; there was such a cry got up that that was put a stop to, and now they repudiate them. If I wish to breed from a Hackney I don't see why I should be prevented.

7468. Do you wish to breed from a Hackney?—I think from the class of mares I see going to the fairs—strong thick little mares that would kick sixpence for a mile along a road—that a cross with the Hackney would do good; I don't think a cross with a Hackney would ever produce a hunter, and as to their being inferior animals I cannot understand it. From what I have seen I think they would not be so bad as they are made out.

7469. From what you know of the Hackney you don't think it would cause any deterioration?—My nephew has brought a Hackney from England, and he is as useful a cob as I have ever seen.

7470. Do you think from what you know that the Hackney blood would be likely to improve the breed of highclass harness and carriage horses?—I don't think it would; but those horses are a small item in proportion to all the horses—one per cent.

7471. What do you look on in your county as the most profitable class of horse to breed?—The good hunter is of course the most profitable, but very few can breed it. For one £30 or £40 horse I saw in the fair at Kilkenny, there were a couple of hundred from £20 to £25.

7472. If you can produce the hunter it would be the most profitable?—Undoubtedly.

7473. You think the introduction of two or three Hackneys would produce a better class hunter?—No, but it would produce a more saleable horse. What the farmer wants is a horse that will go to the dealer and get his money—a horse that there will be a good sale for; to suggest that every horse to be bred by every common farmer is to be a hunter, I cannot see it.

7474. Do you think the Hackney could be kept from contaminating other breeds?—We have admitted Clydesdales and I don't see they interfered. There was a gentleman said he had bred from a Clydesdale and sold it for a very large sum.

7475. I was not talking of Clydesdales—all I want is your opinion. You said you think it would be a good thing if there was a Hackney sire or two in every county, you think at the same time that the Hackney blood would be detrimental to the blood of hunters?—I don't think it would be actually detrimental; I don't think it is going to help the hunter, but I don't think the crossing in 100 years would be appreciable.

7476. Would not the blood be likely to spread largely?—There are 600,000 horses in Ireland; it would take a long time to permeate them.

7477. Are the sires in your part of the country sound in your opinion?—I think so.

7478. Are they good enough?—Quite good enough—I don't know though that £5,000 is going to make any great improvement, and unless we get more money it is very hard to do much with that.

7479. Do you think the system of registration has conduced to the disappearance of any unsound stallions?—I have not heard of the disappearance of one.

7480. Lord Ashtown.—Speaking of the Royal Dublin Society's Scheme, I gather you want to give the money to the mares?—Yes.

7481. How would you manage about settling whether a stallion was sound or unsound—some authority I suppose?—I should say it would be quite sufficient for the owner of the mare to be bound before he could exhibit his mare to procure from the stallion owner a certificate, and be in a position to say that the stallion had been proved for soundness.

7482. Most stallion owners have the certificate, I fancy?—They have; because I should say the Royal Dublin Society would have the right to slip in and have the horse examined.

7483. Would you publish a list of sound stallions?—I would not exactly publish them.

7484. You would have to have some list for the farmer?—I think the local Committees would be competent, and if they had any doubt to call on the Committee of the Royal Dublin Society and certify his examination by a Dublin veterinary surgeon.

7485. You don't approve of inspection on the principle that these sires had been put up and down in the Dublin Show?—Certainly. I don't think the inspection goes further than to say these sires are fit to get hunters. It sometimes has been said a sire is not suitable and when the sire has been shown to others they said he was quite suitable. I have in my mind a sire rejected by the Inspector of the Royal Dublin Society; to my mind he was suitable, and some of the members of the Committee said he was; but he was rejected on the ground of suitability—he was perfectly sound.

7486. You would allow a farmer to send his mare to a half-bred or thoroughbred, whichever he thought most suitable?—I would allow the farmer to be the judge, and in my opinion he is as good a judge as we shall ever get; he judges by produce.

7487. You would not bind him down to go to a thoroughbred?—No, I would not bind him to any particular sire.

7488. Mr. Gardner.—You spoke of breeding very good stock by a halfbred sire that you bought for £35. Can you tell us his breeding?—By a thoroughbred out of a Clydesdale mare. I bought him for the use of the tenants; I was at that time agent on a very large property, but I used him myself for three or four mares.

7489. He is what you call a draft horse?—Better than that—a clean legged horse, a good stepper.

7490. You would approve of that crossing?—If I could get another horse like him, I would never breed from anything else.

7491. Mr. Warren.—Have you ever bred from the produce of a thoroughbred horse, the second cross?—Yes, these very often run light. I think that when a light horse runs anyway contrary with you he is practically worth nothing; if he is a perfect beauty of a thoroughbred horse he is worth a good deal, but he must be a very good one.

7492. Do you think the heavy class of horse like the Clydesdale or Shire is required on Irish farms?—No, I don't think so; I have compared notes with Scotch farmers, I have had as many as fourteen pairs of horses working, and my opinion is that on the light land I had I was able to plough quite as deeply as they were.

7493. Which do you think it pays a small farmer to breed, a hunter or harness horse?—It is very seldom you get a hunter—the harness horse, I think.

7494. You think action is desirable in the harness horse?—Rather; it is most important.

7495. I think you said Ireland had succeeded in breeding better horses than any other country—you did not say to what cause you attributed that?—The Irish farmer has always had a dash of sport in him; he is fond of a good horse, and for that reason they have kept up this class of horse all through.

7496. Do you attribute it also to the soil and climate?—I don't think it has much to do with it—feeding is much more important.

7497. You know a great many parts of Ireland—in the country generally what class of farmers do you think breed the best horses?—Men from £200 to £400 valuation—big men beyond all question; I know a great deal of Cork and Limerick, and there the horses are much in the hands of big men.

7498. They are a small proportion as compared with the others?—They are; the multitude of horses are in the hands of small men, and that is what I want to improve; if I could do that I would be satisfied to allow the few to go on as they are.

7499. You think the few are able to study their own interests?—I think so.

7500. The CHAIRMAN.—The smaller farmer in your locality cannot breed at a profit?—I don't think they can pay for the service of a mare—rear the colt to two years old and sell it for £15 or £20. I would try and give them a horse that will get the £30 to £40—give them more action.

7501. They cannot breed at a profit now; you don't see any reason why they should not with a suitable sire?—Certainly; I think this buying of stallions by the Dublin Society has been rather a mistake. It has been suggested that we should go to England and buy mares. I don't see how that would be better; our experience of bringing over those stallions is not satisfactory. One was killed on the road, and another, bought for £850, was sold for £50, and so on; that sort of thing rather frightens me—I don't like it.

7502. Have you considered the question of Government [illegible]?—I have considered it; I don't know it would be a great advantage; I think it would be a good thing, but at the same time it is doubtful how it can be carried out. If they had not a demand for the refuse horses I don't know what they would do with them. Everybody must have refuse; I don't think any man can breed more than one good horse out of every two; if he does that he is very lucky. The refuse would hardly be good enough for troopers, and what they would do with them I could not tell.

7503. Assuming there was any grant of money, in what way do you think it would be best expended?—I think put in the hands of local committees, to hold shows and encourage the farmers with hunting prizes. It is nonsense giving £5 prizes; it doesn't induce any man to keep a mare. If they gave £15 or £20 in two or three districts it would be such an inducement as to induce a lot of farmers to compete for them. In that way we could get the mares kept, if we could see the chance of getting £30 or £40.

7504. You think the money should be expended in prizes for mares?—Yes; I have thought so for a good many years, and at the show I [illegible] that I thought that was the great thing. I only got second prize because I gave my opinion very strongly. Poor Mr. [illegible] told me that was the reason.

7505. You have nothing else to say?—Thank you. I think I must have exhausted you—I know I nearly have myself.

Mr. P. [illegible], Ballyraskin, Callan, examined.

7506. CHAIRMAN.—You live in the County Kilkenny?—Yes, sir, South Kilkenny, very near the borders of Tipperary.

7507. And are you engaged in farming?—Yes, sir.

7508. Do you breed horses yourself?—I do, three or four foals every year.

7509. And do you buy also?—I do, from twenty to thirty horses every year.

7510. Do you buy all over the country?—Generally in the district I spoke of, South Kilkenny and East Tipperary.

7511. What kind of horses do you breed yourself?—Well, I aim at producing hunters, and I was fairly successful.

7512. What do you consider the most profitable kind of horse to breed?—The thoroughbred horse. Sometimes I have bred from horses that are not in the stud book, but practically thoroughbred horses. There are two or three in the locality I speak of that I consider as good as any thoroughbred horse to breed from.

7513. What kind of mares do you use?—Well-bred mares with size and substance about them.

7514. And you aim at producing hunters?—Yes.

7515. And if they are not good enough for hunters they sell as harness horses?—If not good enough for hunters I sell them as carriage horses, and if not I sell them for troopers.

7516. Do the farmers about you aim at producing hunters?—Yes, the farmers of South Kilkenny and East Tipperary. They are principally sold at the fair of Clonmel. Mr. Milward made an observation about Kilkenny; but in the fair of Kilkenny they only get the refuse, because the best of the colts in South Kilkenny go to Clonmel, and the dealers count the county, so it is only the refuse of the county that goes to Kilkenny.

7517. The animals in the fair at Kilkenny you would not consider a fair sample of the produce of the county?—No.

7518. Do you buy generally in the fairs, or how do you buy?—Sometimes in the fairs and sometimes at the houses.

7519. To whom do you sell?—I make a hunter, and sometimes I sell to gentlemen who make hunters of them and sometimes to dealers.

7520. Do you sell generally to the locality or to dealers?—Both.

7521. How is your part of the country off for stallions?—Well, fairly well off, but we might be better off.

7522. Are there any half-bred stallions?—There are a good number.

7523. Do you approve of them?—If you mean by a half-bred stallion a horse that is got between a thoroughbred horse and a Clydesdale, I certainly would not approve of him under any conditions, but there are a good many horses called half-bred horses that are really almost thoroughbred horses, and I would approve of them; I have used them successfully; there are two or three in the locality at present, very successful ones.

7524. Are there any Clydesdale stallions in your part of the country?—Yes; but they are not used in the south of Kilkenny or east of Tipperary. In north Kilkenny there are some Clydesdale stallions.

7525. Do you think the farmers generally about you take sufficient care to mate their mares to suitable stallions?—Generally speaking I think they do. In south Kilkenny they take an interest in horse-breeding and have bred a good class of horse there for a number of years.

7526. Is the Royal Dublin Society's scheme in operation?—Yes; I am a member of the committee myself.

7527. Do you think it has done good?—Well, I think so.

[illegible]

7569. Have you found that the price of horses has much deteriorated in your district?—The price of a good well-bred horse has not deteriorated at all, but the price of the inferior horse, of the weed or screw, has deteriorated more than 50 per cent. in the last six or seven years.

7570. Has the price of the ordinary light-weight harness horse deteriorated?—No; if it is a really good harness horse it has not.

7571. Then what class of horse do you think has deteriorated, the horse that is a little worse than a screw?—Yes.

7572. Mr. Wrench.—You think the good harness horse has held his own as price?—I think so, sir.

7573. Do you think Hackney bred is improving?—In numbers it has, but in quality it has not.

7574. The other Hackney you mentioned, where did he stand?—Almost in the same district, three or four miles away from that.

7575. Also in Waterford or Kilkenny?—It is in Tipperary, in the town of Carrick-on-Suir.

7576. But you are not sure it is a Hackney?—I am not; I never saw the card of pedigree; it is only hearsay, but I saw Mr. Malcolmson's Hackney.

7577. And they have only been a short time in the country?—Only two years.

7578. You have had no opportunity of judging what their stock would turn out?—Except what I could judge from the foals.

7579. Would you be inclined to go further and examine the stallions; you have heard it suggested that all horses should be registered; do you think that a good thing?—I do.

7580. And do you think that could be carried out in the country without too much trouble?—I think so.

7581. Do you think that would put up the price of horses if you were always able to produce a certificate and if the breeding could be traced?—I think so [illegible]; it is always an object with them to know [illegible].

7582. Chairman.—How do you think such a general system of registration could be carried out?—I think it could be carried out through the County Committees at present—the County Committees appointed under the Royal Dublin Society. Of course, it would need a little more than at present. There would have to be some local officials appointed, but I think it would be carried out through them.

7583. It would have to be compulsory—the universal registration of horses that Mr. Wrench was speaking about?

7584. Mr. Wrench.—Mares and all?—That would involve a great lot of machinery.

7585. Chairman.—Your answer to Mr. Wrench was intended to apply to stallions only?—Stallions only.

7586. Anything else you would like to say to the Commission?—No; I don't think there is.

Mr. H. [illegible], [illegible], examined.

7587. Chairman.—You live in the county Longford, I think?—Yes, sir.

7588. Have you personal experience of horse-breeding?—I have, for over 21 years.

7589. Do you keep stallions yourself?—Yes.

7590. Are they registered under the Royal Dublin Society's scheme?—Three of them.

7591. How many do you keep?—Five.

7592. Three of the five are registered. Do you think the scheme of registration has done good?—I think it has done a lot of good, and it is absolutely necessary to continue it if you want to improve the breed of horses.

7593. Do you think it ought to be carried further—all horses?—All sires, in my opinion, should be registered after passing a veterinary surgeon's examination.

7594. Do you mean that if they did not pass the veterinary surgeon's examination they should not be allowed to serve?—Should not be allowed to serve. It is the only possible way you can relieve the small farmers from these mongrels that almost [illegible] for three months of the year. If you give the farmer any encouragement or assistance he won't [illegible]. Sometimes they make cheaper bargains, and some of these people are caught in the market through [illegible] and they might [illegible] for going in an unsuitable [illegible]. If these sires were cut in the way you would [illegible] suitable [illegible] and would [illegible] on the [illegible] side.

7595. Do you find [illegible] horses more popular with the farmers?—[illegible] a bit more popular.

7596. How many mares do you keep yourself for breeding purposes?—From five to seven, and more than I have eight or nine, according as I breed a [illegible].

7597. What kind of mares are they?—Four thoroughbreds.

7598. And you breed thoroughbred stock?—Yes, and [illegible].

7599. What are the others?—The others are half-bred mares, mares that I work on the farm, and if I get a good filly I make a [illegible], and [illegible] them [illegible] of age.

7600. What do you expect to get out of them?—If I get a good one he will make a hunter, if not he is bound to make a working horse to sell to the English dealers.

7601. Do you breed from two-year-olds yourself?—Occasionally, if I get a good strong one, that is, one well-grown, that develops early. I take a foal off her as a two-year-old and I [illegible] the next year's rest, and I have a foal for her again and a foal comes to [illegible] again.

7602. Are there many horses in your district?—A great number.

7603. What are they mostly?—The majority are hunters. A great number are what you call medium or high class working horses. They are sold to the northern [illegible] who feed them for six or eight months and sell them to Wimbush or [illegible]. They are sold in Mullingar [illegible] and all around, two, three-year-old colts. Sometimes a farmer keeps one until it is a four-year-old. If he has a son [illegible] capable of riding it himself, he will keep him and break him, and sell him for a hunter [illegible]. If a buyer can beat the county Longford and has a fair turn of speed he will go with any hounds in the world.

7604. Do they sell them as hunters or [illegible]?—They sell them to both; but mostly the principal ones with [illegible] anything worth a big one; [illegible] known that they are attended by the principal dealers.

7605. How is your country supplied with stallions?—Fairly [illegible].

7606. Are there any half-bred stallions?—Yes, a good many of them, but they are a [illegible], the [illegible] and those half-breds. I have a half-bred [illegible] myself, and he is a very old horse now and [illegible], he has [illegible] largely [illegible] in any horse in Ireland and has got a good class of hunter and harness horse, a good [illegible] horse.

7607. Are there any pure bred [illegible] or Hackney stallions?—[illegible] there was one Hackney stallion came to [illegible] years ago, but he has gone away.

7608. Why did he go away?—[illegible] it is [illegible] a man changes his stallion, my [illegible] would not have a Hackney; they are very fond of a nice good horse, and [illegible] him as any county in Ireland.

[illegible]
Mr. E. Reynolds.

7609. You never used the Hackney [illegible] yourself?—No, [illegible] not.

7610. Or anything except a thoroughbred?—[illegible] half-bred. I [illegible] years ago to Yorkshire and bought a thoroughbred [illegible] horse; he was a prize taker in the Yorkshire Stud Book; he has done very well in my locality, and [illegible] good [illegible]. I [illegible] a [illegible] of the [illegible]—I have [illegible] as far as my [illegible] goes they are a fair good lot with good [illegible] and plenty of bone, and I consider [illegible] are just as suitable [illegible] to bring [illegible] small fillies—to put strength into them—[illegible] if they were back again to the thoroughbred horse it would not be [illegible] in them as wellness.

7611. You think it would be an improvement?—I [illegible] so. I have [illegible] the [illegible] and a great number of farmers [illegible] have approved of him.

7612. When did you buy this horse?—Five years ago, and some of the [illegible] did [illegible] as [illegible] as [illegible] the [illegible]; [illegible] who did not want to keep them, [illegible] to the [illegible].

7613. And those fillies you have by this horse?—I [illegible] to keep them.

7614. Do you propose to put them to a thoroughbred horse?—I have only one filly, but I will try it.

7615. Your idea would be that the introduction of this strain of blood would improve the mares and [illegible] more likely to produce good [illegible]?—I would not go so far as to say [illegible] that it would bring it back a little more [illegible], so that you can go back again to the thoroughbred.

7616. Are the [illegible] in your district inclined to sell their [illegible] and breed [illegible]?—[illegible] they will sell all their good young mares [illegible] year old and four years old [illegible] I found [illegible] to try to breed from [illegible] the time I [illegible]. I find [illegible] inclined to [illegible] their young mares, [illegible] good [illegible] they were for [illegible] till they go [illegible] to maturity, and if a [illegible] a fairly good [illegible] for [illegible], and the [illegible] more [illegible] to [illegible] when she comes of age.

7617. Do you think the young stock in [illegible] part of the country has improved of late?—I do. They have kept up very well, comparatively speaking. As a proof that they are fairly good, they are [illegible] by [illegible] dealers. They [illegible] in the [illegible] but they [illegible] and very frequently they would [illegible] of two-year olds or one and a half-year olds to bring back to the [illegible] breeder.

7618. Are the prices kept up?—[illegible] a good horse or the making of a good one.

7619. [illegible] prices as good as it used to be?—It is [illegible].

7620. Do the small farmers breed much about you?—They do; they are very fond of breeding, and the very small farmer [illegible] and [illegible] to pay his little [illegible], and his horse [illegible] all the same for him. There are the [illegible] that would require a little assistance, but I don't think that you could expect a [illegible] breed of high-class hunters [illegible] from them, but you would get a useful horse. You might get some of them [illegible], they will [illegible] useful horses [illegible] a good size.

7621. What kind of a [illegible] do you think would be most useful?—I think a half-bred horse—say a horse with one strain or two from the thoroughbred horse, if his mother was of a good family—would be the best. They want to have them to work a little at a two-year old on the farm, and let them grow up for years before they sell them. An English [illegible] who want buy them under four and a half years old, and very few [illegible] in [illegible]. These [illegible] have not [illegible] and a [illegible] of them. If they put a thoroughbred horse [illegible] not [illegible]. They have [illegible] their farms, and worked [illegible] and the thoroughbred is [illegible], the only way they can do is to [illegible] and then they are no use for anything [illegible] wards.

7622. Lord Arthur [illegible].—When [illegible] Three registered thoroughbreds and the half-bred horse and the coaching horse.

7623. Which do you find most patronised?—The half-bred.

7624. You think the half-bred sire is the most useful in your district?—To a farmer he is; they are [illegible] to keep their produce a little longer, and can work [illegible] and use it.

7625. You think it pays a farmer best in your district to breed from a half-bred sire?—It is better for a farmer who has good luck to breed from a thoroughbred horse.

7626. You know a farmer that has bred that [illegible] by a [illegible] and [illegible]?—Yes; but in the small farmer who [illegible] up to the time it is [illegible], and [illegible], a thoroughbred [illegible] the produce of it, because [illegible]; he is [illegible].

7627. When [illegible] you get the Yorkshire coach horse?—I was recommended by some of the principal English dealers. I could not get a half-bred horse, and they said to get [illegible] a pure-bred horse. I went and got a horse in the Yorkshire stud book. I got a [illegible] looking [illegible]. I wanted to get a [illegible] horse, with clean legs, no hair, light [illegible], and good shoulders. He was five year old when I bought him and I gave a long price for him.

7628. You find the farmers patronise him?—They do; they admire him very much. Some of them are more than satisfied with the produce of the first. They have [illegible] and [illegible]; [illegible] good [illegible] a half-year old, and good [illegible] horse.

7629. Mr. C[illegible].—[illegible] the [illegible] of your half-bred sire bred?—There is only one half-bred horse; his dam was by [illegible], by Lord Clonmell's horse.

7630. What sort of [illegible] is the [illegible]?—His dam was by [illegible], and grandam by [illegible] as far as I can [illegible]; the [illegible] is by Lord [illegible] that [illegible], and [illegible] was by [illegible].

7631. You spoke of [illegible] old, what sort are the produce?—They [illegible]; and [illegible] I found the fillies that had [illegible] there were five fillies, and I found the three that I had [illegible] in as good condition and looking as well [illegible].

7632. Mr. La Touche.—What do you do with the [illegible] stock yourself that you [illegible] up to four and a half-year, or if I have a good [illegible] to the [illegible], or a good-looking horse [illegible] and [illegible] him as a hunter.

7633. Which do you find you get the best price for?—The produce of the thoroughbred horse.

7634. Do you think the average value of the produce of the thoroughbred horse is higher than the produce of anything else?—You get as much for one as [illegible] three or four years as for [illegible].

7635. Mr. Watson.—You keep [illegible] stallions [illegible] registered and two [illegible]?—Yes.

7636. Which do you always [illegible]?—The registered horses.

7637. And you think it is an advantage to have them registered?—I believe it is a very great advantage, and I believe it has caused a very great improvement since they began to register.

7638. Would you like to register your [illegible]?—If it was possible I would, but no horse could be registered up to their [illegible] was a thoroughbred in Weatherby's Stud Book.

7639. Would you approve of registering other [illegible]

horses [illegible] would, and I think it is the only way you can possibly protect the small farmer in getting rid of the mongrels.

7640. Which do you find pays best—breeding the thoroughbred or half-bred?—It depends on the class of man who breeds.

7641. I mean yourself?—Oh, thoroughbreds.

7642. You alluded to a Hackney having been in your district; can you tell me his name?—I don't know his name; a gentleman from England brought him over, Mr. Graham; he was supposed to be a prize winner; he had a lot of mares served his work.

7643. You are not sure he was a Hackney?—He was said to be.

7644. The small farmers breed a good deal about you?—They do.

7645. And you think they are the men who want most help?—What is it you want to get rid of bad horses out of the country.

7646. Would it be possible to stop them breeding horses?—I don't think it would; I think they would be quite satisfied to go on breeding, and if there was any encouragement given in the way of giving them a free sire, some little assistance given in that registered sire I think it would help them.

7647. And you think it would be well spent money?—I do.

7648. I suppose you don't think it would be possible for them to breed high class hunters or [illegible] horses?—You might get a few of them, but in an average you would not.

7649. What kind of horses would pay them best to breed?—Useful horses to go in harness or for [illegible] purposes, or the like of that.

7650. Good-sellers?—Good [illegible] light harness horse.

7651. They want a hardy class of horses to get early some?—They do want a hardy class of horse, and the mongrels are fairly hardy; they are not coarse.

7652. Do they leave their foals out in the winter?—The greater part of them let them run out, and if they get enough to eat, I would sooner have that than shut them up in a small house.

7653. They don't take them inside the dwelling house in Longford?—No, but they would not be [illegible] bring in a good one.

7654. CHAIRMAN.—Anything you would like to say to the Commission?—I would register the half-bred horse that would be considered suitable, and would have undergone a veterinary surgeon's examination. Then if it is possible, or there is any means of doing it, the money given at present by the Royal Dublin Society should be increased, because only five or six men will get a portion of it. £50 is given to my county; that is divided among four or five farmers for mares, and then something for foals—that is not worth any man's while to keep his day and go eight or nine miles for the chance of that; you would get a good [illegible] who would spend it all before he got back; it is not worth it.

7655. They want more money?—I think if you gave money for the young mares and then I would give a free nomination to the selected sire; the money you are giving is only going to keep up six men. Under my plan there would be forty or fifty free nominations and the men would take it in preference. I would let them go to any sire if he was registered, but [illegible] you will get those farmers to [illegible] and as good judges what to breed as any man in Ireland; the only thing that prevents them is want of money.

7656. And registration you think should be granted if the horse passes sound?—If the horse passes sound.

7657. The question of suitability ought not to come in?—Certainly, suitability. I would register him if he has all the marks and proper qualities about him to be a sire and had a sound veterinary surgeon's certificate.

7658. And also you would admit half-bred horses provided they passed sound and suitable?—If they passed sound and suitable, for at present you have a very fair foundation with a number of thoroughbred sires, and it is in order to keep that alive and keep it in working order.

7659. Mr. [illegible].—Would you approve of any horse being allowed to serve who is not registered?—If he registered himself as a good, clear and fond [illegible], and his position was good, and his certificate made a representation to the Royal Dublin Society and [illegible] that he [illegible], there is nothing in the world can be under [illegible] that, the good or bad [illegible] of a [illegible] in a district; you cannot keep it going.

7660. I am not referring to the Royal Dublin Society; but would you make it compulsory that every entire horse should be inspected as regards soundness before he was allowed to cover a mare?—I would.

7661. Lord ASHTOWN.—And to keep the entire question alive you would want some other men to refuse the fillies?—Yes.

7662. Do you think the fillies are too light?—A good many of them are too light, and if you have not a fifty £ to make a considerable or every [illegible] is in [illegible] the world; but at the same time a farmer might take a [illegible] out of it for a couple of years, and take a foal out of it, and then some when four or five years old might have useful mare in her class and use live when three years old.

7663. Mr. GAMBLE.—Have you seen any Hackney produce from the west in your district?—I saw some represented to be that. There are a number of them come up, and hundreds of them are sold in the different fairs the last month or so. I asked some of the men why they had not better foals. I generally buy a couple myself and let them run round until they come of age. I said "Why have you not better foals?" "Oh, bad luck to the Hackneys," said he. That was the only answer.

7664. Mr. WILSON.—You could not tell whether they were Hackney produce or not?—No; I only heard that.

Mr. THOMAS M'CORMACK, [illegible], examined.

7665. CHAIRMAN.—You live in the Co. Longford?—I live quite close to it, just on the border, but I have some land in the Co. Longford.

7666. Is your district a horse-breeding district?—Yes.

7667. Do the small farmers breed much?—They do a good deal.

7668. What class of mares are generally bred from in your part of the country?—There are some very good mares in the hands of farmers who are pretty extensive, and the small farmers have a small, weedy bad class of mare, but we have some very good mares in the hands of farmers that have a considerable portion of land.

7669. How is your district off for stallions?—It is fairly well off for thoroughbred stallions, but we have no good half-bred stallions, at least very few.

7670. Have you any pure-bred stallions of any other kind except the thoroughbred?—Not that I know of.

7671. What does your district produce mainly, hunters or harness horses?—Both; that is with the good class of mares.

7672. What do these other farmers produce?—At present they have a wretched class of animals, the fairs are full of them, they cannot be sold, they are apparently useless for any purpose.

7673. Can they produce them at a profit?—Oh, no, they cannot get rid of them at present.

7674. And yet they go on breeding?—They have bred from these mongrel horses for many years past;

man that have seen the filly of it, and I don't think they are breeding so much this last year or two.

7675. Are there any difficulties in the country that would make their horses unfit?—No; they are liable [illegible] for a horse to put more size into them and action into [illegible] the produce.

7676. What kind of a stallion do you think would be most suitable?—I think a good half-bred stallion.

7677. Is the Royal Dublin Society's Scheme in operation about you?—It is.

7678. What has been the effect of it?—I think it has had a very good effect.

7679. You approve of it?—I do, decidedly.

7680. Do you think the farmers have a tendency to sell their best mares?—They have, I think; the foreign buyers have made a lot of harm, buying good fillies for foreigners; they go away, and we never see them again.

7681. Do you know are they kept as brood mares or bought by foreign Governments?—The three-year-olds are bought by foreigners now, as I don't believe this Government will buy from these three-year-olds, and the best three-year-olds are being sent away.

7682. Does that go on to a great extent?—Every good three-year-old filly that is raised is sold; there is plenty of demand for them.

7683. Do you think that the produce generally at your part of the country is worse than it used to be, or better?—I think it is [illegible] the same with a good class of mare served by a thoroughbred horse, but I certainly think the half-bred animals bred from mongrel horses have deteriorated considerably.

7684. Mr. La Touche.—Have you any experience of Hackneys?—No, I have never seen a Hackney in my part of the country, either sire or produce.

7685. Do many dealers of the Connemara ponies come up to the County Longford?—A good many.

7686. Not many now, though?—Yes.

7687. Brought there and sold?

7688. Noticed any marked improvement in them for the last two or three years?—[illegible] for the last two or three years.

7689. Why?—I have heard a good many other horses [illegible].

7690. Have you observed any Clydesdale, Hackney blood, or the crosses?—They always come up as fillies, and I really have not seen where they have been; they come up [illegible], and the people about pick them up.

7691. Do you know if there is any difference in the price?—Well, I have not asked the price this year, I have not seen them sold there.

7692. Chairman.—What do they use these Connemara ponies for?—They make very nice cobs and good trappers, good hardy breed, some of them are sold for very good prices.

7693. What size are they?—They are up to 14 hands, 14.2 some of them.

7694. Do the small farmers breed from them at all?—No, not very much.

7695. Just use them for their own farm purposes?—Yes.

7696. Can you make any suggestion how these farmers could be induced to keep their best mares to breed from instead of selling them?—I would be greatly inclined to give the money that is distributed to the young mares to encourage people to keep them three or four-year-olds if possible, and I think if they were offered a good prize they would keep them, and then there would be a chance of their being bought as hunters when four or five-year-old by men who won't buy them as three-year-olds.

7697. Do you approve of breeding from two-year-olds?—I would on good land, but I would not allow them to be bred from if they are put to work. I think the small farmer that works the animal and breeds from her, produces an inferior animal, and destroys the mare itself.

7698. Anything else you would like to suggest to the Commission?—No, my lord, except I heard a good deal of the registration, and I think that is one of the principal points that should be adhered to. I don't think a horse should be absolutely in the power of the inspector so far as his appearance is concerned, but I certainly would have every horse that a man is getting a prize for having a mare put to, I would have him registered as sound.

7699. You think a man ought not to be allowed to keep a stallion as a matter of profit without a certificate of soundness?—I do; and I think if these men were asked to produce their horses for registration they would do so if they believed him sound, and the unsound horses would soon go out.

7700. Mr. Wrench.—Do you think these small farmers who breed such bad animals now need attention?—I do.

7701. And the class of animal that pays them best is something they can work on the farm with good action, and can sell afterwards?—Yes.

7702. I think you said action is essential?—Oh, certainly.

7703. Helps to sell them?—It does.

Mr. T. M. Cahan, Wildington, Kinnegad, examined.

7704. Chairman.—You live at Wildington, King's County?—It is just in the County Meath, bordering on the King's County.

7705. Are you pretty well acquainted with this district?—The district where I am pretty well acquainted with; I am acquainted with these four counties, Kildare, Westmeath, Meath, and King's County.

7706. You breed horses yourself?—Yes, I do.

7707. Thoroughbreds, mainly?—Yes, and halfbreds.

7708. Have you a number of your own?—I have a half-bred stallion for my own use.

7709. And how many thoroughbred mares?—I have two thoroughbred mares.

7710. And how many others?—I have seven or eight or ten; I had ten foals this year.

7711. And putting aside the thoroughbred stock, what do you aim at producing?—I put the thoroughbred mares to the thoroughbred horse.

7712. Mr. [illegible].—What do you aim at producing [illegible] a thoroughbred?—[illegible] had a thoroughbred [illegible] except I am breeding from by a thoroughbred horse.

7713. Chairman.—What do you put the other mares to?—The principal mares I put to the thoroughbred horse, and the light ones to my half-bred horse.

7714. And what is the produce generally sold as, or do you keep them yourself?—I sell them at [illegible] when they come to five years old mostly as hunters; I sell a few of them at two years old, and keep those till five years old, and then if they are sound and good and make a [illegible]. I think [illegible] but I don't think they specially [illegible] to use them as a trapper or harness horse.

7715. Are there a great many horses bred in your part of the country?—Yes; nearly every farmer about me produces a foal every year.

7716. What class of mares have they got?—The small farmers have very common mares, about 14 hands or 15.2 high, rather [illegible] bad [illegible]; they are bred from halfbred horses. I don't think we have a great half-bred horse in the district.

7717. Are you pretty well off for stallions in that part of the country?—Fairly well off for thoroughbred horses, but badly off for half-breds.

7718. Any think any thoroughbred stallions or Hackneys or anything of that kind in the country?—The

[illegible]

7750. Did you know any [illegible] of the result of that cross yourself?—No.

7751. Have you seen any of those horses of Connemara ponies working up in England?—I have not seen any of them lately; some years ago I used to see them working about the docks.

7752. You have not seen any lately?—I have not.

7753. Do you think that the result of this Hackney cross with the ordinary mare would be to get a good sort of a harness horse in fact?—Yes, I think so, with those [illegible] mares; I am sure they would be valuable.

7754. You have heard that English carriage horse dealers have strongly condemned the introduction of the Hackney blood?—I have heard it; I am only giving my own opinion.

7755. Mr. Carew.—You have no experience of it otherwise?—No more.

7756. Only what you saw at Mr. Wrench's?—Yes, I saw some very nice horses there.

7757. Mr. Wrench.—As a fact, Mr. Green, in my action one of the first things looked for?—It is, I [illegible] again with you.

7758. Then with regard to the class of horses you try to breed, you think that when a dealer comes to your door you want something with size and substance that looks up to a lot of weight?—Exactly.

7759. Unless you have an animal that looks up to the weight you would not get a good price?—No.

7760. And have you found it necessary to introduce cart blood in order to get that?—Yes, and it turned out very successful.

7761. You bring in a Clydesdale mare and cross again with a thoroughbred?—The Clydesdale is the only thing we have to give us size. I [illegible] in my district a pure bred Clydesdale except Chestnut's, and he is not at all so [illegible] or anything like the horses I saw in the Dublin Show; he is a coarser horse, but I can [illegible] he is pure bred, and has produced very good [illegible] from common mares about.

7762. Do you know whether the Clydesdale blood has been in your country for a long time or not?—It has been up in my country at [illegible] for nearly a century; it must be eighty or ninety years ago since the [illegible] came in there.

7763. How were the Clydesdale horses brought over originally?—The [illegible] [illegible], Scotchmen who came over and brought a great lot of them, they are there still; they took a lot of the land and farmed very extensively, and brought over all their work horses and farm horses, and used to import Clydesdale stallions now and again.

7764. And that is really how the Clydesdale blood came into that district?—That is how the Clydesdale blood came into that district, and most of the big horses about me have a drop of it, being descended from them.

7765. And it is in breeding from that class of mares that you have got the biggest prices for the produce?—Yes, when they have a couple of crosses.

7766. And you think that a good half-bred sire is very much wanted in your part of the country?—I [illegible] any more of it.

7767. And you would register them as well as thoroughbreds?—I would register any stallion of any breed, and I would have an inspector going along it; I would insist on having on the certificate whether they are free from hereditary unsoundness; however he is affected I would have it specified there, and would leave it to the breeder then to make his choice to breed from him or not and not be taking it from the veterinary surgeon.

7768. Chairman.—What would the small farmer about you afford to pay for the service?—They will give £1 for a good horse; they are very keen about getting a good marketable horse.

7769. Would it pay a man to buy and introduce thoroughly good half-bred sires such as you would like to see there?—I think it would. I think his mileage fees would fill—a good stout horse of this pattern and good constitution. I don't approve of those big mules and big shoulders and bad hocks and hips. I say I would like them as natural as good shape, like Ingalls' like.

7770. I gather from you then you think that so far as the Hackney blood is concerned it would not be an improvement in the getting of hunters or high class carriage horses?—I think they are not so good for the saddle, carrying a man; but I am certain that [illegible] of action would be of great service, unquestionably.

7771. You think amongst the smaller farmer who has no suitable mare you would get more suitable produce?—Yes; and some of the larger farmers too want it.

7772. Have you ever considered at all whether if the Hackney was once introduced in that way it may not permeate through the country so as to deteriorate the hunters produced there?—I think the people would be keen enough to take care of themselves.

7773. You think it would be possible for men to prevent [illegible]—that it would be easily managed?—I think so; I think they would be very careful; I would very much rather not register the Hackney, but I think the majority of farmers are well able to take care of themselves.

7774. We have had very different opinions?—I am sure there is a diversity of opinion.

7775. Have you any suggestions to make to the Commission as to what you think anything should be done to improve the production of horses?—I think we are pretty well off about thoroughbred horses, and I would like to see more encouragement given to the half-bred, for the purpose of keeping size and bone and strength in the horses; if you breed a good big stout mare and cross her with a half-bred horse you will have plenty of quality in the second generation; no judge, no one could tell that there was any of the cart in them.

7776. What you think is chiefly wanted is substance?—It is.

7777. Is it easy to get the quality back again afterwards?—It is; we want substance.

through Mr. Wrench, to get a Hackney down in my neighbourhood under the Congested Districts Board, and they had not the money at the time.

7784. Mr. Wrench.—You were not sufficiently [illegible] and could not tell you that, but we wanted a horse in that country, for we have some disgraceful [illegible].

7785. Chairman.—What is the general kind of mare that the farmers possess?—The very worst description, low-sized, long-backed mares; they are generally sold to local dealers, and get the pit ponies. You could buy a whole field of them at [illegible] for £3 [illegible]. All the good mares in the country are in the [illegible] district, and they are in the hands of the [illegible] farmers.

7786. What kind of sires do those mares [illegible]?—We had a brute called [illegible] that came over from an English dealer, who swapped him for a good-looking country mare. He was standing at Ballyhaunis.

7787. What sort of a horse was he?—A thoroughbred, and about 15 hands. He had a very long pedigree. I think the service fee was taken out in all kinds—potatoes and everything like that—from the small farmers.

7788. Would you think that a suitable kind of horse to mate with those mares?—Certainly not. I think he was the greatest curse in the country.

7789. What do you think is the most suitable kind of sire?—At the present moment, I think the Hackney for those small mares would be the better, provided the same horse was not left in the country too long—that he got shifted. And I would have given longer time after a time when the old mares were dropping out, the young mares that were springing up would be more suitable for crossing with the Hackney again, and making a larger [illegible] for the same. Having [illegible] left in the country, that they would not [illegible] the [illegible]. And even by the Hackney I would prefer a good half-bred horse, but it is very hard to make any improvement with the mares we have. If there was any way of getting Government assistance to procure good mares for the country, it would be a great improvement. If we had a Government stud there that we could get any kind of mares for the farmers it would be a great improvement.

7790. You think the general type of mares in the country is not worth preserving?—I don't see how they can be improved. They are [illegible] weedy [illegible]—[illegible] of them. There are, of course, among the large farmers some very good and excellent mares, and in one or two cases, among the small farmers, where they have mares that have been known to breed good horses, they can command a [illegible] price for the foals. I know one case where £12 10s. was refused for a foal a few days after birth, and, indeed, more money taken on.

7791. You think, if it was feasible, the best thing would be an importation of new mares into the country altogether?—I think so. We have plenty of good stallions, except round Ballyhaunis and [illegible], but round the good hunting districts, [illegible] and [illegible], we have very good horses. I think we want a very extensive licensing scheme for the stallions.

7792. Would you advocate such a system of licensing stallions as would practically prevent unlicensed stallions from serving at all?—I would not go so far as that; we had a horse there—"[illegible]"—he was abominably unsound; he was a bad roarer. Well I [illegible] him a mare, very true [illegible], and bred her at stud, and she has not the slightest taint of a roarer, and I never heard of any of his progeny being unsound. We had another there [illegible] there who bred a lot of good hunters, and he, I believe, [illegible]; he [illegible] a [illegible] with [illegible] at the Dublin Show; but any man that had a horse like that which was theoretically unsound, and was valuable, I would make him pay certainly a large fee for his license. I would give a free license to any man that had a thoroughly sound horse, and any man that had an unsound horse let him pay for his license.

7793. Would you increase the license in proportion to the unsoundness of the horse?—I would not say that; but anything that did not pass the veterinary surgeon I would make him pay £10 for his license.

7794. Would it not be rather difficult to do that; it is easy enough to say you won't license a horse unless he is passed sound, but rather difficult to say "I will license him if he is theoretically unsound, but appears not likely to transmit it"?—If he did not pass the veterinary surgeon I would leave it then to the owner; if the owner considered he was worth keeping even in spite his own cost it would be worth paying for, and if he did not he would castrate him or do away with him. But I think it would be hard lines if you had a thoroughbred horse that was breeding winners that you would have to do away with him out of the country, or prevent your friends breeding from him.

7795. But you would not allow him to serve for nothing without paying for his license?—I would not; a man would not pay a large fine for a horse unless he was worth something.

7796. Has the Royal Dublin Society's scheme done any good in your part of the country?—I should say it did; it has kept the [illegible] of [illegible] in our [illegible] good horses in the country; [illegible] we had a very [illegible] lot.

7797. Have you any suggestion to make in regard of the Royal Dublin Society's scheme?—No, my lord, I think as far as the Royal Dublin Society, so far as they have done up to the present, they have done their best [illegible], and as far as very skilful men could do.

7798. Have you any idea at all as to any possible way in which, by the aid of Government, or in any other way, possible mares could be introduced into the country—a better class of mares?—I think if there was a Government stud got up in Connaught—supposing there were 50 to 60 of the very typical hunter mares procured, and horses like [illegible], of the [illegible] Stud Company, and the [illegible] as thoroughbreds were Government bred and distributed among the farmers at cost price on the [illegible] system—that would be a great improvement. Of course the colts would be put up for auction, and any man that wanted a good hunter would go there then, and if he was not suitable for a hunter he would make a [illegible] horse.

7799. The farmer undertaking not to sell the mare?—I would not allow him; I would do brand her that she could not be exported, the same way as the Australian horses; I would brand her and number her, and keep a register how she was bred.—I think it would be a great improvement in the country. But it is ridiculous to talk of introducing mares in a country where we have not got the means of exporting.

7800. Would you be in favour of a large scheme of registration, registering mares and foals?—I certainly would register the mares, and I would register the yearlings.

7801. How do you think that could be carried out?—They could be registered by the local committees that are appointed at present under the Royal Dublin Society's scheme.

7802. Would a local committee be able to do that?—I should think they could if there was a paid secretary to aid—you could get a man for £75 or £100 a year that would be very glad to undertake the job.

7803. Mr. La Touche.—You think there should be a Government stud farm in which these mares should be bred for distribution among the farmers?—Yes, on the lines of the [illegible] stud farm where all our good mares have gone to.

7804. What did you mean by saying there was [illegible] in some cases with a dash of the old Irish blood in them?—I have at the present moment [illegible] of old Irish blood, and [illegible] and [illegible].

7805. Why do you call that the old Irish blood

10 Oct. 1895 / Mr. H. B. [illegible]

any more than Favo or Victorian?—My father had it for the last 40 years.

7506. What you mean by old Irish blood is a mare got some years ago by a thoroughbred horse—Cheshut was got by Bandboy?—The Cheshut we had was a Magpie horse, bred by Mr. Waters of Monasterevan, I think, but all the old mares there are three-quarter bred, they have all a touch of Will Scarlet, and in a great many cases of Tom Steele, a half-bred horse by Semilthorpe; in nearly every good hunter in our country the name of Cheshut or Semilthorpe crops up in the pedigree.

7507. I understand you to say for the improvement of the ordinary horse in the country you would prefer a good half-bred to a Hackney?—If I could get a half-bred horse to my liking, that is well-balanced, short-legged, good shouldered, three-quarter bred horse, I would prefer him to the Hackney, but it is very hard to get that stamp of typical horse; every good colt is nearly castrated as a yearling; it is very hard to get one of them unless a man keeps one for racing purposes, and when he has done racing he may go to the stud, but it is more difficult to get a good half-bred than a good hunter sire.

7508. Do you know much about the South?—No my connection is nearly all with the west; I go into the congested districts portion; I buy a good deal of cattle in Swinford, and that part of the country.

7509. It is not the fashion in Roscommon to keep well-bred colts uncut?—No, they are nearly all cut as yearlings.

7510. Mr. Warren.—Is horse-breeding a considerable industry with these small farmers in Connaught?—It used to be, but I think it is dying out greatly; I think they are getting disgusted with the game, the animals have been so bad, they have hundreds on hands; there are hundreds of horses at present in Connaught that you cannot absolutely sell. In the fair of Boyle and in the fair of Athlone I suppose next January you will see hundreds of them that are absolutely worthless, they cannot be tendered; they used to be bought for light van work in London, but the Argentine horse is cutting against them.

7511. It is not very hard to realise how bad mares can be until you see them in the hands of these small farmers?—No person could believe it until you saw them—until you regularly go down and look at them it does not dawn on you how bad a mare can be.

7512. There are very few left of the better class?—Any good mare or any of the good pony type is either picked up the foreigner or large farmer.

7513. Is the land very bad in these districts?—No; I would not say the land is bad in Roscommon.

7514. Take the Swinford district?—It is very bad down there and round Kiltimagh; it is all mountain or lake.

7515. Requires something very hardy to live there?—It wants to be something very hardy; they are not able to feed them in it.

7516. Do you think from what you know of the mares in the hands of the small farmers in Connaught that there is much danger of their produce finding its way into the hands of men who now breed high class hunters?—I should not think there is the slightest danger, they are altogether a different breed, you might as well say you would hunt on a mule as to hunt on one of them. I don't think there is the slightest danger of their mixing; no man will ever try to breed a hunter from the miserable weeds down in that country.

7517. Are not the more intelligent people of Roscommon very much more enlightened now on the subject of breeding horses since this discussion has taken place?—I think they are.

7518. And they would be very careful what they bred from?—Very well able to take care of themselves. Any man who goes to breed a hunter generally knows what he is about. If he does not he soon learns.

7519. If you wished to buy such a half-bred sire as you have described now do you know where to find him?—No; I would find it very difficult, that is why I have great hopes out of a Government stud. If they left the colts unmatched until two years old you could pick the best of them and let them run round as country sires. I don't think a good stamp of half-bred horse exists in the West of Ireland, except in a few isolated cases.

7520. Chairman.—You don't mean he does not exist anywhere?—Well, I don't know. I only speak from my own experience. I should not say that about Kildare or Meath.

7521. You spoke just now about the Government breeding establishments in Hungary. Do you know anything about them yourself?—Except to read articles in the "Field."

7522. You said "where all our best mares have gone to"?—Nearly all the good mares I have sold I have sold to foreigners.

7523. More lately than formerly?—I think there is just as good a demand now for the foreign market as ever there was.

7524. You think it is the case throughout the country, or in that part of the country that you know, that many of the best mares have been bought for abroad?—I think all the best mares, except in cases where a man could afford to keep one of the old strain or a strain he thought a lot of, he kept her for breeding purposes, but everything else was sold that could be turned into cash. I think the Land agitation, too, had a good deal to do with it, because when rents did not come in men had to realise their horses.

7525. You think no one would undertake to breed a hunter from the miserable weeds in that part of the country?—I don't think there is the slightest fear. If he does he will never try it again.

7526. But if these miserable weeds were improved by the introduction of Hackney blood, would they not be likely to get about the country?—Even if they did would it not be a great thing to improve it?

7527. That is another question. Assume, for the sake of argument, that the Hackney blood is considered objectionable in a part of the country where they breed hunters and harness horses, do you think there is no danger if those mares were improved by the introduction of Hackney blood that they would find their way into districts producing hunters?—I don't think they would.

7528. Why should they not?—They are altogether of a different type. Any man who goes to breed a hunter would never take a Hackney as a standard.

7529. No, but I am talking of the produce?—I would recognise that the produce would have the type of the Hackney.

7530. And that the produce would show that type so strongly that no man would breed from them?—I certainly think they would. Of course if I could get a three-quarter bred horse to my liking I would prefer him to the Hackney.

7531. Anything further you would like to say to the Commission?—Nothing; only I think the great thing would be to try and improve the mares. They talk of subsidising owners to keep their mares. They would want to put them in some way to get a mare to start with. They cannot start from nothing. The things they have now are useless for any purpose.

[illegible]

bred; the very best I ever saw in the hunting field were by these half-bred sires; they are hardy and clever and never put a foot wrong.

7868. So which people talk about there being nothing like the thoroughbred sire and the great horses only being got by the thoroughbred sires, they are talking rubbish?—Most decidedly. There was a man living in our country at [illegible] that used to [illegible] half-bred horses [illegible]. His country [illegible] visited him one day, and he asked his groom to tell this gentleman what the horse was got by. "Got by Major Dix out of Jemima," said the groom. The English gentleman thanked him and gave him a half-sovereign. "Major Dix" was not the sire at all, he was a [illegible].

7869. Are there many Clydesdale horses in your country?—There was one in [illegible]; I don't think he would suit there.

7870. You would not have any such blood at all?—I would not have him at all; he is a big soft horse made of lumps and [illegible].

7871. You don't think he is wanted for the farmers' work?—No; he would destroy them and a [illegible] Hackney would a great deal.

7872. Are there many horses sold for foreigners in Roscommon?—Hundreds of them.

7873. Are they bought by the dealers?—Mostly by them.

7874. Do you think it would be an improvement if they would be bought direct from the farmers by Government?—Certainly; if they get good premiums to keep them on, and a kind out of them [illegible], then you would have what with a good crossing of the half-bred horse that you would have a substantial horse with quickness, and not these big soft-legged Clydesdales [illegible], if you [illegible].

7875. Mr. La Touche asked you if Hackneys were bred from and [illegible] think they would do harm to horses—if there was a breed of horses at present, and that they would do harm to breeding, you would be against having them in the country and you said "yes"?—I said I should be against anything that would produce bad stock.

7876. If, on the other hand, there were Hackneys that were bred from good bred blood with plenty of thoroughbred blood in them, would you be against them then?—Certainly not.

7877. Chairman.—I think you told us that you don't really know anything at all about Hackney blood?—No, I have not, except to see them in the show ring.

7878. You have seen one Hackney that you thought a good horse?—That is all, but I have heard them opposed by people who know nothing about them.

7879. Is there anything more you would like to say to the Commission?—Yes; except to keep on giving premiums to the young mares and fillies and get more half-bred sires, and I think it would be very easy to bring the horses back to a standard better than ever they were. Roscommon, I suppose, can produce better horses than any place in the world. If the English people only knew Roscommon, and started there, they would [illegible] to "Red House" over and over again.

7880. Mr. Wrench.—You exhibit very often in the Dublin Show?—Always.

7881. You know at present you are only allowed to foal or with foal at foot to a registered thoroughbred stallion?—I do.

7882. Would you approve of mares being allowed to be shown in foal or with foal at foot to a half-bred stallion?—Oh, surely; I would encourage the half-bred in every way.

The Commission adjourned to next morning.

FIFTEENTH DAY—FRIDAY, DECEMBER 4TH, 1896

Present:—The Earl of Dunraven, K.P., in the Chair; Lord Ashtown, Mr. J. L. Carew, M.P., Mr. Percy La Touche, Mr. F. S. Wrench.

Mr. Hugh Neville, Secretary.

Mr. J. F. Bomford, Drumlargan, Kilcock, Co. Meath, examined.

7883. CHAIRMAN.—Mr. Bomford, you live in the county Meath, do you not?—Yes, sir.

7884. And you have been personally occupied in breeding horses?—Yes.

7885. For some time?—For a great many years.

7886. What class of horse do you breed?—I was breeding hunters or carriage horses, thoroughbred horses, and Clydesdale horses, and a few thoroughbreds.

7887. You have bred, you say, Clydesdales—pure bred Clydesdale horses?—Pure bred Clydesdales.

7888. And for what purpose did you breed them?—I bred them for my own use and for sale. I kept stallions sometimes and sold the mares. I generally sold the colts for stallions, in fact, always.

7889. You keep a thoroughbred yourself?—I keep a thoroughbred stallion.

7890. Any half-bred stallions?—No; I never had a half-bred.

7891. Only a thoroughbred and a Clydesdale?—Only a thoroughbred and a Clydesdale. I have no Clydesdale stallion at present.

7892. And what kind of mares do you breed from for the hunters and high class harness horses?—Well, pretty well-bred looking cleanly mares, with one or more crosses of the thoroughbred in them.

7893. You put them to a thoroughbred?—Put them to a thoroughbred.

7894. Have you crossed the Clydesdale with the thoroughbred at all?—Yes, not with the intention of breeding for a cross. It was when the mares had [illegible] to send them off to the stallion. I just put my own horse on them then, not to lose them altogether [?]. I also crossed a thoroughbred mare on one occasion with a pure Clydesdale horse for the same purpose.

7895. And with what result?—Well, I was very much surprised at the result in that case, because the animal that I bred was an extremely good hunter.

7896. Is that the only occasion on which you tried the experiment?—I think [?] I bred that way from that mare, a colt and a filly. One of them I did not care about, the colt; he was coarse-bred looking; I sold him young and I don't know what became of him. The other turned out very well, and the foals of hers by a thoroughbred horse have turned out particularly good too. I sold one of them for a couple of hundred last year.

7897. That foal would be by a thoroughbred out of this mare?—Out of a mare got by a pure Clydesdale stallion out of a thoroughbred mare.

7898. A great many horses I suppose are bred in your part of the country?—A great number.

7899. Are they mostly hunters?—Mostly first class hunters and [illegible].

7900. How are they generally, thoroughbred horses or what?—Got by thoroughbred horses as a rule.

7901. How would these young horses be bred in general?—The small farmers breed horses from all sorts of stallions. I think it depends greatly on the bargain [?] to them and can be got cheap.

7902. Are they sold all in your part of the country for sires?—Oh yes, there are some very good sires.

7903. Thoroughbred sires?—Thoroughbred sires.

7904. What kind of fees do they charge?—They go from £3 to £10, I think.

7905. I don't think the breeding [illegible] the kind of [illegible] the farmer would put his mare to?—I think the thoroughbreds used that way would average about £3. I think that would be the average.

7906. Are there any half-bred sires?—There are a few.

7907. Are they popular, do you think?—I have known some of them that were.

7908. Would you approve of a good half-bred sire generally for getting hunters?—I think what they produce is very uncertain. It sometimes seems to take one way and sometimes to take another. I know that was my own experience. You cannot rely upon getting any fixed type. But I have seen some very good horses got by half-bred horses. Of course most so-called half-breds are practically thoroughbreds.

7909. Are there any Clydesdale stallions, except the one you had, in the district?—Yes, there is one which is called a pure-bred Clydesdale. I do not know whether he is or not. He is not a good horse. And there is another in the district which may be [illegible] horse; but I do not know much about him. He is near the Enfield side.

7910. What kind of mares do the small farmers generally have?—Fair useful [?] mares, I think.

7911. Do they breed profitably out of them?—I don't think they do. I think it is a mixed lot.

7912. Why do they continue breeding?—I don't know. I could not answer that. [illegible] It has not been always so.

7913. What is your opinion about breeding from Clydesdale mares?—The only time I have practised it, it was very successful. The first time I ever tried it—I think it was 25 years ago—I put a [illegible] Clydesdale mare, a well-grown one, to a Clydesdale horse and I sent her down as a brood mare to the Royal Agricultural Show at [illegible]; she showed against a lot of good mares, and she won the first prize, [illegible]. I exhibited it, and I got a big price for him—very nearly £100 as a three-year-old. I have also tried it with half-bred mares, and they did very well. I think it reduces the quality, [illegible] but I don't think it prevents her from growing to full size if she gets time.

7914. The advisability of doing so would depend, perhaps to a certain extent, on the character of the soil, climate, and things of that kind. It may be profitable in some places and not in others?—I don't think it would at all do to put a half-bred or badly grown mare [illegible] to a horse. I think

Dec. 4, 189[illegible]. Mr. J. P. [illegible].

think that would destroy her. It is the only way I see to induce the farmers keep good mares.

7915. Do you think that the farmers generally about you are alive to the necessity of making their mares suitably?—The smaller farmers I don't think are so at all.

7916. You say that you think the small farmer having from a mare that he cannot sell—do you think they are more inclined to sell their good fillies than they used?—I cannot say that they are, except, perhaps, that they want the money more than they used.

7917. You do not know whether there is any greater foreign demand for our mares than used to be the case?—I have no reason to say that there is. I do not know.

7918. And do you know at all whether the price is as good now as it used to be for what I may call the inferior style of horse?—I think the price for the inferior style of horse for the last two or three years has been as low as ever I remember. I think the price for a good horse is as good at present as ever it was. I think size is wanted more than it used to be.

7919. The demand is more?—I think there is more demand in proportion for the size than there used to be, especially in harness horses. I do not think there is a similar demand for small hacks, particularly during the last few years, and I attribute it very much to cycling. I know numbers of men, good-sized farmers, who do not keep anything like the number of horses they used. I am not speaking of my own district but of all Ireland. I have a great deal to do with that class of people all through Ireland, and I find very generally that numbers of them do not keep half the horses that they used five years ago, and they generally attribute it to cycling, tramways, and that sort of thing.

7920. The demand for size is increasing—how do you think that the requisite size can best be attained?—I think if you encourage any stallions you ought to encourage stallions that have size, or stallions that are known to impart a good deal of size to their offspring.

7921. Do you think that the system of registration of stallions under the Royal Dublin Society's scheme has done any good?—I think it unquestionably has; I think it has enabled men to select a sound stallion.

7922. You think a suitable half-bred mare is more likely to impart size and substance than the ordinary thoroughbred sire that is standing about the country?—Yes, if she is a bigger and stronger beast.

7923. And would you approve of the registration of sound and approved half-bred sires?—I think it might be of use. Let people use their own judgment whether they mind their mares or [illegible]. I do not see in breeding hunters how you can to keep breeding from thoroughbred horses without breeding them into thoroughbreds altogether, and there are not very many men who can keep a thoroughbred except a very strong thoroughbred.

7924. Your experience of the cross of the Clydesdale has been very favourable?—I think I made more money by breeding Clydesdales than any other class of horse.

7925. I do not mean pure-bred Clydesdale but a cross?—In the one instance I have given you I am inclined to think that there was an exceptional instance.

7926. Have you any experience of crossing with any other breed—Hackney blood for instance?—No, I have not. I crossed a pure-bred Clydesdale mare with a thoroughbred horse and the result in that case was that the first foal was a very fine colt with every fine action, a handsome carriage horse, and an excellent fencer, in fact he was a good hunter too, and I sold him at a good price for a carriage horse, and the next foal, a full brother, was more of a cart horse. Any one looking at the two would not suppose that they were brothers at all, and I didn't get half the money for him.

7927. Have you any definite opinion as to the relative importance of the sire or the dam—some witnesses attached more importance to endeavouring to encourage stallions throughout the country; others seemed to attach more importance to endeavouring to improve the breed of mares—what do you think about that?—I would attach much more importance to the stallion for the simple reason that he will produce a great many more foals, but I do not suppose that the produce will take more after the stallion than after the mare provided they are both equally purely bred. My opinion from breeding different kinds of animals is that whichever animal is the purest bred and has the longest pedigree will be the most impressive whether male or female. I never could find that the male was more impressive than the female unless he was purely bred and she was not. And the more an animal is bred an animal is the more impressive he is either for good or evil.

7928. Could you suggest any way in which the farmers could be induced to keep their best mares for breeding from instead of selling them?—I don't know of any practical way.

7929. Mr. La Touche.—Would you approve of the idea, Mr. [illegible], that all stallions should be licensed, and that those that were unsound should be put under heavy penalties before they are permitted to serve?—It has been my opinion that the only way to improve the breed of horses in Ireland is to discourage the breeding of bad ones as much as possible, and bad stallions; and the only way that I can see of coming at that is by having a tax upon all stallions and not allowing any horse to be let to the public without paying a tax.

7930. I suppose you would permit the tax to be remitted in cases where the stallion would be sound and suitable?—I dare say that would be a very good thing; but I think if there was a tax it might be a very small one. I don't think it would be any hardship upon anybody; quite the reverse. I think it would stamp out the horses that perhaps do the most harm. I know it is the habit of many men who keep stallions to have two or three stallions to suit their different class of customers and the prices. They have one good one for the good breeders, and they have generally a cheap Jack for the farmers, who do not care what they breed from as long as they get it cheap. If there was a tax it would tend to make them keep only one, and to keep one best.

7931. You think the regular mares is in need of improvement?—I am sure they are.

7932. How would you suggest that they should be improved?—Well, the only practical way that I know is to encourage breeding from young mares, because I think if a man finds a young mare breeding well he will probably stick to breeding from her.

7933. How do you think that that encouragement should be effected—in what manner?—I think by giving more prizes for young brood mares.

7934. Do you think that £5 and £10 prizes would be sufficient to encourage the farmer and induce him to keep the mare?—I think it would. But the worst of it is that the small farmers who keep the worst class of mares rarely do not exhibit. It made them less much, and shows are too far away.

7935. Do you think, in your experience, that the ordinary light-weight driving horse is very much depreciated in value?—I certainly think he is for the last few years.

7936. And possibly, with the introduction of motor cars to supersede the bicycle, there will be a still further depreciation?—I don't know that the motor car will interfere as much as cycling, which is still only holding its own, but increasing; and I think it likely to do so, not for amusement, but practically, for use.

7937. You don't see any chance to imagine that the

breeding of light-weight small hunters horses is likely to be ever a profitable enterprise?—I would not like to go so far as to say that, but at present I think it [illegible].

7938. Have you any experience of Hackneys?—No, I know nothing of them, except what I have seen at shows.

7939. Have you any experience of the congested districts?—Yes; I know the districts, but I have had nothing to do with the working of the scheme. Of course I saw their ponies when going through the districts, and I asked them how they got on and asked them if they were bred from the Government horses or what.

7940. Have you seen any of the ponies coming down to fairs in the county Meath?—No; not to my knowledge.

7941. You have no personal experience of the produce of the Government horses in the congested districts?—I have seen the foals on the mountains.

7942. The foals?—Yes, both in Donegal and Galway.

7943. Have you seen two-year-olds and three-year-olds?—I have seen two-year-olds, I never saw a three-year-old.

7944. Do you think that they benefit the breed of horses there?—I saw a dozen of them very near the Twelve Pins—the first lot I saw, and I was able to pick out all the foals provided they told me the breed afterwards, and even not following my judgment, I was able to pick out the foals got by the Congested Districts' sires, and I picked them out at the time and told them so, and they said I was right in every instance. However, they might say that to please me.

7945. Were these foals or two-year-olds?—There were some two-year-olds and some foals.

7946. Mr. Watson.—You know the whole of Ireland?—Practically.

7947. And the North particularly well?—I know the North very well.

7948. Do you think that the different parts of the country require different treatment?—Oh, certainly.

7949. You would not suggest the same breed for Meath as for the North of Ireland?—Certainly not.

7950. Do you think that the different breeds of horses, the different classes of horses can be raised in Ireland generally without interfering with each other?—I certainly think so; I do not see why they should interfere.

7951. Do you think there is any danger of the big breeders in Meath breeding from ponies that came up from Connemara and the Twelve Pins, & interbreeding?—No, I think not, breeding hunters.

7952. What class of farmers breed the best horses in Meath?—The large graziers.

7953. Not the small farmers?—Not the small farmers.

7954. No better judges of horses, I suppose, in the world than the Meath graziers?—I fancy they are as good as any going.

7955. And no better mares?—No better mares. I have not seen them better; I have seen them very good in other countries too.

7956. And no better land?—I would not say that. Meath is the best land for raising horses in Ireland.

7957. What would you say is the best land in Ireland?—Where there is some limestone. I think Limerick is better than the [illegible] [illegible], down in Roscommon; I think it grows strong natural bone.

7958. Mr. La Touche.—Roscommon also?—Roscommon is limestone, grows strong and [illegible] bone. I saw a great deal of young stock reared, and though they are very good and in very good condition, I think that is land not so good for breeding purposes they might grow quicker; of course, if you had a horse with once you make up for all that, and as the best horses are fed with oats in Meath.

7959. Mr. Wrench.—I think you said you would be in favour of licensing all stallions?—Yes; I don't think any stallions ought to be let to serve without a licence.

7960. You have seen it suggested that every horse should be registered, mares and all?—I have read it; I cannot see the object of registering the mares.

7961. Do you think it would be a practicable scheme to carry out?—If you register the mares you would find very great difficulty indeed, in preventing a bad stallion from serving them instead of the registered one.

7962. Do you think there are many large graziers and breeders in Meath who could tell you the breed of their mares now?—I am sure they could; most of them know the pedigrees of their mares.

7963. How they are bred?—I am sure **that those** who breed really good ones could tell you.

7964. By the records?—By the records.

7965. Would you be in favour of establishing a Hunters' Improvement Society in Ireland?—I don't know the details, but I dare say it would do a great deal of good.

7966. You don't know the work of the Hunters' Improvement Society in England?—I do not.

7967. But if such a society was started, you think the control would be in the hands of the big breeders in Meath for giving the pedigrees of their mares?—I think so, for a good many reasons.

7968. Chairman.—You know the whole of Ireland pretty well?—Yes, I know it all.

7969. And I think you attributed the falling off in the demand for the lighter description of harness horse a good deal to the influence of the bicycle?—I say that is the principal reason—what you call the hack horse.

7970. Do you think **there is** any danger that the introduction of the motor cars will interfere with the trade in the heavier kind of horse; the farm horse and the dray horse?—I suppose it would. Well, I don't know about the dray horse, but I should think it would interfere with the cross-bred draught horse that would be fit for a team car, but after all that is nothing like such a large class of horse as the hunter.

7971. Speaking generally of Ireland, what class of horse do you think the country is best suited to produce?—I would not confine it to any one class. I think there is a great part of Ireland that is not at all fit to produce hunters; in fact, I would go so far as to say, the greater part of it. There are some counties in Connaught, and a good number of counties in Munster, and a great part of Leinster, where undoubtedly they can produce hunters as good as anywhere else in the world, I suppose; but a great part of Ireland is not fit to produce hunters at all, I think.

7972. And do you think that anything could improve it—any mixture of the blood for instance?—I do not. I would not like the idea of encouraging some small farmers to breed hunters at all. I think it is not profitable to them.

7973. I would like to know your opinion on this point as to whether it is or is not the case, that where the production of hunters or high class weight hunters is concerned, Ireland has not got a reputation for superiority over any other country—is the Irish hunter thought more of than the hunter produced anywhere else?—I should think there is no doubt about that. I know how they speak of them in England, and I know when I have been in England I have been offered a position as a buyer on a larger scale for any man coming to the grazier business; and I have heard them say that they would not get a hunter except an Irish hunter, that they must use in the best Shires in England, in Leicestershire and that part of the country, and I have heard numbers say they would not ride anything but an Irish horse if they could get him.

7974. Do you **think we have the same natural advantages in the production of any other kind of**

Dec. 4, [illegible]

Mr. J. [illegible]

being—do you think we could breed a heavy draught horse, or a cart horse, or an ordinary agricultural horse?—I think the same thing that checked them in the beginning, and all that, would similarly do it for all other breeds.

7975. How do you think that we have established this superiority in the production of hunters?—As far as the highly-bred hacks are concerned, I think a great deal of it comes from this—that in England the thoroughbred horse is set to work when he is two years old. Whereas in Ireland the hunter has been let run loose until he is four or five, and I think that is one reason why the Irish horse, as a rule, beats the English horse in steeplechasing. I think the same class of Irish horse that goes and wins the Grand National in England would have been running his races when he was two years old, and would have been broken down when the Irish horse begins to race. I am sure it brings on unsoundness to work them before they are fully developed.

7976. What I want to get from you is if you have got any opinion on this, assuming that you are quite right that the price of what I may call the inferior horse has greatly declined, and as far as I can judge is likely to keep down, taking Ireland all over, what kind of horse is the most profitable for the country to produce?—Where they can produce a high-class hunter successfully it is the most profitable, because the prices are so very much larger.

7977. And some parts of the country are adapted to producing them, and some parts of the country are not?—That is my opinion.

7977a. I think you said you had no experience yourself of Hackney blood?—I do not know whether you have got any opinion as to what the effect of the introduction of Hackney blood would be upon the production of hunters?—Provided it had got mixed with the hunters?

7977b. Yes, certainly?—Well, I might from what I saw of some of the Hackneys at shows, I think they are a very nice style of horse, but I think they would be an unsuitable cross to breed mares for the purpose of breeding hunters from their mares, and for two reasons. The principal reason is that you want to add in size and the Hackney, although he is a very nice horse, is not calculated to add size to the animal. And the only other reason that I say that he would be unsuitable for breeding hunters from—I may be very wrong in it—But looking at their action as shown, although it is excellent road action, I think it is not field action, it is too high. But it is only from looking at them going round the ring that I have come to form that opinion. I may be entirely wrong.

7978. Assuming for the sake of argument that you are right, and that the Hackney strain would be prejudicial to the production of hunters, do you think if any large quantity of Hackney blood was introduced into the North or West of Ireland, that it would do any harm?—I don't think it would do any harm to the breeding of hunters, because I think the men who breed the best class of hunters would be able to judge the mares suitable to breed them.

7979. You think they would be able to detect the Hackney?—I think they would, the vast majority of them. If there was anything in the mare to make her unfit for breeding hunters I think they would detect it at once. I would be disappointed in them if they didn't.

7980. You do not think that the Hackney blood would be likely to gradually spread all over the country?—I don't think it would. I don't see why the breeds should mix at all. There is one suggestion I would like to make—I think you considered a talk about the breeding of ponies and the improvement of them—I think if any means could be taken to stop the importation of Iceland ponies into Ireland it would be a good thing for the breeding of Irish ponies.

7981. Do a number of them come?—An immense number of them come in. I never saw one of them yet that was not the very worst possible description of animal, and I know that up in the North, in Antrim, it has gone so far that some men have got these Iceland ponies, and have run them upon the hills and sold them as Connemara ponies, which has given the Connemara ponies a very bad name, and I have heard that they have begun to breed them.

7982. Where have they landed these Iceland ponies?—In Dublin very much, and in Belfast.

7983. What age are they?—I think they come over two-year-olds and three-year-olds.

7984. What do they sell for?—Something very small. I think they are brought over for ballast—or they get them for nothing.

7985. Which numbers of them?—Mr. Davis, I saw, has large sales in Dublin of them very frequently, and people get them for very little, thinking they are getting a great bargain. They are generally very sick of them before they have them a month, and they cannot get rid of them. That is my experience.

7986. Do they spread about the country?—They spread very much.

7987. You think it is a bad thing?—I think it is very bad for Irish ponies.

7988. Why don't the people protect themselves from them?—I think the reason is that they are very cheap to buy. You get a big strong looking pony for some very small price; you think he will turn into a good one, when you buy him.

7989. What is the matter with them, why do you object to them?—I don't think they have a single good point about them. They have no action, no shoulders, no strength, whatever.

7990. Do they breed from them in this country?—I fear they do now. I did not know it until lately. They have been breeding them in Connemara, and spoiling them. They are the very worst description of animal I ever saw.

7991. How would you propose to stop their importation by legislation?—I would leave that to the Legislature, but I think it would be a very good thing if it could be done.

7992. Lord Ashbourne.—That would only affect the pony breeding?—That is all.

7993. Would you think pony breeding peculiarly suited the ordinary farmer?—Well, I thought there was a good deal of effort being made to improve the Connemara ponies, and that is the reason I mentioned it at all. I have no experience of pony breeding myself.

7994. Mr. La Touche.—Is it your experience that these Iceland ponies have penetrated different parts of Ireland from Ireland—you don't think that the ponies of Connemara are likely to penetrate Ireland?—I think they do. I think the Iceland ponies would spoil the ponies of Ireland.

7995. Then the cross between the Hackney horse and the mongrel districts more generally might be something bigger than a pony—anything in the prejudicial to the hunter breed, you don't think that that produce is likely to permeate the [illegible] produce?—It may as a lack of course.

7996. You said that the farmer who bred hunters would recognise in the mare that was got by one of those Hackney sires something that would induce him to believe that she would not breed a good hunter. Is it within your experience that you can tell from the outward appearance of a horse what he is likely to produce?—You cannot, I said. The fault is the one, there will be no difficulty about seeing that, and the other in the action; and I think he should be able to judge of that too.

7997. Don't you think that a mare 15 hands high is big enough to breed anything?—I would like to breed from a bigger one.

7998. But it is within possibility that [illegible] mare [illegible] hands high would breed a horse 16 hands high?—Quite.

3000. Do you think that the ordinary farmer would be a sufficiently good judge to condemn a mare 15 hands high with good action?—No; I don't think he would.

3001. Then it is quite possible that many of these animals that were bred by a Hackney horse out of Connemara [illegible] [illegible] mares might find their way into a hunter breeding district?—They might, of course.

3002. And he would breed?—Yes; but I think the produce would be sold as a harness horse, not as a hunter.

3003. Mr. Wrench.—Do you think that the man who understands breeding hunters would select a mare of that class, 15 hands high, as a brood mare?—Not unless she was a very good one. Lots of small mares breed well.

3004. Do not all the horse breeders in North aim at producing a weight-carrying hunter?—Of course they aim at it.

3005. Therefore they would not be likely to select a small animal as a brood mare?—I don't think they would keep a small mare for breeding.

3006. They do not generally breed from small mares in [illegible] [illegible] very many of them.

3007. You think the conditions of the country are calculated to improve every kind of horse?—Yes; it seems to suit them very well.

3008. And that we can grow better horses in Ireland than in England?—I think we do.

3009. What has been the chief reason, up to the present, that we have acquired a name for hunters—[illegible] more suitable than others to encourage hunters than any other breed in England?—Well, I suppose that is only within the last twenty years.

3010. Have not all the shows—[illegible] the hunters [illegible] [illegible] shows throughout the country—as a rule [illegible] [illegible] [illegible] [illegible] [illegible] of hunter [illegible]?—The vast bulk of them have.

3011. There have been very few horses [illegible] in any of the shows up to the present?—I think so.

3012. And if equal [illegible] [illegible] [illegible] to improve the harness horse do you think Ireland could also grow harness horses?—I see no reason why it should not; I think the [illegible] [illegible] as much to do with them [illegible] [illegible] anything.

3013. And they are easily sold?—They easily sold.

3014. But that up to the present there has been [illegible] [illegible] the breeding harness horses?—Not much.

3015. It has been suggested to us that foreign horses should be [illegible] [illegible] into Ireland, would you approve of that—[illegible] your Ireland [illegible] there are also American horses coming into Ireland—would you approve of branding American horses?—I have seen some American horses and they were all very bad; they were no bad sort of [illegible] that I do not understand why anyone wanted a brand to distinguish them.

3016. You think they would be known?—I think they would be known.

3017. We have also had it stated that these American horses were among Irish hunters and were not detected?—I think it is quite possible; they might be better American horses than I have seen.

3018. Would you be in favour of branding American horses?—I don't see what harm it would do. I would be very glad if it would deter horses coming into the country and spoiling the name of what we breed.

3019. You said in answer to Mr. La Touche that you had asked the people in Connemara how they were getting on with their horse-breeding?—I have asked them in different places.

3020. What opinion do they give generally?—Some of them spoke very highly of them, and said they had improved the ponies they raised [illegible]; others told me that it was Government horses they had bred from once or twice, but that they had given back to the others.

3021. What were the classes?—Hackneys.

3022. Larger or smaller?—I think they were getting very small, and when I pressed them as to why they did, and was it that the others were better horses, it didn't appear so to me; but that they went to some fellow who had a horse, and then they didn't like to leave him—they preferred giving their money to their neighbour than to the Government as far as I could make out.

3023. That was the general idea?—That was what I gathered.

3024. Chairman.—I do not think you have yet said, admitting you didn't quite make [illegible]. You said, in answer to a question of Mr. Wrench, that Ireland could produce better horses than were produced anywhere, of all kinds.

Mr. Wrench.—He did not say exactly that.

Witness.—I am very much obliged to you if it wants correcting. I didn't hear some of the questions very clearly, and I may not have answered them.

(Shorthand notes read (Q. 3007–3008).)

3025. Chairman.—But you say that you think we breed better horses in Ireland than in England; that would include the draught horses and everything else?—I think we grow them better. I think there is no difference between the blood of a good Irish horse or anywhere. It is all the same as the English blood.

3026. I want to know whether you think that we produce better carriage horses, better dray horses, better cart horses, and all kinds of horses better in Ireland than in England?—No; I would not say it about the heavy dray horses, but I think we can produce them just as good.

3027. I wanted to make sure you didn't say anything you did not mean?—I don't think we breed better draught horses than they do in England. We do it on a very small scale.

Dec. [illegible], 18[illegible].

Mr. J. O'Connell Murphy.

Mr. J. O'CONNELL MURPHY examined.

8028. CHAIRMAN.—You are also a resident in the county Meath?—Yes.

8029. Do you live at all in the same neighbourhood as Mr. Rowland?—Yes, almost. Two miles from him, between Trim and Summerhill.

8030. Have you heard his evidence?—I have.

8031. Do you agree pretty generally with that?—With some particulars; not with all.

8032. Do you breed horses yourself?—Yes; I breed a good many horses. I have at present 18 brood mares. I have been breeding horses for 30 years on my own account, and all my life I have been looking after them for my father before that.

8033. Do you keep a stallion?—I do not keep a stallion.

8034. Do you breed hunters or carriage horses, or what sort?—Hunters; steeplechase horses.

8035. MR. CHAPLIN.—From thoroughbreds?—Yes.

8036. CHAIRMAN.—Altogether thoroughbreds?—Oh, no; I breed some half-bred.

8037. What class of sire do you use?—The best thoroughbred I can get.

8038. And out of what kind of mares do you breed?—I have generally mares with four or five crosses of thoroughbred. I have only two mares that have only one cross that I know of.

8039. Do you find that the thoroughbred horse and the mare with three or four crosses of thoroughbred blood produce a good hunter?—I think that is the best animal any man breeding can produce. It is the high type of hunter; the steeplechase horse; the Leicestershire hunter.

8040. You think that class of horse gets the best in producing?—I think the sire the best, and the thoroughbred.

8041. You consider the stallions in your neighbourhood of the quality and the kind that suits the neighbourhood?—Some of them are very good.

8042. Are you sufficiently well supplied with suitable stallions?—Yes; I think we are.

8043. Do the small farmers breed much?—They breed a good many; but I think in my estimation it ought to be held out to the farmers to hold and breed from their good young sound mares. I would give as substantial prizes as I could at local shows. I would increase them if possible, and give the farmers good substantial prizes for their filly foals and to retain young ones. I approve of breeding from two-year-olds; I have bred from them myself, with the very best results, but, at the same time, I would give the farmers prizes for mares up to any age. But I would have special prizes for foals at foot, from three to seven years old. There ought to be good sound mares, with good bone and size—good animals having [illegible], equally balanced, with [illegible], and with a good [illegible] that they ought to have them home in [illegible] to be [illegible] by the [illegible] which ought not to commence to serve till the 1st of May; and I think the [illegible] would [illegible] be [illegible]. [illegible] £1 at the most. [illegible] a difference, [illegible] though they get to [illegible] a few [illegible]. [illegible] for the country [illegible], because, no matter how good the colt, he can't sell it being a bad colour. I think that people, when comparing thoroughbred stallions with others, should take into account the quality, bottle, and the [illegible]. It is a well known fact that if we take the cannon bone of a thoroughbred horse's leg and weigh it with the bone of a Clydesdale, the thoroughbred bone will outweigh it, and it is a well known fact that if we bury the bone of a thoroughbred horse and the bone of one of these other horses and take them up in [illegible] years, the bone of the Clydesdale, or of any of those other horses, will be possibly like a sponge, and the thoroughbred bone will be solid as when it was foaled. As Colonel [illegible] described it, one will be ivory and the other bone. I have no prejudice against the Hackney, but I think it is very wrong to lay out Government money on a breed of horse that we don't know are going to improve the breed of Irish horses, and I am quite certain that the blood from the congested districts will permeate through the whole country, as the blood of the Connemara pony and the Barb ponies permeated through it in the past, and I say permeated through it with great advantage. If we could get back something on the type of those ponies into those districts it is the very best thing could be done. I have known some of the best animals I ever saw in my life by Connemara ponies. I have seen some of the best animals I ever saw the produce of Connemara ponies, and their produce were the very best animals. I lived for eight years at [illegible], in the county Kildare, and I saw a Connemara pony with a foal by her side grazing on the road. I liked it and bought it, and the foal was by Fairyland. I sold him to Captain [illegible] for 90 guineas; he sold him to Colonel McCalmont; I don't know for what sum, and he was sold at Tattersall's for 230 guineas. I sold another out of the same mare to [illegible] of Williamstown, and he sold it to Leonard Morrogh, and it was one of the best animals that ever ran with the hounds. In 18[illegible], I exhibited [illegible] at the Dublin Show, and [illegible] and third prize, and the [illegible] of them was a Connemara grey.

8044. Then you have a high opinion of the Connemara ponies?—Wonderful; I never saw as good animals as they were, especially the Connemara ponies that were [illegible], with black [illegible]; they were the best of those that I have seen.

8045. Do you know Connemara yourself?—I don't; but I have seen them coming up for years to Dublin. They are not improving, they are deteriorating.

8046. Have you seen them lately?—Yes.

8047. Can you detect anything of a difference?—I don't think they are the same class at all.

8048. In what way? How are they deteriorating?—They are narrower and lighter, and I don't think they are nearly so well shaped, nor have they as good shoulders.

8049. You have had no experience of Hackneys yourself?—Nothing, except what I saw at the Dublin Show and what I heard and read of, and, from their action and shoulders, I would say they are not at all suitable to improve the breed of hunters. I think all Hackneys ought to be [illegible] of Ireland. We ought to put our [illegible] to the blood and [illegible] as much as possible.

8050. You think we have obtained a certain reputation?—Yes, for breeding hunters.

8051. And you think that horses from some [illegible]?—I [illegible] in the past [illegible]. I don't think the general run of farmers' horses are at all as good as they were.

8052. Can you suggest any way of improving matters?—The only way I see is by giving the prizes at the Shows and the farmers keeping their best mares. I would keep on the cross of the thoroughbred horse with them.

8053. That is to say, a thoroughbred horse with, as you describe?—Yes, a good thoroughbred horse with good shoulders.

8054. A horse to serve at a low fee?—Yes.

8055. I gather from you that you look with some apprehension to the Hackney blood—you don't know what effect it may produce?—I don't know myself but from what I have seen and heard and read I think it would very much deteriorate our hunters. I think the Hackney action would not do at all for hunting; it is quite extravagant, and a waste of energy.

8056. You think the Hackney blood may gradually filter through the whole country?—I haven't the smallest doubt of it but that it will filter as the Connemara blood filtered before, and as I say that blood filtered through the country with advantage.

8057. Have you any experience of Clydesdale blood?—None, I may say; I never bred one. I had a few of them.

8058. Then may I take it, I gather from you that what you think should be done to improve the breed generally is to endeavour to induce the farmers to keep their best mares at home to breed from, and that they should obtain the service at a fee they can afford of a really sound thoroughbred horse?—Yes.

8059. Would you have any objection to a sound and selected half-bred horse?—I would yield to no man in my appreciation of the thoroughbred, but I think a horse with three or four crosses on his dam's side by a thoroughbred horse would be a very good sire—in some cases as good as the others and perhaps more useful. Some of these horses should be in the Stud Book. "Mayboy" and "Fairyland" should be in it too, for they were nearly all thoroughbred. I say a horse with three or four crosses on the dam's side with a good family—I would be most particular about the family—and bred from a thoroughbred could make a first-class sire. I think that every man ought to aim at breeding a high class hunter, and failing that a good harness horse.

8060. Do you think it is possible for the small farmers to breed that class of horse?—I think it is. I think a man with twenty acres and one mare or perhaps two could. I think there should be a prize given at the end of April or May for the best done yearling by the farmers, for I am a firm believer that the best part of a horse is what goes into his mouth.

8061. How do the small farmers generally treat their foals?—Very badly.

8062. They don't feed them?—No.

8063. Have you any opinion about registration? Do you think all stallions should be registered or licensed?—I think they ought to be all registered.

8064. You think the Royal Dublin Society's scheme has been of use in your part of the country?—Yes, I think it has. I think the colts at the fairs in the country, as far as I can see, are not at all as good as they used to be, but I think the shows took a great deal of them away. I think the places where fairs are held in some places are most disgraceful. It is almost as much as a man's life is worth to go into some of them. They are not suitable at all.

8065. I suppose you don't know enough about these Connemara ponies to give to any opinion as to how the breed could be restored to what it formerly was?—I think a Welsh pony stallion would be a good thing through the country.

8066. What?—A Welsh pony stallion. I don't know can they be got now. I think if you had something like the Galloway it would be the very best thing.

8067. Do you know something about these Iceland ponies?—I do, a little.

8068. What do you think of them?—I think they are the most wretched animals you could imagine of the equine race. But I could not understand Mr. Bradford's evidence that they could permeate the country and that the Hackney blood would not permeate the country.

8069. Lord Ardtoney.—Talking about breeding hunters, do you think it is possible to breed the high class hunter in every district of Ireland?—I think it is not possible, but I think you could do as much good for the farmers in those districts by introducing a breed the blood of which, when it permeated through the country, would not deteriorate the hunting blood, but would add to it.

8070. That is not the question I am touching on: I am speaking of breeding hunters. You cannot breed hunters in a great many parts of Ireland?—I think you could breed a hunter of a certain class, decidedly. The Connemara pony was a good hunter, I saw men on them cutting down the field.

8071. Do you believe that as a rule in the poorer districts it pays the farmer to try and breed a hunter, counting misfits and everything?—I think if he does not succeed in breeding a hunter or trying to breed something that will afterwards produce a hunter he had better not try at all.

8072. You think they ought to try and produce riding horses?—Of course now more than ever, when you have the motor car and the bicycle competing with the other classes of horses. Now is the time to try and breed hunters.

8073. In the good districts, I agree with you?—Yes, and bad districts. Tell me any animals that can be bred in Connemara and the congested districts that will do better than the animals they have.

8074. What about medium districts like the North of Ireland?—In medium districts I say you can breed a very good hunter.

8075. You ought to take into calculation the misfits?—I say a misfit hunter would be very much better than a misfit Hackney to my mind. Put the two to a plough and how do you suppose they will manage; the hunter will pull the head off the Hackney. I don't believe any horse with the action of the Hackney even if he got it by chance could stay: it is too extravagant.

8076. Mr. Carew.—Of course what we want to aim at is to get a horse that will plough and do some of the farming work, and what you mean is that the Connemara ponies will be deteriorated by the introduction of Hackney blood?—In my opinion they would.

8077. The droves coming up now are very inferior?—Yes.

8078. And the best thing could be done would be to go back to that breed which is more suited to the Connemara district and to the rest of Ireland?—Yes.

8079. You spoke of breeding from half-bred mares with sufficient dashes of thoroughbred blood to get the best weight carrying hunter?—Yes.

8080. What other blood would you have in the mare?—The old Irish type.

8081. Mr. LaTouche.—You think the stallions are up to the requirements of the country?—I think they are; but I don't think the farmers can get them at a low fee enough.

8082. Would you approve of the idea of the establishment of Government studs for the purpose of disseminating mares amongst the farmers or for putting valuable mares at the service of the farmers at low fees?—Yes; if I knew the breed they were going to establish.

8083. I am taking it for granted that you would advocate thoroughbred sires?—Yes; I would.

8084. Your personal experience of Connemara ponies was that they proved to be a good brood mare when crossed with a thoroughbred horse?—Yes; decidedly.

8085. You attribute that, I am told, to there being no admixture of any English blood in the pony?—I believe there were Arabs at some time or Spanish horses let out in Connemara. I often heard that these cream coloured ponies from Connemara were the descendants of two Spanish stallions—Spanish barbs.

8086. You would hesitate now to breed from a Connemara pony?—I would not hesitate a bit with one of the old sort.

8087. But with the new sort. Would you breed from a three-year-old pony that came from Connemara now, if you were told it was got by a Government stallion?—Not after their being in the district, fearing it might be got from a Government stallion.

8088. Do you think this will depreciate the value of animals coming from the congested districts to the eastern districts?—I think it will make them unsaleable in our country.

8089. Do you think the farmers are buying them now as freely as they used to?—I don't think they are buying them at all.

8090. You would hesitate to buy one **of them for** breeding purposes?—Decidedly.

8091. Mr. Wrench.—You have got eighteen brood mares?—I have, at present.

8092. How many of those are thoroughbred?—About eight, I think.

8093. All except two have four or five crosses of thoroughbred blood?—Yes, and those two are by "Fairyland," out of a very good mare—I think she had a lot of Connemara blood in her.

8094. Is that the only experience you have had yourself of breeding from Connemara blood?—Yes, that is all. I sold you about three, two horses I bought that I had in the Dublin Show last year. I bought them as colts. They come in eight colts every year, if I see a good colt I buy him if I can at all.

8095. Were they bred directly from a Connemara pony?—No, the Connemara pony was their grand-dam in one case, I think, the great grand-dam in the other.

8096. You have never bred from Connemara ponies directly, straight away I mean?—No.

8097. Never in the congested districts?—No.

8098. You can't say the ponies have deteriorated very much in recent years?—No, but I say that the produce coming up here has deteriorated very much.

8099. Do you like a Clydesdale cross?—I don't like him at all.

8100. Do you know they have been using stallions, half-Clydesdales, down there before the Congested Districts Board came there? They might have affected the produce?—Indeed it may.

8101. You have not bought any Connemara ponies lately?—I have not.

8102. I think you said every man ought to aim at breeding a high class hunter?—Yes, I don't speak the small farmers exactly, but I think every man ought to aim at breeding a hunter of some sort, and I think every man who has a fair amount of land and can afford it will find that the horse that will pay him best is the Leicestershire hunter or a steeplechase horse; and if you don't succeed in that you will breed the next best thing to it.

8103. Do you know the North well?—I don't.

8104. Have you ever come across any North of Ireland people?—I think I have.

8105. Are they fairly intelligent?—I **think the** North of Ireland people are intelligent.

8106. If they thought it paid them better to breed another class of horse, you would not disagree with them?—I might alter my opinion, but if I was dealing in the argument I would probably yield; I would not at once change my opinion.

8107. You would not like to tell them what to breed?—Yes, I would.

8108. And you say all North of Ireland men ought to breed a hunter?—I say they ought to try and breed hunters, and if you miss him he will do for a harness horse or a plough horse, or something else.

8109. Do you consider high action a good point in a hunter?—No.

8110. Do you consider that action when with a harness horse?—I think it does; but I think there may be good action and extravagant action. I think there is a lot lost while the horse is carrying his feet through the air in that way.

8110. But in order to get good action that will suit him would you not be obliged to have rather extravagant action on the sides?—I would not say so.

8111. You have not tried breeding harness horses?—I never wish to breed a horse that I don't breed for a hunter.

8112. You have never sold your hunter misfits as harness horses?—I never had a hunter misfit yet.

8113. Then you never sold a harness horse?—I never sold a horse that I had driven myself in harness.

8114. What sort do you consider more suitable for Connemara?—I say if you could get something of the style of the Galloway cob or pony, he was a very suitable animal, fifteen hands high.

8115. Would you be surprised to hear that they had this class of stallion standing there for the past fifteen years?—I would not be surprised.

8116. Then why are you so adverse to buying Connemara ponies?—Fearing there may be Hackney blood in them; it would deter me from doing anything with them.

8117. You would give substantial prizes for encouraging breeders to keep their good fillies?—Yes.

8118. What would you call a substantial prize?—I would say £10 and £5. I would give more if I could.

8119. Do you think that would be sufficient to make them keep their good fillies?—If you could give more I would approve of it. I don't know exactly what you would be prepared to give. I would give them the most I could—that would be my idea.

8120. Then I think you said you would encourage stallions without a single bad point?—I said with no very bad point. I would not have a stallion with one very bad point.

8121. With one specially bad point?—Yes.

8122. Is it hard to find good thoroughbred stallions at present?—I don't think it is.

8123. Where would you go to buy them?—There are several stallions in England, if there was a demand for them. I had two horses operated on myself this year, and there were just two finer hunting stallions in the world; but there was no use for them. One of them was by "Buckler," out of a daughter of "Marchioness," by "Playmate"; and the other by Mr. Malone's horse, "Tragedian."

8124. Mr. Coates.—"Ireland" is a very good stallion that you bred yourself?—I think "Ireland" is one of the best sires in Ireland for hunters.

8125. Mr. Wrench.—Do you consider the Clydesdale blood has filtered through the country?—I think Mr. Bomford was the only man who took Clydesdales through. I didn't think it bad. I know very little about cart stallions.

8126. Do you come across through the country?—Not about our country. There was an old type of sire in Meath—an old Irish sort of horse—and I saw some of those plain-looking horses get good hunters out of mares from thoroughbred sires. There was a horse called "Tom Tug"——

8127. More in the type of a cart stallion, but more legged?—Yes.

8128. You think that all these small farmers in the West ought to aim at breeding hunters of some kind?—Yes.

8129. So that you would turn the whole country into the hunter trade?—I would.

8130. Do you know, as a matter of fact, that the trade in hunters is only a small part of the trade in horses generally?—Yes; but I say in trying to breed the hunter you will breed a good type of horse to trip—the best sort of harness horse I know.

8131. What is the size of a small horse of about 15 or 15.1 hands?—I think he would be a very suitable horse

8152. In spite of pedigree?—That is my argument. I say I would breed nothing but the hunter in spite of the pedigree and the market says.

8153. Would you advise those small men with these small mares, who would not produce an animal of about 15 hands, to breed hunters?—Yes.

8154. Do you find it easy to sell 15 hands hunters?—Very easy.

8155. Would you buy any of pedigree of that sire?—If I thought he was a wonderful animal I would buy him, but I buy and breed the very best I can. I have not seen the animal, but I bought one bred in the [illegible] district this very week, but it is by a "Hackney."

8156. Do you often buy without seeing?—I have bought a great many horses without seeing them, horses I depend on the pedigree.

8157. The Chairman.—As to these Commissions, [illegible] Mr. Murphy, you said to you that you know the district yourself, and then all you judged by is that in your opinion they have [illegible]?—Yes; I think I am coming up I judge by.

8158. You told us which you think would be the best way of improving them. I gather from you that as the whole, from what you have heard and seen, you don't think that the Hackney blood is likely to be of general benefit throughout the country, and I think I understood you to say at the beginning that what you objected to principally, as regards the Hackneys, was that the Government should supply those Hackneys?—Yes; that there should be money spent on a breed that we didn't know who going to improve the breed.

8159. The results being uncertain in your opinion, it is not, in your opinion a wise thing for the Government to expend public money in that particular way?—Yes.

8160. I gather from you also—correct me if I am wrong—that you think, taking it all round, that the most advantageous thing for Ireland, generally, is to keep its attention, as much as possible, to breeding hunters?—Yes; I think the Irish hunter now is a speciality, and I think in years to come it is one of the only things I see to help the farmer in his ever increasing difficulties, which I think are bound to increase as far as I can see.

8161. You think the best way of improving the breed would be to supply—I suppose you mean that the Government should supply—suitable sound thoroughbred stallions at a low fee to walk the country?—Yes.

8162. And that all stallions should be registered, which of course necessitates an examination for their soundness; and that encouragement should be offered to induce farmers to keep and retain their best mares?—Yes.

8163. Is there anything you would like to say to the Commission?—I think that what I said about a prize in the end of April or May, for the best foals, is very important. I think the farmers ought to be encouraged to do their foals well.

8164. Mr. Watson.—You think the best way to meet the agricultural depression in Ireland is to turn the farmers into hunter breeders?—I don't say that. I said it is one of the best ways.

8165. Mr Carew.—What you think is the most paying thing is to produce the hunter; and if they fail in the production of the hunter, they will have the next best thing?—Yes; I am a very large farmer myself, and I don't believe I would be in Ireland at all now but for breeding hunters.

8166. You bred a great many hunters yourself?—Yes; and sold as well as most men.

8167. And got very good prices?—I got £1,000 for a half bred horse.

8168. Mr. Watson.—Do you know a man who breeds as many good hunters as yourself?—Outside these horses, I do not.

8169. Mr. La Touche.—You admit the necessity for harness horses?—A few, of course.

8170. And you acknowledge that there is an enormous sale of harness horses out of Ireland?—Yes.

8171. And the best way to breed these harness horses is to breed the hunters?—Yes; and some of these horses I sold as steeplechase horses would make excellent hunters.

8172. The Chairman.—Are many horses sold at Limerick about you?—Very few.

8173. Mr. Watson.—They are all not good looking I don't think so. I don't know whether Mr. Wrench is thinking one or not, but if he comes down, I will show him the horses I am breeding, the way they are bred, the way they are fed, and, if he disagrees with me, I will consider his views with pleasure.

8174. Chairman.—Any other remarks you would like to make?—Nothing, except if it came within the line of this Commission, I think the present way of handicapping hunters and short distance races, are very much against the thoroughbred horse; and I think that this should be looked to, because there is where we have to go for our stallions. I think there should be a few good long weight-carrying races established through the country. I think it would be a great means of keeping up the sinews of stallions, something on the lines of the Paris Steeplechase.

Dec. 4, 1896. Mr. John Persse.

selling now at that as two-year-olds. Colts that are taken from in the North of Ireland are £30 less than four years ago.

8162. Have you any experience of breeding from Connemara ponies?—Yes; they are useful good animals, no horses. I am talking of ten years ago.

8163. Have you seen any lately?—I did. I saw twenty or thirty of them yesterday in Athboy Fair.

8164. What do you think of them?—A poor looking lot, I thought.

8165. Do you know how they were bred?—I don't —I didn't ask what they were got by.

8166. Mr. La Touche.—You have been in Galway yourself?—Yes.

8167. And did you notice that the mares there have very much deteriorated in late years?—I saw some beautiful mares in spite of Clydesdales, but I think they belong to one man who kept a special breed for generations. He was near Hollymount.

8168. Mr. Wrench.—Was it a man named William Lyons, near Claremorris?—Some miles past it?—Oh, good. Wonderful; they were beautiful mares; I never saw anything nicer; about twenty were in the drove, and foals with them. They were the perfect type of a small thoroughbred mare.

8169. Mr. La Touche.—Have you any personal experience of Hackneys yourself?—Very little; I have seen them in their own country, in England.

8170. Do you think the introduction of any strain of blood into Connemara and the western districts is likely to affect horse-producing districts?—I keep stopping up through the country here and there. Fifty or sixty of them ponies are sold into Meath every year.

8171. And some of them are kept there?—Most of them are kept there, I think.

8172. Do you agree with Mr. Murphy that the best way to improve hunters here is to try to breed hunters?—I think so; and in they will go a long distance on a journey for you, and won't stand up.

8173. Do you agree as to the registration of stallions?—A very useful thing.

8174. Would you advocate the establishment of Government studs for the purpose of sending mares to farmers, and of putting valuable thoroughbred sires in reach of poor farmers at reasonable fees?—That will do away with private enterprise altogether, and then, if the Government got into any little difficulty to-morrow or next day, and the shop is shut up, the farmers will have nothing to fall back upon. If, and people like me, who keep stallions, if this is to be established, will want to be bought out and get compensation for our horses. It cuts both ways. I would not compete against the Government.

8175. You disapprove of Government studs?—I say it does away with private enterprise.

8176. Do you think the action of the Congested Districts Board has done away with private enterprise in the West?—No; I think there is very little private enterprise in the West.

8177. Were there not horses bred there before the Government stallions went down?—Many, indeed.

8178. Then how were they bred?—With their own country stallions, and they got some blood to them strange blood put into it.

8179. Didn't they belong to private individuals?—Some of the landlords down there may have had useful horses. The very ones I talked about just now must have produced very useful stallions and ponies.

8180. But is not private enterprise, even by a landlord, a thing of precarious?—I don't know about the private enterprise of a landlord able to pay any rent.

8181. Whatever is our own desire to interfering with private enterprise in Meath, but you don't see any reason to object to it in Galway?—The people there are poor. I have seen the greatest improvement in their cattle since bulls were sent there. I think that did them more good than horse breeding. The cattle are worth £2 a piece more than they were before.

8182. Have the young horses improved likewise?—In that country?

8183. Yes?—I don't think they are as good as they were. The Connemara pony is not the same pony that I remember.

8184. While the cattle have improved in value?—Very much.

8185. You don't think the horses have done the same?—I don't think so.

8186. Have you acted as a judge at any shows in those districts in the poorer parts of Ireland?—Yes; down at Hollymount.

8187. You didn't see any of these ponies shown?—They have a class for ponies there always.

8188. Do you think that any part of Ireland that you are acquainted with, that is capable of breeding a horse at all, is capable of breeding a hunter?—Well, I don't think that in Connemara you would breed a hunter, but you would breed a thing that might produce a hunter.

8189. Do you think it would be to the advantage of the Connemara horse breeder to endeavour to increase the size of his animal?—I don't know very much about ponies, but I think any pony over 14 hands is not as valuable as one under 14.

8190. For polo, I suppose?—That is the only thing you would get a good price for them for.

8191. Would you approve of stallions being sent down of a larger size with the idea of improving the size and stature of these ponies?—I think they are more useful their own size, and under it.

8192. Mr. Wrench.—What stallion would you think the best to send into Connemara?—You are asking me a thing I don't very well know, because I have not studied pony breeding. I suppose the old type of short-legged useful thing, with good neck and shoulders—a substance thoroughbred horse.

8193. Do you think as a rule that higher prices would be paying prices to breed horses?—I think they do, and they are very useful.

8194. I am not talking about their use, but whether they pay well?—No doubt they pay.

8195. What do polo players generally look for in a polo pony?—Action and ability, and a certain size.

8196. Those are the most important qualifications?—Yes.

8197. Did you ever see any of the country stallions in Connemara?—I did, a good many.

8198. Recently?—Last summer.

8199. Where?—Three or four of them I saw at Oughterard, at a fair, that were brought in to be shown there.

8200. Did you act as a judge at the jumping at Hollymount?—I really forget; I know it was very good there; it was two years ago I think.

8201. Not last year?—I wasn't there last year. I could not go.

8202. The Chairman.—I didn't ask you a great many questions because you agreed generally with Mr. Murphy, and there was no occasion to go over the same ground again; but if you have got any suggestions to make, or anything to say to the Commission, I should like to hear it?—I think the suggestion of Mr. Murphy, of giving prizes for the best three yearling and also for young mares, could not be bettered; I often said the same.

8203. Mr. Gibson.—And for the establishment of long walker races?—I would not like to compete with Mr. Murphy in his long distance races.

8204. The Chairman.—Do you judge thoroughbred horses yourself?—Yes.

8205. Mr. Grene.—You are the owner of "[illegible]"—Yes.

Mr. Charles Ward(?), [illegible], Sligo, examined.

8210. CHAIRMAN.—You live in the county of Sligo?—Yes.

8211. You act as land agent?—Yes; I was land agent to Sir Henry Gore-Booth.

8212. Do you know the county pretty well, generally?—Yes; the north part better than the south, but I know the south too.

8213. Are there many horses bred in the part you know best?—No, not many; it is not a very horse breeding country; it has not many advantages; there are very few sires, and I don't think there is a good one in it.

8214. Is the southern portion of the county better?—Yes. The late Mr. Alexander had some good sires, and there was another one, more towards Tubbercurry—"[illegible]" he was called—that got a wonderful lot of good horses.

8215. What kind of mares do the farmers keep there now?—Small weedy mares; the wonder is how they could pay [illegible].

8216. And what kind of stallions is there?—About as there is one thoroughbred horse, and there is a [illegible]—a Congested Districts Board horse there [illegible]; that is the only one about Sligo. There are two or three others, said to be thoroughbreds; [illegible], but they are unsound; this part of the county is very badly off for sires.

8217. What class of sire do you think is most suitable?—Thoroughbred.

8218. Have you seen any of the produce by the [illegible]?—I did not hear of him getting any—I don't think he was liked; I asked the farmers [illegible] and Major [illegible] that had him told me he didn't like him either; he was not [illegible], I think.

8219. You think that with a suitable thoroughbred sire, assuming that he stood cheap enough, that the farmers about you should breed a valuable class?—I think they could, more valuable than at present. I think it would be a good thing if the Government would grant money to landlords to enable them to buy a good sire to give to their tenants at a nominal price; that would be going against Mr. [illegible]'s private enterprise; but I think the landlords should endeavour to [illegible] their tenants by having the best sires of everything, cattle and sheep. When I went down there Sir Henry had started me to purchase bulls and rams every year for the tenants, and I think if the same thing was done about getting good sires, it would have a good effect.

8220. Are there any half-bred stallions in the county?—There is one that I know of at Sligo.

8221. What kind of a horse is he?—He stands a great deal; he is a fine looking horse got by "[illegible]" [illegible] by "Lord Gough." I know a few foals of his, and one is especially good, the other not quite so good looking; they are both out of good mares.

8222. Is he very popular?—I don't know; his action is against him; he dishes a great deal, but a [illegible]; he has great courage, and if his price is not better; he should get a good carriage horse.

8223. Do you know what fee he stands at?—£1.

8224. Do you know what are the fees of the thoroughbreds of the district?—£2 to £3. A great many, whatever they can get, the cheaper the better; and that is the reason I say the landlords should try to get good sires; if they got money from the Government they could afford to do it without making money out of it. Under the Royal Dublin Society's Scheme the stallion keepers get [illegible] for keeping a stallion so it [illegible].

8225. What do you think the small farmer could afford to pay?—The less the better—half a sovereign or so.

8226. Is the money the great object—supposing he can get a small horse for a sovereign, would he go to the animal for half a sovereign in preference?—Yes. I think you should leave the discretion with the landlord to whom [illegible] the horse, to enable him to give the service to a mare suitable for breeding; the farmers would then see the advantages of having a good mare.

8227. At what age do they sell their horses in your district?—As young ones.

8228. Where do they sell them?—There is a fair at [illegible] where they sell a good many, and a fair at Ballymote, and at [illegible], in [illegible], and some go to [illegible].

8229. What becomes of them?—They are shipped away; they sell them young; there is not many of them are offered to keep, they must keep them until they are two or three years old, and get a little work out of them.

8230. Have you any idea how the sires can be improved?—By giving some substantial prizes, and by offering some inducement to the farmers to keep them, by giving cheap service, or at a small rate for a good horse.

8231. Is the Royal Dublin Society's Scheme in operation in your district?—It is; but it is almost a dead letter; there is only one horse there belonging to the Royal Dublin Society, and I don't think he is [illegible]. I think there is only one good horse in the neighbourhood, and that is at [illegible], a horse called "[illegible]"; I have seen hunters from him recently; he is not very big—15.3, [illegible] a fellow that [illegible]; he is [illegible] by "[illegible]" [illegible] "[illegible]" by "[illegible]."

8232. During your experience of the country, do you think the breed of horses has improved or otherwise?—No, I think it has deteriorated.

8233. Do you attribute that to any known cause?—To the [illegible] away of the mares.

8234. Lord LONDONDERRY.—You think it would not pay a landlord, without Government assistance, to keep a sire?—I don't think he should look for profit.

8235. Could he keep it without losing money?—I don't think landlords should be asked to do it.

3 X 3

Dec. 1, 1896.

Mr. Charles Welsh.

thing; they are asked to do a great deal at present; to get a good sire means laying out a very large sum of money.

6336. You think if a landlord has got a good sire he should be helped?—Yes.

6337. This horse "Red Anchor," how far is he from you?—Seventeen miles.

6338. Is he one of the registered horses?—No, and I don't know why he is not. He ought to be; the owner, I believe, is applying to have him registered now. I don't think he understood about it until I told him.

6339. Mr. Wrench.—Was not a thoroughbred standing at Major Eustace's?—Yes; I don't think he is liked.

6340. He was standing the same as the Hackney?—Yes.

6341. You don't know how many services this thoroughbred got?—I don't think either got many.

6342. They are not a very horse-breeding people then?—Not very. I think they would, though, if more inducements were held out to them. They have to go too far; they have no inducement to breed now.

6343. Mr. Carew.—If inducements were held out would they breed?—I certainly think so.

6344. The Hackney didn't hold out these inducements?—I heard them say they didn't like him.

6345. The Chairman.—Is there any suggestion you would like to make?—I agree with what Mr. Murphy has said; I think his ideas are very good; I think he speaks like a book.

6346. You agree generally with what he said?—Yes.

Mr. R. D. Lawrence, Oxdikugan, Wicklow, examined.

Mr. R. D. Lawrence.

6347. Chairman.—You live in the County Wicklow?—I live in West Wicklow.

6348. Have you any experience yourself in horse breeding?—I have been breeding horses myself for the last twenty years.

6349. What class of horses?—I have been aiming to breed hunters, and have been fairly successful.

6350. What do you do with horses that are not quite good enough for hunters, or are they all good enough for hunters?—I manage to turn them all into hunters.

6351. Do you consider that the most profitable horse to breed in your part of the country?—Certainly the hunter is the most profitable kind to breed.

6352. How many brood mares do you keep?—At present four thoroughbreds and three half-bred mares.

6353. Have you any stallions?—I have two.

6354. What are they?—One is a thoroughbred, and the other a Clydesdale; the Clydesdale I got only last year.

6355. A pure-bred Clydesdale?—Yes, a pure-bred.

6356. You only have the Clydesdale breed?—Yes.

6357. What mares do you put to him?—I did not put any mares of my own except one cart mare.

6358. Do you propose to try thoroughbreds with him or a thoroughbred or half-bred mare?—Certainly not.

6359. Why did you get him?—We want them [illegible], and there are very few Clydesdales about. I got him more as a profitable horse. The farmers want to breed Clydesdales. He answers for this, and they get rid of him earlier than the thoroughbreds.

6360. What kind of mares are there about the country generally?—About [illegible] in the one may fairly well-bred; some descended from the old Irish breed, and some of them descended from a very good horse in that locality forty years ago, called "Midge"; and some of them descended from "Irish Birth October" and [illegible] and grandsons of his.

6361. Is the quality of the mares about the district improving, or the reverse?—They certainly are not improving, inasmuch as good ones have to be sold, and those mares that have to be sold are, of course, all by thoroughbred horses. I would sell them for good money.

6362. How is your part of the country off for sires?—Not as well off as I would like to see it. I have to pay [illegible] thoroughbred horses about here, not [illegible] to my idea.

6363. Are there any half-bred sires?—There are some.

6364. Do you approve of them?—I much prefer the thoroughbred; at the same time the half-bred horse descended from the mare with three pure crosses and that looked like a hunter, I would say would be the next best thing to a thoroughbred horse.

6365. Are there any other stallions of any other breeds?—There are one or two Clydesdales about, and in Carlow there are some shire horses. I live on the border of Carlow.

6366. Have you any experience of the cross of the thoroughbred with the Clydesdale or Shire horse?—I have, one or two cases, but I don't like the cross.

6367. You don't like them?—No; they generally have big heads—heads not stuck on properly. You cannot catch them properly in your hand, and they are deficient in stamina.

6368. What do you prefer?—The thoroughbred horse and the horse fairly approaching the thoroughbred horse.

6369. And the half-bred mare?—Yes; I have seen some good hunters bred from Connemara ponies.

6370. Have you ever done so yourself?—No, but neighbours of mine have.

6371. That has been successful?—Yes; very successful.

6372. Are they doing so now?—There is a neighbour of mine breeding out of a mare from a Connemara pony at present.

6373. Do you know at all—can you offer any opinion as to whether the Connemara pony has deteriorated?—Yes, deteriorated a good deal.

6374. Since when?—Within the last eight or ten years.

6375. Do you know Connemara yourself—have you ever been there?—No, I have never been there.

6376. And you have no opinion as to the cause of the deterioration of the ponies?—The drovers that come to the country are plainer looking; they are more off the pony, and more Clydesdale blood in them, I should say.

6377. Mr. Carew.—Have you any experience of Hackneys?—None, except that I have seen them at Shows.

6378. So far as you have seen them at the Shows you would not care for them?—No; I don't like their action at all. I had a drive in a trap with one and I didn't like him.

6379. He belonged to a neighbour?—Yes.

6380. What didn't you like in him?—He went very well for a few miles, and then died away and wasted about every way.

6381. Mr. La Touche.—There is traffic in ponies

between the Wexford [illegible] and Wicklow [illegible]; they come in large droves to the fairs about—[illegible], [illegible], and [illegible].

8282. Do they breed from them?—The small farmers buy them and keep them to work, and they breed a foal from them.

8283. And anything that affects the blood of the [illegible] is calculated then to affect the breed in the county of Wicklow?—Certainly.

8284. Mr. Wrench.—You think breeding from thoroughbred horses is the most successful way of horse breeding?—I would say it is the most successful way to breed the hunter.

8285. And you think hunters are the best horses to aim at breeding?—Yes, I do; the high class hunter.

8286. And that is what you say yourself?—Yes.

8287. These neighbours of yours, are they not their produce from Connemara ponies as high as you can sell your produce not from Connemara ponies?—I would not go so far as that. I have known one Connemara pony being the grand dam—the produce to go to £150, and [illegible] up to 15 stone.

8288. Have you known more than one instance of that?—Yes, two or three.

8289. Did you sell a short time ago some horses that you bred?—I did.

8290. Did you find they sold at paying prices?—No, I did not. I sold the worst I had.

8291. You sold about twenty, did you not?—I did.

8292. Did you sell a black horse you got by "[illegible]," grand dam by "Old Ridge"?—Yes.

8293. You got 90 guineas for that one?—Yes, the [illegible] pony.

8294. Did you also sell a bay gelding, three years, by "[illegible]," grand dam by "Old Ridge," for 110 guineas?—That was a good price; those two were very [illegible]—much [illegible].

8295. Was a bay mare by "Sylvio," dam by "[illegible]," a pony?—It was not, but "Sylvio" was an [illegible] horse, and the mare was [illegible].

8296. That went for 145 guineas?—Yes.

8297. A bay gelding by "Pakenham," dam by "[illegible]," went for 105 guineas?—Yes; I bought [illegible] at the present time.

8298. At that time didn't you sell your entire stud?—No.

8299. How many did you sell?—About 20.

8300. And you didn't find these pay?—No, that is why I got rid of them.

8301. As a matter of fact in breeding you must lose a good many animals?—Of course, you cannot breed them all to order.

8302. How many brood mares had you at that time?—Four or five, I should say.

8303. Did you find the horses pay as well as cattle?—Yes; I have got some very good prices for hunters.

8304. Do you find altogether that horses pay better than cattle?—I think they do.

8305. In spite of the advice you have [illegible] sum in accordance [illegible]?—I should say so; but I would like [illegible] to note against the [illegible] of public money on [illegible] blood being introduced into Wicklow.

8306. Chairman.—You naturally admit that in breeding horses you cannot always ensure that you will be quite satisfied with the animal you produce?—No, you cannot.

8307. Any more than in cattle breeding or anything else?—No.

8308. I take it you think that horse breeding can be made to pay under certain circumstances, and as far as your opinion is concerned, you think breeding hunters is the most profitable?—I think so.

8309. You don't mean by that that it must be the most profitable everywhere?—No.

8310. Mr. O'Neill.—This sale of yours was not with the object of getting rid of your entire stud?—No.

8311. Only with the object of getting rid of those that did not pay?—Quite so.

8312. The Chairman.—Is there anything else you would like to say to the Commission?—I would like to say that I think encouragement by prizes for yearlings in the spring would be very good. I don't see how very well you can encourage farmers to keep their best mares, because when we want money we must sell the best mares; and I do think that if they are not fed from the weaning stage to the following spring they never turn into anything. In reading the newspaper reports of the Commission last week, I saw that one gentleman wanted to do away with Queen's Plates. I would not at all approve of that. Those are the horses we want to encourage most; they are the ones proved to have stamina. I would rather agree with Mr. Murphy's idea of having long-distance races.

8313. You think the improvement of thoroughbred stock would be of general value throughout the country, because you would have a better chance of size to go so?—Certainly.

8314. Mr. Wrench.—Would you register any stallions except thoroughbreds?—I would register half-bred stallions which have good [illegible] the dam side.

8315. Would you make that a sine qua non?—Yes.

8316. Would you register any suitable looking horse that had that breeding?—Yes, provided he was like a hunter and showed quality enough. I would also suggest that all stallions should be licensed and examined by a veterinary surgeon each season.

8317. Mr. Gibson.—That is, that every stallion should take out a licence before serving a mare?—Yes, in favour for the public, but I would only register the thoroughbred horses, and those half-[illegible] the thoroughbreds.

8318. For the purpose of getting rid of this mongrel stock?—Yes, and unsound ones.

Mr. George Russell, Dundalk, examined.

8319. Chairman.—You live in the County of Louth?—Yes.

8320. Do you wish to speak on behalf of the Committee of the Dundalk Horse Show?—I have not been specially sent here by the Committee; but speaking about coming here to some of the members, they thought if I could come and give evidence on a particular point it would be a good thing, a point that we are all agreed upon.

8321. You are a member of that Committee?—Yes. I may say I have been the one to start the Show from the beginning. I have worked it up, and taken a great interest in it.

8322. What are the particular points you wish to speak about?—Well, all the evidence we have read goes to show that the improvement should be in the direction of the mares; well, we don't think so—at least I don't. I think the improvement should begin with the stallions. At present in the county I don't think we have five thoroughbred weight-carrying hunters.

8323. In the county—you mean in your district?—I don't think I saw more than three in my district that would carry 15 stone to hounds. As long as we are breeding from cast off 5 furlong horses from England what can we have but these miserable mares we see in the fairs? What I would suggest is the establishing of a stud farm for the purpose of breeding thoroughbred weight-carrying hunters to let out for the country.

8324. Hunting [illegible]; the only valuable hunters we have in this country are those carrying 13 to 15 stone; but the want of suitable mares and suitable stallions we cannot produce them in sufficient numbers.

8325. You are in favour of establishing a Government establishment?—It is the only way to improve the thing; it would take a longer time than within the reign of private enterprise.

8326. What would you suggest they should do with the fillies?—If you have a weight-carrying hunter sire you are bound to improve the fillies in time.

8327. What would be done with the fillies at the Government establishment?—Let them out to suitable districts, not to every district; it is a well-known fact that you cannot get some sires you have here [illegible]. I would choose the districts, and [illegible] in suitable parishes; a certain number would have to be kept for the production of the very thing I am advocating.

8328. When you say let out, you mean for pure hire or [illegible]?—Quite so.

8329. And then supposing these sires to be bred and produced?—Then I would let them out on the same terms as under the present scheme. You have horses scattered all over the country fit to be let to good mares—rather a heavy hunter with the bone.

8330. They would have to serve at a low fee?—I think the fee is reasonable at present.

8331. I mean these Government horses?—If they could charge a lower fee so much the better, but they are not unreasonable at present.

8332. You admit, I suppose, that the existence of these mares is detrimental?—Yes.

8333. You tell me the most practical way to improve them would be to improve the stallions?—Undoubtedly, no question about it; what I have noticed at our shows is the few mares that are shown, and those very bad quality.

8334. I suppose you have not thought out in detail anything about it?—No, only I merely wished to state that is the unanimous opinion of some of my friends.

8335. Lord Ashtown.—Do you wish these horses bred at the stud farm to be thoroughbred horses?—Mainly; I want to avoid mixing; we cannot [illegible] all our weight-carrying hunters are mongrels; they have all a cross of the draught in them, for the purpose of getting strength you have to get the draught.

8336. These horses bred in the stud, do you wish them to be what are called half-bred horses or thoroughbreds?—I want them pure bred if possible.

8337. You don't go breeding them as racing horses?—I don't think horses bred for racing purposes are fit to let out for hunters at all.

8338. But you want to buy hunting mares?—You have to begin with the hunting mares; you would not get a weight-carrying thoroughbred mare.

8339. And you would form a breed of hunting sires?—Yes; and endeavour to breed straight instead of as at present by crossing.

8340. Mr. La Touche.—I understood you said those mares might to be purchased, and then you said they should be thoroughbred horses out of hunting mares—that would not be purchased?—You will have to work up the breed. With the present horses I don't think you can get a sufficient number of weight-carrying hunters.

8341. You propose that the Government should manufacture a breed?—Yes.

8342. A breed of sires?—Yes; to get a horse that will carry 13 to 15 stone to hounds.

8343. You don't think that could be done by breeding from thoroughbreds?—Not the sort we have at present.

8344. Do you think it is beyond the bounds of possibility to breed a 13 stone to 15 stone horse with a thoroughbred sire?—If you do you must put them to a draft mare.

8345. Do any of the horses of the congested districts come to you?—None whatever. I don't know anything about it.

8346. Mr. Wrench.—To keep up this breed you would mate the horses with each other?—I think it is the only way.

8347. You would not go on mating with the thoroughbred, but mate the animals with each other?—Yes.

8348. What is your idea of escaping a bastard breed?—Quite so. I don't know how to do it any other way.

8349. Have the mares deteriorated since you?—Yes; they have become lighter in bone, and not nearly such good horses.

8350. Do they breed many hunters here?—Everybody goes in for breeding a hunter if they possibly can, and of course, anything that does not turn out a hunter is sold for harness purposes.

8351. Chairman.—Is there anything else you would like to say?—Nothing, I think.

The Commission then adjourned to January 5th, 1897.

SIXTEENTH DAY.—TUESDAY, JANUARY 5TH, 1897.

Present:—Lord Rathdonnell, in the Chair; Lord Ashtown, Hon. Henry W. Fitzwilliam, Colonel St. Quintin, Mr. Percy La Touche, Mr. F. S. Wrench.

Mr. Hugh Neville, Secretary.

Sir Douglas Brooke, Bart., Colebrooke, County Fermanagh, examined.

8352. Chairman.—You live at Colebrooke, county Fermanagh, and take considerable interest in the subject of horse breeding?—Yes, I have been on the Dublin Society's district committee since it was first started. I did secretary for it for some time, and I have taken a good deal of interest in the local shows there too, and I have been breeding for some years a good many horses myself.

8353. What class of horses do you breed?—I was trying to breed hunters. I was breeding from very good mares. They were all mares in the Hunters' Improvement Society's Record, and there were some of them mares that had taken prizes in England, and I put them to the best thoroughbred horse I could get. I put them to several of the horses sent down under the Dublin Society's first scheme, which were supposed to be the best horses, I suppose, in Ireland at the time; and I put them to all the best thoroughbred horses I could find about the place, and I had a very good thoroughbred stallion of my own, but I did not find that I succeeded in breeding horses of the class that one wanted as hunters.

8354. What class of land is there in your district: what soil?—It is a good deal limestone, but it is rather a poor soil on the whole.

8355. Are there many horses bred in your neigh-

[illegible]-blood?—Oh, yes; there are a good many [illegible], but I don't think quite so many as used to be. I should say that [illegible] out of the [illegible] a foot about [illegible] in [illegible] years.

8856. What class of horse do they breed?—General utility [illegible]; [illegible] else. They did breed [illegible] Clydesdales at one time, but they gave them up, they found it was such an exceedingly bad cross. I am sorry to say there is some of the blood left in the country still. But the other horses they breed are [illegible] sold as remounts for the foreign [illegible] [illegible]. The better class and the others are largely used in the country among the farmers. When I say the better class, the sold better class than that are sold for harness purposes, I think, more than anything else.

8857. Are there suitable mares and stallions in the district for getting that class?—No; there are very few good mares. I don't think there are [illegible] in the whole county that are fit to be put to a thoroughbred stallion at all. The mares are all either these bad horses with half Clydesdale blood in them or else they are bad small and [illegible] altogether, and when put to a thoroughbred they would nothing but [illegible] weeds, and the result of that is that the people put them to what they call half-bred stallions —or what I call a half-bred stallion—I should call them a mongrel stallion, simply to get a little weight and substance for the produce.

8858. Are there many of these stallions in the country?—Yes; a good many, and I don't think very many of them are sound.

8859. A bad class of stallion?—A really bad class of stallion.

8860. And the mares, you say, are——?—Mares are mostly the majority; there are a few good mares, but very few.

8861. Do the farmers in your district [illegible] their foals or sell them young?—They keep them mostly, and a few are sold young when they are weaned.

8862. Where do they sell those horses?—In Clones and Enniskillen, young horses, and at the May fair anything they can [illegible]; but the colts that are sold in, the fair that are horses that are bought in the North of Ireland and brought up and fed by the farmers.

8863. Do they do the feeding business in your district?—Yes, some of them; there are very few horses bred in my district that are fit to send to the May fair at any time of their life.

8864. Do you ever remember any better class of horse in your district than what there is now, in the old [illegible], do you think?—They are certainly not improved, and I was told by men who have more experience than I, farmers who are breeding horses, that in their memory they have decidedly deteriorated, if, about any [illegible] years ago the horses, it [illegible] the horses then, they certainly have not improved within the last [illegible] years.

8865. Have you any scheme that you think would work out well for the improvement of horses?—I should think that the class of stallions that are there at the present time are not suitable, and I have seen the produce of Hackneys with these [illegible] and it certainly has been very successful, they are animals which have [illegible] well and fetched good prices. I had one of them myself out of two half-bred mares that I had, that I only bred from because they happened to be there; I certainly should not have bred from them with a thoroughbred, I tried the experiment with a Hackney and the produce of those two mares sold for more than the produce of [illegible] should be a thoroughbred stallion, and gave me very much less trouble, in fact. I had them [illegible] in the [illegible] [illegible] together, and when the thoroughbred produce was not thriving the produce of the [illegible] Hackneys were as fat as they could stand. There has been one Hackney stallion in the district, only one and he was a very good one, and I have seen the produce of this Hackney and certainly with these mares it has

had a much more suitable and useful article for the small farmers than the thoroughbred did for them. One I believe the only thing really to improve the breed of horses through the country is, as was suggested here before, I believe, to register all horses, in fact, in Ireland, the same as dogs are registered, register them with a full pedigree, so that anybody can see what the pedigree is, and I think it will stop a good deal of false pedigrees that are sometimes put on indifferent animals.

8866. Have you had any opportunity of seeing any of the stock by the horses supplied by the Congested Districts Board?—Oh, yes, I have seen two that are there, or one that were bought at [illegible] there, one of them is a very fine colt about 15.2, with good action, a heavy-[illegible]-everything colt, the other shows more quality, is lighter built and is a very good hunter; it was out hunting the other day, and is a very fine jumper indeed, I have never seen it in very long runs, but what I have seen it do it has done very well. And then I have seen a lot of the produce down at the stud farm, and I have seen some very good ones. There are two colts that are there, those one that would, I think, make a good enough pair of [illegible] [illegible] anyone to have.

8867. What stud farm?—The Congested Districts Board's stud farm, Clonsilla.

8868. You would not have used the half-bred Hackneys?—The half-bred Hackneys, yes, and also there are some of the produce of the Arab stallion, "[illegible] Jolly," they are very nice ponies, but they are absolutely out of the market, as far as I can see; they are only about 13.2 to 13.3, would do for a child's pony, but there is no value in them, which the others have [illegible]. I don't suppose those two colts are [illegible] for harness yet, but they are certainly worth £100 or £120 as they stand.

8869. What age are they?—Rising three. Then I have seen two animals on Mr. [illegible] own farm, one of them bred in Achill Island by a Hackney, a horse of over sixteen hands, and I don't think £100, or £120 would induce him to buy it.

8870. Is there a Hackney stallion standing in Achill Island?—There was I believe.

8871. Has the Royal Dublin Society's scheme been of any benefit in your district?—I think not. I have been watching it the whole time, but I don't think it has been of any real benefit.

8872. Have you any improvement to suggest with regard to that scheme?—I don't think it can be improved on without more money. The money is not there to do any good. The money devoted to each society must be so small that it can do very little.

8873. Do you think with some money the scheme would work beneficially in the country?—Yes, but I should certainly make it a much broader scheme. I should register other horses than thoroughbreds. I should register those according to the desire of the people in each county. You might have it the same as the present scheme, and allow anybody who had a Hackney to have him registered, and anybody who had a thoroughbred to have him registered. You would soon see to which of the registered stallions the majority of the people were going, and would thereby be able to judge which was more required in the country. I certainly think the scheme should be open that way to allow other horses of pure breeds to be registered.

8874. Have you any further observations you would like to make to the Commission?—No, I can not think of anything at the present moment.

8875. Mr. FITZGERALD.—You mentioned some of these horses by—I think you said, Hackneys, that they thrive and did well; you are referring to the first cross of these, I think?—The first cross, yes.

8876. In Ireland a fact that the first cross of any distinct breed generally does show great thriving powers, whether it is horses or whether it is cattle, or anything else? Do you think the [illegible] breeding [illegible] as you describe would [illegible] in [illegible] means? I think so from what I have been told by people who have tried the experiment, both crossing the half-bred produce back to the Hackney or crossing it to the thoroughbred. I have been told that the produce thrives very well, but I have not any personal experience of it.

[illegible]. Then that is your opinion against, I may say, the generally accepted theory?—Yes.

[illegible]. But you know that that is the accepted theory?—Yes, I know it is.

[illegible]. LORD ARDILAUN.—You have tried breeding hunters. Do the horses which you breed [illegible] at all?—No, practically not. They may by an accident get one, but there is no market for a hunter, but in some [illegible] there is [illegible].

[illegible]. When you were breeding hunters you said you failed. Do you mean they did not grow?—They grew tall enough, but not with sufficient bone, and were very weak.

[illegible]. Do you think the soil is not suitable for breeding an animal?—I certainly don't think it is suitable for breeding hunters.

[illegible]. You said a lot of [illegible] were bred in the district; how are they bred?—Mostly off the half-bred stallions.

[illegible]. Of half Clydesdale mares or weedy mares?—Of weedy mares and off Clydesdale mares, too. It is all the Clydesdale [illegible] generally by a thoroughbred horse, and all the weedy class by a half-bred.

[illegible]. Are [illegible] that are bought in your district?—They [illegible] most of them. I think they mostly go to the Continent; they are bought very largely for the [illegible] and Italian Governments.

[illegible]. You say you have seen the produce by the Congested Districts Board's horses, have you seen the horses themselves?—Yes, I have seen them all.

[illegible]. What do you think of them?—I like them very much. I think they are exactly the [illegible] to mate with weedy light mares, especially as I have seen the good [illegible] result of the cross.

[illegible]. You have bred, you say, two horses yourself by a Hackney; have you had any experience of working them, or anything of that kind?—No, I sold them both. But one of them was worked by the farmer who bought it, from the time it was nearly three until it was four, on the farm, and he then sold it and got [illegible] it—a good price considering the animal, something under £[illegible] for it. The other one was not worked at all; it was just fed and sold.

[illegible]. Have you [illegible] any Hackneys yourself, owned or [illegible] experience?—I own one half-bred Hackney at the present moment, a pony of about [illegible]. I have [illegible] her for the last five seasons. I never got her [illegible] on her. I [illegible] her, and I have had [illegible] very long runs. In the [illegible] she has only given me two [illegible], and the [illegible] about as it is very easy to get [illegible]. Talking of that, I knew another Hackney belonging to the local doctor, a Hackney bred in the [illegible] districts, which he bought as a foal; he regularly hunts him [illegible], and not only hunts it but rides it across country [illegible] patients; he [illegible] goes straight across the country, and when he is [illegible] it is a man [illegible] enough to [illegible] the tail of his pony than anything else.

[illegible]. You keep a thoroughbred stallion yourself?—Yes.

[illegible]. Do you get a sufficient number of mares?—No, I do not.

[illegible]. MR. WRENCH.—Have you considered the question of licensing stallions at all, having a licensing stallion [illegible]?—Yes.

[illegible]. Do you approve of that suggestion?—I do most thoroughly approve of it. I should [illegible] very [illegible] penalty on any [illegible] stallion [illegible] any [illegible] that [illegible].

[illegible]. Would you follow the system adopted in (several) foreign countries, of placing on a very heavy penalty unless the horse is properly passed, for covering any mares but the owner's?—Yes.

[illegible]. The [illegible] very [illegible] own mares by [illegible]?—Yes; I think you can hardly prevent a man covering his own mares if he likes, with an unlicensed sire.

[illegible]. Which do you think it would pay the farmers in your district best to breed, hunters or harness horses?—Harness horses unquestionably. There are no dealers coming up into the country to look for hunters; any dealers that are there are looking for harness horses and remounts.

[illegible]. Is there a good demand in [illegible] fairs for a harness horse that has action?—Yes.

[illegible]. And action is the one you want; you want breed for what will bring money?—Undoubtedly; they will look at a horse to see that he has action, and won't look at him again if his action is not pretty good.

[illegible]. When you speak of remounts being bought, do you chiefly refer to foreign Governments?—I think almost absolutely to foreign Governments; there may be a few bought for our own Government, but not many.

[illegible]. There are many in the district who deal largely, quite close to you?—Yes; I [illegible] buy nearly a thousand horses in the year.

[illegible]. And [illegible] one of the horses you bred some [illegible] of the [illegible] in [illegible]?—Yes.

[illegible]. I think you said that there were a great many [illegible] stallions, but what would be your definition of a half-bred stallion that should be registered under the [illegible] Society's scheme?—Well, certainly a horse with at least four crosses of thoroughbred blood. I know Captain [illegible] definition of one for the [illegible] Improvement Society's [illegible] is that the horse should have four crosses of thoroughbred, and the original [illegible] should have been a registered mare at the time. I think that is perhaps rather a strong condition, but certainly there should be not less than four crosses of thoroughbred; whereas these half-bred horses, I very much fear, are [illegible] very often are half-bred horses, and the [illegible] may be [illegible]; I [illegible] a good Clydesdale blood in them.

[illegible]. You don't think that the Clydesdale blood has been a success?—Certainly not.

[illegible]. And it has been very largely [illegible]?—It was largely introduced at one time.

[illegible]. CHAIRMAN.—I would like to know what [illegible] there are in your district?—A good [illegible]; when I say [illegible] they are 21-inch [illegible].

[illegible]. But they [illegible]?—Yes.

[illegible]. [illegible]?—Not [illegible]; I wish there were [illegible].

[illegible]. MR. WRENCH.—There was one thing I think you said in answer to Mr. [illegible], I think he said it was an accepted rule that the first cross from any breed was the [illegible]; you said "yes." Do you simply mean that that [illegible] theory [illegible] Hackneys is [illegible]?—Oh, no, [illegible] I have heard; I have no personal experience of this, but from what I have heard from others I doubt it.

[illegible]. It was only the general theory, not referring to Hackneys specially?—Yes.

[illegible]. CHAIRMAN.—You think the Hackney [illegible] the exception to the rule?—I would not say that, that is the generally accepted idea [illegible] the [illegible], [illegible] the case of [illegible].

[illegible]. But the second cross again?—I think the effect of the fresh blood will still tell.

[illegible]. Although it is generally [illegible] that the second cross is not so good in all other breeds?—Yes.

[illegible]. Except in the Hackney?—Yes.

[illegible]. MR. [illegible].—But would not the Hackney be [illegible] to the mares in your district than a thoroughbred on the [illegible] of [illegible] to [illegible]?—Yes.

Mr. Robert M'Kinley, Stranorlar, Castlefin, Donegal.

Jan. [illegible] 1896. Mr. Robert M'Kinley.

8611. Chairman.—You live at Stranorlar, on the east side of the county Donegal?—Yes.

8612. Are many horses bred in your neighbourhood?—Yes, there are a great many.

8613. What class of mare do the farmers generally breed from?—They are very indifferent at the present time, small light-legged little mares.

8617. Do you consider that horse-breeding can be carried on profitably in Donegal?—Well, to a certain extent it can. Generally the farmers in my neighbourhood, the majority of them are small farmers, varying from 10 to 40 acres of land, and they breed a young mare to do the work of the farm, and then if it turns out well, he is sold to the [illegible] when four or five years old, that is the way breeding is generally carried on.

8618. What class of horses in your opinion should be bred in the district?—Well, to suit the wants of the farmers themselves, to begin with, it requires a strong horse, probably to turn into a van horse or go to the Glasgow trams or something of the sort, when they turn up at a certain age, or a strong harness horse.

8619. Are the mares of the district suited for breeding that class of horse?—Yes, when you get a [illegible] cross with [illegible].

8620. What kind of a stallion do you think the mares of the district should be mated with?—The stallion that gets the most stock in the district is a cross between a Clydesdale mare and a Welsh [illegible], that breed is doing more to the country than any other, whether it is that he is helping to a horse for [illegible] I don't know.

8621. What sort of produce comes from that?—[illegible] [illegible] the light mares and [illegible] of horse [illegible] a van horse or to go to the Glasgow trams, they begin to work those young horses at one and a half year old and they work them up until they are about four, and sell them off; that is the demand in the district for the purposes that I have mentioned.

8622. Are there many hunters bred in the district?—Oh, yes, generally every farmer breeds a few for himself every other year. I myself bred a good many horses, but I go in for a stronger class of horse, my land is very heavy and I go in for a Clydesdale horse generally. I have bred some light horses, but I have given it up, as they did not pay me. I have half a dozen Clydesdale mares at the present time and I am breeding from a Clydesdale horse from them.

8623. What sort of soil is there in your district?—It varies a good deal, my land has a good deal of limestone in it, but the majority of the land is [illegible] [illegible] and boggy land.

8624. Does it require a heavy horse to work it?—Well, the land is very hilly, the horse therefore very [illegible].

8625. Do you think a heavy horse is better for the [illegible]?—It is better for the hills on any farm.

8626. Have you made any observations of the stock got by the Congested Districts Board's horses?—Oh, yes, I have seen some of their produce, there was a horse stood in Ballybofey, six or seven miles from my place, a horse belonging to the Congested Districts Board, "[illegible]," a very good Hackney.

8627. What are the stock like?—The little fellows I saw were a good many of them, but the farmers there would require a stronger horse than a Hackney to mate with their mares, that is the opinion of a good many I have been talking to lately. When I heard I was coming up here to give evidence I asked several that would give me information, and they say they would rather have a stronger horse to mate with their mares, they think the Hackney is too small.

8628. What class of stallion do you yourself recommend?—Speaking for myself I would go in for a Clydesdale, but of course for the neighbourhood there is entirely different. Anything that I have been referring to would be a strong horse up to about 15 to 15.2, something like a carriage horse or a well made hunter, that would be exhibited in the Dublin Horse Show in August, up to eighteen stone weight.

8629. Do you think you would get that from a Clydesdale stallion?—I don't know.

8630. At what age are the young stock usually sold in your district?—Some are sold at one and a half and some of them are sold from that up to five years old.

8631. Has the price of horses [illegible] of late years in your district?—It certainly has.

8632. Are there any thoroughbred sires in your district?—There is only a horse called "Greenhills," standing in the district under the Royal Dublin Society's scheme.

8633. Do you know where he came from?—His name is "Greenhills," he is registered under the Royal Dublin Society.

8634. Mr. Fitzwilliam.—What age is he?—I think he is an aged horse now. He was bred by Mr. [illegible], I think, in the beginning of the [illegible], I [illegible] it now. He has been under the Royal Dublin Society's scheme for a good number of years now. He belongs to Mr. [illegible], of [illegible].

8635. Chairman.—Now with regard to [illegible] of horses, are there many in the district?—Yes, there are a good many horses, very inferior horses too.

8636. How are they mostly bred?—Well, I took some little notes of some of them. There is a man has a horse called "Sir William." The next one is a horse called "Windsor," and "Windsor" was out of a Hackney mare and [illegible] by a Clydesdale horse. That is [illegible] [illegible]. I had it from the owner of the horse himself.

8637. Lord Arthur Hill.—He is by a Clydesdale horse out of a [illegible] [illegible] mare?—No. This horse is by a sire who was by a Clydesdale horse out of a [illegible] mare.

8638. And the dam is anything I suppose?—The dam was anything at all.

8639. Chairman.—What sort of stock does he get?—The stock is not very heavy. I have seen a good many of the stock sired by them. He is very [illegible], and the fee that was charged is £1 for the service and 2s. 6d. to the groom—on bail no money. They [illegible] about [illegible] marks each year. Considerably the fees are [illegible]. [illegible] the [illegible] [illegible]. The farmers are in such a way they are not able to pay high service fees, and they take the cheapest horse they can get. This Welsh horse, I mentioned before, [illegible] [illegible] a Clydesdale mare and the sire was an imported Welsh [illegible].

8640. Mr. Wrench.—A Welsh [illegible]?—Yes.

8641. Chairman.—You don't know anything about the breeding of the Welsh [illegible]?—[illegible] he was a horse up to 14 hands I am sure, and this horse is up to 15 hands, too. This horse with the light [illegible] mares [illegible] [illegible] gets a fairly good [illegible]. It is able to do the work of this small farmers at 1½ year old, and they make it work until four year old, and then they sell it for £15 or £20, and perhaps some would go to £30 when three year old.

8642. Have you any suggestions to make to the Commission with a view to improving horse-breeding in the district?—I would say the [illegible] of the horses in my neighbourhood should be controlled by [illegible].

8643. How would you replace those?—I would [illegible] those men [illegible] those horses from the end of the season until the next season begins. They [illegible] those horses on the farm. I would say, [illegible], [illegible] [illegible] for the use of their horses, and let the Government assist them in buying suitable horses for the districts, subsidise the owner, and compel him to [illegible]

8 N

[illegible]

it as a low enough service fee to suit the wants of the country?

8444. Which stallion would you propose that would produce both stallions—a carriage horse or hunter as I describe, and as well a Clydesdale horse, and give the people their choice?—I am quite sure the two horses would do as much as they would be able to do in the district. I have great confidence in that. I know a friend of mine bought a Clydesdale horse in Scotland, I advised him to buy it. He is a very good horse, and cost a good deal of money. That horse is let at £2 10s. People think it is too high a fee, and if he would put it at 30s. they would patronise him, but his fee at would not pay him to let it at such a low fee.

8445. You said you would also have a carriage or hunter sire. How would you get that class of horse?—That is a difficult question. From a three-quarter Clydesdale mare with a thoroughbred horse. I have bred horses of that description myself. There is one mare in particular that I bred eight foals from with a thoroughbred horse. The first I bred I sold him in the May fair at £80 at three years old, and the gentleman that bought him from me (Mr. McGill) kept him for about three months and sold him at Tweeddale fair in England, and got £130 for him.

8446. Mr. La Touche.—Was he a gelding?—Yes.

8447. Lord Ashtown.—How was he bred exactly, a thoroughbred horse, "Shandarilly," by "[illegible]." He is dead now. He belonged to the same man that has "Guaiacol." He was about the best breeding horse we had in our country. He died this last season.

8448. Mr. Wrench.—He was a small horse?—Oh, no, he was a big horse, up to 16 hands high.

8449. Mr. Fitzwilliam.—What did you say this horse was by, that fetched £130?—He was by "Shandarilly."

8450. A thoroughbred horse?—Yes.

8451. When was he sold, as the year round?—Sold as a hunter to follow foxhounds.

8452. What sort of a mare was he out of?—A three-quarter Clydesdale mare. I bred eight foals in eight successive years from the same mare and the same horse—three fillies and five males—and they all turned out good horses. The third foal that the mare bred was a filly, and at three years old I put her to a thoroughbred horse, "[illegible]" kept by under the Royal Dublin Society—and the foal that I had by that mare I sold it at the mother's foot for £17 when about three months old, to be delivered in November when the foal would be spent. It turned out an inferior horse, whether the man did not treat it well, I do not know, but it is not worth more than £17, and the mare was a good one.

8453. That must have been exceptional, because Shandarilly is particularly well-bred, and an extremely strong horse, and a very good-looking horse too?—Yes, I sold that mare in May fair when coming five year old at £40.

8454. Then on the whole your experience of breeding from a thoroughbred horse has been a success?—Yes, with a very strong mare; but with a light mare, it has not been a success. I would go with a light mare to mill, and I got a horse not worth more than £15 or £20 when three year old. I am sure as a horse would be worth to a considerable, but the majority of the farmers would wish, and when they breed a horse, they want to put him to the plough when he is young, and so they cannot put a light horse they want to breed a strong horse.

8455. Don't you think in Ireland they used to put a horse to work early, no matter by whatever horse they are—don't you think early work in Ireland is a great number of cases is carried too far?—I think so. I don't think a young horse should be put to work until he is coming three year old, and then to light work for the first year.

8456. You say that in your district there are a number of stallions that you describe as being of a very second-rate kind?—Undoubtedly.

8457. Have they been there long, or are they new importations?—They have all been bred in the district.

8458. And used in the district?—Yes.

8459. And in fact, they are to a great extent responsible for the present dearth of good mares that are in the district?—I don't say that that is just altogether the reason.

8460. To a great extent?—To a certain extent it is. I think the cause of the deterioration of the mares of the district is this—that the farmers are not as well off as they used to be, and when a man has a filly that he would like to keep as a brood mare, he has to sell her to meet a pressing demand, and consequently has to keep a worse one in her place, or one that such while as suitable to go in and is not suitable for the market; I think that has more to do with it than anything else.

8461. But still you say on the whole that the horses are very bad?—Yes; they are a bad description, they have deteriorated certainly within the last ten years considerably. And there was a horse registered in the Royal Dublin Society, "[illegible]," is quite a blank altogether, there is nothing using that horse him, sixty five or six mares in the season, they have no notion to put the horse.

8462. Is that on account of the high fee or what?—The farmers don't like to breed from a thoroughbred horse, they think the progeny would be too light for their work, and then it when they look to sell cheaply; and the high service fee has a good deal to do with it too, I think, this horse is let at £3 5s., if you look at the book.

8463. I am not surprised the horse was not very popular if he had a horse let at 30s. or £3, I don't think he would get more to do, the farmers are prejudiced against breeding from a thoroughbred horse in our district.

8464. In fact, no record of that very inferior animal have had a foal in the district for a long time?—I think so, judging from what was said to be done with a thoroughbred horse at all.

8465. You recommend either a hunter stallion or a carriage horse?—Yes.

8466. How ought such a horse in your opinion to be bred?—The most successful breeding I have ever tried is an uncommonly strong mare put to a thoroughbred horse; you will either get a suitable hunter or a very strong harness horse.

8467. How would the mare be bred?—I have told you that I bred myself from a three-quarter Clydesdale mare, the mother of those colts and fillies that I mentioned.

8468. You would not object to Clydesdale blood being introduced into the mare?—I don't think it would do any harm at all; I have bred some pure bred Clydesdale horses myself; I have six or seven pure Clydesdale mares, and I have sold some of their young stock, I sold one horse to Jones last at £30, a pair, to go back to Scotland to keep for a stud horse. I could if I wish to incur trouble expenses in keeping my brood mares; I bought two mares in Scotland at one pony a half guinea, which cost me 70 guineas, I brought another which cost me £40.

8469. Lord Ashtown.—Where is the young stock bred in your district, you say they are bought some them as foals, who buys them?—Very few are bought as foals, I don't think I sold one.

8470. When they are sold, who buys them besides the dealers to sell to the Glasgow market.

8471. They are bought by dealers to go out of the country, they don't come down south?—Oh, no, they go to Glasgow principally.

8472. Mr. La Touche.—Do you think that the heavy stock in your country has deteriorated?—I think so, I think they are.

8473. To what do you attribute that?—To the bad

quality of the mares, because they could not keep good ones.

8473. Who did they sell them to?—They went out of the district altogether.

8474. Do you know the county Fermanagh?—Not much.

8475. You heard Mr. Douglas Brooke's evidence to the effect that he attributed the deterioration of the good horses very much to the introduction of Clydesdale blood?—As far as the county Fermanagh, and the county Donegal, is altogether an agricultural county where I live, there are no tracts of grazing land at all, it is consequently altogether an agricultural country, and the introduction of Clydesdale blood into that country, I think, tends to improve and strengthen the class of mares more than anything else.

8476. You consider that this blood has done good in the county Donegal?—It has not been in existence sufficiently for me to give a decided opinion on that.

8477. You used it yourself, I suppose?—I had nothing from Clydesdales, at least for the last couple of years, but year I had a foal from about a thorough-bred mare, she is quite thoroughbred, although she is half [illegible] for the third time—from a Hackney horse that stood at Ballybofey, "Guy Mannering." I had foal from her this year, a filly, and a nice filly it is too.

8478. Have you seen any thoroughbred by these Congested Districts Board horses?—No, I have not.

8479. You personally?—Well, personally is about the size I have seen.

8480. Your experience of the Clydesdale does not coincide with that of Mr. Douglas Brooke?—Of course I don't know the county Fermanagh sufficiently well to say what would suit the county, I only know what suits my own country.

8481. You don't consider it is calculated to do harm in your country?—Not at all; I think they are nearly as bad as they can be at present, any change at all would be an improvement; of course there are a selected few better than others.

8482. Mr. Wrench.—You live in the good farming part of Donegal, when you talk of Donegal **you** are hardly a fair specimen?—I don't know that.

8483. Is there such a great difference between your part of Donegal and the part of Donegal up here as that which?—Well, so far as the Congested Districts is concerned, I think this is entirely different.

8484. There is a good deal of good farming and land about you?—It is all arable land.

8485. And some very good horses?—Undoubtedly, I [illegible] some of [illegible], all arable land.

8486. Then what you have said I gather, you think, a thoroughbred horse is really as good in your district?—No; the Royal Dublin Society's schemes have been a failure altogether, the last showed we had them over three years and [illegible] we had to give the prizes, and we could not distribute all the money we had to give away, and [illegible] the cups for the last three or four years.

8487. When Knightsbridge was there, was he largely used?—Very largely used.

8488. What was his fee?—Two guineas.

8489. Then possibly he was only used by the [illegible] that [illegible] thing about Stranorlar for third, all the colt foals were [illegible] good, and all the filly foals were small and light and weedy, the filly foals were small and the majority of them marked.

8490. Has the half-bred [illegible] of them kept ended so well, but the majority of the filly foals were useless.

8491. Of course hunter-breeding is quite out of the question. It is simply a question of breeding an agricultural horse or a harness horse?—That is it.

8492. For harness horses it is necessary to breed them with action?—I would say so.

8493. You would say that is the chief thing to aim at?—Yes; but I would not go in for so much action as the thoroughbred Hackney has.

8494. It is not necessary that there should be extravagant action on the sire's side, because the mares have not very much action?—Not very much, but I believe there should be action on the sire's side because it is that which improves the progeny more than the [illegible].

8495. What is the best kind that you say you have seen, a Hackney pony?—I think it is a good one, a good foal, but it was a particularly good mare and the same type bred in the county Fermanagh by Mr. [illegible], of [illegible], I was a judge at [illegible] Show and [illegible] and bought the mare from [illegible] there.

8496. You say there must be a strong horse for the farmers, and, I suppose, a [illegible] horse, do they [illegible] their ponies about in your district?—They do.

8497. They take good care of them?—They don't take good care of them, although they have them. I don't think they are well enough fed in the winter time; a young horse, like a [illegible] amount of growth as [illegible], it will not be to keep **up** the system, and it [illegible] to be well fed.

8498. Have any of the American horses found their way into your district?—No, except a few at the very beginning, but they were not got away again; there are none in my district now.

8499. They did not like them?—[illegible].

8500. You have heard what has been said about registering all horses, would you be in favour of that?—I would, of stallions, but I don't know what you would register [illegible] mares.

8501. Would you be in favour of their being licensed, too?—Yes.

8502. Can you see any plan by which you can improve the breed of mares?—The class of [illegible], I have noticed that, goodness thoroughly, and cannot see any way of improving the mares, except the farmers take it into their own heads to improve them themselves, and keep good [illegible].

8503. Are there any local shows?—Yes, a show at Letterkenny.

8504. Do they give premiums for the best mares?—I got first prize for a mare with foal at a Hackney pony; I got first prize at the Derry Show with that brood mare and the foal by Guy Mannering last year.

8505. Do they give any special premiums, except the prize for good [illegible]?—No.

8506. Then the Derry Show is practically the only show of any size in the district?—The only show.

8507. Can you suggest any plan to encourage farmers to keep mares?—I don't think giving prizes as a few mares would be of any good, unless you could get mares to come up to a certain standard that would suit the judges; I don't think there would be any use in anything else, and I don't see how there would be money available for them.

8508. It has been suggested here that mares should be bought and given out to the small farmers to breed from, do you think that would be practicable?—It might, but I don't see that it would serve any good end.

8509. Supposing a young mare was lent, with a foal for two years, do you think farmers would take good care of it?—I don't think they would; it would be very difficult to work, it would require to be looked after far more than anybody would be able to do.

8510. Do you think you would get as good results in breeding from a half-bred sire such as you suggest, as you would in breeding from a pure-bred sire such as a Hackney or Yorkshire coach-horse, or any other sort?—I think so.

8511. That is, a half-bred sire **by a** thoroughbred horse out of a strong country mare?—Yes.

8512. Chairman.—Mr. Wrench, in putting a question to you just now, said that you had given it as your opinion that a thoroughbred horse was of no use in your district?—Yes.

8513. You did [illegible] possess a very large [illegible] of [illegible] from the produce of a thoroughbred horse?—Yes, but I was only speaking for myself when I

2 N 2

Jan. 8, 1897.

Mr. Robert [illegible].

mentioned that, I was not speaking of the country in general; there are very few farmers in the country farm as much land as I do—I can afford to wait.

8514. If a suitable big-boned, thoroughbred horse was standing at a low fee in your district, would they patronise him?—You would require to have more bone and substance about him than any thoroughbreds I have seen. Hilarion was the strongest horse I saw, and he would require to have more bone.

8515. Do you think the bone of the Clydesdale stallion is as strong as the bone of the thoroughbred horse?—I think so.

8516. You have never heard it was more porous?—There is a great difference in Clydesdales as well as thoroughbreds. I have seen some Clydesdale mares and their bones are quite as hard as any thoroughbreds. The last mare I bought in Scotland I would say her bone was quite as strong as any thoroughbred horse's, and as clean, the legs as can be under any animal; although she has the flesh of hair on her behind, she has not greasy, thick legs you will see in many Clydesdales.

8517. Size for size; the bone of the Clydesdale horse is as heavy as that of the thoroughbred?—Yes, I think so; that is, the real, proper Clydesdale sire—we have very few of them in this country.

8518. Have you anything further to say to the Commission?—Nothing further than I would say that all stallions should be registered in the country, and subsidised by the Government, all correct and proper stallions, and they should pass a veterinary surgeon, and that stallion should be forced to travel in the district and serve mares at a certain low fee—that is the only suggestion I have to make.

Mr. James [illegible].

Mr. JAMES [illegible], [illegible] Road, Derry, examined.

8519. CHAIRMAN.—You are an agriculturist, and live at Londonderry?—Yes.

8520. Have you had any personal experience in horse breeding?—Yes, for the last eight or ten years I have been breeding horses, and paying particular attention to horses in general.

8521. Are there many horses bred in the district with which you are acquainted?—There is a fair number.

8522. What class of horses are mostly bred?—Well, [illegible] horses, Clydesdales, [illegible] ponies, [illegible], and the Hackney; there has been very little breeding of thoroughbreds for the past four or five years.

8523. What class of horses do you think best to breed in your district, with an eye to profit?—With an eye to [illegible] for profit, harness horses are the principal horses used; they generally breed the heavy horses for their own use.

8524. Have they introduced any such stallions to the district for breeding purposes?—No; they have not.

8525. Is there a ready sale for horses?—Yes; there is a fairly good sale for big, good stepping harness horses.

8526. Is the price as high as it used to be?—For a really good horse it is as good as ever it was; for the average, [illegible] horse, it is not quite so good.

8527. Has the Royal Dublin Society's Scheme been beneficial in your district?—No, it has been practically useless for mares; there was but one mare in our district when the inspection was called for—there was one in Limavady, one in Derry, and one in [illegible].

8528. Have you any suggestion to make with regard to that scheme?—I think the Royal Dublin Society has been generally giving the money; they started with £100 or £200 to the owner of the stallion, and the owner of the mare that received a nomination, paid a pound and half-a-crown, so that the owner of the stallion had £200 or £300 for his service, and if he [illegible] have a low pound rate or a twenty pound rate, in any district the Congested [illegible] never [illegible]; the owner [illegible] £3, as they were on giving the Royal Dublin Society's grant, till it eventually dwindled to nothing, and they would not [illegible] thoroughbred stallions to compete for it.

8529. Are there many thoroughbreds in the district?—Only practically none. There are two (2) horses, "[illegible]" and another horse belonging to Lord [illegible], called "[illegible]," but they are very old horses, and have been doing nothing lately; there was a horse called "[illegible]" registered under the Royal Dublin Society, and he was the only thoroughbred horse within forty or fifty miles of Derry. The year before last we had Mr. [illegible]'s "[illegible]," which he [illegible] in the district last year.

8530. Where are the horses sold in your district, and what breeders of them?—A number of them are bought at home by dealers, and a number of dealers go to Derry fair; it is the leading fair for good horses in the principal fair.

8531. Have you had any experience of American horses?—No, we have had no American horses of any consequence in the neighbourhood or district; there were a few some five or six years ago, but I would not call them American horses.

8532. Have you had an opportunity of seeing any of the stock got by the Congested Districts Board's horses?—Yes.

8533. And which, in your opinion, has been the effect of the working of the Congested Districts Board Scheme in your district, as regards horse breeding?—I believe it has been of great benefit to the small farmers; it has put a horse within their reach for a small fee, which they otherwise could not have had; I [illegible] in some of the congested districts a pony stallion for the small pony mares in the district. Of course the congested district I know most of, Carndonagh, I would consider it the most [illegible] district on the list—Carndonagh would be first, and Cushendall(?) second. The mares are very inferior; you would be surprised to see the [illegible] there, and, it would certainly be the effect of the [illegible] some of the stallions [illegible]; that is, some of those you would not give a twenty pound note—you might not take a gift of some of them.

8534. What do you attribute that to?—They are starved from their youth, and they live in wretched out of doors, working from they are fifteen or eighteen months old, they are all spread at their hind quarters.

8535. They are worked out of [illegible]?—Yes.

8536. From being worked too young?—Yes, and too much too heavy, and they are not fed.

8537. You mentioned just now a pony stallion, which do you mean?—[illegible] a Welsh horse, for those small pony mares in the congested districts.

8538. You think that is the best class of animal as a sire?—Yes, for these pony mares, and in this district, but, in my own immediate district, the harness horse—either Hackney or coaching horse—a good half-bred hunting horse with three or four crosses of thoroughbred breeding. My experience is and has been [illegible] that what the farmers want is a big, lefty horse with plenty of bone and substance, with a thoroughbred top, Hackney sometimes have the bone and [illegible] the bone, and Hackney action, with as much quality as you could give them. I could give you an instance of a horse bred in the congested districts that made £77 at a Ferguson sale at the May fair. I bought the horse myself; he was 15 hands high; he was reared in Carndonagh, and he was by a Hackney sire only 13.3 hands high, and his dam was about 15.1.

8539. What was the dam's breeding?—I don't know that I could get you her breeding; I [illegible] that I could give you any pedigree for her; she was a little short-legged mare with a fair leg on her and great bone too.

8540. Have you any suggestion to make to the Commission with a view to improving the breed of horses?—In the first place we are in as much need of some way of [illegible] horses [illegible]; the farmers, if they have a good mare worth £40 or £45 she is sold, [illegible] and [illegible] in a [illegible] In the North of Ireland we are only getting the cast mares of England and Scotland [illegible] both as thoroughbred horses and [illegible]; they [illegible] at a fee that would not pay any man to purchase a really good horse for—a sound and [illegible] and [illegible] to a [illegible].

8541. In the nature of the soil in your part of the country adapted for horse-breeding?—Some of it is very well adapted—a good limestone bottom. You asked me if I had any suggestion to make as to the improvement of the breed of horses. I would suggest that there should be a standard fixed both as to size and quality and in every instance of a [illegible] [illegible] a [illegible] [illegible] up to [illegible] standard—[illegible] [illegible] a foal got, either by a thoroughbred horse, [illegible] horse, or whatever [illegible] [illegible] [illegible] [illegible] [illegible], and that all stallions should get a certificate from a veterinary surgeon, of soundness and also as [illegible] free from hereditary disease, and also some aid from Government.

8542. Would you approve of licensing stallions?—Yes, I would say that a certificate of soundness should be the licence; if such animal [illegible] [illegible] he should not be allowed to travel at all.

8543. Mr. Fitzgerald.—On the whole do I understand you to say that you would prefer the Royal Dublin Society's system to [illegible] [illegible] it was originally, that is of premiums—[illegible] a good [illegible] [illegible] a premium of say £200, and [illegible] [illegible] [illegible]?—Yes, that would be my idea, and I would suggest that at the North-East and North-West [illegible], that [illegible] should have [illegible] of the [illegible] [illegible]. [illegible] the Government and that [illegible] should [illegible]; it is [illegible] [illegible] of [illegible] after itself in that respect.

8544. I think you said you would like to have all stallions registered?—Yes; I think that all distinct breeds of horses, Clydesdales, Hackneys, Shire, Yorkshire [illegible] horses, or thoroughbreds, if a gentleman [illegible] to [illegible] a stallion and [illegible] [illegible] [illegible] [illegible] the horse be registered as a [illegible]—the registration only in [illegible] [illegible].

8545. Did you say too that all mares ought to be registered?—Yes, register the mares, but let there be a certain standard of quality of size and soundness and [illegible] [illegible] [illegible] a mare [illegible] up to that standard, if he breeds off her every year this is shown with a foal at foot he should get aid.

8546. Would not that be rather an expensive [illegible]?—Five thousand [illegible] is a mere drop in the bucket if it is to be the Government aid for horse-breeding in Ireland. There is no [illegible] [illegible] [illegible] of [illegible] [illegible]. The Government has plenty of money; there is no want of [illegible] [illegible] [illegible] [illegible] [illegible] [illegible] [illegible] [illegible], we ought to [illegible] have a good [illegible] [illegible] all.

8547. Have you thought over the idea of registering mares that should be allowed to be bred from. Do you mean to say you would not allow other mares to be bred from?—Oh, yes; it is only to encourage the farmers to keep a really good mare. If a farmer has a mare worth £40 [illegible] [illegible] [illegible] [illegible] [illegible], and then [illegible] to [illegible] as a brood mare. The [illegible] [illegible] [illegible] [illegible] [illegible] Hackneys, and several private people have Hackneys, and they [illegible] [illegible] [illegible] very well in the country; they have been able to compete at small shows favourably with the produce of the thoroughbred. I myself [illegible] [illegible] [illegible] with a [illegible]. [illegible] out of a [illegible] [illegible] mare. A [illegible] Hackney got first prize for a very strong [illegible] in Belfast some years ago, a class of twenty-five.

8548. As to the stallions you would like to see in the district, I think you said you would like to see a good [illegible]?—Yes, I [illegible] that too.

8549. Would you describe the half-bred produce of an agricultural stallion as belonging to the [illegible] class?—What the English people are [illegible] of [illegible] [illegible] is a [illegible] [illegible], and the Hackney and the Yorkshire coach horse; [illegible] [illegible] is a good horse to produce harness horses.

8550. And for the smaller [illegible] a Welsh horse?—I would say a Welsh horse is a good horse for them.

8551. In the main [illegible] [illegible] [illegible] [illegible] [illegible] your [illegible] a great advantage to the [illegible] [illegible] the same may be?—Certainly, a small fee in the [illegible], of course, if you can get a good horse; but you cannot get it unless there is some Government aid. It won't pay a man to give £300 or £400 for a good horse and travel him at a small fee, [illegible] guarantee a foal, and take all the responsibilities and risks.

8552. Mr. La Touche.—This horse that you spoke of as being used in the congested districts that brought £75, he was not [illegible] [illegible] of the Congested Districts Board horses?—He was by a thoroughbred [illegible]—a very good breed of [illegible]—[illegible] [illegible] [illegible] [illegible] [illegible] [illegible] [illegible].

8553. What was he sold at?—He was sold in May for £75.

8554. How what is?—As a hunter; and would give you as [illegible] a [illegible] as any horse could in the saddle, and would answer as [illegible] as a [illegible].

8555. Mr. Wrench.—As a rule are there many hunters bred in your district?—Very few.

8556. Is the breeding of hunters [illegible] [illegible] [illegible] [illegible] in that district as the way of horse breeding?—Yes, the principal.

8557. And the [illegible] horse—agricultural horses?—Agricultural horses and harness horses.

8558. They are the two that it pays to breed best?—Yes, if you get a good strong agricultural horse you can work him from four until five, and then sell him; that horse I spoke of brought [illegible] three-year old.

8559. Where are the most of the horses sold from [illegible] [illegible], a lot of them are sold at [illegible], and a lot of buyers take them in May.

8560. Do many foreign buyers come to May fair?—Yes, a good many.

8561. Do they look for action in the horses they buy?—Altogether for action; if you have a horse with action in the May they [illegible] overlook some other points of quality if he has a [illegible] [illegible].

8562. It is the most saleable [illegible]?—Yes; you will have twenty men pulling you on one side if you have a good stepping horse, and if you have only a [illegible] horse with very little action they don't [illegible] you very much.

8563. Have you ever seen any of the stock of a horse called "Ulmond Arrow" that Lord Castlereagh used to have?—Well, I cannot say I have, but I have heard of the horse; and I have [illegible] anything that came [illegible] [illegible] they wished to [illegible] it a good character they would tell you it was by "Ulmond Arrow."

8564. That was to help to sell it?—Yes.

8565. Excellent "[illegible]"?—Yes.

8566. He was a very uneven horse, had good colts, but bad [illegible]?—Yes, as a rule the mares were light, and [illegible] bone and substance.

8567. And were likely to make?—Yes, they were [illegible] to make.

8568. Have you had any experience of [illegible] the relative soundness of Hackneys and thoroughbreds?—I have had eight or ten Hackney-bred hunters, hunting

[illegible]

between buying them as three-year-olds, and breeding them, and I have not had any unsuccessful one out of the lot as yet.

8569. Carrickmacross is the district you know best?—Yes, I know it well.

8570. Do you know that the Congested Districts Board had a Welsh cob there last year as well as a Hackney?—Yes, I saw him.

8571. You have bred from Hackneys yourself for some time?—Yes, for the last seven or eight years.

8572. Have you ever tried of these Hackney [illegible]?—Very little.

8573. You have put them in Belfast?—I have just seen them; but sold no weanlings to them.

8574. Do they do harm or good?—They do harm in this way; that they are injuring the prices of the ordinary horses; but I believe eventually the [illegible] will get sick of them. I understand from the dealers that they are not horses.

8575. Would you be in favour of having them branded or marked so that people would know what they were buying?—It would be a wise thing to brand them, but when some people are buying a horse they [illegible] of which breed it is if they get what pleases them.

8576. You suggest that Ulster should have control of its own Government grant. You mean by that the North-East and North-West Agricultural Societies?—Yes.

8577. If they had control do you think they would confine the grant to thoroughbreds as it is now confined?—I am very sure they would not. They would go in for both Hackneys and thoroughbreds.

8578. About Belfast are they great breeders of harness horses?—They breed a good many thoroughbreds in the vicinity of Belfast.

8579. And, I think, you said you had seen the progeny of Hackneys at the different shows of the North-East and North-West?—Yes.

8580. And that they held their own in the show ring?—Yes, very favourably against the thoroughbred horses.

8581. Practically you have hardly any thoroughbred horses in Londonderry?—Very few. You can not get off a thoroughbred horse the same bone and substance as off a Hackney unless with a very heavy dam.

8582. It is not a hunter breeding district at all?—No.

8583. Any horses that come there come from the South?—Yes; a great many are bought in the South and fed and sold at May.

8584. And most of the horses out of that part of the country are sold to go to England and Scotland, and not to other parts of Ireland?—Very few. A great many go Dublin way. Tom M'Mahon, of Carrickmacross, attends the May regularly and buys a lot of horses; but he sells them mainly in England.

8585. A lot of horses that are shown in May come from the South and are fed in the North?—Yes a lot of farmers make a trade of going to the South of Ireland and buying horses and then bringing them to the North and then selling them in May fair. It is the best [illegible] in the North of Ireland; it is the only really good horse fair we have in the North of Ireland. We have had several fairs in Derry, several of quarterly fairs; but they have greatly died away. I account for that by the dealing men going into the farms and buying any good colts they see at home, they never come to a fair at all.

8586. The CHAIRMAN.—You said you won prizes with a half-bred Hackney in some shows in the North; in what classes did you exhibit him?—Three-year-old geldings or fillies—the prize was for the best gelding or filly likely to make a hunter.

8587. It has been said that none but a foolish man would try to breed hunters from half-bred Hackneys—would you agree with that?—No, I would disagree with that. Let me choose the mare and I will take a Hackney stallion, and I will breed you a hunter that Dublin will be only too glad of.

8588. Mr. WRENCH.—What kind of mare would you require?—A good [illegible].

8589. You would require a good deal of thoroughbred blood in the mare?—Yes, a good thoroughbred strain. I have a mare that I am breeding from and I sold light weight hunters from her by a Hackney, a very good sort, galloped long and low.

8590. You don't think there is any evil blood in Hackneys?—Any people who talk against Hackneys are only people that do not know them. Lots of people [illegible] Hackneys for fancy and they make and never like a [illegible] and [illegible] to [illegible] on [illegible].

8591. Do you know how these animals are bred?—Yes, they are half-bred. I have bred some myself and bought some. I know their breeding perfectly.

8592. Col. St. QUINTIN.—What class of horses is it that is generally brought from the South and fatten in the North—the thoroughbred or draught?—Riding horses.

8593. Which sells best in May fair, those that come from the South or those that are bred in the North?—At one season of the year there is a demand for the hunter-like horse and at another season for the harness horse.

8594. But as to price, you have seen half-bred Hackney horses to make £80, £90, and £100.

8595. Yes, and I daresay you have also known a hunter to make £80 or £90?—I have known them to make it.

8596. Do you know that the demand for harness horses has greatly decreased in the last year or two?—I would say the demand for harness horses would be double the demand for hunters.

8597. You think it is not an answer to my question?—The demand for the commonplace harness horse is not so good, or the price so good.

8598. It has greatly decreased in the last two or three years?—Yes, I am satisfied of that.

8599. We can all account for that—how do you account for it?—Owing to the introduction of electric trams and bicycles there is not such a demand for cabs and small-priced horses.

8600. Has the higher class harness and riding horse kept the price?—Yes, and so has the high class hunter horse.

8601. Do you think the breeding of the moderate harness horse is likely to be a great industry in the future?—I don't know.

8602. I mean with those electric cars and bicycles, with the low [illegible]?—I think the good riding horse will keep his price in the foreign market as well as the English market. I believe he will.

8603. And the foreigners are keen for [illegible] harness than we are.

8604. Anything as keen for the harness horse?—Yes; they are very keen for a really good harness horse.

8605. Can you breed a really high class harness horse in the North?—We can.

8606. Then why can you not breed a high class hunter?—We don't go in for hunters, and have not the service cheaply.

8607. Because the English dealers tell us that their best high class harness horses are all bred by thoroughbred horses?—The dealers don't really know how they are bred.

8608. Well, they know their own business?—They do, of course.

8609. And they say they cannot buy high class harness horses in Yorkshire and Lincolnshire as they used to, and have to come to Ireland for them?—There is a prejudice against the Hackney here by especially the South of Ireland people. I know we have had southern judges judging here.

8610. Putting the prejudice aside, it is a matter of really [illegible] what [illegible] didn't see if I dams to breed off a Hackney there should be any question by anybody. I have a right to breed what I like.

8611. Nobody says you should not?—According to the Royal Dublin Society we should not have a Hackney in the country at all.

8612. Well, horse-breeding is the industry of this country. Is it not?—Horned cattle is just as great an industry as breeding horses to an extent, if you go into it in that way.

8613. Is it not a large industry?—Yes.

8614. All you want to do is to preserve it in its highest form?—Yes, but by keeping out the Hackney stallion you won't do that.

8615. I am not saying that?—That is what the Royal Dublin Society is constantly wanting to do.

8616. Mr. Wrench.—Do you know, as a matter of fact, that the dealers who have objected to these Hackneys are the big jobmasters in London, who buy horses of from 16 to 16·2 hands high?—No, certainly not. I have known Hotherall, an English buyer, to give a long price for Hackneys.

8617. He knew them to be bred off Hackneys?—Yes.

8618. If a horse has good action in the Moy fair does a dealer stop to ask how he is bred?—He will never stop to ask what he is by.

8619. Is not the breeding of very high class horses in the hands of a very few men?—It is very few can afford to breed high class horses.

8620. And the most of the industry is in the hands of small farmers?—They don't want to bring them to maturity, and if they breed a small class of horse with action it is the one thing that will help them to sell.

8621. Chairman.—You are an auctioneer?—Yes.

8622. And you know a good deal about buying and selling horses?—A little.

8623. And you know that a great many high-class harness horses are bought and sold at Moy fair?—Yes.

8624. Do you know who the chief buyers are?—I know English buyers, Hotherall and Vanderbyl, and there are several buyers from Belfast.

8625. Are there any foreign buyers?—A lot of foreign buyers. At the last Moy fair there were three from Switzerland.

8626. Did you ever hear of Mr. [illegible]?—I cannot say I did; it is only occasionally I go to the Moy fair.

8627. You never heard of Mr. Hurst or Mr. Wimbush buying many horses there?—I cannot say I did.

8628. You don't know the names?—I cannot say I do.

8629. Supposing these buyers like Hurst and Wimbush were to say they objected to the Hackney mare as harness horses, and preferred the thorough-bred cross, would you agree with them?—I cannot say I would agree with them. In a harness horse I think action is a very important thing.

8630. They won't buy without action?—You cannot always put action into a thoroughbred horse; of course you would get it to a certain extent, but not to the extent of the Hackney.

8631. You heard of the Hackney system in the North of Ireland?—Yes.

8632. Where do most of the horses come from that are sold?—A number are bought in the [illegible], and in [illegible] and [illegible] in the north.

8633. Don't most of them come from the north?—A good number.

8634. The chief number?—Yes; but there is a lot bought all round.

8635. Of a high class?—Yes.

8636. Do you think the horses bred in the north fetch as high prices as the horses from the south that are sold in Moy to Hurst and Wimbush?—Yes; and some of them, I daresay, would fetch higher prices than a southern horse.

8637. But, as a general rule, which fetches the higher price?—I suppose there are more horses come from the south to Moy than from the north, because they go in more for horse-breeding, I think, in the south than in the north of Ireland.

8638. Mr. Wrench.—Do you know that Hackney stallions have only been in Ireland a few years?—I don't know that.

8639. Chairman.—Is there anything else you wish to state to the Commission?—I would like to impress on them the desirability of getting the [illegible] registered, so that they will be [illegible], each having a list of [illegible] of approved horses going [illegible] district or county.

Mr. Thomas [illegible], [illegible], Ballinasloe.

8640. Chairman.—You live near Ballinasloe, in the county of Galway?—Yes.

8641. And are you acquainted with horse-breeding there and in the rest of Ireland?—I am acquainted with horse-breeding in Galway and King's county, not very much in other parts of Ireland, except what I have seen in shows.

8642. What class of horses are bred in your immediate neighbourhood?—Hunters principally, and a very bad class of nondescript wretch; I don't know what purpose he is wanted for or what purpose they put him to.

8643. There is a large fair held at Ballinasloe?—Yes.

8644. Where do the horses come from to that fair?—They come from all over Ireland, King's county, Roscommon, Galway, North Tipperary, and from all parts.

8645. Are you acquainted with the subsoil west of Galway?—Yes, I lived in Connemara and lived in the Island of Achill for years.

8646. Have you had an opportunity of observing the effects of the Congested Districts Board Scheme in that country?—Yes, in Mayo.

8647. To what conclusion did you come with regard to that scheme?—From the stock I saw from all ages—from foals up to 3½, I think the Hackney cross is decidedly a failure. In those cases where I could see the sports as well as the stock, in nearly all cases they had been [illegible] they had not got as much bone as the dam, and what action they had is anything but action—no knee action; they had absolutely none.

8648. What class of horse do you think the country is best adapted to breed?—All through the Congested [illegible], I think the country [illegible] is well suited to hunters; it is practically a hunter-breeding country; and in Connemara [illegible] it is only a pony breeding district, [illegible] and big.

8649. Do you object to [illegible] stallions in the county?—A few; [illegible] the prices are too prohibitive; there is no good sire [illegible] standing under about £2, and the best is £3, which is absolutely prohibitive to the farmer of £10 valuation, and he forms the largest number.

8650. What breed of stallions would you advise should be used?—Suitable thoroughbred stallions, and if there is such a thing to be got a good [illegible] type of [illegible], or, if possible, [illegible] I should like to see. I have only known a few [illegible] they have all been [illegible] good. I remember in Leicestershire, when I was a young man, a horse that was [illegible] "[illegible]" belonging to Mr. [illegible], who got very good hunters; and there is a good horse [illegible] standing in Tipperary, "Reliable," for [illegible] in the

Grafton country one time, I don't know how he is bred; he is a good 14 stone blood hunter, I have known some good horses by him; I had one myself, he was bred in the Grafton country; I brought him over here, and I took prizes with him, both jumping and in the hunter class. There is a horse called "Thunderbolt," standing in the county Galway, I believe he is only a second descendant from a thoroughbred horse called "Thunderbolt," and he gets very good stock; indeed I would say there is more good stock going out of the county of Galway by "Thunderbolt," or descended from him than any other thoroughbred.

8651. They show size and bone and quality?—Yes.

8652. Has the Royal Dublin Society scheme had any beneficial effect in your district?—I don't think the last scheme has had as much beneficial effect as the previous one, that is the scheme that gave free service to selected mares. You have to show the foal, and so many farmers neglect to put their mares to a thoroughbred horse at all; they bring them into the show, and you give a prize to the foal and find it is ineligible. The whole thing, as far as the county of Galway is concerned, is the price they can get their mares served for. The small farmer cannot afford to give more than £1; the farmer next to him would give £2; that would be farmers with a valuation between £75 and £200.

8653. At what fee did "Thunderbolt" serve at?—At various fees; the nominal fee is £1, but you can make your own bargain.

8654. You don't know what "Reliable" is serving at?—No, I don't.

8655. Have you any suggestions to make to the Commission with a view to helping the industry of horse breeding?—Well, if funds would admit of it in Galway—part of Galway and King's county—I think we require mares as much as we do anything else. I think it would be quite feasible to work such a scheme if the money were forthcoming.

8656. What scheme?—I think you could give mares to farmers whose valuation does not exceed £60 or £70. Bind them to keep them for two years and keep the stock until two years old; give them the mares free, and give them the service of registered sires at a nominal fee, or free service, if possible. We also want at least six sires in the county Galway, four thoroughbreds; and I should like to see a trial made of hunter sires. I think it would be a great benefit to Ireland if the Royal Dublin Society's certificates were only given to horses that served at a nominal fee. I don't see what good they do except they give a warranty that the sire is sound. We have 13 Royal Dublin Society registered horses serving in the county Galway, and they are not a bit of good to the farmers. There are 25 altogether, and 13 registered. There are 12 what they please to call half-bred sires, which certainly ought to be castrated at once.

8657. Have you any further suggestion to make to the Commission?—One thing I should like to say is this—that I think in selecting stallions for half-bred mares great stress should be laid on their having good shoulders, because in all half-bred mares they are always very much better behind the saddle than in front. As a rule, there is no care taken in selecting the different stallions; one county wants one kind, another county another. We want two classes in the county Galway. In my own immediate neighbourhood we have a great many mares with plenty of blood that only want more bone and substance. With these I should like to see the hunter sire crossed. We have a thoroughbred horse in my neighbourhood, Liscanny, where they have bred a good many horses, "The Sinner" and others.

8658. Lord ASHTOWN.—What is "The Sinner"—a half-bred horse?—No.

8659. Mr. FITZWILLIAM.—You think that in your district a good thoroughbred horse is infinitely the best that can be placed in the country?—Undoubtedly.

8660. I think you said you would like to have what you call a hunter bred sire?—Yes, with as many crosses of blood as possible. I don't think you can get them with more than three to start with.

8661. You would object to having Hackneys placed in your district?—From what I have seen of their gets I certainly would.

8662. Lord ASHTOWN.—You say you would not register any sire except he stood at a moderate fee?—No, I don't see what benefit the country gets.

8663. But what would you call a moderate fee?—£1 for farmers with a valuation not exceeding £30.

8664. If you did that you would have to subsidise the stallion owner?—Oh yes, of course.

8665. I thought you meant without a subsidy?—Oh no, I was looking on these as being Government sires.

8666. The old system of nominations, the owner to get so much and the farmer to pay the rest?—That is the best because it does not interfere with private enterprise.

8667. Colonel ST. QUINTIN.—We have been told that the work of the Congested Districts Board is to benefit the small farmer—do you think the small farmer is capable of expressing a good opinion as to what the real requirements of horse-breeding are?—Not the least in the world, he would not know one horse from another—to begin with he would always take the cheapest, and if any one of local influence told him to go to a certain horse he would go irrespective of whether he is good or bad.

8668. Do you know what the feelings of the larger class of farmers and gentlemen in that district are?—With regard to the Hackney blood you mean?

8669. With regard to the strain of blood required and the conditions of breeding generally in the country?—The feeling amongst the larger farmers undoubtedly is in favour of thoroughbred horses to be given them at a small fee—that is what they all complain of, we have the stallions and they are no use to them, they think that the certificate of the Dublin Society means that the stallion's owner gets something out of it, it is only the larger farmers and the gentlemen who are getting the benefit.

8670. Mr. LA TOUCHE.—You were saying from your experience of the stock of the Hackneys in the congested districts—you thought the effect of the Hackney had been rather to deteriorate the breed of horses there?—Certainly not to improve them; I mean they have had the action of the Hackney, and they have none of their own, and they have lost bone very materially. In the Belmullet district I should say there is the most unique breed of ponies in the British Isles; they are all exactly of one type, and many of them about 14 hands, and many of them I measured with over eight inches of bone, and they are very full of quality, good shoulders and plain heads, but very bad behind the saddle and with sickle hocks.

8671. You are laying great stress on the necessity of good bone, do you think the conformation of the Hackney generally, as far as his neck and shoulders go, is likely to improve the shoulders?—Certainly not, I once rode one as a hack and I hope I won't have to repeat the dose.

8672. You don't think his shoulders are riding shoulders?—Certainly not.

8673. Mr. WRENCH.—You say you lived in Achill?—Yes.

8674. How long?—I was there in 1889-90 for one year.

8675. Did you also live in Connemara?—Yes.

8676. What part?—At Leenane on Killary Bay, that was the year before.

8677. You were there for sporting purposes, not for horse-breeding purposes?—That is so.

8678. And I think you visited Belmullet and Achill recently for the Horse-breeding Association?—Yes.

8679. With Mr. O'Connell?—Yes, in Achill, but not in Belmullet, I had a local stallion there.

8680. How long did your visit take there?—I was there a week.

8681. Going through the district?—Yes.

8682. And what class of stallion do you recommend for Belmullet?—A nice active thoroughbred horse; when he had been in the country one year I would like to [illegible] the best of his stock to serve again in the country. I think the characteristics of the pony are so strong they have gone on for generations with very [illegible], that with at least one or two [illegible] of fresh blood they could keep up the type.

8683. Did you see any of the native stallions there?—Yes, two; "Keel Chief" and Gallagher's horse.

8684. That is near Newport?—No, there are two Gallaghers, one in Achill and also one near Belmullet close to Binghamstown.

8685. I think you said you would approve of horse shows?—Yes.

8686. If you wanted to buy half a dozen horses [illegible] at the present moment where would you first [illegible]?—That is one of the greatest difficulties; I saw one in that district, but I am afraid he is no longer [illegible]. I saw a typical sire in Belmullet.

8687. They are hard to find?—Yes, but they can be found; they go over to England now and again. I have known them to have been sent to England and [illegible] in Lancashire.

8688. Talking of the young stock I suppose you know the [illegible] and the worst [illegible]?—No, I don't think so. I saw one colt at a three and a half years old [illegible] which [illegible].

8689. That may have been a good foal?—It might have been. It was one you gave a prize to as a foal and as a yearling; but the man said he would like to take £10 for it, if he could get it, there was in Newport.

8690. When you talk of large [illegible] in the congested districts, are there many?—I would not say there were any large farmers in the congested districts at all.

8691. And very few graziers?—Very few.

8692. Would you register the horses [illegible] before you [illegible] as to his stock?—Yes, because I think you would have to wait so long.

8693. You would register the horses [illegible] with how many crosses of thoroughbred blood?—Not less than three, four would be better, but I don't think you would get them with four; it would only mean that a pedigree would be [illegible] to suit the [illegible]; there is one very far to go back.

8694. You would be inclined to give the [illegible] to the former?—Yes; I think probably only a few [illegible] in Ireland would require them.

8695. In those counties that would require them?—Yes.

8696. Would you give them [illegible] old or [illegible] old fillies or aged mares?—I would sooner have aged mares.

8697. Have you heard it suggested that [illegible] old fillies should be bought from the army and given out for two years to the farmers and taken back again?—In the hands of the farmers they are much too young to breed from—I think they would require [illegible] feeding.

8698. The only mares that you would give are aged mares?—Yes, with certain restrictions.

8699. What restrictions?—They must be serviceable for the work for a certain number of years and produce [illegible] every year.

8700. Mr. LA TOUCHE.—Do you know anything of what becomes of the foals sold from Connemara?—They mostly go through the country to dealers; the Connemara ponies principally go from that part of Galway and the cream of Connemara into Kings county and North Tipperary, and the Belmullet ponies mostly go through the North of Sligo and into the North.

8701. The [illegible] of the ponies from Connemara stay in East Galway?—Yes, they go through the country and everybody [illegible] and [illegible] are [illegible] bought to [illegible] every year.

8702. Are they only sold for breeding purposes?—No, they are generally sold again when [illegible] years old [illegible] bought to feed.

8703. You are a member of the Ballinasloe Agricultural Society?—Yes.

8704. Is that open to residents all over the county of Galway?—It is now, but it was not until last year. It did not take in Connemara up to last year.

8705. Did you pass a resolution there in reference to the introduction of the Hackney blood into the congested districts?—Yes, we did.

8706. Unfavourable to it?—Unfavourable to it.

8707. Was that passed after Connemara was included in it?—No, before.

8708. Connemara was not represented then?—No, it was not; it would be difficult to get anybody to represent it at any time.

8709. Was it the belief then of this Association that the introduction of this blood into Connemara would do harm to the districts in which they were concerned, or was it out of regard to Connemara?—No, because you cannot shut out the breed; if they are bred in Connemara or anywhere else in Ireland they [illegible]; they are just as likely to be found in Meath or in any other county; the result [illegible].

8710. Then it was out of regard to the general horse-breeding of Ireland you passed this resolution?—Certainly. I think there is a general feeling that the mongrel or [illegible] cross from the Hackney would do more harm than the [illegible].

8711. CHAIRMAN.—Is there anything further you wish to state?—No, I think not.

8712. Mr. LA TOUCHE.—It would be impossible for private enterprise to supply such stallions as you think are required, at fees the farmers are able to pay?—Exactly; we have no stallions there, nothing in any immediate neighbourhood—[illegible] get enough mares to make him pay.

8713. Mr. WRENCH.—Is that Col. Dickie's horse?—It was bred by his brother, Mr. [illegible] Dickie.

8714. Have you seen any of the [illegible] by Hackneys outside Connemara ponies?—No.

8715. Do you know that they had a sale, and they would be [illegible] bred?—No, I don't think they would be by Hackneys.

8716. Col. Dickie said they were?—I don't think he has been into a pony breeding district.

MR. WILLIAM FIELD, V.S., Allington Lodge, Kildare.

8717. CHAIRMAN.—You live in the County Kildare, and are largely interested in the horse-breeding industry, I believe?—Yes.

8718. You also are a Fellow of the Royal College of Veterinary Surgeons?—Yes.

8719. And you have purchased horses for the Government?—Yes, very largely.

8720. Under what [illegible] was that?—I was employed on the Purchase Commission when we were buying horses during the Russian scare in 1878, when the Government required a large number of horses. I was with General Morris. We bought a large number of horses for the Government.

8721. You have inspected stallions, and have bred horses for a great many years?—For thirty years. I have bought a lot of the stallions here, which I inspect [illegible] of the Commissioners in some of the stallions that have been imported by the late [illegible].

8722. You know the stallions [illegible]?—I know [illegible] stallions also. This is the list of the stallions that

Jan. [illegible], 18[illegible].
Mr. William [illegible], v.s.

have been imported and used in my stud. I think nearly fifty.

8723. A great many of those horses were leased out, I suppose?—Some were leased and some were sold; some which I have sold to go abroad have stood in the country as well. I lease a number of horses each year, as well as using a good many horses at my own stud. At present I have eight stallions at the stud.

8724. Do many of the smaller farmers of your district breed horses, and of what class?—In Kildare the farmers breed principally hunters and riding horses.

8725. What stamp of mare do they usually keep for breeding purposes?—Do you mean in Kildare?

8726. Yes; your own district?—Principally half-bred mares; mares got by a thoroughbred horse out of the usual half-bred country mares, generally with one cross of thoroughbred.

8727. In your opinion have brood mares deteriorated of late years or not?—I consider the brood mares quite as good as they have been for years past.

8728. Just now you said you had eight stallions. Are the eight you keep included in this list?—They are included in this list.

8729. Would you mind telling me which they are?—Perhaps you would mark them on this list; you can there mark the ones?—I have imported seven stallions which you see marked here. Those ones marked are the stallions I have at present.

8730. Would you read out the names?—"Brown-[illegible]," "Wales [illegible]," "[illegible]," "[illegible]," "[illegible]," "[illegible]," "[illegible]," and also an Irish pony stallion I use as a teaser. "[illegible]" is a horse that has had five Queen's premiums, and has bred a great many winners, and has done a great deal of good indeed. The year marked on the list is the year in which I brought each horse over.

8731. Outside the stallions you mention here, is there a sufficient number of suitable stallions in the district, standing at fees within the reach of the smaller farmers?—I consider that in Kildare we are well supplied with stallions, but I think of course those districts where stallions are not sufficient is the principal thing to look to. For Kildare, and Dublin, and Cork, and Carlow, and Limerick, and those places I think the present supply of stallions is very good indeed; very fair.

8732. You are well acquainted with a great many parts of Ireland?—All over Ireland I have had horses. Last year I had one in Mallow, in the county Cork, one in Galway, one in Waterford, another at the [illegible] stud in England, and [illegible] at home.

8733. So that you are pretty well acquainted with the country?—Each year I have in different districts—Wexford, Waterford, Wicklow, different places these horses go to. My horses are all registered.

8734. Registered under the Royal Dublin Society scheme?—Yes; I may say that horses suited for one district are not suited for another. Different horses suit different districts.

8735. Have you made that a study in order to guide you when sending out your stallions?—Yes, I study as far as possible to suit the district. Of course the men that lease them the stallions say they suit them, but I know myself from experience that certain horses will not suit certain districts, and I recommend them not to have them. I have at present numbers of applications for the coming season for any horses which I have not done anything with yet. Several gentlemen [illegible] [illegible] to take horses from me for the coming season.

8736. Do you think the fees are all prohibitive in any case you are aware of?—In Kildare.

8737. In any part of the country?—Oh, I think yes; in certain parts the farmers are not able to pay a high fee. Of course in Kildare we have rather a rich peasantry, and in Carlow, Meath, and those places I think they are quite well able to pay for a good horse.

8738. Can you give us any idea of the fees the horses you hire out usually stand at?—The horses hired out from me usually stand at £2 for what we call gentlemen's mares, and £3 for tenant farmers' mares, some at £5.

8739. Have you attended any of the horse shows?—I have, some of them.

8740. Perhaps you could give us some idea of what you saw at some of them?—I am disappointed with the mare shows, because I do not think the farmers have come forward as much as I expected they would at the mare shows. First of all, I do not think the prizes are sufficient inducement to them to do so. I am entirely in advance for substantial money prizes to be given for mares at those shows, and unless that is done the farmers won't come forward. For the sake of a single pound or a sovereign they will not go to the trouble of bringing a horse to shows; and up to this in Kildare—well, perhaps we have no good shows or none—but from what I can gather, the mare shows have not been as good as they might have been, due, I think, to there not being sufficient inducement.

8741. Do you think the farmer have deteriorated at all of late years, that is, among the smaller farmers who are under the scheme of the Royal Dublin Society?—I think the smaller farmers are not breeding as much as they were, while the larger farmers and the men that have places for them are breeding larger. The smaller farmers are not breeding as much as they were, but the larger farmers with good tracts of land will do so, horse-breeding is a remunerative industry, and therefore bound to largely increase. I think the price for a good horse is quite as good as it ever has been in Ireland, and the facilities for selling him his greater than ever it has been. The Royal Dublin Society's Show is one of the largest horse marts in the world, and no doubt has robbed the fairs, such as those held at Ballinasloe and other places, of a number of horses that used to go there. Now, the Royal Dublin Society show has become the chief fair [illegible] in Ireland, and all the people who used to go to those fairs keep their horses for the Royal Dublin Society's Show, where they have a better opportunity for selling and a better opportunity of getting them bought; buyers and sellers have a better opportunity for seeing them than at the fairs, and no doubt that is one of the greatest benefits, in disposal of our [illegible] industry there.

8742. You have heard it stated that the good mares are picked up by dealers in the country and shipped away into England?—There is a certain amount of truth in that. A needy farmer, if he has a very good mare, is tempted to sell it, undoubtedly, but at the same time I know that in Kildare the small farmers are very very slow to part with their good mares. Those that can afford to keep them always do. In the poorer districts of course, the mares are sold, no doubt, because if a poor farmer has a good mare he is tempted to raise the half-year's rent by selling the good mare; perhaps one that is raising a foal, or a mare in a [illegible], and may be an own sister; he sells the one that brings him in the money. I do not think there is any possible remedy to prevent a man from disposing of them, because it is human nature after all. They want the money and dispose of the mare. You cannot bind a man to keep those mares.

8743. Money is at the bottom of it, you think?—That is the truth of it. The only way you can encourage them is by supplying them with a sure to breed from those mares, and provided you can supply them with a sire at a price that is within their reach it will be the means of causing them to retain their mares to breed from. If a man has a good mare and he knows he can get the service of a really good horse for a pound, he will be more inclined to keep her and avail himself of the benefits of this than otherwise, and in that same way the placing of the sires, a good horse within the reach of farmers [illegible] the means of [illegible], of upsetting [illegible] the [illegible] of the horses in the district. I was greatly [illegible] very little with the [illegible] of the [illegible]. It is a very difficult thing to do, and [illegible], I [illegible] within the scope of any Commission. [illegible] it would be a very, very difficult thing to do. It would cause [illegible], [illegible], and [illegible] in the end, probably, in the [illegible] of [illegible]. I think to give [illegible] [illegible] of a high class, [illegible] the class of horses, [illegible] in the strongest [illegible] to [illegible] the [illegible] to keep [illegible] good [illegible] to breed [illegible] in the country.

8744. You know the present scheme of the Royal Dublin Society?—Well, the present scheme of the Royal Dublin Society [illegible].

8745. I ask you this question now because I want to ask you whether [illegible] all my horses are [illegible] under the present scheme.

8746. As regards the [illegible]?—The present scheme of giving prizes for the [illegible] of [illegible] is a very good one.

8747. Well, now are you aware that under the present scheme there are prizes for [illegible] mares that have been entered as registered [illegible]?—I am quite aware of that.

8748. Also prizes for three-year-old mares [illegible] by registered [illegible]?—Yes.

8749. Do you think that would have any tendency [illegible] the [illegible] which is [illegible] to keep the mares in the country? I [illegible] any encouragement you can give in that way would keep the mares in the country.

8750. A [illegible] generally [illegible] three or four years old; therefore if the [illegible] has a [illegible] is not likely to [illegible]?—I have [illegible] of these mares in my [illegible] which have been [illegible] two years old; some of them have come to my [illegible], and they will be [illegible], and when they [illegible] they will have [illegible] the object of the Royal Dublin Society, namely, to give the [illegible] an opportunity of [illegible] a foal from a good mare, and [illegible].

8751. If [illegible] a good [illegible] might have a tendency to [illegible]?—[illegible] I think it is a wise provision on the part of the Royal Dublin Society, [illegible] to [illegible] and [illegible] that have been [illegible].

8752. Of course that is the [illegible] of their scheme?—Yes, that is [illegible].

8753. With regard to [illegible] stallions, what is your [illegible]?—My opinion in connection with half-bred stallions has [illegible] a great many years. I [illegible] in the [illegible], although I [illegible] [illegible] that I [illegible] in [illegible] to [illegible] half-bred [illegible] I [illegible] the [illegible] [illegible] you would find that [illegible] half-bred stallions [illegible] to be registered would be [illegible]. At the same time I [illegible] had a number of half-bred stallions in Ireland [illegible] in [illegible] of [illegible], I [illegible] "[illegible]" [illegible] [illegible] I would say [illegible] [illegible] on the [illegible]. They [illegible]: [illegible] a half-bred horse by "[illegible]" [illegible] "[illegible]" [illegible] "[illegible]" [illegible] with beautiful [illegible] and [illegible]. They [illegible] for a [illegible], [illegible] 20 per cent. They were [illegible] in the [illegible]. The [illegible] of these horses [illegible] thoroughbred [illegible] some of the very best

[illegible]. There are several others by [illegible], "Young [illegible]," out of a half-bred mare by "[illegible]," a very [illegible]. [illegible] horse which [illegible] different horses. There are many half-bred horses through Ireland at present [illegible], and are likely to [illegible]. Of course the [illegible] "[illegible]" under the head of half-bred horses, [illegible] a long way from it. He is nearly a thoroughbred horse. I at present have a very good [illegible] [illegible], got by a horse, "Young [illegible]," a son of "[illegible]," out of a mare [illegible], that is, by a thoroughbred horse. Mr. [illegible] knows him; [illegible] grey horse I [illegible]. He is a wonderfully good horse, and a great [illegible], the [illegible] of "Young [illegible]," which was a son of "[illegible]," out of a [illegible] mare. I [illegible] a good [illegible] of [illegible] of that class would do very much more good in the districts where they [illegible] to [illegible] the [illegible] than any other horse, except, of course, a thoroughbred horse.

8754. Have you any experience as to the breeding of [illegible] from Connemara ponies?—I have very large experience. I [illegible] some of the [illegible] [illegible] [illegible] Connemara ponies with a thoroughbred horse. I am at present [illegible] a horse which I have [illegible] for the last three seasons, "[illegible] of [illegible]." He [illegible] in [illegible], he is out of a pony that was bought out of a [illegible] from Connemara, and by "[illegible]." They [illegible] all the [illegible] and the hardihood of the Connemara pony, with the quality and [illegible] of the thoroughbred horse. They are particularly [illegible]. I [illegible] in the [illegible] Connemara pony, and they [illegible] have a tendency to strengthen any delicacy the thoroughbred [illegible] here. I [illegible] many [illegible] where [illegible] [illegible] have been bred direct from Connemara ponies themselves, or from their [illegible] the first or second generation. I have also a very [illegible], a [illegible] horse, which was got by a thoroughbred horse by "[illegible]," [illegible] a mare, daughter of a Connemara pony.

8755. Colonel St. [illegible].—What size is this horse you speak of—"[illegible] of [illegible]" was a [illegible] [illegible], he is 15 [illegible] high.

8756. Chairman.—You may have heard it [illegible] here [illegible], with regard to the horse of the Clydesdale and the horse of the thoroughbred, that the [illegible] of the Clydesdale was as great as that of the thoroughbred horse. What is your experience?—The gentleman that said it had never [illegible], [illegible] I [illegible] you [illegible] that the [illegible] of the Clydesdale [illegible] or [illegible]. The [illegible] is [illegible], and the difference [illegible] a [illegible]. There is no comparison.

8757. Mr. [illegible].—I did not think it was so much?—Very [illegible], it is just [illegible], [illegible] very [illegible]; the horse in the thoroughbred [illegible] and [illegible]. That of the Clydesdale horse is well [illegible], and no [illegible], and not so [illegible] as much.

8758. That applies not only to the Clydesdale?—To any of those [illegible]—[illegible]. [illegible] the [illegible] of the [illegible] and [illegible] is a very [illegible], [illegible].

8759. Chairman.—I believe the [illegible] of the [illegible] is very [illegible]. [illegible] "[illegible]"?—Yes, [illegible].

8760. I [illegible] it [illegible] what you say, Mr. [illegible], that you would not have any objection to [illegible] half-bred horses, provided there was [illegible] of [illegible] [illegible] horses [illegible]?—I would approve of the use of certain half-bred [illegible] in [illegible] districts, but I would not register them, because I [illegible] a dangerous experiment. You would find [illegible] that you would register horses that would not be half-bred at all. I

Jan. 4, 1897.
Mr. William [illegible]

mean they would be mongrels in the end. At the same time I should approve of good selected half-bred sires being sent to those districts where they need size and strength, and that these horses should be subsidised.

8761. How would you select these?—By a committee of the Royal Dublin Society. I think in the hands of the Royal Dublin Society we are safe; and they have done so much for horse-breeding already I am quite safe under their committee we would be safe in their selection.

8762. You were going to say something about the registration?—Of course, registration has really been one of the most effective checks to diseased horses in the country. It has been a great help to horse-breeding immediately; but I would not wish to say anything about registration of horses in the past, because though I am quite sure the trouble and pains has been spent by the gentleman who has carried it out, and it has been done with every care in every possible way, yet at the same time I think that the registration scheme, to have the beneficial effect it should have, should be carried out in a different way from the present. It should be carried out by a committee appointed by the Royal Dublin Society, that committee to meet in certain large places like Limerick, Waterford, [illegible], and those places, and a horse should be submitted to them for their approval. I would go so far as to say that the owners of horses should be allowed certain travelling fees to present them to the committee, and this committee should see these horses and approve of them; and, if they approve of them, they should then be examined by one or two veterinary surgeons, not local men, but men appointed by the Royal Dublin Society; and then they should be registered, and that registration should entitle them to stand in the country. Of course the present registration has been carried out with a great deal of care and judgment, indeed, by the Royal Dublin Society, and has done endless good, because it has pointed out to local people the sound and unsound horses in the country.

8763. You may have heard it mentioned here by various witnesses that they would prefer to have stallions licensed?—I do not think it is possible. I think the licensing will consist in properly registered horses. It will be quite sufficient if horses are properly registered by the committee of the Royal Dublin Society appointed annually. I think it would be [illegible] licence. I think it would be a very difficult thing to carry, and almost impossible. You should pass an Act of Parliament to stop people from covering mares with a horse that was not licensed; just the same as you do with a public-house or anything else. Unless you bring it under the law, that nobody shall have an unlicensed stallion, the same as he could not have a public-house, you would not do it. With the present system of registration extended and well done, it will ultimately prevent the men who have unsound stallions from keeping them. Now, I was at [illegible] Newcastle fair, and we had [illegible] Irish [illegible] there looking out for stallions. When they saw a horse they came to me and said: "Will this horse be registered?" They do not buy any horses that would not be registered, showing that the registration system has done good already. We will find the unsound horses dying out. There are many unsound horses that are not on the register, and are getting very good horses, and they will be registered. I know many cases at present when [illegible] very well, and people go and breed from them. They are not registered, but they are able to sell their produce, and they go on breeding from them.

8764. On the matter of which do you think there is anything in it—that if a horse is [illegible] the [illegible], and eventually turns into a roarer, would you take that as hereditary, and likely to pass down in the produce?—The point of roaring is very difficult point. There is roaring from accident and roaring from hereditary tendency. If you have an accidental roarer, in many instances I know have gone, possibly they will get sound stock; if hereditary, [illegible] follows their produce if they make a disease—the [illegible] system. At the same time it may also happen that horses that have had the best blood with a family taint or a hereditary predisposition to roaring, when they are put to the stud they become in two or three years [illegible] themselves, simply from the family taint. Those horses would have all the disadvantages of producing roaring stock, while on the other hand you may have a horse coming from a sound family who gets a severe attack of pneumonia, and becomes a roarer during his stud life—that horse will probably never get a roarer.

8765. Conformation has a good deal to do with it?—Yes, and the hereditary taint. We have certain lines of family in the stud book that are tainted with roaring, the same as consumption or any other disease in the human subject, and whenever they get the slightest exciting cause, strangles, pneumonia, or pulmonary disease, they develop the condition.

8766. Although their formation may be against it?—Although their formation may be against it; but such comes from a [illegible] family [illegible].

8767. Mr. FITZWILLIAM.—I did not exactly gather your ideas as to the class of stallion you would recommend for general purposes of breeding in Ireland. Firstly, I understood you to say you preferred the thoroughbred?—I consider there are only two classes of horses you can breed in Ireland, as native the [illegible] farmer can breed. In my remarks I refer particularly to the tenant farmers. The two classes of horses that will pay the tenant farmer to breed are hunters and utility horses. In breeding hunters it is, as far as possible, necessary they should be got by thoroughbred horses. When I say thoroughbred, I do not mean weeds, which the country is full of. I mean a sound, short-legged, [illegible], thoroughbred horse—that is the sort to breed hunters with. The second class, the utility horse, are horses sold for [illegible], carriage horses, or general purposes, and those can be bred very successfully from half-bred horses. By a half-bred horse I mean a horse got by a thoroughbred horse out of a good mare. The bad class of small mares are clean-legged, Irish mares. There is no doubt we had a breed of cart horse before the introduction of the Clydesdale; of course the country was poisoned by other breeds coming in, we had a breed of cart horses in Ireland—an old-fashioned horse, like an enlarged Connemara pony. Every county in Ireland had its own special breed of cart horse according to the requirements. If it was an agricultural country they went in for a heavier class; on other lands they were of a lighter class, and just in the same way it has gone down along, till you come to the West of Ireland and Connemara, where the pony itself has gone down there. I might refer to a breed of horses which were in Clare called Kerry horses; they were called the Kerries, they were originally the descendants of an old Irish stallion in Clare, a son of [illegible]. They were crossed with these clean-legged mares, and produced some of the very best utility horses we had in the country—horses that did plough, go in harness, or do anything. A large number of those horses went into the Army, and were [illegible] troopers; they had good bone, and were quick, sharp horses.

8768. The government of their blood was thoroughbred?—Oh, yes, the top cross was thoroughbred.

8769. In your opinion would the required class of half-bred stallion be procured now?—Yes; I think at the present time you would not get quite the ideal class coming from that clean-legged, straight-going breed; there is no doubt that half-bred horses, the breeding horses would be picked up, horses with bone and size, with good hunting character and [illegible] them, they would be bought and sent to districts where [illegible] horses is essential.

8770. You told me about the mares, though you [illegible] the service where there are subsidised or registered stallions to good or sound mares, or should you allow any mare to go?—I should think surely that [illegible] a subscription to a subsidised stallion produced a certificate of soundness from some veterinary surgeon that she was free from hereditary disease. It would be very easily done, and it would be a protection to the horse as well as to this stock themselves.

8771. Do you think that breeding from a two-year-old in any way damages her in after life?—I think it prevents their growth for the time being. I think breeding from a two-year-old mare [illegible] their growth to a certain extent for a year, but if they do not continue to breed from her she possibly gets it up again or more, as the strain on the system is taken away.

8772. So then, on the whole, you would not advise any breeding from a two-year-old?—No.

8773. Nor one that had [illegible]?—[illegible] I have seen some very good [illegible] from it, but I think it is a mistake. I should not breed from them till they are three years old.

8774. On the matter of these Hackney stallions which have been introduced within the last few years, have you seen a good deal of them?—Yes; I had the pleasure of seeing last week the Congested Districts Board stallions and going over them. Previous to that, I was down in Kenmare in May, 1895, and saw a horse there that was sired by the Board [illegible] him specially, and I think he was perhaps one of the greatest horses I ever saw. Of course he had gone through a very heavy course; had covered perhaps nearly a hundred mares, and there was only the [illegible] of him left. The head and neck and tail and quarters were there [illegible], and he looked like the 'King William' in College Green. I have a letter here I wrote to Captain Taylor, of Kenmare, some time ago. He touches on the points which Mr. [illegible] has asked me. I wanted to find out about these horses, and I wrote to him. This is the letter:—

"The young Hackney horse here are not a bad lot to look at, but, of course, I cannot take [illegible], as for years we had nothing but the very worst type of stallions in this part. In fact I think they should be greatly [illegible] the blood of any of our old [illegible]. The [illegible] of the Hackneys must be looked on as better than [illegible] of the local stallions I [illegible] to; but I find since that if a thoroughbred would [illegible] the [illegible] would be infinitely better. Everyone who knows anything of horses can testify to the staying powers of thoroughbreds. There are great differences of opinion as to the staying power of Hackneys. I am of the same opinion as one of the gentlemen examined lately in Dublin that the thoroughbred can do anything the Hackney can do; but I can go further, the former can do what the latter cannot, therefore why spoil the true blood that cannot be questioned by importing here horses that a serious question arises as to their staying powers."

8775. That is from Captain Taylor, a local man?—I wanted to find out about the produce of these horses there.

8776. What districts is that?—Kenmare. I saw the horses of the Congested Districts Board also last week, and was greatly struck with the excellent management and beautiful arrangements, and the [illegible] I thought, a very good class of horses, a fair class, very good of their class and [illegible]. In fact I thought it a most perfect establishment, with perfect arrangements, and great credit is due to those connected with it, but, as I said before, if the same amount of trouble and pains and expense had been taken with a few thoroughbred horses or [illegible] horses it would have done more good than could possibly be done in years. It is not now, but in years to come we have to look at this Hackney breed; the consequences it will bring into every county in Ireland. It will penetrate into every county. As an old breeder of thirty years experience I tell you, you have it in evidence that no dealer or hunting man will have anything to do with a horse with a Hackney taint if he can get any other sort. The [illegible] is that, as the papers collected by the Horse Breeders' Association testify, the [illegible] in England [illegible], and will [illegible] show the districts where the produce of these horses have been. The [illegible] industry is [illegible] to the greatest extent, and it is [illegible]. That is my opinion. It will penetrate beyond the districts where they [illegible]. They will go into Meath, Carlow, Kildare, and other counties. [illegible] these generations we will find [illegible]; want of [illegible], want of [illegible], and their [illegible] constitutions [illegible] good horses which have made our [illegible].

8777. You think these Hackney stallions, even though they may be introduced to get good [illegible] horses in this first generation will do great damage to the breed of the Irish [illegible] of horses in future generations?—That is thoroughly my view; I consider it is not in their [illegible] they [illegible], and will [illegible], in [illegible] extend all over Ireland.

8778. Have you ever heard of the produce of this Board's stallion?—Yes, [illegible]. I have seen it in Kenmare. I have [illegible] of the produce of the Congested Districts Board's horses, but I have seen the horses themselves.

8779. Have you [illegible] other stallions, Welsh and [illegible]?—Yes, and I think next to [illegible] stallions you could not make a better selection than the Welsh cob horse. He is a hardy horse, a horse with a constitution, and at the Congested Districts Board's [illegible] I saw three very good horses, which I think certainly are more suitable to the wants of the [illegible] farmers in the poorer districts. I had considerable experience on the Purchasing Committee in 1878, in Wales, and we purchased a large number of Welsh horses for exhibition purposes, and [illegible] there a large number of those Welsh stallions of which the produce were very excellent. I bought a large number for [illegible] Welsh [illegible], and I [illegible] these Welsh stallions would be found a most useful breed to cross with our Connemara ponies, because they are something of the same tribe themselves. You know, one of the most [illegible], it seems to me the [illegible] of the Congested Districts Board—the horse they sent to Kenmare last year, I saw him, and [illegible] a horse about 15.1. This idea seems to be that if you [illegible] hands high. That is a most fatal thing. The result is you breed horses with the head of a Hackney, which is not handsome, with the body probably of a pony, and the legs of his grandfather or grandmother. That is practically the result.

8780. As to the Arabs and Barbs, have you any opinion?—I have looked at Arabs for two or three years. I think they are really very useful, and would be very suitable in districts where ponies are wanted. [illegible] is the great thing.

8781. Would you like to see the Welsh horse and the Arab or Barb introduced into many of these districts?—Yes; and placed within the reach of these small farmers.

8782. Amongst Connemara ponies [illegible]?—Yes; I should think you would select excellent [illegible] which have played [illegible] in the country, and that [illegible]. They would make excellent stallions if placed at the disposal of these people.

8783. You put great value on the present prestige

[illegible]

of the Irish bred horse?—I think we are admitted to be the best horse-breeding country in the world. We wish to keep it up. If we do we must breed the very best. The only way to make breeding pay, if we breed horses, dogs, sheep, or anything else, is to breed the very best of its class. You must not breed anything that will deteriorate it. It is exactly the same in breeding Connemara ponies. To improve them will be to produce a horse that will be the best of their own class, which will be the Welsh horse. You do not want to put them to a thoroughbred stallion, or a cart horse stallion, or any other stallion three times their own size. You immediately get an unevenly bred animal.

8784. You think that the loss of the prestige that the Irish bred horse has at the present time would be a great loss to the Irish farmer?—I think it is our strongest Irish industry.

8785. You believe that any experiments as regards the introduction of new breeds, whatever they might be, might be damaging to the prestige of the Irish horse?—I quite agree with you. My idea is that when we have been so successful I do not see why it should be rendered doubtful.

8786. You think that the keeping of stallions that you do not approve of in districts such as the congested districts would eventually filter through into other horse-breeding districts of Ireland?—I am quite sure they will. I am quite sure the result will be this: the dealers won't buy these Hackney horses, and they will ultimately find their way into fairs and horse marts and places, and percolate into other parts of the country, to be used by farmers for breeding purposes, and perhaps in ten or fifteen years' time the mistake will be found out.

8787. Lord Ashtown.—Do you think half-bred sires would be wanted in some parts of the country?—Yes; in connection with thoroughbred sires. There are parts of Ireland where good strong half-bred sires would be the greatest benefit.

8788. Don't you think the Royal Dublin Society should recognise these sires?—Yes.

8789. But you would not register them?—I would have them on a register, but would not register them in the same way as a thoroughbred.

8790. Not on the same footing?—No.

8791. But you would not object to their recognising these horses in certain districts?—No; I should recommend he should have a licence if he passed the committee.

8792. Or a recognition?—Yes, or a recognition from the Royal Dublin Society. I mean to say that the danger of registering a half-bred horse is so great. It is just like letting a half-bred horse into Weatherbys' stud book. Over and over again there are instances of horses which we know are thoroughbred horses, like Morley, but Weatherbys say "No, we cannot take them in." We recognise that.

8793. The Royal Dublin Society does not at present register mares; don't you think they might give premiums to light bred mares, to half-bred horses, and recognise them in that way?—That is the way I would do it. I would give certain selected mares free nominations to these horses, or help them to pay in a certain way. But I would not call a horse fit for registration that had not three distinct crosses of thoroughbred, that was got by a thoroughbred horse, his dam got by a thoroughbred and her dam, after that I would not go back.

8794. Colonel St. Quintin.—I wish to ask you about a subject that has been very lightly touched on up to the present; a few practical questions, with regard to the production of military horses in Ireland. Lord Harberton(?) spoke of remounts; you have had a great deal of experience of government horses, and the government to a certain extent finds itself mixed up in this question of horse-breeding in Ireland. It is to a very small extent, and the question is—I am speaking of the military department—whether they could come forward with any scheme that would assist them in their purchase of military horses. Of course you have to take into consideration the cost of production, but with regard to the question of the Hackney, I should like to know what your idea is as to the first essential point in the construction of a horse from a military point of view?—I have bought two hundred troopers for my regiment, and the first essential in the formation of every trooper is his shoulders. Without shoulders it is impossible to carry a military saddle, it goes over his head. I have never seen a Hackney yet with shoulders to carry a man; that is an admitted fact. On that ground I think Hackneys are quite unsuited to produce horses suitable for riding purposes for military use.

8795. Well then, independent of the riding horses, we have to buy a great number of what you may call different draught horses, which are for the various positions in the teams of artillery and transport. They require a certain amount of weight with activity. Do you think the introduction of the Hackney blood with the mares at present in Ireland, will give us the stamp of utility horse we require for this purpose?—I do not, because I think the Hackney action is an action that is a waste of power. If you want a horse to go twenty miles you want him to be able to get over that twenty miles with the least amount of exertion to himself, and the least loss of material. If a horse takes up his foreleg and brings it up to his chin, and puts it down again in the same place, it is an absolute waste of power. Therefore a horse with that class of action would be absolutely unsuited for your transport. I do not mean to say that you might not possibly find a horse got by a Hackney horse without that class of action; but if they have the artificial action, I should say they would not be suited for the work for which you require them.

8796. Well there is also another question with regard to the possibility of forming Government studs in the country for the purpose of assisting the military horses. I must tell you beforehand there is a mistaken notion as to the influence military horses have on the breeding in Ireland, because a great many people think it has a very large influence whereas it has a small one. The number that is required by our Government is so small, it practically has no effect. At the same time they naturally would be anxious to assist in any way they could the industry of the country, and the question is whether it would be advisable in any way to form depots to buy more directly from the farmers, and to keep the young stock, and as to whether it could be done in an economical way. I don't know whether you have thought this out; it might require consideration?—I have thought it out. I think the present system has worked very well. I do not think Government studs or places to buy young horses, and keep them over for Government use will be successful for this reason, that you may buy a horse as a yearling or a two-year-old, and when he comes to be a three-year-old, when he is wanted he may be a different animal altogether. You will have to shoot away a large number of unsuitable and unsaleable horses, and I think the present system of the purchasing officers attending at the different places, the large fairs, and selecting the horses themselves every three or four months in the year, and sending them on to the regiment, is far the most economical course, and the wisest and most practical that can be adopted. Government breeding studs will never pay. Breeding studs will pay best when managed by private enterprise, and if that private enterprise is assisted by Government it is the way to enable it to do so. When a man's own money is at stake it makes him more careful and more guarded in his selection. I think there is only one way I could say that the Government could give the Commission on the horse-breeding of Ireland assistance, and that would be to make some arrangement, or that the parties should come to some decision with reference

Nov. [illegible], 1896. Mr. William [illegible].

to pleasing the most [illegible] [illegible], any [illegible] [illegible] did, at the disposal of local breeders; disperse them about the country for breeding purposes. I was once with [illegible] regiment [illegible] certainly [illegible]. I know they are sold at Newbridge for remount [illegible], and go to hackney [illegible] and for other purposes. If a certain number of them were placed at £5 each, or £[illegible], at the disposal of those interested in promoting a scheme of local horse-breeding, to give them [illegible] in those districts where they are needed, not in the rich central part of Ireland, but in those districts where the Congested Districts Board is doing good, I think it would be a great benefit, and one of the ways in which the authorities could serve local horse breeding considerably. There are a large number of useful stallions that are broken down, under [illegible] [illegible] that would make excellent [illegible]. [illegible] have the opportunity of seeing or knowing about those horses.

8317. Do you think a farmer would take a mare of that description—broken down, so as to be [illegible] of work?—[illegible] I think they would [illegible] without work, out of them to pay for their keep. I do not think they would keep them to do nothing. Every one of them would plough and cart and do something; and I am sure if recommended by this Commission, it would have a very beneficial effect. [illegible] perhaps a hundred or two hundred [illegible] a year, which would be the very [illegible] in the country. [illegible] pay for them at so much a month or a fixed sum, or in some way or other. That, of course, is [illegible] which would have to be worked out [illegible]. It is an idea which [illegible], and I think something might possibly be done with it.

8318. You said that in breeding hunting dogs, or [illegible], you wanted to breed the best you could?—Yes.

8319. To breed up and not down?—Yes.

8320. And you say that at the present moment there is a particular class of well-bred stock that Ireland possesses which has been [illegible] by the introduction of mixed blood; that Ireland stands almost alone, both as far as the British Islands are concerned and as far as foreign countries are concerned, with that particular class of stock, and that the introduction of any mixed blood is to be deprecated?—Those are my opinions. I think the introduction of any mixed blood into the country is a tendency in the wrong direction.

8321. Mr. La Touche.—Do you think it so absolutely essential that the stallions should be [illegible]?—I think the mares should also be sound. I think it is very essential to have the mare sound as well as the stallion. It is all the better to have them both sound.

8322. As a matter of fact, I was reading the evidence that Admiral Rous gave before the Commission in 1873, and one remark he made was that there is hardly any old stallion of twenty years old that does not become a roarer. They become roarers from [illegible], and fat as a pig. They are not roarers in the same sense as other horses; it is the effect of the life they lead. Of course if you have a horse [illegible] and feed him, [illegible] his respiration becomes impaired.

8323. Colonel St. Quintin.—That is not what you call absolutely a practical [illegible]?—No; there is a [illegible] difference.

8324. Mr. La Touche.—Would you forbid him to [illegible]?—He covers and does no harm.

8325. I say would you forbid him to cover?—No.

8326. But he would be forbidden to serve if [illegible]. Suppose I bought a horse in England [illegible] in Ireland, why, the Veterinary Board would [illegible] him as a roarer? All you say is [illegible]

him, I would pass him provisionally sound for breeding purposes. I think we should be able to detect those horses that are roarers from disease and [illegible] from [illegible] mismanagement. I quite agree with Admiral Rous's remarks that it would be very difficult to find a [illegible] old stallion whose respiration was not more or less impaired from his life.

8327. Admiral Rous goes in the opposite direction in another case. He speaks of the horse named "Favonius," belonging to the Duke of Bedford. He was a roarer, but never got a roarer, and in all human probability, he says, it was hereditary?—Well, we know lots of horses that are roarers that did not get roarers. I know lots of horses that are [illegible] [illegible] [illegible] [illegible] different from the other kind. In fact, Lord [illegible], you know that horse "[illegible]"? He was a [illegible], and his produce are [illegible]. I knew several of them.

8328. Then there was the "Melbourne" [illegible] of a very celebrated family; Admiral Rous and Lord [illegible] agree that he was a roarer. [illegible] think [illegible] to prove that there are great difficulties in the [illegible] of [illegible]?—That is the very [illegible] I [illegible] suggest again. I suggest the advisability of having a committee to [illegible] of these horses, and also [illegible]. It is [illegible] to select [illegible]. It should be done by a committee; they would be able to [illegible] these cases [illegible] important, especially the point as to the advisability of admitting the horse.

8329. Even though he might be a roarer?—Even though he might be a roarer, if it was not likely to interfere with his progeny, or interfere with the [illegible] he was going to be used for.

8330. As regards the soundness of the mares. There would be [illegible] difficulty [illegible]?—Don't you think my suggestion with regard to [illegible] that would be [illegible] to the [illegible] of those horses [illegible] hereditary [illegible] would [illegible] a safeguard to an extent.

8331. That she had not [illegible]?—Yes.

8332. How are you going to examine a brood mare?—The possibility is that she would be examined before she was [illegible] to know that she was not a [illegible].

8333. I can't see the possibility of being able to give [illegible] for [illegible]. For instance, you may get a perfectly sound mare at five years old [illegible] would be perfectly [illegible]?—I would not have [illegible] every year. You get your certificate when two years old, and that [illegible] afterwards.

8334. She may be sound at two years old before [illegible]. On the other hand you may have a mare [illegible] years old [illegible]?—You would [illegible]. [illegible] It is one of the most difficult and most [illegible] points, and all that could be done is to lessen the [illegible] as much as possible.

8335. As regards [illegible] knowledge [illegible] Commission has been [illegible] that there are a very considerable number of so-called half-bred horses [illegible]?—Yes, there are.

8336. I suppose you agree with me that the use of these horses does not tend to improve the breed?—

[illegible] — Mr. William [illegible], v.s.

They don't improve the breed, but unfortunately there are farmers who will breed from them. Many owners of those half-breds have a large circle of relations who all patronise them. But those horses will gradually die out as the neighbourhood improves, and as the better horses are placed at the disposal of the breeders this class of horse will gradually find its own level.

8817. Don't you think these horses are generally used from the fact that they come at much lower fees?—That's the fact. They come at anything they can get.

8818. It is possible those horses would be quite put out of the market if really suitable sires were placed at the disposal of the small farmers at the same fees that those horses come at?—Quite so. But to do so they should be subsidised.

8819. It would be absolutely necessary?—Yes; it would not pay without a subsidy.

8820. It would not pay any private enterprise?—It would not pay any private enterprise to do it.

8821. For the breeding of horses in our country you think the thoroughbred horse is certainly the most suitable?—Certainly the most suitable.

8822. You saw the Hackney stallions of the Congested Districts Board lately?—Last week.

8823. Have you seen any of the stock got by those horses?—I have not, except what I saw at the Congested Districts Board's farm. They were moderate.

8824. Were they bred at the farm?—Some of them were bought, I think, and some were bred there. There were only a very few of them, so that you could scarcely form an opinion about them. They wanted small enough. The horses themselves were very good of their class.

8825. Have you had any experience of the Hackney horse?—Yes, I had personal experience of them in England, driving them. I have also kept a good deal of them in England. I never bought one for the purpose, because I was always strongly prejudiced against something (?) in him. I have liked them in [illegible], but I avoided, as far as possible, ever having a horse with a Hackney strain in him. They don't stay. They are the most constitutional horses in the world, and I may tell you as a professional man that whenever they get sick they die. It is a very extraordinary thing—they have no recuperative power. If you take the horse, say a Hackney and the other thoroughbred, and they both get an attack of inflammation of the lungs and leave the same symptoms, the Hackney horse is sure to die and the other to pull through, because the Hackney has not recuperative power—he has no stamina.

8826. In India had you anything to do with the Government breeding?—I was not in India, but in Africa. I went through a good deal of the horse-breeding in Africa. There are some very large studs there.

8827. You heard some of the witnesses to-day state that the mares of the country were too bad to put to a thoroughbred horse. Do you think the fact of a mare being very bad is sufficient reason for sending her to a worse horse than a thoroughbred horse?—No; on the contrary, I think that those very bad mares should have an opportunity of getting a thoroughbred horse, a thoroughbred horse that would be suitable to the district. If a pony district I would not send to breeding a great big horse, but pick a pony size to them. A little horse called "Whalebone" had done wonderful [illegible]. The produce of this horse with small pony mares are all useful, sharp, quick animals, and sending a small horse to those districts where even the mares are bad would improve them considerably.

8828. I was talking of the county Donegal?—I should send them a good strong master thoroughbred horse and that would improve them, no matter how bad the mares were.

8829. You don't agree with the witnesses who say that the mares are too bad to send to a thoroughbred horse?—I don't agree with them at all. The single reason that they breed from a bad horse is because the Irish farmer in those districts looks at the price the first thing, and the price is what guides them and not the horse. If they got a horse fit for and suitable for him, they will send to the fit horse as because what he is.

8830. A gentleman here this morning said that if a thoroughbred horse was sent to his district in the county Londonderry, to stand at equal fees with another sort of horse, the thoroughbred horse would get nothing to do?—Well, if he were a good, strong thoroughbred horse I am perfectly certain he would be [illegible] in the [illegible].

8831. You think he would?—I think if he didn't, it would be the fault of the owners of the mares, and if they didn't do it the poor thing would send when they saw by the finds of a year that it was a benefit. Of course you would build those everything through in a [illegible].

8832. Mr. Wrench.—You said you would be in favour of Government studs, but would be not being given by Government to private studs?—Not to private studs, but to individual horses belonging to private studs.

8833. Take your own instance. Say you had eight thoroughbred stallions, in what way would you let Government assist you?—I don't want any assistance for my stud, but I mean to subsidise horses that would be sent to those districts. If you wanted to send a horse to a certain district, and the Government subsidised, one asks the owner of the stud, what is it he would not pay him to send a horse whose cost was up to £500 to a district like Donegal to cover mares at two shillings each; so then the horse should be subsidised.

8834. Much on, something on the former plan of the Royal Dublin Society?—Somewhat on the same plan.

8835. On what ground do you form your opinion that each county ought to have a separate breed?—From thirty years living in Ireland.

8836. From experience during the last thirty years?—From experience during the last thirty years.

8837. You have been able to form that up as in some documentary evidence of it?—I have followed the thing very carefully, and I have been [illegible] that you can go to almost any county in Ireland, and like the people that live in the county, the horses belonging to it have their peculiarities.

8838. Did those use at two special [illegible]?—They used from one or two special breeds of [illegible] that have existed in it.

8839. At what period do you think the foreign blood—the English blood like the Clydesdale began to come largely into Ireland?—Beginning the last thirty or fourteen years there has been a large introduction of Clydesdale and other breeds.

8840. And you don't think that before that any one foreign blood brought into the country?—I will not say that there was, but not in the same quantities as there has been since.

8841. Fifty years ago there was very little cart horse blood?—Very little, I think. Fifty years ago the horses were entirely bred in the districts in which they were used.

8842. They were presumably of the pure Irish breed?—Of the pure Irish breed, but the facilities for exporting them out of the country and taking them away didn't exist then that exist now.

8843. Do you know the congested districts?—Yes. I have been through Kerry and Connemara.

8844. And Belmullet?—I have not been to Belmullet.

8845. Or Achill?—No; not to Achill.

8846. Do you know Lisdoonvarna?—No.

6847. Or Clifden?—I have been as far as Clifden.

6848. And Oughterard?—Yes.

6849. Do you know Donegal?—I don't know Donegal.

6850. What sires would you place in the congested districts if you had to purchase sires at the present moment?—I should have three classes of sires. I should have a small, thick, short, thoroughbred horse with action, for certain districts; I should have a half-bred—a strong half-bred horse of the class that I referred to, namely, a horse of three crosses of thoroughbred; and Welsh cobs, similar to the Welsh cobs you have at present, on the same lines as the Congested Districts Board's cobs, which I think are very useful ones.

6851. Would you have any Arabs or Barbs?—I might have them occasionally in some districts. But they don't do so well, I find. I have had an Arab and a Barb pony standing at my stud, crossed with ponies, and I am disappointed in their produce, rather. There is a want of bone in them.

6852. Is it always the case that a small thoroughbred horse will also breed small produce?—Not at all; but still it is more likely to breed an animal (from the small mares) with an equalised conformation.

6853. On what grounds have you formed your opinion that Hackneys are so delicate of constitution?—From the experience that I have had amongst them—a lengthened practical experience.

6854. You have been called in professionally to attend to Hackneys?—Yes.

6855. Where?—In England.

6856. In what part?—When I was quartered in England; I have seen quantities of them.

6857. Where?—In Leeds, Manchester,—and not only from my own opinion, but also from the opinions of several very eminent veterinary surgeons who have been largely called to attend on them.

6858. It is the general opinion of the profession?—It is.

6859. CHAIRMAN.—From what you said, I take it you think a good scheme could be made out of the old scheme of the Royal Dublin Society and the one at present in force?—Yes.

6860. Between the two you could make a good scheme?—Yes. I have written a few suggestions, which, if you allow me, I shall read. They perhaps might be of use.

6861. Would it be well to hand them in?—I will if you wish, but perhaps it would be better for me to read them. My first suggestion is—"To encourage by subsidising good, sound, suitable stallions to stand in certain counties which are not now sufficiently supplied."—That is, referring to districts which are now not supplied with stallions, because I think it is quite unnecessary and would be absurd to subsidise stallions in the congested districts of Ireland, where there are large quantities of stallions. "The object would be to subsidise stallions where they are needed." "Second. The distribution of the prizes, as far as possible, to local societies and committees, to work under the Royal Dublin Society." I am quite sure local societies are really the best judges of what they want in the districts, but they should act entirely under the Royal Dublin Society, and I believe they should have the power of distributing a certain sum of money. "Third. Subsidised stallions to cover a certain number of tenant farmers' mares at low fees, according to certain rules of societies." This I think is a most important thing, so as to enable the stallions to be within the reach of smaller tenant farmers. "Fourth. Subsidise money prizes for brood mares at local shows," which I think is the only way of keeping the mares in the country. "Fifth. The supervision of stallions by the Royal Dublin Society, and to be done for the farmer by commission appointed for each district, with veterinary surgeons attached." I think I have already referred to that. My sixth suggestion is one which the members of the Commission will think a strong one. "Sixth. The elimination from Ireland of the horse known as the Hackney stallion, excepting those kept by private studs."

6862. Mr. [illegible].—You object to having half-bred stallions registered, but don't you think the registration of the half-bred stallions would [illegible] so much as it would give confidence to the farmer or the public that the pedigree of a stallion was exactly what it professed to be?—I quite agree with you; I quite think that, as I already said, the half-bred stallions that would be subsidised should be recognised by the Royal Dublin Society in some way that would give a guarantee to those that breed from them that they were bred in this way and were sound, and had the approval of being deserving of [illegible] prize of the subsidisation.

6863. That would be almost [illegible]?—Yes; it would be, but it [illegible] not let them into the list on the same footing. It is simply this: I am afraid that if you put half-bred stallions on the register it will be an almost impossible thing to draw the line afterwards, and it will be very dangerous. But if you have a stallion with three crosses of thoroughbred in him by a thoroughbred horse himself, but with the make and shape of a hunter likely to breed the class of horse which is required in the district, and that have been subsidised by the Royal Dublin Society, I think he would be a most useful animal. Without unnecessarily [illegible]—Perhaps in some way by registration you will permit me to say that all the half-breds were registered in a separate register it might meet the wants.

Mr. H. A. ROBINSON, Roundstone, Galway, examined.

6864. CHAIRMAN.—You are a land agent, I believe, and you live near Roundstone, which is almost the extreme point of the west of Galway?—Yes, my lord.

6865. You are well acquainted, I presume, with the congested districts, and the horses which are bred in the county Galway?—Yes, my lord, I know them very well.

6866. Will you describe the horses bred in your neighbourhood?—Do you mean the horses belonging to the district, or the stallions the Congested Districts Board have sent there?

6867. The horses native to the place?—The stallions are very bad, indeed; the mares are fairly good. The small country farmers, as a rule, sell the foals at six months, they are sold in the fairs of Clifden and Oughterard, and go away. Some of the mares are very good, and have good bone. They are small, about 14 or 14.2 hands—hardly any higher than that.

6868. Are there many horses bred there?—Yes; a large number.

6869. What sort of stallions are there principally used there?—The native stallions are very bad indeed; nothing could be worse.

6870. A bad class?—Very bad.

6871. What sort are they?—Just anything so all to the shape of a horse.

6872. Are they horses or ponies chiefly?—Ponies, not horses.

6873. Have the ponies deteriorated much in Connemara latterly?—The ponies have deteriorated very much. I would not say there is much change in the ponies. The foals that used to go at £6 a few years ago are now only going at from £2 to £3. I saw them on the 17th December last in the fair of Clifden—plenty of them selling under £3.

6874. At the present moment there is less price for the foals than there used to be?—Yes; much less.

[illegible] Mr. [illegible]

But I don't know what the drop in value is. What the Pony is worth or is anything worth, but the prices for those ponies have gone down very much. I suppose the demand for them is not so great now.

8874. When did you notice that drop take place? —For the last two or three years; certainly for the last two years.

8875. Have you been able to form any opinion as to the stock got by the Congested Districts Boards' Hackneys used in your neighbourhood? —Yes, I have seen a great many of them, but I myself don't care about the Hackney. I have had thoroughbred stallions myself, and I like them much better. I had "Wattlebanging" in Connemara, and I also had another thoroughbred horse called "Hold-Ripple"; he was by "Dutch." I had "Wattlebanging" for three years under the Royal Dublin Society's scheme.

8876. What sort of stock did he get? —They were nicely formed. I have a great many of those stock.

8877. Did many of them go out of the district as foals? —Yes, a good many. Many have been kept, and a good many have been sold as two-year-olds and yearlings. Some gentlemen went down and bought a good many. He bought some from Mr. Berridge the other day, and he would not have anything but "Wattlebanging" with a view to make polo ponies of them.

8879. Have you got the horse now? —No, he is in Connemara. I sold him to Mr. Berridge, a large proprietor there.

8880. Have there been any other thoroughbred stallions down there except those two? —"Goldfinder" and "Wattlebanging" are the only thoroughbred stallions I know of.

8881. Are there any other sort of stallions down there? —No others, except the horses of the Congested Districts Board.

8882. No mongrel stallions? —Oh, I think not; but [illegible] than I think of any use in the world.

8883. What sort are they? —Mongrels of the very worst description. Principally ponies; there is one up in Recess. In some parts of Connemara they just turn a stallion out loose on the mountain with the mares.

8884. One of those goes with them? —Yes.

8885. And just leave it in charge? —Yes; there is a man in Connemara that [illegible]. He has a lot of mares, that is Martin Morgan of Cornia. I think he would agree to the Congested Districts horse. He had [illegible] of those in the last year of [illegible]; he would have sold them for £8 a piece, but he could not [illegible].

8886. Is the habit there to send them up like a [illegible] of sheep and collect the young animals and send them away? —Yes. They used to go away in droves, but we have got a railway now and they go away in wagons.

8887. Do people come down to buy them? —Yes; there was a large number of small jobbers [illegible] the small class of buyers there, and there was great demand for the ponies at low prices.

8888. Were there any of the foals of the Congested Districts Board horses sold down? —They were mixed up with the other foals. They don't seem to make any difference in the price from the others.

8889. What price do they range at? —From about £4 up to £8. £8 was a good price this year for the ordinary foal. Lots of them went at £3. I saw them selling at Clifden; Mr. Jones bought foals at £2 a piece.

8890. Do the farmers [illegible] appreciate the Hackney stallions down there? —I really could not say. I think they appreciate anything they get for breeding [illegible]. I don't think they are judges really about them—most of them.

8891. You think the [illegible] has [illegible] to do with them. You could not get a [illegible] for [illegible] a horse now if you had a "Kendal" down there.

8892. Do you think that hunter-breeding can be made to pay down there? —I think you are [illegible] make breeding for polo ponies pay; that would be certain to pay I think.

8893. You think by that same breed would go into the [illegible]? —Yes, I had one myself by "Gold Finder" a four-year-old. He [illegible] and I only had him for six months and I got £23 for him at the last Ballinasloe show. That [illegible] very well. He was out on a rough mountain that was only worth a half-a-crown an acre.

8894. Do you think the Hackney stallion is likely to produce that class of animal down there? —Not a polo pony.

8895. You think not? —I don't think it, my lord, but I am quite sure of it. He may produce a large [illegible], but he won't produce a polo pony, as far as my experience goes.

8896. What sort of stallion do you think now would be the best to have down there? —A small thoroughbred—he may be even up to 15 hands, with plenty of bone. "Wattlebanging" was a hunter-bred horse; but it is not easy to get a horse like him. He was 15.2, he was beautifully bred, by "Spring Bold." You could not beat him. If you could not get a thoroughbred with enough bone I would not object to a slight cross; but I would rather have a thoroughbred.

8897. Have you any suggestions to make to the Commission with a view to improve the breed of horses in your district? —Certainly; to send down a thoroughbred stallion.

8898. Mr. Fitzwilliam.—Do you think that those Connemara ponies are able to be [illegible] the breed has gone down a good deal? —Oh, yes, I think they are.

8899. The Chairman.—Did I understand you to say the ponies have deteriorated of late? —We have often heard a great deal about the Connemara ponies, but I have been in Connemara for the last forty years, and there are some very good mares in it, and of ponies, there are a lot of very bad ones. The general impression is that they deteriorated; but you can pick some very good mares [illegible] with good bone.

8900. Mr. Fitzwilliam.—I think you said they deteriorated. In your opinion the best way to keep the breed up to its original excellence would be to use these small thoroughbreds, such as you describe "Wattlebanging" to be? —Yes.

8901. Should you object to an Arab as a [illegible] cross? —Yes. There was [illegible] in Connemara that [illegible] "Awfully Jolly"—was, I think, a very good horse, indeed; and [illegible] enough for the [illegible].

8901a. What size was he? —"Awfully Jolly" was about 14 hands.

8902. If you could have a larger one of the same class? —Yes, I would not object. From what I hear, I have no experience of breeding from the Arab myself. I have heard the other.

8903. "Wattlebanging" is out there now? —Yes, at Ballynahinch Castle. Mr. Berridge has him; but I don't know whether the owner [illegible] give him to [illegible] that can be reached by the small men, because he has a good many mares himself. I don't know what his intention is.

8904. But you think the introduction of Hackney blood among the ponies would be [illegible]? —I think it is a mistake, even if it produces a small [illegible], there are no [illegible] of those [illegible] now.

8905. Are there Hackney stallions in that district? —Yes, and Welsh cobs. Welsh cobs and Hackney stallions are in different places through the district.

8906. And in your opinion of the Hackney, the opinion generally among your neighbours who are [illegible] to give an opinion on horsebreeding [illegible] could not say that. I am sorry to say that in Connemara, I think they know very little about horse-breeding.

[illegible]

[illegible]

8934. A very close one?—I didn't say the foals were by the Hackney.

8935. Do you find that people would send to a thoroughbred?—I think they would if they thought they would breed good produce.

8936. Did you get a fair number of mares to "Woodspring"?—I don't know about fifty each year.

8937. You charged £2, I think?—It was 10s. under this scheme; £2 some time.

8938. Do you know that most of the horses that have been sent into Connemara by the Board have been Welsh?—Yes; I know "Rothsmere" is Welsh, that stood at Letterfrack, and "Prince Llewellyn" stood at Oughterard and also at Maam.

8939. And at Clifden?—And a Welsh horse called "Moonstone" stood at Clifden. I am not sure what he was.

8940. I know there have been some Welsh there. Was anything else stood in that district?—Welsh and Hackneys. There was a Hackney at Clifden. "Ecce," I think, was a Hackney.

8941. Was not his stock good?—I wish there [illegible] of "Ecce." The best, I think, I saw there was a big chestnut horse, "Valette"—something "Valette"—the year before last. He was the biggest of them.

8942. CHAIRMAN.—Have you anything further you wish to say?—The only suggestion I wish to make is that I would be most anxious to get a thoroughbred horse—I don't mean a weedy thoroughbred—into Connemara, because no private individual can bring one in. He cannot compete with the Board's horses at 5s. as the price of his fee, otherwise I would try and get a horse myself, but I could not afford to keep him and compete with that price. If the Board would send us one or two thoroughbred horses I think it would be a very good thing indeed.

Adjourned.

SEVENTEENTH DAY.—WEDNESDAY, JANUARY 6TH, 1897.

Present:—RIGHT HON. EARL OF DUNRAVEN, K.P., in the Chair; LORD ASHTOWN, HON. HENRY W. FITZWILLIAM, LORD RATHDONNELL, COL. ST. QUINTIN, MR. PERCY LA TOUCHE, MR. F. S. WRENCH.

MR. HUGH NEVILLE, Secretary.

Mr. GEORGE L. TOTTENHAM, Glenfarne, County Leitrim, examined.

8943. CHAIRMAN.—Mr. Tottenham, you live in the County Leitrim, do you not?—Yes.

8944. You are a deputy lieutenant and magistrate of that county?—Yes.

8945. Are you a member of the Horse Breeding Association?—Yes, I am a member of it; I was one of the original members.

8946. Have you any experience personally in breeding horses?—No, I am not interested personally in horse-breeding; the reason I am on the Committee of the Horse Breeding Association is that we have a common ground of interest—the people who principally started that and I—in putting a stop, if possible, to the action of the Congested Districts Board and their horse-breeding scheme.

8947. To what object in their horse-breeding scheme?—I object to their horse-breeding scheme on other grounds, because I say it is a misapplication of the money of which they are trustees.

8948. That is a question that scarcely affects us here. Well, I suppose in this way it would affect the Commission, that I may show it practically as horse-breeding in those districts at all.

8949. I see, but the question of the application of the money entrusted to them is not one that comes into our purview at all. As far as horse breeding is concerned, are you acquainted with the congested districts in the County Leitrim?—Yes, I am acquainted not only with the County Leitrim, but all the west of the congested districts.

8950. Well, and what have you got to say as to the question of horse-breeding in the districts you are acquainted with?—Well, I have a good deal to say in one way or another.

8951. I should like to get what you want to put before us in your own way?—I am really here as the representative of the Horse Breeding Association, and to advocate their view, which is to take a strong part to this introduction of inferior Hackney blood; and also to show that if any State assistance is given to horse-breeding at all in Ireland, it should be to the particular blood that does good to every other breed and does harm to none, and that is, of course, the thoroughbred blood. There are two public bodies spending what is supposed to be public money on horse-breeding in Ireland; it is a mistake to suppose, as a great many people do, that the Congested Districts Board's money is public money, except as to a very small proportion of it, which I propose to show presently. The Royal Dublin Society's money is, of course, public money. The [illegible] grant of £5,000 a year under the Land Purchase Act, which has been going on for the last six or seven years. And of these two public bodies, it seems to me one is doing as much harm as the other—the Royal Dublin Society encouraging second-class thoroughbred horses, and the Congested Districts Board scattering cheap Hackneys about the country.

8952. You don't approve of the system of the Royal Dublin Society?—No; I don't at all, and I think they made a great mistake in thinking that the country approved of it.

8953. Well, but let us have your reasons for disapproving of it?—The money is simply being thrown away, I think. In the first place, I object to second-rate stallions being registered and subsidised. I think they should have spent their money in buying five or six good horses every year, and planting them out through the country, in the same way that, I think, the Horse Breeding Commission in England does—they give a certain grant every year, which they expend on what they call premium stallions, and place them out through the country; instead of that the Royal Dublin Society—their first scheme was to subsidise, to pay £3, I think, for each mare the [illegible] stallion that they registered, and their standard is said to be low—necessarily must be—because the farmers cannot afford to pay for good stallions that anybody who buys a stallion and gives £200 or £300 for him gets a certificate of soundness, and [illegible]. Their practically they are all registered—both of them are not fit to breed from.

8954. But they have to be sound, have they not?—Yes.

8955. And they are, besides?—Yes; you find the same complaint all over the country that what is wanted is a good strong horse, they don't always [illegible] a thoroughbred, but what they want is a good strong horse, that is what the farmers ask for, [illegible] whether they like a thoroughbred horse, but what they don't want is these light weeds.

8956. I understand you object to the Royal Dublin

[illegible]

great deal of trouble about it, and he has given it up now altogether. The Leitrim Chairman goes on to say—"We recommend going back to the first plan of giving nominations." The merit of that plan was not so much as giving nominations, it was in subsidising stallions; the mares, I think, had only to be approved, but when a stallion was subsidised he got £3, he was supposed to serve at £3, and the Royal Dublin Society paid £3 out of the £3. He probably never got the third pound at all, at all events he was sure of £3 and the mares were practically served for nothing, and it was worth a man's while to buy a moderate stallion, at all events very few could afford to buy a good one, but it was better than the present system. He recommends going back to the former system. What he says is "we found the people would not pay the two guineas fee, as you say, on the chance of a £3 prize." I consider the whole scheme wrong, and he recommends the Hungarian and Australian scheme, which I don't agree with. "It would be better to give a good lump sum down for an improved scheme than go on year after year spending thousands uselessly." In Fermanagh that year they got a special dispensation to give substantial prizes for mares.

6966. Are you saying this yourself or quoting somebody?—No, I know it of my own knowledge, they had great trouble in getting that dispensation from the Dublin Society, but it worked much better. I have here the number of mares shown in Leitrim, there were two only at Carrick-on-Shannon—this is the return from the Secretary.

6967. Secretary of what?—Of the Leitrim committee of the Royal Dublin Society's horse-breeding scheme. Only £36 out of the £60 that was allotted was given in prizes, and the committee objected, as I think I said before, that they have to give prizes to mares that are really not worth giving prizes to.

6968. You say the committee object to that?—Yes.

6969. Who says they object to that?—I say it of my own knowledge from what the Chairman has told me.

6970. You can scarcely speak authoritatively for the committee?—He says "we have neither horses nor mares to breed from."

6971. That is all secondhand evidence, it would be much better to give us your own opinion about it?—I think my opinion is not of so much value. I have not so much experience in horses as the people whose written evidence I have.

6972. I have no objection to your reading anything, but if you say the committee thought so and so, it is a different matter?—I am not a member of the committee myself.

6973. Quite so, and I don't see what authority you have to speak for the committee?—Except from the Chairman.

6974. Well, you can quote from the Chairman what he says in his letter?—Well; but I know from conversation with him.

6975. We can scarcely take that in evidence from you?—This is a written document from the secretary saying there were only two mares presented at Carrick-on-Shannon.

6976. You are quite at liberty to tell us anything you gather from any conversation or your own personal knowledge, but we can scarcely take it from you that the Secretary of the committee thought so and so?—It was from what I gathered in conversation I was giving my last evidence. Then I can give it as my own knowledge of what they do object to. In the same way I know that there is considerable objection to sending back this money to the Royal Dublin Society, supposing there is £80 or £100 allotted to each county, and they only spend £30 or £40, they have to send back the balance, instead of being allowed to accumulate it to buy a good horse for that county. It is all put into a common fund for the Royal Dublin Society, and a horse is bought and sent down to Clonmel for instance, where a horse is not wanted.

[illegible]

Mr. George L. Tulloch.

8877. Then it is where you think a [illegible] is not wanted?—Well, [illegible] in the matter of a horse-breeding industry where all the best horses are, [illegible] they don't want a stallion there. [illegible]

8878. [illegible] Dublin Society's [illegible] Ulster, Munster, and Connaught [illegible] —Major [illegible], Major [illegible], Lord [illegible], [illegible] O'Reilly, Lord [illegible], [illegible] and Frederick Wrench. [illegible] Royal Dublin Society [illegible] Dublin society [illegible] Leinster men. [illegible]

8879. [illegible]

8880. [illegible] Dublin Society [illegible]

8881. Now as to the Congested Districts' Board? [illegible] Congested Districts' Board [illegible] Royal Dublin Society [illegible]

8882. I will give the Committee of the Dublin [illegible] Royal Dublin Society [illegible] Royal Dublin Society [illegible] Committee of the [illegible] Secretary of this Commission. [illegible] Royal Dublin Society.

8883. [illegible]

8884. Have you anything further to say about the Royal Dublin Society?—No, I think not.

8885. The only other body that I think can appear [illegible] Congested Districts' Board?—Yes. [illegible] Congested Districts' Board [illegible] the 31st March, 1895, [illegible]

8886. To whom?—To Parliament. In the statement of the Act it is provided "The Congested Districts' Board shall, once in every year after the year 1891, [illegible] Lord Lieutenant [illegible]

[illegible] Parliament [illegible] the Congested Districts Board [illegible]

8887. Do you know [illegible] October, 1893. [illegible] March, 1895, [illegible] Act of Parliament [illegible]

8888. [illegible]

8889. [illegible] October, [illegible]

8890. [illegible]

8891. I think you [illegible] Commission [illegible]

8892. [illegible] Congested Districts. [illegible] McCormack [illegible] Board [illegible]

8893. [illegible]

8894. We have [illegible] Commission would [illegible] Districts Board.

8895. I don't think [illegible] the Congested Districts [illegible]

[illegible]

[illegible] Mr. [illegible]

9021. You don't know that the [illegible] [illegible] whether they will work the old scheme through the stallion or the later one through the [illegible]?—I don't think they understand that they [illegible] do [illegible].

9022. You referred to the money [illegible] from the different counties, do you know what becomes of that money?—Yes, I understand that goes into a [illegible] fund and that horses are bought with it.

9023. Is not that what you recommend, is it your idea that the best way of improving the breed of horses is the purchase of stallions?—Yes.

9024. And you don't object to the money being spent in that way?—Only in this way that it is rather hard on the county to send such money every year and not to get it back again in the shape of a stallion.

9025. Do you know what would happen if the money was not expended at the end of the financial year?—I know if it is not expended it would go back to the Treasury.

9026. I also understand you to say that you would prefer not to have any registration of stallions whatever?—I don't see the use of it except as a [illegible] of soundness.

9027. That is nothing in your eye, you don't care about the soundness of the stallion?—It is desirable, but some of the stallions [illegible] through the country [illegible] at the [illegible] of their [illegible] [illegible] veterinary surgeon's certificate.

9028. You would not leave any examination of these stallions by any person sent down by the Royal Dublin Society to see whether the horse was a fit horse to serve mares?—Any ordinary stallion or thoroughbred stallion [illegible] the stallions generally in the district.

9029. Any thoroughbred stallion?—Well, if he had a certificate from a competent veterinary surgeon of [illegible] I don't see why that should not be [illegible].

9030. You would not leave the [illegible] to [illegible] if he was likely to improve the breed of horses?—Yes, I would, certainly; but then I think his examined is [illegible] that the inspection is [illegible] [illegible].

9031. Are you aware that any horses were rejected from registration?—Yes, I believe there were some, but I do not know whether it was on the ground that they were unsound or [illegible].

9032. In fact you are not aware of how the process of registration works at all?—Yes, I suppose I know all about it [illegible] in the [illegible]. I know that the Inspector goes down from the Royal Dublin Society and inspects the horse, and there is a veterinary surgeon's certificate given, where a horse applies to have his horse registered.

9033. And you would do away with that, you say it is no use?—I don't see that it prevents any [illegible] being an [illegible] horse from serving through the country.

9034. You know and heard that of any horses having [illegible] [illegible] on account of [illegible]?—No.

9035. Or [illegible] account of their [illegible] not [illegible] [illegible]?—No; I know there were 242 applications this year and only 231 were registered.

9036. You are speaking of a district that you are not thoroughly acquainted with, I fancy?—Yes, as far as the [illegible] of the working, I suppose I am.

9037. Are there many horses bred in your country?—[illegible]. [illegible] there are. There was a thoroughbred stallion there [illegible] your [illegible] [illegible] the old [illegible].

9038. [illegible] when the stallion was [illegible]?—Yes, and then when the [illegible] was taken away the owner sold him. He got very few mares, and it was not worth his while to keep him.

9039. Mr. [illegible].—I think, Mr. [illegible], you are one of the gentlemen who [illegible] [illegible] [illegible] instead of horses for the congested districts?—Yes, I think the money would be [illegible] better spent in that way or in getting mares.

9040. And I think you said there was no horse-breeding in the district at all?—No, I don't say there is no horse-breeding in [illegible] at all, because in all other districts there are [illegible] [illegible] [illegible] those where the larger farmers [illegible] breed horses, and where there are [illegible] [illegible] kept.

9041. You have referred to [illegible], do you [illegible] the same Union [illegible]?—Yes, [illegible].

9042. Do you know the number of [illegible] in [illegible] [illegible] [illegible] the [illegible] of families in that Union [illegible]?—No, I do not at all.

9043. That would be news to you?—It would, certainly.

9044. Do you know the Union of [illegible]?—Yes.

9045. How many families do you think [illegible] in that district?—I don't know, but that is not nearly so congested as [illegible].

9046. No, but you say you know all the congested districts, I want to test your knowledge?—I could tell you about [illegible].

9047. I want to tell you first, about your knowledge, do you know that in [illegible] 34 per cent. of the [illegible] of families keep horses, and do you know that in [illegible] 39 per cent. of the number of families keep horses there?—[illegible] I have no way of checking those figures. You are assuming that those figures are correct.

9048. They are compiled from figures furnished by the [illegible] General. I think you said you knew all the congested districts?—Yes.

9049. Donegal, for example. Do you visit Donegal constantly?—I have been there two or three times.

9050. And you live in Donegal, do you?—No, I live in [illegible], close to Donegal.

9051. Have you been in Mayo?—Yes.

9052. How often have you been in Mayo?—Two or three times.

9053. Do you know whether you have been [illegible] those times there?—Yes, I have.

9054. Each three times all through Mayo?—No, all through Mayo.

9055. What part of Mayo have you been those times in?—In the Westport district.

9056. I am speaking of the congested districts of Mayo. Have you been in all the congested districts of Mayo those times?—No; I don't suppose I have.

9057. How often have you been in the congested districts of Galway?—Two or three times, too.

9058. Do you remember how many times, exactly, at all through?—Well, I have been about [illegible], and all round, three times, I suppose, [illegible] [illegible].

9059. Have you been in the congested districts of Galway or Mayo [illegible] the [illegible] of the [illegible] [illegible] Board?—Oh, yes.

9060. Have you been there since the [illegible] of the Board?—Yes.

9061. And in Kerry?—No, but I have been in Cork, West [illegible].

9062. You have not been in Kerry?—[illegible] the formation of the Congested Districts Board; I have been as far as Bantry, all round by [illegible] [illegible] and that way; that would be in Cork.

9063. You have not been in Kerry?—No.

9064. Chairman.—Not since the formation of the Board. You have been before, and know the country?—Oh, yes.

9065. Mr. Wrench.—You referred particularly to Donegal. I think your correspondence with the Congested Districts Board [illegible] back [illegible] some time?—No; I have had no correspondence with them for the last two or three years.

9066. Did it not begin in November, 1892, when they were formed?—Yes, quite likely.

9067. And went on to January, 1893. Did it not?—I daresay it did. I cannot say.

9068. After that correspondence did you write a great many letters with reference to the proceedings of the Congested Districts Board?—Yes; I did.

9069. Well, you have referred to one, I think, to Dungloe?—Yes; I don't know that I said anything particularly about Dungloe.

9070. Did you say in a letter that out of a population of 12,000 at Dungloe, who were fortunate enough to be the possessors of some kind of pony mare, there were not more than 30?—Served by the Congested Districts Board's horse.

9071. You did not state that. I am referring to your letter of 11th October, 1896?—Was that a published letter?

9072. Yes?—What did I say?

9073. That out of a population of 12,000 there were 30 who were fortunate enough to be the possessors of some kind of pony mare?—There were 30 mares served by the Board's horses; that I have from the District Inspector.

9074. You did not put it that way?—Would you kindly read the context.

9075. "The Board's money must go in prizes for fat sheepkeepers and substantial farmers, who can keep good mares to get good foals, or for keeping a horse at a first cost for purchase of perhaps £300, and at an annual cost for keep of £250 for the 30, for instance this year, out of a population of 12,000 at Dungloe, who are fortunate enough to be possessors of some kind of pony mare?"—Exactly; 30 people only profited by the Board's expenditure there.

9076. Do you know that there are in that district over 300 mares?—No, I do not. The only other stallion, when I was round there I went to see him, I was told he had had twenty-seven mares, that was fifty-seven altogether served in the district this year. I wrote to the Registrar-General to know if there was any return of mares for these districts, because Mr. Ruxton put in a return of 48,000 horses as being in the congested districts from some returns which he said were not yet published, and I wrote to the Registrar-General to know where I could get these statistics and whether he could give the figures of the number of mares in these districts, which seemed to me the important thing to know, but he said he had no statistics of the kind, and that the numbers Mr. Ruxton had stated of horses generally in the district and the returns had been sent in to the Commission and therefore belonged to the Commission and I could not have it.

9077. But when you say there is no horse-breeding in the district you don't know the number of mares in the district?—I know the number of mares that were served in Dungloe.

9078. You don't know the number of mares in the district?—You can pretty well judge from that.

9079. You think that is a test?—Oh, I think so, certainly.

9080. Do you think most of the mares that were served belonged to what you call fat sheepkeepers?—In that district, no, because that is one of the exceptional districts where there are a lot of small ponies kept.

9081. Do you call the Dungloe district an exceptional district?—Yes, in that respect, in respect of there being a number of ponies, but in the districts about me only graziers and sheepkeepers have profited.

9082. In what Union?—Ballyshannon, and various Unions in Leitrim.

9083. Has there been any horse stationed at Ballyshannon?—No, Donegal.

9084. Not there now?—No.

9085. Taken away?—Because there is another man who has a Suffolk Punch which is preferred.

9086. That is the reason, you know that is the reason that influenced the Board?—I imagine so, I have got a letter from the gentleman, he says the Board's horse has been getting nothing to do.

9087. That is what you imagine?—That is what he says.

Mr. [illegible] Tobias.

9088. CHAIRMAN.—Well, I may take it, Mr. Tobias, here, from you, that you think on the whole with the exception of a few favoured spots that there is no use in trying to breed horses in these congested districts?—Yes.

9089. Therefore, as a whole, that the money is wasted?—Nobody there keeps a horse for breeding, and even the larger farmer, he simply takes a foal from his mare just to help her to pay her way, it is a by-product altogether.

9090. You think it is more or less wasting money to spend it in trying to encourage horse-breeding in these districts?—I think it is a monstrous thing that £50,000 should have been spent in that way.

9091. Can you not say yes or no to what I asked you. Do you think it is a waste of money?—Decidedly I do.

9092. But besides that fact, assuming the money is to be spent there, do you think it is spent in the best way, assuming a certain amount of money is to be spent in the congested districts for encouraging horse-breeding, do you think it is spent to the best advantage?—Decidedly not. I object to the kind of horses; the only kind of horse that is suited for that particular part where there are a lot of ponies is some kind of a [illegible]; of course different parts of the congested districts are different. In Inishowen, for instance, they had a sire and a Hackney this year, and they objected to both as being too light for what they have to do there in a certain amount of ploughing, and a good deal of very heavy carting to Derry, twenty miles of a bad road, and they want a larger kind of horse. I believe it was intended to send a thoroughbred up there, a thoroughbred that has been serving at the stud farm at Derry this summer; this would be utterly ridiculous; the people would have nothing to do with him; he would not carry any more than a light Hackney would. Then again, along the coast there are other places, for instance, near Lord Leitrim's, at Milford. The old Lord Leitrim used to keep a Suffolk Punch twenty years ago, and the people there say that was the most serviceable horse for the district, and afterwards when the young Lord Leitrim came in (the late Lord), he kept a Clydesdale, and then an Arab and a thoroughbred, and this year they have gone back again to the Suffolk Punch. Then in, within one and a half miles, the Board has had a light Hackney and the reason they [illegible] the Suffolk Punch they used to [illegible] to this light Hackney of the Board. Then they don't keep ponies in the same kind of way as they do about Dungloe. They are much larger again about Dunfanaghy. It is different too in those places where there is heavy carting, or [illegible] where they [illegible] from Derry, forty miles, there they want a larger breed of horses, but now there is less need for horses owing to these new light railways. There used to be a lot of carting from Letterkenny to Ballyshannon and [illegible], but that has now been knocked off the road. The small occupier used to keep a horse [illegible] for carting purposes.

9093. You don't think that the money that is spent by the Congested Districts Board in encouraging the breeding of horses is spent in the best way?—No, I object of course to the expenditure [illegible], and also to the way in which it is being expended. The number of foals that they say they have got is about 5,000, and the foals have been making this year at 40s., and others have been selling at from £5 to £6, and if the same money had been spent for [illegible]

CHAIRMAN.—We have nothing to do with that, that is [illegible] a question [illegible].

9094. Mr. WRENCH.—You take the Dungloe [illegible] congested [illegible] ponies [illegible] being required, [illegible] Dungloe and Glenties.

9095. That is in the Union of Glenties?—Yes.

Jan. 6, 1898.
Mr. George L. Tottenham.

9096. And you say the people at Carndonagh object to a Welsh cob being sent there?—Yes, they thought that and the Hackney too light.

9097. Do you know that there was a petition from the Board of Guardians to send a Welsh cob?—No; but I know there was a petition from the Board of Guardians to send a Suffolk Punch.

9098. You don't know that there was a petition to send a Welsh cob?—No; I think it is very improbable as they asked for a Suffolk Punch.

9099. Are you forming your own opinion as to the best class of horse to send to these districts, or is it from information received locally?—From what I saw and heard both.

Mr. William Roberts.

Mr. William Roberts, Rigsdale, Ballinhassig, Cork, examined.

9100. CHAIRMAN.—I think you represent the Cork Agricultural Society?—Yes, sir; I was asked to come here.

9101. Can you tell us when that society was formed and what its objects are?—Well, the society is a very old society; I don't know the exact date it was formed, but it is a very old society. As to its objects, one of them is to encourage horse-breeding in the county, and then we take up cattle and all agricultural purposes.

9102. But among its other objects one is to encourage the breeding of horses?—Yes, sir, this is the principal object I think.

9103. What means does it take towards that end?—We hold an annual show and we give a good list of prizes. We gave annually about £500 in prizes at our show. Some ten years ago we were giving about £250 annually in prizes, and we increased that, and this year we gave £520. We have different classes for all sorts of horses, but our principal thing is the hunters; we try to encourage the hunter breeding as far as we can.

9104. Could you tell us to what classes you give prizes?—I can. We give, first of all, a prize for thoroughbred stallions. The best thoroughbred stallion in the Stud Book, calculated to get weight-carrying hunters, and they must stand in the province of Munster for the ensuing year. Then we give a prize for the best gelding or mare, not less than five-years-old, and calculated to carry fifteen stone and upwards.

9105. In the hunter class?—Yes; and then for the best gelding or mare, not less than five-years-old, for the best [illegible] to 13 stone. Light hunter class really, for the same age, from 12 stone to 13 [illegible]; we gave that at equal horses—£80 in prizes. Then we encouraged the four-year-olds, and we give for the best four-year-old gelding or filly, in every different class and up-to-weight first prize, £30; we try to encourage that class as well as we can in Cork; in that class we give £80 in prizes. We also give a class for light weight three-year-olds, that is from twelve stone to thirteen stone seven; and we give prizes for three-year-olds, £37 in that class. For hunting purposes all these are. And then for two-year-olds, the same; and we give a prize for yearlings.

9106. Any prize for thoroughbred stock?—I am just coming to that. And then for brood mares we have two classes, one an open class. I will just read the heading we put to it—"For thoroughbred mares in foal to, or with foal at foot by a thoroughbred horse of a registered hunter size, which in the opinion of the judges is most calculated to produce high-class weight-carrying hunters." We get a medal from the Hunters' Improvement Society of England, and they ask us to put in that the mare might be in foal to a registered hunter sire. We have none of them in Cork; so it does not make much difference there. Then we give prizes for non-thoroughbreds, mares under the same heading for brood mares.

9107. What age are the brood mares?—We don't limit them. The only thoroughbred class we give for the produce of thoroughbred stallions in the yearlings, we give a prize for thoroughbred yearlings.

9108. What is the prize for brood mares?—We give £25 for the two classes, £15 and £10, and besides we get a gold medal from the Hunters' Improvement Society. This year I believe the Hunters' Improvement Society offered silver medals also for stallions. Then we give prizes for cobs and ponies, and a driving class, and we have a class for agricultural horses, but our principal thing is for hunters. This year we had 275 entries for our show, and of this there were 175 entered in the hunting classes, leaving only 85 for all the other classes combined.

9109. How long has your society been in the habit of giving prizes to this value, or expending this sum in this way?—We are about five years increasing in this way; this year, I am sorry to say, we had financial trouble, and lost all our gate money, and I am afraid we will have to reduce our prizes next year unless something turns up.

9110. What has been the effect, in your opinion, of the efforts of your Society during the last five years?—I am an attendant every year of the horse classes, and I feel, as far as I am a judge, that the horses are improving, and since we have increased the prizes the exhibitors have increased likewise, and we have very good sales at our Show. I could give you the entries in each class. In the aged horses we don't have so many entries as in young horses, which shows that the horses are sold out of the country. We have always good entries in light-weight four-year-olds, nearly always our best exhibits; we had twenty entries in that class this year.

9111. Is there anything objectionable in that, it appears to me, the horses going out?—The horses are taken out of the country when four or five years old.

9112. Are many horses bred in your country for purely agricultural purposes?—There are. Besides being connected with the County Cork Agricultural Society I am working on the Royal Dublin Society's scheme, on the committee, since the first year it was started. I was inspecting mares in [illegible] their areas in the Cork, and this year I noticed myself more than I did [illegible] the opinion is [illegible].

9113. Putting aside agricultural horses, what do you consider is the most profitable kind of horse to breed?—In the County Cork there are two classes of farmers. But the principal horse we want in the County Cork is the thoroughbred horse, to breed hunters. In some parts of the country there are small farmers that sell their produce, and in the bad times the extra pay for cart horses sell better than the hunters. But for the general thing for the improvement of horses there the thoroughbred horse would be required more than anything else.

9114. I don't quite understand you?—For the general run of the country we want to breed horses from thoroughbred stallions.

9115. Your object would be to breed hunters?—Yes; I am a farmer myself, and breed hunters. I have to breed them to make the most, and I take an interest in them all over the country.

9116. How is your part of the country off for thoroughbred sires?—In some parts of the County Cork we have plenty of horses, but then there is a district from Bandon, along to Clonakilty and West Cork, and the Macroom district, where there are very bad horses. This year, I am glad to say, Mr. John Aaron is getting in some stallions for the districts, but they may be confined to only one district. When the Royal Dublin Society's first scheme came in they located a horse in West Cork, and I think that did more good than all their schemes since; as far as I could see, the farmers took an interest in it and showed their mares.

[illegible]

June 8, 1897.

Mr. William [illegible].

where that was that you referred to?—Bandon and in the West Cork District. Macroom is one place; there are hardly any stallions there.

9140. Are there good mares in that district?—There are some good mares; plenty of mares to breed good horses in that district and Clonakilty, around the Dunmanway district. There was a stallion located by Dunmanway under the Dublin Society's scheme, that was "York."

9141. How do you account for it that the stallions don't go down there if there are a sufficient number of good mares?—No particular harm comes by going into stallions, I suppose. There is a good stallion sent there now to Bandon; but he is for the owners of the district—"Royal Muzzle." I believe also near Skibbereen Mr. Townshend has got some stallions very lately.

9142. Thoroughbred?—Yes. I think he gave evidence before you.

9143. Mr. Waldron.—"Castlereagh" is his?—He was there, I am not sure but he left it. Mr. Townshend gave evidence before you.

9144. Lord Clonbrock.—Are there any half-bred stallions in that part?—Well, you would not call them half-bred. They are bred some way; you don't know what way they are bred. They call them half-bred. The dams may be what you like; only are got by thoroughbred horses. There are some with three or four crosses in that district.

9145. But they are chiefly got by a thoroughbred horse?—There are some of them got by a thoroughbred horse; and then if they have a good-looking colt out of a common mare some of the farmers keep them on.

9146. How is the common mare mostly bred?—There is some of the Clydesdale in her, and then again back again to the thoroughbred horse.

9147. Are there any Clydesdale horses in the district now?—There are some Shires and Clydesdales in our district and in the county. The distance between Bandon and Skibbereen. They like the Shire horses. They sell their colts as two-year-olds, yearlings, and they sell better than if bred by hunters.

9148. I take it that you think the old scheme of the Dublin Society worked better than the present one—that is, sending the stallions down and subsidising them?—Yes, sir, it certainly did.

9149. Do you think the present scheme is good, also if there was sufficient money to give prizes to mares with an eye to keeping the younger ones in the country?—If the show of mares was held where there would be a good local show going on and give more money it might encourage them; but as it is now, for the money that is given the farmers don't show the mares. You have the same sort, you make your exhibiting the whole country. You don't get any encouragement.

9150. But if a scheme could be worked, an amalgamation of the two schemes together, you think it would be good?—Yes; if a stallion was sent to that part of the district he was wanted in, and there were thoroughbred shows of mares in the other parts of the district; and then the stallion owners should be subsidised in reducing the fee for farmers. They cannot afford to pay for good stallions at the prices they are charging.

9151. That would be something like the old form—the mares went down to the different stallions, and a proportion of the nomination fee was paid by the Royal Dublin Society?—Yes; and when the owners of the mares paid their dues at the show when the nomination was given; because I heard some of the stallion owners saying they never got their share; they got their share from the Dublin Society, but not from the mare owners. I never found it hard to get the money from the farmers in Bandon.

9152. Did you ever know a stallion [illegible] his stallion [illegible] it [illegible]. I think if the

9164. But the £1 1s. 0d. they paid under the first Royal Dublin Society's scheme was the utmost they could pay?—Yes, and they paid that to me very freely in conformity with Mr. [illegible] for Wall(?) Clerk of the Show.

9165. Therefore it would become impracticable for any private individual to undertake to supply this district with good and suitable horses. You would not get a thoroughbred horse of the class of "Rock" for less than two or three hundred pounds. It would not pay a man to keep that horse and take [illegible] at £1 1s.—He could not afford to do it at all.

9166. In fact, if this county is to be served by thoroughbred sires it must be done by somebody, by a public body?—Yes, unless we get rich landlords like Sir John Arnott to keep up the [illegible].

9167. In North Cork there are a lot of good stallions?—Yes, sir.

9168. There are a certain number of half-bred stallions there that breed very useful horses?—Yes, there are some.

9169. There is "Garrett" for instance; I don't know whether he is living?—Yes, and there was a horse called "Old Rockingham" in South Cork, and some by him out of some of the old mares up to 20 years old are knocked out, they are still very good horses.

9170. I think there are some sons of "Garrett" standing too?—I believe there are.

9171. It has been pointed out to us by some of the witnesses that it would be extremely difficult to get half-bred sires, the type of half-bred sires represented by "Garrett" and "Old Rockingham." Do you think it would be possible in the county Cork to get some? Do you see them out hunting?—To get some stallions got by them?

9172. Such stallions as "[illegible]" or sons of "Garrett" or "Old Rockingham"?—You would get a good many of them, of course, but "Old Rockingham," I believe, has gone; but the stock are there got by him.

9173. I mean stallions. Do you, as a dealer of [illegible], see half-bred hunting [illegible] like him in Cork?—There are none like him near Cork. There might be a few in the Duhallow country, but that I don't know.

9174. Then you think it would be an assistance to keeping mares in this country if a certain number of [illegible] given [illegible]?—I believe it would—that is, if it was given at one of the local shows; not to have a separate show. In the autumn, as we have now, it becomes along with carrying the time prize people like to see something besides the [illegible] they are coming to it.

9175. But do you think that if a man was offered £50 for a three year old colt, the fact of its being possible for him to win a prize of £5 would cause him to decline that offer?—The general run would not refuse it.

9176. And still £50 is not an extravagant price for a three-year old?—Well, it is a good price for a three-year old mare; if you [illegible] off the grass it would pay well.

9177. Don't you think that a prize that would be of use in inducing a farmer to keep a good mare, and induce to sell her, would have to be so large that if spread over the whole of Ireland would necessitate the expenditure of a whole lot of money?—It would have to be a considerable amount of money, no doubt. If you gave a prize of £20 or £30 to the cause you might induce farmers to retain them.

9178. For a three-year old?—Of course you would get horses that would breed well, that would be sound and good-looking, that the farmers would keep on [illegible] a smaller price than £30.

9179. They would keep the mare they could not get more than £30 for; and sell the mare they could get £50 for?—That would be honest; it would not pay the farmer to work a mare worth more than £30.

9180. Mr. Wrench.—What class are the agricultural horses you refer to, are they Clydesdale class. You have prizes for it in the class?—The heavy cart horses we have, Clydesdales and Shires; we have not separate classes. [illegible] Mr. William [illegible].

9181. They are all shown in the same class?—Yes.

9182. Do you think they are becoming more popular as the farmers seeing the demand?—I think, as far as I can see of late years, they were getting much less prices for light ones, they were [illegible], they would rather have the heavy horses.

9183. Then you think they are becoming more popular?—I think so, for small farmers to sell their young horses.

9184. In your catalogue do you put in the pedigrees of the horses that are entered—you have a catalogue for the show?—We don't put in the pedigree in full, but just how they are got.

9185. Do you put the breeder in too?—Yes.

9186. You don't get how the horse is got without getting to the breeder?—No, sir; the cases of the heavy horses shown in Cork are imported horses, and their breeding is given.

9187. I was not thinking so much of the heavy horse class as of the hunter class. Do you ever give a horse's pedigree without knowing who the breeder is?—I suppose they do.

9188. That is so pretty much as in the Dublin catalogue?—Oh, it is. A lot of them put down the breeding and the "breeder unknown."

9189. Would it help the sale of high-class hunters if people were able to give the true pedigrees?—I am sure it would.

9190. Have you heard it suggested that all horses should be registered through the petty sessions district?—I heard it suggested in evidence; I approve of registering all horses, and of not registering a horse unless he was sound.

9191. You would approve of all horses, mares, and young stock, being registered?—I would approve of registering entire horses, and if they were inspecting by a committee you would get sound horses. I would not have anything to do with the breeding registered.

9192. And you think that any registration like that would be better carried out through the Cork Agricultural Society than through a central body like the Dublin Society?—I think it would, sir; the Cork Society has members all over the county. Of course the [illegible] committee of the Dublin Society would work it too.

9193. They are all members of the Cork Agricultural Society?—The most of them are.

9194. And the dealers that attend fairs in Cork, are they mostly men who buy hunters and exporters?—There is a lot buy high-class horses, they are, sir. We have a lot of gentlemen from England that come to our show and buy hunters.

9195. What class of men buy agricultural horses?—We have dealers in the small horses, shippers.

9196. Chairman.—Is there in your part of the country, or was there when you recollect, a distinct type of Irish horse, we frequently hear of the old Irish horse, which in your idea of [illegible]?—The horses got by a horse like "Rockingham," they are all well-bred hardy mares, can stay well, with plenty of bone in them, good, long, low, hardy horses.

9197. Are there as many of them in the country now as there were 20 years ago?—I could not tell you 20 or 30 years ago. There are a good many. Some of the people stick to them year after year in their breeding.

9198. Lord Rathdonnell.—There is one question I wanted to ask you. Do you know why the Royal Dublin Society wanted to [illegible] three year old [illegible] registered [illegible]?—They wanted to encourage farmers to breed from young mares so that they would not draft them at three or four years old. By keeping them breed from two or three-year-old mares I should think they thought that they would sell them afterwards, and they would have the good [illegible]. I think that was it.

June 4, 1897. Mr. William Rath, &c.

9199. Partly that. It is probable a dealer would not buy a two-year-old filly if she was stinted, or a three year old with a foal at foot, to take out of the country?—That is it, that when a farmer had his mare stinted he should keep her.

9200. CHAIRMAN.—Anything else you would like to say to the Commission?—Well, the only thing is that as I told you before about our society, that we are pleased we will have to reduce our prizes this year as [illegible] got [illegible] if the Commission [illegible] to improve the breeding of horses in the district. We [illegible] but the weather was awful [illegible] year, and we lost nearly £100 on the show days' [illegible].

9201. You think your local efforts would be attended with more success if you had larger means [illegible]?

Mr. W. R. Rutledge.

Mr. W. R. Rutledge, [illegible] Villa, Hollymount, Co. Mayo, examined.

9202. CHAIRMAN.—You are secretary of the Hollymount Agricultural Society, are you not?—Yes, I am.

9203. Do you live at Hollymount?—Yes, in the neighbourhood.

9204. I presume that society is like the Clare Society just mentioned, that it is concerned with agricultural matters generally, and devotes its attention also among them to horse-breeding?—Yes.

9205. Now, in your part of the country have you got any specimens of the old Irish mare?—Yes, and the Hollymount Society are very anxious to do everything in their power to trace back the old Irish breed, for we know by experience that whatever such a mare [illegible] that there is no better method of getting a high class hunter than a cross between the old Irish mare and the thoroughbred stallion, and, therefore, we are taking steps to trace back and revive the old breed if we possibly can, and we believe that it is not at all impossible to do it.

9206. Have you any idea how the animal you speak of was originated or bred?—Well, you see 60 years [illegible] the old Irish mare, it was a necessity to have one a good hardy active animal. Before railways were established the traffic of the country was carried on from the city of Dublin to provincial towns by carting [illegible] goods, and an animal to [illegible] the goods from day to day drawing 20 to 25 cwts. from Dublin to [illegible] or from Dublin to Castlebar [illegible] [illegible] a hardy animal, and he [illegible] back on the day again [illegible] of something else. When we opened a show [illegible] agricultural [illegible] may [illegible] secretary for the Hollymount Society to make all the inquiry I possibly could about the breed, and those men who knew it, the oldest and most intelligent I could refer to, gave me a great deal of information. At that time they had no cars, and the Irish mares were often obliged to carry two, the head of the house and his better half, and sitting on the back of the old Irish mare, a saddle and pillion behind. It took a good animal to carry two twenty miles. She was a large animal, and there are [illegible] traces of that breed to be found. That continued until after the famine and then the Clydesdales were introduced to the neighbourhood unfortunately, but in the days I speak of it was necessary to get up stallions, and the only way they had to do that was from the [illegible] [illegible] kept by resident gentlemen; it was [illegible] [illegible] the [illegible] [illegible] in their [illegible] business to have [illegible] and they kept in those days some of the good [illegible], and so got [illegible] they had to go to the [illegible] stallion. A great many of these [illegible] the country, and there was a strain of good blood in the old mares, but then when the Scotch farmers came over and took farms in the neighbourhood they introduced the Clydesdale, and the Irish breed was found so valuable that all the high-class dealers [illegible] and [illegible] a high price for it, so that the farmer could [illegible] [illegible] and in that way they have been [illegible] out of the country, and then for [illegible] [illegible] back on the Clydesdale. The Clydesdale was introduced by Mr. Lawrie and Mr. [illegible] [illegible] [illegible]. The Suffolk Punch was introduced by the late Lord Lucan, who farmed extensively, and the Irish breed got crossed in that way, and those breeds that were introduced they are not good for [illegible]

hunters. They will have size but certainly they are not good. And another thing I have found against was the Cleveland Bay, and I was very sorry for it. That was a horse that was introduced by Mr. [illegible] and bought from him by Mr. [illegible], a great looking horse for any [illegible] hunters; he was a dark bay [illegible] [illegible] on black legs with plenty of bone under the knee and well topped, the colt was the good and would [illegible] a fair price on account of his size and appearance, but when you came to work him he was a [illegible]. The man who bought them from one of them [illegible] and said he was very sorry ever to have had anything to do with him. You see in a district breeding hunters that crops [illegible] injurious, for if a colt [illegible] will and you get a good price the buyer won't come back to you again for another. These three crosses, I believe, were injurious in the hunter breeding districts.

9207. Well, the old Irish mare, Mr. Rutledge, you speak of, originated in the necessity for a hardy animal with great [illegible] and endurance, because all the work of the country had to be done by carting, and people rode about a good deal; now that most of things have passed away, do you think that there is any way in which this particular breed could be revived and [illegible]?—Yes, I think there is.

9208. The natural necessity then was a call for it, [illegible] is [illegible] necessity?—No, but in breeding class hunters we think it would be well worth the while of any society to do everything in their power to revive such breed, and there are some means to be found that I think we should follow. I would ask your [illegible] to [illegible] the prize list for 1896, I have it here. We have three classes, first, the thoroughbred class, for the best thoroughbred mare [illegible] [illegible], silver medal and £10; second prize, £5; third prize, £3. The second class is for the half-bred [illegible] calculated to get hunters or [illegible] [illegible] prize, silver medal and £4; second prize, £2; third, £1; [illegible], 10s. More in the class I wish particularly to draw your attention to, class 3, for the best Irish agricultural stallion, measuring not less than 15.3 and under the age of fourteen [illegible] [illegible] to get strong, active, clean-legged Irish farm horses in neighbouring [illegible]. Any stallion entered in Class I or II not eligible. First Prize, silver medal and £4; second, £2; third, £1; [illegible], 5s. 6d. In that class we [illegible] change a [illegible] fee, to encourage the man who keeps them to take them out to the [illegible], in order as [illegible] the old [illegible]. This and three [illegible] classes, and we believe that [illegible] might as well try to do away with the Society if you failed to encourage any one of the three classes on which the Society [illegible]. We want the [illegible], we want the middle classes, and we want the [illegible], and we want the [illegible] [illegible] to breed [illegible]. The farmers say, "If you want us to [illegible] thoroughbreds they are no use to us, they won't be suitable for our work," and if they go the [illegible] [illegible] the [illegible] [illegible] that crop will be [illegible] good. Well, if they keep the foal bred by a thoroughbred horse, and the farmers in any district [illegible] they [illegible] with foals or [illegible] from [illegible] other [illegible] that [illegible] back again to another thoroughbred horse it becomes [illegible] and [illegible] [illegible] [illegible] [illegible] that the animal won't [illegible] for the farmers' purposes. If the Irish agricultural [illegible] could be bred [illegible] the [illegible], and [illegible] [illegible]

[illegible]

[illegible]

Jan. 6, 1897.
Mr. W. T. Rutledge.

would be a very important thing if the local gentry could be helped to get a good sire into the district, there is only the one important sire in the whole district; we would like a good thoroughbred if we could get him.

9266. Anything else, Mr. Rutledge?—Yes; supposing we had that stud farm, and then we had these three classes of horses, I believe it would be well to have a stud of them and [illegible] the farmers' [illegible], that would be likely [illegible] bring good mares, there might be a few free nominations given. If they give a nomination at a low rate, or a free nomination, they consider it is a great feather in their cap, and they are proud of that sort of thing, and they would, I think, value nominations of that kind more than prizes, and it would reach a larger number, whereas, at a show from two or three good mares they will come back two or three years in succession to win prizes. Then with regard to the young colts in the district where that stud farm would be established, supposing it was established that they should be registered, and an account kept of how they were bred, and what sire they were, so that any person coming to the district to buy would at once find the references, and ascertain all about them, and where they could be seen, supposing the farmers themselves reared them, and supposing the society were established, if a farmer wished to go himself to a country fair and select his own mares.

9267. There are details and rules for this particular society?—Yes, but don't you consider them important.

9268. I don't say they are not; but until there is a society, perhaps it is rather premature to go into great detail. I think we have got very fairly your general opinion, but if you have got anything further to say?—No, I have nothing else.

The Commission adjourned to next morning.

Jan. 7, 1897.

EIGHTEENTH DAY.—THURSDAY, JANUARY 7TH, 1897.

PRESENT:—THE RIGHT HON. THE EARL OF DUNRAVEN, K.P., in the Chair; LORD ASHTOWN, HON. H. W. FITZWILLIAM, LORD RATHDONNELL, COLONEL ST. QUINTIN, MR. WRENCH.

MR. HUGH NEVILLE, Secretary.

Mr. H. Johnston, [illegible], Belfast, examined.

Mr. H. Johnston.

9269. Chairman.—You live near Belfast?—Yes.

9270. You are engaged in dealing in horses?—I am, I might say since I was a child. I have been thirty-seven years, more since [illegible], working on my own account, and I was with my father [illegible] years before that.

9271. Do you think the importation of American horses has had any effect upon the trade in horses in your part of the country?—American horses? Not the slightest on hunters, but they have reduced the price of harness horses very much. I may tell you if they had not American horses coming over it would be very difficult to get harness horses in Ireland at all; [illegible]. I have a lot of American horses, I don't approve of them at all. Once they go here you can scarcely ever get them sound again. They are liable to take rheumatism.

9272. You don't like them?—Until they are acclimatised they are not very much use. They are liable to pains in their shoulders and their feet. They are not used to our macadamised roads. Very often a horse is not shod in America. They are never shod until they come over here.

9273. Are they passed off as Irish horses?—Very seldom; any man of judgment would know an American horse. They are not the same formation as the Irish horse at all, and some, as I have very few, that I have ever seen would make a hunter.

9274. However, there are a great many of them imported into the North of Ireland?—There have been I think a dozen sales by persons who brought over American horses, but I don't think they bring the best over here. They have sales in Liverpool and Glasgow and other cities, and I think they only bring over the leavings of what they cannot sell. I don't think the best horses come over here.

9275. What becomes of the American horses after they have been imported into the North of Ireland?—I think they go generally for cab purposes [illegible] and some gentlemen buy them for harness.

9276. You don't think they are passed as Irish horses?—They may look them and sell them as Irish horses, but any man of good judgment and experience would easily know the difference between a Yankee horse and an Irish horse.

9277. What class do you generally deal in, carriage horses?—I deal in the best horses of different classes. I buy hunters, harness horses, and [illegible] horses. I buy my horses in the North of Ireland entirely myself and my sons, buy in the counties of Cork, Waterford, Wexford, Limerick, and all the principal places throughout the south.

9278. You have had a long experience, Mr. Johnston; do you think, generally speaking, the prices are about the same as formerly?—I think a good hunter is worth as much money as ever. In fact if you want a good horse like a hunter, a young [illegible], my experience at the present time is if he is a good horse you must buy him or you will never get the chance again. I remember thirty or thirty-five years ago if you saw a good horse at Cahirmee or some of the big fairs and a man asking an extravagant price you might let him run perhaps a day and buy him the second or third day, but at the present time in all the large fairs there is such competition for a good horse that if you meet a good horse, a really good horse, you must buy it or you will never get the chance again.

9279. The competition then for a really good horse is keener than it was?—A good horse we can sell as well and better than ever, I believe.

9280. Is the reason of the great keenness of competition that the supply of good horses is less and the demand greater?—I think the supply is a very great deal less. It is very difficult to get a good horse.

9281. That is speaking of hunters?—Yes.

9282. Throughout the country generally there are not so many of what would be called first-class hunters bred as formerly?—There are not.

9283. What about high-class harness horses?—You can scarcely get a good harness horse. I have at the present time and for the last two months an order for three pair of carriage horses, and my sons and I have travelled all the fairs and we cannot get them. You can get them at the age of three or four years, but you cannot get five or six-year-old horses. A good horse you can scarcely get at five or six years of age.

6284. Do you attend the fairs in the country in the South?—I buy always and all my life all over Ireland.

6285. Then I take it from you that you think, as far as hunters are concerned, that quality is not as good as it used to be, and that as regards high class hunters they are exceedingly scarce; scarcer than they used to be?—They are.

6286. Can you account for that in any way?—I would account for it that they don't breed the right horse from the right horses or the right mares in the majority of cases. If you go to the Ballinasloe Fair or Cahirmee you will see thousands of horses there, and, perhaps, you would not take one in a hundred that would make a useful hunter, whatever class it may be. My great objection to the farmers is that they are not particular enough in breeding off mares of good straight action, and that they nearly all breed from long-backed weak [illegible] mares that they think will. For instance, if a farmer has two mares he will bring them out to a fair to sell them. If he has a really good mare with a good short back and good shoulders and quarters, that mare will make a good price, and if he has an animal with a long back she is brought home and bred from. Then the majority of the [illegible] stallions are weak and weedy. It is [illegible] to see the [illegible] and very objectionable in their action; and, unless the breeder gets a mare with straight, good action and a good back and strong limbs, the produce is of no [illegible] to be sold at any price.

6287. Have you considered any practical means whereby the farmers can be induced to breed from their best mares instead of their worst mares?—My idea is that you should give them inducements to get them to keep their best mares and breed from them. My idea is—and from my experience I know they did it formerly in the county Meath and in Westmeath, and through that country, the farmers used to keep their three-year-old fillies. They took their best mares and picked them and they would keep a filly at three-year-old and perhaps another at four-year-old, and perhaps another at five-year-old, and then when the mare was coming to six-year-old she might be sold; then the mare can very easily be trained as they have been trained in the meantime, and then they brought her out and they would get as good a price as if the mare had a foal at all. A three-year-old is not too young to have a foal. This was before they got so much into the cattle trade through Meath and Westmeath that they used principally the best fillies commencing with two-year-old fillies. They were wide, strong short-legged nice mares with quality, good head and neck, and shoulders, and good back and loins, and the tail well up, and got by the very best thoroughbred horses produced. They got a very great price for the best of those young mares.

6288. What is your opinion as to the class of thoroughbred stallions about the country?—I think there are a great many inferior horses. There are a great many very good ones privately through the country [illegible], not Government horses as they are called. I have myself seen a great many very good horses.

6289. What kind of horses do they breed from hunters?—They are inclined to breed good horses, but I don't know how it is they never get, at least perhaps one in a hundred. You can scarcely ever get a good horse in the county of Down or the county of Antrim. It is either the fault of the mare, or the stallion, although there are some very good stallions there. They have bred some very good horses for hunters once, or the artillery or general purposes, or half-bred horses. This is a beautiful breed, down there, from "Harkaway" would breed hunters and they have got a very useful breed of horses there that connected with ponies, useful horses, with straight action.

6290. Are those young horses bought by the dealers coming and kept by us the North?—Oh! yes. There is not a fair in the South where there are not dozens of young horses bought in it, taken down to the North, and they keep them, for perhaps six months or twelve months.

6291. To what kind of work are they put?—The majority of those horses work in all kinds of the work of it. They are fed like and fed bullocks. The farmers never give them a bit of exercise, and they are brought out to the fair, and they are good horses spoiled the want of work and exercise, hardly one of them properly conditioned. A three-year-old horse in the North has a neck as heavy as a four-year-old, and if you buy one of those produced in the North they have no brains whatever and no [illegible].

6292. Do you buy horses in England at all?—No. I never bought a horse in England in my life. I always sold them there.

6293. It is immaterial to you whether horses have been broken or ridden before they come to you?—It is a wonderful difference. They are worth a lot more as hunters. You often buy a horse here which is often never ridden a good hunter.

6294. And the opposite takes place I suppose very often.

6295. Do you think anything should be done in any way to induce the farmers to breed more or better horses rather than for hunters?—I think, sir, if you get a good half-bred Irish mare and a really good thoroughbred horse with straight action you will have either a hunter or a hackney horse.

6296. Do many foreign buyers buy here?—The principal customers I have are foreigners—Germans, Swiss, and Italians.

6297. What do they buy for?—I have sold them a lot of horses for both the Swiss and Italian armies. The Germans purchase their own horses. The Government there buy directly from the farmers. I sell a lot of good mares to go to Germany. The best mares go out of Ireland to England, and the foreigners buy them.

6298. More [redacted]

—Yes.

6299. I suppose they give a bigger price for them?—I think they do. A horse named Cognoscente [illegible] from Hanover and he has been more than any man I ever saw. He took nearly a hundred mares from the York Christmas Show. He comes over to me three or four times a year, and he always takes away more than 100 mares.

6300. All mares?—Mares, the best he can get, and the class of mare he buys would be the sort to bring to this country to improve the breed. He will buy from three-year-old to any age.

6301. Do you buy horses at all on the western seaboard, in the congested districts?—No, I do not buy there. I don't care for Connaught at all. I keep as much to the county as possible.

6302. May I take it then that you can give us no idea of the effect the Congested Districts Board's scheme has had on horse breeding?—Not the slightest. The only thing I would suggest about what I know of the class of mare which is there is, that I would suggest they ought to get a small thoroughbred stallion [illegible] a good Welsh cob. I think that would improve the breed very much.

6303. Have you in your dealings come across many cases of improper breeding of Connemara ponies?—No.

6304. Not perhaps the first but the grand dam?—No, I don't think I ever had any.

6305. Do you go to any expense into the pedigree of the horses you buy?—Yes.

6306. Do you think you can generally rely on the pedigrees you get?—I think the farmers through the centre of Ireland are very careful about that. I very seldom or ever got a wrong pedigree. Some people, no doubt, would give a wrong pedigree, but I think they are very few. The people I generally buy off are people I deal with continually.

Mr. J. [illegible]

Mr. [illegible]

[illegible]

Nov. 8, 1896.

Mr. T. [illegible]

9309. Have you any opinion as to the effect of an infusion of Hackney blood in the Thoroughbred [illegible] breed here [illegible]?—I don't like the Hackney myself. I have had several animals got by a Hackney stallion, but they have [illegible] trotting action. That trotting action is [illegible], and I don't think they are very good to use them at all.

9310. As carriage horses, do you object to the Hackney blood?—Well, I don't know. I would not encourage it. I would rather have a good half-bred Irish horse by a sound horse from them.

9311. The only thing that is said in favour of the Hackney blood, that you object to gradually percolating all through the country and deteriorating the breed of hunters, or do you think it would be confined to certain districts?—I tell you that at Roscommon I would not recommend them at all. I know a man in a place like I know, that proved to me that they have a very injurious breed. I bought mare in Mullingar which as good a mare as ever I owned, a good half-bred mare, and I think a man who hunted her for [illegible] said she was a very fast mare, would do a mile in three minutes, she was the fastest [illegible] in my country until the Hackney horse came, and the fact that she was a good hunter and [illegible] too long to ride or drive her, and this mare was induced to take her to Lord Clanmorris's horse "Grand Accord," and no doubt, she bred a good looking horse, true enough for horse. I know gentlemen have ridden and I have never seen a much better horse, but that horse would not stay two miles. They tried to bring him up to see if he could not be made to stay, and they sent him to the Meath under a good trainer, but they never could get him to stay for two miles, and the mare being a very good stayer it must be that that thing came from the horse. I have seen [illegible] bred from "Reasdale," the best Hackney Hackney I ever saw. He was in the county Derry and belonged to the Newtownlimavady Stud Company. I bought several animals got by him in May, and there was never one of them worth anything. They were useless and [illegible].

9312. I would gather from you that you think the old Irish mare is the best class of mare to breed from?—I do.

9313. And you would mate her with a suitable thoroughbred sire?—That is the idea.

9314. You would prefer that to any other?—I would prefer that to any other breed of horse you can have.

9315. Mr. FITZWILLIAM.—I think you said you generally bought from the breeder?—Yes.

9316. If you go to the same breeder from year to year I suppose you get the produce very often of the same mare?—Very often.

9317. And you are able to form pretty accurately the effect produced by particular sires?—I don't often go to the people's houses, I generally buy in the open market; as far as I really can tell what the produce are like when they are young, as I don't often have an opportunity of seeing them.

9318. It would I suppose be an easy thing to make a note of the effect of different crosses upon the produce of the mares, and if you buy the produce of any mare from year to year it would be easy to make such the mare is allowed by different horses?—Yes.

9319. Do you find a good deal of difference between the produce according to the horse the mare is mated with?—There is no doubt there is a lot. If a mare breeds from a really good mare and a thoroughbred horse in hunting or [illegible] to get good produce. There are horses for the service of the mares of the poor, unfortunate farmers in parts of the country and they should not be allowed to serve at all. They should not be in the country. Those horses, I believe are not worth the food of them. I remember once down at Dunkin, a place where they used to breed a lot of good horses, I saw a lot of Hackney there and, I assure you, there was not a horse in the [illegible] [illegible], except [illegible] and [illegible] and bad legged ones, and the poor man who keeps them here, the [illegible] bought his mares thinking they were fit to cover at all.

9320. Can you suggest any remedy for getting rid of this class of horse?—The only thing is to get them away from the people and give them better ones.

9321. CHAIRMAN.—In the absence of the horse inducement to the owner to [illegible] [illegible]. There is, [illegible] great many of the farmers who [illegible] [illegible] never had [illegible] a good horse for the [illegible] except the horse would [illegible] the [illegible] but as the colonel had good horses they [illegible] [illegible] them, and I think that should be promoted by the Government in every way.

9322. Lord ARDILAUN.—The horses that are bred in the Counties brought to the North, where do they go to, and who buys them?—The majority of the horses are brought into the North are bought by English and Scotch people at the different local fairs, and principally at the May fair. The majority are [illegible] of the largest fairs in the country, and there is some other local fairs. These horses are [illegible] bought up by dealers about the country, and taken to the English fairs.

9323. Lord ROSSMORE.—The people around Belfast are very fond of trotting horses?—Yes.

9324. They have rather a fancy for a trotting and pace for trotting races?—Yes, they have got up a race track now on the new North-east Society grounds.

9325. I believe you are fond of the trotting yourself?—No, I never kept a trotter except for my own driving.

9326. Have you ever yourself driven a Hackney as a [illegible]?—Never.

9327. You always go in for thoroughbred breeding as much as possible?—The best horse that I drive I kept him for four or five years for my own driving. I bought in that city, and he was a hackney bred [illegible] a hunter. I think there is no Hackney horse would go twenty miles with him. I have had some Yankee horses myself for my own driving, and they are very good, if you get a good [illegible] horse, you will have as good a horse for harness as any, but they are of the kind that you get a [illegible] of this kind.

9328. They are not good for riding?—No.

9329. Mr. WRENCH.—"Grand Accord" and "Reasdale" are the only two Hackney sires of which you had any personal experience?—Well, there were a lot from "Grand Accord" called "Grand Accord."

9330. He was not a pure-bred Hackney?—I don't know.

9331. I think he was only one of a litter bred some belonging to Mr. Robinson, of Rosehill?—That is the horse, I think.

9332. Those were the only two thoroughbred Hackneys you have owned?—Yes.

9333. They were both Norfolk Hackneys, were they not?—I could not tell you.

9334. You say it is very difficult to get better [illegible] in Ireland?—Very.

9335. Have you any suggestion as to how it would become easier than they would [illegible] have been some time ago a strong thoroughbred horse, or is it a good half-bred horse. In the North of Ireland the "Hackney" breed are both useful and [illegible]. They are principally [illegible] [illegible].

9336. Those "Hackneys" get horses with good action [illegible], all.

9337. It is necessary, I suppose, to have action in a good harness horse?—Yes; it [illegible] been in the [illegible] to [illegible].

9338. Where do you get the [illegible] horses [illegible] over the country.

9339. In any one part of the country more than another?—Only once more in Ireland, [illegible] [illegible] [illegible] the day before and in Mullingar the next day. They buy a good horse when they [illegible].

9338. Do you know how they are bred?—They are principally bred from English horses, from Thoroughbred sires. You think that most of these have Clydesdale blood in them?—They have. There is a great quantity of them [illegible] in those [illegible] for two or three years, it would pay them [illegible] to breed those class of working horses, and when they are good [illegible] in this country [illegible].

9339. Do you know whether many of the [illegible] horses are sold to farmers as brood mares?—I have heard that plenty of them [illegible]. I think there are plenty of the mares would make good brood mares.

9340. Would you [illegible]?—I don't know how they are bred. The mares I have sold to the tramway company, I have bought a great many of them [illegible] good brood mares [illegible] than the majority of tramway horses. The tramway horses generally are [illegible] with [illegible] of them [illegible].

9341. The [illegible] price [illegible]?—[illegible].

9342. What age would they take them at?—At all ages.

9343. Will they take them under four years old?—[illegible].

9344. Will they take them at four years?—No, not until five years old.

9345. Is the [illegible] taking steps in any extent to improve the breeding of [illegible] horses in [illegible]?—[illegible] I think the thing is [illegible] I don't know what is the new [illegible], but they [illegible] very [illegible] in the breeding of horses.

9347. But they have made great strides in the last [illegible]?—Yes, I think they are [illegible] to be [illegible].

9348. Do you know where the big London [illegible], the [illegible] and [illegible], get their horses? Do they get their horses through dealers, or from the [illegible]?—The majority of the London [illegible] [illegible] go to Ireland, buying them at about [illegible] years old, [illegible] as many as they want now, and they are obliged to buy American horses. I know myself one of the [illegible] in London, and he buys nearly all his horses [illegible]. He [illegible] in the largest [illegible] in the [illegible] Kingdom. He seldom [illegible] more than 100 or 150 at a time, and he [illegible] in London. I don't think he has bought an Irish horse for the last two or three years, and he used to be a very big buyer in Ireland.

9349. He would buy them in Ireland if he could?—Well, he could get plenty, but he could not sell them.

9350. He would get them cheaper there in Ireland?—I don't know. If you get good American horses you [illegible] a good price for them.

9351. Then, if these horses [illegible] brought from abroad, Ireland is losing a trade by not being able to produce these horses?—Certainly. I have [illegible] [illegible] of any [illegible] and I have [illegible] to have [illegible] in [illegible], and could not get them.

9352. Do you buy any horses in Aberdeen yourself?—Yes, [illegible] in America [illegible] I have bought [illegible] that have come direct from America.

9353. Do you think the importation of American horses into Scotland is increasing?—How many are brought over in a month?—I could not give you the exact number. They are shipping them now all round the [illegible].

9354. Do you think the importation is taking off [illegible] the [illegible] think [illegible] now than formerly?—[illegible].

9355. [illegible] is bought in Glasgow?—Yes.

9356. There is a large weekly market there?—There is.

9357. In addition to the [illegible] importation, the large foreign [illegible] and Americans also [illegible]?—Yes.

9358. The Germans have been buying their [illegible] for a good many years?—They have.

9359. For twenty-five years?—They have.

9360. They buy their [illegible] horses [illegible]?—I don't know. The majority of them are sold [illegible].

9361. Do you sell [illegible] to the Germans or the Italian [illegible], or in the Government service?—[illegible]. They would [illegible] the [illegible] and I sold them [illegible] for the Italian Government. They were intended for the Italian [illegible]. The [illegible] [illegible] and they bought a lot of [illegible] horses. They have been [illegible].

9362. They were mostly bought for [illegible] than [illegible] the price usually paid for [illegible].

9363. What price would they **have to pay for** them?—Up to £50 or £60 [illegible].

9364. They were all bought for the Government?—Yes.

9365. You were talking of **Mr. Oppenheim, he is one of the biggest dealers in the world?**—Yes.

9366. What class of horses does he buy, riding or harness horses?—He does a very big trade in harness horses, in [illegible] of horses. He sends a lot of them to London, to different [illegible] masters, but he does not buy any harness horses here. He buys nothing but [illegible] and very [illegible] horses.

9367. Do you know what is done with those [illegible] for [illegible] trade [illegible]?

9368. You have heard it suggested [illegible] that all [illegible] should be [illegible] to [illegible] the [illegible]. Do you approve of that?—[illegible] I think [illegible] should [illegible] [illegible] many horses in the country that should not [illegible] at all.

9369. Would you say [illegible] [illegible] from [illegible]?—I would [illegible] to any [illegible].

9370. The [illegible] the [illegible] are [illegible] [illegible]. [illegible] not [illegible].

9371. [illegible] [illegible] that [illegible] people should be [illegible] [illegible] they [illegible] [illegible] [illegible] than [illegible] them [illegible] [illegible].

mares, and the same. I would be as particular about the one as the other.

8372. I would gather from you that you think that the average farmer is not a good enough judge to know the sire that is likely to be best suited for his mare?—A great many farmers do not know what is the right class of mare, or the right class of horse to breed from.

8373. And in that case it would not be sufficient that there should be a subsidised stallion standing at a subsidised price, do you think they would still go to the inferior stallion as it would be cheaper?—Well, I believe if they did not know, they would have neighbours who would advise them to go to the better horse.

8374. As a matter of fact is it the service price that guides them in the choice?—I think with poor people who have not money, the price is the great inducement, and if there was a good horse at £3 and a very bad one at £2, I think they would take the cheaper horse.

8375. Do you sell many horses to the Government for remounts?—No, I don't. I have sold to the Government at times, but that was some time when there was the war. I have sold to the commissariat and the artillery remounts as well, but I have never had a commission from the Government to supply remounts, although I would have got it I think if I applied.

8376. Colonel St. Quintin.—Could you give us any information as to foreign buyers?—Well, there was an enormous exportation to Switzerland within the last ten years and a great many taken by Italy also. The Germans buy their own brand of horses direct from the farmers. They have no agents.

8377. I am speaking of the export from this country, you could not give us any idea as to the annual export?—I could not.

8378. Chairman.—Mr. Johnson, you said that a great number of horses were bought by the Italian Government, but of a superior class to the ordinary remounts, say, a horse that would fetch from £30 to £35?—I think so.

8379. Colonel St. Quintin.—That is rather the class I was dealing with, a lower class of horse. They were chiefly [illegible]?—Certainly.

8380. A good many of the best [illegible] go to foreign buyers at prices from £30 to £50?—Yes. Those are all troopers horses that I mean.

8381. You don't [illegible] young [illegible] of a high class for I should say a good [illegible] them.

8382. Where do they go?—To foreign Armies. They [illegible]. The best [illegible] are bought and taken to [illegible] for the [illegible] there.

8383. Mr. Wrench.—Do you know, Mr. Johnson, whether some of the foreign Governments are now buying, as an experiment, horses in Canada?—Well, I heard they were. They tried it but they don't like it. I know the Swiss people bought a lot, and the Italians too, but they did not like them.

8384. Was that from the States or was it from Canada?—I can't tell you.

8385. You have not heard recently that a good many horses were bought as an experiment from Canada?—I don't know whether they were bought as an experiment. The party I sold troopers to for the Swiss Government used to buy from me for a considerable time, but there was one year, instead of buying Irish horses, he went to America, and he is now getting a supply of Irish horses as they did not like the American horses.

8386. Do you think the American export of horses is affecting the foreign trade as well as the trade with the London jobmasters?—I know several foreigners who used to buy horses here, and they are now living in Chicago, and they are regularly sending them over to buy horses for their people. I know one Belgian and one Frenchman who used to buy a lot of horses in Ireland, and they are now living in America.

8387. Living in America and buying there?—Yes.

8388. When you told about selling the Italian horses at £20 or £30 each, were they chiefly mares or geldings?—They were not particular.

8389. They took either?—Either.

8390. Colonel St. Quintin.—Do the Germans make any distinction between mares and geldings?—Yes; they would rather buy mares. They buy no horses except thoroughbreds or very well bred horses.

8391. I think it was the Swiss Government that you said one man was buying for. Was he buying as a dealer, or did the Government on their behalf [illegible]? Was he buying on his own responsibility and selling to the Government?—He bought on his own responsibility and resold to the Government.

8392. What was his name?—Mr. [illegible] of Bâle.

8393. He is not a Government agent?—He has no order from the Government, and he buys for them, and of course runs the risk as to whether they will take them or not.

8394. He buys as a dealer would?—Yes.

8395. Chairman.—I think you said your trade has been very largely by Americans [illegible]?—Yes.

8396. And your son buys for him in America?—Yes.

8397. Can you tell us how those horses are bred, generally speaking?—I don't know really. Some are beautiful looking horses, and most are [illegible] bred horses, but out of a hundred purchases you would not get one that would make a riding horse.

8398. They are all harness horses?—They are the best harness horses in the world for pairing. They must be got by a thoroughbred horse, for they show a lot of quality. The majority of them have long thighs and crooked hocks, but a great many of them are well made with fine long heads, and they are so well matched that immediately you put a pair together they go right off, and you have no trouble to train them at all.

8399. Mr. Wrench.—Would it be possible to ascertain their breeding when they are put up for sale in Chicago?—It might be possible. They have got very fine blood in England both for mares and horses out there.

8400. Chairman.—Has your particular customer to pay for him?—He had two or three agents, but did not get on so well with them [illegible] a half dozen men who buy horses, and they bring them over and he buys the lot, the same as you would buy sheep. He selects as well as he can the good horses for which he could get a good price, and the [illegible] horses he sells for whatever he can get.

8401. He makes no inquiries as to the breeding?—Never; I don't think he would think of such a thing.

8402. Colonel St. Quintin.—Have you noticed anything in the shape of the American horses that you would take exception to?—As a rule they have peculiar hips, a very peculiar thing.

8403. Is there anything about them that you would object to? Do you notice anything in the general lots of them?—Yes; the majority of them are high at their heart, and they have long backs, straight and crooked hocks.

8404. Peculiar hips, and wanting in power in their second thighs?—Yes.

8405. Chairman.—Where are they landed?—Those I am speaking of are landed at Glasgow, but every week horses are landed in Liverpool and London. There is hardly a market of any consequence where they are not landing American horses.

8406. What is the freight from Chicago to Liverpool?—From Chicago to Liverpool is £6 10s.; it used to be about £12. I may say I bought a horse just landed from Chicago; he was just such a horse as you would buy in Limerick or the county of Cork, again and over like an Irish hunter, a four-year-old. I gave nearly £100 for him. I sold him to a dealer outside London, and he showed him at the Hackney Show and got first prize for him in the four-year-old class.

He sold him to a man that shows horses all round the country in England, and in every place he was shown he got first prize. No one could know that he was not an Irish horse. I don't know, but perhaps he was shown as an Irish horse.

9407. Mr. Wrench.—You never heard his pedigree after he was shown?—No.

9408. Chairman.—What have you to say as to the cost of transportation from Chicago to England?—We pay from the county Cork to Belfast exactly double what it used to be ten years ago, and I know that from New York and Chicago it is half what it used to be at that time.

9409. The price has gone up at home for carriage, and it has gone down abroad?—It has. Then I know the railway companies are bound to clean and disinfect their wagons for cattle, but I don't know how it is they are not bound to cleanse their boxes for horses, and it is very seldom a horse gets out of any of their boxes without some infection.

9410. Mr. Wrench.—Do you mean in Ireland?—Yes; they never think of cleaning or disinfecting their boxes for horses. I have lost over £1,000 through horses taking influenza and going wrong of their wind. We bring our middling horses in wagons, and they are far safer and sounder than the better class of horses, who are put in the boxes, as they do not take influenza or some cold or disease.

9411. What does it cost to take a horse from Cork to Belfast?—If you take a single horse in a box, £3; and if you bring six in a wagon it is £3 a horse.

9412. And supposing you had to take a horse from Cork to Glasgow?—In the boat from Cork to Glasgow it would be 22s., and 7s. 6d. [illegible]

9413. Chairman.—Is there any other suggestion that you have to make to the Commission?—The only suggestion that I would think of making would be to try and induce the farmers to breed from a better class of mares, and to keep them from taking the mares to a bad horse. If they would breed from a good horse out of a good mare, they would be sure to get good produce. That is a thing that everyone knows. And if you could induce them to keep their mares by giving them [illegible] inducement, I think it would be a good job.

9414. I think you said that your principal [illegible] breeding from two-year-old fillies? [illegible] I would suggest that is that the mare is not too young to have a foal at three year old, and it does not check their growth or make them lose their size; and when they are six year old, supposing she had two foals, and missed them, [illegible] it would be as much as if she never had a foal, and the filly is in the condition [illegible], which I consider is a great benefit and points to her.

Mr. Thomas Donovan, Cork, examined.

9415. Chairman.—You live in the county Cork?—Yes.

9416. And you are engaged in dealing in horses?—Yes.

9417. Have you been engaged in that business for a length of time?—Yes, as long as I can recollect.

9418. What class of horses do you generally deal in?—Hunters principally. I sell a great many chargers. I buy a good harness horse occasionally, but not often.

9419. How do you buy your horses; in the fairs, or from the breeders personally, or how?—Formerly I bought principally at fairs; but latterly I find I cannot get what I want at the fairs. The majority sell now at their own houses. Railway travelling has considerably improved lately, and people can come from England; in fact, I believe I get as much opposition now from a man living in London as from a man living in Ireland. You can leave London at 6.30 and go to any part of Ireland and get back again the next day.

9420. Do you sell your horses principally in Ireland or in England?—Principally in England. All more or less to go to England. I would be glad to sell them at home to go to England; but I have to take them over.

9421. Do you generally buy made hunters?—Yes; but I am always anxious to buy a young one that would grow to a hunter. I take a great fancy in breeding a good three-year-old that would get a four-year-old prize in Dublin.

9422. Do you find the price you have to pay for this class of horse about the same or are they becoming more expensive?—High-class horses are just as valuable now as ever they were.

9423. You pay the same and get the same?—I am sorry to say I don't get as much as I did.

9424. You have to pay as much though?—Yes, and I find they are dearer in Ireland than in England; but the influx of horses into England from all parts is so great that when you go into an auction—and there are auctions every day—while you only see an odd one you want in Ireland, you see twenty in England to choose from. The present consumer finds it hard to buy a horse in Ireland.

9425. You buy all over the South?—I do.

9426. And in the North?—No; I never go beyond Gallagher or Ballinasloe.

9427. Do you think the South produces as many good hunters as formerly?—Yes, and more.

9428. And of as good quality?—Quite as good quality. The worst of it is the majority of the good colts are bought by Rest and Wimbush. Rest comes frequently to Ireland, and Wimbush always in the summer. He will only buy three-year-olds unbroken, and he buys regardless of cost. The worst of his colts will make a hunter.

9429. Where does he buy?—In Limerick, Clare, and Cork principally. He buys from dealers who collect them for him, and a great many from graziers in Limerick, who buy them in the county Kerry as two-year-olds and sell to him as three-year-olds. He buys at an average price of £140, and they find that pays them far better than to keep them up to five and hunt them and get half the money.

9430. What does Wimbush buy for?—For carriage horses.

9431. The same class as you buy for hunters?—Oh, yes.

9432. Do you think the farmers about you, and in the South generally, pay as much attention as formerly to horse-breeding?—Farmers in the South pay a great deal more attention to horse-breeding than farmers throughout Ireland generally. They are very fond of it, but unfortunately in West Cork, whether they attempt it or not, their efforts are useless, because they have no sires.

9433. No sires?—They have plenty, but they are quite enough to poison the district. I was not in Dunbon for some time, though it is only twenty miles from Cork, until the 5th of August last, and it was deplorable to see the horses there. It would be a great boon to their owners if they were all destroyed. There is nothing more difficult to sell than an unsaleable horse.

9434. Is it true as has been said here that, though the price of carriage horses and hunters has kept up, the price of the inferior horse has gone down?—The medium class harness horse is considerably lower in consequence of the influx of foreigners, but they have in no way interfered with the value of hunters. I was in Leicester during the month of December, and I think I am safe in saying there were not ten horses in any hunting field I attended except Irish hunters.

9435. Are you particular as to the pedigree when

[illegible] 1, 1896. Mr. Thomas [illegible]

buying a horse or are you content to judge by the appearance and shape?—The first question is the pedigree of the horse you are buying.

9436. Can you help on the pedigree given you?—I am very glad to say I seldom got a false pedigree. I may tell you I have got wrong pedigrees, but it is the exception.

9437. You have spoken about the bad quality of the sires in one particular district. Generally speaking, do you think the country is well supplied with suitable sires?—The district from Limerick Junction to Cork is well supplied, but when you get from Cork to the West it is in a deplorable state. I think the Congested [illegible] are doing their very well in sending the sires through—a horse called "York"; his breed, I think, in Thoroughbred; at the present moment, Mr. John Arnott, who has purchased the Duke of Devonshire's property, is [illegible] a sire for his tenants, [illegible] on part of Ireland so badly off for sires as the west of Cork, and the same remark might apply to the eastern portion of the county Cork, the Youghal and Waterford side.

9438. What raises the quality of mares they breed from?—My opinion is that, if possible, you would make an effort a great improvement in the mares, but the difficulty is how to do it. I, for one, think the way the mare shows are held is a mockery; the system is a total failure. I attended a few in Cork, and I must say if there were only so ones of the description I saw in the south of Ireland we could not produce hunters at all; it is ridiculous giving a lot of miserable prizes; I would only give three prizes, and then any mare exhibiting will be eligible in the hope of getting the first prize. I would give a first prize of £20, a second prize of £15, and £10 to the third, that is, if I had sufficient means to give it, and then the farmers instead of selling their good mares would be looking forward to this first prize.

9439. Do you approve of breeding from a two-year-old filly?—I do not; I have frequently bought [illegible] that had foals when they were young, and when I had the good luck in the [illegible] of riding them myself I thought they were very far from being as good as those that never had a foal. I have heard it stated that it doesn't do them harm, but I am convinced it does, even in selling the animals if they have the sign of having been at stud it detracts from their value.

9440. Have you sold to any foreign government?—I cannot say, I have sold a great many horses to foreigners.

9441. Do you know at all whether of late years there has been a great demand on the part of foreign governments for Irish horses?—I don't think I'd be inclined to hear anything at all, as long as I can see that they are always anxious for buying good mares and fat ones.

9442. Have you any opinion about breeding from half-bred sires?—I mean horses with two or three strains of thoroughbred?—I have a strong opinion on this subject, but at the same time I would be slow in doing away with all half-bred horses. I certainly would not give any portion of government funds towards subsidising them.

9443. You prefer the thoroughbred?—Yes; though I have known some good half-bred sires that have been very useful—those half-breds that are little short of thoroughbred. I think I got a horse from you, Lord Rathdonnell, got by "Harkaway," he won the Wicklow Cup in 1891; a very good horse.

9444. Lord Rathdonnell.—Yes, you are right.

Witness.—That is to the surprise that greatly the [illegible]; he was as good a horse as a man would want to look at.

9445. Chairman.—Do you know the western portion of the county of Cork in the congested districts?—I know a good deal of the west of Cork, but I could not define which part comes under the head of congested. I think it is all congested.

9446. Do you know anything of the other [illegible] [illegible] of the Congested Districts Board scheme has had in those parts of the country in the breed of horses?—I cannot say that I do. I think they have taken no action in the county Cork. I am not aware that they have.

9447. Do you ever come across horses out of Connemara ponies by thoroughbreds as horses with a good strain of the Connemara pony in them?—I consider the Connemara and Kerry ponies are very plucky [illegible] [illegible], and I have seen [illegible] good horses got by a horse called "Applause," out of a Kerry pony, and he was well up to sixteen stone.

9448. What size was he?—Sixteen hands. I have seen a great many extraordinary good hunters got out of very small mares by thoroughbreds.

9449. Have you any knowledge of the Kerry ponies, have you dealt in those at all?—No; but I have seen some very good polo ponies bred in Kerry.

9450. Do they come from Connemara or Kerry to your part of the country?—No; I saw a large drove [illegible] in Clonmel. There was a fair there, and they were driven together like a flock of sheep.

9451. Where did they come from?—I should not say they came from Connemara. I was curious to know and looked at them particularly, but I could not tell where they came from; they were a miserable lot, not worth their travelling expenses. Those unfortunate fellows who had to drive them had them along the road, and drive them from place to place until with the buyer having the choice out of the drove. Whatever district they come from you never will be able to make them; it is waste of money [illegible] trying to breed horses like them.

9452. We had it in evidence that the breed of Kerry pony had deteriorated?—I would not be [illegible] positive. I am sure whoever stated this was accurate. I frequently visited Kerry and bought some of the best horses I ever bought in my life there. A horse bred in Kerry was the Harkaway, two years shipping, and was placed [illegible] another year, a horse called "Cheerion," bred in the adjoining [illegible]. Those were times very good stud in Kerry, and their produce was purchased in Castleisland, and would at the age of three years to Windsor generally. I bought a good many that were bred in Kerry, very good ones.

9453. Mr. Fitzwilliam.—You said that in these shows you would advocate an alteration in the prize list, and give only three substantial prizes to [illegible] [illegible] to a good number?—Yes.

9454. That would help the larger farmer, but would it, in your opinion, tend to help the smaller farmer?—I am certain it would. I find that the smaller the farmer is the more [illegible] he has to devote to horse-breeding; the larger farmer, unless he farms with money, the smaller farmer takes a more interest in horses.

9455. You think it would work better than spending the same amount of money over a larger number of prizes that are not so competitive?—The present prizes are almost nil each, for a larger number. It looks like doling out the relief to a pauper, instead of giving him something he could call his own. It is given haphazard, and as I was on the judging, I may say, having given three prizes, I would advocate having proper judges appointed. I have seen myself a mare that produced the first yearly prize at the Cork show that didn't even get one of those [illegible] premiums—I don't think it is fair to appoint local gentlemen as judges, because you will find generally their [illegible] [illegible] from [illegible] [illegible] of the [illegible]—I would have independent judges.

9456. You mentioned that Lady and Windsor bought a large number of horses between Limerick and Cork every year?—Yes.

9457. And that they give a good price for them?—Yes.

9458. How are those horses bred?—All by thoroughbred sires.

9459. Therefore you would advocate having nothing but thoroughbred sires if you were able to manage it?—Yes, if the Government would only give sufficient money, my suggestion would be not to subsidise the present sires, but to buy the best they could get, and give them to the farmers at a nominal fee say five shillings each. At the present moment, I suppose they will do something; they would not think of troubling you gentlemen, for the paltry sum they are giving now—about £3,500 a year for horses; if they are inclined to give us more, it would be better if they capitalised it for ten years. It would amount to about £35,000, and with that they could buy a certain number of valuable sires, which would do more good than all the agitation they are going on with for the last ten years.

9460. Have you seen any or had any experience of the horses taken down to the congested districts by the Congested Districts Board?—No.

9461. But from what you hear of them are they horses that you think will be a permanent benefit?—From what I hear of them and what everybody says must be true, they are a curse to the country—the unfortunate people will not find out the real mischief until they try to realise cash for them.

9462. You think they will destroy the prestige the Irish horse now holds?—I would not like to say that—I earnestly hope they will not—I am in hopes they will be done away with; it is the only thing we are fighting over its [illegible]. I have already stated that horses are much dearer in Ireland than in England, but at the same time it is owing to the high character of the Irish hunter that we can get more for him than any other horse.

9463. If you alter that you lose that prestige?—Yes, you lose the whole thing.

9464. And if you continue to use cops in the congested districts the stallions brought over at present will you lose that?—No doubt they will, in [illegible], because they won't be saleable, and they will have to [illegible], dealers won't stand them, and these unfortunate fellows [illegible] to breed from these [illegible].

9465. Lord Ardilaun.—You would like the Government to buy sires and station them about the country?—Yes.

9466.—Do you mean the Government should keep these in their own possession?—I certainly think they should have them kept in their own possession.

9467. You think in fact Government studs?—Well, that is a matter of doubt; you could not well have a Government stud, because you would have to distribute the stallions in various districts, they could hardly give them to a man and pay him so much a year. I am of opinion, if the Government take any step at all, they should buy a better class of sire than the present horses that are registered.

9468. You think they are not good enough?—They might be better. "Red Prince II." for instance, is a horse that might be worth buying; he is in the country now.

9469. Lord Rathdonnell.—Do you think there are more good sires in Ireland at the present moment than before, or do you think they are worse than they were?—I think they are considerably increased; I know in my district and all over Tipperary—I have great experience in Tipperary, from Dublin up—there are more good thoroughbred sires than there were formerly.

9470. You say the class of thoroughbred horses you would like to see should be better than at present?—Yes, if possible.

9471. It might be inferred from what you say that you [illegible] the [illegible] of the horses in Ireland?—I would not go so far, there are a great many I would approve of, but a great many others I would have had—notwithstanding that they are registered by the Royal Dublin Society.

9472. Do you think the sires have deteriorated?—I would rather not make any heavy [illegible] but I would say in some exceptions, good, some, and some very bad ones. There was a great temptation a few years ago, when you were giving so much a year for thoroughbreds, lots of fellows went off to Newmarket and other places, and thought anything good enough to bring in if it was in the stud book; some of those beggars should never have been registered.

9473. Do you think people have found that out?—The farmers of Ireland are slow but they find it out when they come to realise the produce.

9474. Then they won't send to them once again?—If you are living in a remote district and have only one horse near you, beggars are hardly to be choosers.

9474a. You are a member of the Cork Agricultural Society?—Yes.

9475. Did that society pass a strong resolution against the introduction of the Hackney?—Yes.

9476. Did you approve of that?—I approved of the resolution.

9477. Colonel St. Quintin.—You told us there are so many [illegible] horses [illegible] now in the country, is the demand equal, or is it as great as [illegible]?—The demand is as great as ever for high class hunters, that is my opinion.

9478. More or less, could you sell more now if you could get them [illegible] than you could [illegible] the year ago?

9479. Can you tell me anything about a subject I am anxious to find out something about—where do all the black horses go to. You say Shorthorns and [illegible] buy at three years old, [illegible] horses for harness—are they not anxious to get hold of the black [illegible] [illegible], what we call [illegible], I expect, a black horse. A black horse is not at all so attractive as a dark brown.

9480. Where do the black horses go to?—If you can only tell me where they come from first, colonel.

9481. You are quite right, but there are a few about that run about any price, and I am told they are bought by the dealers in England at prices from £70 to £100?—I would not say that. Whenever I see a black horse I buy it myself. I sell a good many black chargers to the Guards, and I find they are very hard to get, just as difficult as a white magpie.

9482. What age do you buy at?—Four years and upwards.

9483. You don't buy at three?—No, a man who has a good colt scarcely shows him at three, that is if he be a [illegible] colt. The only people who trade in three year olds are those people who train them, such as [illegible] and Windsor. If they have been at [illegible] [illegible] [illegible] they don't like them. Englishmen are better dealers than Irishmen.

9484. Is it not a fact that the Irish bred hunters now never find their way to the fairs, that they are [illegible] down by yourself and other dealers?—I am glad you mentioned that subject. The first-class horses [illegible] [illegible] [illegible] to find in Ireland. Certainly they are when a man only goes to fairs, because a man that has a good horse sees and wants him outside his own place, except to a show. Lord [illegible] referred to the Cork Agricultural Society, I am glad to say we have a show only second to Dublin, and there were some good [illegible] shown there. It may seem like a [illegible] to say that the horses that won in Cork, and some that didn't win, [illegible] the [illegible] in Dublin. I had a horse that got first prize in Cork and got first prize here, and he was the only thoroughbred horse that ever obtained first prize in the four-year-old class in Dublin. The horse that got third prize in Cork got the champion prize in Dublin. In fact, every horse that was [illegible] in Cork got first or something like it, in Dublin. Mr. Johnson asked this horse [illegible]. They are if a man should go [illegible] they are. They come to the Dublin Show. I recollect when there were about 600 horses shown, now it is up to 1,300, and last year one man bought forty-seven out of the Show, Mr. Hanon, of Leicester. But even if a farmer doesn't get rid of a horse at his own home, and brings it to the fair, he never brings it to the fair ground, he brings it to the stable. You will have to buy a horse the day before the fair. All the good horses are picked up the day before, even if it is a Sunday.

9485. You go about the fairs a good deal; and do you find that if there are a large number of highly-bred small animals standing in bogs and mountains there are quite a sufficient number of horses and animals, but so underbred and misshapen that they are practically useless for anything but the commonest work?—They are well represented in quantity and deficient in quality.

9486. Though you don't come like troopers, you may know something about them. In those fairs there is a great amount of [illegible]. A good many animals sold at much higher prices a month or two before and sold for [illegible], are shipped for troopers. Have you had experience in the remount business?—I had some experience in troopers; I mounted several regiments, and I found I got some good-looking ones and their wind went wrong. Take the last days of those big fairs, like Cahirmee or Ballinasloe, and you see 300 or 400 horses, and there is hardly a sound horse amongst them. They are good-looking animals, and if they had been passed by a veterinary surgeon would have brought £30 or £40 absolutely. It has been said that the last days at Ballinasloe and Cahirmee were made for veterinary surgeons. They see these horses, quite good-looking, take them to a veterinary surgeon, pay a guinea, and the partnership is dissolved at once. I heard a veterinary surgeon say he got nine guineas out of one house during the fair.

9487. Which would you prefer for troopers—a well-bred, light-actioned horse, or a longer-framed, less well-bred charger animal?—I would not have the underbred for a trooper at all. He has a lot of work to do, and if you get him underbred he is a failure.

9488. Mr. Wrench.—You were asked about the black horse. Can you say where the grey horses came from?—A great many from the South. There was an old breed of horses there. They are descended from a horse called "Arthur," and some of the descendants are still there. The fact is they call every grey horse a descendant of "Arthur."

9489. Is it more difficult to buy a good grey horse now than it used to be?—I cannot say it is; it is a colour that is never sought for.

9490. I was thinking of the Irish Greys?—They are wonderfully well mounted, and by some means the greys seem to last for a lifetime.

9491. They are said all to come from Ireland?—I sold a very good grey to Major Higginsby, the Adjutant, and he was [illegible].

9492. Your trade is chiefly in hunters and chargers?—Yes.

9493. Nearly altogether in riding horses?—Yes.

9494. And you generally buy the best horse you can find?—Yes.

9495. What class of men do you buy from—what size are their farms?—I cannot class. It is the last witness, that I buy direct from the breeder. I never buy young horses. I buy them from men who have kept them a season or so.

9496. What age do you generally buy at?—Generally at five.

9497. Do you buy them younger than four?—Very seldom.

9498. You don't sell under five?—I sell them at four.

9499. This time of the year?—At any time.

9500. Do you find it easy to sell hunters at four years?—No, very hard. They won't buy them in England.

9501. They only buy five years old?—That is so.

9502. The majority of the farmers who have no opportunity of breaking them sell them out of the fields, and, as the last witness said, they go to the North and are fed like cattle?—When they are brought out they are useless for six months until the condition wears off; in the South they are kept and hunted.

9503. You find a great disadvantage in a horse fed from at two years old?—I do.

9504. Have you had any experience of a horse that had his bone put to a horse, until three years old; does it make the same difference with him?—I can hardly define whether the animals I refer to were sold as two or three years, but if they had a bad, I have had nearly as [illegible] experience in hunting as dealing. I find they were not as good animals as others in the long run.

9505. I think you said you would not give any Government money to encourage half-bred sires?—I would not.

9506. You would except "Hackenapek" or "May Boy"?—Yes. Any horse that claimed to be a thoroughbred. "May Boy" is as good a sire as you would get.

9507. You know that class of horse you would not get?—I would not.

9508. What would you do for the farmers who cannot breed hunters—those horses that you say are rubbish—what sire would you give them—would you encourage only the big, the thoroughbred?—I would not, unless you want to perpetuate that rubbish. If you want to get rid of it you must get rid of the sire, and the only way of doing that is you cannot compel a man to send his mare to one horse instead of another, but he is sure to send him to the best when he gets it at a small fee.

9509. Would you approve of encouraging the Clydesdale?—No.

9510. Or a cart horse?—Except for cart purposes, none.

9511. If they are encouraged in a neighbourhood how are you going to keep out the blood?—You can't, and keep it out if you bring it in.

9512. Is there a class for cart horses in the Cork Show?—I am not prepared to say, but the class is so small that only two animals were shown last year.

9513. Do you know there are a good many Clydesdale and half-bred Clydesdale stallions standing in Cork?—There are [illegible], but not half so many as twelve years ago. When the trade was brisk, there was a rush made for them and they got sick of them—the [illegible] of bad horses at the [illegible] Shows.

9514. Would you be surprised if there were nearly a third of the stallions in Cork cart horses or half-bred cart horses?—I would be surprised.

9515. But suppose that people are breeding from their mares and find they are breeding the [illegible] from a thoroughbred horse, how would you correct that?—I will give you a case in point which might astonish you. I bought a horse from Mr. O'Connell, of Fethard, by "Bagshot" out of an Arthur mare, two years ago, and three years ago I bought a horse out of the same mare by "Rotastor." This horse is up to 15 stone. I hunted him myself, and sold him in Leicestershire. I put him among a lot with a [illegible] which I got on the following Monday. I think that breeding from inferior horses doesn't always make a bad [illegible], but gives an appearance of [illegible].

9516. You think thoroughbreds can be found to suit any amount?—If you are willing to pay.

9517. And I think you suggested a little way of making a nest-egg of £40,000?—In which the Government give [illegible] for ten years that would make up a considerable amount.

9518. How many horses do you think you could buy for £40,000?—You would not get more than [illegible] of the horses I mean. The horse I spoke of would make thousand pounds to begin with.

[illegible]. You named and have many horses there are in Ireland like "Red Prince"?—There is a horse called "Bushy," a good horse.

[illegible]. There are not many of those?—No; if there were they would not be so dear.

[illegible]. You would not get "Red Prince" for £[illegible]?—No; I say that would cost £1,000.

[illegible]. Have you thought at all how you would help those men who [illegible] the [illegible] of the farm to breed better mares?—If you give a show of mares in every district, and have independent local judges, but outside judges—[illegible] these three farmers, instead of selling their mares at £30 and £25, would be looking forward to this prize. I would like to have a class with a foal at foot, and I would give three prizes of £[illegible], £[illegible], and £[illegible].

[illegible]. That won't go very far?—Nearly as far as good [illegible] [illegible] prizes, and the man that would be [illegible] would want to be [illegible].

[illegible]. Would you let the same mare win a first prize two years running?—No; I would let the second prize mare [illegible] next year; it is not often an animal wins twice.

[illegible]. Do you think stallion owners ought to be compelled to take out a licence?—I do.

[illegible]. You approve of that?—I do.

[illegible]. [illegible].—Do you know at all whether the small farmers breed many of this class of horse you have been talking about in [illegible]?—Yes, a great many.

[illegible]. And do you see any reason why a man, because he is a small farmer, should not breed good horses?—Nothing in the world to prevent him, as I said already. Some of the best horses I ever bought were bred by small farmers. I know one man who has [illegible] acres of land.

[illegible]. You told us what you think ought to be done in the way of encouraging them to keep their mares, and you told us that if the Government did anything in the way of supplying stallions, that they ought to [illegible] [illegible] [illegible] as a [illegible]?—Yes, that would have the effect of [illegible] away this [illegible] of which you are so [illegible] in many [illegible].

[illegible]. Do you think the average farmer capable of choosing the most suitable stallion?—I have heard lots of people say they are not, but my opinion is that they know the [illegible]; whenever I am buying from them, they never ask less than the value. I am certain they are capable of [illegible] themselves. If you [illegible] [illegible] they will avail themselves of it.

[illegible]. The fees being equal, they are quite capable of selecting a suitable stallion?—There is no doubt of that at all.

[illegible]. Lord [illegible].—You say there is no reason why the small farmer should not breed a good horse—would you qualify that by saying he ought to have a suitable mare to breed from?—Yes.

[illegible]. The [illegible] [illegible] & [illegible] buy [illegible] as well as you?—Not many.

[illegible]. Colonel St. [illegible].—Can you tell me where most of the good horses go to?—They are [illegible] [illegible] in the hunting studs of England; the geldings used to be chiefly [illegible] as [illegible]?—Yes, are quite right.

[illegible]. And there is a great export of the [illegible] class [illegible] [illegible] from here?—I really think the majority—well, I would not say the majority—go to Germany, but all the [illegible] are most anxious to buy the mares. As you [illegible] remarked, you will see very few [illegible] [illegible] in England.

[illegible]. Don't you know a **great portion go to Germany**?—I really think so.

[illegible]. Mr. [illegible].—When you talk of a small farmer you allude to a man who would have [illegible] acres?—I consider a man under 100 acres is a small farmer. I have bought horses from men who had under 30 acres, but very few.

[illegible]. But the [illegible] men who breed horses have more than 30 acres?—Yes, and 100 acres. I think the farmers in the North average between 100 and [illegible] acres each.

[illegible]. That is in the districts where they breed good horses?—Yes.

[illegible]. But when you go to the West it is different?—Oh, yes; the farmers hold smaller holdings.

[illegible]. Chairman.—Is there anything you would like to say about the fairs—about the accommodation?—They are not held in proper fields; in a great many districts you have got fields at all. The extraordinary thing about that is, that if these fairs are held in the streets it is almost impossible to get the inhabitants to agree to have them shifted to a proper field, because they derive a benefit much in the way of [illegible]. In [illegible] there is a great row going on the [illegible] [illegible]. They [illegible] the [illegible] to [illegible] the [illegible] and go into the [illegible] field. In my opinion that has ruined the fair. The fair field is a mile out of the town. You don't like going out and [illegible] you might miss something in the [illegible], and the [illegible] are so [illegible] [illegible] in that respect they will summon you if they see you walk a horse in the [illegible]—the street, not the [illegible]. It has absolutely ruined the fair. Something [illegible] has occurred in [illegible] with regard to the [illegible] [illegible] fair. They [illegible] a fair in [illegible], and it [illegible] [illegible] [illegible]. It was worth going to at one time.

Sir Owen R. Slacke, C.B., examined.

[illegible]. Chairman.—You are a Divisional Commissioner of Police at present, are you not?—Yes.

[illegible]. What districts are under your supervision?—The whole of Ulster, and the counties of Meath and Louth—eleven counties.

[illegible]. You are residing in Dundalk?—Dundalk is my headquarters.

[illegible]. You have had a large experience in horse breeding throughout Ireland generally?—Yes; I have had a good deal of experience. For about eighteen years I lived in the South of Ireland after I left the service, and I used to keep a good number of horses then and used a certain number. I always took a very great interest in the subject, for the last six years I have been in the North. I have observed what they do in the counties with which I am connected.

[illegible]. Would it be convenient to you to divide your experience?—My Irish experience is what I would rather to speak to you about and what I am connected with now, though I am quite willing to answer any questions you may put to me regarding the South.

[illegible]. Take the North. What is your experience of it now?—The counties under me differ very considerably in the manner in which they breed their horses. Taking the North of Ireland generally they breed horses more for general utility than for any other purpose. They breed very few hunters in the North, and when you go into districts like Donegal, where they are very poor, the breeding is of a different description altogether. Then Meath and Louth, which you [illegible] [illegible] belong to the North [illegible], are very different. In Meath I consider they breed the best horses in Ireland. The land is suited to it, the farmers are substantial, and they understand it. The big graziers there are very good judges of horses, and they make a regular business of it. In the part of the county Louth adjoining Meath they also breed pretty well, but in the county Louth as you go nearer to the county Armagh you get into

Jan. 7, 1897.

Sir Owen R. Slacke, C.B.

a kind of horses which are more for farm purposes, and for harness and general utility.

9548. And as to those harness horses and general utility horses I gather from you that that part of the country is not suitable to produce the higher class of hunter and carriage horse?—I think that parts of the country are suitable for breeding, but that the people do not go in for it; they don't understand breeding; they have not got the trade for the same class of horses that they have in Meath or in the South of Ireland. Of course, it is a great agricultural country, and a farmer goes in greatly for the breeding of horses for farm purposes, and if he does not want them for that he can always dispose of a big horse as a dray horse for a brewery. They breed an immense number of that description in the North. I should say in Louth, Armagh, parts of Down, about Belfast specially, and in parts of Antrim they breed a great deal of that kind of horse. In other counties, like Monaghan and Cavan, they breed a small and an inferior kind—generally underbred horses, but very few hunters.

9549. How are those dray horses bred?—The dray horses are generally bred from Clydesdale or Shire stallions.

9550. From what class of mare?—From very much the same class of mare with Clydesdale or Shire blood. They are a very different sort from what used to be bred from in the South—a large and rather common looking mare.

9551. Are you acquainted with the western outhouse at all?—Donegal—yes, very well.

9552. What do they produce there?—I think they breed more for their own use than anything else, the work there is very light. It is generally light cart work and their horses are used to carry people on their backs to fairs and markets; their selling is mostly among themselves. There are whole parishes in Donegal where there is not such a thing as plough, and of course they don't want horses very much in those districts, except for cart work, and that is all light cart work. That is in Donegal as it is along the seacoast—the congested districts part. Of course there are parts of Donegal where there are very large farms, and very good land, and there they go in more for the agriculture horse.

9553. And the smaller class of horse—the general utility horse—is there as much demand for that as formerly? Is it a profitable kind of horse to breed?—Well, no; I don't think it is a profitable kind of horse. They generally sell among themselves, but of course if a horse is a good looking harness hack they can sell it; but it is not a district that dealers go to to buy. They are all local men—the smaller people that buy among themselves. In Donegal they sell a good deal of horses quite young as foals before they are a year old.

9554. What becomes of them?—I think they are bought and taken out of the country as harness hacks; some larger farmers buy them and train them, and keep them, and sell them as harness hacks, but I don't think there is a very great trade in that.

9555. Are there not a very considerable number of horses bred in the North and sold out of the country as harness horses?—A great number. I suppose one of the largest fairs in Ireland—the largest country fair—is held in the North of Ireland, in Moy. There all classes of horses are bought; but the hunters you will find in the North all come from the South of Ireland and the West. A great number of harness horses are sold there. It is very much the custom of a certain class of dealers—and there are a great number of dealers in the North of Ireland—to go to the South, and bring up two-year olds and let them out or sell them to the farmers who keep them for a year and work them on their farms, and then make them up and sell them at Moy. There is a great trade in that.

9556. Buying these two year olds?—Yes; and they sell them as three or four year olds at Moy.

9557. For mostly harness purposes?—Harness purposes. They sell some as hunters; but their existence as hunters cannot be very great considering there is no hunting in that country.

9558. One [illegible] thing to inquire into the question of horse-breeding with a possible view to its improvement, what would you suggest as regards the North?—Do you mean as regards the North generally?

9559. Or divide it into any portions you find convenient?—Of course, I think in all breeding the first thing to do is to get suitable stallions, because it is the bad stallions that produce bad horses; and I think the first consideration would be to get a check upon bad stallions being allowed to ply through the country for hire. Do you mean the kind of horse?

9560. I mean, would you rather turn their attention to improve the breed of carriage horses or trying to induce them to breed hunters?—I would always try to induce the farmer to breed as well bred a horse as possible, because they ordinarily pay the best. Taking my experience in the South, they have nearly always bred. In the former days in the South from thoroughbred sires for every purpose, and, taking it all round, they certainly answered the best. I would rather see thoroughbred sires imported into the country and used in the majority than any others.

9561. Even in the North?—Even in the North. That is providing that they are the right sort. At the same time I think that for purely agricultural purposes you would require a heavy class of horse, the same as they use in England. I think you would require horses like Shires or Clydesdales or something of that sort for agricultural purposes. But I think that that is a perfectly distinct thing, and that anyone who is going in for horses, and the object is they are looking to the shape in them. I don't think you could get—at least it would be very exceptional if you could get a dray horse—and there is a great trade in that kind of horse—by a thoroughbred horse. They are two distinct things. For harness horses of a superior class in any part of the country I would prefer a thoroughbred sire, but for agricultural purposes and heavy work I think you could not do better than keep a [illegible] horse. I think you would require them in those cases.

9562. As regards thoroughbred sires, is the country pretty well supplied with them?—Yes, it is. I have got returns from the counties that are under me.

9563. Giving the stallions?—Giving the stallions. I have a return of [illegible]. I can hand in the [illegible] [illegible], which embraces my districts [illegible] there are 181 thoroughbred sires. (I can give them by counties which perhaps would be rather interesting afterwards to show the different counties in which they are located.) There are 168 half-breds, 29 Hackneys (exclusive of the five belonging to the Congested Districts Board), 43 Shires, 136 Clydesdales, and 54 of other breeds, that is, generally rough mongrel horses that people scarcely know how they are bred or all except that they are stallions. There are a good number of those in the country.

9564. Except the thoroughbreds and the half-breds, the Clydesdales are the largest?—The thoroughbreds is the largest. There are 181 thoroughbreds. Then taking them again by counties. In Antrim there are eighteen thoroughbreds and ten half-breds. I can give you a copy of this return if it is any use.

9565. You can put it in afterwards.—(Witness).—I gave a copy to Mr. Neville, this is only a rough copy that I have myself. In Meath there are forty-seven thoroughbred horses; the next largest county is Down with twenty-six thoroughbreds.

9566. Do you suppose the supply of stallions has naturally suited itself to the local demand. I mean the kind of stallion bred?—Yes; I think that they are, but I should rather like to see an improvement. By that what? I suppose you mean thoroughbred or a half-bred?

9567. Thoroughbreds, half-breds, Clydesdales, or whatever they may be?—Yes; I think that in some

Jan. 7, 1897. [illegible]

8878. That is what I want to get at?—I think it is not to stop the growth of the horse, and that in one case in which it might succeed it would fail in twenty others. The people we ought to encourage, in my opinion, as shown, are the small farmers. The small farmers won't feed their young stock, and if you breed from a two-year-old, and don't feed it properly, you cannot expect that the produce would be very excellent. I would not give prizes for two-year-old brood mares at all. I would begin with three.

8879. Three?—I would breed from three-year-olds, for they are more developed then.

8880. Not three-year-olds with a foal?—Oh! no. Because then you think they would breed from a two-year-old. I would not do anything to encourage breeding from two-year-olds.

8881. You think a three-year-old is not too early?—No, I don't. I have seen them breed good stock from three-year-olds. Another thing is that a farmer works his three-year-old always, and a young farmer cannot afford not to breed from his mare if he has one. Of course you cannot prohibit him breeding, in this country, I think it is a good thing to encourage him, if he has a good mare, to breed from her. There are the same recommendations I would make as to our country.

8882. To come for a moment to those harness horses that are largely produced in the North, what is your opinion about the introduction of Hackney blood?—Well, I don't like Hackney blood.

8883. Confine it to harness horses?—Confine it to the harness horse. In the first place I think that it is unfit, and in the second place I think that Hackneys are dangerous, if I may say so; that they make a very good appearance as young horses, but that the blemishes that we find about them is that they don't turn out in the very good manner. I think it is only fair to say I have had little practical experience of Hackneys myself, because there is not all blood I don't go in for very much; but I made inquiries about them from men that I know to be competent judges. I have asked a good many in England about them, and I don't think that any person who studies the subject can ignore the evidence of men like the large dealers in England who have given their written opinions. I see also that everyone knows [illegible] Bass, Brown, and others. Men who came over to this country frequently [illegible], with great experience, and others, have proved the Hackneys are deleterious in the countries where they have been tried, and therefore we must accept that it is not good to breed from. There are other instances. I was in the North of England not very long ago, and I asked a gentleman there about them, in Northumberland, and he told me they always got their harness horses, the hacks, there, hunters, because they didn't want any kind of Hackney blood—they thought it so impure blood. Another reason, and perhaps the chief reason of all against Hackneys is this—I think their blood is doing an injury to what has been one of the greatest industries in the country. Men from all parts have come to buy horses in Ireland, because they believe that the Irish blood is very pure, especially as regards hunters, that it is what is called good jumping blood. Well, if Hackneys are introduced largely into this country, of course it would be a great [illegible] to that industry; and I think it would be a very great pity to do anything that would give the name that Ireland is deteriorating in horseflesh. These are my principal reasons against Hackneys. I have seen Hackneys that, as far as their action goes, are good, I have seen a great number of them; I don't like at all, they are too showy, what is up and down action. I consider they are deceptive, and have no endurance, are showy in action, and that they would do a material injury to the industry of the country.

8884. Do you think the production is falling off in Ireland, speaking generally, of hunters and high-class carriage horses?—I think that is a thing that differs very much. Taking Ireland as a whole, I take it the class of horse has rather improved. It varies both very much to what I was saying about the stallions. In counties where the breeding is not looked after at all it deteriorates; in places where it is looked after it is improving very much. I was down in [illegible] Kilkenny last September, and judged at a show there that I used to judge at ten or fifteen years ago, and that I always attended if I were not a judge; and I think the class of horses has very much improved. This I put down to the interest being taken in the question and by the farmers understanding it better. The class was altogether superior to what it used to be. First of all, I attribute that to the Dublin Show, because its effect penetrates through the whole of Ireland, and I think that the class of horses, and the quality of horses at the Dublin Show is improving every year. But it must be remembered that in the Dublin Show the horses are only sent up by gentlemen, large farmers, and by horsey people that can afford it. The Dublin Show won't get at the small farmers, therefore I think that everything ought to be done to increase and improve all the country shows, and to get the small farmers to come in and show at them. Those men cannot go into the Dublin Show, they cannot afford it, and they don't understand it. In places where local shows are held there is a decided improvement; in places where there are no shows horse breeding is deteriorating.

8885. Taking it all round you think we produce as many good hunters as previously in Ireland?—Yes; I think so. I think that a great number of them go out of the country younger than they used to go; therefore we don't see the development of them. If you take the young stock that goes out of Ireland and that brought at the show, I think there are as many good hunters as there used to be, but the demand is very much greater and therefore people think there are fewer.

8886. And the price?—The price for a good young horse is I think as high as ever, but he must be a good one. I think in the second class and in the third and fourth classes the prices are very much less. That is in reason, for in these days of bicycles, motor cars, &c., there is not the same demand for hacks or harness horses that there used to be.

8887. There is also more competition from the American and foreign horse?—Yes, a good deal; and I would be very glad if it were possible that some check in the way of branding could be put on those American horses. A great number come into Belfast and the North of Ireland, and I am told on very good authority that these horses are made up and sent to [illegible] fairs and sold as Irish horses.

8888. Not being in your opinion as good as Irish horses?—No, those I have seen are certainly not as good. I think that there are good American horses because I have seen some, but I think they are [illegible] in the same way, as there are good and bad Irish hunters.

8889. You think that the fact that American horses may be sold as Irish horses is apt to give a bad name to the Irish hunter?—I do, as to Irish horses being [illegible]. If they were sold as American horses and were good horses, well and good. As long as a horse is a good horse it does not matter where he comes from or how he is bred, but the Americans I have seen I didn't—with very few exceptions—like. I have seen a few I thought were good-looking harness horses, but these good ones had not so much as the similar horse in Ireland.

8890. When you say the demand for the second and third classes is falling off through various causes, do you mean you think the most profitable kind of horse to breed in Ireland would be a high class carriage horse or hunter?—Certainly.

8891. And for that purpose you prefer clean thoroughbred or a selected half-bred sire?—Yes.

8892. Mr. Fitzpatrick.—Talking about the good [illegible] harness horses, the harness horses up in the North of Ireland, do you think they could in any way be improved

June 4, 1896. [illegible]

in the country?—I think that if you establish a system of registration and holding the thoroughbred and good half-bred horses very prominent, that the others will naturally become a thing of their own. Besides I think that the Clydesdale horse has had a change. I have never seen a horse got by a Clydesdale you could mistake for a hunter.

9894. For that reason you would like to see the agricultural farmers breed their half-bred horses, and no Clydesdale or Shire in preference to an animal of an entirely [illegible] that who didn't show the want of breeding so plainly?—Yes, I would. Remember if a farmer can get what he wants from a thoroughbred horse I would rather have it; and I have seen lots of very good cart horses in the South of Ireland got from a good thoroughbred horse out of common mares. But I can quite understand the necessity for having big heavy animals for certain places. I would let them drift into a class of their own by doing everything I could to bring the others forward.

9895. Do you think you could get enough thoroughbred or good half-bred stallions if the demand was created?—I think there would be great difficulty at first but by degrees, when the owners became aware of what only would pay as a travelling stallion in a country, they would buy the sires that would suit, and the check that I would propose to put on them would prevent men buying cheap horses for the purpose of making a travelling stallion in the country to make money, as I have seen done over and over again.

9896. Lord Ardilaun.—About licensing stallions do you propose to license all stallions or only travelling and sound stallions?—I would license all stallions that are to be let out for public hire. If you choose to keep a stallion for your own use or for the use of your friends you are perfectly free to do so.

9897. Do you mean if I bought a stallion, no matter what it was, I should pay my license?—If you were going to let it out for public hire.

9898. Is it to be extended to an examination?—That is to be free from hereditary disease. If the system of licensing were considered too arbitrary the next thing I would come to would be veterinary inspection and registration, then the Royal Dublin Society would step in, for they would not register a horse defective in other respects, though he might be sound technically as regards hereditary diseases.

9899. Every stallion before being let out for service should be suitable to the district and sound?—Yes.

9900. And no other stallions should be allowed to serve any but the own mares?—Yes. I would put a check on them.

9901. Colonel St. Leger.—You said with regard to the veterinary examination of these stallions you would have them passed by an approved veterinary surgeon. Would you leave it to a single veterinary surgeon or have a board of veterinary surgeons?—I said if the party felt aggrieved by the inspector or the veterinary surgeon, I would have an appeal to a board whatever board it might be considered suitable. Of course, I have not drawn out a scheme in any which it would be—but some board. But I would particularly guard against a man bringing up a certificate from a veterinary surgeon in the country and then demanding registration. I think that in that way perhaps through ignorance lots of very unsound horses would be palmed off in the country.

9902. In that you would sub-guard the individual opinion?—I would.

9903. Have you been through many fairs in England of late years?—A great number.

9904. And there has been a great discussion as to the really valuable thoroughbred and to the like, and [illegible] a [illegible] the thoroughbred horse. But have you noticed that in addition to above stallions there are a lot of horses of substance and bone that are very underbred and misshapen, and practically useless for any purpose?—Yes; but in the first place to [illegible] [illegible] giving this kind of stallion you mention, then I would put a restriction on the stallions.

9905. Do you attribute that to the thoroughbred so much as to the unregistered stallions in the country?—I would attribute it to both together—breeding from a bad weedy sire, although thoroughbred, or from a [illegible] animal.

9906. Mr. Wrench.—I think you say in your paper, Sir Thomas, that the bad weedy thoroughbreds have done more harm than anything?—Yes, I do; I think that there is nothing worse than a useless weedy thoroughbred bought simply because the owner thinks he can make a little profit in the country.

9907. With regard to the returns that you put in, do you mind telling us how you had these prepared?—Certainly; you are aware that in every county there are returns of these things for statistical purposes, and I got them from the different [illegible] [illegible] up to this list.

9908. We will take the county Londonderry. You have not checked these eleven stallions returned in Londonderry, as thoroughbred, with the Weatherby's Stud-book to see whether they are right or not?—I have not.

9909. So that they may not be absolutely accurate?—No, I merely got it originally for my own information. I only offer it to you as it is. I have a detailed return of any of these horses that I can give you for your information. I can name every one of these horses in Londonderry, but I have not compared them.

9910. But is not the whole of the country divided into police districts?—Yes, certainly.

9911. And do you think it would be possible to obtain any returns more accurate than these, of the police, each inspector being responsible for the returns of his district?—I think it would be the most accurate way you could obtain it.

9912. You think it would be?—Yes; in the many way that agricultural statistics are prepared now.

9913. And you think a return has been obtained for 1895, though not yet published, in that manner?—I should think so; I don't know it as a fact, it may not go through me.

9914. There could be no prize scheme way of obtaining a return?—I don't think so. This being a non-official one, there may be inaccuracies in it. I really got this for my own information.

9915. In the district which you are speaking of now, by what [illegible] are the best bred mares kept?—Which district.

9916. I am talking of Ulster generally, excluding the congested districts?—By gentlemen, and by what you call gentlemen farmers, and large farmers.

9917. What do you call a large farmer?—Such men as there are plenty of in Tyrone, Armagh, and other counties, with 200 or 300 acres.

9918. Do these men breed the best horses?—I think they breed the best horses for their own purposes. They don't go in very much for hunters but they breed the best class of general utility and farm horses. I may say that it is very exceptional to see a good colt or a filly with a small farmer.

9919. Their mares are of a very low class?—Yes; the large farmers have the best mares, and what is more they can afford to give a higher fee than a small farmer, and what decides the small farmers more than anything else is the price they have to pay for the service. I wasn't asked about fees or else I would have told you.

Chairman.—Don't wait to be asked anything you want to say.

9920. Mr. Wrench.—Did you want to say anything more about fees?—I was going to say that they [illegible] very considerably. For instance, one horse in Meath is standing at £50, "Brown Prince"; "Aconite" is £25. Then you come down to £15 for thoroughbreds, but the ordinary service fee through [illegible] [illegible] Blake, [illegible]

the country for thoroughbred horses is £5 to the farmer and £4 to gentleman. Why they should charge them so[illegible] I don't know, but they do.

9621. There are a good many so-called thorough-bred horses through Ireland that serve at lower rates?—Yes; often come down to £1, and what they call "the sight of a foal," and it is a very common thing through the whole of Ireland that a mare will go to a friend and agree for the sight of a foal; if there is no foal he pays nothing; you can get a thoroughbred horse down to 10s. In the county I come I have put the list of such horses, but of course there is no use troubling you with them.

9622. I think you said you thought the Irish blood was very pure. Did you mean from that there had been no importation into Ireland of anything mixed?—No, I mean what you call the original Irish breed was or horse was combined [illegible] of [illegible] blood and good mixed staying blood.

9623. Have you any idea when first of all foreign blood began to come in?—No; but I remember that about twenty years ago when Lord Kenmare brought a Hackney stallion over to the county Tipperary there was the greatest outcry amongst all horse-breeding people in the country, that he was going to ruin the country.

9624. That was about twenty years ago?—I should think so; it might have been fifteen.

9625. Did you ever hear of any Clydesdale blood being imported into Ireland?—Very often; and I have heard it complained very frequently, among people in the North of Ireland especially.

9626. You dislike Clydesdale blood in a hunter?—No, certainly not.

9627. CHAIRMAN.—The question was, do you dislike Clydesdale blood in a hunter?—I said, "Yes, certainly."

9628. You said the reverse?—Oh, thank you for the correction; it was the way it was put. Oh, certainly I dislike it.

9629. Mr. WRENCH.—You haven't looked up or taken the trouble to find out when Clydesdale blood and cart-horse blood was imported into Ireland?—I don't say. I know it has been long a very long time.

9630. You said Hackneys are not [illegible] [illegible] I had no practical experience, but I gave it from the opinion of men whom I believe to be exceptional judges, and I gave you one or two instances of men who told me so.

9631. But you have not had any personal experience of Hackneys?—I have never had a Hackney.

9632. You don't know how they were bred?—I don't, but I said also that my personal objection is that I consider it dangerous to the great industry of hunter-breeding in Ireland.

9633. Do you think that any of these small mares of Donegal would be likely to breed hunters. Is there any danger of their becoming [illegible] blood mares?—No, certainly not.

9634. No people would dream of breeding hunters from the mares that exist out of Donegal?—No, and giving [illegible] [illegible] [illegible]. I may, though I don't like Hackneys, I think they have done the mares and a certain amount of good in Donegal—I have seen nearly all their sires there—because they were better than what they had before in Donegal. It does not [illegible] in any way upon a breeding country, but, also, at the same time, if I were asked the question I would much rather see a good stock small, [illegible], thoroughbred horse, if you could get him, or a half-bred horse there than the Hackneys, because of the prejudice against the blood.

9635. Do you think the produce of the thorough-bred horse would live and thrive as well in Donegal as the produce of a Hackney?—I think it would.

9636. You are now speaking without experience?—Well, yes. Of course, the experience of the Hackneys is only a few years in Donegal. But remember that there are eleven Hackneys in the county Donegal, besides the five of the Congested Districts Board, so that all the Hackneys in Donegal must not be put down to the Congested Districts Board. I don't know when they came in; I don't know whether the Congested Districts Board encouraged the others to get them or not, but there they are. Colonel St. Quintin was speaking about the troopers, and I see it has been suggested several times about Government studs. If you like my opinion on that——

9637. CHAIRMAN.—We should like your opinion about anything connected with the subject?—I saw it was proposed by one or two witnesses that there should be Government studs. I should be very much against anything of the sort. I think that it would interfere a great deal with private enterprise. I think that they would cost an immense deal of money, and that the money would be a great deal more profitably used by being distributed through the country in the encouragement of shows such as I have recommended—local shows; and I think, looking at it from a financial point of view, the Government studs would have an enormous amount of misfits. And what would become of them? The Government would sell them, and that would be distributing on the part of the Government bad stock through the country.

9638. Of course there is a system of licensing?—Oh, still with all licensing you must have misfits.

9639. Still a system of licensing would be interfering with private enterprise?—Not to the same extent. Every one that put out his horse for hire would be obliged to have a licence, the same as in a great number of other trades—for keeping covering stallions is a trade—so that they would be all in the same boat that way.

9640. I suppose one of the practical effects of that would be to put an end to this class of thoroughbred horse now serving?—That are bought for a few sovereigns for a man to make profit through the country on.

9641. To that extent it would interfere with private enterprise?—Yes. There is another question that has arisen very often, and that is buying horses direct from breeders. I have seen a great deal about it. Troopers, I believe, it is impossible to buy through the country from breeders, except from large men who know their business. With small farmers, if a gentleman, or any person who is respectable or is a stranger, comes to them to buy a horse, they immediately think they have got a treasure, and you can't buy the animal. I don't think you can buy a horse, as a rule, from a small farmer at all until he has had a try at a fair, or perhaps two.

9642. Colonel ST. QUINTIN.—With reference to that, it has been suggested that Government should take up some land and form a depôt, not for breeding, but for buying direct from breeders—buying at three years and keeping the horses for a year or eighteen months until they are fit to go into the service. Do you think that would be a good financial speculation for Government to carry out?—I think you could get the horses, but not direct from the breeders. As to the financial question, one would have to work it out to see what the cost would be before I could give an answer. I should not think it would do. I don't see anything to better the present system.

9643. You don't think it would be advisable for the Government, having a supply at their doors, as they have now, and having all they can take when they require them, to go to the expense of a large establishment to buy young stock, and to take all the risk that must necessarily be incurred until they are enabled to send them into the service?—Certainly not; I think they would be very foolish—that the Government will scarcely ever be able to buy direct from the breeders. I think that a farmer—in fact I

[illegible]

Mr. T. [illegible] Michael R. [illegible]

[illegible]. The Chairman.—It has been suggested before the Commission that, in the case of half-bred stallions they are registered it should be ascertained what kind of stock they have got, in addition to the inspection of the stallion?—Well, I think that would be unfair, because a man might buy a very good half-bred stallion, and he would have to keep him a year before he got him registered, and if you were to make registration a great point, without which you will not give prizes, you would encourage and discourage the horse from the start. I would register him from his appearance and pedigree to begin with.

[illegible]. It has been given in evidence that some districts are without a stallion, probably West Cork. How would you supply those districts with suitable stallions in any scheme you think of?—I would leave it to private enterprise. I would not send a Government stallion down.

[illegible]. Because, Kildare, some time ago the Government did send a horse down?—I am thinking of a different thing from what you are; you are talking now out of a congested district.

[illegible]. No; this is West Cork—the district they call "Poor" [illegible] you are?—Yes; I believe that if the country requires them, stallions will turn up; they may be rather scarce for a year or two, but in any country that wants them, they will turn up because it is a paying business.

[illegible]. Mr. Wrench.—Then you would register half-bred stallions got by a thoroughbred horse out of a good half-bred mare?—Out of a half-bred mare. I would rather [illegible] the mare.

[illegible]. But you would register that?—I would.

[illegible]. I don't quite understand you as to the manner in which you would have the mares registered. What means would you have employed and how would you have it done?—I would have it done under the Royal Dublin Society if possible, because I think they have an organisation ready that if you started you can get into working order.

[illegible]. Would you leave it optional for people to register their mares?—Yes; but as I said at the beginning, I think that the Royal Dublin Society, or whatever society works the horse breeding in Ireland, ought to have more agents through the country, where, while it would be impossible in countries where there are good sporting farmers, as there are in the North, to explain the advantages of the scheme and to register their horses. I think it would be absolutely necessary to establish some system—and I don't think you could do it better than under the Royal Dublin Society—to have agents through the country to show the advantages of registration, and to let it be demonstrated at the shows where the yearlings, sucklings, and foals come in, and where they will see the prices they get.

[illegible]. And you would rather do that through the Royal Dublin Society than through a county committee?—Through the Royal Dublin Society—in conjunction with a county committee. I think all county committees would require a central authority, otherwise they would be fighting amongst themselves.

[illegible]. Did you hear it suggested here by a gentleman from Limerick that all mares should be registered like dogs through the petty sessions clerks, and that a nominal fee should be paid, and that anyone who wanted a certificate of the breeding should be able to get it by paying a shilling for the registering of the horse?—I don't see the object of it.

[illegible]. To keep a record of the way in which every animal was bred. Do you think it practical?—Neither practical nor useful.

[illegible]. It is quite sufficient to enable people to register horses if you wish to register them?—Not only to register but to encourage the registration of brood mares—I would make it compulsory—How would you do so?

[illegible]. How exactly would you encourage it beyond giving prizes in local shows for the produce?—Through the Royal Dublin Society having local committees or agents, and letting the farmers know what half of them don't know.

[illegible]. But the way would be giving prizes at local shows?—Yes; and exhibiting the advantages of registration.

[illegible]. And do you think that the produce of these registered mares would sell for a higher price than the ordinary ones?—A [illegible] of course you will have some exceptions.

[illegible]. But there would be a money advantage?—Yes, with the general buyer.

[illegible]. The Chairman.—Do you think our countries' horse-breeding as regards horse-breeding as an industry in Ireland is sufficiently [illegible] what it is?

[illegible]. It only gets us the numbers in the country and the exports and imports?—Not even the public one. I think you know what was before your own Commission.

[illegible]. No; I mean the public one?—Yes; I think it is. I don't see that any further information we get there would increase the horse-breeding in Ireland. I don't see any object in it, looking at it from a horse-breeding point of view.

[illegible]. Is there anything else you wish to suggest to us?—I don't think there is. May I refer to my recommendation which I made up.

[illegible]. Mr. Wrench.—I don't think you have left anything out.

Witness.—There is one thing that I have a note of here I see. That is that in any country where there is fox hunting, it does a great deal to improve and maintain the breed of horses in the country; and there is one reason that in the South of Ireland—that is south of Dublin—you have a much better class of horse than you have in the North, where you have no fox hunting.

[illegible]. Mr. Wrench.—Do you see any way to enable the Government to establish fox hunts in the North?—No; but I think all these things come out. I said there was a great number of dealers in the North of Ireland who buy an immense number of horses, but I find that all these hunters come from the South or West.

[illegible]. There are dealers all over the North?—A tremendous lot of dealers are in the North, and generally their hunters are bought from the South. I think those are all the points.

The Commission adjourned to next day.

NINETEENTH DAY.—FRIDAY, JANUARY 8TH, 1897.

Present:—THE RIGHT HON. THE EARL OF DUNRAVEN, K.P., in the Chair; LORD ASHTOWN, HON. HENRY W. FITZWILLIAM, MR. P. LA TOUCHE, COLONEL ST. QUINTIN, LORD RATHDONNELL, MR. F. S. WRENCH.

MR. HUGH NEVILLE, Secretary.

Mr. James Daly, Liffey Bank, Dublin, examined.

[illegible]. CHAIRMAN.—Mr. Daly, you live at Liffey Bank?—Yes, sir.

[illegible]. And you have been engaged in horse dealing for a considerable number of years?—Yes.

[illegible]

Jan. 5, 189[illegible].
—
Mr. James Daly.

9719. But in regard to the small, weedy, very light mares that we hear of in some parts of Ireland, would you do them some good by putting a thoroughbred sire, provided that he had sufficient bone and substance?—Certainly, my lord. I think the horses might do for a thoroughbred, and of sufficient strength and substance. In fact I mean a good horse.

9720. Would it be difficult to find that kind of stallion?—No, my lord, if you pay for him. There is a difficulty in ways about finding a good one, but it is wonderful what an [illegible] money does. I have a few of them myself, but I have had to pay for them.

9721. Now, as to harness horses, do you achieve one of the first requirements of a harness horse?—Yes, my lord.

9722. Do you think that the thoroughbred sire is sufficient to give action as well as the Hackney sire?—Yes.

9723. Have you any experience of the produce of Hackney sires, have any passed through your hands?—Well, I have only seen them casually. I have certainly not taken much notice of them.

9724. Have you got any opinion of your own as to the effect likely to be produced by the introduction of Hackney blood?—I think if it were the object of the Government to ruin the horse-breeding industry in Ireland they could not go about it in a more effectual manner.

9725. Do you think that the Hackney blood is likely to spread through the country from the congested districts, even if it is confined to the congested districts?—I certainly think it would spread; in fact, I am sure it would.

9726. And do you think that the strain of the Hackney blood would be more difficult to detect after a generation or two than the strain of, say, the Clydesdale?—There is no difficulty in detecting the strain of the Hackney to any man who knows anything about a horse. I don't see any difficulty about it at all.

9727. Then, if there is no difficulty in detecting the Hackney strain, what danger is there of the Hackney strain ruining the industry throughout the country generally?—I may tell you that the people who come here to buy our horses, will come to detect and the foreigners will not have anything to do with them, because they are already familiar with these [illegible], and know what they are, and there is no use in our breeding horses if we have not customers to buy them. Every man in Ireland who breeds a horse breeds him to sell. Therefore he ought to breed what the customer wants.

9728. Should we not go on breeding what the customer wants in spite of the Hackney blood, if, as you think, everybody can detect the Hackney blood?—I don't think so, my lord. There are only two classes, according to my opinion, to breed—one is the cart horse and the other is the thoroughbred horse; but the thoroughbred sire is of the proper class.

9729. As to what I may call the second class harness horse, the general utility horse, and such like, is the price as good as it used to be few years?—It is not, my lord—nothing like it. We are not only flooded with American horses. Forty thousand American horses come into Great Britain and Ireland every year.

9730. Do many of those come to Ireland?—Yes, a good many of them, my lord. These are [illegible] I took out of the Manchester Guardian [illegible].

9731. You took the figures out of that this year, Mr. Daly?—That is so. I read another account last night, where they said between forty and forty-six thousand [illegible].

9732. Well, of course, I can't discuss the absolute accuracy of the figures, because we have no way of proving it, but I suppose that there is a very large importation?—There is, my lord. If we send horses to America—I sold some horses to America—they charge us 30 per cent. on all horses going out unless they are thoroughbred. We pay [illegible] horses going to America. They charge 30 per cent. on them, and American horses get in free here.

9733. Do you buy those American horses yourself?—No, my lord, I have never bought an American horse.

9734. They are very good, some of them—are they not?—I have never heard of any of them being very good.

9735. Do you think that American horses are imported into Ireland and sold again as Irish horses?—I have heard of such a thing occurring. I think all those horses coming from America ought to be branded, or something done to them.

9736. You think they should be marked in some way?—I do, most decidedly.

9737. And to this importation you largely attribute the fact that the trade in the general utility horse of that breed is very much falling off?—Yes; I should say 30 per cent. at least.

9738. Which, in your opinion, is the most profitable kind of horse for a farmer to breed?—The produce of the best thoroughbred sires to get hunters and harness horses. If the Government encourage this they would cause a great improvement. There is no other way of doing it. There is no use in breeding common horses, because you can get nothing for them. You only breed them to do farming work, but they won't pay you.

9739. Do you know anything of the Kerry ponies or the Connemara ponies?—I have only had one Connemara pony. I had a very good one once—a cob—and I sold it for £[illegible] to Mr. Fox, and he told me that he would not take under £[illegible] for it. I have bought horses from Connemara, ponies—as least I have been told so. Personally I don't know.

9740. They were very good?—They were.

9741. They would be by a thoroughbred?—Oh, certainly.

9742. Do you attach much importance yourself in buying to pedigree?—Well, I always buy a horse and then look out for the pedigree. I would not buy a horse off the book.

9743. Do you think the general run of pedigrees [illegible] are [illegible] reliable?—I should say so. I think they are as a rule are very truthful.

9744. Have you at all considered, Mr. Daly, the advisability or the practicability of licensing stallions or having a more stringent system of registering stallions?—Well, I think that registration or licensing stallions would be a very good thing, my lord; but if they followed it up by a system of sending thoroughbred horses into the country and charging a low fee for them, it would have just the [illegible] effect.

9745. And as to the mares generally throughout the parts of the country that breed hunters and high-class harness horses, what do you say about them?—Yes; I would say there is a very fair supply of mares, not too many, but quite enough.

9746. And as good quality as they used to be?—Well, I think so; they must be, for they breed horses just as well [illegible].

9747. And do they keep up any of the special characteristics that we hear of—of what we call the old Irish mare?—Well, I have found a good deal about the old Irish mare, and I think there are a good many of them left.

9748. It would be rather a difficult animal to draw accurately?—Well, I would say it would, my lord.

9749. And we have had before us that there is a greater tendency now than there used to be formerly among farmers to sell their best mares to foreigners—have you any opinion about that?—Well, if a farmer has a good mare and wants to dispose of her, I don't see why he should not.

9750. The question is, does he do so more than formerly—is there more demand from abroad?—The [illegible] at a stiff [illegible] all the [illegible]; in fact **they** would buy 80 per cent. [illegible].

9751. Do you know are they buying more than they used to—are there more going abroad than formerly?—I should say there were; I should say they go at the rate of about 5,000 a year.

9752. Mostly mares?—Mostly mares—oh, certainly.

9753. Bought for the foreign governments?—A great many are for the foreign governments. A great many private foreign buyers come here too; nearly all the [illegible] stallions are exported from England.

9754. Do you know what prices the foreign governments give—are they far beyond the prices our Government give?—I have never sold any to them, but I believe they give more than our Government does—a little, I have heard so. I don't know.

9755. And they **much** prefer mares?—Yes, I believe so.

9756. I gather, Mr. Daly, that you think that the best thing that could be possibly done to improve horse breeding in Ireland would be the general action of a better class of stallion?—There is no other way of doing it, my lord. There is no other way it can be done.

9757. Do you think it would be a good thing to try to induce the farmers to keep their mares at home instead of selling the best of them?—If you produce a good stallion the farmers will keep the mares. The farmers are open to their own interests, and they know well what suits them best.

9758. Mr. Fitzwilliam.—You rather object, Mr. Daly, to half-bred stallions—do you think you could get the required number of thoroughbred stallions to supply the wants of the country?—I do, sir.

9759. That is at a reasonable rate?—Yes; well, I don't know what you would call a reasonable rate; that private people are prepared to pay for them.

9760. Yes. Do you think you would get [illegible] enough of them?—I don't think you could get them in a great hurry. They would not be in this country in short while in any large quantity, but you would get them.

9761. I gather the way that you would like to help the horse breeding interest would be by allowing good stallions and subsidising them, and obliging them to be that stallion to serve farmers' mares at a low fee?—Yes.

9762. What do you think the large farmers **are able** to pay?—Well, I don't know what they are **able** to pay. They will go where the best horse **is**, independent of the charge. I don't mean **that** there should be such like a district of that kind. **I** thought you wanted to send them into districts where they were required.

9763. Yes, you would. What do you think the smaller farmer could pay?—I don't think any farmer ought to pay more than a pound for a good class of horse, if you want to hold out an inducement to him to breed, be he poor or rich. The only man who's [illegible] it is the big man who [illegible] the [illegible]; I think if the Government is going to do it, sir. They do these things on the Continent. The Government give a couple of thousand pounds for a horse and then let him afterwards to somebody for £100 or £200, and let him out to farmers.

9764. Talking about Hackneys, you said that you thought that any buyer could detect the Hackney strain, or the taint of any of those horses?—Well, I don't think a dealer would have much difficulty about it.

9765. Do you think the general buyer would?—I can only speak for myself.

9766. It is [illegible] **or two—I cannot answer** the question.

9767. You think he could not?—I think he ought to be going and [illegible] buying. But [illegible] they [illegible] people not on that ground.

9768. Well, if you do think that it would be difficult to detect it, in a few generations, if [illegible] would be dangerous to employ it?—Most decidedly.

9769. And for that reason, I suppose, if you do [illegible] any of these [illegible] horses, you would like to have a [illegible] one that would really show his [illegible] breed?—Let him be a [illegible] horse.

9770. A [illegible] or something of that sort?—Yes.

9771. Could you in any way suggest any means of keeping the mares in the country but the only way I could suggest would be to send them good stallions, and they will find it their interest to keep good mares, and they will do so. It is very hard to tell a man not to sell his mare if he wants money and has a saleable animal. You would be a long time talking to him before he did it either.

9772. Lord Arthur Hill.—How much will you have to pay for these thoroughbred sires?—Well, I think you ought to pay from £200 to £1,000.

9773. You want the Government to buy **the sire?** —Certainly.

9774. And you would have the Government **sell to** the private individuals?—No.

9775. The Government would [illegible] the sire **in** [illegible] places?—Where he would be required.

9776. I thought you meant the private individual to buy the sire and the Government to subsidise him?—I think the private individual would hardly do that.

9777. Lord Rathdonnell.—Mr. Daly, you know a part of the North of Ireland?—I know the North well.

9778. What sort of horses do you think they breed up there?—I have not been there for a good many years, but when I was going to the North of Ireland there were some very good ones bought there. There was [illegible], of [illegible], [illegible] a couple of stallions. I often found a good horse near [illegible], [illegible], and [illegible], county [illegible].

9779. Do you know now whether they breed the same class of horses they used?—Well, I think that they do, but I don't go there.

9780. Can you account for that in any **way?** —Well, the thoroughbred horses are got there, I believe. That is the only way I could account for it. I don't know.

9781. Colonel St. Quintin.—Is not the case that it is almost chiefly in the South where the proportion of the big [illegible] are bought?—Yes.

9782. And that is practically the only district to which you can put what you suggest for your [illegible]—[illegible] were [illegible]?—Yes, South, and West.

9783. Well now, [illegible] in former **days was** one of the best [illegible] in Ireland for these **both?—** It was.

9784. Could you get them there now?—In very small quantities. That is just a district where they would want a few good stallions.

9785. Did [illegible] [illegible] [illegible] [illegible] [illegible]?—[illegible].

9786. [illegible] [illegible] [illegible] [illegible] to the half-bred [illegible] of [illegible] [illegible] [illegible] [illegible]?—[illegible].

9787. **You** say that in many counties that are in the congested districts—Connemara, Kerry, and all around—there is [illegible] [illegible] you could [illegible] to get high-class horses?—I have bought many high-class horses out of Kerry, and out of Mayo too.

9788. Then probably a great proportion of that district is capable of producing good horses?—Certainly; I bought from Captain [illegible] and the [illegible], and Dr. [illegible], and other people in Mayo, very good horses.

9789. In regard to the half-bred [illegible], you say that you would have nothing but the thoroughbred horse; would you propose that he should be by the thoroughbred—what would you call "half-bred" and "Hackney," and those horses that you have shown to call them half-bred?—I don't think it is fair to call either of those half-bred; they are not half-bred.

9790. [illegible] say but we are bound to say that they are half-bred, because they are not in the [illegible]?

[illegible]

—You are bound to say they are not in the stud-book, Colonel, but they are not half-bred.

9791. You would not object to those horses?—No, because I know they are thoroughbreds.

9792. But they come under the denomination of half-bred?—Yes.

9793. Simply because they are not in the stud-book?—Yes.

9794. Well, those are around of three horses which, has you count them as thoroughbred?—Yes; what I call a half-bred horse is a hunter.

9795. Well, what I want to arrive at is what degree which you would think is necessary to preserve for the class of horses of that class. Of course with the class bred here in the stud-book you could deal, but you would not have any very fixed idea with regard to horses of that class. I think if the Government is going to send stallions they ought to be thoroughbred and nothing else.

9796. Quite so; but you would count them as thoroughbred horses?—I would.

9797. With regard to the proper class, there have been several schemes put forward at different times which may not have come under your notice—one was for Government to breed the sires themselves—to establish a breeding establishment for breeding horses. Do you think that that would be an advisable thing for the Government to undertake?—I do not, Colonel.

9798. Do you think it would pay anyone to breed hunters?—Certainly not; I don't think anybody ever thought of breeding hunting horses.

9799. Then we practically get our hunters from the horses that are bred with a higher object, and have not come up to the standard?—They are animals that get through the sieve.

9800. And there are plenty of those that we should get with bone and substance and suitable for the purpose with the thoroughbred horse, and the breeding should be as it is now?—I don't think, Colonel, you would buy two-year-olds in the year, the large quantity that they, that would not be by thoroughbred horses; they are all by thoroughbred horses.

9801. I say they may, but I may press on it is more because you thing it—Yes.

9802. And they are all by thoroughbred horses?—Certainly.

9803. And taking the bad ones, there are a great number of them utterly worthless animals there?—Well, of course, they will be, no matter what you do. At least there are a great many of them—unfortunately too many.

9804. Are there not as many that are strong enough, but undersized and misshapen, so that you cannot make them do anything hardly?—Yes; just as much as there are of weeds.

9805. That is from breeding from a second-rated horse?—Yes.

9806. You can only make an approximate estimate of the number of horses taken by the foreign buyers?—Oh, that is all; well, I have made inquiries from people who buy them for them, and I would say about 3,000.

9807. Mr. Wrench.—That is the foreign element for the whole of Ireland?—Yes; that would be the remount horses, bought for foreign governments. That would not at all take in what private people would buy.

9808. Colonel St. Quintin.—Take the breed of horse that you are speaking of, like the Hackney, which it is maintained, that after a number of years it would become difficult to detect except by an experienced man, don't you think that very shortly people would find out for themselves, and leave the stallions which they think worse?—Certainly.

9809. Mr. La Touche.—Do you think it would pay a farmer better to breed from a thoroughbred sire than any other?—Certainly; in fact it is the only horse that would pay.

9810. You said in the old days you used to go to the North of Ireland to buy horses?—Yes.

9811. And you have left off now, because the thoroughbred sires appear to have disappeared out of the district?—Yes.

9812. You have not got a high opinion of the breeders of the North of Ireland already as a horse-breeding?—No, I have not; they don't breed good horses.

9813. You don't think there is anything in the North of Ireland itself, in either climate or soil, which precludes the possibility of their breeding good horses?—Well, I don't see any reason why they might not. Of course it is not a dull district as the South is, but I don't see any reason why they might not, because they have bred good horses there, but they are not used the same as the horses in the South.

9814. How do you mean "good"?—A farmer's son in the South will get upon a horse and ride him to hounds; they would not do that in the North.

9815. Do you think that is a common reason for the disappearance of the thoroughbred sire in the North of Ireland is owing to the absence of fox-hunting up there?—Well, they never had any fox-hunting up there.

9816. But still in old times they used to breed good horses?—It was never a hunter-breeding country, but they bred nice horses, that would be harness or chargers, which would show blood and quality.

9817. You said that you had seen only the produce of Hackney stallions?—Well, very little, sir.

9818. You don't attach much importance to your opinion of these animals—you have seen but few of them?—No; at least I would not wish to see the produce.

9819. Well, you said that the fee charged for the use of these valuable stallions would be all?—I think if you would to encourage the farmers to breed, you must hold out some very good inducement.

9820. I think that, instead of having an inferior horse, would be a detriment to him in a stock. What I should be only 10s. per season, of where there are many thousands in the West of Ireland, where an enormous quantity of horses are bred—where would you propose to get for them, however?—I would sell them a thoroughbred horse in all cases—of course of a different type; you want a short-legged, wiry thoroughbred horse anywhere.

9821. You would put it at a fee, I suppose, of 5l., something like that?—That is as low as you can, sir; they would not object to that.

9822. Do you think that those horses could be provided at from £500 to £1,000, that is the range of those?—I do, and they might be bought for less.

9823. I understood you to say that you considered that the value of an Irish horse was owing to a great extent to the being nearly in every instance got by a thoroughbred horse out of a mare that was got by a thoroughbred horse?—Yes; a clean-legged mare that has continued a thoroughbred to as good a horse as ever I saw, as a rule.

9824. Mr. Wrench.—You are one of the people who practise what they preach; you have one of the best thoroughbred stallions in Ireland?—I have four very good horses.

9825. You don't charge 5l. where the horse is. I think not; I would not afford to give £1,000 for a horse and charge 5l. for him. But I am not the British Government.

9826. But do you think it would be possible to buy the class of horse you recommend for £500 in any considerable numbers on an average?—Well, I think you could. My opinion would be not to buy a good horse, if he cost £1,000. But I say that if the Government are going to do a thing, they ought to do it well; if not they had better not do it at all, and let private enterprise do it.

9827. But is that taking you a good long time to

had a suitable horse?—Well, I was buying my [illegible] young as carefully as I could, and I wanted to get the best animals, and I think succeeded.

8828. While you have been looking for the Dublin Society's stallions, sometimes it has taken you a long time to find the right horse?—The Dublin Society want a very good animal for £200. If they say "Daly, find the horse and we will find the money," I could do it.

8829. You don't think it would be possible to find a horse that would do any good in the country for £200?—I certainly do not.

8830. Do you object to the Clydesdale cross in horses?—I do.

8831. Do you think you could detect it in the animals you buy?—Yes.

8832. Do you know there are a great many Clydesdale and cart horse sires in some of the districts in which you buy?—I suppose there are.

8833. Do you know that in Westmeath, Meath, and Cork there are some cart horses and half-bred [illegible] horses?—I don't know, but it may be possible.

8834. I think you said you had taken the figures, as far as you could, from the foreign governments as to what their purchases in Ireland were?—It was merely what I got from other people who do business with them.

8835. What governments do you think is [illegible]—Swiss, Italian and other Continental people.

8836. Dutch?—Yes, I believe so. I sent, myself, horses to Germany. I sent eight to Berlin the other day, but they were not troopers.

8837. The German government do not buy troopers now from Ireland?—I never sold a trooper to any government but the one.

8838. Are the Dutch the largest buyers?—I really could not tell you.

8839. Therefore, then, the governments you allude to, the Swiss, Italian and the Dutch?—I believe so.

8840. Do you know that all these governments—that the Italian government and the [illegible] governments buy a considerable number of [illegible] horses?—I don't know. I know that all the people from these countries that I have spoken to—the government officials all much want them.

8841. But you don't know that they still buy them?—I do not.

8842. Do you know that the Dutch government have been purchasing some troopers from Canada?—[illegible] me, but I know the English government were there and could not get any, and came back again.

8843. You don't know that the Dutch government have recently made an importation as an experiment?—No, sir.

8844. Do you think that the importation of American horses lessens the price of Irish horses?—Certainly, to a certain extent.

8845. When you refer to buying in Mayo and Kerry, have you ever gone further west than Tralee?—No, I have not.

8846. Have you ever gone further west in Mayo than Westport and Belmullet?—No.

8847. That was the district you alluded to in talking of those animals?—Yes; but I have bought horses that came a bit further. That was the farthest part I have been myself.

8848. And with regard to the class of people who produce the horses that you buy, do you agree with Mr. Roberts in his division of classes? He said that there was a certain lot of small farmers, those below £100 valuation, and that they bred worthless animals; that there were a class from £100 to £500, that bred a fair kind of animal; but that the people who bred the horses for which Ireland had acquired such a high character were the gentlemen and the farmers above £500 valuation. He gave that as a rough classification?—I am very bad at figures. I don't know anything about that part of the subject.

8849. What does generally breed good horses?—[illegible] It is difficult to define them. You might get a very good horse from a very poor man. Very often I did. [illegible]

8850. Do you think it is impossible to make any classification of that sort?—I think whoever's good stallion is standing near to them may produce a good horse from him. I have seen rich men with the worst horses I ever saw as well as poor men.

8851. Chairman.—How many thoroughbred stallions have you got?—Six, my lord.

8852. Do you breed yourself; have you any mares?—I have four of my own that I [illegible] leased.

8853. Thoroughbred mares?—Yes.

8854. What was your blood [illegible] stallions thoroughbred stock?—Thoroughbred stock. I bought a good deal [illegible].

8855. How many mares do you say?—I said I had six horses. I thought you were speaking of horses.

8856. Have you any mares of your own?—Yes, seven.

8857. Well, then, those horses of yours, what are they used for, breeding?—Thoroughbred stock?—And half-bred stock. I bought [illegible] by a horse of [illegible] and I gave the same £300 for a two-year-old by him.

8858. This class of thoroughbred that you think might be bought by the Government and sent about to the poorer parts of the country, I presume, you would not require such an expensive valuable horse as you would if your object was to breed thoroughbred stock?—No. The horse you want is a horse likely to get high-class hunters and harness horses, and useful horses of everything describable. Of course, [illegible] they don't want any racking after at all.

8859. And if there was a demand for that kind of stallion, do you think that horses that are not quite first class for racing might be bought at a fairly reasonable price?—I am not sure. Of course that is the sort of horse you would require to buy, a horse with a certain amount of power, quality, and action.

8860. Now, supposing the Government or some other public institution were to buy thoroughbred horses and locate them about the country at a very low fee, something to the condition of the people, say anything from 5s. to £1, would you not have some kind of inspection or supervision over the class of mares that were sent to them, or would you let any poor man's mare go to them?—Well, I could hardly [illegible] be an open question, because I have [illegible] so many mares that you might think that might be the very best-bred mares. I have a mare myself that I [illegible] back. I gave £300 for her, and she has never had a [illegible] I refused £1,000 for [illegible] unfortunately when I sold her I only got £300 for him. I think I would [illegible] an open question about the mares, my lord.

8861. How would you regulate the fee—would it be according to a man's valuation or how?—Well, I really think I would make it one charge altogether. I do not see why any man would be taxed more than another. If a horse is there, and by the Government as a low fee [illegible] why I would not avail myself of the low fee as well as a poor man.

8862. Then you would have them all stand at the lowest fee, if it was £1?—I don't think you would get so low as that, my lord.

8863. Do you not think that the Government in taking a percentage of the service of the horses should have a choice as to the mares sent to them?—I don't think I would, my lord. I would like, of course, that the mares that were sent should be sound. But I think, in this case many good mares are [illegible] to the [illegible] of [illegible]

[illegible]

Jan. 9, 1897.
Mr. James Daly.

eight kind, I don't think I would have them examined. It would create a lot of bother, and I don't think it would do any good.

9863. With, there would be a [illegible] committee in all these districts for the purpose of these horses?—Well, I would expect that there would be regulations.

9864. That is what I want to try to get at. How do you think it would be regulated?—I really do not know, my lord.

9865. Are your horses registered under the Dublin Society's scheme?—They are, my lord.

9866. In your opinion of the work that the Dublin Society are doing through the country?—I do, my lord.

9867. Have you any suggestions to make as to whether those schemes could be improved in any way?—I just made a few notes here, my lord. I would recommend that money be given to small farmers, giving prizes to young mares from three to six years old, with their foals.

9868. You don't disapprove of breeding from two-year olds?—I don't disapprove of rejecting a mare two years old to the horse. Some of the best horses I have had were the produce of two-year-old fillies. I would suggest the [illegible] of the best suitable thoroughbred horses into the districts where they were registered at a nominal charge; the continuation of registering stallions by the Royal Dublin Society; no Hackney or half-bred stallions to be subsidised by the Government. I would [illegible] out Americans horses. It is the only country in the world where they charge a big tax on horses. If I send a half-bred horse they will charge £5 per cent. I don't see why they should come in here and try to wipe us out.

9869. You don't think it would be sufficient to make them [illegible]—I do not know whether you can do that or not, my lord. I would certainly do it if I could.

9870. Mr. Wrench.—You would make the [illegible] pay by anything else?—If I could I would apply the same I would.

9871. Chairman.—Do you think there is any likelihood that the prices for the thoroughbred horses will continue?—Certainly not, my lord, because as long as the Americans come in they will regulate that.

9872. You think that they have, to a large extent, given up keeping good suitable thoroughbred sires in the North?—Well, I believe they have, my lord. I do not know much of the North now. I have not been there for years, and I don't know.

9873. You don't know that the county Antrim [illegible] at some [illegible] to breed horses other kind of [illegible] had never been looked on as a breeding country at all.

9874. I take it from you that you put into two very broad categories the horses that Ireland may produce—first, the heavy carthorse for heavy work; and for all other purposes horses got by thoroughbred sires?—Certainly, my lord.

9875. And you don't object to a horse nominally a half-bred horse provided he is really a thoroughbred?—No, but [illegible] people keeping a half-bred horse if they [illegible]. What I say is that the Government ought not to have half-bred horses. If a farmer or anyone else wishes to get a half-bred horse I have no objection to him doing so, but I don't think they should be subsidised.

9876. But on the whole, you prefer a thoroughbred sire in any cases?—There can be only one opinion; in fact, there is only one.

9877. Lord Enniskillen.—At former sittings of the Commission, Mr. Daly, there was evidence about the action of Hackneys. Do you care for that action at all?—No, my lord, I don't; they have only got action all one part.

9878. Have you seen many high-class Hackneys at shows and elsewhere?—No; I have not. The best class of Hackney I saw was a black horse shown here from the North of Ireland. I do not know where he came from.

9879. You have not seen many of them; you have not looked for them much, of course?—No, I have not.

9880. Would you prefer to have high action in a horse that you were buying?—Well, I don't think you can find a thoroughbred horse with too much action, because he will carry it along with him. No matter what distance you go with him he won't lose his action.

9881. You mean shoulder action?—Yes.

9882. With fair knee action?—Yes.

9883. And going straight?—Yes.

9884. Colonel St. Quintin.—Do you think that the malformation of the Hackney shoulder would not be almost invariably transmitted through any stock that he might get, and that it would go far to make a good riding shoulder?—I certainly say so. I don't believe anyone gets the Hackney for a riding horse.

9885. It is what he may get eventually?—That is what he might get, Colonel.

9886. Lord Dunraven.—I was going to ask Mr. Daly this very question—whether he ever saw a Hackney with a good shoulder at all?—What we want to breed here is a horse that can be disposed of, and the people who come here to buy them are good judges. They don't grumble at prices, but they want the best. Hackney horses will not produce them.

9887. Colonel St. Quintin.—You say you have got very good horses from two-year-old fillies, because horses of course have been well done and well matured. We are told that in many places the young stock is very badly raised, and there is like two year olds are practically half starved through [illegible]. In those conditions do you think she would throw a good foal unless the filly herself had been exceedingly well done, would it be advisable to breed from her?—I think the farmer is the man who should judge that. The man who rears the horse the animal, if he would breed it, as is his look-out. I think it is very hard to manage him there.

9888. Mr. Wrench.—In the class for mares and foals recommended, but I put this in order to prevent [illegible] and the produce of those mares to be got by thoroughbred sires I would certainly.

9889. Would you adopt the same principle as is now adopted by the Dublin Society [illegible]

9890. You said that you didn't think the Americans horses are the chief cause of the depression in [illegible] trade in Ireland. Do you think if we could get the Americans horses the price of several [illegible] would go up?—Decidedly.

9891. You are not very much afraid of [illegible] and one [illegible]

9892. You don't think they made a good start?—They may do some little harm; but I don't think they would affect us a bit. I think if something could be done with American horses—forty or fifty thousand a year coming into this country and England makes a very difference.

9893. Lord Ardilaun.—What would you call the average price of American horses?—I would be only guessing at it. I should say about £40. Those are more carriage horses—I would not say good carriage horses, but there are carriage horses which sell at £40. I have heard so; I have not seen them. With good thoroughbred horses here they would breed good carriage horses. I have seen carriage horses sold as high as £300 a pair.

9894. Mr. La Touche.—Americans?—No, Irish bred.

9895. Mr. Fitzwilliam.—How were they bred?—By thoroughbred horses. I sold a pair of horses the other day for £300, but they were hunters broken to the harness. I broke them to harness.

9896. Chairman.—Anything else you would like to say to the Commission, Mr. Daly?—Nothing I know of, unless you like to ask me any questions.

9897. Have you any suggestions to make?—Those are the only suggestions that I have.

9898. What you said just now?—Yes, my lord.

Mr. THOMAS O'BRIEN examined.

8899. CHAIRMAN.—You live in Limerick ?—I do, my lord.

8900. And you are engaged in horse dealing ?—Yes.

8901. What class of horses do you mostly deal in ?—Hunters and high class carriage horses. Our business was established in 1833 in Limerick, and we deal very extensively in horses.

8902. Chiefly hunters and high class harness horses ?—Yes ; principally hunters and high class carriage horses.

8903. Where do you buy your horses ?—We attend fairs, but buy most of our horses in districts from the breeders.

8904. In what parts of the country do you buy mostly ?—In the counties of Clare, Limerick, Tipperary, Cork, and Wexford. We also get a good many out of Meath and Mullingar districts.

8905. The most of your horses go to England, or what becomes of them ?—They mostly go to England.

8906. Which do you deal most largely in, hunters or carriage horses ?—About an equal number of each. I think we buy as many of one as of the other.

8907. Where do you sell your carriage horses ?—We used to sell the majority to Windsor of London. During the last four or five years we sold a large quantity to Moses' Bros., who are large jobmasters in Somers-town.

8908. Do they take as large a number as you can give them ?—They would take twice as many if we could find them for them, but we find it very difficult to get the class of horse.

8909. How is the class of horse they require bred ?—They are by thoroughbreds with few exceptions, and those horses, not thoroughbred, are practically speaking thoroughbred, because though some are bred they don't appear in the stud book, such horses as "Mayboy" and "Buckthorn" that Mr. Daly referred to.

8910. The horses are produced in the same way ?—Yes.

8911. The same class of animal only more adapted to harness than hunting ?—Exactly.

8912. Has the quality of horses you get of late deteriorated ?—I should say they are a very fair average, but I don't see any particular improvement in the breed of horses for the last ten years.

8913. Do you see anything the cause may be ?—Any horse by a thoroughbred horse out of a good class of mare, with bone and substance, are always saleable and a good class of horse, and nearly a good many horses the country would be well without, are under inferior thoroughbred horses.

8914. You think some parts are served by inferior thoroughbreds ?—I do, and think the Government ought to substitute these horses with high-class ones.

8915. How about the mares ?—They are fairly good.

8916. As good as they used to be ?—Well, I would scarcely say so. I think the farmers are not encouraged sufficiently by the Government to retain their good mares and would rather to get the first demand, owing to the depression, and also to the competition of American trotting horses have the breeders very much in price, owing to the American horse.

8917. Horses of a certain class ?—Principally harness horses, and mostly horses.

8918. Would that American competition affect the price of the high-class harness horse ?—No, I think not, they cannot compete with the high-class horse, they are not the same class of horse. I am in a position to know that. A short time ago I had an interview with them in England, and with the all dealers from, especially the jobmasters of Windsor firm ; they have been the sole of breeders in Yorkshire.

8919. That is their opinion ?—Yes, and the opinion of breeders in Yorkshire whom I am acquainted with and deal with.

8920. You don't object to state that the stallions are not in the stud book, but might be called thoroughbreds—do you object to the half-bred horse, with one or three crosses of the thoroughbred ?—Certainly, I have a decided objection to horses—what you call the Clydesdale.

8921. Oh no, a horse that is not in the stud book, but not absolutely thoroughbred ?—No. In certain districts we have horses, practically speaking, thoroughbred, and the farmers and gentlemen who breed from them know by experience they are valuable, because their previous connexions pedigreed with.

8922. Do you give any pedigree with your horses ?—I always give the pedigree I get from the breeder or the party I purchase from.

8923. Do they attach much importance to the pedigree ?—Yes, great importance.

8924. And do you attach much importance to it in England ?—I do. If a horse is got by a horse in the stud book, or a horse that escaped the stud book accidentally, I look on him as being far more valuable than if got by a horse not thoroughbred, but I attach no importance to a thoroughbred because he is in the stud book—I look to his make form first and then if he is in the stud book all the better.

8925. Which part of the country do you know best ?—I know every inch of Limerick, Cork, Tipperary, Clare, and Wexford. I had some good horses out of Wexford, and twenty years ago the best horses that used to come to our establishment came out of Kerry. That is a county in a miserable bad state as regards sires.

8926. Don't you get the same class of horse there now ?—No ; all the good sires and the good class of horses that were there for stud purposes are all dead and gone out of it, and have been replaced by a class of Clydesdales, and I believe, I am not so certain about Hackney sires ; but the sires introduced by landlords and others who bought as a speculation have ruined the breed of horses in Kerry.

8927. Have they not found them out for themselves ?—I think now they ought to.

8928. Do they have any stallions ?—No, it has not been ordered.

8929. You have more competition from the foreigner than you used to have ?—Well, yes, many come to Ireland now ; they used to come to England before, but now a great many come here to buy horses.

8930. And we have been told that they buy principally mares ?—Yes ; principally mares.

8931. And what do you think would be the best method of improving horse-breeding generally. Do you think it would be sufficient if the Government or any society supplied the country with suitable stallions at suitable fees, or do you think it necessary also to do something to induce the farmers to keep their best mares ?—I certainly think the farmers of Ireland require protection. Take them as a whole they are bad judges. I have seen, passing on my yard, worthless sires not worth the ground fees. They require protection and to be educated in the class of mares to breed from. They are influenced by friendship. If a gentleman is popular and well liked, and keeps a sire, they send mares to him ; and generally, if the fee is low they will send. If there is a horse standing at thirty shillings they go to him, and pass by a really higher class sire at forty shillings.

8932. Do you know any of the congested districts in any of the counties you deal in ?—Not sufficiently enough to form any opinion of the horse-breeding industry in those districts.

Jan. [illegible]
Mr. Thomas O'Brien.

9932. Have you seen the produce of any of the Hackneys in the congested districts?—I have seen some Hackneys in Ireland and a good many in England.

9933. What is your opinion?—I think if distributed to any extent in Ireland it would mean the ruin of a great national industry; it is a thing that has to be [illegible] if Irishmen are to make horse-breeding remunerative.

9934. You think high class hunters and carriage horses are the most profitable to breed?—I think they are the only two classes worth breeding in Ireland, and then if you breed them you will get a very large percentage of utility horses from that class of sire. Breeding with a high class of horse, even if they don't succeed in producing a high class horse they will get animals suitable for remounts and various other purposes at fairly remunerative prices.

9935. And for this purpose you think a thoroughbred sire is best?—No other is suitable, certainly. I think there can be no second question about it.

9936. I gather from you that if the Hackney blood was to permeate through the country there is a danger that such buyers as came to you would not come to Ireland?—Certainly they would cease coming. They come to Ireland as an absolute necessity, because they cannot find what they want elsewhere.

9937. Do you know any of the districts in England where they breed Hackneys largely?—I know a good many farmers and dealers in Yorkshire and Lincoln and other counties which I have been speaking of, and they condemn in the most emphatic manner the Hackneys, and say they have ruined their counties to such an extent that horse rearing has been discontinued almost altogether. It would appear from information I received that thirty years ago the large [illegible] had no occasion to come here, because they could buy in Yorkshire and in Lincoln: then they bred from thoroughbred sires something similar to ourselves. The Hackneys were effected in [illegible] and then the horse-breeding [illegible] completely ruined.

9938. In your opinion do you think that Ireland has any natural advantages over England in producing the hunter and the high-class carriage horse?—Certainly, the climate has a great deal to do with it, and the limestone land; it is a well-known fact that horses bought two-year-olds in Ireland and taken [illegible] the experiment of leaving them there, and they grew [illegible] proportionately in size and bone, whereas they did not grow in the same way in England.

9939. Do you think there is any danger of the Hackney blood spreading throughout the country?—I think there is every danger. It is quite possible these Hackneys would find their way [illegible] the [illegible] districts in the various counties where good horses are bred.

9940. The produce of them?—Certainly.

9941. Have you any thoroughbred horses of your own?—I have.

9942. Are they registered under the Royal Dublin Society's scheme?—One of them is; one is an old horse; I am really only keeping him because he is an old friend of mine; he is a horse called "Mackintosh," he is twenty-seven years old. "Mackintosh" cannot be registered because they call him a half-bred. He is by "[illegible]," out of "Isabella," by "[illegible] [illegible]," that ought to be good enough. I have a horse I bought from the Duke of Portland, called "[illegible]"; he is registered.

9943. Do you think the Royal Dublin Society's scheme has done good in Ireland?—Yes, I think so.

9944. And you approve of it?—I do to an extent, although there was a good many mistakes made when they were giving premiums to mares; there was a class of unsound stallions distributed through the country. A great many of these horses are still in the country and are patronised by ignorant, stupid people that don't know a horse from an ass.

9945. Mr. FITZWILLIAM.—You say you supply a good many horses to Messrs. East and Wimbush?—Yes.

9946. East principally?—Yes; we supplied Wimbush with a great many horses, but for some years we have been supplying a good many to East.

9947. Both are men who deal in high-class carriage horses?—Yes.

9948. Have you served with the horses they require, and that you have found from them that the action that is necessary is able to be produced by thoroughbreds?—The best actioned horses I ever saw were got by thoroughbreds, and I would not expect to see a horse with superior action got by anything else.

9949. And have Messrs. East ever told you that they don't like for their purposes the produce of the Hackney blood?—They would not have them at all, sir. Furthermore, the American horses they deal are so [illegible], they don't stand up the stones of London, they can only get a year's work out of them; and secondly they are not high-class horses.

9950. In breeding in Ireland you would employ almost entirely thoroughbred horses?—Certainly, as a rule.

9951. What fee do you think the average farmer in Ireland could give and would give?—I consider the farmer in Ireland ought to be supplied with these sires at a small fee. I would agree with Mr. Daly; I think a sovereign would be sufficient. Owing to the depression, times are not very gay with them, and they cannot afford to pay much.

9952. Would you have one fee only, or would you graduate it?—I think the better class people ought to pay more. Valuation ought to have a good deal to do with it, but certainly the tenant farmers ought to get horses at very reduced fees.

9953. Colonel St. QUINTIN.—This horse, "Mackintosh," of yours gets some of the most beautiful stock in Ireland, and you probably take an interest in watching them at fairs?—Yes.

9954. I have seen great fine sixteen hands three-year-old colts by him, and they disappear—is that the class of horse that is bought by East and Wimbush?—That is about the stamp of horse.

9955. They give large prices?—They give large prices when you take into account that they buy the raw material, and that it takes twelve months before they are turned into a carriage horse.

9956. What age do they buy at?—Three year olds off, four and five. They like four-year-olds; three years is rather far away from the market.

9957. Mr. La TOUCHE.—I take it, Mr. O'Brien, that you would approve of Mr. Daly's suggestion that the Government should buy really valuable stallions and place them about the country at the service of farmers?—Under certain circumstances I would approve of that—that is, provided the Government would depute men to buy sires that are thoroughly competent judges. There are a great many things to be looked into in the selection of sires.

9958. If the Government were to take that course don't you think it would interfere with private stallion owners?—As regards that, that is a thing I would not personally object to. You must take the interests of the country all round. It is one of the most remunerative industries we have now, the rearing of high class colts.

9959. You think that if owners like yourself and Mr. Daly are prepared to run this risk, that owners elsewhere ought to be equally prepared for the benefit of the country?—Of course, private individuals can keep sires if they choose, then it will be open competition.

9960. It would not be exactly open competition, if the Government introduce a better class of sire, and if a private individual wants to buy a sire to earn profit by him he will have to be more particular in the selection?—Naturally he will have to be.

9961. You yourself are prepared to run the risk of having the immune derived from your stallions, or [illegible]?—So far as I am concerned, I never derived profit from them—the people never ordinarily pay, and there is only one way in which I ever derived profit, and that is by buying the produce. I get a good deal of money from the produce of some of my [illegible].

9962. Mr. Fitzwilliam.—As well as having Government stallions standing throughout the country, would you advise privately owned stallions to be subsidised also by Government?—Yes, I should say so, horses of merit; they are not very numerous, but there is an additional reason, you will find a horse of two in every county, and a thoroughbred sire with four crosses of the thoroughbred, and in this district you will be able to find out his merits or demerits, and the Government might subsidise him with advantage.

9963. That is a half-bred horse?—I would not say a half-bred horse, he is more than half-bred.

9964. I mean a horse that is not in the stud-book?—Yes.

9965. You would subsidise any thoroughbred horse if he was a good one?—If he was a good one, but there are a great many thoroughbred horses which the Government ought to make an effort to buy up and [illegible]; they are ruining the districts in which they stand.

9966. Mr. Wilson.—"Mackintosh" happens to be almost a typical horse for getting carriage horses; he has been very often quoted as an example?—That is not a very good question for me to answer.

9967. As a matter of fact would you not get more the first to give you a few pounds more for taking [illegible] got by "Mackintosh"?—Yes, certainly.

9968. He has been very successful as a sire?—I must decline to answer that question.

9969. Would you be in favour of licensing all stallions?—I think it would be a good thing.

9970. You think it would be sufficiently good for the people to get something the Government gives?—It would be a good thing for people to know they were sending their mares to sound horses.

9971. You have heard it suggested that brood mares ought to be registered?—I don't think it would work satisfactorily.

9972. Do you think that the foreign buyers pay attention to pedigree?—The buyer never buys a horse by his pedigree. He doesn't think of the pedigree when buying; not until he has him bought, or fairly nearly.

9973. You sell a large number of horses to Messrs. [illegible]?—Yes.

9974. About what height do they buy them at?—At all heights; I have sold them horses 14 hands up to 17 hands.

9975. But the majority, at what height do they buy them?—As a rule they like horses 16 hands; from 15.3 to 16 would be the highest they buy most [illegible].

9976. They only buy a small one when he happens to be exceptionally good?—Yes.

9977. Have you any objection to say how many horses you sell to Messrs. [illegible] in a year?—A good many.

9978. Up to 100?—Sometimes 100, and sometimes less, but we could sell them 200 a year if we could find them.

9979. Do you know the total number they buy all through in the year?—I should say 600 or 800 for the [illegible] in Ireland.

9980. You would be surprised if it was a good deal less?—I would.

9981. You say you think the Hackneys have been the ruin of Lincolnshire and Yorkshire. Do you know Yorkshire well?—Fairly well.

9982. You know the Yorkshiremen well?—Yes.

9983. Can you explain why it is they go on breeding Hackneys when they do so much harm?—I think they have, [illegible] to a great extent; principally the people who did breed have discontinued. Of course there are new people springing up every day who may try to experiment; they much to their own disadvantage.

9984. Your opinion is that they don't breed in Yorkshire so much from Hackneys as they used?—Yes, but my opinion is based on the statements of Yorkshire dealers and farmers.

9985. And when you refer to Kerry you mean the district about Tralee chiefly?—Yes; Castleisland and back as far as Dingle and Castlemaine and Milltown.

9986. You have bought as far back as Dingle?—Yes; my father bought horses there for forty years, and I have a distinct recollection of good horses coming out of Kerry. For ten years I have not seen ten really good horses come out of Kerry.

9987. You know there have been a large number of cart horses introduced there?—A good many.

9988. You don't like the Clydesdale blood at all?—Certainly not.

9989. You would rather have it kept out of Kerry and Limerick?—Yes.

9990. You talked about the limits of valuation. If these stallions were bought you would make a difference to people of different valuations—have you made up your mind as to what the limits should be?—There are persons farming at [illegible] acres, and you can go lower still. I should say that farmers of 100 acres [illegible] should get a concession, and should get something. I think it would be a fair principle that the farmer of 30 acres could more than he would have to pay the same money as the gentleman.

9991. You would be inclined to make a limit of 100, and under that a lower and above of a higher fee?—If the Government want to do the thing on a broad scale they will embrace everyone; but I think if they protect the small farmer it would be a step in the right direction.

9992. Would you ban American horses?—I never could understand why the Government of England tolerated the importation of these horses.

9993. If you could not ban them you would breed them?—That would amount to the same thing. It would not give people an opportunity of bringing them to Ireland and afterwards selling them as Irish horses.

9994. Do you know whether these [illegible] like Kerr buy many American horses?—They have bought a good many; not now, as a rule, they won't buy them.

9995. They chiefly buy high-class horses?—They buy the best horses they can find.

9996. Chairman.—You are not in a position to say how many English Hackney Stallions or anything like them in Ireland?—No.

9997. I gather from you that if the Government subsidise stallions they ought to charge a low fee at the same rate as other on the valuation—that is to say, charge a low fee to a poor man, and a higher fee to a man better able to pay it?—That would be my opinion.

9998. At present, we have been told, there are a great many unsuitable thoroughbreds throughout the country, unsound, worthless animals, serving at low fees—fees that hardly can pay any private owner. That is a state of things you would like to see changed?—The good sires will always earn their own keep. It would be a good thing if the Government saw their way to buy a good lot of those horses and get rid of them before the coming season commences.

9999. Mr. Wilson.—If the Government were to buy too many of these horses, don't you think a desire would spring up in breeding animals to sell them to the Government?—I don't think so; the Government would depute a proper class of men to buy sires. The Government purchase means one more stimulus to the breeding of horses in Ireland than anything else. How many worthless horses were bought in England for

Jan. 5, 18[illegible]

Mr. Thomas O'Brien.

fifty sovereigns by man to bring them over here and get a Government premium of £200 for them, horses with neither character or soundness.

10000. You think the present system is better?—Yes; I should say in the distribution of premiums I would spend the money on mares. You cannot put pressure on a farmer to keep a good mare. If he has a worthless brood mare that is not saleable he will retain her, and sell a good mare for 40 or 50 sovereigns that might be worth a gold mine to him if he kept her.

10001. Would you let the same mare win a prize two years running, or do you think it would be wise to restrict that?—I think it would be hard to stamp her out after one year.

10002. After two years you would draw a limit?—I think so; it might so happen that a mare might be led into the show yard four or five years in succession, and she might win.

10003. CHAIRMAN.—Have you any knowledge of the Kerry ponies?—A slight knowledge, my lord; as a rule they are very good.

10004. We have been told they have deteriorated of late years?—I think that is so.

10005. Have you ever bought horses out of Connemara or Kerry ponies by thoroughbreds?—We had some out of Connemara ponies by thoroughbreds, turned out very good horses.

10006. Were they suitable horses?—Yes, they were.

10007. Is there anything else you would wish to say to the Commission?—No, the only interest I would have is if the Government would see their way to introduce good horses.

10008. Lord ASHBOURNE.—Don't you think there is as much harm done by bad mares as bad sires?—Yes, but there is no way of preventing the farmer selling his mares. We called a meeting of the Agricultural Society in Limerick on the 3rd of October; it was unanimously adopted; it was one of the largest meetings I ever attended, and they were all unanimous in stamping out the Hackney sires. This is a copy of the resolution. (Resolution handed in.)

Mr. John Wright.

MR. JOHN WRIGHT examined.

10009. CHAIRMAN.—You live in Waterford?—Yes.

10010. Are you extensively engaged in dealing in horses?—Yes.

10011. You buy all over the country?—Yes, but the North.

10012. And what class of horses do you deal in generally?—Hunters, harness horses, remounts and chargers.

10013. You heard what the last two witnesses have said, do you agree with them, generally speaking?—Yes.

10014. You think that the country generally is not sufficiently supplied with the proper stallions, and that the Government ought to step in and remedy that state of things?—I think so.

10015. And do you agree also that for the classes of horses you deal in, hunters, high class carriage horses, and remounts, the most suitable sire is the thoroughbred?—Yes.

10016. And would you approve of a half-bred also, provided he was suitable and sound?—Yes.

10017. Which do you suppose you sell most of, harness horses or hunters?—Mostly for hunting, to England.

10018. England and foreign countries?—Dutch and Italians.

10019. Do you send many abroad?—Yes.

10020. To what countries?—Dutch and Italians.

10021. For army purposes?—Yes.

10022. I mean to the Governments or privately?—To the Governments; we sell about 200 a year to the Dutch Government, and 150 or 200 to the Italians.

10023. For remounts for troopers?—The Italian officers' horses; the Dutch remounts.

10024. What age do they buy them at?—Three to five years old.

10025. Do you know how the price the Dutch government pay for remounts compares with what the English pay?—About the same.

10026. I suppose for Italian chargers the price is higher?—Various prices from £50 to £100.

10027. What do they prefer?—Principally mares.

10028. And this kind of horses that you deal in do you think the supply is as good as formerly—do you find it as easy to get them?—Not as easy as years ago.

10029. You think there is a larger demand than there is?—I think so.

10030. And the supply is not larger?—Not sufficient.

10031. Do you think if the supply was considerably increased that the price would keep up?—I think so.

10032. Do you think there is any danger of the supply exceeding the demand?—No.

10033. And as to the inferior style of horse, the general utility horse, we have been told that the prices have gone down very much?—Yes, for a certain class of animal.

10034. Have you any experience of the American horses imported into the country?—I have not.

10035. Does their introduction interfere with you at all?—In the harness horses it does.

10036. Do you sell your harness horses to any particular firm?—No.

10037. Have you any knowledge or opinion as to the effect upon horse-breeding likely to be produced by the introduction of Hackney blood or any blood but thoroughbred?—I think Hackney blood would be the ruination of Ireland.

10038. What would you think as to selling 100 mares go to a fair, ninety would be hunters, and they can turn their hunters into harness horses; only few of them will buy such horses as Hackney horses.

10039. And in your opinion is the quality of the mares as good as it used to be?—Not as well as good as it used.

10040. How do you account for that?—The premiums. If a farmer has got a good mare he will sell her.

10041. Was he not always inclined to sell her?—Not years ago, my lord.

10042. How do you think that could be remedied?—I think if a premium was given for mares it would be a subsidy. Farmers would keep their mares.

10043. You consider it of just as much importance to consider a means of improving the mares as the stallions?—I think so.

10044. You understand the Royal Dublin Society's scheme?—Yes.

10045. Do you approve of it?—I do.

10046. And you think that if there was a large sum of money at the disposal of the Royal Dublin Society that it should be expended according to the present scheme?—I do.

10047. Is there no suggestion you would like to make as to how the system could be improved in any way?—No.

10048. Do you attach much importance to getting a pedigree with the horses you buy?—Oh, certainly.

10049. And you found those who buy from you require a pedigree?—Yes.

10050. Do you approve of any kind of registration of mares, or do you think it would be possible?—I think it would be practicable.

Jan. 3, 1896.
Mr. John Widger.

10047. Do you think it would be useful?—I do.

10048. Do you know any of the congested districts as the western seaboard?—No, not much.

10049. Do you know the congested districts in Cork and Kerry?—Yes.

10050. Do you ever buy any horses there?—Yes.

10051. Have you seen any of the produce of the Hackney sires?—No, my lord, I have not.

10052. Have you ever bought horses out of Kerry ponies?—Yes.

10053. What class?—I have bought horses that grew into hunters, out of a Kerry pony by thoroughbreds.

10054. Do you know what that neighbourhood is standing in Kerry now?—"Rosslare."

10055. Is the county properly supplied?—Not with thoroughbreds.

10056. What has taken their place?—I don't know.

10057. Is it not as well supplied as it used to be?—No.

10058. Do you agree with Mr. O'Brien that it is difficult to get as many horses out of Kerry now as formerly?—You cannot get them.

10059. Mr. Fitzgerald.—Do you think you can trace any of the old strain of Irish mares in Wexford or Waterford?—Yes.

10060. Where you can trace back?—Yes, for four or five generations.

10061. Any number of them?—Yes.

10062. What are they like? Could you describe them,—a working mare; light-like a working Hackney mare; a hunting stamp.

10063. Any particular characteristics?—No, nothing particular.

10064. Lord Rathdonnell.—Did you ever buy a horse in the North at all?—No.

10065. You do not go northward?—No.

10066. Colonel St. Leger.—What would you consider a sufficient premium to offer for mares to induce farmers to keep them?—I think £20.

10067. Do you think that would be sufficient?—I think so.

10068. You would advocate local shows all over the country?—I would.

10069. For small farmers?—Yes.

10070. I wanted to ask you with regard to the question of the remounts—you supply the Government and foreign Governments with a good many?—Yes.

10071. You have your representatives in every fair almost in the South of Ireland?—Yes.

10072. Whenever you see a likely horse you buy it?—Yes.

10073. And you keep for that purpose a large tract of ground on which you store these horses until they are required?—Yes.

10074. Would that be a remunerative business unless it was carried on on a very large scale, with the different classes of horses you buy—because you do not buy all of the one class; you buy higher priced horses and various classes?—Yes.

10075. Without you did that would it pay you to keep that ground, that large tract as a farm to hold horses for the market? You keep your horses there on the same plan as a farmer buys and fattens his bullocks; would that pay you unless you did it on a very large scale, and bought various classes of horses, and had various outlets for them?—No; it would not pay me.

10076. You don't know anything about the foreign countries beyond these two, the Dutch and Italian, especially remounts?—No.

10077. Do you know anything about the Germans?—No.

10078. We are told they take a lot of mares out of the country?—Yes, for private use; I think for the Government that I am aware.

10079. The German dealers are not Government dealers; they are private?—Yes.

10080. Do you think there is a certain amount sold to a number of these to the German Government?—I have never heard.

10081. They take chiefly the mares?—Yes.

10082. We are told that if the Hackney is introduced, that in the course of two or three crosses it will be difficult to sell him?—I don't think so.

10083. Mr. Daly says not, but a great many gentlemen say that it would?—I do not think so.

10084. You have no practical knowledge of the Hackney?—I bought a few in my time.

10085. What is your objection to the Hackney?—My objection is that they are not jumping enough; no shoulders.

10086. With regard to their action?—I could not sell their action at any price.

10087. You consider you could get a sufficiency of action practically for show as well as for useful purposes with a thoroughbred horse?—I think so.

10088. You think for the foreign trade it would be a great mistake to get any of the Hackney blood into it?—Oh, decidedly.

10089. Mr. La Touche.—You are a stallion owner, too?—Yes.

10090. Do you agree with Mr. Daly and Mr. O'Brien in advocating the purchase of high class stallions by the Government?—Certainly.

10091. Although that might to some extent affect your private interest as a stallion owner?—It may and it may not.

10092. In any case you would advocate it?—Yes.

10093. Mr. Wrench.—I think you said you sold 800 horses on an average to the Dutch?—Yes.

10094. All remounts?—Yes.

10095. What are their particular requirements, what size?—From 15.1 to 15.3.

10096. Do they mind whether they are geldings or mares?—They don't mind.

10097. They buy them either way?—Yes.

10098. Would you be in favour of registering mares?—Yes.

10099. What do you mean by that exactly?—To give premiums to every good mare that would show in belonging to the farmers; advertise, and have all these mares shown, and give premiums to the best.

10100. Selected mares at local shows?—Yes.

10101. And these mares considered suitable by a competent committee or by judges you would have registered at the State breeding?—Yes.

10102. That registration you would have carried out in the county?—Yes.

10103. What half-bred stallions would you also register?—Such horses as "Reliable," "After Dark," "Mayboy," and that class.

10104. You keep a half-bred sire yourself, don't you?—No.

10105. I thought you owned a horse called "Morton"?—Not now; a couple of years ago.

10106. You sold him?—Yes.

10107. He got good stock, did he not?—No, that is the reason I sold him.

10108. You did not like him?—No.

10109. How many years did you keep him?—Two years.

10110. Did you sell any of the stock got by him to the Italians?—No.

10111. You did not sell him because his dam happened to be by the Hackney stock sire?—I saw some of his yearlings, that is why I sold him.

10112. Where is he now?—He has gone into the county Cork.

10113. Did you buy him **from Mr. Earling?**—Yes.

10114. He was by a thoroughbred horse?—Yes.

10115. Dam, thoroughbred?—No, half-bred.

10116. You said you bought in the congested districts of Cork. Where did you buy?—All through Cork.

10117. What part of the congested districts, though?—Skibbereen.

10118. That is not [illegible]. Did you go any further than Midleton?—I travelled all over Cork.

10119. Did you go as far as Kinsale?—I go to Bandon.

10120. And in Kerry how far do you buy; do you go beyond Tralee?—No, not beyond Tralee.

10121. CHAIRMAN.—Do you find you can get the horses you require for about the same price now as formerly, or are they dearer or cheaper?—About the same.

10122. The price keeps up?—Yes.

10123. Is there any suggestion you would like to make to the Commission?—The only thing I have to say is that they should not [illegible] horses coming to England.

10124. LORD RATHDONNELL.—With regard to the [illegible] share of mares that have been held under the Royal Dublin Society, you approve of them?—I do.

10125. As those sums of money would you give a few large prizes or spread the money over a greater number of mares, which of those means would you prefer?—I would prefer spreading the money over.

10126. You mentioned a sum of £20 as a prize before?—I would say £20, £10 and £5.

10127. That would be three prizes?—Yes.

10128. You would not advocate spreading the money over in smaller sums?—No.

10129. You would prefer to have three or four large prizes?—Yes.

10129. Colonel ST. QUINTIN.—Do you think £20 would be enough to induce the poorest class of farmers who had a good mare to keep her, on the chance of getting this £20?—I think so.

After the adjournment, LORD RATHDONNELL in the **chair.**

THOMAS HENNESSY, Horse-dealer, Dublin, examined.

10130. CHAIRMAN.—You are a horse dealer, and live in Dublin, I believe?—Yes, sir.

10131. In what part of Ireland do you buy your horses generally?—The principal part of my horses that I buy is in the South, but I travel all parts except the North—I don't travel much in the North.

10132. In your opinion, is it harder to get a high class horse than it was in former years?—It is far harder, sir; I find it a great deal harder—they are very scarce to what they used to be long ago.

10133. To what do you attribute that?—My opinion is this, there are so many foreign dealers come that are judges, and they think which they buy young, and if [illegible] good [illegible] they will bring it for a foreign dealer, and send it away to such as Wurtemburg, or those men that buy these good class mares and fillies, and send them away when they are young.

10134. By foreign dealers, you mean English and foreign?—I mean both.

10135. Do you think the price of high class horses is higher than it used to be in former years?—I think the price of a high class hunter is higher than ever it was.

10136. Do you consider the mares throughout the country generally are as good as they used to be?—They are not, according to me.

10137. How do you account for that?—I will tell you, the poverty of the country, sir. When a poor man that had a good mare was going into a fair to sell his yearling or two-year-old, or three-year-old, he led in the yearling along with the colt, and the dealer met him, or the man that was a judge, and said, "I won't buy your colt, I will buy your mare." The poor man wanted the money, he said, "I will give you £30 or £35," as the case might be. "I will take it, and I will keep my colt." Then, some other man might come and buy the colt, and the owner would buy a cheap mare—[illegible] [illegible], crooked, hollow-backed, as the case might be. He bought something cheap to take home to do his work and to breed, and all the good mares were away—all the best of them that poor men could buy; of course, rich men would not sell their good mares.

10138. Then, I suppose, we may take it that you consider the mares have been taken out of the country on a large scale, and the residents that kept a [illegible] from [illegible] great [illegible]; anything was good enough to breed.

10139. That applies to the breeding class?—I mean that is why there are not many bad horses and poor horses in the country.

10140. Have you had much experience with regard to the Army remount horses?—These last twenty years I had; part of my time I bought 400 to go away to the Dalmatian—400 horses a year. I was the man that principally bought for "French Cavalry," and when he died I bought for them; after that I got an order from the French Government, and I am supplying them since.

10141. Were many of the horses that you have bought taken away out of the country by foreign Governments?—A good many, but not so much these last few years.

10142. Could you tell us how the price given by foreign dealers compares with that given by our own Government for horses?—I can tell you; when I commenced to buy for them first, when French Cavalry died, they gave £45 for cavalry cobs, and £50 for light cavalry.

10143. Mr. WATSON.—That is the Dutch, is it?—Yes, the foreign man; that was my price when I commenced first—£45 and £50.

10144. CHAIRMAN.—Forty-eight pounds for the cavalry horses, and £50 for the highest?—Yes, what they call riding artillery horses.

10145. How does that compare with the price our own Government gives?—Well, our own Government give £41 15s., and you have to deliver them; for the foreign Governments we have not to ship them out of the place, they can pay the man that brings them to the boat.

10146. Colonel ST. QUINTIN.—You don't get £41 15s. to deliver in Ireland?—Not quite so much.

10147. Eighteen shillings to deliver in Ireland?—From you, sir; we have to deliver them, that is the reason the £1 15s. comes in.

10148. That is in England?—Yes, sir.

10149. But it is only 10s. in Ireland?—That is all.

10150. The foreigners buy from you in the yards, and you have no further responsibility?—We have no more to do with them; when they take them at the yard and brand them, we are done with them—they pay the man to bring them to the boat.

10151. CHAIRMAN.—How do the prices of the present day compare with the prices in former days, I mean, as regards the export to foreign Governments?—I have nothing at all to do with that—nothing to do with it now; I have never paid for a horse to go a year unless I sell them to the British, and then I must deliver them, but when a foreign man buys them we never have to pay a penny.

10152. You told us just now that you got £45 and £48 for the horses that you exported to foreign Governments some years ago, how does that compare with the present prices you are getting from foreign Governments?—Well, they don't give us quite so much now, £45 and £48, if they like the horses, they don't make a regular price with you; if they like a lot of horses

[illegible]

you may ask them a price and they won't obtain you, they won't make a deal with you at all, they will say, "Very well, I will leave them."

10153. You mean that formerly there was a set price given?—That was the price they recommend with me.

10154. And now they buy independently of that?—They buy everywhere now.

10155. They make their own bargains?—They make their own bargains in this way, that if they don't like the horse they won't give you so much now. "I will not give you a sovereign," or half a sovereign, as the case may be, and the expenses are as great generally. £32 and fifty the small ones, and the large ones you can charge £45 or £50 for them, if they like them.

10156. What has caused that difference in the price?—I think myself the reason of that is, I am not sure, but my opinion is that these are men who have taken up the supplying of the foreign armies; they want to buy them as cheaply as they can for themselves the way they will have profit—that is my opinion of that.

10157. Then you mean to say that there are middlemen between you and the foreign governments?—I cannot know it—that's you know them to some extent; what will pay their expenses, or how will they come and buy horses here and deliver them there? I am [illegible] different men that take them away.

10158. Colonel St. Quintin.—If you will explain, he does not understand what you mean—there are men between him and the foreign dealers?—There are men got expenses there, and must make both to fill their contract, and they have to make it for the and the like of me to take them to get them.

10159. Chairman.—Do you put that down to any deterioration in the horse itself?—I do not, but you asked me the question, and I am answering it as well as I know how.

10160. Do the foreign dealers take mares in preference to geldings?—They do; money would stop them if they got a mare more than one with a mark on her leg, and carries herself well, and has good shoulders—money won't stop them. Many a time the Chilians come from me that you would get £40 or £50 for from a foreign dealer in a fair.

10161. Have you had any experience of the American horses that have been imported here?—None sir.

10162. Never seen them?—I saw some of them.

10163. What do you think of them?—I could not give any opinion of them, for I had no dealings with them. I would not buy them at all.

10164. Are they likely to affect the breeding of horses in Ireland in any way?—They have affected the price of horses, that is, the middling class of horses.

10165. In what way?—They don't want them so much when they are bringing them to Scotland and London every other day, they don't want middling or lower horses half as much as they used—that is my opinion going about the fairs.

10166. What part of Ireland do you travel in chiefly looking for horses?—Well, there is force years I am going through the county Galway, county Mayo, Wicklow, Wexford, and all parts of the South, or far as Kilkenny; there is not a county or a place that you could mention but I was in—I am all my lifetime going in Ireland.

10167. You know all the West?—I do, sir, well.

10168. Have you any experience with regard to the horses imported by the Congested Districts Board?—The Hackney horses, sir?

10169. The and others?—Not to touch; I never bought many of them and more than one or three in my life; they had not age enough for me during my time there. The ponies I buy in that country must be six or seven years old—I don't think there are many of those there yet, there may be now.

10170. Can you buy many horses in that district?—Sometimes you could, but of course not good horses. Now, if you wanted a nice polo pony, I remember the time you would go down to a fair there and bring one or eleven out of the fair. Many a one I sent into Kildare for eight guineas—five years, and you never would have with less than ten or eleven good polo ponies out of it.

10171. And you say you cannot get them out of it now?—No, not in that country; I left never a good one as it is that ever I saw.

10172. Do you travel down there now?—Not so much; we don't want so many polo ponies, and now they want a different class of polo pony. At that time it was 14 hands and now it is 14.2. Now it is a little thoroughbred horse you want like a "Waterspring" long ago, or those little horses that win races for gentlemen and officers, or that ever might be, when the number is done. A 14.2 pony lower there is seldom a pony or a horse now. If you got a 14.2 pony more would Wicklow or Wexford you would think but you don't want a halfbred one now—they are no way, these would half bred ponies—you must have a thoroughbred pony now. When I went down there first there was a breed of ponies in it that you could get up on and ride them all the game the miles across the mountains, or I often did from Belmullet into Ballina, and they would never tire, without a [illegible] it was, nor did not know what the tails of them was.

10173. Have you any plan in your mind by which you could raise that class of pony?—I have not; only all that time there was a breed of ponies there, wherever they came in—I took the weight of them out of it; they had heads, necks, and shoulders like thoroughbred horses, the finest thing you ever saw, with power, the greatest power you ever saw, but they are gone out of that country altogether. I often spent a week or a fortnight looking for polo ponies there, and you would get good ones, and the moment I came home some of the gentlemen I used to sell them to would say, "This is a Belmullet pony?" They used to call them Achill ponies—they came in from a place called Achill.

10174. You have no idea then of how we revive the breed of ponies there, with an eye to getting the sort of pony you require?—I could indeed, sir.

10175. Well, we would like to hear it?—The mixture of ponies with Scotch horses that got into the county Galway and county Mayo ruined that country, and they are nothing ponies nor horses, and there is a great many through every county in it, for they sell them at fairs, and they went to Wicklow and Wexford and ruined that country. The Scotch horses came here when I was a very young boy; they went very easy to fire, hairy-legged horses, the farmers got those cheap and gave them to mares, and then the foals were ruin hairy-legged kind of ponies and no use, not like the old fresh class of pony I am speaking of them. I used to get in Achill and Belmullet. Get a good-shaped mare, for without a good mould you won't have a good horse, and then give them a good small thoroughbred horse, and you will get a good pony. Don't give them a crooked one, with spavins, with a bad back and loins, but one with good hocks and good legs, legs with good hind, neck and shoulder, and you will pretty soon a good foal. There is a thing, in every place I ever got a "Waterspring" pony I bought it!

10176. I take it you think that a small thoroughbred horse is the sort of animal that ought to be mated with the mares of that district?—In the county Mayo sir, yes; but there is a great deal of money that should not be allowed; there is horses in all the country, and half the people in that country does not know the differ; they think anything is good enough to leave a foal. In a great many counties there should be a regular system of supplying mares, and to get good half-bred thorough—I don't mean thoroughbred—half-bred mares with good legs, and good colours, and good backs, and in every

Jan. 8, 1896. — Mr. Thomas Malody.

with all the rubbish that is eating what good horses should get, and the poor man does not know the differ. Then you might go into a fair and get a remount, where you will have to go to five or six now before you will get two, and some that you think is good they won't take from you.

10177. Have you much experience of high-class harness horses—have you exported much of them from Ireland?—I never did; but my opinion is this, if you give a good mare a good horse, if you have not a hunter you have a harness horse.

10178. With regard to the Royal Dublin Society's scheme, do you think that that has had any beneficial effect or the reverse?—I cannot exactly answer you that question; I don't really understand what you mean.

10179. Well, under the Royal Dublin Society's horse-breeding scheme, do you think that the horse-flesh in Ireland has improved at all?—Well, in parts they have; you know you cannot expect a good horse to get a good foal unless he gets a good mare. Remember, I am telling you, sir, that if you had the best horse that ever walked and gave it to a bad mare you won't get a good foal; you might get one good one and ten bad ones—you must have the dam you must have the mould.

10180. We would like to hear your ideas as to how you would improve the horses in Ireland—can you give us any?—Begor' my opinion is that I would register the mares and the horses, and I would take the bad ones from the poor people and allow them a little for them as the case might be, and give them a good mare and make them keep it, and a good one is as easy to feed as a bad one, and unless you do that you will never change it, because they will be sticking to what they have and they cannot help it, they have not judgment. Some of them are too poor to keep a good mare, and more of them would rather feed cattle. Unless there is something done that way to register the mares and foals and make them keep them, it is the only way that I suggest, sir, for I know poor people who are not able to keep a mare and foal and have very big tracts of land. I do, indeed, sir.

10181. You think there ought to be some inducement held out to make the farmers in Ireland keep their good mares, and that is the way you suggest?—Yes, by giving them to them. I would not want you to give them for nothing. Allow them something for the bad ones, and send them away to work cabs or something, and whatever was over give it to them, for there are some of them really would do those things if they knew how or had judgment enough, and then they would see the differ.

10182. Do you think the class of stallions in the country is fair?—Well, there are a great many of them very good. The class of stallion you must get is a good thoroughbred stallion with good bone, not weedy lads that goes this way and that. You must get them to go straight and well. If you want to improve the hunters and harness horses, as the case may be, you must get that class of a horse or mare; but as long as I remember any mare was good enough to give a horse, and that is what ruined the country.

10183. And you think the thoroughbred horse is the right stamp of horse?—I see a power of them very good in my opinion.

10184. Would you be in favour or not of breeding from a half-bred?—I would, sir. Well, you know, that is for its class. We cannot do without a big draft horse. That is another class, but for a hunter or harness horse a good, big, strong half-bred mare that has good points about it, and goes well, and gets an action, you cannot miss. But the poor people cannot get those things unless they are helped. They are getting nothing for the corn or anything, not as much as would pay the rent.

10185. Mr. Fitzwilliam.—Mr. Malody, from your evidence I rather gather that you look on the mare as being the most important of the two?—I do, sir.

10186. Then, if any public money is to be used for horse-breeding you would rather spend it on the mares—on keeping good mares in the country—than on keeping a good stallion?—I would not say that exactly, sir; but I say there is no use in giving a good stallion to a bad mare. Without the mares you will never improve.

10187. Then the improving of the mares, would you think that would cost a good deal of expense; would not that require a large amount of money?—I think it would, but in the end it would pay; and I will tell you the reason why; for my experience is that the poor countryman is without feeding while there are no good and that they cannot get [illegible], and a great deal of the [illegible] from the American and foreign horses that are coming into this country now.

10188. Colonel St. Quintin.—By cattle you mean [illegible] mares?

10189. Lord Ashtown.—When you say cattle you mean horses?—I do, sir; I mean the bad cattle.

10190. Mr. Fitzwilliam.—What would you suggest with regard to keeping mares in the country; how would you suggest to do it?—I would make the [illegible] keep them; if they had a good mare to register her and make them keep her.

10191. How would you do that?—If she was registered they would have to keep her, unless she died, or sold her. There are people in the country that would breed a horse and keep a good mare if they were able and had plenty of means of feeding her and good land; but they are not able to afford to keep one. If you compel him to buy one and make him keep it that would not be fair, for I don't think the poor man is able to do it; but if he is obliged to buy one, why would it not be subsidised, and make him keep it, and give him the premium of it?

10192. You would be obliged to pay him to keep the mare?—You were asking me my opinion to improve the horses that I see, and that is the way you would improve them.

10193. By spending money and keeping the mares in the country?—Yes, and not let them go away where all our good mares and horses have gone.

10194. Do you advocate entirely thoroughbred horses in the country, or would you advocate any others?—I would like no other but a good thoroughbred and half-bred mare, a good one; and if you do that you will have plenty of good horses—of course I don't mean farmers' horses. If you want a high-class horse that is how you must go get him. I don't want the [illegible] to be thoroughbred at all.

10195. Now, as regards the Hackney blood that we have heard a great deal about, do you believe that if these Hackneys are kept in the congested districts that their blood will not in time permeate the country; it will come through—it will do harm throughout the country?—You ask my opinion and I will give it. I don't think it will improve the country.

10196. Do you think the ordinary buyer in [illegible] will be able to detect the Hackney [illegible] or not?—A judge will.

10197. The dealer will, you think?—Yes.

10198. But you think the ordinary buyer will not?—Well, there are ordinary buyers that want only one horse in a year or two as good horses as anybody; but I would have those horses. They have not the same shoulders, the same neck, or the same way; they have only a harness head, neck, and shoulders. The shoulders are not put on them right; they have not the same [illegible] as our own good thoroughbred horse or good.

10199. And so you think that no Government money ought to be spent on the Hackney blood?—I wouldn't say much about that. That is my opinion; but I am only telling you what I know.

10200. Would you like it to be done or would you not?—To tell you the truth, I would not care much for them.

Apr. [illegible] Mr. Thomas [illegible].

10201. You would rather they were not used in the country?—I would, unless I want them myself.

10202. Lord Arrow[illegible].—You say the foreign dealers have more or less depleted the breed of Irish horses?—The power of our good mares are away.

10203. You mentioned [illegible] that [illegible]?—Yes, there are very good buyers.

10204. Do they buy mares?—Anything that [illegible].

10205. Mares or geldings?—Anything that [illegible] and has good neck, head, and shoulders, they buy them.

10206. You would hardly call them foreign?—No, but they buy for foreign people.

10207. They buy to sell again?—Yes; I am only telling you the people to buy good ones.

10208. Then you bought a lot of [illegible] ponies for polo ponies?—I did.

10209. You don't buy any more?—Not [illegible] so much; that country is [illegible] out of them.

10210. When spoiled them?—I [illegible] the [illegible] on one; I bought all the good ones I saw in it.

10211. You mean you bought all the good ones and spoiled the breed?—I [illegible] [illegible] a week, but the people will call you [illegible] took all the good ponies out of the country.

10212. [illegible] you against the breed yourself?—A good deal.

10213. You think the Scotch horses injured them?—A good deal of it. I remember the time you could go into a fair and buy beautiful mares and horses, but [illegible] in every fair; now you [illegible] to [illegible] in [illegible] of the same good ones.

10214. In that district?—In other districts as well as those.

10215. I am talking specially of the pony district?—The pony district is spoiled; they are not [illegible] as good as they were.

10216. Now I don't want you to say what price you give, but in olden times before the breed was spoiled what price would the average pony go for unbroken?—I suppose you bought them unbroken?—I did not. I would buy them with [illegible] if I saw a good one, but in those days I would not. As soon as we bought them we could sell them.

10217. They were broken then?—Yes.

10218. Now you buy them unbroken?—I do if I saw a good one, but I seldom do.

10219. I think you said a [illegible] could not breed a good horse?—I did not.

10220. I understood you to say so?—I think not.

10221. I understood you to say if a man had a bad mare?—I did not, only [illegible] him.

10222. Chairman.—I think you said it was not much use putting a [illegible] to [illegible].

10223. Lord Arrow[illegible].—You said that people that had a big tract of land sometimes could not keep a good [illegible] [illegible]?—I will tell you; they have a big tract of land, and sometimes they [illegible] [illegible] [illegible], and when they [illegible] the wages and rates and the [illegible] of their horses they find that they have not enough to meet the landlord, and they must [illegible]. It [illegible] [illegible]; they have [illegible] their [illegible] to meet it.

10224. But you think if a farmer kept a good mare and a big farm, that the better the more the better the progeny?—That is all right, sir; what you say is true, but a [illegible] [illegible] [illegible] [illegible] [illegible]; when he wants his rent he must sell something, and if he had a mare and that he had to keep [illegible] [illegible] [illegible] he [illegible] his stock [illegible].

10225. I see what you mean now; you mean if a man has a good mare he will be tempted to sell her to pay the rent?—He would.

10226. Colonel St. Quentin.—The foreign dealers prefer the mares to the geldings?—They do.

10227. And take a great many out of the country. Do you know which country they chiefly go to—is there any country that takes them more largely than others?—I could not suggest that to you, sir.

10228. Do you know anything about the [illegible] buying?—No, sir; I don't know them at all.

10229. Mr. Fitzgerald.—Do you say that there were a good many ponies bought in Wicklow?—I buy them any place I see a good one.

10230. Are their good ones there?—If you see one it is a good one, but it is very seldom you would see a pole pony in those places.

10231. I thought you said you did buy them there?—Or I do any place I meet them I take them.

10232. Colonel St. Quentin.—Do you think any [illegible] [illegible] a thoroughbred horse is a fit animal to breed a hunter or riding horse for any country or [illegible] any [illegible]?—You will see half-bred horses get good [illegible] [illegible].

10233. What do you mean by a half-bred horse—a horse that is not actually thoroughbred?—Yes.

10234. But I mean with a cross of the Clydesdale and Hackney and various other breeds?—Oh, no, no; I would not think of that at all; you are asking me my opinion and I will give it, I [illegible] [illegible] [illegible].

10235. But the ponies that you buy, what are they almost invariably by?—The [illegible] of them would be thoroughbred horses.

10236. Well, the foreign dealers I suppose would not take them unless they got quality and right action, would they?—A foreigner, if you have a good mare, will give you £50 or £60 for her, or £100 if she is a good mare.

10237. But then he would not only like a good mare as [illegible] she had quality and right [illegible], would he?—He would get, [illegible] I have [illegible] if she had not.

10238. You can only get that from the thoroughbred strain?—Yes, sir.

10239. Mr. Watson.—Are the Dutch the largest foreign buyers?—I believe they are.

10240. Do you know whether they have been buying troopers from Canada lately?—I do not.

10241. You know Captain [illegible]?—I do well.

10242. Would he know?—He would.

10243. Is he the chief man for the Dutch Government buying here—does he usually buy from you?—Always.

10244. Have you ever bought any ponies in Donegal?—I never did, but I bought ponies in [illegible].

10245. From Sligo?—Yes.

10246. You have not been further north than that?—No; I was once in Derry.

10247. How did you buy many ponies there?—No; I was [illegible] [illegible] for [illegible], and [illegible] [illegible] [illegible], but I bought none of them.

10248. What price would you give in the old days for [illegible] ponies, roughly speaking?—From £10 to £20, or easy to £30, if I could get a good one.

10249. But an average price of £10 or £15?—Yes; then the expense was dreadful out of it—all this [illegible] [illegible] and bringing them [illegible] miles across a [illegible].

10250. What did it cost you on your head bringing them up to Dublin?—[illegible].

10251. Did you buy them under 3 or 4 years old?—No, I would not buy 4 year old ponies, they would [illegible] [illegible] [illegible].

10252. You would not buy anything under 4 years old?—No.

10253. If the same class of ponies were bred in [illegible] now, could you afford to give a bigger price for them?—I would, if it was a good one—money would [illegible] [illegible].

10254. For the same class would you afford to give a bigger price now than you did then?—Well, yes, not a bit more.

10255. You would not give more than £8 or £10, or £15 to £18—£20 or £25, and taking them up here and feed them for a while, for they would be [illegible].

10256. It would take six months to get them into condition?—It would not—it would take three at least.

10257. I am here [illegible] [illegible] of [illegible] [illegible] [illegible]—do you think it would be [illegible] [illegible] [illegible] from the ponies left there now the class of pony ponies that is now wanted?—If you had a good one as he was you would breed a good pony plenty of them; if you had the good old sort and gave her a thoroughbred horse, you would breed a Grand National winner from them.

10258. Do you think there are many of those good ones left?—Not to my knowledge.

10259. And you had an opportunity of seeing them all in Tipperary?—I had. My son and I are going there thirty years, this [illegible] of every month; until the last two or three years we did not go at all.

10260. And did you go up to the West, and through the country?—We did, every place—Connemara, Roscommon, Ardrahan, and Sligo, and I [illegible] in them to-day.

10261. You are in favour of registering mares?—Yes; if you get a good mare I would make them keep her.

10262. And you think it is important that a mare should be a good goer?—A straight goer; I would not want her to be a high goer.

10263. And you think that a good half-bred mare is the right sort to look for for a brood mare to mate with a thoroughbred horse?—I do, sir, for a hunter or for a harness horse; I don't mean for a draught.

10264. Yes, we are talking of hunters and harness horses now?—Yes, or for a [illegible].

10265. How would you breed those mares?—I will tell you very easy. If I had the ways of doing it I would want a couple of men that would be a judge, and I would buy a good mare everywhere I would see her, and register and give her to a farmer, and tell him he should keep her. Then give him the produce of her and let him work her as he liked, but keep her in a proper condition.

10266. You would buy a good mare and station her in the country with a farmer who would keep her?—Yes, and good big mares, no small ones.

10267. Would there be any dark horse blood in them or Clydesdale?—Very little; all sorts you may buy them with that if you like, but you need not if you don't like.

10268. You think you could get good mares without any Clydesdale blood?—If you like a good half-bred mare.

10269. Would you be in favour of registering Clydesdales?—What occasion would you have of doing that?

10270. I am asking you, would you?—I would not.

10271. You think there is no occasion for them in this country?—Yes, for farmers.

10272. What would you do for the farmers who want to breed work horses?—I don't see what would be going to run away with them, with the blood; there is no [illegible] to run away with them.

10273. But you would not help them to breed better ones?—I don't know where you would get better ones than a good strong mare and draught horse for the work.

10274. You think the draught horses in Ireland are as good as they can be?—I have not much experience of them, only I see them good enough.

10275. You don't think they want any improvement?—They may be improved, but I don't know much of them.

10276. I want to know what you would do for farmers who want to breed that class?—[illegible] horses his own mind; the best working horse is the [illegible] by one horse.

10277. You would not like to advise except about hunters and harness horses?—That is it what I most expect and [illegible].

10278. CHAIRMAN.—I think I understood you to say that in years gone by you had found ponies that had originally come from the West, you found them in Wexford and Wicklow?—I did not, sir; but I said that they went the train out of that country, yearlings and two year olds and six months old foals, all through Wicklow and Wexford and the country, and destroyed it.

10279. Was that from the West?—From the county Galway and the county Mayo; those county dealers did it coming with wagons and selling them yearlings and two-year-olds—that is what I said.

10280. I think that was the question I asked you, whether they came from the West?—They did, sir; they came from the county Galway and county Mayo, anywhere that they brought a poor little thing, they brought it up there and sold them, sold some up to two and three year olds and they only six months old.

10281. That was after they introduced all sorts of Clydesdale and foreign blood in the West?—I am telling you my opinion. Whatever [illegible] in that country was the Clydesdale mixed up through them; of course they have found the sights now and they are not in it at all, for they would not have them.

10282. I take it that it was the mixture of those stallions that came to Wicklow and Wexford and destroyed the ponies?—That is the very thing.

10283. Then you think that the young horses from the West are likely to permeate through all the other horse breeding districts in Ireland?—Well, they did, as long as I remember; they are coming up and going to England too.

10284. Do I understand you to say that you do not approve of Hackney sires?—I did, sir. I said of course that I had no [illegible] of those whatsoever, that I would rather have a good thoroughbred horse than the Hackneys, because you can breed as good a harness one off a thoroughbred horse as you can off a Hackney. A good thoroughbred horse if you have him will stay and go where the other will. [illegible] up the [illegible] when they go a piece, and you would not like to be behind the [illegible] on a dark night.

10285. Have you seen any of the Congested Districts sires in the West?—I did.

10286. What is your opinion of them?—They are very nice horses, carry themselves well and go very well, and what any man would buy, but if he wants to show off, such as to go through a town or [illegible]; their action is too high to stay; I would rather have one that would skim on the ground lower.

10287. What do you think causes that?—Something in their blood, I suppose, makes them step high.

10288. Cow-hocked?—No, if they had they would not step; you never saw a good shouldered one stepping high yet—hardly.

10289. Then are you afraid of the produce of these horses percolating through the other parts of Ireland and doing damage to horse-breeding?—No, I think not.

10290. Have you found ponies in Wicklow?—I did, sir; but what harm will they do?

10291. You do not like the Clydesdale cross in the ponies?—I did not, nor I would not have them at all.

10292. But you don't think the Hackney blood will do any harm among Wexford way in the ponies?—I don't know, sir; I did not prove that yet.

10293. Would you like it?—I would not.

10294. Lord [illegible].—About the cross of the thoroughbred horse and the half-bred mare, you say you are in favour of the thoroughbred stallion?—Yes, sir.

10295. If you keep on crossing with a thoroughbred stallion, won't you in the end get to a thoroughbred mare and thoroughbred stallion, and you will have to keep [illegible]?—Indeed you will, you will have to keep [illegible] up.

10296. Would you not be in favour of a half-bred horse now and then?—Indeed, they will run into very close blood after some years.

10297. How would you remedy that?—I could not suggest that. If I could tell you I would, but I don't know how you could suggest that.

10298. About Hackney blood—did you find only in riding ponies? Do you find in harness ponies as well, stopping ponies?—Yes; I would like a good stopping pony.

10499. Don't they all stop well?—As well as any; but I would like they would stay.

10500. You would not mind buying a stopping pony?—I would not if I could get a fine profit.

10501. Colonel de Crespigny.—Talking about the breeding of polo ponies, it has been brought up here very often, you as a polo pony salesman and I as a polo pony buyer, may possibly have two different ideas, but do you think polo much in any way enters the breeding of polo ponies?—The only way that I could suggest is a small thoroughbred horse.

10502. What is the first essential in these days for a polo pony—an absolute necessity?—The first thing is you must have a polo pony, the mouth is a kindler, with good shoulders and good riding points.

10503. I don't mean the formation, but in his blood in the game?—You must have him ready.

10504. You can make him handy afterwards, but you must have pace?—Yes.

10505. If a polo pony in these days must be galloping like a racehorse, he is not worth anything?—I told you that when you asked me first.

10506. If you get the Hackney in do you think the Hackney would breed anything that could gallop?—I don't think anything of the sort. It has not the ways of keeping back the strain of the weight to the right places.

10507. Do you think it would breed a pony that could gallop?—It might.

10508. He would gallop all shambling in the air?—Yes.

10509. Then it would not gallop?—I told you so before.

10510. You say that you don't object to the Hackney blood getting into the country where you propose the polo pony should be bred. Do you consider that the formation of the Hackney is likely to help in galloping polo pony?—I told you twice, Colonel, that I did not like them.

10511. But you said you had no objection to their coming in?—No I have not, but I would not buy one of them. I would know them by their heads, necks, and shoulders. If you get to cross-questioning, you [illegible], you will make me very cross. I told you I had no objection to them, and I say it still. You have on one side a question and you are asking me too many questions.

10512. Now, Mahomed, answer me. Do you think that the Hackney horse would be conducive to the breeding of polo ponies?—I would not have them at all.

10513. I only want you to answer—you said you would not have them at all.

10514. Mr. Wrench.—Now, Mr. Mahomed, I am not going to bother you much. I am just going to ask you two questions. When you say that the Hackney won't stay, have you formed that opinion from your own experience or merely from what you hear?—I know it; I can prove it.

10515. From what Hackney [illegible] that I [illegible] of my own [illegible].

10516. You assume they were bred from Hackneys?—Yes, sir. They might not be bred Hackneys. They were ready for a while, but could not stay.

10517. But you assume any that at all Hackneys?—I am only telling you, sir, what I know. You don't want me to answer more.

10518. Were they Hackneys by [illegible] I don't know whether they were or not, they were called Hackney horses. I was only told that.

10519. Do you think now it would pay a breeder in the Western and his produce at five years old for £10 or £15, would it pay the small farmer? It would pay them better if they got more, but when they could not get any more what would they do?

10520. Is that an industry that is worth going on with?—I don't think it is.

10521. Chairman.—Have you anything further you wish to say?—Not a [illegible] more, sir. I will answer any question you ask me.

Veterinary-Lieutenant Dunn, 10th Hussars, examined.

10522. Chairman.—You are Veterinary Surgeon to the 10th Hussars, now stationed at Newbridge?—Yes.

10523. You have had considerable experience in India, I think. To what extent does the Government carry on horse breeding there?—They get sires from home and Australia; I cannot say the number of sires they have there now. In the North Punjaub they had about 100; in the South Punjaub they had not so many, eighty, I suppose; in the North-west Provinces they had some, I don't know the number, and some in Bombay, and one or two in Central Provinces—thoroughbreds, Hackneys, Norfolk trotters, thoroughbred Australians, and Arabs. They were put out in the various districts of India under the superintendents of horse-breeding. I was in the North Punjaub. We travelled the districts, branding approved mares for horse breeding, and each stallion was allowed fifty mares. That is the extent to which it was going on when I left.

10524. Can you give us any idea as to the character of the different sort of horses, that is thoroughbreds, Hackneys, and so on, which were the best adapted to suit the country?—In my mind, undoubtedly the strong thoroughbred English horse or the strong Australian horse are infinitely better adapted to the wants of the country than the Hackney.

10525. What sort of mares are they?—They vary all over India. In [illegible] the mares were quite as good as the mares you will see in England or Ireland. The mares in the Punjab district were very good indeed, but as you get further south, they were weedy [illegible], and [illegible] them. But you get fewer misfits, I think, with the thoroughbred than with the Hackney, and when the produce grew up they were certainly better for military purposes, the better-bred ones, that is the thoroughbred ones than the Hackneys. For instance, after leaving the horse breeding department I was in a regiment mounted on country breds, and the better bred horses at field days were very easily distinguished. Fewer cases in the sick lines, less unfit horses, you got fewer bony diseases, such as splints, side-bones, ringbones, and spavins, while the better bred horses.

10526. That is with the thoroughbred and Australians?—Yes, and the Arab. The only fault I could find with the Arab stock was that they did not grow large enough. The best Arabs were, I think, over 14.2, or something like that, the Arab stock, and they did not get the stock quite large enough to carry the weights.

10527. Then did they put these horses out in the different districts with an eye to the nature of the district so as to correct any faults there might be in the mares?—We had to do that, but they varied in themselves a little. We were told to put the Hackneys where the small mares were. We indented for thirty more thoroughbreds than we got. Generally we [illegible] to send out request to England to Sir John Watson as purchaser, but he could never buy a sufficient number of thoroughbreds, and he made up the deficiency with Hackneys, so we had to utilise them, and put them somewhere, and we put them in those districts where the smaller mares were.

10528. We should like to hear your experience of the

produce of the Hackney?—I don't think the produce was nearly as good as the produce of the thoroughbred. Each district has its own show, or the majority of the districts started horse shows; and there the thoroughbreds always came out, taking the prize. The better class of animal was by a thoroughbred, the prize winners as a rule.

10329. In the examination of the produce could you see any difference?—The produce of the Hackney had the Hackney characteristics—more of the rounded neck, not such fine shoulders as the thoroughbred. The quality and the substance was not so good, was not so good. More action, far more action than the thoroughbred.

10330. You think that the Hackney stallion passed down the action to the produce?—Undoubtedly, to a certain extent; but we found the strong, thoroughbred horse the best horse for the country-bred mares. Kathiawar, the Waler mare, I think, mainly in Kach. As the English thoroughbred, and then the Arabs; but the price the Indian Government gave for the stallions from home was £250, and I don't think that was sufficient; but the system they adopted was to encourage the native farmer to keep his brood mare. That was the chief thing we had to do—not to sell the mare, but to keep her for breeding purposes.

10331. What inducement was there in India to encourage the farmer to keep his mare?—At the time there each district had its own horse show, and the majority of the money was given to this class—the brood mares with foal at foot. Good mares in foal to stallions.

10332. That is, in foal to the Government stallions?—Yes; but in those districts every mare that was put to a thoroughbred stallion was branded "F.T." on the shoulder. Those were the only animals, and the produce of those mares the only animals allowed to be shown at the show, and to keep those mares, more money was given in prizes in that class. For instance, more money was given in the brood mare class than in the yearlings or two-year-olds.

10333. What did that represent in English money for each prize by the show?—It varied as in the different districts; some were richer than others and gave more money; in some they would give as much as £10—and in India that would represent a lot to the natives—to the zemindar—and then private individuals would give prizes. They would leave it to us, the superintendent of horse-breeding, to arrange how it should be given, those sort of things—and we always gave them to the brood mare class.

10334. Colonel St. Quintin.—Will you kindly describe on what principle it was carried out—the whole thing was by [illegible]. Each district had its own money allowed to it by the Government to spend in various ways and things in the district. A certain portion of that money was given for horse breeding in the district. It varied according to the district, whether it was a rich district or a poor district. The Rawal Pindi district was a rich district, and the prizes were very big indeed; and then there they had many private individuals who were interested in horse-breeding, and they themselves would give large prizes and silver medals in the fashion—and put them a medal is thought a lot of by a farmer; and all these private prizes were always given to the brood mare class. That was the way we encouraged them to keep their brood mares. We would never give an extra prize in the gelding class or anything. They might be sold, in fact, the sooner they were sold the better, and the bigger prices they got the more it encouraged the people to breed.

10335. Chairman.—Had these shows anything [illegible] like what you have in [illegible]?—Either the Deputy Commissioner of the District and the Superintendent of the Horse-breeding Department. I don't think there is anything in Ireland or England that would represent it.

Mr. La Touche.—I understood that the Government of India were the proprietors of a number of stallions?—Yes.

10336. How did the private owners of stallions like having Government horses put there in the districts, compete there with people who owned stallions there too?—Yes, with these animals.

10337. Did they show any resentment?—Yes, they did not like it; the ones who kept a private stallion [illegible] enough for his own business—the people who had land under him—he used to keep a [illegible] sort of mongrel animal, and the Government stallion prevented mares going to him.

10338. As a matter of fact was the effect of putting these Government stallions in the districts to drive a number of these mongrel or inferior animals out of the districts?—Oh, undoubtedly.

10339. They disappeared?—Yes, they were very few; I don't think I had more than ten in the North Punjaub.

10340. Ten, the property of private individuals?—Yes.

10341. But there were, I suppose, considerably more before the Government horses were put down?—Oh, yes, sufficient to get all the horses of India.

10342. When these Government horses were placed in these districts was any compensation given to private owners of stallions?—None at all, none whatever. What was recommended several times was to give a tax on the private stallions. It was suggested two or three times to encourage the farmer to keep an approved brood mare by letting him off so much land tax.

10343. Did the owners of mares just pay that [illegible] to the Government stallions?—None whatever, approved mares; anyone was allowed to put a mare that was not branded by a horse on payment of 10 rupees, but so the case did, one or two a year, they'd get their mares branded.

10344. And they were covered free?—They were covered free.

10345. And the military authorities or the Government had no claim upon the produce?—None whatever.

10346. The farmer could sell the produce to whoever he liked?—Yes; except in India it is peculiarly situated, the buyer always happens to be a Government official, the remount department or the Bengal native cavalry; but they could sell their produce to whoever they liked.

10347. You have had considerable opportunities of looking at Irish horses and Irish mares—do you consider that it would be possible to draw any analogy between the ordinary Irish bred mare and the country bred mare of India?—Well, I think the country bred mare of Baluchistan is a mare quite as good as an Irish mare; at the Horse Show, at a place called Dera Ghazi Khan, the brood mare class there was a splendid class—I think 200 brood mares—and there was hardly a bad one in the class.

10348. Colonel St. Quintin.—Did you [illegible] quite as high, a little lower, but very much the same stamp?—Yes, a little lower, well-bred mares of substance and carrying weight.

10349. Mr. La Touche.—You said one of the principal objects of these brood shows was to encourage farmers to keep their mares?—Yes.

10350. Was there any special demand for mares in India, was there any market, any means, as in Ireland, the farmers would sell their mares?—Yes, there is a market in India for them—Calcutta, Bombay, and Madras; in all these places you can sell them. The [illegible] dealers would buy them to send to the places—they are the biggest dealers in the world.

10351. Is a mare as a matter of fact more valuable than a gelding?—In certain parts of India they are; in Baluchistan they are; money would not buy them, they would not sell them there.

10352. Then you don't require to give them prizes in Ireland there to keep them?—Not in that part [illegible].

10353. Colonel St. Quintin.—Would you just [illegible] an instance? Could you tell the prizes that will [illegible] thing as a four year old colt up in the North-West provinces in the fairs, because when I left there was hardly such a thing to be found. They were all taken down to the South of India at one and a half years old and filtered away into the native states.—You you could find them, but not a very good sort. The Bengal cavalry now buy their own. Five years ago the Remount took them up, and now they buy the four year old geldings, and I am sorry to say many mares as well. Branding was chiefly for the purpose of preventing the Bengal cavalry buying mares. That was the only restriction on the sale, that Government officials were not allowed to buy the mares. Recently I put a brand on a mare the owner could not sell that mare to a Government official.

10354. Mr. Le Trobe.—Since you have been in Ireland you have bought a certain number of horses in the country?—Yes.

10355. And you have visited many of the local places and the Dublin show, and have had occasion of seeing the way in which horses are bred in Ireland. Could you make any suggestion as to the way in which—perhaps I ought to say that, that has been suggested to us by a general officer, and other witnesses have suggested similar things, that mares should be taken from the cavalry regiments and artillery regiments and distributed among the farmers for breeding purposes in Ireland?

Colonel St. Quintin.—Cast mares?

Mr. Le Trobe.—No, selected mares.

Witness.—They would be over age, over fifteen years.

10356. Mr. Le Trobe.—No, I beg your pardon. The scheme I alluded to was suggested by a general officer and submitted to this Commission, that the mares were to be between six and ten years old, selected mares from regiments and in the First Army Corps. Do you think that that would be calculated to improve the breed of horses in this country?—These mares were to be given to the farmers, and they would be to keep them?

10357. They are not allowed to sell them?—Suppose they could not keep them properly.

10358. Well, then it is stated, they would be under a certain inspection then, I suppose. Government officials, and the idea is that they pay [illegible], a price for the use of the mares, the produce to be the property of the tenant and be disposed of at his will?—I don't think if the mare was [illegible] she would stay [illegible] on a tenant [illegible] after that. It is very doubtful whether they would hold or not.

10359. Do you think such a suggestion as that, in the first instance would possibly meet with the approval of the colonels of cavalry regiments?—It certainly would not, after they have trained them and everything to have them taken away to be given to the farmers.

10360. At the same time if it could be carried into execution it would certainly place a number of useful mares at the disposal of the farmers?—Oh, I think it would, but I think the disadvantage to the regiments would be great.

10361. What do you think of the brood mares of Ireland from what you have seen of them?—I think they are useful mares. I think the great thing is to get good stallions to mate them with, and I think there ought to be some encouragement, something the same way as they did in India, to keep the brood mares. The prizes now in the brood mare classes are absurdly small, £10 and that sort of thing. The prize ought to be £50 or something like that. You will get higher prizes than that in England at some of the shows.

10362. Do you think, on the whole, supposing there was a sum of money at the disposal of a department in horse breeding in Ireland, do you think it would be better that a large proportion of that money should be devoted to the purpose of the stallions or the mares?—I think in the present time we should have a great [illegible] stallions to begin with.

10363. And given a sound stallion, you would spend the money on the mares?—Yes, I should spend the money certainly on the mares, and the stallions ought to be registered and ought to be sound. There is no encouragement to the farmers to keep a good mare.

10364. Mr. Wrench.—How long were you in India?—Six years.

10365. All that time were you engaged in this horse breeding?—Three years.

10366. And part of that time in the North Punjab?—Always in the Punjab, for part of the time I had the whole of the Punjab, and for part of the time I had the North Punjab, it was found to be too big for one.

10367. During part of that time were you partly under Colonel Queripel and partly under Colonel Hallen?—Yes.

10368. When you speak of thoroughbred Australians, you mean thoroughbred horses bred in Australia?—Yes.

10369. They were practically of the same breed as our own thoroughbred?—I suppose so, if you trace their pedigree back.

10370. Does Sir John Watson buy for the Indian Government in England?—Yes.

10371. And is there a regular requisition sent to him each year, telling him what stallions to buy?—Yes.

10372. As a matter of fact, I think they don't take thoroughbred stallions for India over 15·3?—I had many over.

10373. But I mean for the last three years?—I could not say for the last two years; certainly the last year I sent in my indent I did not restrict them to 15·3; it was never mentioned.

10374. You don't know that at present they don't buy them over 15·3?—No; in fact, I always, in my annual report, asked for big stallions, and the big stallions I had I know got better produce than the smaller ones.

10375. And you thought the Arab stock too small?—That was the only objection I had to them.

10376. Are not the Hackneys at present imported into India, chiefly Norfolk trotters?—There were some Norfolk trotters and some Hackneys; they came out in the descriptive roll as Hackneys or Norfolk trotters, and some as roadsters, and I could see very little difference in any of them.

10377. They were largely bought from Norfolk?—I could not say; they were all of the same stamp.

10378. Do you know what price they are paying for thoroughbreds—what the limit is at present?—I think it was £300.

10379. You don't know now that it goes up to 350 guineas?—No, I hope it does; it was not enough in those days. There was no limit for the Arab stallions.

10380. Do you know what the numbers were last year purchased of each breed, thoroughbred and Hackney?—I have no idea since I left the Department what they are doing.

10381. You don't know that Sir John Watson had been out there lately?—I had a letter saying he was out there lately inspecting the studs.

10382. Did you ever see any good native-bred stallions?—A very few; we were ordered to purchase them if we could; I purchased one or two in the three years.

10383. Did you see any special native breed that would be worth preserving or trying to improve?—I think the Beloochistan breed if we could get stallions there, but they won't keep stallions; they insist on having them castrated.

10384. Are there not stallions of the same class as those mares?—The Belooch stallions are of the same breed as the mares.

10385. It has never been tried breeding them pure with stallions of their own breed?—They did it themselves before the Government interfered.

Apr. 8, 1897.

Vet.-Lieut. Dunn.

10386. And have the Government by interfering improved the breed?—I think they have; the majority of this enormous breed now there were by English sires.

10387. They were not by the original Beloochi?—No.

10388. But no attempt has been made, except by supplying an exceptionally good stallion, to keep the breed?—No, in no part of India.

10389. CHAIRMAN.—I think you said that you saw as many as 300 mares with their produce at one of the shows in India?—Yes.

10390. How far have the farmers to bring in their mares and foals?—Many miles, I could not say how many; all over the district, and the district is an enormous area.

10391. They travel an immense distance?—An immense distance; the same as if they brought mares from all over Ireland to Dublin.

10392. It was the prizes that were given that induced them to bring the mares in to the show?—The prizes, and you see they bring their young stock in to sell to the remount department, or to the Bengal cavalry, or to private buyers.

10393. And you select their mares, too, I suppose, for next year?—I branded on that occasion two or three hundred young mares; it was like an immense fair or horse show—it was in India like the Dublin Horse Show.

10394. I take it that your method for improving the breed of horses would be to use a big, sound thoroughbred stallion, and to encourage farmers to keep their sound brood mares by subsidising them?—That is so.

10395. That is what you recommend?—Yes, to work in Ireland.

10396. Mr. LA TOUCHE.—And a very substantial subsidy?—Yes, I think the present is absolutely useless; the little paltry prizes they give now I would rather give it in increased money for premiums. I think you want to give more money for brood mares.

10397. CHAIRMAN.—Have you anything else you would like to say?—[illegible] you want the big thoroughbred stallions in Connemara and those places, you want the very small thoroughbred stallion to mate with the mares; I am not speaking from experience, but I should imagine that would be so.

10398. Well, you would stick to the thoroughbred?—I would stick to the thoroughbred for the polo pony. In India in the districts, not through the Government but privately by each district, they buy Arab ponies from the Bombay market, and place them all over the district to improve the breed of ponies in India.

10399. Where do those Arabs come from?—Bombay market; from [illegible] ponies.

10400. Where do they import them from?—From Arabia; it is quite a sight in Bombay, the Arab market.

10401. Colonel ST. QUINTIN.—I should like to ask you one question touching on the trooper question, don't you consider that for the trooper it is absolutely necessary you should have quality and staying power, and light even under?—I think it is absolutely necessary; I think it is essential for a troop horse to be well bred to be a good one.

10402. And he wants light easy action, not extravagant?—I think so, that was what I always found with the [illegible] in India; [illegible] the Norfolk trotter, and [illegible] the thoroughbred, and the thoroughbreds always were down the hill-tracks.

10403. You would advocate nothing but the thoroughbred for troopers, certainly.

The Commissioners adjourned.

TWENTIETH DAY—WEDNESDAY, MARCH 3RD, 1897.

Sitting at 18, Hanover Square, W., London.

PRESENT:—THE RIGHT HON. THE EARL OF DUNRAVEN, K.P., in the Chair; THE RIGHT HON. LORD ASHTOWN; THE MOST NOBLE THE MARQUESS OF LONDONDERRY, K.G.; MR. J. L. CAREW, M.P.; RIGHT HON. LORD RATHDONNELL; HON. H. W. FITZWILLIAM; COLONEL ST. QUINTIN; MR. PERCY LA TOUCHE; MR. F. S. WRENCH.

MR. HUGH NEVILLE, Secretary.

The LORD TREDEGAR examined.

10404. CHAIRMAN.—You live in Monmouthshire, do you not?—Yes.

10405. And you have been for a long time interested in the subject of horse breeding?—Yes, I have.

10406. Could you tell us what classes of horses you breed, and what classes of stallions you keep?—I keep three classes, thoroughbreds, Shire horses, and Hackneys.

10407. Would you tell the Commission your experience in breeding from these three classes of stallions?—Do you mean experience of breeding generally as a [illegible] sort of operation, do you mean that?

10408. I rather wanted to know the results?—I suppose I am here merely with a brief for the Hackney people because I am on the Council of the Hackney Society, and have been now for three years, and therefore I have taken a great interest in the Hackneys, more particularly.

10409. How many Hackney stallions do you keep?—Two.

10410. What class of mares do you put them to?—Almost anything that comes to them. All of my tenants have the use of them, and all the farmers near where I reside may have them, as many as they can. I find a Hackney is a very useful animal that way.

10411. Lord LONDONDERRY.—What kind of a mare do they send, as a rule, to them?—Small mares, 15 hands, used for light plough work and light trap work into the markets.

10412. Do you keep good Hackney mares yourself?—I have only one. I don't keep any mares really to breed from them; I have enough to do with the tenants who send their mares to the horse. I have no stud [illegible], and I [illegible] my country suitable for a stud of that description. I don't think it is suitable for breeding horses in a large way. The soil is not good for it.

10413. CHAIRMAN.—Do you know the [illegible] districts in Ireland at all?—No, I don't at all.

don't know that I ever was there; it is a long time ago since I was in Ireland. I don't think I was ever in what may be called a congested district, but I imagine they are rather similar to our mountain districts in Wales.

10414. I dare say you have heard that the ordinary class of mares in the congested districts is a very small and rather inferior animal?—Yes, I have heard that.

10415. Would you think that the Hackney stallion would be the best class of stallion to be put to such a mare in order to breed a useful animal?—I should say so decidedly, looking at my own district, a good part of it is Brecknockshire, where I own mountain lands, where the ponies are reared on the mountains, Welsh ponies. I think the cross likely to improve them is as a rule good Hackneys, pure-bred Hackney stallions.

10416. Do you think the Hackney crosses well with the Welsh pony?—I think so. I am very strongly impressed that way myself. Some five or six years ago a large district came into my possession, about 16,000 acres of moor, cliff-covered land in Brecknockshire, which adjoins my manor, where Welsh ponies graze, and I did intend to have gone in largely for improving the breed by buying four or five of the very best Hackney stallions I could, and putting them there. It so happened that some dispute arose and I gave it up. But I was so impressed with the idea of how useful it would be to support Hackney stallions into pony rearing countries that I was fully intending to have gone in for it there.

10417. Could you tell us at all about the produce of the Hackney sire and the Welsh pony?—It breeds the best of animal in the world, for ladies driving in Bath-carts, victorias and broughams, small dog-carts. I had a Hackney stallion called "Young Denmark," five or six years ago, an extraordinary fine goer, with high action, and all round me all the farmers have little stepping horses by him that they drive to market now, and which they can sell quite easily to dealers.

10418. What age can they sell them at?—About three years old, as soon as they can; you soon find out that they want to make money as soon as they can nowadays, so it does not pay to keep them.

10419. What do they get for them?—£40 or £50 for three-year-olds, they can sell them if they only at all.

10420. Do you know where they go to?—Mostly to London and the other big towns.

10421. Do they sell direct to dealers?—Direct to dealers, I think; they come down so soon that they come I don't see them.

10422. Do they sell them by fairs, or do the dealers come round?—I think the dealers come round. I think it would be absolutely useless to send a thoroughbred stallion into that part of Brecon I first alluded to, the thoroughbred stallion would be absolutely useless unless he was very small, and they could thoroughbred stallion in a neck of hiring your can only pick up by chance.

10423. You would prefer the Hackney sire to the thoroughbred sire at equal prices?—Certainly; but there are districts like Carmarthenshire, Pembrokeshire, and Cardiganshire, where they breed big boned horses. I should never think of sending a Hackney stallion into that district, they have got really good thoroughbred horses there, and breed very good hunters. I imagine I am here to say what I think would be useful for the congested districts of Ireland.

10424. Our inquiry is not confined to the congested districts, we are dealing with the whole of Ireland. I should gather from what you have said that you would consider a suitable thoroughbred sire would be the best sire in the country capable of breeding high-class hunters?—Yes, for countries which are in the habit of breeding hunters I should stick to the thoroughbred stallion.

10425. And from your experience of Wales, you should think that in the congested districts the Hackney sire would be the most suitable?—A good Hackney sire would certainly be the best, certainly for producing animals that would enable the farmers to sell readily; I don't see what you can do with the thoroughbred horse and a small pony, except to get racing ponies, which of course are unsaleable to a certain extent if they are not like a racehorse, but where you breed one that can run you breed forty that cannot.

10426. Have you any idea of how the Welsh pony was originally produced?—No, I cannot say, I think they have been there from time immemorial in the Welsh hills, they run wild and loose, not looked after as they ought to be, the stallions particularly.

10427. How about the Welsh cob?—It would be very difficult to define the Welsh cob. I gave a prize at my show for pony stallions, I never got more than one or two shown there, and these are certainly not animals I should care to see to improve the breed; that is one of the reasons why I am so fond of the Hackney stallion for improving it, for I think the breed itself is neglected, bred as it is not, by running loose on the mountains, that they want some fresh blood, and it should be a stallion that has not only knee action, but hind action and riding shoulders.

10428. The congested districts, as you know, extend all over the western seaboard of Ireland, from north to south; and assuming that the Hackney sire would be the most useful class of sire in that part of the country; and assuming, secondly, that the greater part of the rest of the country is adapted for producing hunters, would you, from your experience, think that there would be any danger to the rest of the country from introducing Hackney blood into the congested districts?—I should think not, certainly not, if you mean that the blood would get spread about it. It would be a better breed than is there now.

10429. You think if the Hackney strain permeated through the districts devoted to breeding high-class hunters it might do no harm?—No, I think not, it would do good, you would have better mares from them spread about the country than you have now.

10430. Have your local shows been beneficial, do you think?—Perhaps there was originally started as a fat stock show, or fat cattle show, it has very little to do with horses until lately. I give prizes for cattle, chiefly one of my farms, it is held at a very bad time of the year, just before Christmas, farmers don't show very many, I don't look upon it as much use in the horse-breeding line, it is more for cattle.

10431. Do you do anything to try and induce farmers to breed from their best mares?—Of course I reserve the right of refusing any mares that come to my stallion, that is all.

10432. I mean in the shape, in the way of prizes?—There are prizes for brood mares; but I find the same animal generally wins every year. There are not many shown—two or three. The farmers look upon it as cigarettes or shooting, they always say, "there is some sharp man or big farmer that is going to take it." That is my experience of local shows.

10433. Lord Londonderry.—Do you yourself keep these stallions at Pentegarth?—Yes.

10434. That is where you hunt?—Yes.

10435. Do the farmers in the country hunt to a great extent?—No, not many of them. Very few farmers hunt.

10436. They don't breed hunting mares—they have not hunting mares of their own?—No, except just now they have a few of them since I got these stallions.

10437. Are they a large class of farmer?—No, small. Most of them work on the farm.

10438. And they have these ponies you have been speaking of?—Yes; a sort of light cob horse. They prefer the Hackney a good deal to the thoroughbred.

[illegible]

10439. Mares of 15 hands?—Yes.

10440. Well-bred sort?—No, not well-bred, because they are used as leaders in the plough in the hilly parts.

10441. Where do you suppose they have been got by originally?—By anything they can get. Have they taken any care in breeding them?—No; they get got by any stallion that came around.

10442. Do they send them to the Hackney?—Yes, by choice. They have twice the work the thoroughbred has.

10443. And the result you say, the produce of those mares is sold on to the London dealers?—Yes, that is where they go.

10444. Have you ever seen the result of those mares by your Hackneys crossed with a thoroughbred stallion?—No, I don't know that I have noticed it. There is my own hunting stallion and two of my best servants' horses which are by one of my Hackneys.

10445. Out of what kind of mares?—Out of the very commonest mares—one that came to the kennel.

10446. Of course, you know that in Ireland the great fear of the hunter-breeding people is that the get of these Hackneys will get out of the districts in which these Hackneys are found, and will be the means of ruining hunters in the hunter-breeding parts of Ireland. From your knowledge of the Hackneys and hunters do you think they are justified in maintaining that fear?—That is not to be feared I think myself; but I cannot tell about a particular district. I fancy the complaint in Ireland is you have got so few good mares.

10447. Do you limit your horse at all in the number of mares he does in a year, or as many as he gets?—I should be obliged to limit them, otherwise there would be too many. I don't limit them, only my man says he cannot do any more. We have another stallion now.

10448. In fact, they are intensely popular in this district?—Yes. The thoroughbred has hardly enough to do, and the Hackneys have more than they can do.

10449. In fact, they don't really take advantage of the thoroughbred stallion because they have not got mares of the proper shape to send to them?—Yes; they breed a light, leggy, weedy thing that does not sell at all. A [illegible] is worth about 50 [illegible] as a four-year-old.

10450. Mr. Fitzwilliam.—What, as a rule, are the mares about you?—Oh, mostly about 15 hands, light [illegible]. I believe originally from a Welsh pony.

10451. And there is no great amount of hunter-breeding there?—No.

10452. You say you think that if you introduced a Hackney stallion the [illegible] would not persuade the adjoining country where there are hunters breeding?—No, I don't think so. I don't think it would do any great harm, if it did. The really good Hackney is a beautiful animal. He goes back to the Darley Arabian and "The Shales" and "[illegible]" very old stock.

10453. Lord Rathdonnell.—Have you ever seen any of the ponies that come from the west of Ireland?—No, I don't know that I have. I don't know the breed at all.

10454. You don't know how they compare with [illegible]?

10455. Mr. La Touche.—You have bought Irish hunters I suppose, Lord Middleton?—Yes, I suppose so, what are called Irish hunters.

10456. I suppose you acknowledge, like most people, that the Irish hunter is a very excellent animal?—Oh, yes.

10457. But you don't think that the excellence is due to the fact of its having no Hackney blood in the pedigree, nothing but thoroughbred blood?—Oh, I should think that probably it was.

10458. But at the same time you don't think that a mixture of Hackney blood would have a prejudicial effect upon the horse?—Well, that is rather a difficult question to answer, I think.

10459. Some people in Ireland maintain that the excellence of the Irish hunter, the superiority to the ordinary horses as bred in England, is greatly due to the fact of his dam and grand-dam being descended from thoroughbred horses from time immemorial, and they consequently kept with great care [illegible] fresh blood being mingled with the pedigrees of their horses?—Well, I have just said that two of my best hunters are by a Hackney stallion, and that being the first cross I don't see why it should hurt, if you went on breeding; supposing those had been mares, I don't think you would have a worse style of hunter from them, they happened to be geldings otherwise I could have bred from them.

10460. I am afraid that in breeding horses, like any other animal, where the first cross might come out fairly well, in the second and third crosses you get out all the bad points and lose all the good ones of the original strains?—Yes, I know that is very often said, but I never found it myself either in hounds or horses. It was said that a first cross between a Welsh and English hound was first-rate, but if you bred it again it was bad, but I never found it myself.

10461. I don't say in hounds, but in dogs if you cross a pointer and setter you will get a very useful animal, but if you breed from that again then will the produce be useless?—You probably breed a mongrel, I don't see why it should be useless unless it is a [illegible].

10462. Do your Hackney stallions serve at the same fees as the thoroughbred ones?—Yes, they have all to serve for nothing, I may say.

10463. Lord [illegible].—Do you find the Hackney which has improved with the pony increases the size, the mount?—Oh, yes, most certainly.

10464. Then it makes any other noticeable difference?—Of course a Hackney is bigger than a pony to start with.

10465. You may get a small Hackney, but a big one do you find it gives substance?—Oh, yes, that is one of the greatest advantages they have, such splendid forelegs and feet; of course the very [illegible] a good Hackney, a bad Hackney is about as bad a thing as you can have.

10466. You say you have two horses in your own stable by your own Hackney stallion?—Yes.

10467. Are they good serviceable horses?—Most serviceable, bold and splendid hunters, they have got just the ideal action that the [illegible] back, and they can jump [illegible] some horses can do out of a gallop.

10468. Do a day's work and stay?—Yes, and all day too, and don't look like doing it, they don't look like being great powerful horses.

10469. Mr. [illegible].—What is the average extent of the holdings in your district?—About 50 acres to 100 acres.

10470. Then they are pretty well off?—They don't say so.

10471. Do they use the produce of the Hackney mares for farming purposes—for drawing purposes?—Oh, yes, and for light plough work and light traps into market.

10472. And they are sold about three years old in the London market?—Yes.

10473. You don't think they are suitable then for heavy farm work such as ploughing and carting?—No, I don't think so.

10474. Mr. Wrench.—When you talk of fifty acre holdings, about what rent per acre are they, what class of land, is it very good land?—It is rather good grass land, but it is mainly a [illegible], and it is not suitable for breeding horses.

10475. Have they mountain run with the right to moor-land, any rough land with it?—The moorland farmers have fields on the land to get their stock in in winter.

10476. Then they don't winter them on the hills?—Oh, no, they all come down from the hills.

10477. But they leave the young stock out all the winter?—Yes, entirely.

10478. And do you find the produce of these Hackneys are very hardy?—Yes, I think so; considerably hardy you mean?

10479. Yes?—Yes, I think so, just as hardy as any other.

10480. Have you been able to see if there is any difference between the produce of the thoroughbred and the produce of the Hackney in the way of hardiness?—Oh, yes, certainly, the produce of the thoroughbred cannot stand out in the winter like the produce of the Hackney.

10481. Then in these cases where the horses would be liable to great hardships, do you think a Hackney would be the best cross?—Oh, yes, certainly.

10482. I think Mr. La Touche asked you if you thought the excellence of Irish hunters was due to the fact that nothing but thoroughbred blood was in their pedigrees. Do you know, as a matter of fact, that numbers of the stallions in Ireland are draught horses or half-bred draught horses?—No, I didn't know that.

10483. You don't know that for a great many years cart-horses have been introduced into Ireland and been all over the breeding districts?—No, I don't know anything about Ireland that way.

10484. Have you bred many hunters yourself from thoroughbred horses?—Yes, a good many, but not with much success. I have never been very particular in the mares; I have used some that were broken down, or favourite mares.

10485. Is it your experience that a pretty harder makes a good harness horse, a horse not good enough for a hunter?—It depends upon what you call a good harness horse.

10486. Does he make a valuable harness horse?—A useful sturdy, but not a valuable harness horse.

10487. Do you think action is a great thing?—Yes, everything in a harness horse.

10488. Do you think action is one of the most valuable things that a horse, horses can say be?—I think so.

10489. You think a horse with action will sell much better than any other horse?—I think so undoubtedly.

10490. How many years have you had these Hackney stallions in Wales?—Fourteen or fifteen years now.

10491. Did the farmers use them much at first?—No, I don't think they did.

10492. What has made them so popular now?—Because they found that they can sell their produce I think. When a horse gets . . . mares you will find a sale for the animals by that horse.

10493. Do you think it would pay them at all as well to try and breed polo ponies?—No, I don't think so. I don't think my country is suitable for that.

10494. But I suppose there are the mares, are there not?—No, not suitable for breeding polo ponies.

10495. There have been very good polo ponies, half-bred Welsh ponies, have there not?—Well, I am talking about my own district near me; there are no mountain ponies bred near me at all, which is very cut off.

10496. They are rather a larger size, but still the mountain pony blood comes into a good deal?—I suppose it does down there.

10497. We have heard a great deal about the soft blood in Hackneys, as you call it, where the soft blood in Hackneys comes in?—No, I don't know at all about that.

10498. Is it your experience that Hackneys are soft or not?—No, certainly not. I buy nearly all my carriage horses, driving horses and hack horses from Norfolk, and I find they can trot on as long as any other horse.

10499. And do a good journey?—Oh yes. There are of course useful bad horses of Norfolk Hackneys.

10500. I suppose you have seen a great many thoroughbred horses?—Yes.

10501. Do you think there are as many bad horses in proportion among thoroughbreds as there are among Hackneys?—I should say more.

10502. Have you been able to form an opinion as to their soundness, whether the Hackney is a sound horse or not?—I think they are very sound. I should say as sound as any breed, roadsters or cart-horses.

10503. And their produce generally sound?—Generally sound. I think they have very good feet and limbs, which so many other breeds don't have.

10504. *Chairman.*—Have you any preference for any particular locality as regards Hackneys, Norfolk or Yorkshire?—Yorkshire I prefer to the Norfolk. I think they are more riding horses, the Norfolk are more driving.

10505. Yours came from Yorkshire, do they?—No, I have only one from Yorkshire. The ones I had before were from Norfolk, but I think they are more riding-looking horses in Yorkshire than in Norfolk.

10506. And how many generations of the produce of the Hackney stallions have you had experience of, you have kept Hackney stallions a great number of years?—About fourteen or fifteen years, it has been going on now for that time.

10507. And putting the progeny of the Hackney to the Hackney again, I suppose?—Yes, I think so. Do you mean putting a mare by a Hackney to the same Hackney again or to a Hackney.

10508. To a Hackney?—Oh, yes, I think so, and with a good Hackney they go on getting just the same.

10509. I think you said you considered that the Hackney was a hardier animal than the thoroughbred, and could stand more vicissitudes of climate?—Yes, stand more climate, more bad weather, out-of-doors. I don't think a thoroughbred can stand any; you cannot leave a thoroughbred out in the fields all through the winter, he would fall away in condition, and die probably.

10510. But the cross between a thoroughbred and a half-bred mare for instance in Ireland. I am not talking of the stallion, either Hackney or thoroughbred stallion, but the produce?—Oh, I should think he would be softer than the produce of the Hackney because the Hackney comes from a hardier strain, a rougher strain like the cart-horse.

10511. Can you say that from practical experience, your own experience?—Yes, I think so, I have seen things on my own farm, that I have left out, falling away, while your cart-horse and Hackneys were doing well.

10512. Is there any other information you can give us or anything you would like to say?—No, I don't think so.

sole idea of saving time, and keeping the matter clear.

10515. I think it would be convenient if you give us your information according to the order of subjects which you put down in this document. You were consulted, were you not, by the Congested Districts Board as to what class of stallion would be suitable to the congested districts?—I was. I have the letter in which I was consulted, and my reply is here. I don't know whether you would care to hear it. My only reason for submitting it is that the letter which I wrote before my tour of inspection might just as well have been written after it.

10516. CHAIRMAN.—We have had your reply?—Yes.

Mr. LA TOUCHE.—We have not had the letter Mr. Burdett-Coutts replied to.

10517. CHAIRMAN.—I am not sure; I think we have.

Mr. NEVILLE (Secretary.)—No; we have not got it.

Witness.—It was the first communication I ever received on the subject from Mr. Wrench. It ran:—

"31st December, 1891.

"DEAR SIR,—The Congested Districts Board for Ireland are about to make the experiment of locating stallions in a few stations in the congested districts for the purpose of improving the breed of ponies. They propose to limit the price which they will give for the stallions to £150, and would be glad if they could purchase under that price. May I venture to ask you where it is possible to obtain stallions from 14.2 to 15 hands high, best calculated to produce cobs and ponies. The stallions must have good shapes, notably good shoulders, and good action. Perhaps you will kindly at the same time say whether you think the objects of the Board will best be attained by purchasing Arabs, small thoroughbreds, or small Hackneys? There is no doubt but that the latter would be the most popular in the districts, if they could be had. I trust you will kindly excuse the liberty I have taken in writing to you, but feel sure that the scheme of the Board is one in which you will take an interest.

"Believe me, truly yours,

"FREDERICK WRENCH."

10518. Perhaps you better read your reply and read pertinent points of any reply which you will think fit in full in the printed document.—"It is a little difficult for me to advise you definitely without being acquainted with the exact type of ponies [illegible] which it is desired to breed, and without knowing what class of animals will find the best market in the special districts. Assuming, however, on these two points—(1) That the animals will consist of under-sized stock, those of hardy quality and courage, and in addition mostly [illegible] light of bone, and (2) That it is desired to raise the standard of excellence, that while the stock produced will be more serviceable for the various purposes which are at present to be served, breeders will also have an opportunity of getting more and better horses with the action and shape which would fetch good prices from the harness dealers, and so gradually draw a better class of dealers into the districts,—I have no hesitation in strongly advising the use of the Hackney stallion. I do not believe in the Arab; nor do I think the result just mentioned would be in any way advanced by the use of a small thoroughbred. The thoroughbred is not the horse to get harness stock, because in 99 cases out of 100, his action is deficient in knee, which now makes the price of the harness horse all over the world; and besides, because his tendency is to get them high on the leg and light of bone. The Hackney corrects the latter deficiencies, gives width, strength, weight-carrying and draught power; and in addition gives action. It goes without saying that you must get the right sort of Hackney, because there are a great many of the wrong sort. There are very many important considerations in choosing a Hackney, such as bone, blood, suitability for conformation, [illegible], which [illegible] and shapes."

10519. You subsequently made a report?—Yes, three months afterwards I visited [illegible], of which the following is a paragraph:—Oughterard, Clifden, Recess, [illegible], Leenane, Westport, Newport, Mulranny, Achill Sound, Belmullet, Bangor Erris, [illegible], Crossmolina, Ballina, Foxford, and Swinford, [illegible] the neighbouring [illegible] their [illegible] and I carefully examined them. I should rather like to read this because I visited the district which I gave [illegible] this Board and the small thoroughbred for a particular reason which was disclosed during the tour. This is an extract from my report on the tour:—

"I proceed briefly to explain the principles which have guided me in the opinions I have placed before the Board. It would, I think, have been unwise to attempt to make any violent change in the kind of horse produced in these wild districts, where there exists a common type of pony or little horse, greatly deteriorated in some respects, but still possessing many valuable points which can be [illegible] on, in conjunction with new and improved features to be acquired by the use of a superior class of stallion. To attempt to produce heavy cart or draught horses from these ponies [illegible] long [illegible], or (by the use of the ordinary thoroughbred sire) to look for a supply of the high priced hunters for which other parts of Ireland are justly famed, would [illegible]. Such an attempt would result in the loss of most of all the valuable features of the existing breed, while none of the advantages aimed at would be attained. Moreover neither the land, nor the means of the farmers, nor the conditions under which horses are at present raised, would support big horses. The object should therefore be to improve the existing type by the introduction of quality, substance, and action; that while the horses produced will be as good, if not better, for the work they have to do in the country, they will also include many specimens which will bring to the breeders a higher price than that at present obtained. In addition to [illegible] cobs and [illegible] harness [illegible], the production of the special [illegible] as the polo pony will be another direction and by providing suitable stallions [illegible]. In my opinion there is no reason why Connemara and Mayo should not in a few years become the recognised breeding ground of the best cobs and polo ponies to be found in Ireland."

With [illegible] to a [illegible] of the districts which I visited that there had been [illegible] a supply of polo ponies, [illegible]. I do not consider the Hackney stallion suitable for the production of polo ponies, and I therefore advised Arabs or very small thoroughbreds, as, when one [illegible] further in [illegible] opinion, [illegible] of polo [illegible] I am given to understand that this was done, but that generally where both a [illegible] and a Hackney were [illegible] the [illegible] preferred the Hackney. Of course I cannot speak of that for a certainty. I don't know if I may explain a little further my advice with regard to type. I found in those districts what I call a "fixed type," and it may be taken as [illegible] that whenever you have a fixed type you can [illegible] with [illegible] the results of [illegible] that type with another fixed type. What I mean by a fixed type is a horse whose characteristics of shape, substance, action, quality, and so on, have come to him by virtue of heredity, have been repeated over and over again in his ancestors on both sides [illegible] they have become fixed; and by reason of his having [illegible] them by heredity he [illegible] characteristics, and he is able to hand them on to his stock. I found certain deficiencies in that fixed type, since my [illegible] experience has grown [illegible] and I believe that these deficiencies would be best supplied by the use of the Hackney stallion. The fixed type in the West is a small pony with great courage and stamina, good limbs and feet, and some signs of quality, but lamentably deficient in bone, action, shape, and substance. I should like to state a somewhat curious fact. Those farmers who had never been out of the district and who appeared to know very little, when they were asked what sort of stallion they wanted—I think Mr. Wrench will remember this, I asked them over and over again—replied, in varying terms, giving a very emphatic description of the sort of stallion they wanted. They had never seen a Hackney, they had never heard of a Hackney, but their description tallied almost exactly with the Hackney type. I advised small Hackneys because I understood that small horses were wanted in the district for local work. When the hilly part of my tour brought me to a district, which in the "Minutes of Evidence" I have called the "Borderland" between the pony district and the interior, there was a pitiable mixture of every description of bad horse, mainly produced from the offspring of ponies by Suffolks, Clydesdales, and thoroughbreds. They were either shapeless lumps or undersized weeds about 15 hands high, with absolutely nothing to recommend them. The thoroughbred cross had been almost without exception the result of sending thoroughbred sires to the districts of the West which I had visited. There was obviously more hope from the extreme West with its poor but fixed type than from the outlying districts with their poor and promiscuous [illegible]. I believe it would have resulted in permanent advantage to the country side if the whole of the latter had been carted off and knocked into the sea. But the best I could do was to apply my second scheme which was that where you have a promiscuous type of horse produced by promiscuous breeding from every kind of sire. If you put a fixed type upon that promiscuous type, the fixed type having a prepotency with regard to its characteristics will counteract the promiscuous type and to a certain extent obliterate the promiscuous type. I advised the Hackney stallion again for this district, but in that case I advised a full-sized Hackney stallion. I think it will be obvious from the description I have given of the mixed stock in the districts I visited, that my advice to introduce Hackney stallions applied to material from which there was no possibility of producing a hunter. That is all I have to say about my tour.

10520. Before going to another subject perhaps it would be convenient for the Commissioners to ask you some questions upon these points. I should like to ask you one or two questions myself. The fixed type you speak of, I understand, is indigenous?—Yes.

10521. That is, the aboriginal horse, or the aboriginal horse improved by means we don't know of?—By experience I should think the fixed type of pony had been very little crossed with anything that could improve it for a very long period back. Where I saw the cross which I considered that of a thoroughbred horse upon the pony it was what I have described, namely, a 15 hands horse without any bone or any action. I cannot imagine to what purpose such a horse could be put.

10522. We have had it in evidence that the Connemara pony crossed with thoroughbred sires produces very valuable hunters?—That I could not say myself nor could I find it by exhaustive inquiry; I asked about it.

10523. In your opinion this fixed type has deteriorated?—I should think it had gradually deteriorated; I don't know what it has deteriorated from—that is rather a speculation, but from the testimony of the inhabitants I should imagine it had deteriorated. They ride these animals at two years old sometimes, two people ride on their backs. Their backs were their great defect.

10524. I understand you to say that you think the small Hackney sires put to this fixed type of ponies would be apt to produce polo ponies?—I beg your pardon, that is exactly what I did not say. I said my opinion was that the Hackney stallion was not a sire for the polo pony. Nov. 4, 1896. Mr. [illegible] [illegible]

10525. A small thoroughbred sire or any sire that is known to get a polo pony?—I don't know what would get a polo pony. The polo pony has to be bred from a sire that has proved himself a getter of polo ponies.

10526. There is much of a chance in breeding a polo pony?—I should think so.

10527. Have you seen the thoroughbred sires in those various districts that you are describing?—Yes, I think if I remember rightly I saw three or four. I don't think we saw more. I did not like any of them. I don't remember what they were.

10528. I want to ask you whether in your opinion the class of thoroughbred sires in these poor districts are at all fair specimens of what a thoroughbred sire ought to be?—That I could not say.

10529. Do you know at all what kind of fees the farmers will pay for a thoroughbred sire in these congested districts?—I think they wanted to pay five shillings.

10530. Do you think that private enterprise would be likely to supply a thoroughly sound thoroughbred horse for a fee of five shillings?—As a private enterprise, no, no.

10531. What I want to gather is whether you think the thoroughbred sire has, in those districts, had a fair chance of his being represented by a suitable description of thoroughbred sire?—That I am not able to say.

10532. And did many of the farmers describe to you the sort of horse they wanted?—Many of them over and over again.

10533. What kind of a description did they give?—They said they wanted horses with a lot of bone, with short legs, with substance and with action, particularly action; and at the same time they wanted them to [illegible] on them.

10534. Do you think they were capable of giving a description of what they thought to be a suitable thoroughbred sire?—I don't think that their description would possibly apply to the thoroughbred class.

10535. They had never heard of or seen a Hackney, but they evolved the image of him out of their own consciousness?—I think they evolved an image of the requirements which they thought would sell well.

10536. Then leaving the pony district you came to a district which is more or less infected with a very inferior promiscuous [illegible] of animal?—Yes. I was very much impressed to find that the cart horse, the Clydesdale, the Suffolk, and the Shire horse had been used, and used I should imagine on the light mares and on these ponies. I thought the result was deplorable, but I am not sure that it was quite so bad in my opinion for market purposes as the stock out of these ponies by thoroughbred stallions. Because, whereas I call the produce of the cart horse "lumps," a lumpy sort of horse, but the other produced [illegible] 15 hands horses with little bone of legs, no action, and faulty shapes. I myself would not say for what purpose the could be used or sold.

10537. And you think that there also the Hackney would have the best effect, in a larger class of stallion?—Yes; of course it is very difficult to make a silk purse out of a sow's ear, but I think they would give better [illegible] and [illegible], and more uniformity of type.

10538. In both cases you would prefer, I gather, the Hackney to the thoroughbred, even supposing the thoroughbred was equally good of its kind to the Hackney?—Yes.

10539. Lord Londonderry.—About this fixed type of ponies—you consider them a very poor class?—I entirely agree with that. There was something rather advantageous in their quality, and also in the knowledge one had of the enormous amount of work they did.

10540. What do you suppose to be their worth?—Their worth is a market where a buyer is necessarily

[illegible], 1896.

Mr. [illegible], M.P.

sold from some consideration of his appearance would, I should say, be very low.

10541. Then I gather it is the result of these ponies crossed with thoroughbreds that you consider such a very poor class of [illegible]?—Yes.

10542. Were you able to gather at all what kind of a thoroughbred horse it was that had crossed those mares?—Lord Dunraven [illegible] [illegible] to me; my view on that point was rather limited. I think we saw three or four thoroughbred stallions. I didn't like them.

10543. Were they animals locally known in [illegible], or were they animals that you ever heard anything about?—No; I had not heard anything of those [illegible] animals.

10544. They were owned by whom?—By small people in the district?—I think they were owned rather on a speculation, I fancy—by local proprietors. I don't want to go into any evidence beyond my own actual experience, although I may [illegible] opinions. I think probably, if I may say so with all respect, that this might be got from other sources with greater accuracy than from me.

10545. Well, I was only asking you about the animals you said you thought had been a failure with the thoroughbred cross—have you any idea of what the thoroughbred was?—I think I would rather express my opinion about the stock which I saw than about the sire which I did not see. I only know the stock I am speaking of were by a thoroughbred.

10546. They are very hardy, I suppose?—The small ponies are very hardy; yes, the fixed type were very hardy.

10547. I suppose that really they would, as a rule, be crossed with any other pony that happened to be there?—As far as I could make out they were mated with stallions of their own type. If a man lived a little with a little more bone, perhaps, and a little more size, he would keep him as a stallion. I saw some of them. They were kept by people there—rather [illegible] looking animals, and certainly some of them were un-[illegible]. I could not imagine them being used in their [illegible] having produced even this fixed type of horse.

10548. They are a very small class of farmers up there that own those animals?—Very small and very poor.

10549. And I suppose would rather send their ponies to any sire they could get for nothing, or as cheaply as possible?—They would be willing to try it, most of them.

10550. Did they hold out any idea that if stallions of the class they described were sent, they would gladly send their ponies to them at a fee, or was it merely in their imagination?—I think the prospect of having stallions of the character that were afterwards put there was received with the greatest enthusiasm. It created a great deal of interest, and these people came to great distances from the mountains to us. I talked to them; some of them could hardly understand me.

10551. Lord RAVENSWORTH.—I think I understood you to say it would be foolish and useless to use a thoroughbred horse in the west of Ireland. I may have misunderstood you?—No; I don't think I said that. I described the horses I saw, I divided them into two classes; one a fixed type of pony, and the other a promiscuous, small, shapeless horse. I said I thought it would be useless and hopeless to attempt to breed profitable horses by the use of a thoroughbred sire upon that type.

10552. Upon which type?—Upon the promiscuous type.

10553. Was the promiscuous type in greater numbers than the fixed type?—Well, that I can't say because when my tour over the pony districts was completed that was all really I had to do, and when I went on to the "borderland" between the pony districts and the interior, I only covered a small amount of ground, and I only speak exactly of what I saw.

10554. Have you ever heard that ponies in the west of Ireland when crossed with a thoroughbred have frequently produced good hunters?—Shortly after my tour I had a letter which I have been trying to find, but cannot, from someone in the North of England, saying that he had had one of the best hunters he ever rode by a thoroughbred horse out of a West of Ireland pony; that is the only instance that I have ever heard. My inquiries in the district did not lead me to the same conclusion.

10555. Do you keep any thoroughbred stallions?—Not now; I used to. I am not speaking of my stud at Newmarket. I have thoroughbred stud at Newmarket.

10556. Have you sold any Hackney stallions to the Congested Districts?—Not one; I felt that having given the advice I did, my connection with the Board was closed.

10557. Mr. FITZWILLIAM.—Can you divide locally where what you call the fixed type and the promiscuous type exist?—I could do so, but I don't say that I am prepared to do so to-day. I must make this excuse to the Commission that I have had a great deal else to do, and this evidence has taken me a good deal of time. It would require me to go over—which I should be very happy to do and to send a statement on that subject to the Commission—a number of memoranda pencil notes which I made during my tour.

10558. You can't say whether you consider the fixed type to exist, perhaps, in Connemara or in any particular place?—Certainly. The fixed type exists on the sea-board and towards the West; it was when I came inland in the "borderland" that I found the promiscuous type of animals. Roughly speaking, I should imagine that the fixed type exists entirely to the west of the blue line on the map.

10559. Do you remember where you saw what you call the mongrel?—Certainly; I remember the two places where we saw what I call the mongrels. They were Foxford and Belmullet.

10560. Does your remark apply to Donegal?—I didn't go to Donegal.

10561. CHAIRMAN.—You didn't go to the north districts?—No, I didn't go to the North.

10562. Mr. La TOUCHE.—You had expressed an opinion in favour of the Hackney sire before you made this tour?—I had expressed no opinion, and the Hackney sire to carry out the object explained to me is the latter.

10563. And the result of your tour was to confirm you in this previously expressed opinion?—Entirely.

10564. And you were influenced to some extent, I conclude, by the description that the farmers gave of the horse they wanted?—No, I don't think I was influenced by that at all. I considered that only as a fact. I was asked to form an opinion, and I formed it independently of all considerations except what I thought was to the advantage of the country.

10565. Had you taken into consideration the possibility of breeding by a stallion that was got by a thoroughbred horse out of a mare that was got by a thoroughbred horse?—Twelve years ago I expressed a very strong opinion upon that subject with regard to hunter-breeding—in favour of it. I may, perhaps, be anticipating, but at the end of the [illegible] which I supply I state that, "from the point of view of true hunter-breeding only, I have no other suggestion to make; it is as asked for by the thoroughbred. I do not pretend to be a hunter-breeder."

10566. I take it that for these districts you would consider the Hackney sire would be a more suitable animal than the horse bred as I have described?—Yes.

10567. Why?—Because I think the stock would be more really saleable.

10568. You mean on account of the action?—Yes.

10569. You found the mares there very deficient in action?—The mares were deficient in action.

10570. Do you think the action of the Hackney which some people would characterise as extravagant would be likely to become good cart horses when crossed with an animal with no action at all?—I don't think it would be as high as the Hackney action, but I think it would be both good and true as long as you have been within in your Hackney. Of course there are Hackneys that have bad action; I am prepared to deal with the question of Hackney action from that point of view.

10571. I was only asking a question with reference to the evidence you have given as regards your tour in these congested districts. The horse required for the work there in the congested districts is not a very high-class one I take it?—I should think not for the local work.

10572. Do you think that high action is at all essential for an animal that has got to go along mountain paths and carry creels on his back and draw seaweed?

Chairman.—Mr. Burdett-Coutts goes into all these questions a little later on.

Witness.—May I be permitted to answer that question, because it deals with certain propositions which I should like to submit to the Commission, as regards profit in horse-breeding, and the most important of them is that my efforts to make horse-breeding pay can be successful unless the production of the highest type of horse for any particular purpose is aimed at. I think you will see the bearing of that proposition upon your question.

Chairman.—I am only anxious to keep the questions as far as possible within the various headings we have put them down.

Witness.—My object in the advice I gave was to enable the people in those districts to breed a horse which would do their country work, but at the same time give them an opportunity of breeding—and the more often the better—more valuable specimens which they would sell well.

10573. Mr. Fitzwilliam.—Do you think the ordinary mares you saw in your tour were capable of breeding the highest type of any sort of horses?—I think the mares were capable of breeding very largely a better type than they do now. You cannot of course jump to the highest class at once in the horse-breeding.

10574. Lord Rathdonnell.—The type you proposed to breed there was the stepping pony?—Yes, the stepping pony or stepping cob.

10575. Trotting is much something to the native breed?—Yes; and improving the substance of the native stock.

10576. Mr. Cassidy.—You say that the Hackney is only fit for getting harness produce? I think that is one of the conclusions you give in this statement?—I should like to explain that at some greater length when I come to that part.

10577. Mr. Wrench.—Might not the small type that you allude to as the ponies that you saw largely arise from the conditions under which these animals have lived for years?—I should think the change in the type might arise, and probably they may have diminished in size from their treatment; but I don't think the type arose from that.

10578. You think that the type arose from some Spanish breed or some special cross originally?—I think so.

10579. And you think that the best results would be obtained from those mares by crossing them with a prepotent sire?—Yes; I think that is very important.

10580. Do you think that a Hackney or such a horse as you described would be the most prepotent?—A Hackney decidedly.

10581. Have you had any experience of breeding from Irish mares?—Yes, I have. I have a very elaborate analysis of all the crossing that I have done in my stud. I am perfectly willing to answer any question that is asked me.

10582. Supposing that a really good thoroughbred was stationed in the districts you saw what do you think would be the result?—I am inclined to think that it would be very much the result I did too from the best thoroughbreds with some slight improvement perhaps and with more brilliance, but I still think that you would get a lot harder horses without much trot and probably with no action, and without what I call substance.

[illegible] Mr. Burdett-Coutts, M.P.

10583. Do you think that it would pay those small farmers to try breeding polo ponies as well as it would pay them to breed the animal you have described from a Hackney?—That I am not able to say. I imagine that the value of a polo pony depends very largely, like the value of a hunter, upon his character, that is upon his performances; whereas there is a very marked difference from the market point of view between that and a stepping cob. In order to sell a stepping cob you need know nothing about him except his shape and his action.

10584. And do you think there is a demand for the class of cob which could be bred from the mares you saw?—Yes. I think there is always a demand for a good cob. I should like to say that what I call the best specimens—the glamour-brilliant sort—would sell well in England, whereas the rank and file would do the local work as they do it now.

10585. You think that the produce of the Hackney with the mares you saw would be quite competent to do any work that would be asked on the farms in these districts?—I should think so.

10586. Would crossing the native mares with the Hackney produce mares from which more valuable animals would be bred afterwards?—Yes. Decidedly you can build a breed up.

10587. So that in addition to producing saleable animals a better breed of horses would be built up in time?—I should think that the second crop would be better than the first.

10588. And the third time you would cross again with a Hackney?—Decidedly.

10589. And you think that that would produce a still more saleable animal?—Yes; I think the improvement would be progressive.

10590. Chairman.—Have you ever visited these districts since your tour?—Never.

10591. You know nothing about the actual results?—Nothing, except from hearsay.

10592. You have a stud at Brookfield?—Yes; and I also have a large farm of about a thousand acres in Herefordshire and a large farm in Yorkshire.

10593. Can you give us some information about those studs?—I perhaps may be permitted to mention very briefly the origin of my stud. I felt the truth of the two propositions which I have submitted to the Commission. In the first place, that in a horse-breeding country it is economically wrong to exclude from the purview of breeders the possibilities of the harness horse, and secondly, that to confine the aims of a horse-breeding industry to thoroughbreds is uneconomical by excluding the profitable production of the harness horse. Side by side with that, I found that foreign governments had for thirty or forty years been acquiring our stallions of the harness breeds, and that, whereas thirty years before I had founded my stud, England or Ireland used to supply [illegible] harness horses, that we [illegible] a vast number of good harness horses—I am not speaking of the [illegible] horses—were coming over from abroad, that we had been exporting the raw material and were taking it back in the shape of a manufactured article for harness purposes. I found that some of these breeds were in danger almost of being extinguished, and at that without any idea of what the stud would grow to, and certainly without any commercial object or any idea that it would turn into a business, I started it, being determined to preserve a number of each of these breeds and try experiments in crossing. The whole subject attracted a great deal of publicity, and the value of these breeds as breeds, as other breeds are bred by family with hereditary characteristics of their own, became

18 Jan. 1899.
Sir Walter Gilbey, Bart.

so important that I rather abandoned the idea of breeding for some years in order to get a strong ... of each breed and to be able to find out which ... and families, as it were, the best ... I am not qualified to say whether my stud is a good or bad one, but it may ... that, though it is five times as large, I should think, as any other stud in England; that people come to it and have continuously come to it from all parts of the world to purchase stallions and mares for breeding purposes; and that I am generally satisfied with obtaining the highest prices for my harness horses. The fundamental basis of my stud has been the Hackney stallion, and at least 90 per cent. of the horses I have sold have been by a Hackney. Now with respect to the number.

10890. That is not Sandringham?—It is all the more. ... I put out of these ... the thoroughbred which I kept at ... I have ... thoroughbred mares in my Brookfield stud. Since its foundation, roughly speaking, 1,500 horses have passed through my hands, including those now in my stud. My stud now consists of 507 horses which for the information of the Commission I have divided according to the breeds of the sires. Of Hackneys pure-bred there are 314, by Hackney stallions out of coaching mares 36, by Hackney stallions out of other mares 18, total for the Hackney sire division 368. Of coach horses pure bred I have 34, of thoroughbreds pure bred 8, of horses by thoroughbreds out of other mares 7, of ponies pure bred 15, of American trotters, that is the only foreign animal I have in my stud, I have 3 sports which I have kept for use, but I am beginning to breed from them; and of animals of unknown breeding I have 6. Now as to prices, I submit the average of prices obtained at my sales by public auction. These sales are annual and are composed almost entirely of harness horses. There have been three, viz., 1896, 1897, and 1898. At these three sales 172 horses were sold for a total of £23,324 4s., making an average of £135 for each horse. Of these 172 horses eleven were by thoroughbred sires; their average was £104—while the general average was £135. Eight were by coaching stallions; their average was identical with the general average; all the rest—viz., 153—were by Hackney stallions. I also submit a statement of the value of pure Hackneys. It is in my ... to the Commission, the average of prices obtained for stock by my leading Hackney stallions as collected from my auctions book for 1897. Money realised by the stock is after all the ... criterion of the value of a sire. Of Candidate's stock sold from the Brookfield stud up to the present time for breeding purposes the stallions have averaged £1,072 6s. each stallion, and the mares £174 13s. 6d. each mare. The total average for all the horses sired by Candidate and sold from this stud has been £237 6s. 10d. each animal. The harness horses included in this average made an average price of £168. I now submit an analysis of the horses that I have bred myself which I have carefully prepared for the information of the Commission. The result of it is that, eliminating the 101 thoroughbreds which are not pertinent to the inquiry, there remain 453 horses bred by myself, of which 319 have been by Hackney stallions, 289 pure Hackneys; 30 out of coaching mares, 6 out of thoroughbred mares, 38 out of half-bred mares, 8 out of pony mares; sixty-three have been by coaching stallions (58 pure coachers, 2 out of hackney mares, 3 out of half-bred mares); eleven have been by pony stallions (nine pure ponies, two out of hackney mares); and ten have been by thoroughbred stallions (excluding pure thoroughbreds, 2 out of hackney mares, 5 out of half-bred mares, 3 out of pony mares). I only give this analysis in order to show the extent and variety of my horse-breeding operations. These do not include about 100 mares in my stud served by my stallions in 1898 and due to foal this year.

10891. Mr. Wrench.—When you allude to the average of a particular horse what horse are you referring to?—I was referring to "Candidate." I will now deal with the two propositions upon which I have stated my stud was founded. The first is that in a horse-breeding country it is economically wrong to exclude the production of the harness horse. This I support by the fact that the demand for harness horses is constant and universal. It may be so for fashion, that I cannot say, but for harness horses they are wanted all over the world, and there is a constantly increasing demand for the best harness horses of all sorts in England. I suppose it is mostly by that that harness horses are brought to saleable age and condition with the minimum of risk to the breeder. The harness horse has simply to be taken up from grass at three off, fed for a few weeks in a loose box, then put on a halter, and if he has good action and shape there will be plenty of dealers to buy him. The hunter has got to make high-class harness ... and, without any experience in those ... a ... price to the breeder for a horse ... know whether he can hunt or not; secondly, that the breeder has ... as a rule, to ... the risk of ... into a hunter, which are very serious risks. I support this proposition thirdly by the position of other countries. Their whole attention has been to improve their harness or general purpose horse. On ... horse breeding is carried on under government departments there, and they have all the help of ... experience and government money, and so on, and I believe the practice of most countries has been to endeavour to improve their harness horses or general purpose horses. When I was in Italy I found many stallions that there were Hackney stallions entering there. Then the system which I have always thought a thoroughly sound ... in this country or in any other country: the system of the foreign farms, of supplying a variety of stallions in order to enable the breeder to make a choice, is a much better position than to attempt to confine him to any particular breed. Fourthly and finally I support this proposition by reference to the state of things horse-breeding in the Eastern Counties and in Yorkshire—with respect to which I don't know if the Commission has had evidence. Of that I have a very large and extensive experience, and I should say that there is no part of England where the farmers of the horse-breeding have been so very successful as those by the farmers of Yorkshire and the Eastern Counties from the use of Hackney stallions. ... bred stallions have been located there. They have, to a large extent, disappeared under the ... of the demand for harness horses. I read in a paper which I believe has been before the Commission, a statement from a London dealer to the following effect:—"Men who buy the highest class of harness horses for the London market do not go into Yorkshire breeding countries of England to find them." My experience would be quite contrary. In my opinion and experience, putting aside what is called the "jobbing" horse in London, at least 90 per cent. of the highest priced horses in London come from Yorkshire or the Eastern Counties. In those districts the harness horse-breeder knows that it would spoil him to use the thoroughbred stallion. But he has always had the choice of doing so. That is all I have to say upon my first proposition, viz., that of the value of harness horse-breeding to a country.

10892. Chairman.—Have you any figures on that point?—It would be impossible for me to give any except from my own stud. The whole of the breeding operations of my stud have been entirely under my own hand. No mare has ever been put to a stallion in my stud except at my discretion. In the whole ... I had never bought a brood ... up to two or three years ago except by seeing it myself; of late years

I have to. lower the [illegible] of [illegible] horses to a great extent to my knowledge. This experience of the [illegible] in [illegible] has [illegible] me to adopt, apart from my own purchases, what horses were bought, the prices paid for them, and the class to which they belonged. And I have no hesitation in saying that if [illegible] the highest priced harness horses, [illegible] from 1[illegible] or [illegible] hands in 18[illegible], the horses you see in the [illegible] in Hyde Park in phaetons or Victorias, [illegible] horses, landaus in [illegible], &c., [illegible] per cent. of them are from these [illegible] which are confined to harness horse-breeding.

My second proposition was that the Hackney is [illegible] the breed for producing harness horses. I come to that point with a very long and extensive experience of the Hackney.

[illegible]. You say that in [illegible] the aims of a horse-breeding society to thoroughbreds is [illegible] to [illegible] the profitable production of the harness horse?—That is my opinion. With [illegible] I will place this evidence in the hands of the Commission. There is a great deal of it I need not go through now. There is a point about the Hackney type which I should like to mention, and that is that the Hackney type is the correct one in relation to the draught of carriages. There are two forms by which draught can be effected. The first is the application of weight to [illegible]. Of those an obvious instance is the cart horse. A cart horse by simply [illegible], the greater part of his weight is the [illegible] of his centre of gravity will draw an ordinary vehicle. The second is [illegible] or muscular energy. [illegible] to see plenty of instances in the streets of London where omnibuses were drawn by [illegible], weedy horses [illegible] by thoroughbred stallions; and it is found all over the [illegible] of Europe, where light, weedy horses are seen struggling and fighting with the weight behind them. A very distressing spectacle it is. The only proper method of draught, and that which is least exertion to the horse, is the combination of these two forces, or the force between them. That you have in the Hackney when applied to harness work. He has substance enough not to put an undue strain upon his muscular energy, and he has energy enough to make full use of his substance. There is a point with regard to action which I was asked——

[illegible]. Mr. Le Touche.—Yes, as regards the probable result of a cross between an animal with high action and an animal with no action at all?—I should like to state, in the first place, with regard to a point that was made by Lord [illegible] about high action. I myself [illegible] thinking that the [illegible] of the [illegible] which is commonly a hereditary property of the Hackney and which no other breed possesses in anything like the same degree in [illegible], would be a very valuable attribute to the horse. It would enable the hunter to jump off his hind legs and to extricate himself better in a cramped place. I myself have ridden several horses that I [illegible], thoroughbred hunters, and nearly thoroughbred hunters, good galloping horses, very [illegible], but if you got them into a cramped place it was exceedingly difficult to collect them on their [illegible]. If you could give more [illegible] the bending of the hock to hunters it would be better and advantageous. I was going to speak on this question of the utility of this high action, and, in my opinion, high action although [illegible] in the Hackney has been developed by his [illegible]. He was originally a trotting horse. He was a horse that was put to long fast work, and [illegible] he always had to [illegible] in the old [illegible] and [illegible] which [illegible] the [illegible] in the country—great [illegible]; [illegible], a natural propensity to throw his legs forward a great distance, and to a certain extent to raise his knees, certainly a great deal more than the American trotter does. When the necessity for this long work disappeared, and the value of the showy properties of the Hackney increased, the [illegible] in the [illegible], and [illegible]

as [illegible]. His natural propensity to throw his feet [illegible] to expand their [illegible], and [illegible] more [illegible] he was [illegible] he threw his knees up to satisfy the [illegible]. That was only the development of a natural property. Now, if you take the [illegible]; if you [illegible] from a horse with high action and you drive him for a long distance the natural result will be [illegible] the less [illegible], it will [illegible] his knees and [illegible] his stride. This valuable value of this high action has been found out in America. The American trotter undoubtedly has a large admixture of Hackney blood, in my opinion, to start with; the high action has [illegible] for the purpose of [illegible] speed bred out of him, but now, when they see the valuable value of high action, they are [illegible] by what they call "[illegible] and [illegible] the horse to be a knee action" to produce high action. I don't think that this explanation leads me to the conclusion that high action is detrimental in any way to work, but that if you put a horse to long work you will lower the knee action. It is, therefore, valuable for fast and for show [illegible]. It is a hereditary property; there is no question about that. If you take a Hackney mare and [illegible] of [illegible] the [illegible] you will find that the foal will have [illegible] high [illegible], while a thoroughbred foal will [illegible]. It is a very valuable property of course for selling harness horses. The [illegible] of [illegible] between the Hackney [illegible] their value to [illegible]. That is my experience, but I will submit to the Commission a letter from a man who is one of the leading veterinary surgeons in Yorkshire, where it may [illegible] be [illegible] giving his opinion of the Hackney breed, based on a very full experience of [illegible] years.

[illegible]. Mr. [illegible].—What is his name?—[illegible]. I consider him one of the best veterinary surgeons and one of the best authorities on horses in England.

[illegible]. Chairman.—What is the letter?—I will read it if you like:—

"Pocklington, Yorks.,
"February [illegible], 18[illegible].

"Dear Sir,—In answer to your letter asking me for my opinion of the Hackney, based on my long experience of the breed, I beg to say that I have been in practice as a veterinary surgeon for [illegible] years, and have always had [illegible] going, and [illegible] for the last fifteen years. During that time I have [illegible] all breeds—thoroughbred, half-bred, [illegible], [illegible], and [illegible] that have not found any animal to [illegible], either for quality or [illegible] work, as the Hackney, and for style and endurance [illegible] can equal them. I have found [illegible] horses to do better in [illegible] than in [illegible]; they [illegible] the best [illegible] during the winter months, [illegible] and [illegible] the work. The best animal for all purposes, in my opinion, is the [illegible] Hackney, [illegible] by a thoroughbred. I have [illegible] some of the best of hunters with a cross of Hackney, the latter giving them more bone and [illegible] without [illegible] their [illegible] powers. I have also known many [illegible] harness horses by a big bold Hackney from half-bred mares. [illegible] old [illegible] got some very valuable horses from [illegible] and [illegible] [illegible] the same district for nearly twenty years); the same might be said of many other Hackneys. Then as to soundness, we have far more [illegible] than we have [illegible]. A [illegible] is very rarely found in a Hackney, and no [illegible] on the [illegible]. Then as to [illegible], whistling and roaring, you have amongst the [illegible] and [illegible] in [illegible] of the Hackney. Then the Hackney is more hardy than any other breed [illegible] the [illegible], as [illegible] more suitable for a cold climate. As to the financial part, they [illegible], and they are either ready for sale at three off, or [illegible] year they can do light work or a farm.

March 8, 1893.
Mr. Burdett-Coutts, M.P.

earning their food and at the same time getting muscles and stability for their work in after years. The demand also for the Hackney is greater than any other animal, being equally suitable for both saddle and harness, having taken the place of the old fashioned coach-horse for driving purposes."

On the question of soundness I think the Hackney breed is the most healthy of all. Then there is the question of endurance. I should like to preface what I have to say upon the question of the endurance of the Hackney with this observation—that of course a great many of the finest harness horses are kept all their lives for show purposes. Not for the show ring; but I mean, if a man has got a beautiful stepper he likes to keep it as such, and he does not ride or drive it long distances for the very reason I mentioned, that to do so would be to lower the horse's action. To ask a horse so kept and used to do a long journey in thirty miles, if he cannot do it, is no argument against him. In my opinion you might just as well ask an overdressed lady, unaccustomed to walking or trained at all, to live with the Derwent Harriers from Oxford Circus to Woolwich Town and back again, as to ask show Hackneys which had been used every day for town work to go thirty miles at ten miles an hour. It has become quite an imputation upon a Hackney that he is not a horse of endurance, because people take him entirely unconditioned for long work and put him to it without thinking that a long distance sometimes requires special condition. Endurance is unquestionably an old property in the Hackney breed. They were the horses, of course, that used to perform all the road work in the North and the East of England, and if you take the route by which the great horses were tried in those days you will find them instances of endurance continually. Those miles assured in nine minutes, and something resting in fifty-six minutes carrying thirteen stone —this was "Norfolk Phenomenon" one of the great early sires of the Hackney; sixteen miles in one hour carrying sixteen stone—this was Wroot's "Pretender," in the early part of the century. I can give you others, and these are perfectly authenticated cases. Very often they went thirty miles to market and thirty miles back, and I can give you hundreds of specific instances of endurance in the Hackneys in former and in recent times.

10001. Lord ARTHUR CECIL.—Was that any particular breed of Hackney or the Hackney generally?—I have taken three noted Hackney sires, just as you would take the thoroughbred.

Mr. CHAPLIN.—Those stallions?—Three different stallions. All more or less about the same time. Now, the necessity for all that long work disappeared after the introduction of railways. I would undertake in any case of individuals amongst my own Hackneys—certainly after two generations of training and practice—to train and condition them to do any work and go any pace that could reasonably be asked of a horse. I want to give a specific instance of my own experience. I have driven Hackneys, and high stepping Hackneys, for the past seventeen years. I have constantly driven a pair out to my farm in Hertfordshire, which is nineteen miles from my town house and twelve miles from my stud, and driven them back the same day at nine-ten miles an hour. And these same horses after a day's rest I could bring out in Piccadilly or the Park, and put them in the saddle too and they would be the show horses of the town. Last summer I took with me on a tour of visits in the North of England a team of what I call purely all bred by myself. The leaders were 15.2, and were by my first pony stallion, "Tommy"; the wheelers are 15.2, and are pure bred Hackneys, bred in the purple. After driving them for some 300 miles, generally from twenty-five to thirty miles a day, I finished up with a journey in which I met the members of this Commission. It was made in the Lake district, which, as everyone knows, is hilly. The whole distance compassed in the day by the team was forty-eight and a half miles. I take off three and a half miles of slow work going to the station. The remaining forty-five miles were done with two stoppages of an hour each at a decent point over ten and a quarter miles an hour. The last five miles were done in twenty-two minutes, and the horses were fit and well the next day. These are heavy Hackneys—horses with high action; horses I can sell at a very high price. Finally, I say that a few Hackney strains are undoubtedly soft. The same thing exists with thoroughbreds and with most other breeds. In the Hackney blood there have been strains where cart blood has been taken in to get greater size. This can be detected in the shape, and where it exists, it is, in my opinion, a fatal bar for breeding purposes. What I say about the Hackney is that he is not in his general type a riding horse. My opinion on this point differs no doubt from that of so-called Hackney men. The riding type has been greatly developed in recent years, and in my own stud I have paid special attention to quality and shoulders. If you get a Hackney with fine shoulders he is a very good horse to ride on the road; he is also a good horse to canter; he is rarely good to gallop. As a road back, where the child gets in the saddle, he is safer than the thoroughbred, but his action, although more showy, is not so smooth or stable. The articulation of both the fetlock and the shoulder is stiffer. I can show many specimens which do not deserve this criticism, but in the main I believe it to be correct. I spoke in the riding horse to both hind at the top; at the same time it must be remembered that from the earliest times one of the chief uses of the Hackney was as a weight-carrying hack, and in that capacity some specimens fetch very long prices in the present day. I have added a remark about the classification and judging of Hackneys in-hand at English shows. I consider it deserves the strongest possible censure. Unless a hack is something else than a riding horse, the classes of the horses in such classes have no business to be there at all; they are merely harness horses shown in the saddle, and the first prize is given to the highest stepper. That is all I have to say about the Hackney.

10002. CHAIRMAN.—These horses you speak of were they called Hackneys in those days or what?—No; I consider the name Hackney is ridiculous and misleading. What happened was this:—Before the Stud Book was established these horses used to be called in Norfolk, Norfolk trotters, or cobs, and also Hackneys; in Yorkshire they were called Roadsters and Nags. Well the two sections of breeders of this class of horses had a tremendous dispute, and the Yorkshire side were going to break away and adopt a society of their own, because they could not get those horses called Roadsters—and in my opinion Roadster was the only name for the breed. It was the old name in Yorkshire, and in all the old papers and programmes of shows fifty years ago, that I have seen, the classes were Roadster classes or Roadster mares and foal. And the word is the proper name for the Hackney; that is the difference between the Hackney and the thoroughbred horse, and for the road in my opinion the Hackney is the best horse.

10003. When was the Hackney Stud Book instituted?—I think in 1884.

Lord ARTHUR CECIL.—I think volume III. is just out, that would make it 1883.

10004. CHAIRMAN.—These were so called in Yorkshire or Norfolk before that?—Not breeding roadsters. That was the date of the Stud Book movement—the movement, so to speak, which followed these breeds into Stud Books.

10005. Then the Hackney of those days you speak of was somewhat a different animal to the Hackney of the present time?—I don't think you will find he had so much high action, and I think they probably he was smaller than the horse which I want to put

[illegible]

March 8, 1898.

Mr. [illegible], M.P.

production of the highest type of some kind must be aimed at?—Yes.

10618. To return to the western districts of Ireland, do you think it is possible to produce anything of a very high type of animal in those congested districts?—I should think it would be a long and difficult task, but I think you could improve the type.

10619. In your opinion would it not be likely that the highest type that you could successfully produce would be something in the nature of the type of the aboriginal pony that is there?—Oh, no; I think you might greatly improve that, and breed stepping cobs with quality from a great many of these ponies.

10620. An animal that would fetch a good price?—Oh, yes; over there. If he would fetch a good price here he ought to make a price over there. This Connemara pony was an animal that sold as a foal for £4 10s.

10621. I am not talking of the commercial value, but that class of animal having developed itself there naturally, I should have thought, that to endeavour to improve it and get a superior breed of ponies might, perhaps, have enabled you to arrive at the highest type of animal that the district can produce; not looking at it from a commercial point of view?—I don't like to argue the question on a basis that does not look at it from a commercial point of view.

10622. When you talk of the highest type you don't mean the animal that would sell for the highest money?—I think the two are identical. I think the animal which sells for the most money is the best animal of its type.

10623. Quite so; of its type?—I don't want to alter the type.

10624. But not as selecting the one type against another, you don't mean that the type suitable for any country or district is the type of horse that would produce the most money for the time being?—Oh, no; I don't mean that, of course not.

10625. What do you think would become of the misfits resulting from the Hackney blood in Ireland, we have had a good deal of evidence that in the best horse-breeding part of the country—I am not talking of the congested districts—the result of the half-bred mare crossed with the thoroughbred stallion was either to produce a high-class hunter or a high-class and valuable carriage horse, or failing that, a good remount, always worth money, the misfit fetches money as a general utility horse or remount; what would become of the misfit between the Hackney sire and the half-bred mare?—They would fetch as much as misfits.

10626. For what purpose would they be used?—The low draught purposes of towns.

10627. In Ireland?—Yes; well, I suppose every horse gravitates to England if it is good enough.

10628. Do you think they would fetch a considerable price in England?—No, I don't think misfits of any kind make a profitable price, you must aim at the best and make a profit out of your best, you make a loss on your misfits in all breeds.

10629. You think so?—Unquestionably.

10630. Do you know what price they give for cavalry remounts in Ireland?—I suppose they give about £35.

10631. Lord Londonderry.—£35 for the light and £40 for the heavier?—I don't think I have ever bred horses by a Hackney stallion that I could not sell or get from £30 to £40 for.

10632. Chairman.—I am not talking of you or your stud, I am talking of the small farmers?—I was not at the moment talking of pure-bred Hackneys either. I was talking of horses that come out without any action out of half-bred mares, and I think the small farmers could get about that for his Hackney misfits. I should think so. Of course you are speaking, I believe, of hunter-breeding districts where the mares have size, and where the misfits would probably have a certain amount of size.

10633. Of course what I want to get from you is your opinion as to what the effect of the introduction of this Hackney blood would be among the small farmers and breeders in Ireland. I gather from you that you think the best of their produce would fetch a good price, and the misfits would at any rate be about the same value as the misfits from a thoroughbred horse?—Yes, I should think so. If you can tell me or if anybody can tell me that in Ireland there is a district where there are nothing but hunter mares, and mares thoroughly capable of producing good hunters, why then I should say keep the Hackney stallions out of those districts, but I do not recognise there is any such district, and in every district wherever you were to draw a circumference you would find a certain amount of farmers who had mares that would not cross well with thoroughbreds.

10634. It appears to be the fact that over a very large portion of Ireland the country from some natural cause or other seems to be particularly adapted to breeding hunters, at any rate they have succeeded in producing a very superior class of animal of that kind, and I gather from you that that being so you think it would be economically correct that in those parts of the country they should continue to direct their attention to the producing of the kind of animal that has been proved to be most valuable?—Yes, but I would not compel them to breed one class of horse exclusively.

10635. No, certainly not?—By confining the stallions to thoroughbreds you do so compel them.

10636. You would like them to have their choice?—I would like them to have their choice.

10637. Then you do not think that the introduction of the Hackney blood would have any bad effect upon the superiority which Ireland has attained in the production of high-class hunters?—I cannot say that I am prepared to say that. I should be very chary of saying that without personal experience. I have, as I shall show you, in eight specific crosses, bred fillies from hunter mares by Hackney stallions, which fillies I consider in their shape and action and size look suited to produce hunters. I cannot say that they would produce hunters. I cannot say how the hunters would gallop, or jump, or last, but I do find in the Hackneys certain properties of great value to the hunter, whatever properties they may possess which could deteriorate the hunter.

10638. Are there not many hunters bred in England by Hackney sires?—I myself don't consider the Hackney a hunter sire; but there is no doubt about it. You had the evidence to which I listened of Lord Tredegar, and there is no doubt about it that "Old Fireaway," a great Hackney stallion, got some very good hunters, long low horses that had considerable staying power. This letter of Johnson's, to which I referred, states also that he has known capital hunters—"I have known some of the best of hunters with a cross of Hackney." I should suppose that crossed by thoroughbred stallions out of a mare by a Hackney, "the latter giving them more bone and build and greatly improving their staying powers."

10639. Are there do you know as a matter of fact many hunters bred in the same parts of the country where Hackneys are largely bred?—I think not, not by Hackneys.

10640. I mean bred at all—are as many hunters bred for instance in Yorkshire as formerly?—The Hackney district in Yorkshire is rather circumscribed. In that district there are a certain number of hunters bred and all over Yorkshire.

10641. As many in that district as there were before?—I should think not, I should think the Hackney had pushed the hunter-breeding out, in the Eastern Counties and in parts of Yorkshire, certainly.

10642. Do you think its introduction into the hunter-breeding parts of Ireland would be likely to be followed by the same results, or I will put it in this way, if it did produce the same results would you think it was from natural economic causes and the

[illegible] 5, 1896.

Mr. Burdett-Coutts, M.P.

therefore economically sound?—If it did I should think it was sound, but I don't believe it would, because I believe you have a very valuable article in the Irish hunter. I think myself that there are certain weaknesses in the thoroughbred sire, increased by constantly mating with a thoroughbred sire, which require some careful consideration with regard to correcting those weaknesses, but whether those corrections should be applied in pure hunter districts by the introduction of Hackney blood, I am not prepared to say. I do firmly believe that the introduction of Hackney blood would enable the farmer to breed some profitable harness horses, but I am not prepared to say that from the point of view of hunter-breeding alone the introduction of the Hackney into a pure hunter-breeding district would be a good thing.

[illegible]. When you say you think the farmer should have a chance you mean that they should have an opportunity of mating their mares to a good thoroughbred sire or a good Hackney sire as they think?—Yes.

[illegible]. Of course you are aware that at present nearly all the Hackney sires in Ireland are licensed sires?—Yes.

[illegible]. And that therefore the question of choice has never been put before the farmer. For instance, in the congested districts there are no thoroughbred sires at all to be compared with the Hackney sires standing at the same fee?—Well, the largest experience of my regiment would be [illegible] there and let them try both. I have very little doubt myself that if you were to put a first-class Hackney alongside the best sire you could get, farmers would go to the Hackney in those districts.

[illegible]. Do you know at all whether buyers for foreign Governments buy many Hackneys or Hackney bred horses for remounts in England?—I believe they buy most of their remount horses in England, and I have already stated [illegible] the question of their [illegible] having a valuable commodity [illegible] the thoroughbred is a better sire for [illegible] than a Hackney. I have some very interesting specific instances of remounting.

[illegible]. Lord [illegible].—I want to ask you if I am correct in gathering from your answers that [illegible] pure hunter-breeding districts like Westmeath, Cork, Tipperary, it would be running a considerable risk to have a Hackney stallion standing there with the chance of farmers preferring that stallion to the hunter sire for their mares?—I think there might be a risk, a very great risk, of the breeders using the Hackney.

[illegible]. It would militate very much against the hunter-breeding?—That is what I rather meant [illegible] my opinion.

[illegible]. When I asked if you thought there might be a risk with the two you thought that the Hackney might appear the more attractive [illegible] the breeding, and consequently the mare that had perhaps bred good hunters to a thoroughbred horse would be transferred to the Hackney stallion?—I think very likely that the Hackney stallion would be tried and my whole remarks upon this subject—it is a difficult subject to express a fixed opinion on—[illegible] led me to this conclusion, that where you have a pure hunter district I should put the thoroughbred horse and not the Hackney. Where you have a district [illegible] the congested districts I should [illegible] Hackneys, [illegible].

[illegible]. Chairman.—You say that you think that the farmer should have a choice as to the sire?—Yes.

[illegible]. And that, speaking broadly, in districts specially adapted to producing hunters, you think the proper proportion would be one thoroughbred sire to one Hackney horse, and that in other districts not specially adapted to producing a hunter the proportion should be reversed, and should be [illegible] Hackneys to one thoroughbred?—That was not quite, I think, what I said. The first part of it is quite right. In districts like the [illegible] districts I think there should be no Hackneys [illegible] thoroughbred; in the [illegible] districts, where the [illegible] I believe myself a big Hackney stallion is the most suitable sire, but I should give perfect freedom of choice there to the breeder, and put one Hackney to one thoroughbred.

[illegible]. What I want to ask you is, not as to whether you think the [illegible] intelligence of the average farmer in Ireland can be sufficiently trusted in that matter. You see we have had a certain amount of evidence before us that the farmer, especially the small farmer, is influenced by all kinds of motives in choosing the sire, the popularity of the owner, and [illegible] things of that kind come into play. And we have had a large body of evidence to the effect that Ireland [illegible] a sort of pre-eminence in producing the class of horse that [illegible] happen to make a hunter is making a carriage horse, practically equally valuable, and then if it does not turn into a [illegible] first-class carriage horse of that kind, it has a [illegible] value, [illegible] sired by thoroughbred sires, [illegible] thoroughbreds, and by animals not in the Stud Book, [illegible] great many thoroughbred strains in them, very nearly thoroughbred; [illegible] the introduction of the Hackney strain is likely to interfere with that sort of pre-eminence that this country generally has gained in producing that class of horse. There are two questions I should like to ask you, first of all whether, so far as your experience goes, you think that the average farmer in Ireland can be trusted to choose what is really the best kind of sire, best for the general interests of the country; and, whether if the Hackneys were introduced in the way you suggest, granting that they might be very valuable in certain districts of the country, whether the Hackney, when spread through the country generally, might not be detrimental to the general industry of horse-breeding?—With regard to the first question, I think that the Hackney has certain external attractive properties which may dazzle the hunter breeder, but I think [illegible] of his being supplied, and I do not think that the supply of a [illegible] number of such Hackney stallions to a hunter district would materially interfere with the hunter stock as a breeding stock. I think it possible on that subject—I have carefully [illegible] a definite opinion—I think it possible that the introduction of the Hackney blood might improve the breeding stock for harness-breeding, although I do not believe in the first cross of the hunter by a Hackney stallion.

[illegible]. You do not approve of it?—No.

[illegible]. But you think eventually?—I think eventually it might introduce valuable properties. I [illegible] the introduction of a Hackney stallion is not what I would suggest from the point of view of hunter-breeding [illegible] if the industry of hunter breeding is so valuable that [illegible] profitable horse-breeding, I think that the Hackney stallion should be introduced only with the greatest care; [illegible] the opportunity of producing the type of very profitable horse, and [illegible] I think

[illegible] Mr. [illegible]

that the Hackney stallion might be introduced with the result of greatly improving the harness stock and without materially injuring the hunter stock. From the point of view of pure hunter-breeding it is not what I would suggest.

[illegible]. Well, there is another question arises out of that. I don't know whether you or anybody would give a very definite opinion about it, and that is whether there is anything in the climate or soil or natural [illegible] in Ireland which enables Ireland to compete very successfully, say with England, in the production of hunters, and whether the same causes would operate in the same direction in the production of harness horses; that is to say, whether Ireland naturally has any advantage over England in producing harness horses that it has over England in producing hunters?—That, of course, would be very difficult to give an opinion about; my own opinion is that there can be nothing in the climate or the soil of Ireland which would interfere with the production of the best harness horses, but what you want in the hunter is jumping power, speed, bone, and substance, and while Ireland does produce these they can also be produced in other countries of the [illegible] [illegible]. I believe the real explanation of Ireland being hunter-breeding country is that they have always bred hunters and they have the hunter stock. I believe also that the tendency of the thoroughbred stallion is towards certain deficiencies, while it possesses the essential properties of the hunter there are certain deficiencies which it [illegible], certain defects which ought to be remedied. Now whether they could be remedied by the introduction of the Hackney stallion I am not prepared to give a decisive opinion.

[illegible]. Well, assuming that Ireland has achieved a certain prominence in producing hunters, the question is whether the Irish [illegible] [illegible] is peculiarly favourably situated to produce that particular type of horse?—I should think the only [illegible] [illegible] [illegible] the hunter stock and kept it.

[illegible]. By accident?—I would not say by accident, I would not say [illegible], but there it is.

[illegible]. It would be rather natural to suppose that as regards the industry of horse-breeding it had developed in that direction, because it was the direction of least resistance, or the most favourable direction that it could develop in?—Well, what does Ireland give to hunters that it would not give to other horses, what does the climate and soil of Ireland give to hunters that it would not give to harness horses, what does the climate and soil of Ireland give to thoroughbreds that it could not give to other breeds of horses. It gives to those horse, quality, and [illegible]—all those things are of value to other breeds. I myself believe that the character of Ireland as a hunter-breeding country is owing to the fact that breeders have always been hunter breeders.

[illegible]. You think if equal attention had been paid to breeding good harness horses she would have equal advantages over England?—Oh, certainly.

[illegible]. I am assuming that experience shows she is able to produce a better class of hunter as a rule than England?—Yes, I think the operation of the same forces under the more [illegible] would enable her to produce better harness horses. I think so, I [illegible] [illegible] the reason why not. You have asked me—perhaps it is going back a little—as you put to the same questions about the value of harness horses bred in Ireland, and I answered that you will remember by stating that the whole of what I call the middle of the trade was left out of the question of Irish breeding, and the two classes of harness horses that are bred in Ireland, the Irish carriage-horse, the [illegible] [illegible], of course, by thoroughbred stallions. The reason why, in my opinion, the thoroughbred stallions are never to a safe or profitable sire of a harness horse is [illegible] deduced from my own experience but from the fact that you have bred the thoroughbred horse for [illegible] years or more with the view of producing one thing—speed in the gallop. Now you don't want speed in the gallop, you don't want the gallop at all for a harness horse. If a thoroughbred horse has action you don't like him, you say his gallop "round," he does not get over the ground. Therefore your whole harness-stock, with regard to the thoroughbred has been to breed action out of him, and action being essentially the property of producing harness horses and action being essentially absent from the thoroughbred, that is the reason why I say you cannot in the long run breed harness horses profitably, harness horses, from the thoroughbred. Now the thoroughbred sire answers that the endurance of the thoroughbred is of great value in the harness horse. I reply to that: The endurance of the Hackney, which has the hereditary property of action, is sufficient for all practical purposes to which the harness horse is put, and to that I would like to add that while I admit frankly the courage of the thoroughbred, in my opinion, the two-year-old training of racehorses and short races have resulted in reducing that courage, so to speak, for the purpose I am speaking of, simply to an exhibition of the greatest possible expenditure of muscular energy in a very short space of time and over a very short distance. If by genetics, which would have made it breeding, the thoroughbred had been trained to distribute his muscular energy over a longer space of time and a longer distance it would have increased the fine sense of value for staying and endurance, and would have been more valuable than it is now for the purpose of harness horses. It has been so, that the effect of racing has been to aim at producing great speed for a comparatively short distance it would be equally fair to say that the effect of the aim of the Hackney breeder is to produce action in an excessive degree and for a short distance possibly. I think that that peculiarities might be [illegible] what you want to mix the two together with mutual benefit, that is to say that if you want to get a harness horse that will go a very long distance at a good speed, for very long distances I would take the Hackney to speed and distance and so modify the height of his action. If you wanted to carry with the Hackney a thoroughbred that would improve him and produce great endurance and speed I would take two or three generations of thoroughbreds in very long distance races.

[illegible]. To revert for a moment to the question I asked you, may I assume, that if it was desirable to breed more extensively for harness purposes in Ireland and from Hackney sires, it would be necessary in order to be successful that it should be done somewhat on the same scale and manner as it has been in England, that is to say you would require a certain number of the best Hackney horses and the Hackney mares?—I think not; that would be simply breeding the pure Hackney, that would be simply taking the Hackney breed into Ireland, and you would still have to start your crosses whenever you crossed him out on to the hunter stock. My remarks have been directed to the value of the Hackney in crossing. I have very carefully kept [illegible] of the pure Hackney except in one or two cases I spoke.

[illegible]. May I take it from you that you think that if anything should be done by the Government towards encouraging horse breeding in Ireland that in the districts proved to be specially suitable for producing hunters they ought to get a larger amount of suitable thoroughbred stallions at the same price as Hackney stallions; and that, in the districts which at present have been assisted by the Government and the Congested Districts Board you think that a certain number of suitable thoroughbred stallions should stand alongside of a larger number of Hackney stallions, and that in view of the general interest of the industry in Ireland the farmer can be trusted to discriminate, and decide which sire he would send his mare to?—I think in the first case a farmer would be trusted, and [illegible] ... give the [illegible] ... [illegible] ... in the pure trotting districts [illegible] ... [illegible] ... light-legged [illegible] a very valuable [illegible].

[illegible] ... produce a valuable [illegible] ... produce a valuable [illegible].

[illegible] Mr. [illegible] ... of the [illegible] ... [illegible] ... Yes.

[illegible] ... for the purpose of [illegible]? ... Yes, I qualified the [illegible] ... [illegible]

[illegible] Do you think you can [illegible] high [illegible] ... [illegible] ... No, I don't think that. I agree with you. I think you can have a horse that would [illegible] ... [illegible]

[illegible] ... [illegible]

[illegible] Don't you think that [illegible] ... [illegible]

[illegible]

[illegible] ... Yorkshire ... [illegible]

[illegible]

[illegible] ... Very little [illegible].

[illegible] And you think [illegible] ... [illegible] ... [illegible]

[illegible] ... Very [illegible] ... [illegible] ... Yorkshire [illegible] ... [illegible]

[illegible] But the [illegible] ... Well, yes; [illegible] ... [illegible]

[illegible] ... [illegible]

Hackney stud-book has anything like the authority of the general stud-book would, of course, be advised.

10822. Then, as horses were introduced into it and what you may call Registered horses?—That was a system on which I am hardly qualified to speak, because I was the greatest opponent, and carried on a very bitter fight against the practice of registration, and by the help of the Yorkshiremen, who were opposed to it, who had been in favour of [illegible]—we completely beat the inspection, and [illegible] it. It is [illegible] [illegible] the stud-book. What I did not like was that we [illegible] [illegible] [illegible] Yorkshire and the Eastern Counties [illegible] good mares [illegible] to [illegible] and kept it three or four years, that it was upon [illegible] that the stud-book was founded, and that there was attached no entry or pedigree in the stud-book a very great value as [illegible]—they [illegible] than I think it really [illegible]. Then there were among them people—a number of people—who said, "Oh! but you [illegible] know that [illegible] the Hackneys [illegible] [illegible] that [illegible] [illegible] ought to be admitted to the stud-book, and [illegible] would [illegible] [illegible] [illegible] [illegible] of the old Hackney [illegible], and it was [illegible] [illegible] by myself and Lord Londesborough. The great advocate was a member of this Commission, who is not here to-day, whom I expected to see here. We won the day, and that utterly [illegible] system of inspection has never been [illegible] again. There were, I admit, during the period when it obtained—I think two years—[illegible] of mares admitted to the stud-book by inspection which are in the [illegible] now, and [illegible] remained in the stud-book and have been bred from, and by the [illegible] of the value of the stud-book it is possible to [illegible] [illegible] [illegible] [illegible] [illegible] [illegible] pure [illegible] Hackney—a [illegible] registered Hackney; therefore, while I think I don't want to be misunderstood about this [illegible] registration with regard to [illegible] has been of [illegible] value to the [illegible] of these horses, and [illegible] the value of the animal, in [illegible] [illegible] [illegible] that the stud-book [illegible], at the [illegible] [illegible] I should be very sorry to say that [illegible] an animal is in the stud-book it is a good Hackney or a [illegible] Hackney to breed from.

10823. There is one other thing quite apart from that, you mentioned before we adjourned, which was [illegible] long distances. You say that long distances more [illegible] [illegible] [illegible] [illegible] [illegible] of [illegible]?—I did say so.

10824. That is the case in England I [illegible], but [illegible] [illegible] [illegible] [illegible] [illegible] [illegible] [illegible] in Ireland, and the long distances [illegible] [illegible], for instance, [illegible] to [illegible], and [illegible] [illegible] [illegible] [illegible], do you think that quite applies as much to Ireland as it does to England?—My whole argument was that the Hackney did not do long distances, because he was not asked to, and you could trust him with the greatest care to do long distances.

10825. I thought you said they were not required?—Yes, but that does not imply that they can[illegible] do it.

10826. No, I was not supposing that, but the long distances you will allow in Ireland are still required?—Oh, yes, and could be performed by the Hackney.

10827. *Lord Rathdonnell.*—There is a question I would like to ask you in reference to Hackneys. Do you take action into consideration before the [illegible] [illegible] of the animal itself?—I should say that action is the very first thing. I would put this remark, that the action of the Hackney, and the [illegible] of the Hackney, which [illegible] and the [illegible] [illegible] in the best combination for [illegible], ought to be [illegible]. One associates the Hackney type with fine action.

10828. With regard to action do you look very carefully, when you breed, to the shoulders of the Hackney?—I have always myself [illegible] I have paid great attention to shoulders and quality. I think that they are extremely valuable, both for the [illegible] horse and the riding horse. I think they are valuable for the harness horse, because I think good shoulders make less [illegible] of the [illegible], [illegible] [illegible] [illegible] [illegible] [illegible], and my definition of good action in the Hackney is that the knee should be raised as high as you like, the higher the better, but the shoulder should carry it there and the foot follow out. Then you get elegant action, and [illegible] of action if you drive the [illegible] [illegible] [illegible], a beautiful effect, because the [illegible] [illegible] for a moment before putting it down. I place a high value indeed on shoulder action in the Hackney.

10829. I believe it is rather hard to tell shoulder action unless you get on the back of the animal. In a [illegible] form of action, you can test the shoulder action to a certain extent. How can you test it as the harness horse [illegible] [illegible] [illegible] [illegible] [illegible] [illegible] [illegible] of the front action. I think you can see pretty well when you see a horse [illegible] whether his shoulder is really working as his knee. A good many Hackneys have, I [illegible] [illegible] bad shoulders, but the point of the shoulder is fixed in its place, they don't raise it enough, they raise the knee without working the shoulder, and that produces the pumping action, which is a very bad feature to my mind. But I think the most beautiful action you can have in a horse is that of the Hackney with good shoulder action.

10830. As a rule do you think they have good shoulders, taking the whole of the Hackney breed at [illegible]?—If you ask me whether they have good riding shoulders I should say no. I should say that very often, [illegible] [illegible] [illegible], their shoulders are very well placed. But I make a very great difference between a well-placed shoulder and a riding shoulder. For riding the shoulder of the Hackney would probably be not thick on the top and perhaps a little too loaded on the point, but the place of the shoulder in relation to the [illegible] is good in the Hackney.

10831. Some people judge shoulders pretty much by the height of the withers, do you think withers have anything to do in the shoulders?—Yes, I think I do, I may be ignorant, but I am very fond of a good wither.

10832. High withers?—Not an abnormally high wither for the Hackney, because that would make him awkward to look at, but I very much dislike a horse that is flat on the wither.

10833. Do you find in Hackneys [illegible] to be light in the forearm?—I should say not, not as a characteristic.

10834. Do you think that as a rule they stand well on their knees or back-[illegible]?—They stand on their knees. There is a certain breed of horses, the most fashionable and, from a market point of view, one of the most profitable breeds in the Hackney [illegible] that had a peculiarity, they were not exactly back at their knees, I distinguish between that and having them out away a little underneath the knees. These horses had the best [illegible] [illegible] [illegible] [illegible] with their work. I should say Hackneys stand very well on their knees, perhaps it is one of their strongest points. There is no [illegible] family of Hackneys which you would say is back at their knees, and another family [illegible] [illegible] [illegible] [illegible], but they only represent two strains of the whole Hackney blood.

10835. Do you think as a rule they have strong, [illegible] thighs?—Their thighs are, [illegible] well into their backs. I should say they are splendidly [illegible] horses. I should not like a specimen that had not got good second thighs, I should not say they were weak in that respect, certainly not.

10836. I think you said with regard to Hackney-breeding in Ireland that you would give the farmer a choice of stallions, that is a choice of the Hackney

10714. You say you use a hunting seat? You would not get us to an animal with a bit shoulders and nothing else that knee action would give?—No; but I thought you were talking about the private which hunting men don't ride—horses which were going into able.

10715. You mights go into the different Governments?—Take a hobby rule to use at particular.

10716. I am speaking of the cavalry entirely.—I have seen a great many horses in the cavalry that had not very good shoulders and seats in the artillery. My point in this stand for the cavalry you want have a [illegible] position with horses and you might as have short legs, and so on; and if you have got all those things—although I should prefer the horse with good shoulders, but as a great many Hackneys have good shoulders there is no reason at all why the use of the Hackney stallion should counteract bad shoulders, you have done well.

10717. Did you think the Hackney stallion has a better head and tail than the good thoroughbred horse?—For weight-carrying I should think by far.

10718. Do you think he is a better hunter horse than the thoroughbred?—He is very much shorter between his joints.

10719. [illegible] may be a little shorter in a [illegible]—I think he has good bone.

10720. If he does not possess as much ground he has not good bone?—This I will say, that many horses with the bone possessed by thoroughbred stallions, of which you see hundreds working in England and Ireland, would be absolutely rejected as Hackney stallions.

10721. I quite agree with you, but I am speaking of the high-class thoroughbred, if you can get him, and the high-class Hackney?—But I don't admit that the high-class thoroughbred necessarily has good bone. My experience has been with regard to the thoroughbred that he has been bred for one thing, speed on the gallop.

10722. Then in defects, and if you take the high-class horse then you would breed from to get the hunter type—if you get a thoroughbred with as much bone as any animal in the world?—I don't think you get him with more bone than the Hackney.

10723. Not more bone, but if you can get the thoroughbred bone is it as good or better bone?—Of its quality it is better bone, because it is denser in substance, but it is a long way between the joints, and puts the horse a long way up in the air, and the body is shelly.

10724. CHAIRMAN.—As regards the bone itself, if the length was equal, the thoroughbred bone would be better?—Yes, and that makes the Hackney, the [illegible]. The other [illegible] bone of course in [illegible] of the Hackney would [illegible].

10725. Colonel ST. QUINTIN.—You spoke of the beautiful action of the Hackney, can you have more beautiful action than that of the thoroughbred horse with [illegible]?—Oh! I think so.

10726. Mr. FITZWILLIAM.—The best thoroughbred?—Yes; for driving purposes.

10727. Colonel ST. QUINTIN.—For any purpose?—Ah! that would. I must have a definition of this action. When I speak of action I mean what is commonly called knee-action, that is action which shows as well as [illegible]. If you ask me about riding action, can you have better riding action than in the thoroughbred? I should say not.

10728. Do you prefer knee action to that beautiful action of the thoroughbred with sweep and length like [illegible] very easily see it. If you see it in a [illegible].

10729. I have seen it very often?—I should be very glad to see a thoroughbred stallion who can give it, whereas every Hackney stallion can give his action.

10730. You say a light shoulder gives light action, and prevents the horse from hammering his legs?—I did not quite say that. I said that a horse with good shoulder action that prevented him hammering his legs; but the thoroughbred, while he hardly puts his foot on the ground, does not raise his knee.

10731. Oh! he does?—Well, it is a question of experience. I keep to my experience.

10732. But not in the same extravagant manner, I mean?—If we are talking about profit to the breeder I have given my manager some [illegible] to buy horses with the [illegible], and the result has been that out of the 170 horses sold by my [illegible] only [illegible] by thoroughbreds, and whereas the [illegible] average was £[illegible], the average of the horses by thoroughbreds was £[illegible]. Now that is a direct appeal to the market, which I believe after all is one of the safest guides ultimately.

10733. Quite so, if you can [illegible] that class of horse, but can the poor Irish farmer who has a very indifferent mare, even be supposed that [illegible] by getting an indifferent, well, I don't like to say that, getting a [illegible] high class of [illegible] than the thoroughbred horse?—For what purpose, hunting.

10734. To sell out in the market?—There is no question about it that the introduction of the Hackney here may [illegible] in [illegible] would enable a man to breed horses for use [illegible] of in the country. I know many and the question about the introduction of the Hackney into the [illegible] [illegible] with a great deal of success.

10735. Mr. CAMPBELL.—Then again comes the recommending the introduction of the Hackney blood as to improve the breed of harness horses in Ireland?—Yes.

10736. That in that line produce would [redacted] valuable [illegible] mainly?—Yes.

10737. Don't you think it would be a dangerous experiment to limit the breed to the particular type which in England now they successfully breed from the thoroughbred animal through [illegible], they get the hunter, they get the harness, and they get the [illegible]?—I am all against limitation, and I consider that adhering alone to the thoroughbred is a greater limitation than adding the thoroughbred and a Hackney sire.

10738. Your contention is that the Hackney will produce only a harness animal?—I never suggested that; I think the Hackney might produce extremely valuable mares, which, if you put them to thoroughbred sires, would produce better hunters than the original mares would.

10739. You spoke of the introduction of Hackneys into Italy; are you aware the Italian Government buys [illegible] largely in Ireland?—Oh, yes, certainly.

10740. That has been given in evidence before the Commission?—Oh, I know that very well, but that remains that when they wanted—they are [illegible] Italy having [illegible] [illegible] what they wanted to improve their [illegible] they bought, as I have said, gradually, 100 Hackney stallions, and they [illegible] now, [illegible] use only thoroughbred stallions.

10741. When was that introduction made?—That would be [illegible] years ago, and I should think they have been introduced gradually from the time of King Victor Emmanuel, he was extremely fond of English horses, he introduced a certain number of Hackneys at the same time. Victor Emmanuel and the present king have bought their [illegible] driving horses in Ireland. The present King of Italy has the finest stud of weight-carrying hunters that has ever existed in the world, you could see nothing like it in this country. This does not reach, but he has brought the first prize weight-carrying hunters at the Dublin Show at Royal, and so on, the riding horses. They would probably suppose that Ireland was a capital place to get them from, but when it comes to the providing their [illegible] blood they do not introduce the thoroughbred stallion but the Hackney stallion, and such information as I have, and such experience as I have gained in travelling abroad, which is not very extensive, but I have gone thoroughly into the [illegible] of this [illegible] where I have been, is that whereas the hunting [illegible] will always come to Ireland to buy his hunters, he will never take part in any effort to improve hunter-breeding in his own country.

10742. Chairman.—They don't hunt, do they?—Why then do they buy hunters?

10743. They hunt here?—I beg your pardon, an immense number of hunters are taken abroad.

10744. Lord Ardilaun.—Riding horses would be the same?—Well, they call them hunters, they hunt in Austria, and France, and in Italy to a certain extent.

10745. Mr. Wrench.—Do you know that all the hunters in Ireland now are chiefly bought by dealers, the breeder does not get the top price at all, there is a profit between him and the army?—I believe that is the case.

10746. I don't know whether you have read in the Press any of the evidence that has been given before us?—No, I have not. I should have been very glad to have read it, but I could not get it, and I have been extremely busy, otherwise I could perhaps give more useful rebutting evidence.

10747. You don't know that the people who are credited with producing the best hunters hardly form 1 per cent. of the population, have you got those statistics at all?—No, I don't exactly know what that would mean.

Mr. La Touche.—I should like to know how Mr. Wrench arrives at these statistics?

Chairman.—I don't think Mr. Burdett-Coutts can be in a position to answer that question.

Witness.—I am extremely anxious to give all the information to the Commission that I can.

10748. Mr. Wrench.—Do you think, from what you have said to Lord Dunraven, that Ireland is specially adapted to produce every kind of horse?—I should think so.

10749. And do you think that the trade in harness horses or the trade in hunters is the most certain to the breeder?—I have already pointed out that there is far less risk to the breeder of the harness horse than there is in the hunter. The buyer of the harness horse has to take all the risk of breaking him, and making him, and keeping him sound during the most critical part of his existence. Whereas—I am not sure of the practice in Ireland, so I speak with diffidence—but certainly in England, the man who breeds a hunter as a rule has to make him, ride him, and show him as a hunter, and possibly give a trial of him to a buyer before he can make a profitable price of him.

10750. Mr. Fitzwilliam.—May I ask when you are comparing the two whether "hunter" applies to the riding horse and not exclusively to the made hunter?

10751. Mr. Wrench.—I am talking of hunters alone?—I should also like to say, as bearing on that question, that I do think it is a matter for somewhat grave consideration whether you are wise in confining or doing anything to confine the horse-breeding of the country to the production of the hunter, because while the demand, as I have already pointed out, for the harness horse is absolutely certain and permanent and must always exist, the demand for hunters depends upon conditions which have already once or twice been seriously interfered with, and which may hereafter be interfered with again, and it is possible that hunting might be either stopped or greatly diminished in England. Then you would have committed your country—you would have confined your country—to a class of horse, the hunter, which if hunting disappeared it would be extremely difficult to make a profit out of.

10752. Mr. La Touche.—What about the motor cars?—I don't mind them.

10753. Mr. Wrench.—You are not alarmed about the motor cars?—I am not, and I certainly hope that hunting will never be interfered with, but at the same time the hunter is a more perilous basis for trade than the harness horse.

10754. Do you know that there is a good demand for harness horses in England at present, in that they [illegible] by [illegible]. The [illegible] of the present experience [illegible] that of the [illegible] London dealers' stables, eighty per cent. [illegible] from abroad. He had great experience and great knowledge of foreign horses and of the English trade with foreign countries, and I should be inclined to believe that was the case. [illegible]

10755. Do you know anything about the American trade, whether any horses have recently come in [illegible]?—I don't know from personal knowledge very much about it. I think you might find someone who knew a great deal more. I have seen [illegible] in the papers, and [illegible], which are common property, about large [illegible] of horses coming over.

10756. I wanted to ascertain if you thought there was any trade which the foreigners have now that Ireland could get hold of in the way of producing harness horses?—I don't know [illegible] a very large trade that Ireland might get hold of, granting I am right in what [illegible] the matter of [illegible] a good [illegible] [illegible]. I think that probably the result would be to produce a harness horse which would be bigger than the Hackney, and [illegible] with the great mass of foreign carriage horses, which now come over here. I can [illegible] the question of the effect of the Hackney upon [illegible], but [illegible] would be the result. I have no doubt that [illegible] produce a class of horse which is now supplied to a great extent by foreigners.

10757. We have had it suggested to us several times that all the horses that come from America, especially from Canada, [illegible] all the horses that come in from abroad, should be branded or marked in some way to distinguish them as foreign horses, do you think that would be a practical measure?—I think it would be extremely unpopular with the dealers.

10758. [illegible]?—[illegible]

10759. Then it is not one of the remedies you would suggest?—No. In Italy they are [illegible]

10760. [illegible]?—Yes, I should say that [illegible] they give very high prices, and for some of the very best horses [illegible].

10761. Chairman.—I should like to ask you to make me understand a little more clearly, if you can, about what you call the middle of the harness horse trade. That is in Ireland the trade which lies between the two extremes, the farm horse on the one hand and the superior carriage horse or hunter. You say [illegible] that there is very little [illegible] the two extremes?—Yes, that sort of [illegible] between the extremes.

10762. And there is no great demand for them, no great [illegible] as a [illegible] price. I understand you to say that although there is a demand and consequently a [illegible] price for the animal which will do for the [illegible] and [illegible] a demand for the hunters and high-class carriage horses, yet that between [illegible] there is not any demand?—I am afraid I must have explained myself badly if you have got that impression. My two categories were horses of [illegible] size, namely, the little [illegible] horse, which would not go [illegible], and the big horse, which I have called [illegible] to which you have had evidence. There are [illegible] produced in Ireland [illegible]. I say that the whole of the [illegible] which [illegible] those two [illegible] the most valuable portion [illegible].

10763. Do you mean that they are actually or ought to be?—Oh, no, that they are. They are not

March 1, 1900.
Mr. [illegible], M.P.

produced in Ireland, there are some, they don't exist. That was my whole argument. I mentioned a case where I sent a thirteen-pound horse to that middle range who was a high first-class price.

10763. That is vacant?—That is vacant in Ireland and within that lie by far the most valuable harness horses.

10764. There are large possibilities you think within that range?—Very large.

10765. And those possibilities might be filled by the introduction of suitable sires which you think are the Hackney sires?—Undoubtedly.

10766. What I would like to get from you is why you think so, and in that direction, what grounds have you got for so thinking, that the produce, say, of good Hackney sires in this heterogeneous and very mixed type of mares that exists on the southern of the congested districts for instance, what reason have you to think that their produce could in any way compete with the animal that at present in England fills up that gap in Ireland, that middle class which does not exist in Ireland, that could compete with England?—You will remember that I gave an explanation, that a fixed breed would be prepotent and predominant over a mixed and promiscuous breed, and that the Hackney is a fixed breed, that he has his characteristics, which are valuable to him as a harness horse, by heredity, and when he is crossed with a promiscuous mare, the result would have more of the characteristics of the fixed breed than of the promiscuous breed; so I think in Ireland you would gradually—perhaps not by the first cross—but you would gradually work up to the production of a horse which would be within the range I have described as the great middle range.

10767. That range being pretty well filled in England?—I don't think it is, I think there is plenty of room within that range for other horses. I think the price of those horses is very high, I am very glad it is.

10768. Just putting the matter practically and taking that class of animal that you describe as lying latent in the congested districts, this sort of class of animal that could be improved by the introduction of the Hackney stallion, how many generations do you think it would take before you could produce an animal that could fairly compete in the open market with the animal which already exists and is being produced in England and by what means?—It would be difficult for me to say how long. I don't think anybody could say in how many crosses, and I have never suggested that out of that frightfully inferior stock, which I describe as being located in those special districts, you could breed the highest type of horse, but I think you could breed a far more valuable horse than they do now, and possibly in cases that might work up to a fine harness horse. I may say myself—as I did say when I came to the question of single produce crosses—that in two generations I have worked up some beautiful horses from a small pony by the use of the Hackney stallion.

10769. Now, as regards the riding horse, the circumstances are entirely different because for the middle animals, not good enough to make a hunter and perhaps not good enough for a high class carriage horse, there is a demand for them as troopers?—Yes.

10770. Assuming there was a certain amount of public money available, in which way do you think it could be more profitably expended, in endeavouring to improve the riding horse or in endeavouring to produce in Ireland, which does not exist at all at present, what you term the middle between the Irish tax horse and the few high class carriage horses, the middle of the harness class?—I think for the profit of the breeder it would be better to introduce the Hackney.

10771. For the profit of the industry generally?—Yes, guarded by the conditions which I have already stated.

10772. I think you said the profitable nature of breeding high class Hackneys depends a good deal upon the demand for horses with showy action?—Yes, undoubtedly.

10773. In your opinion is that likely to be a constant demand?—I should think, looking at the course of the last 2,000 years, it is bound to be, because you see action is as old as the first representation of the horse; in the old sculptures and figures you will see the horse with his legs up, and every picture you see of a horse in the days when they wanted to make a horse attractive he is always shown with action. The love of action has been greatly on the increase within my memory and I think it is likely to remain so, because I think in the Hackney we are improving the class of action and getting away from the unpleasant character of up and down, pounding action, which I never liked and never would have.

10774. Is the demand for a high class Hackney with superior action a large demand or comparatively limited?—I cannot exactly say—I know it is greater than the supply.

10775. That may be, but perhaps the supply is not very great?—I think you must look upon this matter with which we are dealing. The breeding of horses in Ireland is a very important industry, relatively more important there as compared with other industries. I want to know whether you consider the supply of hunters is an important factor as connected with horse-breeding in Ireland?—I think it is tremendously important, and the greater importance of the place that horse-breeding holds in Ireland in the economy of agriculture, the greater the importance of increasing the strings to the breeder's bow by enabling him to breed all the kinds of horses he can.

10776. There is a great deal in reputation, the name for producing a good article?—I don't think you can get the name without producing a good article.

10777. Ireland having the name for producing a good hunter that has a strictly commercial value?—Yes, the good will is very important.

10778. And anything that proved detrimental to the production of the animal would tell against the country as a horse-producing country?—Yes; I think it would be very unfortunate to do anything to interfere with the production of hunters in Ireland. I believe it is possible to largely increase the scope of horse breeding without interfering with the production of hunters in Ireland.

10779. And you, I gather, attach no importance to the bicycle and tricycle, and motor cars, as affecting the horse industry?—I do not in reference to the high class expensive horses, but the ordinary animal that the middle classes in England used to drive about. All our cabs and broughams will be driven by motor cars; they are all hired from jobmasters now, and I think you are sure to have the action of the motor car; it will no doubt interfere with a good many light draught horses I should think.

10780. You mean driving horses?—I [illegible] the horses that trot round with parcels.

10781. Don't you think it may become common for a man—instead of keeping a horse and gig as you have at times—bicycles for himself and his daughter instead?—Oh, I don't think so. I will tell you exactly where bicycles interfered with. They interfered with high class park hacks, because the people who rode high class park hacks took to bicycling; it was the fashionable thing to do, and the blow was fell—I found that on my last sale. That is all changed now. Then, I think, as a rule, the great body of people who now ride bicycles did not formerly ride horses; the people who form the great mass of customers for the bicycle are people who will give up a trip at the seaside for a year in order to get a bicycle; they never kept a horse at all.

10782. You spoke of the Indian government buying Hackney stallions; have other governments bought these largely?—Oh, yes; Austria has bought them very largely; France has bought them largely and Germany has bought.—I am not sure to what extent.

10785. Do you know of your own knowledge what class of horses they have [illegible]?—They have [illegible] them all round the country, on the principle of the foreign [illegible], to give people a choice. A government stud will consist of five or six different varieties of horses, so as to enable the farmer to attune his breeding operations according to the [illegible] of his market, his own soil, or his mares.

10786. Have you any knowledge of what the result has been?—I believe myself that we, in this country, buy very largely in those horses that are now coming [illegible] to us.

10787. The German horse?—Yes, an improved type of horse.

10788. As a matter of fact, do these foreign governments buy so many cavalry remounts as ever they did?—That I don't know.

10789. I presume the governments did not keep their stallions solely with a view of benefiting farmers?—I think the foreign governments always have at the back of their heads some idea about their military purposes.

10790. I think you have not told us about your experiments in crossing?—Of course these questions have brought out a good deal of what I wanted to say generally on the subject of crossing. I desire to make one or two explicit observations with regard to the Hackney stallion used for crossing on other breeds. You should be certain that his blood is old, as you cannot always tell from the Stud Book—you can tell from local knowledge—and that it comes of a line in which his characteristics—that is to say, those which you wish to reproduce—have been constantly repeated. That is the first thing, pedigree; the second is quality. It is essential that he should have quality. The Hackney has greatly improved in late years in this respect, and an enormous amount of harm has been done to the reputation of the Hackney by a coarser class which was pushed in the trade when the boom first came into prominence, the horse with "chunky" shapes, short neck, and meaty quarters. You might see at the first Hackney show the type of horse that was shown, and won prizes the first two years, did a great injury, and I think reflected great discredit upon the Hackney breed. Yorkshire horses were hardly shown. Then the Yorkshire horse came to be shown, and the Yorkshire type was fixed more or less as the type which won the prizes. And then the Norfolk breeders worked up to that type and produced a horse which they thought [illegible]. Also he must have size. It is a mistake to suppose that Hackneys are necessarily little horses, 15.1 or 15.2 hands. I have already spoken about the size of these older horses, the [illegible] being lost. I have [illegible] myself with some success to raising the size in the pure breed; but it can only be done by the most careful selection and the most systematic and patient [illegible]. I make this observation with regard to size for the general purposes of horse-breeding. Of course you may have, as in the case of the [illegible] [illegible], small [illegible] which it would be foolish to put to big horses. My conclusion with regard to the Hackney stallion as a getter of [illegible] [illegible] is this:—given good pedigree, good quality, and good size, the Hackney is infinitely more valuable for that purpose than the thoroughbred stallion—that is from half-bred mares. Well, then, I will just give you one or two [illegible] specific instances of crossing in my own stud. I already gave, at the beginning of this [illegible], an analysis of this subject, and I now deal with them [illegible]. When I first began horse-breeding, I began as other people breed. I bought [illegible] mares, more or less hunter mares, [illegible] I knew were hunter mares, and I chose them for their looks as brood mares, for their shape and bone and [illegible], and so on; they were mares that any judge of a horse would say were fine brood mares. I put them to thoroughbred stallions, not the result, [illegible] that I put them to Hackneys and [illegible] by breeding from a thoroughbred stallion. I used a very beautiful thoroughbred stallion, a horse that had every [illegible] that a weight-carrying hunter can have, a horse called "[illegible]." He got a good many very fine horses, but he never got weight carriers. I used him a few times, then, as I explained before, there came in the demand for pure Hackney blood, came to my stud and wanted pure blood, and I rather gave up crossing and stuck to the pure breeds. I have not yet begun it again, because I have a sufficient number of each pure breed. I will begin now with the Hackney and thoroughbred stallions on half-bred mares, that is a matter of [illegible] breeding and [illegible] what I have called [illegible]. I did not know the breeding of the mare. I take a mare, one of the greatest hunters any man ever rode. I rode her five years in Leicestershire. She could jump anything and gallop as long as hounds would run, and was up to weight. I put her twice to a thoroughbred. The first foal I sold at six years old for £24. This mare was not [illegible] to "[illegible]." The second I sold for £3. She did not breed for three years, but last year had a foal by a Hackney which is worth at least double what I got for the two foals by thoroughbreds; it was a very fine foal.

10791. What horse did you put her to?—The two thoroughbred horses. One was a horse which I think I would rather not mention, because he is living now; the other was a horse called "Lord Melton," who was winning. He was a very good looking horse but he was [illegible]. The other horse's foal was a good [illegible].

10792. Mr. [illegible].—A foal [illegible] out of an old mare would not be likely to be a very good one in any case?—Here I had two foals—the first sold for £24 and the second for £3.

10793. Lord [illegible].—What age were they when you sold them?—They were full age. Of course they were not successful horses. I don't want to lay too much stress on these instances; I am giving them as only individual cases, but I [illegible] to place all the information I could at the disposal of the Commission. Here is another instance: [illegible] who was made to harness and driven. I put her to a thoroughbred, I think that was "[illegible]." The only foal was sold at five years of age for £36. The same mare was put to a Hackney, the colt was a good harness horse, but he had a bad [illegible], and sold as a four-year-old at Tattersall's for £66. Now, I take a big brown mare, 16 hands, still in my stud, which I bought at Tattersall's, [illegible] [illegible], in a [illegible] from [illegible]. She is a fine type of an Irish hunter, but without the [illegible] [illegible]. I don't mean that Irish hunters have not good shoulders, but I mean this one did not happen to have the best of shoulders. I bred from her by a Hackney, a fine, great harness horse, splendid, and with plenty of action and big bone, which was sold as a four-year-old for £125. The next foal, also by a Hackney, was a big horse with equally good action and a [illegible] worker. He was sold as a [illegible] after two years' hard work, for £[illegible]. Then she was put to "[illegible]," and the foal was a good looking [illegible] without the [illegible] of a hunter and without the action of a harness horse. I should say I could not get more than £30 for her. Since then the old mare has been put to Hackneys continuously, and there is a three-year-old mare out of her by a "[illegible]" stallion, which is one of the best in my stud. I take a rather smaller mare bought [illegible] at Tattersall's, with rather better shoulders, breeding unknown. I found out by subsequent inquiry that she was a hunter, and a very good one. I bred her to a Hackney, and the foal was a very fine harness horse, 15.3, sold for £130. This mare stopped breeding and I sold her. I take a very big mare, something between a hunter and a harness horse, 16.1, big frame and fair action

[illegible]

Mr. Burdett-Coutts, M.P.

Mr. Burdett-Coutts, M.P.

I put her to Hackney stallions, and she has bred me some of the finest mares in my stud—great striding mares with big bone, roomy frames, and very fine action. I should imagine that if you were to see these mares, you would say they would breed fine hunters to thoroughbred stallions. Now I take the thoroughbred and the Hackney on the Irish hunter mare of known breeding. This was an Irish mare, which I reared in Leicestershire, by "Else Fortune" out of a mare by "M. D." She was a very beautiful hunter, rather under my weight. I put her to a good thoroughbred, still living, whose name I will not mention, whose fee was 25l. And I obtained a thoroughbred with good bone. She bred a substantial horse, which was sold as a four-year-old for £150. That was her first foal, and then in that legitimate direction. I then put her to my own Hackney stallion, "Candidate," and she bred me a beautiful mare, 15.3, with good shapes, clean bone, and fine pattern—a perfect type of a park hack. I put this mare that was by the Hackney out of the nearly thoroughbred hunter again to a Hackney stallion, and she has bred me a very fine horse, with more action than the dam, and with all the original quality of the grand-dam. This is a case which is about with a hunter mare with quality, of which many are to be found in Ireland, and bred to the second generation with a Hackney stallion with successful results. Now, I take a case, which is perhaps not so very pertinent to this inquiry. It is that of the Hackney stallion on the thoroughbred mare. I take three thoroughbred mares first—"Arabella," a mare by Mandrake out of Family by Chevalier d'Industrie, out of Jon des Mots (dam of Duquesne, winner of the Grand National in 1869), by King Tom. Arabella is a typical steeplechase mare up to fourteen stone. She won the Open Hunters' race at Kempton Park. I have put her to my Hackney stallion, Sir Peter, and she has produced a charming filly, deep, with plenty of quality and fine action. "May," a much lighter thoroughbred mare by Beeswax out of Bonibel by Blanche out of [illegible] by Rattlin. She bred me in the first instance a filly to a horse whose fee was fifty guineas, which was sold for thirty guineas. To Dorado she bred a pony, of which I will speak afterwards. Again to another thoroughbred she bred a gelding of no value. To a Hackney stallion she bred me a beautiful filly, which is entered in the Hackney Stud Book; a perfect park hack, with the shape and quality of a thoroughbred, and a great deal more action, easy and from the shoulder. You will remember you asked me about the action that Hackneys would get out of mares with quality. This last mare I put again to a big Hackney stallion, and she has bred me a really magnificent mare with good size, long sloping back shoulders, big flat bone, and high swinging action, [illegible] I should think be made one of the finest brood mares in my stud. With regard to the pony above mentioned by the thoroughbred stallion out of the thoroughbred mare, I put her to a Hackney pony stallion, and she has bred me a distinctly stepping pony with great quality. The third thoroughbred mare that I take is "Start," bred in Ireland by Cassidy. She was bought in 1878 in [illegible] to "Junior," and third in the Newmarket Hackney Club Cup to "Stirk" and "Isonomy." She was one of the finest types of a big thoroughbred mare I ever saw, with great size and depth, clean flat bone, and a certain amount of action. She produced a horse whose fee was a hundred guineas a thoroughbred foal which was sold as a yearling for 25 guineas. For five years afterwards she either was barren or slipped or her foal died, to thoroughbred stallions. I then put her to one of my Hackney stallions. She bred me a fine foal, now a yearling, somewhat too light of bone for my purpose, but with fine action in both the trot and gallop. This mare herself had very good bone; the Hackney, of course, has; but the thoroughbred blood throws back to some lighter bone in spite of her own and the Hackney's excellence in that respect. I may say generally speaking that the bone is an enormous difficulty in dealing with the thoroughbred blood, whether pure or whether seven-eighths or whatever it may be. I would have crossed the thoroughbred with the Hackney over and over again, years ago, if every time I tried it it had not diminished the bone and lengthened the leg. That is my general experience of crossing with the thoroughbred. There are three instances, which are perhaps hardly to the point, of the Hackney stallion on harness mares with action but of unknown breeding; they have bred some very valuable animals indeed. I don't know the breeding of these mares, but they have got action. There is now a case which I particularly want to call your attention to, the Hackney stallion on the pony mare with quality. This was a beautiful mare; she is dead now, but if you saw her I think you would say she was a mare, that it was not impossible to find the type of—although you might not find anything quite so handsome to buy—in Ireland. You could either call her a pony mare or a very small thoroughbred mare, her breeding was quite unknown to me, she had great quality, rather light of bone and very little action. I put her always to Hackneys. She bred me a stallion, which after serving for a year at my stud was sold for 600 guineas. That was in the days of the Hackney boom, at the same time he was a wonderfully valuable horse, he served for a year at my stud. This stallion bred great quality and action. I put him to a strong Yorkshire mare, a Hackney, a Norfolk mare with the oldest and purest Hackney blood I could get, and he bred me a far better stallion than himself, which again has bred some beautiful stepping horses with great quality. This mare is of a type not unfrequently to be seen in Ireland. Whether you would call her a pony with quality or a small thoroughbred, she is an admirable instance of the value of the Hackney cross upon small mares with quality. During the last eight years from 200 to 300 mares have been sent annually to my Hackney stallions.

10787. CHAIRMAN.—Hackney mares?—My stud is located outside the recognised Hackney districts, and roughly speaking, 80 per cent. of the mares sent to my Hackney stallions have been non-Hackney mares, hunters, harness mares, hacks, &c., old favourites of people that live about London. Year after year I have seen their foals at my stud by my own stallions, and these have comprised a great number of beautiful and valuable animals with good size and quality, and action running through them as the predominant feature. Most of the dams have been devoid of action. There is only one more thing with regard to crossing I should like to call the attention of the Commission, and I will explain why, to the cross of the Hackney stallion and the coaching mare; the mare Mr. FitzWilliam was mentioning. In my breeding operations I have looked ahead for some method of supplying the demand for harness horses of 16 hands, more or less with fine shapes and action; a demand now very largely supplied to the dealers by harness horses from abroad. I find the pure Hackney as a rule not big enough to supply in any number the type of horse from ordinary-sized mares, the coach horse, except in the case of my own horse Sultan, has not sufficient action. In this class of horse you have to compete with the French coach horse (carrossier) that has a good deal of action and fair shapes, and the German coach horse which has shocking bad shapes, soft bone, bad feet, no action behind, but who "flops" it up in front. Again, the buyers of this class of horse, which is chiefly used in the towns, are very often people who do not know anything about horses, and their eye is taken by this action in front. I believed from the first that the best cross to produce the required type was the Hackney stallion on the coaching mare, and I have used that cross with great success. The produce have, as I have stated above, more size than the Hackney, and more action [illegible] the cleaner horse. They have just that extra length of shoulder and quality which are necessary when you mate a Hackney to it, to produce [illegible] being a vulgar harness horse. Now I call the attention of the Commission to this point, because the most [illegible] big hunting horses now bred in Ireland from the thoroughbred stallion than any other breed [illegible], except [illegible], in England. Moreover, they are used for the same purpose, and supply a [illegible] purpose, [illegible] and elegant, and [illegible] harness work. They are the true English "carriage" horse, and an old and [illegible] breed. Formerly, as I have already stated, the great London jobmasters got most of their horses from this breed in Yorkshire. Their carriers would not have been profitable to the breeders, and the class of horses they bought could not stand alongside of the Hackney, with his higher action and his greater market value. Consequently much [illegible] breeding [illegible]. They were generally produced by crossing big thoroughbred stallions on Cleveland mares. This is the origin of the Yorkshire coach horse, and the thoroughbred blood was since taken in again and again. I do not wish to [illegible] as [illegible], but I would show the Commission [illegible] of them, with respect to which I think any judge of horses [illegible] would say "[illegible] a quick, short-legged horse standing with [illegible] shoulders, and she would breed a fine horse." I put her to the Hackney, and she breeds me a fine harness horse. The [illegible] to which I have pointed is not absolutely clean, but I feel sure it is a sufficient guide to [illegible] that [illegible] of the Irish hunter mares would breed very good harness horses to the Hackney stallion. That is all I want to say about crossing, the relation between the breeding from the Hackney stallion and the breeding from the [illegible] which I have found extremely successful, would, in my opinion, be carried into Ireland with [illegible] with very good effect [illegible] 15 hands harness horses.

19733. You spoke just now about the quality of the Hackney having been much improved of late; how, by what means?—The only means by which I have been able to improve it has been by careful selection.

19734. Among Hackneys?—Among Hackneys entirely.

19735. I have a vague idea of what quality means as regards a thoroughbred horse, but I am not sure what it means as regards a Hackney?—It is a somewhat subtle property residing in the neck and head and quarters.

19736. And produced by careful selection?—Produced by careful selection. Undoubtedly my principle has been with regard to the produce that you are bound to stick to the breed in order to have a [illegible], and the closer you stick to the breed, the more you will be able to produce the result of [illegible] in other breeds.

19737. Lord [illegible].—Have you ever seen any of the stallions that were purchased by the Congested Districts Board in Ireland?—Between the letter which I wrote and my [illegible] three months elapsed, and when I was coming back from my tour I saw, I think, seven or eight stallions which had been purchased.

19738. Do you know the names of any of them?—I don't know that I could quite remember their names now, but I know there were some very nice horses amongst them, and there were one or two, I think, very bad horses—only one bad horse. [illegible] of them, although very [illegible] them.

19739. [illegible] you approved of the horses?—[illegible] them I saw.

19740. Did you find many of them [illegible] back of the knee?—I don't remember [illegible]. There was one bad horse—I think he had a very [illegible] than he [illegible].

19741. A horse standing that way would probably be standing more on his fore tendons than if he were properly placed?—Yes, I think he would. I don't know quite whether you mean "calf-kneed," or simply the bone set in under the knee, which is sometimes loosely called "back of the knee." I have seen a lot of good working horses made like that, but I don't like it—in my opinion. I think it is far less objectionable than a calf-kneed horse, a horse whose knee is really bad. The horse I mean does not stand back of his knees, but puts his foot in relation to the knee, and the knee in relation to the shoulder, as if he had good legs, but there is, so to speak, a little of the bone scooped out [illegible]—it is a great question, and I always try to avoid it. There was one famous strain, perhaps more than one, amongst the Hackneys of which that was a characteristic.

19742. Did you notice that at all in the Congested Districts Board's horses?—I don't remember that I did. If I were to say [illegible] I should find out, because it is a thing I would [illegible] on the look out for; I have had it in my own stud.

19743. Do you object to a horse having long pasterns and standing back on them?—Personally I am rather fond of long pasterns, that is, I would rather have a pastern too long than too short.

19744. You would rather [illegible] on the [illegible] than [illegible]?—A good deal [illegible] having the pasterns too sloping, rather than having them too upright. I would rather have them too sloping than upright pasterns, particularly for riding.

19745. Mr. Wrench.—Do you know whether there was a great trade in those coach-horses to America at one time?—Well, there has been a great trade in everything in America; they are the most extraordinary people for rushing at a fancy. [illegible] they got very fine specimens of that breed and got rid of it. There was at one time a very considerable export of these coach-horses.

19746. [illegible] there has not been much trade in coach-horses to America?—I think not.

19747. Why were they given up?—Because [illegible] jobmasters bought them, the use of that class of horses has gone so enormously into the hands of the jobmasters, and out of the hands of private persons. A great proportion of the people in London that have only a landau and brougham, job their horses, and they are the jobmasters' horses exclusively.

19748. You have been about Yorkshire a good deal?—Yes.

19749. And has not horse-breeding there been of great use to the farmers, have not some of the farmers made a good deal of money by it?—Yes; I have already said there was no counties in England to my experience where horse-breeding has been anything like the profit to the breeder that it has been in the Hackney business of Yorkshire and the Eastern Counties.

19750. And they are a fairly intelligent lot of people?—Very much so, particularly the Yorkshire men, sharp as a needle.

19751. And they would not take up the Hackney breeding unless it paid them?—No.

19752. Mr. La Touche.—With reference to the Yorkshire Hackney breeding, are they the same people who bred the Hackneys in Yorkshire some years ago?—Oh, I should think not.

19753. [illegible] £1,500 twenty years ago [illegible] for £50, we might [illegible] the Hackney?—Yes; and so there was a sudden boom in the Hackney breed, as there has been a great [illegible] in [illegible]. [illegible] responsible for it in a great measure. [illegible] for three years, and brought a tremendous lot of money into the Eastern Counties and Yorkshire, and I think it did more harm to this breed. I think it gave people the idea that if they bred anything they could get it into the Stud Book only through sale. That I knew that was all thing which would have been shut down in Ireland, and it was for that reason I turned my attention to the business department of my stud, because I felt I must have an outlet for my horses, to avoid depending on the natural course of trade. And therefore when I speak on this subject, I speak not only as a theorist but as a person who has had to face the question. I have certain advantages, of course.

10814. Mr. Fitzwilliam.—Don't you think the "boom" was unavoidably in a sport country, for the large way in which the men of the East Riding of Yorkshire suddenly went in for Hackneys?—I think a great many more men went in for Hackneys, but the Hackney has always been limited to the districts about Hull and Driffield.

10815. Yes, but to a comparatively limited extent?—No doubt, there has been an increase in Hackney breeding.

10816. A very large increase?—A very large increase.

10817. And don't you think the boom in Hackneys a few years ago was greatly accountable for that?—I suppose it was, when the demand increased at such the supply will increase.

10818. Do you know that a great number of farmers in that district would be very glad to get back again, if they could now, to hunter breeding?—I did not know that.

10819. That is what they tell me, I live in the middle of the district?—I think, as I say, that the boom did this harm, it gave people the idea that no matter what Hackneys they bred, good or bad, they could always sell them, and they did go in rather foolishly, but as a steady industry in that district, I think the old residents always remained.

10820. Chairman.—Is there anything else you would like to tell the Commission?—There is nothing else I have to say myself, unless I may explain my suggestion with regard to hunter-breeding in Ireland. It applies to the points in which I believe that [illegible] of the thoroughbred [illegible]. There are to be found in Ireland weight-carrying stallions, which [illegible] properties essential to the hunter—bone, substance, good shoulders, short legs, big [illegible], quality, pace, and staying power, sound all over, and with good [illegible]. Some of these are thoroughbred, and from [illegible] hunter stock known for generations in the country. Some are even [illegible] the thoroughbred. These horses have resisted for generations the deteriorating operation of the thoroughbred cross with regard to substance, while they have retained those properties necessary to the hunter which the thoroughbred alone possesses. This shows that they must have a strong force of prepotency with respect to the properties also essential to the hunter which the thoroughbred does not possess, and which you want to ingraft into hunter stock. Keep some of these horses as stallions. Make sure before you use them that they like jumping and have pace and endurance. That will enable you also to decide if they are sound in the wind, and free from any other transmissible weakness. Take this cross in wherever or whenever the native stock becomes light and weedy, and while keeping to the true hunter you will greatly improve his type. This, of course, would have to be the work either of a public-spirited individual or of a system aided by Government. Had I been a hunter-breeder I should have adopted this method twelve years ago, when I suggested it, and should have patiently worked it out. Like the other theories which I put forward with regard to the breeding of harness horses and have carried out in practice with successful results, this one, I believe, would have attained its object. That is my suggestion, and I believe it is better than the introduction of the Hackney stallion, better infinitely than the constant, excessive, sole use of the thoroughbred stallion, and a suggestion which if carried out would cause a great improvement in the breed of weight-carrying hunters. Now there is only one other thing I want to say, that is, I, myself, consider—although I have talked a great deal and written a great deal on these subjects—I myself consider one ounce of experience worth twenty tons of theory, and one minute of sight-seeing worth a week of talking, and if it would be within your scope, and would be possible for you to see my stud, I would endeavour to arrange for a view of it with the special object of illustrating such of these crosses and questions as have arisen in the course of my evidence to remain in my stud. I may state that it is divided into three parts, many of the horses which would illustrate these points are away in Yorkshire, and if you did like to see the horses I should so arrange the show that it would be useful to illustrate the evidence.

Chairman.—It is very kind of you to suggest that.

The Commission adjourned to next day.

TWENTY-FIRST DAY.—THURSDAY, MARCH 4TH, 1897.

Sitting at 12, Hanover Square, London, W.

Present:—The Earl of Dunraven, K.P., in the Chair; Lord Ashtown, Marquess of Londonderry, K.G., Hon. H. W. Fitzwilliam, Lord Rathdonnell, Sir Walter Gilbey, Colonel St. Quintin, Mr. Percy La Touche, Mr. F. S. Wrench.

Mr. Hugh Neville, Secretary.

General Sir John Watson, V.C., K.C.B., examined.

10821. Chairman.—What position do you hold under the Government, Sir John?—My duties are to purchase stallions in England, and send them out to the Indian studs.

10822. And how long have you been engaged in doing that?—Four years.

10823. Could you tell the Commission what class of stallions you send out?—I send out stallions such as are indented for by the Indian Government, sometimes thoroughbreds, Hackneys in different proportions, occasionally half-breds.

10824. What do you mean by half-breds?—It is difficult to know what the Indian Government means by half-breds, but if I meet with a stallion, not a pure Hackney, not a pure thoroughbred, but who has his lines of race blood in his pedigree, that is what I take to be a half-bred horse indented for by the Indian Government, and send him accordingly, but very few are asked for.

10825. That is a cross between the thoroughbred and the pure-bred Hackney?—Either that or a horse bred by a thoroughbred out of a mare that is not in the thoroughbred Stud Book.

10826. And you send it?—In the proportions asked for annually by the Indian Government.

10827. Could you tell us what proportion of

thoroughbreds, half-breds and pure-bred Arabs, Hackneys or other breeds, you mean? — Yes. In the last four years I have sent out 153 stallions, sixty of those were thoroughbreds, sixty-six Hackneys, and some Arabs.

10510. Are you limited to price? — I am limited to 250 guineas, but if I see a horse of a higher price that I think worth buying, I have to make special application to the Secretary of State for India, which is usually granted.

10511. And what are the principal objects of the Government establishments in India? — The Government of India maintains 300 to 370 which are called Imperial stallions scattered over the country, and any owner of a mare who can get it inspected by the Civil Veterinary Department as fit to produce a remount can obtain the services of that Imperial stallion free. The local governments also maintain what are called District Board stallions, but they are chiefly small Arabs for breeding ponies and mule animals.

10512. Then so far as the Imperial stallions are concerned, am I right in supposing that the main object is to secure a sufficient supply of suitable animals for remounts? — Entirely, the only object is remounts for the army.

10513. And for that purpose both thoroughbred, pure-bred Hackneys, and half-bred stallions have been sent? — Yes, Arabs are also used, and a few thoroughbred Australian horses have been used lately.

10514. I suppose the class of mares varies a good deal in different parts of India? — Very much indeed.

10515. Are these different classes of stallions sent to localities where it is supposed they would particularly suit the class of mare? — They are distributed by the Inspector-General of the Civil Veterinary Department to such districts as he thinks best, with regard to the class of mare in the district.

10516. Can you tell the Commission at all where the Hackney stallions are placed, and the kind of mares they are put to? — No, because they are entirely under the direction of the Stud officers.

10517. Have you formed any opinion as to whether the produce of the Hackney stallion with the native mare has been successful and proved useful as remounts? — I think the produce of the Hackney stallion has been very successful.

10518. And how about the thoroughbreds? — When I was in India last winter I endeavoured to come to a decision as to which class of sire was the most suitable, but I was unable to give the preference to either one or the other. The produce of the Hackney appeared to me to be quite as good as the produce of the thoroughbred, but I had complaints from many cavalry officers that the legs and bone of the Hackney-bred remount was not so lasting, although it was larger than the bone and leg of the thoroughbred produce, but still that evidence was not very decisive, and I came home with the conviction that there was no credit to be given to the one above the other, and that the one was quite as useful as the other, employed by the staff officers in the districts where they were used.

10519. You think the produce of the Hackney is equal to the produce of the thoroughbred in endurance and staying? — I could not answer that question, because it can only be decided on a campaign, and the question arises whether we have in India any sufficient test for a point of endurance.

10520. Can you tell us when Hackneys were first introduced into India; how long have they been there? — Certainly for the last twenty-six years, and I think a few were sent thirty-five years ago.

10521. Then there has been plenty of opportunity of testing the results? — Yes.

10522. What is your opinion about that? — My opinion is that the introduction of the Hackney stallion upon the Indian mare has been attended with great advantage.

10523. Improved the breed, the result, I take it? — I should not say that it had permanently improved the Indian mare, but the produce of the Indian mare, and the remounts from the Indian mare by the Hackney stallion are very good looking. Maj.-Gen. Sir John Watson, V.C., K.C.B.

10524. Do you think that the introduction of any European blood at all is calculated to improve generally the Indian horse? — My opinion is that it does not create any permanent improvement.

10525. How have you formed that opinion? — That is my private opinion only. I don't think I am supported much in that view.

10526. You would think that well-selected native stallions would be as useful as Imperial stallions for Government purposes. — I must maintain, and so does [illegible] with them that if pure-bred country were introduced in India, that either the thoroughbred or the Hackney stallion would produce from them the best remounts, but that they would not permanently improve that class of Indian mares, and I hold that to be supported by our knowledge of remounts in India we acquire many of the pure and ancient Indian races, many of which there are in India now.

10527. Are the owners of such animals careful in preserving their pedigree? — Many; few of them have written pedigrees, but they have traditions.

10528. I gather from you that the qualification necessary for free service of the Imperial stallion is a certificate that the mare is suitable to produce remounts? — Yes, it is required on the certificate if she is approved of by the civil officers as a mare likely to produce a remount, likely to breed a remount.

10529. And is that all that is done by the Government in the way of encouraging good animals? — Yes, that is all, with the exception of prizes given at horse shows. Horse shows are held all over the country, and prizes are distributed to mares and produce.

10530. Has that been found to answer well? — Yes, undoubtedly.

10531. Lord Londonderry. — You have seen, I suppose, the second [redacted] of these Hackneys put to Indian mares. Have you ever [redacted] the produce of this again? — The third cross?

10532. Yes? — I may or may not have [redacted], but I have no record of having seen them.

10533. I think you said that you thought there was no permanent improvement by means of crossing the Hackneys with the Indian mares. Does that mean that you think that the third cross would not be so advantageous as crossing that with a different class of horse? — I apply that idea to all English blood, whether Hackney or thoroughbred, exactly the same.

10534. Chairman. — Australian also? — Exactly the same. There is a difference in that point. We have used thoroughbred stallions for 100 years, and I think they have left no permanent mark of improvement in India. The Hackneys we have used for five-and-twenty or thirty years. I don't think they have left any permanent improvement in the breeds of India. The best and handsomest remounts I saw in India last year were the produce of Hackney stallions out of mares whose sires were Arabs.

10535. Lord Londonderry. — Are the remounts, as what are the sizes usually by Imperial stallions? — Between 14.2 and 15 hands, as a general rule.

10536. And what is the height required for remounts, what is the smallest you take? — For European troops, 15 hands the minimum, for native cavalry, 14.2.

10537. And I suppose a great many animals are bred considerably smaller than that, that are no use to you for remounts? — Yes, there are many animals under 14.2, such as I remember last year the District Boards maintain 700 stallions, and their produce does [illegible] much more than 14 hands.

10538. Is there a market for that class of animal or what becomes of them? — There is a civilian market.

10539. Do they fetch anything like remunerative prices? — Oh, they fetch very good prices. The prices of all the horses in India have much increased in the last 25 years.

Major-General Sir John Watson, V.C., K.C.B.

10840. And you tell them that, in the importation of these Hackney and thoroughbred horses, I can hardly say much, because we have imported thoroughbred stallions for 100 years, but the system of Hackneys has only come in for the last 20 years.

10841. Of course you see a good many Hackneys in England when you are making your selection before you send them?—Yes.

10842. Do you see a great deal of difference between them, some very good ones and some very bad ones, that you come across frequently at the shows which you visit every year among those that they bring you?—There are good and bad of course, but I see a very great number, a very largely preponderating number of good Hackney stallions than I can of good thoroughbred stallions, that is to say, I could more easily select 10 or 20 good Hackney stallions than I could select ten good thoroughbred stallions, which I want.

10843. Mr. Pennington.—At the price you are allowed?—Yes.

10844. Lord Londonderry.—Which would you think, if you were limited to one or the other, either Hackney or thoroughbred—would breed the best class of horse for your purpose in India, if you were limited to one or the other?—I never expected to be limited, and therefore I have never considered the question.

10845. You think the results are equally good from both, you have no data to find which either is better in relation to which they are most suited?—I think they are equally good.

10846. You have not, I suppose, seen any of them actually serving and doing work in the congested districts?—No, I have not seen them.

10847. Mr. Pennington.—I suppose from the number of years that the Hackney has been in India that there has been a certain number of generations of them already there?—Oh, yes.

10848. But I gather that you think that the second and third and fourth generations have not improved, and there is no great improvement?—I think there is no great improvement in the breed of Indian horses permanently made either by the Hackney or the thoroughbred.

10849. Then should you like in breeding to go back with those half-bred mares to the Indian horse as a stallion?—No, I should like to breed pure bred mares, pure Indian mares of pure breeds, and breed remounts from them by English horses.

10850. Then what you prefer is the first cross?—The first cross.

10851. Pure Indian mares and pure English stallions?—Yes, for remounts, first cross.

10852. What size of Hackney do you prefer for India?—From 15 to 15.1.

10853. Lord Londonderry.—I think you mentioned Arabs and Hackneys and thoroughbreds as being stallions chiefly used in India; is there not another, the Waler?—There are a few. I believe that Veterinary Colonel Hallen is coming here. He is provided with all the statistics as to the numbers of horses in India in their proportions.

10854. Have you ever seen any of the Walers?—Yes I have; I have two last year, Australian stallions with thoroughbred English pedigrees, that is to say descended from thoroughbred horses imported into Australia.

10855. Is that what you call the Waler?—That is what they call the Waler.

10856. How do they compare with other stallions?—The English thoroughbred stallions?

10857. Yes, and the Hackneys?—You cannot compare them with the Hackney, but comparing them with the English thoroughbred they have bigger bone, and hence from the Australian character of the English thoroughbred than much better bone and much better feet.

10858. Did you see any of the produce of these Walers?—No.

10859. Sir Walter Gilbey.—Are those Walers that you allude to pure thoroughbred on both sides, are and from English stock?—Yes.

10860. But the Waler that is known in India as remounts, he is not pure bred, is he?—No.

10861. The horse commonly termed the Waler is not a thoroughbred horse?—No, he is a horse bred in the great runs of Australia from any sort of sires, but they are all descendants of English horses.

10862. But not from the registered thoroughbred horse?—There is an enormous mixture of them.

10863. It is rather important to the evidence that you should define the difference between the Walers that are known as Walers in India, and those that you are alluding to when you said they were the sons of the thoroughbred horse. I want to know are the sire and dam thoroughbred?—Yes, those imported to India for stallion use. The question I think was regarding Waler stallions; the Government have lately imported a few from Australia, thoroughbred Australian stallions with as pure pedigree as any thoroughbred horse in this country; the pedigree is maintained in Australia in their stud book, there is an Australian Stud Book.

10864. It is necessary that the horses that are bred there should be for endurance in India in case they should be wanted for an emergency. Do you, therefore, you have had an experience as to how these different strains with the native mares from different stallions turn out?—Yes, as I have said, we have been breeding for one hundred years, and in many of our Indian wars the stud-bred horse, as they call them, has been well tested. There has been diversity of opinion as to their endurance, but I think the evidence prevails that the Australian horse does not surpass the stud-bred horse in endurance. You will find one commanding officer of a regiment say: "Give me the Australian Waler," and another say, "Give me the stud-breds," but there has been no definite and decided preponderance of opinion in favour of one over the other.

10865. Have there been reports published every year from India on the results of the breeding in the various districts, I think you said. Mr. Hallen would produce them, it would be very useful that we should be furnished with those reports?—The annual report of the Civil Veterinary Department of India gives all the statistics every year, and minute particulars. Mr. Hallen, no doubt, will have the books with him.

10866. Colonel St. Quintin.—Are you able, Sir John, to get the number of thoroughbreds, as a rule, that are indented for by the Indian Government?—Perhaps I have, but I have never been asked for more than twenty; I think that if I was asked for more than twenty I should have great difficulty in procuring them. When Lord Mayo was Viceroy of India he took a great interest in the studs, and he said he was perfectly certain that the thoroughbred stallions suitable to the Indian studs could not be found in one year in England and Ireland. I think I might find twenty but not many, because the perfection of bone, and limb, and hoof, which is required for the Indian studs is very rarely found among the thoroughbreds at the present day, except in large horses and very expensive horses.

10867. When you were in Persia, from what you saw of the Australian horse, what did you think of them, had I many of the Australian stallions?—I saw eight or ten very good ones.

10868. They were all of thoroughbred English blood?—Yes.

10869. Speaking of endurance and the test of endurance, did you ever hear that, according to the statistics of the Afghan War and of the Russian Commission, where they had every class of horse, the stud-bred, the Barb, the Waler, and the Arab, that they came to the conclusion that it was the age rather than the breed of the horses that determined how they stood the hardships?—I have not heard that.

10870. That the horse between six and ten years old is best?—I have not heard that.

10871. Mr. WESTCOTT.—Before you had this appointment of buying stallions for the Indian Government, had you previous experience of India?—Yes; I have, as a cavalry officer, been always very much interested in the breeding stock of India all my life.

10872. And were you many years in India?—Thirty-eight.

10873. Do you find great opportunities of seeing, of the stock of native horses there?—Yes.

10874. To what do you attribute the reversion of all the horses to the native type in India?—I won't say that they revert to the native type, but my belief—a belief which I am not supposed to try away—my belief is that the cross between the European blood and the Asiatic blood always does revert in the third and fourth generation. I consider that this is the reason why, although we have been breeding from English horses for a hundred years, yet we have not so far as I can see any [illegible] permanent improvement in the Indian horses.

10875. Were you recently in India inspecting studs?—Yes, last winter.

10876. Did you inspect many of the stud-horses, and many of the stations where the Government stallions are located?—Yes; a good number of them, and attended several fairs.

10877. At the fairs do they give prizes, as you then give stallions for sale?—Very considerable prizes are given, and rates are also offered.

10878. Can you say what proportion of the prizes, as if you were able to distinguish whether one breed takes them another won prizes?—The last Veterinary-Colonel [illegible] can give you the exact statistics of the prizes won by each class of horse.

10879. Did you make any experiment in any stations you could see the appearance, whether you could tell what stallions the different horses were got by?—I did try once, in company with the Inspector-General at [illegible]. We ordered the [illegible] officer to take out ten four-year-old geldings [illegible] by Hackneys, ten by thoroughbreds, and ten by Arabs, and mix them all together, and then we went to the [illegible] and selected what we thought the best horses [illegible], and then sent for their pedigrees, and I think one was by Hackneys, four by Arabs, and one by a thoroughbred: but I should not consider that a very reliable test, though I think it is quite sufficient proof that the Hackneys used in the proper districts give quite as good remounts as the thoroughbred. This test showed, of course, a great superiority, but I don't think it is a test you can rely upon altogether, because we had no record of the mares that they came from.

10880. In purchasing stallions you have tried to purchase what you term half-bred stallions?—Yes.

10881. Have you looked at many of these half-bred stallions, or [illegible] to that breed?—I [illegible] found one that I would [illegible] send out to India, but because they were asking [illegible] I bought one [illegible] or three.

10882. Did you have looked at prize [illegible]?—No, I don't find a great number.

10883. They don't exist, so far as you are aware?—I don't think they exist; I never find them. Occasionally I have sent out five stallions bred by a thoroughbred out of Hackney mares; I don't think that they were so good as the pure Hackney or the pure thoroughbred.

10884. Do you know at all which the result has been?—No, I don't; they have not been there long enough.

10885. In the course of buying horses, have you been over most of the Hackney studs in England?—I have seen a great many; not all, it would be a long job.

10886. There you saw the horses belonging to the Congested Districts Board in Ireland, the stallions?—I have.

10887. Did you form any opinion of those generally?—I thought they were a wonderfully good class.

10888. You looked over them carefully?—Yes.

10889. CHAIRMAN.—I suppose, Sir [illegible], in buying these Hackney stallions you would be guided by your choice as to shape and quality and so on by the knowledge that they were intended to get horses suitable for cavalry [illegible]. I always select, if I can, a Hackney stallion that looks likely to produce a riding horse, rather than a driving horse.

10890. And I take it that your general opinion is, that from natural reasons the Western horse, the European horse, produces no permanent effect upon the native blood in India, but I gather as you did not include it in the same category that the other Eastern horses would. Has the Arab produced any permanent effect [illegible] has not some [illegible] in his or not.

10891. And you consider the most suitable animal for remount purposes is the first cross between the native mare and the thoroughbred or nearly pure-bred English horse, whether thoroughbred or Hackney?—If the mare is herself [illegible].

10892. In granting licences there [illegible] may [illegible] mares do the Government exercise any right over the produce of the mare?—No.

10893. None whatever?—None; the only restriction is that remount officers are not to buy licensed mares, excepting these in my [illegible].

10894. Do the Government keep any record of [illegible] sires in breed [illegible]?—Yes they could try but they have [illegible] given it up.

10895. Since when?—Colonel [illegible] can explain the exact date when that branding was given up.

10896. All that the Government try to do is to provide those imported and [illegible] stallions?—That is all.

10897. Do they recruit the remounts?—No, they have fixed stands, and the remount officers attend the fairs, buy the young ones, and turn them out to large runs until they are four years old, when they take them up and stable them and mount them, and make them fit for the army.

10898. What is the price they give for remounts?—For young ones?

10899. What age do they generally buy them?—At eighteen months.

10900. That would not lead to very much—but what price do they give then?—Between 200 or 300 rupees, I think, according to the value of the animal.

10901. Do they buy any three or four year olds?—No, the cavalry officers buy the horses at four years old.

10902. What is their price?—About 500 rupees.

10903. I don't know, Sir [illegible], whether you have formed any opinion or can give us any opinion on the subject of the most suitable animal for remounts at home, in England and Ireland, whether the cross with the Hackney is likely to be useful or [illegible] other people know more about that than I do.

10904. Mr. [illegible].—Do I understand you to say that in the case of breeding you would like to put an English stallion to a pure-bred Indian mare for the purpose of producing a remount, with the one [illegible] the breed.

10905. But as a half-bred mare you would prefer to put on an Arab. I thought you had said that. I was not speaking. I thought you had said that, the Hackney [illegible] to answer for a remount?—No, I don't think I said that. I said that the best remounts I saw were bred by Hackney stallions out of mares sired by Arabs.

10906. CHAIRMAN.—Is there any other information you would like to give us?—I think not; it is my opinion upon any general subject that I might have left otherwise.

10907. I don't know whether you have formed any definite opinion as to the fitness of the Hackney sires for getting an animal suitable for horse purposes?—I should be guided in this country by what the nature of the animal to do, and I think that is very fit animal to get riding horses, and I think you can get the sound and useful Hackney stallions at a great deal less than the thoroughbred stallions at the same price, of course.

[illegible]

[illegible]

Mr. Charles Hutchinson, M.R.C.V.S., Newcastle-on-Tyne, examined.

10608. Chairman.—You live at Newcastle-on-Tyne?—I do.

10609. Where you practising as a Veterinary Surgeon?—I do. I am not in general practice now. I gave up general practice in October, 1893. I only do work of a special kind now. Consultations and examinations and inspection work. I am Chief Inspector for Northumberland and also for the city of Newcastle-on-Tyne.

10610. And you know that part of the country pretty well?—Very pretty well; I do.

10611. I mean pretty well as regards horses?—Yes.

10612. Are there many horses bred in that part of the country?—No, sir, it is not a great breeding country; it is a large manufacturing district.

10613. Have you got any opinion as to the general character of the mares that are bred there?—We have not a good class of brood mares, that is the great trouble and the great cause of all the disappointments in breeding, the want of good brood mares. I think there is the ordinary farmer who has got a moderately good mare, and breeds from a half-bred sort of mare or a little hackney mare.

10614. Are you speaking of that district generally?—Generally, in reference to the whole of the Kingdom, I believe that.

10615. Has not the Duke of Portland a scheme for the breeding of half-bred horses?—He has.

10616. Do you know anything about that?—Yes. I took a little interest in it. I was at the Duke's show at Welbeck last summer, and I was also at Bothal, near Morpeth, where that he gives up [illegible] which he gives prizes for the benefit of the tenantry. They have to show horses that are sired by the Duke's horses. The Duke finds the very best sires. And at the luncheon at Welbeck he said that the great trouble was the want of good mares and to remedy that he bought a Yorkshire Hackney stallion with a view of the [illegible] got by the Yorkshire Hackney stallion being kept to breed from.

10617. What is the character of the mares?—I cannot tell you that.

10618. I mean the mares complained of?—A great want of size, want of character, being weedy small animals and not good enough to put thoroughbreds to. I may say in connection with that that when I saw the Duke's scheme in the papers some two or three months ago, that he was buying mares to lend to his tenantry to breed from, I wrote to Mr. Turner, his agent at Welbeck, and asked him what was the result of the buying of the Hackney stallion, and he replied. That is his letter.

10619. Will you read it?

Witness reading—"Dear Sir,—Referring to your letter of the 9th inst., the Yorkshire Hackney stallion the Duke of Portland bought last year, served between thirty and forty of his tenants' mares, and we hope that the fillies, the produce of these mares, will in time be put to one of His Grace's thoroughbred horses. Of course it will be several years yet before we would be able to see the effect, but I will not fail to let you know about it. In the meantime you may be interested to read the enclosed which is rather a brief scheme on the Duke's behalf." That is this scheme, which perhaps you have seen, that was sent out to all his tenantry. "It is determined if possible to make the tenants breed good animals, and now we are purchasing mares for them, we are going in for the Yorkshire coaching mares and I think they should do very well with the thoroughbred horses." Upon the receipt of this letter I wrote back to Mr. Turner and told him that I had been asked to give evidence before this Commission, and perhaps he had also been asked. I said, "If you are not asked may I make use of this letter?" He replied, "I have not the slightest objection to your making any use of my letter to you, if you think it will be of service to your evidence. I do not think the Commission are likely to ask my opinion." That was Mr. Turner, the Duke's [illegible] agent.

10620. I was going to ask you, up to the formation of this scheme from what class of mares did the tenantry [illegible] breed?—[illegible] from the Coach [illegible] thoroughbreds.

10621. And that is still the object eventually?—Yes.

10622. The introduction of the Hackney being merely to give bone and substance?—Substance and action.

10623. Is there anything more you would like to say on that point?—No, except that you will observe that they are buying coaching mares, and of course you probably understand there is a difference between the Yorkshire coaching horse and the Cleveland horse; the Yorkshire coaching horse has a cross of thoroughbred blood in him, he is much lighter with more action, stands up high, very valuable harness horse.

10624. Have you formed any general opinion as to the usefulness of the Hackney as a cross?—I think as a sire they are remarkably fine harness animals.

10625. And as to their soundness and character?—I have not much experience of the soundness of the Hackney except this, I have examined for about three years three horses coming into Newcastle, one in single harness and a pair, certainly the three best horses that come into Newcastle driving, pedigreed Hackneys. I spoke about a fortnight ago to the owner and asked how they were bred, thinking I was in some fear that I should, they were all pedigreed Hackneys and all by "Wildfire." They step high, go fast and keep on going, certainly the three best harness horses I know of, and show a great deal of quality.

10626. Have you had much experience of half-bred Hackneys?—No, I have not; there are very few bred in my country. I know nothing about the soundness of the Hackneys, well, I have examined these Hackneys for a long time, I have examined for the Royal Agricultural Society of England several times, and for the Royal Commission; I am acting for them again next week. I have also examined at the great Yorkshire Show for the last three years, along with Mr. Cope, Chief Veterinary Officer of the Board of Agriculture. Well, in examining horses at the shows we examine by number, I don't know any of them, therefore, I keep no record, but I knew that Mr. Cope did keep a record of the Yorkshire examinations, and I wrote to him asking if he would give me the record of the Hackneys for the last three years, and I got this from him:—In 1894 we examined 75 Hackney stallions and rejected 3; in 1895 we examined 82 and rejected 3; in 1896 we examined [illegible] were rejected, that is we examined 41 Hackney stallions, and rejected 4, and [illegible] only one of these horses rejected was afterwards passed sound at other shows.

10627. Lord Londonderry.—Who was the [illegible]?—I got that information from Mr. Cope, of the Board of Agriculture, he has acted for a long time for the Yorkshire Society, and for three years I have assisted him at times.

10628. Chairman.—I don't know whether you have any knowledge of Ireland?—I have been over there three times. Some years ago I used to go over there to purchase horses.

10629. Lord Londonderry.—There would be hunters?—Yes, and thoroughbreds.

10630. Chairman.—Have you sufficient knowledge to form an opinion as to which breed of stallions should be encouraged in Ireland in order to generally improve horse-breeding in the country?—I think the first thing to settle upon is what sort of mares have you to put the stallions to. It is little consequence what stallions you send if the mares are not adapted

[illegible]

[illegible] **Do you think that hunter would be as good** [illegible] **ones we breed now?—It might not be so fast;** [illegible] **would be a valuable animal. I am sure of** [illegible]

[illegible]

March 4, 1897. Mr. [illegible]

bred from the base of the thoroughbred, that one seems quite narrow and light, and the other like heavy and thick, and weighs more. I should very much like to have your opinion on that, whether you have examined the bone of the various breeds?—Only in an ordinary way, with the naked eye and hand. I have heard that theory years ago, but I have yet to know that it is a fact.

10964. Is it possible without a microscopic examination to know the bones of different animals?—They can be seen without that if you wish, only some one accustomed to anatomy [illegible] would say there is no difference in the bone, but it would only settle that question to employ a very good microscopist to make sections and examine them under the microscope, and examine them as to the amount of earthy matter in the consistency of the dense.

10965. You don't think any one who was not an expert could give an opinion on that matter that was worth having?—Certainly not.

10966. That it could only be ascertained by a microscope?—Yes.

10967. Do you know whether there has ever been a test of that kind made?—I cannot say that it has.

10968. Have you consulted any special authority on that point?—I have not. I am not aware that any books or from the best anatomists or physiologists I could consult.

10969. Therefore any expression of that kind is not of much value?—I should say none at all.

10970. We have been also told that Hackneys are very liable to roaring and curby hocks?—That is not my experience. I cannot remember ever having seen a Hackney with curb.

10971. Do you think they are sound generally in their legs and feet?—They are the soundest breed of horses I know of.

10972. And we have also been told that they have defective constitutions, that they don't recover from illness as easily as thoroughbred horses?—Well, I cannot speak very much as to their recovery from illness. I have not been in general practice since 1880, but I have no reason to think he is slower to recover from illness than any other breed.

10973. Is his constitution hardy?—What I know of them have been hardy, the three horses I know of in my district, and the three best horses I have seen on the road.

10974. Do you know generally anything as to the origin of the Hackney?—I know that they are a very old breed.

10975. If you were breeding a hunter, do you think Clydesdale or Hackney blood would be most objectionable?—The Clydesdale by all means; there is far more danger in Ireland of getting a mixture of cart-horse blood than there is of the Hackney. It is more than twenty-five years since I saw changes in Ireland [illegible] I saw there.

10976. Do you think Clydesdale blood would [illegible] than the Hackney?—Yes.

10977. And do you know that a number of the stallions in Ireland are Clydesdale or half-bred cart-horses?—I am very sorry to hear you say so.

10978. Dealing with small farmers who have not the means to breed hunters, do you think it would pay them best to breed hunters with [illegible], or to try to breed harness?—I should try to breed Hackneys and small [illegible], ride and drive, harness, [illegible].

10979. Do you think that would pay them better?—I am certain it would, particularly if they had action, nothing enhances the value of a horse more than action all round, and that you would get from the Hackney.

10980. There is one question we have had debated at the Royal Dublin Society lately, with regard to the hereditary soundness of horses, and that is on the question of [illegible]; do you think [illegible] is a hereditary unsoundness or not?—I think it is an unsoundness.

10981. Is it hereditary, in your opinion?—I have no doubt that [illegible] is very closely allied to roaring, and [illegible] roaring is hereditary, and therefore it follows that [illegible] must also be hereditary; they are closely allied.

10982. Perhaps if you were asked your opinion you would say it was hereditary unsoundness?—Certainly, and I would never pass a horse that [illegible]. I have known a horse that you could not make [illegible], and I have known a horse that [illegible] that did not make a noise in his paces, but my opinion is that a horse that [illegible] takes the first opportunity to become a roarer.

10983. And you would not breed from a grunter?—I would not breed from such an animal.

10984. CHAIRMAN.—Would not the specific gravity [illegible] of the bone, [illegible] of the family [illegible] would be one of the tests.

10985. Would not the difference between the specific gravity of the bone of the thoroughbred and the bone of the Clydesdale give you a rough and ready notion of the relative densities?—Before you mapped out this test you would have to take corresponding bones of the different horses; if you take the [illegible] bone of the horse, you would have to have the corresponding bone from another horse, you would have to have the bone from horses of the same age, they would have to be [illegible] horses, about six years old, because as they get older, they get [illegible]. If you took a five year old bone and a fifteen year old the analysis would show differently.

10986. We have had it in evidence [illegible], and a good many people think, as a matter of fact, the bone of the thoroughbred is denser than the bone of any other horse?—I have heard it said so. I don't disagree. I only say I am not aware of it; but I have looked up all the authorities I could, and I consulted one of the very best anatomists in the South of England, Professor Macalister, of the [illegible] College of Medicine. I put it to him and he could not say it. It is a question you will have to get settled by a microscopist. My own opinion is that there's no difference.

10987. You think, for instance, that the [illegible] bone that was mentioned to us yesterday as being particularly narrow and light, then probably it is just as dense and heavy as the thoroughbred?—They [illegible] I was not thinking of the [illegible] horse or the Hackney horse. I was thinking of the Hackney bone and the thoroughbred bone. I got two bones sent from Newcastle; but they were bones of a two year old, that would be utterly [illegible] to compare with the bones I had, old bones, so I didn't go any further.

10988. It was suggested by Mr. [illegible] a large proportion of the sires in Ireland are Clydesdales or [illegible] Clydesdale. You have no knowledge of that yourself?—No, sir. I hope it is not so, because if you have got any Clydesdale blood in your hunting mares it is [illegible] up with the character of the Irish hunter.

10989. But still the Irish hunter [illegible] the character?—Not with Clydesdale blood.

10990. But still it has not lost its character, and you would deduce from that that there are not many of the Clydesdale blood?—I cannot think it possible.

10991. Mr. [illegible].—The majority of the [illegible], I think, [illegible]?—They are kept away from the [illegible] now.

10992. CHAIRMAN.—Do you think the Hackney is a suitable sire to get a riding horse?—I should [illegible] the [illegible].

10993. I mean in the first cross?—There is [illegible] blood [illegible] blood. [illegible] the animal I would [illegible]

[illegible]

[illegible]

Veterinary Lieutenant-Colonel J. [illegible], C.I.E., [illegible], examined.

[illegible]

[illegible]

March 4, 1898.

Vet. Lieut.-Col. J. H. B. Hallen, C.I.E.

they generally get them, because they give the highest price as a rule. The only exception is where a native chief may come in with a big purse, and give anything for a horse he likes; but as a rule the English Government have the pre-emption, because they give a good price.

11049. Would the returns show what prices were for horses and what the horses four years old?—No, but there are returns in them also reports which show the different ages and the prices at the different ages.

11050. (Chairman.) What reports would they be in?—In the annual report of the Civil Veterinary Department; there are in another report, an appendix to this, which gives several hundred horses and foals, and I think you might get a copy of this from the India Office, and you will be able to get exactly the information you want.

11051. (Mr. La Touche.) It is very important we should know the ages of the horses when the prizes are awarded to them?—I can tell you that they are awarded to foals, yearlings, two years old, three years old, four years old; all different ages get prizes.

11052. Do you find as a matter of experience that the animal that gets prizes as a foal often gets prizes as a four year old?—It depends a good deal on how he has been fed in the meantime, if he has not changed hands, if he has been cared for he has got a good chance; but if he gets changed or sold he falls very bad off and become worth nothing, though he may have been the best at a year or eighteen months old.

11053. (Col. St. Quintin.) Before the present system of breeding was inaugurated the Indian Government had a system of Government breeding establishments of their own?—Yes.

11054. And they bred their own horses—can you tell us what class of horse and stallions were chiefly used in those—do you remember the historical old establishment before the Mutiny, were brought up to.—Yes.

11055. How were they bred?—Chiefly out of the country-bred mares, but later on the mares were imported; some mares were imported from England and some from Australia, but as a rule the country-bred mares were the produce of the stud themselves.

11056. What were the stallions chiefly?—The English and Arabs, stud-bred, half-breds (English imported) stallions very in early years ago, and occasionally an Australian thoroughbred.

11057. They were chiefly thoroughbred?—About half and half, half Arabs and half thoroughbred.

11058. When you indented for these Hackneys for the stud did you do so with the view of getting cavalry or artillery horses, or for both?—The aim was for the general improvement of horses in the country, the feeling of the military people was that we were getting weeds up solely to [illegible] them; [illegible] we hoped to [illegible] think [illegible] also wished to improve the breeding of horses in India. We hoped that the military people would get the best of the stock; we went in for getting both riding and draught horses.

11059. Do you agree with Sir John Watson that the Hackney is equally good for breeding for cavalry as for artillery purposes?—It depends on the shape of the Hackney, if he has good shoulders and shape, good action, action that will take a horse over the road well, and not too high knee action.

11060. You consider that by one get a good riding horse?—I have seen some excellent riding horses by Hackneys.

11061. The first class?—I am going so rapidly that by saying I think a great mistake that there is not more care taken with regard to shoulders in the breeding of Hackneys. I think that you are my opinion about shoulders, the shoulder of the thoroughbred is a grand shoulder as a rule, and there are some very poor shoulders in thoroughbreds, but look how that shoulder has been made, he has been going at a walk or a gallop over the most lovely ground, a billiard table racecourse for how many generations, how many years, and therefore he has got into a most beautiful shape so far as shoulders and [illegible] powers, and becomes well fitted to go over turf and level ground at a tremendous pace with a light weight on his back. That is his work at the present day, and that is really what he is raised for. Now a Hackney has to do different work altogether, and I will put the Arab in with the Hackney as far as shoulders are concerned. The Arab, what does he do? In his native country he has to go through deep sand, and to have a very powerful shoulder to pull himself along and pick his feet out of the sand, his pasterns grow long as a rule from the weight dwelling in the sand, and his shoulder gets very thick and clumsy because he has to use it in that particular way. At the same time when a man comes on he has to go at a very fast pace to raise the property, [illegible] and his shoulder is fair, not a good shoulder, but well suited for his work. Now, a Hackney has not a riding shoulder, because he is principally used for driving purposes. I am not an admirer of fancy horses. I know Mr. Burdett-Coutts describes something the fashionable action for a Hackney, but for a general utility horse we do not require that kind of action.

11062. Do you think the thoroughbred horses that were sent to India for many years were good of their type?—As good as they could be obtained.

11063. For the money?—I must tell you that the late Inspector-General, General Thornhill, and the present one, General Watson, if they saw a good horse above 300 guineas, they would always buy him. General Thornhill told me he had not any horses fitted for the India stud as a rule above 300 guineas; except you get hold of a really good horse that you would get for £1,000, £1,500, or £2,000, there are exceptions, but as a rule the thoroughbred obtainable for any [illegible] ought to be [illegible] and we always receive fine bred treatment in the breeding district [illegible] by General Thornhill, and by General Watson up to a certain number. I think Lord Hope [illegible] quite right. I quite agree with him when he said we should not get anything more than ten or twelve of the perfect horses we want in India, and there are very few perfect horses amongst thoroughbreds as regards bone and conformation. I have seen some grand thoroughbreds out in India, but we know the most perfect looking horses does not always get the best stock.

11064. If you could get plenty of stallions in thoroughbreds would you prefer them to the Hackney for military purposes, for cavalry purposes?—If you could get a sufficient number of what we call a perfect military horse, thoroughbred, up to eighteen or twenty stone, you would be better satisfied than you would be on Hackneys, but I say they are not to be had.

11065. You said that the Australian horses a great many of which come to India, are really from highly bred English horses, that they were not so good as the country bred, according to the Inspector-General?—No, only the imported ones.

11066. You are not talking of the stallions?—No.

11067. Do you know the native cavalry ever prefer the small Australian horse to the country bred?—No; I know one or two regiments [illegible] I know what [illegible] were and there they took kind of you for Australians.

11068. (Mr. Watson.)—Had you an opportunity of seeing the condition of the horses got by these different stallions after they had done work, when they were on the regiments, to see how they stood the wear [illegible] the work of the regiment. Did you ever inspect the horses in the regiment to see how they stood, whether those got by thoroughbreds stood better than those got by Hackneys, or vice versa?—No, I never examined it with that view.

11069. Have you any knowledge of the results that way?—No; in this report I have, [illegible] one of the assistants gives his opinion on that subject.

11070. But you have not yourself?—No.

Mr. [illegible] examined.

11064. CHAIRMAN.—You are, I believe, a partner, are you not, in the firm of Messrs. [illegible] and Co.?—No, I am managing, my lord.

11065. They are jobmasters?—Yes, my lord.

11066. Can you give the Commission an approximate idea of the number of horses you let out on jobbing?—Well, I could not say exactly that, my lord. I can tell you the number we buy every year and the number we sell when out of the job work.

11067. Well, how many do you sell?—It averages 800.

11068. But you let out horses besides?—Oh, yes, my lord.

11069. Have you any idea of how many you let out?—I should think somewhere about 1,500 to 2,000.

11070. Where do you get your horses from?—All parts; mainly from Ireland.

11071. What parts of Ireland?—South of Ireland chiefly, some in the North.

11072. Do you buy them yourself through your own agents?—Yes.

11073. Do you buy them individually yourself or employ agents to buy them?—We have people over there, agents who pick them up at two and three years old and we buy them just when they are coming four years old.

11074. And you have been in this business for a large number of years?—I have been in Mr. [illegible]'s business for the last six years, but I have been in the jobbing business for the last thirty five years.

11075. Do you find that you can obtain the class of horse you want as easily in Ireland now as you used to do, is the supply as good as it used to be?—I don't think it is.

11076. Do you have to give more money for them?—No, there is not very much difference in the prices.

11077. But you think there is not so large a supply?—Not quite; I think [illegible] the same price, but horses are fewer than they used to be; I used to buy [illegible] originally; they are very much dearer than they used to be.

11078. Do you buy hackneys now?—No, we only buy harness ones.

11079. And you buy principally you say in Ireland?—Yes.

11080. And in England also?—Yes, a few in England.

11081. And from abroad?—Yes, we get a few Americans.

11082. What is the class of harness horse you buy in Ireland?—Horses from 15.3 to 16.1 or 16.2.

11083. Do you know at all how they are bred?—They are all by thoroughbred sires, I think. We have bought a few by a horse I think called "[illegible]" in Ireland, a Hackney stallion, we have had a few by him, that is the only horse I know of, of that breed.

11084. Do you attach much importance to the pedigree of the horses you buy?—Oh, yes, my lord.

11085. Do you get pedigrees with them?—[illegible] by thoroughbred horses.

11086. Do you get pedigrees with them?—Yes, as a rule.

11087. And you think the pedigrees are generally correct?—Oh, I think so, because we know the horses that are coming in the different districts of Ireland, they are a kind of [illegible] quality of horse, and they must be by some thoroughbred horse or another. We buy them from the men, as a rule, that keep the stallions, so they must know pretty exactly what they are by.

11088. Are your horses generally bought at fairs or privately?—They are originally picked up at the fairs by the men we buy them from, we don't go so much to fairs ourselves, because [illegible] we could not get them that way. They are selected horses, we go and buy horses with such [illegible] and we could not get them by going about to fairs, for they are picked up before the time. The men we get them from buy them as three-year olds and hold them and keep them for us.

11089. And as compared with the American and English horses, do you think the Irish horses suit your purpose as well as the others, or better?—Better, I think, they wear better.

11090. What are they used for, the horses you let out?—Oh, carriage work.

11091. In London?—Yes, a good many of them, some in the country.

11092. Do you find that these horses got by thoroughbred sires have got sufficiently good action?—Well, that is the difficulty very often, they have not got action enough.

11093. But when you do get one with action it is much better than anything else I think?—They can do work, they can keep on going.

11094. I presume I should be right in saying that it is the same class of horse that is turned into a hunter?—Yes, my lord.

11095. It may not be particularly adapted for making a hunter, and it makes a [illegible] harness horse?—Yes, my lord.

11096. Do you agree that the action could be obtained from the Hackney blood?—The action you might get some action from it, but I don't think you will get the height and breadth [illegible]. I have never seen any Hackney horses of the size we require them. For [illegible], we let a great many horses for [illegible] work, you must have a horse of good length and size for that class of work, unless they have got [illegible], they are no use for it.

11097. Then for your purpose you think the thoroughbred is as good as the Hackney sire?—Better, I should say.

11098. The [illegible] of Hackneys in this [illegible] comparatively very recent, do you know anything of Hackneys in Yorkshire and other parts of England?—We used years ago to buy a good many more horses in Yorkshire than we do now, we have a great difficulty in buying thirty or forty a year, we used to buy a great many more years ago.

11099. Do you attribute that to the fact that they have turned their attention more to breeding Hackneys?—Certainly.

11100. In fact the Hackney does not breed what you want?—No.

11101. What do you think the Hackney is suitable for?—I think they are very suitable for small [illegible], they [illegible], but I have not had very much experience of the Hackney horse myself, I don't think you can make them into carriage horses.

11102. [illegible] you find it easier to get the class of horse you require in Yorkshire?—[illegible] in Yorkshire [illegible].

11103. But still they are not quite extinct in Yorkshire?—No, there are still a few people breeding Cleveland Bays and [illegible] bigger horses, but they are [illegible] them in Yorkshire, that is one of the great difficulties in our being able to get horses now, you hardly ever see a horse with [illegible].

11104. Then as regards Ireland, in your particular district, am I right in supposing that you think that the thoroughbred sire is the class of sire you prefer?—Oh, yes, my lord.

11105. Mr. [illegible].—You talk about wearing qualities, do you think the strain of the Hackney would be a [illegible] action in harness as a useful harness horse?—[illegible] I have seen [illegible].

March 4, 1897. Mr. Henry [illegible].

11106. Have you noticed that their [illegible] is an extra age of action?—They are [illegible] in [illegible] very often and are no good behind, most of them.

11107. Don't [illegible] you think it does? I don't think they do [illegible] than the others when they have gone out half [illegible].

11108. Where in Ireland used you to get the majority of your [illegible]?—Limerick and the South of Ireland.

11109. And you get them there still?—Oh, yes.

11110. But [illegible] Mr. [illegible] of Yorkshire, you have almost given up going there?—We have very nearly given up going there, I think we got twenty horses there this year.

11111. And this is entirely since the introduction of the Hackney blood?—Yes.

11112. Can't you go and get a great many?—Not in the last [illegible] years since I have been with this Mr. [illegible], but before that, they used to buy a great many in Yorkshire.

11113. Mr. [illegible].—I suppose you do occasionally buy a [illegible] horse got by a Hackney sire?—Occasionally.

11114. Do you find that he can do anything that a horse got by a thoroughbred sire cannot do?—No.

11115. And don't you think that a thoroughbred sire can do things that a Hackney sire cannot do?—They are not always such fine goers, you cannot perhaps get them in such large numbers; but they do the riding part which a Hackney can not do, and you cannot get Hackneys of such a size. They do [illegible] or [illegible], but when you want to put them into a [illegible] or large carriage you cannot get them big enough.

11116. I don't wish to ask you a personal question, but do you give prices for those who [illegible] in breeding?—I think so.

11117. You say the supply is not so large as it used to be, to what do you attribute that?—I could not say, except that perhaps the demand is larger. I dare say you know the statistics better than I do, a great many more people go to Ireland now than twenty-five years ago to buy horses.

11118. Why do they go to Ireland?—Because I think they find the best there; thirty years ago we used to go and stop in Dublin and buy twenty or thirty horses in three days within a radius of eighteen or twenty miles of Dublin and buy them at five or six years old, you cannot do it now.

11119. You have to buy four year olds?—I gave up [illegible] dealing, only because I could not buy the horses at a price that would pay to bring them over here, and make a living out of them.

11120. Do you think a [illegible] of Hackney blood would have any effect on horse-breeding in Ireland?—I think it would.

11121. A good effect?—The reverse. There [illegible] is a better [illegible] the [illegible] than a [illegible] in Ireland.

11122. Do you think the mixture of Hackney blood in the pedigree of the horse would be perceptible to the eye?—I cannot say. It may or may not.

11123. We have a better chance of detecting the mixture of Clydesdale or Shire blood?—Yes, I should think you would.

11124. Lord Arthur.—When you used to buy in Yorkshire what class of horses used you to buy, the Cleveland Bay or coaching [illegible]?—Yes.

11125. They don't breed so many of them now?—Not half so many.

11126. Do you find many horses docked that would have been good enough for you if they had not been docked?—Yes, I rejected horses so many this last year because they were docked.

11127. The Bell of [illegible] having given up the breeding of Cleveland Bays also [illegible]?—Yes.

11128. Mr. Warren.—You buy about 300 horses in the year altogether?—Yes.

11129. How many of those do you think come from Ireland?—I should think 150 to 200.

11130. You buy them chiefly from dealers who buy them in the South and North, and they practically feed them and sell them to you as long tails, at four years old?—Yes.

11131. I don't want you to answer any question that would do your trade any harm. Would you say the price you give on an average?—£60 or £100 apiece.

11132. Do you know whether any of the horses you buy are American horses brought over and sold in Ireland?—I should not think they were.

11133. You are not aware of having bought any American horses in Ireland?—Not in Ireland.

11134. But you do buy them when landed here in this country?—Yes, sir.

11135. When you buy these horses, do you make inquiries as to how they are bred?—Yes.

11136. And do you think you get reliable pedigrees. Don't you find, for instance, that a great many are got by some particular horse noted for getting [illegible] horses, like "[illegible]"?—I don't think so. I think we get them pretty straight as a rule.

11137. But you only get the pedigrees from those men who buy them from the farmers?—Yes.

11138. Do you think the superiority of the Irish horse is from their thoroughbred blood, or the way they are brought up, the soil and climate of Ireland?—Both.

11139. Do you object to [illegible] blood in your horses?—Yes.

11140. Do you know that there are a great many cart horses to Ireland?—No; I was not aware of that.

11141. What is your opinion as to the number of stallions in Ireland. Did you think they were chiefly thoroughbred?—I should have thought so.

11142. And that is why you think buying there is so safe?—Yes.

11143. Do you know anything of the trade outside your own trade in Ireland, the lower class trade?—No; I don't.

11144. You don't know the class of men who breed those horses you buy?—Not except that those that I have seen at fairs with the horses.

11145. But you don't often go to fairs now. You chiefly buy from these private people?—Chiefly.

11146. When you come to Ireland you go round to three or four of your friends in different parts of the country and look at the horses they have collected for you?—Yes, sir.

11147. And very often buy twenty or thirty from one man?—Yes.

11148. Have you any acquaintance with the [illegible] of Ireland?—Not much.

11149. The men that you buy from, are [illegible] their chief business is in the hunter trade mostly?—No; I think they buy a great many [illegible].

11150. At this time of the year they are selling harness horses, but as a rule they sell more hunters than harness horses?—I don't think so.

11151. Then there is as big a trade in harness horses as in hunters?—I think so.

11152. Do you buy a lighter class of horse now than you used to [illegible] or four years ago. Do you find the carriages getting lighter?—They were lighter two or three years ago, but now they are getting heavier again. Nearly all the carriages are made to go with 16 [illegible], and we [illegible] not get any big enough.

11153. How what size do you think he buy?—Not less than 15.3.

11154. You buy them as low as 15.3?—Yes.

11155. And you never buy docked horses?—Occasionally we do. We might buy a horse that was docked, but he might have a good leg and at the same time.

11156. You have not been in the West of Ireland at all?—No.

11157. You don't know what the poor farmers do then?—No.

11158. You would not recommend anything for these people?—I don't know that part of the business at all.

11159. Why do you think they have given up breeding the class of horse that you look for in Yorkshire?—I think because so many of them have taken to breed Hackneys.

11160. Yes, but I mean why do they breed Hackneys?—I suppose they think it will pay them better.

11161. Are they all fairly intelligent people in Yorkshire?—I should think they are.

11162. Then you think if they have adopted this they have done it with some good reason?—I should think so, they are the best judges of that.

11163. And I think you said the supply of the horse you want is not as good as it used to be; can you explain that?—I cannot, except that perhaps the demand is greater. I don't know whether there are as many horses bred in Ireland as twenty years ago, but they are harder to get I know.

11164. Have you bought American horses for many years?—Oh yes, for a great many years. Our [illegible] Mr. [illegible], was over there fifteen years ago, and sent horses over. Then they gave them up.

11165. Are American horses coming over in large numbers?—Very large numbers.

11166. Do you think the American horse is improved to what he was five years ago?—I could not tell you. I did not see many American horses five years ago.

11167. Are there good horses coming then now?—Yes, a few.

11168. And you can buy them at an age?—Yes, five or six years old and more broken to harness, than in this [illegible].

11169. Perfectly trained?—Not perfectly trained, but you can get them into work in three or four months.

11170. Do you think the American trade is cutting into a good deal of the trade that might be kept in this country?—Certainly.

11171. It is doing harm to the Irish breeders?—Yes.

11172. Can you suggest any remedy to help the breeders?—Unless you can stop them coming.

11173. Would you be in favour of marking American horses?—I think if they were branded they would not be so saleable.

11174. Would you yourself object to buying branded horses?—Yes.

11175. And supposing as a measure of [illegible] branding was suggested, would you as a large buyer, be against it?—It might prevent us buying some.

11176. But you would be patriotic enough to support it for the sake of the Irish breeder?—I don't know about that.

11177. Chairman.—It would not make any difference to you as a buyer if all the American horses were branded, for other buyers would be in the same position?—It would not matter if they branded them on their feet, but if they branded them on their sides and quarters it would make a difference, because there are a great number of [illegible] horses and other horses that were branded, and people would not look at them.

11178. Would it make any difference to you if all the foreign horses were excluded?—It would make the other horses dearer.

11179. You would pay more for those and would ask more for them?—I suppose that would be the whole.

11180. But it would make no difference to you individually as against any other man in the same business?—We would be all the same, I suppose.

11181. You used to buy at one time a good many horses in Ireland?—Yes.

11182. I think you said you could formerly get twenty good horses within a short distance of Dublin, and that you cannot now?—No.

11183. How do you account for that?—They are more sought after. Everybody, more people in Ireland [illegible] horses now than [illegible] years ago. Ever since the Dublin Show started horses have gone up very much in price.

11184. Could you say that the breeding of the hunter and the carriage horse you buy is an important part of the industry of Ireland?—I should think very great.

11185. Would you say it is the most important?—I should think it is.

11186. Would you say that anything that was to be done to keep the industry as an industry in Ireland should be directed to the production of that kind of animal?—Yes, my lord, certainly. I think the important thing, if we could only get the farmers to keep the better mares, that is where the failing is, I think. If you could hold out some inducement to get them to keep a better class of mares, this would get better horses.

11187. Mr. Fitzwilliam.—Do you suggest any means for doing that?—The only thing is to give them prizes at agricultural shows, buy mares for them, let them have them and keep them. I think what the Duke of Portland is doing at the present moment is a very good thing.

11188. Chairman.—Would you agree with me that Ireland has achieved a certain amount of pre-eminence in the production of high class hunters?—Oh, yes, my lord, no doubt about that. I don't know any other country you can go to where you can get the [illegible].

11189. How do you account for that?—There is a great deal in the soil. The country is better adapted for breeding horses than any other I have ever heard of or know of.

11190. And that would apply equally to breeding any kind of horse?—I think so. What makes bone for one makes it for another I think.

11191. Have you much experience of Hackneys in England?—No, I have not. I know very little about them.

11192. And if the production was largely increased in Ireland of the kind of horses you buy, do you think there would be still a demand for them? Could you dispose of a great many more if you could get them?—We should buy more there if we could get them instead of buying horses from other countries.

11193. Lord Rathdonnell.—With regard to mating, it has been stated here to-day that a mare sired by a Hackney would produce a hunter if put to a thoroughbred. Would you like that crossing?—It would depend a good deal on the animal [illegible] I think.

11194. Do you think it would produce a hunter?—I don't think so, if it was a very fine one. I should not pick out a Hackney mare as a dam for a hunter.

11195. Perhaps you don't understand quite what I mean. If you put a Hackney stallion to what they call a weedy, well-bred mare in Ireland, and cross the produce of that with a thoroughbred horse again, do you think that would be good crossing for hunting purposes?—I don't think it would be so good as having a regular hunting [illegible], without the Hackney cross.

11196. Perhaps you would be able to tell us something with regard to the ages at which horses are taken out of Ireland. Are not most [illegible] horses taken out at a very early age?—I should think [illegible] yearlings and three-year-olds, a great many of them.

11197. Do you think it would be likely that a dealer would buy a two-year-old horse that was [illegible] or a three-year-old mare that was [illegible] or had a foal at foot?—I could not tell you, it would just depend upon what the horse was. I should not have thought any ordinary horse-dealer would have bought one so young as that.

11198. [illegible] of the Royal Dublin Society's [illegible] prizes are given to mares [illegible] have a [illegible] all these ages. You don't think that a [illegible] would take away [illegible]?—I should not have thought it at that age.

11199. Do you think that would be a good way of managing to keep the sound mares in the country?—It might. I would not say. It is not the class of [illegible] I am acquainted with.

11200. Mr. [illegible].—You said that you considered the hunter trade most important. Do you mean as [illegible] or in number? [illegible] you [illegible] the number? Do you know the number of hunters that [illegible] Ireland every year?—No.

11201. But you think it might produce a good horse of any kind?—Yes.

11202. Therefore there might be a trade to produce harness horses which it does not produce now?—Yes.

11203. Is there a large trade, below years, in horses with action to ride and drive in lighter carriages, horses from 15.2 to 15.3?—There are a great number of that size used no doubt.

11204. Is there any falling off in the demand for that class of horse?—I don't think so. I think there are plenty of those horses about. I think the smaller horses are easier to get than the bigger ones.

11205. But there is a demand for them, a fair trade?—I think so.

11206. In these horses is action a desirable paying quality?—No doubt about it.

11207. It is a thing that sells a horse quicker than anything else?—Yes.

11208. When you are talking about breeding hunters with a mare got by a Hackney stallion, and then crossed again with a thoroughbred, would you consider the Hackney cross the worst, or a cart-horse cross in that mare?—I should think the cart-horse would be the worst cross. I should put the Hackney before the cart-horse.

11209. You like the Hackney better than the Clydesdale?—Yes.

Professor [illegible] examined.

11210. CHAIRMAN.—You are a member of the Royal College of Veterinary Surgeons?—Yes, my lord.

11211. Have you a professional experience of Hackneys?—Yes, a very large one.

11212. Have you any information you could give the Commission as to their [illegible], formation, and so on?—My opinion is that they are particularly sound, compared with thoroughbred horses or cart horses. I think they are sounder, their joints are particularly clear from disease, particularly of a bony character. Of course my experience has been more particularly with those that have come in to the show ring, and have to come under [illegible] before they come under my notice. [illegible] I have had experience of them to [illegible] considerable [illegible] in [illegible], and that is the impression that I have obtained that they are perfectly free from disease.

11213. Would it be correct to say that in both the case of the cart-horse and the thoroughbred, the probability is that the [illegible] you have seen of them have been [illegible] gone through any description of work that would tend to [illegible] them unsound to a greater degree than the Hackneys?—With regard to the thoroughbred horse there is no question that that would apply because he is put to excessive work very early in life, and the process of [illegible] [illegible] is a very considerable [illegible], but that does not apply to the cart horse.

11214. And to what do you attribute the [illegible] [illegible] of the cart-horse?—Hereditary predisposition.

11215. [illegible] all, hereditary disease [illegible] [illegible] to [illegible]?—Oh, yes, [illegible], and I think it has originated in the cart-horse from [illegible] breeding, years back.

11216. Have you long experience of Hackneys?—Twenty-five years.

11217. And what is called a Hackney now, is it much the same as the [illegible] twenty-five years ago?—It has been very very much improved upon in [illegible]

11218. Improved in action or what?—Both, in make and shape, and action.

11219. By careful breeding?—Yes, selection.

11220. Have you any opinion or any knowledge as to the commercial value of the Hackneys, I don't mean Hackney stallions of course, but as ordinary driving or riding horses?—Well, I know this that they are fetching very much more money at the present day than they did years back, but beyond that I don't think I could give you anything definite.

11221. Have you got any opinion as to the relation of the bone of the thoroughbred and the Hackney, either as to size or density?—I have long held an opinion that the quality of the bone has as much to do as the quantity in the value of it.

11222. How do they compare as to quality?—The quality of the bone [illegible] is better in the thoroughbred than in the Hackney.

11223. And as to quantity, the measurement?—As a rule, I should say, the Hackney would measure more than the thoroughbred.

11224. Do you mean measuring round the bone itself or round the leg?—That is the way it is usually measured, round the leg below the knee.

11225. But then that measurement would depend on more than the [illegible] of the bone [illegible] thinking, my lord.

11226. If the covering of the bone was larger and thicker in one case than the other than would alter it, you measured the leg, skin, and [illegible]?—[illegible] but we don't [illegible] the difference in the size of the ligaments and tendons that [illegible] in the bone, [illegible] of the leg measures larger it is [illegible] to be attributed to the bone then, to the ligaments and tendons.

11227. I take it that the bone is [illegible] in size in the Hackney, and the quality is superior in the thoroughbred?—That is so.

11228. Could you say whether they [illegible] and [illegible] in that respect, as to the difference in favour of the Hackney or thoroughbred?—I should say in favour of the thoroughbred.

11229. LORD [illegible].—With regard to breeding, it has been stated by a breeder of Hackneys that action in the [illegible] is to be considered in preference to formation, do you think this sound?—If the action is not sound, as is commonly explained, I should prefer that to the formation, but if the action is confined to simply knee action then I should prefer the formation to the action.

11230. Do you think that, taking the Hackneys all round as a type of horses, that they are apt to be [illegible]?—I have not noticed that. I should say that is not so.

11231. Have you ever noticed any [illegible] to short back ribs in the Hackney type?—No, I cannot say that I have.

11232. In general have they strong thighs?—They have, and good hocks.

11233. Mr. [illegible].—You say the Hackney horse has improved both in conformation and action in twenty-five years. In what points of conformation has he improved?—I think the limbs and action and thighs are better than they used to be.

11234. [illegible] [illegible] [illegible]—I cannot say that I have noticed that particularly.

11235. I take it that the Hackney horse is [illegible] from the old riding horse that used to [illegible] in Yorkshire?—He came from Norfolk and Yorkshire.

11236. Chiefly used for saddle purposes?—Yes.

11237. Do you think the modern Hackney is of a saddle type?—No, I do not; I think he is more of a harness horse.

11238. Then it is a matter of question whether he has improved or whether you value a harness horse higher than a riding horse?—It is a question which article you want. I think he is a better looking harness horse than he was a long while ago.

11239. But it is a question whether it is an improvement to turn a riding horse into a harness horse?—It is a matter of opinion.

11240. At any rate his type has changed to some extent from this selected breed?—I think so; I think he has improved very much in his arms and thighs.

11241. Not in his shoulders?—Not in his shoulders, but in his quarters he has.

11242. Mr. Walrond.—We have had it stated in evidence before us, Professor Pritchard, that Hackneys were specially liable to curbs and curby hocks. Is that your experience?—No, the reverse of that.

11243. Which would you say had the soundest hocks as a rule, a Hackney or a thoroughbred?—I should say a Hackney.

11244. And his hocks are not of a formation that is more objectionable than curbs?—Predisposition to curbs, certainly not.

11245. You have had a very large experience in examining horses, both at the shows and at horse breeders' own places for a great number of years?—Yes.

11246. A great number have come under your observation?—Yes, many thousands.

11247. Do you think a Hackney is a horse of a delicate constitution or the reverse?—The reverse, decidedly.

11248. Have you ever attended Hackneys in illness?—Yes, but most frequently when shown under circumstances calculated to give rise to illness.

11249. It has been also stated to us that they are of a delicate constitution, and have not the same power to recover from illness as a thoroughbred horse, do you agree with that?—I think not.

11250. You think they have the same recuperative powers?—I think so.

11251. Have the Hackneys been carefully bred for a long period now?—Unquestionably.

11252. When you first went among the Norfolk and Yorkshire farmers did you find they were working their Hackneys more than they do now?—I could not give an answer to that question; I am not aware.

11253. Have you formed any opinion as to why they are not worked now?—I think they are more kept for show purposes; that probably is the reason. The majority of the best Hackneys are kept for show purposes or for sale, and therefore they would not be worked to any great extent beyond serving mares. I have one myself that I have driven fourteen years now. She is in the Stud Book, and she has never been ill.

11254. Do you find that she is soft or unable to do a journey?—She is a little too hard for me sometimes.

11255. Is it your experience that they are a soft breed or the reverse?—The reverse I should say.

11256. You would say they still possess staying powers?—On that point I should like to say—Well, my own experience is, there is that they have staying powers, but I think what I have heard people say there are many of them, since going a distance, this.

11257. But you have no experience of them, and have no experience of that.

11258. Is that confined to special strains?—That I could not answer.

11259. Do you know at all why Yorkshire men have given up breeding coach-horses and taken to Hackneys in preference?—I think it is a matter of pounds, shillings and pence.

11260. Do you know as a matter of fact, the Yorkshire men have made a great deal of money lately by breeding Hackneys?—I think there is no doubt about it.

11261. Then you were asked as to the riding and harness horse—which horse do you think is the most certain for a farmer to attempt to breed?—I should select the harness horse if I were going to supply the market.

11262. And you think that would be the wisest trade for small farmers to breed who had only an indifferent mare?—I do, indeed.

11263. And their action is the essential point?—Yes.

11264. Do you know whether the Hackneys have a shorter canon bone than a thoroughbred?—I should think there is not much difference, taking a number of them. I should not think there is much difference relatively to the height.

11265. And you have never made any experiments to test the length or shape of the Hackney's shoulders compared with the thoroughbred?—Only by vision.

11266. Chairman.—When you say you think that breeding for harness purposes would be the most profitable thing for a farmer to do—what part of the country do you allude to?—Anywhere, of course.

11267. But I mean for Ireland?—Well, of course the breeder would sell to the dealer who brings the horse to London. There is always more demand than supply in London for harness horses.

11268. We are talking of what is the most profitable thing for a farmer to turn his attention to—do you mean that universally all over the United Kingdom it would be better for him to turn his attention to harness purposes, or are you speaking of a particular locality?—Oh, no; I am speaking of the whole kingdom throughout.

11269. Do you know Ireland at all?—I cannot say I know Ireland. I have been there many times, but it has always been flying visits. I have been to Dublin Show officially, and I have been through Ireland for pleasure, but I don't know Ireland.

11270. Are we to understand that, for instance, in Meath, Limerick, Cork, and other localities, you think it would be more profitable for the farmers to turn their attention to breeding for harness purposes than to breeding for hunters?—I should think if I were in Ireland, certainly.

11271. Anything you would like to say to the Commission?—No, my Lord, I don't know that there is; but I should rather lay stress on one answer I gave with regard to the tendency to curbs in the Hackney's hock. I don't think that is so at all; I am sure it is not.

March 4, 1896.
[illegible]

March 8, 1897. Mr. John Hope.

so I must go back to the time when I first took in hand my late father's first Hackney show mare, being then a youth of nineteen or twenty. This mare was a daughter of Bond's "Sir Charles" by Taylor's "Fire Away," and was sold to a nobleman in London when four years old.

11274. Is this a statement of how you have bred your Hackneys?—Yes; this old mare was the ancient stock.

11275. Do you not think it would be better to hand that in, as does it refer to anything at the present day?—We still retain the same breed, and I was going to show the durability and the staying powers. She came to London when four years old, and by constantly going and from her London owner until she was fourteen, when she was brought back, within three months, and made up for showing in both saddle and harness. The first time given she never was beaten, and was during that time about sixty first prizes, which are pretty good, but is taking a back seat. It was always easy to know from the public when a riding or driving class had just entered the ring: "Wait till Major's 'Polly' comes on the scene, with her knees-up-to-her-eyes and feet from the London stones; she'll soon polish the lot;" and so she did. This statement can be verified by scores of Yorkshire horsemen still living that witnessed so many of her fine exhibitions, showing style and action in all her paces, as well as a perfect model in shape. She was then put to the stud, and won the Great Yorks at York, in 1859 or 1860, as a Hackney brood mare with foal at foot; first prize foal, three years later, winning the first prize for the best Hackney stallion under fifteen hands at the Horse Show at the Agricultural Hall in London. I also exhibited at the same Yorkshire show, as a three-year-old mare, "Miss Giles," recorded in Vol. I. She also took first prize in her class, and was sold the spring following to a partner in the Hartford and Bristol Brass Company, Liverpool, London, where she was giving fine. This gentleman drove her along with a black cob, from London to York in three days, when the black pony broke down. Mr. Reed, the gentleman's cousin, hired a gig and drove "Miss Giles" in single to Scarborough the fourth day, stayed a week, drove her back to York, bought another hunter at Walker's, and reached London again in three more days, where he wrote and told me "Miss Giles" had given him the greatest pleasure in his over 400 miles' drive, and was as fresh as paint, with legs as clean as glass, after tiring her less reliable companions perfectly useless. This gentleman afterwards made me a present of the mare, when a good lot worse: and unfortunately stuck to her thrown up breeding such horses as Mr. Smith's "Satisfaction," Mr. Mark Pearson's "The Marian," and others, which have done more to pay a landlord his rent the last twelve or fourteen years than all the corn-growing put together. I have letters from friends, which I shall be pleased to submit, bearing out my own statements as to the endurance of a good-bred Hackney. I don't object at all having a cross of blood in the third or fourth dam, nor do I think Hackney breeding has at all interfered with hunter breeding, only in cases where the hunter breeder has adopted the Hackney breeder lacking his head off to utilise his produce; hence a good many discarded hunter breeding for the Hackney, and I find are sticking to it yet. I don't think for one moment that all the cycles and motor cars in the world, after the novelty is gone, will ever cause our English gentry, or their sons and daughters, to turn their backs on a beautiful typical riding or driving horse, such as we Yorkshire men are trying to produce, not only because we admire them so much, but also I take them to be a great saving value towards keeping at a distance that man who may be called Yank doctor, give his mark on all you have and oblige you to choose your own conveyances. For ones which I shall go on trying to produce a nice Hackney, and would advise Ireland to do the same.

11276. I take it your experience has been chiefly in connection with pure-bred Hackneys?—We try to keep them as pure as possible.

11277. Do you consider that Hackney stallions are suitable animals to mate with common inferior mares?—May I ask what class of mares?

11278. The ordinary common mares?—Oh, you get very often get good harness horses, very good selling horses.

11279. In your part of Yorkshire has the hunter breeding decreased?—Yes, I believe it has.

11280. To what do you attribute that?—We have such a superior Hackney now that we find so much more ready a sale for it, and whereas like the hunter, the hunter has to belong to a gentleman that can ride it and make it before it is remunerative.

11281. You get a readier sale for your Hackney?—I have always found it so.

11282. Is there a demand in your country for horses got by a Hackney stallion?—Yes, sir.

11283. That is from half-bred mares or ordinary mares?—Yes, where the mare is producing a good harness horse.

11284. Do you think that the crossing of the Hackney has had any effect on the breed of hunters in your district?—I scarcely know how to answer that question. I have seen some very beautiful hunters by a Hackney sire out of a common mare, but I have no experience of hunter breeding.

11285. You don't know whether they have proved themselves good in the field afterwards?—A good many of our Hackneys at the present day are as good hunters as ever went into the field.

11286. Are there many Cleveland Bays and Yorkshire coach horses bred in your country?—Very few indeed; it is very rare I believe.

11287. I take it from what you have said that you think the Hackney is a most good horse?—Yes, I do.

11288. Well, now, as regards his stamina, do you think he is a delicate horse at all or the reverse?—The reverse, taking it all round and the way we have got in our Hackneys now they cannot possibly be delicate.

11289. Mr. Fitzwilliam.—You say you never did breed hunters?—Only an odd one now and again.

11290. Therefore your experience in horse breeding seems to be almost entirely confined to Hackney breeding of a high class?—Yes; I try to keep them as high-class as possible. I breed nothing else except cart horses for my own land work.

11291. Then you have had no experience of half-bred stallions and Hackneys of a less good type?—Oh, yes, I have.

11292. What have you found with regard to them?—I found that that it behoved me to stick as much as possible to the best class of Hackney I could get because I could command about treble the amount of money for it, a companion bred Hackney generally goes for harness purposes.

11293. Then the high class Hackney goes only for show purposes?—No, I think mostly show purposes, but for riding purposes. We go in to get the pattern riding shoulders, giving beautiful depth of girth and placing its rider and saddle in the proper position where he can sit without sitting on its haunches and plenty of room for the hands to rise.

11294. Do you ride your best Hackneys yourself?—Oh, yes, and drive them too occasionally. We always take it we can drive a Hackney when we like but we cannot always make a Hackney a riding horse.

11295. But as for the worst class of Hackneys do you find there is a good sale for them too?—Oh, yes, they can be sold favourably, with other classes of horses, not of the best class, you know.

11296. They are easy to sell?—Yes.

11297. On your farm do you work Hackneys?—Very often. We are very careful with them; we often make them perfectly gentle to either ride or drive by light chaining for parts of their practice time. We don't go in for hiring them.

11298. Mr. Wrench.—Do you know how the Hackneys were originally bred; I mean in the early part of the century did you learn from your father the animals they were descended from?—My father used to tax my memory as to whether I ever remembered a horse called Hazeyboy, [illegible]. I got all the date of Hazeyboy I found I was only a little boy two or three years old, so I could not remember him. He wanted me to remember him and he [illegible] my memory and carry it in my eye so as to remember it when I was going about to buy, to keep that type in my eye so that I should never go far wrong.

11299. What were the old nags used for in former days riding or driving?—They did both, but there was a deal more riding then than there is at the present day.

11300. Did **they do long distances?—Very long** indeed.

11301. And are the Hackneys at the present day bred from the animals that did the long distances?—Yes.

11302. Is a great many of the best strains of Yorkshire Hackneys there are a good many crosses of thoroughbred blood?—Not a great many. I know several that have a cross of blood in the third and fourth dam.

11303. That is what I mean; that was common in the Yorkshire Hackneys?—Yes, the people rather advocated it.

11304. Why have the Yorkshire farmers given up breeding the big class of horses that Messrs. Burdett look for?—Well, there is a good many like myself. We have found that the Hackney paid us so much better, and it was a question of pounds, shillings, and pence as well as having a fancy for the Hackney.

11305. Then the real reason that Hackneys are bred so much in Yorkshire now is because they pay?—Quite so.

11306. And if the Yorkshire men found the coaching horse or [illegible] paid better they would turn back to them?—It is evident.

11307. They have no prejudice when their pockets are concerned [illegible] not.

11308. Mr. Fitzwilliam.—Would it be easy to get the mares now if they desired to turn back to the large well-bred thoroughbred; would it be very easy for them in East Yorkshire to breed them now?—Yes.

11309. Where would they go to get them?—I dare say would be happy indeed to get them or [illegible] on the market tomorrow.

11310. I [illegible] larger mares than Mr. [illegible] was talking about, that he says he cannot find now in the East Riding of Yorkshire, you say they do exist?—I beg your pardon, I mean the Hackney mares.

11311. Mr. Wrench.—When you are not breeding absolutely pure Hackneys, with what class of mares do you think that a Hackney stallion produces the best results?—Well, I have had very [illegible] experience of that class of breeding. I have had a few half-bred mares [illegible] that have bred beautiful horses to a Hackney stallion.

11312. But with thoroughbred blood in them?—Yes, two crosses of blood perhaps.

11313. Have you tried any experiments, breeding from the same mare with a thoroughbred horse and then with a Hackney stallion; have you any opinion as to the different results from the same mare?—No, I have tried sometimes a thoroughbred stallion with a Hackney mare.

11314. What was the result?—It never suited me.

11315. And can you explain at all why it is that Yorkshire farmers don't work these Hackneys at the present day as much as they used to?—I don't know that I am able to explain it.

11316. Is it because they have become more valuable?—One thing is, we put such a great value on them, and we try as much as possible to take care of them, and put them to a little light field work. I never allow one of mine to go, as I send any one with it.

11317. Then they are so valuable it pays you to use them in nothing except breeding?—Yes, sir.

11318. Chairman.—I think you said that the Hackneys you have are [illegible] Hackneys?—Yes, sir.

11319. Are they all registered in the Stud Book?—Yes, sir.

11320. Can you tell me when that Stud Book was formed?—I believe it is fourteen or fifteen years ago. I am [illegible] to the year. I became a member the first year.

11321. Do you know whether **the Stud Book is** closed or not?—It is partly closed.

11322. It is not closed altogether?—I **have** been **on** the Hackney Council now for three years, and every time I go to our meetings we try and get the very greatest and utmost care we possibly could that we should have these pedigrees. There is no doubt in the first formation of the Hackney Society there were some very imperfect pedigrees admitted into the book, that is, at the commencement.

11323. Is there any other way of getting a nominal entry in the Stud Book without perfect pedigree?—You cannot get an animal in the Stud Book now unless the sire and dam are both already registered, it is so far closed as that.

11324. There is no [illegible] of inspection?—There is no [illegible] of inspection now only for pony mares. The book is just [illegible] now altogether for pony stallions. The pony mares are let [illegible] the inspection, the mares are for the last three or four years—[illegible] pony not to exceed 14 hands and not to be under four years old.

11325. What other qualifications have they to have?—I suppose nothing but their pedigree. As far as inspection goes my instructions have been when I was sent to inspect ponies to take the type and the age. We look upon a pony having the usual Hackney type as the [illegible] Hackneys.

11326. What amount of pedigree must they have to get in?—I am sure I could not answer you that question just now.

11327. But when you go on your tour of inspection are you passing these animals don't you [illegible] report with them?—Yes. I have already said I give the type, the shape of the animal, the age as correct and the height correct, and my inspection is always attended by a veterinary surgeon. [illegible] as well as myself. He reports on the general soundness of the animal.

11328. As to pedigree, how do you refer them in the Stud Book. I believe the inspection is where you cannot get at the true pedigree of the animal?—Certainly.

11329. Therefore you only [illegible] that do not go into the book?—In the pony mare classes.

11330. But the same thing was done, was it not, in the larger classes?—It was, sir.

11331. Mr. Ll. Tanner.—Would the produce of one of these admitted pony mares by a registered Hackney stallion be eligible for admission into the Hackney Stud Book?—Yes; in a certain sense. They go in as inspected mares. There are three grades before they get a full register.

11332. As a matter of fact, the mare, as you say, that is got into the Pony Stud Book is practically in the Hackney Stud Book?—Yes, and called a pony.

11333. Mr. Wrench.—But it is in the pony part of the Stud Book?—Yes. It is [illegible] appear in the Hackney Stud Book the reason that is explained is [illegible] will make the word "pony."

11334. Mr. Ll. Tanner.—These ponies are 14 hands. They are not to exceed 14 hands; but a 14 hands pony mare may be put to a registered Hackney stallion of 15.2. The produce might be 15 hands high?—Very easily.

11335. Would that produce be eligible for admission into the Hackney Stud Book?—I believe they would take it in and call it "entered," before that it is by "inspection."

11336. CHAIRMAN.—Then the produce of that again? —It would get full registry, provided the sires that had been used in the different crosses were registered horses.

11337. Mr. FITZWILLIAM.—So it is really the fact that an animal can get into the Stud Book even now through the pony classes through an inspection at the present moment?—I don't see what is to hinder, if you go on raising a sire that you feel certain will increase the height by nearly a hand.

11338. Colonel ST. QUINTIN.—You said you got some very good animals on one or two occasions by a Hackney stallion out of a blood mare. What sort were they?—Chiefly driving. If you get the action and the breeding that way out of a blood mare, you very often have a very valuable animal as a harness horse.

11339. You would not advocate a Hackney stallion with a blood mare for riding horses? -They might do. They would get both classes of horses according to the stamina of the mare.

11340. But you prefer a thoroughbred horse to get a riding horse out of a well bred mare?-Oh! no, sir, I would prefer a Hackney.

Mr. GEORGE GALE, Atwick Hall, Seaton, Hull, examined.

11341. CHAIRMAN.—You are a large purchaser of horses, and I think have tried various experiments in breeding, have you not?—Yes.

11342. Would you give the Commission an account of the various experiments you made, and the reason you tried?—I think if I commence at the commencement of my career as horse breeder, forty-five years ago, I commenced from a mare by Philip Hasselgrove's "Old Phenomenon," out of a blood mare. That was the first Hackney sire, and the produce of that was the best hunter I ever crossed in my life. More than I have bred from that mare and from her offspring by a Hackney stallion, and crossed again with blood. I have had some extraordinary good hunters, in fact I have two now that I am hunting by "[illegible]," out of a mare by "Taliesin," and they go back to Hackney blood.

11343. I take it from that that you think the Hackney blood does not damage hunter-breeding?—I think in one cross you would get so much better [illegible] and jumping power.

11344. Mr. WRENCH. "[illegible]," of course, was a thoroughbred?—Yes; he is by "[illegible]."

11345. CHAIRMAN.—But I am right in supposing you think the Hackney more a cart [illegible] to hunters? I rather prefer the Hackney cross to a cart horse. I would much rather breed from a Hackney mare and put a blood horse to her to produce a hunter.

11346. Are you acquainted with the horses bought in Ireland?—I am not. I have ridden in Irish hunters brought over from Ireland.

11347. What sort of horses are bred in your district chiefly?—There is nothing but mongrel [illegible], [illegible] by cart horses out of light mares. No one goes in particularly for breeding. The old coach horses are extinct. When I was a lad there were those in that country had the right kind of coaching breed [illegible], but they are all extinct now. Crossed by breed.

11348. Mr. FITZWILLIAM.—You began, you say, forty-five years ago with these Hackneys?—Yes.

11349. In those days, the Hackney, I think, was a riding horse. He was called, I think, a [illegible] [illegible] then, yes.

11350. And you yourself have tried to keep up that type of animal, to keep the Hackney as a riding horse?—Quite so.

11351. But you would not quite say that the Hackneys that you see in the shows in the north of England are riding horses now?—I consider very many of them are harness horses, and horses I would not use as any [illegible] [illegible] to them.

11352. You would not like to ride?—Yes, I would not ride them and I would not use them for getting riding horses.

11353. Therefore the type of Hackney at the present day is not at all the same type as he was when you began to breed forty-five years ago?—The best type, the riding Hackney, there are a few of them, but they are so [illegible] out. I don't know. [illegible] that I have always gone in for riding horses with good shoulders and good hind action, and that is the way you will get the propelling power for getting hunters. I may say I rode a mare with strains of Hackney blood, one of the finest jumpers I ever crossed in my life, with jumping power, [illegible] more [illegible] hands.

11354. I imagine from what you say that there is a considerable difference now between the Hackney that you bred and the type of Hackney that we see in the show-yards in Yorkshire, you think a riding horse?—I won't see a horse that I think is not [illegible] getting a riding horse with beautiful [illegible] action and [illegible] the [illegible], I [illegible] that you can ride for fifty miles with them and fifty more if you wish.

11355. That would not apply to those [illegible] high-actioned horses that you see in the shows?—Certainly not.

11356. So that when you advocate the best class of Hackney animals, you are speaking of the class you bred yourself, not of the class you see at the show-yards?—Not the majority of them, a good number of them are not riding horses, you [illegible] get a saddle on them, it goes up the neck. I had an old Hackney mare, [illegible], I would always tell [illegible] if [illegible] had been a thousand [illegible], if I could not see her I would tell her by the peculiar sound of her feet.

11357. Lord ARTHUR(?)—This horse you are talking about by "[illegible]" would he be in the Hackney Stud Book?—No, I don't think there is [illegible] [illegible] with him in the Hackney show, his dam was by "[illegible]," out of a mare by "[illegible]" and "[illegible]" was by "[illegible]."

11358. Mr. FITZWILLIAM.—An American horse is that one in the Hackney Stud Book?—Oh, no, she is not eligible. I rode a mare by "[illegible] [illegible]" out of a [illegible] mare, and she was as fine a huntress as a man could cross, a good jumper with staying power.

11359. Col. ST. QUINTIN.—Do you think the present Hackney with his extravagant action is a desirable cross for riding purposes?—I don't approve of those myself, as an instance of that, I think yesterday in the Champion Cup class one horse was a perfect model of a riding horse, and the other if you [illegible] [illegible] in two, the hind legs are five years old and the front [illegible] [illegible] the other is the wrong way.

11360. Mr. WRENCH.—You live in a Hackney breeding district?—I do.

11361. And you have been a breeding man all your life?—Yes.

11362. And have a good deal now?—Yes.

11363. Keep hunters and follow hounds?—Do you think that the Hackney [illegible] to [illegible] [illegible] his [illegible] any [illegible] to hunter breeding?—I don't think so; I don't think it has interfered with it at all.

11364. You think it is possible to keep the two quite distinct?—Oh, yes.

11365. Is the Hackney a cart horse or a hardy blood?—I think the [illegible] horse.

11366. Do you think he is a horse that can say

long distances?—I am quite certain of that. I have [illegible] it in my own case.

11867. You have had a good many going—you cannot be mistaken?—I have got into the saddle at seven o'clock in the morning, and [illegible] twenty miles to a meet, and hunted all day, and ridden back in the evening not a bit the worse. I was riding a four-year-old mare the other day, we had a tremendous run over a very deep country, she was by a [illegible] horse out of a Hackney mare, the whip asked me what I was riding, I said "a four-year-old mare." "You have not been riding that all day." "Yes, I have." "Well," said he, "I never saw anything like it; my second horse is tired." I rode her all day, and I rode her [illegible].

11868. Do you know what the origin of these Hackneys is—were they bred from the old roadsters that the Yorkshire farmers used to ride long distances?—I have no doubt.

11869. Has much care been taken in the breeding of Hackneys?—Not until recently, [illegible] years ago. I remember the time of the old-fashioned [illegible], the old trotting horse.

11870. And did they ride those long distances then?—Very long distances; they were noted for their speed and [illegible].

11871. Why do you think the Yorkshire farmers have given up breeding [illegible] and taken to Hackneys?—Because the fashion changed, there were no people to buy coach horses twenty years ago, and they became extinct; now there is a demand, but the supply is not equal to the demand.

11872. Are there not plenty of good riding Hackneys still to be found in the back stocks in Yorkshire?—Oh, yes.

11873. Having your ideal [illegible] of a good riding type?—Yes.

11874. Descended from those old roadsters?—Quite so.

11875. Without any [illegible] in them to spoil their riding shape?—I must admit the riding shape has been lost of late, because people have gone in for big horses to try to supply the [illegible] you cannot very well sell a horse to-day under 15.2, not as a riding horse, for exportation, they will have them big—they are not riding horses.

11876. You think that the older stallions were smaller horses than this, the [illegible] horse [illegible] "Old [illegible]" was not a very big horse, they

came from Norfolk, there is more quality in the Yorkshire.

11877. CHAIRMAN.—Do you sell your own [illegible] riding horses pure-bred Hackneys?—Yes; I have some as good bred Hackneys as anybody.

11878. Are they entered in the Stud Book?—Oh, yes.

11879. It has been stated here that the first point to be considered in breeding Hackneys is action, and that the conformation is to be considered after that—is that the way you would think right to breed?—Yes, if you had not the riding action, it is the not having the conformation; you must have the action, that is the most important point—after that get the beautiful riding shoulders.

11880. How are you going to get the riding shoulders, if you don't breed from an animal with good shoulders?—If you find that it is for want of properly crossing.

11881. You think the crossing gives the shoulders?—Oh, yes; in every animal—whatever it is, sheep or shorthorns, or whatever it is you want to cross them—if the dam is deficient in one point, try to get the sire good in that point.

11882. In all this conformation—do you consider that before the action?—I consider the action is produced by getting the right conformation.

11883. How can the right conformation, surely it is the conformation brings the action, unless you brought the action artificially—do you believe in that?—I think there is a great deal of artificial action.

11884. Then, if you saw an artificially [illegible] horse, as he goes, you would look twice at his shoulders, if he was a stallion, before you would put a mare to him?—If I was judging one I would tell you what I should do; I would say, "You go there miles an hour and let his head loose, let him walk, and then put him into a slow trot of five miles an hour." That is the way to get at a riding horse's action.

11885. Without putting on his back?—Yes, it will tell you his conformation; I think it is a great mistake in the showing that horses are allowed to be shown as they are. It depends entirely on the man; if you have a man that can run fast and make a great show, and [illegible] shape, it is taken that the horse has action.

11886. Is there anything else you would like to state to the Commission?—No; I do not think there is anything further.

The Commission adjourned to next morning.

TWENTY-SECOND DAY.—FRIDAY, MARCH 5TH, 1897.

March 5, 1897.

Sitting at 12, Hanover-square, London, W.

PRESENT:—THE EARL OF DUNRAVEN, K.P. (In the Chair); LORD ASHTOWN; MARQUESS OF LONDONDERRY, K.G.; MR. J. L. CAREW, M.P.; LORD RATHDONNELL; HON. H. W. FITZWILLIAM; COLONEL ST. QUINTIN; MR. PERCY LA TOUCHE; MR. F. S. WRENCH.

MR. HUGH NEVILLE, Secretary.

Mr. WILLIAM [illegible] examined.

Mr. William [illegible].

11887. CHAIRMAN.—You live in Lincolnshire, do you not?—Yes, [illegible].

11888. You are Secretary of the Lincolnshire Agricultural Society?—Yes.

11889. And do you deal in horses?—Yes.

11890. Have you had experience of horses?—Yes; I do a large [illegible] business, but I don't get any horses to buy and sell.

11891. What class of horses?—Shires, Hackneys, hunters.

11892. Both riding and driving horses?—Yes.

11893. Are you at all acquainted with Ireland?—I have been there a good deal.

11894. Buying horses?—Yes.

11895. Do you know the congested districts of the western seaboard?—I was there [illegible] for about a fortnight, once [illegible] and [illegible], and rode about there.

11896. Are you able to give any opinion as to the class of mares that the horses bred in those western districts?—Well, I was [illegible] to the class, and bought a few of their progeny whilst I was out there, seven or eight [illegible], one of them [illegible] mare, and [illegible] horses. I did not find anything that was better that I could always, and I bought a few [illegible] ones.

[illegible]
Mr. William [illegible].

11397. How are they bred?—Mostly by Mr. [illegible]'s Hackney, and what was got by him I didn't know how they were bred; it was evidently a good horse, and not a thoroughbred, and, therefore, I had no idea what the strain of horse was. I did not make further inquiries, except that he was not a Hackney or a thoroughbred.

11398. How did those turn out?—Well; I sold some of them to a man that was with me at the time. Only one mare I know of that was sold and did very well. She is now breeding.

11399. Was she by the Hackney?—She was by the Hackney pony "Star of the West," that used formerly to stand in Enniskeen.

11400. Do you think generally from what you saw that the class of mares there would be suitable to unite with a Hackney?—Quite so.

11401. To produce what?—To produce a good all-round animal, horses from 14 to 15 hands. I don't think the first cross would be likely to produce anything good enough for either hunting or riding; but perhaps a good tradesman's horse.

11402. And if the best of the fillies were kept and crossed again they would probably be something of a better class?—Crossed again with a Hackney, yes.

11403. Would you prefer the Hackney or a second or third thoroughbred horse for that kind of mare?—I think a thoroughbred horse would be too much going for the mares I saw round about Crossmolina and that neighbourhood.

11404. You would not expect much from the first cross?—I would not.

11405. But after a time you would think they would turn into a fairly suitable, valuable description of horse?—I do.

11406. Do you consider those districts capable of producing hunters or high-class horses?—They have not size at present in the mares I have seen to produce either size or strength.

11407. Do you know Ireland pretty well generally?—Not the South of Ireland, except just from visits to fairs.

11408. Then you probably would not be able to give us any information as to the question of the improvement of horse-breeding in Ireland generally?—I have bought a good many horses from the fairs in Ireland, but I have not been round about much amongst the farmers. I don't know much of the conditions under which they are raised. I only know the horses when they are raised and brought to a marketable place.

11409. We have had a certain amount of evidence to the effect that the Hackney is not a suitable sire, at any rate to get hunters, have you any opinion on that point?—I don't think he will ever be used for that purpose, will he?

11410. We have had some evidence also to the effect that the breeders in those portions of Ireland where the hunters are principally bred are afraid that the use of Hackneys in any part of the country, to a large extent, would result in the Hackney blood percolating gradually through the country and would interfere with the production of high-class hunters for which Ireland is rather celebrated, have you any opinion on that?—I don't think they need fear much. It depends solely on the selection of the Hackney they put into Ireland.

11411. Have you seen the Hackneys of the Congested Districts Board?—I have.

11412. Have you any opinion about them?—Yes, on the whole they are very suitable for the country, and I think some of them would be very likely to get high-class valuable horses.

11413. Do you think the demand for what has been called the middle, between the high-class carriage horse of today and the class of animal that goes in back cars and things of that kind, do you think the demand for that sort of general utility horse is likely to increase or diminish?—I don't think there is likely to be any [illegible] in any way.

11414. There is a good demand for that class of animal now?—Certainly.

11415. You don't think other classes of locomotion, bicycles and motor cars, are likely to interfere with it?—I don't think so.

11416. Do we gather from you that to produce that kind of animal ought to be profitable?—Yes.

11417. Do you know America at all, have you ever been there?—I was there last year but once.

11418. Are there many Hackney sires in America?—There are a few, but it is such a large country that they are considerably scattered.

11419. And do they breed generally pure bred Hackneys?—I made it my business more particularly to visit some of the Hackney studs there, and did not see much of the carrying business where horses were largely travelling.

11420. To what use do they put the produce of the Hackney in America, riding or driving?—I believe they have not used them a sufficient length of time, scarcely to say, except in a few isolated cases. Men like Mr. Cassatt, of the Pennsylvania Railway, and Mr. Fairfax, of Virginia, and Mr. Webb have used them, but apart from these men, I don't think many people have an opportunity of using them to any great extent, not the full pedigreed Hackney.

11421. Have you seen in Ireland any of the produce of the Congested Districts Board Hackneys?—I cannot say that I have, except what I have seen at the farm. I have not been in the congested districts. I have seen several that were bred from ponies from those districts. I understand that they are now at the Board's farm.

11422. Have you seen much of the produce of private Hackney stallions?—I have seen some of "[illegible]'s" stock, and a great many of "Lord Raddlier's," "[illegible]" in the North, and "Lord Rattler" in Tyrone. A good many of the latter have come over to England.

11423. To what purpose are they put?—Harness horses.

11424. What do you think of the produce which you have seen?—I think they are very good indeed.

11425. Do you think the Hackney strain ought to be wholly devoted to a breed, supposing, for the sake of argument, that it would be [illegible] to introduce it into the parts of Ireland that breed hunters generally, do you think the average farmer would be able to choose it for a mare?—I think probably he would.

11426. So if they chose they could practically exclude it?—Yes, and if they chose they could go on with it.

11427. Lord Londonderry.—I think you told the Chairman you pass a good many horses through your hands every year, I suppose so?—Oh, yes. I buy on commission. I don't buy any to trade on.

11428. Which class of horse of the lot that go through your hands do you think realises the greatest market?—A horse with action.

11429. And you think that is combined in the Hackney more than any other class?—I think so to a greater proportion.

11430. You think they are more suitable for the English market than any of the other class of horses?—Yes.

11431. I think you said you bought some mares in the congested districts?—Yes, some foals and some young stock.

11432. What sorts of mares were they?—Just the first cross of the native pony.

11433. Crossed with what?—The Hackney "Star of the West" and "Lord Rattler." "Star of the West" was a Norfolk bred Hackney, "Lord Rattler" was by "Lord Derby II."

the Week," a good stamp of
tone horse.
the result of "Star of the
, pony mare you got, what
weight on the legs and very

decided improvement in the

I crow you say you are looking.
e any results of that?—I
years old when I got her,
Champion Ganymede," so she

improvement on the dam?—
engtish mare, that is the

it was in an improvement on
e three years old and went
country, and the horse and

ponies?—Yes.
I first about?—It was mild.
Mitchell and he said hes
by "Champion Ganymede."
then would be give for their
motion?
enough I mean?—That many
a coming to England just
was trained and put into
in the months.
a many in the hunting
and sent them at home
to the regular hunter breed-
ture, and Tipperary?—Yes,
a have.
the mares from which most
breed that are bought by
were not from the mares.
up the roads of the world?
up fine and ridden them.
but one that was got by
mare?—No.
got by thoroughbred horses?

because of the animal bred
is a good horse?—Yes, but
ughbred because it was by

ridden any horse yourself
by out of a hunting mare?—
a horse myself of Hackney
other too. By Sir a Hackney,
said Charles said he advised
it, but not for saddle, ex-
ghton, I think he said, have
Hackney has been crossed the
nothing but bred, and the
and the best number of young
gallop, and I think it would
see your Irish mares with
ney, but I don't think you
a Hackney cross into them,
I anything action, and those
if they were crossed and had
on by such wild conditions
ey as well as hunters.
a hunting if you were told it
I sure by a Hackney?—I
said I had seen it and had
a trial.
did you it your either by a
ering, or by a thoroughbred,
g, or by a Hackney, which
as either been a Hackney
nes.
where buy the result of the
e hunting those that of a
ing mares?—I don't approve
ing more for a Station

11455. Then, if the Hackney got out of the one, ... out and put into the hunting districts of Ireland they might be detrimental to the breed of hunters sent over to England?—I don't believe so. I think the Hackney cross is the one with them bones. I would not advise the Hackney as the sire cross as to the trade.

11458. Mr. Fitzwilliam.—What is the objection to the thoroughbred horse?—Because I don't know how he is bred; but we do know that the Hackney ... of a great many—he comes from "Flying Childers." You may have a Clydesdale or Cleveland in the thoroughbred horse.

11459. You may, but may you not also in the Hackney?—I don't think so. We have a pedigree which proved it is as pure bred as any other breed.

11460. Is not the Hackney stud-book very recent?—Yes, but we had the help of Wetherby's stud-book to look to—nearly all the best animals can trace back to Wetherby's in the direct male line.

11461. Is it not the case that you can introduce mares into it now?—No, except ponies under 14 hands.

11462. But eventually they get into the book?—If they breed good stock, but they are not likely to have any cart-horse blood in them.

11463. I don't think a thoroughbred horse bred in Ireland is likely to have much cart-horse blood?—You have got a good many cart-horses in Ireland, and they are the very kind likely to produce poor ones. You must have a certain cross of thoroughbred horses, and I don't think they have used Hackneys long enough to produce a thoroughbred stallion with Hackney blood; therefore you must have cart-horse blood—an Arab would not give strength enough.

11464. Would not an Arab be a useful thing amongst the ponies of the country?—I don't think anything better in Ireland would be likely to be ... successful ... to sell.

11465. When you were there you saw some of the Hackney stallions and blood there, at least?—Yes; I know both ... before they went to Ireland.

11466. Did you see any of the thoroughbred stallions that were standing about in the country?—I saw one horse—I cannot remember his name—at Birdy, about four or five years ago.

11467. Belonging to the Board?—No, I don't think so.

11468. You only saw one?—I only saw one.

11469. Lord Rathdonnell.—Have you ever heard of the old Irish breed of horses that have not been crossed with imported cart-horse blood?—I have, and but I don't doubt it is so.

11470. You did not see it given in evidence at a former stage of the inquiry?—I have not seen any of the evidence you have taken.

11471. Have you ever seen what they call thoroughbred stallions in Ireland?—I have, only that and also close to Dublin.

11472. Those few places, I suppose, would only have horses crossed with either Clydesdale or Shire?—I should think not about Dublin. The horse I saw there, I don't remember what he was, but he was a very good-looking horse.

11473. You don't know anything about Tipperary or that part?—I don't.

11474. If you had a three-quarter bred horse, with two or three crosses of thoroughbred on both sides, ... would you object to that kind of horse?—If he were a riding type or a horse that had quality I would not. Take a horse from "Hermit" they would get good purpose, but take the "Galopin" blood through "St. Simon," you would not have horses that looked like a good riding horse.

11475. The thoroughbred sire I was alluding to would be of the former strain?—Not necessarily, because he had two or three crosses of thoroughbred.

11476. Certainly not; but if he had been a hunter mare, with two or three crosses of breeding in him and the sire was thoroughbred, would you object to that class of horse?—Not at all.

Mr. W. ...
Hetherington.

11477. Mr. Carew.—You spoke of buying foals by a Hackney of the Congested Districts Board?—Yes.

11478. What became of those?—They were sold at a sale in Yorkshire.

11479. Did they fetch good prices?—They brought profitable returns on the prices I paid for them.

11480. Do you think they would be useful for farm work if kept by the breeders?—They were not like farm horses.

11481. They would not be useful for doing the ordinary work of the farm in the district?—In that district they would, because their mothers were doing farm work, and they were better proportioned and stronger animals than their mothers.

11482. They were all first cross horses?—Yes, and therefore had no pedigree that admitted them to any stud book and were therefore useless.

11483. Do you know the Congested Districts sires?—Yes, I saw three six weeks ago, and I saw several in England before they became the property of the Congested Districts.

11484. Mr. Wrench.—Have you been a hunting man most of your life?—Yes, I have ridden to hounds ever since I was seven years old.

11485. And have you judged at a great many shows in different parts of the United Kingdom?—Yes.

11486. Do you know much about Mr. Mitchell's farm at Tourmakeady?—I paid a fortnight or three weeks' visit to it at one time.

11487. Do you know whether before he tried the Hackney breeding there he made other experiments to breed hunters?—Yes, he got a thoroughbred horse there.

11488. Did he breed many animals by that hunting horse?—Yes, a good many.

11489. Do you know why he gave it up for the Hackney?—Because they did not pay to bring to England to sell, and he had no use himself for them except to sell.

11490. He bred them for the market?—Yes.

11491. And you know they did not pay?—Yes.

11492. And then he put a Hackney there, do you know with what result?—It has done very well.

11493. And he constantly sells animals bred in Ireland in English markets?—Yes, every two years; he is regular still.

11494. Do you know do they fetch paying prices?—Yes, they pay very well, and he brings some of his tenants' foals across the first year to help to sell for them.

11495. Have you ever gone into the question of statistics at all as to what number of hunters there are brought from Ireland every year?—Well, I don't know what number of horses would be brought. I can only say the Government statistics of the number of horses that do come from Ireland of all classes, and you may take it from the number of hunts in England the probable number of hunters that are required every year.

11496. Have you at all made any calculation as to the probable number required?—I could not say distinctly. I did go into it some time ago.

11497. Do you know whether it is a large proportion of the general horses bred in the country?—I think it is, but not nearly so large as the general trade of the country. It is a larger proportion than the first-class harness trade, but not nearly so large as the ordinary riding and driving tradesman's trade in the country.

11498. Then there is a large trade in Ireland outside the hunter in high class carriage horses?—A very large trade. I have some statistics of the Board of Agriculture which gives the number of horses which have come from Ireland. This is taken from the last return we have, 1896—34,540 were exported from Ireland to England in 1896; we have not got the 1898 return.

11499. Do you know that in 1898 it has gone up to 40,000; it was in the *Times*?—No; I have not seen it.

11500. Do you know at all what proportion of those 34,000 would be the ordinary ride and drive horses below the high class hunter and harness horses?—I should think 20,000 at least.

11501. Do you think from your knowledge of the trade in England that there is a good trade in that class of horses which can be obtained by the Irishmen if they had any help in that direction?—I do.

11502. Do you find the demand for that class of horse increasing or decreasing in the North of England?—I think it would increase from your country considerably if you could get horses with straighter action and better and stronger hind quarters which the Hackney will give to you.

11503. Are the Irish horses deficient in action at present?—They are deficient in that kind of action which really sells well for harness horses.

11504. You don't find in the North of England that bicycles and the idea of motor carriages is lessening the trade in that class of horses?—Not at all.

11505. Has that trade increased in late years?—Oh, yes, considerably; more people drive in carriages now than did, I am told by coach builders—nearly 100 per cent.

11506. You have made inquiries from the coach-builders?—Yes.

11507. And the trade in small carriages is very much larger?—Yes.

11508. I suppose in that class of horses the one thing that tells is action?—Straight action; it does not matter whether it is high or not, but it must be straight action, and that is a peculiarity of the Hackney horse that he has been bred with straight limbs and straight action, and I do not think it will do harm if he gets into the hunter in that way.

11509. Do you think that any of these large dealers in England, if they saw a horse that in appearance suited them, say by a thoroughbred horse, would refuse to buy it because its dam happened to be by a Hackney sire?—Not at all.

11510. You know their trade and know a good many of the dealers?—Yes. I know good horses breeding at present with the Hackney strain.

11511. How were they bred?—One was by "Sportsman," not a very well bred Hackney and out of a well-bred mare.

11512. What is he as a hunter?—Perhaps one of the best that ever looked through a bridle; he was sold for £200 and went to Leicestershire, sold for £400 there and is now back in our country, seventeen or eighteen years old, hunting regularly and carrying fifteen stone.

11513. There is no doubt about his breeding?—Not at all; I bought him myself as a three years old.

11514. Mr. Carew.—Not in Ireland?—No, bred in Westmoreland. I know the Master of the Ullswater Hounds is riding a horse by a Hackney. I don't know his dam's breeding.

11515. Mr. Wrench.—Is that a good horse?—Very good. He stays all day with the stag hounds and stags go very fast, and over is a rough undulating country.

11516. Are there many instances like that?—I only know another. Mr. Sawrey Cookson's mare, by a thoroughbred horse out of a registered Hackney mare, won at the Yorkshire and other Royal Shows and was a galloping good hunter.

11517. It has been stated to us in Ireland that the Hackney horse is soft?—I have not been able to ascertain where the softness comes in. I have gone into the pedigree of several of the leading strains of horses, and unless the softness comes from the thoroughbred I don't see where it is. I have gone into the leading strains of horses whose produce is most likely to be used. If Hackneys are to be used there was "Lord Derby II."

11518. How does he trace back?—He traces back in the sixth generation to no less than eight crosses of the "Fireaway" (249), who was by Jenkinson's "Fireaway" by "Shales" by "Blaze" by "Flying

[illegible] Mr. [illegible]

"Chickens," "Fireworks," dam mostly "Shropshire" by "Highflyer," a son of "Flying Childers," that was a thoroughbred horse, besides a more remote cross of "Dutch Stars," going back to the "Godolphin Arabian." You could not get much better breeding than that.

11519. Is it a fact that the principal Hackney blood of the present day traces back to the thoroughbred blood you have mentioned?—Yes. The horse "Lord Derby II." traces back to "Blaze" on one hand and "Sampson" on the other by "Joseph Andrews," by ......

11520. Was there much thoroughbred blood also in "Fireaway" and "Danegelt"?—"Danegelt" (174) traces back to Lord Fitzwilliam's "Blacklegs," by "Mambrino," a lot of thoroughbred blood; whilst "Petrel," who was a champion horse, his grandsire was by "Tamworth" by "Outlaw," the sire of his dam was by "Lucas's Wentworth" out of a thoroughbred mare.

11521. So that practically in that early breeding there was a large admixture of thoroughbred blood in the best Hackneys?—Decidedly.

11522. I don't know whether you know any of the pedigrees of the horses belonging to the Congested Districts Board, but did it come under your notice that a large amount of that blood is in the pedigrees of those horses?—Yes.

11523. Have you formed any opinion from actual experience as to the endurance of Hackneys?—Yes, I have seen a good deal of them, and I have one or two letters here I have received on the subject from men who have tried them.

11524. On the particular point of endurance?—Yes. I have a letter here from Mr. Anderson, of Brown Hill Stud Farm, Cadley, Preston:—

"I wish to give you the following facts respecting a Hackney mare, sire 'Lord Derby II.' (417), dam, breeding unknown, which I bought in 1896. She was then rising three-years-old and unbroken. I broke her myself, and in 1899, the Saturday before Whit-Monday, I drove her from Accrington to Harrogate, which is just fifty-one miles, in just nine hours, and I stayed in [illegible] and [illegible], and also on Whit-Monday the same, having just six hours' travelling or eight and a half miles per hour, and she did the last eighteen miles in an hour and fifty minutes. Sunday, Monday, Tuesday, Wednesday, Thursday, Friday, Saturday, and Sunday again following, the average miles per day driven was just over thirty, and on the Monday I drove her back again the fifty-one miles in nine and a quarter hours, [illegible] again, having [illegible] in ten days just 361 miles. I have now a mare ('Lady,' dam 'Cheerful [illegible]' (1704), dam by 'Sir Charles' (740)), that has been driven seventy-eight miles between eight o'clock in the morning and eight o'clock at night. These are only two mares out of many I could give. I have a colt by 'Performer' (1,385), dam 'Minnie' by 'Telegraph' ([illegible]), that I am sure would do thirty to forty miles a day the year round."

I have another letter from Mr. Crump, of Wolverhampton. He was saying that he wants a Hackney mare, particularly. He was a judge of the Shire Horse Society last year, and he [illegible]. I bought a very good Hackney mare from this gentleman, and [illegible] from Mr. Robertson that she had [illegible] to hounds. He writes:—

"Mr. Robertson recommended her. I did not think 'Hackney' breeding, but he declared her [illegible] and good for everything you could wish as a riding Hackney. I may have told him that I felt sure she would carry anyone to hounds all day, and I still think so. My reason for not hunting her was that I always had the mare in foal, and did not think it safe to do so. My brother, one of the hardest riders in this neighbourhood, is now riding and hunting regularly a three-year-old by our Hackney stallion 'Grand II.' (2,878) out of a three-parts-bred mare, and he says he never rode a better stayer, and that he is fast enough to ride to any hounds. I am of opinion that the Hackney stallion on blood mares will get the best all-round riding horse you can produce."

I have another from Mr. Taylor:—

"The mare 'Cullingworth Shamrock' is still in my possession, and ready to do anything. I drove a horse-dealing farmer in a trap [illegible] and nearly scared him to death, and you may [illegible] as a thing, and [illegible] in the world to [illegible]. When we had arrived he couldn't speak, only he grasped my hand as though he never expected to see me again. The mare (3,693) 'Cullingworth Shamrock,' was turned out to grass on [illegible], and until the day before [illegible], was [illegible] and had nothing but grass. She was then [illegible], well groomed and fed, and [illegible] and at [illegible] the following morning myself and a friend drove her in a rather heavy gig to the [illegible], a distance of forty-one miles in under four hours. Of course we were not trying against time, and the mare was never urged on. Returning the day following we [illegible] (by a [illegible]) in the journey, and were about three hours and forty-five minutes on the road. At the time she was about three months advanced in foal, and while the [illegible] without [illegible], the sudden change from grass to dry [illegible] having apparently [illegible] her digestive organs. She, however, [illegible] and [illegible] in the morning following [illegible] of the [illegible]."

11525. Do you know how that mare was bred?—She was bred in Ireland, at [illegible].

11526. Have you any other special instance?—Mr. Ackworth, Master of Hounds, has two Hackney mares which he rides [illegible] regularly, and [illegible] back again at night. They are by a Hackney [illegible] and [illegible] their breeding.

11527. [illegible] they stay?—They can stay all day, and carry him back without [illegible] their [illegible] on the ground or anything.

11528. Chairman.—With the exception of one of the animals you mentioned, you know nothing of them yourself?—I do not; not in the least.

11529. And the account, especially in the first letter you read, of the distance these animals travelled, would you think that was a fair average of what an ordinary Hackney can do?—Yes; I think it is a good Hackney. It is rather above the average.

11530. I [illegible] the distance travelled in a day [illegible] miles in the same [illegible].

11531. You think that would be a little above the average?—Oh! yes. I don't think that it would be likely that every horse could do it.

11532. You hunt a good deal yourself?—Yes; I have always hunted.

11533. Have you ever ridden a Hackney yourself hunting?—Never.

11534. What kind of hunter do you generally hunt with?—Generally a thoroughbred one.

11535. Where do you get him from?—I bought a good many in Ireland.

11536. For your own hunting you prefer an Irish hunter by a thoroughbred sire?—I don't know if I prefer it, but it has been always my practice to come over, and I am rather a heavy weight, and except the one I am riding now, I think I have always had high-bred ones, and he won the jumping at Dublin.

11537. I suppose the Hackney type was particularly well established and distinguished before the institution of the stud-book?—Decidedly; they had kept a very good record of the [illegible] then, but not of the [illegible] type.

11538. Do you know if there was in Ireland a fairly distinct type [illegible] the old Irish hunter?—I am not sufficiently acquainted with it to say.

11539. Assuming for the sake of argument there was such a type of animal and crossed frequently with a thoroughbred sire, would you object to the stallion being half-bred under these circumstances, provided any strain of **cart horse blood** or Cleveland blood has been mixed.

11540. Your objection to the half-bred I gather is that probably the utility work of the cart-horse would?—Yes.

11541. I think you said that of your own horses you are not quite sure whether one of them had a Hackney strain in him or not?—From his appearance I would think so, but not from his sire and grandsire; I am not quite sure; he won the jumping at Dublin some five years ago.

11542. I think you also said that, in your opinion, the average Irish farmer would be able to detect after several generations the strain of Hackney blood?—Not after several generations.

11543. I did not know whether you credit the average Irish farmer with a greater facility for the detection than you possess yourself?—No, it was in the first cross that he would not have much difficulty; they are a horse with strong powers of hitting their action that I think they would be very likely to show.

11544. You made an estimate of the total number of horses imported from Ireland in 1895, as to the proportion that the hunters and high class horses would bear to it, that is from your own general knowledge of the trade, I suppose?—Yes.

11545. Have you formed any estimate in your own mind of what the relative value would be, in round numbers you say 10,000 would be hunters and high class horses, and 20,000 general utility horses, have you any idea of the relative value of the 10,000 against the 20,000?—I have not figures; I don't think that many of the horses that are eventually sold for high prices are sold for a lot of money in Ireland; it is a question of education or getting them into the hands of men who can place them.

11546. At any rate you cannot give us the relative values?—I don't think the relative value is very different in Ireland between a fairly middle-class hunter and an ordinary cob or road horse; it is the man in England who gets it, or the man who brings them over to English fairs; the breeder does not reap a large amount of benefit.

11547. Do you know anything about cavalry remounts?—I do not.

11548. I suppose horses bred in Yorkshire and other parts of England have passed through your hands?—A good many.

11549. Can you form any opinion whether the breeding of Hackneys in Yorkshire has interfered with the breeding of hunters?—No, I don't think so.

11550. Not at all?—I don't think so.

11551. You think as many good hunters come out of Yorkshire as before?—Yes, there are more men breeding, there are more horses wanted.

11552. And in your opinion the value of the general utility horse keeps up as good as ever?—It does, as good as ever.

11553. Lord Londonderry.—These 34,000 horses, are they all bred in Ireland?—Well, I could not say; there are no statistics given, except that they come from Ireland to England, and that includes also the horses that pass through England to go to France and Belgium.

11554. Lord Ancaster.—It would also include horses that had gone over to shows in Ireland and come back again?—Yes.

11555. Mr. Fitzwilliam.—How did you say "Sportsman" was bred?—He was by a Hackney, but very little was known of the breeding of his dam. He was out of an ordinary countrybred mare; it might be an Irish mare or anything. We get a great number of Irish horses into Westmoreland and Cumberland. It might be an ordinary hill and farm mare of the country or an Irish horse.

11556. Was he by a studbook Hackney?—Yes.

11557. Lord Rathdonnell.—With reference to the 34,000 horses, do you know whether with a cavalry regiment moving from Ireland to England the horses of that regiment would be in that number?—There are horses that are traded in. The cavalry remounts would be included, but not the horses of a cavalry regiment.

11558. Mr. Fitzwilliam.—How would they ascertain them in the statistics?—The Government would do that.

11559. Lord Rathdonnell.—I wanted to know how you got those figures?—From the Board of Agricultural Returns.

11560. Lord Ancaster.—Are these horses that have been bought and sold?—They are horses that have been bought and sold and shipped. I don't think they would include the Government horses.

11561. In Mr. Andrews's horse, the dam mare you mentioned, I think he said, was by a Hackney?—By a Hackney, dam unknown.

11562. Then that constituted Hackney?—No, she is not in the stud-book.

11563. May I ask you did you buy or [illegible] him only since for the [illegible] Show?—None.

11564. Mr. Le Tresch.—Are you a member of the Hackney Society's Council?—No, sir.

11565. But you are nominated by the Hackney Horse Society as an expert in Hackney horses to give evidence to this Commission. I noticed that when you were talking on the pedigree of these Hackney sires you seemed to put a considerable stress on their being descended from thoroughbred horses, why is that?—I don't know that I lay particular stress upon it, but it was a point that they were bred from a good line of horses.

11566. You acknowledge that the thoroughbred horse is a good line?—Decidedly.

11567. Is there any advantage in being bred from a thoroughbred horse, surely the nearer you can get to the thoroughbred horse the better?—I believe that.

11568. I noticed that those thoroughbred horses you referred to in the pedigree of these Hackney stallions were horses that were about contemporary with the Darley Arabian and "Flying Childers"?—Yes.

11569. By this time you must have pretty nearly effectively worked out the thoroughbred blood from the Hackney?—I don't think it has been worked out, because fresh thoroughbred blood has been brought in at other times. I don't know that we are beginning to keep in the thoroughbred blood, but for a horse of trotting action.

11570. You consequently bring in **thoroughbred** blood again?—It has been done so.

11571. Why?—That I don't know.

11572. It is admitted then by the lovers of the Hackney that thoroughbred blood is of advantage to the Hackney?—Certainly; it gives him quality, and some of them are wanting in slope of shoulder, and are perhaps too upright in their shoulder, rough-looking horses, and they are admittedly very much improved by a cross of thoroughbred blood.

11573. It comes to me that if you follow that to a logical conclusion, if you eradicate the Hackney and stick to the thoroughbred, you would get a better horse than you have?—I grant you that for some purposes, but you would not get weight and substance.

11574. I have not seen many Hackney stallions, but I have never seen one half the size of a thoroughbred?—You would have seen yesterday [illegible] Hackney stallions, [illegible], and many of them up to 16 hands, and many of them are able to take a big carriage. "Sportsman" is a good big thoroughbred. Take on the other hand all the little weeds you have.

11575. Mr. Watson.—Do you know anything about the American trade in horses?—I know a good deal of it.

11576. Are they not sending over a large number of horses to England and Ireland now?—Yes.

11577. It has been suggested to us that American horses should be branded in order that they may be known when they come to this country, do you think that would be a good plan or not?—For what is the purpose of branding, simply for the purpose of knowing them?

11579. Yes, to distinguish them as American horses?—I would not approve of branding anywhere where it would disfigure the horse.

11580. You think there ought to be an opportunity of buying them no matter whether they came from America or Ireland?—I don't think a man who gets an American horse should have him branded and destroy his chance of getting a good home because other good horses come from America.

11581. Do you know that many American horses have been sold as Irish horses?—Yes, and sold as English horses too, I know you have a good many in Ireland now. I would suggest branding, but not very strongly, not so that it would depreciate the animal in appearance, it should not be in any conspicuous place.

11582. How would you brand?—Underneath his mane.

11583. With a hot iron?—Yes, branding the foot is no use.

Mr. Fitzwilliam.—A bog-trotting horse would get the worst of it.

11584. Mr. Wrench.—You have been talking of thoroughbred horses as opposed to hunters, now put them out of the question and think of the small farmers, what do you think would be the best sire for their market?—A horse with some Hackney blood in him, because he will give good action and good shape and rather strong muscular development, a horse that they will be able to sell.

11585. Have you ever seen the same action from horses got by a thoroughbred as you have from horses got by Hackneys?—Not consistently. I have seen some thoroughbred horses that have got horses with a good deal of action and have been very beautiful-moving horses, but they don't get them consistently.

11586. And is the saddle class horse's action the chief selling quality?—Yes.

11587. Chairman.—What are these American and foreign horses used for, mostly harness?—Yes, many of them are being trained for private work, and taking the place in London of some of our Yorkshire horses that used to be, and of your Irish horses that are good green horses in ... [illegible] for horse ...

11588. Looking at the matter, as we are bound to do from the point of view of the industry in Ireland, would you say, that in breeding for harness purposes in Ireland, the breeder would be subjected to greater competition than, in breeding for hunting purposes?—I don't know anybody who does breed especially for hunting purposes either in England or Ireland.

11589. There are certain districts in Ireland where the object of the breeder is to produce a hunter?—Yes.

11590. I am asking you generally what your opinion would be, whether in trying to produce harness the competition would be less than in breeding for harness purposes?—I think either would have a good sale and would not be affected by any foreign horses of a high class.

11591. Is not nearly the whole of Great Britain more or less devoted to breeding for harness purposes and are not the greater number of these foreign importations used for harness purposes?—The foreign importations are used only for harness work. But with regard to England they are devoting considerable attention to the breeding of cart-horses and Hackneys, and horses especially just at present.

11592. Do you suppose the majority of horses used for hunting in England are bred in England or bred in Ireland?—I should say about two-thirds of them are bred in Ireland.

11593. Lord Londonderry.—You have bought horses for a good many years in Ireland?—Yes.

11594. Should you say at the present time that the breed of horses taken generally is as good or better or worse than it was when you began to buy horses?—There are not as many horses with size and substance as there were, there are more weeds, unsaleable horses until they know their business, if they are good enough for hunters. When I went there first, which is some twenty-five or twenty-three years ago, we could find a good many big upstanding horses with quality.

11595. Then you think the breed of horses has deteriorated in the last twenty years?—Decidedly.

11596. In special classes?—I am taking your light horse as a class, and the hunters we don't know very much about the hunters until they are made, but hundreds of horses that are bought as hunters never see a hound as long as they live in your country.

11597. Your experience is that the breed of horses as a whole has deteriorated?—Decidedly, there is a want of substance and bigger class than was not the case some twenty-three years ago.

11598. That is over the whole of Ireland?—Yes, it is more particularly the counties past.

11599. Mr. Fitzgerald.—Should you think the bad times had anything to do with forcing the farmers to sell their mares more than they did years ago?—I don't think bad times have done it so much as the extra prices the foreigner gives for a good-looking mare to take abroad, and there is no chance of getting them back again, we can get geldings from abroad, but not mares.

11600. Mr. Gamble.—It is the bad times that have induced the farmers to sell to the foreigner?—I don't think so; a man will sell the most valuable article on his farm whatever the times are, whether he is well off or ill off unless he is fond of it.

11601. Mr. Wrench.—Do you think that has prevailed in England, have the good mares been sold in England?—Decidedly.

11602. Has the Horses' Improvement Society not had an effect in England yet?—It has not had that effect that one would expect to see come of it. The stallions chosen have in many instances not been acceptable to the farmers.

11603. Mr. La Touche.—I suppose the foreigners offer the same inducements to the farmers in the South of Ireland as in the North?—Probably, but the foreigner likes a mare with a little action, and in the North of Ireland the mares have always had a little more action than the hunter mares in the South.

11604. Then it is in the North of Ireland you see this deterioration of the mares?—Yes.

11605. You don't think it is in any way due to the great popularity of a horse called "Broad Arrow" that the farmers in the North of Ireland say is the best horse that came to them?—I don't think one horse can change the breed of the whole of the country.

11606. He got a great many there, I understand?—I never saw a horse by "Broad Arrow;" I have seen a good many "Broad Arrow" mares.

11607. And then "Bounding Willow" for instance?—"Bounding Willow" I don't know; I think he is in Scotland, he would not be in Ireland very long.

11608. Mr. Wrench.—When you speak of the North of Ireland, what parts do you mean?—Mayo, Armagh, Monaghan, and round about there.

11609. When you are buying there, what aged horses do you buy?—Four and five year olds.

11610. And do you know that a good proportion of those horses come from the South of Ireland?—I am led to understand that a great many are bought there and brought to the North as foals or two and three year olds.

Mr. James M'Kinley, Carnlough, Derby, examined.

11611. Chairman.—You live at Derby?—Yes.

11612. That is near Glasgow?—Yes. I should like to read the little evidence I wish to give, and then shall be glad to answer any questions. I am a horse and hunt agent in Glasgow, and a breeder of Hackneys at my house at Carnlough, Derby. I was one of the judges of Hackneys at the

Mr. James M'Kinley.

[illegible]

London Spring Show in 1895, and last November I was one of the judges of Hackneys at the National Horse Show of America at New York. I wish to state at the outset that I have had no experience in my own stud of crossing Hackneys, or their produce with other breeds. Any evidence therefore I can give on this branch of the subject is necessarily limited to observation of such animals at agricultural shows, and throughout the country generally. I am well acquainted with the ordinary ride and drive horses of Scotland, and I can speak very distinctly to a marked improvement in this class of young stock since the introduction of Hackney stallions in the north. I am a member of the "Scotch Committee" of the Hackney Horse Society which was formed in 1890 for the purpose of encouraging the breeding of Hackneys in Scotland, and the separation into different classes of Hackneys and hunters at Scotch shows. This Committee has subscribed about £1,000 within the last five years. The money is spent in giving contributions towards the prizes to agricultural societies under certain conditions as to classes, judges, etc. Prior to the existence of the "Scotch Committee," hunters and roadsters were for the most part classed and exhibited together at Scotch shows. This practice was a most discouraging one to breeders, both of hunting stock and roadster stock. Now, however, through the efforts of the "Scotch Committee" each breed of horses is exhibited in its own class; and breeders can see by comparison what progress they are making in the improvement of their respective breeds. In place therefore of the introduction of the Hackney into Scotland proving detrimental to the breed of hunting horses there, the very reverse has been the result, as hunting young stock have now separate classification at most of the principal shows in consequence of the introduction of the Hackney and the operations of the "Scotch Committee." In my opinion there is no real ground for supposing that the introduction of the Hackney horse into Ireland will interfere with the breeding of hunting stock there. The Hackney stallion has not interfered with the breeding of hunting or other thoroughbred stock in Scotland. If all the Queen's premium thoroughbred stallions were handed round me I would never think of using one of them in my Hackney stud; and I presume the same thing would apply to the owners of thoroughbred studs in regard to Hackney stallions. In my opinion the one class of animal does not clash with the other in the least. I have observed that objection has been taken to the Hackney on the allegation that he is a soft blooded animal without staying power; and therefore is not a breed to be encouraged. If this was true I would agree with objectors, but in my opinion the charge is entirely unfounded, except as regards perhaps one particular strain of blood. However, I think it has been clearly proved by Mr. Euren, the Secretary of the Hackney Horse Society, that one of the progenitors of this strain, although registered as of good Hackney blood, is really of foreign descent. The get of this horse some years ago were largely introduced into Scotland by dealers, and they have done incalculable harm to the true interest of Hackney breeding in Scotland. In my opinion, however, the staying power of such strains of Hackney blood as Danegelt 174, Denmark 177, Lord Derby II. 417, and Fireaway 249 cannot be disputed. I believe there is no breed of horses in the world so sound and generally serviceable to the use of man as the Hackney, and while there is plenty of room for all classes of horses (even the pleasure race horse and pleasure hunting horse) there ought in my opinion to be special encouragement given to Hackney sires throughout the country, both because of the soundness and utility of the breed, but also because the Hackney stallion is the most likely animal to produce out of the ordinary mares of the country a valuable class of carriage horses, which at the present moment this country is much in need of, and is largely dependent on America for its supply. When I was in America I had an opportunity of seeing the result of crossing the Hackney horse on American native bred mares. At the New York show the Hackney stallion Cadet came into the ring with four of his get out of such mares following him. I had also an opportunity of seeing a large number of native mares themselves. When I say native mares I do not mean their fast-trotting stock, but the ordinary ride and drive animals of the country. These mares are very blood-like, but with very light and puny limbs and small joints and seem too heavy on the underside. The produce I refer to by Cadet were big strong animals with big limbs and joints and nicely shaped necks, and appeared to me to be like growing into very handsome and powerful carriage horses. After the show was over I had an opportunity, on the invitation of Mr. Cassatt, the President of the Hackney Horse Society of America, of viewing his large stud at Philadelphia. I saw there a considerable number of youngsters by Cadet out of native mares, and a finer lot of Hackney shaped animals I have seldom seen. The result of crossing the Hackney stallion on these native mares, so far as I had an opportunity of judging, was a great improvement on the native animal itself, and I would say as soon as the Americans overcome their unnatural prejudice against things English, and go in generally for the use of the Hackney stallion, they are likely to produce, in my opinion, probably the best carriage horses in the world for size, quality, and pace. Then with regard to native Scotch pony mares bred to Hackney stallions, I can speak with the greatest confidence. I am decidedly of the opinion that no cross has produced such good results in Scotland as the Hackney stallion on such mares. The prepotency of the well bred Hackney stallion for producing his own type and good qualities out of weedy thoroughbreds, ordinary cold farmer's light-legged mares or nondescript ponies, is one of the marked characteristics of this breed of horses.

11613. Lord Londonderry.—I notice you state that you yourself if you were surrounded with thoroughbred stallions would not cross them with a Hackney; in the same way you would not expect that anybody connected with Hackneys would cross thoroughbred or hunter-bred mares with them?—I think so. I limit my remarks entirely to thoroughbreds—I mean the pure-bred thoroughbreds. I did not include any half-bred animal in that. I mean those gentlemen who own studs that are pure in breed—all thoroughbred—they would never think of using a Hackney in such. The same thing applies in America where the 2.10 and 2.8 trotting horse is. These gentlemen would not think of using a Hackney stallion on these mares, and my remarks there again apply to the ordinary mare of the country.

11614. The great fear of the hunter breeders in Ireland is that the smaller farmers might be tempted to send the mares that breed good hunters to Hackney stallions instead of sires that have got good hunters. Do you think there would be any danger of that?—I think not; the price would regulate that and the shape to a large extent; there is no mistaking the Hackney in the first cross.

11615. Do you think yourself that it would do harm?—I am not a hunting man, and prefer not to speak about hunters.

11616. But so far as you yourself are concerned you would keep the Hackney distinctly in its own class of mare?—As far as my own stud is concerned.

11617. And you think that would be generally supported by gentlemen you have talked to about it?—By owners of pure-bred studs.

11618. Mr. Fitzwilliam.—As far as your remarks are concerned they don't apply to hunter breeding to any extent?—No.

11619. Lord Ravensworth.—I think in your

discussed that you said so, as you state that the ponies in Scotland had been improved by the introduction of Hackneys?—[illegible] about that. They have been improved, and by using Hackneys to produce hunters, but by the operation of the Scotch Committee of the Hackney Society in providing classifications for such horses and enabling those who want to see the breeding hunters to see the effect of the operations at those shows. Previous to this Committee being formed there was great trouble in exhibiting the Hackneys and cobs together. If a Hackney judge went into the ring to judge, as there was a majority of Hackney judges, the high-stepping ones went to the top; but if it happened that a majority of thoroughbred or hunting men were into the ring, the other class went to the top, and both classes of breeders were discouraged and had no means of seeing how they progressed in their breeding. To that exhibit only my remarks apply.

[illegible]. Lord Arthur.—You mean to say that if Hackneys were given separate classes, and hunters got by Hackneys likewise, then the hunter class, people would keep the two breeds more separate?—Yes, I do, distinctly; if that was done there would be no danger whatever in Ireland.

1161. If young horses got by Hackney stallions were not forced to compete in the classes for hunters you think it would encourage the men who use Hackneys not to cross them on mares likely to go into the hunter classes?—Quite so.

1162. Mr. Carew.—Is there much hunter-breeding in Scotland?—I would not say there is much; there are very good classes exhibited, principally [illegible] where young stock come [illegible] in some of the principal shows.

1163. Do you know how they are bred?—No, I don't; but I presume they are got by thoroughbred horses from the best of them.

1164. Mr. Wrench.—Do you think that the American trade, to which you referred in your evidence when you spoke of their preferring [illegible] English horses, do you think when they acquire that, that the American trade will be very favourable for native breeders here?—I think it will.

1165. You think it will increase very largely?—I think so.

1166. **And their horses will continue to improve?**—I think so.

1167. Have you thought in any way if there is any remedy for this [illegible] in this country?—Yes; I think we have the remedy in our own hands, and can compete with America if we set ourselves to work [illegible] on the ordinary course of [illegible]. We have a type of ordinary mares in Scotland, and there is another class in Ireland, [illegible] altogether from the breeding of thoroughbred mares that we can improve in an animal—I think we can compete successfully with America if we use a proper breed of Hackney, and we have plenty of those in our country.

1168. Of course the American trade is practically only up to the present in general utility horses and harness horses?—Yes; I think they have hardly discovered where they are; [illegible]. I think this class of horses ready for breeding [illegible] America, and I have a [illegible] that [illegible] got by the Hackney [illegible] because they are more near the type of our [illegible], and those are the animals which we have to beat, not the other ones.

1169. Are they coming in as increasing numbers now?—I think so.

1170. Would you approve of breeding **horses** [illegible] from America?—I should not think so; **the** best way of [illegible] is to compete with them.

1171. You think that is possible?—I think it is thoroughly possible.

1172. Have you any instances of the same [illegible] being put to a thoroughbred horse and being put to a Hackney horse, with the result?—Yes; I think I have some notes here on that point. There is one mare I have noted, owned by Mr. Wm. Scott, of [illegible]. It was imported and entered in the Hackney Stud Book, 3,584 "[illegible]"; the sire of the mare was "Royal Grand," and the dam "Kate," a 14.3 pony only, which I have seen, by the thoroughbred horse "Knockie" by "Hermit." This [illegible] winner of many prizes, and being the champion gold medal at Chester against first [illegible] Hackneys. Then there is another one out of the same mare, a very good one, by the same horse, which is now in the stud of the Marquis of Londonderry at Seaham Harbour. I have also seen this, it is a nice one. The mare was a little mare worth about £[illegible], and this mare "[illegible]," if I was asked to value at the present moment I would put her at not less than £[illegible].

1173. Lord Arthur.—Was that mare crossed with a thoroughbred?—No. But I know instances of that. Another instance of a mare belonging to Mr. Watson Mackay, one of the Factor of [illegible]; he owned a mare called "Black Bess" [illegible]. She was imported, her sire was "Lord of the Isles," dam "Betty" by "Devil," thoroughbred, winner of first prize at Cleveland, Dumfries, Ayr, Glasgow, and Edinburgh. Then I have another instance, Mr. Adams, a gentleman in our neighbourhood, [illegible] bred "Prince Confidence," [illegible], whose sire was "King Confidence," and dam "[illegible]" an Irish mare, 14.1, [illegible]. Mr. Adams purchased this mare when in foal for £[illegible], and sold her produce, a filly by a thoroughbred horse, when four years old, in the Horse Guards for £[illegible]. The next foal, "Prince Confidence," took third prize at Glasgow when a yearling, and was sold when two years old to a dealer for £[illegible] for America. He informs me the dealer refused £[illegible] for him. Probably the best specimens of this crossing that I have seen was a pair of [illegible] carriage horses owned by Mr. Morton, got by the Hackney stallion "Lord Derby II." [illegible], out of high-legged Yorkshire coach mares. These horses **are** 15.3, and were sold at a sale for £[illegible].

1174. Mr. Wrench.—Then you think that Hackneys can get high-class carriage horses?—Decidedly.

1175. Have you any experience as to their shoeing and endurance?—Not personally, except from my own driving. I drive a pair of Hackneys and [illegible].

1176. Chairman.—As to the crossing of the Hackney on the pony mare, have you any experience of that?—Not in my own stud; I have seen it.

1177. Can you tell us anything about it?—We have one very marked instance in Scotland of this. The celebrated pony stallion "Mars" is about 13.2 hands high, he is now owned by Mr. Mitchell, of [illegible], he was got by the Hackney stallion "Dalby" ([illegible]), [illegible], out of a mare from the Isle of Skye. He was a winner all along the line and took [illegible] at York, where Mr. Christopher Wilson's wonderful pony appeared as his opponent, and he was seldom beaten except when he met him.

1178. Where is this pony?—He is living at Millfield, near Edinburgh.

1179. Do you know anything of his produce?—He has made a most marked improvement in the breed of ponies round our district. You can tell a "Mars" pony anywhere. He can stick up to his sire, and go with [illegible]. There is a bit of strength [illegible] for pulling machines.

1180. What kind of mares has he been put to?—All kinds. The rough little mares that come from the Highlands, and all round. Then I have a very extraordinary instance of his crossing—Mr. [illegible]'s famous pony "[illegible]." It has gone all round England and taken very many prizes. It is 13.2 hands high. It was got by "Mars" out of a little mare 13 hands high by the thoroughbred horse "[illegible]." Those were the sires of this pony, a little

3 K

[illegible]

sense of a thing. "Hungarian" was sold at Mr. Macbeth's sale, after a most spirited competition, for 180 guineas, and I believe it would bring double the money now if put into the market.

11641. Lord Ardilaun.—The dam was a Irish mare?—Yes.

11642. Chairman.—The dam was by a thoroughbred horse. Do you know out of what family?—By "Speciality." I don't know what out of.

11643. Are you acquainted with Ireland as well as a horse-breeding country?—No.

11644. Are there any districts in Scotland particularly devoted to producing hunters?—There are a lot of hunters produced round the district of Ayr, for instance, but I don't know that in Scotland there is any one district specially marked for producing hunters. It is rather a general thing spread all over.

11645. Would you say that the production of hunters was a small or a large part of the whole of horse-breeding as an industry in Scotland?—I would say it was a fair proportion, judging from the numbers that appear in the classes at the shows.

11646. I gather from you, you think the introduction of the Hackney into Scotland benefited the hunter in so far as a separate class was given for them?—Yes, my lord.

11647. How do you think that the use of the Hackney sire is beneficial in producing hunters?—I do not.

11648. Then may I take it that you consider the Hackney principally as a harness horse?—Saddle and harness.

11649. You mean by saddle not including hunters?—Not including hunters.

11650. Mr. Wrench.—Do you know whether a large number of horses are taken from the North of Ireland to Scotland now?—I believe there are.

11651. And do you think that if Hackneys were introduced into the North of Ireland where they don't breed hunters, that Scotchmen would give more for the produce than they do for the animals they now are buying there?—I think they would. I believe if Hackney stallions were used there it would create a revolution in the character and style and type of the animal sent over, and it is in that way that I hope we can compete with America successfully.

11652. When you talk of a revolution you are not talking of hunters, but of the bad class of horses that now come from Ireland?—Yes. I don't interfere with the thoroughbred. There is room for them all, and I believe that is the basis on which we must go for the breeding of horses in Ireland—keeping the lines separate. We have done that most successfully in Scotland, and I believe in Scotland there has already been a marked improvement, and there will be more from year to year as we go on.

11653. Have you ever considered whether it would be possible to keep a registration of horses in different districts so that the breeding of all the horses might be known—do you think the foreigner would give a bigger price if he could ascertain the true pedigree of a horse?—I think he might. I think he would, in fact. But most men look at the type of the animal, not his pedigree—I mean for ordinary work; but for export it would be an improvement if horses could be certified to be bred a certain way, if they had any thoughts of breeding them again.

11654. But you think the ordinary buyer does not think much about pedigree?—Not for carriage work; for instance for a gelding, I don't think it matters how he comes if he is of the right stamp and type.

11655. Chairman.—As far as you are concerned you breed only pure-bred Hackneys?—The purest blood I can get.

11656. But you approve of crossing them; you have given us some instances where they have been crossed very successfully?—Yes.

11657. What becomes of the misfits in the main, say of the cross of the Hackney stallion with the ordinary mare of the country; they cannot always be successful, what are they used for?—They find their way, I presume, into trams, and buses, and cabs.

11658. Have you any idea what their market value would be?—No, I cannot speak of the value of these ordinary horses, because I do not deal in them as they are, if they happen to have any of them.

Mr. W. E. Thorburn, Stocksfield-on-Tyne, examined.

11659. Chairman.—You live at Stocksfield-on-Tyne?—I do.

11660. Are you occupied in horse-breeding?—Yes.

11661. Do you buy horses at all?—Yes.

11662. What class of horses do you breed?—All kinds.

11663. For all kinds of purposes?—Yes.

11664. You keep stallions of your own?—Yes, about twenty.

11665. Of what breed?—Pony stallions, Hackney stallions, thoroughbred, hunters, Clydesdale, and Shires.

11666. What do you mean by hunters—half-bred?—Yes.

11667. What do you understand by a hunter sire?—I understand by a hunter sire a horse of a hunting type that can be hunted.

11668. I mean how bred?—Well, I have only had one hunter horse I bought at Kildare Royal Show; he was not a clean thoroughbred; I bought him out of the weight-carrying class. He was of a [illegible] hunter type—only three years old. I took him to the North. There was a show where there was a prize given for the best hunter, and I showed him against "[illegible]," and I thought he was going to beat him, but the age rather [illegible] from him. I hunted him for two seasons, and he left more good hunters in the two seasons than any horse I ever had.

11669. Lord Ardilaun.—What was his name?—"Lord [illegible]."

11670. Chairman.—In buying a hunter sire of that kind would you consider at all what blood was flowing [illegible] of, whether cart horse, Cleveland, or Hackney?—I would not care so very much where it came from so long as he got it, but I should certainly buy a hunter stallion off a hunter mare that proved himself a good class hunter, because I consider any stallion is more likely to reproduce the features of his mother than anything else.

11671. How many Hackney sires do you keep?—I have three or four just now.

11672. How many thoroughbreds?—I have one thoroughbred.

11673. Do you use him for breeding thoroughbreds?—No, simply for hunters; at least when I say simply for hunters people can use him for any sort of thing they like.

11674. Do you keep mares yourself, too?—Yes.

11675. A number of mares?—I should say pretty near to about twenty.

11676. Of various breeds?—Yes, all breeds.

11677. And those you put your own stallions to, I suppose?—Yes.

11678. Can you tell us what breed of mare you put to what breed of stallion?—I am breeding from my hunter mares now by "Carlisle" by "[illegible]," out of "Zodiac's" dam. He is four crosses from a Welsh pony; his dam bred "St. Gatien," "[illegible]," "Marmaduke," and this one of mine.

11679. Mr. Fitzwilliam.—"Carlisle" is not thoroughbred?—No, but he has won three steeplechases, and carried 13½ stone over the Aintree course. He is absolutely sound.

11680. How old?—He was nearly years in mid[illegible]

I don't know his exact age. I was talking to a gentleman the other day that had one of the same breed descended from the same mare, and he says they are the bravest and best horses he ever saw, and this [illegible] of mine is absolutely clean on his legs.

11681. CHAIRMAN.—And you put most of your [illegible] mares to him?—I put them all to him.

11682. And have for some time?—I have had him only two seasons; this is the third season.

11683. And you are satisfied with the produce?—Perfectly.

11684. You put none of your hunter mares to the Hackney or thoroughbred?—I put one mare to a thoroughbred horse two years ago, but judging from the produce I would not think of using anything else than this horse now.

11685. Then I judge, as far as breeding for hunting purposes is concerned, you have no objection at all to the half-bred horse?—Certainly not.

11686. Do you think that type could be sufficiently defined? Supposing there was a system of registration for them, could you define what you mean?—There are a great many people breed hunters, and a lot of people breed good ones. My idea would be to breed, a hunter stallion out of a first-class hunter mare which has been hunted and remained absolutely sound.

11687. Then in a system of registration, as far as the half-bred sire is concerned, do you think it necessary that before allowing him to be registered his past performances should be considered as a [illegible] of [illegible], and the produce he got?—Well, to a certain extent that may hold good. I have used Hackney stallions on hunter mares, high-bred Hackney stallions, and they have left some excellent hunters, so that it would be altogether unfair to condemn these horses for hunter breeding simply on their own merits. If there is to be a system of registration I should certainly take individual merit as the leading consideration. Of course I mean by individual merit an animal good in itself and any [illegible], because I think the essential [illegible] of the hunter are undoubtedly hereditary.

11688. You have put hunter mares to Hackney stallions?—Yes. Well, I have kept Hackney stallions and seen their produce off hunter mares.

11689. Off your own mares?—My own mares, as I have only a small place, and cannot keep a great lot.

11690. What is your opinion of the produce?—Well, I have had Hackney stallions get some very good hunters indeed.

11691. Out of what kind of mare?—I saw a hunter by a Hackney the other day hunting with the [illegible] going remarkably well. I followed him. There was four of us going pretty sharp, and he kept with us to the [illegible]. He is a bad horse; has never given his owner a fall; he is fourteen years old, and absolutely sound.

11692. Do you know what his dam was?—Yes, a hunter mare.

11693. What do you mean exactly by a hunter mare?—A mare that has been hunted and has been breeding hunters to thoroughbred stallions. The first hunter she bred was a remarkably good hunter by the horse of mine, "[illegible]."

11694. Taking it generally, do you approve of the Hackney idea for the purpose of getting hunters in Ireland?—I believe the Hackney stallion to be the best almost every class of horse.

11695. For hunting and for all purposes?—For hunting, and for all purposes. I advised a friend of mine to put a thoroughbred mare to a Hackney stallion of mine two years ago. She is by "[illegible]." She had been put to a fashionable thoroughbred stallion and broke. He said to me one day—"I want you to cover her with any horse you like." I put her to a top-sized Hackney stallion, and he replied in my enquiry:—"I have every reason to be satisfied with my yearling filly got by your Hackney stallion. She has big bone, correct shoulders of a hunting type, and gives promise of being a high-class weight-carrying hunter."

11696. Do you know Ireland at all?—Yes, I have been to the Dublin Show a few times.

11697. You don't know the country generally?—I cannot say that I know the country generally, but I have a general idea of the horses that come from it.

11698. Would you think that the introduction of Hackney blood into those districts of the country that breed hunters principally would be beneficial or prejudicial?—I should think it would be beneficial certainly.

11699. Lord RATHDONNELL.—You say the cross of the Hackney stallion with the hunter mare produces a good hunter?—I know so to my own knowledge.

11700. But you say you do not cross your hunter mares with a Hackney stallion at the present time; why, if the produce is so good?—Because I have a hunter stallion which I like better. You see I keep a lot of stallions. I am the [illegible] [illegible] [illegible] [illegible] to them, and can see the effect that these horses have on the mares, and I unhesitatingly say that for light mares a Hackney stallion will get always a much more marketable animal than a thoroughbred.

11701. Why would you [illegible] Hackney stallions in Ireland to improve the breed of hunters?—For the very good and sufficient reason that there appears to be a unanimity of opinion that there are too many weedy horses in Ireland, and if you put the mares to a Hackney stallion you are sure to get a great deal more bone, and if you don't breed a hunter you will probably breed something which will pay you a good deal better, a high-class harness horse; and if you put your filly produce back to the thoroughbred again you are sure to breed a better hunter.

11702. Would such a horse such as "[illegible]" be a better cross to put in Ireland?—My horse has four crosses of blood, and I hope he is getting first-class hunters in places with strength, but if you have mares that are already too light you want something stronger.

11703. What sire is "[illegible]"?—He is a little full on his legs, I think. I think it would be better if he were an inch lower.

11704. What sire of horse?—The best you ever put your hand on, big bone and marvellous quality; there is a little more, and his knees are so big.

11705. Still you think that he would not make with a small mare?—I would rather risk a Hackney stallion to breed a marketable animal, because the "[illegible]" has too many crosses of blood already.

11706. If you had a horse of the same breeding as "[illegible]," with plenty of bone and muscle, and altogether a hunter-shaped animal, would you use that horse in preference to a Hackney?—I would use him in preference to any horse living, because I think you ought to breed hunters from hunters.

11707. Mr. [illegible].—Do you keep your stallions at your own place?—They travel.

11708. But they travel from your own place?—The headquarters are at home, but they are sent out of home. During the season I have them all over the country.

11709. You have [illegible]?—I have [illegible] and [illegible], too.

11710. Lord ARDILAUN.—To what sort of mares do you put your thoroughbred sire?—Of course there are a certain number of people who will have a thoroughbred, it does not matter whether he is a really good one or not.

11711. You say people came to you and ask you to put them to which you think best?—That all depends on the mare; if a man sends a [illegible] mare to my place and leaves the selection of the stallion to myself, then I select a horse that I think is likely to give the mare [illegible].

11712. What [illegible] would you put in [illegible] which sire you would use the Hackney, or which you would put the half-bred, and to which you would put the thoroughbred?—If a first-class hunter mare was sent to me I should certainly put her to a hunter stallion; but if a mare on the light side was sent to me I would put her to a horse with bone and substance, and you may get a Hackney with good shoulders and as much bone and substance as you want.

11713. In breeding from a thoroughbred you are bound to get some weeds—do you think if that filly was put again to a Hackney the produce would be saleable?—I have had weedy mares sent to me, and the owner says:—"Tell Mr. Tasker to put this mare to anything he likes;" then I sent her to a big Hackney stallion, and she often breeds a first-class foal.

11714. They will breed a saleable animal?—Yes; it is the weeds eat the profit up.

11715. There are big coarse heavy mares—you would not put a half-bred stallion to those?—Oh, no. I have had thoroughbred stallions that left very good stock indeed from the coarser mares in the country, such a horse as "King Harold" and "[illegible]," but I never bought a thoroughbred stallion yet unless I knew he was a good getter before I bought him.

11716. A mare that was known to breed well to a thoroughbred, you would not change her?—No; if she succeeded in breeding well to one thoroughbred horse, I would keep her at it. I don't believe in changing if you once hit the right nail on the head.

11717. Mr. Green.—You said you were in favour of registration of half-breds?—Yes; I think registration is a very useful thing if you are only registering individual merit, which [illegible].

11718. What do you mean by merit?—I mean, of course, if you had a really first-class hunting mare that you had owned for years, and knew she was sound, although you knew nothing of her breeding, you would have to adopt either show-yard success or [illegible] or something of that sort.

11719. Then you don't mean by merit performance in the hunting field?—Oh, yes, I said performance. I think you could easily get at the stallion part of it by giving prizes for hunter stallions, or by giving prizes for, say, the best two-year-old hunter colt; you should have those from sound parents.

11720. Mr. Wrench.—What class of farmers use your Hackney stallions now?—As a rule they are the smaller farmers. You will get a large number of mares from the North and West of Ireland into Newcastle and the North of England; there are a lot of these mares with long tails, and the farmers buy up little mares, young mares, and when after they have been worked in a town [illegible] they come back to the farmers—and those are the mares that are put to Hackney stallions.

11721. You know that there are a large number of mares that come from Ireland put to Hackney stallions?—Yes.

11722. What do they produce?—Nearly all of them produce an animal having their [illegible].

11723. Do they produce a saleable animal, an animal that pays?—Yes.

11724. When you talk of a small farmer in your district, what is his rent?—Tyneside, and practically the whole of Northumberland, is a country where there are various classes; you have the big farmers in the valleys, and when you get into the hills away from the seaboard, you get amongst the smaller farmers, who are farming one hundred acres, and perhaps more hill land with it.

11725. What would be their rent?—They often have a small piece [illegible] ground in connection with it; they get often a little three-bred mare to work their grass and do any carting they may have to do, and often put her to a Hackney stallion.

11726. And those are the men that chiefly use your Hackney stallion?—No, not necessarily; some of them are large farmers [illegible].

11727. Are many high-class harness horses bred from them?—Yes.

11728. If you wish to breed for the London market high-class harness horses, what stallion would you use?—I would rather use a large-sized Hackney or a Yorkshire coach-horse.

11729. Would you use a thoroughbred?—No.

11730. Do you keep any Yorkshire coach-horses yourself?—I have used them.

11731. Why would you not use a thoroughbred?—Because he has not got the action.

11732. Do you think it is necessary to have the action?—Undoubtedly.

11733. I suppose the farmers you talk about are hardly as small as the farmers in Ireland?—No; a lot of the small farmers from the West of Ireland come to us and work all the summer to get money to pay the rent with.

11734. Do you know that seventy-five per cent. of the farmers of Ireland are under £10 valuation?—No, I did not know that; that is news to me.

11735. Putting hunter breeding aside altogether from such men as that, what sire do you think would be most useful to them?—Undoubtedly a Hackney.

11736. Why?—My idea of the small mares kept by these men are, that they are mares probably from fourteen to fifteen hands, not extra good-looking or extra good movers; if you use a Hackney stallion you get the Hackney type and the Hackney action, and if you have that you have a saleable animal.

11737. Then you think for [illegible] they would make a good deal more breeding from a Hackney to the other horse you describe?—I have seen remarkably good results from using a Hackney stallion, for this very good reason, you have got more bone and length, and you have a short leg with fine flat legs, which is an advantage, and you have almost as much width.

11738. How big are Hackney stallions as a rule?—I bought a horse the other day that won first prize at Lancaster Royal Show, 15.1 hands at three years old, a whole coloured black bay.

11739. Would you be inclined to put him to fourteen hands mares?—When you come down to fourteen hands, I should certainly say a Hackney, but for a fifteen hands mare I would prefer a thoroughbred. There is this disadvantage in using a Hackney, you sometimes get a good deal too much white, and if you use a coach-horse, you often get an animal that is whole-coloured, which is a decided advantage for the London trade.

11740. You think the cross of 14.1 hands and 15 hands is not too great?—Certainly not.

11741. I think you said that you had experience of hunters yourself got by Hackney stallions?—Yes.

11742. Did you find those deficient in staying power?—Certainly not.

11743. Do you think there is anything in the allegation that Hackneys are soft?—I think they are the hardiest animals I have.

11744. And you have considerable experience, are they hardy in constitution?—Very, and very sound.

11745. Have you seen the [illegible] got by Hackneys living out in those hills you said?—Oh, yes.

11746. How do they stand the climate there?—They do very well; and we have a much more severe climate in the North-east coast of England than you have in Ireland.

11747. And they remain out all the winter?—Oh yes.

11748. Then take those small farmers—what do you think is the most remunerative thing for them to go in for, for the harness market or the hunting market?—Certainly to cater for the harness market from the [illegible] mares.

11749. I am not referring to the good mare of [illegible] course. I am assuming that my idea of the average mare in your country [illegible] is correct, that is, about [illegible] an animal from 14 to 15 hands without much breeding, without much action.

11750. Assuming such an animal, do you think they would get the best results from a Hackney stallion as a horse like "Clydesdale"?—Certainly, from a Hackney stallion. I think you would get a much better-paying animal for this reason—that you can sell a Clydesdale [illegible] hairy with the long tail on for a lot of money. London men will buy those, and give £100 for a harness horse, without taking tights. But if you breed a hunter you must make him before you can sell him to any advantage.

11751. Do these London dealers care how the animal is bred?—Not a copper, if they can get them.

11752. They would not object if they were by a Hackney?—No. I know a gentleman who is willing to give £2,000 for fifty high-class harness horses if he can get them.

11753. Is it easy to find harness horses of the type of "Cheltenham"?—I have not seen any but [illegible].

11754. You know "New Century"?—He is by the same stallion, and Mr. Wilson tells me he is a very good horse.

11755. Mr. FITZGERALD.—Is there not a horse of the same kind called "Magnum"?—There was a thoroughbred horse called "Magnum." At the Dublin Show there was an animal got second prize in the harness class by "Excelsior." I have every reason to believe that was got by the Limerick Stud Hackney. You were asking Mr. Bainbridge about a crossing of the Hackney. Now, "Excelsior" was got by "Reality," and "Reality" was out of a mare by a thoroughbred horse. That "Excelsior" himself was bred from a thoroughbred mare, so he is very nearly thoroughbred, but a first-class animal.

11756. Mr. WATSON.—Is there much thoroughbred blood in the best breeding of the best strain of Hackneys?—I know of some Hackney stallions which have thoroughbred blood in them already.

11757. You hunt a great deal yourself?—As much as ever I can.

11758. Which blood would you dislike most in the hunter—Clydesdale blood, Shire blood, or Hackney blood?—I should certainly take Hackney. I have seen some stunning good hunters got by Clydesdales.

11759. When you say you would take Hackney, would you dislike that the least or most?—The least.

11760. Would you prefer Hackney blood in the hunter to Clydesdale or Shire?—Undoubtedly.

11761. Is it necessary sometimes in order to get weight in hunters to bring in cart blood?—I know four or five of the best [illegible] hunters I have seen got by such stallions out of thoroughbred mares.

11762. Have you tried breeding hunters with thoroughbred horses?—Oh, yes. I have kept thoroughbred stallions for over twenty years, twenty-three or twenty-four.

11763. Used you to keep more than you keep now?—I have never kept more than one or two.

11764. What results had your breeding from thoroughbred stallions?—There have been some very good animals indeed from thoroughbred mares.

11765. Were those mares with any cart blood in them?—Oh, yes.

11766. But I mean from mares without any cart blood in them, have you ever bred any with thoroughbred horses from those mares?—Yes, I have bred some very good hunters. According to Mr. John Henry Stokes' opinion, he buys in the North of England, he says he gets no horses like them—Melton, or Market Harborough.

11767. How are these bred?—Most of them by thoroughbred stallions off the average mares of the country.

11768. And the average mares of the country have cart blood in them?—Undoubtedly.

11769. Have you any other instances of the results of Hackney crosses from other people?—I have a note of seven Hackney stallions that I have traced, and all of these have got some good hunters amongst good horses, and I just kept him standing at home. I don't know of a good hunter by him, but all the rest have got hunters, all the six.

11770. And with what class of mares did they get them?—Well, "Caspian" got a very good horse out of a [illegible] mare, a bloody hunter mare, he is seventeen years old and still serviceable. "Norway Charley" got that hunting [illegible] hunter I told you about, he has been hunted ten years and still serviceable. "Masterpiece," a big-sized Norfolk horse, a neighbour of mine got a rather weedy [illegible] mare to him, and the first I bought at four years old and sold it to Mr. Bowlby to Kenilworth, it was a striking good hunter. "Wroxham [illegible]," I have only had him four seasons, I saw a three-year-old grey horse by him the other day, out of a little plain pony-bred mare, and he is going very well. His mother was only 14.2 hands, he is not a big one. "Perfection IV.," I only travelled that horse a season, I had him three seasons, but I saw a black brown gelding by him shown at our show last year, a very good horse, and I asked one of the judges how he liked it, and he said "very well, he gallops very fast; he is got by your old horse, is he not?" "What mare do you think?" "A Hackney?" "No," I said, "he is got by a Yorkshire coach-horse, 'Charmer,' that is the way he is bred."

11771. Lord ARDILAUN.—What was the mare by the Yorkshire coach-horse out of?—Out of a mare by a thoroughbred horse.

11772. Mr. WATSON.—You say you have been to the Irish shows and bought Irish horses on several occasions?—Yes.

11773. Would you suggest for the improvement of hunters in Ireland that such horses as "Cheltenham" should be registered?—I leave yourself about registration, but I should certainly say that more of them you use the better.

11774. Better than a thoroughbred horse?—Yes, decidedly.

11775. CHAIRMAN.—When you say better than a thoroughbred horse, do you mean better than any thoroughbred horse, a thoroughbred equal in bone and substance to your horse?—The bulk of thoroughbred horses are not of the hunter type, and if you are breeding from animals of a dissimilar type from the animal you want to breed, the chances are you don't succeed, but if you breed from hunter stallions which are of the type you want to breed the chance is you will succeed.

11776. That is to say if you could find a thoroughbred of the same type would you still prefer the half-bred to the thoroughbred?—I should certainly do so for this reason, that unless I know the pure thoroughbred. There was not as it is a logic in the [illegible], because we know many thoroughbred mares with skinny legs on them and likely to breed; they may breed a big horse, but I should say that that horse would be unreliable, because he had not a good [illegible].

11777. Then to breed a hunter out of any sort of mare you prefer a half-bred to a thoroughbred?—I don't say so; for legitimate hunter breeding I should breed from a hunter stallion and hunter mare, because by that time and then you have [illegible] mares at the state of perfection you wish to attain, but in going back to the thoroughbred you are bringing in a class of animal that perhaps you don't want.

11778. There is some sense in what I say, that for only [illegible] of [illegible] for breeding hunters you would prefer a half-bred or hunter sire to a thoroughbred?—I don't mean that; for a horse of understood excess I should pick a nice type of stout-boned thoroughbred horse.

11779. I take it you are not personally acquainted with the congested districts in Ireland?—Well, I have never been in them, but we have had the same. I can remember men coming from there to work, and very intelligent men, too, and I got to know pretty well the sort of horse they breed, and I may say that these men told me that their Hackney stallions are doing a great deal of good, but personally I have not seen the result.

11780. You have only a general idea of their condition and the holdings they have. You were asked

Mr. W. E. Trotter.

about their rental, you cannot speak authoritatively? —I have talked to these men about the rents they pay, but I have not a good memory for figures. I know they are small farmers, and nearly all keep a little mare. I have seen the animals that come from the district. I can form a general idea of the stallions that should be put to them.

11781. You say that judging from the class of mare they have and the circumstances of these farmers you think that with a Hackney sire they can produce a more saleable animal?—A much more saleable animal.

11782. You mentioned a first-class harness horse that would fetch £100. Do you think these small farmers would, under any circumstances with the mares they have, with any kind of sire, be likely to produce a harness horse worth £100?—Well, I don't see why they should not. I know there was a Frenchman paid £300 for a 14.3 hands mare in the Hall yesterday. She is got by a Hackney stallion out of a mare of unknown breeding. If you get them good enough looking and fine goers you will always get customers.

11783. We have had evidence before us from some people interested in that business that for certain purposes the highest class carriage horses they can get are got by thoroughbred sires?—I have that to learn yet.

11784. As far as you know you would prefer to use the Hackney?—I would prefer to use the Hackney or Yorkshire coach horse, because you have the animal there pretty nearly what you want.

11785. Mr. Fitzwilliam.—With regard to breeding, from all you have said I have gathered that you prefer, or rather you put greater stress on the appearance of the animal than you do on the blood of the animal?—The appearance and the performance of the animal.

11786. As a stallion?—Well, I said I would prefer to use a hunter stallion from a really first-class hunting mare, assuming he was a first class horse himself. It is not a mere theoretical opinion. It is based upon my own experience of hunter stallions.

11787. But still your preference is for appearance? —If you leave individual merit out, you leave the principal factor out.

11788. Lord Ravensworth.—Are your Hackney stallions of the hunter type?—All my Hackney stallions have good shoulders and good loins.

11789. Then do you go in for very high action?—Get as much action as ever you can, because they are sure to breed plenty with too little.

11790. Do you like the pounding?—I like them to go up and go on.

11791. Besides breeding, do you buy and sell many horses?—A few.

11792. Do you know Ireland well yourself?—Well, I cannot say I know Ireland well myself, but I have been at the Dublin Show many times, and got a fair idea of the animals produced there, and also from seeing a lot of horses that come from Ireland.

11793. How do you know that the small farmers in Ireland have only small mares?—Judging from the animals they sell to us.

11794. That is, from the produce of their animals you think the mares must be small?—I have asked Mr. Wrench if my idea of the average mare in the West of Ireland was correct, a plainish mare of 14 to 15 hands, and not a good mover.

11795. That is the West of Ireland. But all over Ireland do you mean to say the generality of small farmers have small mares?—I understand that most of the small farmers keep a mare, and they are not very big.

11796. How do you form that idea. Why?—From a variety of sources.

11797. By hearsay?—I have seen a lot of them myself, and spoken with them—small farmers.

11798. From hearsay? I don't know whether it is correct to say from hearsay, because it is not strictly speaking from hearsay. I see two or three hundred horses that come from Ireland every year, and can form my own idea.

11799. Do you see many brood mares?—Well, you see these undersized mares that are subsequently put to breeding.

11800. In England?—Yes, plenty of them. I have seen men bring forty at a time of these small Irish mares.

11801. Do you believe a prize in a showyard is a proof of a good hunter?—Certainly not.

11802. Lord Arthur.—With reference to this half-bred cross that Mr. Fitzwilliam asked you about, you say although you like personal appearance you would be still better pleased if you had personal appearance and breeding?—Oh, yes, I am not at all an advocate for underbred animals, but the hunter stallions I use have both been first-class performers. I hunted one and the other had won eleven steeplechases, so there was a propensity to jump undoubtedly.

11803. You would prefer that animal to an animal that was only good looking and of which you did not know his breeding?—Undoubtedly, because I am certain of this that the propensity to jump is an hereditary accomplishment.

11804. When you say you prefer these half-bred stallions to the thoroughbred you mean from a commercial point of view?—That is the thing from a profitable point of view.

11805. You would breed a better average of profitable horses?—Undoubtedly.

Mr. Alexander Morton, J.P.

Mr. Alexander Morton, J.P., Darvel, Ayr, examined.

11806. Lord Ravensworth.—You live at Darvel, Ayrshire?—Yes, my lord. This morning I put my evidence on paper and if you will take it I will—it puts my views better than I could give them orally. I am a lace and carpet manufacturer, and employ about one thousand hands. Since my earliest days I have been a lover of the horse. When a boy of eleven I knew every horse in the parish by name and look. For twenty years afterwards I confined myself strictly to my business, but after getting a little out of the wood and requiring some relaxation, my old love for the horse sprang up anew. I bought a few half-bred mares or mares bred on the hunter lines by a thoroughbred horse. Following this I bought a thoroughbred stallion from Mr. Tattersall, named "Clansman," which I for several years used. The production of these mares by this horse I showed over the West of Scotland with moderate success. As far as I can remember I sold them at from forty to sixty pounds at four years of age. One reached seventy pounds, but unfortunately when put to work she went wrong in her wind, and I had to give twenty pounds back. About this time there was exhibited at the Highland and Agricultural Show in Glasgow a blue roan mare called "Lady Pairlington," by "Lord Derby II.," one of his very first gets. I was so captivated with the quality, action, and style of this mare, that I resolved to trace her to the bottom, and before a week's end I was found at Waxholm, Withernsea, Yorks, inspecting "Lord Derby II." and Collingson's old grey blood mare. I bought two out of her, and purchased in all nine young ones—colts and fillies—by "Lord Derby II." These laid the foundation of the Hackney in Scotland, which has now grown to over 1,000 for breeding purposes, my own stud being considerably over 100. My yearly increase in foals now runs from forty to fifty. These animals I exhibited over Scotland against those bred in the country by thoroughbred horses, under the name of "Blood or Bold." This we found very unsatisfactory, as judges that want the hunting cob, those by the thoroughbred, and those who want [illegible] horses [illegible] [illegible] for stepping hacks, but in a year or two [illegible] [illegible] me to [illegible] Hackneys, and on the forming of the Hackney Committee in Scotland (which I am chairman), we [illegible] the [illegible], namely, the [illegible] and the Hackney, which have worked very [illegible] there, [illegible] being from twenty to thirty [illegible] of yearlings, two year and three year old. Now, the leading gentlemen confine themselves to [illegible] by the thoroughbred, and [illegible] interested in horses and [illegible] [illegible] [illegible] to the Hackney. During [illegible] years I [illegible] [illegible] the [illegible] of the Hackney, and found that his blood was as pure as that of the thoroughbred, and that both, to the extent of about three-fourths (of their blood) sprang from the imported Arabian and Barb horses. I am the author of two or three papers bearing on this point, which I beg to hand in for your consideration. I also had the pleasure of drawing up a [illegible] from the year 1908, showing the beginning of the breed and its growth to the present day, which I also hand in for your perusal. I may say that this paper and [illegible] have been [illegible] [illegible], and that [illegible] [illegible] have [illegible] been [illegible] and circulated all over the English speaking [illegible] [illegible] for the introduction of the Hackney into Scotland. It may, however, be more to the present point of consideration to say something about how these Hackneys have done in Scotland and to inquire whether they have paid. I am not prepared to say that I have made money by them, indeed I do not know of any hobby that does pay, but I feel convinced, if I had to make a business of Hackney breeding and which every [illegible], as business men do, the balance would be on the right side of the ledger. There is a [illegible] market for this animal, and it can be bred with greater safety to type and sell better than any horse in the country. I may be allowed in this connection to say that I have sold within these last five years over 200 Hackneys and ponies [illegible] all bred by myself. The ponies averaged over fifty guineas each, and the Hackneys over one hundred guineas each [illegible]. I have sold a number of [illegible] out of hunting mares by Hackney stallions at 120 to 150 guineas each, and in several cases I have obtained from 400 to 500 guineas for [illegible] [illegible] bred in this way and out of light [illegible] and [illegible] by a pure Hackney stallion. During these last ten or twelve years I have kept for my own and the district's use one Hackney pony and three or four large pure-bred Hackney stallions. I charge from two to five guineas each mare, and I am very pleased indeed to see the great improvement of the horses here all over Scotland. Every year I get mares sent to my stud from distances of two to three hundred miles, and I can see that in a few years we will supply the growing demand for our own light [illegible] harness work, and may even be able to sell some to our neighbours, while up till this time nearly all have been imported. I might here be excused for referring to [illegible] breeding in Ireland. I have [illegible] the Dublin Horse Show, and was [illegible] pleased with the hunters I saw there. I [illegible] and [illegible] they were the cleverest and finest animals I had ever seen. I was told of the [illegible] [illegible], and I wish them good luck. If the introduction of the Hackney into Ireland were in any way to interfere with these beautiful hunters I would be at one with those opposed to the Hackney being introduced into the country, as I do not believe the Hackney blood mixed with the hunters would improve their hunting qualities. In Great Britain we have no difficulty in keeping our breeds of horses and cattle pure and distinct, especially since the establishment of stud books, and I cannot see why the same should not be done [illegible] in Ireland. In visiting a number of the breeding establishments in the West of Ireland I found a great many very light blood mares being kept for breeding and still being used with thoroughbred horses. Most of their stock was unsuitable for the hunting field, and had to be sold for what they could bring say from £15 to £25, to go into a harness or [illegible] car. Now I feel sure if these mares were put to a powerful, [illegible], high-stepping Hackney they would produce the finest carriage horses in the world, and they would find a ready market alongside the best and highest class London dealers at remunerative prices on account of their quality and action. In Ireland drawing stock [illegible] use of the Hackney stallion. [illegible] [illegible] [illegible] of [illegible] or no use for breeding purposes, and it [illegible] [illegible] the production of the horse which would find the best and readiest market in this or any other country. I think I am safe in saying that for every hunter sold there are at least twenty harness and carriage horses, and why should the best breeding country in the world be closed against this large and valuable business, for surely Ireland can do with some of it, and [illegible] good money, large [illegible] [illegible] for animals not half so valuable for the purpose.

11807. I take it from that document that you have been chiefly promoting Hackneys?—Yes, all recent years I have been promoting Hackneys, but in the earlier part I had and exhibited ponies as well and I [illegible] [illegible] [illegible] [illegible] with my Hackney stallions. I have been [illegible] [illegible] [illegible] few years I have dealt greatly with Hackneys. A great many of my friends in the district have now half-bred animals out of my stallions.

11808. What class of half-bred [illegible] is a rule?—They are mostly mares that [illegible] over from England that were unfit for hunters, they might be carriage [illegible] in breeding or [illegible] [illegible] [illegible] a high-class [illegible] and were bought for £30 or £50, and sold in our district for harness work.

11809. What is the produce like?—My neighbour within half a mile of my house bred two or three out of one of these mares by a thoroughbred horse and never could make much out of them, because they came out rather light, but he then used them for five years to my stepping stallions, and I was pleased to say the first produce he had he sold for eighty guineas.

11810. Lord [illegible].—What age?—Four years of age. I could [illegible] several times. I have bought myself a good many of these animals [illegible], given £30 and more for them when just coming four, to handle and break and bring them on for my own driving, and those that I refer to [illegible] in having sold at from £150 up to £400 were animals that I really bought, young animals, but know the class of mares they were out of.

11811. Lord [illegible].—Are there any hounds near you?—The [illegible] hounds hunting within three or four miles of my place, it is rather wet.

11812. How far are you from Glasgow?—Twenty miles south. I live in [illegible] parish; the [illegible] hounds come up as far as [illegible].

11813. Are the [illegible] hounds near you?—They are further south; I never see them.

11814. You referred to [illegible] breeding stock in the West of Ireland, what breeding studs do you refer to?—I stayed a week in that district. I went there by Carlow, Limerick, by Killarney, and Cork. I had one or two of my family with me, they were enjoying themselves at the Lakes, but I was going through the country seeing the mares. I could not give you the names of the farmers, but I just went from Cork to [illegible], one day one place, and the day another, and saw a lot of mares, they were beautiful mares in good [illegible], but rather light.

11815. You have used the word "islands," I think [illegible] you mean large breeding studs?—It was more [illegible] [illegible] [illegible], there might be two or three in each of those places I visited.

March 4, 1896. Mr. Alexander Morton, jr.

11846. Did you mention Cork?—Yes; I was not as far down as Cork. I was down in the district between Limerick and Cork; it is a matter of ten or twelve years since I was down there, it was chiefly selling Lomaknaxt with the Hackneys. I went to Kildare, it is a interesting quiet village with an old round tower where a fine we were told had been burning for 500 or 600 years. Of course it was not burning when I was there.

11847. Did you go to any farmers in the neighbourhood of Kildare?—I went to see at home different farmers, and I saw two lovely mares, thorough-bred; beautiful quality, deep bodies, fine mares, but the young stock were too light for producing hunters.

11848. You did not go to any of the raising establishments at the Curragh?—No. I know little about raising racing stock. I had been induced previous to that with those Irish hunters being brought over year after year and bothering me when I was breeding from my own "Cleveland" horse, and I went over to see if I could see the dams, and perhaps buy one or two. They seemed to be too light, and then I could not find out the right strain. I have visited the Dublin Horse Show three several times.

11849. With regard to your own breeding, you say you breed a good many every year?—Yes.

11850. Can of that number I suppose all of them are not prize?—No; we never have that.

11851. What do you do with those that are misfits?—We sell them the best we can. We don't continue to breed from them. We sell them for from £40 to £60. What I gave there was my average, putting bad and good together. I have sold them as low as £30, and as high as 2,000 guineas, Hackneys, but I put the good and bad together of five years production.

11852. Where do the misfits go to?—They are used for farmers' purposes, and ordinary jobbing trades that do not go to such a high class. For instance, Glasgow, in Ayr, buys one or two occasionally, and I sold to Griffin, and he would sell them for jobbing purposes.

11853. Are they not good for agricultural purposes?—Yes; in light land. I use myself two or three mares constantly during the winter for light work, making out manure and ploughing. I keep one big strong mare for very heavy work. But all the ordinary work is done by Hackney mares. "Old Dinah" and "Lady Dunnegian" are ploughing within a day of foaling.

11854. Are the Hackneys you use for driving purposes or riding horses?—I drive myself Hackneys.

11855. There are Hackneys and Hackneys; some people call them roadsters?—It is a loose term. The Hackneys which I have used for some years are pure Hackneys. I drove one last year for a fortnight all over the South of Scotland.

11856. What strain of Hackney?—Pure Yorkshire Hackneys. I have scarcely a drop of Norfolk blood in my stud. I had one or two at first. I was carried away by their action, and after I got them home I could not take them, having no staying power or stamina.

11857. You think the Yorkshire Hackney is superior to the Norfolk?—Yes, I don't say why it should be so. I find in the early part of the seventeenth century there were a great many Arabian horses spread over Yorkshire. I think that has had the foundation of the superior class of Hackneys they have in Yorkshire. We commence the stud book with "Blaze." Well, "Blaze" was used on mares that were, perhaps half Arabian before that, from the large infusion of the Arabian blood introduced fifty or sixty years previous to "Blaze's" time. You will find that there were forty Arabian stallions introduced into Yorkshire in Queen Anne's reign.

11858. To come down nearer to our times what is the difference in the quality and conformation of the Yorkshire Hackney from the Norfolk Hackney?—I find that the Norfolk Hackney is very much more narrow about his shoulder and his head, he is not a riding horse, and I don't think he is even a proper driving horse, that is, in the strain of them, and I have driven one or two and thought shame of the name of Hackney belonging to them. They are not true, the infusion of foreign blood having got in among the Hackneys in Norfolk and done a great deal of injury to the name of Hackney. I feel sure myself that the true Hackney is just as pure and genuine after a careful examination of the early pedigrees of the horse as the thoroughbred is himself. He is from the same foundation and the same strain, and we have thus two lines from the same original one producing the fast racer, and the other ending in a riding and driving horse.

11859. Is there not now a Hackney Stud Book?—It has been compiled for the last dozen years, going back to about the year 1750 for our foundation. We had to struggle with several things, and no doubt one or two have got in which, had we known what they were, would not have been allowed in.

11860. Is that Stud Book closed?—No, every year they are still going on, the membership is higher than ever, and the entries are still increasing. It is closed for new animals and has been for a number of years.

11861. The English Hackney Stud Book?—Yes, as far as Hackneys are concerned it has been closed for five or six years, but they still allow Hackney ponies.

11862. Still it is not closed if they admit Hackney ponies?—They still admit what may be called ponies under a certain size inspected by competent judges, suitable to be bred with Hackney sires.

11863. Supposing that mare was put to a Hackney sire and bred a larger animal than the height at the present moment for entry, can that animal get into the Stud Book?—I believe that animal would be allowed into the Stud Book as having descended from the pony.

11864. Then it would come from the pony class and go into the actual Stud Book?—Being admitted as the production of a certain pony they had inspected.

11865. It would not require inspection to go in?—No.

11866. Therefore the Stud Book is not closed?—It is not closed in that side way. For several years after it was established we had what was called inspected mares. We had a council over England and Scotland, and I believe Ireland, for inspecting mares that were suitable for breeding Hackneys. For some four or five years, that has been stopped, so that it is closed as far as ordinary mares are concerned. But there is a motion tabled by Sir Gilbert Greenall now to stop even the inspection of pony stallions.

11867. What has been your experience of the Hackney as regards staying power?—I was going to say that I drove last year one for a fortnight, on a driving tour I had round the south and west of Scotland, Peebles, Dumfries, Kirkcudbright, and Wigtown, and when I got home I had done an average twenty-eight miles per day while I was out. It was a cob by "Lord Derby" out of a little Danmark mare, a little mare 14.2 to 14.3. He went as cocky and sharp the whole time that it was a perfect pleasure to sit behind him.

11868. I suppose you did not take the worst one?—No, it is the one I like to drive. I had just as much pleasure to sit behind him when he was walking as when he was going fast.

11869. As a general rule have you found the worst thing?—Yes, of the Hackneys of Yorkshire, as compared with Norfolk Hackneys, a great proportion of which have been bred by "Confidence," and those who have bred from him have cursed the name of that horse. It would have been worth thousands of pounds to the Hackney world if that horse had been killed the day he was born. I [illegible]

[illegible]
Mr. Alexander Morton.

driven the Yorkshires, on the other hand, one by "Lord Derby" out of an old mare that had a strain of thoroughbred in her by her dam. I have driven her time after time to Lanark and back, which is thirty-two miles, making over sixty miles in a single trip. I have also driven that mare to Motherwell and back in a day, and to Glasgow and back. Her mother was by a thoroughbred horse and her sire was a pure Hackney, her name is "Nancy."

11840. You think a cross of thoroughbred is rather a good thing?—I don't think it is an objection for staying powers. I don't prefer it for continuing the breed, because I am sure to get action if I stick true to the Hackney; but we get as good results from a stallion out of a mare that is by a thoroughbred to sell the produce, not to lay the foundation of a stock.

11841. Lord Arrow.—You mean a Hackney put on a mare by a thoroughbred?—Yes.

11842. Lord Barrymore.—Do you think it is a good thing to go on breeding from the produce of that?—It does very well, but you would not have the certainty of getting everyone to come like pure as I have got of my own Hackney mares.

11843. That is pure-bred, but the cross breeding?—If you have a stud of good mares and don't want to reproduce them again but to sell the produce, they will pay very well.

11844. But the produce of them?—Only for mares, and use always the pure-bred Hackney stallion; not to use the stallion that is half-bred, but a pure-bred, and rather inbred. I always like to have him a little inbred, to stamp himself, and give character and give action.

11845. Have you seen the produce of these half-bred mares?—I have just said that I have sold them for £400 the pair.

11846. That is the produce of the half-bred mares?—Of the mares by a thoroughbred horse out of either a Hackney mare or a carriage mare.

11847. And crossed again by a Hackney?—And crossed again by a Hackney. This mare that I drove from Lanark and back, and used as a mare for many years, is bred in that way; her grand-dam was by "Old Wildfire," her mother was by a thoroughbred horse, and she herself was by "Lord Derby," she has been the best mare I ever owned for stud value.

11848. Have you put her to the stud?—I have bred two out of her.

11849. What is her produce?—One of them is a gelding by "Goldfinder." He has taken to his grand-dam, and has a little more of the thoroughbred in him, and does not bend his knees.

11850. Lord Arrow.—About the stud book, although things are passed in still as inspected, still any man who looks back in the stud book can trace that they do come from the inspected mares?—Oh, yes; they are always mentioned.

11851. So that it is entirely optional with you if you wish to buy the produce of an inspected mare?—Oh, yes; there is a bracket put on to show that the horse has a stain.

11852. That would not throw a permanent stain on the Hackney?—I find in reading Joe Osborne on "Eclipse," that there are thirteen parts out of thirty-two that they cannot account for even in his breeding.

11853. But still you would not be buying that stain with your eyes shut?—No, they would see there were so many crosses that they could not tell.

11854. You have had experience of crossing Hackneys and ponies?—Yes, I have done a good deal of that, perhaps more than any man in Scotland or England. I bred some from our own ponies, the Scotch ponies; these were not so good. I went to Wales, and picked up a good many Welsh ponies. I bought thirty-six in one lot, four or five years ago, and I put my Hackney stallion "Goldfinder" on these ponies, and I have some of the loveliest ponies coming on, in fact I sold one the other day, a gelding not broken, for £60, in the rough I may say. I will have fifty coming up. Of course I am picking the Welsh mares. I think I have sixteen of these still. The ponies are 13.2 hands from the Hackney stallion and these little mares, and I would them to form the foundation of the pony breeding.

11855. Do you find these ponies hardy?—I have not had a great deal of experience.

11856. Not for work but for keep?—Oh, yes, I have them on the hill, and we only give them hay and a little linseed mixed with hay chopped up.

11857. What sort of pasture; ordinary hill pasture?—It is pasture that has really been wrought with, perhaps ploughed; a little heathery, but not bad; pretty dry. Then I have a big shed outside where they can run in at night, if it is very rough.

11858. We know about "Confidence," but there are other good strains in the Norfolk Hackney?—Yes, I don't connect all Norfolk Hackneys. There is a family belonging to Fenwick, that amongst to "Old Kitty" and "Norfolk Gentleman," a most useful strain I believe to use for Irish mares. I say, after carefully thinking it over, that if I was in Ireland that is the strain I would use. They are true-bred for three or four generations, and when they go back to anything else it is to the thoroughbred. They are great goers, with powerful limbs and deep shoulders, and would make beautiful carriage horses with the light Irish mares. I have several in my stud. I am trying to raise the standard of height of my Hackneys, and I am pleased to say with the using of Fenwick's strain, I have now eight or ten Hackneys from 15.2 to 16 hands.

11859. That is "Rufus'" strain?—Yes, but the old "Norfolk Gentleman" is better, he was "Rufus'" grandfather.

11860. "Confidence" was of a capital Norfolk strain?—I am pleased to say that Fenwick's father would not be mixed with his nation, and they only used that strain twice.

11861. They used "Reality"?—Yes, but I believe his stock is now clear of the "Confidence" blood.

11862. Mr. Wrench.—You have been a great deal about Yorkshire?—Yes, many and many a time.

11863. When you were there you inquired a good deal about the way in which Hackneys were bred from the old farmers there?—Yes, of course, from the old men. It was really a passion with me. I got so fond of them that anybody that could bishop to me about Hackneys I was there. My business brought me up to Yorkshire a good deal. I went to Leeds and Bradford in the way of business, and I made it convenient to go down and see the farmers.

11864. Then although the Stud Book was only formed comparatively recently, have you any reason to believe that the pedigrees given in it are in a rule not correct?—I believe myself that there are mistakes, as there are errors in the old original thoroughbred stud book, but mainly I believe it is correct, and my greatest proof is this, that I have bred now for twelve or fifteen years from these Yorkshire strains, and they come year after year almost exactly alike. I could tell them just by seeing them what they were. Now, if they were cross-bred and mongrel-bred and bad blood they would produce all sorts of things. I was in America last back-end, spent a month there, and I went to see some of the studs. I went up to Chenoweth and saw the stud of him. I saw in one field about seventeen or eighteen colts by "Cadet" out of these pure native mares, and he had such power by the purity of his own blood that they were like a handful of peas. I never saw a finer lot much alike. They were all chestnuts, and the mares were different colours, browns and bays. The colts all took to himself in colour and type.

11865. And were there not a good many families in Yorkshire specially celebrated for their breeds of horses?—Yes, old Mitchells and Covingtons and Smith; it was quite a pleasure to stay and listen to them talking of their favourite Hackneys, and how they were kept sixty years back sixty or seventy years.

[illegible]

Mr. Alexander [illegible]

11866. Were those animals that they had from there noted for doing long distances and hard work in those days?—They spoke of going to market and doing great journeys. I did not pay so much attention, but they used to sing how they walked with their head and tail up, and the old men would get up and show you by his walk their gait and style.

11867. Were you able to find out that there was any cold blood in Yorkshire Hackneys?—I have never seen it or heard of it. I have had a great deal to do with what we call the leading blood, "Lord Derby II." I have sold 100 horses by him, I have sent them to America and Australia, and I have had nothing but the best reports. I have had a great many of the "Denmark's" and of "Fireaway's," these are the principal strains that have built the foundations of Hackneys in Yorkshire. I would like to say regarding Burdett's horses in Norfolk, and comparing them with the Hackneys, that while they are big, strong, useful horses for hackney purposes, they are not the horses for the show ring like the other horses. I am speaking of commercial value as regards breeding horses to put into the market to sell.

11868. Lord Ardilaun.—You mean non-pedigreed Hackneys to sell as carriage horses?—But the Hackneys we are judging in the show ring were nine out of ten come from these three strains, "Lord Derby," "Denmark," and "Fireaway."

11869. Mr. Watson.—Do you know whether there is a large trade between Scotland and Ireland?—There are still a good many brought.

11870. Do you think by the improvement of your breeding in Scotland you would injure that trade in Ireland?—They would pay me a much larger price, double in fact to the price they would pay for those coming over from the North of Ireland. I have no difficulty in selling them at good prices.

11871. I am referring entirely to half-breds?—I am speaking of those horses that are bred by my Hackney sire, I mean that which the mare is if the foal happens to be of the Hackney type and can go as it is a gelding. When I am going to have a sale I gather in two or three from my neighbours and am glad enough to buy one from a small farmer here and another from a farmer there, because if price holds for them, and induced them to go on breeding. I can break them better and put them in better shape, and they come and see at my sale that they have made good money.

11872. Do you find that there is any prejudice among the Scotch dealers against the Hackney blood except so far as "Clydesdale" is concerned?—No. I think there is one man has spoken pretty strongly against the Hackneys going into Ireland on account of being interested in keeping the pure hunters; but the same gentleman is very fond of getting a pair of Hackneys when I can sell them at his price, and he is always ready when I have a pair to come and see them, and offer me a price. I won't mention his name, for he is a customer, and will be a customer.

11873. He does not find any fault with you on that account?—No, he would give me a much larger price for those than for ordinary carriage horses, either coming from the Hackney or from Ireland, because they have more action.

11874. In the case of animals that a small farmer with a small weedy mare can breed do you think there is any better stallion than the Hackney?—Certainly not. I would tell you several instances where this has been most valuable. The mare I am speaking of, that I first saw, of Collingson's, was a little grey mare, by a thoroughbred horse under 15 hands, and the production of that mare to these sires was over £1,000. There was £600 realised for this very mare that I saw first chance.

11875. That was nearly extra-bred?—This was one of this little blood mare by "Lord Derby II." I gave him a very good price for the tree Lyon, and within 200 yards of the place from I bought two from Mr. Atkinson, of W——, one I called "Adam Bede" and the other "Lord Lyon." I sold both when two years of age; one for £150, and the other for £150. "Lord Lyon" went to America as a stallion, and he carried the gentleman that bought him from me 500 guineas. He got nearly £1,000 for him. He has been used in that country, and has spread a lot of breeding, riding and driving horses there. "Adam Bede," strange to say, in the year following followed him to America, but he was kept by the gentleman's brother that bought him from me, and he never went out to the public properly. These were both from a mare by a horse called "Sportsman Hall," a big, roaring thoroughbred horse. The mare was a breeding type, showing the class of animal that would be bred from using a pure Hackney. They came out nearly 15.3 hands high, although "Lord Derby" himself was not over 15.1 hands.

11876. Have you ever bred Hackneys from thoroughbred mares at all?—Not pure thoroughbred mares. I never had a pure thoroughbred mare.

11877. Do you think that Hackneys are improving now or the reverse; is more trouble taken with their breeding or are they going back?—I mean the general run of Hackneys?—I think there is a great improvement. I judged in London four years ago, and I judged this week again. I have also judged at the Royal and the Royal Lancashire, and I think there is a great increase in the merit and quality of the Hackney generally. I think our yearling class this year was not so good as I have seen it, but that will happen. Next year they may come up quite different. The three-year-old stallions over 15 hands was the best young class I ever saw in a show ring.

11878. Do you know at all whether there has been much trade in the show, whether there is a large demand for Hackneys?—I believe there have been several sold; they were in the parade, and my place as judge was to stand in the ring. I asked one or two were they sold, and they said, "Yes, I am pleased to say I have got mine sold," "and mine sold," and several have been sold there. Last year about twenty of these valuable stallions were sold; I cannot tell what quantity this year, but several have been sold both to home and foreign buyers. I might say regarding the Americans, if I be allowed, that I was at the New York Show, and I saw several of the trotting horses and a lot of fine horses in America, but I thought from my standpoint they were a little bit light of bone and a little bit leggy, and I am sure in time the Americans will find that nothing can improve the value of their horses so much as using a Hackney stallion. The real trotting men are very jealous of interfering with their fast trotters, the same perhaps as hunting men would be; but for general utility horses, to sell for carriage and harness work, nothing could do them so much good as using our Hackney stallions on their own home mares.

11879. Do you think if they do that, they will, to a great degree, cut out the home trade in horses here?—I cannot tell; if they can breed a good horse and sell a good horse, somebody will get the benefit of it. I would not object, it is like the cattle and wheat. I am glad to see the good blood going into the country. I think they will breed some good horses; I met a great many farmers west of Chicago that made a great trade in horses.

11880. Were you ever at one of the big sales in Chicago?—No; I did not go there.

11881. It is one of the largest horse markets in the world?—Yes; I met one of the auctioneers, and spent a night or two with him; he staggered me with a statement of the number of horses that passed through their hands.

11882. A number of American horses are come over to Scotland and affect the breeders?—Yes, they affect a certain class; but they are not appreciated, they are too leggy, they would not be bought. I had a long talk with a West End dealer here; he is a very extensive importer and dealer; he generally brought to Ireland to buy, and he had made up his mind, he said, never to buy an American horse again; he had nothing but disappointment, and it affected his position with his customers. I saw a team in New York of Hackneys by a Hackney horse out of their own mares, I thought they were as fine a team as ever I saw; that was in the New York Show—they were really charming.

11883. Lord RATHDONNELL.—There is one question I would like to ask you—I understood you to say that there is no soft blood in the Yorkshire Hackney?—Well, I have not found any myself. If there is any particular strain you would name, I could tell you whether I had experience of it.

11884. But it is rather a broad statement to make that there is no soft blood in any breed, because I suppose there is hardly any breed of horse, thoroughbred or anything else, that has not some soft strain in it?—I have not found myself in the Yorkshire Hackney soft blood; of course, I have not driven so many myself, I have driven half a dozen different mares or horses—as many as I have used—but we break them mostly all in, and know before we give them finished whether they are soft or not.

March 9, 1897.
Mr. Alexander Morton, J.P.

11885. Mr. WRENCH.—Have you had any complaints from the people you sell them to?—Never a word; the pair of brown horses I sold them to a Michigan manufacturer, he is a millionaire; I met him in the store, and he said, "Those horses have given me more pleasure than any I ever had, I should like to have another to make them, so that I could rest one if anything went wrong with it." These are some out of light Yorkshire cart mares by "Lord Derby."

11886. Is there anything else you wish to state?—No; I have made my statement on that paper.

The Commissioners adjourned.

TWENTY-THIRD DAY—WEDNESDAY, MARCH 10TH, 1897.

March 10, 1897.

Sitting at 13 Hanover-square, London, W.

PRESENT:—THE EARL OF DUNRAVEN, K.P. (in the Chair); MR. J. L. CARew, M.P.; HON. H. W. FITZWILLIAM; MR. PERCY LA TOUCHE; MR. F. S. WRENCH; MARQUESS OF LONDONDERRY, K.G.; LORD RATHDONNELL; COLONEL ST. QUINTIN.

MR. HUGH NEVILLE, Secretary.

The EARL OF COVENTRY examined.

The Earl of Coventry.

11887. CHAIRMAN.—You are Master of Her Majesty's Buckhounds?—Yes.

11888. And for some years you were Master of fox hounds?—Yes, for many years.

11889. And you have judged horses in shows in England and Ireland?—Yes.

11890. Are you pretty well acquainted with Ireland generally as far as horse-breeding is concerned?—Yes, I am; I know Cork, Limerick, Tipperary, and Waterford.

11891. And the special parts of the country principally devoted to breeding hunters?—I think so.

11892. Have you yourself bought many Irish hunters?—Yes, I have bought a good many during the last 30 years, almost entirely hunters.

11893. Have you bought any horses in Ireland for harness purposes?—I cannot remember having bought, perhaps, more than half a dozen for harness.

11894. In your opinion has the Irish horse any special value as a hunter?—Yes, I think he has; I think they are the best horses I know.

11895. To what do you attribute that?—Principally to their superior breeding and to the effect of the climate and soil of the country, which are so well adapted to the raising of horses.

11896. The soil and the climate would be equally well adapted, I presume, to the raising of harness horses or any kind of horses?—They may be so.

11897. Am I right in saying that you attribute the success of Ireland in breeding hunters largely to the blood?—Certainly, yes.

11898. That would be to a very large admixture of the thoroughbred blood?—Yes.

11899. Have you bought any horses as hunters which had any strain of cart-horse or Hackney in them?—In Ireland, as I don't know that I have; I have in England, but not in Ireland to my knowledge.

11900. Am I to infer from that that you would not buy them in Ireland if to your knowledge they had Hackney blood or cart-horse blood in them?—No; if I knew it.

11901. You bought horses yourself in Ireland from the breeders?—Generally from the breeders. I used at one time when I was a Master of Hounds to attend a great many of the fairs in Ireland—Limerick, Cahirmee, Clonmel, Kilkenny, several of the principal fairs.

11902. Do you get pedigrees of the horses?—Nearly always, I always like to have a pedigree if I can.

11903. And you think they are reliable?—Oh, I think so; speaking generally.

11904. Are you able to form any opinion as to whether the supply is falling off in the last few years, I have rather given up going to the fairs. I have not been for the last seven or eight years. I have not had to buy so many horses, and in consequence I have abandoned going to the fairs.

11905. Have you bought hunters in England with Hackney blood in them?—I think I can conscientiously say that I have bought with Hackney blood in them.

11906. Were they satisfactory?—No, they were not.

11907. We have a good deal of evidence to the effect that the Hackney blood is not only not detrimental to the production of a good hunter, but that a great many good hunters are the result of the first cross of the Hackney blood; have you any opinion about that?—No; I can only judge from the two animals I am speaking of just now that I possessed; they were very smart, fine horses, and jumped very well; as long as hounds ran with a cold scent they could get on very well, but in a burst they failed to keep their place.

11908. You have not had any particular experience except of those two animals of your own?—No, I have not.

11909. Do you think the introduction of the Hackney blood in Ireland would have a detrimental or beneficial effect upon the production of hunters?—Oh, a most detrimental effect in my opinion.

11910. Do you think the introduction of the Hackney blood would be beneficial in the congested districts and those parts of the country?—Well, I have had no experience of that part of the country, and I would hardly say; I don't like the Hackney.

March 12, 1896.

The Earl of [illegible].

11911. Assuming that it would be beneficial there, do you think there would be any danger of the blood gradually permeating through the country and doing damage?—I should say there would be great danger of its filtering out and so on.

11912. We have had a good deal of difference in evidence as to the value of the half-bred sire; I think by half-bred sire a sire that is not in the Stud Book, but with many crosses of thoroughbred blood—as to whether they are suitable or not for getting hunters and high-class carriage horses out of the half-bred mares; have you got any opinion about that?—Oh, I have a very strong opinion. I should be very sorry to see them to get hunters. My own idea of the thing is if you want to breed a hunter I think you should have a pure strain of blood on one side, and that remark would apply to the breeding, in my opinion, of cattle or sheep too; but for carriage horses I dare say a half-bred horse would do; I might say as well, but that he might do.

11913. Have you formed any opinion as to the class of thoroughbred stallions in Ireland generally, I am not speaking of Meath and that kind of counties, but more of the West, and so on?—I have not seen many during the last few years; I was so much engaged at the last Dublin Horse Show in my ring that I did not see the thoroughbred stallions there, but when I have seen them it has been a source of surprise to me that so good a collection could be got together; I had not thought there were so many good horses in Ireland.

11914. We have had a good deal of evidence to the effect that in the poorer parts of the country the description of the thoroughbred horse is very inferior indeed, which, perhaps, is not strange, if they are not able to pay more than a fee?—In the West of Ireland?

11915. Yes, all over the north and south and the poorer parts of the country with the small farmers, and the question would be if anything is to be done to try and improve the horse-breeding in those parts of the country, what kind of a sire would be most suitable?—I have no knowledge of the mares; I should hardly like to express a positive opinion, but I am always in favour of the thoroughbred stallion.

11916. That is to say, if a sound thoroughbred stallion with sufficient bone and substance could be obtained, you would prefer that to anything else?—Certainly.

11917. Even for those parts of the country where the mares are very small and light and weedy?—Yes.

11918. I don't know whether you could give the Commission any information as to breeding for harness purposes?—No, I am afraid I cannot.

11919. And we have had a good deal of divergence of opinion also, assuming there was money to be laid out in the improvement of the industry in Ireland, as to how it could be best applied, how the better class of mares generally could be obtained, whether it should be entirely confined to the question of providing superior stallions, or whether anything could be done to induce farmers to keep their best mares to breed from, or supply them with better mares, or anything of that kind?—It strikes me that the best way to improve the breed of horses in Ireland would be to send over a few more superior stallions if you could get them; unquestionably Ireland is worse off for stallions than England.

11920. Then you would not suggest that anything special should be done in respect of the mares, a scheme of registration, or prizes, or anything of the kind?—No; I am afraid I could offer no suggestion, except, perhaps, that I should always encourage the giving of prizes for four-year-old mares with foal at foot.

11921. Can you give us any opinion as to the ponies?—No, I know nothing of ponies.

11922. Have you any information as to the Royal Dublin Society's scheme in Ireland so far as horses are concerned, its methods, and so on?—As far as I can judge from what I heard it seems to be working uncommonly well.

11923. Lord Londonderry.—I gather from what you told the Chairman that you consider the best hunters you had originally came from Ireland?—Yes.

11924. You attribute the goodness of those animals to the soil, and to the climate in a great extent?—I think, to their superior breeding first, and then to the soil and climate which are so well adapted for the raising of young horses. In my experience it seems to me that the Irish horses have always so much more bone than those bred in England, and better quality of bone.

11925. Have you had the biggest and best and experience of from any particular districts that you have confined yourself to buy, to buy mostly all my horses in Cork, Limerick, and Tipperary.

11926. Have you judged at any Shows in Ireland besides the Royal Dublin Society's Show?—Yes, I have judged at Clonmel and Limerick.

11927. You were struck there by the superior class of horses that you have seen shown there?—Yes, generally all through the shows the young horses have been particularly good.

11928. Comparing the Dublin with the Islington Show, and the local shows in Ireland with those in England, would you say that the horses shown in Ireland were superior to the class shown in England at similar shows?—Yes, a far superior class; you see a far larger number of superior horses than you see in England.

11929. When you were judging in England, have you seen superior horses to which you have given prizes that you have known to come from Ireland and taken prizes there?—Yes, many.

11930. And those horses by their appearance were by thoroughbred horses?—Certainly; I should think so.

11931. And from a superior class of mare?—Yes.

11932. Such as you see in those hunter-breeding centres to which you have alluded—Meath, Kildare, Tipperary, and Waterford?—Yes.

11933. In your experience of judging horses at shows, you would be able to tell—very likely you would notice—probably by shape and action whether there was anything of the Hackney strain in horses shown as hunters?—I think I should detect it, the action is so very different.

11934. Would you give a horse of that sort, however well shaped, a prize as against a horse perhaps not so well shaped, but showing qualities and action which he could only get by a thoroughbred sire?—I should not; certainly not. I should give the preference to the breeding type of horse. To my mind the action of the Hackney is not suited to get over the country.

11935. You have seen of course a good many of these Hackneys. I don't know whether you have seen any of the Congested Districts Board—you know some of those horses?—I have seen them in London and at different places in the country, too.

11936. They are to a certain extent very taking in their action when they are walking through the town?—Yes.

11937. Do you think that these animals standing about parts of Ireland, and their appearance being more taking than the true hunter sire, might induce the farmers to send their mares to such a type?—Yes; the action of the Hackney would be sure to fascinate the farmer; he would like to see him run up and down the street in a neat sort of way, and he would send his mare to him in preference to a thoroughbred sire.

11938. And that you think would be disastrous to maintaining the present superior breeding of the horses which now prevail?—Certainly, I do; I don't think you can improve the lines on which the principal hunter breeders are going now in Ireland.

11938. And if these Hackneys were used in certain parts of Ireland, whether they would be an advantage you would draw a hard and fast line to prevent their getting into those parts of Ireland in which you think the present breed of hunters?—I should like to see that done very much.

11939. You have not seen those parts of Ireland in which it is proposed to produce a better class of animal horse, those parts worked by Hackney stallions?—No, I have not.

11940. Have you been in South Wales, in Lord Tredegar's park, at all?—Yes, I have been there.

11941. He told us, I think, that one of the best hunters he or his man had, was by a Hackney. Have you seen the produce by the Hackney stallions from the poorer class of animals that he reared in those poorer districts of South Wales?—Yes, I think I have. I have seen ponies got by Hackneys in most of them.

11942. Did they give you the idea that they would be animals that would fetch a certain price in the open market?—I think they would have been useful for harness purposes.

11943. Then, as far as I gather, your opinion is that if these Hackneys, so far as your experience in Lord Tredegar's district, could be kept perfectly pure and confined to these poor districts they would be of use, but that if they were allowed to get down to those hunter-breeding counties they would ruin the breeding of hunters?—Quite so.

11944. Mr. Fitzwilliam.—Talking about stallions, particularly thoroughbred stallions, and as the number of [illegible] to get the required number of thoroughbred stallions in Ireland, should you object to a well-bred half-bred stallion?—I think I should on principle.

11945. How would you supply his place?—I think the people who live in the locality ought to try and buy to get the thoroughbred horses.

11946. What do you think a thoroughbred horse suitable for the purposes can be obtained for now-a-days?—I should think a very suitable horse might be obtained at from £100 to £150. I am speaking of the ordinary run of horses, nothing out of the common. I don't mean a special horse such as "Wellington," but horses which have broken down, with no particular character on the turf, but who are good-looking, well-shaped horses. I think they might be got at from £100 to £150. But I have had no experience myself in buying lately.

11947. Do you object at all to breeding early from a mare that is going to be used afterwards for other purposes?—No, I see no objection to it. I think very often a mare takes more than to recover from it, and that her appearance is not so good for two or three years perhaps.

11948. But you don't think **it would injure her in her growth**?—I think not.

11949. Your remarks as to hackney and hunter breeding, do they apply also to riding horses generally throughout Ireland?—I hardly understand your question.

11950. Do the remarks that you have made with regard to the qualities of the hunter apply to horses for general purposes?—Oh, I think so. It seems to me, from my experience of Ireland, that the horses are generally very well bred. Certainly in the South they are a very well bred type.

11951. Lord Rathdonnell.—From what you have seen of Irish shows where you have judged, do you think that the high class horses in Ireland have deteriorated, or the reverse?—I don't think you see any more good horses than you did eight or ten years ago. I should think the supply keeps pretty much the same. I do not see any great improvement as far as I was judge in the classes.

11952. As to quality?—I think I see more under-bred horses in the show now than I did fifteen or twenty years ago, but all the best horses are still of the same quality.

11953. About **the same in** number?—I should think so.

11954. You say you would not have a half-bred sire in Ireland on principle—do you know how the winner of the last Grand Military at Sandown was bred?—I don't know his name.

11955. Do you know he is by a horse called "Mackintosh"?—I have heard the name.

11956. He is a half-bred horse?—I speak of him as a half-bred horse; he is not in the Stud Book.

Mr. Wrench.—He is practically thoroughbred, included in the Stud Book.

Witness.—Then, he is probably what they call a contrast; nearly as thoroughbred as "Eclipse," but never registered.

11957. Lord Rathdonnell.—I think he is a half-bred horse.

Lord Londonderry.—The **famous "Mrs. Taffe"** was half-bred.

Witness.—Yes, and "Rosiere," who ran second in the Derby, but I believe they were as thoroughbred as "Eclipse," only they have never been registered.

11958. Lord Rathdonnell.—Still you would not object to using a horse of that class?—Possibly the dam of that horse might have been a thoroughbred mare, and in that case I should not object to it. My contention is that you must have a pure strain of blood on one side.

11959. Mr. La Touche.—I conclude you would have the same objection to a Hackney stallion as to a half-bred?—Certainly.

11960. Would you or would you not consider that the Hackney strain was a pure strain of blood?—I should not consider them a pure strain.

11961. Have you ever judged Hackneys at local shows in England?—No, never; I frequently had horses that came before me, got by Hackneys, no doubt.

11962. The leading characteristic of the **Hackney** horse is action I suppose?—I think so.

11963. Do you think that he adds much of shape and good hunter action?—Very often they are well made horses. I don't think they show much quality.

11964. You said you thought you could detect the Hackney blood in a hunter from the Hackney action, but I suppose it would be quite possible that a Hackney horse might transmit his shape without his action to his progeny?—Oh, I should think so. I should say that three out of four would have the action more or less of the Hackney, but I should not like to speak positively on that point, because I have had no experience in breeding them.

11965. You say that Ireland is badly off in the matter of stallions—did you mean in the number or quality of the stallions?—I should say the quantity in the rural districts. I was judging last year in Limerick. There were very nice horses shown, but I don't think there were more than four or five stallions at the show. There were very nice horses, but not in my opinion a sufficient number for the district.

11966. It has been represented to us that a great many stallions in the country districts are unsound from disease, and that it is possible that the disease would be hereditary—would you approve of practically prohibiting such stallions from serving?—Oh, I think I should like to see it done, but of course it would be a very difficult matter to carry out.

11967. I take it that in your opinion there is nothing that a Hackney horse can do that a thoroughbred cannot do better except lifting his knees?—Yes. That is so.

11968. You fully recognise the importance of breeding harness horses—how would you propose that these harness horses should be bred in Ireland?—I don't think they do breed; as far as I can see from my experience I don't think they do go in for breeding harness horses in Ireland, do they?—I don't see many.

11969. There are something like 40,000 horses exported from Ireland to England—a very large proportion of those must go in for harness horses?—Yes, I think so. I think there are more, as far as I can judge, that are bought in two or three years old at Cahirmee fair, but a great many of those which are taken over to London for harness purposes would make very useful hunting animals.

11970. You have probably heard of these mares the property of farmers in the poorer parts of Ireland, do you think they would be capable of breeding an animal of any utility by a thoroughbred sire—do you think these very [illegible] mares would be capable of producing an animal of any value or utility?—I have had no experience of them, but I am a great believer in the thoroughbred blood. I think it is very possible that a thoroughbred sire might get some very good offspring from these mares, but I have not seen them, so I cannot say.

11971. You think they would be just as likely to produce a useful stock by a thoroughbred sire as any other sire?—I should say so.

11972. Mr. Carew.—You know that a great want in Ireland is some inducement to the farmer to retain his mares to breed from?—Yes, I have heard that.

11973. What would you recommend as an inducement to them?—I think you might do like the [illegible] that you would establish prizes for four-year-old mares with foals at foot at the shows?—Yes. I think that would be a step in the right direction.

11974. Would you have prizes for three-year-olds with foals at foot?—I don't think so.

11975. You would not object to breed from two-year-olds?—I don't think so. I will give an instance. I bred from a mare who was only two years old, I sent her to a horse called "Pulmonal." The result was a colt that won a race yesterday.

11976. That was "Pulmonal," the winner of the Two Thousand guineas?—Yes. Many of my friends thought the mare was too young to send to the horse, but I did. [illegible] and it certainly turned out pretty well. That is the only time I put a two-year-old to the horse.

11977. You know that the farmers breed from two-year-olds, and very successfully, in Ireland?—Yes.

11978. And if prizes were given to three-year-old mares with foals at foot, it would be a great inducement?—I think that would be a step in the right direction.

11979. Then your qualification for the Irish hunter is due to the superior breeding?—Yes.

11980. And to the absence of Hackney blood?—Certainly.

11981. And if you were a buyer in Ireland, you would object to the introduction of the Hackney blood?—Certainly.

11982. You think that they would taint the hunter breed?—Certainly; they would destroy, in my opinion, the character of the Irish hunter altogether.

11983. You have considerable experience yourself in the shows in England and Ireland of the different qualities of the horses exhibited there?—Yes.

11984. And it is in favour of Ireland?—Certainly.

11985. And if Ireland had the same facilities for getting thoroughbred stock she would still maintain the superiority in the breeding of horses?—I think the horses are now greatly superior in Ireland to what they are in England.

11986. Mr. Wrench.—Do you breed horses very much?—Not very largely. I have always had three or four mares for the last thirty years.

11987. No Hackney mares?—No, never.

11988. If you had to try to improve the very miserable animals in the very poor districts, what class of sire would you be inclined to use?—I have faith in the thoroughbred blood. I should like to try a small thoroughbred sire. I imagine they are of little value there, the mares, are they not?

11989. They are horses dwarfed by starvation, do you think that a small thoroughbred would produce the [illegible] [illegible]?—I cannot say that, because generally speaking I do not know what their points are. It may be so, unless the thoroughbred horse has very little or action either, and the result would be that perhaps the animals would, but for a valuable for that reason.

11990. Do you think that action is a valuable commodity for a poor man's horse?—Oh, I think so for certain purposes; for harness, I have horses in my mind.

11991. Do you think that a thoroughbred horse as well as good [illegible] action would be likely to transmit action to a breed of horses that had it [illegible] to them for generations?—Oh, I think so. I think if the thoroughbred has good action himself he would probably transmit it to his offspring.

11992. As much as the Hackney?—Yes. I do not see why he should not.

11993. Have you any experience of that?—There was "Q.C.," a thoroughbred horse with the finest action I ever saw.

11994. You saw him yesterday?—I did not know that he was at the show. That was a horse with very fine action indeed, and I have understood that he [illegible] that through his produce, but I have never seen any of them, so that I cannot speak of my own experience.

11995. And would you object more or equally to the cross of the Suffolk Punch on a hunter as the cross of the Hackney?—I don't like the Suffolk Punch.

11996. You dislike him as much for hunting blood as you do the Hackney?—Certainly as much as the Hackney.

11997. And do you dislike the Clydesdale as much?—I dislike the Clydesdale. I should prefer to breed from a Shire or cart horse and put him with a thoroughbred than, I would from a Hackney.

11998. But I was talking of half-bred mares—would you object to Clydesdale blood in them?—I don't like it.

11999. Do you think it would be easier to breed out Clydesdale in horses than Hackney blood?—I think it would be much easier to breed Hackney blood than cart blood in the hunter.

12000. Have you known instances of horses with cart blood in them very good hunters?—Very good indeed.

12001. And sold at a very big price?—And sold at a very big price. I knew one horse sold for five hundred guineas, and I have known several sold at four hundred and three hundred, out of cart mares. But the gentleman who bought them I don't think knew them to be out of cart mares. But I knew, because they were bred in my neighbourhood. There was a horse called "Nell in the Pen," who was a very good hunter galloper. The local farmer sent their cart mares to him and he was very successful in getting good horses. There was a horse of my own, called "Umpire," I remember his getting three exceedingly good hunters out of a cart. One was found the very [illegible] [illegible] a very good horse indeed, it had been bought by a dealer and sold to this gentleman, and the gentleman wrote to me for the pedigree of the mare, and he asked me if she was a thoroughbred, he had such a high opinion of the horse, and when I told him the pedigree I could hardly get him to believe it, the horse showed so much quality almost as a thoroughbred horse.

12002. He was sold at a very big price?—Five hundred guineas. He was by "Umpire" out of a cart mare.

12003. Mr. Carew.—Was "Umpire" thoroughbred?—Yes.

12004. Mr. Wrench.—You think that the prizes given by farmers at Irish fairs might be fairly evened out?—I think so.

12005. And you think it is infinitely easier to breed Hackney blood in an animal?—I do.

12007. If there are these two circumstances what danger is there of the Hackney blood being used by people who do not wish to use it?—Oh, well I think the danger would be if the Hackneys found their way into the South of Ireland. I think they would be very largely used possibly.

12008. Have you ever heard that it is suggested that Hackney stallions should be sent into the hunter-breeding districts?—I have never heard it—no.

12009. My point was that if you can detect the Hackney blood, and also if you can ascertain the pedigrees, what danger is there of animals with Hackney blood in them being used as hunter brood mares?—I suppose the farmers would use them.

12010. Yes; but then if you are told that there is a Hackney cross in a hunter, if you don't like the Hackney cross you would not buy the animal?—Perhaps after the second cross it would not be so easy to detect it.

12011. Would you object to the second cross?—Oh, certainly.

12012. The cross of the Yorkshire Hackney if he had thoroughbred blood in him?—I should not have called the Hackney a thoroughbred myself, but I have no experience of them.

12013. Have you any preference for the Norfolk or Yorkshire Hackneys?—I have not studied the breed very much. I have seen them, but have never had anything to do with them.

12014. Do you think that the Hunter Improvement Society has done good in England?—Oh, I think so.

12015. Would you like to see a similar Society started in Ireland?—I rather think I must qualify that opinion by saying I have not followed the proceedings of the Hunter Improvement Society very much lately, but I understand that they rather sanction the use of half-bred sires. I object to that very much indeed, to half-bred sires with a certain number of strains of thoroughbred blood in them.

12016. Do you object to half-bred sires, limiting them as they limit them?—I do.

12017. You would not have that blood?—I would never use them at all unless for thoroughbred mares. My contention is that you must have the pure blood on one side to be successful.

12018. Do you know as a matter of fact that in Ireland there are a very large number of cart horses—half-bred cart horse stallions standing even in the best hunter-breeding districts?—No; I do not. In my visits to the South of Ireland I never see them. Probably I should not be in the way of seeing them perhaps. I never recollect to have seen many cart horses in Ireland.

12019. Has it ever been brought to your attention that many of the best hunters in the Dublin Show are by half-bred horses?—No.

12020. Do you believe the pedigrees given in the Dublin Show Catalogue as well as the pedigrees given by the farmers at fairs?—I do. I believe they are generally correct.

12021. Do you think it is a curious fact that there are a number of horses with pedigrees, and there is a note attached that the breeders are unknown?—No doubt a great many mistakes are made, but generally I believe the pedigrees are correct.

12022. Substantially correct?—I think so.

12023. And therefore if an attempt was made to start a Hunter Improvement Society in Ireland it would not be difficult to obtain material?—I think not.

12024. Do I understand you to say that the thoroughbred horse is practically the only sire you would encourage in Ireland by public money?—With a view to breeding hunters.

12025. Would you turn the whole country into hunter breeders?—Oh, I incline to the hunter more than to any other class of horse.

12026. Would you try and encourage all the horse breeders in Ireland to breed hunters, or do you think there is a large opening for breeding harness horses?—There is room for all. I don't see why farmers should not breed harness horses if they like. I think they would find hunters more profitable. [illegible]

12027. Do you think that the hunter is as profitable to the poor small farmer who cannot raise them but merely sell them really [illegible]; he would probably sell them as foals, yearlings, or two-year-olds.

12028. Do you think it is as profitable as selling harness horses with action?—I think so. I think a hunter of good quality, two or three years old, would fetch much more money than a harness horse got by a Hackney, that is my opinion.

12029. Do you know the North of Ireland at all?—No, I don't.

12030. You don't know what class of horses they breed there?—No.

12031. Then you are not prepared to say that there is no opening for breeding harness horses in Ireland as well as for breeding hunters?—No.

12032. Do you consider Ireland the best country in the world for breeding horses of every kind?—I think it is the best I know of.

12033. It has been suggested to us that all stallion owners should be obliged to take out a licence, and that the licence would only be granted to sound stallions, would you approve of such a recommendation?—Oh, I think I should, certainly.

12034. Do you think with regard to mares that it is feasible to give any sufficiently large prizes to induce the farmers to keep their best mares, and not sell them if they get a good offer?—I think so. As I was saying before, I should encourage the two or three year old classes by giving good prizes.

12035. What do you call good prizes?—I mean the amount?—I hardly know; I think prizes of £50 and that sort of thing.

12036. CHAIRMAN.—You attach great importance, absolute importance, to the existence of a pure strain on one side or the other in breeding horses, saddle, and so on?—Decidedly.

12037. As regards Hackneys, do you consider that the pure strain is established by the horse being in the Hackney Stud Book?—I should not have said so myself.

12038. How would you define as regards Hackneys and Clevelands and a variety of horses, what do you understand by a pure strain in anything except a thoroughbred?—I should think there were none of them pure, clearly, in my view.

12039. And practically either the dam or sire should be a thoroughbred?—Yes.

12040. As to the pedigrees, some apprehension has been expressed before us in evidence that the horses of these Western ponies, the animals that Mr. Wrench described as half starved animals, and the Hackney sire would be sold in the guise of the ordinary mare or less of [illegible] hunters, and that they were not suitable for breeding hunters. You said then you think that the pedigrees given to you by the farmers and others from whom you bought might be generally relied upon, but that would not affect this particular class; it would be a question whether the farmer buying a mare to breed from would be sure of its pedigree. Do you think that in the case of, say, these horses coming from Connaught and the Western districts into the open market, do you suppose the farmer buying a mare to breed from would make any particular inquiry as to its pedigree, or would pick up the animal he thought best suited to him?—I should say that he would make inquiries, but I have not sufficient knowledge of your countrymen to say that; but I should think he would; they always seem to take an interest in the pedigree, and nearly always when I have been buying horses I invariably ask for the pedigree, and I generally find that they give me a pedigree that I can trace whenever I try to check, and they are correct generally speaking.

12041. You don't disapprove of thinking them trustworthy yourself?—No, I think not. As I was saying, I only breed once from a two-year-old mare.

12042. The result would depend a good deal upon how the mare was treated?—Yes, this mare had been in training and well done all her life.

12043. And you told us that you thought that, as far as the breeding of hunters was concerned, the present lines on which the breeders were acting in Ireland were satisfactory, what do you mean by the present lines?—I think that as to the present lines that they use in the South of Ireland they breed from well-bred mares and from thoroughbred horses. I don't think they could proceed on better lines than those.

12044. And you think that a certain number of sound and suitable thoroughbred stallions with, we will say, not speed enough for racing, or perhaps broken down from some comparatively immaterial cause, can be had for about £150?—I should think so.

12045. Do you know what price the Government paid on an average for their Hackney stallions?—I don't know.

12046. Assuming it to have been on an average £300, you think a *fortiori* suitable half-bred stallions could be obtained at the same price?—I should say so, but I am taking your figure.

12047. Speaking very generally—I do not know whether you could express any opinion about it—would you say that the breeding of hunters and high class carriage horses, which are bred in some numbers in Ireland, is probably the most profitable branch of the industry of horse breeding in the country?—I should think certainly it is.

12048. And would you think it dangerous to encourage the production of harness horses by say the introduction of Hackney stallions—do you think that would be likely to be followed by any consequences which would deteriorate the hunters?—I think it would be most dangerous to the interests of the farmers—most dangerous.

12049. Mr. Wrench.—You referred to two horses that you recollected with Hackney blood—do you remember what Hackney stallion they were by?—Oh, no; it was years ago; I don't remember what they were by.

12050. Or whether they were bred in Yorkshire or Norfolk?—I don't remember; I know they were by Hackney horses.

12051. But you don't know any particulars?—No.

12052. And in the fairs that you attended in Ireland, do you think the preponderance was of good or bad horses?—Oh, largely of bad horses. I should think a great many bad ones of course. In a fair like Cahirmee you see a great many.

12053. Yes, but that is a picked fair?—Yes, there are two or three thousand horses there. There must be however a very large number of bad ones.

12054. Do you think that it is the duty of any public body to try and improve the best class or try to help the poor people?—I should try to improve the best class of horses. I should try to improve both. I think it is the duty of every landlord to do what he can to try to improve the breed generally.

12055. You think the poor farmers would have an equal claim at any rate with the big farmers to be improved?—Certainly.

12056. Do you know that in Ireland the very poor farmers form a large preponderance of the population?—I have no doubt that they do; yes.

12057. Chairman.—Do you know that prizes are given by the Hunters Improvement Society for hunter sires, half-bred sires—do you know the conditions?—I think my friend who is going to be examined can probably tell you, Mr. Legard. I think they must have four crosses of the thoroughbred blood, but I was very sorry such a rule was ever allowed to pass.

12058. You don't approve of it?—I don't approve of it at all.

12059. I only wanted to get from you whether you disapprove of it, subject to those rules?—Yes, I disapprove of it.

12060. Lord Ravensworth.—In your travels through Ireland, have you ever privately bought hunters from small farmers, breeders?—Oh, frequently.

12061. You think the small farmer is a pretty sharp man as a rule about breeding?—I think so. I used to buy cob hunters, and I found I could buy them from small farmers better than anywhere, generally small horses.

12062. A good class?—A very good class.

12063. Mr. Wrench.—What do you call a small farmer?—I could not say.

12064. You did not take the acreage of the farm?—They were not what you would call strong farmers.

The Rev. Cecil Legard examined.

12065. Chairman.—You live at Cottesbrooke Rectory, Northampton?—Yes.

12066. You have had a large experience in horses, and have acted as a judge at shows for many years?—I daresay twenty-five years.

12067. Have you judged in Ireland at all?—Yes; on three or four occasions in Dublin and once in Limerick; not more than that.

12068. Then your only comparative knowledge would be as regards the Dublin show?—Yes.

12069. Have you formed any opinion as to the utility of the Royal Dublin Society's scheme, and the benefits it has produced, if any?—I am afraid I do not quite understand it: I have not been told what it was.

12070. When did you judge first at the Dublin show—do you remember the date?—Probably it might be ten years ago, perhaps.

12071. And when last?—Perhaps about three years ago.

12072. Did you attend the show last year?—No.

12073. You have not been there for the last three years?—Not since I judged about three years ago.

12074. What opinion did you form during those seven or eight years as to the improvement or deterioration of the horses shown, and so on?—Well, there were a great number that I think ought not to have been shown at all, and were not shown with any idea of getting prizes. They were sent there with more of the idea of getting customers.

12075. The numbers were greater in the last years than in former years?—I am afraid I cannot tell you that. I remember the class I judged; there were 253 horses in one class.

12076. What class was that?—I think the class 12 st. to 13 st. 7 lb.

12077. Mr. Wrench.—Light-weight hunters?—Yes, as well as I can remember.

12078. Chairman.—Would you approve of the registration of half-bred sires under the Royal Dublin Society's scheme?—Well, I should.

12079. How would you define them—in the same manner as they are defined by the Hunters' Improvement Society?—I should give, I believe, rather more latitude than they are inclined to give. According to their conditions they are practically thoroughbred. They are race horses with a cock-tail strain only according to the Hunters' Improvement Society.

12080. And you think that a thoroughbred sire, sound and otherwise suitable, is a suitable stallion to use in Ireland for getting hunters?—Yes, undoubtedly, for hunters.

12081. I am not speaking at all, of course, about thoroughbred stock. Do you know Ireland pretty well in the way of horse-breeding?—No, I don't.

12082. You don't know the South at all?—No, with the exception of being in Limerick, and lately in Kildare, I really know nothing.

12083. You only judged once at Limerick?—No. That was probably about five or six years ago.

12084. What opinion did you form as to the quality of the animals shown in the various classes?—Full of quality—very good.

12085. I mean quality in the more general sense?—Yes, there was not so inferior a class, I should say, as what there was in the Dublin Show.

12086. Were there a large number of stallions exhibited?—Oh, I don't think there were any stallions.

12087. Have you bought many horses yourself in Ireland?—In England I have bought horses from Ireland—one or two from Capt. Bland, but, as a rule, I have not bought horses in Ireland.

12088. We have had in evidence further on that the breed of hunters and high class carriage horses, and so on, are deteriorating in Ireland, and that a great deal owing to the fact that so many of the best mares are sold out of the country and go abroad. Have you any opinion whether that is the case?—I quite agree with that. I think that is at the root of it.

12089. If that be so, can you suggest any means by which the best mares would be retained in the country?—I am afraid hardly. The only chance would be to give very good prizes to young mares—two, three, and four-year-old mares. I doubt that that would stop the foreigners.

12090. It would put the prices up?—Yes. If a mare won these prizes that would enhance her value and the foreigner would give an extra price in proportion. I don't think anything would stop them buying the best mares. They buy with public money. My experience is confined to the East Riding of Yorkshire. I know what the mischief has been there from foreigners, from what I see there and from what I have heard from older men who are now dead.

12091. Do you think that the system of the registration of mares is practicable?—Oh, yes.

12092. Do you think it would be useful?—It would be useful, and, I should say, would enhance their value.

12093. In both cases I gather from you the enhancement in the value of the animal would not be sufficient to keep it in the country—the foreigner would probably give more for it?—I think so.

12094. It would only benefit the farmer?—Yes.

12095. It would not benefit the industry in the country?—No; nor would it benefit the breeder in the long run as he would have to sell his good mare.

12096. Do you think that the Irish hunter or high class carriage horse commands a better price in the market from the fact that he is an Irish horse?—Well, I think, perhaps, as a hunter he does, because I think people buy hunters as much from having better performances over the country. They are better horses than the English hunter.

12097. Do you think the greater purity, or supposed greater purity of blood in Ireland would have anything to do with the predilection of people for Irish hunters?—No, I think not. I think it is from their performances they would give more money, not from their being better bred.

12098. Have you a knowledge of the Hackney sire as a sire?—I don't know in Ireland, but in England?—Yes, I have seen a good deal of them in the East Riding of Yorkshire.

12099. Do you think they are suitable sires to get hunters?—Oh, no, not to get hunters. I have known one horse which was by a Hackney—a very good horse—but that is the only one I can remember.

12100. That would be an exception?—Quite an exception.

12101. We have had it in evidence that for a certain class of carriage horse the thoroughbred sire is the best, whilst another says that the Hackney has been brought to Ireland, and that they are superior to anything produced by the Hackney sire. Do you think that that is the case?—Yes. I should say that for a high class carriage horse but not for the ordinary run—the smaller class that many people drive now in the lower carriages, the 15.1 horse or 15.2 horse; but certainly to be the sire of the bigger, finer, dark bay or brown horse, the thoroughbred would be the best sire.

12102. But for a smaller class of harness horse, for which the Hackney would be suitable?—Quite so.

12103. Hackneys are very largely bred in Yorkshire, are they not?—Yes, in the East Riding.

12104. Much more so now than formerly?—Yes.

12105. What effect has it had on the industry of breeding horses in the East Riding—has it made it more profitable to the farmer?—Yes; it has brought thousands and thousands of pounds to the East Riding of Yorkshire.

12106. Used more hunters to be bred there formerly than now?—Very many more.

12107. Is that owing to the introduction of the Hackney, that decrease?—No. I should say not. I should say that it is not that the Hackney has ousted the hunter breeders. I should say it is the foreigners that I have mentioned before, because [those] who have always for generations bred hunters, have sold and sold all their good mares, till at last they could not breed anything worth buying; and then those men have taken to breeding the Hackney.

12108. And Hackneys proved more profitable?—Well, it has proved profitable.

12109. Your opinion is that they have ceased to be able to produce the hunter?—Yes; through having been tempted to sell their best mares.

12110. Do you know Ireland well enough and the condition of the horse breeding there to give us any general opinion as to how, in your opinion, the industry of horse breeding could be encouraged, assuming that State money was devoted to that purpose?—I do not know enough of the districts. But if there are districts where they do not produce in blood hunters, where there are small, little cobs, I would not say ponies, but weedy, well-bred little things, there I should say that they would do much better to have Hackney stallions in those districts than thoroughbred horses, simply with the idea of breeding suitable animals for harness. They would breed enough for carriage purposes and that class of horse.

12111. Do you think the horse got by a Hackney is a suitable country horse?—I don't, except when out of those little, well-bred, very well-bred mares.

12112. Would you anticipate any danger to the breeding of hunters in those parts of the country which are devoted to breeding hunters, from the Hackney blood gradually dribbling into it?—I should be rather afraid that it might in the course of time.

12113. You think it would be difficult to keep the two districts separately distinct?—I should be a little bit afraid of it.

12114. Lord Londonderry.—You have judged a good deal at English shows as well as at shows in Ireland?—More in England.

12115. Have you the same admiration for the Irish hunter as Lord Carnarvon has—would you put them above the English hunter?—Not above the best English hunters.

12116. You think you have seen first rate hunters from both?—Yes.

12117. The horses you were chiefly struck with for their quality were at Limerick—more so even than what you saw at Dublin in proportion to their numbers?—Yes. In Dublin probably more were sent, and with the idea of winning prizes, but to sell, whereas in Limerick those that were sent were exhibited chiefly with the idea of getting prizes.

12118. Do you think the horses which won prizes in Dublin would fetch prices that would be remunerative to the people who bred them?—Yes.

12119. I think you told the Chairman that you thought one of the reasons of the deterioration in the breed of hunters was the fact that all the best mares went out of Ireland?—Yes.

12120. And if prizes of a substantial character were given, they would enhance the value of those mares so that they would fetch bigger prices?—Yes.

12121. Those mares that would fetch these high prices must be very well bred?—Yes.

12122. Supposing that they bred a foal, and that foal instead of being by a thoroughbred horse had

[illegible]

Mr. [illegible]
The [illegible]
[illegible]

again by a Hackney and turned her way into those districts, supposing that that mare a filly, do you think she would be as valuable as a mare by a thoroughbred horse?—No.

12123. Therefore the value of those mares if crossed with a Hackney would decrease?—The produce would not be so valuable as those by a thoroughbred horse.

12124. Supposing one of those well-bred mares which has had a filly foal, to go on breeding with a Hackney, would you consider that she would be capable by that Hackney cross of breeding a good hunter again in the future?—Yes, she might if put back to the thoroughbred horse again; but I think if she breeds were mostly bred you would find not the [illegible].

12125. You would rather not have the Hackney cross?—Not for a hunter.

12126. Was I right in gathering that you thought that the old-fashioned breed of hunters had very much died out in the East Riding of Yorkshire, and their place had been taken by the Hackneys?—Yes.

12127. Do you think that was due to the Hackney Society being more attractive?—No, I think not. I think it was simply because the Yorkshire farmers are naturally lovers of horses, and they took to the breeding of Hackneys because all the old hunting blood had gone; it is not that they prefer a Hackney.

12128. Just where the North Riding adjoins the East Riding, above Malton they breed a certain number of hunters still?—Yes.

12129. Are there Hackney horses about there as well?—I should say not. I am not living in Yorkshire now, but I should say they are breeding more Hackneys in that part along the southern boundary of the North Riding.

12130. I mean where the North Riding and the East Riding adjoin, you think there is a hard and fast line, that the Hackneys are kept in the East Riding, and they breed hunters in the North Riding?—I think so.

12131. Mr. [illegible].—Do you think that there is so good a sale now for individual Hackneys as there was a few years ago?—I really cannot tell you that.

12132. Do you think that the age for Hackneys that existed a few years ago is as great still?—I think the demand for those has been decreasing.

12133. That is for the high class Hackney?—For medium horses, for small carriage horses.

12134. But yet from what you know of the East Riding of Yorkshire you believe that a great many of those old farmers, if they had the opportunity and had the means, would be glad to go back to their old style of breeding hunters and high class carriage horses?—I think so; I think they would.

12135. Lord Ribblesdale.—You said that the Yorkshire farmers lost their mares and good mares by selling them to foreigners or dealers?—Chiefly foreigners.

12136. That, of course, after a time, ruined the country of the good hunting mares?—Yes.

12137. It has been given in evidence before us that something of the same sort is going on in Ireland—have you heard that?—I have heard it, yes.

12138. That the young mares are taken away and the [illegible] left?—All the buyers will [illegible] they will buy.

12139. I think you stated, just now, that you thought nothing would stop the foreign dealer from taking away the good fillies?—I don't think that anything will stop him.

12140. You have got no idea of how to stop them?—No, except by prohibiting the exportation of mares, which I should like to see done.

12141. Do you think if the fillies were to be in foal at two, three, and four years old, that that would stop the dealer buying them?—Well, very possibly, it might. Very often they would buy a mare that was not in foal, when they would not buy a mare in foal.

12142. If they were in foal, or had foals at foot, they would be less likely to buy them?—It had not occurred to me, but I think that would be so.

12143. Therefore, if any scheme could be devised whereby you could induce the farmers to put their mares in foal at two or three years old, it might prevent the dealers taking the young ones?—I think it might. I do not think that I should quite advocate the breeding from two-year-olds, for the reason that it depends upon whether the animal is thoroughly well kept. If a filly is covered at two years old, and then turned into a poor pasture, then, I think, it might injure her for years. I don't think I should advocate putting them to a horse at two years old.

12144. It was more as to the question of keeping so many [illegible] in the country that I was speaking of [illegible]. I think you live in Northamptonshire now?—Yes.

12145. Do you think a hunting with Hackney blood in his veins, would be likely to cross Northamptonshire, in sight with hounds running fast?—Not after the first twenty minutes, I should say certainly not.

12146. Mr. Wrench.—Would you be in favour of starting a Hunters' Improvement Society in Ireland?—I believe it has been a great incentive to breeding in England. I hardly know enough about the Irish to say.

12147. Do you think that hunter breeders are being bred in England since the inception of the Hunters' Improvement Society?—I think more are bred in districts where hardly any were bred before.

12148. You think it has given an impetus to breeding hunters?—I do, and that it has given an impetus to breeding hunters in England.

12149. And, good as the Irish horses are now, might they not be made still better if a society were started there?—I am afraid I cannot tell you; I have little or no experience in Ireland.

12150. Do you think it would send up the prices of [illegible] to foreign buyers if they could obtain reliable pedigrees?—I think it would, if they would depend upon those pedigrees.

12151. And do you think if Irish hunter sires, such as you appear to be in favour of, could be produced, that there would be a foreign demand for them to get cavalry horses?—I think they very likely might produce good stock out of the small mares, the mares which are not good enough to themselves to breed hunters. I think very likely, that those stallions, not thoroughbred, but [illegible] horses, I think their prices would [illegible] better prices from foreign buyers.

12152. Do you think that foreign buyers would be keen to buy stallions of the weight-carrying hunter type for improving their cavalry?—I cannot say; they might not be [illegible] to buy anything that was not thoroughbred.

12153. You have not experience of the foreign breeding much?—No.

12154. Do you think it would be possible to produce a race of weight-carrying hunter sires without establishing a stud book, as it would naturally follow that you would have a stud book. Stud books have been started within the last few years. In all these Clydesdale and Hackneys, and various breeds there were no stud books, I believe, a few years ago, at all.

12155. And do you think the establishment of these stud books has sent up the value of the breed?—I think it would, among foreigners.

12156. You think the starting of stud books among Clydesdales, Hackneys, and Shires has set up the value of those various breeds?—I do think so, certainly.

12157. Therefore, there would be a good chance of the value of Irish hunters increasing if a stud book were established?—Yes, I do think so.

12158. Do you object to the cart horse cross in hunters?—Oh! yes.

12159. As much as you do to the Hackney, or a Suffolk Punch?—I should not like it.

12159. **You object to that equally with Hackney?** —[illegible]

[illegible]—Object to which?

12161. Mr. Wrightson.—The Suffolk Punch. And you object to the Clydesdale, more or less?—Well, I should object to them equally with a Suffolk Punch.

12162. You would object to both more than you would to a Hackney?—Certainly, yes.

12163. Then if Ireland has obtained its present pre-eminence in hunter-breeding with a large number of these stallions in the country, what do you think is the danger of having the Hackney there, as the hunter men have been able to keep clear of these other breeds, where is the danger of the Hackney?—I object to the Hackney also, but not to the same extent that I should to the Suffolk or Clydesdale.

12164. You think he is less objectionable?—He is less objectionable. I would not say but what occasionally you might find an animal that is worth more money which is by a cart horse, simply because it might be bought by a more heavy man who would want a 15-stone horse. He might find occasionally a good horse by a cart horse out of [illegible] mare—a lovely 15-stone horse; whereas the same mare put to a Hackney would probably breed a 13 or 14-stone horse, which would not command anything like the same price as that by the Shire horse.

12165. Have you been in any of the Hackney studs in the East Riding?—Yes, I was a native of the country. I have been among them all my life.

12166. Do you know that a great many of these horses have a large amount of thoroughbred blood in their pedigrees?—No; not a large amount. The "Denmark" strain, I think, would breed to an old mare that John Hunt crossed, a mare by "Gladiator." I am not aware that the others do.

12167. You have not gone into their pedigrees?—No; I know simply because that this particular breed of horses went back to the old chestnut more than [illegible].

12168. Do you say that the East Riding is the best district for breeding Hackneys?—I mean that the best Hackneys are bred in the East Riding?—Yes; I should say with more quality and better backs and shoulders than what I see from other districts.

12169. Then, if all the horses that have been brought over to Ireland, to serve as those pure animals come from the East Riding they come from the right spot?—I like the East Riding Hackneys better than those from other places—Suffolk or Norfolk.

12170. You think there is a distinction between the Yorkshire horse and the Norfolk Hackneys?—I do; they have better shoulders in Yorkshire. Yorkshire horses have better action and backs and shoulders, and more quality than the Norfolk horses.

12171. Do you think it would pay supposing the Yorkshire farmers would go back to breeding hunters—do you think they would like to do—that it would pay them as well as does the breeding of Hackneys?—They used to go back; but more have gone [illegible] lately.

12172. Would it pay them as well?—Oh, yes; I was not speaking of more than 20 or 30 years ago, hunter horses were able to command £200 a piece.

12173. They get good hunter prices for two-year-olds and three-year-old Hackneys there that now in the East Riding?—For a stallion, perhaps, they do. I know there has been an enormous amount of money brought into the Riding from breeding Hackneys.

12174. Could you find a shrewder lot of people than the farmers in the East Riding? Have you ever come across a shrewder people?—Would you not call them a very capable and intelligent people?—One thinks; most capable and most intelligent.

12175. Then, if they have taken up a particular line of breeding they have done so for some good reason?—Because they like horse breeding and their business has grown. They have taken it up as their business.

12176. Do you think a thoroughbred horse would get foals with as good action as a Hackney stallion?—Do you mean action for harness.

12177. I am talking now of thoroughbred harness horses, the smaller harness horses?—I think the Hackney would get more with more action.

12178. He would be more certain to get action?—Certainly, unquestionably.

12179. You say you don't know anything as to how the cavalry and artillery horses are bred in some of the foreign countries now?—No.

12180. Do you think that any of these dealers if he saw a fine horse that suited him would stop buying if he heard the dam was by a Hackney?—As a hunter do you mean.

12181. Simply as a harness horse?—No, it would not stop the dealers buying them for harness purposes.

12182. Then only fear is that it might come into the hunters and not be detected?—It might or might not be detected. The dealer might detect it when he bought it, but when the purchaser bought from the dealer he might not detect it.

12183. Then some registration in Ireland or in any country would be desirable?—Yes, certainly.

12184. If registration were adopted what danger would there be of hunter breeders using these Hackneys?—[illegible] you mean, by saying Hackney [illegible] that didn't exist there?

12185. If hunter breeders object to using any animals of Hackney blood and if registration were adopted so that you could see which blood was in each animal?—There would not be the danger because they would know how the animals were bred.

12186. Then you think that registration would meet any danger of that kind?—I do.

12187. Chairman.—That is registration of sires?—I suppose you mean registering all these persons [illegible] from [illegible] and a filly the same.

12188. Would you not have to register all the [illegible], horses, and geldings of all the horses in the country?—I think you would have to do that; the same as in the Stud Book, I think you would not [illegible] the mares.

12189. Do you think that would be practicable?—I think so.

12190. What authority would you suggest to undertake the registration of all the horses in the country?—With regard to here in England it is done simply voluntarily, and mares are placed by the Hunters' Improvement Society for the purposes of registered mares.

12191. I merely mention this as an assumption—assuming that the foreign buyers of remounts would prefer to buy an animal that had no Hackney blood in it; for instance, it would not be probable, would it, that the owners would be voluntarily registering them. Would it not have to be compulsory?—It would be better to be compulsory, no doubt; but I think you would find in most of the cases they would do it voluntarily and be glad to do it. I should not charge them any fee for doing it. In England I think they do charge a fee of 5s. or so, but it might be well done without I should say. I would give every inducement to the breeders and small farmers to register their mares.

12192. But in England this is a purely private matter and they voluntarily register in certain societies. If you had a system of registration obligatory universally all over the country it would have, would it not, to be undertaken by the State?—It would be better to be done so.

12193. Would it not be the only possible way in which you would ascertain that it was done?—Well, it might be done by the local agricultural societies in the various counties.

12194. Providing the State gave them sufficient powers to enforce it?—Yes.

12195. You don't know the West of Ireland personally, I suppose; don't know the congested districts at all?—I don't.

Monday, 12th, [illegible]

The Rev. David Legard.

12195. I am going to ask you a vague question. Have you such a general idea of the climatic conditions and the conditions of soil and the class of farmers that inhabit the country and so on, as to be able to say that there is any corresponding district in those Islands where, by the introduction of Hackney stallions, a profitable class of carriage horses has been produced?—I am afraid I have not very much opinion, in fact I am no believer as to the suitability of soil for breeding horses.

12196. I am exceedingly anxious if possible to ascertain the kind of place that these small carriage horses—these rather inferior carriage horses got by Hackneys—would finish in the breeder, and where they all go to, where they are used, and so on. I don't know whether you could give any opinion. We have had a good deal of evidence before us that the introduction of Hackneys into the congested districts might result in producing a valuable class of horses, but I never yet could entirely in any capacity see what the gain would be?—Well, there is a great demand for them now. You see twenty carriage horses driving through the streets of London to every one you did perhaps thirty years ago, and that is the very class of horse that goes in those carriages. The carriages are also lower and lighter and smaller than they used to be. They drive them single in broughams and little phaetons, bays and chestnuts with white legs, while formerly people only drove big carriages and good horses, not Hackneys at all.

12197. Have you any idea of what this animal is worth to the breeder?—It would depend upon the age at which he sold it.

12198. What age are they generally sold at?—I think the dealers buy them through their agents in the districts. I cannot really tell you that. I should think they buy them probably at from £30 or £40 and upwards, get them into condition and sell them in pairs and get whatever they like for them.

12199. Buying them as three-year-olds?—I should think so, probably.

12200. Where are they kept?—They would be well kept in Yorkshire.

12201. You don't know the congested districts well enough to say whether you think the mares there with Hackney sires would produce that kind of foal—whether they would be sufficiently well kept to finish anything like that price. You could not give an opinion about that?—I am afraid not. I believe the people on the land there know how to keep their youngsters much in view.

12202. You have no personal knowledge of that part of the country?—No.

12203. Where are most of these light carriage horses bred—chiefly in Yorkshire?—I should think so—in the East Riding of Yorkshire.

12204. Do you know any part of England or Scotland where they are bred by very small farmers?—No; my experience is simply confined to that place.

12205. Do you think they could be profitably produced in the Highlands of Scotland?—They are good constitutioned animals.

12206. They can stand the climate?—Certainly; they are good constitutioned hardy animals.

12207. Are they used in Yorkshire for farm purposes?—Oh, no, not for working on the land; they might drive them a little, they are not heavy enough for that.

12208. Lord Enniskillen.—In answer to Mr. Wrench you said in your opinion the East Riding of Yorkshire is about the best district to get Hackney horses from?—Yes.

12209. Now, why?—I think they are a better class than what I have seen of the Norfolk and Suffolk horses. They have more quality. They are better animals; they have better hocks and ribs and middles.

12210. Are you talking now of **pure-bred** Hackneys?—Yes, the pure-bred Hackneys.

12211. Do you think because a horse comes from such a district it necessarily makes a horse a good one?—No; I don't mean that. I mean that you can breed a better horse in that district than in another.—Is that what you mean?

12212. No, I mean this—because a horse comes from a certain district does that necessarily make the horse a good one?—If he comes out of good stock he is bound to be a better one than one who comes from a district where the stock was inferior.

12213. Regardless of conformation or anything else?—Well, if there is a good breed of horses in one country, we will say in the East Riding of Yorkshire, you will be safer in sending for a stallion from there, in my opinion, than you would if you sent for a stallion from Norfolk.

12214. They are all in the same stud book, are they not?—I don't know the Hackney Stud Book at all.

12215. Mr. Fitzgerald.—With regard to the other breeds of horses that are shown in Yorkshire, the Cleveland and the Yorkshire coach horse, have you any experience with regard to those two breeds?—Very little.

12216. Would they be in your opinion suitable or unsuitable to be crossed for large harness horses or hunters?—Much more suitable to cross than with the high knee action; you would be disappointed if you crossed them with hunting mares with the idea of getting hunters.

12217. But for the large harness horse—carriage horse?—Yes, yes; they would be most valuable.

12218. Which do you prefer, the Cleveland or the coach horse for breeding the kind of horses you see driven in London?—I think the Bay Cleveland; they have a little more quality, I think, than what is called the coach horse, but I think there is very little difference in their quality. The Cleveland is longer, and has his tail set on higher; he is a brighter bay than the coach horse; although the coach horse, I think, has the best bone and size.

12219. You would not like that introduced as a cross into hunter breeding to get weight and size?—No; I should not like that introduced. I think you would get more valuable animals from those than you would with a Hackney cross as a hunter; but I don't approve of it at all.

12220. To get weight and size as hunters you would perhaps prefer them to Hackneys?—Oh, yes; I would prefer them; for where there has been one hunter got by a Hackney or by a thoroughbred horse out of a Hackney mare, there are numerous instances of very good hunters by thoroughbred horses out of Cleveland mares.

12221. The headquarters of both the Cleveland and the coach horse are more in the extreme North Riding of Yorkshire, and the other chiefly in the East Riding?—Yes; there are a few places in the East Riding where they breed the big carriage horses, but it is chiefly, I think, confined to the North Riding and farther north still.

12222. Mr. Carew.—You would not recommend the introduction of Hackney blood into a district where the farmers would be obliged to use the produce for farm purposes?—Well, a great deal depends upon what the land is like that they would have to work. They would not do for ploughing in England; they are not heavy enough, but I could not say on Irish farms.

12223. You don't think they would be useful for ploughing?—Not in England.

12224. Mr. Wrench.—Do you know that the horses that do much of the work on the small farms in Ireland now are very small. Has that ever come under your notice? You don't know that?—I don't know that.

12225. When you talk of the East Riding being a good district or not, of course a district does not make any difference in the horse, but would you think that a Hackney that had a large proportion of "Denmark" and "Fireaway" blood in him had a certain value from his blood?—Certainly I do.

12226. There is some with that strain of blood would be the right strain?—I do.

12227. Do you think England is one of the best countries for breeding horses?—It always had that reputation, and I have no doubt that it is so.

12228. And do you think, therefore, that horse breeding in England is a sufficiently important industry to warrant a system of State supervision being introduced?—Oh, certainly. In England [illegible] people who buy horses for hunting rely almost entirely upon Ireland for their supply.

12229. And therefore, you think any steps in that direction would be warranted by the importance of it?—Most decidedly.

12230. Chairman.—There are many horses in Yorkshire breeding these light carriage horses by Hackneys who cannot always be sold, [illegible]—what becomes of the others? What are they used for? How are they worked?—They are still driven. They will come down to [illegible] purposes of [illegible]—light conveyances, I imagine—tradesmen's carts, and things of that sort.

12231. Mr. Walrond.—Don't misfits of thoroughbreds sell very badly, too?—Oh, yes.

12232. When you get a misfit of that light carriage class the case is [illegible], except that a misfit of a Hackney would be really more serviceable for light [illegible] and other things, whereas a thoroughbred misfit would be [illegible].

12233. Chairman.—We have been told in evidence in Ireland that in breeding hunters and light-legged carriage horses, the misfits are very serviceable as [illegible]. That is why I asked you particularly as to what would be the value of the misfits of this light kind of carriage horse?—Well, if they were big enough, they might do for omnibuses; if not, they would have to go for small [illegible] purposes.

12234. You don't know whether the Hackney blood is considered suitable for [illegible]?—I don't know as a fact.

12235. I don't mean as a matter of opinion, but as a matter of fact?—I can't speak as a matter of fact. No.

Mr. Hobby.

Mr. Hobby examined.

12236. Chairman.—You live in the neighbourhood of Hull?—Yes.

12237. Are you engaged in breeding horses?—I am.

12238. What kind do you breed?—Almost all classes. I have several years bred Hackney mares, two or three thoroughbreds, and then I have some half-bred mares that I breed from.

12239. Half-bred mares?—Of all classes.

12240. You keep a stallion or stallions of your own?—I always keep two, a Hackney, a Shire, and a thoroughbred.

12241. And of your own mares, what mares do you put to the thoroughbred, and which to the Hackney?—I only breed pure-bred Hackneys from the Hackney, but all kinds of mares I put to the thoroughbred. The best Hackneys, those that are in the Hackney book—they are very expensive, these that make £15, £20, and £10, and nothing less than £5; the third-class ones at less money, £3s. and £2.

12242. You breed only pure-bred Hackneys?—Pure-bred Hackneys. I may have occasionally, just for a trial, put a Hackney horse on a young cross-bred mare, just to see what they will breed.

12243. And what has been the result of that?—I would not give an opinion, because some of them never breed twice alike. The same cross-bred mare won't breed twice alike from the same horse.

12244. Do you look upon the breeding of the pure-bred Hackney as a profitable part of your business?—It is now. You get a good name, it is the most profitable, but many men have done very badly by trying to breed the wrong horse.

12245. Would you recommend the Hackney stallion to cross with the ordinary mares of the country about you?—It is every way, depends upon what you want the produce to do; for a working animal the thoroughbred in every sense of the word.

12246. What class of mares do you put to your thoroughbred horse?—I have two thoroughbred mares, and I [illegible] mares to those, and the breeding hunters.

12247. Do you sell any horses as carriage horses that is got by a thoroughbred?—Yes, when they don't fill for hunters, they generally make useful carriage horses. I breed those very classes, by [illegible] thoroughbred with good action, good colour, and good limbs, and I find I have generally a useful carriage horse if they don't fill for a hunter.

12248. Yorkshire men are devoting themselves a good deal more than they used to breeding Hackneys?—Yes.

12249. What is the effect?—The effect is, that where they have got these horses they have done pretty well—very well indeed—with many of them; but with some of them badly. If they are not thorough enough to produce these horses, which foreigners and every one else come to buy, they get a very poor price indeed.

12250. We have been told that the reason why they have given up to a considerable extent the breeding of hunters in Yorkshire is, that the class of mare that they had, the hunter mare, has disappeared?—Yes; but I don't altogether agree with Mr. Legard in the way they disappeared. I think when the high prices came for the Hackney, when some would have to pay the little farmer looked to the first thing he could part with to realise his expenses in any way, or to raise a little money, and he found that the old thoroughbred mare, the old blood mare he had got about the place, could be parted with by him. And there was some one who had a little money left, and he knew the mare, and saw what she had, and he would not part with her. That is the way they went, and he has never been able to get her back.

12251. And then he turned his attention rather to the Hackney?—Yes. The inducement that people were getting rather large prices for [illegible], and they got a Hiley or Bell, and the young ones have begun to breed from them; and some of the old ones have done very well, and others badly.

12252. When you produce a high class animal it gets a big price?—Yes; very well.

12253. You don't consider the price very profitable if you can only breed a light carriage horse or that kind of animal?—Certainly not.

12254. You say that in breeding with the object of getting hunters you breed a misfit as likely to become valuable, and sell at a fair price as a carriage horse?—If he has got the size.

12255. What opinion of the misfits of the Hackneys? I mean not the pure bred but the ordinary?—There is a very good thing about them; so long as they are [illegible] work they are very useful ones, we are not troubled with them very long, they don't last.

12256. Lord Tweedmouth.—You have three stallions, I understand, a Hackney, Shire, and thoroughbred, do you limit them to a definite number of mares a piece?—They rarely have more, I cover very few but my own.

12257. Which is the more popular?—The Hackney is more popular in Yorkshire than the thoroughbred.

12258. Do you sell the produce of your breeding yourself?—Oh, yes.

12259. Direct to dealers, or do you supply customers?—For my hunters I have good customers.

June 8, 1888.
Mr. Bobby.

amongst gentlemen. I "make" them myself and my son "makes" them, and I ride them until they are five or six years of age, and if they are good enough I can get plenty of gentlemen to buy them. Several gentlemen have come to me six years in succession for weight-carrying hunters.

12259. You would not yourself think of crossing a hunting mare with a Hackney to get a hunter?—It would be the worst you could have to ride across country.

12260. You think Hackneys should be kept entirely to their own lines?—Well, I have occasionally bought—I never bred one from a blood mare by a Hackney horse—very beautiful riding horses and beautiful harness horses, and occasionally you can get a very superior animal now from a superior class of Hackney—a blood-looking Hackney from a blood mare.

12261. It must be a great chance?—You have a fair chance, but the best mares don't always breed the best. You find the commonest mares it will breed breed the best animals.

12262. Have you been in Ireland at all yourself?—No.

12263. You don't know the class of mares there it is proposed to improve the breed of in the west by crossing with these Hackneys?—No; I have bought many Irish horses, but been never been there.

12264. Do you think a Hackney crossed with a poor class of mare is likely to breed an animal worth money in the market?—I should have very poor faith in breeding from a Hackney in that case.

12265. From a poor underbred pony you would not get much?—I am afraid not, but I would not give an opinion because I have never seen the mare. I am afraid you would not get size enough.

12266. Which market are your Hackney stallions?—I have bred all my own, but of course I cannot use my own because they are from my own blood, and I have to use other people's. I like a Hackney stallion that breeds for riding purposes with good colour and good action, because I could look for the [illegible] market. I want one that for the little trotting things which would not sell at all.

12267. Do they go out of England, abroad?—Do the foreigners buy them?—Yes, I have to make geldings of those and sell them to dealers. I don't know what they do with them.

12268. Mr. Fitzwilliam.—You say that Hackneys don't race?—Certainly, they don't hunt.

12269. And for that reason you think that they don't remain in the country long—in the East Riding?—They don't stick to work.

12270. In the main the high class Hackney at the present moment is a class animal taken to long?—Yes, exactly.

12271. Is it the case that mares with Hackneys and the half-bred mare do not sell now as well as some few years ago?—I think not, for the reason that we are getting more of them. A few years ago there were not so many bred, and the consequence was there were not quite so many of the class you speak of. Now you are getting more of them, and they make less money.

12272. And I suppose other people besides you discovered that they didn't sing, and that might affect them?—Yes, but there is a difficulty in getting rid of them at all.

12273. Do you think that the breed of the Hackney will remain in the East Riding now it has got a firm hold there, and that will make it very difficult in after years to return again to the high class hunter breeding or the high-class carriage horse breeding?—No, it is not so difficult as that; some just [illegible] again into the other breeds. As soon as ever the craze for the Hackney goes over they will return to breeding other horses, but it will take some time of course.

12274. I haven't any doubt you would clear out of them altogether if you found they were not remunerative; but still there are a great many men that would not be able to clear out of them entirely, and they would go on with the mares they had, with the taint in their blood?—There is no doubt about that.

12275. If the public know of the taint, and thought it to be a bad case, it would damage the prestige and the sale of the East Riding horses?—As hunters, there is no doubt of it.

12276. You find you can get size enough with the thoroughbred close for what you want in breeding?—My experience has been that I get more size with the thoroughbred horse than with any other horse; you get more power and more substance.

12277. And if you select thoroughbred sires with action you find the produce out of half-bred mares has action enough for all useful purposes, generally speaking?—There are thoroughbred horses to be got with as good action as any Hackney in the world. I have mentioned several with as fine action and more quality of action. The action I speak of is not action up and down, but it is a horse with liberty of shoulder action and hock action. If you can get that in a thoroughbred horse, it gives as much as a Hackney to show in what he gets.

12278. You think that liberty of shoulder action is a valuable thing in harness horses as well as in a hunter?—In every horse, because it makes him able to trot fast with action in his walk as well as in his trot, with liberty of shoulder action, will do more work by half than the one who has not got action.

12279. Usually, has the Hackney got that liberty of action?—I know he has got very extravagant knee action, but has he got that shoulder action that you require?—Certain breeds have. There are two or three sorts of action with the Hackney's quality of action, in the action I speak of.

12280. Then all the Hackneys that you go the stud book are not of this particular breed; and it is shown that there are certain sorts of Hackney?—Some people like one class of action, and some another; it is the shoulder action and liberty of action and quality of action that I want. I don't care whether it is of a thoroughbred or Hackney or cart horse, or any other sort.

12281. Lord Ribblesdale.—What strain of blood are your Hackney sires?—I have five Hackney mares at stud at the present time. I bred one mare I got a second prize with at Windsor, she is of the "Denmark," "Triumph," and "Fireaway" blood; she is in foal to "His Majesty." I have had two foals from her; one by "Agility," and another by a horse of Mr. Moore's, "Rufus." I have one in foal to "Reveller," another to "His Majesty," and another to a horse Mr. Moore sold last year, "Chieftain," for two or three thousand pounds. These are good bred Hackneys.

12282. Do you think the breeding of the pure bred Hackneys pays badly (now) because it is if you go in the pure bred blood you must have fashionable blood on both sides?

12283. Do you think the breeding of the half-bred Hackneys pays bad all round and that is so?

12284. That is the cross of the Hackney with the ordinary mare?—I would not like to say so.

12285. With the ordinary mares of the country. Supposing you had a mare that was a little deficient in bone, would you go to the Hackney to get the deficiency in bone?—I would rather take the thorough bred.

12286. Taking the Hackneys all round, as a general rule—I don't allude merely to the Yorkshire Hackneys—but taking them as a rule, do you think that they have good shoulders—that is as a breed?—Yorkshire Hackneys have, they are the best type, and they have better quality and better shoulders than any other class of Hackney.

12287. All Hackneys are included in the Stud Book, are they not?—Yes.

12288. Therefore, when I speak of the Hackneys I speak of the Hackneys generally. Do you think as a general rule that the shoulders are good?—One

Yorkshire Hackneys, and the Hackneys from all other places are quite a separate animal. I have seen breeding between the Norfolk and the Yorkshire Hackney, but I never saw a cross from the Norfolk to the Yorkshire that ever did good to my idea, and I have never seen one from Yorkshire back to the Norfolk that ever did any harm; it always did good. Crossing, I think they are two different animals altogether. The Yorkshire animal has very much more quality than the Norfolk Hackney has, but when they have a large type of the Yorkshire animal with them it is improving to the quality of their shoulders, and makes them more riding horses.

12290. What objection has a Yorkshire man then to using a Norfolk sire, or the Norfolk man use the Yorkshire sire there?—It has been tried, and it has been done. It has been tried many times. They lose the quality; the Yorkshireman loses the quality; he gets all the thickness of hock and the rough neck which our Hackneys never had before.

12291. Do you find any difference in the shoulders?—There are some classes of our breeds have uncommonly good shoulders; most of the Yorkshire Hackneys have, and the Norfolk have a little deficient in the shoulders; they are thick across the top.

12292. Do you find the crosses of the Hackney strong and large, or apt to be light?—I could not say that; they vary so much. One will be light and another won't be. As a breed I would not give an opinion.

12293. Is it a strong point in the Hackneys as a rule to have good action and fair height?—Yes; I think they are fairly good shape.

12294. In Yorkshire?—Yes. I think they are fairly good, when they come to age, you know.

12295. And in Norfolk?—I haven't found fault with them there. It is more with the shoulders and the quality and the hock and necks that I have found fault in the Norfolk, thick in the throat, rough undoubtedly, [illegible] in their breeds.

12296. From your experience of horse-breeding and what you have seen in Yorkshire do you think there is great danger of losing the mares' good mares out of the country?—Oh, yes.

12297. A great danger of that?—Yes.

12298. It would be almost impossible to replace them if you once let the good mares out of the country?—It would be very difficult to do, because the farmer would not have money. They like farmers are not [illegible] for them, and those who do haven't [illegible] to keep them.

12299. Do you think in any horse-breeding countries they ought to be very careful in not letting the good mares go out of the country?—Certainly; that is the first thing they should care for.

12300. Mr. Clarke.—Have you ever tried the horse race with the thoroughbred and the Hackney?—I haven't, but I have an experience of a person who has.

12301. With what result?—Some of you gentlemen will know a horse that Mr. Walter Gilbey bought called "Danegelt"; I suppose he gave the highest price for any Hackney horse for that one—£5,000. He [illegible] for many years. He served three mares of my own that I know; one was a Cleveland bay, another a Yorkshire cart mare, and the third was one [illegible] or two crosses of blood.—I think then I had a little thoroughbred horse that came from Lord Dunsley, and I think he never cost more than £20. I gave £20 for him, and sold him again for £25. The [illegible] colts from the same three mares. I got two of them made; one made £125 and the other £100. The one from the cart mare was sold to Mr. [illegible] for £210. Now, those same mares were put to "Danegelt." I won't be certain, but I know they bought them cheap, and I think they brought five. There never was one of them that made £30.

12302. Chairman.—As to the latter part of the answer, are you certain about that; of course you have to explain what you got for your own horses?—Perhaps I ought not to go so far as that. I saw two of them at a fair, and the man who had them said he was asking £35 for the best; and what he got for them I don't know, but he had not sold it.

12303. Mr. Clarke.—Was your horse a Hackney?—No, a little thoroughbred.

12304. Have you ever put the same mares to a Hackney and to a thoroughbred?—These mares were put to the Hackney and to the thoroughbred.

12305. Oh! I see; your own was a thoroughbred and not a Hackney?—Mine was a thoroughbred horse, and he got on to the same three mares. He got the three first, and "Danegelt" got on to those afterwards. I won't say those were bad foals—I had better say that—but there wasn't one of them I would have bought at any price, and the others were three useful horses.

12306. Mr. Walker.—What sire were those mares?—One was a mare I think by "Tom Bowler"—a blood mare, about 16 hands high—and the other was a half-breeding Cleveland mare, 15.3½; the third was a cart mare—a little undersized cart mare. I bought two myself, and a neighbour of mine bought the other.

12307. Your experience is that a Hackney cross is much better with a blood mare than with a cross-bred mare from what you said before?—I would not put a Hackney horse up to a cross-bred mare at any price. I think you have a fair chance to get a good animal from a blood mare or a very good one from a Hackney mare by a blood horse. I happen to have two or three very superior animals out of a nice quality Hackney.

12308. And I suppose what happened in this experiment with "Danegelt" might happen to any horse?—Certainly; it was a one-sided trial, that is what it was. "Danegelt" has got some of the best horses we ever bred and I should say he has got some of the very worst.

12309. You say the Hackneys are not worked now. Is not the reason that so many horses they are becoming so valuable?—There might be something in that. But I always notice that our farmers who have Hackneys, if they want to ride or drive, they buy horses with a strain or two of blood.

12310. Are they bred from animals that used to drive long distances and do a great deal of work?—I heard of it.

12311. Have you any reason to doubt it?—I have never seen them do it.

12312. It was before your time?—Before my time.

12313. Do you think if any other style of horse-breeding paid the Yorkshire farmers better that they would not turn to it?—Of course they would.

12314. They breed Hackneys because they find it pays best?—They get the price.

12315. You don't like Norfolk Hackneys nearly as well as the Yorkshire?—I do not.

12316. And still you own a couple of your success to "Agility"?—Yes; when a three-year-old, but he was a finer type than any one I had ever seen; but he has not improved, and it is my impression that he is not going as quick looking as he was.

12317. Do you think, as a rule, that thoroughbred horses produce stock with as good action as Hackneys?—Not quite so high, but with quite as much liberty, and rather more so.

12318. When you go to a fair, does not action help you to sell a horse?—I should think so; you are right.

12319. If you are dealing with horses that have no action, would it not considerably be desirable to have extravagant action, so that one of the two sorts would get pretty good action?—Yes; but I consider you can get action in the thoroughbred—you must have action.

12320. If you want to sell?—Yes.

12321. Chairman.—I gather from you generally that you think it profitable to breed the pure bred Hackney?—Certainly.

12322. But that you should not think it particularly profitable to breed the half-bred Hackney for light harness purposes?—I don't.

[illegible]

13349. Not the pure-bred Hackneys, but I am talking of the general run of horses which inherit the Hackney for carriage purposes?—I don't think we properly realise how badly our small Hackneys are so sold. I think we have never been asking for working purposes, or very little up to the present time, but we find that the small, clean and [illegible] are wanting.

13350. What I wanted to get at from you is, putting aside the breeding of those larger high-class pure-bred Hackneys, whether the Yorkshireman breeds Hackneys for harness purposes because it is more profitable than any other kind of breeding, or because he thinks it more profitable [illegible] to breed harness as well as [illegible] the hunter having disappeared—in other words, has the production of hunters been replaced to a considerable extent by the production of harness horses, because the latter was more profitable, or because the hunting [illegible] have largely disappeared?—None of us try to breed harness horses. We try to breed something better, and many of them turn out to be harness horses, and we have to make the best we can of them.

13351. Mr. Fitzherbert.—Don't you think it is rather the case that they breed these Hackneys and half-bred Hackneys now because there are in the East Riding such a large number of first-class Hackney stallions in the country that they are really obliged to go to them—the smaller men, I mean?—I think it is to a certain extent the reason, but we are not breeding many cross-bred Hackneys. Most of the Hackneys that are bred in Yorkshire are all bred with the idea of getting into the show-yard. There are very few cross-bred Hackneys bred in Yorkshire. No farmer that I know of is breeding cross-bred Hackneys at all. The mothers and fathers are all entered in the Hackney book, or they would not breed them. Only a very small proportion are by any but pure-bred Hackneys.

13352. Do you think the reason of that is, to a certain extent, that, as you say, like does breed—that is, the produce out of a half-bred mare by a Hackney stallion—is unreliable; you do not know what you are going to get?—Certainly you cannot be sure of what you are going to get; in fact, out of the cross-bred mares you mostly [illegible]. You must have purity of blood to [illegible] this uniformity to breed with any fair chance of getting a useful animal.

Hackney mares, were they purebred?—Yes, and I put them to the most fashionable—well I won't say most fashionable—to fashionable sires of the day, and selected the sires to the best of my judgment. I did not take the first I saw, but I looked to the conformation of the sires, and compared them with the mares I proposed to put to them, and then compared the pedigrees, so that I used a fair amount of caution in mating my mares.

12251. The object being to breed high-class animals?—I did not expect to breed high-class animals at first, because they were not high-class mares, they were not fashionably bred, they had not the conformation.

12252. And what was the result?—Nothing encouraging; they will be what your last witness described, they will soon wear out. I don't know what will become of them eventually.

12253. Did you discontinue that?—I have one mare left now, and I don't think I shall breed from her again.

12254. Out of what kind of mares have you bred your hunters?—The mares I began from first were mares with at least four crosses of blood, and I have had some very serviceable animals from them, horses that have carried me well in Holderness, which is a very heavy country.

12255. With what kind of sire?—Thoroughbred; I have used some sires that have not been Queen's Premium winners, but I have used a good many of the Queen's Premium winners, notably, "Peppermint," "Sherbrooke," and "Monkscroft."

12256. You have bred them for your own use?—Yes, I have tried the experiment of putting a hunter mare, a mare with four known crosses of blood that I could positively trace, and there were more behind which I could not really verify, and therefore never gave her credit for, but from the conformation of the mare herself I should judge she had several more crosses than those four I knew of, she was rather light of bone, and as an experiment I put her to a strong Hackney in the hope of getting more bone. It was a theory that I think Mr. Burdett-Coutts started a great many years ago now. I thought it was worth trying, that was the idea of putting a thoroughbred or nearly thoroughbred mare to a Hackney horse, and in the produce you would get more bone and increased action, so that in case it did not turn out to be a hunter it would prove a very useful and saleable harness horse. Well, my first venture at that was a failure. I put it to a horse called "Darlington" by "Denmark," who was at that time thought a good deal of. After that I went to blood, and used a thoroughbred horse called "Lambton."

12257. What was the result of the Hackney cross?—A little underbred thing with no action; well it had a nice trotting action but it had not size, it took after the mare's action; I sold it for a park hack. After that I went to blood, and this mare bred me several very good foals, the eldest is ten years old; I am riding it now. Five or six years ago the mare bred me rather a smaller foal, but the thoroughbred there I liked, and I thought I would try the experiment again, and that time I picked out a very strong Hackney horse that had a strong suspicion of a carting cross on one side. The result of that cross was even lighter than my "Darlington" one, a very nice pretty little mare, but nothing more than a hack, and not more than a twelve stone one at that. The following year I put her to the thoroughbred horse again, and she has bred me a very promising colt. I also tried the Hackney cross, the same strong horse I spoke of, to a mare by "Peppermint," a three-stone hunting mare, one I bred, that was out of a mare by "Sea Rock," that I had hunted, and the result of that was a nice upstanding horse, but I tried to hunt him and found he was so soft he could not go beyond two fields, and I then reduced him to harness, in which he did fairly well.

12258. This particular Hackney you say had a strong suspicion of carting blood?—Yes, he was the strongest horse I could find in the district. One horse was full of the purest Hackney blood, and the other horse was a horse that was in the Hackney Stud Book; but still there are bad [illegible] of breeding, and there was a strong suspicion that there was a strain of cart-horse blood. [illegible]

12259. Was it a suspicion in his appearance?—It was a suspicion in his appearance, and as a matter of fact as well; these things are hardly stated, but they [illegible] to prove.

12260. Did you give us the name of the horse?—The second horse was "Carlton," the strong horse.

12261. Mr. Watson.—Was he not by "Foreign Fireaway," belonging to a man named Kirby?—I think [illegible] the horse; he was a very strong horse, and I thought would make an excellent cross with this light Premium mare.

12262. Chairman.—And the result was unsatisfactory, principally on account of the soundness?—Yes, there was not a great deal wrong with the conformation; he had [illegible], but it was his [illegible] made me drop him.

12263. Then I gather you don't think highly of the Hackney cross as far as riding horses are concerned?—I don't think so at all; they have not the riding shoulders.

12264. As to harness purposes?—I have often noticed that the Hackneys that you see in London up and down Piccadilly and once round the Park in a day's work, and they don't want to do more than three days a week.

12265. And your objection to them as harness horses would be the same, that they are not [illegible]?—I think so; I have had them two or three, and when I drive them to the [illegible] a [illegible] miles from the house on a nice fine road they would go beautifully and keep their heads up, but when I wanted to go to Beverley, twelve miles off, and when I was [illegible] miles on the journey, they would drop their heads, and the action was gone, and when you got half way you had to get your whip out.

12266. In the Beverley district you breed mostly?—Yes, a great deal, principally Hackneys; that Driffield district is given over to Hackneys now.

12267. What kind of Hackneys do they breed?—Very nearly all pure; with the large farmers they are all pure bred with a few exceptions. Some of the smaller ones, like [illegible] and pig dealers and so on, when there was this boom in Hackneys if they had a nice quick stepper or anything in the shape of a light animal that would in these hard times, they put it to the Hackney and thought they were going to get something that would be worth perhaps £100.

12268. When you say "a large farmer," do you imply that they [illegible], it was a great disappointment.

12269. What do you call a small farmer about you?—A small farmer there would be a man farming from thirty to fifty acres, and there are very few small farmers about Driffield.

12270. Don't you consider that breeding these pure bred Hackneys, high class Hackneys is a profitable business?—The earliest ones, such as have been in the business since it started, but I think ones who have gone into it lately [illegible] they will not have found it so profitable an occupation.

12271. As to breeding Hackneys from the ordinary country mares by Hackney stallions, do you consider that a paying business?—I don't think it is if they have not a Hackney mare or a strain of the Hackney again. I am speaking of pure bred Hackney stallions, because I don't think there are any known half-bred ones, but if a man had a mare of the Hackney type and put her to a pure bred Hackney stallion he might expect to get a good-stepping horse. Then if he had a mare of a rather hunting type he would be inclined to put her to a

3 K

thoroughbred horse. Had I known that I should be asked to appear before this Commission I would have brought up some particulars with me, because I had the Queen's Premium stallion "Newbury" with me for two years, five or six years ago, and I kept a very careful record of the class of mares that were put to him, and if it would be thought interesting I think I could look up the papers when I get back and tell you exactly the class of mares that were put to him.

12370. I think that would be very interesting?—The groom was an intelligent man, and I was deeply interested in the subject, and I told him to be very particular to note down in the book. I had a book ruled, and for him; he had to take down, among other things the stamp of mare put to the horse, whether hunting mare, Hackney mare, or cart mare; of course if there was no doubt about it he would put it down, but if there was any doubt I inquired into the matter and went and saw for myself.

12371. Do you know Ireland at all?—No, I have never been there.

12372. Well, putting on one side for a moment the question of breeding pure bred Hackneys for show purposes and so on, have you any experience at all in Yorkshire of the results of the Hackney sire with the country mare?—I know of very few instances where he has been used on anything but thoroughbred, or what I will call half-Hackney mares. I have only my own experience as to the results of the Hackney stallion on anything but hack mares.

12373. I suppose you could not very well give us an opinion as to whether the Hackney stallion—the pure-bred stallion—put to a small light class of mares, such as exist in the West of Ireland, would be likely to breed a valuable [illegible]?—Not having seen the cross I would not like to express that opinion, but I may mention that a friend of mine interested in horse-raising in the North-west of Canada had a light weedy class on his ranch, and thought to improve the [illegible] produce of his ranches by introducing the Hackney blood. He came over to the East Riding of Yorkshire, bought two stallions there, and I have never heard that the experiment was a success. I have never heard of his getting more than about £40 for any one horse. He sent a consignment over one time and I should not like to say what he got for them, but the price was disappointing and not remunerative.

12374. But about you in Yorkshire, they do not breed this kind of horse?—I have not heard of any; I don't think that cross is practised at.

12375. You cannot say whether there is any great demand for that class of animal?—I should say there would be none.

12376. Mr. FITZWILLIAM.—In your opinion from what you know, should you think that the cross of the Hackney would be calculated on a breed that is more closely thoroughbred [illegible]; I am speaking of the Irish mares?—From my experience I should be inclined to think so.

12377. And for the reason that you gave, that they are soft?—Yes, they are soft and they are not riding horses, and the present craze in breeding these Hackneys is to sacrifice everything to extravagant action. They are losing their bodies and they seem to look at nothing but action, so that I think [illegible] the Hackney might have they are fast losing [illegible] out of him.

12380. And therefore for general purposes you would expect us to [illegible] as to the Irish mare?—I think so. I think as a general purpose horse the Hackney is [illegible].

12381. Of course our inquiry does not relate to the high class Hackney to any great extent, but to the pure Hackney, it really relates to the sorts to what would be the [illegible] produced both in the first cross and in [illegible] breeding?—Well, from my own knowledge in the [illegible] Hackney horses that are not quite good enough for show are a poor sort drug in the market. You don't know where to place them, and you don't know what price you may get for them.

12382. And have you any experience, as one of the witnesses told us that you cannot depend on breeding true from from the Hackney out of the half-bred?—[illegible] it may come to nothing.

12383. And you think you can to a great extent rely on breeding true from when breeding from a pure bred, a thoroughbred?—To a great extent. I think when you have seen the first foal from a mare by a thoroughbred horse you can to a certain extent calculate what the produce may be.

12384. You don't think that there are such a great many half-bred Hackney-produced animals in the East Riding?—I don't know of any.

12385. Lord DUNRAVEN.—It has been given in evidence that Hackney breeders breed mainly for action, and that they have left conformation out of the question. Is that in your opinion a sound method of breeding horses?—Very much the reverse. I should breed for conformation first. I like a good top piece, a place for the heart to work in, plenty of [illegible] and a back, and I like [illegible] particularly fond of shoulders, which is a thing you very seldom find in these modern Hackneys. I say modern advisedly, because the Hackney of to-day is very different from what I remember him twenty-five years ago. They used to call them roadsters then at the local shows, and some of those roadsters had good action, not the extravagant action you see nowadays. I should say they would be pleasant horses to ride twenty years ago, but these have been destroyed [illegible] the East Riding. You don't see them there now.

12386. Then you think in breeding horses, as in breeding anything else, that conformation is the first thing?—Constitution and conformation, and if a horse has true conformation I hold his action will not be very far wrong. One is [illegible] whatever [illegible] you have [illegible] to mate her with. That has been my object in breeding. I have not taken the first horse that came up, but I have gone out of my way to try and find—I don't say that I have succeeded—but to try and find horses that by their conformation would correct the weak points in my mares.

12387. Mr. WRENCH.—Do I understand you to say in answer to Lord Dunraven that the [illegible] breeders do not take conformation into account?—I should not like to go quite so far as that. Hackney breeding now has become a sort of system; they look to the blood. Certain strains of blood are very successful in the show yard, and men will go to that strain of blood or mare in the hopes of getting a winner.

12388. About Driffield you have seen very good examples of Hackney breeding?—Yes.

12389. Do you think Mr. Nixon does not breed well?—He does, but he will take conformation and the breeding, the line of blood into account.

12390. You would say that he is intelligent in the mating of [illegible]?—I think he takes great pains in mating his mares.

12391. You don't condemn all Hackneys, even at the present day, do you?—There are some good ones, but I take it that they are not riding horses.

12392. I mean for harness?—Well, I think they are more for show than for work.

12393. I am not talking of what the tendency of the show is to produce these extravagant goers, but I mean in the Hackney in the East Riding. Can you get bad horses that are descended from the old roadsters?—Yes, that is what I mean. [illegible] the class of mares I speak of which had good riding shoulders, and you could ride them for ten or twenty miles without your being tired, or their being tired either. Mr. Nixon is one of the few men who have got these old stock, in them, and then to his [illegible] cropped out, so I should say you would get as good Hackneys with Norfolk as you could find. At the same time I should not like to say that a great many of them were not a bit soft, did not like long journeys, or that many of them.

12386. You think they have bred out the old type?—More people have.

12387. Do you find that there are many good Hackney mares to be given away? You said you had two given to you?—Oh, yes, under peculiar circumstances, but I have seen many sold at a pretty good [illegible] price.

12388. Do you know anything how they were bred?—They were Norfolk bred. They are in the book.

12389. Do you know what stallion either of them was by?—I could tell you in a moment, if you allow me to look.

12390. It does not matter. When you say you went out of your way to find good horses, do you think you were rather unfortunate in selecting "Darlington" and "Clarence"?—I may.

12391. Do you know "Darlington" was sold a short time ago for a very small price?—That was "Darlington II.," not "Darlington" himself.

12392. How long ago was this experiment you made?—These mares were put to "Darlington" in 1880 or 1881.

12393. I thought it was [illegible]?—She would be put to "Clarence" seven or eight years ago.

12394. Now take "Clarence." You say he has some strain of cart blood in him?—Well, it was strongly suspected.

12395. Do you know that he was not considered good enough to keep as a stallion?—I don't know about good enough.

12396. His owner did not keep him?—No, he had not the same [illegible] for him.

12397. He was a common-looking horse?—Yes. They are plenty common, I mean, that is hardly a test. My idea was going to start a breed as I could find.

12398. Even though he had a trace of cart blood in him?—Yes. A suspicion, I think, I said.

12399. Have you ever seen the produce of Hackney stallions with thoroughbred mares? The produce of a thoroughbred mare by a Hackney stallion?—No, I cannot call it to mind.

12400. Then when you talk of the country-bred mares in Yorkshire, are they really many of them thoroughbred with a certain amount of half-bred mares in Yorkshire?—It would be very difficult to say how many of those were bred.

12401. But there are a good many animals there under that class also really quality that you find [illegible]?—They have what I call under-bred carriage horses, but of the carriage type—not of the higher type at all—probably they have not been big enough to work as those large, strong-built horses, and they are sold for what they will fetch.

12402. Lord Londonderry.—Have you ever seen anything of the strain of mares that is in the west part of Ireland?—No, I have not. I have never been in Ireland.

12403. Have you seen Hackneys **crossed with a** pure class of mare?—No, I have not.

12404. You have no idea of what result would be obtained by crossing the Hackney with a light mare?—No, I merely knowledge this only of a friend of mine who was in Canada and crossed some of the [illegible] they had on the prairie—half thoroughbred, [illegible] mares, and so far as he has ever told me, the cross was not a success.

12405. Chairman.—You have not seen those [illegible]?—No, I have not seen those. It is only hearsay.

12406. I should gather from what you have said is, that if you wanted to breed Hunters you would not [illegible] Hackney blood introduced?—No, I don't think so.

12407. We have [illegible] don't **know whether it** is the case about Driffield—that in Yorkshire generally the supply of hunters and the highest class of carriage horses has fallen off. That the large carriage horse in Yorkshire [illegible] from.

12408. That has been attributed in various quarters to the introduction of the Hackney breed, and to the fact that the hunter mares have disappeared, and so on. Have you any opinion on these points?—Yes. I think it is quite true that the hunter mares have disappeared, and since the Hackney breeding industry got such a lift a few years ago, men who had been breeding these Hackneys in a small way got such encouragement, and high prices were given for stallions, and very high prices were given for mares. Then there arose a foreign demand, so everybody rushed into breeding Hackneys. Now, the law of supply and demand comes in. People have got supplied. People who wanted to start studs have got their foundation stock, and there is not the demand for the ordinary animals for breeding purposes, and, therefore, unless you have got anything quite first-rate—good enough to show—it is a drug in the breeder's hands. So, I fancy, in the Driffield district there have been some very great disappointments from the Hackney breeding. It is going up suddenly and has died away.

12409. It has been suggested to us that the Yorkshiremen in general, the farmers, would be glad enough to revert to breeding hunters and that class of animal if they could, but they cannot, because the mares have disappeared. Is that, as far as you think of it?—I am afraid it is. And, you see, they have learned a lesson in this way, that in the breeding of Hackneys there is more money in profit than the hunter, and there was so much less risk to run. A promising Hackney they can get rid of at a good price from two to three-year-old. I am speaking of the good Hackneys, and there is no more risk, as he can then be taken to the show and run up and down in a string, or if they keep him a little longer, he can [illegible] to the stud. Whereas with the hunter you must keep him to four years old, and he must have as much [illegible] as to "make" him. That is hardly a theory of my own. They find that the Hackney comes to mature quicker, and there is so much less risk attending the bringing up. But then they would be glad to go back to breeding hunters, and, of course, in that Driffield district, from Scarborough Road to Spurn Point, and right up to Bridlington and York, with very magnificent [illegible], there were some very good horses bred. In that Holderness district there were some hunters bred.

12410. I should gather from you that you think the producing a very valuable Hackney is still a paying business, but does not pay so well as it did because the demand has rather fallen off?—That is so. If you can produce the best animal in the Hackney line, you will get a remunerative price for it, although the price is not so remunerative as it used to be, and one thing that proves this is that so many of these men who were [illegible] have reduced their [illegible] fees. A few years ago there was nothing under five guineas, and anything that had anything of a record had ten guineas. Now this has got down at five guineas and three guineas, which shows the demand has slackened.

12411. As to the inferior Hackney, [illegible] the cross of the Hackney with the country mares, you don't think there is much demand for that?—There is very little demand for the inferior Hackney, and I don't know any good where the country-bred mare has been mated with a Hackney.

12412. Do you know of [illegible] Hackneys being bought as remounts?—I have never heard of them. I think there is very little remount buying in our part of the country. The only time I [illegible] about the [illegible] buying remounts. They bought

[illegible] Mr. [illegible]

[illegible] Mr. Bryant.

very few entries—did not take at all, so I gather there is very little army-buying done in our part of the country.

13421. Have you ever considered at all any steps that could be usefully taken to keep good mares in the country, to induce the farmers not to sell them?—Well, there is the giving of prizes at local shows. I have often thought about it, but it would be a difficult scheme to work, if it could be done, where a man had a good mare and was breeding from her every year to give him a bonus on her foal. But all these schemes are so difficult to work out. But I think that having numerous local shows and giving prizes there of fair value, and if possible to give several prizes of equal value, would have the effect of rather encouraging breeding. I am sure of one thing, that the Royal Commission on Horse Breeding has given horse breeding somewhat of an impetus, because it has put a sound horse at the command of anyone who cares to use him at a low fee, and, of course, the horse's whereabouts is well advertised, so anyone who takes any interest in really producing good horses always knows where he can command the services of at least a sound horse.

13422. We have had a great deal of evidence before us that Ireland has been considerably denuded of the best mares which are bought to go abroad, and some witnesses think the only remedy is to provide the country with sound and suitable stallions, and others, that something should be done to keep the mares in the country?—I am afraid it would have to be a very big scheme to induce men to keep mares in the country. Because when a buyer comes and offers a poor man a very good price for a mare it is a very great temptation to him to part with her, and one that very few men can resist.

George Richardson.

GEORGE RICHARDSON examined.

13423. CHAIRMAN.—You live near Leeds?—I live in Leeds.

13424. Are you engaged in dealing in horses?—I am.

13425. And have been for some time?—Twenty-five years.

13426. What class of horses do you deal in?—Hunters principally and harness horses, riding horses.

13427. And where do you buy them?—In Ireland.

13428. Buy all your horses in Ireland?—Yes. I am obliged to go to Ireland. I cannot get them in Yorkshire. I used to buy them in Yorkshire. Could get plenty twelve years ago, but now there are none left.

13429. Plenty of hunters, and the class of carriage horses you wanted?—Yes.

13430. What kind of carriage horses?—Sixteen hands to say 16.2 hands.

13431. In former days where used you to buy them?—From the breeders in Yorkshire.

13432. What age did you buy?—Fours and fives.

13433. Have you any objection to tell us at what kind of average prices?—It all depends on the animal; the lowest price we gave was about £40.

13434. What would you call a high price?—Oh, £120, that is for hunter horses. I give a great deal more for hunters; £200 to £300 very often.

13435. And now you say you cannot get them in Yorkshire?—It is impossible to find them.

13436. How do you account for that?—Because they are breeding Hackneys. They have given over breeding hunters, and they have gone in for breeding what they call Hackneys.

13437. Do you suppose they have done that because it pays them better?—I think they have made a great mistake, it paid just at first; it was a fashion, everybody wanted Hackneys because they were the fashion, but it is only a small section for the [illegible] that want; if you ride or drive them four or five miles they tire, they are worthless.

13438. And in your opinion you think the farmers breeding horses has made a mistake?—I am sure of it; they have ruined all the farmers in Yorkshire, except a few that have got stallions and made three or four.

13439. Why do they not go back to breeding hunters?—They have not got the mares; they have sold their best mares. I remember fifteen or twenty years ago you could buy from ten to fifteen horses a week in Yorkshire; now you could not buy one good horse.

13440. Where have those mares gone to?—They have gone abroad; the foreigners have bought them all.

13441. And your opinion is that the horse breeder has done himself a good deal of harm?—I am sure of it; they thought well about inferior Hackneys; they cannot give them away; they cannot breed them, they only ruin.

13442. I suppose the pure-bred, the best Hackney you can breed is a valuable article, but there is no such thing as a pure-bred Hackney. You can get anything into the book; you can get anything in if it has taken a prize at the show, no matter how it is bred. If the man steps a bit and gets a prize, the man gets him into the book.

13443. The Hackney that would win a prize at a show, is that a valuable animal to breed?—My experience of show horses is very bad; about the worst horses you can find.

13444. Would it pay the breeder to produce him?—I cannot say as that. If you can get a good one it pays him, but how many do they get, not many.

13445. What happens to all the inferior Hackneys?—They are walked about the country from fair to fair; they are very bad to sell.

13446. Have the Yorkshire farmers to your knowledge made any attempts to try and get back again to breeding hunters?—I am afraid they are too poor. They have lost their best mares and cannot replace them.

13447. Can you suggest any means by which if they were able to afford it they could replace them?—I don't know, I am sure, the farmers are very poor in Yorkshire in my experience.

13448. But assuming they are not very poor or could be assisted by some one? Where would the mares be got from into this country?—They could be bought in Ireland. There are plenty of good mares in Ireland to be bought. What you want is strong, thoroughbred mares, as strong as you can get them, and you cannot get them but with bred ones though. There are plenty in Ireland.

13449. You have since bought these horses in Ireland?—Yes.

13450. Whereabouts?—All parts, principally in the South and West.

13451. Not much in the North?—There are not many good horses bred in the North.

13452. Have you attended the principal fairs?—All the principal fairs all over Ireland except in the North.

13453. And you did find what you wanted there?—Well, they are getting rather difficult to find now. I remember the time when it was quite easy to find them, but it is not so easy now. Everybody is going over there to buy, and probably the hunters in Yorkshire are bought in Ireland as young ones and brought over and schooled and sold as hunters. Nearly all the hunters that are sold in Yorkshire are bred over here. What are sold to go as bred in Yorkshire are none.

13454. And the supply in Ireland has not kept up to the demand?—I am afraid it has not.

13455. Can you form an opinion as to whether the supply is as good as it was ten years ago?—I am sure it is not.

12336. Then not only in numbers [illegible] absolutely there are not so many good ones?—I am sure there are not so many. It is a great mistake of Ireland to allow the good horses to go out of the country; everything ought to be done to stop it.

12337. You said a while ago that there were plenty of good mares?—Yes. Something ought to be done to prevent foreigners getting them. I have often seen a foreigner riding a horse along the fair [illegible] and I offer him a good price [illegible].

12338. You [illegible] think it objectionable for the foreigners to bring the good mares, but you would not think it objectionable to take them to Yorkshire?—[illegible] should not keep them out of the country. A premium ought to be given at the show to farmers for keeping good mares [illegible]. At present they give prizes [illegible].

12339. Assuming [illegible] was done by the Government in the way of a grant of money towards horse breeding in Ireland, you think [illegible]?—[illegible] You [illegible] blood horses without [illegible].

12340. How do you think that could be best done practically?—It would be rather hard to say. [illegible]

12341. Have you any opinion as to the effect of the introduction of Hackney blood into Ireland?—I think Hackneys are not any good at all. [illegible]

12342. You think he is not much use as a light [illegible]?—No; if you drive them three or four miles they hang their heads [illegible]. It is a misery to drive them.

12343. Do you know the [illegible] West of Ireland?—I go all over Ireland.

12344. You know the kind of mares, the small [illegible]?—I do quite well.

12345. Would it not be a great advantage if [illegible] could be introduced [illegible]?—[illegible] thoroughbred horse with strength and action. [illegible] if you only get strength with it.

12346. Don't you think a suitable Hackney would give them [illegible]?—[illegible] They would be breeding back instead of breeding forward with Hackneys. You cannot get a horse too well bred if you only get strength with it. [illegible] the Hackney and the thoroughbred [illegible] and drive twenty miles. You will get through with the thoroughbred; you won't get through with the Hackney [illegible].

12347. Talking of the [illegible] districts of Ireland, do you think by any means they could breed hunters?—It would take some time, but they would improve [illegible] thoroughbred horses. [illegible]

12348. Supposing they turned their attention to breeding for harness purposes, what [illegible]?—Thoroughbred. There is no horse in the world [illegible] harness or riding horse, as good as the thoroughbred.

12349. Have you seen any of the thoroughbred stallions standing in remote parts of the country?—I have seen them travelling about. [illegible] in Ireland. I think it would be a [illegible] in Ireland if they were to [illegible] and not allow them to travel unless they passed [illegible] for soundness and strength and [illegible]. A great many of the stallions [illegible] in Ireland [illegible]. Of course [illegible].

12350. Would you be inclined [illegible] Hackney [illegible]?—I should certainly not send the Hackney [illegible]. I [illegible] thought. I [illegible] Hackneys in the country."

12351. How did you form that opinion?—I have [illegible] and bought a good many. I [illegible] of the best of Hackneys [illegible] a great deal [illegible].

12352. I take it what you think would be necessary for Ireland [illegible] in the country?—If you possibly could.

12353. And secondly, the introduction of suitable sound thoroughbred sires?—Yes, with plenty of strength.

12354. And that for any purpose the introduction of Hackney blood would be bad?—[illegible] I think.

12355. Do you consider the Hackney blood to be worse than [illegible]?—[illegible]

12356. Have you ever seen a good hunter out of a thoroughbred mare or out of a half-bred mare by a Hackney stallion?—Never in my life. [illegible] I will guarantee he will trace back to thoroughbred blood.

12357. Don't they all trace back eventually to thoroughbred blood?—A great many of them [illegible]. [illegible]

12358. A great many horses go through your hands that you buy in Ireland?—About [illegible] a year.

12359. And the price you pay [illegible]?—I don't think there is much difference.

12360. Do you buy at fairs?—I buy from dealers and at fairs [illegible].

12361. Have you agents over there?—Oh, no, I go there myself. I [illegible].

12362. You have never been in the [illegible]?—Oh, yes, [illegible] they are kept in the [illegible] and [illegible] thought [illegible] and [illegible] they get ill, you have to get them [illegible] in the [illegible] west of Ireland the horses are [illegible] and many [illegible] with [illegible].

12363. Do you think the [illegible] for Ireland [illegible]?—[illegible] you could buy plenty at [illegible] apiece.

12364. Where would you get them?—All parts of Ireland. You don't want a horse that could win the Derby or Leger; what you want is a thoroughbred horse with strength and bone and [illegible] and good action.

12365. And you think they could be obtained?—For [illegible] each, quite easily, plenty of them.

12366. Lord Londonderry.—I gather that you are not an admirer of Hackneys?—Well, I have had a great many of them; my experience is very bad.

12367. One gentleman stated that he had driven long distances with a Hackney, that they did not tire; you have tried them yourself and found they do?—I have [illegible]. The Hackneys they call now used to

March 10, 1897.
Mr. [illegible] Robinson.

[illegible] Yorkshire coaching mares, they were very good, they used to cross them with thoroughbred horses and they would stay; but these they have at present cannot stay at all, they are no good only just for show, just for about ten minutes and then they are tired.

12489. Then your idea would be that if these Hackney stallions get into the horse-breeding districts and are crossed with mares that bred good hunters, they would ruin the breed of hunters there? —I am certain of it.

12490. You would not expect to buy a hunter from one of these well-bred mares by a Hackney stallion? —Certainly not, you cannot breed a hunter too well bred if he has strength. If you put blood into a good strong mare he has more blood in him. If you take a common horse, the first place he crosses up he lies down and you cannot kick him up.

12491. You think a Hackney cross would do this? —No quality in it at all.

12492. Have you bought horses in Ireland? —Yes, all over Ireland.

12493. I suppose in Limerick, in Kildare and Westmeath you bought mostly? —No, I bought plenty in Cork and Limerick.

12494. Of what sort and class? —Yes, 15.3 hands.

12495. And up to carrying weight? —Yes.

12496. As a rule do you know anything about pedigree? —I don't care much about pedigree, he shows his pedigree himself as soon as you look at the horse.

12497. But you would not buy a horse unless it gave you the idea that it was by a well-bred horse and by a well-bred mare? —Certainly not, it is quite easy to tell a well-bred horse from a bad one.

12498. Do you find a large number of people go over from England? —Yes, a great many.

12499. Do you find that they will buy a horse that pleases you [illegible]? —I cannot say that.

12500. Is the supply diminishing in the [illegible]? —It is not, the demand is growing than the supply. I remember, ten years ago when I went to Ireland, it was very easy to buy horses. Now you have to travel a great deal about Ireland before you get a good horse.

12501. You buy a great many horses that you require? —I am sorry that are too young for me, that I cannot do with. I would have them four years old or older. I could buy plenty of young horses if I could afford to keep them, but I have no means of keeping them. I must buy them ready for sale.

12502. Is there a market for those young horses? —Oh, yes, there are plenty of markets for them.

12503. Those are by what sort of sires? —By thoroughbred horses.

12504. And there is a demand for them? —A good demand.

12505. And they fetch a good price? —A very good price. Plenty of farmers in England go over there to buy them and make hunters of them. I know farmers in Yorkshire who buy eight or ten at a time.

12506. Would they buy them if they were by bad horses or Hackneys? —They would not, they would not bring them to Yorkshire at all.

12507. Therefore, so far as Yorkshire is concerned, these animals would be a drug in the market? —Certainly, they would not sell them.

12508. You rather imagine that there are not the same number of good horses in Ireland as there used to be? —Yes, I think the foreigners have taken the best mares out of the country, and it would be a good thing to stop them, although it is a good thing in Ireland. But if they are [illegible] we shall soon be without horses.

12509. Why do you think they sell them? —Because they want to get the money, making a few. I buy a mare that is famous in Ireland into the fair, he does not want to sell the mare; I say "if you get a good price won't you sell her?" and then they begin to waver, and when I offer a good price they sell, but if you offer them a price that they would [illegible] if they sold the mare it would induce them to keep the mare.

12510. Supposing a better class of stallion were introduced into Ireland, do you think it would be worth the while of the farmer to keep that good mare, because the weight of the first a good breeder, may be ensured by the produce that he would sell to people like yourself? —I think so. I think the stallions want to pass a Government inspection in practical form; I have a great many of the stallions that are sold to go to different parts of the country and these Thoroughbred horses were supposed to be kept to improve the breed of horses, but they are simply machines for [illegible]. If they were bred with more strength and substance, if they could get more money, they would do much good for a breeder of hunters; but as they are now they are [illegible], a great many of them, they are little weeds.

12511. I think you said in reply to the Chairman that you could buy any number of stallions that you think would be capable of doing what is required in Ireland at £200 a piece? —Buy them in England, there are plenty to be bought.

12512. What class of horse would you suggest? —A horse of 15.3 hands, to carry 13 stone, I like, in weight, of build, you want them that strength.

12513. What breed? —It does not matter so long as they are thoroughbred.

12514. Do you insist on their being thoroughbred? —Certainly.

12515. And you would not advocate any other class of horses being introduced? —Certainly not.

12516. You deprecate Clydesdale, Shire horses and Hackneys? —I would not have anything but a thoroughbred; if you put a strong thoroughbred and work horse together to plough, the thoroughbred horse would tire the other horse, if you keep ploughing all day.

12517. Have you seen any stallions in Ireland? —I have seen a great many, nearly all.

12518. Are they good or bad? —Some are good and some are bad.

12519. In the districts where thoroughbred stallions [illegible], have you bought some good hunters, animals you would like? —I bought some very good hunters all over Ireland, and sometimes you cannot believe how the farmers say a horse is bred, because if a horse is [illegible] at getting good animals, they ask more to buy the horse if he is that kind.

12520. But still you would not buy a horse unless you liked his appearance? —Unless I liked his appearance and strength.

12521. The Chairman asked you if you had seen some of those mares in the congested districts, which, after all, the Hackneys were intended to benefit? —I have seen a great many of them coming into fairs, they are very poor rosses.

12522. Do you think they are capable of being improved? —I am sure if they got thoroughbred stallions it would improve them, they would breed better horses than those are now to the Hackney.

12523. What would they breed by the thoroughbred stallion? —Riding horses, polo ponies, and Hackney horses.

12524. The first cross? —Perhaps not the first, the second one.

12525. You think it is a question of time? —Yes.

12526. You don't think in those poor districts they would get more chance by being crossed with the Hackney? —I think not; there are plenty of thoroughbred horses, with more bone, than the Hackney, and the bone is much better. If you drive the Hackney twenty miles, next morning his legs are filled like [illegible], if you drive a thoroughbred horse the legs are as fine as silk.

12527. The ponies of the poorer classes in the West of Ireland have not much action [illegible]; I have not much chance of judging their action. [illegible] with them in carts.

[illegible] You would be careful in selecting a thoroughbred with action?—Certainly, I would buy [illegible] with good bone and [illegible]. In all horses you want [illegible] such action. [illegible] If you [illegible] a horse [illegible] and [illegible] to get behind [illegible]. If you [illegible] will always [illegible] that way.

[illegible] As far as I gather your opinion from your experience of Ireland in all parts is that there ought to be nothing imported to improve the blood but thoroughbred horses?—Certainly not; I would not [illegible] but the thoroughbred.

[illegible] Mr. [illegible].—Would you really mind [illegible] bred in the country [illegible]?—I would rather have a thoroughbred one.

[illegible] Suppose you were not able to get the [illegible] number of horses?—I would prefer [illegible]; I think there are plenty to be got [illegible]; it is not necessary he should be a [illegible] as long as he is thoroughbred and has [illegible] and quality.

[illegible] The Hackney in Ireland [illegible] there is no doubt that if you [illegible] great action [illegible] a very [illegible] thing; do you think that the [illegible] is likely to be taken [illegible] as a stallion?—They would certainly, but [illegible] they would not [illegible].

[illegible] But that will place them [illegible] the farm [illegible]?—Of course; the Hackney stallion [illegible] they [illegible] and [illegible] for the [illegible] if you [illegible] their [illegible] and [illegible] their heads, you will have to [illegible].

[illegible] You think if the Hackney is introduced into Ireland, it will produce a [illegible] class of animal which will be [illegible]?—Certainly, and the [illegible] of the Hackney—as they call [illegible] very [illegible]. If you [illegible] a Hackney [illegible] or [illegible] we a thoroughbred, [illegible] legs [illegible].

[illegible] Colonel St. Quintin.—You are speaking [illegible] of the riding class?—I buy a good [illegible] horses.

[illegible] [illegible]?—No.

[illegible] You say you buy very few horses in the North of Ireland?—Very few.

[illegible] Why is that?—Because they [illegible] in the South and [illegible] in the North, [illegible]. They bring them [illegible], and when you get [illegible]. They [illegible] a great number of horses in the North of Ireland, but they are different [illegible] in the South [illegible] they have [illegible].

[illegible] Any horses [illegible] that you see in the [illegible] and [illegible] in your [illegible].

[illegible] You have travelled about the North of Ireland [illegible]?—I have been all over it.

[illegible] Don't you think the North of Ireland is [illegible] of producing the same class of horses as the [illegible]?—[illegible].

[illegible] [illegible] the [illegible] do you think the Hackney blood [illegible] for [illegible] purposes?—I think it is [illegible].

[illegible] It may be [illegible] but [illegible] give [illegible]. If you buy [illegible] If you put a [illegible] and thoroughbred horse in harness one will kill the other. You want horses for usefulness; people don't buy them to look at.

12544. You don't think the Hackney is useful blood to introduce for the harness horse independent of the riding horse?—Certainly not; they used to breed good horses in Yorkshire, because they used to have the old Yorkshire mares and cross them with thoroughbred sires; but now they are breeding from these Hackney stallions—they are simply between a cart-horse and these Yorkshire mares. There is a horse, "Star of the East," that used to take a great many prizes. He was a Hackney stallion; I believe he was from a cart mare.

12545. You have seen a great deal of what they call the [illegible] class in Ireland?—I have.

12546. You know the class of horses I buy for remounts. We have had several gentlemen who have advocated the Hackney as a useful horse to cross for military purposes—more for riding than driving—are you of that opinion?—Certainly not.

12547. Do you think that his formation and action is useful?—I think it would be entirely useless.

12548. Lord Rathdonnell.—I think you said you bought several mares in Ireland?—Yes; I buy more mares than horses.

12549. Do you buy for the foreign market?—Yes. I buy for the English market too, but I send a great many abroad, I sent 600 abroad last year.

12550. What age do you usually buy them at?—Four-year-old and upwards, nothing younger, unless it is a thoroughbred that has run—a racehorse.

12551. But you don't buy half-bred ones earlier than four?—No.

12552. Do you ever buy mares that are in foal?—Never; well, I have bought a few thoroughbred mares, but not half-bred mares.

12553. But if a half-bred mare happened to have a foal at foot, would you leave her alone?—I would not buy her at all.

12554. Did I understand you to say that your opinion was asked regarding the introduction of Hackneys into Ireland?—Yes, Mr. Jackson travelled over with me from Holyhead one night, he lives near me, and buys his horses from me, he asked me about it, and I told him then—it was a great mistake if he brought Hackneys in.

12555. Chairman.—You were not consulted by the Congested Districts Board?—Oh, no; we were just speaking as we travelled along.

12556. You gave no opinion in writing?—No; he just asked me for information and I told him what I thought.

12557. Lord Londonderry.—Have you spoken to any of the dealers in the South of Ireland and ascertained their opinion on the introduction of Hackneys?—I never mentioned it.

12558. Mr. La Touche.—Would you buy horses with the same confidence in Ireland if you knew the Hackney horse had been largely introduced?—Certainly not.

12559. Have you ever seen any of the produce of these mares, that you bought, by a Hackney stallion?—I never bought any Hackney mares in Ireland to my knowledge.

12560. No, but you say you bought Irish mares, and probably sold some of them to people who live in your neighbourhood?—Yes.

12561. Have you ever seen them bred from?—I cannot say I have, but the mares I sell they breed from them after they have done for riding purposes.

12562. But you have never seen any of the produce of the Irish mares and the Yorkshire Hackney stallions?—No, I cannot say I have. Yes, I have, I sold Colonel Charlesworth a grey mare, he rode her for nine or ten seasons and put her to a Hackney stallion, but she bred nothing any good, and he gave the mare away to a farmer in the end.

12563. Chairman.—What did the farmer do with her?—I don't know; she was a very good mare, I bought her at Ballinasloe.

12564. Mr. Wrench.—Do you breed any horses yourself?—I do not.

12565. Have you ever bred any?—I have not.

12566. When you talk of being in the West of Ireland, what fairs have you attended?—I go to all the principal fairs in Ireland.

12567. Just name the fairs you go to in Munster, if you [illegible] mention [illegible].—I go to all the principal ones.

12568. Do you go to Ballinasloe?—I do not.

12569. Do you go to [illegible]?—I do not.

12570. Do you go to Clifden?—I did not. I never heard of the name of that fair.

12571. Or Oughterard?—I never heard of it.

12572. Ballinrobe?—There are very likely fairs there.

12573. Do you go to Westport?—Yes; I have been there.

12574. And you have been to Galway?—Yes; I go to Galway every year, to Ballinasloe, and I go to Boyle.

12575. But not to any of the other fairs I have mentioned?—None of the others mentioned.

12576. Do you go to Donegal at all?—No; I have not been to Donegal.

12577. Not into the county?—No; I have been in the county but not to any fairs there.

12578. Do you go to Kerry?—Yes.

12579. Which?—I forget the name of the fair, it was some years ago.

12580. Killorglin, was it?—I could not tell you.

12581. Tralee?—I have been to Tralee many times.

12582. Do you know Cahirciveen or Dingle?—No; I have not been there.

12583. Have you been to Castletown Bere?—No.

12584. Skibbereen?—Yes.

12585. Bandon?—No; I have not been there.

12586. So practically your experience relates to the more inland fairs?—Yes; I go to the principal fairs, but those little fairs I don't go to, it would not pay me.

12587. You have not been to any of the places I mentioned?—I have not been to all the places you mentioned, they are not very large fairs.

12588. It merely exactly includes the Congested Districts. Then, Sir, I understood you to say that you would introduce nothing but thoroughbred horses into Ireland?—Certainly.

12589. Was I correct when I thought you said you had seen nearly all the stallions in Ireland?—I have seen a great many of them.

12590. What do you think they mainly consist of?—There are some very good ones and some very bad ones.

12591. But what breed?—I have seen most of the thoroughbred stallions, but I have not seen any of the Hackney stallions.

12592. Have you seen any of the half-bred stallions?—I have not seen one in Ireland in my life.

12593. You don't know that a great many exist there?—I don't think so.

12594. Do you know at all the number of stallions there are in Ireland?—I don't know at all.

12595. You say you have seen nearly all of them?—I go to the principal shows and the stallions exhibit there, and I have seen the stallions that stand in the fairs round the towns serving mares; I see them very often. Of course I have not been to private places to see the stallions.

12596. You would be surprised to hear that there are many such stallions in Ireland?—I should be very much surprised.

12597. When you say that any horse can get into the Hackney Stud Book I suppose a horse would get in that would have no pedigree?—They could get in with a pedigree which I could [illegible] that would give him a pedigree.

12598. Do you say that the pedigrees in the Hackney Stud Book are false?—They are not worth the paper they are written on.

12599. You don't think they are genuine?—I am certain a good many are not, I know some; I have had and sold, and after taking prizes they have been put into the book, and I could not tell the pedigree because I did not know it.

12600. Do you object to the blood of the Hackney breed in hunters?—I would not have that blood at all.

12601. Or Clydesdale?—Certainly not.

12602. Or Shire?—None of them.

12603. You think they would all be equally prejudicial in the better breeding?—Certainly; you cannot get a hunter too well bred.

12604. Do you think there is any danger if nothing but the thoroughbred is used of the produce being too light and weedy?—Certainly not, if you select the stallions, not [illegible] stallions; of course if you buy those weeds of stallions you are sure to have weeds of horses. You must select bigger, stronger stallions, not worse than 16.2 hands.

12605. And you say those stallions are easy to find?—Quite so.

12606. Do you know that the Indian Government have great difficulty in finding them?—Because they don't go to the right place and the right people.

12607. Chairman.—Do you know as a matter of fact that that is so?—I know they say so, but I could find them plenty if they gave me the order.

12608. Mr. Wrench.—Do you think that thoroughbred polo ponies pays the breeder?—I think so; a good polo pony is worth a lot of money.

12609. And if a great many of the Irish mares that we have had sent into the good sorts were so, of course you would not agree with them?—[illegible]

12610. No good mares in Ireland generally, [illegible] there are a good many good mares in Ireland.

12611. You said there were plenty of good mares?—Yes; but of course if you keep draining the [illegible] they are sure to get fewer in time; they are shipped out of Ireland every day, a great number of them leave the country.

12612. What is your trade chiefly, in hunters or harness horses?—Both.

12613. About equal?—About equal.

12614. And is there as much trade do you think in harness horses as there is in hunters?—Oh, yes, quite as much.

12615. A trade that Ireland could supply?—Certainly.

12616. Do you know anything about the trade in horses from America?—I have seen a great many of them.

12617. Are they coming over in increasing or decreasing numbers?—About twenty-five years ago they used to bring some of the best harness horses in the world from America; now they bring the worst; a great many [illegible] he said.

12618. They compete with the second-class horses from Ireland, do they not?—I should think they do.

12619. Can you suggest any remedy by which this competition could be lessened or prevented in any way?—No, I don't think that I could.

12620. Do you think that the American horses that come over now are bad horses?—Yes; [illegible] Ireland; I think it is the produce of those [illegible] stallions they have taken over.

12621. Do you know that American horses are sold in England as Irish horses?—I know they are, but they are very easy to tell.

12622. Then you think [illegible] old [illegible] prizes [illegible] have seen them take prizes at the Dublin Show.

12623. Then we must have had some bad judges?—Judges don't think; half the judges don't [illegible], they just see the horse [illegible] and [illegible] have a different opinion.

12624. The American [illegible]

could only go a short way as bred from Hackneys, were they pure-bred Hackneys?—I don't think there is such a thing as pure-bred.

12625. Were they from what we call pure-bred Hackneys?—They were what they call the Hackney of the present day.

12626. Those that you drove were what they call pure-bred?—Yes. I gave over £300 a-piece for them, so they ought to be some of the best.

12627. CHAIRMAN.—I don't exactly remember what you said about the stallions in Ireland, but I don't suppose you meant us to understand that you had seen them all?—I could not possibly see them all, but of what I have seen I have seen some very good stallions. I think what you want to do is to induce the farmer to keep his best mares to breed from, and to license the stallions that are travelling. It does not matter if you don't charge them much for the license, then it would stop these weeds. The Board would never pass these weeds to travel. I think there is no horse you can get, it does not matter where you buy him, so good as the thoroughbred horse if you can only get strength, that is the only difficulty.

March 22, 1897.

Mr. George Richardson.

12628. Just to be certain about your opinion on one other point. I gather you think that anything except of thoroughbred blood is rather detrimental?—I think there are only two breeds of horses, cart horses and thoroughbred ones.

12629. In speaking to breed hunters I want to know if you think that every strain except the thoroughbred is equally bad, do you think the introduction of the Hackney or Cleveland Bay or Yorkshire coach-horse is all equally bad?—The Hackney is the very worst blood of the lot, because any riding man that rides to hounds does not want a horse to step in the air but to go from his shoulders.

12630. Are there not a considerable number of Hackneys used for riding purposes?—No riding man will ride a Hackney because he is a very uncomfortable animal to ride. He will shake you to death, and when you have ridden him a mile or two he is tumbling on his head if you don't hold him up.

Mr. [illegible] examined.

Mr. Joseph Dawson.

12631. CHAIRMAN.—You live in Yorkshire [illegible]?—Yes, I live in York at present, but I lived the most part of my life in the north of Yorkshire.

12632. Are you breeding horses?—I have not bred any horses for the last six or seven years. I bred for several years.

12633. Are you engaged in dealing in horses in any way now?—No, I don't deal at all now. I did deal at one time and was a good deal in the horse trade, dealing in all classes of horses, but I have not done any dealing for the last eight years.

12634. Can you tell the Commission what kind of horses you bred yourself?—I bred hunters and harness horses, and of course occasionally a cart horse.

12635. Did you keep stallions of your own?—I never had one [illegible]; the stallions I kept were either Hackney stallions or Cleveland stallions.

12636. Did you keep a number of mares?—Yes, I kept just a few mares.

12637. What class of mares did you breed your hunters from?—Hunter-bred mares. I had [illegible] myself, and sometimes I bred from a Cleveland mare—occasionally.

12638. What did you put them to?—A thoroughbred always. I preferred a little thoroughbred horse, if I was breeding from a half-bred mare, I would prefer him [illegible].

12639. What has been the result of your breeding hunters from the Cleveland Bay?—When I had the right class of Cleveland Bay I could not find any fault; if I did not get a good hunter, I got a good harness horse, but unfortunately there are so many Cleveland Bays that are not Cleveland Bays at all, and so many Hackneys that are not the old Yorkshire Hackney we used to know, and there might be all sorts of blood. But if you get a good one you can breed a great animal. I had one I rode [illegible] with the York and Ainsty hounds, as good a hunter as you could get, from a coaching mare. I have one that was by "Knight Templar," he is one of the best I ever rode.

12640. You don't object to the Cleveland Bay or the Yorkshire coach horse?—No, I don't object to them, but I should be very sorry to say that I advocate breeding from those [illegible]. Really the Cleveland Bay was almost [illegible] of knowledge when the Cleveland Bay stud book was started. I started then and tried to get the old breed back; but I found a great deal of difficulty, as owing to the foreign trade, there was a tremendous demand; you could sell horses for almost any price you liked to ask for them, and there were a lot of mares got into the stud book that had [illegible] breeding, their pedigree [illegible] the book and perhaps after two or three generations it throws back again, and the breed gets a bad name. But when I was a lad I can remember Mr. Tom Parrington, he and his brother kept [illegible] some of the best hunters ever seen from Cleveland mares. "Lady [illegible]" was the [illegible] dam from a Cleveland, and the foreigner got that class of horse.

12641. Was your principal object to breed hunters?—I bred either hunters or harness horses.

12642. If it was not quite good enough for a hunter it made a valuable carriage horse?—Yes.

12643. Got about the same price for either?—No, I could get a better price for the hunter, if the hunter could carry weight and was rather good to ride.

12644. And the farmers generally about you, what did they breed?—In the north of Yorkshire, they bred principally cart-horses, and the whole thing turned over when the [illegible] was started. There was a very big demand for a short-legged powerful cart-horse for town work; there are not very many large farms in Cleveland, and they do good [illegible] at that sort of thing. If they could sell a yearling gelding at from £30 to £40 guineas it was good, and they started to breed the Clydesdale. Since, I don't think there are half a dozen good [illegible] in the district [illegible] breeding light horses.

12645. There has been no demand for horses there from a purely financial reason?—Yes, the foreign demand was one thing, and then they lost their mares.

12646. They lost their mares on account of the great foreign demand?—Yes; they sold them to the foreigners.

12647. Was there any particular foreign demand at any particular time?—There was always a steady demand for a good stamp of carriage horse which I can remember as [illegible] very much fifteen or sixteen years ago.

12648. Are many Hackneys bred in the North?—Well, there are not so many bred in the North as in the East Riding, there are a few bred. When I say the North riding I am not quite correct. I am speaking of the Cleveland district. I don't think there are so many Hackneys bred there. The reason [illegible], it is [illegible] breeding district.

12649. You bred yourself?—Yes.

12650. Have you any practical experience of Irish horses?—Yes, I have ridden a great many Irish horses. I have got now a very good horse. I have [illegible] there. I want a big blood horse to carry me; I must have some blood or I cannot get there at all.

12651. You require the blood for the [illegible]?—Yes.

12652. Have you ridden any half-bred Hackney

[illegible]

[illegible]

thoroughbred blood?—Yes, certain lines of Yorkshire Hackneys. [illegible]

[illegible]

[illegible]

Mr. [illegible].

12713. Do I understand you to object more or in the same degree to the Suffolk or Clydesdale, as compared with the Hackney, for hunters?—I don't think there is anything to choose among the three; I think they are all equally hopeless.

12714. You don't think the fact of the Hackney having thoroughbred blood in his back breeding is any advantage?—I don't think so, his action is sure to tire.

12715. Do you know there was a great demand for Hackneys at the late show for foreign Governments?—I heard that.

12716. When you refer to the Church Stretton ponies, are you quite certain a Hackney was tried there?—I would not be certain without my notes; I think it was either there or at Dartmoor.

12717. I suppose Mr. John Hill would be a good authority as to anything at Church Stretton?—Yes, but I would not stand on that; they tried something at Church Stretton that did not answer.

12718. Are they not very small ponies there?—Yes, 11.2 or 12 hands.

12719. CHAIRMAN.—Have you any opinion, supposing there to be a grant for improving the breed of horses in Ireland, whether it should be devoted to trying to improve the mares?—I should certainly do that, I think the mare is the more important animal of the two; I think it is utterly hopeless to expect any very great advantage to be derived from the stallion if you are breeding from a moderate class of mares—it is a very wide and difficult question to know how best to deal with. It is one I have talked over with many practical men. The Duke of Portland's scheme is, I think, a very good one in lending mares to his tenantry, but it is a very wide one and costs a good deal of money. There is one thing might be done, and it would tend to encourage horse breeding, and that is, I would give prizes for groups—foals and yearlings—by a certain sire, let three or four farmers join together, give a good prize, and let them divide it, pro rata, as to the number of foals they showed—that would be a better object-lesson than any show of stallions. It is a difficult thing to say from looking at a stallion what sort of sire he is going to be.

12720. At any rate, I gather you think it would be very important to do something to try and improve the mares, and to keep the good mares in the country?—That is of the very greatest importance; I am very sorry to see so many good mares going away.

The Commission adjourned.

March 11, 1897.

TWENTY-FOURTH DAY—THURSDAY, MARCH 11TH, 1897.

Sitting at 12 Hanover Square, London, W.

Present—THE EARL OF DUNRAVEN, K.P. (in the Chair); MR. J. L. CAREW, M.P.; SIR T. H. G. ESMONDE, M.P.; SIR WALTER GILBEY; LORD RATHDONNELL; MR. F. S. WRENCH; EARL OF ENNISKILLEN; HON. H. W. FITZWILLIAM; MR. PERCY LA TOUCHE; COLONEL ST. QUINTIN.

MR. HUGH NEVILLE, Secretary.

Mr. Wimbush.

MR. WIMBUSH examined.

12721. CHAIRMAN.—You live in London and are in business as a horse jobber, are you not?—Yes, my lord.

12722. Do you sell horses, or only let them out?—Only let them out; we do not sell at all.

12723. Have you any objection to tell the Commission about what number of horses go through your hands in a year?—I thought I would like just to explain to your Lordship that I have no objection to tell you, but, I presume, it would not go, necessarily, very much further than this room.

12724. Well, you see, the publication of the evidence [illegible]. I don't think it is material. I take it for granted a considerable number of horses go through your hands during the year?—Yes.

12725. Can you tell us at all what proportion of those horses you obtain from Ireland?—Yes, my lord, I can; I think, I may say, we have been buying horses in Ireland since 1871; that was the first time we went there. Of course, when we first went there, we had no connections, and, therefore, we did very little; but by degrees it grew, and, after a few years, we came to buy nearly half our horses. Generally these would be about 1880. In 1888 we bought 240 horses altogether, and 101 of them were bought in Ireland; of course the number varied sometimes. I think you may take it that we have been buying nearly half our horses in Ireland; but, in the last few years, we have not been buying quite so many, for two reasons—one is, we have not required quite so many horses. There has not been quite so much demand for them, and then I have found another place where we could meet with horses—that is, in Normandy. I began to go there about ten years ago, and that has rather grown; therefore, we get a certain number from there and do not require so many from Ireland, still we get very nearly quite one-third of our horses from Ireland, and we used to get much more. We should still get more but for this other opportunity, and this not having quite the same demand for them.

12726. What class of horses do you buy?—Chiefly first-class carriage horses; we do not buy anything else.

12727. Do you go over yourself to Ireland, or any member of your family, or have they [illegible] buy your horses?—As I say, I went in 1871, which is a good many years ago. I then went myself, and went every month for many years to work up a connection among the farmers, and latterly I have not gone quite so much myself, but until two years ago I have been going regularly myself.

12728. And you buy direct from the farmers generally or at fairs?—We do not buy at fairs. When I first began to go I used to attend the fairs and go among the farmers, and in those years I bought almost invariably off the farmers and occasionally at the fairs. But as time went on I made the acquaintance of men who were colt buyers, and by degrees it rather dropped into that, and we have been buying [illegible] at first I was not inclined to take their [illegible], but when they get a certain number together I used to go over to see them. Sometimes I used to go, to see every month; he was constantly in Ireland; he sold the horses [illegible], and we used to deal very largely with him; but only took what we approved; he bought with a view of selling to us, we had the first show. He has rather dropped into that; than we have two or three men [illegible] buying, whom we visit periodically, and they do not sell any horses until we have seen their stock.

12729. What age do you buy them at?—Three years old in the summer, and in the spring, if moved, they are coming four.

12730. I think you said you went to Ireland first in 1851?—Yes.

12731. Prior to that where did you get this class of horse?—Yorkshire; we never went further than Yorkshire or Lincolnshire.

12732. Do you buy any there now?—Yes, a few up to within the last year or two; it has not answered [illegible], but I bought a few last year at the [illegible] [illegible].

12733. How do you account for Yorkshire failing to produce that class of horse?—Principally I have been of [illegible] I noticed how the foreigners kept buying young mares. If a farmer had a good colt we should buy him; if he had a good filly the foreigner would take it. They have been doing that for the last forty years, buying every good mare, and then the introduction of Hackney stallions.

12734. You think the breed in Yorkshire has diverted [illegible] to another [illegible]?—Yes; if we go to the [illegible] where we used to buy these colts, we see nothing but short-tailed Hackneys.

12735. Are you particular in getting the pedigree of the horses you buy in Ireland?—Yes, I always like to know it. I always inquire if I am buying of the [illegible], among the breeders you can always ascertain it, but sometimes those [illegible] who have the colt brought on a farm or [illegible] have not taken much notice of it, and you don't always get it from them.

12736. How are they generally bred?—Nearly always by a thoroughbred horse.

12737. Have you in your mind any particular [illegible]?—There was a very good horse called "Victor," which stood in Kilmallock for many years, a thoroughbred, a splendid horse for getting harness, and we had many of his stock too; he is dead now, but there is a young "Victor" called by the name of [illegible] "Victor." I suppose that was the cross; he is dead a year ago, but "Victor" is there still; he is a son of old "Victor"; there is a little [illegible] in him. He is sold in the [illegible] book.

12738. Then the horses you buy are either by thoroughbred stallions or by stallions which are practically speaking considered to be thoroughbreds?—Certainly.

12739. What class of horse do you buy in Normandy?—Well, the horses there are not very large; 15.3 or 15.3 hands, and occasionally up to 16 hands, but they are horses of a beautiful appearance, very handsome and splendid goers.

12740. Do you know how they are bred at all?—I cannot say I do. The great thing in Normandy is for horses to trot in trotting races, and these young horses are tried before we buy them, indeed they are kept as entire horses until they are, whether they are likely to make good [illegible], and if they cannot do the [illegible] in a certain time they take them over and [illegible] [illegible].

12741. You don't know what kind of sire?—I cannot tell, but I do not think they are thoroughbred, but these horses have breeding, so far as you can judge by their appearance, indeed when [illegible] [illegible], if we get them all [illegible], they do not do [illegible], they [illegible] show a good deal of blood.

12742. Lord [illegible].—And those only?—Yes, we have no complaint in that respect, [illegible] of course they are very carefully selected and apparently very highly bred.

12743. Chairman.—Do you think there is a good supply in Ireland at the [illegible] of the class of carriage horses you want?—Ever since I have been there the saying always is there are no horses, and our [illegible] is a very common [illegible] used [illegible] has been, but I must [illegible] say that I think there is very much falling off.

12744. You have to give about the same price?—Yes, we have.

12745. The price has not gone up?—It has not gone down for the best horses, I think in [illegible] the second class horses for I know they are less expensive than they were. I must say I think, if anything, the better class are dearer; people always tell you so.

12746. I suppose you have been over a good deal of Ireland?—I have.

12747. Where have you principally bought?—The best horses in the county Limerick and county Cork. There are no good [illegible] except in the south; there are two going north of the Boyne. But there are some very good horses bred in Meath, some of the most valuable and expensive horses, both Cork and Limerick, there [illegible] good [illegible].

12748. I suppose you don't know the western way [illegible] of Ireland?—Slightly; I have been there, but it is not a good horse country.

12749. Lord [illegible].—Did you ever buy any horses in Armagh?—I have, but there much of the [illegible] you meet with in Armagh are bought in the south as colts and brought up to the north and [illegible] [illegible] very highly.

12750. Chairman.—And you think that the demand for higher carriage horses is falling off?—What I mean rather is this: we find that our old [illegible] customers, the nobility and so on, as they die off, the younger generation do not take horses in the same way their predecessors did. People [illegible] are more in the habit of just getting horses for the season. The old customers used to have horses all the year round, and that class of customer is rather dying out.

12751. In your business have you any horses to your knowledge with any Hackney blood in them?—I don't think so, an occasional one might be bought in Yorkshire.

12752. Do you think it is or is not suitable?—I am very much against it.

12753. And why?—You do not get the size, colour, or body, or blood that you want.

12754. How about the action?—Well, those [illegible] in said that these [illegible] horses, bred by thoroughbred horses, are deficient in action, most of course if you were to buy them [illegible] without [illegible] probably in [illegible] to a [illegible] extent, but I have bought horses in the south of Ireland by thoroughbred horses with as much action as you wish to see and it is a very remarkable thing that you may see horses that step very high, you may put them to work [illegible] in no greater [illegible] than [illegible] the action away, and [illegible] they have no action. You may buy a beautiful [illegible] horse who does not appear to have much action, but by the time you have had him a few years and got him [illegible] you will be astonished to see his step; if they have not action and [illegible] behind they can move [illegible] go in [illegible] with weight behind.

12755. Mr. [illegible].—As regards the action of the Hackney, do you think his legs with his action are good wearing legs?—I think I could hardly tell [illegible] [illegible] [illegible], every horse differs in that respect, they may have good wearing legs, and no doubt you have in a very marked [illegible] these thoroughbred horses, they are rather apt to be deficient in that respect, and they tend in their pasterns, [illegible] to be a little deficient there, and that is a very great drawback in a carriage horse.

12756. When you were in Normandy did you see any of the stallions that the horses you bought there got by?—I do not think I did, because I went to see [illegible] the Government [illegible] and I saw a good many of these [illegible] [illegible] that is some years ago.

March 12, 1897. — Mr Wickham.

and I cannot say I have any recollection of what the stallion gets like.

12757. Lord ENNISKILLEN.—Did you ever buy any horses by a horse called "Macintosh," in Ireland?—Yes.

12758. He was half-bred?—Is he. I did not know. He stands at [illegible]. You know the horse perhaps?

12759. I have never seen him, but I have seen his stock?—I have seen him many times, I had the impression that he was thoroughbred.

12760. Lord RATHDONNELL.—Have you ever attended any of the fairs in the North of Ireland at all?—Yes, there is a fair at Armagh and at the Moy every month, and I used to go and stay at Armagh a good deal in those days before any of these [illegible] had grown up, and when I had [illegible] to buy for me, he did not make at Armagh, so when I used to go down to see his horses I would stay there, and I went to [illegible] of [illegible] one. But I did very little at those fairs. It is a very bad place to buy horses in, for two reasons; one because a good many of the horses there are bred in the North, and they are generally wanting from my experience of them, and the other reason is—that the [illegible] in the North, as a rule, feed their horses on turnips and potatoes and every kind of [illegible] you can think of. The then thing is that when you [illegible] them you have a few horses to [illegible] up a feeding [illegible], these horses are [illegible] and [illegible], and always certain to die on your hands.

12761. We have had some evidence given of this feeding system. I rather wanted to ask whether you had found it out?—Yes, and the man who lives in the North (I will swear of this) will be [illegible] [illegible] [illegible] he is perhaps the only man who does well.

12762. Then the class of horse that you would pick up in that part of the country chiefly come from the South, you say?—Yes, they do. In those [illegible] in the South which are constantly going on, you will see a contingent of men from the North, a [illegible] [illegible], [illegible] of [illegible] going there regularly and buying the young horses, and bringing them back and feeding them in this way. I may [illegible] [illegible] a very [illegible] trade. Therefore a good many of those horses that are shown in the Moy and Armagh are brought from the South.

12763. Mr. LA TOUCHE.—You say that many of those horses you buy in Normandy are 15.2 or 15.3?—Yes, and up to 16.

12764. There are plenty of horses with action got by Hackney stallions of that size?—There may be, but when I say 15.3 I mean a horse with length and scale, not those short Hackneys.

12765. You get great class by blood on the sire's side?—Yes.

12766. Is your objection to those Hackney horses their lack of [illegible]?—They are not the horses that we want; we want beautiful, superior, [illegible] horses, such as you would put into the Royal carriages.

12767. There are horses over 15.3 or 16?—Yes, but I say 15.3, from [illegible], the horses we get in Ireland and Yorkshire are generally 16 hands.

12768. I wanted to know in what way you considered the Normandy horses of 15.3 hands were superior to the Hackney horses of 15.3?—Well, when I say 15.3, for instance, what I [illegible] there [illegible] [illegible] [illegible] we brought twenty horses there, out of those there were perhaps four or five that were only 15.3, but others were more, 16.3, 16.3½; they measure those [illegible], but I think we get a big size [illegible] [illegible] [illegible] [illegible], if [illegible] 15 hands we generally find [illegible] them [illegible].

12769. The Normandy ones?—Yes, they [illegible] [illegible] and there.

12770. You have not really got much personal experience of the Hackney horse?—No, because we do not want Hackneys.

12771. They are not good enough looking?—No, they are not carriage horses.

12772. If they are not carriage horses they don't appear to be [illegible] horses; then you disapprove of the breed in general?—Well, we want a [illegible] horse and the Hackney is no good to us. If we go into Yorkshire, I [illegible] the [illegible] very well, [illegible], and instead of finding a beautiful carriage horse, [illegible] as a [illegible] Hackney without the [illegible] we want.

12773. Have you the same objection to the Cleveland Bay and the Yorkshire coaching horse stallion that you have to the Hackney stallion?—I am not quite sure that I understand you. I remember in the Yorkshire coach horse we used to get a beautiful animal that is now no [illegible]. It was bred from a Cleveland mare by a thorough-bred horse.

12774. I think there is an actual breed called the Yorkshire coach horse with a stud book?—Certainly, there are a good many coach horses bred in Yorkshire that are not thoroughbred.

12775. They have established themselves into a breed now, that, I believe, is considered by the Yorkshire coach horse breeders to be thoroughbred. They have a stud book of their own. Do you like the Cleveland Bays?—I do not like a Cleveland Bay, not [illegible] [illegible], but I think the Cleveland Bay is very valuable if you get crossed with sufficient thorough-bred blood as well. The Cleveland Bay is too heavy and slow by itself.

12776. A Cleveland Bay mare crossed with a thoroughbred horse?—Yes, and then the [illegible] [illegible] not be too [illegible]; she should have a little blood as well. I do not think she should be pure Cleveland.

12777. In fact, you think the thoroughbred sire is the best to cross with anything?—I do, most certainly.

12778. You are great [illegible] for [illegible]?—Yes, [illegible] other things. I would not buy a horse for his colour, but it is a great thing to have a good horse with beautiful colour.

12779. Col. ST. QUINTIN.—You say there are no horses that are any good south of the Thames that are bred there. Well take, from the [illegible] [illegible] in [illegible] [illegible]. Was that always the case?—Of course you can understand that it is a general [illegible]. I [illegible] it [illegible] [illegible], and I have heard men like Perry, whom you may know, who [illegible] for the [illegible] a good deal. I have heard him say he would never [illegible] a horse south of the Thames.

12780. Can you, in your own mind, give any reason for that. Is it the nature of the soil or the [illegible] of other [illegible]?—[illegible]. The South of Ireland is nearly all [illegible], delightful country for growing horses. They can lie out all the year round with advantage, the [illegible] is [illegible]. In the North it is nearly all arable land, or little small farms, and it is very [illegible] [illegible]. In addition to that, the best thoroughbred ones are in the south. They have very few [illegible] [illegible] in the North.

12781. Sir WALTER GILBEY.—May I ask have you had any experience in breeding race horses?—No.

12782. When you buy horses, or [illegible] so they are of the shape and make you want, and would you say not at [illegible] as to know how they are bred?—I always like to know, but one can not [illegible] [illegible] [illegible] you [illegible]. I have been told by my father that he did not like my finding out. He said, "You are apt to be prejudiced by horses of the blood. You better see the animal you want, and see what they." But at the same time, no doubt, it is a very important thing, as I like to know how they are bred.

12783. You don't find the same difficulty now in getting horses for your business that you did, going back ten or fifteen years ago, at the time of the Franco-German War when there was a great scarcity of horses throughout the United Kingdom?—I do not know that we have found it. About what date was that?

12784. 1870. I think you told your examination having in 1871?—Commenced buying horses in 1871. We [illegible] [illegible] [illegible], [illegible]. We [illegible] our stock very much from that date onward, because my people were still buying in Yorkshire. These horses I bought in Ireland were entire horses, and I found every year the same number we bought were let, so we kept on going. Our stock was larger in those years than it had ever been before.

13785. Have you had any experience in Canadian or American or foreign horses generally?—Very little in Canadian. I have a great horror of American horses. I have had one or two pretty good Canadians, but I do not think it is a trade likely to do very much.

13786. You say you think very favourably of the Normandy horses?—Well, as far as my experience of them goes. Our horse is a scarce animal anywhere; you cannot go and buy them wholesale, either in Normandy or anywhere else, they require careful selection. The first year I went I bought there; they take a great deal of finding, and it is only here and there you get one.

13787. Were you inquisitive to know how they were bred in Normandy?—I did ask the question, and I generally found they were bred by some trotting racer.

13788. Are you aware that the foundation of the blood of this Normandy horse is the Norfolk Hackney?—No, I cannot say I know anything about how he is bred.

13789. Well, I have made inquiries in various parts of France where they have trotting races, and you will see at the haras there the pedigrees of all these horses, no difficulty in getting them; you see the very horses you speak of traced back to that, you are not aware of that?—Well, I think I once heard that they got "Norfolk Phenomenon" over there.

Sir WALTER GILBEY.—No; no!

13790. CHAIRMAN.—I think Mr. Wimbush said he did not know how they were bred?—No, except the man tells me—he questions some French horse—I do not know how he is bred.

13791. Sir W. GILBEY.—You know nothing of the Yorkshire supply of horses previous to 1871, your experience only goes back to that date?—Oh, yes; a great deal further back than that.

13792. Up to what date back?—We will say 1854.

13793. When you bought horses at that time in Yorkshire were not many of them got by the very horse you have alluded to—"Norfolk Phenomenon"?—I do not think so, as far as I could tell.

13794. Mr. WRENCH.—Your trade, Mr. Wimbush, is rather a special one, you only go in for a big, lengthy, blood-like carriage horse?—It is special in this way, we only go in for a very superior carriage horse, but not necessarily a very big one.

13795. You don't buy them much under 15.3½?—No; true enough, that is quite so, 15.2½ to 16.1 hands.

13796. And when you talk of buying from the collectors, I suppose, practically, the same you buy from are dealers?—Well, they are dealers in a certain sense, for instance, the man that I was most connected with in Ireland, I met him constantly in the fairs, you know, and knew that he was a man who bought colts and took them home, and what he used to do when he got home. He lived near Armagh, and his neighbours used to come round next morning, he would perhaps bring twenty colts home, and say to these men, "That is for you," and "this is for you," and show what he had given for them, and they were to give him £5 more, and they did not pay him until they sold them. Then I made his acquaintance, and got him to promise to give me his colts. I used to visit him, and he would take me round to these farmers, and if I saw a horse I liked I bought him. When times became bad these farmers became broken and failed to pay this man. I told him he would lose his money, and then it came to this that I used to see his horses in Dublin before he took them to the North, and take two or three, or none, as the case might be. Afterwards he took these home, and [illegible] I went there and saw [illegible] at a time, but he would [illegible] sell them until I saw them.

13797. You would not call him a dealer?—Well, you know. When I [illegible] Ireland or [illegible] there [illegible].

13798. When you were alluding to what one man you are alluding to [illegible] of this where you do business in the North of Ireland?—Yes.

13799. And he lives fairly close to Armagh [illegible].

13800. I suppose you remember being in some of the fairs in the North of Ireland where "Victor" was [illegible], very well, indeed.

13801. If all the horses that were said to be by "Victor" were really got by him how many mares do you think he must have served in a season?—That may have been so. "I know you have to be careful about that, but at the same time I knew Dundee very well indeed, who owned 'Victor,'" and I knew all these farmers, and looked I got my information from Mr. [illegible]. He said "There is a 'Victor' colt [illegible]."

13802. [illegible] it is a fact that a large number were said to be by "Victor"?—Yes, it is exceedingly probable.

13803. Do you know the [illegible] in Ireland, [illegible], at all. I [illegible] on the west coast of Ireland?—I do not know [illegible].

13804. Have you been in Donegal?—Yes, but not horse buying. I have been there fishing.

13805. Have you been to Connemara and [illegible]?—Yes. I know Connemara very well.

13806. Fishing?—Yes.

13807. But not buying horses?—No, I never saw a colt there I would buy.

13808. You don't think the mares in that district could produce any animal that would be of use to you?—Certainly not.

13809. Can you give any opinion as to what would be the best class of animal to [illegible] the poor animals of that district?—It is such a subject, I am [illegible] to know [illegible], but considering the nature of the country I should imagine the most useful horse would be a sort of pony.

13810. Would you think it would be extremely [illegible] that [illegible] where should be very hardy?—I certainly should.

13811. The [illegible]?—They [illegible] the cob on the hill.

13812. Mr. CHAMBERS.—You don't think the Hackney would be suitable there?—I should think not; they [illegible] I should think the Hackneys are [illegible], but I do not know anything about them.

13813. Mr. WRENCH.—You would not say that the Hackney [illegible] from your knowledge?—If I had to give an opinion I should not go to the Hackney. I think a [illegible] animal [illegible] with the people.

13814. [illegible] that the Hackney [illegible] would [illegible] what the Hackney is good for. They would [illegible].

13815. To [illegible] the Hackney a [illegible] than the animals you have seen [illegible] I am not an authority on such a subject, but I should not think so if you ask me.

13816. You don't think the Hackney is a stronger animal than the animal you saw in their parts?—No, and [illegible] quite suitable for their purpose.

13817. [illegible], but [illegible] I should not think he is [illegible].

13818. Have you any idea [illegible] animals [illegible] I [illegible] are small [illegible] though.

13819. What [illegible] I think about [illegible].

March 11, 1897.

Mr. Wimbush.

12820. Do you think they are as much as that?—Perhaps most of them are less. I should think that is the outside one for them.

12821. You have no experience of the lower class of harness trade below your own trade?—No, none at all.

12822. Do you think action is a consideration in selling a small harness horse?—Oh, yes; I don't think any horse is good for carriage purposes unless he has action.

12823. But a small horse with action will sell at a very much higher price than a small horse without action?—I think he would, but it is very important that a small horse to be valuable should have a good deal of bone, and a good deal of strength.

12824. Do you dislike the cross of the Suffolk Punch or Clydesdale in your horses?—Most decidedly; I object very strongly to it. Clydesdale blood has been introduced into the North of Ireland; it is most ruinous.

12825. Do you know that there is a good deal of Clydesdale blood in the South of Ireland?—I am very sorry to hear it. If it is so, it is very injurious wherever it is.

12826. Have you heard anything about American horses being brought over to Ireland?—I know some Irishmen have been over and bought some.

12827. You don't know that any horses are sold now as Irish horses that really came from America?—No; it has not come under my notice.

12828. Do you think that many of the people in your position, dealing in the class of carriage horses that you buy, have also gone to Normandy and other countries for their supplies?—People in our business—there are not very many in our business in an extensive way—but I am aware that one firm has.

12829. Gone to Normandy?—Yes.

12830. When you were attending fairs in Ireland was the proportion of good horses or bad horses the largest?—Oh, the bad ones, you might go to Mullingar fair, the streets would be crowded with horses, and it was a marvel to me whatever these horses could go to ultimately, with the greatest care and exertion, and knowing people if you got one or two it would be as much as you could do, and generally not that.

12831. Then in any expenditure of State aid do you think the people who breed the horses that you want are those to be encouraged first, or the people that breed that rubbish which you see in the fair?—The people that supply the horses that we want.

12832. You would say "help the rich people"?—Not the rich. I would help the people to get rich. I would encourage the farmers to keep a pretty good mare, and then if they can breed a colt that is worth £60 or £70 at three year old, and pretty nearly £100 at four year old without any risk to them, it must be much more profitable than breeding those little wretched things that are valueless.

12833. Do you think a thoroughbred horse would be the best horse to cross with those mares?—With a good mare.

12834. I am not talking of a good mare, but of the wretched mares?—I think you cannot have anything to do with them.

12835. You would not encourage them at all?—I should not.

12836. And if they still went on breeding horses you would not give them any help?—They will get plenty without any help; there will be plenty of bad horses whatever you do.

12837. Those men who have the bad horses are probably the poorest men?—Yes. I should imagine the object of this Society or the Government would be to get some good horses into the country.

12838. Yes, but how would you do it?—By buying good thoroughbred mares, I don't know how you are to keep the good mares in this country, but you can certainly get good thoroughbred sires there, that in itself would be an immense help.

12839. And there is no other step you would recommend?—No; I have never seen any way through the subject of course, how you are to manage those. The old hunting Irish mare is a wonderful animal; they are rather scarce now. I have seen beautiful colts from them, and though they are not all very handsome, I have no doubt they have plenty of blood; they are very strong with short legs.

12840. Your experience in buying harness horses in Ireland is that they have action enough?—Yes; if you buy none that have got, you must be very careful.

12841. That is what makes your trade comparatively small, as I understand it, about eighty or ninety horses a year?—Yes, only to me.

12842. If you could find the horses you wanted there, you would prefer to buy them than in Normandy?—I don't say that.

12843. You must fetch?—When you get the good Irish horse there is no better horse in the world; he is very handsome and lusty, he begins to come out when other horses are giving off. You may buy a Yorkshire horse and an Irish horse, both in appearance the same, and you will find when you have the Yorkshire horse two or three years his legs begin to get puffy, while your Irish horse is only beginning to come out.

12844. Do you attribute that to the soil and climate, or the way he is brought up?—Partly to that; and especially to the blood.

12845. CHAIRMAN.—I take it that your visits to the West of Ireland have been more visits for pleasure and fishing?—Yes.

12846. And you think yourself more competent to give an opinion on the capabilities of that country from a fishing than a horse breeding point of view?—Yes, I do.

12847. I take it you buy good horses wherever you can find them—Normandy, Yorkshire, Lincolnshire, or anywhere else?—Though that is so, there are only four places we go to generally for them; we can again do go anywhere we can get the right animals.

12848. You mentioned Yorkshire, Ireland, and Normandy, where is the fourth place?—North of Germany.

12849. What class of action have these horses you buy in Normandy?—Very good, good all round. They do not only step well, but go down sufficiently on them fairly high.

12850. I understood you to say that they are bred for racing purposes?—I rather believe they are.

12851. But as to how they are bred you don't know?—No.

12855. Where do you get your horses mostly?—We get about a quarter from Ireland; we replace about a quarter—we replenish in my business as nearly as possible 200 horses a year. I am speaking now not of the hunter trade, because we buy hunters as well, and these are almost all bought in Ireland.

12856. I will ask you a question or two about that afterwards?—We replenish about 200 horses a year in our stock—that is, in the ordinary course of things 200 horses get either worn out or incurably lame or meet with accidents, and we buy about 200 and sell about 200. The 200 horses sold go to Aldridge's, and are sold as horses without any warranty or any reserve. We don't sell carriage horses privately; there may be an exceptional case where a customer says, "I want to buy that horse," then we put a good, fair price upon him, and get it.

12857. Of these 200 horses you get about a quarter from Ireland?—About a quarter.

12858. Where do you get the three-quarters?—At English fairs—York, Horncastle, Lincoln (that is a large fair), and other English fairs.

12859. Do you require a pedigree, or do you know how these horses are bred that you buy?—Whenever I buy a horse I say "How is he bred?" and I make a note of it at the time, but you cannot always get correct pedigrees about horses—people don't know them—unless you buy them from some English farmer who has bred the horse himself. I had a hard week's travel the week before last, for instance. I went from London to Hanover, where I bought six horses; from there I went to Brussels, and did not buy anything. From Brussels I went to Ghent, where there is a very large dealer—one of the largest dealers in the world—named Schmidt, and I bought four horses of him—one a French horse (which was the best horse I bought all through my journey) and three American horses. That man has a buyer in Chicago, and he gets consignments of American horses; he is very fond of American horses. I bought three Americans, and I am quite satisfied now that they have come home and the French horse. From there I went to Lille, where there is a very large dealer, named De Longueville. I did not buy anything there. I went to Paris and spent a day there, where I saw a large quantity of Norman horses. I bought two horses—one a French horse and the other an American horse.

12860. A great number of American horses find their way there?—In Paris I saw a great number of Irish horses—at Lille I saw several Irish horses, at Ghent I did not see any.

12861. Do you know at all as a matter of fact how most of the horses you buy in England are bred?—They are supposed to be—they are as a rule by English thoroughbred horses.

12862. Have you any preference; would you prefer to buy a horse by a thoroughbred to a horse by any other sire?—No, I don't know that I would. I belong to the Hunter Improvement Society, and we are very particular about our thoroughbred horses, but if it is a well-bred English horse I would not say I would prefer them there, there are so many good horses in England that are covering that are not quite thoroughbred horses.

12863. How about the Hackneys?—I have had no experience of them. I saw some very beautiful Hackney horses at the show last week, and I admired them very much; but as to their working capabilities I know nothing, and I am not aware that I have ever had in my stock a horse that has had Hackney blood in him. If I saw a horse that was my type of horse—a Hackney is sure to be a good goer—but if it was my type of horse, if a man told me it had Hackney blood, and I thought his carriage was good and his other points were in my favour, I should not hesitate though he had got Hackney blood, but at the same time I have no experience of them. I have never seen a Hackney horse that is so quite what we call a London carriage horse.

12864. You sell hunters too?—Yes.

12865. Do you let them out or sell them?—Sell them. [illegible]

12866. Is that a large branch of your business?—Yes, I should think my brother has bought from Ireland 100 this year, all bought in Ireland at the Dublin Show and other places.

12867. Do you buy all your hunters in Ireland?—[illegible] in the number of Irish hunters we buy.

12868. You buy them elsewhere?—Yes, a [illegible], but not many.

12869. Principally in Ireland?—We always think them the best for hunters.

12870. What age do you buy them?—Four, five, and six, if the horse has a good character.

12871. Direct from the breeders?—No, we buy them at the Dublin Show, perhaps get a few direct from the breeders; but as a rule they are bought from dealers who have bought them from the farmers.

12872. Does your brother go over himself, or do you go over?—My brother always goes; I don't know much of Ireland.

12873. Where does he buy them do you know?—From Wright of Waterford; you would know him by repute.

12874. In the South of Ireland?—Yes.

12875. Have you ever bought in the North?—I think not.

12876. Do you consider Ireland produces a better [illegible] hunter?—Oh, yes.

12877. Mr. [illegible].—[illegible] think that [illegible] would [illegible] the [illegible] type of [illegible] horse you suggest?—Well, I think not, [illegible], and [illegible]. I should [illegible] the experiment, but I have had no experience.

12878. You don't want to try it yourself?—I don't want to try it myself. Before you got a horse to our type, breeding him myself, I think I should have to go through a good deal of experience; I [illegible] it in my [illegible], but if [illegible] [illegible] a [illegible] for my business would be. I [illegible] them and their [illegible].

12879. Do you think that the Irish hunter as he is at present is the best to the [illegible]?—That is my opinion. I have [illegible] what is called a hunting [illegible] and that is my experience.

12880. If you think that, I suppose you also think that the introduction of any new blood into that breed would be risky?—Oh, certainly, risky, but I am not going to say it would be a failure.

12881. But it would be a risk?—I think so, as it would be in changing any type of horse.

12882. Lord [illegible].—[illegible] that [illegible] you have no experience of [illegible] a Hackney [illegible]?—I have no experience.

12883. The risk is [illegible]?—[illegible] I [illegible] that I would not like to [illegible].

12884. You would leave well alone?—It may be [illegible] [illegible] my [illegible]. I have only [illegible].

12885. But with regard to the Hackney, you have [illegible], but [illegible] it is only your opinion?—I have no experience.

12886. Lord Ribblesdale.—Why do you dislike the Hackney type of horse?—I am only saying that I [illegible] [illegible] [illegible]; [illegible] a London carriage horse, and I have [illegible] in my [illegible] the London carriage horse.

12887. Chairman.—I think you said you very much admired the horses?—Very much admired the Hackney at the show.

12888. Lord Ribblesdale.—I understood you to say you did not like the type?—Not for my business.

12889. Then you admire his type?—Very much as a horse. I saw some beautiful horses the other day at the show, but I did not admire them so much as the thoroughbred horses that were shown at the

[illegible] 11, 1897.

Mr. W[illegible].

beginning of this work. I like the thoroughbred horse, because he has brought grace to our stock by breeding good carriage horses and good hunters.

12890. What do you think the Hackney does in its [illegible] by his type?—For farming purposes.

12891. Altogether?—I have no experience of their riding.

12892. Did you ever attend any shows in Ireland?—Yes. I went a few years in Limerick, but my brother goes to Ireland and goes to the different fairs, and he always attends the Dublin Show, and knows a great number of people in Ireland.

12893. You have no experience of the Irish?—No.

12894. Mr. La Touche.—Have you much experience of the working of the [illegible] Improvement [illegible], Mr. W[illegible]?—I know, but have very small experience. The Society is an improving one in its kind, and more attention are [illegible] to. In addition a greater number of [illegible] than there was. A greater number of [illegible] have passed than last year than I think ever [illegible] in one single year, and I think it [illegible] give [illegible] to the country—the working of it—about it would not have been the success it is.

12895. I gather that one of the parts of the scheme is that they subsidise thoroughbred stallions which are [illegible] in England, and they subsidise them to the extent of £100 a year?—Yes.

12896. Do you think there would be [illegible] to a [illegible] the horse [illegible] if [illegible]?—I should rather give them, if it could be done, I should give them another £100 each, and make it £200 instead of £100.

12897. You think you would get a better class of stallion?—I think you would; I think it would be a [illegible] improvement to a stock.

12898. Have you formed any idea of a feasible plan for keeping mares in the country?—Yes. Up to my hunting [illegible] forty years ago, and [illegible] I was [illegible] and I said to my brother, "[illegible] are [illegible] in the [illegible]." He said "They are [illegible] as they have been [illegible] for a long time." He said, "You [illegible] that when an Englishman will give 200 [illegible] the [illegible]," and, in [illegible] of my experience [illegible], that [illegible] been practically [illegible] and great number of [illegible] have [illegible].

12899. You consider that, possibly, the best way of [illegible] the breed of horses is to try and improve the stallions as much as possible, and to get good stallions within the reach of the farmers?—As much as possible, and to [illegible] the [illegible] from [illegible] and [illegible]. They know the country, and they want to find the [illegible], and are quite ready to give money for them.

12900. It would be very difficult to induce the farmer to keep the best mares?—Yes; it has been tried by a great number of people. "While the [illegible] [illegible], all the better; they [illegible] money in this country." There is a difference. [illegible] I know they [illegible] the [illegible] in England. In one of the places I went [illegible] in Ireland and the other one [illegible] in England.

12901. Mr. W. [illegible].—Your purchases in Ireland are principally for hunters, are they not?—Yes.

12902. You said one-fourth came from Ireland?—About one-fourth of the carriage horses; but all our hunters—with two or three exceptions—are bought in Ireland, and they have been bought by my brother.

12903. I think you said 300 horses you purchased in the year, and about one-fourth from Ireland?—Yes.

12904. [illegible] of carriage horses in [illegible]—[illegible].

12905. You have [illegible] your [illegible] of the Hackney breed. Have you seen any animals bred by the Hackney out of a thoroughbred mare or [illegible]?—[illegible] I don't think I have, Sir [illegible]. I don't [illegible] the Hackney, because I know nothing about them. I like the Hackneys from their action and their type, but they [illegible] to be my type for a horse or carriage horse.

12906. My question was whether you had seen any animals bred by the Hackney out of a thoroughbred mare or a [illegible]?—I have not; it has not come across me.

12907. Sir Thomas [illegible].—What would your definition be of a [illegible] carriage horse?—Well, a true class carriage horse should be a [illegible] horse, with a good back and neck, and good shoulders—and good shoulders, perhaps, so you want for a [illegible] horse with good back and loins and short [illegible] and [illegible] well.

12908. Are many horses of that description brought to London from Ireland, speaking generally?—No; I think not. The Irish horses that find their way to London are either bought by people in my own business or by dealers who buy them in Ireland and bring them over here; that is the only way [illegible] horses could [illegible] to be sold.

12909. Then you said there were not very many of those brought from Ireland—not very many Irish horses—is that what you meant?—That are sold in London.

12910. You mean there are not very many first-class carriage horses imported from Ireland to England?—They are imported, but they don't find their way to be sold in London. They are bought [illegible] Irish dealers who take them in there. You cannot go to an English fair without seeing Irish horses, taking them in these very [illegible].

12911. What class of [illegible] do you think the most likely to be a good carriage horse, assuming there is good [illegible] in them?—[illegible] and [illegible], 400 horses [illegible], I have no [illegible] carriages, and [illegible] of one type [illegible] horses I should only have a [illegible] of [illegible] for their particular horses; you must buy your [illegible] 15.3 to 16.3 or 17 hands, but as a rule they are bought of one type.

12912. And generally a large-sized horse?—Generally a large-sized horse.

12913. Sir W. Gilbey.—Going back some ten or twelve years, there was a great scarcity in the United Kingdom for years perhaps after the Franco-German war, going up to eight or ten years ago; there is not the difficulty now to get the horses you would find [illegible] then?—There is not the difficulty now to buy the horses that there was ten or twelve years ago.

12914. That was previous to the societies that you know are in existence now being established?—Yes.

12915. And at that date, both you were obliged to go abroad, mostly for your horses, to Germany and Canada, were you not?—We were obliged a great deal, and we have two or three years we had our horses [illegible] England, and the other horse [illegible] New York, and we used to get a good many horses from there, but partly because the supply is better in England, and partly because the supply is [illegible] as good there [illegible] they are [illegible]—we have stopped [illegible] so many American horses as we did.

12916. And although there is a decrease in the number you buy now in Ireland, you would not get the same number of horses from Ireland as then [illegible] you purchase?—I don't think it has varied so much.

12917. But you would not get those in Yorkshire or England?—[illegible] we used to buy [illegible] we had had to [illegible] great many [illegible] English horses we could not have supplied them with English [illegible] we want in the best market we could—in America.

12918. You will look forward—I hope you will do so—to the future being able to buy your horses in the United Kingdom, instead of going to America [illegible]

[illegible]?—We don't want to go to America or to go abroad if we could only buy them in England or Ireland, but American horses are that fine, and they have . I remember buying ten horses that just came off the boat at Liverpool, and gave £110 a-piece for them. I bought ten American horses once at [illegible] [illegible], from a man who had gone over to America and gave us the [illegible] when he returned,—they cost £110 a-piece.

12919. Was there any pedigree with these horses; do you know how they were bred?—No; you could not tell.

12920. As long as they sold you you did not care in particular to know how they were bred?—No, we would rather know the breeding of an animal.

12921. Mr. Clarke.—What did you buy these for that cost you £110 apiece?—Carriage horses.

12922. Did they turn out well?—Yes, the record of our books show it was a very good purchase, the [illegible] and they [illegible].

12923. Mr. Walrond.—Have you any experience of breeding horses?—So far as our experience of breeding horses it has been rather [illegible], because it has been from [illegible] mares that have been in the stock; [illegible] but our [illegible] "Well, there is old [illegible] there, let us breed from her before she gets too old," and bred or [illegible] we bred from her that, but we [illegible] with them, and twice or three [illegible] I have broken myself that I bred them. I am one of the [illegible] people in breeding, and so I have given it up.

12924. What class of horse did you use?—Thoroughbred horses for the hunters, and one carriage horse was, I think, by one of the Mr. [illegible] I forget the names of the horses.

12925. Have they did not turn out well?—They did not turn out well because we had not got proper accommodation for them; ours was not a breeding establishment.

12926. You have been obliged a good deal buying, horses?—Not a good deal.

12927. Have you been abroad to more than the place you mentioned; did you buy there Mr. [illegible] horses?—I bought them also from Mr. Oppenheimer, but they were not German horses.

12928. He has a very large establishment?—Yes.

12929. And he owns the horse trade of [illegible]?—Well, [illegible] of New York used to be the largest dealer in the world, but he does not sell so many horses now. Mr. [illegible] of [illegible] used to be Oppenheimer; now I think [illegible] and Oppenheimer may be considered the greatest dealer in the world.

12930. And he buys his horses all over the world?—Yes, from Russia.

12931. Russian horses are very good indeed, are they not?—Yes; they are.

12932. Have you ever heard what you have been abroad how the French Government breed their horses?—No, I have not; I should like very much to go to some of their breeding establishments; I have [illegible] the time or [illegible] there.

12933. You don't know that they breed a great many artillery and cavalry horses from Hackneys?—I do not.

12934. Do you know whether there was a considerable sale of good Hackney stallions at the show last week?—I did not hear that.

12935. You were not buying any yourself?—No.

12936. Do you dislike the blood of the Suffolk Punch or the Clydesdale in your horses?—I am very fond of a good Norfolk horse or a good Suffolk horse. I think he is a good one; it is not quite the type of the Suffolk Punch, because the Suffolk Punch is a horse with more cross, there are many good horses bred in Norfolk.

12937. But I am talking of the Suffolk Punch, the big [illegible] cart-horse; do you like the blood of that in your horses?—Oh, no.

12938. Do you dislike the blood of the Clydesdale?—No, I have not had much experience of the Clydesdale horse, but I don't like the blood.

12939. But if you were buying horses would you prefer that they should have a strain of Hackney blood in them to a strain of cart-horse blood for your purpose?—For my purpose I should say yes, but I have no experience of them from which I have could [illegible] the two types.

12940. When you come to a lower class of harness horses than you buy; do you think the Hackney type would be a suitable horse to produce those horses?—Well, I should very much like to see the influence of some breeding before I ventured an opinion on that.

12941. Do you think the Hackney horse would get animals, which, did you have objection, would be the Hackney blood in because of [illegible] of the carriage type, but horses for ordinary purposes, would not be [illegible], but I would not speak without experience.

12942. And in the lower class of horses having the action of great importance?—If you get a horse with action it will be a good deal more money.

12943. I come simply as a buyer of [illegible] a matter of [illegible] in [illegible].

12944. Is it the thing that perhaps tells most when you come to deal with the lower class of business horses?—Yes, certainly.

12945. I think you said you were a member of the Hunter Improvement Society?—Yes.

12946. Can you speak at all whether there has been any improvement in the breeding of hunters in England since the establishment of the Society?—Yes, I wish I had my records in my own mind from three or four, seeing here a little horse bred and still here, looking at the hunters and the registered [illegible]; I have accounts of them, but I don't go to Horse-breeding on a scale.

12947. And you think it has done good?—I think so; [illegible] a great many of persons at the [illegible] yesterday, where I was acting as referee judge. A great number of farmers and people from there, they said they [illegible] regularly, and I don't think they would continue if it was not a success.

12948. Would you approve of a [illegible] stallions being let out under such exclusive terms as the thoroughbred stallions you select?—No, I would go for the thoroughbred horse here, but there are a certain breed of horse that are called registered hunter class.

12949. Under what conditions?—Under the one condition, that they have to have certain pedigrees.

12950. But would you make those conditions at all?—Well, do you know I think I would, for any purpose of [illegible].

12951. To what degree?—Well, there are many horses that [illegible] upon the registered [illegible] now, which in my opinion would be no good for any purpose.

12952. Would you require any certain number of crosses of thoroughbred blood in such horses?—I would not for my purpose, but for the Hunter Improvement Society they are very jealous of blood.

12953. But for your purpose you would not be a [illegible] class of horses?—For my purpose I would.

12954. Chairman.—In what you say about the horses are you referring to Ireland or England or both?—I am referring to both.

12955. The remarks you make are equally applicable to both countries?—Quite.

12956. In your business do you deal at all in what have been called the lower class of harness horses?—No; we deal that our horses, I [illegible] as good as they can be; [illegible] with what [illegible] our lower class; our endeavour is to keep the standard up as high as possible.

12957. I wanted to ask you whether, in the opinion you have given the Commission in reference to the lower class of harness-horses, there are dealers that have been deterred from experience in your business?

3 K 2

Sept. 11, 188[illegible].

Mr. [illegible].

[illegible] Mr. Walters

...From what I have seen, **other horses do, and the** trade I have been doing **with the lower class of** horses.

[illegible]. In that you have had no practical experience?—No practical experience. I never deals in them.

[illegible]. Can you tell us, Mr. [illegible], whether the supply of hunters in Ireland is falling off or increasing?—Well, I am not quite certain about the number. I should like to have looked up the number of hunters that were imported from Ireland [illegible]. I believe it is [illegible].

[illegible]. I was asking you rather from your own experience [illegible] you always go and buy your hunters, but a first class horse [illegible] very difficult [illegible] always [illegible] a good deal of money in Ireland.

[illegible]. But do you think **there is as good a supply** [illegible] **of twenty years ago?**—I think so.

[illegible]. And you think the quality is as good?—I can only [illegible]. [illegible] hunters come here from Ireland, and the [illegible] they come from, I mean that are bought by English dealers, [illegible] of [illegible], and other [illegible]. They are got as a rule from people like Mr. Wright, Mr. [illegible], and other [illegible] buyers, who buy them from farmers and make them [illegible] then they **are** ready for the English market.

[illegible]. **Then I take it that in your opinion there** has been no marked change in Ireland as regards **the** quantity or the quality of the horses you buy **for** hunting purposes?—I think not.

[illegible]. Would that apply also to the horses you buy in Ireland for carriage purposes? My opinion about carriage horses is that we don't get quite as good horses as we used to, that is my own opinion about carriage horses.

[illegible]. Can you account for that?—No, I cannot account for it, [illegible].

[illegible]. I suppose [illegible] to [illegible] what you want, [illegible] that they [illegible]. [illegible] horses [illegible]. For instance, a lady said to me [illegible] the other day, "We shall only take this [illegible] into the country this year [illegible] **my** [illegible] **top** [illegible] instead of [illegible].

[illegible]. Can you form any opinion as to the [illegible] in Ireland for the improvement of horse breeding as an industry, [illegible]?—Yes, I have thought about it in this way, as Mr. [illegible] said just now [illegible] Ireland and [illegible] the breed [illegible] in the quality. I don't think the fault is in the thoroughbred horse, [illegible] Ireland in the same way that they have taken them from England. A great number of horses go from the English [illegible].

Mr HAWES examined.

Mr. Hawes.

[illegible]. CHAIRMAN.—You live in [illegible]?—Yes, my lord.

[illegible]. And are engaged in horse dealing?—Yes.

[illegible]. What class of horses?—Nearly all **of** [illegible].

[illegible]. Where do you buy your horses?—Nearly all of them in Ireland.

[illegible]. Do you buy them yourself?—Not for the last few years. I have a man who lives in Ireland all the time.

[illegible]. The whole year round? Does he buy **for** you from the farmers generally?—Yes, as far **as** possible I like to save the [illegible] between the [illegible].

[illegible]. How long have you been buying horses in Ireland?—Well, since I first commenced—[illegible] and my father and brother bought a few horses there, but nothing like [illegible]. I remember going to [illegible] [illegible]—I can't tell you quite what year, but it would be two or three years before then.

[illegible]. And previous to that do you know where your hunting horses were bought—which part of England?—Our business was nothing like so large, but my father had always a very good liking for the Irish horses, and he always bought them [illegible]. A very much better class of horses come to our [illegible] than then.

[illegible]. To English dealers?—Yes.

[illegible]. As to Ireland, do you think the horses have improved in your experience or deteriorated? I mean the class of horse you buy?—Well, I think the class is very much the same, but I think it is far more [illegible]. I think that is because of the [illegible], and because of the [illegible].

[illegible]. The demand in England?—Certainly.

[illegible]. And the supply, perhaps, where [illegible]?—Yes, of course, the really good horses are very difficult to get [illegible], but I think that is more [illegible] people go to Ireland, knowing where they [illegible] horses there are there.

[illegible]. Then I take it, in your opinion the supply has not kept up with the demand—that is to say, the demand for a larger number of these good, high class horses is greater than can be easily and easily met by the supply?—Yes. I would not [illegible]. I would only find them. The difficulty is in finding them.

[illegible]. There is no likelihood, in your opinion, that if the supply [illegible] the price would fall very much?—No, I don't think so.

[illegible]. I suppose you buy some hunters in England?—Very few, but I am very prejudiced, and those which I do buy, if you could trace them, are originally Irish horses. There are very few English horses bred.

[illegible]. Are you particular about ascertaining the breeding of what you buy in Ireland?—As far as I can possibly. I never pick a pedigree [illegible], I buy from the [illegible]. [illegible] the [illegible] of you buy three or four horses [illegible]. You can always [illegible] the horse is [illegible] as a [illegible]. A [illegible] will show it.

[illegible]. How are the horses by thoroughbreds?—Yes. I reckon the thoroughbred [illegible] good [illegible] very good [illegible] there. There was a very good one, "[illegible]," who, perhaps, got as many good horses as any [illegible] I ever [illegible], and I believe he was not [illegible]. You might remember "[illegible]." I don't believe he was quite thoroughbred, but I would always buy a horse by him, and I think "[illegible]" was another [illegible]. [illegible] Lord [illegible] [illegible].

[illegible]. CHAIRMAN.—Do you know anything about the Royal Dublin Society's scheme?—No.

[illegible]. Do you think the introduction of [illegible] would be beneficial in any way in the production of the class of hunters you require?—I should think it would be very mistaken.

[illegible]. You would not approve of [illegible]?—[illegible] would possibly [illegible].

[illegible]. Do you equally disapprove of the [illegible] of the Cleveland Bay or the old Yorkshire [illegible] [illegible]. The weight carrying hunter originally in Yorkshire [illegible] [illegible] horses.

13989. You do a certain amount of business in harness horses?—Yes, but more particularly of this special pattern. I never buy a real typical harness horse. I don't like them. They are not the sort I am able to sell. I always like a hunting harness horse.

13990. At what age do you buy these horses in Ireland?—I like to buy them as young as possible, but I have to buy a great number at four, and I keep them out in Ireland. I never take a good horse over till he is old.

13991. If you buy them as four-year-olds do you keep them in Ireland?—Yes, a great number. I have them with two or three farmers—one in Kildare, another in Meath. There was one farmer in a central position, and he has the same with his horses, and he rides them, and he has an opportunity to go to different hunts and then he is able to buy a horse that he is expecting and having to get a horse of good character. That is why I [illegible] them there.

13992. Do you know whether he buys any in the North of Ireland?—None, very rarely. I think there is only a very very rare exception. They are all southern bred horses. I believe there are a few good horses bred in the North, but very few.

13993. Then we may take it from you that you think that the South of Ireland has in some way attained a certain amount of eminence in producing hunters?—Most certainly.

13994. To what do you attribute that?—First of all, I think the blood you get there are so horses so purely bred as hunting horses, and then I should think whether it is the soil or not I don't know, but they are able to school them as young ones with greater [illegible]. Those I think whether they are trained from their youth to jump or not I don't know; but I often said that if I found a really good English horse I would send him to Ireland to be schooled, because they jump as many as twenty times there to one in England, they are able to use their feet more quickly.

13995. Mr. FITZWILLIAM.—I gather from your evidence that you require a highly courageous and highly bred horse?—Yes; they must be well-bred.

13996. And you consider that the thoroughbred blood is the blood which produces that?—Most undoubtedly.

13997. And therefore you would be averse to the introduction of any blood which did not produce it in the same degree?—Most certainly.

13998. Do you think that if any other breed which did not produce the highly courageous and thoroughbred animal was introduced it would damage the prestige of the present Irish breed?—Oh! very much.

13999. And, in that way, I presume it would damage the horse breeding?—Yes, I think it would be the most damaging thing that could happen to Ireland in my opinion.

14000. Lord RATHDONNELL.—Have you been to the West?—Yes, I have been down as far as Galway.

14001. Have you any horses there?—I bought some, but they are not West of Ireland horses, I have not bought there further than Roscommon.

14002. But Galway and Roscommon horses?—Yes.

14003. You never noticed the class of horse in the West, in the Congested Districts?—No.

14004. You have never been to Donegal?—No.

14005. Therefore you have no idea of the class of mare they have got, or what would be the best sire for those?—No.

14006. Your experience is in the horse-breeding districts of the hunting districts?—Yes; more particularly.

14007. Lord RATHDONNELL.—It has been said that the horses in the fairs in Ireland have rather deteriorated. Can you give any cause for that?—No, only that if there is a good horse in a place, Dublin, any man, [illegible] them the whole way to go and see it, and in days gone by, I suppose the travelling was very much worse and one had to wait till they would be [illegible] to the fair to see the fair would be.

14008. You think that you yourself are not the only man doing the same thing?—Oh! there are several others. Wherever there is a good horse, a buyer is of an importance to go and look at it.

14009. We may take it then all the good animals are bought up before ever arriving at any fair?—Most certainly.

14010. And the farmers have received considerable prices from the [illegible] and try to get rid of them?—Yes.

14011. I think you said that no matter how many good horses were bred in Ireland of the right sort, there would be quite as good a demand for them as the present one?—I don't think you could produce a supply sufficient for the demand.

14012. Had the supply increased, the demand would be the same certainly.

14013. Mr. LA TOUCHE.—Have you ever been in the North of Ireland?—Yes.

14014. As [illegible]?—I have never been to buy them.

14015. Do you know any reason why there should not be as good horses in the North as in the South?—No, I don't, except that I think there is a very great deal to do with the peculiar soil. Horses are reared better on certain parts. I don't think it is a [illegible] the North quite so good.

14016. Have you ever seen a good hunter from the North?—They have been seen through and well done. In the North, Lord Rathmore has some, and Morton, of Castlederg. I don't think they have the experience of [illegible] them, but I have had one or two well-bred horses from that part that were bred in the North.

14017. If the farmers in the North were to devote their attention to breeding horses like the farmers in the South, from thoroughbred horses, do you think they would do it?—I don't see why they should not, but I don't think they would have the opportunity of [illegible] them—to finish them off.

14018. Do you think the horse-breeding in the South is more profitable to the breeder than the other breeding in the North?—Yes; most certainly.

14019. Sir WALTER GILBEY.—You came to the last Dublin Show. In the middle-weight hunters, you bought the first prize horse?—Yes.

14020. He was bred in the North?—Yes.

14021. You don't buy horses in the [illegible] [illegible]?—No.

14022. Have your trade been chiefly with hunters?—Very nearly, entirely for hunters.

14023. Colonel ST. QUINTIN.—Did you ever buy any horses formerly out of Yorkshire or Lincolnshire?—A few.

14024. Can you get them now?—No.

14025. Why?—I think the farmers don't breed them; they have not their mares; I don't think they have the money to keep the mares to breed from.

14026. Is there the same class of horse bred in any in Yorkshire and Lincolnshire that were formerly bred there?—I don't think there are. I don't think you can buy as good a horse now.

14027. In former days, as far as my memory goes, there were no part of the United Kingdom that produced better clean hunters and high-class horses [illegible] than Yorkshire and Lincolnshire?—They had a very great reputation, I know, and so had Northampton particularly.

14028. Chairman.—But you have never bought anything there?—No, I have always found the Irish horse with a little experience, and more, has always improved and grown the right way. I have always noticed that simply in the good blood. If you buy a Yorkshire horse they are exceptionally well-bred horses, but as a rule they generally grow [illegible]. You will buy a horse in Yorkshire that shows exceptional amount of quality, and you would say he would be a very fine horse, and would grow up a useful animal, until you [illegible], yet you would find the Irish horse would be grow[illegible] would go the [illegible] 1896. [illegible]

But one might say better than this very good-looking Yorkshire horse. I mean, from appearance, one would look comparatively a handsome, and the other a very useful animal; a half-bred sort of a horse. But compare the two and the one is a much better horse than the other, and a very much better hunter.

13029. Mr. Dudley Ransome.—You say there is a difficulty in getting the number of hunters from England now that you used to get formerly?—Yes, I think there is a far greater difficulty now, but that is not because of the supply, but I think English people have found out the goodness of the Irish horse, and so the people go there.

13030. There is a greater demand for them, that is the real reason?—Yes.

13031. And there is no difficulty in finding good horses any more than there was before, so far as the mission of those who [illegible]. But that the demand is greater now than it was?—I should be inclined to think that that is the reason.

13032. You have no idea, even approximately, what would be the number of Irish bred hunters that come into your country every year—I mean Irish hunters?—I could not say that. I know how many I have imported during the last four or five years. I thought I would just look it up.

13033. Could you give the figures?—For the last five years the smallest number was 300 in one year, not quite the 300.

13034. Your average would be about 300 every year?—Yes.

13035. Mr. Gibson.—You confine it to the South of Ireland, Meath and Kildare?—Yes, most certainly.

13036. Have you ever been in the West, to Ballina, to buy?—Rarely.

13037. Or to Kerry?—Never.

13038. You might always bought any horses that were bred in the West or the South?—I bought one horse that I shall for ever remember, that came from Ballina. He was one of the most expensive and the best animals I ever did buy. I bought him from a very decent gentleman, I remember. I can remember the transaction quite well. I had better not mention his name.

13039. How was he bred?—I have forgotten. I know there was a very good horse raised there, by some farmer that got some very good stock. I had perhaps one good horse, and perhaps I may go down to it there to get very good stock.

13040. You give very high prices for your hunters?—Well, I try to buy them as well as I can, but I never have a good one for the money.

13041. You have been all over the country to select the yearlings from the farmers and keep them?—One becomes pretty well known. We have certain men in neighbourhoods where we have to give something to when we purchase a horse. They write to me and tell him, and of course he is well known, and if anybody who has a good horse, we are only too glad to accept his offer, and they are generally too pleased to sell it to me. It is a very, very quick transaction, and we don't give a very great deal of trouble if they have only got a good sound horse.

13042. What do you consider the breed of horse that makes the best hunter?—Oh, a thorough-bred one, most certainly. If you had to drive one, I think you would agree with me.

13043. Mr. Wrench.—Principally you haven't been into the congested districts in Ireland at all?—No.

13044. Westport?—No.

13045. Or Donegal at all?—No.

13046. You don't know the general horse trade of the country; you don't know whether there is a horse which the hunter could?—No; I do not. I have no experience of that.

13047. Lord Dunraven asked you if you would approve of Hackney blood being introduced to improve the class of horse you buy, and you said distinctly not. Have you ever heard of any such suggestion?—Have you ever heard it suggested that Hackney blood should be introduced into Ireland to improve high class hunters?—I don't think I did.

13048. Mr. [illegible].—I thought from your answer that you had. Do you think the conditions of Ireland, soil and climate, and the nature of things, and the natural way in which the horses are brought up has anything to say to the goodness of these horses?—Certainly; but I think that the breeding is the main thing. It would not matter about all the other things, unless you had the right blood to begin with. I think all the other attributes would be lost.

13049. You think it is possible to be fairly certain of the pedigree of the horses you buy from the farmers?—Yes.

13050. Therefore, if there was any blood to which you objected you would be able to find it out?—I should, if there was a Hackney, most certainly.

13051. You think there is no difficulty about that?—No, I think they are very careful.

13052. If a horse had Hackney blood you would be able to detect it?—I think I could, of course, but some particular strain might be got by a Hackney; I don't think there would be any difficulty in anybody being able to say there is Hackney blood.

13053. Do you object to cart-horse blood, or Clydesdale blood or English Shire?—I do; but I don't say Suffolk Punch; I know nothing about it. But I would rather have Clydesdale blood than Hackney blood.

13054. Why?—To begin with, it is always an impossibility to put a Hackney with anything like riding attributes, and I think they would break down quite quickly. Then they not only go all one way, and that is the worst part for a hunter.

13055. But when you talk of riding something, do you mean length, or what do you mean by—[illegible] of the point of the shoulders. If you were only to ride one once you would not require any explanation of what I mean.

13056. Have you often ridden Hackneys?—I don't say I did; but I have seen these ridden and understand what the movements are like.

13057. You don't speak from experience?—No.

13058. You judge from what you have seen in them?—Yes.

13059. You haven't bred Hackneys?—No.

13060. Chairman.—I don't think that the question I asked just now was quite accurately expressed. I put it in a different shape. I asked you whether you think the introduction of Hackney blood into England is likely to prove beneficial or the reverse to the industry?—I should say it would certainly be unfavourable.

13061. I will simplify that. Do you think it would be possible to confine the Hackney blood to any part of Ireland, and if there are a number of Hackney stallions in the congested districts would you think it probable that the strain would gradually spread about through the country?—I am afraid it would.

13062. You would not object to the Hackney if its blood could be kept away from the part of the country that produces the hunter?—I think it would be a very great mistake to introduce it into the country at all.

Mr. George [illegible] examined.

13063. CHAIRMAN.—You are interested in polo ponies?—Yes.

13064. Do you breed them?—I am trying to breed a few now, but they are not old enough to know very much about them yet. The oldest is three years old.

13065. Where are you breeding them?—In Ireland.

13066. In what part of the country?—In Wexford.

13067. And what stallions and what mares have you used?—I am using a stallion I bought at the [illegible] sale, a thoroughbred stallion, 14.3, "[illegible]" by "[illegible]" out of "[illegible]," and the mares are nearly all old polo ponies, either broken down or mares that were not [illegible] up [illegible] in one way or another. They are about 14 to 14.2½ hands.

13068. As to their breeding, are you particular?—As far as I can be. Whenever I am buying I always find out anything I can about the breed.

13069. Have you entered into this as a matter of business?—Yes; and the breeding is as much as the buying. The breeding is an experiment. I buy ponies largely in Ireland.

13070. Where?—In a great many districts; but mostly Wexford and around there, and in Sligo and [illegible].

13071. What kind of ponies are they?—I find the [illegible] ponies are the best, generally, that I have been among. They are all generally by thoroughbred stallions, and are really the polo pony of the present day in a [illegible]—the [illegible]. [illegible] and [illegible] up in that land of theirs [illegible], and [illegible] to find they are [illegible].

13072. What age do you buy them at?—Mostly at four [illegible]. I buy them as [illegible].

13073. And you keep them [illegible]?—[illegible] them, and sell them as five years old or [illegible].

13074. I suppose a polo pony is [illegible] any price [illegible] "made"?—[illegible].

13075. Have you tried and bought any of these [illegible] ponies?—[illegible] [illegible] [illegible] I have got [illegible] [illegible] [illegible], [illegible]. [illegible] [illegible] [illegible].

13076. Do you know the [illegible] districts—the western parts of Ireland generally?—No, I have never been in Donegal, but I have been in Sligo.

13077. [illegible] in Kerry?—No.

13078. Do you employ anybody to buy?—I employ men to look out for them for me. I have got one man there [illegible] [illegible], and when I go to him and [illegible].

13079. How long have you been buying and selling these ponies [illegible]?—[illegible].

13080. And you find it on the whole successful?—Yes. I [illegible] [illegible] [illegible] [illegible].

13081. What about [illegible] ponies [illegible] [illegible] to say, because it is so hard to breed a pony. You have to [illegible] breed a pony [illegible] [illegible] and a half, but certainly I think that [illegible] [illegible] [illegible] breeding [illegible] a lot of [illegible]. As a rule I find that the ponies I buy have been bred [illegible] to be [illegible], and there is [illegible] a good [illegible] for a good pony [illegible] [illegible] [illegible] [illegible] [illegible].

13082. Your experience of breeding of course has not been long enough as yet?—No.

13083. What do you expect to do with the [illegible] that are [illegible] too big or too small—what kind of [illegible] do you expect?—[illegible] [illegible]. You [illegible] [illegible] them into a fair in Ireland and get for a four-year-old about £15 probably, [illegible] [illegible] [illegible] [illegible] [illegible] [illegible] [illegible] them in England at [illegible] [illegible].

13084. I gather from you that for your purpose you prefer a small thoroughbred sire?—Yes.

13085. In addition?—Yes; [illegible] [illegible] [illegible] small size. I mean my best [illegible] have [illegible] by well known [illegible], such as "[illegible]" and "[illegible] One."

13086. Mr. [illegible].—You say the best [illegible] you have [illegible] have been "[illegible]" and "[illegible] One"?—Yes; and "[illegible]" was a very good polo pony sire. [illegible] stallions seem to get good [illegible].

13087. They have all, I suppose, been thoroughbred stallions?—Yes.

13088. And for that particular purpose would you like to go to any other breed?—No.

13089. Do you think that the small farmer in the West of Ireland would make those polo ponies as [illegible] [illegible]—they are able to do it no doubt—[illegible] [illegible] [illegible] [illegible] [illegible] [illegible] [illegible]?—It is very hard to say, because I found from my experience of breeding that to breed to the height is the great difficulty. [illegible] [illegible] the polo pony [illegible] [illegible] [illegible] [illegible], [illegible] [illegible] [illegible] [illegible] it; but [illegible] [illegible] [illegible] [illegible] [illegible] [illegible] [illegible], and I don't think that people have [illegible] [illegible] [illegible] [illegible] [illegible] [illegible].

13090. Then from what you know, what sort of stallions should you send into the congested districts [illegible] [illegible] [illegible] [illegible] to breed their polo ponies?—I should send small thoroughbred stallions of a high class [illegible], not a Barb.

13091. What is your objection to a Barb?—My experience is, that a Barb [illegible] [illegible], has not as good shoulders—they have generally bad shoulders—and [illegible] [illegible] [illegible] [illegible]. There is a great difference between an Arab and a Barb, [illegible] [illegible] between an English thoroughbred and, I was going to say, a [illegible] [illegible].

13092. You would like everything that is sent into the West of Ireland [illegible] [illegible] [illegible] [illegible] be thoroughbred, with a view of getting both courage and [illegible] [illegible]?—Yes.

13093. Should you be afraid of [illegible] blood being [illegible] into the West of Ireland [illegible] [illegible] [illegible] the breed for the polo pony?—Yes.

13094. And should you think [illegible] [illegible] [illegible] [illegible] [illegible] [illegible] [illegible] [illegible] [illegible] [illegible] [illegible] [illegible] [illegible]?—I should [illegible] country and [illegible] [illegible] [illegible] [illegible], and [illegible] [illegible] [illegible] [illegible] [illegible] [illegible].

13095. Have you ever [illegible] any [illegible] [illegible] [illegible] [illegible] [illegible] [illegible] [illegible] [illegible] [illegible] [illegible] [illegible] [illegible] [illegible] [illegible] [illegible] [illegible]?—I have not formed any [illegible] opinion, but I [illegible] [illegible] [illegible] [illegible] [illegible] [illegible] [illegible] [illegible] [illegible] [illegible] [illegible].

13096. Then if you only had a limited amount of money [illegible] [illegible] [illegible] [illegible] [illegible] [illegible] [illegible] stallions, [illegible] [illegible] [illegible] [illegible] [illegible] [illegible]?—I think it would [illegible] [illegible] [illegible] money [illegible] [illegible] [illegible] [illegible] the mares in the [illegible] and that the best thing is to make sure of [illegible] [illegible] stallions.

13097. Mr. WALTER GILBEY.—Your breeding is confined principally to polo ponies?—Yes.

13098. You have not been breeding?—I have been breeding polo ponies four years. I [illegible] [illegible] [illegible] [illegible] [illegible].

13099. You are hopeful of establishing a breed of polo ponies?—I won't say I am hopeful. I am experimenting. I should not be satisfied till I tried, and I am trying to see what I can do.

13100. You are trying very small thoroughbreds?—[illegible].

13101. And the mares?—About 14 or 14.1½.

March 11, 1897.

Mr. George [illegible].

13102. Not under that.—I have got two: 13.3 they are, I think.

13103. The standard of the polo ponies is under 14.2?—Yes.

13104. Do you think you will be able by [illegible] to breed animals with any certainty [illegible] as an experiment?—No; I think I will [illegible]—I am afraid neither animal [illegible] it depends so very much on the sire. I had the first [illegible] and [illegible] big black [illegible] [illegible] to get small stock [illegible] [illegible] the right size, but he [illegible] big black.

13105. You prefer the thoroughbred and Arab, not the Barb?—Yes.

13106. But there has been a Barb very successful in breeding?—Lord Harrington's "Awfully Jolly" bred some good ponies, but I don't think he ever bred ponies that were equal to the thoroughbred ponies at all.

13107. Equal to the Arab, do you think?—Well, his ponies were [illegible] [illegible], and I only [illegible] two of them and I only [illegible] one of them, and I rode that when it was rather old. I don't like them as well as Arabs.

13108. Colonel St. Quintin.—With regard to breeding polo ponies, do you think anybody can breed a polo pony with any certainty at all as the height and the [illegible] qualities?—I don't think you can yet. I don't think you can say that out of [illegible] you can breed a pony 14.2.

13109. You profess to be buying with very great care and trouble to breed a polo pony. Do you think they in [illegible] breeding that the small mares in size, West of Ireland [illegible] have could breed a pony that would be of very great value to them?—I think they would get a [illegible] of them that would be very good ponies if they had the right sire.

13110. How do you think they would get rid of their ponies, because a polo pony is not a polo pony until he is made, and therefore they would only be able to sell [illegible] ponies at very small prices?—There are a great many men [illegible] in Ireland who will always give a [illegible] price for a pony that in their opinion would make a good polo pony, and I think that the [illegible] would be given for the [illegible] pony now, which has happened [illegible] [illegible] would pay for breeding in the poor districts.

13111. You consider the thoroughbred and the Arab. Do you think that the Hackney is capable of getting the right stamp of polo pony?—Certainly not.

13112. Why not?—Because the Hackney, in my opinion, [illegible] for [illegible] breeding. I have [illegible] [illegible] heavy in the shoulder, which [illegible] makes [illegible] for polo.

13113. Then you don't want the high action in the polo pony, I presume?—No.

13114. You want him for speed?—You want him for speed.

13115. Sir Thomas Esmonde.—Do you say you are breeding or buying ponies in Wexford?—I am doing both.

13116. Do you get many ponies there to buy?—Yes, a good many ponies come from the county Wexford.

13117. Mostly bred in the country?—Mostly in Wexford and Carlow.

13118. Which is the district where you get most of your ponies from?—I should say I get more from Wexford than anywhere else, because it is handier and I know it very well, and I hear of every good pony in it.

13119. What sort is the sire of your own?—A small thoroughbred called "Springfield"; he is one of the Yardley stud.

13120. Mr. Wrench.—If you think the breeding of a polo pony is more or less of a fluke, do you think it would be at all a certain business for farmers to engage in?—No; it can't be.

13121. Would you prefer what we call a dwarfed thoroughbred as a polo pony to any other breed?—The best polo pony is what I call the dwarf 11 stone hunter—a miniature Irish blood hunter.

13122. As nearly thoroughbred as possible?—As nearly thoroughbred as possible with substance.

13123. Do you buy many polo ponies in Ireland in the year?—Yes, fifty or sixty in the year.

13124. Do you think that animals bred for polo ponies if they attempted to breed them for polo ponies would be as useful for the people to work on their farms as animals bred from a stronger breed?—They would not make good plough horses I should say, if that is what you mean.

13125. I mean in places where they have to use their produce to work on the farm—do you think they would be as useful as stronger animals?—They are as useful as most animals. I see them working, but in Ireland they don't use the strong animals in the districts I have been to.

13126. I don't mean very strong?—But as a rule they are using weedy animals about 15 hands or that sort of thing. At least I see a lot of those used, and I think a good well-bred strong pony 14.2 would be more useful than a weed of 15 hands.

13127. But it might not be so useful as a stronger built animal?—No, certainly not.

13128. Chairman.—You don't know the western seaboard yourself personally?—No.

13129. And from personal experience you don't know what kind of animal is wanted to do the farm work, such as it is?—No, not in those parts.

13130. I gather from you that the price you can get for a good made polo pony is such that it might pay as a business, even although of course a considerable number of the produce are not fit for polo ponies at all?—Yes.

13131. That is your general idea. You would not expect to get a very large proportion of polo ponies?—No.

The Commission adjourned.

TWENTY-FIFTH DAY—FRIDAY, MARCH 19TH, 1897.

Sitting at 18, Hanover-square, London, W.

Present:—THE EARL OF DUNRAVEN, K.P. (in the Chair); MR. J. L. CAREW, M.P.; HON. H. W. FITZWILLIAM; MR. PERCY LA TOUCHE; COLONEL ST. QUINTIN; EARL OF ENNISKILLEN; SIR WALTER GILBEY; LORD RATHDONNELL; MR. F. S. WRENCH.

MR. HUGH NEVILLE, Secretary.

Captain Fife, Langton Hall, Northallerton, examined.

Captain Fife.

[illegible]. CHAIRMAN.—You were a Captain in the 5th Lancers?—Yes, my lord.

[illegible]. And you are a member of the Hunters' Improvement Society?—Yes.

[illegible]. You have taken a great interest in horse-breeding for a number of years?—Yes; in fact all my life I have been interested in it.

[illegible]. You originated the Compton Stud Farm?—Yes.

[illegible]. When was the Stud Farm started?—In 1886. We have been going on ever since.

[illegible]. Could you tell us the general principles on which it has been founded, and how it has been carried out?—Dorsetshire, I must tell you, was a country in which hunters were not bred. Nobody used to breed them in that country. The farmers used to buy them from the Irish dealers, make them, and sell them again. [illegible] we would get a thoroughbred horse for the farmers. We got two, "Master Ned" and "King Charley." They both did very well in the country, especially "Master Ned." [illegible] We hold an annual show. [illegible]

[illegible] I think you might give them?—[illegible]

[illegible]. How do you account for the large fluctuations in the prices?—[illegible]

[illegible]. All your stallions are thoroughbred?—[illegible]

[illegible]. What kind of mares did you put him to?—[illegible]

[illegible]. Are there plenty in that part of the country?—[illegible]

[illegible]. What kind of mares are they generally?—They have improved [illegible]

[illegible]. Are they bred there?—[illegible] "King Tom" [illegible] "King Charley" [illegible]

[illegible]. Can you tell us what kind of fees you charge the farmers?—We charge the farmers half [illegible] for the ordinary horses, but for an exceptional horse like "[illegible]," we charge five guineas.

[illegible]. Do you exercise any selection of the mares; do you let any man put any mare to one of your horses if he pays the fee?—We never prohibit; we [illegible]

3 E

March 11, 1896. [illegible]
Captain Fife.

fresh, but they do now. I think they have learned a good deal, and this is the principle of one horse rather than another. We generally have some strong horses suitable for well-bred mares, and we have some blood-like horses that we consider are suitable for smaller mares. At first they would not listen to advice. They all went for the big horse and probably [illegible], but now they [illegible] as to the matter.

13137. Of the stock of these stallions that you have told us of, what proportion do the hunters bear to the others?—They are all bred for hunting, but, of course, the majority are harness horses. When you put a thoroughbred horse with mares not so good as a [illegible] horse, you may get a harness horse if he is not a hunter, owing, perhaps, to his having moderate shoulders or something of that sort. Some very good harness horses are bred in that way.

13138. The object of the Society **is to breed a** hunter?—Yes, to breed a hunter.

13139. How many classes have you in your show?—We divide cobs and Welsh, and we divide gentlemen's classes and farmers' classes. We think the gentlemen have more opportunity of getting their animals up into show form, so that we generally put them apart separately, and we follow that right through in foals, yearlings, two-year-olds, and three-year-olds. We have a large class every year of brood mares; we have sometimes had over 150 brood mares exhibited in the show, and we throw out [illegible] every year by our best horses—the best brood mares in the country are exhibited there. We find this a great encouragement to the man who would keep a good mare. Many mares have gone on, year after year, getting the premium then.

13140. Are many of these horses bought privately?—What I mean principally are bought [illegible] the [illegible], or perhaps some of them are bought privately on the show ground. They give no notice to the [illegible] of their being sold. They sometimes sold the day after or the day before [illegible], but in connection with the show.

13141. Do you know whether many of the mares are bought to go abroad?—No; I don't think we have had any instances of people coming down to buy mares to take abroad.

13142. Could you tell us any more about the Compton Stud before we go into some general questions?—As regards financial or any particulars of that sort—well, financially we have always made it cover its expenses, but in making this calculation Captain Hornby and myself, who work it, don't make any pay as directors. If it was done by a Society or by Government you would have to pay the people who look after it—we charge nothing for that and in that way it pays. We have made it clear its expenses by making horses very often in the Stud [illegible], we always buy the best horses we can and perhaps we keep them for three or four years, and if we have an opportunity of selling the horse at a good profit we do, and are obliged [illegible] the benefit of him for a certain number of years. The farmers very often say—"We are very sorry you sold such and such a horse, we were just getting good stock by him, and it is a great disappointment to us." I always say—"We never could afford to give the country, we have given the stallions just for their benefit unless we can get it back again." If you give £1,000 for a horse to begin with, and keep him a certain number of years, he will rapidly depreciate till he is worth only a couple of hundred pounds, therefore we try to sell him before that has happened, and in that way make both ends meet.

13143. Do you think it has been a benefit to the country?—A considerable benefit to the country; there were no good hunters bred in the country, or all horses that bought, and now there are some first class hunters to be bought every year at our shows, with a good many strains of blood, and there have been [illegible]. I can confidently meeting people who say—"Oh, I bought a horse at your sale two years ago and he is as good a horse as I could wish." They have always given satisfaction, where they have gone to.

13144. And if that advantage could be established in many you would say the whole thing has paid very well; it has absolutely paid its expenses, and besides that it is a great advantage to the people?—Oh, yes. Actually the show is not against this, it costs us a good deal of money.

13145. Could you tell us what you give in prizes?—The first year we gave £40, then we gave £75, then we gave £100, £100, £110, £120. We have given away £1,070 in the nine years. Then we have been out of pocket for the show £1,400 in nine years; it costs us a little over £150 a year; we have sold altogether £26,000 worth of stock, the property of the farmers.

13146. Have you any mares of your own?—Not that we count in the stud account. I have mares of my own, and Captain Hornby has mares, but we don't enter them on the account at all, we pay for them privately ourselves, and deal with the produce. I only just have enough mares to breed horses for my own riding. I am now breeding thoroughbred stock; I have between thirty and forty thoroughbred mares, and it takes me all my time to look after those with the further responsibility.

13147. Mr. La Touche.—What mares, as a rule, do the farmers in the Compton Stud district breed from, big mares or small mares?—As a rule, as one comes with, cross-bred, underbred mares, but we have had much more success since we have got more blood in the mares. The mares that are out of the common mares by our thoroughbred horses make very much better mares than the first lot.

13148. What sort of stock did these mares produce before your stud was started?—Oh, there were hardly any horses bred in the country.

13149. They did not try to breed hunters of any sort or description hardly?—Hardly, I think. Before we commenced at the shows in the neighbourhood there were no classes for young stock, there was so little breeding, and at the Ringwood Show in 1886 probably, or 1887, it was just before our own young stock came out, I proposed that there should be a class for young stock; they said they thought there would not be enough to make a class. I said—"Let us have a class for yearlings, two-year-olds, and three-year-olds together, the best of the three ages," and I think we only had **seven** or eight entries for the three ages combined.

13150. I take it you **charge the farmers 50s.**?—Yes.

13151. Had you ever any experience of half-bred stallions in the Compton stud?—No, never.

13152. You never bought anything that was out of a half-bred?—Never, except one pony; his dam was by [illegible]; I think he was good [illegible] himself.

13153. Do you see any similarity between the mares of the Compton district and the Irish mares?—The Irish mares have great quality and more quality, but I must say our general mares that they are breeding from are rather similar to the Irish mares; our principal mares have been produced by our own stallions, and the farmers have come round to the way of thinking; they find that the better bred mares breed better stock.

13154. Was there any resemblance between the Compton mare in the unimproved condition and the bad sort of mare you encounter in Ireland?—Oh, well, perhaps the bad sort, but they were coarser, commoner, underbred, mixed with the cart. While they had a mare kept to ride or drive into market, and that sort of thing, they were in the habit pretty often of putting her to a cart stallion, as there was that cross about.

13155. Of considerable cart blood?—Oh, yes.

13156. Since the operation of your stud there

[illegible]
Captain [illegible]

in Ireland?—Yes, I bought him in Ireland, and he went back to Ireland, he has gone back there again. If you ever have a chance of buying a "Master Ned" hunter, he is a good hunter, he never has to be taught to jump.

13191. Mr. Wrench.—You think that because there is an absolute certainty about the pedigree in your sales it has put the price up?—Oh, yes, certainly.

13192. I think you said the ordinary mares in the district were really the produce of the roadster mare crossed with a cart horse?—No, I don't think they had any roadster blood in them.

13193. What was the original animal they were bred out of?—I don't know, and I don't suppose the owners knew themselves.

13194. Cart-horse blood in them?—Very often when they got what they call a nag mare, a thing that they could ride and drive. Their idea of breeding was to put her to a cart-horse, to get something to go in milk carts.

13195. I suppose those mares were mostly up to 15.2, were they?—Oh, yes.

13196. Or more?—Yes, they would be of all sorts and sizes.

13197. You think that the Hunters' Improvement Society in England has effected a considerable improvement in the breeding of hunters in England?—I am sure it has.

13198. Would you like to see a Hunters' Improvement Society started in Ireland or your Hunters' Improvement Society extended largely to Ireland?—I should like to see it extended to Ireland.

13199. Chairman.—Do your horses travel the country?—We travel through the districts, our own establishment is in the centre, and when we send a horse out he goes by train. We never allow him to try or serve mares on the road; if he is walking from the station and has a mile to go we never allow our man to try or serve mares at any but the appointed places. We consider there is a great risk of accidents, we consider it leads men into the temptation of getting drunk and all that sort of thing, and also we know that everything is done in a regular manner if the mare is served at a certain place; there is generally a man there responsible for what does happen. Horses go out by train and stop perhaps a couple of nights at one place, and go on by train to another and stop a couple of nights, and they take about three places which are the centres of districts, and we have two horses out in different directions, and then our own four horses stand in the centre and mares are [illegible] into them.

13200. In that way you occupy a considerable range of country?—Yes, I should think we cover about twenty miles by thirty with our stallions and mares outside that come to meet them.

13201. You live yourself in Yorkshire?—Yes.

13202. Why did you select Dorsetshire?—I had a yeomanry appointment, I had the North Somerset Yeomanry for five years, and I was living there during the time I held my appointment, and having a house there I went on living there until I came up to Yorkshire.

13203. It was not on account of any particular advantages?—No.

13204. On the contrary, I gather from you that you thought the class of mares were not very suitable for breeding hunters?—No, we could not have a worse start than we had.

13205. Can you tell us anything about the pony stallion—I think you said he got produce from 13½ to 14.2?—Yes.

13206. What becomes of them?—They drive about in traps, and they are sold at our sales for general purposes.

13207. Are any of them turned into polo ponies?—No, I don't think so; they had not quite quality enough.

13208. You know Ireland well, don't you?—Yes.

13309. The whole of the country?—No, I cannot say the whole of the country; my experience of Ireland was more in the South. I was quartered at Cahir when I first joined my regiment, and my experience of Ireland is more confined to that district and to Cahirmee fair and the Dublin Horse Show. I used to buy horses there a good deal at one time. When I was buying hunters I always bought my hunters in Ireland before I took to breeding my own.

13310. Taking the parts of the country that produce these high-class hunters, roughly say the South, I think you said that the general quality of the mares is superior to that of the mares at any rate that you found in Dorsetshire?—Oh, certainly.

13311. Much superior?—Much superior.

13312. And for them would you recommend the same class of stallion as you have got in Dorsetshire?—Yes, I should recommend the same class of stallion.

13313. I take it you would recommend the thoroughbred?—Recommend the thoroughbred.

13314. What is your opinion about the half-bred hunter sire?—When I use the word half-bred I mean the ordinary half-bred horse, that is by a thoroughbred horse out of an ordinary animal without any particularly authenticated pedigree. I don't believe in him at all, but I believe strongly in the horse that we have recently approved of in the Hunters' Improvement Society, that is a horse with four crosses of blood commencing with a registered mare. If that is put on paper it is found that he cannot be less than 31 parts out of 32 thoroughbred—he is virtually a thoroughbred horse. In introducing a horse of that description you might get some horses of extra power, which I think is a great advantage. The farmers invariably complain that where they have well-bred mares in putting them to a small thoroughbred they lose size and get something that is not saleable, and unfortunately in consequence of that they go and put their mares in some cases to Clevelands, in some cases to Hackneys, and in some cases to these half-bred horses that they don't know how they are bred, and they breed a lot of common useless animals. I think it would be a great advantage to provide what the Hunters' Improvement Society are now trying to carry out, that is these registered sires with four crosses from registered mares, they would be virtually thoroughbred, and you should get the extra size. I don't mean to say that a thoroughbred horse may not be, and in some cases is, quite as powerful as any horse you will breed in the way we have proposed. For instance, there is no half-bred sire we can produce that will have more power than "Yardarm," and he is clean bred. There is "Royal Meath" in Ireland, he is another of those powerful horses. But there is not a general supply of horses of equal power, and I think it would be a great advantage to the farmers—it is of more importance to the farmers—the introduction of these horses, than it is to the gentlemen, because the gentlemen can afford to send his mare a long distance. As I say, we have mares sent from all parts of England to "Yardarm"; a gentleman can afford that, but a farmer cannot; he must go to the horse within reasonable reach of him, and then if there is only a small horse at hand he leaves the thoroughbred altogether, and he goes to some breed that was bred not for quality but for either pulling weight, such as a cart horse, or for the purpose of getting harness horses.

13315. How do you define a farmer?—I think the Secretary of your Commission helped me to find a definition of it—that is, a person who farms as a business and as his sole business.

13316. And if he was engaged in any other business at all?—He would not be a farmer.

13317. Have you bought any hunters in Ireland

lately?—No, I have not. I always have some of my own breeding coming on every year.

13218. Have you formed any opinion as to whether Ireland produces as many good hunters as it used to?—I could hardly give you a good opinion on that. When I have been over at the shows I have been judging thoroughbred stock always for the last few years, so that I have not been so much in the hunter line.

13219. Could you give us any opinion—have you formed any opinion as to whether the hunter-breeding parts of Ireland are properly supplied with stallions?—No; I am afraid my opinion is not worth much.

13220. You have attended a good many of the Dublin Shows?—Yes; I could give you an opinion as to the quality of the thoroughbred stallions. I think that they have improved considerably. I think the thoroughbred stallions have improved in Ireland, but I cannot give you an opinion as to whether the supply is equal to the demand.

13221. The general evidence we have had is that probably the supply is about the same, but the demand is greater?—Yes.

13222. Do you know the Western parts of Ireland at all, the congested districts?—No, I cannot give an opinion as to that.

13223. Or the North?—No.

13224. Do you think that Ireland has succeeded somehow in producing a very superior class of hunter?—I think that it has done so, and not only that but I think the whole of the world acknowledges it. I think Ireland has got a well deserved name as being the best country in the world to produce hunters, and I think it is of very great importance that Ireland should keep up its individuality as the country to breed hunters in.

13225. Do you attribute that to anything special in the climate or soil?—Well, no doubt both the climate and the soil are suitable to it, but I consider the fact that hitherto the thoroughbred has been so largely used in Ireland has had a good deal to do with it. Years ago there was an absence of cart-horse blood. I have observed that in nearly all of those countries where a class of light cart-horse has been used, like in Devonshire, there have been good hunters bred. In Devon there have been good hunters bred which is attributable I think a great deal to the Devonshire pack mare. Where you have that light description of cart-mare you find that good hunters are bred, very often the cross of the thoroughbred on these animals. Northumberland had a breed of little light active cart-mares—the black mares—good hunters were bred, descendants from them, and I think that the old horses of the country in Ireland that used to do the work of that time had little or no cart blood in them, and I think the success of Ireland is due to the fact that their animals are better bred; they have more of the thoroughbred in them as a rule than they have in other countries where they have got mixed up with the cart blood, and as they have got mixed up with the Hackney in parts of Yorkshire and Norfolk, and in other parts of Yorkshire they have got too much of the Cleveland and coach-horse. All that I think is bad and tends to depreciate the soundness of the hunter.

13226. Do you think it very important in breeding that there should be absolute purity on one side or the other?—Yes, I do; but when I talk of purity of blood I should call "Ox-vestry," for instance, a thoroughbred horse, although some people would call him a half-bred. Looking at it in that light, the same thing as the Hunters' Improvement Society has suggested in bringing forward four crosses from a registered mare; I look upon him as a thoroughbred horse. But I would rather have a cross of the thoroughbred mare with a horse of that description, either "New-Oxvestry" or the Hunters' Improvement Society's horse, than the cross of a thoroughbred horse out of a cart-mare, or mare than in a cart mare, for you have a lot of bad blood by that process, whereas in the other case you have good blood on both sides.

13227. We have had a good deal of evidence to the effect that there is a deterioration going on in Ireland, attributable to a great extent to the fact that the foreigners bought so many of the best mares to go abroad. Assuming that to be so, could you suggest any way in which that could be stopped?—No, I don't think it could be possible to stop it, and it would be very wrong to attempt to do so, for it appears to me it is hard enough for people to make horse breeding pay, and anything you can do to help to make it pay should be done, and there should be no stop put to their trade in any way. If we were to say they were not to sell their thoroughbred mares, it would damage their trade, and consequently they would breed less horses. What you would gain by keeping good mares in the country you would lose by giving a check to horse-breeding. And although people think it has been drawn there are in the country plenty of good brood mares to be got if a person really knows how and is able to get them.

13228. Would you try to induce them by giving them premiums and prizes?—Oh, yes, certainly, by all means. I think that would be the greatest benefit in the world. That would be no check, it would be an encouragement and would induce them to go and get good mares. I frequently hear people coming to me and saying "I have an old brood mare that I would like to sell if I can get a good home for her. I will sell her for a moderate sum, but I cannot get anyone to buy her." I don't think there is a want of brood mares in the country. If I had a commission to buy good brood mares I could get them, and at a very small price.

13229. And in England?—I rather think it would be the same in England, if you like to buy them young. The best time to buy from a brood mare is when she is three year old to make it pay; there are plenty of good three-year-olds to be bought cheap now in Ireland, and if they were put to the horse you may get a foal next year, which, at four years old with the foal, would be worth a half year older, and if you sold her she would give the her keep. But I think your suggestion of giving premiums or anything to induce them to breed from good mares instead of bad ones would be of the greatest benefit in the world.

13230. Some of the witnesses have attached very great importance to trying to induce the farmers to keep their good mares, looking upon the mares as almost of vital importance, and others seem rather to have thought that the best thing to do would be to devote more attention to providing a better class of stallion?—If you provide a good mare she only provides one foal in the year; if you provide a good stallion he breeds 30 or 40, and by supplying good stallions you produce good brood mares; if you have bad stallions they produce bad brood mares. Therefore I think the stallion is of the greatest importance in comparison with, and the breeder has always in his option the power of choosing his brood mares, but he has not the option of the stallion unless it is provided for him. Unless he has a good stallion within reach, if he has ever such a good mare he is fairly [illegible], but I think a man, if he really wants to, can get a good brood mare, and if he has a good stallion he ought to have a fair chance of success.

13231. You don't know the congested districts in Ireland, personally, I think you said?—No, my lord, I do not.

13232. Could you give us any opinion from your general experience as to what class of stallion ought to be put to those small, light, weedy mares in that part of the country?—Well, I have had them described [illegible] that they are undersized, and that they are well bred. What I should think would be the best cross really would be the thoroughbred with

[illegible]

extremely good action, that is the type I would suggest as being of greatest [illegible]; I should think it would be no earthly use sending a thoroughbred down there that had not extremely good action, because if you breed a small animal, if it has not action, it is not worth much as a hack. Thoroughbreds with exceedingly good action would get nice hacks, nice little ponies, and useful cobs, in that way, and if their blood were sent in some such manner it would not be the cause of deterioration. I think, in dealing with the congested districts you would always have to consider the general good of the whole of Ireland. I think Ireland has acquired a name as being the finest country in the world for breeding hunters, and I think you have got to consider very carefully about what you do in any particular portion of Ireland, that it is not injurious to the general good of the country, and in introducing the thoroughbred in the shape of a stepping thoroughbred or otherwise it would not interfere with the general good of the breeding in the rest of the country, as it would if the Hackney blood was introduced. But I should like to see in the future—it would take a few years to produce—some, say a dozen, Hackney mares, crossed with a horse like "[illegible]," that, perhaps, a great many of you may have seen at the Horse Show this week, a thoroughbred horse with very beautiful action, beautiful shoulders, knee, and hock action, and if their female produce are kept and crossed again with another thoroughbred horse of similar characteristics, and the male produce kept as stallions, I think that that horse would be a most useful horse to use for the congested districts; they might be a little broader, and have a little more bone than the thoroughbred; that would be good in the first instance, and I think they would have just as good action as the Hackneys have at present—I mean, flying action,—and they would breed a class of animal from those mares in the congested districts that would not only be useful as harness horses, but they would be useful as riding horses, and if ever the produce of these animals I have just recommended was to be crossed with a thoroughbred to breed a hunter, I don't think there would be sufficient Hackney blood to show in the horse.

19333. I gather you think the system of registration is very useful in Ireland?—Yes.

19334. That it would be useful, anyhow?—I don't quite understand what you mean by registration. When we talk in England of registered horses, they are those horses that have got their names in the stud book; we don't register the thoroughbred horses.

19335. Under the Hunters' Improvement Society?—We only register those that have a stamp, which are admitted under certain rules, which guarantee their being sound and thoroughbred.

19336. Have you ever considered the question of registration of mares?—I think it would be a very good thing, we have it in England as much as we possibly can. The Hunters' Improvement Society registers all the best mares in the country; I think it is of the greatest importance in the world, as it is an inducement to owners to keep their mares and take a little pride in them. If they are in the book they don't like to sell them, and they think a good deal of them; it has done good in England, and I think it would do good in Ireland if that was extended. I am sure the Hunters' Improvement Society would be very glad, indeed, to lend any assistance in their power to extend this book, to include Ireland as well as England. There are some Irish mares registered in that book as it is, but they could be registered either mixed with the English mares, or they could be registered separately and in the general stud book, as an appendix at the end, of Irish mares entirely, whichever was the wish of the Irish people.

19337. Some witnesses have given evidence to the effect there ought to be a compulsory registration of all [illegible] in Ireland, horses, asses, and their progeny, supposing it to be practical, do you think it would be valuable?—I am always adverse to trying to force people; you asked me the question at the very beginning of my examination, as to whether we prohibited certain mares coming to our stallions, I have never done it, I always find I can do more with the people by leading them rather than driving them; I think if you provide them with a lead, and give them every encouragement to go on, you would do more than by anything compulsory.

19338. Would you object to the system of licensing stallions, it has been stated in evidence that in the poorer districts the class of thoroughbred stallions was decidedly inferior and unsound, and that they ought to be all licensed and not allowed to stand unless they had a licence?—I prefer in any other way than, to any subsidising stallions in that particular district where the stallions are very bad, I think if there was a subsidised stallion in that particular district at a fee which the people would pay, so that horse is [illegible] to be sufficiently like an existing compulsory registration. If you have compulsory registration, you must have a committee and [illegible], it must be [illegible]; there are many good horses which are passed, and then they are [illegible] the same [illegible] in London [illegible] one year and next year they [illegible], it would be [illegible] that perhaps the most successful horses in the world and perfect in every respect except this, which after all is a [illegible], should be wiped out altogether; you would not register a horse without a voluntary [illegible] certificate.

19339. Lord Rathdonnell.—They would be registered, but not compulsorily.

19340. No premiums given by the Society?—Oh, yes, that is the best way to do it, you are getting the thing all in your own hands. The Society then get everything in their own hands, and if you won't come under their rules they will not give you prizes. It is the same thing if you like, to make sure that you won't have a horse at the Dublin Show unless he is [illegible], and you are not obliged to do so—I should prefer that to compulsory registration.

19341. Chairman.—I gather from you generally that you think that Ireland having achieved a considerable reputation for producing hunters it would be wise to keep her attention directed to producing that kind of horse?—I think it is of equal importance to Ireland as regards horses as it is in Jersey and Guernsey, which have a celebrated breed of Channel Island cattle; and it is equally so that the introduction of [illegible] and Hackney horses and Hackneys and Cleveland stallions should be imported into Ireland as it would be to the disadvantage of Jersey and Guernsey if a shorthorn bull was sent there. A lot of people might argue why should we not breed shorthorn cattle in Jersey, or breed what we like, but no doubt for the benefit of the whole country, they have a law that no cattle can be allowed on the island except that which is pure bred, and the whole world knows that is one of the most valuable animals that you can get.

19342. And I think you are of opinion that foreign competition interferes a good deal with the hunter trade?—I think it has tremendously, the fact, a large quantity of these [illegible], they cannot sell horses in America now, it costs very little bringing them over here, they cannot get rid of them in their own country, and they are sending them over here as fast as they can, at whatever price they fetch. They are selling animals at £25 a piece—the same class of animal that we used to be buying in England for £30 or £40—and it is ruining our trade in the cheap horses; and in [illegible] harness horses, too, they are getting them from the Continent. We have got a speciality in England and Ireland—Ireland especially—for breeding hunters; no country can touch us in that at all.

13213. We have not the same competition in hunters from abroad?—No. They would always give more for an Irish or English hunter than for one they knew had been bred in America or on the Continent; but if it came on with a [illegible] horse—they will give [illegible] for a [illegible] [illegible] if he [illegible], wherever he is bred.

13214. Assuming a Government grant for the improvement of the industry in Ireland, have you any opinion as to how it would be best applied, whether in subsidising or in the institution of stud farms?—The institution of stud farms is a tremendously costly affair always. If things are done by private enterprise people do them in a much more economical way, and it is also necessary in dealing [illegible] to [illegible] [illegible] very careful; it is very difficult to be sure that you have got a suitable man, and even if you have got one when he comes to [illegible] that you got a [illegible] that is capable, so that it is a very difficult thing to carry on Government studs economically and with economy. I should rather see that experiment tried for these congenial districts of the Hackney mares with two crosses of the thoroughbred, the thoroughbred being primarily chosen for action. I should like to see their produce used in the congenial districts, and I believe that would do a great deal of good, and I believe it would meet the want that exists more or less. The people in the country want something suitable for breeding horses, and I think it would meet that, and I don't think it would injure the prospects of the country in general as regards breeding hunters. I think it is too large a question to go into that of a Government stud, but if one was kept at all it might be kept for thoroughbred mares particularly chosen for their suitability of producing hunters, and the thoroughbred sires chosen for the same reasons, and their produce kept entirely; those that were not quite good enough might be sold for [illegible], and the sales paid—[illegible]—would be [illegible]. An establishment of that sort might do a great deal of good, and those that were chosen [illegible] might be sold in Ireland, with a reserve that they were never to leave the country. I think, however, each one are required, might be bred true to type. Undoubtedly in breeding thoroughbred stock you don't want to breed a horse too much like a trotter, too big; you get him there, and if you have a big mare you [illegible] of getting her to a big horse, then you are likely to breed a great clumsy brute. I think in the [illegible] way he would be a [illegible] clumsy horse, though in the breeding way he would be a weight-carrying hunter. That might be carried on by a Government stud, and it might bring paying [illegible]; of course it would cost a certain amount of money.

13215. What would you do with the mares?—I would breed from them again, and you would have the two crosses, and when you have [illegible] from those and [illegible] a third or [illegible] you would [illegible].

13216. You would not distribute the mares or sell them cheap?—Oh, no, because they would all be thoroughbred. I think you would get a price for them that would very nearly pay for breeding them.

13217. Mr. [illegible].—You think you could [illegible] up a breed of stallions out of these thoroughbred mares chosen for action—[illegible]—[illegible] that if you were given the opportunity to do it at the [illegible] you would in a short time be able to produce a class of stallion that you would like to see [illegible] in Ireland?—Oh, yes, certainly.

13218. But I presume you would require help from Government, because you would have to keep these stallions?—Yes.

13219. Of course you would buy good, cheap thoroughbred mares of good pedigree and shape, although they might not have the [illegible] at Doncaster or at Newmarket. I think you could get them for £40 to £50 a piece?—Yes, and there is always a demand for [illegible]. If you had a certain number all of [illegible] [illegible] of any that you thought good enough for keeping for stallions, and those you thought not quite good enough for that would [illegible] a price of from £100 to £200 a piece as thoroughbreds for hunters, and the young mares might be [illegible], and that would go some way towards paying for their breeding.

13220. But as it is now, do you think that with a reasonable price you can buy suitable stallions, suitable for Ireland—thoroughbred ones?—Oh, yes.

13221. With action and short legs?—They are to be bought, but there is a great deal of trouble to find them; they are not to be bought in large numbers. That is really why I have [illegible] of the [illegible] of these horses with a view to their [illegible]. Suitable thoroughbreds are not to be bought in large numbers, but there are a certain number of them. It was always [illegible] to give £300 or so for them; they are to be got every now and then.

13222. Do you think you can find as good action in a thoroughbred horse as in any other breed?—I do, in individual ones. I do not say that the thoroughbred, taking him all round, would be celebrated for his action.—I mean as taking the best of the world. Say the very horse we happen to have mentioned, "Erskine." I think he is quite as beautiful a mover as any Hackney I ever saw, because he moves with such [illegible], and his shoulders and every joint he has got are all action.

13223. Should you say that having produced "Erskine," or any other thoroughbred he is more likely to transmit his qualities than an animal that had not been so long bred on one particular line, the thoroughbred horse has been bred as a thoroughbred now for a large number of years?—More likely to transmit his action, or his knee action and general quality than a horse bred the same way that did not possess those qualities; he would be more likely to transmit his qualities in that direction than [illegible], but he would be less likely [illegible] than a horse that had been bred for it. "Erskine" is a horse that I would recommend purely as a cross with a Hackney to produce action and quality. I would not recommend him as a cross with a thoroughbred for breeding hunter stallions for Ireland.

13224. I only said "Erskine" because you [illegible] his name?—Yes, I mean a horse like "Royal Meath," [illegible] in Ireland, crossed with thoroughbred mares, and their produce again crossed with a thoroughbred horse of equal size and substance; but it is on [illegible] account of the size you would want [illegible] to have more size than one [illegible]. [illegible] these mares were bought specially to suit that size; then [illegible] that want, [illegible] to be entirely different class of stallion to what other mares would. I think that is the reason why we have been rather successful in Devonshire at the Compton Stud, in having the stallions we use confined to a certain district, to get breeders to choose their stallions, and they all belong to the same class, as there is nothing like [illegible]. "I must go to so and so because he is a friend of mine," which is very often the case with a farmer, he puts his mare to a particular horse just because it suits him [illegible] the owner of the stallion is a relation of his wife's or something of that sort.

13225. You were talking about old mares being sometimes offered to you, do you approve of breeding from old mares?—I have known them to breed some very good stock.

13226. At what age do you begin breeding?—I have a very good mare that I rode until she was

his own, and she has bred me two beautiful foals, but of course I would rather breed from young mares.

13357. Have you formed any idea of the best way of trying to induce the farmer in Ireland to keep his good mares in the country?—I should think there would be nothing better than subsidising the mares and registering them, putting people to select them in the book and to give those prizes or free services; we find it very beneficial.

13358. Would not subsidising the stallion be a cheaper way?—Of course giving them a free service is subsidising them. I think if a man can get a free service it ought to be an inducement to him to keep a good mare instead of a bad one.

13359. Lord Enniskillen.—In what way? Any man who registered his mare would get given him a free service?—Oh, no, they are given free nominations every year in my country to the ten best mares; they are shown in competition, and the ten best mares, they think a great deal more of the free service than if you gave them £5 10s., the price of the service; then they would think nothing of it.

13360. Chairman.—Much as what you charge for the service?—Yes, and they think a lot of the free service, and will go to any trouble to enter their mares in competition.

13361. Mr. Fitzwilliam.—But with limited means would you spend your money on the horse or on the mare?—I think the stallion is the direct way to do more benefit to the country, because he leaves more behind him, but you can always regulate your expenditure by giving these subsidies or free services; you can always regulate them the same as we have; you could either set four services in the country, or twenty or five according to your means, and that might be done perhaps in not very great sums; you might do a little of both.

13362. Lord Dunraven.—You mentioned a certain class of stallion that, in your opinion, would suit the congested districts in Ireland, that is a stallion with two crosses of thoroughbred out of a Hackney mare; how many years would it take you to produce that stallion?—You would have a three-year-old mare there put to him, and you would put the two-year-old to the horse, and that [illegible] into the world, so that you would have it as a two-year-old in six years' time.

13363. Not breeding from two-year-olds?—No. There is nothing against breeding from two-year-olds. I have done it both in half-bred and thoroughbred stock.

13364. I understand that three-year-old was the year you thought best?—No, I have not been asked the question, I have given no evidence about the age.

13365. Sir J. Colthurst.—You said a three-year-old mare?—Yes, you buy a three-year-old mare to commence with.

13366. Lord Enniskillen.—That would be a Hackney mare?—Yes, as a two-year-old; if I was beginning a stud I should breed from my two-year-olds, then if [illegible] you have got to observe about breeding from two-year-olds—if you breed from two-year-olds you must do your mares better, as I may very likely have mentioned, three-year-olds, [illegible] generally, with the exception I don't think [illegible] enough to breed from a two-year-old. I don't think they are sufficiently forward and matured.

13367. At the very earliest it would take six years?—Yes.

13368. Would you not have to keep a great number of mares in order to produce a certain number of stallions?—To do that in quantity you would, supposing you started with a dozen mares.

13369. It would be rather a costly business and an expensive one?—It would be an experiment; and one I only recommend if it is decided to continue the introduction of Hackney blood to Ireland.

13370. Mr. Fitzwilliam.—Do you think a small thoroughbred could be bought now for use in the congested districts?—I think so; there were several horses I noticed here, particularly "Chibiabos," "Krishna," and "First Flight II."—he would be a very nice horse for that purpose.

13371. Lord Enniskillen.—Have you ever been in the congested districts?—No.

13372. Have you ever seen the class of mare that is there?—No, I have only taken it from description.

13373. Have you ever seen the class of horses they used there in their carts?—No; I have taken it for granted when Lord Dunraven told me, that they were well-bred small mares.

13374. Pony mares?—Yes.

13375. Do you think that a thoroughbred horse, however good his action, is likely to impart the same action as he has himself?—Oh, I think so.

13376. As much as a horse that has been bred for action for years?—No, certainly not, you would rely more on the action in the case you mention.

13377. Has it been your experience that if you breed from small half-bred mares, or nondescript bred mares, and put a thoroughbred on them—have you ever found that the result is a weedy sort of a useless description, you cannot use it for any good?—No. I have known some of the best hunters in the world bred from pony mares.

13378. Yes, Welsh pony mares; but these are little weedy mares. My experience of breeding from a thoroughbred horse and these mares in the north-west of Ireland is that you get an animal that is absolutely useless?—All depends on the stallion you use; that horse, "First Flight II.," took a premium, and he is made like a Hackney, but he is a thoroughbred and has got as good action as a Hackney.

13379. That is an exceptional horse?—Yes, but there are exceptional horses you can pick out of the stud book.

13380. What sort of a price could that horse be bought at?—I don't like to state in public what I think is the value. There was another horse there that answered the description, though not such a [illegible] horse, "Touchwood"; he is just in the form of a Hackney, but he is thoroughbred—those are the horses I should like to send down now to the congested districts during the time that the others are being built up.

13381. Have you ever seen the stock of any of these?—No.

13382. You said you thought that subsidising the stallion was a better thing than subsidising the mares?—Yes; I think the benefit is larger.

13383. Have you any idea of the number of stallions in Ireland?—No. My idea is you would not subsidise every stallion you think suitable, but by giving a certain number of subsidies, it is not only the horse that wins the subsidy that is improved thereby, but it is the number of horses that are bought with a view of winning the subsidy. I see Irishmen over at Newmarket buying horses, they won't buy an unsound one as long as they think there is a chance of getting a premium. If you give these prizes in districts, it makes them try to buy good horses with a chance of winning—everybody that buys a horse in that district is buying with a view of winning £100 or £150 prize. The benefit is not confined to the one horse you subsidise in the district, but everybody who buys a horse in that district buys a good one, with the view of winning the subsidy.

13384. Colonel St. Quintin.—You say you have used the Hackney in its present condition; you would require two crosses of the thoroughbred before you would introduce it into Ireland?—I think so. I would much prefer to use the thoroughbred horse specially selected, like the horse that I have mentioned, "First Flight II."

13385. There are two classes with which you are acquainted, and there has been a certain discussion about them; one is the cavalry horse for the service

[illegible]

13300. Mr. WRENCH ORMSBY.—You said you have no experience in breeding Hackneys, but have you had them in your own stable to look after?—We had my friends' horses.

13301. Then you speak partly from hearsay?—From reliable hearsay—from friends of mine who bred and had the animals and drove them.

13302. You have recommended experiments to be tried of Hackney mares with thoroughbred horses?—No, I don't recommend the experiment to be tried; I recommend the Hackney mares with thoroughbred horses.

13303. I said so; and you don't think the same result would arise from a Hackney sire and a thoroughbred mare?—It might, if a suitable animal, but the result I don't suggest is this, that if you were to commence by getting thoroughbred mares and getting Hackney stallions your stallions would be serving mares of the country which, I think, would be doing harm. If you bring the Hackney mares they will not cross with the mares of the country—they will do no harm; if you bring the mares to Ireland and mate them with a thoroughbred horse, he can mate other mares as well as the Hackney mares he is doing them no harm in any way.

13304. You have never taken the trouble to post yourself up as to the breeding of the Hackney—as to the origin of them, and the proportion of blood on the dam's side?—I have noticed that there are one very celebrated horse that comes back to "Ratler."

13305. Mr. WRENCH.—"Ditto"?—Yes, it was bred over and over again to "Ditto"—a thoroughbred—a thoroughbred. "King Tom" and a thoroughbred.

13306. By "Fireaway"?—Exactly, he is a thoroughbred horse.

13307. Mr. WRENCH ORMSBY.—Have you had no experience in buying Hackney horses or driving horses in London, and of knowing from the various dealers' experiences in the style of animals they have, and the prices that they get?—No, I have not done that, but I know that they export a tremendous lot of horses from the Yorkshire—very high class animals, horses that fetch very long prices—a great quantity of them.

13308. Don't you think there is plenty of room to breed in England, or in the United Kingdom, horses of that sort without going abroad, taking the great issue we have of being exterminated by our breeds, that we should not keep to the breeding of these horses?—Yes, the way I should do it would be to improve the Hackney; I think the Hackney wants more thoroughbred blood in him. It is not for me to dictate to the Hackney Society, but I would say that that is what the Hackneys want, more stamina, more quality, and more lightness of action, which would enable them to go through longer journeys, much less exertion to themselves. And I think that that might be produced by infusing a greater quantity of thoroughbred blood into the Hackneys. I think it would be a great advantage; they would then be a useful riding horse as well as a better class of driving horse.

13309. You say you have no experience with regard to driving, it is the possibility of Hackney crossed with thoroughbred, but then you expect that from the cross of the Hackney with the thoroughbred horse there a breed of horses suitable for driving might be bred, the Hackneys themselves having a considerable quantity of thoroughbred blood already in them?—I think if you give them a thoroughbred mare you might breed some very nice animals, because you would be doing exactly what I would like to see, mixing the thoroughbred blood with the Hackney. But I think that giving the Hackney an extra chance you would be breeding clumsy, ugly animals.

13310. From your experience are known, like a "Yorkshire" mated with big thoroughbred horses likely to produce a steady kind of thoroughbreds and not just something like the [illegible] and with no encouragement to continue the breeding, and thoroughbred blood, as horses of that class would be likely to be suitable for racing purposes?—Yes, the kind of, which shows and proves what a big powerful class of thoroughbred horses can be produced, that he found exactly what I said and what I found myself not what I knew to be the case, that if you want to breed, combining your racing and blood horses of that character, then the course and chasing; you want to breed something more robust, he must be and be finished. I think that the experiment is most useful than such horses could be produced by careful mating, and I think such horses would be of great value to sell, to horses for breeding hunters, provided they were mated to well-bred mares and not, in cases where I don't think "Yorkshire" as a suitable horse to put his stock away, a half-bred mare or a common mare, you would get a very clumsy brute. You want a good mare of thoroughbred blood and then you will get something of size and quality combined.

13311. You have frequently judged at the Dublin Show. Do you think any benefit would accrue if a little more information could be given of the breeding of the various animals that are sold there?—Yes, more information placed on the catalogue, I think so. I think I noticed on the catalogue all the time there that the information of the pedigree was not always given. I think it would be a great improvement that it should be. We have an instance also in the Hunters' Improvement Society this year at the judging. The money they received in one show was because the breeder of the animal was not known, and we shut out the pedigree of the animal unless the breeder is known. I think that would be a very good thing, and I think you see some instances of that in the Dublin catalogue where the breeder is not given and the pedigree is given. If the breeder is not given you don't know the pedigree. And that really was the object in the class for Irish-bred brood mares, the particular class at the show this year. I think there were some thirteen or more entries there, and in only a very few instances there, or less I think, could any particulars be obtained at all.

13312. Don't you think it would be very important to know something of their pedigrees?—It is very important to know them if they can be obtained, but there are instances in which they buy mares out of a fence and that sort of thing—instances in which they are unable to obtain information of what is the breeder, and if they cannot obtain the information it is better not to give it at all than to put it in only by hearsay.

13313. Mr. WRENCH.—When you talk of crossing Hackney mares with a thoroughbred horse do you think Hackney mares in their conformation have any special qualification for being mated—I do, to mate with a thoroughbred horse.

13314. You think they are of the right shape and shape?—To mate with the thoroughbred [illegible] with the common horse.

13315. If you know that in the Hackneys that have been imported into Ireland there was a good deal of thoroughbred blood in the same way as the horse that was alluded to to-day, would that lessen your objection to them, to have mixed crosses of thoroughbred blood back?—No, I mean them horses I am recommending.

13316. I am not talking of those horses. If the Hackneys imported into Ireland can have shown their several crosses of thoroughbred blood would that alter your objection, or would you prefer them to be bred with no cross of blood?—Certainly, the more blood the better.

13317. You would not object so much to them if you knew they had thoroughbred blood in them?—My objection would be in want of action. We have got to go through all this exchange here to get some four or five stallions when the particular animal I would recommend in a cross to mate with a Hackney. If you had a suitable horse he will improve the quality as healthy or sturdy mares, but if you had an ill-bred [illegible]

[illegible] [illegible]. Captain Fife.

13349. You think it would keep the breeders?—I think so, certainly; I think it would prevent importation.

13350. When you talk of breeding thoroughbreds as sires and not for racing purposes—do you think if such horses were bred there would be a good demand for them from foreign Governments?—Oh, yes; there would be. But then if they were bred by a Government stud, of course they would not allow them to go to foreign Governments; they would sell them or let them, on the conditions that they were never to leave the country.

13351. But still they would be a marketable commodity?—Certainly.

13352. And capable of paying prices?—Yes.

13353. Do you think it is possible now to buy horses in any number that would be good in Ireland—thoroughbred horses at from £200 to £300 each?—Well, I should like a higher limit than that; I might buy one or maybe two for £250, but I should like [illegible] of £500.

13354. Mr. Fitzwilliam.—At auction?—No, a limit. I might be able to go to £350. I think you would do more good by buying one first class horse if you paid £1,000, than if you bought two you gave £750 a piece for, for those would be no better than they are in Ireland already.

13355. Mr. Wrench.—When you talk of some of the mares in the Dublin Show being got by a Hackney sire, you don't say they came from the congested districts?—If they were, my knowledge of the congested districts is different from what I have been led to understand.

13356. These were fine mares?—Yes.

13357. You don't know the pedigrees?—No.

13358. Was it more than one mare?—I think there were two.

13359. You reported it to the Dublin Society?—I mentioned it in my report.

13360. When you talk of shoulders, what do you consider the great requisites in a horse's shoulders?—Slope and the placing of the forelegs, which is far more important really than anything.

13361. The placing of the forelegs and slope?—And slope combined.

13362. You think that Hackneys are deficient in slope?—I think they are chiefly at fault in [illegible] of the shoulders which makes them roll in their action.

13363. You are speaking chiefly from what you see in the show?—Yes; and the placing of the forelegs. I mean in measuring length of shoulder; length of the same measuring is from the point of the body; it should be guided really from where the foreleg goes in. If a horse had a great prominence there you must not measure it in with the shoulder to show the slope.

13364. The shoulder blade?—Yes, but the shoulder blade really extends into the breast. You should measure from where the legs go in.

13365. You would not object to use in any part of Ireland where they produce a marketable animal a horse with any Hackney blood with two crosses of thoroughbred blood?—I don't think it would do much harm, but it would not breed the best hunters.

13366. I am not talking of hunters?—I think it would do good; of course the same time I should be consistent, supposing in the first instance you want to send thoroughbred sires, possibly there, to go down to the congested districts you would [illegible] a different class of horse to what there is now to what you would desire to cross with the [illegible] to produce a [illegible]. For instance, the sort of horse I should send to the congested districts would be a horse—"First Flight II." It is like a Hackney, but is a thoroughbred horse, and has got greater length and quality, and very likely the Hackneys would. But to produce these animals, as cheap a horse to mate with a Hackney mare, I should prefer "Flash Boy" [illegible].

13367. But when you say a Hackney mare is a suitable shape as a brood mare to mate with a thoroughbred horse, is it not possible that mares got by a Hackney stallion may not also grade up to animals suitable to cross with thoroughbred horses out of a thoroughbred mare?—It depends upon how much quality [illegible].

13368. I mean a very well bred mare. If you say a Hackney is the right shape to a brood mare may not a mare got by a Hackney be of the right shape as a brood mare?—It might, but it would have the blood; I am recommending it as second cross.

13369. I am talking of the existing stock. Supposing you have to deal with a lot of weedy, well-bred mares in a poor district you cross with Hackneys, and may not that grade up those animals?—You might grade up, but you do a great deal of harm in the meantime. The Hackney stallions would be infusing their blood into animals that would breed horses for riding purposes.

13370. Have you heard it suggested that there should be a general registration of horses in Ireland?—No; I have not heard that.

13371. That all horses should be registered with the Royal Dublin Society?—You mean all sires?

13372. Everything entered it would be possible for any buyer to know the pedigree?—I think it would be an excellent thing. It is done here to a certain extent. It should be done all over the country.

13373. Don't you think Ireland practically is the best country in the world for producing horses?—Yes.

13374. If it is, would it not be worth while for the State to spend some money on registration of that kind?—Certainly.

13375. If a registration of that kind were adopted of mares it would then be practically possible to trace the pedigree of every horse?—Yes, it would be a very great advantage.

13376. Therefore those people who don't wish their [illegible] to Hackney blood could avoid having any?—Yes; they would do so, but if you place horses like that indiscriminately before small people who don't study and who don't know much about it, they will send to any horse. There is always a greater run on the new horse, because it is a new horse.

13377. With poor farmers the chief thing is what they can get?—Yes.

13378. [illegible] they will soon come back?—Yes, but they don't know till they have tried it.

13379. Would you interfere with their choice then?—I should never interfere with their choice.

13380. That would give them a choice between?—No; I should only spend public money on the production of the thoroughbred that we know has certainly done good. I have no objection to the test being made of the thoroughbred being tried on the Hackney mare. I think you would there get animals that would get some very good riding and driving animals.

13381. You would not object to horses got out of a thoroughbred mare by a Hackney stallion?—It depends upon what sort is the thoroughbred mare, and what you want her for.

13382. Would you object to use an animal as a sire that had been bred out of a good thoroughbred mare by a Hackney stallion, with much thoroughbred blood in him?—What do you want to produce?

13383. To produce a horse with action?—I should want to know what sort of a thoroughbred mare it was out of.

13384. A mare with action?—Well, if you had got a mare with as good action as "Hermit," and got it by a Hackney stallion, it would be a very good experiment. But the produce by a thoroughbred horse and that one would be all right.

13385. Have you formed any opinion as to whether [illegible]?—No, I never particularly observed that.

13386. You don't know the [illegible] [illegible]

[illegible]

[illegible] is the very best in the world?—Yes.

[illegible]

[illegible] had failed in the [illegible] they [illegible] the animal.

[illegible] The question I asked was [illegible] would [illegible]

[illegible]

[illegible] examined.

[illegible]

13410. You were once master of the Devon and Somerset Staghounds?—Yes, for six years, '81 to '87.

13411. You know all the Exmoor country?—Yes, pretty well.

[Margin notes: "[illegible] Capt. [illegible]" (top right); "[illegible]" beside 13410]

Viscount Ebrington.

13413. And the breed of ponies?—Yes.

13414. Is it a large tract of country in which these Exmoor ponies are bred?—Well, the true Exmoor ponies are only bred by Sir Thomas Acland, but the Exmoor type of pony is found in all the Devon and Somerset country, right away to Dartmoor, in all that hilly country. In all the hill country there they breed ponies which are more or less of the Exmoor type and Exmoor blood.

13415. How have they been bred?—Anyhow—the great part of them anyhow. Sir Thomas Acland for the last twenty-five years has headed a lot of ponies with his herding; he keeps the breed pure, and takes the best mares with their suckers down to Killerton, near Exeter, every year and brings the young ones back. They go down there as soon as they are weaned with the mares, and the suckers with the mares until it is nearly two years old and then is gone back to the hills. In that way he has improved the shape and the size of these ponies very much. There are some [illegible] who [illegible] with the same trouble with their ponies and know their pedigrees and keep up their own, but, to a great extent, they have been bred in a very haphazard sort of way.

13416. You don't exactly know what the sires are?—The Master of the Stag-hounds has had for some time one or two thoroughbred horses, and they cover a certain number of ponies. I had a Hackney horse for two years and he had a certain number of ponies. Mr. [illegible], who succeeded me, had a Hackney horse for three or four years and he covered a certain number of ponies; I had two Arabs at different times. Sir Frederick Knight has had an Arab for several years past, and many years ago his father had a Kingsley horse.

13417. That is a long way to go for a horse?—It was an experiment.

13418. What does Mr. Thomas Acland use?—He brings in his own ponies.

13419. Exmoor ponies?—Yes, pure Exmoor ponies.

13420. You have crossed them with the thoroughbred, the Hackney, and the Arab?—I say that I have personally. The only pony I ever bred from was one who had already a cross of thoroughbred blood.

13421. You have experience of the produce?—Yes.

13422. And which do you prefer?—Depends on what you want to make. I have known some extraordinarily good ponies with one-quarter thoroughbred blood, and a second cross of thoroughbred blood very often answers very well. A pony got by my Hackney took first prize as an Exmoor pony at Plymouth, Exeter, and other shows although it was no more an Exmoor pony than a cab-horse, only that it was bred on the borders of Exmoor and was a very clever pony. The Hackneys give them style and action and are apt to improve their shoulders and put in some very useful ponies.

13423. What kind of prices do the farmers get for the ponies they breed?—I have made inquiries of the two principal auctioneers. A great many ponies are sold every year at Bampton fair. One auctioneer sold 100 suckers and 50 other ponies. The suckers on an average realised £2 10s. 6d.; 20 yearlings £4 [illegible] each, and a pair of ponies that were made £33 10s. From that auctioneer, in my opinion, that the prices at Bampton fair are rather low; as a rule the best ponies don't go there, and he generally makes their own price. He has just sent a batch of ponies to [illegible] and they averaged £17 10s. Another auctioneer sold by order on nearly similar, and they averaged from £4 10s. for a lot of five belonging to a man at Exmoor, to £8 17s. 6d. The best £20 is all, and his opinion is that the demand is not so strong as it was in former years.

13424. Not so high, thereabouts?—No.

13425. What are they used for?—The suckers are mostly bought by dairymen and tradesmen in a small way, but some by gentlemen, and a certain number of them go across to polo country for use in the towns. Other ponies are bought by dealers who take them to Reading and Brighton and Chichester; a few go to Hampshire and a few to the New Forest.

13426. Are any of them turned into polo ponies?—The Exmoor pony is too small for that. The true Exmoor pony is under twelve hands. Sir Thomas Acland's ponies don't certainly exceed twelve hands. By crossing with the thoroughbred you would get them up in size a lot.

13427. You don't know whether they have ever been bred at all specially for the purpose of polo ponies?—A number of polo ponies have been bought in North Devon at different times. I know some of them have turned out very well indeed. Still at our Exmoor Horse Show this year we had no [illegible]. We had classes mostly by height, and this year we had a class for children's ponies and a class for ponies likely to make polo ponies and we had there a considerable number of entries for the polo pony class.

13428. Lord Ravensworth.—Were they bred in the country?—Yes; they had to be the property of farmers living within twenty miles of the Exmoor, and we [illegible] because we had to see them ourselves entirely in the show.

13429. Chairman.—How long have you had that show?—It has been going on for thirteen years. I started it first when I began hunting as Master of the Hounds, and I thought I would try and get a better class of horse. We began in a very small way offering small prizes at local shows. Then they got up a subscription to the Horse and they asked me to get up a general show, and now we have a very successful show in the same way every year.

13430. Could you give us any particulars of the classes?—That is the list of prizes we offered this year (producing), and I put in the margin the number of entries in each class.

13431. Read them?—The first class was for the best mare with foal or foal submitted for agricultural purposes; there were only five entries, although we offered £10 in prizes. The second class was for brood mares not exceeding 15 hands, with foal at foot. There were seven entries and the prizes amounted to £9 10s. Then was a class for breeding ponies not exceeding 14.2 hands, and in this class there were entries, the prizes being £7 10s. In the class for yearling colts or fillies by hunter sires with foal at foot there were seven entries, prizes £15. Then we had three prizes for cart horses which have not done well lately. I think partly owing to the time of the year in which they are all at hard work and are in show condition. We give a prize for the mare whose horse [illegible] A class for the best hill pony not under three years old, not exceeding 13 hands, really quiet, and to be ridden by boys and girls not [illegible] years, and in this there were twenty entries. For geldings or mares calculated for riding or driving and exceeding 14.2 there were twenty entries. For ponies calculated to make polo ponies there were twenty-six entries; there was an extra prize of £5 given in that for the best pony, the property of a small farmer; this was not very successful. Then we had prizes for pony stallions £5 and £3 10s., in which class we had three entries; we have had this class for the last three years and it has not been a success. We never had more than three or four entries, and they are not very good ponies. They don't take the trouble to bring them up all the hill for the purpose of bringing them in. The pony that won the [illegible] years was a horse I used myself by a thoroughbred horse out of a very good pony, but the same was not a good one and the pony was not of very much account. Still the pony was good enough to win the prize two years running. I sold him as a two-year-old because I didn't like to keep him. We had a class for the best weight-carrying cob not exceeding 15 hands high, thirteen entries. Class for hunters, any size, 15 entries. Class for three-year-olds, 8 entries.

[illegible]

March 25, 189[illegible]
[illegible]

13463. CHAIRMAN.—According to your experience you say that the pure pony stands the climate and exposure better than any cross?—Yes.

13464. And you think—though you don't know the congested districts—it might possibly be the same there?—You can improve the Exmoors, and it has been done, and you can get them bigger, stronger, and more useful, but you have got to take care of the young stock.

Colonel F. Henry, [illegible], Tetbury, Gloucestershire, examined.

Colonel F. Henry.

13465. CHAIRMAN.—You live in Gloucestershire, do you not?—Yes, my lord.

13466. And you are a member of the Hunters' Improvement Society?—I am on the council at the present time.

13467. Have you bred horses yourself at all?—Yes, I have for a considerable number of years.

13468. Have you any acquaintance with Ireland as a horse-breeding country?—No, further than that I know that three-fourths of the horses supplied to our hunt in Gloucestershire come from Ireland, for I have made particular inquiry from horse dealers that supply hunters. They tell me that, at least three-fourths of the horses they sell come from Ireland, and they consider them superior in every way to English-bred horses. They have more stamina, and come to the hand more readily. They take less schooling they consider. I have asked three or four of them the question.

13469. Do you know at all whether they can get as many good hunters in Ireland now as formerly?—I asked that question particularly, and one man told me he could get as many horses as he liked if he would pay for them, and gave the high prices. Another man said [illegible]. The [illegible] in the County Waterford, in that neighbourhood at least, and he told me he was there last spring and he saw [illegible] mares brought to Waterford [illegible], and he could not say there were more than three good mares among the thirty-six.

13470. Who told you that?—A man who buys very largely in Ireland.

13471. Do you think they attach any importance to the fact that the horse was bred in Ireland, owing to the mere fact that it was bred in Ireland?—They do. As soon as they hear a hunter is bred in Ireland, they prick up their ears and think the horse is worth more money than if it was bred in England. I know myself when I am buying horses, if I heard a horse was from Ireland, I should be much more likely to buy him.

13472. Do you know Ireland yourself?—I was quartered there a great many years ago, but I have not been there of late years.

13473. Do you attach any importance to having pedigrees with the horses?—Yes, very. I bought a horse the other day. A man told me he was by "Ascetic;" he said, "I consider 'Ascetic' the best sire standing in Ireland." I asked him could he prove it. He proved it to my satisfaction, and it certainly made a difference in my purchasing the horse.

13474. I suppose you cannot say whether the pedigrees that the dealers give in Ireland are generally accurate or not?—No.

13475. You have not been buying horses yourself in Ireland lately?—No; I [illegible] of what I want.

13476. What have you done in the way of breeding yourself?—I have bred, and I have bought [illegible] and brought them on as hunters; but my experience of breeding is [illegible] other people [illegible] half-bred mares. I have always bred from good mares, and have been able to sell them well in London or locally.

13477. What kind of stallions?—[illegible] thoroughbred horses.

13478. What kind of mares?—Hunting mares; mares that one would think would bring bigger foals than they [illegible].

13479. You have bred with the object of getting hunters?—Yes.

13480. What did you do with those that were not good enough for hunters?—They have all been sold [illegible] hunters. I have good facilities for breaking them in, and have made them handy, and sold them as hacks in London.

13481. Without going into particulars, did you get a price for them for that particular purpose that pays?—Yes; I got a good deal of [illegible] out of them between four and six years old, after [illegible] them. I break them to [illegible].

13482. And the six years old, they are fit to sell?—I sold a five-year-old, only 14.3 hands, for £80 in London, and he had done a good year's work before.

13483. Is that a horse suitable for driving and riding, both?—Yes.

13484. That is what he is used for?—I believe he is used entirely for riding where he has gone.

13485. Was that by a thoroughbred sire?—Yes. I never [illegible] anything but a thoroughbred horse.

13486. Do you think these [illegible] of registered sires would be beneficial in Ireland?—Yes, I think it would, most certainly, for I find that farmers who have got mares registered near [illegible] get a better price for their offspring. [illegible] You take the trouble to go and look at a horse [illegible] you know he is entered in the [illegible]; [illegible] that was not, you would not take the trouble to go and see.

13487. And about stallions—do you think registration would be sufficient, or that there ought to be something more stringent in the way of licensing stallions in Ireland?—I don't think I could give an opinion.

13488. Do you know the West of Ireland at all?—No, not at all.

13489. You use nothing but the thoroughbred sire?—Nothing.

13490. You never bred anything else?—A great many years ago I bred what I looked upon at the time as an Exmoor cob, with the old pack horse blood in it. I put him on to a thoroughbred mare and I got a very good animal.

13491. As a hunter?—Yes. [illegible] that was [illegible] twenty years ago I am talking of.

13492. You have never used Hackney sires?—No, but I have [illegible] two Hackneys.

13493. What kind of Hackney?—One was bred by Mr. Walter Gilbey, and the other by Lord Londesborough's "Young [illegible]." They are beautiful goers, and my wife is very fond of them, but I don't like to drive them myself. I happen to have a pair of horses by a thoroughbred stallion. When I want to go hunting [illegible] I always take the [illegible] by the thoroughbred horse, and leave the Hackneys at home. I think they [illegible]; they [illegible] to drive [illegible]. [illegible] for my own comfort and driving long distances

[illegible]

[illegible] Mr. [illegible] [illegible].

with [illegible]?—No, I don't think so. He would [illegible] about [illegible] and the type of [illegible] to [illegible] and I don't know very much about them.

18491. It is rather with reference to what he said about Ireland, to [illegible] horse-breeding there; do you generally agree with him in that respect?—Well, I hardly know that I should agree with what he said about a stallion bred by a thoroughbred horse out of [illegible] mare. I should hardly perhaps agree with that.

18492. You think that might be rather risky?—Well, it would be an experiment, would it not?

18493. Mr. FITZWILLIAM.—Do you know Ireland?—I do not, personally.

18494. Do you breed at all?—No, I do not. I see a good deal of other people's breeding. I have taken a great interest in our Society. I don't breed myself; I have not a suitable place to do it.

18495. CHAIRMAN.—You live in [illegible]?—Yes.

18496. Mr. FITZWILLIAM.—As far as breeding goes for general purposes, what breed do you prefer?—I should think that the way to improve the breed of horses is certainly to have lots of suitable sires travelling stallions [illegible]. I think the [illegible] of the Royal Commission are right, but at the same time there are so few horses that it is a drop in the ocean. When you find there have to go from a mile and a half of where we stand to the [illegible] that it is a drop in the ocean, but the principle is right.

18497. But still you think that the fact of having those one or two good animals in a district is encouraging, as rather it is an incentive to other people to keep a good class?—Oh, yes; I think it does a great deal of good. I think the Royal Commission and the [illegible] Improvement Society have called attention to horse-breeding, and I am certain there are many more people [illegible] to breed; but of course there is in some districts a great deficiency of suitable horses. That is to be found, [illegible] particularly.

18498. How would you propose to increase the number?—I take it it is impossible without more money.

18499. Mr. LA TOUCHE.—You have heard some witnesses talk about the [illegible] of mares and the [illegible] of mares. Did your Council consider in any way which would induce farmers to retain [illegible] mares?—They gave additional prizes to local societies. They give as much as a local agricultural or horse show society gave to assist in prizes for brood mares. We gave them an additional prize which makes it better worth winning and so keeping the mares.

18500. Has it come under your observation that the prospect of winning one of these prizes has induced a farmer to refuse to sell his mare?—I think it induces them to keep the mares; but if a high price was given, I think most of them would jump at it, except in the case of farmers who are so well off to whom the [illegible] is not a matter of much importance.

18501. Are there many of those in [illegible]?—No, I am sorry to say there are not many anywhere, I know.

18502. You cannot speak personally as to farmers refusing to sell their mares for the purpose of winning a prize?—No; I should only say it tends to induce farmers to keep brood mares, for if some fellow came along to the show and offered the farmer a high price for his mare he would let it go, and very probably he would go and get another one. I think it induces farmers to keep the mares, but not to refuse a high price for one.

18503. Do you think the class of mares have improved owing to the action of the [illegible] Improvement Society?—I think the mares are what they are.

18504. The stallions have been travelling for some years?—Oh, yes; I think that was the best way to improve horse-breeding. We cannot [illegible] the mares. If they are going to be kept from it it would [illegible] that they should be [illegible] [illegible] [illegible] in [illegible] [illegible].

18505. You think the best way of getting up the [illegible] is to put them to thoroughbred horses?—Generally, except in the case of light [illegible] mares, then I should like to see a good [illegible] sire.

18506. Do you prefer them to a Hackney stallion?—Decidedly; I don't think the Hackney suitable for [illegible].

18507. Mr. WRENCH.—[illegible].—I may take it that you are in favour of the Councils money grant [illegible] the [illegible] being diverted from racing, and giving stallions those premiums under the Royal Commission?—Most decidedly.

18508. Do you think that any further grant should be given?—Certainly, if possible.

18509. Has it occurred to you that if a further grant were asked for the thoroughbred it would also be asked for other breeds of horses and there would be no end to subsidising breeds of animals generally?—I don't know about that exactly, but if the object is to improve the breed of horses in this country generally, I certainly think the way to do it is to go on the basis of the Royal Commission, and give very many more stallions. Instead of there stallions to [illegible] I should like to see three stallions to one county.

18510. Private enterprise has that entirely failed?—Does stallions for a district [illegible] in a district where there are numerous horses owned by noblemen and gentlemen that are at the service of [illegible] farmers and others who wish to breed.

18511. Which district do you speak of—the New [illegible]?—Yes, but the horses there are all [illegible] high [illegible], and it is not a hunter-breeding district. The distribution is wrong. In [illegible] there is no stallion, and the farmers breed [illegible] [illegible] animals. Then, again, with Leicestershire and Northamptonshire, there are [illegible] stallions there, [illegible] [illegible]. It [illegible] altogether depends on private enterprise we get unequal distribution.

18512. Then would you [illegible] the [illegible] of horse-breeding [illegible]?—I personally should [illegible]. I am only interested in [illegible].

18513. Have you had occasion to see very many [illegible] horses, have you found any difficulty in getting them?—I have seen [illegible] good many at [illegible] [illegible].

18514. Are they English or foreign?—There are a great many foreigners, and the [illegible] been bred in Ireland. I saw once a particularly fine pair of carriage horses that came from Dublin, and I asked the dealer who brought them over how he thought they were bred. He said he believed that the people had bred [illegible] horses, and then bred the [illegible] of carriage horses, and they were true Irish horses, and in [illegible] they had sold them for carriage horses.

18515. When [illegible]?

18516. In that [illegible]?—Five years ago. They were a particularly beautiful pair of horses.

18517. But you have only his statement that they were Irish horses?—Yes, but I think he knew.

18518. Yes, but you have only his statement?—Yes; I saw them in his yard, and asked him.

18519. Mr. WRENCH.—I think you said you don't breed horses yourself?—No.

18520. And you don't know Ireland?—I do not.

18521. CHAIRMAN.—Those questions as to the distribution of stallions have been asked in reference to England. Our inquiry is in reference to Ireland. There are a great many gentlemen in Ireland, but there are not a great many that have a great deal of money. Is there anything else you would like to tell the Commission?—Except this, that I have seen some [illegible] of horses got by Hackneys out of hunting, and the [illegible] has not been favourable. The best that I have seen were in [illegible] [illegible] horses, but he was a horse that [illegible] after a long day.

13865. Where do you hunt?—In Essex and also in Leicestershire. I saw this horse in Essex. I have seen two horses by Hackneys in hunting stables. The best was a very useful hunter by one of the Walter Gilbey's [illegible] out of a [illegible] mare, and [illegible], but he could not stay.

13866. Have you seen any of them in [illegible]?—No.

Mr. H[illegible], Edgware Road, London; examined.

13867. *Chairman.*—You live in the Edgware Road?—Yes, my lord.

13868. And are engaged in dealing in horses?—All sorts of horses.

13869. Do you deal in any particular breed of horses more than another?—No; I have had a great many hunters all my life and a great many harness horses, of course, all my life.

13870. But you are not particularly devoted to hunters?—I am not devoted to anything especially.

13871. What does the bulk of your business consist of?—Harness horses.

13872. Where do you buy your horses mostly?—In Ireland and in England.

13873. Do you buy many horses from abroad?—[illegible]

13874. May I take it then you buy what suits you without any particular reference to [illegible]?—I would not buy a horse [illegible] Germany or any [illegible] whatever. I never [illegible], and I [illegible] them, and I know the country as well as I do England. I bought a great many there [illegible], but I never bought horses there to send to England.

13875. Have you any objection to say why?—Because I don't like them. They [illegible] to look at and not [illegible] to me.

13876. How [illegible] kind of horses bred, do you know?—Yes, I know [illegible]. [illegible] the old Mecklenburg horse, which is the foundation of the [illegible] coach horse.

13877. As a [illegible]?—[illegible] in Mecklenburg [illegible] horses [illegible]. They [illegible] and [illegible] they [illegible] you [illegible] the [illegible] horses.

13878. What is the matter with those horses?—They are no use.

13879. What were they crossed with in Yorkshire to make the Yorkshire coach horse?—The Yorkshire [illegible] must have [illegible] a hundred years ago [illegible] Yorkshire, but [illegible] in Yorkshire. I [illegible] than that is [illegible] thoroughbred. They have got their blood from our thoroughbred horses in [illegible] in my own mind.

13880. How do you know?—I [illegible] them in Mecklenburg.

13881. You don't know whether they brought the [illegible] of the [illegible]?—I don't know [illegible].

13882. You approve of these horses [illegible] in every respect, except that they have not [illegible]?—Yes.

13883. They have good action?—Yes.

13884. And you don't buy them because they have not got [illegible]?—Yes.

13885. Where do you buy your horses?—In the South of Ireland, of course.

13886. Principally?—Well, principally.

13887. Do you buy any in England?—Not very few.

13888. Have you been buying there long in Ireland?—Since 1840.

13889. And in those thirty odd years do you find much difference in the supply of the quality of the supply?—[illegible] is good enough to [illegible]. I [illegible] think that the horses thirty years ago were as good as they are today; but whether my memory [illegible] I can't say. But my impression is that I used to find horses in those days at half the price I give now, and they were as good. Whether that is right or not I should [illegible] to say.

13890. As to the demand is the demand bigger than it was?—The demand is double what it was in those days, I think.

13891. How do you buy them?—I buy them myself and I go over very often.

13892. Have you anybody buying for you?—No.

13893. I suppose your buyer collects a certain number of them?—Oh, no. I sometimes go to the fairs, otherwise he collects half a dozen and sends them over.

13894. Do you find that you buy more horses from the [illegible] himself and less in the fairs than formerly?—No; there are as many at the fairs now, if you take them as a whole, as there were formerly. In England we go to fairs and buy horses, but you buy a great many more privately; you can't in Ireland [illegible] about all over the place. You go to the fair and get what you can, and the best are supplied [illegible] with what you [illegible] of.

13895. Have you bought any horses in the North of Ireland?—Not many; a few.

13896. Where have you bought them?—At Armagh. I have bought them there, and [illegible] collected them from the South; they take them up there to sell.

13897. Can you explain to me how they could pay them?—Oh, yes; it pays them very well. They buy them horses at the fairs in the South at £40, £50, up to £60—that is about as much as they give for a three-year-old. They [illegible] him [illegible] him [illegible] and [illegible] him up and feed him on potatoes, and he is sold to [illegible].

13898. Why then are the men in the South [illegible] they?—I don't know, but he is a man I look on with great respect—the man in the South—because he exercises his horses. The man in the North does not; he [illegible] like a pig and [illegible]; that is one of the reasons I never go to the North. When you go to the South you see what your horse is, but when you go to the North you only buy a fat pig, that you can't tell how he will turn out, and he generally dies in the process of getting him fit. Those dealers in the North always buy the best horses early, and give more for them than anybody else.

13899. Did you ever buy any hunters in England?—Not many; I have bought some. Formerly I used to buy more than I do now. If I see one I buy it of course, but I go to Ireland if I want half a dozen or twenty. I know where to find them.

13900. Don't you know where to find them in England?—No, or if you do you only get an Irishman imported. The horses in Yorkshire are as good-looking as they are in Ireland, but they are a different sort.

13901. And as to their harness horses?—I used to buy a great many harness horses in Ireland, and I sometimes [illegible] there now, for my experience tells me they are the very best. They are, however, [illegible] on account of their blood, but for [illegible] they are not so good. I [illegible] unfortunately I have had to pay for it, and that [illegible] you a [illegible] horse; the more blood you get [illegible] the same [illegible] is to [illegible]; [illegible] the Hackney, and the Hackney is the best harness horse in the world, take him all round; but keep him to himself—don't mix him more than you can help.

13902. What has been described to us in evidence

3 N 2

[illegible] [illegible] the Hackney [illegible]

[illegible] a [illegible] horse, [illegible] quality, and [illegible]. Do you think the Hackney will produce that?—The Hackney is worth most money.

13900. And can you find him?—I have no doubt [illegible] the Irish horse, but when I have got him I would rather have him as a [illegible] horse.

13901. Have you much experience in Hackneys?—A great deal.

13902. Is the bulk of your business in London horses or Hackneys?—Oh, no. I have [illegible] myself in Hackneys since 1874, when I have been agent for the French Government here, and I bought all their Hackney stallions.

13903. Have they bought many Hackney stallions?—Yes; I bought all that were at the show the other day that were suitable.

13904. What do they do with them?—They breed artillery horses with them.

13905. Have you any objection to saying what price they pay for them?—Not the slightest. I gave 400*l.* a piece last week for seventeen.

13906. Have you been buying them for some years?—Since 1874.

13906. Principally Hackneys?—I buy thoroughbred horses sometimes. I bought a few—what you would call country stallions but not [illegible]—perhaps fifty in the whole time, not more—but I bought every year about twenty Hackney stallions for them. Thirty [illegible] years, I bought many Hackneys for Hungary.

13907. **Ever since 1874?—Yes, ever since 1874.**

13908. **Have you been in France yourself?—Oh,** yes.

13909. Where do they put them?—We put them all over France—north, south, and in the middle, in Normandy, and right down to the south to Nice.

13910. What kind of mares do they put them to?—In the North of France they have a [illegible] [illegible] [illegible], [illegible] kind of things, but [illegible] their produce [illegible] any [illegible] and no [illegible], then they have these Hackney stallions, the best little Hackneys that I can get, and put them in the North to correct the faults of their own mares. In Normandy we send the Hackney stallions as long as we can get them. They must have the type of the Hackney; but we get them stronger [illegible]. I bought some last week 16.2; it is not an easy matter to get a pure Hackney 16.2; I got two chestnuts, very good horses that took the first prize last year; they go to Normandy. These mares in [illegible] class of horses 16.2, he goes to the East of France about [illegible] and that country; and these horses cover the farmers' mares and they are [illegible] to get artillery horses. They always use the thoroughbred horse a great deal, but the artillery horses they prefer bred from the Hackney, because they [illegible] and [illegible] in [illegible], which is the great fault in pure bred horses in harness.

13911. What kind are the mares in the South?—Very [illegible] [illegible] of little mares with short legs, what you can see in the [illegible] in the North of France; [illegible] [illegible] they call the Boulonnais; they are 15.2 and 15.3, short horses without [illegible], and they take the Hackney stallions to improve their [illegible].

13912. What do you say?—If they found it not to pay, they would not go on doing it, and they have been doing it since 1868.

13913. And therefore we may presume that in their opinion it is successful?—And every year they [illegible] more. It proves to a certain extent that the Hackney is [illegible] in [illegible] [illegible] in a very [illegible] [illegible].

13914. Have you a sufficiently long experience in France to know if the Hackney does give the requisite strength?—They would not go on if they did not approve of him.

13915. I am asking you if you know yourself?—I go there, and of course I am an official in the French service, and so I get to the [illegible] of everything; and the breeders there think a very [illegible] [illegible] to see Hackneys arrive, and keep saying they wished they had more [illegible]. It might be the [illegible] of the breeder or that the breeder would [illegible] [illegible] [illegible].

13916. I should **not like to press you for your opinion?—Oh, yes; my own opinion, it does not** matter.

13917. It might be **so** the [illegible] of the breeder but in the [illegible] of the artillery?—What would you call [illegible] [illegible] [illegible] [illegible] [illegible] [illegible] a horse that [illegible] [illegible], and [illegible] [illegible] [illegible]?

13918. Well, I don't know; I can only tell you?—I suppose they find the horses are better than they were or they would not get them.

13919. Have they used the thoroughbred in that part of the country?—Yes; [illegible] [illegible] [illegible] side of the Hackney, and they prefer the Hackney.

13920. I suppose you have seen the results of all those horses in different parts of France?—Of course I have.

13921. What do you think of them?—Well, I have seen some better got by the Hackney [illegible] [illegible] [illegible] [illegible] I saw in Normandy, [illegible] [illegible] [illegible] [illegible] [illegible].

13922. Would you say at all that that is the class of horse that we have had in evidence as bought in the London market for carriage purposes?—Yes. [illegible] the breeder has the opportunity to get [illegible] [illegible] to a Hackney [illegible] [illegible] [illegible] [illegible] to [illegible] [illegible] [illegible], and he takes the [illegible] to the Hackney [illegible] in preference to the French [illegible].

13923. What is the French [illegible]?—The [illegible] that is [illegible] from the old [illegible] [illegible] [illegible] old Norfolk [illegible] that went [illegible] [illegible] [illegible] the [illegible] [illegible]. He was the first man to take the English [illegible] Hackney [illegible] to France.

13924. For the saddle?—For the action. The [illegible] [illegible] [illegible] a very [illegible] [illegible] a very good looking horse, [illegible] [illegible] [illegible] anything we can get in England, but he has not the activity; he [illegible] [illegible], and our Hackney is supposed to give him [illegible] action.

13925. Do you think [illegible]?—I think so.

13926. They breed them for [illegible] and [illegible] of [illegible]?—I [illegible] [illegible], of the [illegible] horse. If you [illegible] a [illegible] in Normandy you [illegible] [illegible] [illegible] [illegible] [illegible] [illegible] a [illegible] [illegible]; [illegible] [illegible] [illegible] [illegible] [illegible] [illegible] [illegible] to [illegible] [illegible] [illegible] [illegible] to [illegible] Hackney.

13927. How do they manage with these Government stallions—what kind of fees do they charge?—I bought a very good horse last week at the show, I gave 350*l.* for him. As soon as he was bought all the [illegible] [illegible] [illegible] [illegible] [illegible] [illegible] [illegible] [illegible] [illegible] [illegible]—that is [illegible] [illegible] [illegible] [illegible] will pay.

13928. Where is he going to?—To Normandy.

13929. Do the Government select the mares?—Not that the Government would not allow a horse as good as I spoke about to serve a very inferior mare. The [illegible] at the station who has charge of the horses has a right to say—"No, I won't serve your mare; you can put it to so-and-so. That mare is not good enough."

13930. How many mares would that horse be limited to?—Forty or fifty—not a hundred like they [illegible] here.

13931. Do the Government have any call upon the produce?—None at all; they buy them in open market.

13932. Where did you say their cavalry [illegible] were bred?—In the South?—[illegible] [illegible]; they are [illegible] of [illegible]; but in the South of France they have a [illegible] [illegible] light cavalry horse [illegible] [illegible] [illegible] to [illegible] [illegible] [illegible], are very [illegible]—so that you would not have thought they could carry the men they have [illegible] [illegible], but they [illegible] [illegible] [illegible] [illegible] [illegible] [illegible] [illegible] [illegible] [illegible] and they find the Hackney [illegible]

[illegible] [illegible] [illegible]

[illegible]

[illegible]

13606. CHAIRMAN.—Do you think the carriage adapted itself to the horse, or the horse to the carriage?—The horse to the carriage, certainly. If a farmer has a big good horse about 16.2 and takes it to a fair, he cannot sell it; if he has a Hackney 15.2 he can sell it at a good price.

13607. MR. FITZWILLIAM.—You don't go in to a great extent for hunters?—I have had a great many hunters.

13608. Did you buy them in Ireland, too?—Yes; always.

13609. You think they are the best that's sold?—To my opinion they are; I would not think of buying hunters anywhere else. If I found a hunter when I was travelling about in Yorkshire I should buy it, but I never think of looking for one; wherever the season, during June, July, I am in Ireland every three weeks.

13610. You would not like to introduce the Hackney cross in the hunter?—No; I would not think about it.

13611. And therefore you would not like to introduce the Hackney cross in the South of Ireland?—Certainly not. I would not listen to it in the South of Ireland. Most unfortunately up to this year I was very much in believing a Hackney would gallop; I had a hunter this year got by "[illegible]," and I never rode a slower horse in my life.

13612. But as a practice, you should not like the cross introduced into the hunter-breeding district?—If the South of Ireland ever were to go all gammons to the thoroughbred horse, I contend that all your foreign trade, which is a great thing in Ireland, would be lost. The foreigner gives nearly as much for a hunter as an Englishman does, and he always goes to Ireland for it.

13613. And he goes there because of the reputation that Ireland has got for breeding that horse?—He does not get the reputation. He begins by buying English hunters, and after he has been buying them for five or six years, he gradually finds his way to Ireland, because he finds he gets better there than in England.

13614. Then any admixture in the breed would be a pity, so far as you think?—I should think it would be a curse.

13615. Colonel ST. QUINTIN.—I should like to ask you when the Percheron mares were [illegible]—I have asked many times and I have seen a great many of them, and they are very good, but where they [illegible] from I have never been able to find out. Mr. Gilbey can—just know where I [illegible] from that Percheron mares, put them to the thoroughbred horse, and produce the finest carriage horses you could possibly imagine, and he won't breed from anything else. When I am over there I always try to bring him back a mare or two, and I have often asked to find out what was the history of them, but I never can. It is a race that has been in France for two hundred years. It is a big and animal with beautiful looks and beautiful goods, and the feet are so well, and the body is as strong as a barn board, which is a very good thing in a foreign horse.

13616. And good action?—And good action.

13617. What sort of height?—15.2½ up to 16 hands, but they have altered the old Percheron horse. He used to be a sharp fastened horse; they used to drive him twenty-five or thirty miles; but now he has been crossed into a heavier horse, and what you see in the Yorks counties is supposed to be a Percheron, but he is not a Percheron.

13618. Is not the Hungarian supposed to be about the best of the Continental horses?—I don't know, but I have heard a great many people speak of them.

13619. I thought you said they were very good?—The smaller horses that they mount the light cavalry on, are better than the light-cavalry horses in the South of France; they are much about the same height—15.2.

13620. Do you ever get any big upstanding carriage horses out of the Mey?—Oh, yes.

13621. How are they chiefly bred and before they bring them from the South?

13622. But they are the big upstanding London carriage horses?—Yes; but there are a great many horses which in the Mey that are very common horses.

13623. They say I was asking when you buy—you should not buy them?—No.

13624. But you do buy some of the other class from the Mey, but they are from the South?—They are from the South and West. I don't think they are bred in the North—at least not many of them.

13625. SIR WALTER GILBEY.—You have been visiting France for the last twenty years?—Yes.

13626. And you have been buying horses there since '73, and previous to that time in France?—Yes.

13627. From your experience in travelling over France, do you consider there is a great improvement in [illegible]—I am speaking of the Percheron horse as a horse suitable for country purposes?—Yes, for the [illegible]. The [illegible] horse that is bought at [illegible] has improved generally in the last twenty-five years. I think they have more an [illegible] horses in the hussy regiments in France as we have in England.

13628. We had one witness yesterday, a Yorkshire dealer, who has spoken very unfavourably of the Normandy horse. You have made some mention of the Normandy horse. Have you any knowledge of his breeding?—Yes, he is bred from the Percheron unquestionably, because they have the great Percheron mares, what they call the poitou, a broad, good-looking animal. Then they have the Percheron horse, which is a great heavy bodied horse, and he has been crossed with the horse of Normandy all round and about. I should bring the thoroughbred, because the rule of the Norman horse is that above fifty years old.

13629. Will the Norfolk trotter, has he found his way into Normandy?—Oh, yes, and he is supposed to a great deal more there than anywhere else.

13630. Do you think he is the foundation of these carriage horses we see, in Paris?—I don't know, I haven't been able to find out. There were some big horses in Normandy before Napoleon's time, and Napoleon was the first man to import Hackneys into France in any quantities.

13631. Have you been attending many of the local shows in the Percheron in France, where they give prizes for trotters?—Yes.

13632. And they call them the Norfolk trotter?—Yes.

13633. How is that horse bred?—They have been bred for years from the trotter and by a thoroughbred horse. The old horse he trained has been called to a thoroughbred horse, "Flair of [illegible]." He was imported there thirty years ago, in fact when I was in the Administration as a boy, by Mr. de Saillard.

13634. The CHAIRMAN.—How long have you acted for the administration?—About 1868.

13635. SIR WALTER GILBEY.—You supplied horses considerably you said. Previous to that date which you mentioned, who preceded you in your purchasing office?—Phillips.

13636. And he was the introducer of the Norfolk Hackney to Yorkshire?—In France.

13637. But I am speaking of Yorkshire?—It was Ramsdale who was the first man.

13638. Did you ever hear from Mr. Phillips that he took the Norfolk horse to Mr. Ramsdale—did you ever hear that?—Yes.

13639. He had great experience with regard to the importation to France and Germany, and he was then, I suppose more largely than you have done since?—Certainly. In those days they paid no thoroughbred in France in large values. He was the man who imported the original thoroughbred stallions. In fact, I was taking for Mr. Phillips at that time

13700. Mr. Wrench.—Personally, you commenced your career in Hungary?—No, I did not.

13701. I thought you were born there?—No, I was pretty nearly born there.

13702. You know every part of the Continent?—Yes.

13703. Mr. Philips at that time was by far the largest and most important dealer of horses in England?—Certainly.

13704. You succeeded to his foreign business, and were with him a great deal, and knew what his business was?—Yes.

13705. Did you hear he gave evidence before a Royal Commission some twenty-five years ago?—Yes, I believe he did; but I did not take any interest in it in those days. Mr. Philips and Mr. East were examined.

13706. Any evidence Mr. Philips gave would be absolutely accurate?—I should think so. He had great knowledge.

13707. Had he gone abroad himself?—He was educated in France.

13708. Do you remember his buying a horse called "English Champion"?—No; that was twenty years before my time.

13709. Do you know yourself whether that horse went into Yorkshire?—I don't know it at all. I haven't the slightest idea.

13710. You don't know when the Hackneys had been introduced in Yorkshire?—When I was quite a young man, old Philips used have horses brought from Market Weighton that he used to show at the Yorkshire Show. He took some horses from Norfolk into Yorkshire, and tried to breed there Hackneys, and did breed them I believe.

13711. Do you know before you began to buy yourself did Philips import Hackneys into France?—Yes.

13712. Was the importation of Hackney stallions in Ireland going on before your time?—Yes; before my time. It is forty years since the first Hackney stallion went into France.

13713. Have you formed any opinion as to whether there are Hackneys in Yorkshire now with staying blood?—Oh, no, I have not; but I know some very good hunters have been got by Hackneys.

13714. Do those horses show any [illegible]?—No.

13715. Can you say then why the Yorkshiremen have given up breeding coach-horses?—Because they did not find a market for them.

13716. Do they find a market for the Hackneys they breed there?—Yes, and harness horses got by Hackneys.

13717. Do you think the thoroughbred horse with action himself would produce action in his progeny in the same, greater way as the Hackney?—I don't know that.

13718. Have you tried it?—Yes. I should not breed from a thoroughbred unless he has action.

13719. Does the Hackney, if he is well bred, produce action in his stock?—Yes, unquestionably. The only point in my view of the Hackney is whether he is old enough as a race to give a type. The thoroughbred horse is a much older breed, but I don't know whether the Hackney is old enough himself as a race to give a stamp, or what I wish to say is to show himself so much in his progeny as the thoroughbred.

13720. But do you find that the produce of the Hackney with these trotting mares in France is fairly uniform?—Certainly fairly uniform. The Hackney as we used to know it in England certainly did not give uniformity in his produce, because of the mares. If you breed from a Hackney mare and a Hackney stallion I believe it is a very good progeny, but I am a great believer in the Hackney getting every sort of mare.

13721. What class of horses are Hackney-bred horses bred from?—I don't know what they are. They are all sorts of things. They want that the Hackney [illegible] giving the progeny or they would not be giving them.

13722. You think they have good reason for going on using them?—Of course they must have reasons.

13723. When you refer to being able to get less harness horses from Ireland, is it because they lack weight or trotting power?—No; they lack trotting power. We find we can get good horses in a better market than Ireland now.

13724. When you take Ireland and draw a line across the hunter-breeding district, do you know anything of the country North and West of that line?—Yes, I know something, but I have never been able to find any other class. They are put only to [illegible] in the North of Ireland.

13725. Do you think there may be a demand for breeding harness horses in that district that would pay the farmers?—Certainly a demand for harness horses, but not in breeding hunters.

13726. Do you think there would be room in the country to breed both hunters and harness horses?—I don't know that; I can't tell that. I would not like to say.

13727. Would you be in favour of having the pedigrees of horses registered? Would you start a Hackney Improvement Society in Ireland, the same as the Hackney here?—Quite so.

13728. You would be in favour of that?—I would not use anything but thoroughbred horses in Ireland.

13729. Do you think it would add to the value of the horses now bought in Ireland by foreigners if they were able to get an authenticated pedigree with them?—No, I don't think it would be valuable; the horse speaks for himself.

13730. You don't attach importance to pedigree?—You attach importance to pedigree, but you attach much more importance to the form of the horse.

13731. If you saw a horse that would give satisfaction to you, and heard that his dam or grand-dam had been got by a Hackney, would that stop you buying it?—I should not buy him as a hunter; if a harness horse it would not stop me at all—on the contrary.

13732. You say those horses have been sent to France to [illegible] in that [illegible]?—Yes.

13733. Do you think the Hackney has lost any of his power to give [illegible] his not being [illegible]? As a matter of fact [illegible] brought [illegible] and [illegible] in the stock, and do you think he has lost any of his power of imparting [illegible]?—Every horse that goes [illegible] a horse that has done nothing at all. They bring [illegible] to France [illegible].

13734. Are they [illegible] afterwards in the [illegible]?—Yes. If a Hackney is [illegible] as a thoroughbred, and if he were not [illegible] the French [illegible] he would not be asked for.

13735. And if he was not you would find it out?—Oh, wouldn't they? They would not buy, but they would show.

13736. And you would hear of it?—Of course I should.

13737. You haven't heard complaints this year?—No; if I had I should not [illegible] orders from the Ministre.

13738. Did you buy many Hackneys in the show in '98?—Forty-six.

13739. About the usual price?—No; I don't think they cost as much as this year.

13740. In your opinion would Hackneys then be suitable to mate with such sorts of mares as you have described in the North of France, which have thoroughbred and trotting blood?—I presume they would.

March 16, 1897.

Mr. [illegible]

13741. Have you seen any of the produce from these?—Yes.

13742. Is the produce better than the sires there showed?—Yes, [illegible].

13743. You have never seen the produce of these mares crossed with a thoroughbred horse?—Yes, I have.

13744. What was the result?—The first cross was better with the thoroughbred horse than with the Hackney.

13745. Then would they get too weedy?—I don't know afterwards. I only saw the first crossing and the produce of the thoroughbred horse was absolutely bigger in [illegible] than the produce by the Hackney.

13746. Do you know whether any foreign Governments buy sires from Normandy, France?—Every Government in Europe buy out of Normandy.

13747. What do they buy?—In October every year 800 stallions are brought before the commission, and twenty [illegible] officers in the [illegible] they give out perhaps 150 out of the 800 stallions which are shown to us in three years [illegible]. After we have picked what we want the Italians come in, after the Italians the [illegible]; and after the [illegible] the Russians. Normandy is a great depot for the supply of these people.

13748. And these horses are used for the breeding of cavalry horses?—Yes.

13749. Do you know whether any other Governments were buying Hackneys at the last show?—Yes, they were buying for Austria-Hungary, Switzerland, and Norway and Sweden.

13750. The CHAIRMAN.—How many stallions are there owned by French Administration?—[illegible].

13751. Are they all Hackneys?—Oh, no. The Hackney begin the [illegible] of [illegible].

13752. Where would the [illegible] be [illegible] Trotters, Hackneys, thoroughbreds, and horses of the country. In [illegible] there is a [illegible]. There is a station at [illegible], and at [illegible], and in [illegible], and if they have a horse there [illegible] [illegible] this country is [illegible] to another station.

13753. And who settles all that?—There is a Minister, and he has [illegible] of eighty-four people under him.

13754. And they have to decide as to the suitability of the sires?—Each man at his station has a horse there, and he says: "I want so many horses, so many Hackneys, or so many thoroughbreds, or so many of this kind or the other."

13755. Can you tell the proportion of thoroughbreds you have would have of those stallions?—About one hundredth.

13756. That is about the same proportion as Hackneys?—I should think so.

13757. You talk of Mr. Phillips introducing Hackneys forty years ago. Is that the same sort of animal you call the Hackney now?—No. I was talking only the other day with a friend of mine at the show, a Frenchman, and he said to me: "Where is the old Hackney we used to get?" I said, "We don't want him now." "Yes," he said, "I would like to find him now. He was enormous and stronger, with splendid action, and a good big head and neck;" he says. "[illegible] Hackneys are short small [illegible], [illegible] with their tails out, with little heads and little feet comparatively to what we used to see in the former [illegible]." He has been improved upon, but the question is whether he has been improved upon for the purpose for which he was intended. We don't have all the big horses that you get from Mr. Walter Gilbey, because we want horses for £200 or £400, and when we go to Mr. Walter it is about £1,000 and then we shut off.

13758. I gather from you that, so far as Ireland are concerned you don't approve of Hackney blood?—Certainly not.

13759. Do you think it would be injudicious to introduce it largely into any part of Ireland?—I don't know. I don't think I am the person to give an opinion on that subject. They are, perhaps, worse horses than Hackneys in Ireland—much worse—but I don't think it would be wise ever [illegible] to get the Hackney and the [illegible] to improve the breeding. If you have a good mare and a [illegible] it might be very advantageous in certain parts of Ireland, but you may get Hackneys 15 hands or 14.2. That size, surely, would not be of advantage to Ireland. As all [illegible] it would not be any good for [illegible].

13760. You think generally the character of the horses in France has been improved during your [illegible] as far as [illegible] and [illegible] [illegible]?—They have been improved in every thing. They hadn't have horses fifty years ago, and now they send over here, and compete with us at Newmarket with their race horses, and they have improved in every other degree. We have in all about 45 [illegible] there that is not [illegible]. Formerly we have a horse that [illegible], if he is the [illegible] [illegible], and [illegible] with no [illegible], he is [illegible] the [illegible] and [illegible]. It would not do [illegible]. That must [illegible] in the [illegible]. If I have a Hackney stallion that makes a [illegible] he is [illegible]. He is [illegible] as a stallion.

The Commission adjourned.

APPENDIX.

APPENDIX A.

REPORTS ON HORSE-BREEDING AND AID GIVEN BY THE STATE IN AUSTRIA AND HUNGARY, FRANCE, ITALY, AND PRUSSIA.

REPORT ON HORSE-BREEDING IN AUSTRIA.

Answers to Questions of the Commission on Horse Breeding in Ireland.

Question 1.—Amount of money spent by the Government on Horse-breeding.

The Estimates of the Austrian Ministry for Agriculture for 1897, give the following figures under the head of Horse-breeding :—

—	Expenditure.		
	Ordinary.	Extraordinary.	Total.
	£	(Fl. at 12 gulden to £1.)	
1. State Studs (Radautz and Piber),	32,450	851	33,304
2. State Stallion Depots,	84,575	5,508	92,083
3. Farms for Colts bought by the State,	6,755	—	6,755
4. Additions to State Breeding-stock by purchase from private breeders,	25,875	—	25,875
5. Encouragement of Horse-breeding,	10,063	—	10,063
6. Foal-farm in Nestwerna (for Fillies bought by the State),	1,108	1,108	2,216
Total,	162,588	7,770	170,298

From the foregoing figures it appears that the Ministry of Agriculture actually disburses £170,298 in the maintenance of the State Studs, and in the encouragement of horse-breeding generally.

The receipts of this branch of the Ministry, for 1897, are estimated as follows :—

Income from Horse Breeding Establishments.

Ordinary Income	—
	£
1. State Studs (Radautz and Piber),	5,843
2. State Stallion Depots (Covering Fees, &c.),	18,166
3. Colt-farms,	678
Total,	27,966

The amount of the receipts (£27,966 as estimated for 1897) is paid over the Ministry of Finance by the Ministry of Agriculture.

Question 2.—The system on which the money is spent.

1. *State Stud Farms.* 2. *Stallion depots.*

There are two State Studs in Austria, viz., Radautz and Piber. The object of these establishments is to provide stallions for use throughout the country. These stallions are first sent to the Central depots, and then distributed to the various stations in the country, where they remain during the covering season. Care is taken that each stallion should be suited to the requirements of the district where his services are to be placed at the disposal of farmers and private breeders. For the use of the country stallions (Landbeschäler) a very small covering-fee is charged per mare, which varies from one to ten gulden ([illegible]) for ordinary stallions.

In some districts, where the peasants are very poor, and the breed of horses is in danger of degenerating, mares are covered by State stallions free of charge.

The Commission of Inquiry on Horse-breeding, which sat in 1876, resulted in the division of the whole Cis-Leithan territory into five districts, with a view to the distribution of stallions especially suited to existing local breeds, viz. :—

(*a*) The Noric district, i.e., Kell, St. Johann, and the neighbouring districts where the heavy Noric breed prevails.

(*b*) An Alpine district, including Tyrol, Salzburg, Styria, Upper Austria, and a part of Carinthia, where the "*Pinzgauer*" horses, and crosses of that hardy breed, are mostly used.

(*c*) A mountain district, including parts of Bohemia, Moravia, Silesia, and Lower Austria, where various lighter types of horse are bred.

(*d*) Galicia and Bukowina, where the local breed (Galician peasant horse) is small and light.

(*e*) Dalmatia and parts of Carinthia and the coast districts, where small hardy Italic horses are wanted as pack animals.

The following classes of stallions where decided upon for use in these various districts :—

(*a*) The Noric district.—The local breeds to be kept as pure as possible, and in Salzburg, especially, only "Pinzgauer" stallions to be used.

(N.B. The Pinzgauer breed is extremely useful for draught purposes in hilly districts. The colour is peculiar—white or light colour "splashed" with dark spots. The Pinzgauer horses are very strong and hardy, and have good action; the lighter class trot quite well enough for heavy carriage work over bad ground).

(*b*.) Stallions similar to the prevailing local breeds.

(*c*.) Strong heavy stallions, suitable for the production of a heavy cart breed.

(*d*.) Light stallions of the carriage or riding-horse class.

(*e*.) "Lippizaner" stallions, i.e. an excellent class of horse bred at the Imperial Stud in Lippiza, and which is of mingled Spanish Italian and Arab descent.

2 O

The leading principles by which the Austrian Ministry for Agriculture is guided in selecting stallions for distribution to country stations are:—

1. To encourage good local breeds, such as the Noric horse, the Pinzgauer, and the Huzulen, or small Carpathian breed. All these are to be kept pure.

2. To improve, by judicious crossing, any local breeds which have degenerated, or are in danger of doing so.

The stallions used are of the following classes:—

1. Stallions of English origin—

(a.) Thoroughbred stallions to be used in districts where the majority of the mares are big and strong, but not over-bred. These thoroughbreds are mostly bred in the country.

(b.) Hackney, Clydesdale, and Suffolk stallions for the production of heavy carriage and riding horses, also remounts.

2. Oldenburger stallions for the production of medium carriage horses and artillery horses.

3. Belgian stallions are used to improve and give character to the heavy draught breeds.

4. The lighter class of Ardennes stallion is used to give size to the small local breed in Galicia.

MANAGEMENT.

The State horse-breeding establishments have a military organisation, and a Military Department (Militär-Abtheilung)—which is an integral part of the standing army—is entrusted with the management of the studs, stallion depôts, and covering stations.

This Military Department is subordinated to the Imperial Ministry for War in matters purely military; to the Ministry for Agriculture in regard to everything connected with the horse-breeding establishments; and to the Commander of the Local Military Division in matters of discipline.

The purely clerical and civil part of the stud-farms is worked by civilians; otherwise both management and service are military—civil departments having been tried, and having failed utterly, owing to constant changes among the employés who were attracted by higher wages elsewhere.

As it is found that the State studs of Radautz and Piber cannot supply all the stallions required for the country districts, entire colts are purchased by the State, and reared on farms kept especially for this purpose. (See Item No. 6 in Estimates for 1897.) These colts are usually bought as yearlings.

The State breeding-stock is also added to by purchase from private breeders, either in the country or abroad, and the animals bought are distributed to the studs, to the stallion depôts, or to the colt-farms, according to circumstances. (See No. 4 in the Estimates).

Item No. 6 in the Estimates includes expenditure for rearing young stock on commission; for prizes given at the various race-meetings (£4,000); prizes given to breeders (£3,300); subventions to licensed stallions, the property of private owners (£3,850); subventions to prizes at horse shows, &c., and subventions to private owners for rearing foals.

Item No. 6 in the Estimate represents the cost of the foal farms in Niederösterreich, where fillies purchased by the State are reared for eventual distribution to the peasants in the poorer parts of Galicia (free of charge), on condition that they should be used for breeding purposes.

Question 3.—The amount of money spent on the encouragement of farmers and other private breeders of horses.

Speaking generally, it may be said that the whole expenditure of the Ministry for Agriculture on horse-breeding is a direct encouragement to farmers and private breeders, as they obtain the use of suitable stallions at an almost nominal fee.

The more direct advantages offered come under heads Nos. 5 and 6 in the Estimates, amounting to £13,718.

In these are included as above stated:—

Prizes given at race-meetings.

Prizes given at horse shows and to breeders.

Subventions to owners of licensed stallions.

Subventions to private owners for rearing foals with a view to breeding.

The possibility of obtaining a State stallion, on hire, for use in a private stud under very favourable conditions.

The sale of mares at a price far below their actual value, in the poorer parts, on condition that they are used for breeding, and last, but not least, the ready market offered to private owners by the frequent purchases, made by the Government of animals suitable for the State studs, and for cavalry and artillery remounts.

To give a better idea of the great advantages offered to private breeders, a statement is annexed showing the number and breed of the State stallions at present standing in the covering stations, in private hands, and hired out:—

SUMMARY OF STALLIONS AT THE COVERING STATIONS, IN PRIVATE HANDS, OR ON HIRE

—	No. of Covering Stations.	No. of Stallions.	English Thoroughbred.	English Half-bred.	Norfolk.	Arab Thoroughbred.	Arab Half-bred.	[illegible]	[illegible]	[illegible]	Cart Horses.	Heavy Draught Stallions.	[illegible]	[illegible]	[illegible]
a. In Covering Stations,	533	2,763	55	127	192	10	309	69	10	121	261	261	643	825	30
b. In Private Hands,	–	276	1	1	9	–	10	1	–	–	254	254	5	1	18
c. On Hire,	–	99	38	18	5	3	20	1	–	1	–	–	26	77	–
Total,	533	3,138	94	146	206	13	339	71	10	122	515	515	674	903	48

From the foregoing table it appears that the State possesses no less than 3,138 stallions, of which 94 are English thoroughbreds, 146 English half-breds, and 206 Norfolk. This shows how much English blood is appreciated, though most of the animals in question are bred in the country.

Question 4.—Inducements, if any, held out to private breeders with regard to keeping brood mares.

This question has practically already been answered.

The easy terms on which the services of suitable stallions are available are, of course, a direct inducement to private owners to keep brood mares.

As an additional inducement, prizes or premiums are distributed by a regularly appointed Prize Committee, according to the regulations laid down in 1878, viz.:—

1. For brood mares with foal at foot, from five years old and upwards, if their foal is by a State stallion, by a licensed stallion in private hands, or by a stallion belonging to the owner of the mare so qualified.

* "Noted" mares can obtain prizes as four-year-olds.

2. For young mares (two years and three years) when in foal to a State licensed or private stallion.

3. For colts of two and three years, if they give promise of being suitable for stud purposes.

4. For stallions (licensed stallions belonging to private persons).

No stallion for which a State subvention has been granted can compete.

In 1878 premiums were also established for one and two year old fillies.

The prizes consist of:—

1. Prizes in cash (1–25 gold ducats). **Ducat** = 5 fls.
2. Silver medals.
3. Certificates of commendation.

Each recipient of a State prize has to undertake to keep the animal in question for another year, failing which the amount has to be refunded.

In 1891, 5,871 prizes were granted.

Question 5.—The system, if any, of registering or of licensing stallions, the property of private owners.

Private owners are encouraged to keep stallions to cover their mares, and also those of others, as by this means it is hoped that horse-breeding may gradually be emancipated from State assistance.

Private stallions are only encouraged if they are suitable for stud purposes, and their fitness is established by licence.

The Committee on Horse-breeding, which sat in 1878, recommended the following amendments of existing laws:—

1. That all stallions used for covering mares, not owned by the proprietor of the stallion, should be obliged to have a licence, even if no covering fee were charged.

2. The establishment of a regular **system of** Licensing Commissions.

3. The cost of veterinary examination of stallions for which a licence is demanded to be charged to the State.

4. The use of unlicensed stallions to be a punishable offence.

5. Owners of brood mares allowing their mares to be covered by an unlicensed stallion to be punished.

6. That stallions and colts should not be pastured with mares and fillies, especially in Galicia, Bukowina, and Dalmatia, where the horse breed is small and light.

These recommendations were adopted by the various provincial diets at different dates, excepting by those of Carinthia, Bohemia, Silesia, and the coast district, where the previously existing laws of 1855, 1869, and 1875 are still in force.

The regulations in the other provinces are all based on the following principles:—

1. No private owner may allow his stallion to cover mares owned by others, whether for a covering fee or gratis, unless he has taken out a licence for his stallion for the covering season in question. An exception is sometimes made in favour of owners of English thoroughbreds and stud owners who possess their own stallions. They may be relieved by the local authorities from the obligation of taking out a licence.

2. Any owner is free to have his own mares covered by his own stallion.

3. An owner wishing to take out a licence for his stallion must notify his desire to the chief local authorities within a specified period.

4. In order to obtain a licence the stallion must be brought before a Licensing Commission for examination. The Commission must then declare the stallion "fit" or "unfit" for stud purposes, and must grant or refuse the licence accordingly.

The decision of the Commission is final, and from it there is no appeal.

5. The owner of a stallion which is declared "fit" for stud purposes receives from the Commission gratis a licence in the form fixed by the regulations. This licence entitles the stallion to stand at a fixed place, and to cover the class of mares described in the licence certificate, for the period of one year.

In Galicia and Bukowina, however, in view of local conditions, licences are granted for periods of one to three years.

6. The Licensing Commissions are appointed by the competent local authorities for periods of from one to four years, according to the various provincial regulations.

7. The number of members and formation of these Commissions vary in the different provinces.

The number of members varies between three and five. In each province a representative of the local authorities is attached to the Commission, and a representative of the State Stallion Depôt must be on the Committee, as well as a veterinary surgeon, either as a voting member or merely in order to give his professional opinion on the stallions brought before him. The other members are experts appointed by the local authorities in an honorary capacity.

8. The owner of a licensed stallion is obliged to give a certificate (Deckschein) to the owners of mares covered by his stallion, and to keep an accurate register of such mares.

The form of these certificates and registers are defined in the licensing regulations, and are similar to those of the certificates issued, and of the registers kept by the managers of the Government covering stations.

9. The amount of the fee to be charged per mare covered by a licensed stallion is left to be arranged by the parties concerned.

10. Throughout the covering season every licensed stallion is to be examined once a month, at Government expense, by a veterinary surgeon or further appointed for the purpose.

11. Whoever uses an unlicensed stallion to cover mares other than his own, whether gratis or for a covering fee; whoever knowingly allows a mare in his possession to be covered by an unlicensed stallion, or whoever allows his stallion colts of from one year old and upwards to be pastured with mares or fillies their age, or otherwise infringes the licensing regulations in any other respect, is to be punished according to the provisions of the regulations applicable to the case by a fine not exceeding 100 gulden (= 8l. 6s. 8d.)

The licensing regulations also contain provisions for the application of these penalties, and for appeals against the same.

The Ministry for Agriculture is charged with the execution of the licensing laws.

The local authorities are charged with the necessary surveillance, and with the prevention of any infringements of the laws in question.

The authorities of the State Stallion Depôts have to report any case of an unlicensed stallion being used for stud purposes (except for the owner's mares) to the Ministry of Agriculture; the local authorities are

they [illegible] with a view to [illegible] premature [illegible] of the case.

As already stated, licensed stallions are sometimes granted a State subvention when considered as specially suitable for stud purposes in a given locality. This is especially the case with regard to cart stallions. The cases suitable for subvention are brought to the notice of the authorities of the Land Stud Book, and by them to that of the Ministry of Agriculture.

Subventions are granted of 100 guldens (£8 6s. 8d.) for a period of three years; or of 150 guldens, with yearly increase of 50 guldens, for a period of four years. The owner of the stallion obliges himself to keep him well, and to use him for his own and other people's mares during the period for which the subvention is granted. The stallion must cover a specified number of mares yearly, the covering fee being fixed by the owner.

In 1891 Subventions granted to [illegible] stallions belonging to private owners, by which 10,215 mares were covered—i.e., [illegible] mares per stallion.

In the same year subventions were granted to 133 licensed stallions.

Division 5.—Success, or otherwise, of Government Stud Farms.

The Austrian Government first began to take an active interest in horse-breeding in the reign of the Emperor Charles VI.

By a decree of 1728 the provincial authorities were directed to provide stallions suitable for getting remounts, and the working of very young horses was forbidden.

But the first great impulse to horse-breeding in Austria was given by a decree drawn up by the Empress Maria Theresa with her own hand in 1763; and since that time the State has continued to encourage horse-breeding as far as possible.

By the above-mentioned decree Baron von [illegible] was appointed superintendent in all matters connected with horse-breeding.

The existing State Studs at *Radautz* and *Piber* were established in 1792 and 1798 respectively. So their history extends over the last century.

Count [illegible] of Hungary, who [illegible] after the conclusion of Peace in 1815, was the first to systematise horse-breeding as carried on by the State, and to manage it on fairly scientific principles. He imported at various times a number of thoroughbred Arab stallions, as well as English horses, bought either in England or in Germany. He organised the studs at Kisber and Mezőhegyes (in Hungary), and at the former he commenced breeding English thoroughbreds. Premiums were established for both stallions and mares, and stallions were distributed throughout the provinces. [illegible] almost [illegible] to [illegible] all remounts for the army from the country itself, and succeeded so well that, in 1849, the 21,000 horses required were all home bred.

[illegible] was a great believer in Arab blood, but after his death in 1854 his successors began to use English thoroughbred blood more and more.

The following figures show that the efforts of the Government to encourage horse-breeding were successful.

In the Cis-Leithan territories (exclusive of Lombardy and Venice) there were:—

In 1819, [illegible] horses, giving 187 per square mile.
In 1880, [illegible] " " 193 " "

In Hungary there were:—

In 1819, 941,872 horses, or 160 per square mile.
In 1870, 2,158,819 " " 365 " "

Import and Export of Horses and Foals.

	Imported.	Exported.
In 1803,	18,788	6,352
In 1842,	[illegible]	28,345
In 1880,	[illegible]	51,517

Austrian horse-breeding was also greatly improved by the occasional supply of stallions from the Imperial studs at *Kladrub* and *Lippiza*.

In 1869 the care of the State studs and horse-breeding establishments was transferred from the Ministry of War to the Ministry of Agriculture.

The object of the preceding historical sketch is to show that the Government has, at any rate, been successful in increasing the stock of horses in the country, and in improving their quality—thereby ensuring a good supply of remounts for the army, and rendering great service to the agricultural class.

It is doubtful, however, whether the existing State studs at *Radautz* and *Piber* can be regarded as successful from all points of view. It appears that the percentage of foals (*i.e.*, the increase on the breeding stock) varies between 60 and 70 per cent., whereas in a stud the increase should be about 80 per cent. This may be partly due to the severity of the climate, and the great extremes of heat and cold. On the other hand, the increase of breeding-stock in the hands of farmers is much smaller. As the chief object of the State studs is to supply stallions for the various covering stations, and as both these, and the stallions at the studs, cover at an almost nominal fee, it is difficult to say, from a commercial point of view, whether they are successful or not. (At Radautz the Stud thoroughbred stallions cover at 30 guldens (£2 10s.) for thoroughbred, and 15 guldens for half-bred mares). There is no doubt, however, that the State studs have done much in raising the quality of the horses bred throughout the country, in preserving good local breeds, and in spreading the knowledge of breeding on scientific principles among the farmers.

Imperial Studs at Kladrub and Lippiza.

The Imperial Studs at *Kladrub* and *Lippiza* are restricted to producing two very fine types of carriage horses. The Kladrub horses are very large, showy animals, with good action, and are chiefly used in the Court carriages on State occasions. They are descended from Spanish and Italian stock; they are either black, or white, and stand as high as 17 h. 2 in. (17½ hands). Attempts to improve the breed by crossing with English thoroughbreds have failed.

English thoroughbreds are also successfully reared at Kladrub, and for ten years the Imperial colours were much honoured on the turf. The racing establishment there was given up in 1876, partly so as not to compete so heavily with private owners, and partly on account of the great expense entailed thereby.

Lippiza.

The Imperial Stud at Lippiza is situated at about an hour's drive from Trieste. The property was bought by the Archduke Charles in 1580; an Imperial stud was soon after established there, which is still flourishing, and which has produced the celebrated "Lippizaner" breed. The first breeding stock consisted of three "Brioni," six other selected stallions, and twenty-four brood mares, all of which were bought in Spain. To these were added Italian, Danish, and a few Arab sires. During the stormy years between 1797 and 1815 the stud suffered much from constant removals. In 1826 a considerable number of Arab stallions were imported, but stallions, belonging to the local "karst" breed, were also used. In 1857 two more Arab stallions and sixteen mares, purchased in the Syrian desert, were added to the stud, and with these pure Arab stock was bred. It was found, however, that the pure Arab was not so good for severe carriage work as the Lippizaner, and the Arab thoroughbred stock was therefore applied to cross the stud-breed. English thoroughbreds were also used for the same purpose, especially a stallion called "Northern-Light" by "Chanticleer," out of "Sunflower" by "Bay Middleton." The latter's

REPORT ON THE BREEDING OF HORSES IN HUNGARY.

The enclosed report, published in 1896, by the Hungarian Minister of Agriculture, gives an account of the origin, progress, and present state of the Hungarian State Studs and the items connected with these establishments.

There are four studs in Hungary which form State property, and are maintained by the Government for the promotion of horse-breeding.

When the stallions have reached the necessary age, they are brought to the stallion depôts from whence they are yearly sent for a certain period of time to the covering stations.

There are eighteen stallion depôts and 836 covering stations distributed in the different parts of the country.

There were in total 2,998 stallions kept in 1896 at the State stallion depôts, of which about [illegible] were bred in the State studs and almost [illegible] has been purchased from private breeders.

The covering fees paid to the Government at the covering stations vary between 1 to 10 florins (1s. 8d. – 16s. 8d.) per stallion.

Breeders are also at liberty to hire stallions from the stallion depôts for covering purposes.

The hire paid for the hire vary between 300–1,200 florins = about £25–£100.

Committees are formed in the different parts of the country with the view to encourage the breeding of horses by making acquainted the farmers with the object and the principles of rational breeding, and thus constituting a connecting link between the breeding establishments of the Government and the private farmers.

A further mode adopted by the Government for the encouragement of private breeders is continually to purchase from them a certain amount of stallions to be employed in the State establishments.

The Military authorities contribute to this encouragement by trying to avoid middlemen and to procure the necessary supply of horses directly from private breeders.

It has proved to be a useful mode for the promotion of horse-breeding to sell a certain part of the stallions, purchased by the Government from private breeders, to communities at low prices and at convenient payment conditions.

Facilities for the transport of breeding stock are granted at all times by the Hungarian State railways.

Prizes are distributed among the farmers for their encouragement to keep mares and foals.

Subsidies are granted by the Government for the creation of spacious pastures (foal gardens) in the poorer communities of the country.

The Government has raised a fund for the promotion of horse-breeding, deriving its income from the tax imposed upon the "totalisateur" at the racing courses.

The State Budget for 1897 shows the following figures in connection with horse-breeding:—

—	Expenditure.		Receipts.	
	Flor.	£	Flor.	£
State Studs,	1,[illegible]4,249	96,18[illegible]	518,579	43,608
Stallion Depôts,	1,870,781	155,898	518,830	43,2[illegible]
Subsidies for Racing purposes,	30,000	2,500	—	
Subsidies for Breeding purposes, and for the creation of Foal-gardens,	40,000	3,333	—	
For the purchase of Covering Stock,	14,000	1,166	—	
Receipts from the Fund created for the promotion of Horse-breeding,	......		14,000	1,166
Stud Farms, including the Crown Domain from Gödöllő,	3,08[illegible]	256,996	3,376,121	281,343

Remarks.

Register stud books are kept at the State studs.

The Hungarian Agricultural Society at Buda-Pesth is charged stud-books to be kept at their offices for the registration of the stallions and mares of private breeders.

The registration is not compulsory.

Supplementary details are to be found in the printed [illegible], published by the Hungarian Agricultural Society, on the stud-book, and the regulations relating thereto.

HUNGARY.

It appears that the system of State encouragement to horse-breeding in Hungary and of managing the State studs is very similar to that followed in Austria.

In Hungary, however, thoroughbred stock is bred in the State studs, which is not the case in Austria.

There are four State studs in Hungary, viz.:—

Kisber.
Babolna.
Mezőhegyes.
Fogaras.

The estimates for the Department of the Hungarian Ministry for Agriculture charged with horse-breeding amount to 2,800,000 gulden for 1897 (£233,333).

As the official returns are only published in Hungarian it has not been possible, so far, to obtain further details.

M. de C. Findlay,

Vienna, March 19th, 1897.

REPORT ON HORSE-BREEDING IN FRANCE.

1. The French Government spends annually about £88,000 on the encouragement of horse-breeding. The exact figures for the last two years are 2,207,200 francs (£88,288) in 1896, and 2,193,890 francs (£87,755) in 1895.

The above sums do not include an annual grant of 50,000 francs (£2,000), made to Algiers.

In addition to the above, various Towns and Departments in France spent 1,313,570 francs (£52,543) in 1895—probably about £54,000 last year—on shows and other purposes connected with encouraging the breeding of horses.

2. The money granted by the Government was distributed in 1896 in the following manner:—

—	Francs.	£ sterling.
Flat Races,	171,985	6,844
Trotting Races,	248,500	9,940
Races open to Colts only,	66,250	2,650
Races open to Fillies only,	84,100	3,364
National and Public Horse Shows,	49,600	1,984
Premiums to private Stallions,	600,000	24,000
Premiums to Colts and Fillies,	123,000	4,920
Premiums to Brood Mares,	651,500	26,060
Premiums to Thoroughbred Mares devoted to the production of Arab or Anglo-Arab stock,	54,000	2,160
District Shows,	110,000	4,400
Expenses incurred in marking private Stallions whose services are open to the public,	27,000	1,080
	fcs. 2,153,890	£86,161

Various Towns and Departments assisted the breeding of horses as follows in 1895:—

—	Francs.	£ sterling.
Flat Races, Steeplechases, and Trotting Races,	817,530	32,700
Harness and Saddle Horse Shows,	16,600	664
Local Shows,	489,440	19,577
	fcs. 1,323,570	£52,941

It is probable that the above subsidies were more than maintained last year, but the returns are not yet procurable.

3. The amount of money spent by the Government in the encouragement of Societies and other private breeders of horses is not noted in the above statement, since there are no special subventions made to them directly. Private breeders and farmers benefit, however, more especially from the premiums given to colts and fillies, brood mares and private stallions, as set forth in the preceding schedule of expenditure. They are also the chief gainers by the large grants in prizes at the District Horse Shows.

4. It will have been observed above that, under the headings of premiums to brood mares (651,500 francs), and premiums to thoroughbred mares devoted to the production of Arab or Anglo-Arab horses (54,000 francs), a grand total of 705,500 francs (£28,220), is expended as an inducement to keeping brood mares. The Report of [illegible] of money given in premiums to brood mares [illegible], the latter given the total value of the premiums, varying from 300 to 600 francs, granted to thoroughbred mares in certain districts of the Pyrenees, where they are too scattered about for it to be possible to assemble them in a show yard. The premiums in this instance are given on the recommendation of the Government Stud Officials.

The Government does not give any other special premiums or aid for this purpose to private breeders.

5. Stallions, the property of private owners, whose services are open to the public, are examined by the technical Veterinary Commission, whose duty it is to determine whether or not they are afflicted with roaring or intermittent ophthalmia. Only stallions that have been passed free of these two blemishes are authorised to cover public mares. It is the duty of the Prefects of the Departments to bring the mares to the notice of the breeders.

Such stallions are merely registered as "Accepted." There are, however, two other classes of private stallions, namely:—

(a.) "Approved" stallions which are recognised as capable of improving the breed of horses, and which receive an annual premium from the Government, varying from 300 francs (£12) to 2,000 francs (£80). It is these premiums which make up the total of 600,000 francs (£24,000) quoted in the expenditure schedule under the heading "Premiums to private stallions"; and

(b.) "Authorised" stallions which are judged good enough to maintain the breed of horses, though incapable of improving it. These horses do not receive premiums, but they have an official status which enables their products to take part in Shows subventioned by the State.

6. The Haras de Pompadour, in the Department of the Corrèze, is the only regular Government Stud Farm in France. Sixty thoroughbred mares are kept there which are solely intended for the production of Arab and Anglo-Arab horses. It is stated that the results are satisfactory.

In addition to the Stud Farm of Pompadour, the French Government possesses 22 stallion depots, containing 3,500 horses. These stallions stand during the covering season in the country districts in towns and threes, and their services are reserved—at a very small covering fee—the sires belonging to private breeders. It is said that, thanks to this system, the production of horses in France is amply sufficient for the requirements of the army and trade.

Although not actually coming within the scope of the questions asked by the Commission on Horse-breeding in Ireland, it may be of interest to them to have certain supplementary data concerning horse-breeding in France laid before them.

The law of January 29, 1892, fixes the number of Government sires at 3,000, and this figure is maintained as nearly as possible in the following proportions:—[illegible] thoroughbred sires (Arab, English, and Anglo-Arab), [illegible] half-bred sires, and [illegible] draught stallions. In 1895, the Government stallions covered 157,187 mares, as against [illegible] during the preceding season, a satisfactory increase, and a larger number than has been previously recorded. The receipts derived from the services of Government stallions amounted to [illegible] francs ([illegible]), equivalent to a fee of about six shillings per mare.

The official returns for 1895 show that [illegible] sires belonging to private owners received certificates of approbation; of these [illegible] were thoroughbred, [illegible] half-bred, and [illegible] draught horses. A stallion standing at a higher covering fee than 300 francs (£12) is not entitled to a premium, though accorded a certificate of approbation. Eighty-seven thoroughbred and eight half-bred stallions came under such higher conditions for this reason. These "approved" sires covered [illegible] mares, an average of about [illegible] mares per horse.

One hundred and twenty-eight sires belonging to private persons were officially "authorised," a distinction which [illegible] them to take part in shows supported by Government. These horses covered [illegible] mares in 1895, an average of about 54 mares per horse.

Of the private stallions presented to the Military Commission for examination in 1895, [illegible] were rejected as unfit from the [illegible] (roaring and intermittent ophthalmia) prohibited by the law of August 14, 1885. The statistics do not state how many mares they covered.

The total number of mares covered in 1895 by (1) Government, (2) "Approved," and (3) "Authorised" stallions amounted to [illegible], an increase of [illegible] over the [illegible] mares covered by these three classes of sires in 1894.

The above figures would seem to show that horse-breeding is in a flourishing condition in France, but nevertheless, the official returns give a decrease on the exportations of 1895 over those of 1894, and an increase on the importations. The exact totals for all classes of horses are:—

1894,	Importations,	21,031
1895,	"	26,457
1894,	Exportations,	23,238
1895,	"	21,464

It is said that this increase in the importation of horses may be partly ascribed to the large numbers of cheap animals lately sent to Europe from America and Canada. The Director of Government Studs points out in his Report for 1895, however, that 212,[illegible] mares were covered that year by Government "approved" or "authorised" stallions, as against [illegible] mares in 1886. He therefore concludes that either the number of horses used in France becomes larger and more considerable every year, or that the supplementary production, that is to say, the number of horses bred from mares merely passed as sound by the Military Commission, keeps on diminishing. The returns, however, do not give a sufficiently large reduction in this class to account for the fall in exportation, and the extraordinarily large rise in importations.

WALTER TOWNLEY.

Paris, 3rd March, 1897.

REPORT ON HORSE-BREEDING IN ITALY.

British Embassy, Rome,
February 25th, 1897.

SIR,—In compliance with instructions from Your Excellency, I have the honour to enclose a Preliminary Report on Horse-breeding in Italy, together with a sketch-map of the country indicating the situation of the central and other depots.

This report will furnish some of the information asked for in Lord Salisbury's Despatch, No. 1, marked Commercial, of the 30th January. I propose to send a further report after personally visiting the Stud-farm at Pisa, and the Army Remount Depot at Grosseto. The information has been collected from the Annual Official Report for 1895, of the Minister of Agriculture; unfortunately, the report for 1896 has not yet been published, but will be ready shortly. I will notify any changes of importance that have taken place during the year, and at the same time forward a copy of the Italian Hand-book.

I have the honour to be, Sir,
Your obedient servant,
CHARLES NEEDHAM, Colonel,
Military Attaché.

H. E. The Right Honourable
Sir Clare Ford, G.C.B., &c.

REPORT ON HORSE-BREEDING IN ITALY.

Ministry of Agriculture and Commerce.—Horse Breeding Department, 1896.

Number of Stallions.

There were 563 stallions in the Government Horse Depots on January 1st, 1896. These were divided, according to their breeds, as follows:—

Breeds.

Thoroughbreds,	English,		73	13·04 per cent.
	Eastern,	80	86	11·77 per cent.
	Anglo-Eastern,	6		
Three parts bred,			97	—
Half-bred,			377	67·68 per cent.
American Trotter,			1	—
Heavy Draught,			26	4·61 per cent.
Total,			563	

Classes.

For breeding purposes they were divided as follows :—

Saddle Horses,	167	American and Russian Trotters,	24
Carriage Horses,	63	Heavy Draught,	28
Saddle and Light Draught,	120		
		Total,	402

Losses.

During 1886 there was a loss of 44 stallions, of which 19 died, and 25 were cast for the following causes :—

Breeds.		Died.	Cast.	Total.	Percentage.
Thoroughbreds,	English,	2	3	5	7·33 per cent.
	Eastern,	4	2	6	
	Anglo-Eastern,	1	–	1	
Three parts bred,		3	8	11	
Half-bred,		5	11	16	
American Trotters,		–	1	1	
Heavy Draught,		1	–	1	
Total,		19	25	44	

Causes of Loss.

The causes of death, or reasons for casting, were as follows :—

Died, or were slaughtered for		Cast for	
Apoplexy,	3	Various defects,	1
Pleuro-pneumonia,	3	Unsaleable,	4
Colic,	4	Age and exhaustion,	4
Typhus,	3	Blindness,	11
Fracture of Limbs,	2	Amaurosis,	1
Hernia,	1	Ophthalmia,	1
Castration,	1	Inflammation,	1
Operation,	1	Blood poisoning,	1
Glanders,	1	Bad temper,	1
Total,	19	Total,	25

Purchase of Stallions.

To replace these stallions, some were purchased in the country, and others abroad. The proceedings to regulate the purchase of stallions are described in the following order of the day, approved by the Council in 1882, and confirmed in 1883 :—

"In order to procure stallions for service in Italy, as far as possible in the country, the Commission will indicate the places at which thoroughbred stallions may be offered for sale; the Government will not haggle over the price, but will offer what they consider fair. Half-bred stallions will be purchased in the same manner. Half-bred stallions purchased abroad will be procured, as far as possible, in England, failing the requisite numbers, in Germany or France."

Conditions of Purchase.

In June, 1886, the usual notice was issued for the purchase of three parts half-bred and Eastern stallions; the following conditions are worthy of notice :—

"With the exception of horses that have run in public races under the management of a recognised club, all horses must be tried under saddle, or in harness. The trial, which must be made at the greatest speed of which the horse is capable, will be directed by the Government Commission, and will extend to one mile and three furlongs. Grey horses will not be purchased, unless of exceptional merit. The Government will state the price they are ready to give for any stallion found suitable for their purpose."

Numbers Purchased.

One hundred and thirty-four stallions were shown for sale to the Government, being 35 less than in 1894.

The following table shows the number of stallions purchased and the places where they were shown to the Commission :—

In Italy.	English Thorough-breds.	[illegible]	[illegible]
Cremona,	–	3	–
Ferrara,	–	3	–
Reggio Emilia,	–	4	–
Casalina (Borgata Perugia),	–	–	1
Pisa,	2	–	–
Roma,	–	3	6
Santa Maria Capua Vetere,	–	–	1
Salerno,	–	–	1
Sicily,	–	1	1
Sardinia,	–	–	2
Total,	2	11	13
In England,	–	11	–
Totals,	2	22	13
General Total,		37	

Cost of Stallions.

The 26 stallions purchased in Italy cost £3,437, an average of about £132 each; the 11 purchased in England cost £2,868, an average of £259 each.

Proportion of Breeds.

The number of stallions at the Depots on December 31, 1895, was 575. The proportion of different breeds was established by the Council as follows :—

English Thoroughbreds,	13 per cent.
Thoroughbred Eastern and Anglo-Eastern,	14 "
Heavy Draught Horses,	5 "

Ages.

The ages of the stallions were :—

2 Year Olds,	1	7 Year Olds,	87	12 Year Olds,	38
3 "	13	8 "	83	13 "	17
4 "	64	9 "	93	14 "	85
5 "	34	10 "	60	16 "	81
6 "	94	11 "	86		
					575

Inspection of Colts.

The Administration, acting on the advice of the Council, in 1893, as to the most efficacious means of increasing the number of stallions in the country, so as to assist the Government Depots, ordered in 1895 an inspection of the colts that had been shown as two-year-olds in 1894, and had been considered likely to become good stallions; of the 46 shown in 1894, 13 had been selected for further inspection; of these 13, 4 were not shown, and 5 were purchased by the Government. In June, 1895, a special notice was issued to owners and breeders of horses, informing them of the conditions under which two-year-old colts would be inspected. The Administration assumes no responsibility at this preliminary inspection. The colts considered likely to become useful stallions are, if kept by the breeders, examined the following year, and may be purchased, if funds are available, if the colt continues to show the same qualities, and if he passes the prescribed trials.

SERVICE OF GOVERNMENT STALLIONS.

Number of Stallions serving Mares.

Five hundred and eighty-two stallions served mares in 1895; they were posted at 377 different stations. They covered in all 19,546 mares, an average of 31·09 mares to each stallion.

The following table shows the names of the central depots, and the number of stallions at each station :—

Name of Depot.	Number of Stations with 1 Stallion	2	3	4 or more.
Cremona,	10	37	9	5
Reggio Emilia,	18	13	6	–
Ferrara,	37	23	6	1
Pisa,	40	15	3	–
Santa Maria Capua,	63	15	4	–
Catania,	43	14	3	–
Chieri,	25	11	1	1
Total,	236	118	32	10
	377 Stations.			

The following is the report on mares covered :—

Breed of Stallion.			Stallions.	Mares.	Average.
Thoroughbred,	English,	73	156	[illegible]	33·23
	Eastern,	78		2,161	27·61
	Anglo-Eastern,	6		204	34·00
Three parts and half-bred,			[illegible]	13,800	34·81
American Trotter,			1	33	33·00
Heavy Draught Stallions,			29	[illegible]	13·15
			563	19,843	34·09

Number of Mares refused.

During the season in the seven central depots, 319 mares were refused for the following reasons: 60 were under-sized, 40 were malformed, with serious defects, 16 had ophthalmia, 13 were broken-winded, 13 had tumours, 25 were got in use, 13 were vicious, 73 had infectious diseases, 1 was too young, 3 were already in foal, 1 was too in-bred. Besides these, 18 could not be served, because the stallion refused to cover them, 57 because the stallion was otherwise employed, 1 because the stallion was sick.

Service Fees.

The amount received for service of 19,848 mares was £11,819, divided as follows :—

		£	s.	d.	£
5	Mares at	64	0	0	320
37	"	32	0	0	1,184
6	"	2	2	0	12
258	"	1	12	0	413
1,071	"	1	0	0	1,071
18,520	"	0	9	7	8,869
Total, 19,848					£11,819

[illegible]

New Stations.

"A new station cannot be established except in unusual circumstances, unless it be at least 12 miles distant from one already existing. The Directors of Depots should ascertain whether, in the locality where a new station is asked for, there is a sufficient number of good-sized mares to justify the detachment of one or more stallions. These stations should not be retained where less than 35 mares are brought for service, especially if there are other stations in the neighbourhood where mares can be conveniently taken. When at the end of a season it is found that at a station where one stallion is kept, and the number of mares is less than 35, and the cause is not attributable to any defect in the stallion, and is not of a transitory nature, the Director should warn the Mayor that the following spring the station will only be kept up on trial, and will be suppressed, if the limit of numbers is not attained. Or, he may suggest to the Ministry the immediate abolition of the station. An increased number of stallions may be allowed, when it has been ascertained that during the season more than 45 mares have been brought to the station."

Uniform** [illegible] **Private

[illegible]

[illegible]

No. I.—Staff.

Officers.		Veterinary Surgeons.		Soldiers.	Farriers.		Total.
Pay and Allowances.	Travelling Expenses.	Pay and Allowances.	Travelling Expenses.	Pay.	Pay.	Travelling Expenses.	
£ 1,990	£ 207	£ 338	£ 7	£ 10,309	£ 1,584	£ 293	£ 17,848

Cost for each Stallion, £31 (circa).

No. II.—Forage.

Oats.	Barley.	Straw Feeding.	Straw Bedding.	Bran.	Meal.	Beans.	Green Food.	Hay.	Total.
£	£	£	£	£	£	£	£	£	£
6,853	1,369	50	2,639	569	194	344	1,354	3,108	16,839

Daily Ration, about 1s. 6d. Cost of each Stallion, £37 10s.

No. III.—General Expenses.

	£		£
Shoeing,	414	Special visits to Sick Horses,	3
Saddlery and Harness,	826	Allowances to Members of Council,	24
Stables and Coach Houses,	418	Fire Insurance,	112
Lighting,	184	Inspections and Journeys,	84
Fuel,	337	Medicines,	329
Lodgings,	181	Sundry Expenses,	2,166
Carriage,	983	Total,	£8,653

Cost of each Stallion, £12.

In all each stallion cost for 1895—

	£	s.	d.
Expenses of Staff,	31	0	0
Forage,	27	10	0
General Expenses,	12	0	0
Total,	£70	10	0 (circa)

The expenses of the seven depots were fixed at £1,353 for 1896; these expenses are borne three-fourths by the provinces included in the management of each depot, in proportion to the number of stations, and one fourth by the commune in the commune district of which the depot is situated.

General prosperity.

On the whole the condition of horse-breeding may be considered satisfactory. The breeders are doing better, and there is more trade in horses, which is essential to the prosperity of the industry.

Sardinia.

In Sardinia, for instance, the Director writes: "That many more foals are bred there, the breeders are employing a better system; certainly, there is but little stabling, but that does not apply to horses only, other animals have to live in the open. Consequently, the breeders are anxious to sell their foals as two-year-olds. If they do not sell them, there is great difficulty in keeping the foals in the enclosures. The Government Depot is, whatever may be said to the contrary, an encouragement, and even a necessity in Sardinia."

Sicily.

Horse-breeding in Sicily is also doing well. The Director at Catania writes: "The Military Commission bought 185 good foals, and might well buy 250 more excellent two-year-olds."

Pisa.

In the District of Pisa, and especially in the Provinces of Pisa, Grosseto, and Rome, the breeding of horses continues to improve. It is true, private breeders, and those who have sufficient [illegible] and technical knowledge, [illegible] the Military Commission buy really good colts; we must not forget that the greater portion of these breeders are [illegible] owing to the [illegible] of their [illegible]. Another reason for [illegible] prosperity in this district is the number of good mares, mostly bred by Government stallions.

Cremona, Ferrara, Reggio.

Good progress is also being made in the three districts of Cremona, Ferrara, and Reggio d'Emilia. Cremona is the most important, that of Reggio the least. In these districts, which include, besides the Marche, the whole valley of the Po, breeders care less for selling horses to the army than in other places. In a great part of Lombardy, and to a certain extent in Venetia and Upper Emilia, a good market is found for their horses, both in the country, and for exportation; the best of these are sold at good prices, and make a fine show in the largest Italian towns, where they are passed off as coming from abroad, and are doubtless paid for as such.

S. Maria di Capua.

The reports from Santa Maria di Capua are less satisfactory; this district includes the whole southern Mediterranean and Adriatic provinces, except Aquila, which belongs to the Pesaro district; the Abruzzi will henceforward belong to it. The Director writes: "Breeders of horses do not consider their profession [illegible]; they have an idea that the Government ought to buy all the good horses fit for the army, forgetting that though many are required, all cannot be disposed of. Hence, many neglect the breeding of horses for that of mules, which is more profitable. A mule, at twelve months old, is worth from £6 to £8, whereas a foal of the same age will rarely fetch more than £4. A three-year-old mule is worth more than £20, a horse of the same age can seldom be sold for that amount in the place where it is bred. The breeding of mules is also of great importance in Sicily, where a quiet and hardy beast of burden is a necessity."

Ferrara.

The Director at Ferrara writes: "Whilst in Lombardy, and especially in the province of Cremona, [illegible] of horses are bred for exportation, the [illegible] in the province of [illegible]; though a [illegible] of [illegible] are reared there. The [illegible] in [illegible] several months of the year, go to Cremona, [illegible] number of foals, which they [illegible] there. The result is very satisfactory, [illegible] in Cremona soon become weak and [illegible], and are [illegible]; whereas, with change of food and climate, they become more lively, and develop good [illegible], [illegible], and endurance."

Croatian Horses.

The Directors at Reggio mention the importation of small horses from Croatia and Dalmatia. Depots from Ferrara and Capua also allude to these. These small horses have certainly some advantages: their low price, some at £4, the better class at from £8 to £10, their endurance, speed, good temper, and ability for saddle or light draught. The freight from Dalmatia to Italy is under £1; they are brought over in boat loads, 40 at a time, and are much used by farmers and peasants, as also for drawing the public carriages in almost all the towns of the southern Adriatic provinces.

Exportation.

The Director at Pisa mentions the exportation of horses of all ages suitable for light draught or saddle, and which increases annually. They are purchased by French dealers, and the trade is of benefit to owners, who, for various reasons, have been unable to sell their horses to the Government.

Brabant and Ardennes Stallions.

In Lombardy, the best market, and the highest prices are found for foals got by stallions from Brabant and the Ardennes. At six months old they are very well grown; but it does not follow that this type of stallion is most suitable for the whole district.

Hackney Stallions.

For the district of Cremona, and the greater part of Ferrara, especially along the River Po, the best stallion is the Hackney—stout, strong limbed, and well-shaped.

Eastern Stallions in Sardinia.

The best type of stallion for Sardinia is undoubtedly the Eastern, either pure or cross-bred; they do well there, and are popular.

The same remark should apply to Sicily, but great difficulty is found in using them there; breeders compare them to mules, and prefer a larger animal, whose produce makes better prices. The Anglo-Norman cross, which is somewhat larger, is the most popular.

English Thoroughbreds.

In Pisa and Sicily the English thoroughbred is increasing in popularity; in the former district no less than 16 stallions of this breed served in 1895.

SERVICE OF STALLIONS BELONGING TO PRIVATE OWNERS AND APPROVED BY GOVERNMENT.

Regulations.

The regulations passed in 1888 for the approval of stallions belonging to private breeders remain in force; the following article was added in 1893:—"The provincial Commissions may refuse to pass a stallion on account of vice, or any malformation likely to cause deterioration in the breed."

Numbers.

In 1895 there were 715 stallions belonging to private owners approved for public service. Of these there were:—

Breeds.

Thoroughbred English,	37
Half bred,	112
Italian,	325
Eastern,	71

and the remainder of every other breed and country. From the 715 must be deducted 3 that died, and 67 that did not serve public mares, leaving 645, which served 17,945 mares, an average of 27·83 for each stallion. In 1894 there were 875 stallions shown for approval, of which 148 were rejected. In 1895 there were 875 shown, and 160 rejected.

The following table shows the names of the seven central Government depôts, of the provinces connected with them, the number of approved private stallions, and of mares served by them in 1895:—

TABLE showing numbers of approved private Stallions, and of Mares served by them in 1895.

Depots.	Provinces.	Stallions.	Mares.
Crema,	*Cuneo, *Turin, *Alessandria, Novara, Pavia, Milan, Como, Sondrio, Bergamo, Brescia, Cremona, *Porto Maurizio, *Genoa.	81	3,502
Reggio d'Emilia,	Piacenza, Parma, Reggio, Modena, Bologna, Ravenna, Forli, Pesaro, Ancona, Macerata, Ascoli, Mantua.	54	1,753
Ferrara,	*Massa, Verona, Vicenza, Belluno, Udine, Rovigo, Venice, Padua, Treviso, Ferrara.	103	2,094
Pisa,	Massa, Carrara, Lucca, Florence, Pisa, Arezzo, Siena, *Leghorn, Grosseto, Perugia, Rome, Aquila.	87	2,703
Santa Maria di Capua,	Teramo, Chieti, *Campobasso, Foggia, Bari, Lecce, Caserta, *Naples, Benevento, *Avellino, Salerno, *Potenza, Catanzaro, *Cosenza, *Reggio, Calabria.	138	2,310
Catania,	Palermo, Messina, Catania, Syracuse, Caltanisetta, Girgenti, Trapani.	109	2,173
Ozieri,	Cagliari, Sassari,	73	2,488
	Total,	645	17,945

N.B.—In Provinces marked * there was no public service.

Causes of Reduction in Numbers of Private Stallions.

The number of approved private stallions is considerably less than in previous years. This may be explained by the fact that since 1893 the provincial Commissions have been more strict in their requirements. There were many complaints against their decisions, but the Central Administration were convinced they had not exceeded their duties. Formerly many owners could get their horses passed, even if they were not considered likely to improve the breed; now, the quality of horses is far superior, though the number is smaller, and the Government is bound to provide stallions. There is no fear of horses being [illegible] by the concurrence of Government and private stallions, always provided that the latter are really good animals, and not only free from malformation but [illegible]. The Government are glad enough, if there are sufficient private stallions for the use of breeders, to send the few they have at their disposal elsewhere. There are so many places where stallions are in demand, that there is no fear of the supply exceeding the demand.

Reports from various Districts.

The reports from the different districts on this subject vary considerably. It is reported from Chieti that private breeding, which is regarded with greater [illegible] than the Government [illegible] the stallions is [illegible], and the [illegible] with the Government stud by [illegible].

Ferrara.

From Ferrara it is reported that among the private stallions there are many excellent thoroughbreds and good American trotters, but they do not compete severely with Government horses. At Reggio the private stallions are "fairly satisfactory."

Pisa.

From Pisa the report says:—"The co-operation of private breeders has been of immense use in improving the produce, especially since the new regulation has been in force; it is a great pity their number should be decreasing, at a time when we cannot increase the numbers of our stallions."

S. Maria di Capua.

From Santa Maria di Capua it is reported that private breeding is prejudicial in consequence of the inferior class of the stallions, and is besides injurious to the service of the good animals provided by Government.

Catania.

At Catania the opinion is that the Commissions approve of stallions not calculated to improve the breed.

Sardinia.

There is no report from Ozieri, in Sardinia, as to private breeding, so we may conclude there is no deterioration. From another part of the island we hear that owners appreciate the Government horses, and are anxious to use them; this would be satisfactory, if we did not also know that small owners frequently have recourse to private stallions on account of the low fee and easier payments.

General Remarks.

However much some of the over-zealous officials may deprecate private breeding, there is no doubt the conditions are far more satisfactory than formerly. There is only one fact to be deplored—the law is too often evaded, and it is impossible to exercise sufficient vigilance to prevent offences against the law increasing in number.

GENERAL RESULTS OF SERVICE.

The number of mares covered by Government and private stallions was 912 more than in 1894. In 1895, 19,848 mares were covered by Government stallions, and 17,943 by private stallions, total 37,791.

TABLE showing Results of Government Stallions' Service, 1894:—

Mares Covered.	Live Foals.	Slipped Foals.	Pregnant Mares — Sold.	Pregnant Mares — Died.	Total Pregnant.	Barren Mares.	Not reported.
19,786	8,468	1,703	486	407	11,164	6,030	2,548

From this we gather that the proportion of foals to mares covered was 43·37 per cent., and that 56·40 per cent. of the mares were in foal. But if we count those not reported, we may assume that 64·65 per cent. of the mares were in foal, and 43·77 per cent. of foals born.

As the number of mares covered in 1894 by Government and private stallions was 36,879, we may estimate the produce at about 16,400.

ARMY REMOUNTS.

Purchases for Army.

In 1895 the military authorities purchased 3,543 young horses, of which 2,980 were foals, for re-stocking the young horse depots, and for remounting the cavalry, artillery, and engineers.

Horses fit to join regiments were posted as follows:—

Cavalry,	40
Artillery,	457
Engineers,	66
Total,	563

Young Horse Depots.

The remaining 2,980 were distributed among the young horse depots, of which there were then six, but four of these have since been done away with. On December 31st, 1895, the depots contained 3,983 young horses; this was after the remounts had been posted to the regiments.

INDIRECT ENCOURAGEMENT OF HORSE-BREEDING, RACES AND HORSE SHOWS.

Encouragement of Horse-breeding.

In consequence of the state of public finances in 1894 no prizes were offered by the Ministry in 1895. The following were the sums granted in 1894:—

To	By Racing Clubs.	By Ministry.
	£	£
Flat Races,	12,673	1,600
Steeplechases,	2,318	1,600
Trotting Races,	1,600	560
Total,	16,590	3,960

The amount given to race meetings managed by recognised racing clubs in 1895:—

Subscriptions.	Flat Races.	Steeplechases.	Trotting Races.	Total.
	£	£	£	£
The King and Royal Family,	1,150	600	—	1,750
Jockey Club,	1,050	—	—	1,050
Steeplechase Club,	—	1,712	—	1,712
Racing Clubs,	11,897	2,440	1,580	15,917
Municipalities,	350	90	103	543
Entrance Fees, &c.,	5,350	524	3	5,877
Total,	19,997	5,366	1,685	27,166

IMPORTATION AND EXPORTATION OF HORSES FROM 1885 TO 189[illegible].

The figures are taken from "The Commerce of the Kingdom of Italy," published by the Ministry of Finance.

Year.	Importation.	Exportation.	Year.	Importation.	Exportation.
1885	[illegible]	[illegible]	[illegible]	[illegible]	1,387
1886	[illegible]	[illegible]	[illegible]	[illegible]	[illegible]
1887	[illegible]	[illegible]	[illegible]	[illegible]	1,107
1888	[illegible]	[illegible]	[illegible]	[illegible]	1,561
1889	[illegible]	[illegible]	[illegible]	[illegible]	3,481
1890	[illegible]	[illegible]			

[illegible]

ITALIAN STALLIONS IN OTHER COUNTRIES.

The following Table shows the number of Government stallions exported from Italy, and mares covered by them in various countries that have State-breeding studs.

Table showing number of Italian stallions in other countries.

Country.	Year.	[illegible]	[illegible]
France,	[illegible]	[illegible]	157,000
Prussia,	[illegible]	[illegible]	136,138
Austria,	[illegible]	[illegible]	94,265
"	[illegible]	[illegible]	94,265
Hungary,	[illegible]	[illegible]	94,265
Bavaria,	[illegible]	[illegible]	12,930
Saxony,	[illegible]	[illegible]	830

Rome, January [illegible], 189[illegible].

II.—REPORT ON HORSE-BREEDING IN ITALY.

[illegible]

Distribution to regiments.

The horses are generally kept in droves of about twenty-five, and are of every breed, size, and colour; [illegible] are sent to the [illegible], the [illegible] to the [illegible], while the heaviest are detailed to the artillery, engineers, and transport corps.

The officer commanding the [illegible] has the right to select any horse he may require for the school; then the officer commanding the regiment of [illegible] takes his choice, the remaining horses are distributed to the regiments by the officer commanding the depot.

Condition.—Disease.

The horses I saw (about 150), were probably looking at their worst, having only just recovered from the effects of a severe winter in the open, during which they have run absolutely wild, sometimes up to their knees in snow; this might, however, [illegible] the result being many [illegible] of [illegible]. The [illegible] (about [illegible] per cent) is caused chiefly by [illegible] and the [illegible] of [illegible], the [illegible] to [illegible] the [illegible] and expense of castrating their colts before they are sold to the Government.

Methods of [illegible].

The horses, though in poor condition, looked hard and healthy, and most of them had fairly good action; their very existence is an [illegible] of the [illegible] of the [illegible], for [illegible] in the open will not suffer from exposure to the most [illegible] weather. The chief defect in most of [illegible] is [illegible] of [illegible]. It is [illegible] that in a mountainous country like Italy, large horses are useless. There is no doubt the [illegible] have great powers of endurance when carrying heavy weights and doing long marches, as I observed during the manoeuvres in 1895, and [illegible] in [illegible]. Though [illegible] in their [illegible] when four and a half years old, they are [illegible]. They are [illegible] from the depot perfectly [illegible] having [illegible] a halter on them. When it is necessary to [illegible] them for [illegible] at [illegible] times, they are [illegible] into an [illegible] from which a narrow passage leads to a [illegible] made of [illegible], with a padded roof, just wide enough to hold a horse in single file, with a door [illegible] the end of the [illegible], [illegible] through [illegible] and [illegible] to prevent it moving in any direction, the [illegible] which by a pulley [illegible] the height [illegible] the wall of a shed, [illegible] a [illegible] and [illegible] a full description of the [illegible], the door in front of the [illegible] is then opened, the [illegible] and [illegible] the door is closed, and the next horse takes his place under the [illegible].

[illegible].

[illegible] that are found to be unsound, or in any way defective, are [illegible] at the depot for the use of the [illegible] on the farm work; [illegible] are not [illegible].

Other remount depôts in Italy.

I mentioned in my report of [illegible] that four of the six horse depôts in Italy had been suppressed, but the original intention [illegible] has [illegible] been carried out, and the other [illegible] still exist, though on a smaller scale than formerly; they are at Persano, near Naples; Grosseto, in Maremma; [illegible], near [illegible]; [illegible], near [illegible]; and [illegible] near Catania, in Sicily.

Stallion depot at Pisa.

The Government stallion depot at Pisa is situated on the [illegible] at the end of one of [illegible] thoroughfares of the town. The building for 120 horses originally belonging to Leopold, Grand Duke of Tuscany, stands in a large riding ground, about [illegible] acres in extent, laid down in turf and gravel roads, where the horses are exercised for an hour and [illegible] daily.

"[illegible]" and "Washington."—[illegible] stallions.

At the time of my visit, March, 1897, there were two thoroughbred English stallions, "[illegible]" and "Washington," which have been bought by the Government to replace "[illegible]," who was for years [illegible] by [illegible], to the great regret of all good judges of horses in Italy. Many of the other stallions had been sent to their stations in the district, but some [illegible] remained, all of which will be sent in [illegible] [illegible] before the end of the month; [illegible] every variety of breed was represented, including English, [illegible], English and [illegible], Italian and Arab, [illegible]; Hackney and Italian, American [illegible], &c., but I cannot say that, in my opinion, there was a really good-looking horse amongst them, excepting the two English thoroughbreds.

Defects in system of breeding.

The great fault of [illegible] appears to be the tendency to [illegible]; the [illegible] are [illegible], [illegible], but they have bad shoulders, [illegible] quarters, and are deficient in substance, all of which defects are [illegible] in the [illegible], except in the [illegible], and of these there were [illegible] in the [illegible]. The [illegible] of the Arab, [illegible] of [illegible], is already [illegible] by the [illegible] race, and it would [illegible] unnecessary to reproduce it in [illegible]. Probably the [illegible] type of animal to breed from in the first instance would be "Washington," and by crossing his descendants with a [illegible] [illegible] some [illegible] of animal [illegible] the standard. Unfortunately the [illegible] for "Washington," [illegible] is [illegible] for the Italian [illegible], whose [illegible] will not permit him to spend more than [illegible] or at the most [illegible] lire [illegible]. The thoroughbreds are only used by [illegible]; they have [illegible] the [illegible], and it is doubtful whether they will [illegible] [illegible] altogether. "[illegible]" [illegible].

[illegible].

"[illegible]," the English thoroughbred, is [illegible] at Pisa; he is now [illegible] years of age, and though he [illegible] has [illegible], he is [illegible] [illegible].

[illegible] of improvement in Breeding.

[illegible] be [illegible] [illegible] will be made in horse-breeding in Italy until the Government [illegible] [illegible] some really good, [illegible] [illegible], and [illegible] [illegible] to [illegible] in [illegible] than [illegible].

Rural Station at Vecchiano.

I drove out to Vecchiano, the nearest rural station, about five miles from Pisa, where two stallions are kept during the season; they are cross-breds, one by an English Hackney, out of an Italian mare, the other by an American trotter; they are probably useful for producing small harness horses. The arrangements are very primitive; the stallions are kept in two fairly good loose boxes, which open on to a yard some thirty feet square; they are under the care of a horse-keeper, who keeps the register, and reports to the Director at Pisa, who makes occasional inspections of all the stations in the district.

CHARLES NEEDHAM, Colonel,
Military Attaché.

British Embassy, Rome,
March 23, 1897.

REPORT ON HORSE-BREEDING IN PRUSSIA.

Introductory.

In a memorandum published by the Royal Ministry of Agriculture in 1896, the position held by the Government in regard to horse-breeding is described as follows:—

"Horse-breeding in Prussia is mainly dependent upon the stud established by the Government, which provides stallions for stock supplied by private breeders.

"According to the cattle census in 1892, the total number of foals born in 1892 was 194,184, to produce which about 400,000 mares must have been covered. The stallions belonging to the Government rural studs (Landgestüte) covered in 1893, 151,687, and in 1895, 128,348 mares. The task of the stud administration has become from year to year more extensive and more difficult; as it is no longer merely a question of providing stallions suitable for the breeding of horses for military purposes, but also of considering other requirements, notably the demand for heavy draught horses, apart from the fact that the military authorities themselves now require greater variety for different arms of the service—from the light cavalry to the heavy artillery horse.

"In addition to this the depressed condition of agriculture has led many land owners to devote greater attention to horse-breeding, in order to cover the losses caused by the fall of prices in other branches of production. To meet this increased interest in horse-breeding, the Government Stud Department has found it necessary to increase the number and [illegible] of their studs, and the number of stallions kept for service in the country."

Expenditure included in Estimates of Ministry of Agriculture.

The sums expended by the State in Prussia for the encouragement of horse-breeding fall under two different heads, viz.:—(1) those included in the General Estimates of the Ministry of Agriculture for prizes and [illegible], &c.; and (2) the separate estimates for the Government Stud Department.

The Estimates of the Ministry of Agriculture for 1895–96, contain the following items in this respect under ordinary expenditure:—

		£
1.	Fund for awarding prizes at horse shows,	10,000
2.	Fund for grants for the improvement of the breed of stallions, and mares which are the property of Associations or of private persons; also for bounties on the importation of thoroughbred stud horses and kindred objects,	9,000
3.	For foal shows,	171
	Total,	19,171

Note.—Any surplus remaining over from the former fund is added to the second; and can be carried forward, together with any surplus in the latter, for use in the following year.

The amount voted in the Budget for 1896–97 was identical.

Under the heading of "Non-recurrent and Extraordinary Expenditure," the voted Estimates for 1895–96 and 1896–97, each contain an item of £3,000 as an "extraordinary supplement to the fund for prizes for the improvement of the breed of stallions, &c." (No. 2 above). This brings the total of money voted for such purposes in each of those two years up to £22,171, and in the Estimates for 1897–98, which have recently been laid before the Landtag, the same amount is demanded.

The reasons which moved the Ministry of Agriculture to ask for the extraordinary supplement are stated in the Estimates for 1895–96, as follows:—

"The present depressed condition of agriculture renders it necessary to give all possible encouragement to efforts directed towards the improvement of (among other things) horse and cattle breeding.

"The Horse-breeding Fund is almost entirely handed over to the Agricultural Associations for prizes at horse shows, and for assisting the importation of good breeding material for general purposes. A very small portion of it is assigned to the importation of thoroughbred horses.

"In all the branches for which this extraordinary vote is asked, the necessity of increased expenditure has made itself felt.

"As regards horse-breeding, the object must be to make the country as independent as possible of importation from abroad in regard to horses for ordinary use, and at the same time to encourage in certain provinces the breeding of horses suited to military purposes.

"As it is impossible to foresee whether the conditions which make this increased expenditure necessary will be permanent ones, the amount required is claimed under Extraordinary Expenditure."

Mode of application of money granted through the Ministry of Agriculture for the encouragement of horse-breeding.

The prizes granted by the Ministry of Agriculture take the form of (1) money prizes, (2) [illegible] medals, and (3) [illegible]. It is customary to give money prizes in the large associations and [illegible] for the smaller breeders. In the provinces of [illegible] all the money available is distributed in the form of [illegible]. In some parts of the country a large part of the money granted by the State for the encouragement of horse-breeding is applied to assisting private breeders to purchase good brood mares and foals. As a consequence of these grants [illegible] the establishment of districts [illegible] breeding to [illegible], and has led to the establishment of stud-books and to the formation of associations of horse-breeders. Grants have also in many districts been effected with a view to breeding towards a special regional type, and good results have been attained in this way in the breeding of heavy cart horses in the Rhine Province.

Grants are also made out of Government funds to assist breeders to purchase [illegible] and [illegible], and to maintain public breeding establishments, which enable the breeders to get their young horses properly broken for riding or driving without the intervention of a dealer.

The Government grants distributed through the local agricultural associations for all the above-mentioned purposes amounted on each foal born to an average of 1s. 10d. in 1895–96 and [illegible] in 1896–97.

Government Stud Farms.

The Government Stud Department administers four principal stud farms and seventeen provincial establishments or rural studs (Landgestüte), where stallions only are kept for service in the district.

At the time when the Estimates for 1893–94 were drawn up the principal Stud farms possessed :—

—	Stallions.	Brood Mares.	Colts and Fillies.
Trakehnen,	15	[illegible]	1,048
Graditz,	10	[illegible]	434
Beberbeck,	6	[illegible]	259
Neustadt a/Dosse,	3	30	–
	34	[illegible]	1,[illegible]

In the Estimates for 1897–98 the number of brood mares at Neustadt a/D. is given as 30, and there are 32 colts and fillies. The number of the latter at Beberbeck had fallen to 205, and their total number to 1,664. The remaining figures are the same.

The seventeen rural studs had a total of 2,603 stallions, the number varying from 235 in the Hanover [illegible] to 86 in the Westphalian stud, and averaging 153 for each.

The Estimates for 1897–98 give the total number of stallions as 2,670.

In 1867 the principal stud farms then existing owned the following areas of land :—

TRAKEHNEN (founded in 1732) :—

Arable,	6,577	acres.
Meadows,	2,733	"
Pasture,	230	"
Total,	9,540	"

GRADITZ :—

Arable,	1,238	acres.
Meadows,	1,693	"
Pasture,	15	"
Total,	2,946	"

BEBERBECK :—

Arable,	425	acres.
Meadows and Pasture,	1,621	"
Forest-land,	128	"
Total,	2,174	"

The acreage occupied by the stud farms has not changed materially since 1867. To the newly re-established stud farm at Neustadt-on-the-Dosse 741 acres were assigned from domain and forest lands which originally belonged to it. (It was founded in 1788, suppressed in 1876, and re-established in 1886.)

The following Tables show the general results of the working of the three principal Government Stud Farms during the years 1893–95 :—

TRAKEHNEN.

Year.	Stallions.	Brood Mares.	Living Foals Born: Colts.	Living Foals Born: Fillies.	Kept as Stallions for Rural Studs.	Kept as Brood Mares.	Supplied to Royal Stables.	Horses Sold: Old.	Horses Sold: Young.
1893,	15	331	130	106	61	53	26	25	96
1894,	17	334	151	129	47	44	22	16	78
1895,	17	350	104	110	62	37	28	43	83

GRADITZ.

Year.	Stallions.	Brood Mares.	Living Foals Born: Colts.	Living Foals Born: Fillies.	Kept as Stallions for Rural Studs.	Kept as Brood Mares.	Supplied to Royal Stables.	Horses Sold: Old.	Horses Sold: Young.
1893,	10	165	66	60	21	17	1	20	48
1894,	10	178	64	68	20	14	1	14	85
1895,	10	165	42	64	13	10	–	6	64

BEBERBECK.

Year.	Stallions.	Brood Mares.	Living Foals Born: Colts.	Living Foals Born: Fillies.	Kept as Stallions for Rural Studs.	Kept as Brood Mares.	Supplied to Royal Stables.	Horses Sold: Old.	Horses Sold: Young.
1893,	5	97	44	33	17	12	3	13	33
1894,	6	97	33	38	9	11	5	7	27
1895,	6	96	31	31	6	11	1	10	52

The Landgestüte or Rural Studs.

The rural studs distribute their stallions by twos and threes to stations in different parts of their districts, according to the demand for their services.

The statistics for 1895 show that 17 rural studs had 3,551 stallions in use, divided among 839 stations.

The following is an abstract of the table of foaling results of the rural studs for 1894–5, published in the Agricultural Year-books :—

Number of Stallions employed in 1894,	3,516	
Number of Mares covered by them,	134,905	
Of which	41,345	remained barren.
	93,560,	or 70 per cent., became pregnant.
Living Foals born in 1895,	78,146	
Of which	8,679	were branded with the Stud mark.

Each stallion produced on an average 22 living foals.

At the end of 1895 the total number of stallions employed by the rural studs amounted to 2,567, divided into three classes, with sub-divisions of the 3rd class:—

—	Number of Stallions.
Class I.—Light Riding Horses,	419
Class II.—Heavy Riding or Light Draught Horses,	1,165
Class III.—Heavy Draught Horses,	681
Percherons,	9
Belgian and Ardennes Horses,	94
Clydesdales,	14
Shire Horses,	55
Do., Belgian cross,	1
French Farm Horses,	7
Normandy do.,	8
German Farm Horse Type,	161
	2,567

In the first class were included 100 thoroughbred stallions, of which 94 were pure English, 5 Anglo-Arabian, and 1 pure Arabian blood.

Of the above stallions 1,969 had been purchased, the remainder — 598 — bred in the Government Studs.

The following Table shows the progress made in the work of the rural studs within the last twelve years:—

—	Prussia.			Prussia.		
	[illegible]	[illegible]	[illegible]	[illegible]	[illegible]	[illegible]
Total number of Stallions,	2,151	2,236	2,396	2,463	2,502	2,567
Number of Stations,	738	799	820	874	690	695
Total Number of Mares Covered,	111,151	120,145	116,839	134,076	134,834	145,133
	348,133			414,043		

Military Remounts.

The principal object of the Government Stud Department is to provide remounts for the Army. With this object in view, the Provinces of East and West Prussia, Posen, Hanover, and Brandenburg, which offer the most favourable conditions for the purpose, have been selected as the so-called "Remount Provinces," and the stallions stationed in these are exclusively strong thoroughbred. The effect of this has been to increase the speed and endurance of the breed. In these Provinces all forms of State aid for the encouragement of horse-breeding, prizes at horse shows, &c., are given only for the type of horse required for military purposes.

The annual number of horses purchased by the Prussian Remount Commission increased from 7,183 in 1885 to 8,371 in 1890, and 8,758 in 1895. The Bavarian and Saxon cavalry is also almost exclusively remounted from East Prussia.

Of the remounts in 1895, about 6,000 were intended for the cavalry, and of these 588 were from thoroughbred sires. Under existing arrangements this proportion will increase, and is expected shortly to reach 10 per cent.

Estimates of Government Stud Department.

The separate Estimates of the Government Stud Department for 1896-97 show a total revenue of £123,699, and a total expenditure of £362,999, of which only £16,070 are under the heading of "non-current and extraordinary expenditure."

The revenue is divided as follows:—

	£
On the four principal stud farms—	
Horses and Cattle sold,	14,437
Covering Fees and Foal Money,	1,670
Farming Receipts,	14,496
Value of the Emoluments of Officials, &c.,	2,350
Other sources of Revenue, including Racing Prizes won by the Graditz Stud,	3,110
Total of Principal Studs,	36,995
On the Royal Stud Farms (Landgestüte)—	£
Covering Fees and Foal Money,	83,104
Farming Receipts,	634
Value of Emoluments to Officials, &c.,	192
Other sources of Revenue,	1,328
Total of Royal Studs,	85,154
Total of Receipts from Stud Farms,	121,149
In the Central Administration—	£
Sale of Superannuated Stallions and other items,	2,550
Total Revenue,	123,699

The expenditure may shortly be divided as follows:—

	£
Salaries and Allowances of Officials,	13,976
Wages and Clothing at the principal Stud Farms,	12,288
Do. at the rural Stud Farms,	83,918
Material Expenditure at the principal Stud Farms (including Transport, Office Expenses, Forage, Farming Expenses, Maintenance of Buildings, Rents, Rates, and Taxes, &c.),	47,300
The same for the rural Studs,	78,888
	£236,[illegible]
Expenses of the Central Administration and various Expenditure (including an item of £50,000 for the purchase of horses and for large transporting),	60,[illegible]
Total of Permanent Expenditure,	£246,[illegible]
Extraordinary Expenditure (for Drainage and Purchase of Land, &c., with a Special Supplement to the Fund for purchase of Horses),	16,073
Total Expenditure,	**£262,[illegible]**

A note to the item of £50,000 [illegible] should be added £3,[illegible] in the extraordinary expenditure [illegible] the purchase of horses, &c., explains that from this fund horse-breeding associations can obtain advances bearing no interest, which must be repaid within six years. Such repayments, except they are partly or wholly remitted for special reasons, are added to the fund, and any surplus can be carried forward from one year to the next.

Note.—At the end of 1895, there were [illegible] horse-breeding associations in Prussia, which had taken advantage of such loans, the total sum lent by the Government amounting to £[illegible].

The annual amount of the loans granted was as follows:—

1890–91,	**£1,[illegible]**
1891–92,	**800**
1892–93,	**1,180**
1893–94,	**[illegible],770**
1894–95,	**1,080**
1895–96,	**[illegible],440**

The deficit to be made good from public funds is, therefore, for the principal and rural stud farms:—

Expenditure,	**£186,[illegible]**
Less,	**131,[illegible]**
	£[illegible]

Or the vote required for the whole Government Stud Department, including the Central Administration and the extraordinary Estimates:—

Expenditure,	£262,[illegible]
Less,	[illegible]
	£[illegible]

The Estimates of the Government Stud Department for 1897–98 show an increase on these figures both in receipts and expenditure. Briefly stated they are:—

Total Receipts,	£[illegible]
Total ordinary Expenditure of Government Studs,	[illegible]
Central Administration,	[illegible]
Extraordinary Expenditure,	[illegible]
Total Expenditure,	£[illegible]
Less Receipts,	[illegible]
To be supplied from Public Funds,	£[illegible]

Total Expenditure for Encouragement of Horse-breeding.

Taking both heads of expenditure together, the total amount voted by the Prussian Parliament for the encouragement of horse-breeding was:—

—	18[illegible]	18[illegible]
	£	£
In Estimates of Ministry of Agriculture,	[illegible]	23,171
Government Stud Department,	[illegible]	160,103
Total Expenditure,	[illegible]	**183,[illegible]**

Financial position of Government studs.

With few exceptions all the stud farms work at a loss—that at Trakehnen being estimated at £[illegible] for 1896–97. The exceptions are the two Lithuanian rural studs at Insterburg and Gudwallen, the former credited with a profit of £[illegible] and £[illegible], the latter with one of £[illegible] and £[illegible], in the Estimates of 1896–97 and 1897–98, respectively.

Licensing ordinances for stallions.

In all the provinces of Prussia so-called "Körordnungen" are now in force—i.e., Ordinances for the establishment of licensing commissions for stallions, bulls and boars. These commissions are appointed locally, but their decisions are [illegible] from the Ministry of Agriculture as their composition and [illegible].

During the year 1895–96 the number of stallions presented amounted to [illegible], of which [illegible] were licensed. Of the latter [illegible] were light riding or draught horses (so-called warm-blooded), and [illegible] heavy and cart horses, [illegible] were [illegible].

The object of these ordinances is to prevent poor stallions being produced to good mares [illegible]. A knowledge of these [illegible] of [illegible] economy in covering fees. They all take the form of simple Police Ordinances, in order that they may be more easily altered to suit the varying requirements of horse and cattle breeding in the different districts.

The licensing Police Ordinance for the Province of Brandenburg is one of the latest issued, and is given as an example.

Police Ordinance respecting the Licensing of Private Stallions in the Province of Brandenburg.

On the basis of the powers conferred by § 137 of the Law respecting the General Administration of the Kingdom of the 30th of July, 1883, and by §§ 6, 12 and 15 of the Law respecting the Police Administration of the 11th of March, 1850, and repealing all previous regulations relative to licensing private stallions, it is decreed for the extent of the Province of Brandenburg, with the consent of the Provincial Council, as follows:—

§ 1.—Private stallions may only be employed to cover mares belonging to other persons, if the competent Licensing Board (Schaukommission) has certified their fitness by the issue of a license (Deckerlaubnisschein).

§ 2. Each Administrative District (Kreis) shall form a licensing district (Körbezirk), the towns of Potsdam and Spandau being included in the district of East Havelland, Brandenburg in that of West Havelland, Charlottenburg in the district of Teltow, Frankfurt a. Oder in the district of Lebus, and the towns of Guben and Kottbus in the districts of the same name. If in future a town is separated from the administrative district in which it is situated, the boundaries of the licensing district shall not thereby be altered.

For each licensing district a licensing board (Schaukommission) shall be established, and one or more licensing stations (Schaustationen) shall be appointed and publicly made known.

§ 3. The licensing board shall consist of:—

1. The Royal District Commissioner (Landrath) or a deputy elected for six years by the District Assembly (Kreistag) as Chairman;

2. The Director of the Royal Stud concerned;

3. A member to be elected by the Principal Board of Management of the Provincial Agricultural Association for the Mark Brandenburg and Nieder Lausitz, who may belong to several licensing boards;

4. A member to be elected for six years by the District Assembly.

5. A Veterinary Surgeon to be selected, if possible, from among the veterinary officials of the district, and appointed by the President of the Government (Head of an administrative division or "Bezirk") concerned.

This Veterinary Surgeon shall have a consultative voice only.

For each member of the Board pair of sub-deputies shall be elected or appointed in the same manner.

§ 4. The licensing board shall meet in the months of October, November, and December of each year. The place, day and hour of each meeting shall be notified by the District Commissioner, after consulting the members named in § 3, under 2 and 3, at least 14 days before the date in the District Gazette [illegible] regards towns, in any papers which may be used for the publication of official notices.

§ 5. The owner of a stallion who wishes to use it for covering mares belonging to other persons, must notify the fact to the District Commissioner (Landrath) concerned before the end of September of each year, presenting at the same time a schedule according to the annexed model A, duly filled in, and stating the place where the stallion is permanently stabled.

§ 6. Only such stallions may be licensed as have completed their third year, and are without hereditary faults.

§ 7. The licensing board, the decisions of which are only valid when all the members (§ 3) are present, decides by majority of votes.

In case an equal number of votes are given for and against granting a license, it shall be refused.

If a member of the licensing board be unable to attend the meetings at the appointed time, he must notify the fact, as soon as he can know such inability, to his deputy and to the Landrath. Such notification shall be considered as a summons to the deputy to appear at the meeting.

The decisions of the licensing board are final and are recorded. Every voting member of the Board may obtain a copy of the records from the Landrath on application.

Stallions which have been licensed in one year may be presented again in the following year.

§ 8. If a stallion is found fit for service by the licensing board, the owner shall receive a license (Deckerlaubnisschein), signed by the Chairman of the Board in the form of the annexed model B. The amount of covering fee which is noted on the license, is fixed by the owner, but cannot be altered (raised or lowered) during the covering season, for which the license is issued.

The Royal District Commissioner (Landrath) shall publish the descriptions of the licensed stallions, together with the place where they stand and the amount of the covering fees.

§ 9. The license (§§ 1 and 8) is valid for the covering season following the date of its issue; and each licensed stallion must again be presented and examined at each succeeding annual meeting of the Board, if it is again to be used for covering mares belonging to other persons.

§ 10. If the owner of a stallion wishes the licensing board to meet before the dates fixed in § 4, he must communicate with the Landrath and refund any expenses which may arise.

§ 11. Each licensed stallion must remain during the covering season, at the place indicated by the owner at the meeting of the board. If the stallion is meanwhile sold, and the place where it stands consequently altered, the fact must be notified to the Landrath, or, if it is thereby transferred to another district (Kreis) of the province of Brandenburg, to both the District Commissioners concerned. If a licensed stallion belongs to several owners it may be taken to their various places of residence for the purpose of covering their own mares.

A non-licensed stallion which is the common property of several owners can only be used by one of the same, whose name must be notified in writing to the chairman of the licensing board, for covering his own mares.

§ 12. Every owner of licensed stallions must keep a covering register according to the annexed model C, in which the mares covered by each stallion are to be entered. This register shall be closed at the end of the covering season—at latest on the 31st of July—in each year, and must be forwarded to the Landrath with the expired license.

§ 13. The following fees are collected for stallions presented to the licensing board to meet the expenses of the same:—

1. For each stallion licensed—
   - (a.) The first time, 10 Marks;
   - (b.) On each further occasion, 5 Marks.
2. For each stallion not licensed, 3 Marks.

§ 14. Infractions of §§ 1, 5, 11, and 12 of this Police Ordinance are punishable by fines up to 60 Marks (£3). The same penalty applies to the owners of mares who allow them to be covered by non-licensed stallions belonging to other persons.

§ 15. This ordinance comes into force on the 1st of October, 1891. The requisite elections for the licensing boards and other preparations (§§ 2, 3, 4, and 5) are to be carried out in good time.

Potsdam,

April 14, 1891.

The Ober President.

(Signed). Von Achenbach.

MODEL A.

DESCRIPTION OF STALLION TO BE USED AS SIRE.

Name and Residence of Owner—

No.	Name of Stallion.	Pedigree.	Size.		Colour and Marks.	Age. Years.	Covering Fee. Marks.	Observations of the Licensing Board.
			H.	Cm.				

MODEL B.

LICENCE.

The Stallion (name) , years old, out of dam by sire, metres centimetres high, colour, with marks, is licensed to cover mares belonging to persons other than its owner during the year . The covering fee amounts to marks.

Date .

The Licensing Board of the District of .

Signature of the Chairman.

MODEL C.

REGISTER OF THE PRIVATE COVERING STATION BELONGING TO , AT

No.	Name and Residence of Owner of Mare.	Mares.				Covered by (Name of) Stallion.	Date.	Observations.
		Size.		Colour and Marks.	Age. Years.			
		H.	Cm.					

APPENDIX B.

RESOLUTION passed by the COUNTY KERRY GRAND JURY at the Spring Assizes, 1897.

Proposed by Arthur Blennerhassett; seconded by Sir J. H. Dobbyn.

Resolved—"That we hope that the Congested Districts Board will not this year, or for the future, send any Hackney sires to County Kerry, as we do not consider them suitable. The largest dealers and most experienced horse breeders both in England and Ireland condemn them in every way.

"And that in place of the Hackneys, thoroughbred or Arab sires be sent."

(Signed), E. A. De Moleyns, Foreman.

PETITION PRESENTED to the COMMISSION by a DEPUTATION at DINGLE on 28th May, 1897.

Resolved—"That we, the Ratepayers of the Dingle Union, [illegible] the Commission [illegible] Horse-breeding [illegible] the Representative, Mr. Thomas R. [illegible], [illegible] the absolute necessity of [illegible] of Stallion for this District which is purely agricultural."

2nd: "From our experience of Hackney breeding of horses in this part of the country, the most suitable class of stallion would be a [illegible] thoroughbred and a [illegible] if possible."

3rd: "That we consider the progeny of the Hackney stallion unfit to realise a profitable price."

David Watson (Chairman).
John [illegible].
Richard Talbot.
Patrick M'Donnell.
[illegible].
Michael M'Donnell.
John [illegible].
Michael F. [illegible].
Timothy O'[illegible] (Secretary).

RESOLUTION of AGRICULTURAL and other SOCIETIES.

Clonmel, Co. Tipperary.
6th August, 1896.

We, the Members of the Committee of the Clonmel Horse Show Society [illegible] to [illegible] against the [illegible] of the breed of Hackney horses into Ireland by the aid of State funds as being detrimental to the best interests of farmers and the good of the country at large, tending to deteriorate that breed of horses for which Ireland has hitherto been just celebrated.

Passed unanimously.

(Signed), [illegible],
Chairman of the Committee.

Mullingar, 11th August, 1896.

We, the Members of the "Mullingar Horse Show Committee," desire to enter our strongest protest against the introduction of State Funds in Hackney Stallions to Ireland, the introduction of which breed we consider calculated to injure the Horse-breeding industry of Ireland.

Passed unanimously.

(Signed), [illegible],
Chairman and President.

Navan, 17th August, 1896.

We, the Members of the Committee of the Navan Horse Show, protest in the strongest manner against the introduction of the breed of Hackney horses into Ireland, by the aid of State Funds, as being detrimental to the best interests of farmers and the good of the country at large, tending to deteriorate the breed of horses for which Ireland has hitherto been justly celebrated.

Passed unanimously.

Signed on behalf of "Meath Horse Show Committee."

R. H. Fowler,
J. R. G. Pollock,
Hon. Secs., Meath Horse Show.

Resolution passed at a Meeting of the County Cork Agricultural Society.

Cork, 16th September, 1896.

R. H. [illegible], President, in the Chair.

We, the Members of the Committee of the "Cork Agricultural Society," protest in the strongest manner against the introduction of the breed of Hackney horses into Ireland, by the aid of State funds, as being detrimental to the best interests of farmers and the good of the country at large, tending to deteriorate that breed of horses for which Ireland has hitherto been justly celebrated.

Passed unanimously.

Signed on behalf Co. Cork Agricultural Society,
[illegible], Secretary.

Limerick Horse Show and Agricultural Society.

Limerick, 3rd October, 1896.

Resolved,—That we, the Members of the Committee of the Limerick Horse Show and Agricultural Society, protest most strongly against the State-aided introduction of Hackney stallions into any portion of this country, as we believe the blood will seriously deteriorate the class of horses now bred in this country, and in this opinion we are supported by the best judges in England, where the experiment has been tried and proved a failure, and we suggest the substitution of thoroughbred horses with bone and substance, or of sires as nearly thoroughbred as possible, which have proved good sole getters.

Passed unanimously.

(Signed), Jas. P. Gaffney,
High Sheriff, Chairman.

"Ballinasloe District Agricultural Society."

Ballinasloe, 12th October, 1896.

Resolved,—That we, the Members of the Committee of the Ballinasloe Horse and Agricultural Society, wish to place upon record our objection to the introduction of Hackney blood in any form into Ireland.

We believe that it will be most injurious in results to the maintenance of the character of high class horses which have been produced in this country, whether as hunters, carriage horses, army remounts, or polo ponies.

(Signed), R. J. Gill, Secretary.

APPENDIX C.

LETTER FROM COLONEL St. QUINTIN.

Island Bridge Barracks, Dublin,
June 6th, 1897.

Sir, [illegible] Commission on Horse breeding in Ireland, [illegible] Government [illegible] at your request [illegible] Remount Department, [illegible] Government [illegible] This is [illegible] Between the middle of February and the end of March [illegible] horses [illegible]

This could not have been done by personal purchase from the breeders [illegible] of well-known reliable dealers [illegible] demand [illegible] and guarantee our supply, and [illegible] free trade in the horses of this country [illegible] more than [illegible] With reference to our Army demand, [illegible] the large continental and private demand in the horse market, [illegible] [illegible]

[illegible]

I have the honour to be,

My Lord,

Your obedient servant,

T. A. St. Quentin,

Colonel,

A. Y. & R. Ireland.

To the Earl of Dunraven, K.P.,
&c., &c., &c.

APPENDIX D.

CONGESTED DISTRICTS BOARD FOR IRELAND.

STATEMENT showing the Expenditure in connection with the Scheme for Improvement of Horses and Asses up to 31st March, [illegible].

Expenditure to 31st March, [illegible]					Amount.	Total.
Capital Expenditure:—					£ s. d.	£ s. d.
To Purchase of [illegible] Stallions,					[illegible]	
Do. [illegible] Mares,					[illegible]	
Do. [illegible] Asses (including [illegible] Ass Stallions),					[illegible]	
Do. 1 Mule,					[illegible]	
Do. 1 Stallion Pony (purchased at Arran),					[illegible]	
Do. 1 Farm Horse for Stud Farm,					[illegible]	
Do. [illegible] Foals (Half-breeds),					[illegible]	
Hire of Stallions,					[illegible]	
Clothing and Equipment of Stallions,					[illegible]	
Cost of Stud Farm Buildings,					[illegible]	
" " " Furniture,					[illegible]	
" " " Implements, etc.,					[illegible]	
" " " Water Supply,					[illegible]	
" " " Fencing,					[illegible]	
Cost of Fittings on Stables in Country,					[illegible]	
Total Capital Expenditure,						[illegible]
	Year [illegible]	Year [illegible]	Year [illegible]	Year [illegible]		
Annual Maintenance:—	£ s. d.	£ s. d.	£ s. d.	£ s. d.		
Transport Expenses (to and from Country Stations),	[illegible]	[illegible]	[illegible]	[illegible]	[illegible]	
Keep in Country and Forage while at Central Stud Farm,	[illegible]	[illegible]	[illegible]	[illegible]	[illegible]	
Shoeing, Veterinary Fees, &c.,	[illegible]	[illegible]	[illegible]	[illegible]	[illegible]	
Managers and Grooms,	[illegible]	[illegible]	[illegible]	[illegible]	[illegible]	
[illegible] to R.I.C.,	[illegible]	[illegible]	[illegible]	[illegible]	[illegible]	
Stud Farm—Repairs, Painting,	—	—	—	[illegible]	[illegible]	
" Rent and Taxes,	—	[illegible]	[illegible]	[illegible]	[illegible]	
" Labour on Farm,	[illegible]	[illegible]	[illegible]	[illegible]	[illegible]	
Coal, Oil, &c.,	[illegible]	[illegible]	[illegible]	[illegible]	[illegible]	
Inspections of Mares, Advertising for Tenders, Insurance of Horses, &c., &c.,	[illegible]	[illegible]	[illegible]	[illegible]	[illegible]	[illegible]
Total Maintenance Expenditure,	[illegible]	[illegible]	[illegible]	[illegible]	[illegible]	
Grand Total Expenditure,						[illegible]

Wm. L. Micks.

SCHEDULE SHOWING NUMBER, BREED, NAMES, PEDIGREES, AND DISTRIBUTION OF STALLIONS

No.	Breed.	Name.	Pedigree.	Distribution. [illegible]	[illegible]	[illegible]	[illegible]	[illegible]	Date of Purchase.	Observations.
1	Hackney.	[illegible]	[illegible]	[illegible]	[illegible]	[illegible]	[illegible]	—	[illegible]	[illegible]
2	Do.	[illegible]	[illegible]	[illegible]	[illegible]	[illegible]	—	—	[illegible]	[illegible]
3	Do.	[illegible]	[illegible]	[illegible]	[illegible]	[illegible]	[illegible]	—	[illegible]	[illegible]
4	Do.	[illegible]	[illegible]	[illegible]	[illegible]	[illegible]	—	—	[illegible]	[illegible]
5	Do.	[illegible]	[illegible]	[illegible]	[illegible]	[illegible]	[illegible]	[illegible]	[illegible]	
6	Do.	[illegible]	[illegible]	[illegible]	[illegible]	[illegible]	[illegible]	[illegible]	[illegible]	
7	Do.	[illegible]	[illegible]	[illegible]	[illegible]	[illegible]	[illegible]	[illegible]	[illegible]	
8	Do.	[illegible]	[illegible]	[illegible]	[illegible]	[illegible]	—	—	[illegible]	[illegible]
9	Do.	[illegible]	[illegible]	[illegible]	[illegible]	—	—	—	[illegible]	[illegible]
10	Do.	[illegible]	[illegible]	[illegible]	[illegible]	[illegible]	[illegible]	—	[illegible]	[illegible]
11	Do.	[illegible]	[illegible]	[illegible]	[illegible]	[illegible]	—	—	[illegible]	[illegible]
12	Do.	[illegible]	[illegible]	[illegible]	[illegible]	[illegible]	[illegible]	[illegible]	[illegible]	
13	Do.	[illegible]	[illegible]	—	[illegible]	[illegible]	[illegible]	—	[illegible]	[illegible]
14	Do.	[illegible]	[illegible]	—	[illegible]	[illegible]	[illegible]	[illegible]	[illegible]	
15	Do.	[illegible]	[illegible]	—	[illegible]	[illegible]	[illegible]	[illegible]	[illegible]	
16	Do.	[illegible]	[illegible]	—	[illegible]	[illegible]		—	[illegible]	[illegible]
17	Do.	[illegible]	[illegible]	—	—	[illegible]	[illegible]	[illegible]	[illegible]	
18	Do.	[illegible]	[illegible]	—	—	—	[illegible]	[illegible]	[illegible]	
19	Do.	[illegible]	[illegible]	—	—	—	[illegible]	[illegible]	—	[illegible]
20	Do.	[illegible]	[illegible]	—	—	[illegible]	—	—	[illegible]	[illegible]
21	Do.	[illegible]	[illegible]	—	—	—	[illegible]	[illegible]	[illegible]	
22	Do.	[illegible]	[illegible]	—	—	—	[illegible]	[illegible]	[illegible]	
23	Do.	[illegible]	[illegible]	—	—	[illegible]	[illegible]	[illegible]	[illegible]	
24	Do.	[illegible]	[illegible]	—	—	—	[illegible]	—	[illegible]	[illegible]
25	Do.	[illegible]	[illegible]	—	—	—	[illegible]	[illegible]	[illegible]	

SCHEDULE SHOWING NUMBER, BREED, NAMES, PEDIGREES, AND DISTRIBUTION OF STALLIONS—*continued.*

No.	Breed.	Name.	Pedigree.	Distribution. [illegible]	[illegible]	[illegible]	[illegible]	[illegible]	Rate of Purchase.	Observations.
[illegible]	Hackney,	"Lord [illegible],"	Book [illegible], p. [illegible]	—	—	—	Letterkenny,	Newport,	[illegible]	Died, [illegible] May, [illegible]
[illegible]	Do.	"Merry Lad."	„ [illegible]	—	—	—	—	Newport.	—	[illegible], [illegible]
[illegible]	Do.	"Lord [illegible],"	„ [illegible]	—	—	—	—	—	—	[illegible], [illegible]
[illegible]	Do.	"[illegible]."	„ [illegible]	—	—	—	[illegible]	[illegible]	[illegible]	
[illegible]	Do.	"[illegible],"	„ [illegible]	—	—	—	[illegible],	Achill Sound.	[illegible]	
[illegible]	Do.	"[illegible]."	„ [illegible]	—	—	—	[illegible],	[illegible],	[illegible]	
[illegible]	Do.	"[illegible]."	[illegible], Vol. [illegible]	—	—	—	[illegible].	—	—	Sold for [illegible], [illegible]
[illegible]	Do.	"[illegible] Chief,"	[illegible], Vol. [illegible]	—	—	—	[illegible],	—	—	Sold for [illegible], [illegible]
[illegible]	Do.	"Lord [illegible],"	Book [illegible], p. [illegible]	—	—	—	[illegible].	[illegible].	[illegible]	Died, [illegible] July, [illegible]
[illegible]	Do.	"[illegible]."	„ [illegible]	—	—	—	[illegible],	[illegible].	[illegible]	
[illegible]	Do.	"[illegible],"	[illegible], Vol. [illegible]	—	—	—	—	[illegible],	[illegible]	
[illegible]	Cleveland Bay,	"[illegible]."	Book [illegible], p. [illegible]	[illegible].	[illegible].	—	—	—	[illegible]	Sold, March, [illegible]
[illegible]	Barb,	"[illegible]."	„ [illegible]	[illegible].	[illegible] ([illegible]).	[illegible],	Achill Sound.	Achill Sound.	[illegible]	
[illegible]	Arab,	"[illegible],"	Imported,	[illegible],	—	—	—	—	—	Sold for [illegible], [illegible]
[illegible]	Do.	"[illegible],"		Achill Sound,	—	Achill Sound.	[illegible].	[illegible].	[illegible]	Do. [illegible]
[illegible]	Do.	"[illegible],"	Book [illegible], p. [illegible]	[illegible],	[illegible],	[illegible],	—	—	Presented by H.M. the Queen [illegible]	Removed to Windsor, [illegible]
[illegible]	Welsh Cob,	"[illegible],"	„ [illegible]	—	[illegible].	[illegible].	[illegible],	[illegible],	[illegible]	
[illegible]	Do.	"[illegible]."	„ [illegible]	—	[illegible],	[illegible],	[illegible]	[illegible].	[illegible]	
[illegible]	Do.	"[illegible] IV.,"	„ [illegible]	—	[illegible].	[illegible],	[illegible], Achill Island.	[illegible], Achill Island,	[illegible]	
[illegible]	Do.	"Prince [illegible],"	„ [illegible]	—	[illegible],	Arran Island.	Arran Island.	[illegible],	[illegible]	
[illegible]	Welsh Pony,	"Welsh [illegible],"	„ [illegible]	—	Achill Sound,	[illegible],	[illegible].	[illegible].	[illegible]	
[illegible]	Do.	"[illegible],"	„ [illegible]	—	[illegible].	[illegible],	Clare Island,	Clare Island,	[illegible]	
[illegible]	Thoroughbred,	"St. [illegible],"	[illegible],	—	—	—	—	[illegible].	[illegible]	
[illegible]	Do.	"[illegible]."	Do.	—	—	—	—	[illegible].	[illegible]	
[illegible]	Welsh Pony.	"[illegible],"	Book [illegible], p. [illegible]	—	—	—	—	—	[illegible]	Sold January, [illegible]

WM. L. MICKS.

SCHEDULE

SHOWING the NUMBER of MARES SERVED by each of the BOARD'S STALLIONS since [illegible] inclusive.

No.	Name of Stallion.	Breed of Stallion.	No. of Seasons Used.	Mares Served.	
				Total No.	Average No. each Season.
1	"Rokeby,"	Hackney,	4	178	43
2	"North Riding,"	"	3	183	61
3	"Real Gentleman,"	"	4	196	49
4	"Callis Fireaway,"	"	3	261	87
5	"Bray,"	"	5	214	43
6	"Fashion III.,"	"	3	240	79
7	"Lord Go Bang,"	"	5	220	44
8	"Zeus,"	"	3	189	63
9	"Lord Derwent,"	"	3	183	61
10	"Fireaway II.,"	"	4	237	59
11	"King Fireaway,"	"	3	197	66
12	"Lord Tennyson,"	"	5	337	67
13	"Highgate Performer,"	"	3	137	46
14	"Romulus II.,"	"	4	191	48
15	"Gay Lad III.,"	"	4	255	64
16	"Earl of Eskdale,"	"	2	152	76
17	"Flying Fireaway,"	"	3	188	63
18	"Ireland's Duke of York,"	"	2	108	54
19	"Chantilly I.,"	"	2	64	32
20	"Matchless Fireaway,"	"	1	63	63
21	"Baron Performer,"	"	2	81	40
22	"Bay Malton,"	"	2	118	59
23	"Lord Loppington,"	"	3	130	43
24	"Proud Dane,"	"	1	15	15
25	"Lord Gaunt,"	"	2	101	50
26	"Lord Sheridan,"	"	2	46	23
27	"Merry Lad,"	"	1	6	6

Schedule showing the Number of Mares served by each of the Board's Stallions since 1892 inclusive—*continued*.

No.	Name of Stallion.	Breed of Stallion.	No. of Seasons Used.	Mares Served.	
				Total No.	Average No. each Season.
28	"Lord Durraville,"	Hackney, .	–	–	–
29	"Carnaccum,"	" .	2	103	51
30	"Derwent,"	" .	2	82	41
31	"Eastburn Duke," . . .	" .	3	109	36
32	"Grimston Performer," . . .	" .	1	71	71
33	"Flookburgh Cadet," . . .	" .	1	33	33
34	"Lord Middleton," . . .	" .	2	90	45
35	"Sir Tatton,"	" .	2	83	41
36	"Conroy,"	" .	1	77	77
37	"Bay Bonadico,"	Cleveland Bay,	2	86	43
38	"Awfully Jolly,"	Barb, .	5	231	46
39	"Ali Baba,"	Arab, .	1	19	19
40	"Desert Born,"	" .	4	140	35
41	"Tiresome,"	" .	3	112	37
42	"Electricity,"	Welsh Cob, .	4	276	69
43	"Sunbeam,"	" .	4	200	50
44	"Express IV.,"	" .	4	115	29
45	"Prince Llewellyn," . . .	" .	4	150	37
46	"Welsh Tommy,"	Welsh Pony, .	4	340	85
47	"Movement,"	" .	4	104	26
48	"St. Aidan,"	Thoroughbred,	1	10	10
49	"Uncle Sam,"	" .	4	48	12

Wm. L. Mears.

APPENDIX F.—RETURN OF STALLIONS IN THE HANDS OF PRIVATE OWNERS STANDING IN IRELAND IN 1896.

(Compiled by the Land Commission from Reports furnished by the Constabulary.)

Province and County	[illegible]	[illegible]	[illegible]	[illegible]	[illegible]	[illegible]	[illegible]	[illegible]	[illegible]	[illegible]	[illegible]	Total.
ULSTER.												
Antrim	[illegible]	[illegible]	[illegible]	7	–	[illegible]	–	–	–	–	1	[illegible]
Armagh	[illegible]	[illegible]	[illegible]	[illegible]	–	–	–	–	–	–	–	[illegible]
Cavan	[illegible]	[illegible]	[illegible]	–	–	–	–	–	–	–	–	[illegible]
Donegal	[illegible]	[illegible]	[illegible]	[illegible]	–	–	–	–	–	–	–	[illegible]
Down	[illegible]	[illegible]	[illegible]	[illegible]	[illegible]	[illegible]	–	1	–	–	–	[illegible]
Fermanagh	[illegible]	[illegible]	[illegible]	[illegible]	–	–	–	–	–	–	–	[illegible]
Londonderry	14	[illegible]	[illegible]	–	[illegible]	[illegible]	–	–	–	–	–	[illegible]
Monaghan	1	[illegible]	[illegible]	[illegible]	–	–	[illegible]	–	–	[illegible]	[illegible]	[illegible]
Tyrone	[illegible]	[illegible]	[illegible]	–	–	–	–	–	–	–	–	[illegible]
Total	[illegible]	[illegible]	[illegible]	[illegible]	[illegible]	[illegible]	1	1	–	[illegible]	[illegible]	[illegible]
LEINSTER.												
Carlow	1	[illegible]	[illegible]	1	[illegible]	[illegible]	–	[illegible]	–	–	–	[illegible]
Dublin	–	[illegible]	[illegible]	[illegible]	[illegible]	[illegible]	–	–	[illegible]	–	[illegible]	[illegible]
Kildare	[illegible]	[illegible]	[illegible]	[illegible]	[illegible]	[illegible]	[illegible]	–	[illegible]	1	[illegible]	[illegible]
Kilkenny	[illegible]	[illegible]	[illegible]	[illegible]	–	[illegible]	–	–	–	–	–	[illegible]
King's	[illegible]	[illegible]	[illegible]	[illegible]	–	–	–	–	–	–	[illegible]	[illegible]
Longford	[illegible]	[illegible]	[illegible]	[illegible]	–	–	–	–	[illegible]	–	–	[illegible]
Louth	7	[illegible]	[illegible]	[illegible]	[illegible]	[illegible]	–	–	–	–	–	[illegible]
Meath	[illegible]	[illegible]	[illegible]	[illegible]	[illegible]	[illegible]	[illegible]	–	[illegible]	–	[illegible]	[illegible]
Queen's	[illegible]	[illegible]	[illegible]	[illegible]	–	[illegible]	–	–	[illegible]	–	[illegible]	[illegible]
Westmeath	[illegible]	[illegible]	[illegible]	[illegible]	–	[illegible]	–	–	–	–	–	[illegible]
Wexford	[illegible]	[illegible]	[illegible]	[illegible]	–	7	–	–	–	–	[illegible]	[illegible]
Wicklow	[illegible]	[illegible]	[illegible]	[illegible]	1	–	–	–	–	–	–	[illegible]
Total	[illegible]	[illegible]	[illegible]	[illegible]	[illegible]	[illegible]	[illegible]	1	[illegible]	1	[illegible]	[illegible]

Province and County	[illegible]	[illegible]	[illegible]	[illegible]	[illegible]	[illegible]	[illegible]	[illegible]	[illegible]	[illegible]	[illegible]	Total.
CONNAUGHT.												
Galway	[illegible]	[illegible]	[illegible]	[illegible]	[illegible]	[illegible]	–	–	–	–	–	[illegible]
Leitrim	[illegible]	[illegible]	[illegible]	–	–	–	–	–	–	–	–	[illegible]
Mayo	[illegible]	[illegible]	[illegible]	[illegible]	–	–	[illegible]	–	–	–	–	[illegible]
Roscommon	[illegible]	[illegible]	[illegible]	[illegible]	[illegible]	1	–	–	–	–	–	[illegible]
Sligo	[illegible]	[illegible]	[illegible]	[illegible]	[illegible]	[illegible]	–	–	–	–	–	[illegible]
Total	[illegible]	[illegible]	[illegible]	[illegible]	[illegible]	[illegible]	[illegible]	–	–	–	–	[illegible]
MUNSTER.												
Clare	[illegible]	[illegible]	[illegible]	–	1	–	–	–	–	–	–	[illegible]
Cork	[illegible]	[illegible]	[illegible]	[illegible]	[illegible]	[illegible]	–	–	–	–	[illegible]	[illegible]
Kerry	[illegible]	[illegible]	[illegible]	[illegible]	–	–	–	–	–	–	–	[illegible]
Limerick	[illegible]	[illegible]	[illegible]	[illegible]	1	[illegible]	–	–	–	–	1	[illegible]
Tipperary	[illegible]	[illegible]	[illegible]	[illegible]	[illegible]	[illegible]	–	–	–	–	–	[illegible]
Waterford	[illegible]	[illegible]	[illegible]	[illegible]	[illegible]	–	–	–	–	–	–	[illegible]
Total	[illegible]	[illegible]	[illegible]	[illegible]	[illegible]	[illegible]	–	–	–	–	[illegible]	[illegible]
SUMMARY.												
ULSTER	[illegible]	[illegible]	[illegible]	[illegible]	[illegible]	[illegible]	[illegible]	[illegible]	–	[illegible]	[illegible]	[illegible]
LEINSTER	[illegible]	[illegible]	[illegible]	[illegible]	[illegible]	[illegible]	[illegible]	[illegible]	[illegible]	[illegible]	[illegible]	[illegible]
CONNAUGHT	[illegible]	[illegible]	[illegible]	[illegible]	[illegible]	[illegible]	[illegible]	–	–			[illegible]
MUNSTER	[illegible]	[illegible]	[illegible]	14	[illegible]	[illegible]	–	–	–	–	[illegible]	[illegible]
TOTAL	[illegible]	[illegible]	[illegible]	[illegible]	[illegible]	[illegible]	[illegible]	[illegible]	[illegible]	[illegible]	[illegible]	[illegible]

Provinces and Counties.	THOROUGHBREDS.																HUNTER SIRES.						
	No.	Highest.	Lowest.	Highest.	Lowest.	Highest.	Lowest.	No.	Highest.	Lowest.	Highest.	Lowest.	Highest.	Lowest.	Total		No.	Highest.	Lowest.	Highest.	Lowest.	Highest.	Lowest.
CONNAUGHT.																							
Galway,	[illegible]	[illegible]	[illegible]	[illegible]	[illegible]	[illegible]	[illegible]	[illegible]	[illegible]	[illegible]	[illegible]	[illegible]	[illegible]	[illegible]	[illegible]		[illegible]	[illegible]	[illegible]	[illegible]	[illegible]	[illegible]	[illegible]
Leitrim,	—	—	—	—	—	—	—	—	—	—	—	—	—	—	[illegible]		[illegible]	[illegible]	[illegible]	[illegible]	[illegible]	[illegible]	[illegible]
Mayo,	[illegible]	[illegible]	[illegible]	[illegible]	[illegible]	[illegible]	[illegible]	[illegible]	[illegible]	[illegible]	[illegible]	[illegible]	[illegible]	[illegible]	[illegible]		[illegible]	[illegible]	[illegible]	[illegible]	[illegible]	[illegible]	[illegible]
Roscommon,	[illegible]	[illegible]	[illegible]	[illegible]	[illegible]	[illegible]	[illegible]	[illegible]	[illegible]	[illegible]	[illegible]	[illegible]	[illegible]	[illegible]	[illegible]		[illegible]	[illegible]	[illegible]	[illegible]	[illegible]	[illegible]	[illegible]
Sligo,	[illegible]	[illegible]	[illegible]	[illegible]	[illegible]	[illegible]	[illegible]	[illegible]	[illegible]	[illegible]	[illegible]	[illegible]	[illegible]	[illegible]	[illegible]		[illegible]	[illegible]	[illegible]	[illegible]	[illegible]	[illegible]	[illegible]
	[illegible]	[illegible]	[illegible]	[illegible]	[illegible]	[illegible]	[illegible]	[illegible]	[illegible]	[illegible]	[illegible]	[illegible]	[illegible]	[illegible]	[illegible]		[illegible]	[illegible]	[illegible]	[illegible]	[illegible]	[illegible]	[illegible]
MUNSTER.																							
Clare,	[illegible]	[illegible]	[illegible]	[illegible]	[illegible]	[illegible]	[illegible]	[illegible]	[illegible]	[illegible]	[illegible]	[illegible]	[illegible]	[illegible]	[illegible]		[illegible]	[illegible]	[illegible]	[illegible]	[illegible]	[illegible]	[illegible]
Cork,	[illegible]	[illegible]	[illegible]	[illegible]	[illegible]	[illegible]	[illegible]	[illegible]	[illegible]	[illegible]	[illegible]	[illegible]	[illegible]	[illegible]	[illegible]		[illegible]	[illegible]	[illegible]	[illegible]	[illegible]	[illegible]	[illegible]
Kerry,	[illegible]	[illegible]	[illegible]	[illegible]	[illegible]	[illegible]	[illegible]	[illegible]	[illegible]	[illegible]	[illegible]	[illegible]	[illegible]	[illegible]	[illegible]		[illegible]	[illegible]	[illegible]	[illegible]	[illegible]	[illegible]	[illegible]
Limerick,	[illegible]	[illegible]	[illegible]	[illegible]	[illegible]	[illegible]	[illegible]	[illegible]	[illegible]	[illegible]	[illegible]	[illegible]	[illegible]	[illegible]	[illegible]		[illegible]	[illegible]	[illegible]	[illegible]	[illegible]	[illegible]	[illegible]
Tipperary,	[illegible]	[illegible]	[illegible]	[illegible]	[illegible]	[illegible]	[illegible]	[illegible]	[illegible]	[illegible]	[illegible]	[illegible]	[illegible]	[illegible]	[illegible]		[illegible]	[illegible]	[illegible]	[illegible]	[illegible]	[illegible]	[illegible]
Waterford,	[illegible]	[illegible]	[illegible]	[illegible]	[illegible]	[illegible]	[illegible]	[illegible]	[illegible]	[illegible]	[illegible]	[illegible]	[illegible]	[illegible]	[illegible]		[illegible]	[illegible]	[illegible]	[illegible]	[illegible]	[illegible]	[illegible]
	[illegible]	[illegible]	[illegible]	[illegible]	[illegible]	[illegible]	[illegible]	[illegible]	[illegible]	[illegible]	[illegible]	[illegible]	[illegible]	[illegible]	[illegible]		[illegible]	[illegible]	[illegible]	[illegible]	[illegible]	[illegible]	[illegible]
SUMMARY.																							
Ulster,	[illegible]	[illegible]	[illegible]	[illegible]	[illegible]	[illegible]	[illegible]	[illegible]	[illegible]	[illegible]	[illegible]	[illegible]	[illegible]	[illegible]	[illegible]		[illegible]	[illegible]	[illegible]	[illegible]	[illegible]	[illegible]	[illegible]
Leinster,	[illegible]	[illegible]	[illegible]	[illegible]	[illegible]	[illegible]	[illegible]	[illegible]	[illegible]	[illegible]	[illegible]	[illegible]	[illegible]	[illegible]	[illegible]		[illegible]	[illegible]	[illegible]	[illegible]	[illegible]	[illegible]	[illegible]
Connaught,	[illegible]	[illegible]	[illegible]	[illegible]	[illegible]	[illegible]	[illegible]	[illegible]	[illegible]	[illegible]	[illegible]	[illegible]	[illegible]	[illegible]	[illegible]		[illegible]	[illegible]	[illegible]	[illegible]	[illegible]	[illegible]	[illegible]
Munster,	[illegible]	[illegible]	[illegible]	[illegible]	[illegible]	[illegible]	[illegible]	[illegible]	[illegible]	[illegible]	[illegible]	[illegible]	[illegible]	[illegible]	[illegible]		[illegible]	[illegible]	[illegible]	[illegible]	[illegible]	[illegible]	[illegible]
	[illegible]	[illegible]	[illegible]	[illegible]	[illegible]	[illegible]	[illegible]	[illegible]	[illegible]	[illegible]	[illegible]	[illegible]	[illegible]	[illegible]	[illegible]		[illegible]	[illegible]	[illegible]	[illegible]	[illegible]	[illegible]	[illegible]

[illegible]	No.	Highest	Lowest	Highest	Lowest	Highest	Lowest	No.	Highest	Lowest	Highest	Lowest	Highest	Lowest	[illegible]	No.	Highest	Lowest	Highest	Lowest	Highest	Lowest
ANTRIM.	[illegible]	[illegible]	[illegible]	[illegible]	[illegible]	[illegible]	[illegible]	[illegible]	[illegible]	[illegible]	[illegible]	[illegible]	[illegible]	[illegible]	[illegible]	[illegible]	[illegible]	[illegible]	[illegible]	[illegible]	[illegible]	[illegible]
ARMAGH.	[illegible]	[illegible]	[illegible]	[illegible]	[illegible]	[illegible]	[illegible]	[illegible]	[illegible]	[illegible]	[illegible]	[illegible]	[illegible]	[illegible]	[illegible]	[illegible]	[illegible]	[illegible]	[illegible]	[illegible]	[illegible]	[illegible]
CAVAN.	[illegible]	[illegible]	[illegible]	[illegible]	[illegible]	[illegible]	[illegible]	[illegible]	[illegible]	[illegible]	[illegible]	[illegible]	[illegible]	[illegible]	[illegible]	[illegible]	[illegible]	[illegible]	[illegible]	[illegible]	[illegible]	[illegible]

Counties and Royal Irish Constabulary Districts.	Hackneys: Registered in the Hackney Road Book: No.	Fee: Highest.	Fee: Lowest.	Which do not appear in the Hackney Road Book: No.	Fee: Highest.	Fee: Lowest.	[illegible]: No.	Fee: Highest.	Fee: Lowest.	[illegible]: No.	Fee: Highest.	Fee: Lowest.	[illegible]: No.	Fee: Highest.	Fee: Lowest.	[illegible]: No.	Fee: Highest.	Fee: Lowest.	[illegible]: No.	Fee: Highest.	Fee: Lowest.	[illegible]: No.	Fee: Highest.	Fee: Lowest.	Total No. of [illegible]
		s. d.	s. d.		s. d.	s. d.		s. d.	s. d.		s. d.	s. d.		s. d.	s. d.		s. d.	s. d.		s. d.	s. d.		s. d.	s. d.	
ANTRIM.																									
Antrim,	-	—	—	-	—	—	[illegible]	[illegible]	[illegible]	-	—	—	-	[illegible]	[illegible]	-	—	—	-	—	—	-	—	—	[illegible]
Ballymena,	[illegible]	[illegible]	[illegible]	[illegible]	[illegible]	[illegible]	[illegible]	[illegible]	[illegible]	[illegible]	[illegible]	[illegible]	[illegible]	[illegible]	[illegible]	-	—	—	[illegible]	[illegible]	[illegible]	-	—	—	[illegible]
Ballymoney,	-	—	—	-	—	—	[illegible]	[illegible]	[illegible]	[illegible]	[illegible]	[illegible]	[illegible]	[illegible]	[illegible]	-	—	—	-	—	—	[illegible]	[illegible]	[illegible]	[illegible]
Larne and Carrickfergus,	-	—	—	[illegible]	[illegible]	[illegible]	[illegible]	[illegible]	[illegible]	[illegible]	[illegible]	[illegible]	[illegible]	[illegible]	[illegible]	-	—	—	[illegible]	[illegible]	[illegible]	[illegible]	[illegible]	[illegible]	[illegible]
Lisburn,	-	—	—	-	—	—	[illegible]	[illegible]	[illegible]	-	—	—	[illegible]	[illegible]	[illegible]	-	—	—	-	—	—	-	—	—	[illegible]
Belfast: East District,	-	—	—	-	—	—	[illegible]	[illegible]	[illegible]	-	—	—	[illegible]	[illegible]	[illegible]	-	—	—	-	—	—	-	—	—	[illegible]
North District,	-	—	—	-	—	—	-	—	—	[illegible]	[illegible]	[illegible]	[illegible]	[illegible]	[illegible]	-	—	—	-	—	—	-	—	—	[illegible]
North-West District,	-	—	—	-	—	—	-	—	—	-	—	—	-	—	—	-	—	—	-	—	—	-	—	—	-
West District,	-	—	—	-	—	—	-	—	—	-	—	—	-	—	—	-	—	—	-	—	—	-	—	—	[illegible]
South District,	-	—	—	-	—	—	-	—	—	-	—	—	-	—	—	-	—	—	-	—	—	-	—	—	-
	[illegible]	[illegible]	[illegible]	[illegible]	[illegible]	[illegible]	[illegible]	[illegible]	[illegible]	[illegible]	[illegible]	[illegible]	[illegible]	[illegible]	[illegible]	-	—	—	[illegible]	[illegible]	[illegible]	[illegible]	[illegible]	[illegible]	[illegible]
ARMAGH.																									
Armagh,	-	—	—	-	—	—	[illegible]	[illegible]	[illegible]	-	—	—	-	—	—	-	—	—	-	—	—	-	—	—	[illegible]
Lurgan,	-	—	—	-	—	—	[illegible]	[illegible]	[illegible]	[illegible]	[illegible]	[illegible]	-	—	—	-	—	—	-	—	—	-	—	—	[illegible]
Newry,	-	—	—	-	—	—	[illegible]	[illegible]	[illegible]	-	—	—	[illegible]	[illegible]	[illegible]	-	—	—	-	—	—	-	—	—	[illegible]
Portadown,	-	—	—	-	—	—	[illegible]	[illegible]	[illegible]	-	—	—	-	—	—	-	—	—	-	—	—	-	—	—	[illegible]
	-	—	—	-	—	—	[illegible]	[illegible]	[illegible]	[illegible]	[illegible]	[illegible]	[illegible]	[illegible]	[illegible]	-	—	—	-	—	—	-	—	—	[illegible]
CAVAN.																									
Bailieborough,	-	—	—	-	—	—	[illegible]	[illegible]	[illegible]	[illegible]	[illegible]	[illegible]	[illegible]	[illegible]	[illegible]	-	—	—	-	—	—	-	—	—	[illegible]
Cavan,	-	—	—	-	—	—	[illegible]	[illegible]	[illegible]	-	—	—	[illegible]	[illegible]	[illegible]	-	—	—	-	—	—	-	—	—	[illegible]
[illegible]	-	—	—	-	—	—	[illegible]	[illegible]	[illegible]	[illegible]	[illegible]	[illegible]	[illegible]	[illegible]	[illegible]	-	—	—	-	—	—	-	—	—	[illegible]
[illegible]	-	—	—	[illegible]	[illegible]	[illegible]	[illegible]	[illegible]	[illegible]	-	—	—	[illegible]	[illegible]	[illegible]	-	—	—	-	—	—	-	—	—	[illegible]
Virginia,	-	—	—	-	—	—	[illegible]	[illegible]	[illegible]	[illegible]	[illegible]	[illegible]	[illegible]	[illegible]	[illegible]	-	—	—	-	—	—	-	—	—	[illegible]
	-	—	—	[illegible]	[illegible]	[illegible]	[illegible]	[illegible]	[illegible]	[illegible]	[illegible]	[illegible]	[illegible]	[illegible]	[illegible]	-	—	—	-	—	—	-	—	—	[illegible]

[illegible]	[illegible]															[illegible]						
	[illegible]														[illegible]	[illegible]						
	[illegible]							Other Thoroughbreds														
	No.	[illegible]		[illegible]		[illegible]		No.	[illegible]		[illegible]		[illegible]			No.	[illegible]		[illegible]		[illegible]	
		Highest	Lowest	Highest	Lowest	Highest	Lowest		Highest	Lowest	Highest	Lowest	Highest	Lowest			Highest	Lowest	Highest	Lowest	Highest	Lowest
LONDONDERRY.		[illegible]	[illegible]	[illegible]	[illegible]	[illegible]	[illegible]		[illegible]	[illegible]	[illegible]	[illegible]	[illegible]	[illegible]			[illegible]	[illegible]	[illegible]	[illegible]	[illegible]	[illegible]
[illegible]	[illegible]	—	—	—	—	—	—	[illegible]	—	—	—	—	—	—	—	[illegible]	[illegible]	[illegible]	[illegible]	[illegible]	[illegible]	[illegible]
[illegible]	[illegible]	—	—	—	—	—	—	[illegible]	—	—	—	—	—	—	[illegible]	[illegible]	[illegible]	[illegible]	[illegible]	[illegible]	[illegible]	[illegible]
[illegible]	[illegible]	—	—	—	—	—	—	[illegible]	—	—	—	—	—	—	—	[illegible]	[illegible]	[illegible]	[illegible]	[illegible]	[illegible]	[illegible]
[illegible]	[illegible]	—	—	—	—	—	—	[illegible]	[illegible]	[illegible]	[illegible]	[illegible]	[illegible]	[illegible]	[illegible]	[illegible]	[illegible]	[illegible]	[illegible]	[illegible]	[illegible]	[illegible]
	—	—	—	—	—	—	—	[illegible]	[illegible]	[illegible]	[illegible]	[illegible]	[illegible]	[illegible]	[illegible]	[illegible]	[illegible]	[illegible]	[illegible]	[illegible]	[illegible]	[illegible]
MONAGHAN.																						
[illegible]	[illegible]	[illegible]	[illegible]	[illegible]	[illegible]	[illegible]	[illegible]	[illegible]	[illegible]	[illegible]	[illegible]	[illegible]	[illegible]	[illegible]	[illegible]	[illegible]	[illegible]	[illegible]	[illegible]	[illegible]	[illegible]	[illegible]
[illegible]	[illegible]	[illegible]	[illegible]	[illegible]	[illegible]	[illegible]	[illegible]	[illegible]	—	—	—	—	—	—	[illegible]	[illegible]	[illegible]	[illegible]	[illegible]	[illegible]	[illegible]	[illegible]
[illegible]	[illegible]	[illegible]	[illegible]	[illegible]	[illegible]	[illegible]	[illegible]	[illegible]	[illegible]	[illegible]	[illegible]	[illegible]	[illegible]	[illegible]	[illegible]	—	—	—	—	—	—	—
	[illegible]	[illegible]	[illegible]	[illegible]	[illegible]	[illegible]	[illegible]	[illegible]	[illegible]	[illegible]	[illegible]	[illegible]	[illegible]	[illegible]	[illegible]	[illegible]	[illegible]	[illegible]	[illegible]	[illegible]	[illegible]	[illegible]
TYRONE.																						
[illegible]	[illegible]	[illegible]	[illegible]	[illegible]	[illegible]	[illegible]	[illegible]		—	—	—	—	—	—	[illegible]	[illegible]	[illegible]	[illegible]	[illegible]	[illegible]	[illegible]	[illegible]
[illegible]	[illegible]	—	—	—	—	—	—		—	—	—	—	—	—	[illegible]	[illegible]	—	—	—	—	—	—
[illegible]	[illegible]	—	—	—	—	—	—	[illegible]	[illegible]	[illegible]	[illegible]	[illegible]	[illegible]	[illegible]	[illegible]	[illegible]	[illegible]	[illegible]	[illegible]	[illegible]	[illegible]	[illegible]
[illegible]	[illegible]	—	—	—	—	—	—		—	—	—	—	—	—	[illegible]	[illegible]	—	—	—	—	—	—
[illegible]	[illegible]	[illegible]	[illegible]	[illegible]	[illegible]	[illegible]	[illegible]	—	—	—	—	—	—	—	[illegible]	[illegible]	[illegible]	[illegible]	[illegible]	[illegible]	[illegible]	[illegible]
[illegible]	—	—	—	—	—	—	—	[illegible]	—	—	—	—	—	—	[illegible]	[illegible]	[illegible]	[illegible]	[illegible]	[illegible]	[illegible]	[illegible]
	[illegible]	[illegible]	[illegible]	[illegible]	[illegible]	[illegible]	[illegible]	[illegible]	[illegible]	[illegible]	[illegible]	[illegible]	[illegible]	[illegible]	[illegible]	[illegible]	[illegible]	[illegible]	[illegible]	[illegible]	[illegible]	[illegible]

Counties, and Royal Irish Constabulary Districts.	Hackneys: Registered in the Hackney Road Book. No.	Fee. Highest.	Fee. Lowest.	Hackneys: Which do not appear in the Hackney Road Book. No.	Fee. Highest.	Fee. Lowest.	[illegible] of any kind. No.	Fee. Highest.	Fee. Lowest.	Draught: [illegible] No.	Fee. Highest.	Fee. Lowest.	Draught: [illegible] No.	Fee. Highest.	Fee. Lowest.	[illegible] No.	Fee. Highest.	Fee. Lowest.	[illegible] No.	Fee. Highest.	Fee. Lowest.	[illegible] No.	Fee. Highest.	Fee. Lowest.	Total No. of Horses and Ponies in Constabulary District.
LONDONDERRY.		£ s. d.	£ s. d.		£ s. d.	£ s. d.		£ s. d.	£ s. d.		£ s. d.	£ s. d.		£ s. d.	£ s. d.		£ s. d.	£ s. d.		£ s. d.	£ s. d.		£ s. d.	£ s. d.	
Coleraine,	-	—	—	[illegible]	[illegible]	[illegible]	[illegible]	[illegible]	[illegible]	[illegible]	[illegible]	[illegible]	[illegible]	[illegible]	[illegible]	-	—	—	-	—	—	-	—	—	[illegible]
Limavady,	[illegible]	[illegible]	[illegible]	[illegible]	[illegible]	[illegible]	-	—	—	[illegible]	[illegible]	[illegible]	[illegible]	[illegible]	[illegible]	-	—	—	-	—	—	-	—	—	[illegible]
Londonderry,	-	—	—	-	—	—	-	—	—	[illegible]	[illegible]	[illegible]	[illegible]	[illegible]	[illegible]	-	—	—	-	—	—	-	—	—	[illegible]
Magherafelt,	[illegible]	[illegible]	[illegible]	-	—	—	[illegible]	[illegible]	[illegible]	-	—	—	[illegible]	[illegible]	[illegible]	-	—	—	-	—	—	-	—	—	[illegible]
	[illegible]	[illegible]	[illegible]	[illegible]	[illegible]	[illegible]	[illegible]	[illegible]	[illegible]	[illegible]	[illegible]	[illegible]	[illegible]	[illegible]	[illegible]	-	—	—	-	—	—	-	—	—	[illegible]
MONAGHAN.																									
Castleblayney,	-	—	—	[illegible]	[illegible]	[illegible]	[illegible]	[illegible]	[illegible]	[illegible]	[illegible]	[illegible]	[illegible]	[illegible]	[illegible]	-	—	—	-	—	—	-	—	—	[illegible]
Clones,	[illegible]	[illegible]	[illegible]	[illegible]	[illegible]	[illegible]	-	—	—	[illegible]	[illegible]	[illegible]	[illegible]	[illegible]	[illegible]	-	—	—	-	—	—	-	—	—	[illegible]
Monaghan,	-	—	—	-	—	—	[illegible]	[illegible]	[illegible]	-	—	—	-	—	—	-	—	—	-	—	—	-	—	—	[illegible]
	[illegible]	[illegible]	[illegible]	[illegible]	[illegible]	[illegible]	[illegible]	[illegible]	[illegible]	[illegible]	[illegible]	[illegible]	[illegible]	[illegible]	[illegible]	-	—	—	-	—	—	-	—	—	[illegible]
TYRONE.																									
Aughnacloy,	-	—	—	-	—	—	[illegible]	[illegible]	[illegible]	[illegible]	[illegible]	[illegible]	[illegible]	[illegible]	[illegible]	-	—	—	-	—	—	-	—	—	[illegible]
Cookstown,	-	—	—	-	—	—	[illegible]	[illegible]	[illegible]	[illegible]	[illegible]	[illegible]	[illegible]	[illegible]	[illegible]	-	—	—	-	—	—	-	—	—	[illegible]
Dungannon,	[illegible]	[illegible]	[illegible]	-	—	—	[illegible]	[illegible]	[illegible]	[illegible]	[illegible]	[illegible]	-	—	—	-	—	—	-	—	—	-	—	—	[illegible]
Newtownstewart,	-	—	—	[illegible]	[illegible]	[illegible]	[illegible]	[illegible]	[illegible]	-	—	—	[illegible]	[illegible]	[illegible]	-	—	—	-	—	—	-	—	—	[illegible]
Omagh,	[illegible]	[illegible]	[illegible]	-	—	—	[illegible]	[illegible]	[illegible]	[illegible]	[illegible]	[illegible]	[illegible]	[illegible]	[illegible]	-	—	—	-	—	—	-	—	—	[illegible]
Strabane,	-	—	—	-	—	—	[illegible]	[illegible]	[illegible]	-	—	—	-	—	—	-	—	—	-	—	—	-	—	—	[illegible]
	[illegible]	[illegible]	[illegible]	[illegible]	[illegible]	[illegible]	[illegible]	[illegible]	[illegible]	[illegible]	[illegible]	[illegible]	[illegible]	[illegible]	[illegible]	-	—	—	-	—	—	-	—	—	[illegible]

COUNTIES and Poor Law Unions	[illegible] No.	[illegible] Highest	[illegible] Lowest	[illegible] No.	[illegible] Highest	[illegible] Lowest	[illegible] No.	[illegible] Highest	[illegible] Lowest	[illegible] No.	[illegible] Highest	[illegible] Lowest	Half-bred No.	Half-bred Highest	Half-bred Lowest	[illegible] No.	[illegible] Highest	[illegible] Lowest	[illegible] No.	[illegible] Highest	[illegible] Lowest	[illegible] No.	[illegible] Highest	[illegible] Lowest	[illegible]
CARLOW.	[illegible]	[illegible]	[illegible]	[illegible]	[illegible]	[illegible]	[illegible]	[illegible]	[illegible]	[illegible]	[illegible]	[illegible]	[illegible]	[illegible]	[illegible]	[illegible]	[illegible]	[illegible]	[illegible]	[illegible]	[illegible]	[illegible]	[illegible]	[illegible]	[illegible]
DUBLIN.	[illegible]	[illegible]	[illegible]	[illegible]	[illegible]	[illegible]	[illegible]	[illegible]	[illegible]	[illegible]	[illegible]	[illegible]	[illegible]	[illegible]	[illegible]	[illegible]	[illegible]	[illegible]	[illegible]	[illegible]	[illegible]	[illegible]	[illegible]	[illegible]	[illegible]
KILDARE.	[illegible]	[illegible]	[illegible]	[illegible]	[illegible]	[illegible]	[illegible]	[illegible]	[illegible]	[illegible]	[illegible]	[illegible]	[illegible]	[illegible]	[illegible]	[illegible]	[illegible]	[illegible]	[illegible]	[illegible]	[illegible]	[illegible]	[illegible]	[illegible]	[illegible]

[illegible]	No.	[illegible] Highest	[illegible] Lowest	[illegible] Highest	[illegible] Lowest	[illegible] Highest	[illegible] Lowest	No.	[illegible] Highest	[illegible] Lowest	[illegible] Highest	[illegible] Lowest	[illegible] Highest	[illegible] Lowest	[illegible]	No.	[illegible] Highest	[illegible] Lowest	[illegible] Highest	[illegible] Lowest	[illegible] Highest	[illegible] Lowest
[illegible]																						
[illegible]	[illegible]	[illegible]	[illegible]	[illegible]	[illegible]	[illegible]	[illegible]	[illegible]	[illegible]	[illegible]	[illegible]	[illegible]	[illegible]	[illegible]	[illegible]	[illegible]	[illegible]	[illegible]	[illegible]	[illegible]	[illegible]	[illegible]
[illegible]	[illegible]	[illegible]	[illegible]	[illegible]	[illegible]	[illegible]	[illegible]	[illegible]	[illegible]	[illegible]	[illegible]	[illegible]	[illegible]	[illegible]	[illegible]	[illegible]	[illegible]	[illegible]	[illegible]	[illegible]	[illegible]	[illegible]
[illegible]	[illegible]	[illegible]	[illegible]	[illegible]	[illegible]	[illegible]	[illegible]	[illegible]	[illegible]	[illegible]	[illegible]	[illegible]	[illegible]	[illegible]	[illegible]	[illegible]	[illegible]	[illegible]	[illegible]	[illegible]	[illegible]	[illegible]
[illegible]	[illegible]	[illegible]	[illegible]	[illegible]	[illegible]	[illegible]	[illegible]	[illegible]	[illegible]	[illegible]	[illegible]	[illegible]	[illegible]	[illegible]	[illegible]	[illegible]	[illegible]	[illegible]	[illegible]	[illegible]	[illegible]	[illegible]
[illegible]	[illegible]	[illegible]	[illegible]	[illegible]	[illegible]	[illegible]	[illegible]	[illegible]	[illegible]	[illegible]	[illegible]	[illegible]	[illegible]	[illegible]	[illegible]	[illegible]	[illegible]	[illegible]	[illegible]	[illegible]	[illegible]	[illegible]
[illegible]	[illegible]	[illegible]	[illegible]	[illegible]	[illegible]	[illegible]	[illegible]	[illegible]	[illegible]	[illegible]	[illegible]	[illegible]	[illegible]	[illegible]	[illegible]	[illegible]	[illegible]	[illegible]	[illegible]	[illegible]	[illegible]	[illegible]
	[illegible]	[illegible]	[illegible]	[illegible]	[illegible]	[illegible]	[illegible]	[illegible]	[illegible]	[illegible]	[illegible]	[illegible]	[illegible]	[illegible]	[illegible]	[illegible]	[illegible]	[illegible]	[illegible]	[illegible]	[illegible]	[illegible]
[illegible]																						
[illegible]	[illegible]	[illegible]	[illegible]	[illegible]	[illegible]	[illegible]	[illegible]	[illegible]	[illegible]	[illegible]	[illegible]	[illegible]	[illegible]	[illegible]	[illegible]	[illegible]	[illegible]	[illegible]	[illegible]	[illegible]	[illegible]	[illegible]
[illegible]	[illegible]	[illegible]	[illegible]	[illegible]	[illegible]	[illegible]	[illegible]	[illegible]	[illegible]	[illegible]	[illegible]	[illegible]	[illegible]	[illegible]	[illegible]	[illegible]	[illegible]	[illegible]	[illegible]	[illegible]	[illegible]	[illegible]
[illegible]	[illegible]	[illegible]	[illegible]	[illegible]	[illegible]	[illegible]	[illegible]	[illegible]	[illegible]	[illegible]	[illegible]	[illegible]	[illegible]	[illegible]	[illegible]	[illegible]	[illegible]	[illegible]	[illegible]	[illegible]	[illegible]	[illegible]
[illegible]	[illegible]	[illegible]	[illegible]	[illegible]	[illegible]	[illegible]	[illegible]	[illegible]	[illegible]	[illegible]	[illegible]	[illegible]	[illegible]	[illegible]	[illegible]	[illegible]	[illegible]	[illegible]	[illegible]	[illegible]	[illegible]	[illegible]
[illegible]	[illegible]	[illegible]	[illegible]	[illegible]	[illegible]	[illegible]	[illegible]	[illegible]	[illegible]	[illegible]	[illegible]	[illegible]	[illegible]	[illegible]	[illegible]	[illegible]	[illegible]	[illegible]	[illegible]	[illegible]	[illegible]	[illegible]
	[illegible]	[illegible]	[illegible]	[illegible]	[illegible]	[illegible]	[illegible]	[illegible]	[illegible]	[illegible]	[illegible]	[illegible]	[illegible]	[illegible]	[illegible]	[illegible]	[illegible]	[illegible]	[illegible]	[illegible]	[illegible]	[illegible]
[illegible]																						
[illegible]	[illegible]	[illegible]	[illegible]	[illegible]	[illegible]	[illegible]	[illegible]	[illegible]	[illegible]	[illegible]	[illegible]	[illegible]	[illegible]	[illegible]	[illegible]	[illegible]	[illegible]	[illegible]	[illegible]	[illegible]	[illegible]	[illegible]
[illegible]	[illegible]	[illegible]	[illegible]	[illegible]	[illegible]	[illegible]	[illegible]	[illegible]	[illegible]	[illegible]	[illegible]	[illegible]	[illegible]	[illegible]	[illegible]	[illegible]	[illegible]	[illegible]	[illegible]	[illegible]	[illegible]	[illegible]
[illegible]	[illegible]	[illegible]	[illegible]	[illegible]	[illegible]	[illegible]	[illegible]	[illegible]	[illegible]	[illegible]	[illegible]	[illegible]	[illegible]	[illegible]	[illegible]	[illegible]	[illegible]	[illegible]	[illegible]	[illegible]	[illegible]	[illegible]
	[illegible]	[illegible]	[illegible]	[illegible]	[illegible]	[illegible]	[illegible]	[illegible]	[illegible]	[illegible]	[illegible]	[illegible]	[illegible]	[illegible]	[illegible]	[illegible]	[illegible]	[illegible]	[illegible]	[illegible]	[illegible]	[illegible]

Counties and Baronies	Paupers: No.	Highest	Lowest	Paupers: No.	Highest	Lowest	No.	Highest	Lowest	Traders: No.	Highest	Lowest	Traders: No.	Highest	Lowest	No.	Highest	Lowest	No.	Highest	Lowest	Pedlars: No.	Highest	Lowest	[illegible]
KILKENNY.																									
[illegible]	[illegible]	[illegible]	[illegible]	[illegible]	[illegible]	[illegible]	[illegible]	[illegible]	[illegible]	[illegible]	[illegible]	[illegible]	[illegible]	[illegible]	[illegible]	[illegible]	[illegible]	[illegible]	[illegible]	[illegible]	[illegible]	[illegible]	[illegible]	[illegible]	[illegible]
[illegible]	[illegible]	[illegible]	[illegible]	[illegible]	[illegible]	[illegible]	[illegible]	[illegible]	[illegible]	[illegible]	[illegible]	[illegible]	[illegible]	[illegible]	[illegible]	[illegible]	[illegible]	[illegible]	[illegible]	[illegible]	[illegible]	[illegible]	[illegible]	[illegible]	[illegible]
[illegible]	[illegible]	[illegible]	[illegible]	[illegible]	[illegible]	[illegible]	[illegible]	[illegible]	[illegible]	[illegible]	[illegible]	[illegible]	[illegible]	[illegible]	[illegible]	[illegible]	[illegible]	[illegible]	[illegible]	[illegible]	[illegible]	[illegible]	[illegible]	[illegible]	[illegible]
[illegible]	[illegible]	[illegible]	[illegible]	[illegible]	[illegible]	[illegible]	[illegible]	[illegible]	[illegible]	[illegible]	[illegible]	[illegible]	[illegible]	[illegible]	[illegible]	[illegible]	[illegible]	[illegible]	[illegible]	[illegible]	[illegible]	[illegible]	[illegible]	[illegible]	[illegible]
[illegible]	[illegible]	[illegible]	[illegible]	[illegible]	[illegible]	[illegible]	[illegible]	[illegible]	[illegible]	[illegible]	[illegible]	[illegible]	[illegible]	[illegible]	[illegible]	[illegible]	[illegible]	[illegible]	[illegible]	[illegible]	[illegible]	[illegible]	[illegible]	[illegible]	[illegible]
[illegible]	[illegible]	[illegible]	[illegible]	[illegible]	[illegible]	[illegible]	[illegible]	[illegible]	[illegible]	[illegible]	[illegible]	[illegible]	[illegible]	[illegible]	[illegible]	[illegible]	[illegible]	[illegible]	[illegible]	[illegible]	[illegible]	[illegible]	[illegible]	[illegible]	[illegible]
	[illegible]	[illegible]	[illegible]	[illegible]	[illegible]	[illegible]	[illegible]	[illegible]	[illegible]	[illegible]	[illegible]	[illegible]	[illegible]	[illegible]	[illegible]	[illegible]	[illegible]	[illegible]	[illegible]	[illegible]	[illegible]	[illegible]	[illegible]	[illegible]	[illegible]
KING'S.																									
[illegible]	[illegible]	[illegible]	[illegible]	[illegible]	[illegible]	[illegible]	[illegible]	[illegible]	[illegible]	[illegible]	[illegible]	[illegible]	[illegible]	[illegible]	[illegible]	[illegible]	[illegible]	[illegible]	[illegible]	[illegible]	[illegible]	[illegible]	[illegible]	[illegible]	[illegible]
[illegible]	[illegible]	[illegible]	[illegible]	[illegible]	[illegible]	[illegible]	[illegible]	[illegible]	[illegible]	[illegible]	[illegible]	[illegible]	[illegible]	[illegible]	[illegible]	[illegible]	[illegible]	[illegible]	[illegible]	[illegible]	[illegible]	[illegible]	[illegible]	[illegible]	[illegible]
[illegible]	[illegible]	[illegible]	[illegible]	[illegible]	[illegible]	[illegible]	[illegible]	[illegible]	[illegible]	[illegible]	[illegible]	[illegible]	[illegible]	[illegible]	[illegible]	[illegible]	[illegible]	[illegible]	[illegible]	[illegible]	[illegible]	[illegible]	[illegible]	[illegible]	[illegible]
[illegible]	[illegible]	[illegible]	[illegible]	[illegible]	[illegible]	[illegible]	[illegible]	[illegible]	[illegible]	[illegible]	[illegible]	[illegible]	[illegible]	[illegible]	[illegible]	[illegible]	[illegible]	[illegible]	[illegible]	[illegible]	[illegible]	[illegible]	[illegible]	[illegible]	[illegible]
[illegible]	[illegible]	[illegible]	[illegible]	[illegible]	[illegible]	[illegible]	[illegible]	[illegible]	[illegible]	[illegible]	[illegible]	[illegible]	[illegible]	[illegible]	[illegible]	[illegible]	[illegible]	[illegible]	[illegible]	[illegible]	[illegible]	[illegible]	[illegible]	[illegible]	[illegible]
	[illegible]	[illegible]	[illegible]	[illegible]	[illegible]	[illegible]	[illegible]	[illegible]	[illegible]	[illegible]	[illegible]	[illegible]	[illegible]	[illegible]	[illegible]	[illegible]	[illegible]	[illegible]	[illegible]	[illegible]	[illegible]	[illegible]	[illegible]	[illegible]	[illegible]
LONGFORD.																									
[illegible]	[illegible]	[illegible]	[illegible]	[illegible]	[illegible]	[illegible]	[illegible]	[illegible]	[illegible]	[illegible]	[illegible]	[illegible]	[illegible]	[illegible]	[illegible]	[illegible]	[illegible]	[illegible]	[illegible]	[illegible]	[illegible]	[illegible]	[illegible]	[illegible]	[illegible]
[illegible]	[illegible]	[illegible]	[illegible]	[illegible]	[illegible]	[illegible]	[illegible]	[illegible]	[illegible]	[illegible]	[illegible]	[illegible]	[illegible]	[illegible]	[illegible]	[illegible]	[illegible]	[illegible]	[illegible]	[illegible]	[illegible]	[illegible]	[illegible]	[illegible]	[illegible]
[illegible]	[illegible]	[illegible]	[illegible]	[illegible]	[illegible]	[illegible]	[illegible]	[illegible]	[illegible]	[illegible]	[illegible]	[illegible]	[illegible]	[illegible]	[illegible]	[illegible]	[illegible]	[illegible]	[illegible]	[illegible]	[illegible]	[illegible]	[illegible]	[illegible]	[illegible]
	[illegible]	[illegible]	[illegible]	[illegible]	[illegible]	[illegible]	[illegible]	[illegible]	[illegible]	[illegible]	[illegible]	[illegible]	[illegible]	[illegible]	[illegible]	[illegible]	[illegible]	[illegible]	[illegible]	[illegible]	[illegible]	[illegible]	[illegible]	[illegible]	[illegible]

[illegible]	No.	[illegible] Highest	[illegible] Lowest	[illegible] Highest	[illegible] Lowest	[illegible] Highest	[illegible] Lowest	No.	[illegible] Highest	[illegible] Lowest	[illegible] Highest	[illegible] Lowest	[illegible] Highest	[illegible] Lowest	Total No. [illegible]	No.	[illegible] Highest	[illegible] Lowest	[illegible] Highest	[illegible] Lowest	[illegible] Highest	[illegible] Lowest
KERRY.																						
[illegible]	[illegible]	[illegible]	[illegible]	[illegible]	[illegible]	[illegible]	[illegible]	[illegible]	[illegible]	[illegible]	[illegible]	[illegible]	[illegible]	[illegible]	[illegible]	[illegible]	[illegible]	[illegible]	[illegible]	[illegible]	[illegible]	[illegible]
[illegible]	—	—	—	—	—	—	—	[illegible]	—	—	—	—	—	—	[illegible]	—	—	—	—	—	—	—
[illegible]	—	—	—	—	—	—	—	[illegible]	[illegible]	[illegible]	[illegible]	[illegible]	[illegible]	[illegible]	[illegible]	[illegible]	[illegible]	[illegible]	[illegible]	[illegible]	[illegible]	[illegible]
[illegible]	[illegible]	[illegible]	[illegible]	[illegible]	[illegible]	[illegible]	[illegible]	[illegible]	[illegible]	[illegible]	[illegible]	[illegible]	[illegible]	[illegible]	[illegible]	[illegible]	[illegible]	[illegible]	[illegible]	[illegible]	[illegible]	[illegible]
	[illegible]	[illegible]	[illegible]	[illegible]	[illegible]	[illegible]	[illegible]	[illegible]	[illegible]	[illegible]	[illegible]	[illegible]	[illegible]	[illegible]	[illegible]	[illegible]	[illegible]	[illegible]	[illegible]	[illegible]	[illegible]	[illegible]
MEATH.																						
[illegible]	[illegible]	[illegible]	[illegible]	[illegible]	[illegible]	[illegible]	[illegible]	[illegible]	[illegible]	[illegible]	[illegible]	[illegible]	[illegible]	[illegible]	[illegible]	[illegible]	[illegible]	[illegible]	[illegible]	[illegible]	[illegible]	[illegible]
[illegible]	[illegible]	[illegible]	[illegible]	[illegible]	[illegible]	[illegible]	[illegible]	[illegible]	[illegible]	[illegible]	[illegible]	[illegible]	[illegible]	[illegible]	[illegible]	[illegible]	[illegible]	[illegible]	[illegible]	[illegible]	[illegible]	[illegible]
[illegible]	[illegible]	[illegible]	[illegible]	[illegible]	[illegible]	[illegible]	[illegible]	[illegible]	—	—	—	—	—	—	[illegible]	[illegible]	[illegible]	[illegible]	[illegible]	[illegible]	[illegible]	[illegible]
[illegible]	[illegible]	[illegible]	[illegible]	[illegible]	[illegible]	[illegible]	[illegible]	[illegible]	[illegible]	[illegible]	[illegible]	[illegible]	[illegible]	[illegible]	[illegible]	[illegible]	—	—	—	—	—	—
[illegible]	[illegible]	[illegible]	[illegible]	[illegible]	[illegible]	[illegible]	[illegible]	[illegible]	[illegible]	[illegible]	[illegible]	[illegible]	[illegible]	[illegible]	[illegible]	[illegible]	—	—	—	—	—	—
[illegible]	[illegible]	[illegible]	[illegible]	[illegible]	[illegible]	[illegible]	[illegible]	[illegible]	[illegible]	[illegible]	[illegible]	[illegible]	[illegible]	[illegible]	[illegible]	[illegible]	[illegible]	[illegible]	[illegible]	[illegible]	[illegible]	[illegible]
	[illegible]	[illegible]	[illegible]	[illegible]	[illegible]	[illegible]	[illegible]	[illegible]	[illegible]	[illegible]	[illegible]	[illegible]	[illegible]	[illegible]	[illegible]	[illegible]	[illegible]	[illegible]	[illegible]	[illegible]	[illegible]	[illegible]
QUEEN'S.																						
[illegible]	[illegible]	[illegible]	[illegible]	[illegible]	[illegible]	[illegible]	[illegible]	[illegible]	[illegible]	[illegible]	[illegible]	[illegible]	[illegible]	[illegible]	[illegible]	[illegible]	[illegible]	[illegible]	[illegible]	[illegible]	[illegible]	[illegible]
[illegible]	—	—	—	—	—	—	—	—	—	—	—	—	—	—	—	—	—	—	—	—	—	—
[illegible]	[illegible]	[illegible]	[illegible]	[illegible]	[illegible]	[illegible]	[illegible]	[illegible]	[illegible]	[illegible]	[illegible]	[illegible]	[illegible]	[illegible]	[illegible]	[illegible]	[illegible]	[illegible]	[illegible]	[illegible]	[illegible]	[illegible]
[illegible]	[illegible]	—	—	—	—	—	—	[illegible]	[illegible]	[illegible]	[illegible]	[illegible]	[illegible]	[illegible]	[illegible]	[illegible]	—	—	—	—	—	—
	[illegible]	[illegible]	[illegible]	[illegible]	[illegible]	[illegible]	[illegible]	[illegible]	[illegible]	[illegible]	[illegible]	[illegible]	[illegible]	[illegible]	[illegible]	[illegible]	[illegible]	[illegible]	[illegible]	[illegible]	[illegible]	[illegible]

Counties and Royal Burghs (Constabulary District).	Hackneys: [illegible] — No.	Price: Highest	Price: Lowest	Hackneys: [illegible] — No.	Price: Highest	Price: Lowest	Half-bred of any breed — No.	Price: Highest	Price: Lowest	Draught: Clydesdale, [illegible] — No.	Price: Highest	Price: Lowest	Draught: Half-bred — No.	Price: Highest	Price: Lowest	[illegible] — No.	Price: Highest	Price: Lowest	Arabs or Eastern Horses — No.	Price: Highest	Price: Lowest	Ponies — No.	Price: Highest	Price: Lowest	Total No. [illegible]
LOUTH.		£ s. d.	£ s. d.		£ s. d.	£ s. d.		£ s. d.	£ s. d.		£ s. d.	£ s. d.		£ s. d.	£ s. d.		£ s. d.	£ s. d.		£ s. d.	£ s. d.		£ s. d.	£ s. d.	
Ardee,	-	—	—	[illegible]	[illegible]	[illegible]	[illegible]	[illegible]	[illegible]	[illegible]	[illegible]	[illegible]	-	—	—	-	—	—	-	—	—	-	—	—	[illegible]
Collon,	-	—	—	-	—	—	-	—	—	[illegible]	[illegible]	[illegible]	[illegible]	[illegible]	[illegible]	-	—	—	-	—	—	-	—	—	[illegible]
Drogheda,	-	—	—	-	—	—	-	—	—	[illegible]	[illegible]	[illegible]	[illegible]	[illegible]	[illegible]	-	—	—	-	—	—	-	—	—	[illegible]
Dundalk,	-	—	—	[illegible]	[illegible]	[illegible]	[illegible]	[illegible]	[illegible]	[illegible]	[illegible]	[illegible]	[illegible]	[illegible]	[illegible]	-	—	—	-	—	—	-	—	—	[illegible]
	-	—	—	[illegible]	[illegible]	[illegible]	[illegible]	[illegible]	[illegible]	[illegible]	[illegible]	[illegible]	[illegible]	[illegible]	[illegible]	-	—	—	-	—	—	-	—	—	[illegible]
MEATH.																									
Athboy,	-	—	—	-	—	—	[illegible]	[illegible]	[illegible]	[illegible]	[illegible]	[illegible]	[illegible]	[illegible]	[illegible]	-	—	—	-	—	—	-	—	—	[illegible]
Dunshaughlin,	-	—	—	-	—	—	-	—	—	-	—	—	[illegible]	[illegible]	[illegible]	-	—	—	-	—	—	-	—	—	[illegible]
Kells,	[illegible]	[illegible]	[illegible]	-	—	—	-	—	—	[illegible]	[illegible]	[illegible]	[illegible]	[illegible]	[illegible]	-	—	—	-	—	—	[illegible]	[illegible]	[illegible]	[illegible]
Navan,	-	—	—	-	—	—	[illegible]	[illegible]	[illegible]	[illegible]	[illegible]	[illegible]	[illegible]	[illegible]	[illegible]	-	—	—	-	—	—	-	—	—	[illegible]
Slane,	-	—	—	-	—	—	-	—	—	[illegible]	[illegible]	[illegible]	[illegible]	[illegible]	[illegible]	-	—	—	[illegible]	[illegible]	[illegible]	[illegible]	[illegible]	[illegible]	[illegible]
Trim,	-	—	—	-	—	—	[illegible]	[illegible]	[illegible]	[illegible]	[illegible]	[illegible]	[illegible]	[illegible]	[illegible]	-	—	—	-	—	—	[illegible]	[illegible]	[illegible]	[illegible]
	[illegible]	[illegible]	[illegible]	-	—	—	[illegible]	[illegible]	[illegible]	[illegible]	[illegible]	[illegible]	[illegible]	[illegible]	[illegible]	-	—	—	[illegible]	[illegible]	[illegible]	[illegible]	[illegible]	[illegible]	[illegible]
QUEEN'S.																									
Abbeyleix,	-	—	—	[illegible]	[illegible]	[illegible]	-	—	—	-	—	—	[illegible]	[illegible]	[illegible]	-	—	—	-	—	—	-	—	—	[illegible]
[illegible]	-	—	—	-	—	—	-	—	—	[illegible]	[illegible]	[illegible]	[illegible]	[illegible]	[illegible]	-	—	—	-	—	—	[illegible]	[illegible]	[illegible]	[illegible]
Maryborough,	-	—	—	-	—	—	[illegible]	[illegible]	[illegible]	[illegible]	[illegible]	[illegible]	[illegible]	[illegible]	[illegible]	-	—	—	-	—	—	[illegible]	[illegible]	[illegible]	[illegible]
[illegible]	-	—	—	-	—	—	[illegible]	[illegible]	[illegible]	-	—	—	[illegible]	[illegible]	[illegible]	-	—	—	-	—	—	-	—	—	[illegible]
	-	—	—	[illegible]	[illegible]	[illegible]	[illegible]	[illegible]	[illegible]	[illegible]	[illegible]	[illegible]	[illegible]	[illegible]	[illegible]	-	—	—	-	—	—	[illegible]	[illegible]	[illegible]	[illegible]

Counties, and Royal Dublin Society's District.	THOROUGHBREDS. — Thoroughbreds entered in Weatherby's Stud Book. — Thoroughbreds Registered by the Royal Dublin Society for the purposes of their Scheme. — No.	Fee, Thoroughbred Mares. Highest.	Fee, Thoroughbred Mares. Lowest.	Fee, Gentlemen's Half-bred Mares. Highest.	Fee, Gentlemen's Half-bred Mares. Lowest.	Fee, Farmers' Half-bred Mares. Highest.	Fee, Farmers' Half-bred Mares. Lowest.	Other Thoroughbreds. — No.	Fee, Thoroughbred Mares. Highest.	Fee, Thoroughbred Mares. Lowest.	Fee, Gentlemen's Half-bred Mares. Highest.	Fee, Gentlemen's Half-bred Mares. Lowest.	Fee, Farmers' Half-bred Mares. Highest.	Fee, Farmers' Half-bred Mares. Lowest.	Total No. of Thoroughbreds.	HUNTER SIRES. — Horses returned as Thoroughbreds, but which do not appear to be entered in Weatherby's Stud Book. — No.	Fee, Thoroughbred Mares. Highest.	Fee, Thoroughbred Mares. Lowest.	Fee, Gentlemen's Half-bred Mares. Highest.	Fee, Gentlemen's Half-bred Mares. Lowest.	Fee, Farmers' Half-bred Mares. Highest.	Fee, Farmers' Half-bred Mares. Lowest.
WESTMEATH.		£ s. d.	£ s. d.	£ s. d.	£ s. d.	£ s. d.	£ s. d.		£ s. d.	£ s. d.	£ s. d.	£ s. d.	£ s. d.	£ s. d.			£ s. d.	£ s. d.	£ s. d.	£ s. d.	£ s. d.	£ s. d.
Ballymore[illegible]	[illegible]	[illegible]	[illegible]	[illegible]	[illegible]	[illegible]	[illegible]	[illegible]	[illegible]	[illegible]	[illegible]	[illegible]	[illegible]	[illegible]	[illegible]	[illegible]	[illegible]	[illegible]	[illegible]	[illegible]	[illegible]	[illegible]
Castlepollard,	[illegible]	[illegible]	[illegible]	[illegible]	[illegible]	[illegible]	[illegible]	[illegible]	[illegible]	[illegible]	[illegible]	[illegible]	[illegible]	[illegible]	[illegible]	[illegible]	[illegible]	[illegible]	[illegible]	[illegible]	[illegible]	[illegible]
Delvin,	[illegible]	[illegible]	[illegible]	[illegible]	[illegible]	[illegible]	[illegible]	-	—	—	—	—	—	—	[illegible]	-	—	—	—	—	—	—
Kilbeggan,	[illegible]	[illegible]	[illegible]	[illegible]	[illegible]	[illegible]	[illegible]	[illegible]	[illegible]	[illegible]	[illegible]	[illegible]	[illegible]	[illegible]	[illegible]	-	—	—	—	—	—	—
Moate,	[illegible]	[illegible]	[illegible]	[illegible]	[illegible]	[illegible]	[illegible]	[illegible]	[illegible]	[illegible]	[illegible]	[illegible]	[illegible]	[illegible]	[illegible]	[illegible]	[illegible]	[illegible]	[illegible]	[illegible]	[illegible]	[illegible]
Mullingar,	-	—	—	—	—	—	—	[illegible]	[illegible]	[illegible]	[illegible]	[illegible]	[illegible]	[illegible]	[illegible]	-	—	—	—	—	—	—
	[illegible]	[illegible]	[illegible]	[illegible]	[illegible]	[illegible]	[illegible]	[illegible]	[illegible]	[illegible]	[illegible]	[illegible]	[illegible]	[illegible]	[illegible]	[illegible]	[illegible]	[illegible]	[illegible]	[illegible]	[illegible]	[illegible]
WEXFORD.																						
Enniscorthy,	[illegible]	[illegible]	[illegible]	[illegible]	[illegible]	[illegible]	[illegible]	[illegible]	[illegible]	[illegible]	[illegible]	[illegible]	[illegible]	[illegible]	[illegible]	[illegible]	[illegible]	[illegible]	[illegible]	[illegible]	[illegible]	[illegible]
Gorey,	[illegible]	[illegible]	[illegible]	[illegible]	[illegible]	[illegible]	[illegible]	[illegible]	[illegible]	[illegible]	[illegible]	[illegible]	[illegible]	[illegible]	[illegible]	[illegible]	[illegible]	[illegible]	[illegible]	[illegible]	[illegible]	[illegible]
New Ross,	-	—	—	—	—	—	—	[illegible]	[illegible]	[illegible]	[illegible]	[illegible]	[illegible]	[illegible]	[illegible]	[illegible]	[illegible]	[illegible]	[illegible]	[illegible]	[illegible]	[illegible]
Taghmon,	-	—	—	—	—	—	—	[illegible]	[illegible]	[illegible]	[illegible]	[illegible]	[illegible]	[illegible]	[illegible]	[illegible]	[illegible]	[illegible]	[illegible]	[illegible]	[illegible]	[illegible]
Wexford,	[illegible]	[illegible]	[illegible]	[illegible]	[illegible]	[illegible]	[illegible]	[illegible]	[illegible]	[illegible]	[illegible]	[illegible]	[illegible]	[illegible]	[illegible]	[illegible]	[illegible]	[illegible]	[illegible]	[illegible]	[illegible]	[illegible]
	[illegible]	[illegible]	[illegible]	[illegible]	[illegible]	[illegible]	[illegible]	[illegible]	[illegible]	[illegible]	[illegible]	[illegible]	[illegible]	[illegible]	[illegible]	[illegible]	[illegible]	[illegible]	[illegible]	[illegible]	[illegible]	[illegible]
WICKLOW.																						
Arklow,	[illegible]	[illegible]	[illegible]	[illegible]	[illegible]	[illegible]	[illegible]	[illegible]	[illegible]	[illegible]	[illegible]	[illegible]	[illegible]	[illegible]	[illegible]	[illegible]	[illegible]	[illegible]	[illegible]	[illegible]	[illegible]	[illegible]
Bray,	[illegible]	[illegible]	[illegible]	[illegible]	[illegible]	[illegible]	[illegible]	-	—	—	—	—	—	—	[illegible]	-	—	—	—	—	—	—
Dunlavin,	-	—	—	—	—	—	—	[illegible]	[illegible]	[illegible]	[illegible]	[illegible]	[illegible]	[illegible]	[illegible]	-	—	—	—	—	—	—
Wicklow,	[illegible]	[illegible]	[illegible]	[illegible]	[illegible]	[illegible]	[illegible]	[illegible]	[illegible]	[illegible]	[illegible]	[illegible]	[illegible]	[illegible]	[illegible]	-	—	—	—	—	—	—
	[illegible]	[illegible]	[illegible]	[illegible]	[illegible]	[illegible]	[illegible]	[illegible]	[illegible]	[illegible]	[illegible]	[illegible]	[illegible]	[illegible]	[illegible]	[illegible]	[illegible]	[illegible]	[illegible]	[illegible]	[illegible]	[illegible]

Counties and Royal Irish Constabulary District.	Hackneys: Registered in the Hackney Stud Book: No.	Fee: Highest	Fee: Lowest	Hackneys: Which do you approve to the Hackney Stud Book: No.	Fee: Highest	Fee: Lowest	Half-bred of any kind: No.	Fee: Highest	Fee: Lowest	Draught: Clydesdale, Yorkshire Coach Horse, Shire, Clydesdale and Suffolk Punch: No.	Fee: Highest	Fee: Lowest	Draught: Half-bred: No.	Fee: Highest	Fee: Lowest	Thoroughbred: No.	Fee: Highest	Fee: Lowest	Arabs or Eastern Horses: No.	Fee: Highest	Fee: Lowest	Ponies: No.	Fee: Highest	Fee: Lowest	Total No. of Mares and Ponies in Constabulary District.
WESTMEATH.		£ s. d.	£ s. d.		£ s. d.	£ s. d.		£ s. d.	£ s. d.		£ s. d.	£ s. d.		£ s. d.	£ s. d.		£ s. d.	£ s. d.		£ s. d.	£ s. d.		£ s. d.	£ s. d.	
[illegible]	[illegible]	[illegible]	[illegible]	[illegible]	[illegible]	[illegible]	[illegible]	[illegible]	[illegible]	[illegible]	[illegible]	[illegible]	[illegible]	[illegible]	[illegible]	[illegible]	[illegible]	[illegible]	[illegible]	[illegible]	[illegible]	[illegible]	[illegible]	[illegible]	[illegible]
Castlepollard,	[illegible]	[illegible]	[illegible]	[illegible]	[illegible]	[illegible]	[illegible]	[illegible]	[illegible]	[illegible]	[illegible]	[illegible]	[illegible]	[illegible]	[illegible]	[illegible]	[illegible]	[illegible]	[illegible]	[illegible]	[illegible]	[illegible]	[illegible]	[illegible]	[illegible]
Delvin,	[illegible]	[illegible]	[illegible]	[illegible]	[illegible]	[illegible]	[illegible]	[illegible]	[illegible]	[illegible]	[illegible]	[illegible]	[illegible]	[illegible]	[illegible]	[illegible]	[illegible]	[illegible]	[illegible]	[illegible]	[illegible]	[illegible]	[illegible]	[illegible]	[illegible]
Kilbeggan,	[illegible]	[illegible]	[illegible]	[illegible]	[illegible]	[illegible]	[illegible]	[illegible]	[illegible]	[illegible]	[illegible]	[illegible]	[illegible]	[illegible]	[illegible]	[illegible]	[illegible]	[illegible]	[illegible]	[illegible]	[illegible]	[illegible]	[illegible]	[illegible]	[illegible]
Moate,	[illegible]	[illegible]	[illegible]	[illegible]	[illegible]	[illegible]	[illegible]	[illegible]	[illegible]	[illegible]	[illegible]	[illegible]	[illegible]	[illegible]	[illegible]	[illegible]	[illegible]	[illegible]	[illegible]	[illegible]	[illegible]	[illegible]	[illegible]	[illegible]	[illegible]
Mullingar,	[illegible]	[illegible]	[illegible]	[illegible]	[illegible]	[illegible]	[illegible]	[illegible]	[illegible]	[illegible]	[illegible]	[illegible]	[illegible]	[illegible]	[illegible]	[illegible]	[illegible]	[illegible]	[illegible]	[illegible]	[illegible]	[illegible]	[illegible]	[illegible]	[illegible]
	[illegible]	[illegible]	[illegible]	[illegible]	[illegible]	[illegible]	[illegible]	[illegible]	[illegible]	[illegible]	[illegible]	[illegible]	[illegible]	[illegible]	[illegible]	[illegible]	[illegible]	[illegible]	[illegible]	[illegible]	[illegible]	[illegible]	[illegible]	[illegible]	[illegible]
WEXFORD.																									
Enniscorthy,	[illegible]	[illegible]	[illegible]	[illegible]	[illegible]	[illegible]	[illegible]	[illegible]	[illegible]	[illegible]	[illegible]	[illegible]	[illegible]	[illegible]	[illegible]	[illegible]	[illegible]	[illegible]	[illegible]	[illegible]	[illegible]	[illegible]	[illegible]	[illegible]	[illegible]
Gorey,	[illegible]	[illegible]	[illegible]	[illegible]	[illegible]	[illegible]	[illegible]	[illegible]	[illegible]	[illegible]	[illegible]	[illegible]	[illegible]	[illegible]	[illegible]	[illegible]	[illegible]	[illegible]	[illegible]	[illegible]	[illegible]	[illegible]	[illegible]	[illegible]	[illegible]
New Ross,	[illegible]	[illegible]	[illegible]	[illegible]	[illegible]	[illegible]	[illegible]	[illegible]	[illegible]	[illegible]	[illegible]	[illegible]	[illegible]	[illegible]	[illegible]	[illegible]	[illegible]	[illegible]	[illegible]	[illegible]	[illegible]	[illegible]	[illegible]	[illegible]	[illegible]
Taghmon,	[illegible]	[illegible]	[illegible]	[illegible]	[illegible]	[illegible]	[illegible]	[illegible]	[illegible]	[illegible]	[illegible]	[illegible]	[illegible]	[illegible]	[illegible]	[illegible]	[illegible]	[illegible]	[illegible]	[illegible]	[illegible]	[illegible]	[illegible]	[illegible]	[illegible]
Wexford,	[illegible]	[illegible]	[illegible]	[illegible]	[illegible]	[illegible]	[illegible]	[illegible]	[illegible]	[illegible]	[illegible]	[illegible]	[illegible]	[illegible]	[illegible]	[illegible]	[illegible]	[illegible]	[illegible]	[illegible]	[illegible]	[illegible]	[illegible]	[illegible]	[illegible]
	[illegible]	[illegible]	[illegible]	[illegible]	[illegible]	[illegible]	[illegible]	[illegible]	[illegible]	[illegible]	[illegible]	[illegible]	[illegible]	[illegible]	[illegible]	[illegible]	[illegible]	[illegible]	[illegible]	[illegible]	[illegible]	[illegible]	[illegible]	[illegible]	[illegible]
WICKLOW.																									
Arklow,	[illegible]	[illegible]	[illegible]	[illegible]	[illegible]	[illegible]	[illegible]	[illegible]	[illegible]	[illegible]	[illegible]	[illegible]	[illegible]	[illegible]	[illegible]	[illegible]	[illegible]	[illegible]	[illegible]	[illegible]	[illegible]	[illegible]	[illegible]	[illegible]	[illegible]
Bray,	[illegible]	[illegible]	[illegible]	[illegible]	[illegible]	[illegible]	[illegible]	[illegible]	[illegible]	[illegible]	[illegible]	[illegible]	[illegible]	[illegible]	[illegible]	[illegible]	[illegible]	[illegible]	[illegible]	[illegible]	[illegible]	[illegible]	[illegible]	[illegible]	[illegible]
Dunlavin,	[illegible]	[illegible]	[illegible]	[illegible]	[illegible]	[illegible]	[illegible]	[illegible]	[illegible]	[illegible]	[illegible]	[illegible]	[illegible]	[illegible]	[illegible]	[illegible]	[illegible]	[illegible]	[illegible]	[illegible]	[illegible]	[illegible]	[illegible]	[illegible]	[illegible]
Wicklow,	[illegible]	[illegible]	[illegible]	[illegible]	[illegible]	[illegible]	[illegible]	[illegible]	[illegible]	[illegible]	[illegible]	[illegible]	[illegible]	[illegible]	[illegible]	[illegible]	[illegible]	[illegible]	[illegible]	[illegible]	[illegible]	[illegible]	[illegible]	[illegible]	[illegible]
	[illegible]	[illegible]	[illegible]	[illegible]	[illegible]	[illegible]	[illegible]	[illegible]	[illegible]	[illegible]	[illegible]	[illegible]	[illegible]	[illegible]	[illegible]	[illegible]	[illegible]	[illegible]	[illegible]	[illegible]	[illegible]	[illegible]	[illegible]	[illegible]	[illegible]

Counties and Royal Irish Constabulary Districts.	Thoroughbreds. Thoroughbreds entered in Weatherby's Stud Book. Thoroughbreds Registered by the Royal Dublin Society for the Purposes of their Scheme. No.	Fee, Thoroughbred Mares. Highest.	Fee, Thoroughbred Mares. Lowest.	Fee, Half-bred Mares. Highest.	Fee, Half-bred Mares. Lowest.	Fee, Farmers' Half-bred Mares. Highest.	Fee, Farmers' Half-bred Mares. Lowest.	Other Thoroughbreds. No.	Fee, Thoroughbred Mares. Highest.	Fee, Thoroughbred Mares. Lowest.	Fee, Half-bred Mares. Highest.	Fee, Half-bred Mares. Lowest.	Fee, Farmers' Half-bred Mares. Highest.	Fee, Farmers' Half-bred Mares. Lowest.	Total No. of Thoroughbreds.	Hunter Sires. Horses returned as Thoroughbreds, but which do not appear to be entered in Weatherby's Stud Book. No.	Fee, Thoroughbred Mares. Highest.	Fee, Thoroughbred Mares. Lowest.	Fee, Half-bred Mares. Highest.	Fee, Half-bred Mares. Lowest.	Fee, Farmers' Half-bred Mares. Highest.	Fee, Farmers' Half-bred Mares. Lowest.
GALWAY. West Riding.		£ s. d.	£ s. d.	£ s. d.	£ s. d.	£ s. d.	£ s. d.		£ s. d.	£ s. d.	£ s. d.	£ s. d.	£ s. d.	£ s. d.			£ s. d.	£ s. d.	£ s. d.	£ s. d.	£ s. d.	£ s. d.
Clifden,	—	—	—	—	—	—	—	—	—	—	—	—	—	—	—	—	—	—	—	—	—	—
[illegible],	—	—	—	—	—	—	—	—	—	—	—	—	—	—	—	—	—	—	—	—	—	—
[illegible],	[illegible]	[illegible]	[illegible]	[illegible]	[illegible]	[illegible]	[illegible]	—	—	—	—	—	—	—	[illegible]	—	—	—	—	—	—	—
Gort,	—	—	—	—	—	—	—	[illegible]	[illegible]	[illegible]	[illegible]	[illegible]	[illegible]	[illegible]	[illegible]	—	—	—	—	—	—	—
Oughterard,	—	—	—	—	—	—	—	—	—	—	—	—	—	—	—	—	—	—	—	—	—	—
[illegible],	[illegible]	[illegible]	[illegible]	[illegible]	[illegible]	[illegible]	[illegible]	—	—	—	—	—	—	—	[illegible]	—	—	—	—	—	—	—
Spiddal,	—	—	—	—	—	—	—	—	—	—	—	—	—	—	—	—	—	—	—	—	—	—
Tuam,	[illegible]	[illegible]	[illegible]	[illegible]	[illegible]	[illegible]	[illegible]	—	—	—	—	—	—	—	[illegible]	—	—	—	—	—	—	—
Galway Town,	—	—	—	—	—	—	—	—	—	—	—	—	—	—	—	—	—	—	—	—	—	—
East Riding.																						
Athenry,	[illegible]	[illegible]	[illegible]	[illegible]	[illegible]	[illegible]	[illegible]	—	—	—	—	—	—	—	[illegible]	[illegible]	[illegible]	[illegible]	[illegible]	[illegible]	[illegible]	[illegible]
Ballinasloe,	[illegible]	[illegible]	[illegible]	[illegible]	[illegible]	[illegible]	[illegible]	—	—	—	—	—	—	—	[illegible]	—	—	—	—	—	—	—
Loughrea,	[illegible]	[illegible]	[illegible]	[illegible]	[illegible]	[illegible]	[illegible]	[illegible]	[illegible]	[illegible]	[illegible]	[illegible]	[illegible]	[illegible]	[illegible]	—	—	—	—	—	—	—
Moylough,	[illegible]	[illegible]	[illegible]	[illegible]	[illegible]	[illegible]	[illegible]	—	—	—	—	—	—	—	[illegible]	[illegible]	[illegible]	[illegible]	[illegible]	[illegible]	[illegible]	[illegible]
Portumna,	—	—	—	—	—	—	—	—	—	—	—	—	—	—	[illegible]	[illegible]	[illegible]	[illegible]	[illegible]	[illegible]	[illegible]	[illegible]
Woodford,	—	—	—	—	—	—	—	[illegible]	[illegible]	[illegible]	[illegible]	[illegible]	[illegible]	[illegible]	[illegible]	—	—	—	—	—	—	—
	[illegible]	[illegible]	[illegible]	[illegible]	[illegible]	[illegible]	[illegible]	[illegible]	[illegible]	[illegible]	[illegible]	[illegible]	[illegible]	[illegible]	[illegible]	[illegible]	[illegible]	[illegible]	[illegible]	[illegible]	[illegible]	[illegible]
LEITRIM.																						
[illegible],	—	—	—	—	—	—	—	—	—	—	—	—	—	—	—	—	—	—	—	—	—	—
Carrick-on-Shannon,	—	—	—	—	—	—	—	—	—	—	—	—	—	—	—	—	—	—	—	—	—	—
[illegible],	—	—	—	—	—	—	—	—	—	—	—	—	—	—	—	—	—	—	—	—	—	—
Manorhamilton,	—	—	—	—	—	—	—	—	—	—	—	—	—	—	—	[illegible]	[illegible]	[illegible]	[illegible]	[illegible]	[illegible]	[illegible]
Mohill,	—	—	—	—	—	—	—	—	—	—	—	—	—	—	—	—	—	—	—	—	—	—
	—	—	—	—	—	—	—	—	—	—	—	—	—	—	—	[illegible]	[illegible]	[illegible]	[illegible]	[illegible]	[illegible]	[illegible]

[illegible]

Thoroughbreds entered in Weatherby's Stud Book.														Horses entered as Thoroughbreds but which do not appear to be entered in Weatherby's Stud Book.						
Thoroughbreds Registered by the Royal Dublin Society for the purposes of their Schemes.						Other Thoroughbreds.							Total No. of Thoroughbreds.							
Fee, Thoroughbred Mares.		Fee, Cart/Half-bred Mares.		Fee, Farmers' Half-bred Mares.		No.	Fee, Thoroughbred Mares.		Fee, Cart/Half-bred Mares.		Fee, Farmers' Half-bred Mares.			No.	Fee, Thoroughbred Mares.		Fee, Cart/Half-bred Mares.		Fee, Farmers' Half-bred Mares.	
Highest.	Lowest.	Highest.	Lowest.	Highest.	Lowest.		Highest.	Lowest.	Highest.	Lowest.	Highest.	Lowest.			Highest.	Lowest.	Highest.	Lowest.	Highest.	Lowest.
£ s. d.	£ s. d.	£ s. d.	£ s. d.	£ s. d.	£ s. d.		£ s. d.	£ s. d.	£ s. d.	£ s. d.	£ s. d.	£ s. d.			£ s. d.	£ s. d.	£ s. d.	£ s. d.	£ s. d.	£ s. d.
—	—	—	—	—	—	—	—	—	—	—	—	—	[illegible]	—	—	—	—	—	—	—
—	—	—	—	—	—	1	[illegible]	[illegible]	[illegible]	[illegible]	[illegible]	[illegible]	1	—	—	—	—	—	—	—
—	—	—	—	—	—	1	[illegible]	[illegible]	[illegible]	[illegible]	[illegible]	[illegible]	1	—	—	—	—	—	—	—
—	—	—	—	—	—	—	—	—	—	—	—	—	—	—	—	—	—	—	—	—
—	—	—	—	—	—	—	—	—	—	—	—	—	—	—	—	—	—	—	—	—
[illegible]	[illegible]	[illegible]	[illegible]	[illegible]	[illegible]	—	—	—	—	—	—	—	1	1	[illegible]	[illegible]	[illegible]	[illegible]	[illegible]	[illegible]
—	—	—	—	—	—	—	—	—	—	—	—	—	—	—	—	—	—	—	—	—
—	—	—	—	—	—	—	—	—	—	—	—	—	—	—	—	—	—	—	—	—
—	—	—	—	—	—	—	—	—	—	—	—	—	—	1	[illegible]	[illegible]	[illegible]	[illegible]	[illegible]	[illegible]
[illegible]	[illegible]	[illegible]	[illegible]	[illegible]	[illegible]	[illegible]	[illegible]	[illegible]	[illegible]	[illegible]	[illegible]	[illegible]	[illegible]	[illegible]	[illegible]	[illegible]	[illegible]	[illegible]	[illegible]	[illegible]
[illegible]	[illegible]	[illegible]	[illegible]	[illegible]	[illegible]	—	—	—	—	—	—	—	1	—	—	—	—	—	—	—
—	—	—	—	—	—	1	[illegible]	[illegible]	[illegible]	[illegible]	[illegible]	[illegible]	1	[illegible]	[illegible]	[illegible]	[illegible]	[illegible]	[illegible]	[illegible]
[illegible]	[illegible]	[illegible]	[illegible]	[illegible]	[illegible]	—	—	—	—	—	—	—	[illegible]	[illegible]	[illegible]	[illegible]	[illegible]	[illegible]	[illegible]	[illegible]
[illegible]	[illegible]	[illegible]	[illegible]	[illegible]	[illegible]	—	—	—	—	—	—	—	[illegible]	[illegible]	[illegible]	[illegible]	[illegible]	[illegible]	[illegible]	[illegible]
[illegible]	[illegible]	[illegible]	[illegible]	[illegible]	[illegible]	[illegible]	[illegible]	[illegible]	[illegible]	[illegible]	[illegible]	[illegible]	[illegible]	[illegible]	[illegible]	[illegible]	[illegible]	[illegible]	[illegible]	[illegible]
[illegible]	[illegible]	[illegible]	[illegible]	[illegible]	[illegible]	[illegible]	[illegible]	[illegible]	[illegible]	[illegible]	[illegible]	[illegible]	[illegible]	[illegible]	[illegible]	[illegible]	[illegible]	[illegible]	[illegible]	[illegible]
[illegible]	[illegible]	[illegible]	[illegible]	[illegible]	[illegible]	[illegible]	[illegible]	[illegible]	[illegible]	[illegible]	[illegible]	[illegible]	[illegible]	[illegible]	[illegible]	[illegible]	[illegible]	[illegible]	[illegible]	[illegible]
[illegible]	[illegible]	[illegible]	[illegible]	[illegible]	[illegible]	[illegible]	[illegible]	[illegible]	[illegible]	[illegible]	[illegible]	[illegible]	[illegible]	[illegible]	—	—	—	—	—	—
—	—	—	—	—	—	[illegible]	[illegible]	[illegible]	[illegible]	[illegible]	[illegible]	[illegible]	[illegible]	[illegible]	[illegible]	[illegible]	[illegible]	[illegible]	[illegible]	[illegible]
[illegible]	[illegible]	[illegible]	[illegible]	[illegible]	[illegible]	[illegible]	[illegible]	[illegible]	[illegible]	[illegible]	[illegible]	[illegible]	[illegible]	[illegible]	[illegible]	[illegible]	[illegible]	[illegible]	[illegible]	[illegible]

[illegible]						[illegible]			[illegible]						[illegible]			[illegible]			[illegible]			[illegible]
[illegible]			[illegible]						[illegible]			[illegible]												
No.	Fee		No.	Fee		No.	Fee		No.	Fee		No.	Fee		No.	Fee		No.	Fee		No.	Fee		
	Highest	Lowest		Highest	Lowest		Highest	Lowest		Highest	Lowest		Highest	Lowest		Highest	Lowest		Highest	Lowest		Highest	Lowest	
[illegible]	[illegible]	[illegible]	[illegible]	[illegible]	[illegible]	[illegible]	[illegible]	[illegible]	[illegible]	[illegible]	[illegible]	[illegible]	[illegible]	[illegible]	[illegible]	[illegible]	[illegible]	[illegible]	[illegible]	[illegible]	[illegible]	[illegible]	[illegible]	[illegible]

[illegible]	[illegible]
CLARE.	
[illegible]	[illegible]
[illegible]	[illegible]
[illegible]	[illegible]
[illegible]	[illegible]
[illegible]	[illegible]
[illegible]	[illegible]
[illegible]	[illegible]
[illegible]	[illegible]
[illegible]	[illegible]
	[illegible]
CORK.	
East Riding.	
[illegible]	[illegible]
[illegible]	[illegible]
[illegible]	[illegible]
[illegible]	[illegible]
[illegible]	[illegible]
[illegible]	[illegible]
[illegible]	[illegible]
[illegible]	[illegible]
[illegible]	[illegible]
[illegible]	[illegible]
[illegible]	[illegible]
[illegible]	[illegible]
[illegible]	[illegible]

[illegible]	[illegible]
CLARE	[illegible]
CORK	[illegible]

Counties, and Royal Irish Constabulary District.	Thoroughbreds. Registered by the Royal Dublin Society: No.	Fee, Thoroughbred Mares: Highest	Fee, Thoroughbred Mares: Lowest	Fee, Gentlemen's Half-bred Mares: Highest	Fee, Gentlemen's Half-bred Mares: Lowest	Fee, Farmers' Half-bred Mares: Highest	Fee, Farmers' Half-bred Mares: Lowest	Other Thoroughbreds: No.	Fee, Thoroughbred Mares: Highest	Fee, Thoroughbred Mares: Lowest	Fee, Gentlemen's Half-bred Mares: Highest	Fee, Gentlemen's Half-bred Mares: Lowest	Fee, Farmers' Half-bred Mares: Highest	Fee, Farmers' Half-bred Mares: Lowest	Total No. of Thoroughbreds	Hunter Breed: No.	Fee, Thoroughbred Mares: Highest	Fee, Thoroughbred Mares: Lowest	Fee, Gentlemen's Half-bred Mares: Highest	Fee, Gentlemen's Half-bred Mares: Lowest	Fee, Farmers' Half-bred Mares: Highest	Fee, Farmers' Half-bred Mares: Lowest
[illegible]—continued. [illegible]		£ s. d.	£ s. d.	£ s. d.	£ s. d.	£ s. d.	£ s. d.		£ s. d.	£ s. d.	£ s. d.	£ s. d.	£ s. d.	£ s. d.			£ s. d.	£ s. d.	£ s. d.	£ s. d.	£ s. d.	£ s. d.
[illegible]	1	[illegible]	[illegible]	[illegible]	[illegible]	[illegible]	[illegible]	–	–	–	–	–	–	–	1	1	[illegible]	[illegible]	[illegible]	[illegible]	[illegible]	[illegible]
[illegible]	–	–	–	–	–	–	–	–	–	–	–	–	–	–	–	–	–	–	–	–	–	–
[illegible]	–	–	–	–	–	–	–	–	–	–	–	–	–	–	–	–	–	–	–	–	–	–
[illegible]	–	–	–	–	–	–	–	1	[illegible]	[illegible]	[illegible]	[illegible]	[illegible]	[illegible]	1	1	[illegible]	[illegible]	[illegible]	[illegible]	[illegible]	[illegible]
[illegible]	–	–	–	–	–	–	–	–	–	–	–	–	–	–	–	1	[illegible]	[illegible]	[illegible]	[illegible]	[illegible]	[illegible]
[illegible]	–	–	–	–	–	–	–	2	[illegible]	[illegible]	[illegible]	[illegible]	[illegible]	[illegible]	2	–	–	–	–	–	–	–
[illegible]	–	–	–	–	–	–	–	–	–	–	–	–	–	–	–	[illegible]	[illegible]	[illegible]	[illegible]	[illegible]	[illegible]	[illegible]
[illegible]	[illegible]	[illegible]	[illegible]	[illegible]	[illegible]	[illegible]	[illegible]	–	–	–	–	–	–	–	[illegible]	[illegible]	[illegible]	[illegible]	[illegible]	[illegible]	[illegible]	[illegible]
[illegible]	–	–	–	–	–	–	–	–	–	–	–	–	–	–	–	1	[illegible]	[illegible]	[illegible]	[illegible]	[illegible]	[illegible]
	[illegible]	[illegible]	[illegible]	[illegible]	[illegible]	[illegible]	[illegible]	[illegible]	[illegible]	[illegible]	[illegible]	[illegible]	[illegible]	[illegible]	[illegible]	[illegible]	[illegible]	[illegible]	[illegible]	[illegible]	[illegible]	[illegible]
[illegible].																						
[illegible]	–	–	–	–	–	–	–	–	–	–	–	–	–	–	–	–	–	–	–	–	–	–
[illegible]	–	–	–	–	–	–	–	1	[illegible]	[illegible]	[illegible]	[illegible]	[illegible]	[illegible]	1	1	[illegible]	[illegible]	[illegible]	[illegible]	[illegible]	[illegible]
[illegible]	–	–	–	–	–	–	–	–	–	–	–	–	–	–	–	–	–	–	–	–	–	–
[illegible]	–	–	–	–	–	–	–	–	–	–	–	–	–	–	–	–	–	–	–	–	–	–
[illegible]	–	–	–	–	–	–	–	1	[illegible]	[illegible]	[illegible]	[illegible]	[illegible]	[illegible]	1	1	[illegible]	[illegible]	[illegible]	[illegible]	[illegible]	[illegible]
[illegible]	1	[illegible]	[illegible]	[illegible]	[illegible]	[illegible]	[illegible]	1	[illegible]	[illegible]	[illegible]	[illegible]	[illegible]	[illegible]	2	1	[illegible]	[illegible]	[illegible]	[illegible]	[illegible]	[illegible]
[illegible]	–	–	–	–	–	–	–	–	–	–	–	–	–	–	–	1	[illegible]	[illegible]	[illegible]	[illegible]	[illegible]	[illegible]
[illegible]	[illegible]	[illegible]	[illegible]	[illegible]	[illegible]	[illegible]	[illegible]	–	–	–	–	–	–	–	[illegible]	–	–	–	–	–	–	–
	[illegible]	[illegible]	[illegible]	[illegible]	[illegible]	[illegible]	[illegible]	[illegible]	[illegible]	[illegible]	[illegible]	[illegible]	[illegible]	[illegible]	[illegible]	[illegible]	[illegible]	[illegible]	[illegible]	[illegible]	[illegible]	[illegible]

[illegible]	No.	Fees. Highest	Fees. Lowest	No.	Fees. Highest	Fees. Lowest	No.	Fees. Highest	Fees. Lowest	No.	Fees. Highest	Fees. Lowest	No.	Fees. Highest	Fees. Lowest	No.	Fees. Highest	Fees. Lowest	No.	Fees. Highest	Fees. Lowest	No.	Fees. Highest	Fees. Lowest	[illegible]
[illegible]		[illegible]	[illegible]		[illegible]	[illegible]		[illegible]	[illegible]		[illegible]	[illegible]		[illegible]	[illegible]		[illegible]	[illegible]		[illegible]	[illegible]		[illegible]	[illegible]	
[illegible]	[illegible]	[illegible]	[illegible]	[illegible]	[illegible]	[illegible]	[illegible]	[illegible]	[illegible]	[illegible]	[illegible]	[illegible]	[illegible]	[illegible]	[illegible]	[illegible]	[illegible]	[illegible]	[illegible]	[illegible]	[illegible]	[illegible]	[illegible]	[illegible]	[illegible]
[illegible]	[illegible]	[illegible]	[illegible]	[illegible]	[illegible]	[illegible]	[illegible]	[illegible]	[illegible]	[illegible]	[illegible]	[illegible]	[illegible]	[illegible]	[illegible]	[illegible]	[illegible]	[illegible]	[illegible]	[illegible]	[illegible]	[illegible]	[illegible]	[illegible]	[illegible]
[illegible]	[illegible]	[illegible]	[illegible]	[illegible]	[illegible]	[illegible]	[illegible]	[illegible]	[illegible]	[illegible]	[illegible]	[illegible]	[illegible]	[illegible]	[illegible]	[illegible]	[illegible]	[illegible]	[illegible]	[illegible]	[illegible]	[illegible]	[illegible]	[illegible]	[illegible]
[illegible]	[illegible]	[illegible]	[illegible]	[illegible]	[illegible]	[illegible]	[illegible]	[illegible]	[illegible]	[illegible]	[illegible]	[illegible]	[illegible]	[illegible]	[illegible]	[illegible]	[illegible]	[illegible]	[illegible]	[illegible]	[illegible]	[illegible]	[illegible]	[illegible]	[illegible]
[illegible]	[illegible]	[illegible]	[illegible]	[illegible]	[illegible]	[illegible]	[illegible]	[illegible]	[illegible]	[illegible]	[illegible]	[illegible]	[illegible]	[illegible]	[illegible]	[illegible]	[illegible]	[illegible]	[illegible]	[illegible]	[illegible]	[illegible]	[illegible]	[illegible]	[illegible]
[illegible]	[illegible]	[illegible]	[illegible]	[illegible]	[illegible]	[illegible]	[illegible]	[illegible]	[illegible]	[illegible]	[illegible]	[illegible]	[illegible]	[illegible]	[illegible]	[illegible]	[illegible]	[illegible]	[illegible]	[illegible]	[illegible]	[illegible]	[illegible]	[illegible]	[illegible]
[illegible]	[illegible]	[illegible]	[illegible]	[illegible]	[illegible]	[illegible]	[illegible]	[illegible]	[illegible]	[illegible]	[illegible]	[illegible]	[illegible]	[illegible]	[illegible]	[illegible]	[illegible]	[illegible]	[illegible]	[illegible]	[illegible]	[illegible]	[illegible]	[illegible]	[illegible]
[illegible]	[illegible]	[illegible]	[illegible]	[illegible]	[illegible]	[illegible]	[illegible]	[illegible]	[illegible]	[illegible]	[illegible]	[illegible]	[illegible]	[illegible]	[illegible]	[illegible]	[illegible]	[illegible]	[illegible]	[illegible]	[illegible]	[illegible]	[illegible]	[illegible]	[illegible]
[illegible]	[illegible]	[illegible]	[illegible]	[illegible]	[illegible]	[illegible]	[illegible]	[illegible]	[illegible]	[illegible]	[illegible]	[illegible]	[illegible]	[illegible]	[illegible]	[illegible]	[illegible]	[illegible]	[illegible]	[illegible]	[illegible]	[illegible]	[illegible]	[illegible]	[illegible]
	[illegible]	[illegible]	[illegible]	[illegible]	[illegible]	[illegible]	[illegible]	[illegible]	[illegible]	[illegible]	[illegible]	[illegible]	[illegible]	[illegible]	[illegible]	[illegible]	[illegible]	[illegible]	[illegible]	[illegible]	[illegible]	[illegible]	[illegible]	[illegible]	[illegible]
[illegible]																									
[illegible]	[illegible]	[illegible]	[illegible]	[illegible]	[illegible]	[illegible]	[illegible]	[illegible]	[illegible]	[illegible]	[illegible]	[illegible]	[illegible]	[illegible]	[illegible]	[illegible]	[illegible]	[illegible]	[illegible]	[illegible]	[illegible]	[illegible]	[illegible]	[illegible]	[illegible]
[illegible]	[illegible]	[illegible]	[illegible]	[illegible]	[illegible]	[illegible]	[illegible]	[illegible]	[illegible]	[illegible]	[illegible]	[illegible]	[illegible]	[illegible]	[illegible]	[illegible]	[illegible]	[illegible]	[illegible]	[illegible]	[illegible]	[illegible]	[illegible]	[illegible]	[illegible]
[illegible]	[illegible]	[illegible]	[illegible]	[illegible]	[illegible]	[illegible]	[illegible]	[illegible]	[illegible]	[illegible]	[illegible]	[illegible]	[illegible]	[illegible]	[illegible]	[illegible]	[illegible]	[illegible]	[illegible]	[illegible]	[illegible]	[illegible]	[illegible]	[illegible]	[illegible]
[illegible]	[illegible]	[illegible]	[illegible]	[illegible]	[illegible]	[illegible]	[illegible]	[illegible]	[illegible]	[illegible]	[illegible]	[illegible]	[illegible]	[illegible]	[illegible]	[illegible]	[illegible]	[illegible]	[illegible]	[illegible]	[illegible]	[illegible]	[illegible]	[illegible]	[illegible]
[illegible]	[illegible]	[illegible]	[illegible]	[illegible]	[illegible]	[illegible]	[illegible]	[illegible]	[illegible]	[illegible]	[illegible]	[illegible]	[illegible]	[illegible]	[illegible]	[illegible]	[illegible]	[illegible]	[illegible]	[illegible]	[illegible]	[illegible]	[illegible]	[illegible]	[illegible]
[illegible]	[illegible]	[illegible]	[illegible]	[illegible]	[illegible]	[illegible]	[illegible]	[illegible]	[illegible]	[illegible]	[illegible]	[illegible]	[illegible]	[illegible]	[illegible]	[illegible]	[illegible]	[illegible]	[illegible]	[illegible]	[illegible]	[illegible]	[illegible]	[illegible]	[illegible]
[illegible]	[illegible]	[illegible]	[illegible]	[illegible]	[illegible]	[illegible]	[illegible]	[illegible]	[illegible]	[illegible]	[illegible]	[illegible]	[illegible]	[illegible]	[illegible]	[illegible]	[illegible]	[illegible]	[illegible]	[illegible]	[illegible]	[illegible]	[illegible]	[illegible]	[illegible]
[illegible]	[illegible]	[illegible]	[illegible]	[illegible]	[illegible]	[illegible]	[illegible]	[illegible]	[illegible]	[illegible]	[illegible]	[illegible]	[illegible]	[illegible]	[illegible]	[illegible]	[illegible]	[illegible]	[illegible]	[illegible]	[illegible]	[illegible]	[illegible]	[illegible]	[illegible]
	[illegible]	[illegible]	[illegible]	[illegible]	[illegible]	[illegible]	[illegible]	[illegible]	[illegible]	[illegible]	[illegible]	[illegible]	[illegible]	[illegible]	[illegible]	[illegible]	[illegible]	[illegible]	[illegible]	[illegible]	[illegible]	[illegible]	[illegible]	[illegible]	[illegible]

[illegible]	No.	Highest	Lowest	Highest	Lowest	Highest	Lowest	No.	Highest	Lowest	Highest	Lowest	Highest	Lowest	[illegible]	No.	Highest	Lowest	Highest	Lowest	Highest	Lowest
LIMERICK.																						
[illegible]	[illegible]	[illegible]	[illegible]	[illegible]	[illegible]	[illegible]	[illegible]	[illegible]	[illegible]	[illegible]	[illegible]	[illegible]	[illegible]	[illegible]	[illegible]	[illegible]	[illegible]	[illegible]	[illegible]	[illegible]	[illegible]	[illegible]
[illegible]	[illegible]	[illegible]	[illegible]	[illegible]	[illegible]	[illegible]	[illegible]	[illegible]	[illegible]	[illegible]	[illegible]	[illegible]	[illegible]	[illegible]	[illegible]	[illegible]	[illegible]	[illegible]	[illegible]	[illegible]	[illegible]	[illegible]
[illegible]	[illegible]	[illegible]	[illegible]	[illegible]	[illegible]	[illegible]	[illegible]	[illegible]	[illegible]	[illegible]	[illegible]	[illegible]	[illegible]	[illegible]	[illegible]	[illegible]	[illegible]	[illegible]	[illegible]	[illegible]	[illegible]	[illegible]
[illegible]	[illegible]	[illegible]	[illegible]	[illegible]	[illegible]	[illegible]	[illegible]	[illegible]	[illegible]	[illegible]	[illegible]	[illegible]	[illegible]	[illegible]	[illegible]	[illegible]	[illegible]	[illegible]	[illegible]	[illegible]	[illegible]	[illegible]
[illegible]	[illegible]	[illegible]	[illegible]	[illegible]	[illegible]	[illegible]	[illegible]	[illegible]	[illegible]	[illegible]	[illegible]	[illegible]	[illegible]	[illegible]	[illegible]	[illegible]	[illegible]	[illegible]	[illegible]	[illegible]	[illegible]	[illegible]
[illegible]	[illegible]	[illegible]	[illegible]	[illegible]	[illegible]	[illegible]	[illegible]	[illegible]	[illegible]	[illegible]	[illegible]	[illegible]	[illegible]	[illegible]	[illegible]	[illegible]	[illegible]	[illegible]	[illegible]	[illegible]	[illegible]	[illegible]
[illegible]	[illegible]	[illegible]	[illegible]	[illegible]	[illegible]	[illegible]	[illegible]	[illegible]	[illegible]	[illegible]	[illegible]	[illegible]	[illegible]	[illegible]	[illegible]	[illegible]	[illegible]	[illegible]	[illegible]	[illegible]	[illegible]	[illegible]
[illegible]	[illegible]	[illegible]	[illegible]	[illegible]	[illegible]	[illegible]	[illegible]	[illegible]	[illegible]	[illegible]	[illegible]	[illegible]	[illegible]	[illegible]	[illegible]	[illegible]	[illegible]	[illegible]	[illegible]	[illegible]	[illegible]	[illegible]
	[illegible]	[illegible]	[illegible]	[illegible]	[illegible]	[illegible]	[illegible]	[illegible]	[illegible]	[illegible]	[illegible]	[illegible]	[illegible]	[illegible]	[illegible]	[illegible]	[illegible]	[illegible]	[illegible]	[illegible]	[illegible]	[illegible]
TIPPERARY.																						
North Riding.																						
[illegible]	[illegible]	[illegible]	[illegible]	[illegible]	[illegible]	[illegible]	[illegible]	[illegible]	[illegible]	[illegible]	[illegible]	[illegible]	[illegible]	[illegible]	[illegible]	[illegible]	[illegible]	[illegible]	[illegible]	[illegible]	[illegible]	[illegible]
[illegible]	[illegible]	[illegible]	[illegible]	[illegible]	[illegible]	[illegible]	[illegible]	[illegible]	[illegible]	[illegible]	[illegible]	[illegible]	[illegible]	[illegible]	[illegible]	[illegible]	[illegible]	[illegible]	[illegible]	[illegible]	[illegible]	[illegible]
[illegible]	[illegible]	[illegible]	[illegible]	[illegible]	[illegible]	[illegible]	[illegible]	[illegible]	[illegible]	[illegible]	[illegible]	[illegible]	[illegible]	[illegible]	[illegible]	[illegible]	[illegible]	[illegible]	[illegible]	[illegible]	[illegible]	[illegible]
[illegible]	[illegible]	[illegible]	[illegible]	[illegible]	[illegible]	[illegible]	[illegible]	[illegible]	[illegible]	[illegible]	[illegible]	[illegible]	[illegible]	[illegible]	[illegible]	[illegible]	[illegible]	[illegible]	[illegible]	[illegible]	[illegible]	[illegible]
[illegible]	[illegible]	[illegible]	[illegible]	[illegible]	[illegible]	[illegible]	[illegible]	[illegible]	[illegible]	[illegible]	[illegible]	[illegible]	[illegible]	[illegible]	[illegible]	[illegible]	[illegible]	[illegible]	[illegible]	[illegible]	[illegible]	[illegible]
[illegible]	[illegible]	[illegible]	[illegible]	[illegible]	[illegible]	[illegible]	[illegible]	[illegible]	[illegible]	[illegible]	[illegible]	[illegible]	[illegible]	[illegible]	[illegible]	[illegible]	[illegible]	[illegible]	[illegible]	[illegible]	[illegible]	[illegible]
[illegible]	[illegible]	[illegible]	[illegible]	[illegible]	[illegible]	[illegible]	[illegible]	[illegible]	[illegible]	[illegible]	[illegible]	[illegible]	[illegible]	[illegible]	[illegible]	[illegible]	[illegible]	[illegible]	[illegible]	[illegible]	[illegible]	[illegible]

Counties and Royal Irish Constabulary Districts	Thoroughbreds.						Half-bred [illegible]			Agricultural.						[illegible]			[illegible]			Ponies.			Total No. of Stallions and Ponies in Constabulary Districts.
	[illegible]			[illegible]						[illegible]			Half-bred.												
	No.	Fee. Highest.	Fee. Lowest.	No.	Fee. Highest.	Fee. Lowest.	No.	Fee. Highest.	Fee. Lowest.	No.	Fee. Highest.	Fee. Lowest.	No.	Fee. Highest.	Fee. Lowest.	No.	Fee. Highest.	Fee. Lowest.	No.	Fee. Highest.	Fee. Lowest.	No.	Fee. Highest.	Fee. Lowest.	
CORK—continued.																									
WEST RIDING.		£ s. d.	£ s. d.		£ s. d.	£ s. d.		£ s. d.	£ s. d.		£ s. d.	£ s. d.		£ s. d.	£ s. d.		£ s. d.	£ s. d.		£ s. d.	£ s. d.		£ s. d.	£ s. d.	
[illegible]	[illegible]	[illegible]	[illegible]	[illegible]	[illegible]	[illegible]	[illegible]	[illegible]	[illegible]	[illegible]	[illegible]	[illegible]	[illegible]	[illegible]	[illegible]	[illegible]	[illegible]	[illegible]	[illegible]	[illegible]	[illegible]	[illegible]	[illegible]	[illegible]	[illegible]
[illegible]	[illegible]	[illegible]	[illegible]	[illegible]	[illegible]	[illegible]	[illegible]	[illegible]	[illegible]	[illegible]	[illegible]	[illegible]	[illegible]	[illegible]	[illegible]	[illegible]	[illegible]	[illegible]	[illegible]	[illegible]	[illegible]	[illegible]	[illegible]	[illegible]	[illegible]
[illegible]	[illegible]	[illegible]	[illegible]	[illegible]	[illegible]	[illegible]	[illegible]	[illegible]	[illegible]	[illegible]	[illegible]	[illegible]	[illegible]	[illegible]	[illegible]	[illegible]	[illegible]	[illegible]	[illegible]	[illegible]	[illegible]	[illegible]	[illegible]	[illegible]	[illegible]
[illegible]	[illegible]	[illegible]	[illegible]	[illegible]	[illegible]	[illegible]	[illegible]	[illegible]	[illegible]	[illegible]	[illegible]	[illegible]	[illegible]	[illegible]	[illegible]	[illegible]	[illegible]	[illegible]	[illegible]	[illegible]	[illegible]	[illegible]	[illegible]	[illegible]	[illegible]
[illegible]	[illegible]	[illegible]	[illegible]	[illegible]	[illegible]	[illegible]	[illegible]	[illegible]	[illegible]	[illegible]	[illegible]	[illegible]	[illegible]	[illegible]	[illegible]	[illegible]	[illegible]	[illegible]	[illegible]	[illegible]	[illegible]	[illegible]	[illegible]	[illegible]	[illegible]
[illegible]	[illegible]	[illegible]	[illegible]	[illegible]	[illegible]	[illegible]	[illegible]	[illegible]	[illegible]	[illegible]	[illegible]	[illegible]	[illegible]	[illegible]	[illegible]	[illegible]	[illegible]	[illegible]	[illegible]	[illegible]	[illegible]	[illegible]	[illegible]	[illegible]	[illegible]
[illegible]	[illegible]	[illegible]	[illegible]	[illegible]	[illegible]	[illegible]	[illegible]	[illegible]	[illegible]	[illegible]	[illegible]	[illegible]	[illegible]	[illegible]	[illegible]	[illegible]	[illegible]	[illegible]	[illegible]	[illegible]	[illegible]	[illegible]	[illegible]	[illegible]	[illegible]
[illegible]	[illegible]	[illegible]	[illegible]	[illegible]	[illegible]	[illegible]	[illegible]	[illegible]	[illegible]	[illegible]	[illegible]	[illegible]	[illegible]	[illegible]	[illegible]	[illegible]	[illegible]	[illegible]	[illegible]	[illegible]	[illegible]	[illegible]	[illegible]	[illegible]	[illegible]
[illegible]	[illegible]	[illegible]	[illegible]	[illegible]	[illegible]	[illegible]	[illegible]	[illegible]	[illegible]	[illegible]	[illegible]	[illegible]	[illegible]	[illegible]	[illegible]	[illegible]	[illegible]	[illegible]	[illegible]	[illegible]	[illegible]	[illegible]	[illegible]	[illegible]	[illegible]
	[illegible]	[illegible]	[illegible]	[illegible]	[illegible]	[illegible]	[illegible]	[illegible]	[illegible]	[illegible]	[illegible]	[illegible]	[illegible]	[illegible]	[illegible]	[illegible]	[illegible]	[illegible]	[illegible]	[illegible]	[illegible]	[illegible]	[illegible]	[illegible]	[illegible]
KERRY.																									
[illegible]	[illegible]	[illegible]	[illegible]	[illegible]	[illegible]	[illegible]	[illegible]	[illegible]	[illegible]	[illegible]	[illegible]	[illegible]	[illegible]	[illegible]	[illegible]	[illegible]	[illegible]	[illegible]	[illegible]	[illegible]	[illegible]	[illegible]	[illegible]	[illegible]	[illegible]
[illegible]	[illegible]	[illegible]	[illegible]	[illegible]	[illegible]	[illegible]	[illegible]	[illegible]	[illegible]	[illegible]	[illegible]	[illegible]	[illegible]	[illegible]	[illegible]	[illegible]	[illegible]	[illegible]	[illegible]	[illegible]	[illegible]	[illegible]	[illegible]	[illegible]	[illegible]
[illegible]	[illegible]	[illegible]	[illegible]	[illegible]	[illegible]	[illegible]	[illegible]	[illegible]	[illegible]	[illegible]	[illegible]	[illegible]	[illegible]	[illegible]	[illegible]	[illegible]	[illegible]	[illegible]	[illegible]	[illegible]	[illegible]	[illegible]	[illegible]	[illegible]	[illegible]
[illegible]	[illegible]	[illegible]	[illegible]	[illegible]	[illegible]	[illegible]	[illegible]	[illegible]	[illegible]	[illegible]	[illegible]	[illegible]	[illegible]	[illegible]	[illegible]	[illegible]	[illegible]	[illegible]	[illegible]	[illegible]	[illegible]	[illegible]	[illegible]	[illegible]	[illegible]
[illegible]	[illegible]	[illegible]	[illegible]	[illegible]	[illegible]	[illegible]	[illegible]	[illegible]	[illegible]	[illegible]	[illegible]	[illegible]	[illegible]	[illegible]	[illegible]	[illegible]	[illegible]	[illegible]	[illegible]	[illegible]	[illegible]	[illegible]	[illegible]	[illegible]	[illegible]
[illegible]	[illegible]	[illegible]	[illegible]	[illegible]	[illegible]	[illegible]	[illegible]	[illegible]	[illegible]	[illegible]	[illegible]	[illegible]	[illegible]	[illegible]	[illegible]	[illegible]	[illegible]	[illegible]	[illegible]	[illegible]	[illegible]	[illegible]	[illegible]	[illegible]	[illegible]
[illegible]	[illegible]	[illegible]	[illegible]	[illegible]	[illegible]	[illegible]	[illegible]	[illegible]	[illegible]	[illegible]	[illegible]	[illegible]	[illegible]	[illegible]	[illegible]	[illegible]	[illegible]	[illegible]	[illegible]	[illegible]	[illegible]	[illegible]	[illegible]	[illegible]	[illegible]
[illegible]	[illegible]	[illegible]	[illegible]	[illegible]	[illegible]	[illegible]	[illegible]	[illegible]	[illegible]	[illegible]	[illegible]	[illegible]	[illegible]	[illegible]	[illegible]	[illegible]	[illegible]	[illegible]	[illegible]	[illegible]	[illegible]	[illegible]	[illegible]	[illegible]	[illegible]
	[illegible]	[illegible]	[illegible]	[illegible]	[illegible]	[illegible]	[illegible]	[illegible]	[illegible]	[illegible]	[illegible]	[illegible]	[illegible]	[illegible]	[illegible]	[illegible]	[illegible]	[illegible]	[illegible]	[illegible]	[illegible]	[illegible]	[illegible]	[illegible]	[illegible]

[illegible]	[illegible]
Athy	[illegible]
Naas	[illegible]
Kildare	[illegible]
[illegible]	[illegible]
[illegible]	[illegible]
[illegible]	[illegible]
[illegible]	[illegible]
Total	[illegible]
TIPPERARY.	
North Riding.	
[illegible]	[illegible]
[illegible]	[illegible]
[illegible]	[illegible]
[illegible]	[illegible]
[illegible]	[illegible]
[illegible]	[illegible]
[illegible]	[illegible]

[illegible]	HACKNEYS: [illegible]			HACKNEYS: [illegible]			[illegible]			[illegible]: [illegible]			[illegible]: [illegible]			[illegible]			[illegible]			[illegible]			[illegible]
	No.	Highest	Lowest	No.	Highest	Lowest	No.	Highest	Lowest	No.	Highest	Lowest	No.	Highest	Lowest	No.	Highest	Lowest	No.	Highest	Lowest	No.	Highest	Lowest	
LIMERICK.																									
[illegible]	[illegible]	[illegible]	[illegible]	[illegible]	[illegible]	[illegible]	[illegible]	[illegible]	[illegible]	[illegible]	[illegible]	[illegible]	[illegible]	[illegible]	[illegible]	[illegible]	[illegible]	[illegible]	[illegible]	[illegible]	[illegible]	[illegible]	[illegible]	[illegible]	[illegible]
[illegible]	[illegible]	[illegible]	[illegible]	[illegible]	[illegible]	[illegible]	[illegible]	[illegible]	[illegible]	[illegible]	[illegible]	[illegible]	[illegible]	[illegible]	[illegible]	[illegible]	[illegible]	[illegible]	[illegible]	[illegible]	[illegible]	[illegible]	[illegible]	[illegible]	[illegible]
[illegible]	[illegible]	[illegible]	[illegible]	[illegible]	[illegible]	[illegible]	[illegible]	[illegible]	[illegible]	[illegible]	[illegible]	[illegible]	[illegible]	[illegible]	[illegible]	[illegible]	[illegible]	[illegible]	[illegible]	[illegible]	[illegible]	[illegible]	[illegible]	[illegible]	[illegible]
[illegible]	[illegible]	[illegible]	[illegible]	[illegible]	[illegible]	[illegible]	[illegible]	[illegible]	[illegible]	[illegible]	[illegible]	[illegible]	[illegible]	[illegible]	[illegible]	[illegible]	[illegible]	[illegible]	[illegible]	[illegible]	[illegible]	[illegible]	[illegible]	[illegible]	[illegible]
[illegible]	[illegible]	[illegible]	[illegible]	[illegible]	[illegible]	[illegible]	[illegible]	[illegible]	[illegible]	[illegible]	[illegible]	[illegible]	[illegible]	[illegible]	[illegible]	[illegible]	[illegible]	[illegible]	[illegible]	[illegible]	[illegible]	[illegible]	[illegible]	[illegible]	[illegible]
[illegible]	[illegible]	[illegible]	[illegible]	[illegible]	[illegible]	[illegible]	[illegible]	[illegible]	[illegible]	[illegible]	[illegible]	[illegible]	[illegible]	[illegible]	[illegible]	[illegible]	[illegible]	[illegible]	[illegible]	[illegible]	[illegible]	[illegible]	[illegible]	[illegible]	[illegible]
[illegible]	[illegible]	[illegible]	[illegible]	[illegible]	[illegible]	[illegible]	[illegible]	[illegible]	[illegible]	[illegible]	[illegible]	[illegible]	[illegible]	[illegible]	[illegible]	[illegible]	[illegible]	[illegible]	[illegible]	[illegible]	[illegible]	[illegible]	[illegible]	[illegible]	[illegible]
[illegible]	[illegible]	[illegible]	[illegible]	[illegible]	[illegible]	[illegible]	[illegible]	[illegible]	[illegible]	[illegible]	[illegible]	[illegible]	[illegible]	[illegible]	[illegible]	[illegible]	[illegible]	[illegible]	[illegible]	[illegible]	[illegible]	[illegible]	[illegible]	[illegible]	[illegible]
	[illegible]	[illegible]	[illegible]	[illegible]	[illegible]	[illegible]	[illegible]	[illegible]	[illegible]	[illegible]	[illegible]	[illegible]	[illegible]	[illegible]	[illegible]	[illegible]	[illegible]	[illegible]	[illegible]	[illegible]	[illegible]	[illegible]	[illegible]	[illegible]	[illegible]
TIPPERARY.																									
[illegible]																									
[illegible]	[illegible]	[illegible]	[illegible]	[illegible]	[illegible]	[illegible]	[illegible]	[illegible]	[illegible]	[illegible]	[illegible]	[illegible]	[illegible]	[illegible]	[illegible]	[illegible]	[illegible]	[illegible]	[illegible]	[illegible]	[illegible]	[illegible]	[illegible]	[illegible]	[illegible]
[illegible]	[illegible]	[illegible]	[illegible]	[illegible]	[illegible]	[illegible]	[illegible]	[illegible]	[illegible]	[illegible]	[illegible]	[illegible]	[illegible]	[illegible]	[illegible]	[illegible]	[illegible]	[illegible]	[illegible]	[illegible]	[illegible]	[illegible]	[illegible]	[illegible]	[illegible]
[illegible]	[illegible]	[illegible]	[illegible]	[illegible]	[illegible]	[illegible]	[illegible]	[illegible]	[illegible]	[illegible]	[illegible]	[illegible]	[illegible]	[illegible]	[illegible]	[illegible]	[illegible]	[illegible]	[illegible]	[illegible]	[illegible]	[illegible]	[illegible]	[illegible]	[illegible]
[illegible]	[illegible]	[illegible]	[illegible]	[illegible]	[illegible]	[illegible]	[illegible]	[illegible]	[illegible]	[illegible]	[illegible]	[illegible]	[illegible]	[illegible]	[illegible]	[illegible]	[illegible]	[illegible]	[illegible]	[illegible]	[illegible]	[illegible]	[illegible]	[illegible]	[illegible]
[illegible]	[illegible]	[illegible]	[illegible]	[illegible]	[illegible]	[illegible]	[illegible]	[illegible]	[illegible]	[illegible]	[illegible]	[illegible]	[illegible]	[illegible]	[illegible]	[illegible]	[illegible]	[illegible]	[illegible]	[illegible]	[illegible]	[illegible]	[illegible]	[illegible]	[illegible]
[illegible]	[illegible]	[illegible]	[illegible]	[illegible]	[illegible]	[illegible]	[illegible]	[illegible]	[illegible]	[illegible]	[illegible]	[illegible]	[illegible]	[illegible]	[illegible]	[illegible]	[illegible]	[illegible]	[illegible]	[illegible]	[illegible]	[illegible]	[illegible]	[illegible]	[illegible]
[illegible]	[illegible]	[illegible]	[illegible]	[illegible]	[illegible]	[illegible]	[illegible]	[illegible]	[illegible]	[illegible]	[illegible]	[illegible]	[illegible]	[illegible]	[illegible]	[illegible]	[illegible]	[illegible]	[illegible]	[illegible]	[illegible]	[illegible]	[illegible]	[illegible]	[illegible]

Counties and Royal Irish Constabulary Districts.	Thoroughbreds. Thoroughbreds entered in Weatherby's Stud Book. Thoroughbreds Registered by the Royal Dublin Society for the purposes of their Scheme. No.	Fee, Thoroughbred Mares. Highest.	Fee, Thoroughbred Mares. Lowest.	Fee, Gentlemen's Half-bred Mares. Highest.	Fee, Gentlemen's Half-bred Mares. Lowest.	Fee, Farmers' Half-bred Mares. Highest.	Fee, Farmers' Half-bred Mares. Lowest.	Other Thoroughbreds. No.	Fee, Thoroughbred Mares. Highest.	Fee, Thoroughbred Mares. Lowest.	Fee, Gentlemen's Half-bred Mares. Highest.	Fee, Gentlemen's Half-bred Mares. Lowest.	Fee, Farmers' Half-bred Mares. Highest.	Fee, Farmers' Half-bred Mares. Lowest.	Total No. of Thoroughbreds.	Hunter Sires. Sires returned as Thoroughbreds, but which do not appear to be entered in Weatherby's Stud Book. No.	Fee, Thoroughbred Mares. Highest.	Fee, Thoroughbred Mares. Lowest.	Fee, Gentlemen's Half-bred Mares. Highest.	Fee, Gentlemen's Half-bred Mares. Lowest.	Fee, Farmers' Half-bred Mares. Highest.	Fee, Farmers' Half-bred Mares. Lowest.
TIPPERARY—con.																						
[illegible]		£ s. d.	£ s. d.	£ s. d.	£ s. d.	£ s. d.	£ s. d.		£ s. d.	£ s. d.	£ s. d.	£ s. d.	£ s. d.	£ s. d.			£ s. d.	£ s. d.	£ s. d.	£ s. d.	£ s. d.	£ s. d.
Borrisokane, ...	[illegible]	[illegible]	[illegible]	[illegible]	[illegible]	[illegible]	[illegible]	[illegible]	[illegible]	[illegible]	[illegible]	[illegible]	[illegible]	[illegible]	[illegible]	[illegible]	[illegible]	[illegible]	[illegible]	[illegible]	[illegible]	[illegible]
Nenagh, ...	[illegible]	[illegible]	[illegible]	[illegible]	[illegible]	[illegible]	[illegible]	[illegible]	[illegible]	[illegible]	[illegible]	[illegible]	[illegible]	[illegible]	[illegible]	[illegible]	[illegible]	[illegible]	[illegible]	[illegible]	[illegible]	[illegible]
Newport, ...	—	—	—	—	—	—	—	—	—	—	—	—	—	—	—	[illegible]	[illegible]	[illegible]	[illegible]	[illegible]	[illegible]	[illegible]
Roscrea, ...	[illegible]	[illegible]	[illegible]	[illegible]	[illegible]	[illegible]	[illegible]	[illegible]	[illegible]	[illegible]	[illegible]	[illegible]	[illegible]	[illegible]	[illegible]	[illegible]	[illegible]	[illegible]	[illegible]	[illegible]	[illegible]	[illegible]
Templemore, . . .	[illegible]	[illegible]	[illegible]	[illegible]	[illegible]	[illegible]	[illegible]	[illegible]	[illegible]	[illegible]	[illegible]	[illegible]	[illegible]	[illegible]	[illegible]	[illegible]	[illegible]	[illegible]	[illegible]	[illegible]	[illegible]	[illegible]
Thurles, ...	—	—	—	—	—	—	—	[illegible]	[illegible]	[illegible]	[illegible]	[illegible]	[illegible]	[illegible]	[illegible]	[illegible]	[illegible]	[illegible]	[illegible]	[illegible]	[illegible]	[illegible]
	[illegible]	[illegible]	[illegible]	[illegible]	[illegible]	[illegible]	[illegible]	[illegible]	[illegible]	[illegible]	[illegible]	[illegible]	[illegible]	[illegible]	[illegible]	[illegible]	[illegible]	[illegible]	[illegible]	[illegible]	[illegible]	[illegible]
WATERFORD.																						
Cappoquin, . . .	[illegible]	[illegible]	[illegible]	[illegible]	[illegible]	[illegible]	[illegible]	[illegible]	[illegible]	[illegible]	[illegible]	[illegible]	[illegible]	[illegible]	[illegible]	—	—	—	—	—	—	—
Dungarvan, . . .	—	—	—	—	—	—	—	[illegible]	[illegible]	[illegible]	[illegible]	[illegible]	[illegible]	[illegible]	[illegible]	[illegible]	[illegible]	[illegible]	[illegible]	[illegible]	[illegible]	[illegible]
Portlaw, ...	—	—	—	—	—	—	—	[illegible]	[illegible]	[illegible]	[illegible]	[illegible]	[illegible]	[illegible]	[illegible]	[illegible]	[illegible]	[illegible]	[illegible]	[illegible]	[illegible]	[illegible]
Waterford, . . .	[illegible]	[illegible]	[illegible]	[illegible]	[illegible]	[illegible]	[illegible]	[illegible]	[illegible]	[illegible]	[illegible]	[illegible]	[illegible]	[illegible]	[illegible]	—	—	—	—	—	—	—
	[illegible]	[illegible]	[illegible]	[illegible]	[illegible]	[illegible]	[illegible]	[illegible]	[illegible]	[illegible]	[illegible]	[illegible]	[illegible]	[illegible]	[illegible]	[illegible]	[illegible]	[illegible]	[illegible]	[illegible]	[illegible]	[illegible]

[illegible]	[illegible]			[illegible]		
	No.	Fee		No.	Fee	
		[illegible]	[illegible]		[illegible]	[illegible]
[illegible]—						
Montrose		£ s. d.	£ s. d.		£ s. d.	£ s.
[illegible]	[illegible]	—	—	[illegible]	—	—
[illegible]	[illegible]	—	—	[illegible]	—	—
[illegible]	[illegible]	—	—	[illegible]	—	—
[illegible]	[illegible]	—	—	[illegible]	—	—
[illegible]	[illegible]	—	—	[illegible]	—	—

www.ingramcontent.com/pod-product-compliance
Lightning Source LLC
Chambersburg PA
CBHW022128020426
42334CB00015B/809
9783742805157